Expert Oracle Database 11*g* Administration

Sam R. Alapati

Apress®

Expert Oracle Database 11 g Administration

Copyright © 2009 by Sam R. Alapati

ISBN-13 (pbk): 978-1-4302-1015-3

ISBN-13 (electronic): 978-1-4302-1016-0

Printed and bound in the United States of America 9 8 7 6 5 4 3 2

Lead Editor: Jonathan Gennick
Developmental Editor: Douglas Pundick
Technical Reviewer: John Watson
Editorial Board: Clay Andres, Steve Anglin, Mark Beckner, Ewan Buckingham, Tony Campbell,
    Gary Cornell, Jonathan Gennick, Michelle Lowman, Matthew Moodie, Jeffrey Pepper,
    Frank Pohlmann, Ben Renow-Clarke, Dominic Shakeshaft, Matt Wade, Tom Welsh
Project Manager: Richard Dal Porto
Copy Editor: Ami Knox
Associate Production Director: Kari Brooks-Copony
Production Editor: Laura Cheu
Compositors: Susan Glinert Stevens, Ellie Fountain
Proofreader: April Eddy
Indexer: John Collin
Cover Designer: Kurt Krames
Manufacturing Director: Tom Debolski

Distributed to the book trade worldwide by Springer-Verlag New York, Inc., 233 Spring Street, 6th Floor, New York, NY 10013. Phone 1-800-SPRINGER, fax 201-348-4505, e-mail orders-ny@springer-sbm.com, or visit http://www.springeronline.com.

For information on translations, please e-mail info@apress.com, or visit http://www.apress.com.

Apress and friends of ED books may be purchased in bulk for academic, corporate, or promotional use. eBook versions and licenses are also available for most titles. For more information, reference our Special Bulk Sales–eBook Licensing web page at http://www.apress.com/info/bulksales.

To my dear wife, Valerie, as a small token for her immense help and support

Contents at a Glance

PART 1 ■■■ Background, Data Modeling, UNIX/Linux, and SQL*Plus

PART 2 ■■■ Oracle Database 11*g* Architecture, Schema, and Transaction Management

PART 3 ■■■ Installing Oracle Database 11*g*, Upgrading, and Creating Databases

PART 4 ■■■ Connectivity and User Management

PART 5 ■■■ Data Loading, Backup, and Recovery

PART 6 ■■■ Managing the Database

PART 7 ■■■ Performance Tuning

Contents

PART 1 ■■■ Background, Data Modeling, UNIX/ Linux, and SQL*Plus

PART 2 ■■■ Oracle Database 11*g* Architecture, Schema, and Transaction Management

■CHAPTER 7   **Schema Management** 261

PART 3 ■■■ Installing Oracle Database 11*g*, Upgrading, and Creating Databases

PART 4 ███ Connectivity and User Management

■CHAPTER 12   User Management and Database Security

PART 5 ■■■ Data Loading, Backup, and Recovery

■CHAPTER 14 Using Data Pump Export and Import 677

PART 6 ▪▪▪ Managing the Database

PART 7 ■■■ Performance Tuning

■CHAPTER 19 **Improving Database Performance:**
SQL Query Optimization 1041

About the Author

SAM ALAPATI is currently an independent Oracle consultant, working at ERCOT (Electric Reliability Council of Texas). Prior to this, Sam was an Oracle DBA at the Boy Scouts of America, Sabre, Oracle Corporation, NBC, and AT&T. Sam has previously written *Expert Oracle9i Database Administration* and *Expert Oracle Database 10g Administration*, both for Apress, as well as three OCP certification books for Oracle Press. Sam has also coauthored *Oracle Database 11g RMAN Recipes* and *Oracle Database 11g New Features for DBAs and Developers*, both published by Apress. Sam has been working with relational databases since 1985, starting with the Ingres database.

About the Technical Reviewer

JOHN WATSON has spent 20 years hacking away at the Oracle product set, some of those years working for Oracle Corporation (in Internal Support and for Oracle University). Now he works for BPLC Management Consultants, consulting and teaching Oracle server technologies throughout Europe and Africa. He has written and edited several books for Apress and Oracle Press. He currently lives in Oxfordshire with his wife, two Chow Chows, six cats, and a parrot.

Acknowledgments

A book is never the product of a single-handed effort by the author. All books, especially technical books, are the product of intensive effort and care by a number of people, and the author is invariably the beneficiary of the hard work and help of a team of people who labor behind the scenes. So, let me start from the beginning and acknowledge my debts to all those who contributed to making this book a reality. First, I must acknowledge the book's Lead Editor, Jonathan Gennick, well known to many folks in the Oracle field, for explaining complex new topics to Oracle DBAs and developers in several articles and best-selling books. Jonathan is unique among editors: he always makes the author feel like his or her book is the only one he is working with, whereas the truth is that at any given time, Jonathan is probably grappling with a number of books at various stages of writing. Not only has Jonathan given freely of this time and counsel over the last year, but his unfailing courtesy and concern for this author has helped quite a bit. I am forever in the debt of the marvelous technical editing performed by John Watson, who was the technical reviewer for the book. John, as he has done before for some of my other books, has saved me from committing several errors—not only has he pointed out errors, but in most cases, he also pointed out what might work. John's exceptional consciousness and his painstaking testing of various features has truly enhanced the quality of the book. Any errors that have eluded John's keen eye are, alas, my own, and I must take responsibility for them.

This is a long book by any standards, and big books test the patience and the stamina of the best of the people who work on them. I must say that the Apress team came out with flying colors, handling potential problems with aplomb and moving the production process along through a long and arduous period lasting about a year. Project Manager Richard Dal Porto made sure none of us dropped the ball, by gently coaxing us to deliver the chapters on schedule. Richard, thanks for your patience and the skill with which you have led us over this long course. Douglas Pundick, Developmental Editor, had to labor through the extra long chapters, a task he performed with great distinction. I've benefited from Douglas's suggestions regarding chapter styling and ordering of topics. Copy Editor Ami Knox is in a class all by herself. I've had the fortune over the years to work with several good copy editors, but Ami is by far the best. The truly great copy editors don't merely catch errors in style and substance and typos—as Ami has shown me for the past several months, they also have an innate sense of what the author is trying to say and whether the author has managed to convey that message to the readers. Ami's brilliant copyediting has helped me produce a final book that is more readable and, hopefully, contains few errors. I've worked with Production Editor Laura Cheu before, and her crisp professionalism and meticulousness has always enhanced my books and I'm thankful to her. April Eddy, the proofreader, has, as usual, performed a sterling job, catching some hard-to-find potential errors, and I thank her for her hard work. Thanks also to the rest of production team as well as the marketing team for producing this book.

Moving on to friends and colleagues, I gratefully acknowledge the support of David Campbell, Technical Services Director at Boy Scouts of America (where I've worked until recently for many years). Dave's confidence in me and his helpful nature has always provided an incentive for me to do the best job I could at work and on my books. David Jeffress has been a wonderful manager and a valuable friend over the years and I appreciate all the help David gave me. I'd like to acknowledge Dan Nelson for his warm friendship and support. Jerry Hasting has always been a great role model, and I appreciate his support (and his sense of humor) over the years. I'd also like to acknowledge the following colleagues from the Boy Scouts of America: Nate Langston, Rob Page, Lance Parkes,

Myra Riggs, Debra Kendrick, Carla Wallace, and Carol Barnes, all of whom have helped make my stay there one I'll always cherish. My special thanks to my friend Dabir Haider for helping with various issues time and again. I appreciate the enormous help provided by Letica Salazar over the last year.

As with all my prior books, my friend Mark Potts has helped me immensely by troubleshooting and fixing problems with my computer as well as helping with several other things. Thanks, Mark, for all the help! I'd also like to acknowledge the friendship and support of Sabrina Kirkpatrick and Al Wilson during my tenure at the Boy Scouts.

I've been working at ERCOT for only a short period, but I've benefited from the warm atmosphere and the challenging work environment. My thanks to Shawna Jirasek and Bryan Hanley for bringing me here and for their understanding and support. Thanks to the trio of exceptionally good Oracle DBAs I'm privileged to work with every day: Sudhir Mahableshwarkar, Ben Groenewald, and Bhavesh Rathod. Friends Durga Viswanatha Raju Gadiraju, Sankara Krishnaswamy, Jai Kanuri, and and Nannapaneni Sandeep also have indirectly contributed to the book by helping out in many ways in settling in at ERCOT, and I thank them for that.

I'd like to take the opportunity to thank, from the bottom of my heart, the selfless help given me by Peter Ronald, Pamela Kruger, and Angela Shoup.

My father, Appa Rao, and my mother, Swarna Kumari, have always been a source of strength and joy, and as with all my books, they have provided the inspiration for me to write. I owe my academic and professional achievements to the support and encouragement my parents have provided me over the years. My brothers, Hari and Siva Sankar, although they live far me, are close to me in spirit and inspire me every day. I'm grateful to my sisters-in-law, Aruna and Vanaja, for their support and affection. I cherish deeply the love and affection of my nephews, Teja and Ashwin, and my nieces, Aparna and Soumya. Last but not the least, I appreciate the kindness and love shown by Sobbanna Boppanna, whose well wishes have been a source of support.

Finally, I acknowledge the enormous debt I owe to all the members of my immediate family: my wife, Valerie, and children, Shannon, Nina, and Nicholas, since it's really they who have enabled me to write all of my books, by cheerfully taking care of the numerous things that fall on the wayside when one embarks on a book-writing endeavor. The children have forgiven my frequent absences (figuratively) from home as I immersed myself in this book. Without their help, love, and support, I simply couldn't have written this book. Yet again, Valerie has supported me by making numerous sacrifices so I can write. I thank her for practicing the greatest virtue of all—patience—during the long time I spent working on this book.

Introduction

GRATIANO: . . . As who should say "I am Sir Oracle, And when I ope my lips, let no dog bark!"

—The Merchant of Venice, act 1, scene 1

Oracle Corporation used to print the preceding quotation from Shakespeare at the beginning of one of its chapters in the database administrator (DBA) manual for an earlier release of the Oracle database (Oracle version 6). I always thought the quote was interesting. If you proceed a little further in the play, you'll find this quotation:

BASSANIO: Gratiano speaks an infinite deal of nothing, more than any man in all Venice. His reasons are as two grains of wheat hid in two bushels of chaff: you shall seek all day ere you find them . . .

—The Merchant of Venice, act 1, scene 1

Bassanio counters that, in truth, Gratiano speaks too much: from two bushels of chaff, two grains of wheat may be recovered. And that's the *raison d'être* for this book: to separate the wheat from the chaff. The second quotation is even more apt when you consider the difficulty of extracting the right database management procedures from the tons of material available for the Oracle Database 11*g* database. Oracle Corporation publishes copious material to help you manage its increasingly complex databases. Oracle Corporation also conducts a variety of in-person and web-based classes to explain the vast amount of subject matter that you need to understand to effectively work with the Oracle database today. Yet users will have a good deal of difficulty finding the essential material for performing their jobs if they rely exclusively on Oracle's voluminous (albeit well-written) material in the form of manuals, class notes, web-based seminars, and so on.

The goal of this book is to provide you with a single source for most of your day-to-day Oracle database management tasks. Of course, it isn't feasible to cover each and every DBA topic in detail. What I've done in this book is focus on the topics that are common to most enterprises, such as installing the Oracle Database 11*g* software, creating and upgrading databases, exporting and importing data, backing up and recovering data, and performance tuning. I place a lot of emphasis in this book on explaining all of Oracle's automatic management solutions. Using Oracle's automatic management features will keep you from reinventing the wheel each time. It also turns out that after several years of development, Oracle has finally placed in your hands a set of powerful management advisors and other tools that make a lot of traditional DBA work obsolete.

How to Become an Oracle DBA

As you start out on your journey to become a proficient Oracle DBA, you have many sources of information on the Oracle database:

- Oracle Database 11*g* database administration classes, which have now been boiled down to a pair of five-day long classes

- Oracle manuals—an entire library of which are available on the Oracle web sites

- Books from various publishers that impart the various pieces of knowledge you need to become an accomplished Oracle DBA

You'll also need to acquire the necessary operating system knowledge. Most of the large Oracle databases are based on the UNIX (or Linux) operating system, so you'll need to have a reasonably good understanding of UNIX. Again, you have many sources of information available. You can attend a class or two from the leading UNIX system vendors, such as Hewlett-Packard and Sun Microsystems, you can read the manuals, or you can buy some books. Microsoft Windows is another popular operating system for Oracle databases, so you need to have a basic understanding of the Windows Server operating system as well.

As many of the new entrants to the Oracle Database 11*g* field find out, the Oracle DBA world is exhilarating, but alas, it's also exhaustive in its reach and scope. It isn't uncommon for DBAs to have an entire shelf full of books, all explaining various facets of the DBA profession—modeling books, UNIX texts, DBA handbooks, backup and recovery guides, performance-tuning manuals, and networking and troubleshooting books. The amazing thing is, even after you run through the whole gauntlet of courses and books, you aren't really assured of being fully prepared to handle complex, day-to-day database administration chores. There are many people who have taken all the requisite classes to become an Oracle DBA who won't or can't be competent Oracle DBAs based solely on their training. The reason? Refer back to that quotation from Shakespeare at the beginning of this introduction: you need to separate the grain from the chaff, and all the coursework and manuals, while excellent in their content, can serve to muddy the waters further.

The experienced Oracle DBA can find his or her way through this baffling amount of material, but how's the neophyte DBA to cope with the overwhelming amount of information? That's where this book comes in. This text will not only educate you in the theory and principles involved in managing relational databases, it will also help you translate that theory into the useful, practical knowledge that will enable you to manage real-life Oracle Database 11*g* databases with real-life data and real-life issues.

Oracle Database 11*g*

The *g* in Oracle Database 11*g* stands for "grid." The idea is to enable software to access spare processing power across networks (grids) of inexpensive servers. Traditionally, database systems have been run on large servers capable of running several very large databases at once. However, there are distinct disadvantages inherent in the single-server model. For example, resources tied up in the large servers can't be redistributed among the various databases and other services to ensure an optimal allocation of resources. If you need a massive amount of resources to handle your database's peak needs, chances are that you'll run with identical resources throughout the day, thus guaranteeing that you are going to waste critical resources during low-utilization periods.

Grid computing provides a means of harnessing the power of a large number of cheaper servers to supply the computing power you need in a flexible manner. This hardware would be servers like the Intel-based blade servers, and the software would include the free (or almost free) open source Linux operating system. By choosing small, generic servers, your system will cost much less than a traditional large server system, and because you can dynamically reallocate or provision resources based on actual needs, you'll be using resources efficiently.

Grid computing (also referred to as *computing on demand* and *utility computing*) isn't a new innovation invented solely by Oracle. The idea of grid computing has been around for a while, primarily in the academic world. In fact, grid computing arose out of the academic community's need for extremely fast and scalable computers to perform complex, massive research tasks. Another over-riding goal of the academic community was to permit the sharing of computing resources among large numbers of researchers. Of course, the academics also aimed to keep the cost as low as possible. Grid computing emerged out of these efforts as a viable way to create huge sharable computing environments that are dynamically adjustable to changes in the demand for computing power.

When we talk about harnessing the power of a number of commodity servers, realize that the number of computers may not be limited to just a handful. We are talking about combining the power of a fairly large number of small servers linked together to form a grid. Obviously, the key idea here is that the sum is far greater than the individual components. Enterprise grid computing, as envisioned by Oracle, uses large pools of modular storage and commodity servers. Underutilization of resources will be cut down, because capacity could be altered from the centralized pool of resources as necessary.

Here is a summary of the key benefits of grid computing:

- *Flexibility*: Since you are creating a single logical entity from a bunch of small servers, you can, of course, add or remove individual components as your computing needs dictate.

- *Efficiency*: The concept of *dynamic provisioning* underlies grid computing. Dynamic provisioning means that the allocation of resources for various services is not rigidly fixed, but changes according to the need for resources and the availability of the resources. Ideally, a well-run grid will channel resources to where they are needed the most by diverting them from under-utilized sources.

- *Easy manageability*: It is far easier to manage a single logical combination of your computing resources (which may include several databases and application servers), rather than monitoring each one as a completely independent unit.

- *Economy*: The total cost of a grid environment could be considerably lower than a traditional single, big server environment. Oracle strongly recommends the use of Linux-based commodity servers, which Oracle says offer the best price/performance ratio.

Key Components of Oracle Database 11*g*

Following are the essential components of Oracle's grid-based systems:

- Real Application Clusters (RAC)

- Information sharing

- Easy server manageability

- Extensive instrumentation

- The advisory framework

- Automatic performance tuning

- Automatic Storage Management (ASM)

- Automatic memory management

- Scheduling and resource management

- Real Application Testing

Note that you most certainly don't have to use a "grid" platform to be able to use the Oracle Database 11*g* server. In either case, you can take advantage of all the new features of the database system.

Real Application Clusters

Oracle has had a feature called the Oracle Parallel Server (OPS) for many years, which enabled people to access the database from more than one instance, thus providing for scalability as well as high availability. Oracle has refined the parallel server technology considerably over the years, eventually renaming it Real Application Clusters (RAC) a few years ago.

■**Note** This book concerns itself exclusively with the "mainstream" Oracle Database 11*g* DBA concepts and techniques. You'll not find any discussion of the Oracle Real Application Clusters in this book. If you are interested in RAC, you may want to take a look at Oracle manuals or refer to one of the many good books devoted to RAC.

Information Sharing

In order to efficiently share information over a grid spanning many heterogeneous systems, you need to share information efficiently. Data exchange can be occasional (such as when you perform data loads for a new system), or it could be regular and instantaneous (updating one part of the system when something changes in another part). In order to facilitate either type of information sharing, Oracle Database 11*g* provides *transportable tablespaces* and *Oracle Streams*.

Transportable Tablespaces

The transportable tablespaces feature enables high-speed transport of huge amounts of data from one database to another, even if the databases are running on different operating systems. The ability to move huge amounts of data across platforms, and even to rename the tablespaces during the process, makes information exchange far easier.

Oracle Streams

Oracle Streams is a feature that enables you to effortlessly capture changes made in one database and propagate them to subscriber nodes in the grid. The Oracle Streams feature can keep all the copies in sync while the changes are being applied.

Easy Server Manageability

Through its Database Control and Grid Control interfaces, Oracle Enterprise Manager enables the management of either a single database or all databases, application servers, hosts, listeners, HTTP servers, and web applications as well.

The prevailing view among IT organizations is that Oracle is a complex, difficult-to-manage database, especially when compared with the Windows server database, SQL Server. Oracle Database 11*g* makes a conscious effort to simplify management, right from the installation process through to daily monitoring and performance tuning. There is a new common infrastructure for storing workload- and performance-related information. You can now use powerful SQL tuning tools to determine ways to improve performance.

Oracle Enterprise Manager (OEM), which includes the single database-level Database Control, and its enterprise-wide counterpart, the Grid Control, provide unsurpassed capabilities for managing the database. Traditionally, Oracle DBAs relied on complex SQL scripts to monitor the database as well as diagnose and fix performance problems. OEM now can help you do all those things and a lot more, without having to spend enormous amounts of time writing lengthy scripts to help manage the database.

■Note I've reduced the use of DBA scripts to the bare minimum in this book. Instead, I show you how to use the OEM Database Control effectively to perform all your tasks quickly and with far less effort.

Extensive Instrumentation

Oracle Database 11*g* provides instrumentation of its code base that ranges further than any prior release of Oracle, providing accurate metrics about database performance that weren't available until now. Oracle's own instrumentation and metrics, since they are embedded in the database code, provide better information without any measurable performance degradation, compared to third-party performance-measurement tools.

The Advisory Framework

Oracle Database 11*g* contains several highly useful *advisors* to help you optimize the performance of the various components of the database. Here are some of them:

- The *Automatic Database Diagnostic Monitor* (ADDM) helps you analyze current and past instance performance.

- The *SQL Tuning Advisor* helps you tune SQL statements.

- The *SQL Access Advisor* tells you whether you should add (or drop) indexes and materialized views.

- The *Segment Advisor* helps you figure out the necessary space for new tables and to reclaim unused space assigned to segments, among other things.

- The *Undo Advisor* helps you configure the critical undo tablespace.

- The *Memory Advisor* provides recommendations for memory-related parameters.

Each of these advisors has a similar look and feel, and this consistency will help you learn how to use them effectively. Using the advisors isn't mandatory, of course—you can also tune space and memory by using Oracle-supplied packages and various dynamic performance views—but it's more efficient to simply invoke the necessary advisor.

Automatic Performance Tuning

Oracle Database 11*g* provides you with automatic performance diagnosis and tuning recommendations. An expert diagnosis tool called the Automatic Database Diagnostic Monitor uses the new Automatic Workload Repository contents to analyze instance performance. The ADDM's analysis includes a summary of database problems ranked according to the amount of database time they're costing, as well as a list of recommendations to eliminate these problems. The ADDM's recommendations may include modifying configuration settings or running one of the advisors listed in the previous section.

Automatic Storage Management

A significant component of the Oracle's push toward easier management is the Automatic Storage Management feature. Traditionally, database administrators relied on third-party vendors, such as VERITAS and EMC, to provide storage management tools for larger systems. ASM enables the automatic management of disks without resorting to third-party Logical Volume Managers (LVMs).

You can use Oracle's storage virtualization layer to automate and simplify the layout and management of all Oracle database files, when you use ASM. Instead of directly managing numerous files and disks, you can pay attention to a relatively small number of *disk groups*. If you need additional storage, you simply add new physical disks to the logical disk groups.

Automatic Memory Management

The Oracle Database 11*g* server provides you with an easy way of managing the memory needs of your databases. Automatic memory management and automatic program global area management use information collected from the instance to efficiently allocate both the major components of Oracle's memory allocation—the system global area (SGA) and the program global area (PGA).

Scheduling and Resource Management

It's common for enterprise users to share computing resources, and there needs to be a way of scheduling the users and sharing the enterprise's resources efficiently. Oracle Database 11*g* DBAs can use the *Database Resource Manager* to control and channel scarce database resources among the various users of the grid. You can also use the *Oracle Scheduler* to manage and monitor jobs as well as prioritize them.

Real Application Testing

Two major features of Oracle Database 11*g*—Database Replay and the SQL Performance Analyzer—facilitate change management by letting you replay database activities and SQL workloads, respectively. You can thus test the impact of a potential database or server upgrade, for example, by invoking the Database Replay and the SQL Performance Analyzer tools.

Why Read *This* Book?

What sets this book apart from the others on the market is the constant focus on the practical side of the DBA's work life. What does a new DBA need to know to begin work? How much and what SQL does the new DBA need to know? What UNIX, Linux, and Windows commands and utilities does the new DBA need to know? How does a DBA perform the basic UNIX administration tasks? How does a DBA install the Oracle software from scratch? How does the DBA use all the powerful new performance tuning features of the Oracle Database 11*g* server?

This book provides the conceptual background and operational details for all the topics a professional Oracle DBA needs to know. The following sections outline other reasons to choose this book over its competitors.

Delivers a One-Volume Reference

This book's specific purpose is to serve as a one-volume handbook for professional Oracle DBAs—as a book that covers both the theory and practice of the DBA craft. As I mentioned before, most newcomers to the field are intimidated and bewildered by the sheer amount of material they're confronted with and the great number of administrative commands they need to have at their fingertips. Well, everything you need to know to run your databases efficiently is right here in this one book.

How did I manage to achieve the difficult feat of providing comprehensive instruction in just one book? Well, although there *is* a lot of terrain to cover if you want to learn all the DBA material, you must learn to separate the critical from the mundane, so you can identify what matters most and what you merely need to be aware of, at least in the beginning.

I'm definitely not suggesting that this one book will supplant all of the other Oracle material available. I strongly recommend that inquisitive readers make it a habit to refer to Oracle's documentation for the 11*g* database. You can obtain this documentation on the Web by getting a free membership to the Oracle Technology Network (OTN), which you can access through the Oracle web site at http://technet.oracle.com.

It's extremely important to read the Oracle database manuals and to understand how the database works. However, nothing can replace working on an actual database when it comes to mastering DBA techniques, so if you have a Windows desktop, you can easily install the freely downloadable Oracle Database 11*g* software. If you want, you can do the same on a Linux system as well. One of the great things about the Oracle database software is that it runs virtually identically on each operating system. In fact, your production system will operate exactly the same as the free "toy database" on your desktop machine, so go ahead and practice to your heart's content on the Oracle Database 11*g* database.

READING THE ORACLE MANUALS

Whether you use this or some other DBA handbook, you will still need to refer to the Oracle database manuals frequently to get the full details of complex database operations. I can't overemphasize the importance of mastering the fundamentals of Oracle Database 11*g* that are presented in the *Oracle Concepts* manual. Mastering this volume is critical to understanding many advanced DBA procedures.

The Oracle manuals are invaluable if you need a lot of detail. For example, the chapters on backup and recovery (Chapters 15 and 16) are good starting points in your attempt to master the Oracle procedures in those areas. Oracle has several manuals covering the backup and recovery material. Once you finish the two relevant chapters in this book, you'll find going through those manuals a pretty easy task, because you'll already have a good understanding of all the important concepts. This book provides a foundation on which you can build using the Oracle manuals and other online help available from Oracle.

In addition to the online manuals, Oracle provides an excellent set of tutorials that contain systematic instructions on how to perform many useful Oracle Database 11*g* tasks. You can access these tutorials, the *Oracle by Example* series, by going to http://www.oracle.com/technology/obe/start/index.html.

Emphasizes New Methods and When to Use Them

One of the fundamental difficulties for a neophyte in this field is determining the right strategy for managing databases. Although the essential tasks of database management are pretty similar in Oracle Database 11*g* compared to earlier versions of the software, the database contains several innovative techniques that make a number of routine tasks easier to perform than in the past. Oracle Corporation, however, has shied away from firmly recommending the adoption of the new methods and techniques to manage databases. The reason for this is twofold. First, Oracle rarely discards existing techniques abruptly between versions; features advertised as being destined for obsolescence are made obsolete only after many years. Thus, old and new ways of performing similar tasks coexist in the same version. Second, Oracle isn't very effective in clearly communicating its guidelines concerning contending methods. Thus, when more than one method exists for performing a task, you as a DBA have to exercise caution when you select the appropriate methods to use.

In this book, I clearly emphasize the newer features of Oracle that have been refined in the last few years and encourage you to move away from older techniques when the new innovations are clearly superior. I help you in formulating a solid strategy when multiple choices are offered. A good example is performance tuning: it was common to employ a traditional SQL-script approach to guide performance tuning efforts, but this book comes down squarely on the side of using the latest Oracle Enterprise Manager (OEM) GUI techniques to perform all your performance tuning and other DBA tasks.

Covers UNIX, SQL, PL/SQL, and Data Modeling

Some people who are motivated to become Oracle DBAs are stymied in their initial efforts to do so by their lack of training in UNIX/Linux and SQL. Also, sometimes DBAs are confused by the whole set of data modeling and the "logical DBA" techniques. This book is unique in that it covers all the essential UNIX, SQL, PL/SQL, and data modeling that a DBA ought to know to perform his or her job well.

As a DBA, you need to be able to use a number of UNIX tools and utilities to administer an Oracle database. Unfortunately, up until now many books haven't included coverage of these vital tools. This book remedies this neglect by covering tools such as telnet, FTP, and the crontab. Many developers and managers want to have a better understanding of the UNIX system, including the use of the vi file editor, file manipulation, and basic shell-script writing techniques. This book enables you to start using the UNIX operating system right away and shows you how to write solid shell scripts to perform various tasks. Of course, you can take a specialized class or study a separate book in each of the previous areas, but that's exactly what you're trying to avoid by using this book.

In addition to learning all the UNIX you need to start working with the UNIX operating system right away, you can get a good working knowledge of SQL and PL/SQL from a DBA's perspective in this book. Of course, I strongly recommend further study of both UNIX and SQL to strengthen your skills as an Oracle DBA as you progress in your career.

Offers Hands-On Administrative Experience

Although a number of books have been published in the last decade on the subject of Oracle database administration, there has been a surprising lack of the blending of the concepts of the Oracle database with the techniques needed to perform several administrative tasks. A glaring example is the area of backup and recovery, where it's difficult to find discussions of the conceptual underpinnings of Oracle's backup and recovery process. Consequently, many DBAs end up learning backup and recovery techniques without having a solid grasp of the underlying principles of backup and recovery. As you can imagine, this split between theory and practice proves expensive in the middle of a recovery operation, where fuzziness on the concepts could lead to simple mistakes.

Your success as a professional database administrator is directly related to the amount of hands-on experience you have, and to your understanding of the concepts behind the operation of the database. To get this practice, you can experiment with all the commands in this book on a UNIX- or a Windows-based Oracle Database 11g database. Oracle Database 11g is loaded with features that make it the cutting-edge database in the relational database market, and this book covers all the new additions and modifications to database administration contained in the 11g version. It's a lot of fun for an experienced DBA to have the opportunity to use all the wonderful features of the new database, but beginning- and intermediate-level DBAs will have *more* fun, because they're embarking on the great endeavor that is the mastery of Oracle database management.

Who Should Read This Book?

This book is primarily intended for beginning- and intermediate-level Oracle Database 11*g* DBAs. Prior experience with Oracle databases isn't assumed, so if you've never managed databases and intend to master the management of the new Oracle Database 11*g* database, you can do so with the help of this book.

More precisely, the audience for this book will fall into the following categories:

- Oracle DBAs who are just starting out
- Oracle developers and UNIX/Linux or Windows system administrators who intend to learn Oracle DBA skills
- Managers who want to get a hands-on feel for database management
- Anybody who wants to learn how to become a proficient Oracle DBA on his or her own

A Note About UNIX, Linux, and Windows

I personally like the UNIX operating system and use it at work. I'm familiar with the Windows platform and I think it's a good operating system for small enterprises, but my favorite operating system remains UNIX, which stands out for its reliability, scalability, and speed. For medium and large organizations, the UNIX system offers wonderful features and ease of use. As a result, you'll find this book heavily oriented toward the use of Oracle on UNIX systems.

If you happen to admire the Linux operating system, there isn't a new learning curve involved, as most of the operating system commands will work the same way in the UNIX and Linux systems. If you need to find out how to use the Oracle Database 11*g* database on a Windows platform, here's some interesting news for you: the database commands work exactly the same way in both the UNIX and Windows environments.

How This Book Is Organized

I have organized the contents of this book with the new DBA in mind. My goal is to provide you with a decent background in data modeling, SQL, and UNIX, while providing a thorough course in the essentials of Oracle Database 11*g* database management skills. I know it's unusual to provide UNIX and SQL background in an Oracle DBA book, but this inclusion is in line with the goal I set when I decided to write this book: there ought to be a single book or manual that has all the necessary background for a reader to start working as an Oracle Database 11*g* DBA.

I strove to write the chapters to mirror real-life practical training. For example, you should understand basic database modeling and fundamental UNIX operating system commands before learning to manage Oracle databases. I therefore start with a discussion of database modeling and UNIX. You'll install the Oracle database software before learning how to create an Oracle database. After you install the software and create a database, you can create users and establish connectivity. Subsequent chapters deal with the loading and unloading of data, backup and recovery, day-to-day database management, and performance tuning.

I advise beginning DBAs to start at the beginning of the book and keep going. A more experienced user, on the other hand, can pick the topics in any sequence he or she desires. Throughout the book, I've provided detailed, step-by-step, tested examples to illustrate the use of data concepts and features of Oracle Database 11g. I strongly recommend that you set up an Oracle Database 11g database server on your PC and follow along with these examples. Doing so will teach you the relevant commands and help you build confidence in your skill level. Moreover, the examples are a whole lot of fun! The following sections briefly summarize the contents of the book.

Part 1: Background, Data Modeling, UNIX/Linux, and SQL*Plus

Part 1 provides a background on the Oracle DBA profession and offers an introduction to data modeling and the UNIX operating system as well as SQL*Plus. In Chapter 1 I discuss the role of the Oracle DBA in the organization, and I offer some advice on improving your skill set as a DBA. I also discuss the basics of relational databases. Chapter 2 provides an introduction to both logical and physical database design, including the use of entity-relationship diagrams. You'll learn about the Optimal Flexible Architecture (OFA) with regard to disk layout. Chapter 3 provides a quick introduction to UNIX/Linux operating systems, including the most common commands that you need as an Oracle DBA, the rudiments of shell scripting, and how to use the vi text-processing commands. You'll also explore the essential UNIX system administration tasks for Oracle DBAs. This chapter finishes with coverage of disks and storage systems, including the popular RAID systems. Chapter 4 provides a thorough introduction to the use of SQL* Plus, the main interface to the Oracle database. In addition, Chapter 4 also describes how to use the powerful Oracle Enterprise Manager to monitor and manage your databases as well as your entire system. You'll learn how to install and use the Database Control, which you use for managing a single database, and the Grid Control, through which you can manage your enterprise, including application servers and hosts.

Part 2: Oracle Database 11g Architecture, Schema, and Transaction Management

Part 2 is in many ways the heart of the book—it covers the important topics of Oracle Database 11g's architecture, schema management, and transaction management. In Chapter 5 you'll learn about the important components of the Oracle database architecture, such as how the database processes and memory work. It also covers the conceptual foundations of the Oracle database. Chapter 6 provides a detailed introduction to the management of tablespaces. Chapter 7 covers schema management in Oracle Database 11g, and it contains a quick review of the important types of Oracle objects, such as tables and indexes, and shows you how to manage them. Chapter 8 provides you with a thorough understanding of how Oracle databases conduct transaction processing.

Part 3: Installing Oracle Database 11g, Upgrading, and Creating Databases

Part 3 includes two chapters that show you how to install the Oracle Database 11g software, create Oracle databases, and upgrade databases. Chapter 9, which covers Oracle software installation, shows how to install the Oracle Database 11g database server. In addition, Chapter 9 also shows you in detail how to upgrade to Oracle Database 11g. Chapter 10 shows you how to create an Oracle database from scratch, both manually as well as by using the Database Configuration Assistant (DBCA).

Part 4: Connectivity and User Management

Part 4 explains how to establish connectivity to the Oracle database and manage database users. Chapter 11 covers connecting to Oracle databases, and Chapter 12 shows you how to manage users and discusses ways of securing your database.

Part 5: Data Loading, Backup, and Recovery

Part 5 deals with loading data and performing backups and recovery. You'll learn how to use SQL*Loader in Chapter 13, and Chapter 14 covers the Data Pump technology, which enables you to load and unload Oracle data. Chapters 15 and 16 deal with the crucial topics of database backups and recovery, respectively.

Part 6: Managing the Database

Part 6 covers managing the operational Oracle Database 11g database. Chapter 17 focuses on the important Oracle Database 11g automatic management features, as well as exploring several powerful online capabilities of the Oracle database. Chapter 18 shows you how to manage data files, tablespaces, and Oracle redo logs, and how to perform undo management. The chapter also provides an introduction to the Oracle storage solution, Automatic Storage Management.

Part 7: Performance Tuning

Part 7 covers Oracle Database 11g performance tuning and troubleshooting issues. Chapter 19 discusses the Cost-Based Optimizer and provides tips on writing efficient SQL queries. You'll also see how to use Oracle's Automatic SQL Tuning Advisor to improve query performance. In Chapter 20, you'll learn how to optimize the use of Oracle's memory, disk I/O, and the operating system. You'll also learn about the Oracle wait interface in this chapter. A basic approach to performance analysis and troubleshooting production databases is explained as well.

Appendix: Oracle Database 11g SQL and PL/SQL: A Brief Primer

In the Appendix, I introduce Oracle SQL and PL/SQL, provide an introduction to Oracle XML DB, which helps you deal with XML data, and include an introduction to using the Java programming language with Oracle.

Salud!

I truly enjoy working with the Oracle database, because of its amazing range of capabilities and the intricate challenges it throws my way as I explore its wide-ranging capabilities. I hope you derive as much satisfaction and fulfillment from the Oracle database as I do. I leave you with the following observation, adapted from the introduction to the famous economics textbook by Paul A. Samuelson, the great economist and Nobel Laureate:[1]

> *I envy you, the beginning Oracle DBA, as you set out to explore the exciting world of Oracle Database 11g database management for the first time. This is a thrill that, alas, you can experience only once in a lifetime. So, as you embark, I wish you bon voyage!*

---

1. Paul A. Samuelson and William D. Nordhaus, *Economics, Seventeenth Edition* (New York: McGraw-Hill, 1998).

## PART 1

Background, Data Modeling, UNIX/Linux, and SQL*Plus

## CHAPTER 1

The Oracle DBA's World

There are many types of Oracle databases, and there are many types of Oracle database administrators (DBAs)—this chapter discusses the role of the Oracle DBA as well as the training that Oracle DBAs typically need to be successful. You'll look at the daily routine of a typical DBA, which will give you an idea of what to expect if you're new to the field. This chapter also covers ways you can improve your skill level as an Oracle DBA and prepare to keep the databases under your stewardship performing optimally. Toward the end of the chapter, you'll find a list of resources and organizations that will help you in your quest to become a top-notch DBA.

The Oracle DBA's Role

The main responsibility of a DBA is to make corporate data available to the end users and the decision makers of an organization. All other DBA tasks are subordinate to that single goal, and almost everything DBAs do on a day-to-day basis is aimed at meeting that single target. Without access to data, many companies and organizations would simply cease to function.

Note Imagine the chaos that would ensue if a company such as Amazon.com no longer had access to its customer database, even for a short time. The entire company could cease to function. At a minimum, it would lose perhaps thousands of online orders. As a DBA, your job is to ensure access to your organization's data. You are also responsible for protecting that data from unauthorized access—just think of the commotion caused by well-publicized security lapses at well-known consumer data–based organizations.

That's not to say that availability of data is the only thing DBAs have to worry about. DBAs are also responsible for other areas, including the following, all of which further the key goal of making data available to users:

- *Security*: Ensuring that the data and access to the data are secure
- *Backup*: Ensuring that the database can be restored in the event of either human or systems failure
- *Performance*: Ensuring that the database and its subsystems are optimized for performance
- *Design*: Ensuring that the design of the database meets the needs of the organization
- *Implementation*: Ensuring proper implementation of new database systems and applications

In a small organization, a DBA could be managing the entire information technology (IT) infrastructure, including the databases, whereas in a large organization there could be a number of DBAs, each charged with managing a particular area of the system.

You can put the tasks you'll perform as an Oracle DBA in the following three categories:

- Security

- System management

- Database design

I discuss each of these broad roles in more detail in the following sections, outlining what you could consider the bare minimum level of performance expected of a DBA. Although the lists in each section may seem long and daunting, the tasks are really not that difficult in practice if you follow certain guidelines. Proper planning and testing, as well as automating most of the routine tasks, keep the drudgery to a minimum. All you're left with to do on a daily basis are the really enjoyable things, such as performance tuning or whatever else may appeal to you.

The DBA's Security Role

As a DBA, you'll be involved in many different areas of system security, mainly focusing on the database and its data. Several potential security holes are possible when you implement a new Oracle system out of the box, and you need to know how to plug these security holes thoroughly before the databases go live in a production environment. In Chapter 12, which deals with user management, you'll find a fuller discussion of standard Oracle security guidelines and other Oracle security-related issues.

Protecting the Database

For an Oracle DBA, no task is more fundamental and critical than protecting the database itself. The Oracle DBA is the person the information departments entrust with safeguarding the organization's data, and this involves preventing unauthorized use of and access to the database. The DBA has several means to ensure the database's security, and based on the company's security guidelines, he or she needs to maintain the database security policy (and to create the policy if it doesn't already exist). A more complex issue is the authorization of users' actions within the database itself, after access has already been granted. I address this topic in depth in Chapter 12.

■**Note** Some organizations don't have a general security policy in place. This is particularly true of smaller companies. In that case, it's usually up to the DBA to come up with the security policy and then enforce it within the database.

Creating and Managing Users

Every database has users, and it's the DBA's job to create them based on requests from the appropriate people. A DBA is expected to guide the users' use of the database and ensure the database's security by using proper authorization schemes, roles, and privileges. Of course, when users are locked out of the database because of password expiration and related issues, the DBA needs to take care of them. It's also the responsibility of the DBA to monitor the resource usage by individual users and to flag the heavy resource users.

The DBA's System Management Role

Another of the DBA's major roles is the day-to-day management of the database and its subsystems. This daily monitoring is not limited to the database itself. As a DBA, you need to be aware of how the system as a whole is performing. You need to monitor the performance of the servers that host the database and of the network that enables connections to the database. The following sections describe the various facets of the system management part of the Oracle DBA's job.

Troubleshooting

One of the Oracle DBA's main job responsibilities is troubleshooting the database to fix problems. *Troubleshooting* is a catchall term, and it can involve several of the tasks I discuss in the following sections. Two important aspects of troubleshooting are knowing how to get the right kind of help from Oracle support personnel, and how to use other Oracle resources to fix problems quickly.

Performance Tuning

Performance tuning is an omnipresent issue. It's a part of the design stage, the implementation stage, the testing stage, and the production stage of a database. In fact, performance tuning is an ongoing task that constantly requires the attention of a good Oracle DBA. Depending on the organizational setup, the DBA may need to perform database tuning, or application tuning, or both. Generally, the DBA performs the database tuning and assists in the testing and implementation stages of the application tuning performed by the application developers.

Performance requirements for a living database change constantly, and the DBA needs to continually monitor the database performance by applying the right indicators. For example, after migrating to a newer release of the Oracle database, I found that several large batch programs weren't completing within the allotted time. After much frustration, I realized that this was because some of the code was using cost-based optimizer hints that were no longer optimal under the new Oracle version. A quick revision of those hints improved the performance of the programs dramatically. The moral of the story: make sure you test all the code under the new Oracle version before you switch over to it.

You can say that all database tuning efforts can be grouped into two classes—proactive and reactive tuning. *Proactive tuning*, as the name indicates, means that the DBA heads off potential trouble by careful monitoring of necessary performance indices. As we all know, prevention is always better than any cure, so proactive tuning will always trump reactive tuning efforts. However, most Oracle DBAs in charge of production databases don't have the luxury of proactively tuning—they are too busy reacting to complaints about a slow-performing database or some similar problem. You are likely to encounter both kinds of database tuning efforts in your day-to-day life as an Oracle DBA.

Monitoring the System

Once a database is actually in production, the DBA is expected to monitor the system to ensure uninterrupted service. The tasks involved in monitoring the system include the following:

- Monitoring space in the database to ensure it is sufficient for the system
- Checking to ensure that batch jobs are finishing as expected
- Monitoring log files on a daily basis for evidence of unauthorized attempts to log in (something DBAs want to keep close tabs on)

Minimizing Downtime

Providing uninterrupted service by eliminating (or at least minimizing) downtime is an important criterion by which you can judge a DBA's performance. Of course, if the downtime is the result of a faulty disk, the company's service-level agreements (SLAs), if any, will determine how quickly the disk is replaced. DBAs may or may not have control over the maximum time for service provided in the SLAs. For their part, however, DBAs are expected to be proactive and prevent avoidable downtime (such as downtime due to a process running out of space).

Estimating Requirements

Only the DBA can estimate the operating system, disk, and memory requirements for a new project. The DBA is also responsible for coming up with growth estimates for the databases he or she is managing and the consequent increase in resource requirements. Although some of the decisions regarding physical equipment, such as the number of CPUs per machine and the type of UNIX server, may be made independently by system administrators and managers, the DBA can help during the process by providing good estimates of the database requirements.

In addition to estimating initial requirements, the DBA is responsible for planning for future growth and potential changes in the applications. This is known as *capacity planning*, and the DBA's estimates will be the basis for funding requests by department managers.

Developing Backup and Recovery Strategies

Adequate backups can prevent the catastrophic loss of an organization's vital business data. The Oracle DBA needs to come up with a proper backup strategy and test the backups for corruption. The DBA also needs to have recovery plans in place, and the best way to do this is to simulate several types of data loss. Proper testing of backup and recovery plans is sorely neglected in many companies, in spite of its critical importance for the company.

Loss of business data not only leads to immediate monetary damage in the form of lost revenue, but also costs customer goodwill in the long run. Unplanned database downtime reflects poorly on the firm's technical prowess and the competency of the management.

When disasters or technical malfunctions keep the database from functioning, the DBA can fall back on backed-up copies of the database to resume functioning at peak efficiency. The DBA is responsible for the formulation, implementation, and testing of fail-safe backup and restoration policies for the organization. In fact, no other facet of the DBA's job is as critical as the successful and speedy restoration of the company's database in an emergency. I've personally seen careers made or broken based on one backup- and recovery-related emergency; an emergency can test the true mettle of an Oracle DBA like no other job requirement can.

During those times when disaster strikes, the seasoned DBA is the one who is confident that he or she has the necessary technical skills and can remain calm in an emergency. This calmness is really the outcome of years of painstaking study and testing of the theoretical principles and the operational commands necessary to perform sensitive tasks, such as the restoration and recovery of damaged databases.

Loading Data

After the DBA has created database objects, schemas, and users, he or she needs to load the data, usually from older legacy systems or sometimes from a data warehouse. If the data loads need to be done on a periodic basis, the DBA needs to design, test, and implement the appropriate loading programs.

Overseeing Change Management

Every application goes through changes over time to improve features and fix bugs in the software. There is a constant cycle of development, testing, and implementation, and the DBA plays an important role in that cycle. *Change management* is the process of properly migrating new code, and the Oracle DBA needs to understand the process that's in place in his or her organization.

In addition to updating application code, the Oracle DBA is also responsible for ensuring that all the latest changes to the database software are also evaluated and adopted. These so-called software patches are usually made available through Oracle's MetaLink service. In fact, the latest Oracle Enterprise Manager (OEM) enables you to connect directly to MetaLink and download and apply software patches.

In Oracle Database 11*g*, you can use two new change management features, Database Replay and SQL Performance Analyzer, to find out ahead of time the impact of system changes, including a database or server upgrade, on SQL and database performance. I discuss both of these important features in Chapter 20.

The DBA's Database Design Role

Many Oracle DBAs spend at least part of their time helping design new databases. The DBA's role may include helping create entity-relationship diagrams and suggesting dependencies and candidates for primary keys. In fact, having the DBA actively involved in designing new databases will improve the performance of the databases down the road. It's a well-known fact that an improperly designed database thwarts all attempts to tune its performance.

Designing the Database

Although designing databases is probably not the first thing that comes to mind when you think of a DBA's responsibilities, design issues (whether concerning the initial design or design change) are a fundamental part of the Oracle DBA's job. Administrators who are particularly skilled in the logical design of databases can be crucial members of a team that's designing and building brand-new databases. A talented DBA can keep the design team from making poor choices during the design process.

Installing and Upgrading Software

The Oracle DBA plays an important role in evaluating the features of alternative products. The DBA is the person who installs the Oracle database server software in most organizations; the UNIX system administrator may also handle part of the installation process. Prior to actual installation, the DBA is responsible for listing all the memory and disk requirements so that the Oracle software and databases, as well as the system itself, can perform adequately. If the DBA wants the system administrator to reconfigure the UNIX kernel so it can support the Oracle installation, the DBA is responsible for providing the necessary information. Besides installing the Oracle database server software, the DBA is also called upon to install any middleware, such as the Oracle Application Server and Oracle client software on client machines.

Creating Databases

The DBA is responsible for the creation of databases. Initially he or she may create a test database and later, after satisfactory testing, move the database to a production version. The DBA plans the logical design of the database structures, such as tablespaces, and implements the design by creating the structures after the database is created. As the DBA plays a part in creating the new database, he or she needs to work with the application team closely to come up with proper estimates of the database objects, such as tables and indexes.

Creating Database Objects

An empty database doesn't do anyone a whole lot of good, so the DBA needs to create the various objects of the database, such as tables, indexes, and so on. Here, the developers and the DBA work together closely, with the developers providing the tables and indexes to be created and the DBA making sure that the objects are designed soundly. The DBA may also make suggestions and modifications to the objects to improve their performance. Through proper evaluation, the DBA can come up with alternative access methods for selecting data, which can improve performance.

■**Note** As a DBA, you can contribute significantly to your organization by explaining the alternatives available to your application team in designing an efficient database. For example, if you explain to the application team the Oracle partitioning option, including the various partitioning schemes and strategies, the team can make smarter choices at the design stage. You can't expect the application team to know all the intricacies of many Oracle options and features.

Finally, remember that the organization will look to the DBA for many aspects of information management. The DBA may be called upon not only to assist in the design of the databases, but also to provide strategic guidance as to the right types of databases (OLTP, DSS, and so forth) and the appropriate architecture for implementing the organization's database-driven applications.

DBA Job Classifications

Given the diverse nature of business, a DBA's job description is not exactly the same in all organizations. There are several variations in the job's classification and duties across organizations. In a small firm, a single DBA might be the UNIX or Windows administrator and the network administrator as well as the Oracle DBA, with all job functions rolled into one. A large company might have a dozen or more Oracle DBAs, each in charge of a certain database or a certain set of tasks.

Sometimes you'll hear the terms "production DBA" and "development" (or "logical") DBA. *Production* DBA refers to database administrators in charge of production databases. Because a production database is already in production (meaning it is already serving the business functions), such DBAs aren't required to have design or other such developmental skills. DBAs who are involved in the preproduction design and development of databases are usually called *development* or *logical* DBAs. Ideally, you should strive to acquire the relevant skill sets for both development and production administration, but reality demands that you usually are doing more of one thing than the other at any given time. In general, large establishments usually have a number of DBAs and can afford to assign specialized tasks to their personnel. If you work for a small organization, chances are you'll be doing a little bit of everything.

Individual preference, the availability of financial and technical resources, and the necessary skill sets determine whether a DBA is doing production or development work. A DBA who comes up from the developer ranks or who's happiest coding is usually more likely to be a development or logical DBA. This same person also may not really want to carry a pager day and night and be woken up in the dead of night to perform a database recovery. On the other hand, a person who likes to do production work and to work with business analysts to understand their needs is less likely to enjoy programming in SQL or in any other language.

Although all of the preceding is true, both development and production DBAs are well advised to cross-train and learn aspects of the "other" side of Oracle database administration. Too often, people who characterize themselves as production DBAs do not do much beyond performing backups and restores and implementing the physical layout of databases. Similarly, development DBAs, due to their preference for the programming and design aspects of the job, may not be fully cognizant of the operational aspects of database management, such as storage and memory requirements.

Types of Databases

In many organizations, you will be working with different types of databases daily, and thus with different types of data and management requirements. You may find yourself working on simple SQL queries with users and simultaneously wrestling with decision-support systems for management.

Databases perform a variety of functions, but you can group all of those functions into two broad categories: online transaction processing (OLTP) and decision-support systems (DSSs; sometimes also called online analytical processing, or OLAP). Let's take a quick look at some of the basic classifications of Oracle databases.

Online Transaction Processing and Decision-Support System Databases

Online transaction processing databases are the bread and butter of most consumer- and supplier-oriented databases. This category includes order entry, billing, customer, supplier, and supply-chain databases. These databases are characterized by heavy transaction volume and a need to be online continuously, which today (given the use of the Internet to access such systems) means 24/7/365 availability, short maintenance intervals, and low tolerance for breakdowns in the system.

Decision-support systems range from small databases to large data warehouses. These are typically not 24/7 operations, and they can easily manage with regularly scheduled downtime and maintenance windows. The extremely large size of some of these data warehouses necessitates the use of special techniques both to load and to use the data.

There isn't a whole lot of difference between the administration of a DSS-oriented data warehouse and a transaction-oriented OLTP system from the DBA's perspective. The backup and recovery methodology is essentially the same, and database security and other related issues are also very similar. The big difference between the two types of databases occurs at the design and implementation stages. DSS systems usually involve a different optimization strategy for queries and different physical storage strategies. Oracle Database 11*g* provides you with the choice of implementing an OLTP database or a DSS database using the same database server software.

Performance design considerations that may work well with one type of database may be entirely inappropriate for another type of database. For example, a large number of indexes can help you query a typical data warehouse efficiently while you are getting some reports out of that database. If you have the same number of indexes on a live OLTP system with a large number of concurrent users, you may see a substantial slowing down of the database, because the many updates, inserts, and deletes on the OLTP system require more work on the part of the database.

Development, Test, and Production Databases

Applications are developed, tested, and then put into production. A firm usually has development, test, and production versions of the same database in use at any given time, although for smaller companies the test and development versions of the database may be integrated in one database.

Development databases are usually owned by the development team, which has full privileges to access and modify data and objects in those databases. The *test databases* are designed to simulate actual production databases and are used to test the functionality of code after it comes out of the development databases. No new code is usually implemented in the "real" *production databases* of the company unless it has been successfully tested in the test databases.

When a new application is developed, tested, and put into actual business use (production), the development and production cycle does not end. Application software is always being modified for two reasons: to fix bugs and to improve the functionality of the application. Although most applications go through several layers of testing before they move into production, coding errors and the pressure to meet deadlines contribute to actual errors in software, which are sometimes not caught until the application is already in use. In addition, users continually request (or, more appropriately, *demand*) modifications in the software to improve the application's functionality. Consequently, application code does not remain static; rather, developers and testers are always working on it.

Training and Certification

Your strength as an Oracle DBA is directly related to the amount of effort you put into understanding the conceptual underpinnings of Oracle Database 11*g*. As you're assimilating the database concepts, it's vital that you implement the various techniques to see if they work as advertised and whether a particular technique is suitable for your organization.

■**Tip** There's no substitute for hands-on playing with the database. Download the most recent Oracle Database 11*g* server software, install it, buy some good Oracle DBA books, access the Oracle manuals on Internet sites, and just start experimenting. Create your own small test databases. Destroy them, bring them back to life, but above all have fun. I had great trainers who lived and breathed databases; they made it fun to learn and always had the time to show me new techniques and correct my errors. You'll find database experts willing to share knowledge and skills freely both in the workplace and on the Internet.

In this section, I discuss the help and services that professional organizations and other resources can provide to enhance your credentials.

Training

There's no ideal background for an Oracle DBA, but it's highly desirable that one have a real interest in the hardware side of databases, and also have a decent knowledge of operating systems, UNIX and NT servers, and disk and memory issues. It also helps tremendously to have a programming or development background, because you'll be working with developers frequently. The most common operating system for the Oracle database is UNIX, with the Hewlett-Packard (HP) and Sun Microsystems (Sun) versions being the ones commonly adopted. IBM supplies the AIX variant of the UNIX operating system, but it has its own proprietary database, the DB2 Universal Database.

If you want to study to become a full-fledged Oracle Database 11*g* DBA, you need to take these two classes from Oracle or another provider:

- Oracle Database 11*g*: Administration Workshop I
- Oracle Database 11*g*: Administration Workshop II

There are three levels of Oracle certification for DBAs. You must start with the Oracle Certified Associate (OCA) certification first, followed by the Oracle Certified Professional (OCP) certification, which is the most common certification sought by Oracle professionals. The final certification level is the Oracle Certified Master (OCM) certification, which involves a lengthy practical exam over two days. All Oracle Database 11*g* DBA certification candidates are required to take one in-class or online class from an approved list of courses, in order to meet the new hands-on course requirement. If your firm uses Oracle Real Application Clusters (RAC) or distributed databases, you need to take additional, specialized courses. If your firm uses the UNIX operating system and you don't have experience using it, you may be better off taking a basic class in UNIX (or Linux) from HP, Sun, Red Hat, or another vendor. You don't need to take such a course for Oracle DBA certification purposes, but it sure will help you if you're new to the UNIX or Linux environment. Oracle itself provides several courses in Linux administration and even a certification path for managing Oracle under Linux, under the Oracle Certified Expert Program. Of course, if your databases are going to use the Windows environment, you may get away with not taking a long and formal course in managing

Windows, assuming you are relatively familiar with the Windows operating system, unless you also happen to be a Windows system administrator.

■**Note** Remember that Oracle Corporation is not the only source of Oracle classes. Although Oracle University is a large entity with fine courses, other private vendors offer courses that are just as good or better than those that Oracle University offers. As is true of all courses, the quality of the teaching depends directly on the teacher's experience and communication skills. And remember that you really don't have to go anywhere to take a class; you can purchase self-study CD-ROMs and learn by yourself, at a fraction (one-fifth) of the cost for the instructor-led in-class training.

An even better strategy might be to subscribe to Oracle's online learning program, known as Oracle iLearning (http://ilearning.oracle.com). It's cheaper than buying the DVDs, and you get access to hundreds of Oracle University courses. If you're planning to take the Oracle courses, make sure you're also working on a server with an actual database. Oracle supplies very well-designed sample schemas that you can use to sharpen your SQL skills, whether your database is a development version on a UNIX server or a free downloaded Windows version of Oracle Database 11*g* Enterprise Edition on your desktop computer. You'll go further in a shorter time with this approach.

Once you get started as an Oracle Database 11*g* DBA, you will find that the real world of Oracle databases is much wider and a lot more complex than that shown to you in the various courses you attend. As each new facet of the database is revealed, you may find that you are digging more and more into the heart of the software, why it works, and sometimes why it doesn't work. It is at that point that you will learn the most about the database and the software used to manage it. If you really have read everything that Oracle and other private parties have to offer, do not worry—there are always new versions coming out, with new features and new approaches, practically guaranteeing an endless supply of interesting new information.

After the first year or two of your DBA journey, you'll know enough to competently administrate the databases and troubleshoot typical problems that occur. If you've also worked on your programming skills during this time (mainly UNIX shell scripting and PL/SQL), you should be able to write sophisticated scripts to monitor and tune your databases. At this stage, if you dig deeper, you'll find out a lot more about your database software that can enhance your knowledge and thereby your contribution to your organization.

Oracle is constantly coming up with new features that you can adopt to improve the performance of your production databases. Although the developers, testers, and administrators are also striving mightily in the organization's cause, it is you, the Oracle DBA, who will ultimately lead the way to new and efficient uses of the new features of the database.

Certification

In many IT fields, certification by approved authorities is a required credential for advancement and sometimes even for initial hiring. Oracle has had the Oracle Certification Program in effect for a number of years now. The OCP is divided into three levels: Associate, Professional, and Master (the Master level requires a lab test in addition to the other requirements). Traditionally, certification was not a big issue with most organizations, especially in the face of the severe shortages of certified DBAs in the field for many years. In today's environment, though, that certification will help tremendously in underlining your qualifications for the job.

Oracle provides DBA certification at the following levels—Oracle Database 11*g* Administrator Certified Associate, Oracle Database 11*g* Administrator Certified Professional, and Oracle Database 11*g* Administrator Certified Master (OCM). Oracle provides the following descriptions of their certification programs:

- *OCA*: The Oracle Certification Program begins with the Associate level. At this apprentice skill level, Oracle Associates have a foundation knowledge that will allow them to act as junior team members working with database administrators or application developers. The two exams you are required to take expect knowledge of basic database administration tasks and an understanding of the Oracle database architecture and how its components work and interact with one another. The OCA is also a prerequisite to becoming an OCP.

- *OCP*: The exam ensures that the OCP with the 11*g* credential can competently address critical database functions, such as manageability, performance, reliability, security, and availability using the latest Oracle technology. The OCP is a prerequisite to becoming an Oracle Certified Master.

■ Note New Oracle Database 11*g* OCP candidates who wish to obtain the Oracle Database 11*g* DBA OCP credential must attend one instructor-led course, either in-class or online, from the approved list of Oracle University courses.

- *OCM*: The Oracle Database 11 OCM credential is for the Oracle database guru—the senior database professional with both classroom and on-the-job experience. The prerequisites are that candidates earn an Oracle Database 11*g* OCP credential and complete advanced-level coursework. The final stage requires that candidates prove their skills through an intensive two-day hands-on practical examination.

My views on certification are really very practical. Preparing for certification will force you to learn all the little details that you've been ignoring for some reason or another, and it will clarify your thinking regarding many concepts. Also, the need to certify will compel you to learn some aspects of database administration that you either don't like for some reason or currently don't use in your organization. So if you're not already certified, by all means start on that path. You can get all the information you need by going to Oracle's certification web site at http://www.oracle.com/education/certification. Believe me, that certificate does look nice hanging in your cubicle, and it's a symbol of the vast amount of knowledge you've acquired in the field over time. You can rightfully take pride in obtaining OCP-certified DBA status!

SYSTEM ADMINISTRATION AND THE ORACLE DBA

There's a clear and vital connection between the Oracle DBA's functions and those of the UNIX (or Windows) administrator in your organization. Your database and the database software will be running on a physical UNIX (or Windows or Linux) server and a UNIX (or Windows or Linux) operating system. Depending on the size of your organization and your role within it, you may need anything from a basic to a thorough understanding of operating system administration. In small firms where there's no separate UNIX system administrator position, you may need to know how to configure the UNIX server itself before you actually install and manage an Oracle server and the data on it. Fortunately, this situation is very rare, and most organizations have one or more UNIX administrators in charge of managing the UNIX servers and the data storage systems. Some small entities adopt Windows as an operating system, as it isn't quite as complex to manage as the UNIX operating system.

Although the system administrators usually are very helpful, it's in your best interest to acquire as much skill in this field as you can. This will help you in more ways than you can imagine. It will help you in working effectively with the UNIX administrator, because you can both speak the same language when it comes to fancy topics such as the logical volume manager and subnet masks. More important, a good understanding of the UNIX disk structure will help you make the proper choice of disks when you design the physical layout of your database. By understanding concepts such as UNIX disk volumes and the usage of system memory, you can improve the performance of your databases and avoid bottlenecks that slow databases down. You can also write excellent monitoring scripts by being well steeped in the UNIX shell scripting and the related awk and sed programming languages.

You'll find that UNIX is a fun operating system, with interesting commands and scripting languages that can contribute to your being a highly effective Oracle DBA. One of the marks of an accomplished Oracle DBA is his or her expertise in the way the operating system works. By acquiring system administration skills, you'll become a well-rounded professional who can contribute significantly to your organization's IT needs. There are several web UNIX (and Linux) shell accounts available. Get one of these free accounts and start practicing common UNIX commands, if you think you need to practice your skills in this area.

Resources and Organizations for Oracle DBAs

As you progress in your career as an Oracle DBA, you'll need to refer to various sources for trouble-shooting information and general Oracle and database knowledge. I have a couple of recommendations for organizations you may want to make a part of your professional DBA practice:

- The Oracle Technology Network (OTN) at `http://otn.oracle.com` or `http://technet.oracle.com` is highly useful for DBAs and Oracle developers, and even better, it's free! You'll find every-thing from online documentation to copies of all Oracle software available freely for download on the OTN. The site offers a complete set of Oracle documentation.

- The International Oracle Users Group (IOUG), which you can find on the Web at `http://www.ioug.org/`. Membership to this organization will set you back $125 currently, an expenditure that most organizations will reimburse their DBAs for. The IOUG holds annual conventions where practitioners in the field present literally hundreds of extremely useful papers. IOUG makes these articles available to its members, and the organization also publishes a monthly magazine. In addition to the international group, there are several regional Oracle user groups, where users meet in their hometowns and discuss relevant DBA topics. For example, the group located in Dallas, Texas, is known as the Dallas Oracle Users Group (`http://www.doug.org/`). Oracle Corporation also holds an annual Oracle OpenWorld conference, where several inter-esting and useful papers are presented. You can find session papers from recent OpenWorld conferences by going to the Oracle OpenWorld Archives web site at `http://www.oracle.com/openworld/archive`.

There are also dozens of sites on the Web today where you can find all kinds of useful informa-tion and scripts for managing your databases, as well as help in certifying yourself as an OCP DBA. Just go to your favorite search engine, type in the relevant keywords, and you'll be amazed at the amount of help you can get online in seconds. Before the proliferation of DBA-related web sites, DBAs had to rely on printed materials or telephone conversations with experts for resolving several day-to-day issues, but that's not the case anymore.

A great way to enhance your knowledge is to maintain a network of other practicing Oracle DBAs. It's amazing how useful these contacts can be in the long run, as they provide a good way to compare notes on new releases and difficult troubleshooting issues that crop up from time to time. There's really no need to reinvent the wheel every time you encounter a problem, and chances are that most of the problems you face have already been fixed by someone else. Especially when you're starting out, your friendly Oracle DBA contacts will help you avoid disasters and get you (and your databases) out of harm's way.

You can find many excellent resources on the Internet to help you when you're stuck or when you need to learn about new features and new concepts. The Oracle DBA community has always been a very helpful and cooperative group, and you'll probably learn over time that you can resolve many troublesome issues by getting on the Internet and visiting DBA-related sites. You can find hundreds of useful scripts on the Internet, and you're invited to use them. The following is a brief list of excellent sites for Oracle DBAs. Of course, any omissions from this list are purely unintentional—my sincere apologies to any other great sites that I either don't know about yet or have just plain forgotten about. These sites just happen to be some of the ones that I visit often:

- *Hotsos* (http://www.hotsos.com/): The redoubtable Cary Millsap, well-known creator of the Optimal Flexible Architecture (OFA) guidelines and the main author of the best-selling Oracle performance book *Optimizing Oracle Performance* (O'Reilly, 2003), is the person behind the Hotsos site. Visit this site for sophisticated, cutting-edge discussions of performance tuning and other issues.

- *Oracle-Base* (http://oracle-base.com/): This site contains extremely useful and very well written Oracle DBA articles. The site provides free help for preparing for the Oracle DBA certification exams.

- *Ixora* (http://www.ixora.com.au): Oracle internals expert Steve Adams is the main force behind this site. Ixora offers first-rate discussions about many Oracle and UNIX performance issues, although not much new material has been put up on this web site in recent years.

- *OraPub* (http://www.orapub.com/): This is another top-notch site led by an ex-Oracle employee. It provides consistently high-grade white papers on key database administration topics.

- *DBAsupport.com* (http://www.dbasupport.com/): This is another useful site that offers many scripts and a "how-to" series of articles on a variety of topics.

- *Burleson Consulting* (http://www.dba-oracle.com/): Popular Oracle writer and editor Don Burleson runs this web site (and well-known author Mike Ault is a regular contributor). This site is packed with terrific articles covering a broad range of DBA topics.

- *Oracle FAQ* (http://www.orafaq.com/): The Oracle FAQ site, run by Frank Naude of South Africa, provides a lot of question-and-answer–type discussions of relevant topics.

There are several other sites that are useful, including dbazine.com (http://dbazine.com/), Mark Rittman's Oracle Weblog (http://rittman.net/), and Database Journal (http://www.databasejournal.com), whose authors, Steve Callum, Jim Czuprinski, and James Koopmann, present solid articles on various Oracle features. Also, Tom Kyte, the well-known Oracle expert, maintains an extremely popular web site at http://asktom.oracle.com.

Oracle by Example

Oracle Corporation has been providing a highly useful (and absolutely free) set of step-by-step implementations for many of the important features of the Oracle server software. I'm referring to the Oracle Corporation's Oracle by Example (OBE) series (http://www.oracle.com/technology/obe/start/index.html), which provides authoritative hands-on experience with many features of the Oracle database, including installation. I strongly recommend that you go through the OBE series carefully and save yourself quite a bit of frustration when installing and using the database software. Check it out!

Oracle Database Two-Day DBA Course

One of the most useful, if not the most useful, of the Oracle manuals for a beginning DBA is *Oracle Database 2 Day DBA* (Oracle, 2008). The *Oracle Database 2 Day DBA* book is designed to provide new DBAs with sufficient information to manage small to medium-sized databases. So, you if ever wanted an online, self-paced, complete DBA program that's free, you don't have to look any further!

Oracle By Example has a complete series dedicated to the *Oracle Database 2 Day DBA* book. You can go right from the installation of the database to performance turning using the Enterprise Manager rather than the command line as the administrative interface. The Oracle by Example series covering the course content of the *Oracle Database 2 Day DBA* manual, providing an unsurpassed introduction to DBA hands-on tasks. In fact, Oracle refers to the *Oracle Database 2 Day DBA* manual as "actionable documentation" because of its emphasis on practice rather than concepts and theory.

Oracle MetaLink

When you buy the Oracle server software and licenses from Oracle, you can choose from various levels of service support. Support that requires a quick response and round-the-clock attention costs more. Years ago, the only way to get Oracle to help you was by calling and talking to an analyst by phone. Once an analyst was assigned to your technical assistance request (TAR), you and the analyst would try to resolve the issue over the phone. If the analyst couldn't fix the problem right away, there would be a delay until the analyst found a solution to the problem.

For the last several years, Oracle has emphasized the use of a Web-based service called MetaLink to help resolve TARs from customers. The MetaLink service is of enormous importance to the working DBA, as it not only facilitates the exchange of important files and other troubleshooting information through the File Transfer Protocol (FTP), but it also provides access to the actual database of previous customer issues and the solutions provided by Oracle for similar problems. Thus, in many cases, when you are dealing with problems of a small to medium degree of complexity, you can just log onto the MetaLink web site (http://metalink.oracle.com/) and resolve your problem in minutes by typing in keywords or the Oracle error number.

If you have a real problem and need Oracle troubleshooters to help you out, MetaLink is the usual way to get that help. In most cases, the Oracle troubleshooters will ask you to upload several files that'll help diagnose the problem. In some cases, they may ask you to send in quite a lot of information using a tool they call the RDA (remote diagnostic assistant), which helps the professionals understand your system well. All this, of course, saves a bundle of money for Oracle, but more important from the DBA's point of view, it saves a tremendous amount of time that the DBA would otherwise have to spend resolving garden-variety troubleshooting issues.

Oracle Web Conference

Oracle Web Conference (OWC), the latest means of support from Oracle, provides for collaboration between you and Oracle Support. OWC allows the Oracle Support engineers to monitor the issues and problems within your own environment using both telephone and the Web to troubleshoot. You can download the archives of the web conference afterward.

■**Note** You can also look into Oracle Advanced Customer Services, which focuses on providing continual operational improvement of the Oracle environment in your organization.

The Daily Routine of a Typical Oracle DBA

Many of the daily tasks DBAs perform on a database involve monitoring for problems. This can mean running monitoring scripts or using the Oracle built-in tools, such as Enterprise Manager, to keep track of what's actually happening with the database.

A good example of something you'll want to monitor closely is space in the database. If you run out of space on a disk where a database table resides, you can't insert any more new data into the table, and the transactions will fail. Of course, you can fix the problem by adding the requisite amount of space and rerunning the transaction. But if you were properly monitoring the database, you would have been alerted through a page or an e-mail that the particular table was in danger of running out of space, and you could have easily avoided the subsequent Oracle errors.

You'll normally check the reports generated by your monitoring scripts on a daily basis to make sure no problems are developing with regard to disk space, memory allocation, or disk input and output. Enterprise Manager is a handy tool for getting a quick, visual idea about various issues, such as memory allocation and other resource usage. The monitoring scripts, on the other hand, can provide summarized information over a lengthy period of time; for example, they can provide interval-based information for an entire night.

It's also worthwhile to study the *alert log* (the log that Oracle databases maintain to capture significant information about database activity) on a regular basis to see if it's trapping any errors reported by Oracle. You may do this alert log monitoring directly, by perusing the log itself, or you could put a script in place that monitors and reports any errors soon after their occurrence in the alert log.

You will need to take some action to fix the Oracle errors reported in the alert log. Based on the nature of the error, you may change some parameters, add some space, or perform an administrative task to fix the problem. If the problem has no fix that you are aware of, you may search the MetaLink database and then open a new TAR with Oracle to get help as soon as you can.

Oracle, like every other software company, is constantly improving its software by releasing upgraded versions, which usually have newer and more sophisticated features. It's your responsibility as a DBA to be on top of these changes and to plan the appropriate time for switching over to new versions. Some of these switches might be to completely upgraded versions of software and may require changes in both the applications and the DBA's configuration parameters. Again, the right approach is to allow plenty of time for testing the new software to avoid major interruptions in serving your customers.

Some General Advice

As you progress in your journey as an Oracle DBA, you'll have many satisfying experiences as well as some very frustrating and nerve-racking moments. In the following sections, I make three important suggestions that will help you when you are going through the latter.

Know When You Need Help

Although it's always nice to figure out how to improve performance or recover an almost lost production database on your own, know when to call for help. It doesn't matter how much experience you gain, there will always be times when you're better off seeking advice and help from someone else. I've seen people lose data as well as prolong their service disruption when they didn't know what they didn't know. You can't successfully manage production databases by basing your decisions on incomplete knowledge or insufficient information.

Remember You Are Not Alone

I don't mean this in any philosophical way—I just want to remind you that as an Oracle DBA, you're but one of the people who have the responsibility for supporting the applications that run on your databases. You usually work within a group that may consist of UNIX and Windows administrators, network administrators, storage experts, and application developers. Sometimes the solution to a problem may lie in your domain, and other times it may not. You can't take all the credit for your application running well, just as you don't deserve all the blame every time database performance tanks. Today's enterprises use very sophisticated servers, storage systems, and networks, and you need the help of experts in all these areas to make your database deliver the goods. Oracle isn't always the cause of your problems—sometimes the system administrator or the network expert can fix your problems in a hurry for you.

Think Outside the Box

Good DBAs constantly seek ways to improve performance, especially when users perceive that the database response may be slow. Sometimes tinkering with your initialization parameters won't help you, no matter how long you try. You have to step back at times like this and ask yourself the following question: Am I trying to fix today's problems with yesterday's solutions? There's no guarantee that things that worked well for you once upon a time will serve you equally well now. Databases aren't static—data changes over time, users' expectations change, load factors increase with time, and so on. As a DBA, it pays not to rest on your laurels when things are going fine; rather, you should always be looking at new database features that you can take advantage of. You can't constantly increase memory or CPU in order to fix a performance problem. For example, you may have a situation where memory usage is very high, response times are slow, and the user count is going up steadily. Maybe you should rethink your architectural strategies at times like this—how about replacing the dedicated server approach with the Oracle multithreaded server? It's a big switch in terms of the way clients connect to your database, but if the new strategy has great potential, the effort will pay off big.

Primum Non Nocere

The ancient medical admonition *primum non nocere* (first, do no harm) could also serve for us DBAs, when we are confronted with a database that needs recovery or some such critical operation.

In critical situations, it's better to gather vital facts and clarify the conceptual basis of your impending changes before actually typing commands in a hurry. Your goal is to resolve the issue at hand, of course, but at a minimum, you shouldn't do any further harm! Slow down, make sure you really understand what's at stake, and then proceed further or call for additional help.

CHAPTER 2

■ ■ ■

Relational Database Modeling and Database Design

Aside from dealing with tables and the queries that are based on them, many DBAs don't have a detailed understanding of database topics, such as normalization, functional dependency, and entity-relationship modeling. However, a good database is the bedrock on which you can create a good application. The ability to design a database is particularly useful to DBAs working in smaller organizations, where they'll need to know how to do everything from working with the UNIX file system to resolving networking issues. Even if designing databases isn't a part of your job description, however, understanding database design will help you when performance tuning the database.

Because the needs of organizations differ, you can't take a "one size fits all" approach to databases. This makes database design one of the most interesting and challenging areas available to you when working with databases, and large corporate database systems in particular. Someone in the organization needs to first model the needs of the organization on a conceptual level and then use this conceptual design to physically design and build the database. Even though it's not absolutely necessary that you, as a DBA, be an expert in database design, your knowledge as a competent Oracle DBA isn't complete until you learn at least the rudiments of database modeling and design.

In this chapter, you'll first learn the conceptual basis of a relational database, which is what an Oracle Database 11g database is. After you explore the basic elements of the relational database life cycle, you'll learn how to perform conceptual or logical data modeling. Data normalization is very important when dealing with relational databases, and this chapter discusses this topic in detail. Finally, you'll learn how to translate the logical data model into a design you can physically implement. Oracle Corporation refers to its databases as "object-relational" databases, so the chapter concludes with a brief discussion of object-relational databases.

Relational Databases: A Brief Introduction

Oracle Database 11g is a leading example of a relational database management system (RDBMS), although Oracle prefers to call its database an *object-relational database management system* (ORDBMS). (As you'll see toward the end of this chapter, you derive the object-relational model by combining object-oriented design with the traditional relational model.) Relational databases have become the pervasive model of organizing data in the last three decades, and they have revolutionized how companies manage their data. Relational database management systems use relationships among data to answer complex queries.

■Note Thanks to the many RDBMS wizards that walk users through the database creation process step by step, even novices can set up a database; the very ease with which you can create a database sometimes contributes to poorly designed databases. My own general rule of thumb is that if database design isn't your forte, find a person who is good at database design to help you. Putting some effort into good design up front will pay rich dividends later on.

The relational model's domination of the database market is expected to continue into the foreseeable future, given the massive investment many large organizations have made in both the databases themselves and the staff required to manage them. The powerful and easy-to-understand relational databases are indeed the mainstay of a vast majority of organizations in today's world economy.

Relational databases are based on the precepts laid down by E. F. Codd in the 1970s, when he was working for IBM. Codd's paper, which outlined the model, "A Relational Model of Data for Large Shared Data Banks," was published in June 1970 in the Association of Computer Machinery (ACM) journal, *Communications of the ACM*, and Codd's model is accepted as the model for RDBMSs. D. L. Childs presented a similar set-oriented relational model in 1968, but it is Codd's exposition that made relational databases popular.

There were (and still are) nonrelational database models that preceded the relational model—specifically, the hierarchical and the network models. Both the network model and the hierarchical model use actual data links called *pointers* to process queries issued by users. These models, although powerful as far as performance goes, lead to a very complex database, and they are no longer adopted by most organizations. You can call relational databases *second-generation* database management systems.

The Relational Database Model

Three key terms are used extensively in relational database models: relations, attributes, and domains. A *relation* is a table with columns and rows. The named columns of the relation are called the *attributes*, and the *domain* is the set of values the attributes are allowed to take.

The basic data structure of the relational model is the table, where information about the particular entity (say, an employee) is represented in columns and rows (also called *tuples*). Thus, the "relation" in "relational database" refers to the various tables in the database; a relation is a set of tuples. The columns enumerate the various attributes of the entity (the employee's address or phone number, for example), and the rows are actual instances of the entity (specific employees) that is represented by the relation. As a result, each tuple of the employee table represents various attributes of a single employee.

All relations (and thus tables) in a relational database have to adhere to some basic rules to qualify as relations. First, the ordering of the columns is immaterial in a table. Second, there can't be identical tuples or rows in a table. And third, each tuple will contain a single value for each of its attributes. (Remember that you can order the tuples and columns in any way you wish.)

Tables can have a single attribute or a set of attributes that can act as a "key," which you can then use to uniquely identify each tuple in the table. Keys serve many important functions. They are commonly used to join or combine data from two or more tables. Keys are also critical in the creation of indexes, which facilitate fast retrieval of data from large tables. Although you can use as many columns as you wish as part of the key, it is easier to handle small keys that are (ideally) based on just one or two attributes.

Database Schemas

The database *schema*, a set of related tables and other database objects, is a fundamental concept in relational databases, and it is part of the logical database structure of an Oracle database. A schema is always associated with a user, and it can be defined as a named collection of objects owned by a user. That is why the terms "user" and "schema" are used almost synonymously in Oracle databases.

A relational database schema consists of the definition of all relations with their specific attribute names, as well as a primary key. The schema further includes the definition of all the domains, which are the ranges of values the attributes can take.

All work on a relational database is essentially performed through the use of a database language called *Structured Query Language* (SQL).

Relational Algebra

Relational databases are founded on basic mathematical principles (set theory). The very first line of E. F. Codd's seminal paper that outlined the relational database model makes this clear:

> *This paper is concerned with the application of elementary relation theory to systems which provide shared access to large banks of formatted data.*[1]

Relational algebra consists of a set of operations for manipulating one or more relations without changing the originals. The following are the basic operations that you can perform on a relational database using relational algebra; these are called unary operations, because they involve the manipulation of tuples in a single relation.

- *Selection*: A selection operation extracts (or eliminates) a set of tuples from a relation based on the values of the attributes of the relation.

- *Projection*: A projection operation extracts (or eliminates) a specified set of columns of a relation.

Besides these unary operations, relational algebra supports *binary* or *set* operations to manipulate the relations themselves. (Remember that a relation is a set of tuples.) Binary operations merge elements from two relations into a new relation. The set operations are as follows:

- *Union*: A union combines two relations to produce a new, larger relation.

- *Intersection*: Intersection creates a new relation that has only the common tuples in two relations.

- *Difference*: Difference creates a new relation that has only the noncommon tuples in two relations.

- *Cartesian product*: The Cartesian product creates a new relation that concatenates every tuple in relation *A* with every tuple in relation *B*. The Cartesian product is just one example of a join operation.

■**Note** *Join operations* combine two or more relations to derive a new relation based on identical values in the columns (join columns) on the basis they are joined. The resulting relation would be a Cartesian product *if you include all the tuples in both relations*. However, you usually need only a part of this Cartesian product, based on all tuples in both relations that share a common value for the join column. A *natural join* is where you combine tuples from two relations, *A* and *B*, by combining all rows in *A* and *B* that have identical values for all common attributes. A *theta-join*, on the other hand, pairs tuples in two relations, based on an arbitrary condition.

---

1. E. F. Codd, "A Relational Model of Data for Large Shared Data Banks," *Communications of the ACM*, vol. 13, no. 6 (June 1970): 377–87.

It looks as if relational algebra, which is based on set theory principles, should be sufficient to retrieve information from relational databases, which are also based on set theory. The problem with relational algebra is that though it's based on correct mathematical principles, it relies on a mathematical procedural language. So if you want to use it for anything but the simplest database queries, you're apt to run into quite complex, messy mathematical operations. Only highly skilled professional programmers can use such a database. To avoid the complexity of relational algebra and to focus on the queries without worrying about the procedural techniques, you use relational calculus.

Relational Calculus

Relational calculus does not involve the mathematical complexity of relational algebra; it focuses only on what the database is being queried for, rather than how to conduct the query. In other words, it is a declarative language. You focus on the results you expect and the conditions to be satisfied in the process, and you ignore the sequencing of the relational algebra concepts. Relational calculus is based on a part of mathematical logic called *propositional calculus* or, more precisely, *first-order predicate calculus*. Relational calculus involves the use of operators such as AND and OR to manipulate relations in logical expressions.

SQL

Relational calculus is far easier to use than relational algebra, but it still is based on the principles of logic and it is not easy for most people to use. You thus need an easy-to-use implementation of relational calculus. Structured Query Language (SQL) is one such implementation, and it has become hugely popular as the predominant language for the relational database model. SQL is considered a "relationally complete" language, in the sense that it can express any query that is supported by relational calculus.

Structured English Query Language (SEQUEL), the precursor of SQL, was developed by IBM to use Codd's relational database model. Oracle introduced the first commercially available implementation of SQL in 1979 (when Oracle was known as Relational Software), and SQL has since become the standard language for RDBMSs, although not all implementations adhere completely to the official standards. Oracle has its own implementation of SQL, which is very close to the American National Standards Institute (ANSI) standard (visit http://www.ansi.org/ for more information).

SQL is an English-like language that enables you to manipulate data in a database. Using SQL, you can derive any relation that can be derived using relational calculus. You can formulate queries in easy-to-format structures, which are then processed by sophisticated database servers into complex forms to get the queried data. Its intuitive appeal, ease of use, and tremendous power and sophistication have made SQL the language of choice when working with any relational database.

You can divide SQL statements into two major categories: data definition language (DDL) and data manipulation language (DML). DDL statements are used to build and alter database structures, such as tables, and to define and construct database schemas. DML statements are used to manipulate data in the database tables; with DML statements, you can delete, update, and insert tuples that are part of a relation.

The Appendix provides a quick introduction to the Oracle Database 11*g* SQL language as well as to PL/SQL, Oracle's procedural extension to standard SQL that provides the power of traditional programming languages along with SQL's ease of use.

Relational Database Life Cycle

The essential steps of a typical relational database life cycle are as follows:

1. Requirements gathering and analysis
2. Logical database design
3. Physical database design
4. Production implementation

I will examine each of these stages in detail in the rest of this chapter. You could, of course, forget about using any methodology, and just design your database any way you want, create the structures, load the data, and be in business. However, improper database design has serious long-term performance implications, and you risk ending up with an inadequate database or simply with one that is wrong for your company's information and analysis needs.

One thing to bear in mind is that databases tend to grow, and the better the database, the bigger it tends to get as more and more users rely on it. In addition, it won't take long for your application developers to begin to expand upon the core data, especially with today's requirements to make as much data as possible available on the Web.

Requirements Gathering and Analysis

The requirements-gathering stage is the first step in designing a new database. You must first find out, through an iterative process, the requirements of the organization for the database. The preliminary stage of the database life cycle addresses questions of this nature:

- Why is this new database necessary?
- What objective is this database going to help achieve?
- What current systems is the database going to replace?
- What systems (if any) will the database have to interact with?
- Who are the target users of the database?

This stage should yield a clear idea of the expectations of all concerned parties regarding the new system to be supported by the yet-to-be-created database. Requirements analysis for the firm involves extensive interviewing of users and management. The design team should also evaluate both the data that will go into the database and the expected output of the database.

It's common practice to use graphical representations of the application systems to better understand the flow of data through the system. Data-flow diagrams (DFDs) or process models are commonly used at this stage to capture the data processes within and outside the application.

Let's use an educational institution as an example to identify the processes. Say that a college has four processes: Manage Student Records, Manage Course Information, Manage Enrollment, and Manage Class Schedules. The Manage Student Records process maintains all student records, and it updates that information as necessary. The Manage Course Information process takes care of collecting all future course information from the various departments of the college. It is also responsible for making changes in the course list when departments add or drop courses for any reason.

The Manage Enrollment process is more complex than others because it receives inputs from several processes. For example, when a student attempts to enroll in a new course, the Manage Enrollment process needs to first verify from the Manage Student Records process whether the student is in good standing. Next, it has to find out from the Manage Course Information process whether the course is indeed being offered. Then the Manage Enrollment process will enter this new student and course information in its part of the data flow. Only after the successful completion of all these processes can the Manage Class Schedules process send the new schedule out to the student.

As complex as the brief description of data flows and business processes sounds, the use of sophisticated tools such as ERWin Data Modeler or PowerDesigner makes it easy to come up with fancy DFDs and process models with a minimum of frustration. You can find a list of data modeling tools, including all the popular ones as well as some free ones, at http://www.databaseanswers.com/modelling_tools.htm.

Logical Database Design

Database design is both an art and a science. The science part comes in the form of adherence to certain rules and conditions, such as normalization (more about this later in the chapter). Database design is also an art, because you need to model relationships using your understanding of the real-world functioning of the organization.

You can formally define *logical database design* as the process of creating a model of the real world for the database, independent of an actual database system or other physical considerations. Accuracy and completeness are the keys to this activity. One of the best things about this stage is that it's easy to take a draft design, throw it away, and start again, or simply amend it. It's a whole lot easier to tinker at the design stage than to deal with the production headaches of an already implemented database that isn't designed well.

The logical design stage is sometimes broken up into a conceptual part and a logical part, but that's merely a distinction based on nomenclature. The conceptual database design is usually a precursor for the logical design phase and involves the modeling of the information without reference to any underlying data model. The logical design phase explicitly uses a specific data model, like the relational data model, for example—you focus on the logical relationships involved in your conceptual design at this stage. Logical design involves conceptually modeling the database and ensuring that data in the tables passes integrity checks and isn't redundant. To satisfy these requirements, you need to implement data normalization principles, as you'll see shortly.

Entity-relationship modeling (ER modeling) is a widely used methodology for logically representing and analyzing the components of the business system, and it is commonly used to model the enterprise after the requirements analysis is completed. The entity-relationship models are easy to construct, and their graphical emphasis makes them very easy to understand. However, you can't build a real-life RDBMS using the entity-relationship model of an enterprise. ER modeling's utility lies in *designing* databases, not *implementing* databases. ER modeling can't form the basis of a high-level data-manipulation language like SQL, so the model that designers build using the ER modeling approach is translated to the relational model for implementation. By converting the abstract entity-relationship design into a relational database schema, the relational model helps convert the entity-relationship design into a relational DBMS.

Entity-Relationship Modeling

Before you can proceed to actually create databases, you need to conceptually model the organization's information system so you can easily see the interrelationships among the various components of the system. Data models are simple representations of complex real-world data structures, and the models help you depict not only the data structures, but also the relationships among the components and any constraints that exist. Conceptual modeling of the enterprise leads to clear indications regarding the tables to be built later on and the relationships that should exist among those tables. ER modeling involves the creation of valid models of the business, using standard entity-relationship diagrams (ERDs). Note that the conceptual model is always independent of both software and hardware considerations.

ER modeling was originally proposed by Peter Chen in 1976, and it is now the most widely used technique for database design. (You can download Chen's original proposal document as a PDF file at http://citeseer.ist.psu.edu/519283.html.) Nevertheless, there are several design methodologies other than ER modeling available for you to use. For several years, researchers have struggled to model the real world more realistically by using *semantic data models*, which try to go beyond the traditional ER modeling methodology.

■**Note** The World Wide Web Consortium (W3C) is leading a collaborative effort called the Semantic Web, which provides a common framework to share data and reuse it across applications as well as community boundaries. The Semantic Web is based on the Resource Description Framework (RDF), which allows it to use common formats for integrating data drawn from diverse sources. The Semantic Web also is a unified language that helps you record how data relates to real-world objects. The general idea is to try to bring some meaning to the massive amount of data and information available. Information on the Web is designed for and presented to humans, but on the Semantic Web, data and information will be designed so that it can be understood and manipulated by computers as well as humans. On the Semantic Web, you will use software agents to go off in search of data and information on your behalf. Please go to http://www.w3.org/2001/sw/ for more about the Semantic Web initiative. An excellent article on this exciting approach is "The Semantic Web," by Tim Berners-Lee, James Hendler, and Ora Lassila, available at http://www.scientificamerican.com/article.cfm?articleID=00048144-10D2-1C70-84A9809EC588EF21&catID=2.

You can use the conceptual model of your organization as a communications tool to facilitate cooperative work among your database designers, application programmers, and end users. Good conceptual models can help resolve the differing conceptions of data among these groups. Conceptual models help define the constraints that your organization imposes on the data and help clarify data processing needs, thus aiding in the creation of sound databases.

ER modeling views all objects of the business area being modeled as *entities* that have certain attributes. An entity is anything of interest to the system that exists in the business world. An entity can be real (for example, a student) or it can be conceptual (a student enrollment, which does not actually exist until the entity's student and course are combined when the student signs up for a particular course). Conceptual entities are generally the hardest to discover, but ER modeling, as you shall see, assists in their discovery.

Attributes of entities are simply properties of the entities that are of interest to you. For example, a student entity may have attributes such as Student ID, Address, Phone Number, and so on.

ER modeling further describes the *relationships* among these business entities. Relationships describe how the different entities are connected (or related) to one another. For example, an employee is an entity that possesses attributes such as Name and Address, and he or she is, or may be, related to another entity in the model called Department through the fact that the employee *works* in that department. In this case, "works" is the relationship between the employee and the department.

Types of Relationships

You can depict two or more entities in a relationship, and depending on the number of entities, you may describe the degree of relationship as binary, ternary, quaternary, etc. The most common degree of relationship in real life cases is binary, so let's examine a binary relationship in more detail.

The *cardinality of* a relationship indicates how many instances of one entity can be related to an instance of another entity. Just because a binary relationship reflects a relationship between two entities doesn't mean that there is always a one-to-one relationship between them—cardinality in ER modeling expresses the number of occurrences of one entity in relation to another entity. Entity relationships can be one-to-one, one-to-many, many-to-many, or some other type. The most common relationships are the following (assume there are two entities, *A* and *B*):

- *One-to-many (1:M) relationship*: In this case, each instance of an entity *A* is related to several members of another entity, *B*. For example, an entity called Customer can check out many books from a library, but one and only one Customer can borrow each book at a time. Thus, the entity Customer and the entity Book have a one-to-many relationship. Of course, the relationship may not exist if you have a Customer who has not yet borrowed a Book. So the relation is actually "one Customer *may* borrow none, one, or many Books."

- *One-to-one (1:1) relationship*: This relationship is a situation where only one instance of either entity can be related to an instance of the other entity. For example, a person could have only one legal social security number (SSN), and each SSN should refer to just one person.

- *Many-to-many (M:M) relationship*: In this situation, each instance of entity *A* is related to one or more instances of entity *B*, and an instance of entity *B* is related to one or more instances of entity *A*. As an example, let's take an entity called Movie Star and an entity called Movie. Each Movie Star can star in several Movies, and each Movie may have several Movie Stars. In real life, a many-to-many relationship is usually broken down into a simpler one-to-many relationship, which happens to be the predominant form of "cardinality" in the relationships among entities.

Accurately determining cardinalities of relationships is the key to a well-designed relational database. Duplicated data, redundancy, and data anomalies are some of the problems that arise when you don't model relationship cardinalities correctly.

Candidate Keys and Unique Identifiers

Candidate keys are those attributes that can uniquely identify a row in a table, and a table can have more than one candidate key. For example, it's fairly common for an employee table to have both a uniquely generated sequence number as well as another identifier, like an employee number (or social security number). (Of course, any whole row, itself, could serve as a candidate key, because by definition a relational model can't have any duplicate tuples. However, a whole row is rarely used as the key, since the point of a key is to easily access the row.)

The *primary key* is the candidate key that's chosen to uniquely identify each row in a table. You should always strive to select a key based on a single attribute rather than on multiple attributes, for simplicity and efficiency.

Keys are vital when you come to the point of physically building the entity-relationship models. A *natural* primary key is one that consists of data items or entity attributes. Almost all modern relational databases, including Oracle databases, also offer simple system numbers or sequenced numbers that are generated and maintained by the RDBMS as an alternative to a natural primary key (such as a sequence number to identify orders). Such keys are often referred to as *surrogate* or *artificial* primary keys.

Whatever method you choose—a natural key or a surrogate key—certain rules apply:

- The primary key value must be unique.
- The primary key can't be null (blank).
- The primary key can't be changed (it must remain stable over the life of the entity).
- The primary key must be as concise as possible.

■Note Later in this chapter, I provide some guidelines about selecting keys (primary keys in particular).

Step-by-Step: Building an Entity-Relationship Diagram

You can build logical diagrams by using tools such as the Oracle Designer, or the Oracle Warehouse Builder if you are building a data warehouse. If you wish, you can create rudimentary logical diagrams with nothing more than a pencil and paper. In this section, you'll build a simple entity-relationship diagram describing a university, using entities called Student, Class, and Professor. You'll use a rectangle to depict an entity, and a diamond shape to show relationships (as is common practice), although you could use different notations.

Let's assume the following relationship between two entities, Student and Class:

- A Student can enroll in one or more Classes.

- A Class has one or more Students enrolled.

Data modeling starts out easy and then rapidly gets complex as you begin to ask questions and discover the various rules and constraints in force on the data.

Here are the steps you need to follow to create the entity-relationship diagram:

1. Define your entities—Student, Class, and Professor.

2. Draw the entities using a rectangle to represent each one.

3. For each of the entities in turn, look at its relationship with the others. It doesn't matter which entity you begin with. For example, look at the Student and the Professor. Is there a relationship between these entities? Well, a Professor teaches a class, and a student attends one or more classes, so at first glance there is a relationship between these entities. But in this case it is an indirect relationship via the Class entity.

4. Examine the Student and Class entities. Is there a relationship? Yes, a Student may attend one or more Classes. One or more Students may attend a Class. This is a many-to-many relationship.

5. Now look at the Class and Professor entities. One Professor teaches each Class and each Professor can teach many Classes. However, if a Professor is absent (due to illness, for example), do you need to record the fact that a different Professor taught his or her Class on that occasion? What if two Professors teach the same Class? Do you need to record that information? As a modeler, you need to address all questions of this nature so that your model is realistic and will serve you well.

6. Assign the following attributes to the various entities:

   - *Student*: Student ID, First Name, Last Name, Address, Year

   - *Professor*: Staff ID, Social Security Number, First Name, Last Name, Office Address, Phone Number

   - *Class*: Class ID, Classroom, Textbook, Credit Hours, Class Fee

Look at the Textbook attribute in the Class entity. You can use this attribute to illustrate an important point. As the entity stands right now, you could assign only one Textbook per Class. This could be the case, depending on the business rules involved, but what do you do if you need to record the fact that there are several textbooks recommended for each Class? The current model would not permit you to do this unless you stored multiple data items in a single field. To resolve this, you could add a new entity called Textbooks, which could then be related to the Class entity. This way, you could associate many different Textbooks with each Class.

7. The cardinality of a relationship, as you saw earlier, dictates whether a relationship is one-to-one, one-to-many, many-to-many, or something else. Define the cardinality of the system at this point. Assign the one-to-many or many-to-one cardinality indicators. Break down any many-to-many relationships to simpler relationships (such as two one-to-many relationships). For example:

    • A Student can enroll in one or more Classes.

    • Each Class can have many Students enrolled.

    This is a many-to-many relationship, which you must break down by using a link table. In this case, the link table turns out to be an entity in its own right. This new entity contains the individual enrollment record for each Class attended by a single Student.

8. Translate the relationships into an actual entity-relationship diagram by using rectangles for entities, diamonds for relationships, and ovals for the attributes of the entities.

Your entity-relationship diagram should be able to address all the functional requirements of the database in order for it to be adopted as a valid model. In the preceding example, I used some straightforward relationships among the various entities, but in real life, you may encounter more complex relationships like the *recursive* relationship, when data within an entity has a relationship to itself. For example, in a Staff table, a member of the staff may report to a higher level member of the staff. If this is the case, then the table is said to have a recursive relationship with itself.

I have barely scratched the surface of ER modeling, which is an art in itself—one at which you will improve with practice. As with anything else, the more time you spend actually practicing data modeling, the more proficient you will get at it.

■**Tip** The Internet is a great source for both simple and complex case studies you can use to try out your modeling skills. You can find anything from simple order processing databases to full-fledged personnel systems on the Web. One of the best resources I've found is the web sites of major universities. Find the descriptions of computer science courses and pay special attention to the contents of database design courses, many of which have tutorials on creating entity-relationship diagrams.

Normalization

Normalization is the procedure through which you break down and simplify the relations (tables) in a database to achieve efficiency in retrieving and maintaining data. The most common reason for normalizing table data is to avoid redundancy, which reduces data storage requirements and leads to more efficient queries. Another reason to normalize data is to avoid data anomalies.

Why Normalize?

You've probably heard discussions about normalization that range from treating it like the Holy Grail to viewing it as a feature that adversely affects performance. What is it about normalization that gets people going so? You can put all your data somewhere in a table, and as long as you can write SQL code to retrieve the necessary data, and you have a good RDBMS running on a machine with plenty of fast processors, you shouldn't have a slow-performing database, right? The truth is that poorly designed relations and tables in a database can have serious effects, not only on the efficacy of your database, but also on the validity of the data itself.

Let's look at an example of an ordering system in a warehouse. Imagine a simple table with each customer's information contained in a single tuple or row. What happens if customer *A* has 1,000 transactions and customer *B* has only one or two transactions? Either customer *A*'s transactions will not all fit in the row, or customer *B*'s row will be mostly empty. Either you will not be able to cater to the customer, or you will waste a tremendous amount of space in the database. Simple queries turn into terrible resource wasters under this design.

You can try another variation on the previous design by creating a much more compact table by allowing repeatable values of the attributes. That is, for each transaction, each customer's complete information would be repeated. Now you have just traded one set of problems for another. If customer *A*'s information changes, each of that customer's rows in the table would need to be updated. For such repeated groups, when you perform updates, you have to make sure to update all occurrences of the particular customer's data, or you will end up with an inconsistent set of data.

Data Anomalies

You can see on an intuitive level that designing without a solid design strategy, based on sound mathematical principles, will lead to several problems. Although it is easy to see the inefficiency involved in the unnecessary consumption of storage space and longer query-execution times, other, more serious problems occur with off-the-cuff design of tables in a database—these are the so-called data anomaly problems.

Three types of data anomalies can result from improperly designed databases:

- *The update anomaly*: In this well-known anomaly, you could fail to update all the occurrences of a certain attribute because of the repeating values problem.

- *The insertion anomaly*: In this anomaly, you are prevented from inserting certain data because you are missing other pieces of information. For example, you cannot insert a customer's data because that customer has not bought a product from your warehouse yet.

- *The deletion anomaly*: In this anomaly, you could end up losing data inadvertently because you are trying to remove some duplicate attributes from a customer's data.

■**Note** The debate between database developers and designers continues over denormalization. Many believe it's okay to break almost all design rules and denormalize for performance gains. However, others believe that this isn't correct and that the act of denormalization reduces the integrity of the database by removing the controls that lie at the heart of RDBMS design.

The Normal Forms

Before you embark on the normalization process, it's a good idea to understand the concept of *functional dependence*, which is defined as follows:

> *Given a relation (table) R, a set of attributes, B, is functionally dependent on attribute A if at any given time each value of attribute A is associated with a given value of B.*

In simple terms, functional dependency is denoted symbolically as A ➤ B (meaning that entity A determines the value of entity B), and it turns out to be crucial in understanding the normalization process.

Normalization is nothing more than the simplification of tables into progressively simpler forms to get rid of undesirable properties, such as data anomalies and data redundancy, without sacrificing any information in the process. E. F. Codd laid out the normalization requirements succinctly by requiring the elimination of nonsimple domains and then the removal of partial and indirect dependencies. As the tables are taken through simpler *normal forms*, the preceding problems are eliminated.

You can take a table through several levels of simplification, called the first normal form (1NF), second normal form (2NF), third normal form (3NF), Boyce-Codd normal form (BCNF), fourth normal form (4NF), and fifth normal form (5NF). Each successively higher stage of the normalization process eliminates a particular type of undesirable dependency that you saw earlier.

Non-Normalized Data

In this and the following sections, I'll show you a set of data that is non-normalized and then show you how you can make it conform to various normal forms.

In the initial list of data shown in Table 2-1, each employee's information is accompanied by the skills that the employee has. Some employees may have a single skill, and some may have several. In order to answer a simple question, such as "Does John Thomas have accounting skills?" you have to first find John Thomas's record and then scan the list of skills associated with that employee. Obviously, this is inefficient and leads to the maintenance of redundant data.

Table 2-1. *Non-Normalized Table*

Employee Number
Employee Name
Department Number
Department Name
Department Location
Skill ID
Skill Name
Skill Level

First Normal Form (1NF)

A table is said to be in 1NF if it doesn't contain any repeating groups; that is, no column should have multiple values for any given row. This definition, of course, implies that a non-normalized table contains one or more repeating groups. A repeating group occurs when there are multiple values for a single occurrence of an attribute in a table.

To summarize, a table (relation) is in 1NF if

1. There are no duplicated rows in the table.

2. Each cell is single-valued (that is, there are no repeating groups or arrays).

3. Entries in a column (attribute, field) are of the same kind.

■**Note** The order of the rows and columns doesn't matter. The requirement that there be no duplicated rows in the table means that the table has a key (on one column or a combination of columns).

Thus, to put your tables in 1NF, you must first eliminate repeating groups, which can generally be identified by multiple values being stored at the intersection of a row and column. For example, if an employee has several skills, you might have to specify multiple values in the Skill ID column for that employee. Or you may be using several rows for the same employee, one for each skill. Neither is an attractive option. The way to simplify this table into a 1NF table is to break it down so there are only single, atomic values for each attribute or column. Create a separate table for each set of related attributes, and give each table a primary key.

In our example, moving the skills attribute into a separate table helps considerably. Separating the repeating groups of skills from the employee data results in two tables in first normal form. The Employee Number in the Skills table matches the primary key in the Employees table, providing a foreign key for relating the two tables with a join operation (see Tables 2-2 and 2-3).

Table 2-2. *Employees Table in First Normal Form*

Employee Number
Employee Name
Department Name
Department Location

Table 2-3. *Skills Table in First Normal Form*

Employee Number
Skill ID
Skill Name
Skill Level

Now we can answer our question about whether John Thomas has accounting skills with a direct retrieval: look to see if John Thomas's Employee Number and the Skill ID for accounting appear together in the Skills table. Note that in the Skills table, the primary key is a multivalued, or *composite*, key, consisting of both Employee Number and Skill ID.

Second Normal Form (2NF)

A table is said to be in 2NF if it is already in 1NF and every non-key attribute is fully functionally dependent on the primary key. Since a partial dependency occurs when a non-key attribute is dependent on only a part of the (composite) key, the definition of 2NF is sometimes phrased as follows:

A table is in 2NF if it is in 1NF and it has no partial dependencies.

First, let's look at a case where a table is in 1NF but not in 2NF. Table 2-4 satisfies 1NF, since it contains no repeating groups. However, there is redundancy in the data, since the same Skill Name (accounting, for example) appears for every employee who possesses that skill. Just the Skill ID column by itself will suffice to indicate the skill in this table. Recall from the previous section that in the Skills table the primary key is a multivalued (composite) key that consists of both Employee Number and Skill ID. However, Skill Name depends on only a part of the composite key (the Skill ID).

Table 2-4. *Table in 1NF but Not in 2NF*

Employee Number	Skill ID	Skill Name	Skill Level
22	130	Accounting	9
23	140	Marketing	9
24	130	Accounting	7

In the Skills table in the previous section, the primary key is made up of the Employee Number and the Skill ID. This makes sense for the Skill Level attribute, since it'll be different for every employee-skill combination. But the Skill Name depends only on the Skill ID. A partial dependency is said to exist when a column depends on only a part of the primary key. Skill Name reflects a partial dependency, because you can identify it with just the Skill ID, which is only a part of the primary key—Skill Name doesn't depend on the Employee Number, which is the other part of the primary key. Therefore, the same Skill Name will appear redundantly every time its associated Skill ID appears in the Skills table. This redundancy would lead to update and delete anomalies.

For example, suppose you want to reclassify a skill by giving it a different Skill ID. In this case, you have the headache of ensuring that you make the change for every employee who has this skill. If you miss some of the employees, you'll end up with several employees having the same skill under different IDs—this is an *update anomaly*. If only one employee has a certain skill, and this employee happens to leave the organization, that employee's data will be removed from the database, and the skill will disappear entirely from your database—this is a *delete anomaly*.

To avoid problems such as these, you must put your tables in 2NF. Break down the table into simpler versions to get rid of any partial key dependencies. That is, all non-key attributes should be fully functionally dependent on the primary key. In order to do this, you must separate the attributes that depend on both parts of the key from those that depend only on the Skill ID. This results in two tables: the Skills table, which lists the name for each Skill ID, and the Employee Skills table, which lists the skills actually learned by each employee (see Tables 2-5 and 2-6). In the Employee Skills table, the Skill Level attribute is clearly dependent on both parts of the key, since the attribute is based not only on which particular skill is being referred to, but also on the particular employee's level in that skill.

Table 2-5. *Skills Table in Second Normal Form*

Skill ID
Skill Name

Table 2-6. *Employee Skills Table in Second Normal Form*

Employee Number
Skill ID
Skill Level

Now skills can exist in your database without any corresponding employees having that skill, and you can reclassify a skill in a single operation—just look up the Skill ID in the Skills table and change its name. You can also delete any information about employees without losing information about the skills themselves.

Third Normal Form (3NF)

A table is said to be in 3NF if it is already in 2NF and every non-key attribute is fully and *directly* dependent on the primary key. To enforce 3NF, you must eliminate the columns that aren't dependent on the key. If an attribute doesn't contribute to a description of the key, remove it to a separate table.

The Employees table (Table 2-2) satisfies 1NF, since it contains no repeating groups. It satisfies 2NF, since it doesn't have a composite key. However, the table's key is Employee Number, and you can see that the Department Name and Department Location columns aren't dependent on the Employee Number (the primary key for the table)—they are dependent on Department Number column values. To achieve 3NF, you must now move the department information into a separate table. You can make Department Number the key for your new Departments table.

The motivation for the decomposition of the Employees table is straightforward—you want to avoid delete and update anomalies. Suppose there is no employee hired for a new department yet. Under the present setup, you can't have a record of the department in the Employees table. Table 2-7 shows your tables in the third normal form.

Table 2-7. *Tables in the Third Normal Form*

Employees Table	Departments Table	Skills Table	Employee Skills Table
Employee Number	Department Number	Skill ID	Employee Number
Employee Name	Department Name	Skill Name	Skill ID
Department Number	Department Location		Skill Level

If all of the preceding information seems a bit confusing to you initially, don't lose heart. The following is an easier way to remember and understand this whole process of putting a relation in 3NF:

A relation is said to be in the third normal form if all the non-key attributes are fully dependent on the primary key, the whole primary key, and nothing but the primary key.

Although there are more advanced forms of normalization, it is commonly accepted that normalization up to the 3NF is adequate for most business needs. For completeness, though, the other popular normal forms are outlined briefly in the next sections.

Boyce-Codd Normal Form (BCNF)

The Boyce-Codd normal form (BCNF) is based on the functional dependencies that exist in the relation. The BCNF is based on candidate keys.

A relation is said to be in BCNF if, and only if, every determinant is a primary key.

BCNF is a more strongly defined relationship than the 3NF. BCNF requires that if A determines B, then A must be a candidate key.

Fourth Normal Form (4NF)

The 4NF is designed to take care of a special type of dependency called the *multivalued dependency*. A multivalued dependency exists among attributes X, Y, and Z if X determines more than one value of both Y and Z, and the values of Y and Z are independent of each other.

> *A relationship is defined as being in the 4NF if it is in the BCNF and contains no nontrivial, multivalued dependencies.*

Fifth Normal Form (5NF)

When a relation is decomposed into several relations, and then the subrelations are joined back again, you are not supposed to lose any tuples. This property is defined as a *lossless-join dependency*.

> *5NF is defined as a relation that has no join dependency.*

Even if you don't know much about the concept of normalizing data, by following a set of simple rules, and with the help of ER modeling tools, you can design sound databases.

ER Modeling Tools

Although you can design the basics of a system without the help of any tools per se, for most real-world systems it is better to use a modeling and designing tool. There are several excellent tools that can help you in your data-modeling efforts. Oracle provides the Oracle Designer as part of the Oracle Developer Suite. ERWin, PowerDesigner, and ER/Studio (from Embarcadero Technologies) are well-known ER modeling tools. Quest Software (http://www.quest.com/) produces many useful tools, including the well-known TOAD software, both for Oracle developers and DBAs.

Physical Database Design

After you finalize the logical model, you can get down to designing the database itself. You first review the logical data model and decide which data elements you'll need for your physical database. Next, you create a first-cut physical data model from your logical data model using a tool such as ERWin Data Modeler or Oracle Designer. In the physical database design stage, your concern is about specifying how you store the data and what methods you'll use to access the data. You can work on tuning this initial physical model for better performance later on. Remember that physical database design is based on a specific DBMS (for example, Oracle Database 11*g*).

DENORMALIZATION

Should you always work toward normalizing all your tables to reduce redundancy and avoid data anomalies? Well, theoretically yes, but in reality you don't always have to be obsessed with the normalization process. When it comes to actual practice, you'll find that larger databases can easily deal with redundancy. In fact, the normalization process can lead to inefficient query processing in very large databases, such as data warehouses, because there will be more tables that need to be joined in order to retrieve information. Also, operations such as updates take more time when you have a completely normalized table structure. Thus, you end up having to decide between potential data anomalies and performance criteria.

The purpose of physical database design is to *implement* your logical design. Following are some of the key tasks in the physical design stage:

- Translating the logical database model to fit your specific DBMS
- Choosing the storage setup with an eye on maximizing efficiency
- Creating tables (by transforming entities into tables) and the columns for each of the tables
- Creating primary keys, foreign keys, and constraints (thus formalizing the relationships among the objects)

Transforming Entities and Relationships

In the first stage of the physical design process, you transform the entity-relationship diagrams into relational tables. You create the tables based on the different groups or types of information that you have in the database. For example, you may create a table called People to hold information about the members of an organization, a table called Payments to track membership payments, and so on.

What if you want to ensure that the data in your tables is unique, which is a basic assumption in most cases? How about establishing relationships among tables that hold related information? You can use primary keys and foreign keys to ensure uniqueness and valid relationships in your database. You'll examine these two types of keys in detail in the following sections.

Primary Keys

A *primary key* is a column or a combination of columns that uniquely identifies each record (or row) in a table. In tables that have records for different people, it is common to use social security numbers as primary keys because it's obvious that every person has a unique social security number. If there is no appropriate column you can choose as a primary key, you can use system-generated numbers to uniquely identify your rows. A primary key must be unique and present in every row of the table to maintain the validity of the data.

You must select the primary keys from among the list of candidate keys for all the tables in your database. If you are using software to model the data, it is likely that you will already have defined and created all the keys for each entity. The application team determines the best candidates for the primary keys.

Foreign Keys

Suppose you have two tables, Employees and Departments, with the simple requirement that every employee must be a member of a department. The way to ensure this is to check that all employees have a Department column in the Employees table. Let's say the Departments table has a primary key named Department ID—you need to have this primary key column in the Employees table. Remember that the Employees table will have its own primary key, such as SSN. However, the values of the Department ID column in the Employees table must all be present in the Departments table.

This Department ID column in the Employees table is the primary key in the Departments table, and you refer to it as a *foreign key* in the Employees table. Foreign keys ensure that only valid data is entered in your tables.

Designing Different Types of Tables

You should determine which of your tables are going to be your main data tables and which will be your lookup tables. A *lookup table* generally contains static data, such as the Departments table discussed in the previous section. Usually when you have a foreign key in a table, the table from which the foreign key comes will be your lookup table.

One of the ways to ensure good performance later on is to spend a lot of time at the design stage thinking about how your users are going to use the database. For example, whereas normalization may be a technically correct way to design a database, it may require reading more tables for a single query. The more tables you need to join for any query, the higher the CPU and memory usage, which may hurt database performance.

If you perform the appropriate amount of due diligence at the design stage, you can depict your organization's process flow accurately while you design your tables. When you consider the cost and frustration involved in tuning poorly written SQL later on, it's clear that it's worth putting some effort into carefully designing tables and fields.

Table Structures and Naming Conventions

The table structures and naming conventions for your database should be finalized during the physical design stage. However, in many organizations, these elements are predetermined and you may need to use a standard convention. It is important to give tables short, meaningful names—this will save you a lot of grief later when you need to maintain the tables.

Column Specifications and Choosing Data Types

You should now have a good idea about the exact nature of the columns in all your tables. You should also now determine which data types you'll use for your column specifications. For example, you need to specify whether the data in each column is going to be integers, characters, or something else.

The nature of your application will dictate the data types. For example, if you're creating a hospital visitor's database, the number of visitors will always be an integer rather than a floating-point number, since you can't have a person visiting a hospital 2.5 times a year.

Business Rules and Data Integrity

Good database design should adhere faithfully to the company's business rules. Your data design must satisfy any business rules that will be enforced by your application, and incorporating these rules into the design will help you model information that is usually not captured by database models.

When you enforce data integrity, you are essentially ensuring that the data in the tables is correct, and that it doesn't involve any inconsistencies, which can occur either during the data entry process itself, or later, through modifications. The design should also ensure data integrity through the proper use of constraints provided by the RDBMS. The entity-relationship model provides you with an opportunity to note necessary constraints and plan ahead.

The following four methods are commonly used to enforce data integrity and business rules in the entity-relationship model:

- You can use the primary keys to enforce uniqueness of data in the tables. Note that the primary key values should be *unique* as well as *non-null*. The primary key should also not change its value over the life of the entity instance.

- You can use foreign keys to enforce referential integrity, thus guaranteeing the integrity and consistency of data. *Referential integrity* refers to maintaining correct dependency relationships between two tables. *Declarative referential integrity* refers to ensuring data integrity by defining the relationship between two different tables.

- You can ensure the validity and meaningfulness of data by enforcing domain constraints, such as check constraints. *Domain constraints* ensure valid values for certain entities. For example, in a banking-related database, you could have a constraint that states that the withdrawal amount in any transaction is always less than or equal to the total balance of the account holder.

- You can use *database triggers,* which will perform certain operations automatically when predetermined actions occur, to ensure the validity of data.

A fifth way to enforce business rules is programmatically, through the use of built-in database constraints. For example, a simple line of code could be used to require that an insert actually complete a data field, rather than adding a not-null constraint on the column. You'll learn details about the various types of constraints in an Oracle database in Chapter 5.

Implementing the Physical Design

Implementation of the physical design involves creating the new database and allocating proper space for it. It also involves creating all the tables, indexes, and stored program code (such as triggers, procedures, and packages) to be stored on the server.

Database Sizing and Database Storage

You need to estimate the size of your tables, indexes, and other database objects at this stage so you can allocate the proper space for them. You can follow some basic rules of thumb or use some fairly elaborate sizing algorithms to size your database.

You also have to choose the type of storage. Although most systems today are based on hard disks, you have several choices to make with regard to disk configuration and other issues, all of which could have a significant impact on the database's performance down the road. Chapter 3 discusses details of disk configuration and related issues.

Implementing Database Security

Before you actually implement your new system, you need to make sure you have a security policy in place. There are several possible layers and levels of security, and you should ultimately ensure that the system is indeed secure at all these levels.

Normally, you need to worry about security at the system and network levels, and you will usually entrust the system and network administrators with this type of security. You also need to ensure security at the database level, which includes locking up passwords and so forth. Finally, in consultation with the application designers, you also have to come up with the right application security scheme. This involves controlling the privileges and roles of the users of the database. Chapter 12 discusses user management and database security in detail.

Moving to the New System

During this final implementation stage, you establish exact timings for the actual switch to the new business system. You may be replacing an older system, or you may be implementing a brand-new business system.

In either case, you need a checklist of the detailed steps to be undertaken to ensure a smooth transition to the new system. This checklist should also include fallback options if things don't go quite as planned. Chapter 16 discusses recovery techniques that help you restore an older database in case you need to scrap the new one for some reason. You can also run ad hoc queries at this stage to fine-tune your system and find out where any bottlenecks lie.

Reverse-Engineering a Database

This chapter has provided you with an introduction to the art of database design and normalization, and this information will help you when you are designing and implementing a database from scratch. However, what do you do when you walk into a company to manage its databases and you have no idea of the underlying physical data model or entity-relationship diagrams? Not to worry; you can use any of the data-modeling tools discussed earlier in the chapter to reverse-engineer the underlying database model.

The process of generating a logical model from an actual physical database is called *reverse engineering*. By using the reverse-engineering feature in a database design tool, you can quickly generate the physical model or the entity-relationship model of your database. Reverse-engineering a database can help you understand the underlying model. It can also serve to provide documentation that may be missing in situations where the DBA or the lead developer has left and nobody can find the entity-relationship diagram.

Reverse-engineering diagrams can be crucial in tracking the foreign key relationships in the data model. Developers can also make good use of entity-relationship diagrams when making improvements to the application.

Object-Relational and Object Databases

This chapter has dealt with the relational database model, where all the data is stored in the form of tables. Relational databases have been accepted as the superior model for storing most kinds of "simple" data, such as ordinary accounting data. For modeling complex data relationships, however, the object database management system (ODBMS) has been put forward as being more appropriate. ODBMSs are still not at the point where they can seriously compete with traditional relational databases.

The relational model and the object model can be seen as two different extremes in data modeling, and a newer extension of the relational model has come forth to bridge the gap between the two. This new model is the object-relational database management system, and Oracle has adopted this ORDBMS model since the Oracle8 version of its server software. Oracle defines the 11g version of its database server as an ORDBMS.

The following sections compare and contrast the three database management system categories: relational, object, and object-relational.

The Relational Model

The relational model has several limitations. One of its biggest problems is its limited capability to represent real-world entities, which are much more complex than what can be represented in tuples and relations. The model is especially weak when it comes to distinguishing among different kinds of relationships between entities. You can't represent and manipulate complex data in traditional relational databases—the set of operations you can perform in relational models isn't adequate for many real-world applications that include objects with non-numerical attributes.

The limitations of the traditional relational model in modeling several real-world entities led to research into semantic data models and the so-called extended relational data models. Two data models now compete for the mantle of successor to the relational model: the object-oriented data model and the object-relational data model. Databases based on the first model are called object-oriented database management systems, or OODBMSs, and databases based on the second model are called object-relational database management systems.

The Object Model

Object (or object-oriented) databases are based primarily on object-oriented programming languages such as C++, Java, and Smalltalk. ODBMSs are created by combining database capabilities with the functionality of object-oriented programming languages. In this sense, you can view an ODBMS as an extension of the object-oriented language with data-concurrency and data-recovery capabilities added on to it. The object-oriented language is used both for application development and data storage. Object-oriented languages are used to create objects, which are the basic components of the ODBMS.

Several terms have special meanings in object-oriented environments:

- *Objects* are defined as entities containing the attributes of a real-world object and its associated actions.
- *Properties* are the various attributes of an object.
- *Methods* are functions in the object world, and they define the behavior of the object.
- Objects communicate by means of *messages*.
- A *class* is a grouping of objects that have the same attributes.
- *Instances* are the actual incarnations of objects in the class.
- Classes can be divided into *subclasses*, with the parent class being called the *superclass*.

The following three concepts are fundamental to understanding object-oriented systems:

- *Polymorphism*: Polymorphism is the ability of objects to react differently when presented with different sets of information (in the form of *parameters*). Object-oriented languages allow different methods to be run depending on the set of parameters that you specify. In a non-object-oriented programming language, the only way to complete two different tasks is to have two functions with different names.
- *Encapsulation*: This term refers to objects including information about both what they are (their properties) and what they can do (their methods). Thus, code and data are packaged together. For example, if a person were an object in the model and there were a method to calculate the person's annual salary, the code (or method) for calculating the salary would be "encapsulated" with the instance object, which is the person.
- *Inheritance*: Inheritance allows one class to extend another—to *inherit* some characteristics from another class and to add more characteristics of its own. For example, a Student object could be a subclass of a Person class.

The Object-Relational Model

Although pure object methodology is appealing, in actual practice it is quite difficult to implement. ORDBMSs strive to combine the best that relational models have to offer while adding as much of the object-oriented methodology as possible. Oracle says that its ORDBMS model seeks to put complex business data in the basic relational database; the fundamental tabular form of the relational model is retained. The basis for Oracle's (and other vendors') ORDBMS offerings is the SQL standard named ANSI/ISO/IEC 9075:2003 (also called the SQL:2003 standard).

The ORDBMS is somewhat of a hybrid between the traditional relational and the pure object-oriented databases. It doesn't quite achieve the implementation of all the key precepts of an object-oriented database, such as encapsulation. The ORDBMS is really the relational model with a few object-oriented features added on. You can choose to ignore the object-oriented features completely and use the database as a purely traditional relational database. All the database information is still in the form of tables.

ORDBMSs mainly depend on abstract types to bring object-oriented methodology to relational databases. Objects are simplified abstractions of real-world objects, and they encompass both the structure of the data and the methods of operating on data. An object type consists of its name, attributes, and methods, which can be stored within the database or outside of it. Two more object-oriented features, type inheritance and polymorphism, are also enabled in the new Oracle Database 11*g* ORDBMS.

Certain database vendors have maintained for a while now that they have really merged the relational and object-oriented databases and come up with an integral ORDBMS. This claim is motivated mostly by marketing concerns and isn't based on true technical criteria. Real object-oriented databases are still far from becoming commercially viable on a large scale. For the foreseeable future, the relational or the object-enhanced relational model (such as Oracle's ORDBMS) will hold sway as efficient, well-developed, and proven products. You can also expect more and more object-oriented features to be gradually added to databases.

There is an ongoing debate over the merits of the relational database system versus the object-oriented database system. It is accepted by all parties that relational databases do certain chores extremely well, such as those required by business applications, for which they are currently used. Object-oriented databases, though they are more realistic than relational databases, are quite difficult to implement and are many years away from being as mature and sophisticated, operationally speaking, as relational databases. Although object-oriented databases have been increasing in popularity over the years, their market share is still miniscule. The real question is whether object-oriented databases can supplant relational databases.

It seems unlikely, in the near future, that object-oriented databases can become as powerful as well-established RDBMSs in performing most business operations. It seems more practical for relational databases to be extended to make them more closely model the real world. ORDBMSs attempt to bridge the gap between the relational and pure object-oriented systems by incorporating object-oriented features such as encapsulation, inheritance, user-defined data types, and polymorphism into the relational model. Business processing involves a lot of data processing, and the new hybrid will continue to support these activities while also serving the more complex data-modeling needs. ORDBMSs seem like a smart way to progress into the object-oriented world, because their adoption doesn't involve abandoning the tremendous amount of RDBMS know-how developed over the last 25 years or so. All that knowledge can be enhanced to incorporate more of the object-oriented data model. In other words, you can get both higher operational efficiency and the benefits of realistic object type modeling by using ORDBMSs.

Oracle Database 11*g* is an ORDBMS. It evolved over the years from a traditional pure relational system to one with an increasing number of object-oriented features, such as these:

- *User-defined data types*: Oracle supports both object types and collections. Oracle provides a built-in data type called REF to model relationships between row objects belonging to the same type.

- *Methods*: Oracle implements methods in PL/SQL or Java.

- *Collection types*: The collection types include array types known as *varrays* and table types known as *nested tables*.

- *Large objects*: Oracle supports the use of binary large objects (BLOBs and character large objects (CLOBs).

Semi-Structured Data Models

The newest frontier in data models is the emphasis on "semi-structured" data models. Semi-structured data models are much more flexible than traditional relational and object-relational models. This inherent flexibility ensures a more realistic representation of the complex real-world phenomena that DBAs deal with every day. Semi-structured data modeling looks at schemas from a different point of view than the relational and other models you saw earlier in the chapter. Semi-structured data models really aren't based on any strict notions of traditional database schemas—rather, the data in these models is self-describing. This type of data model is useful mainly for document-based information systems. If you are trying to integrate data in several databases, each with its own unique schema, you'll appreciate the use of semi-structured data modeling.

The use of Extensible Markup Language (XML) is but one of the new implementations of the semi-structured data models—XML implements semi-structured data in document form. Oracle Database 11g includes excellent XML capabilities that are better than those of any other commercial database. XML uses tags to mark up documents, somewhat like the HTML pages we are all familiar with now. However, XML tags are more critical from a semantic point of view than HTML tags, which merely control the format and layout of a web page—XML tags tell the document what the contents of the document *mean*. XML documents use Document Type Definitions (DTDs) to find out what tags can be used and how.

Oracle Database 11g has powerful XML capabilities, which enable it to manage large amounts of XML data. Of course, you can use all of Oracle's features, including high performance and scalability, while using the XML data stored within the database.

■■■

## CHAPTER 3

Essential UNIX (and Linux) for the Oracle DBA

If the only thing you needed to learn about were Oracle database administration, your life would be so much easier. However, to ensure that your database performs efficiently, you'll also need to understand the operating system. In this chapter, you'll examine UNIX.

The first part of the chapter covers the most important UNIX/Linux commands for you to know. Most of the UNIX and Linux operating system commands are identical, but I'll show you the differences where they exist. You'll learn about files and directories and how to manage them, as well as UNIX processes and how to monitor them. You'll then learn how to edit files using the vi text editor and how to write shell scripts.

As an Oracle DBA, you'll need to know how to use UNIX services such as the File Transfer Protocol (FTP), which enables you to easily exchange files between computers; telnet, a program that lets you enter commands on a remote computer from a local computer; and the remote login and remote copy services. This chapter provides you with an introduction to these useful features. You'll also learn the key UNIX administrative tools for performing system backups and monitoring system performance. There's also some discussion of the basics of RAID systems and the use of the Logical Volume Manager (LVM) to manage disk systems. Toward the end of the chapter, you'll find some coverage of data storage arrays and new techniques to enhance availability and performance.

Overview of UNIX and Linux Operating Systems

The UNIX and Linux operating systems are similar in many ways, and users can transition easily from one to the other. From the DBA's point of view, there are few differences in commands and utilities when you migrate from one variant of the Linux/UNIX operating system to the other, since they all share common roots.

UNIX

UNIX became the leading operating system for commercial enterprises during the 1980s and 1990s. Although IBM mainframes still perform well for extremely large (multiterabyte and multipetrabyte) databases, most medium to large firms have moved to UNIX for its economy, versatility, power, and stability. IBM itself has made a successful transition to the new computer market, by dramatically reducing the size and cost of its mainframes. The IBM System z series can run Linux software and multiple virtual servers.

UNIX has a rich history, progressing through several versions before reaching its current popular place in the operating system market. I could spend quite a bit of time discussing the history and variants of the UNIX system, but I'll simplify the discussion by stating that, in reality, the particular UNIX system variant that a DBA uses doesn't make much difference. UNIX has become well known as a multitasking, multiuser system, and it is currently the most popular platform for major Oracle implementations. The most popular UNIX flavors on the market are Sun Solaris, HP-UX, and the IBM AIX versions. The basic commands don't vary much between the UNIX variants, and the different flavors mainly distinguish themselves on the basis of the utilities that come packaged with them.

Contrary to what newcomers to the field might imagine, UNIX is an easy operating system to learn and use. What might put off many developers and others who were weaned on the graphical Windows framework are the terse and cryptic commands commonly associated with the UNIX operating system. Take heart, though, in the knowledge that the essential commands are limited in number, and you can become proficient in a very short time.

Sun Microsystems (Sun), Hewlett-Packard (HP), and IBM sell the leading UNIX servers—the machines that run each firm's variation of the Berkeley UNIX system V. IBM is also a big UNIX supplier with its AIX server. Sun and HP currently run the vast majority of UNIX-based Oracle installations.

Linux

Developed by Linus Torvalds, Linux is constantly under development because it is released under an open source license and is freely available for download from the Internet. Many users prefer to use Linux because more programs and drivers are available, it's free (or close to free, as the commercial versions are fairly cheap), and bug fixes are released very quickly. Oracle Database 11*g* was developed on the Linux platform, and that's why the Linux-based version was the first to be released for production use. Oracle has certified and supports Red Hat Enterprise Linux AS and ES (either the 4.0 or the 5.0 version), SUSE LINUX Enterprise Server 10, Asianux 2 and 3, and the Enterprise Linux, versions 4 and 5.

■**Note** I used a Linux 4.0 distribution from Red Hat to run Oracle Database 11*g* on my Windows XP desktop for the purposes of this book. I used the VMware virtual operating system tool (`http://www.vmware.com`) to run the Linux operating system alongside Windows.

Oracle was the first company to offer a commercially available database for the Linux operating system. Oracle even offers a full suite of clusterware for Linux, which makes it possible to use Oracle's Real Application Clusters (RAC) on Linux without the more costly and complex raw file systems.

Do all these moves toward the Linux operating system foreshadow the demise of the UNIX operating system? Although the market for UNIX systems has dropped in recent years, you have to interpret this fact cautiously; most of the movement toward the Linux operating system is intended for low-end machines that serve network and other desktop applications. For the foreseeable future, UNIX-based systems will continue to rule the roost when it comes to large, company-wide servers that run large and complex databases such as Oracle Database 11*g*.

IT organizations are moving to Linux and open source software to solve a wide variety of business problems. The Linux platform often plays the central role in establishing a low-cost computing infrastructure. Oracle's grid initiative relies on using massive numbers of cheap commodity servers based on the Linux platform. Although Linux is growing very fast as a viable operating system for Oracle databases, the consensus among the IT industry is still that Linux is mainly useful for services, and not for mission-critical databases. This leaves UNIX and Windows as the two leading operating systems for Oracle databases. Oracle provides support to the Linux community by offering code for key products and itself uses the Linux platform extensively. Oracle's suite of clusterware links a number of separate servers into a single system, and low-cost Linux servers are an inexpensive choice for these file systems.

Midrange Systems

Just a few years ago, you had to invest in behemoths like the Sun E10K, with its hard partitions and multiple processors, if you wanted a system to support heavy workloads. Today, much smaller midrange UNIX servers come with features like soft partitioning, high amounts of memory, hot-spare processors, and capacity-on-demand features that were once the exclusive preserve of the high-end systems.

The main competition among the midrange servers is between Intel-based servers and RISC-based (reduced instructor set computer–based) servers using the UNIX or the Linux operating systems. The choice of the particular operating system will depend on the workload you plan on supporting as well as on the availability, reliability, and response time requirements.

The rest of the chapter, while formally oriented toward UNIX-based systems, applies almost verbatim to any Linux-based operating system as well.

Understanding the UNIX Shell(s)

In UNIX systems, any commands you issue to the operating system are passed through a command interpreter layer around the kernel called the *shell*. When you initially log in, you are communicating with this shell. The *kernel* is the part of UNIX that actually interacts with the hardware to complete tasks such as writing data to disk or printing to a printer. The shell translates your simple commands into a form the kernel can understand and returns the results to you. Therefore, any commands you issue as a user are *shell commands*, and any scripts (small programs of grouped commands) that you write are *shell scripts*.

The UNIX shell has many variants, but they are fundamentally the same, and you can easily migrate from one to another. Here's a list of the main UNIX and Linux shell commands and the shells they run:

- sh: The Bourne shell, which was written by Steven Bourne. It is the original UNIX shell, and is quite simple in the range of its features.

- csh: The C shell, which uses syntax somewhat similar to the C programming language. It contains advanced job control, aliasing, and file-naming features.

- ksh: The Korn shell, which is considered a superset of the Bourne shell. It adds several sophisticated capabilities to the basic Bourne shell.

- bash: The "Bourne Again Shell," which includes features of both the Bourne and the C shell.

For the sake of consistency, I use the Korn shell throughout this book, although I show a couple of important C shell variations. Most UNIX systems can run several shells; that is, you can choose to run your session or your programs in a particular shell, and you can easily switch among the shells.

The Linux default shell is BASH, the Bourne Again Shell, which includes features of the Bourne shell as well as the Korn, C, and TCSH shells.

■**Note** Most of the basic commands I discuss in the following sections are the same in all the shells, but some commands may not work, or may work differently, in different shells. You need to remember this when you switch among shells.

Shells act as both command interpreters and high-level UNIX programming languages. As a command interpreter, the Korn shell processes interactive user commands; as a programming language, the Korn shell processes commands in shell scripts.

It is possible to invoke any available shell from within another shell. To start a new shell, you simply type the name of the shell you want to run, ksh, csh, or sh. It is also possible to set the default startup shell for all your future sessions. The default shell for your account is stored in the /etc/passwd file, along with related information about your account. To change your default shell, use the chsh command.

Accessing the UNIX System

You can manage the Oracle databases that run on UNIX systems in several ways:

- Directly from the server hosting the database
- Via a UNIX workstation
- Through a Windows Server

Most DBAs use the last approach, preferring to use their regular PCs to manage their databases. If that's what you choose, you again have several choices as to how exactly you interact with the databases running on the remote server:

- Log directly into the server through the telnet or Secure Shell client.
- Log into the server through a display framework such as Virtual Network Computing (VNC), which enables you to interact with a server using a simple client program on another desktop anywhere on the Internet; or a Reflections X-Client, which provides an X Window System that emulates the look and feel of a UNIX workstation.
- Connect through a GUI-based management console, such as the Oracle-supplied Oracle Enterprise Manager (OEM) or through a tool from a third-party supplier, such as BMC Software (http://www.bmc.com/) or Quest Software (http://www.quest.com/).

Regardless of whether you choose to log into the UNIX box through the server or another interface, the first thing you will need is an account and the appropriate privileges to enable you to log in and actually get something done. The UNIX system administrator, with whom you should become very friendly, is the person who will perform this task and give you your password. The system administrator will also assign you a *home directory*, which is where you will land inside the UNIX file system when you initially log in.

You can log into a UNIX machine in several ways. You can always log into the server directly by using the terminal attached to the machine itself. However, this is not a commonly used option for day-to-day work. You can also use telnet to connect to the UNIX server, and you'll learn about this in the "Using Telnet" section later in this chapter. One of the most common ways to work with UNIX, though, is through your own PC by using what's called a *terminal emulator*—a program that will enable your PC to mimic a UNIX terminal. Several vendors produce emulators, including Hummingbird (http://www.hummingbird.com/) and WRQ (http://www.attachmate.com/), which produce the popular Hummingbird and Reflections emulators, respectively. These emulators, also called X Window emulators, emulate the X Window System, which is the standard graphical user interface (GUI) for UNIX systems. The emulators use special display protocols that will let you use your Windows terminal as an X terminal to access a UNIX server.

The general idea behind many of these interfaces is to try and make working with UNIX as easy as possible by providing a familiar GUI. Figure 3-1 shows a basic X session connected to the UNIX operating system.

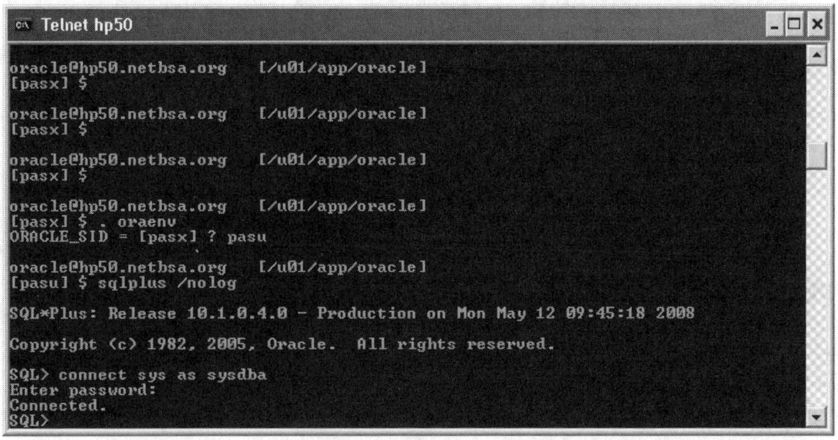

Figure 3-1. *An X session*

For now, let's assume you are equipped with a terminal emulator. You need to know a couple of things before you can log in and use the system. First, you need to know the machine name, which can be in either symbolic or numerical form.

■**Note** All UNIX machines (also called UNIX *boxes* or UNIX *servers*) have an Internet Protocol (IP) address, usually in a form like this: 162.15.155.17. Each IP address is guaranteed to be unique. By using a special system file (/etc/hosts), the UNIX administrator can give what's called a *symbolic name* to the machine. For example, the machine with the IP address 162.15.155.17 can be called prod1, for simplicity. In this case, you can connect by using either the IP address or the symbolic name.

Next, the system will ask you for your password. A shell prompt indicates a successful login, as shown here:

$

The shell prompt will be a dollar sign ($) if you are using the Bourne shell or the Korn shell. The C shell uses the percent sign (%) as its command prompt.

Once you log into the system, you are said to be working in a UNIX *session*; you are automatically working in what's known as your home directory (more on this later on). You type your commands at the shell prompt, and the shell interprets these commands and hands them over to the underlying operating system.

The UNIX directory structure is hierarchical, starting with the root directory at the top, which is owned by the UNIX system administrator. From the root directory, the other directories branch out, and the files are underneath them. Let's say you are in the /u01/app/oracle directory when you log in, and you want to refer to or execute a program file located in the directory /u01/app/oracle/admin/dba/script. To specify this location in the hierarchy to the UNIX system, you must give it a *path*. If you want, you can give the complete path from the root directory: /u01/app/oracle/admin/dba/script. This is called the *absolute path*, because it starts with the root directory itself. You can also specify a *relative path*, which is a path that starts from your current location. In this example, the relative path for the file you need is admin/dba/script.

■**Note** Included among these directories and files are the system files, which are static, and user files. As a DBA, your main concern will be the Oracle software files and database files.

You end your UNIX or Linux session by typing the word **exit** at the prompt, as follows:

```
$ exit
```

Overview of Basic UNIX Commands

You can execute hundreds of commands at the command prompt. Don't get overwhelmed just yet, though: of the many commands available to you, you'll find that you'll only use a handful on a day-to-day basis. This section covers the basic commands you'll need to operate in the UNIX environment.

■**Note** If you need help using a command, you can type **man** at the command prompt, along with the name of the topic you're trying to get help with. For example, if you type in the expression **man date**, you'll receive information about the date command, examples of its use, and a lot of other good stuff. For more details, see the "Getting Help: The man Command" section later in this chapter.

The UNIX shell has a few simple, built-in commands. The other commands are all in the form of executable files that are stored in a special directory called *bin* (short for "binary"). Table 3-1 presents some of the more important UNIX commands that you'll need to know. The UNIX commands tend to be cryptic, but some should be familiar to Windows users. The commands cd and mkdir in Windows, for example, have the same meaning in UNIX. Many UNIX commands have additional options or switches (just like their MS-DOS counterparts) that extend the basic functionality of the command, and Table 3-1 shows the most useful command switches.

Table 3-1. *Basic UNIX Commands*

Command	Description	Example
cd	The cd command enables you to change directories. The format is cd new-location. The example shown here takes you to the /tmp directory from your current working directory.	`$ cd /tmp` `$`

date	The date command gives you the time and date.	`$ date`
		`Sat Mar 26 16:08:54 CST 2005`
		`$`

echo	With the echo command, you can display text on your screen.	`$ echo Buenos Dias`
		`Buenos Dias`
		`$`

Table 3-1. *Basic UNIX Commands (Continued)*

Command	Description	Example
grep	The grep command is a pattern-recognition command. It enables you to see if a certain word or set of words occurs in a file or the output of any other command. In the example shown here, the grep command is checking whether the word "alapati" occurs anywhere in the file test.txt. (The answer is yes.) The grep command is very useful when you need to search large file structures to see if they contain specific information. If the grepped word or words aren't in the file, you'll simply get the UNIX prompt back, as shown in the second example.	`$ grep alapati test.txt` `alapati`

history	The history command gives you the commands entered previously by you or other users. To see the last three commands, type **history -3**. The default number of commands shown depends on the specific operating system, but it is usually between 15 and 20. Each command is preceded in the output by a number, indicating how far back it was used.	`$ history -3`
		`4        vi trig.txt`
		`5        grep alapati`
		`test.txt`
		`6        date`
		`7        history -3`
		`[pasx] $`

passwd	When you are first assigned an account, you'll get a username and password combination. You are free to change your password by using the passwd command.	`$ passwd`
		`Changing password for`
		`salapati`
		`Old password:`
		`New password:`

pwd	Use the pwd command to find out your present working directory or to simply confirm your current location in the file system.	`$ pwd    $/u01/app/oracle`

uname	In the example shown here, the uname command tells you that the machine's symbolic name is prod5 and it's an HP-UX machine. The -a option tells UNIX to give all the details of the system. If you omit the -a option, UNIX will just respond with HP-UX.	`$ uname  -a`
		`HP-UX prod5    B.11.00  A`
		`9000/800      190    two-user`
		`license`
		`$`

whereis	As the name of this command suggests, whereis will give you the exact location of the executable file for the utility in question.	`$ whereis who`
		`who:  /usr/bin/who`
		`/usr/share/man/man1.z/who.1`
		`$`

which	The which command enables you to find out which version (of possibly multiple versions) of a command the shell is using. You should run this command when you run a common command, such as cat, and receive somewhat different results than you expect. The which command helps you verify whether you are indeed using the correct version of the command.	`$ which cat` `/usr/bin/cat`

Table 3-1. *Basic UNIX Commands (Continued)*

Command	Description	Example
who	If you are curious about who else besides you is slogging away on the system, you can find out with the who command. This command provides you with a list of all the users currently logged into the system.	```$ who
salapati   pts/0   Nov
8   08:31
rhudson   pts/1   Nov
8   09:04
lthomas   pts/3   Nov
9   15:54
dcampbel   pts/7   Nov
8   16:27
dfarrell   pts/16   Nov
5   07:00```
whoami	The whoami command indicates who you are logged in as. This may seem trivial, but as a DBA, there will be times when you could be logged into the system using any one of several usernames. It's good to know who exactly you are at a given point in time, in order to prevent the execution of commands that may not be appropriate, such as deleting files or directories. The example shown here indicates that you are logged in as user Oracle, who is the owner of Oracle software running on the UNIX system.	```$ whoami
oracle
$```

■**Tip** It is always worthwhile to check that you are at the right place in the file structure before you press the Enter key, to avoid running any destructive commands. The following commands will help you control your input at the command line. Under the Korn shell, to retrieve the previous command, all you have to do is press the Esc key followed by typing **k**. If you want an older command, continue typing **k**, and you'll keep going back in the command sequence. If you have typed a long sequence of commands and wish to edit it, press the Esc key followed by typing **h** to go back, or type **l** to go forward on the typed command line.

Getting Help: The man Command

There are many operating system commands, most with several options. Therefore, it's convenient to have a sort of help system embedded right within the operating system so you have the necessary information at your fingertips. UNIX and Linux systems both come with a built-in feature called the *man pages*, which provide copious information about all the operating system commands. You can look up any command in more detail by typing **man** followed by the command you want information on, as follows:

```
$ man who
```

This command will then display a great deal of information about the who command and all its options, as well as several examples (see Figure 3-2).

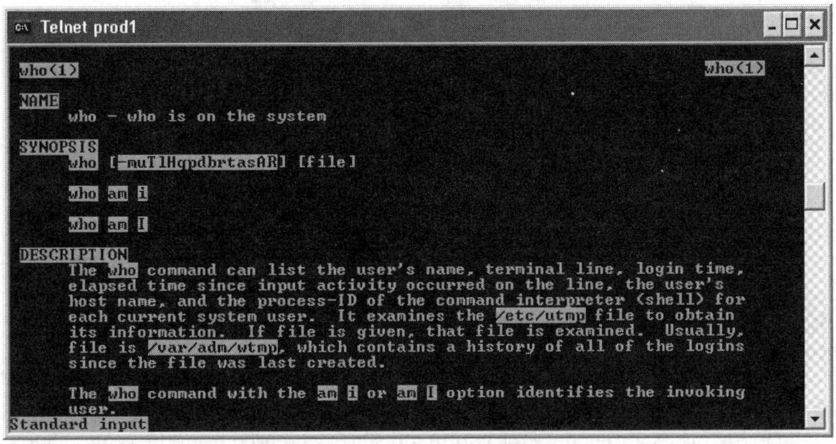

Figure 3-2. *Output of the man command*

In Linux-based systems, you can also use the nifty whatis command to find out what a certain command does. Like the man command, the whatis command is followed by the name of the command you want information about. Here's a simple example:

```
$ whatis whereis (1) -locate the binary, source, and manual page files
for a command
```

As you can see, the whatis command offers a quicker and easier way to locate summary information about any command than the more elaborate man pages.

Changing the Prompt

Every shell has its own default prompt. The default prompt for the Korn shell is the dollar sign ($). You can easily change it to something else by changing the value of the PS1 shell variable.

In the following example, I first check the value of the PS1 variable by issuing the command echo $PS1. I then use the export command to set the value of the ORACLE_SID environment variable to my database name, finance. Using the export command again, I set the value of the PS1 environment variable to be the same as the value of the environment variable ORACLE_SID ($ORACLE_SID). Now the shell prompt is changed to my database name, finance. Since I only exported the ORACLE_SID variable value but didn't place it in my environment files, the value I exported is good only for the duration of the current session.

```
$ echo $PS1
$
$ export ORACLE_SID=finance
$ export PS1=[$ORACLE_SID]
[finance]
```

■**Note** If you add the PS1 variable to your .cshrc file (I explain how to do this later in the "Customizing Your Environment" section), every time you open a new shell, it'll have your customized prompt. The ability to change the prompt is useful if you're managing many different databases via UNIX. You can amend the prompt to reflect the database you're working on at any given time. For example, when you're working in an inventory system, the prompt can display invent>. That way, you won't accidentally execute a command in the wrong database.

Finding Files and Directories

Sometimes you want to locate a file, but you aren't sure where it might be located in the file system. The whereis command, of course, is of help only if you are locating commands, not files. To find out where a file or a directory is, you can use the find command, as shown here:

```
$ pwd
/u01/app/oracle
$ find . -name bill.sql -print
./dba/bill.sql
$
```

In this example, the find command informs you that the bill.sql file is located in the /u01/app/oracle/dba directory. Note that there is a dot after the find keyword, indicating that a recursive search is made from the present directory—every directory and subdirectory under the present directory will be searched. If you want to search from a specific directory, you need to specify that in the command. In the following example, the find command starts its search from the root (/) file system and prints the location of the test.txt file to the screen, if it finds it:

```
$ find / -name test.txt  -print
```

Controlling the Output of Commands

Sometimes a command will produce more output than can fit on the screen. You can control the output of a command in a couple of ways.

The more command will show you the contents of a file, one screen at a time. Just press Enter to see the next screen of the file:

```
$ more test.txt
```

The pipe command (|) enables you to pass the output of one command as input to another command. In the following example, the | operator takes the ps -ef command's output (which is the list of all processes that are currently running on your system) and passes it to the grep command as a list, to search for all processes that contain the word "Oracle":

```
$ ps -ef | grep Oracle
```

This example also demonstrates the use of multiple commands at once.

Showing the Contents of Files

As you know, you can use the vi editor to read a file as well as write to it. However, in some cases you may want to just read the contents of a file. The cat command lets you do so, as shown here:

```
$ cat  test.ksh
#!/bin/ksh
VAR1=1
while  [ $VAR1 -lt 100 ]
do
     echo "value of VAR1 is : $VAR1"
     ((VAR1=VAR1+1))
done
$
```

■Note You can also use the `page` command to peruse files.

Comparing Files

The `diff` command compares two files, returns the line(s) that are different, and tells you how to make the files the same. Here's an example:

```
$ diff test.one test.two
0a1
> New Test.
```

This `diff` command output tells you that if you add the line `New Test.` to the `test.one` file, you can make it identical to the `test.two` file. The first character, "0," is the line number to edit in `test.one`; the "a" indicates that the line should be added to `test.one` to match the first line, "1," of `test.two`.

Understanding Operating-System and Shell Variables

There are two main types of variables in a UNIX or Linux system: user-created variables and shell variables. Let's briefly look at how you use both kinds of variables.

User-Created Variables

A user can create a variable and initialize it by providing a value for it. The variable name must consist of letters and numbers, and it must start with a letter. You can also use the `export` command to export variables, so that any shell you create in your current session can make use of your variables.

Here's an example of a user-created variable (note how echoing the variable itself prints just the variable, not its value—to show the variable's value, you must precede the variable's name with the $ sign in your `echo` command):

```
$ database=nicko
$ echo database
database
$ echo $database
nicko
$
```

In this example, I first created a new variable called database and assigned it the value of nicko. I then used the `echo` command to print the value of the database variable, and the `echo` command just prints the string "database". The second time I used the `echo` command, I added the dollar sign ($) in front of the name of the variable (`$database`). When I did this, the value of the variable database was shown as nicko.

To remove the value of the database variable, simply set it to null, as shown here:

```
$ database=
$ echo $database
$
```

Shell Variables

Shell variables are variables whose values are set by the shell itself, instead of by a user. Shell variables are also called *keyword variables*, since short keywords are used to represent some of these variables. When you first log into a UNIX system, you must make several bits of information available to the shell, such as the name of your home directory, the type of editor you prefer to use for editing text, and the type of prompt you want the system to display while your session is active. Each of these is determined by values assigned to shell variables. These are some common shell variables:

- *HOME*: Identifies a user's home directory.

- *PATH*: Specifies the directories in which the shell should look when it tries to execute any command. It's common to include both the binary (`bin`) directories for UNIX and Oracle software as part of the PATH variable.

Fortunately, you don't have to manually set up the environment every time you log into the system. There is a file, named `.profile` or `.login`, depending on the type of UNIX shell you are using, that automatically sets the environment variables for all users at login time. When you log in, the shell will look in the appropriate file and establish the environment by setting the values of all shell variables.

Using the export and setenv Commands

Both user-defined and shell variables are local to the process that declares them first. If you want these variables to be accessible to a shell script that you want to execute from your login shell, you need to explicitly make the variables available to the calling environment of the child process.

You can make a variable's value available to child processes by using the `export` command in the Korn and BASH shells. In the C shell, you use the `setenv` command to do the same thing. Here's an example that shows how to use the `export` command to make the value of a variable available to a child process:

```
$ export ORACLE_HOME =/u03/app/oracle/product/11.1.0/orcl
```

The following sequence would achieve the same results as the preceding `export` command:

```
$ ORACLE_HOME =/u03/app/oracle/product/11.1.0/orcl
$ export ORACLE_HOME
```

In the C shell, you use the `setenv` command to set a variable's value, as shown here:

```
$ setenv ORACLE_HOME= /u03/app/oracle/product/10.2.0/orcl
```

■**Note** UNIX programs and commands can be run in two entirely different ways: *interactive mode* is when you log in and type your commands directly to the screen; *batch mode* is when you run your commands or an entire program at once, usually by using executable shell scripts in the form of UNIX text files.

Displaying the Environment

Type **env** at the system prompt, and your entire set of environment variables will scroll by on the screen. Here's an example:

```
$ env
PATH=/usr/bin:/usr/ccs/bin:/user/config/bin
ORACLE_PATH=/u01/app/oracle/admin/dba/sql
ORACLE_HOME=/u01/app/oracle/product/11.1.0/db_1
ORACLE_SID=prod1
TNS_ADMIN=/u01/app/oracle/product/network
TERM=vt100
$
```

To see the value of one specific environment variable, rather than the entire set (which can be a fairly long list in a real-world production system), you can ask the shell to print the variable's value to the screen by using the echo command:

```
$ echo $ORACLE_HOME
 /u01/app/oracle/product/11.1.0/db_1
$
```

Note that in the echo command, the $ precedes the environment name so that the command will print the value of the variable, not the name of the variable itself.

Customizing Your Environment

Both the Bourne shell and the Korn shell use the .profile file to set the values for all shell variables. The .profile file executes when you first log into the UNIX or Linux system.

The C shell executes the .cshrc file every time you invoke a new C shell. The .cshrc file is a short file with generic C shell commands that should work with any flavor of UNIX with only minor modifications. This means that you could have essentially the same .cshrc file on all UNIX systems you use. The operating system executes the .cshrc file whenever you open a terminal window in a UNIX or Linux environment, or when you execute a script. You can add commands in the .cshrc file (using a text editor like vi) that will make your work in UNIX more productive. The C shell also executes the contents of the .login file when you log in and start a new session. The .login file is located a user's home directory; for example, /home/oracle for the Oracle user on most UNIX systems.

Here's a list of the various scripts executed under each of the main UNIX and Linux shells, to set the shell's environment:

- *Bourne shell* (sh): The operating system executes only the .profile file when a user logs in. The .profile file is located in the user's home directory.

- *C shell* (cshrc): The shell executes the .login file after it first executes the .cshrc file. When you create a new shell after logging in, the .cshrc script is executed, but not the .login file.

- *Korn shell* (ksh): The .profile file in your home directory is executed.

- *BASH shell* (bash): The .bash_profile is executed at login time, and the .bashrc file is executed when you start a new shell.

To change an environment variable permanently, you can edit the .profile or .login file and insert the necessary values for a variable. For example, for the .login file you would add a line like this:

```
setenv VARIABLENAME value_of_variable
```

For the .profile file, you could add lines like the following:

```
VARIABLE=value_of_variable
EXPORT VARIABLE
```

The changes will come into effect the next time you log in or invoke an instance of the C shell. You can change your environment immediately in the Bourne and Korn shells in order to effect immediate environmental changes, by using the following command:

```
$ . .profile
```

Similarly, you can use the source command in the C shell, to put the environment variable changes into immediate effect:

```
$ source .cshrc
```

Redirecting Input and Output

When using a UNIX window on your PC or a UNIX workstation, the keyboard is the standard way to input a command to the shell, and the terminal is the standard location for the output of the commands. Any resulting errors are called *standard errors* and are usually displayed on the screen.

■**Note** It's common to use the terms *standard input*, *standard output*, and *standard error* to refer to the standard input and output locations in the UNIX shell.

However, you can also use a previously written file as input, or you can have UNIX send output to a file instead of the screen. This process of routing your input and output through files is called *input and output redirection.*

You can redirect output to a special location called /dev/null when you want to get rid of the output. When you use /dev/null as the output location, all messages issued during the execution of a program are simply discarded and not recorded anywhere on the file system. The following example shows how redirecting a file's output to /dev/null make its contents disappear.

```
$ cat testfile1
$ This is the first line of testfile1
$ cat testfile1 > /dev/null
$ cat /dev/null
```

In this example, the first cat command shows you the output of testfile1. However, after redirecting the cat command's output to /dev/null, the output of the cat command disappears.

■**Note** Redirecting the output of the cat command tends to defeat the purpose of running the command in the first place, but there will be other situations, such as when running a script, when you don't want to see the output of all the commands.

Table 3-2 summarizes the key redirection operators in most versions of UNIX.

Table 3-2. *Input/Output Redirection in UNIX*

Redirection Operator	Description
<	Redirects standard input to a command
>	Redirects standard output to a file
>>	Appends standard output to a file
<<	Appends standard input to a file
2 >	Redirects standard error

In the following example, the date command's output is stored in file1, and file2 in turn gets the output of file1:

```
$ date > file1
$ file1 < file2
```

You can achieve the same result with the use of the UNIX pipe (|):

```
$ date | file2
```

The pipe command, which uses the pipe symbol (|), indicates that the shell takes the output of the command *before* the | symbol and makes it the input for the command *after* the | symbol.

Protecting Files from Being Overwritten

You can use the noclobber shell variable to avoid accidentally overwriting an existing file. It's a good idea to include this variable in your shell startup file, such as the .cshrc file, as shown here:

```
set noclobber
```

The noclobber command is very handy when you're redirecting output to a file.

Navigating Files and Directories in UNIX

As you might have inferred, files and directories in UNIX are pretty much the same as in the Windows system. In this section, you'll learn all about the UNIX file system and directory structure, and you'll learn about the important UNIX directories. You'll also learn some important file-handling commands.

Files in the UNIX System

Files are the basic data storage unit on most computer systems, used to store user lists, shell scripts, and so on. Everything in UNIX/Linux, including hardware devices, is treated as a file. The UNIX file system is hierarchical, with the root directory, denoted by a forward slash (/), as the starting point at the top.

■**Tip**   In Oracle, everything is in a *table* somewhere; in UNIX, everything is in a *file* somewhere.

Files in a typical UNIX system can be one of the following three types:

- *Ordinary files*: These files can contain text, data, or programs. A file cannot contain another file.

- *Directories*: Directories contain files. Directories can also contain other directories because of the UNIX tree directory structure.

- *Special files*: These files are not used by ordinary users to input their data or text; rather, they are for the use of input/output devices, such as printers and terminals. The special files are called *character* special files if they contain streams of characters, and they are called *block* special files if they work with large blocks of data.

Linking Files

You can use the link command to create a *pointer* to an existing file. When you do this, you aren't actually creating a new file as such; you are creating a virtual copy of the original by pointing a new filename to an existing file. You use symbolic links when you want to conveniently refer to files from a different directory, without having to provide their complete path. There are two types of links: hard links and symbolic links. You can create *hard links* between files in the same directory, whereas you can create *symbolic links* for any file residing in any directory. The previous example shows a symbolic link. A hard link is usually employed to make a copy of a file, while a symbolic link merely points to another file (or directory). When you manage Oracle databases, you often create symbolic links for parameter files, so you can refer to them easily, without having to specify their complete paths.

You use the following syntax when creating a symbolic link:

```
$ ln –s <current_filename> <link_name>
```

The following command creates a symbolic link called test.sql, which refers to the original file called monitor.sql:

```
$ ln -s /u01/app/oracle/admin/dba/sql/monitor.sql        /u01/app/oracle/test.sql
```

Once the test.sql symbolic link is created, the status of the new file can be checked from the /u01/app/oracle directory, as shown here:

```
$ cd /u01/app/oracle
$ ls -altr test.sql
lrwxr-xr-x   1 oracle      dba                41 Mar 30 10:13 test.sql -> /u01/app/oracle/
admin/dba/sql/monitor.sql
$
```

Managing Files

You can list files in a directory with the ls command. The command ls -al provides a long listing of all the files, with permissions and other information. The command ls -altr gives you an ordered list of all the files, with the newest or most recently edited files at the bottom. Here are some examples:

```
$ ls
catalog.dbf1     tokill.ksh     consumer
$ ll
total 204818
-rw-rw-r--- 1 oracle  dba   104867572  Nov 19  13:23  catalog.dbf1
-rw-r------ 1 oracle  dba         279  Jan  04  2008     tokill.ksh
drwrxr-xr-x 1 oracle  dba        1024 Sep  17  11:29     consumer
$ ls -altr
-rw-r------ 1 oracle dba 279       Jan 04    2008     tokill.ksh
drwrxr-xr-x 1 oracle dba 1024      Sep 17    11:29     consumer
-rw-rw-r--- 1 oracle dba 104867572 Nov 19    13:23    catalog.dbf1
$
```

You can view the contents of a file by using the cat command, as shown in the following code snippet. Later on, you'll learn how to use the vi editor to view and modify files.

```
$ cat test.txt
This is a test file.
This file shows how to use the cat command.
Bye!
$
```

But what if the file you want to view is very large? The contents would fly by on the screen in an instant. You can use the more command to see the contents of a long file, one page at a time. To advance to the next page, simply press the spacebar.

```
$ cat abc.txt | more
```

You can copy a file to a different location by using the `cp` command. Note that the `cp` command, when used with the `-I` option, will prompt you before it overwrites a previously existing file of the same name.

```
$ pwd
$ /u10/oradata
$ cp test.txt /u09/app/oracle/data
$ cp -i sqlnet.log output.txt
overwrite output.txt? (y/n) y
```

The `mv` command enables you to move the original file to a different location, change the file's name, or both. The following example uses the `mv` command to change the name of the `test.txt` file to `abc.txt`:

```
$ ls
$ test.txt
$ mv test.txt abc.txt
$ ls
abc.txt
```

If you want to get rid of a file for whatever reason, you can use the `rm` command. Watch out, though—the `rm` command will completely delete a file. To stay on the safe side, you may want to use the `rm` command with the `-i` option, which gives you a warning before the file is permanently obliterated. Be careful with the `rm` command, as it's easy to inadvertently remove your entire file system with it!

```
$ ls
abc.txt  careful.txt  catalog.txt  sysinfo.txt
$ rm abc.txt
$ rm -i careful.txt
careful.txt: ? (y/n) y
$ ls
$ catalog.txt   sysinfo.txt
```

Permissions: Reading from or Writing to Files in UNIX

A user's ability to read from or write to files on a UNIX system depends on the permissions that have been granted for that file by the owner of the file or directory—the user who creates a file is the owner of that file.

Every file and directory comes with three types of permissions:

- *Read*: Lets you view the contents of the file only.
- *Write*: Lets you change the contents of the file. Write permission on a directory will let you create, modify, or delete files in that directory.
- *Execute*: Lets you execute (run) the file if the file contains an executable program (script).

Read permission is the most basic permission. Having the execute permission without the read permission is of no use—you can't execute a file if you can't read it in the first place.

Determining File Permissions

Use the `ls -al` command to list the file permissions along with the filenames in a directory. For example, look at the (partial) output of the following command:

```
$ ls -al
-rwxrwxrwx  1  oracle  dba    320    Jan 23    09:00    test.ksh
-rw-r---r-  1  oracle  dba    152    Jul 18    13:38    updown.ksh
-rw-r---r-  1  oracle  dba    70     Nov 22    01:30    tokill.ksh
$
```

You'll notice that at the beginning of each line, each file has a combination of ten different letters and the blank sign (-).

The first letter could be a blank or the letter d. If it is the letter d, it's a directory. If it's a blank, it's a regular file.

The next nine spaces are grouped into three sets of the letters rwx. The rwx group refers to the read, write, and execute permissions on that file. The first set of rwx indicates the permissions assigned to the owner of the file. The second set lists the permissions assigned to the group the user belongs to. The last set lists the permissions on that file granted to all the other users of the system.

For example, consider the access permissions on the following file:

```
$ -rwxr-x--x 1 oracle dba Nov 11 2001 test.ksh
```

Because the first character is a hyphen (-), this is a file, not a directory. The next three characters, rwx, indicate that the owner of the file test.ksh has all three permissions (read, write, and execute) on the file. The next three characters, r-x, show that all the users who are in the same group as the owner have read and execute permissions, but not write permissions. In other words, they cannot change the contents of the file. The last set of characters, --x, indicates that all other users on the system can execute the file, but they cannot modify it.

Setting and Modifying File Permissions

Any file that you create will first have the permissions set to -rw-r--r--. That is, everybody has read permissions, and no user has permission to execute the file. If you put an executable program inside the file, you'll want to grant someone permission to execute the file. You can set the permissions on the file by using the chmod command in one of two ways.

First, you can use the *symbolic notation,* with the letter o standing for owner, g for group, and u for other users on the system. You grant a group or users specific permissions by first specifying the entity along with a plus sign (+) followed by the appropriate symbol for the permission. In the following example, the notation go+x means that both the group and others are assigned the execute (x) permission on the test.ksh shell script:

```
$ chmod go+x   test.ksh
```

The next example shows how you can use symbolic notation to *remove* read and write permissions on a file from the group:

```
$ chmod g-rw  test.ksh
```

Second, you can use the *octal numbers* method to change file permissions. Each permission carries different numeric "weights": *read* carries a weight of 4, *write* a weight of 2, and *execute* a weight of 1. To determine a permission setting, just add the weights for the permissions you want to assign. The highest number that can be associated with each of the three different entities—owner, group, and all others—is 7, which is the same as having read, write, and execute permissions on the file. For example, consider the following:

```
$ ls
$ -rw-r--r-- 1 oracle dba      102   Nov 11 15:20 test.txt
$ chmod 777 test.txt
$ ls
$ -rwxrwxrwx 1 oracle dba      102   Nov 11 15:20 test.txt
```

The file test.txt initially had its file permissions set to 644 (rw, r, r.) The command chmod 777 assigned full permissions (read, write, and execute) to all three entities: owner, group, and all others. If you want to change this so that only the owner has complete rights and the others have no permissions at all, set the octal number to 700 (read, write, and execute permissions for the owner, and no permissions at all for the group or others) and use the chmod command as follows:

```
$ chmod 700 test.txt
$ ls -altr test.txt
-rwx------ 1 oracle    dba             0 Mar 28 11:23 test.txt
$
```

Table 3-3 provides a short summary of the commands you can use to change file permissions. By default, all files come with read and write privileges assigned, and directories come with read, write, and execute privileges turned on.

Table 3-3. *UNIX Permissions in Symbolic Notation and Octal Numbers*

Symbolic Notation	Octal Number	Privilege Description
---	0	No privileges
--x	1	Execute only
-w-	2	Write only
-wx	3	Write and execute, no read
r--	4	Read only
r-x	5	Read and execute, no write
rw-	6	Read and write, no execute
rwx	7	Read, write, and execute (full privileges)

The UMASK environment variable determines the default file and directory permissions. Issue the following command to see the current defaults on your server:

```
$ umask
022
```

When you create a new file, it'll have the default permissions allowed by the UMASK variable. In the preceding example, the UMASK is shown to be 022, meaning that the group and others don't have write permissions by default on any new file that you create.

Changing the Group

You can change the group a file belongs to by using the chgrp command. You must be the owner of the file to change the group, and you can change the file's group only to a group that you belong to. Here's how you use the chgrp command:

```
$ chgrp groupname filename
```

Directory Management

There are two facets to directory management. One is that you simply need to know the commands involved in creating, moving, and deleting directories. The other is that you need to know about certain standard directories that you tend to find on just about every UNIX and Linux system that you will encounter.

Manipulating Directories

There are several important directory commands that enable you to create, move, and delete directories.

The mkdir command lets you create a new directory:

```
$ mkdir newdir
```

You can use the mkdir command with the -p option to create any necessary intermediate directories if they don't already exist. The following example creates the directory /u01/, the directory /u01/app, and the directory /u01/app/oracle, all with a single command:

```
$ mkdir  -p  /u01/app/oracle
```

The command for removing directories is not the same as the command for removing files. To remove a directory, you can use the rmdir command, as in the following example (but first make sure you have removed all the files in the directory using the rm command):

```
$ rmdir testdir
```

The rmdir command only removes empty directories. To remove a directory that contains files, use the rm command with the -R (or -r) option. This command will recursively delete the entire contents of a directory before removing the directory itself:

```
$ rmdir -r newdir
```

To move around the UNIX hierarchical directory structure, use the cd command (which stands for "change directory").

```
$ pwd
/u01/app/oracle
$ cd  /u01/app/oracle/admin
$ cd  /u01/app/oracle
$ cd admin
$ pwd
/u01/app/oracle/admin
$
```

Notice that you can use the cd command with the complete absolute path or with the shorter relative path. You can also use it to change to a directory that is indicated by an environment variable. For example, cd $ORACLE_HOME will change your current directory to the directory that happens to be the location for ORACLE_HOME.

Important UNIX Directories

There are several directories that you'll regularly come across when you're using the UNIX system as a DBA:

- /etc: The /etc directory is where the system administrator keeps the system configuration files. Important files here pertain to passwords (etc/passwd) and information concerning hosts (etc/hosts).

- /dev: The /dev directory contains device files, such as printer configuration files.

- /tmp: The /tmp directory is where the system keeps temporary files, possibly including the log files of your programs. Usually you'll have access to write to this directory.

- home: The home directory is the directory assigned to you by your UNIX administrator when he or she creates your initial account. This is where you'll land first when you log in. You own this directory and have the right to create any files you want here. To create files in other directories, or even to read files in other directories, you have to be given permission by the owners of those directories.

- *Root*: The root directory, denoted simply by a forward slash (/), is owned by the system administrator and is at the very top level of the treelike directory structure.

Editing Files with the vi Editor

The vi editor is commonly used to write and edit files in the UNIX system. To the novice, the vi editor looks very cryptic and intimidating, but it need not be intimidating. In this section, you'll learn how to use the vi editor to create and save files. You'll find that vi really is a simple text editor, with many interesting and powerful features.

Creating and Modifying Files Using vi

You start vi by typing **vi** or, better yet, by typing **vi** *filename* to start up the vi editor and show the contents of the *filename* file on the screen. If the file doesn't exist, vi allocates a memory buffer for the file, and you can later save the contents into a new file.

Let's assume you want to create and edit a new file called test.txt. When you type the command **vi test.txt**, the file will be created and the cursor will blink, but you can't start to enter any text yet because you aren't in the input mode. All you have to do to switch to input mode is type the letter **i**, which denotes the "insert" or "input" mode. You can start typing now just as you would in a normal text processor.

Note If you need to create a file but don't want to enter any data into it, you can simply create a file with the touch command. If you use the touch command with a new filename as the argument, touch simply creates an empty file where none previously existed (unless you specify the -c flag). If you use an existing filename as the argument to the touch command, the last-accessed time of the file is changed to the time when the touch command was run. Here's an example: touch program.one

This command sets the last access and modification times of the program.one file to the current date and time. If the program.one file does not exist, the touch command will create a file with that name.

Table 3-4 shows some of the most basic vi navigation commands, which enable you to move around within files.

Table 3-4. *Basic vi Navigation Commands*

Command	Description
h	Move a character to the left.
l	Move a character to the right.
j	Move a line down.
k	Move a line up.
w	Go to the beginning of the next word.
b	Go to the beginning of the previous word.
$	Go to the end of the current line.
^	Go to the start of the current line.
:G	Go to the end of the file.
:1	Go to the top of the file.

In addition to the cursor-movement commands, there are numerous vi text-manipulation commands, but unless you are a full-time system administrator or a UNIX developer, the average DBA can get by nicely with the few text commands summarized in Table 3-5.

Table 3-5. *Important vi Text-Manipulation Commands*

Command	Description
i	Start inserting from the current character.
a	Start inserting from the next character.
o	Start inserting from a new line below.
O	Start inserting from a new line above.
x	Delete the character where the cursor is.
dd	Delete the line where the cursor is.
r	Replace the character where the cursor is.
/text	Search for a text string.
:s/old/new/g	Replace (substitute) a text string with a new string.
yy	Yank or move a line.
p	Paste a copied line after the current cursor.
P	Paste a copied line above the current cursor.
:wq	Save and quit.
:q	Exit and discard changes.

For further information on vi navigation and text manipulation commands, you can always look up a good reference, such as *A Practical Guide to the UNIX System* by Mark Sobell (Addison Wesley).

Moving Around with the head and tail Commands

The head and tail UNIX file commands help you get to the top or bottom of a file. By default, they will show you the first or last ten lines of the file, but you can specify a different number of lines in the output, by specifying a number next to the head or tail command. The following example shows how you can get the first five lines of a file (the /etc/group file, which shows all the groups on the UNIX server):

```
$ head -5 /etc/group
root::0:root
other::1:root,hpdb
bin::2:root,bin
sys::3:root,uucp
adm::4:root
$
```

The tail command works in the same way, but it displays the last few lines of the file. The tail command is very useful when you are performing a task like a database software installation, because you can use it to display the progress of the installation process and see what's actually happening.

OTHER EDITORS

In addition to the UNIX vi editor, there are several other alternatives you can use, including pico, sed, and Emacs. Most are simple text editors that you can use in addition to the more popular vi editor. It's worth noting that Emacs works well in graphical mode when you use the X Window System, and there are also specific editors for X, such as dtpad. For useful information on the various UNIX editors such as the Emacs, pico, and the vi editors, please go to http://www.helpdesk.umd.edu/systems/wam/general/1235/.

Vim (or Vi improved) is an enhanced clone, if you will, of vi, and it is one of the most popular text editors among Linux administrators. You can download Vim from http://www.vim.org/download.php. For an excellent introduction to the Vim editor and its use with SQL*Plus, see David Kalosi's article "Vimming With SQL*Plus" at http://www.oracle.com/technology/pub/articles/kalosi_vim.html.

Extracting and Sorting Text

The cat and more utilities, which you've seen earlier in the "Overview of Basic UNIX Commands" section, dump the entire contents of a text file onto the screen. If you want to see only certain parts of a file, however, you can use text-extraction utilities. Let's look at how you can use some of the important text-extraction tools.

Using grep to Match Patterns

I described the grep command briefly earlier in the chapter—you use the grep command to find matches for certain patterns in a string, using regular expressions. (For a good introduction to regular expressions, see the tutorial at http://www.regular-expressions.info/tutorial.html.) The word "grep" is an acronym for "global regular expression print," and it is derived from the following vi command, which prints all lines matching the regular expression re:

g/re/p

You can think of regular expressions as the search criteria used for locating text in a file; grep is thus similar to the find command in other operating systems. grep searches through each line of the file (or files) for the first occurrence of the given string, and if it finds that string, it prints the line. For example, to output all the lines that contain the expression "oracle database" in the file test.txt, you use the grep command in the following way:

```
$ grep 'oracle database' test.txt
```

In order to output all lines in the test.txt file that don't contain the expression "oracle database", you use the grep command with the -v option, as shown here:

```
$ grep -v 'oracle database' test.txt
```

In addition to the -v option, you can use the grep command with several other options:

-c: Prints a count of matching lines for each input file

-l: Prints the name of each input file

-n: Supplies the line number for each line of output

-i: Ignores the case of the letters in the expression

In addition to grep, you can use fgrep (fixed grep) to search files. The fgrep command doesn't use regular expressions. The command performs direct string comparisons, to find matches for a fixed string, instead of a regular expression.

The egrep version of grep helps deal with complex regular expressions, and is faster than the regular grep command.

Cutting, Pasting, and Joining Text

Often, you need to strip part of a file's text or join text from more than one file. UNIX provides great commands for performing these tasks, as I show in the following sections.

Outputting Columns with the cut Command

The cut command will output specified columns from a text file. Let's say you have a file named example.txt with the following text:

```
one two three
four five six
seven eight nine
ten eleven twelve
```

You can specify the fields you want to extract with the -f option. The following command will return just the second column in the example.txt file:

```
$ cut -f2 example.txt
two
five
eight
eleven
```

You use the -c option with the cut command to specify the specific characters you want to extract from a file. The following two commands extract the tenth character and then characters 10–12 from the password.txt file:

```
$ password.txt | cut -c10
$ password.txt | cut -c10-12
```

You can use the -d option in tandem with the -f option to extract characters up to a specified delimiter. The following example specifies that the cut command extract the first field (f1) of the passwd file, with the -d option specifying that the field is delimited by a colon (:). (The passwd file, located in the /etc directory, is where UNIX and Linux systems keep their user account information.)

```
$ cut -d":" -f1 /etc/passwd
root
daemon
bin
sys
adm
uucp
mail
```

Joining Files with the paste Command

The paste command takes one line from one source and combines it with another line from another source. Let's say you have two files: test1.txt contains the string "one two three" and test2.txt contains "one four five six". You can use the paste command to combine the two files as shown here:

```
$ paste test1.txt test2.txt
one two three    one four five six
```

Joining Files with the join Command

The join command will also combine the contents of two files, but it will work only if there is a common field between the files you are joining. In the previous section, test1.txt and test2.txt don't have a common column, so using the join command with those two files won't produce any output. However, suppose you have two files, test.one and test.two, with their contents as follows:

```
test.one                      test.two
11111    Dallas       11111    High Tech
22222    Houston      22222    Oil and Energy
```

By default the join command looks only at the first fields for matches, so it will give you the following result, based on the common (first) column:

```
$ join test.one test.two
11111        Dallas           High Tech
22222        Houston          Oil and Energy
```

The -1 option lets you specify which field to use as the matching field in the first file, and the -2 option lets you specify which field to use as the matching field in the second file. For example, if the second field of the first file matches the third field of the second file, you would use the join command as follows:

```
$ join -1 2 -2 3 test.one test.two
```

You use the -o option to specify output fields in the following format: *file.field*. Thus, to print the second field of the first file and the third field of the second file on matching lines, you would use the join command with the following options:

```
$ join -o 1.2 2.3 test.one test.two
```

Sorting Text with the sort Command

You can sort lines of text files, whether from a pipe or from a file, using the sort command. If you use the -m option, sort simply merges the files without sorting them. Let's say you have a file called test.txt with the following contents:

```
$ cat test.txt
yyyy
bbbb
aaaa
nnnn
```

By using the sort command, you can output the contents of the test.txt file in alphabetical order:

```
$ sort test.txt
aaaa
bbbb
nnnn
yyyy
```

By default, sort operates on the first column of the text.

Removing Duplicate Lines with the uniq Command

The uniq command removes duplicate lines from a sorted file. This command often follows the sort command in a pipe. By using the -c option, it can be used to count the number of occurrences of a line, or by using the -d option, it can report only the duplicate lines.

```
$ sort -m test.one test.two | uniq -c
      1 New test.
      2 Now testing
      1 Only a test.
```

In the preceding example, the sort command merges the two files, test.one and test.two, using the -m option. The output is piped to the uniq command with the -c option. What you get is an alphabetized list, with all duplicate lines removed. You also get the frequency of occurrence of each line.

Shell Scripting

Although the preceding commands and features are useful for day-to-day work with UNIX, the real power of this operating system comes from the user's ability to create shell scripts. In this section, you'll start slowly by building a simple shell program, and you'll proceed to build up your confidence and skill level as you move along into branching, looping, and all that good stuff.

What Is a Shell Program?

A shell script (or shell program) is simply a file containing a set of commands. The shell script looks just like any regular UNIX file, but it contains commands that can be executed by the shell. Although you'll learn mostly about Korn shell programming here, Bourne and C shell programming are similar in many ways. If you want to make the Korn shell your default shell, ask your system administrator to set it up by changing the shell entry for your username in the /etc/passwd file.

Before you begin creating a shell program, you should understand that shell programs don't contain any special commands that you can't use at the command prompt. In fact, you can type any command in any shell script at the command prompt to achieve the same result. All the shell program does is eliminate the drudgery involved in retyping the same commands every time you need to perform a set of commands together. Shell programs are also easy to schedule on a regular basis.

Using Shell Variables

You learned earlier in this chapter how shell variables are used to set up your UNIX environment. It's common to set variables within shell programs, so that these variables will hold their values for as long as the shell program executes.

If you're running the shell program manually, you can set the shell variables in the session you're using, and there's really no need for separate specification of shell variables in the shell program. However, you won't always run a shell program manually—that defeats the whole purpose of using shell programs in the first place. Shell programs are often run as part of the cron job, and they could be run from a session that doesn't have all the environmental variables set correctly. By setting shell variables in the program, you can make sure you're using the right values for key variables such as PATH, ORACLE_SID, and ORACLE_HOME.

Evaluating Expressions with the test Command

In order to write good shell scripts, you must understand how to use the test command. Most scripts involve conditional (if-then, while-do, until-do) statements. The test command helps in determining whether a certain condition is satisfied or not.

The test command evaluates an expression and returns a 0 value if the condition is true; otherwise it returns a value greater than 0, usually 1.

The syntax for the test command is as follows:

```
test expression
```

You can use the test command in conjunction with the if, while, or until constructs or use it by itself to evaluate any expression you like. Here is an example:

```
$ test "ONE" = "one"
```

This statement asks the test command to determine whether the string "ONE" is the same as the string "one".

You can use the test command in the implicit form (with an alias), by using square brackets instead of the test command, as shown here:

```
$ [ "ONE" = "one" ]
```

To find out whether the test command (or its equivalent, the square brackets) evaluated the expression "ONE" = "one" to be true or false, remember that if the result code (same as exit code) is 0, the expression is true, and otherwise it is false. To find the result code, all you have to do is use the special variable ?$, which will show you the exit code for any UNIX or Linux command. In our case, here is the exit code:

```
$ test "ONE" = "one"
$ echo $?
0
```

You can use exit codes in your shell scripts to check the execution status of any commands you use in the script.

You can use the following relations with the test command while comparing integers:

-ne: Not equal

-eq: Equal

-lt: Less than

-gt: Greater than

-ge: Greater than or equal to

-le: Less than or equal to

Executing Shell Programs with Command-Line Arguments

It's common to use arguments to specify parameters to shell programs. For example, you can run the shell program example.ksh as follows:

```
$ example.ksh prod1 system
```

In this case, example.ksh is your shell script, and the command-line arguments are prod1, the database name, and system, the username in the database. There are two arguments inside the shell script referred to as $1 and $2, and these arguments correspond to prod1 and system.

UNIX uses a *positional system*, meaning that the first argument after the shell script's name is the variable $1, the second argument is the value of the variable $2, and so on. Thus, whenever there's a reference to $1 inside the shell script, you know the variable is referring to the first argument (prod1, the database name, in this example).

By using command-line arguments, the script can be reused for several database and username combinations—you don't have to change the script.

Analyzing a Shell Script

Let's look at a simple database-monitoring shell script, example.ksh. This script looks for a certain file and lets you know if it fails to find it. The script uses one command-line argument to specify the name of the database. You therefore will expect to find a $1 variable in the script.

When the shell program is created, UNIX has no way of knowing it's an executable program. You make your little program an executable shell script by using the chmod command:

```
$ ll example.ksh
-rw-rw-rw-  1  salapati   dba   439   feb  02   16:51  example.ksh
$ chmod 766 example.ksh
$ ll example.ksh
4-rwxrw-rw-  1  salapati   dba   439   feb  02   16:52  example.ksh
$
```

You can see that when the script was first created, it wasn't executable, because it didn't have the execution permissions set for anyone. By using the chmod command, the execution permission is granted to the owner of the program, salapati, and now the program is an executable shell script.

Here are the contents of the example.ksh shell script, which looks for a certain file in a directory and sends out an e-mail to the DBA if the file is not found there:

```
#!/bin/ksh
ORACLE_SID=$1 export ORACLE_SID
PATH=/usr/bin:/usr/local/bin:/usr/contrib./bin:$PATH
export PATH
ORACLE_BASE=${ORACLE_HOME}/../..;
```

```
export ORACLE_BASE
export CURRDATE='date +%m%dY_%H%M'
export LOGFILE=/tmp/dba/dba.log
test -s $ORACLE_HOME/dbs/test${ORACLE_SID}.dbf
if [ 'echo $?' -ne 0 ]
then
    echo  "File not found!"
mailx  -s "Critical: Test file not found!"  dba@bankone.com  <  $LOGFILE
fi
```

Let's analyze the example.ksh shell script briefly. The first line in the program announces that this is a program that will use the Korn shell—that's what #!/bin/ksh at the top of the script indicates. This is a standard line in all Korn shell programs (and programs for other shells have equivalent lines).

In the next line, you see ORACLE_SID being assigned the value of the $1 variable. Thus, $1 will be assigned the value of the first parameter you pass with the shell program at the time of execution, and that value will be given to ORACLE_SID. The script also exports the value for the ORACLE_BASE environment variable.

Next, the program exports the values of three environmental variables: PATH, CURRDATE, and LOGFILE.

Then the script uses the file-testing command, test, to check for the existence of the file test*prod1*.dbf (where *prod1* is the value of ORACLE_SID) in a specific location. In UNIX, the success of a command is indicated by a value of 0 and failure is indicated by 1; you'll also recall that echo $?variable_name will print the value of the variable on the screen. Therefore, the next line, if ['echo $? ' -ne 0], literally means "if the result of the test command is negative" (which is the same as saying, "if the file doesn't exist"). If that's the case, the then statement will write "File not found" in the log file.

The then statement also uses the mail program to e-mail a message to the DBA saying that the required file is missing. The mail program lets you send mail to user accounts on another UNIX server or to a person's e-mail address.

All you have to do to run or execute this shell script is simply type the name of the script at the command prompt, followed by the name of the database. For this simple method to work, however, you must be in the Korn shell when you run the script.

Now that you've learned the basics of creating shell scripts, let's move on to some powerful but still easy techniques that will help you write more powerful shell programs.

Flow-Control Structures in Korn Shell Programming

The Korn shell provides several flow-control structures similar to the ones found in regular programming languages, such as C or Java. These include the conditional structures that use if statements and the iterative structures that use while and for statements to loop through several steps based on certain conditions being satisfied. Besides these flow-control structures, you can use special commands to interrupt or get out of loops when necessary.

Conditional Branching

Branching constructs let you instruct the shell program to perform alternative tasks based on whether a certain condition is true or not. For example, you can tell the program to execute a particular command if a certain file exists and to issue an error message if it doesn't.

The most common form of conditional branching in all types of programming is the if-then-else conditional structure. In UNIX and Linux programming, this conditional structure has the syntax if-then-else-fi. This conditional structure will perform one of two or more actions, depending on the results of a test.

The syntax for the `if-then-else-fi` structure is as follows:

```
if  condition
then
        Action a
else
        Action b
fi
```

Make sure that the `then` is on the second line. Also, notice that the control structure ends in `fi` (which is `if` spelled backwards).

Here's an example of the `if-then-else-fi` structure:

```
#!/usr/bin/sh
LOGFILE= /tmp/dba/error.log
export LOGFILE
grep ORA- $LOGFILE > job.err
    if [ `cat job.err|wc -l` -gt 0 ]
      then
            mailx -s "Backup Job Errors" salapati@netbsa.org < job.err
        else mailx -s " Backup Job Completed Successfully" salapati@netbsa.org
    fi
```

This script checks to see whether there are any errors in an Oracle backup job log. The script uses the mailx program, a UNIX-based mail utility, to send mail to the DBA. The -s option of the mailx utility specifies the subject line for the e-mail. The contents of the `job.err` file will be sent as the output of the e-mail.

Looping

In real-world programming, you may want to execute a command several times based on some condition. UNIX provides several loop constructs to enable this, the main ones being the `while-do-done` loop, which executes a command while a condition is true; the `for-do-done` loop, which executes a command a set number of times; and the `until-do-done` loop, which performs the same command until some condition becomes true.

The next sections examine these three loop structures in more detail.

A while-do-done Loop

The `while-do-done` loop tests a condition each time before executing the commands within the loop. If the test is successful, the commands are executed. If the test is never successful, the commands aren't executed even once. Thus, the loop ensures that the commands inside the loop get executed "while" a certain condition remains true.

Here's the syntax for the `while-do-done` loop:

```
while condition
do
    commands
done
```

In the following example of the `while-do-done` loop, note that the command inside the loop executes 99 times (the `lt` relation ensures that as long as the value of the variable `VAR1` is less than 100, the script will `echo` the value of the variable):

```
#!/usr/bin/ksh
VAR1=1
while [ $VAR1 -lt 100 ]
do
        echo "value of VAR1 is: $VAR1"
        ((VAR1 =VAR1+1))
done
```

A for-do-done Loop

You can use the for-do-done loop when you have to process a list of items. For each item in the list, the loop executes the commands within it. Processing will continue until the list elements are exhausted.

The syntax of the for-do-done loop is as follows:

```
for var in list
do
    commands
done
```

Here's an example of a for-do-done loop (the for command uses the letter F as a variable to process the list of files in a directory):

```
#!/usr/bin/sh
##  this loop gives you a list of all files (not directories)
## in a specified directory.
for F in /u01/app/oracle
do
    if [ -f $F]
    then
            ls    $F
    fi
done
```

An until-do-done Loop

An until-do-done loop executes the commands inside the loop until a certain condition becomes true. The loop executes as long as the condition remains false.

Here's the general syntax for the until-do-done loop:

```
until condition
do
    commands
done
```

The following is a simple example that shows how to use the until-do-done loop. The print command outputs the sentence within the quotes on the screen. The -n option specifies that the output should be placed on a new line. The UNIX command read will read a user's input and place it in the answer variable. The script then will continue to run until the user inputs the answer "YES":

```
until [[ $answer = "yes" ]];do
   print -n "Please accept by entering \"YES\": "
   read answer
   print ""
done
```

Branching with the case Command

The case structure is quite different from all the other conditional statements. This structure lets the program branch to a segment of the program based on the value of a certain variable. The variable's value is checked against several patterns, and when the patterns match, the commands associated with that pattern will be executed.

Here's the general syntax of the case command:

```
case var in
pattern1)
          commands
           ;;
pattern2)
          commands
           ;;
...
patternn)
          commands
           ;;
esac
```

Note that the end of the case statement is marked by esac (which is case spelled backwards). Here's a simple example that illustrates the use of the case command:

```
#!/usr/bin/sh
echo " Enter b to see the list of books"
echo " Enter t  to see the library timings"
echo " Enter e to exit the menu"
echo
echo "Please enter a choice": \c"
read VAR
case $VAR in
b/B) book.sh
        ;;
t/T) times.sh
        ;;
e/E) logout.sh
        ;;
*)    echo " "wrong Key entry: Please choose again"
esac
```

Dealing with UNIX Processes

When you execute your shell program, UNIX creates an active instance of your program, called the *process*. UNIX also assigns your process a unique identification number, called the *process ID* (PID). As a DBA, you need to know how to track the processes that pertain to your programs and the database instance that you are managing.

Gathering Process Information with ps

The ps command, with its many options, is what you'll use to gather information about the currently running processes on your system. The ps -ef command will let you know the process ID, the user, the program the user is executing, and the length of the program's execution.

In the following example, the ps -ef command is issued to display the list of processes, but because the list is going to be very long, the pipe command is used to filter the results. The grep command ensures that the list displays only those processes that contain the word "pmon". The pmon process is an essential Oracle background process, and I explain it in Chapter 5. The output indicates that three different Oracle databases are currently running:

```
$ ps -ef | grep pmon
oracle 10703        1    0   09:05:39  ?         0.00   ora_pmon_test
oracle  18655       1    0   09:24:00  ?         0.00   ora_pmon_prod1
oracle 10984        1    0   09:17:50  ?         0.00   ora_pmon_finance
$
```

Running Processes after Logging Out

Sometimes, you may want to run a program from a terminal, but you then need to log out from it after a while. When you log out, a "hangup" signal is sent to all the processes you started in that session. To keep the programs you are executing from terminating abruptly when you disconnect, you can run your shell programs with the nohup option, which means "no hangup." You can then disconnect, but your (long) program will continue to run.

Here's how you specify the nohup option for a process:

```
$ nohup test.ksh
```

Running Processes in the Background

You can start a job and then run it in the background, returning control to the terminal. The way to do this is to specify the & parameter after the program name, as shown in the following example (you can use the ps command to see if your process is still running, by issuing either the ps -ef or ps -aux command):

```
$  test.ksh &
[1]    27149
$
```

You can also put a currently running job in the background, by using the Ctrl+Z sequence. This will suspend the job and run it in the background. You can then use the command fg%jobnumber to move the job that's running in the background back to the foreground.

Terminating Processes with the kill Command

Sometimes you'll need to terminate a process because it's a runaway or because you ran the wrong program. In UNIX, signals are used to communicate with processes and to handle exceptions. To bring a UNIX process to an abrupt stop, you can use the kill command to signal the shell to terminate the session before its conclusion. Needless to say, mistakes in the use of the kill command can prove disastrous.

■**Note** Although you can always kill an unwanted Oracle user session or a process directly from UNIX itself, you're better off always using Oracle's methods for terminating database sessions. There are a couple of reasons for this. First, you may accidentally wipe out the wrong session. Second, when you're using the Oracle shared server method, a process may have spawned several other processes, and killing the dispatcher session could end up wiping out more sessions than you had intended.

There is more than one kill signal that you can issue to terminate any particular process. The general format of the kill command is as follows:

```
kill -[signal] PID
```

The *signal* option after the kill command specifies the particular signal the kill command will send to a process, and *PID* is the process ID of the process to be killed. To kill a process gracefully, you send a SIGTERM signal to the process, using either the signal's name or number. Either of the following commands will kill the process with a PID of 21427:

```
$ Kill -SIGTERM  21427
$ Kill -15  21427
```

If your SIGTERM signal, which is intended to terminate a process gracefully, doesn't succeed in terminating the session, you can send a signal that will *force* the process to die. To do this, use the kill -9 signal:

```
$ kill -9 21427
```

UNIX System Administration and the Oracle DBA

It isn't necessary for you to be an accomplished system administrator to manage your database, but it doesn't hurt to know as much as possible about what system administration entails. Most organizations hire UNIX system administrators to manage their systems, and as an Oracle DBA, you'll need to interact closely with those UNIX system administrators. Although the networking and other aspects of the system administrator's job may not be your cup of tea, you do need to know quite a bit about disk management, process control, and backup operations. UNIX system administrators are your best source of information and guidance regarding these issues.

UNIX Backup and Restore Utilities

Several utilities in UNIX make copies or restore files from copies. Of these, the dd command pertains mainly to the so-called raw files. Most of the time, you'll be dealing with UNIX file systems, and you'll need to be familiar with two important archiving facilities—tar and cpio—to perform backups and restores. The command tar is an abbreviation for "tape file archiver," and was originally designed to write to tapes. The command cpio stands for "copy input and output." Other operating system–specific backup and recovery techniques such as fbackup/frecover, dump/restore, and xdump/vxrestore exist, but they are mainly of interest to UNIX administrators. You most likely will use the tar and cpio commands to perform backups. The tar command can copy and restore archives of files using a tape system or a disk drive. By default, tar output is placed on /dev/rmt/0m, which refers to a tape drive.

The following tar command will copy the data01.dbf file to a tape, with the format /dev/rmt/0m. The -cvf option creates a new archive (the hyphen is optional). The c option asks tar to create a new archive file, and the v option stands for verbose, which specifies that the files be listed as they are being archived:

```
$ tar -cvf /dev/rmt/0m    /u10/oradata/data/data01.dbf
```

The following tar command will extract the backed-up files from the tape to the specified directory:

```
$ tar -xvf/dev/rmt/0m     /u20/oradata/data/data01.dbf
```

The x option asks tar to extract the contents of the specified file. The v and f options have the same meanings as in the previous example.

The cpio command with the -o (copy out) option copies files to standard output, such as disk or tape. The following command will copy the contents of the entire current directory (all the files) to the /dev/rmt/0m tape:

```
$ ls | cpio -0 > /dev/rmt/0m
```

The cpio command with the -i (copy in) option extracts files from standard input. The following command restores all the contents of the specified tape to the current directory:

```
$ cpio -i < /dev/rmt/0m
```

The crontab and Automating Scripts

Most DBAs will have to schedule their shell programs and other data-loading programs for regular execution by the UNIX system. UNIX provides the cron table, or crontab, to schedule database tasks. In this section, you'll learn how to schedule jobs with this wonderful, easy-to-use utility.

You can invoke the crontab by typing in **crontab -l**. This will give you a listing of the contents of crontab. To add programs to the schedule or change existing schedules, you need to invoke crontab in the edit mode, as shown here:

```
$ crontab -e
```

Each line in the crontab is an entry for a regularly scheduled job or program, and you edit the crontab the same way you edit any normal vi-based file. Each line in the /etc/crontab file represents a job that you want to execute, and it has the following format:

```
minute        hour       day       month     day of week       command
```

The items in the crontab line can have the following values:

- minute: Any integer from 0 to 59
- hour: Any integer from 0 to 23
- day: Any integer from 1 to 31 (this must be a valid date if a month is specified)
- month: Any integer from 1 to 12 (or the short name of the month, such as jan or feb)
- day of week: Any integer from 0 to 7, where 0 and 7 represent Sunday, 1 is Saturday, and so on
- command: The command you want to execute (this is usually a shell script)

Here's a simple example of a crontab line:

```
#-------------------------------------------------------------------------
minute        hour     date    month    day of week        command
30            18       *       *        1-6                analyze.ksh
#-------------------------------------------------------------------------
```

The preceding code indicates that the program analyze.ksh will be run Monday through Saturday at 6:30 p.m. Once you edit the crontab and input the lines you need to run your commands, you can exit out of cron by pressing Shift+WQ, just as you would in a regular vi file. You now have "cronned" your job, and it will run without any manual intervention at the scheduled time.

It's common practice for DBAs to put most of their monitoring and daily data-load jobs in the crontab for automatic execution. If crontab comes back with an error when you first try to edit it, you need to talk to your UNIX system administrator and have appropriate permissions granted.

■**Note** You'll use crontab for all your regularly scheduled database or operating system jobs, but if you want to schedule a task for a single execution, you can use the at or batch command instead. Look up the man pages for more information on these two scheduling commands.

Using Telnet

Telnet is an Internet protocol for accessing remote computers from your PC or from another UNIX server or workstation. Your machine simply needs to be connected to the target machine through a network, and you must have a valid user account on the computer you are connecting to. To use telnet on your PC, for example, go to the DOS prompt and type **telnet**. At the telnet prompt, type in either the UNIX server's IP address or its symbolic name, and your PC will connect to the server. Unless you are doing a lot of file editing, telnet is usually all you need to connect and work with a UNIX server, in the absence of a terminal emulator.

The following example session shows a connection to and disconnection from a server named hp50. Of course, what you can do on the server will depend on the privileges you have on that machine.

```
$ telnet hp5
Trying...
Connected to hp5.netbsa.org.
Escape character is '^]'.
Local flow control on
Telnet TERMINAL-SPEED option ON
login: oracle
Password:
Last   successful login for oracle: Tue Nov  5 09:39:45
CST6CDT 2002 on tty
Last unsuccessful login for oracle: Thu Oct 24 09:31:17
CST6CDT 2002 on tty
Please wait...checking for disk quotas
...
You have mail.
TERM = (dtterm)
oracle@hp5[/u01/app/oracle]
$
```

Once you log in, you can do everything you are able to do when you log directly into the server without using telnet.

You log out from your telnet session in the following way:

```
$ exit
logout
Connection closed by foreign host.
$
```

Remote Login and Remote Copy

Rlogin is a UNIX service that's very similar to telnet. Using the rlogin command, you can log into a remote system just as you would using the telnet utility. Here is how you can use the rlogin command to remotely log into the server hp5:

```
$ rlogin hp5
```

You'll be prompted for a password after you issue the preceding command, and upon the validation of the password, you'll be logged into the remote server.

To copy files from a server on the network, you don't necessarily have to log into that machine or even use the FTP service. You can simply use the rcp command to copy the files. For example, to copy a file named /etc/oratab from the server hp5 to your client machine (or to a different server), you would use the rcp command as follows:

```
$ rcp hp5:/etc/oratab/  .
```

The dot in the command indicates that the copy should be placed in your current location.

To copy a file called test.txt from your current server to the /tmp directory of the server hp5, you would use the rcp command as follows:

```
$ rcp /test/txt  hp5:/tmp
```

Using SSH, the Secure Shell

The Secure Shell, SSH, is a UNIX based command interface and a protocol that enables secure remote logins to a system. Net administrators use SSH widely to control web servers as well as other servers remotely. The big difference between the ssh command (which uses the SSH protocol) and rlogin is that SSH is a secure way to communicate with remote servers—SSH uses encrypted communications to connect two untrusted hosts over an insecure network and also encrypts the passwords.

Here's an example of using the ssh command to connect to the hp5 server:

```
$ ssh prod5
Password:
Last    successful login for oracle: Thu Apr  7 09:46:52 CST6CDT 2005 on tty
Last unsuccessful login for oracle: Fri Apr  1 09:02:00 CST6CDT 2005
oracle@prod5   [/u01/app/oracle]
$
```

Just as SSH is a secure alternative to traditional telnet, the scp service is a secure alternative to rcp, for transferring files between servers. The syntax for the scp command is similar to that of the rcp command:

```
scp [-r] [[user@]host1:]file1 [...] [[user@]host2:]file2
```

The -r option copies files recursively.

Using FTP to Send and Receive Files

FTP, the File Transfer Protocol, is a popular way to transmit files between UNIX servers or between a UNIX server and a PC. It's a simple and fast way to send files back and forth.

The following is a sample FTP session between my PC and a UNIX server on my network. I am getting a file from the UNIX server called prod5 using the ftp get command.

```
$ ftp prod5
connected to prod5
ready.
User (prod5:-(none)): oracle
331 Password required for oracle.
Password:
User oracle logged in.
ftp> pwd
'/u01/app/oracle" is the current directory.
ftp>  cd admin/dba/test
```

```
CWD command successful.
ftp> get analyze.ksh
200  PORT command successful.
150  Opening ASCII mode data connection for analyze.ksh
 (3299 bytes).
226 Transfer complete.
ftp: 3440 bytes received in 0.00Seconds  3440000.00Lbytes/sec.
ftp> bye
221 Goodbye.
$
```

If, instead of getting a file, I wanted to place a file from my PC onto the UNIX server I connected to, I would use the put command, as in put analyze.ksh. The default mode of data transmission is the ASCII character text mode; if you want binary data transmission, just type in the word **binary** before you use the get or put command.

Of course, GUI-based FTP clients are an increasingly popular choice. If you have access to one of those, transferring files is usually simply a matter of dragging and dropping files from the server to the client, much like moving files in Windows Explorer.

UNIX System Performance Monitoring Tools

Several tools are available for monitoring the performance of the UNIX system. These tools check on the memory and disk utilization of the host system and let you know of any performance bottlenecks. In this section, you'll explore the main UNIX-based monitoring tools and see how these tools can help you monitor the performance of your system.

The Basics of Monitoring a UNIX System

A slow system could be the result of a bottleneck in processing (CPU), memory, disk, or bandwidth. System monitoring tools help you to clearly identify the bottlenecks causing poor performance. Let's briefly examine what's involved in the monitoring of each of these resources on your system.

Monitoring CPU Usage

As long as you are not utilizing 100 percent of the CPU capacity, you still have juice left in the system to support more activity. Spikes in CPU usage are common, but your goal is to track down what, if any, processes are contributing excessively to CPU usage. These are some of the key factors to remember while examining CPU usage:

- *User versus system usage*: You can identify the percentage of time the CPU power is being used for users' applications as compared with time spent servicing the operating system's overhead. Obviously, if the system overhead accounts for an overwhelming proportion of CPU usage, you may have to examine this in more detail.

- *Runnable processes*: At any given time, a process is either running or waiting for resources to be freed up. A process that is waiting for the allocation of resources is called a *runnable process*. The presence of a large number of runnable processes indicates that your system may be facing a power crunch—it is CPU-bound.

- *Context switches and interrupts*: When the operating system switches between processes, it incurs some overhead due to the so-called context switches. If you have too many context switches, you'll see deterioration in CPU usage. You'll incur similar overhead when you have too many interrupts, caused by the operating system when it finishes certain hardware- or software-related tasks.

Managing Memory

Memory is one of the first places you should look when you have performance problems. If you have inadequate memory (RAM), your system may slow down due to excessive swapping. Here are some of the main factors to focus on when you are checking system memory usage:

- *Page ins and page outs*: If you have a high number of page ins and page outs in your memory statistics, it means that your system is doing an excessive amount of *paging*, the moving of pages from memory to the disk system due to inadequate available memory. Excessive paging could lead to a condition called *thrashing*, which just means you are using critical system resources to move pages back and forth between memory and disk.

- *Swap ins and swap outs*: The swapping statistics also indicate how adequate your current memory allocation is for your system.

- *Active and inactive pages*: If you have too few inactive memory pages, it may mean that your physical memory is inadequate.

Monitoring Disk Storage

When it comes to monitoring disks, you should look for two things. First, check to make sure you aren't running out of room—applications add more data on a continuous basis, and it is inevitable that you will have to constantly add more storage space. Second, watch your disk performance—are there any bottlenecks due to slow disk input/output performance?

Here are the basic things to look for:

- *Check for free space*: Using simple commands, a system administrator or a DBA can check the amount of free space left on the system. It's good, of course, to do this on a regular basis so you can head off a resource crunch before it's too late. Later in this chapter, I'll show you how to use the df and the du commands to check the free space on your system.

- *Reads and writes*: The read/write figures give you a good picture of how hot your disks are running. You can tell whether your system is handling its workload well, or if it's experiencing an extraordinary I/O load at any given time.

Monitoring Bandwidth

By measuring bandwidth use, you can measure the efficiency of the transfer of data between devices. Bandwidth is harder to measure than simple I/O or memory usage patterns, but it can still be immensely useful to collect bandwidth-related statistics.

Your network is an important component of your system—if the network connections are slow, the whole application may appear to run very slowly. Simple network statistics like the number of bytes received and sent will help you identify network problems.

High network packet collision rates, as well as excessive data transmission errors, will lead to bottlenecks. You need to examine the network using tools like netstat (discussed later) to see if the network has any bottlenecks.

Monitoring Tools for UNIX Systems

In order to find out what processes are running, you'll most commonly use the process command, ps. For example, the following example checks for the existence of the essential pmon process, to see if the database is up:

```
$ ps -ef | grep pmon
```

Of course, to monitor system performance, you'll need more sophisticated tools than the elementary ps command. The following sections cover some of the important tools available for monitoring your system's performance.

Monitoring Memory Use with vmstat

The vmstat utility helps you monitor memory usage, page faults, processes, and CPU activity. The vmstat utility's output is divided into two parts: virtual memory (VM) and CPU. The VM section is divided into three parts: memory, page, and faults. In the memory section, avm stands for "active virtual memory" and free is short for "free memory." The page and faults items provide detailed information on page reclaims, pages paged in and out, and device interrupt rates.

The output gives you an idea about whether the memory on the system is a bottleneck during peak times. The po (page outs) variable under the page heading should ideally be 0, indicating that there is no swapping—that the system is not transferring memory pages to swap disk devices to free up memory for other processes.

Here is some sample output from vmstat (note that I use the -n option to improve the formatting of the output):

```
$ vmstat -n
VM
    memory              page                    faults
  avm      free     re   at pi po fr de sr   in  sy   cs
1822671  8443043 1052 113 2  0  0  0  0   8554 89158 5272
CPU
    cpu          procs
 us sy id     r    b    w
 23  7 69     8   23    0
 22  8 70
 21  7 72
 22  7 71
$
```

Under the procs subheading in the CPU part of the output, the first column, r, refers to the run queue. If your system has 24 CPUs and your run queue shows 20, that means 20 processes are waiting in the queue for a turn on the CPUs, and it is definitely not a bad thing. If the same r value of 24 occurs on a machine with 2 CPUs, it indicates the system is CPU-bound—a large number of processes are waiting for CPU time.

In the CPU part of vmstat's output, *us* stands for the amount of CPU usage attributable to the users of the system, including your database processes. The *sy* part shows the system usage of the CPU, and *id* stands for the amount of CPU that is idle. In our example, roughly 70 percent of the CPU is idle for each of the four processors, on average.

Viewing I/O Statistics with iostat

The iostat utility gives you input/output statistics for all the disks on your system. The output is displayed in four columns:

- *device*: The disk device whose performance iostat is measuring
- *bps*: The number of kilobytes transferred from the device per second
- *sps*: The number of disk seeks per second
- *msps*: The time in milliseconds per average seek

The iostat command takes two parameters: the number of seconds before the information should be updated on the screen, and the number of times the information should be updated. Here is an example of the iostat output:

```
$ iostat 4 5
        device          bps       sps       msps
        c2t6d0          234       54.9      1.0
        c5t6d0          198       42.6      1.0
        c0t1d1          708       27.7      1.0
        c4t3d1          608       19.0      1.0
        c0t1d2          961       46.6      1.0
        c4t3d2          962       46.1      1.0
        c0t1d3          731       91.3      1.0
        c4t3d3          760       93.5      1.0
        c0t1d4           37        7.0      1.0
$
```

In the preceding output, you can see that the disks c0t1d2 and c4t3d2 are the most heavily used disks on the system.

Analyzing Read/Write Operations with sar

The UNIX sar (system activity reporter) utility offers a very powerful way to analyze how the read/write operations are occurring from disk to buffer cache and from buffer cache to disk. By using the various options of the sar command, you can monitor disk and CPU activity, in addition to buffer cache activity.

The output for the sar command has the following columns:

- *bread/s*: The number of read operations per second from disk to the buffer cache

- *lread/s*: The number of read operations per second from the buffer cache

- *%rcache*: The cache hit ratio for read requests

- *bwrit/s*: The number of write operations per second from disk to the buffer cache

- *lwrit/s*: The number of write operations per second to the buffer cache

- *%wcache*: The cache hit ratio for write requests

Here's the output of a typical sar command, which monitors your server's CPU activity, using the -u option (the 1 10 tells sar to refresh the output on the screen every second for a total of ten times):

```
$ sar -u 1 10
HP-UX prod5 B.11.11 U 9000/800    04/07/08

16:11:21    %usr      %sys      %wio      %idle
16:11:22    34        6         56        4
16:11:23    31        7         55        7
16:11:24    45        9         43        4
16:11:25    45        9         44        2
16:11:26    45        11        40        3
16:11:27    46        11        40        4
16:11:28    48        10        40        3
16:11:29    56        11        31        2
16:11:30    50        12        36        3
16:11:31    45        12        39        4
```

| Average | 44 | 10 | 42 | 4 |

$

In the preceding sar report, %usr shows the percentage of CPU time spent in the user mode, %sys shows the percentage of CPU time spent in the system mode, %wio shows the percentage of time the CPU is idle with some process waiting for I/O, and %idle shows the idle percentage of the CPU. You can see that the percentage of CPU due to processes waiting for I/O is quite high in this example.

Monitoring Performance with top

The top command is another commonly used performance-monitoring tool. Unlike some of the other tools, the top command shows you a little bit of everything, such as the top CPU and memory utilization processes, the percentage of CPU time used by the top processes, and the memory utilization.
    The top command displays information in the following columns:

- *CPU*: Specifies the processor
- *PID*: Specifies the process ID
- *USER*: Specifies the owner of the process
- *PRI*: Specifies the priority value of the process
- *NI*: Specifies the nice value (nice invokes a command with an altered scheduling priority)
- *SIZE*: Specifies the total size of the process in memory
- *RES*: Specifies the resident size of the process
- *TIME*: Specifies the CPU time used by the process
- *%CPU*: Specifies the CPU usage as a percentage of total CPU
- *COMMAND*: Specifies the command that started the process

To invoke the top utility, you simply type the word **top** at the command prompt. To end the top display, just use the Ctrl+C key combination.
    Here's an example of typical output of the top command on a four-processor UNIX machine. The first part of the output (not shown here) shows the resource usage for each processor in the system. The second part of the output, shown in the following snippet, gives you information about the heaviest users of your system.

```
$ top
CPU   PID   USER     PRI    NI   SIZE    RES    TIME    %CPU   COMMAND
21    2713  nsuser   134    0    118M    104M   173:31  49.90  ns-httpd
23    28611 oracle   241    20   40128K  9300K  2:20    46.60  oraclepasprod
20    6951  oracle   241    20   25172K  19344K 3:45    44.62  rwrun60
13    9334  oracle   154    20   40128K  9300K  1:31    37.62  oraclepasprod
22    24517 oracle   68     20   36032K  5204K  0:55    36.48  oraclepasprod
22    13166 oracle   241    20   40128K  9300K  0:41    35.19  oraclepasprod
12    14097 oracle   241    20   40128K  9300K  0:29    33.75  oraclepasprod
$
```

Monitoring the System with GlancePlus

Several UNIX operating systems have their own system-monitoring tools. For example, on the HP-UX operating system, GlancePlus is a package that is commonly used by system administrators and DBAs to monitor memory, disk I/O, and CPU performance.

Figure 3-3 shows a typical GlancePlus session in text mode, invoked with the following command:

```
$ glance -m
```

The CPU, memory, disk, and swap usage is summarized in the top section. The middle of the display gives you a detailed memory report, and at the bottom of the screen you can see a short summary of memory usage again.

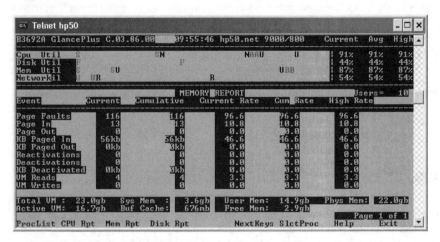

Figure 3-3. *A typical GlancePlus session in text mode*

Note that this session shows memory usage in detail because GlancePlus was invoked with the -m option (glance -c would give you a report on CPU usage, and glance -d would give you a disk usage report).

GlancePlus also has an attractive and highly useful GUI interface, which you can invoke by using the command gpm.

Monitoring the Network with netstat

Besides monitoring the CPU and memory on the system, you need to monitor the network to make sure there are no serious traffic bottlenecks. The netstat utility comes in handy for this purpose, and it works the same way on UNIX as it does on the Windows servers.

Disks and Storage in UNIX

The topic of physical storage and using the disk system in UNIX is extremely important for the DBA—the choice of disk configuration has a profound impact on the availability and the performance of the database. Some Oracle databases benefit by using "raw" disk storage instead of disks controlled by the UNIX operating system. The Oracle Real Application Clusters (RACs) can only use the raw devices; they can't use the regular UNIX-formatted disks.

All the UNIX files on a system make up its *file system*, and this file system is created on a *disk partition*, which is a "slice" of a disk, the basic storage device.

Disk Storage Configuration Choices

The choices you make about how you configure your disk storage will have a major impact on the performance and the uptime of your database. It's not a good idea to make storage device decisions in a vacuum; rather, you should consider your database applications and the type of database that is going to be located on the storage systems when making these decisions.

For example, if you have a data warehouse, you may want your system administrator to use larger striping sizes for the disks. If you are going to have large numbers of writes to or reads from the database, you need to choose the appropriate disk configuration. Compared to the technologies of only a few years ago, today's ultra-sophisticated storage technologies make it possible to have both a high level of performance and high availability of data simultaneously.

Still, you have plenty of choices to make that will have an impact on performance and availability. The nature of the I/Os, database caches, read/write ratios, and other issues are fundamentally different in OLTP and DSS systems. Also, response-time expectations are significantly different between OLTP and DSS systems. Thus, a storage design that is excellent for one type of database may be a terrible choice for another type, so you need to learn more about the operational needs of your application at the physical design stage to make smart choices in this extremely critical area.

Monitoring Disk Usage

When setting up an Oracle system, you will typically make a formal request to the system administrator for physical disk space based on your sizing estimates and growth expectations for the database. Once the general space request is approved by the system administrator, he or she will give you the location of the mount points where your space is located. *Mount points* are directories on the system to which the file systems are mounted. You can then create all the necessary directories prior to the installation of the Oracle software and the creation of the database itself.

Once space is assigned for your software and databases, it's your responsibility to keep track of its usage. If you seem to be running out of space, you will need to request more space from the system administrator. Ideally, you should always have some extra free disk space on the mount points assigned to you so you can allocate space to your database files if the need arises. There are a couple of very useful commands for checking your disk space and seeing what has been used and what is still free for future use.

The df (disk free) command indicates the total allocation in bytes for any mount point and how much of it is currently being used. The df -k option gives you the same information in kilobytes, which is generally more useful. The following example shows the use of the df command with the -k option:

```
$df -k /finance09
/finance09 ( /dev/vgxp1_0f038/lvol1) :
7093226 total allocated Kb
1740427 free allocated Kb
5352799 used allocated Kb
75% allocation used
$
```

The preceding output shows that out of a total of 7.09GB allocated to the /finance09 mount point, about 5.35GB is currently allocated to various files and about 1.74GB of space is still free.

Another command that displays how the disks are being used is the du command, which indicates, in bytes, the amount of space being used by the mount point.

```
$ du -k /finance09
          /finance09/lost+found
          /finance09/ffacts/home
. . .
5348701    /finance09
$
```

As you can see in the preceding example, the du command indicates the actual space used by the various files and directories of the mount point (/finance09 in this case) and the total space used up by it.

I prefer the df command over the du command, because I can see at a glance the percentages of free space and used space.

Disk Storage, Performance, and Availability

Availability and performance lie at the heart of all disk configuration strategies. The one thing you can be sure of when you use disk-based storage systems is that a disk will fail at some point. All disks come with a mean time between failures (MTBF) rating, which could run into hundreds of thousands of hours, and you can expect an average disk with a high rating to last for many years. As we all know, though, averages can be dangerous in situations like this because an individual disk can fail at any time, regardless of its MTBF rating. Disk controllers manage the disks, and a controller failure can doom your system operations. It is common now to build redundancy into your disk systems (and other key components of the entire system) to provide continuous availability.

Performance is also an issue when you are considering the configuration of your storage devices. In systems with highly intensive simultaneous reads and writes, you can quickly end up with disk bottlenecks unless you plan the disk configuration intelligently from the beginning.

To improve performance, the common strategy employed is *disk striping*, which enables you to create a single logical unit out of several physical disks. The single logical unit is composed of alternating stripes from each disk in the set, and data is divided into equally sized blocks and written in stripes to each disk at the same time. Reads are done in the same way, with the simultaneous use of all the disks. Thus, you can enhance I/O operations dramatically, because you are now using the I/O capacity of a set of disks rather than just one.

Disk Partitioning

Raw disks aren't amenable to easy data access—you need to impose a structure on these disks. The first thing you need to do before using a hard disk is to partition, or slice, the disk. Partitioning enables you to store system and application data in separate sections of the disk, as well as manage space issues easily. Sometimes these partitions themselves are called disks, but they are all really parts of a single physical disk. Once you partition a disk, you can create operating system file systems on it.

Creating File Systems

Even after partitioning the whole disk, you still don't have a convenient way to access data or to store it. You can further refine your access methods by using file systems. File systems provide you with the following benefits:

- Individual ownership of files and directories
- Tracking of creation and modification times
- Data access control
- Accounting of space allocation and usage

Disk Striping

It's important to realize that you can place the file system on a single physical disk or you can put it across several "striped" physical disks. In the latter case, although the file system is on several disks, the user will see the files as being on one so-called logical volume. UNIX systems offer several ways of combining multiple disks into single logical volumes.

One way to create a logical device on many UNIX systems is to use a utility known as the Logical Volume Manager. Using an LVM, you can combine ten 72GB disks into a single 720GB logical disk. Thus, disk striping can also enable you to create a much larger logical disk that can handle a larger file system. File systems can't traverse disks, so logical disks offer an easy way to create large volumes.

Logical Volumes and the Logical Volume Manager

Let's briefly look at the two basic methods of configuring physical disks. Although you may never have to do this yourself, it's a good idea to have a basic understanding of how disks are managed by system administrators. You can configure disks as whole disks or as logical volumes.

Whole disks are exactly what their name implies: each physical disk is taken as a whole, and a single file system is created on each disk. You can neither extend nor shrink the file system at a later stage.

Logical volumes, on the other hand, are created by combining several hard disks or disk partitions. System administrators usually employ the sophisticated LVM to combine physical disks. A set of physical disks is combined into a volume group, which is then sliced up by the LVM into smaller logical volumes. Most modern systems use the LVM approach because it is an extremely flexible and easy way to manage disk space. For example, it's no problem at all to add space and modify partitions on a running system by using the LVM tool.

Once you create logical volumes, you can designate disk volumes as mount points, and individual files can then be created on these mount points.

RAID Systems

A redundant array of inexpensive (sometimes also referred to as independent) disk (RAID) device is a popular way to configure large logical (or virtual) disks from a set of smaller disks. The idea is simply to combine several small, inexpensive disks into an array in order to gain higher performance and data security. This allows you to replace one very expensive large disk with several much cheaper small disks. Data is broken up into equal-sized chunks (called the *stripe size*), usually 32KB or 64KB, and a chunk is written on each disk, the exact distribution of data being determined by the RAID level adopted. When the data is read back, the process is reversed, giving the appearance that one large disk, instead of several small disks, is being used.

RAID devices provide you with redundancy—if a disk in a RAID system fails, you can immediately and automatically reconstruct the data on the failed disk from the data on the rest of the devices. RAID systems are ubiquitous, and most Oracle databases employ them for the several performance and redundancy benefits they provide.

When it comes to the performance of disk systems, two factors are of interest: the transfer rate and the number of I/O operations per second. The *transfer rate* refers to the efficiency with which data can move through the disk system's controller. As for I/O operations, the more a disk system can handle in a specified period, the better.

Compared to traditional disks, which have an MTBF of tens of thousands of hours, disk arrays have an MTBF of millions of hours. Even when a disk in a RAID system fails, the array itself continues to operate successfully. Most modern arrays automatically start using one of the spare disks, called *hot spares*, to which the data from the failed drive is transferred. Most disk arrays also permit the replacement of failed disks without bringing the system itself down (this is known as *hot swapping*).

RAID Levels

The inherent trade-off in RAID systems is between performance and reliability. You can employ two fundamental techniques, striping and mirroring the disk arrays, to improve disk performance and enhance reliability.

Mirroring schemes involve complete duplication of the data, and while most of the nonmirrored RAID systems also involve redundancy, it is not as high as in the mirrored systems. The redundancy in nonmirrored RAID systems is due to the fact that they store the parity information needed for reconstructing disks in case there is a malfunction in the array.

The following sections describe the most commonly used RAID classifications. Except for RAID 0, all the levels offer redundancy in your disk storage system.

RAID 0: Striping

Strictly speaking, this isn't really a RAID level, since the striping doesn't provide you with any data protection whatsoever. The data is broken into *chunks* and placed across several disks that make up the disk array. The *stripe* here refers to the set of all the chunks.

Let's say the chunk or stripe size is 8KB. If we have three disks in our RAID and 24KB of data to write to the RAID system, the first 8KB would be written to the first disk, the second 8KB would be written to the second disk, and the final 8KB would be written to the last disk. All writing to the disks is done simultaneously.

Because input and output are spread across multiple disks and disk controllers, the throughput of RAID 0 systems is quite high. For example, you could write an 800KB file over a RAID set of eight disks with a stripe size of 100KB in roughly an eighth of the time it would take to do the same operation on a single disk. However, because there is no built-in redundancy, the loss of a single drive could result in the loss of all the data, as data is stored sequentially on the chunks. RAID 0 is all about performance, with little attention paid to protection. Remember that RAID 0 provides you with zero redundancy. RAID 0 may be a good solution in a lot of test environments, where performance is more critical than the safety of the data, and provides the great advantage of making the entire disk array capacity available for storage.

RAID 1: Mirroring

In RAID 1, all the data is duplicated, or mirrored, on one or more disks. The performance of a RAID 1 system is slower than a RAID 0 system because input transactions are completed only when all the mirrored disks are successfully written to. The reliability of mirrored arrays is high, though, because the failure of one disk in the set doesn't lead to any data loss. The system continues operation under such circumstances, and you have time to regenerate the contents of the lost disks by copying data from the surviving disks. RAID 1 is geared toward protecting the data, with performance taking a back seat. Nevertheless, of all the redundant RAID arrays, RAID 1 still offers the best performance.

It is important to note that RAID 1 means that you will pay for *n* number of disks, but you get to allocate only *n*/2 disks for your system, because all the disks are duplicated.

Read performance improves under a RAID 1 system, because the data is scanned in parallel. However, there is slower write performance, amounting to anywhere from 10 to 20 percent, since the operating system has to write to both disks each time. You use RAID 1 when the value of your data is more critical than the performance, which is the case in most production environments.

RAID 2: Striping with Error Detection and Correction

RAID 2 uses striping with additional error detection and correction capabilities built in. The striping guarantees high performance, and error-correction methods are supposed to ensure reliability. However, the mechanism used to correct errors is bulky and takes up a lot of the disk space itself. This is a costly and inefficient storage system.

RAID 3: Striping with Dedicated Parity

RAID 3 systems are also striped systems, with an additional parity disk that holds the necessary information for correcting errors for the stripe. Parity involves the use of algorithms to derive values that allow the lost data on a disk to be reconstructed on other disks.

Input and output are slower on RAID 3 systems than on pure striped systems, such as RAID 0, because information also has to be written to the parity disk. RAID 3 systems can also only process one I/O request at a time.

Nevertheless, RAID 3 is a more sophisticated system than RAID 2, and it involves less overhead than RAID 2. You'll only need one extra disk drive in addition to the drives that hold the data. If a single disk fails, the array continues to operate successfully, with the failed drive being reconstructed with the help of the stored error-correcting parity information on the extra parity drive. Streaming large files and video applications make use of RAID 3, although it remains a rare configuration in general.

RAID 5 arrays with small stripes can provide better performance than RAID 3 disk arrays.

RAID 4: Modified Striping with Dedicated Parity

The stripes on RAID 4 systems are done in much larger chunks than in RAID 3 systems, which allows the system to process multiple I/O requests simultaneously. In RAID 4 systems, the individual disks can be independently accessed, unlike in RAID 3 systems, which leads to much higher performance when reading data from the disks.

Writes are a different story, however, under this setup. Every time you need to perform a write operation, the parity data for the relevant disk must be updated before the new data can be written. Thus, writes are very slow, and the parity disk could become a bottleneck.

RAID 5: Modified Striping with Interleaved Parity

Under this disk array setup, both the data and the parity information are interleaved across the disk array. Writes under RAID 5 tend to be slower, but not as slow as under RAID 4 systems, because it can handle multiple concurrent write requests. Several vendors have improved the write performance by using special techniques, such as using nonvolatile memory for logging the writes.

RAID 5 gives you virtually all the benefits of striping (high read rates), while providing the redundancy needed for reliability, which RAID 0 striping does not offer.

RAID 0+1: Striping and Mirroring

These RAID systems provide the benefits of striped and mirrored disks. They tend to achieve a high degree of performance because of the striping, while offering high reliability due to the fact that all disks are mirrored (duplicated). You just have to be prepared to request double the number of disks you actually need for your data, because you are mirroring all the disks.

Choosing the Ideal Disk Configuration

Table 3-6 outlines the basic conclusions you can draw about the various RAID systems described in the preceding sections.

What's the best strategy in terms of disk configuration? You, the DBA, and your system administrator should discuss your data needs, management's business objectives, the impact and cost of downtime, and available resources. The more complex the configuration, the more you need to spend on hardware, software, and training.

Table 3-6. *Benefits and Disadvantages of Different RAID Systems*

System	Benefits	Disadvantages
RAID 0	Offers high read and write performance and is cheap	Not very reliable (no redundancy).
RAID 1	Provides 100 percent redundancy	Expensive, and all writes must be duplicated.
RAID 2		Expensive and wastes a lot of space for overhead; it is not commercially viable because of special disk requirements.
RAID 3	Provides the ability to reconstruct data when only one disk fails (if two disks fail at the same time, there will be data loss)	Expensive and has poor random access performance.
RAID 4	Provides the ability to reconstruct data when only one disk fails (if two disks fail at the same time, there will be data loss)	Expensive and leads to degraded write performance as well as a potential parity bottleneck.
RAID 5	Offers high reliability and provides the ability to reconstruct data when only one disk fails (if two disks fail at the same time, there will be data loss)	Involves a write penalty, though it is smaller than in RAID 4 systems.
RAID 0+1	Offers great random access performance as well as high transfer rates	Expensive (due to the mirroring of the disks).

The choice essentially depends upon the needs of your organization. If your database needs the very highest possible performance and reliability at the same time, you may want to go first class and adopt the RAID 0+1 system. This is an expensive way to go, but several companies in critical data-processing areas, such as airline reservations systems, have adopted this as a company standard for data storage.

If data protection is your primary concern, however, and you can live with a moderate throughput performance, you can go with the RAID 5 configuration and save a lot of money in the process. This is especially true if read operations constitute the bulk of the work done by your database.

If you want complete redundancy and the resulting data protection, you can choose to use the RAID 1 configuration, and if you are concerned purely with performance and your data can be reproduced easily, you'll be better off just using a plain vanilla RAID 0 configuration.

To make the right choice, find out the exact response-time expectations for your databases, your finances, the nature of your applications, availability requirements, performance expectations, and growth patterns.

■**Caution** Once you configure a certain RAID level on your disk, you can't easily switch to a different configuration. You have to completely reload all your applications and the databases if you decide to change configurations.

In general, the following guidelines will serve you well when you are considering the RAID configuration for your disks:

- RAID 5 offers many advantages over the other levels of RAID. The traditional complaint about the "write penalty" should be discounted because of sophisticated advances in write caches and other strategies that make RAID 5 much more efficient than in the past. The RAID 5 implementations using specialized controllers are far more efficient than software-based RAID or RAID 5 implementations based on the server itself. Using write caches in RAID 5 systems improves the overall write performance significantly.

- Allow for a lot more raw disk space than you figure you'll need. This includes your expansion estimates for storage space. Fault tolerance requires more disks under RAID systems than other systems. If you need 400GB of disk space, and you are using a RAID 5 configuration, you will need seven disks, each with 72GB storage capacity. One of the seven drives is needed for writing parity information. If you want to have a hot spare on the system, you would need a total of eight disks.

- Stripe widths depend on your database applications. If you are using OLTP applications, you need smaller stripe sizes, such as 128KB per stripe. Data warehouses benefit from much larger stripe sizes.

- Know your application. Having a good idea about what you are trying to achieve with the databases you are managing will help you decide among competing RAID alternatives.

- Always have at least one or two hot spares ready on the storage systems.

Redundant Disk Controllers

If you have a RAID 5 configuration, you are still vulnerable to a malfunction of the disk controllers. To avoid this, you can configure your systems in a couple of different ways. First, you can mirror the disks on different controllers. Alternatively, you can use redundant pairs of disk controllers, where the second controller takes over automatically by using an alternative path if the first controller fails for some reason.

IMPLEMENTING RAID

You can implement RAID in a number of ways. You could make a fundamental distinction between software-based and hardware-based RAID arrays.

Software RAID implementation uses the host server's CPU and memory to send RAID instructions and I/O commands to the arrays. Software RAID implementations impose an extra burden on the host CPU, and when disks fail, the disks with the operating system may not be able to boot if you are using a software-based RAID system.

Hardware RAID uses a special RAID controller, which is usually external to the server—host-based controllers can also be used to provide RAID functionality to a group of disks, but they are not as efficient as external RAID controllers.

RAID and Backups

Suppose you have a RAID 0+1 or a RAID 5 data storage array, which more or less ensures that you are protected adequately against disk failure. Do you still need database backups? Of course you do!

RAID systems mainly protect against one kind of failure involving disks or their controllers. But what about human error? If you or your developers wipe out data accidentally, no amount of disk mirroring is going to help you—you need those backups with the good data on them. Similarly, when a disaster such as a fire destroys your entire computer room, you need to fall back upon reliable and up-to-date offsite backups. Do not neglect the correct and timely backing up of data, even though you may be using the latest disk storage array solution.

RAID systems, it must be understood, do not guarantee nonstop access to your mission-critical data. The way to ensure that is to go beyond the basic RAID architecture and build a system that is disaster-tolerant.

RAID and Oracle

Oracle uses several different kinds of files as part of its database. You may need a combination of several of the RAID configurations to optimize the performance of your database while keeping the total cost of the disk arrays reasonable. An important thing to remember here is that when you use a RAID 3 or RAID 5 system, there is no one-to-one correspondence between the physical disks in the array and the logical disks, or logical unit numbers (LUNs), that are used by your system administrator to create logical volumes, which are in turn mounted for your file systems. Advise your system administrator to try and create as many logical volumes on each LUN as there are physical drives in the LUN. This way, the Oracle optimizer will have a more realistic idea about the physical disk setup that the database is using. Logical volumes are deceptive and could mislead the optimizer.

Other Storage Technologies

Today's storage technologies are vastly superior to the technologies of even five years ago. Disk drives themselves have gotten faster—it is not difficult to find disks with 10,000 RPM and 15,000 RPM spindle speeds today. These disks have seek speeds of about 3.5 milliseconds.

In addition, advanced SCSI interfaces and the increasing use of fiber channel interfaces between servers and storage devices have increased data transfer rates to 100MB per second and faster. The capacity of individual disks has also risen considerably, with 180GB disks being fairly common today. The average MTBF for these new-generation disks is also very high—sometimes more than a million hours.

New technological architectures for data storage take advantage of all the previous factors to provide excellent storage support to today's Oracle databases. Two such storage architectures are Storage Area Networks (SANs) and Network Attached Storage (NAS) systems. Let's take a closer look at these storage architectures.

Storage Area Networks

Today, large databases are ubiquitous, with terabyte (1,000GB) databases no longer a rarity. Organizations tend to not only have several large databases for their OLTP work, but also use huge data warehouses and data marts for supporting management decision making. SANs use high-performance connections and RAID storage techniques to achieve the high performance and reliability that today's information organizations demand.

Modern data centers use SANs to optimize performance and reliability. SANs can be very small or extremely large, and they lend themselves to the latest technologies in disk storage and network communications. Traditionally, storage devices were hooked up to the host computer through a SCSI device. SANs can be connected to servers via high-speed fiber channel technology with the help of switches and hubs. You can adapt legacy SCSI-based devices for use with a SAN, or you can use entirely new devices specially designed for the SAN. A SAN is enabled by the use of fiber channel switches called *brocade switches*. By using hubs, you can use SANs that are several miles away from your host servers.

The chances are that if you are not using one already, you'll be using a SAN in the very near future. SANs offer many benefits to an organization. They allow data to be stored independently of the servers that run the databases and other applications. They enable backups that do not affect the performance of the network. They facilitate data sharing among applications.

SANs are usually preconfigured, and depending on your company's policy, they could come mirrored or as a RAID 5 configuration. The individual disks in the SANs are not directly controllable by the UNIX system administrator, who will see the LUN as a single disk—the storage array's controllers map the LUNs to the underlying physical disks. The administrator can use LVMs to create file systems on these LUNs after incorporating them into volume groups first.

When you use RAID-based storage arrays, the RAID controllers on the SAN will send the server I/O requests to the various physical drives, depending on the mirroring and parity level chosen.

Networked Attached Storage

Put simply, NAS is a black box connected to your network, and it provides additional storage. The size of a NAS box can range from as small as 2GB up to terabytes of storage capacity.

The main difference between a NAS and a SAN is that it is usually easier to scale up a SAN's base storage system using the software provided by your supplier. For example, you can easily combine several disks into a single volume in a SAN. A NAS is set up with its own address, thus moving the storage devices away from the servers onto the NAS box. The NAS communicates with and transfers data to client servers using protocols such as the Network File System (NFS).

The NAS architecture is really not very suitable for large OLTP databases. One of the approaches now being recommended by many large storage vendors for general storage as well as for some databases is to combine the SAN and NAS technologies to have the best of both worlds.

InfiniBand

One of the latest network technologies is InfiniBand, a standards-based alternative to Ethernet that seeks to overcome the limitations of TCP/IP-based networks. One of the driving forces behind network storage is to reduce the I/O bottlenecks between the CPU and the disks. InfiniBand takes another approach and works between a host channel controller on the server and a special adapter on the storage machines or device, thereby not requiring an I/O bus. A single link can operate at 2.5GB per second. InfiniBand provides higher throughput and lower latency and CPU usage than normal TCP/IP and Ethernet solutions. You can find a full discussion of this new technology at http://www.infinibandta.org/ibta/.

Given the high-profile companies involved in developing this concept (Microsoft, IBM, Sun, HP, and some of the main storage vendors), you can expect to see considerable push in the storage area. InfiniBand supports its own protocol, called Sockets Direct Protocol (SDP).

Automatic Storage Management

Remember that whatever RAID configuration you use, or however you use the Logical Volume Manager tools to stripe or mirror your disks, it's the operating system that's ultimately in charge of managing your datafiles. Whenever you need to add or move your datafiles, you have to rely on operating system file-manipulation commands. Oracle overcomes the raw device limits and partition limits by using the OCFS (Oracle Cluster File System), which is a shared storage system released under the GNU General Public License. OCFS also avoids the performance hits associated with SANs.

Oracle Database 10g introduced the innovative Automatic Storage Management (ASM) feature, which provides the DBA with the option (option, because you don't have to use ASM) of managing the database datafiles directly, bypassing the underlying operating system. When you use ASM, you don't have to manage disks and datafiles directly. You deal with disk groups instead, which consist of several disk drives. Disk groups make it possible for you to avoid having to deal with filenames when you manage the database.

Using ASM is like having Oracle's own built-in logical manager manage your disks and file systems. ASM lets you dynamically reorganize your disk storage and perform rebalancing operations to avoid I/O contention. If you're spending a significant proportion of your time managing disks and file systems, it's time to switch to the far more efficient ASM system.

Chapter 15 shows you how to use the powerful ASM feature.

Oracle and Storage System Compatibility

Oracle Corporation actively works with vendors to ensure that storage arrays and other technologies are compatible with its own architectural requirements. Oracle manages a vendor-oriented certification program called the Oracle Storage Compatibility Program (OSCP). As part of the OSCP, Oracle provides test suites for vendors to ensure their products are compatible with Oracle Database 11*g*. In this certification program, vendors normally test their storage systems on several platforms, including several variants of the UNIX operating system, Linux, and Windows.

Oracle has also been responsible for the Hardware Assisted Resilient Data (HARD) initiative. HARD's primary goal is to prevent data corruption and thus ensure data integrity. The program includes measures to prevent the loss of data by validating the data in the storage devices. RAID devices do help protect the physical data, but the HARD initiative seeks to protect the data further by ensuring that it is valid and is not saved in a corrupted format. Availability and protection of data are enhanced because data integrity is ensured through the entire pipeline, from the database to the hardware. Oracle databases do have their own corruption-detecting mechanisms, but the HARD initiative is designed to prevent data corruption that could occur as you move data between various operating system and storage layers. For example, EMC Corporation's solution to comply with the HARD initiative involves checking the checksums of data when they reach their storage devices and comparing them with the Oracle checksums. Data will be written to disk only if the two checksums are identical.

■**Note** New technologies have come to the fore in recent years that enable businesses to operate on a 24/7 basis as well as to provide data protection. Backup windows are considerably reduced by the use of these new technologies, which enable nondisruptive backup operations. These backup technologies include the *clone* or *snapshot* techniques, which enable a quick copy to be made of the production data onto a different server. Compaq's SANworks Enterprise Volume Manager, Hewlett-Packard's Business Copy, Fujitsu's Remote Equivalent Copy, and Sun's StorEdge Instant Image all allow data copying between Oracle databases at a primary site to databases at remote locations. The key thing to remember is that these techniques take snapshots of live data in very short time periods, so these techniques can be used for backup purposes as well as for disaster recovery.

CHAPTER 4

■■■

Using SQL*Plus and Oracle Enterprise Manager

You can connect to and work with Oracle databases in many ways. Chances are, though, that you'll spend a lot of time using the Oracle SQL*Plus interface and a set of commands known as SQL*Plus commands. The SQL*Plus interface provides you with a window into the Oracle database, and Oracle developers use the interface extensively to create SQL and PL/SQL program units. The interface is a valuable tool for Oracle DBAs for several reasons:

- You can use it to run SQL queries and PL/SQL (Oracle's procedural language extension to SQL) code blocks and to receive the results.
- You can issue DBA commands and automate jobs.
- It enables you to start up and shut down the database.
- It provides you with a convenient way to create database administration reports.

This chapter covers the use of SQL*Plus to perform typical database administration tasks, and you'll get a chance to learn the important SQL*Plus commands, if you aren't already familiar with them. There is also a brief discussion of building reports using SQL*Plus. Although you probably won't use the SQL*Plus interface to produce a lot of reports, it's nice to know how to work with its many report-building features.

Starting a SQL*Plus Session

SQL*Plus is the utility most commonly used to connect to and work with an Oracle database. SQL*Plus is included with your Oracle Database 11g server software, and the Oracle Client software also contains the SQL*Plus executables. You can also use the new Oracle Instant Client (discussed in Chapter 11) to connect to a database using SQL*Plus.

Once you ascertain that the SQL*Plus software is installed on your server or client machine, it's a straightforward process to log into the server or client and start a SQL*Plus session. Since every SQL*Plus session involves a connection with a database (unless it's a NOLOG connection, as explained in the "Connectionless SQL*Plus Session with /NOLOG" section of this chapter), all you'll need is a valid username/password combination to start a SQL*Plus session and connect to a database.

Setting the Environment

Before you can invoke SQL*Plus, you must first set your Oracle environment correctly. You must set the ORACLE_SID, ORACLE_HOME, and LD_LIBRARY_PATH environment variables. In addition, sometimes you may have to set the NLS_LANG and ORA_NLS11 environment variables as well.

If you don't have the correct environment variables set, you'll see an error. For example, not setting the ORACLE_HOME variable correctly before starting SQL*Plus will lead to the following error:

```
$ sqlplus
Error 6 initializing SQL*Plus
Message file sp1<lang>.msb not found
SP2-0750: You may need to set ORACLE_HOME to your Oracle software directory
```

If you get the preceding error, simply set the value of the ORACLE_HOME environment variable, as shown here:

```
$ export ORACLE_HOME= /u01/app/oracle/product/11.1.0/db_1
```

SQL*Plus Instant Client

You don't always have to install the entire Oracle Database server software in order to use SQL*Plus. If you just want to interact with an Oracle database that's running on a different server through the SQL*Plus interface, all you need is the SQL*Plus Instant Client. Using this software, you can remotely connect to any Oracle database running on any type of operating system platform. You simply specify the name of the remote database using an Oracle net connection identifier. The only requirement for connecting to a remote database is to specify the remote database in your tnsnames.ora file. That's why you must specify the ORACLE_HOME environment variable for the SQL*Plus Instant Client. There is also a method to connect that doesn't require you to ever use the tnsnames.ora file on the client server. This method is called the *easy connect* method. Using an easy connection identifier, you can connect as a user OE to the database testdb running on the server named myserver by using the following command:

```
$ sqlplus oe/oe@//myserver.mydomain:1521/testdb
```

In this example, 1521 is the port being used by the listener for incoming connections. Chapter 11 explains all the connection methods in detail.

Starting a SQL*Plus Session from the Command Line

Before you can connect to a SQL*Plus session, you first need to set up the environment correctly so you can connect to the default database on a server. You can do this by using the environmental variable ORACLE_SID. Here's an example:

```
$ ORACLE_SID=orcl
$ export ORACLE_SID
```

Once you set up the default database (orcl in our case) using the ORACLE_SID environmental variable, you can access SQL*Plus from the command-line prompt by typing **sqlplus** without providing either the username or the password. SQL*Plus will then prompt you for your username and password. If you provide the username with the command (for example, sqlplus salapati), SQL*Plus will prompt you for the password. As a DBA, you should log in with one of your administrative accounts.

■**Note** On UNIX servers, be sure to type in lowercase letters. On Windows, the interface is not case sensitive. Other than this minor detail, the SQL*Plus command-line interface works the same way on Windows and all variants of the UNIX and Linux platforms.

You can also type in the username/password combination when you invoke SQL*Plus, but your password will be visible to others when you do this. Here's an example:

```
$ sqlplus salapati/sammyy1
SQL>
```

The SQL prompt (SQL>) indicates that the SQL*Plus connection is initiated, and you can start entering your SQL, PL/SQL, and SQL*Plus commands and statements.

In order to connect to a database other than the default database, you must enter the following at the operating system command line:

```
$ sqlplus username@connect_identifier
```

Certain operations, such as startup and shutdown, are permitted only if you log into SQL*Plus with SYSDBA or SYSOPER credentials. If you have the SYSDBA (or the SYSOPER) privilege, you can log into SQL*Plus as follows:

```
$ sqlplus sys/sammyy1 AS SYSDBA
SQL> SHO USER
USER is "SYS"
SQL>
```

The AS clause allows privileged connections by users who have been granted the SYSDBA or SYSOPER system privilege.

If you've created an operating system authenticated user account (previously known as the OPS$name login; see Chapter 12) in your database, you can connect by simply using a slash (/), as shown here:

```
$ sqlplus /
SQL> SHO USER
USER is "OPS$ORACLE"
SQL>
```

You can also connect through the operating system authentication method, by including the Oracle software owner as part of the DBA group, as follows:

```
$ sqlplus / AS SYSDBA
SQL> SHO USER
USER is "SYS"
SQL>
```

Notice that in all the preceding cases, we didn't have to use the database name when connecting through SQL*Plus. That's because we were connecting to the default instance—the database indicated by the value of the ORACLE_SID environment variable. You don't have to specify the database name when you use SQL*Plus to log into the default database. If you wish to connect to a nondefault database that's accessible through your network, however, you must use a connection identifier (net service name).

■Note The instance name, database name, and service name could be either the same or different. I explain the relationship among the three entities in Chapter 11.

Theoretically speaking, you can connect to a database using the complete connection identifier syntax, as shown here, where you use the complete address for the database named orcl:

```
$ sqlplus salapati/sammyy1@(DESCRIPTION =
(ADDRESS=(PROTOCOL=tcp)(HOST=sales-server)(PORT=1521)
(CONNECT_DATA= (SERVICE_NAME=orcl.mycompany.com)))
```

However, by using a net service name defined in the network file tnsnames.ora, you can use a simpler way to connect to the orcl database, as shown here:

```
$ sqlplus salapati/sammyy1@orcl
```

You can also use the easy connect method to connect to a database. The easy connect method has the following syntax:

```
$ [//]host[:port][/[service_name]]
```

For our database, orcl, using the easy connect method, you can connect as follows:

```
$ sqlplus hr/hr_passwd@sales-server:1521/orcl.mycompany.com
```

Note that you don't need a network file (tnsnames.ora) if you're using the easy connect method.

No matter which of these methods you use, you'll open a successful SQL*Plus session to either the default database or the database specified in your connection identifier.

Connecting by Using the CONNECT Command

The SQL*Plus CONNECT command helps you connect as a different user, once you're logged into SQL*Plus. You can also log into a different database after you're connected to one database by using the CONNECT command. In the following example, I use the CONNECT command to connect as a different user:

```
SQL> CONNECT newuser/newuser_passwd
Connected.
SQL>
```

In the following example, I connect to a different database from within SQL*Plus by providing the connect identifier as part of the CONNECT command:

```
SQL> CONNECT salapati/sammyy1@orcl
Connected.
SQL>
```

Just make sure that you have the remote database connection information in your tnsnames.ora file before connecting to the different database.

You can use the CONNECT command from within SQL*Plus with the / AS SYSDBA and / AS SYSOPER syntax, as shown here:

```
CONNECT sys/sammy1@prod1 as sysdba
CONNECT / AS SYSDBA
CONNECT username/password AS SYSDBA
CONNECT / AS SYSOPER
CONNECT username/password AS SYSOPER
```

Connectionless SQL*Plus Session with /NOLOG

You can also start a SQL*Plus session without connecting to a database by using the /NOLOG option with the sqlplus command when starting a new SQL*Plus session. You may do this, for example, when you're starting the database, or if you just want to use SQL*Plus editing commands to write or edit scripts. Once the SQL*Plus session starts, you can connect to a database using the CONNECT command.

Here's an example using the NOLOG option:

```
$ sqlplus /NOLOG

SQL*Plus: Release 11.1.0.6.0 - Production on Wed Jan 2 18:35:25 2008
Copyright (c) 1982, 2007, Oracle.  All rights reserved.
SQL> SHO USER
USER is "
"
SQL> SHO SGA
SP2-0640: Not connected

SQL> CONNECT salapati/sammyy1
Connected.
SQL>
```

Connecting to SQL*Plus Through a Windows GUI

If you are using the SQL*Plus GUI on a Windows machine, click the SQL*Plus icon, and the interface will prompt you for your username. As long as your connection to the database is established through the proper entries in the tnsnames.ora file (see Chapter 11 for more information on this file), you are all set to use the SQL*Plus interface.

You can use the SQL*Plus utility in both manual and scripted noninteractive modes. It stands to reason that you would want to perform sensitive administration tasks, such as database recovery, in an interactive mode. On the other hand, you can automate routine processing of SQL with scripts, and your SQL commands will then run noninteractively. In either case, the commands are the same—it is just the mode in which you issue the commands that is different.

The SQL*Plus connect command has the following syntax:

```
CONN[ECT] [{ logon | / } [AS {SYSOPER | SYSDBA | SYSASM}]]
```

■**Note** In Oracle Database 11*g*, the SQLPLUS command has a new -F argument to enable SQL*Plus to receive Fast Application Notification (FAN) events from a RAC database.

You can connect as a user with the SYSOPER, SYSDBA, or SYSASM privileges to perform privileged operations such as shutting down the database and starting it or backing up and recovering the database. The SYSASM privilege is new in Oracle Database 11*g* and is meant as a device to separate normal database administration and Automatic Storage Management (ASM) tasks. You'll learn more about the SYSASM system privilege in Chapter 17, which discusses ASM.

Operating in SQL*Plus

Once you're logged into the SQL*Plus interface, you can type in any SQL*Plus, SQL, or PL/SQL commands. As explained later in this chapter, a SQL statement is terminated by a semicolon (;) or a slash (/), and a PL/SQL code block is terminated by a slash (/). You can see the output on the screen, and you can also spool it to a file if you wish. A SQL*Plus command is always terminated by a newline character. If you enter a SQL*Plus command, the SQL*Plus client program will handle it, and if it's a SQL or a PL/SQL statement, it's sent on to the database server for processing.

You can use the hyphen (-) as a continuation character, although it's not necessary to use a continuation character when you finish the first line. You can type an arbitrary number of characters or words in each SQL line and just press the Enter key to continue on the next line. SQL*Plus will automatically number each line.

In some cases, however, the continuation character (-) comes in handy. In the next example, I'm trying to enter the SQL statement, SELECT 200 - 100 FROM dual:

```
SQL> SELECT 200 -
  > 100 from dual;

select 200  100 from dual
              *
ERROR at line 1:
ORA-00923: FROM keyword not found where expected
SQL>
```

In the preceding example, when I started the second line after the hyphen (-), which is also the minus sign, SQL*Plus automatically interpreted it as the continuation character and issued an error because the statement was syntactically incorrect (select 200 100 from dual). You can avoid this problem by using a second hyphen (minus sign) at the end of the first line as a continuation character.

```
SQL> SELECT 200 - -
  > 100 FROM dual;

  200-100
----------
      100
SQL>
```

The dual table is necessary in Oracle so as to enable certain queries, since in Oracle's SQL, you must use the FROM clause in a SELECT statement (for example, SELECT sysdate FROM dual;). Microsoft SQL Server database, on the other hand, doesn't use a dual table because you can have a SELECT statement without a FROM clause in SQL Server.

Exiting SQL*Plus

You exit a SQL*Plus session by simply typing **EXIT** in either lowercase or uppercase letters. You can also type **QUIT** to exit to the operating system. Again, case doesn't matter.

■**Caution** If you make a graceful exit from SQL*Plus by entering the EXIT (or QUIT) command, your transactions will all be committed immediately. If you don't intend to commit the transactions, make sure you issue the rollback command before you exit.

SQL*Plus and SQL Commands

Remember that the SQL*Plus interface lets you interact with the Oracle database. You can use two basic types of commands in SQL*Plus:

- *Local commands*: These are executed locally with SQL*Plus and are usually not sent to the server. They include commands such as COPY, COMPUTE, REM, and SET LINESIZE. These SQL*Plus commands all end with a new line, and they don't need a command terminator as such.

- *Server-executed commands*: Server-executed commands aren't locally executed in SQL*Plus, but are processed by the server instead. This group includes all other commands, including the CREATE TABLE and INSERT SQL commands, and PL/SQL code that is enclosed in BEGIN and END statements. All SQL-type commands end in a semicolon (;) or a slash (/). All PL/SQL-type commands end with a slash (/).

SQL*Plus Security

Beyond the mandatory username/password requirement for using the SQL*Plus interface, Oracle provides an additional security mechanism that involves the use of a special table called product_user_profile. This table is owned by the System user, one of the two super users of the Oracle database. By using the product_user_profile table, you can limit access to SQL*Plus and SQL commands, and to PL/SQL statements as well.

When a user logs into the SQL*Plus session, SQL*Plus checks this table to see what restrictions are supposed to be applied to the user in the SQL*Plus session. How Oracle administers this security layer is a little bit tricky. The user may have an insert or a delete privilege in the database, but because the SQL*Plus privileges override this privilege, Oracle may deny the user the right to exercise the privilege.

After you create a database, you should execute a special script, pupbld.sql, which is used to support SQL*Plus security. This script is located in the $ORACLE_HOME/sql/admin directory, and it should be run as the System user. This script will build the product_user_profile table, which is actually a synonym for the sqlplus_product_user_profile table. Listing 4-1 shows the format of this table.

Listing 4-1. *The product_user_profile Table*

```
SQL> DESC product_user_profile
Name                               Null?             Type
---------------------------------- --------  -----------------------
PRODUCT                            NOT NULL          VARCHAR2(30)
USERID                                               VARCHAR2(30)
ATTRIBUTE                                            VARCHAR2(240)
SCOPE                                                VARCHAR2(240)
NUMERIC_VALUE                                        NUMBER(15,2)
CHAR_VALUE                                           VARCHAR2(240)
DATE_VALUE                                                   DATE
LONG_VALUE                                                   LONG
SQL>
```

■**Note** By default, SQL*Plus imposes no usage restrictions on any users, so when the product_user_profile table is first created, there are no rows in it. The System user has to explicitly insert rows into the product_user_profile table if some users need to be restricted in SQL*Plus. You can choose to restrict a user from executing the following commands: ALTER, BEGIN, CONNECT, DECLARE, EXEC, EXECUTE, GRANT, HOST, INSERT, SELECT, and UPDATE. If you get errors stating "INVALID COMMAND" when a user issues one of these statements, even though your product_user_profile table is empty, run the pupbld.sql script as the System user.

Listing 4-2 shows how you can use the product_user_profile table to prevent the user OE from deleting, inserting, or updating any data in the database.

Listing 4-2. *Using the product_user_profile Table*

```
SQL> INSERT INTO product_user_profile
     VALUES
     ('SQL*PLUS','OE','INSERT',NULL,NULL,NULL,NULL,NULL);
1 row created.
SQL> INSERT INTO product_user_profile
     VALUES
     ('SQL*PLUS','OE','DELETE',NULL,NULL,NULL,NULL,NULL);
1 row created.
SQL> INSERT INTO product_user_profile
     VALUES
     ('SQL*PLUS','OE','UPDATE',NULL,NULL,NULL,NULL,NULL);
1 row created.
SQL> COMMIT;
Commit complete.
SQL>
```

You can see the entries pertaining to user OE by querying the product_user_profile table as follows:

```
SQL> SELECT product, attribute FROM
     product_user_profile WHERE userid='OE';

PRODUCT                     ATTRIBUTE
-------------------------------------
SQL*PLUS                    INSERT
SQL*PLUS                    DELETE
SQL*PLUS                    UPDATE
SQL>
```

If the user OE tries to delete data from a table, the result would be the following error, even though the orders table belongs to the OE schema:

```
SQL> CONNECT oe/oe
Connected.
SQL> DELETE FROM oe.orders;
SP2-0544: invalid command: delete
SQL>
```

If you want to grant to user OE the right to delete data through SQL*Plus, you can do so by *deleting* the relevant line from the product_user_profile table, as follows:

```
SQL> DELETE FROM product_user_profile
     WHERE userid='OE' and attribute = 'DELETE';

1 row deleted.
SQL> COMMIT;
Commit complete.
SQL>
```

The ALTER, BEGIN, DECLARE, EXECUTE, and GRANT commands are data definition language (DDL) and PL/SQL commands. The INSERT, SELECT, and UPDATE commands are, of course, data manipulation language (DML) commands. The HOST command is used in SQL*Plus to access the operating system and issue operating system commands. You really don't want your users to be able to issue operating system commands by simply using the HOST command, so if you want to deny user salapati this dangerous privilege, this is what you have to do to the product_user_profile table:

```
SQL> INSERT INTO product_user_profile
     (product,userid,attribute)
     VALUES
     ('SQL*Plus','salapati','HOST');

 1 row created.
SQL>
```

If you want to restore to user salapati the right to use the HOST command, you can do so by deleting the row you just inserted. For example, you would need to issue the following command to restore the HOST privilege to user salapati:

```
SQL> DELETE FROM product_user_profile WHERE userid='SALAPATI';
```

■**Note** Remember that users will retain any privileges you grant them, even though they can't exercise the privileges in the SQL*Plus session. This means you can grant application owners privileges on the data objects when they are using packages and procedures that are stored and executed in the database, while at the same time denying them these same privileges when they log into SQL*Plus.

Controlling Security Through the set role Command

As you probably know, it is better to grant and revoke database privileges through the use of roles, rather than granting the privileges directly, for several reasons. The use of roles, however, carries with it a potential security problem, because any user can change his or her role by simply using the set role command in SQL*Plus. You can shut down this security loophole by using the product_user_profile table to disable any user's ability to use the set role command.

Using the RESTRICT Command to Disable Commands

As an alternative to using the product_user_profile table, you can use the RESTRICT command to prevent users from using certain operating system commands. The net effect is the same as using the product_user_profile table, except that the RESTRICT command disables the commands even where there are no connections to the server.

You can use the RESTRICT command at three levels—Level 1, Level 2, and Level 3. The following example illustrates the use of the command at Level 1:

```
$ sqlplus -RESTRICT 1
```

Table 4-1 shows the commands that are disabled by using th RESTRICT command and the differences among the three restriction levels.

Table 4-1. *The Three Restriction Levels for SQL*Plus*

Command	Level 1	Level 2	Level 3
EDIT	Disabled	Disabled	Disabled
GET			Disabled
HOST	Disabled	Disabled	Disabled
SAVE		Disabled	Disabled
SPOOL		Disabled	Disabled
START			Disabled
STORE		Disabled	Disabled

If you issue the RESTRICT -3 command, Oracle doesn't read the login.sql script. It reads the glogin.sql script, and any restricted commands that are used will not work.

Setting the SQL*Plus Environment with the SET Command

Of all the commands that you can use in SQL*Plus, the SET command is probably the most fundamental, because it enables you to set the all-important environment for your SQL*Plus sessions. Environment settings include the number of lines per page of output, the width of the numeric data in the output, the titles for reports, and the HTML formatting, all of which are enabled, disabled, or modified with the SET command.

The SET command is but one of the commands that you can use in SQL*Plus, and you can see the entire list of available commands by typing **help index** at the SQL prompt, as shown in Listing 4-3.

Listing 4-3. *Using the HELP INDEX Command to Show Help Topics*

```
SQL> HELP INDEX
Enter Help [topic] for help.
   @                COPY          PAUSE                  SHUTDOWN
   @@               DEFINE        PRINT                  SPOOL
   /                DEL           PROMPT                 SQLPLUS
   ACCEPT           DESCRIBE      QUIT                   START
   APPEND           DISCONNECT    RECOVER                STARTUP
   ARCHIVE LOG      EDIT          REMARK                 STORE
   ATTRIBUTE        EXECUTE       REPFOOTER              TIMING
   BREAK            EXIT          REPHEADER              TTITLE
   BTITLE           GET           RESERVED WORDS(SQL)    UNDEFINE
   CHANGE           HELP          RESERVED WORDS(PL/SQL) VARIABLE
   CLEAR            HOST          RUN                    WHENEVER OS_ERROR
   COLUMN           INPUT         SAVE                   WHENEVER SQLERROR
   COMPUTE          LIST          SET
   CONNECT          PASSWORD      SHOW
```

If you want to see the entire set of environment variables that you can control with the SET command, type **help set**. For performing your day-to-day tasks in SQL*Plus, you need to be familiar with several of these commands, and I will explain them briefly in the next section.

Setting Common SQL*Plus Variables

Variables are key attributes whose values you can change while using SQL*Plus. Table 4-2 summarizes the most common variables you will need to know. Practice with the variables will enhance your comfort level and help you become a skilled practitioner of SQL*Plus in a relatively short time.

Beyond what is shown in the table, I haven't provided examples of the use of these variables, so it's important you actually try them out in your SQL*Plus session. Refer to the Oracle SQL*Plus manuals for usage guidelines for all the variables, including many variables that aren't listed in Table 4-2.

■**Note** In Table 4-2, the options inside square brackets show the alternative full name of the command. You can specify either the shortened version of a command or its long version. The options inside the curly brackets, { }, show the possible options you can choose and the default values. The value listed first inside the curly brackets is the default value. You can either leave it as is by not doing anything or change it to the other possible values by using the SET variable value notation.

Table 4-2. *Common SQL*Plus Environment Variables*

Variable	Function	Usage
ARRAY[SIZE]	Determines the number of rows fetched from database at one time.	SET ARRAY 50
AUTO[COMMIT]	Specifies whether commits of transactions are automatic or manual.	SET AUTO ON
COLSEP	Specifies the text that you want printed in between column values.	SET COLSEP
COPY[COMMIT]	Sets the frequency of commits when using the COPY command.	SET COPY 10000
DEF[INE]{&/C/ON/OFF}	Sets the prefix character used during variable substitutions.	SET DEFINE ON
ECHO {OFF/ON}	Specifies whether echo is on or off. If you have ECHO ON, each command will be displayed before its output onscreen.	SET ECHO ON
EDITF[ILE]	Sets the default filename when you use your default editor.	SET EDITFILE draft.sql
FEED[BACK] {OFF/ON}	Specifies whether SQL*Plus shows the number of records returned by your query.	SET FEEDBACK OFF

Table 4-2. *Common SQL*Plus Environment Variables (Continued)*

Variable	Function	Usage
FLUSH {OFF/ON}	Determines whether output is buffered or flushed to the screen.	SET FLUSH OFF
HEA[DING] {OFF/ON}	Specifies whether the column headers are printed or not.	SET HEAD OFF
LIN[ESIZE] {80|n}	Specifies the number of characters displayed per line.	SET LINESIZE 40
LONG {80/n}	Specifies the maximum width of the LONG, CLOB, NCLOB, and XMLType values.	SET LONG 100000
NEWP[AGE] {1/n/none}	Specifies the number of blank lines at the top of each new page.	SET NEWPAGE 0
NUM[WIDTH] {10/n}	Specifies the format for displaying numbers.	SET NUM
PAGES[IZE] {24/n}	Specifies the number of lines in each page.	SET PAGESIZE 60
PAU[SE] {OFF/ON/TEXT}	Specifies the amount of output that is printed to the screen.	SET PAUSE ON
SERVEROUT[PUT]	Specifies whether output of PL/SQL code is shown.	SET SERVEROUTPUT ON{OFF/ON}[SIZE n]
SQLP[ROMPT] {SQL> |TEXT}	Specifies the command prompt for SQL*Plus sessions.	SET SQLPROMPT 'salapati >'
TERM[OUT] {OFF/ON}	Specifies whether command file output is displayed or not.	SET TERMOUT OFF
TI[ME] {OFF/ON}	Displays time if set to on.	SET TIME OFF
TIMI[NG] {OFF/ON}	Controls the display of timing for SQL commands.	SET TIMING OFF
VER[IFY] {OFF/ON}	Specifies whether SQL text is displayed after variable substitution.	SET VERIFY OFF

■**Tip** If you don't want the "X rows selected" and "PL/SQL procedure successfully completed" messages after you execute code in SQL*Plus, use the following command:

```
SET FEEDBACK OFF
```

You can have all your preferred session settings stored in a file, which you can execute like any other SQL file whenever you want to change a bunch of variable values at once. You can also have several of these files saved for different tasks, if your job involves a lot of reporting using the SQL*Plus interface.

If you are using the Oracle SQL*Plus interface on Windows, you can change the environment variables for your session by using the Options menu and choosing Environment. You are shown all the current environment variables for your session, and you can modify them as long as you stay within the limits. If you are logged into SQL*Plus through a UNIX server's X Window Session, you lose this easy way to change the values of your environment variables.

SET SERVEROUTPUT Command

One of the most important commands that you'll use is the SET SERVEROUTPUT command, which determines whether the output of a PL/SQL code segment or a stored procedure is displayed on screen. If you set SERVEROUTPUT ON, you'll see the output. By default, the SERVEROUTPUT variable is set to OFF, and you may be caught by surprise when you run a PL/SQL block that should output something on the screen, but you don't see anything there.

Here's an example that shows how you can use the SERVEROUTPUT variable to display the output from the DBMS_OUTPUT package. This package contains a procedure named PUT_LINE, which outputs a line. By setting SERVEROUTPUT ON, you can see the output printed by the PUT_LINE procedure:

```
SET SERVEROUTPUT ON
BEGIN
dbms_output.put_line('This is the first line');
dbms_output.put_line('This is the second line');
dbms_output.put_line('This is the last line');
END;
SQL> /
This is the first line
This is the second line
This is the last line
PL/SQL procedure successfully completed.
SQL>
```

If you hadn't set the SERVEROUTPUT variable to the value of ON in the preceding example, you wouldn't have seen any of the output of the PUT_LINE procedure.

You can use the FORMAT clauses of the SERVEROUTPUT command to determine how the output is formatted. The FORMAT clause can take the values WRAPPED, WORD_WRAPPED, or TRUNCATED. The default is WRAPPED, meaning that the output is wrapped within the length specified by LINESIZE, and new lines are started as required. Let's look at a short example for each of the other two FORMAT clauses, WORD_WRAPPED and TRUNCATED.

The WORD_WRAPPED option for FORMAT wraps each line to the length specified by the value of the LINESIZE variable, and if an entire word won't fit at the end of a line, the line ends before the word.

```
SQL> SET SERVEROUTPUT ON FORMAT WORD_WRAPPED
SQL> SET LINESIZE 20
SQL> BEGIN
2 > dbms_output.put_line('After the first 20 characters please');
3 > dbms_output.put_line('continue on the second line');
4 > END;
5 > /
After the first 20
characters please
continue on the
second line
```

When you use the TRUNCATED formatting option, each line of the displayed output is truncated exactly at the length specified by the LINESIZE variable.

```
SQL> SET SERVEROUTPUT ON FORMAT TRUNCATED
SQL> SET LINESIZE 20
SQL> BEGIN
2 > DBMS_OUTPUT.PUT_LINE('After the first 20 characters please');
3 > DBMS_OUTPUT.PUT_LINE('continue on the second line');
4 > END;
5 > /
After the first 20 c
continue on the seco
```

Specifying Global Preferences with the glogin.sql File

Users don't have to manually set their SQL*Plus environment each time they log into SQL*Plus—Oracle allows you to specify your variable preferences in a *site profile file,* called `glogin.sql`. You can use the `glogin.sql` file to configure identical environment settings for all users.

■**Note** The `glogin.sql` file applies to all the users of the system, and therefore it is called a *site profile.* If you want all SQL*Plus sessions to have a specific set of environment variable values upon logging in, all you have to do is edit the `glogin.sql` file. Only DBAs, not individual users, can access the `glogin.sql` file.

The site profile is created during installation, and the file is placed in the `$ORACLE_HOME/sqlplus/admin` directory. Listing 4-4 shows the default `glogin.sql` file, which is read by Oracle every time you log into SQL*Plus. You can add various settings to the `glogin.sql` file to suit your needs.

In previous versions of the Oracle database, the `glogin.sql` file contained various formatting commands for the SQL*Plus interface that automatically configured environmental variables for any user who logged into SQL*Plus. The database would run the `glogin.sql` file first when you logged into SQL*Plus, followed by the running of the `login.sql` file. In Oracle Database 11*g*, the `glogin.sql` site profile file is invoked automatically as before, when you log into SQL*Plus. However, the file is blank now, as shown in Listing 4-4.

Listing 4-4. *The Default glogin.sql File*

```
-- Copyright (c) 1988, 2005, Oracle. All Rights Reserved.
--
-- NAME
--   glogin.sql
--
-- DESCRIPTION
--   SQL*Plus global login "site profile" file
--
--   Add any SQL*Plus commands here that are to be executed when a
--   user starts SQL*Plus, or uses the SQL*Plus CONNECT command.
--
-- USAGE
--   This script is automatically run
```

Specifying Individual Preferences with the login.sql File

Users can set their own particular preferences for variables for their sessions, by specifying the preferences in the `login.sql` file, another file checked by Oracle, to set their own customized SQL*Plus environment. Because the login.sql file lets you set individual user variables, it is also known as the *user profile file*. The commands in the login.sql file are executed automatically when you connect to SQL*Plus.

SQL*Plus will look for login.sql in your current directory. The file is usually located in your home directory. You can use the login.sql file for both SQL*Plus command-line and Windows GUI connections. Listing 4-5 shows a sample login.sql file.

Listing 4-5. *A Sample login.sql File*

```
--   login.sql
--   SQL*Plus user login startup file.
--   This script is automatically run after glogin.sql
--   To change the SQL*Plus prompt to display the current user,
--   connection identifier and current time.
-- First set the database date format to show the time.
ALTER SESSION SET nls_date_format = 'HH:MI:SS';
-- SET the SQLPROMPT to include the _USER, _CONNECT_IDENTIFIER
-- and _DATE variables.
SET SQLPROMPT "_USER'@'_CONNECT_IDENTIFIER _DATE> "
-- To set the number of lines to display in a report page to 24.
SET PAGESIZE 24
-- To set the number of characters to display on each report line to 78.
SET LINESIZE 78
-- To set the number format used in a report to $99,999.
SET NUMFORMAT $99,999
```

■**Note** When you connect to the database using SQL*Plus, the site profile file, glogin.sql, is executed first, followed by the user profile script, the login.sql file. All SQL*Plus variable values you specify in the login.sql file will override the settings in the glogin.sql file. Any changes you make in the session itself will override everything else and last for the duration of that session only.

When Do the Login Files Take Effect?

The glogin.sql file, which contains systemwide settings, takes effect after you log in successfully through a SQLPLUS or CONNECT command. It also comes into effect when you use the /NOLOG option when you connect to SQL*Plus.

The login.sql file, which is applicable only to the individual user's session, is automatically run right after the site profile file, glogin.sql, is run.

SQL*Plus Error Logging

You can execute the show errors command in SQL*Plus to view the errors that might occur when you execute a PL/SQL statement. However, these errors aren't logged by the database. In Oracle Database 11g, you can use the new SQL*Plus command-set error logging to store SQL, PL/SQL, and SQL*Plus errors in a special error logging table. When you issue the SET ERRORLOGGING ON command, the database writes all subsequent errors resulting from a SQL or PL/SQL statement to a table called sperrorlog. You can specify your own table name for storing the errors, instead of using the default table sperrorlog.

The error logging table contains the following information about errors that it logs:

- Username
- Time of the error
- Name of the script, if there is one
- An identifier defined by the user
- The error message
- The statement that resulted in the error

Error logging isn't enabled by default, as shown here:

```
SQL> show errorlogging
errorlogging is OFF
SQL>
```

To set error logging on, issue the following command in SQL*Plus:

```
SQL> set errorlogging on;
```

Once you turn error logging on, confirm that by issuing the following command:

```
SQ> connect hr/hr
Connected.
SQL> show errorlogging
errorlogging is ON TABLE HR.SPERRORLOG
SQL>
```

Notice that the database not only confirms that error logging is turned on, but also shows the table (hr.sperrorlog) that'll store the error messages. The database grants ownership of the error logging table to the user who turns error logging on. In this case, the user is HR.

Once you turn error logging on as shown here, you can query the error logging table to check the error messages and other information connected to an erroneous SQL or PL/SQL statement. Here's an example:

```
SQL> select username,statement,message
     from sperrorlog;
```

USERNAME	STATEMENT	MESSAGE
---------	--------------------------	-------------------------
HR	create table employees as select * from employees	ORA-00955: name is already used by an existing object
HR	select names from employees	ORA-00904: "NAMES": invalid identifier

```
SQL>
```

The first error message shows that the create table statement issued by the user HR failed because there's already a table with the name EMPLOYEES. The second error message shows that a SELECT statement errored out because it was referring to a nonexistent column in the EMPLOYEES table. As you can see, the error logging table can be very useful when you're troubleshooting SQL and PL/SQL code errors.

SQL*Plus Command-Line Options

As you saw earlier in this chapter, you can start a new SQL*Plus session by merely typing **sqlplus** at the command prompt. However, you can specify several command-line options to customize the SQL*Plus session. Listing 4-6 shows how you can find all the command-line options available to you in SQL*Plus.

Listing 4-6. *SQL*Plus Command-Line Options*

```
$ sqlplus –help
SQL*Plus: Release 11.1.0.6.0 - Production

Copyright (c) 1982, 2007, Oracle.  All rights reserved.

Use SQL*Plus to execute SQL, PL/SQL and SQL*Plus statements.

Usage 1: sqlplus -H | -V

   -H              Displays the SQL*Plus version and the
                   usage help.
   -V              Displays the SQL*Plus version.

Usage 2: sqlplus [ [<option>] [<logon>] [<start>] ]

  <option> is: [-C <version>] [-L] [-M "<options>"] [-R <level>] [-S]

   -C <version>    Sets the compatibility of affected commands to the
                   version specified by <version>.  The version has
                   the form "x.y[.z]".  For example, -C 10.2.0
   -F              Enables the failover mode for a RAC environment.
   -L              Attempts to log on just once, instead of
                   reprompting on error.
   -M "<options>"  Sets automatic HTML markup of output.  The options
                   have the form:
                   HTML [ON|OFF] [HEAD text] [BODY text] [TABLE text]
                   [ENTMAP {ON|OFF}] [SPOOL {ON|OFF}] [PRE[FORMAT] {ON|OFF}]
   -R <level>      Sets restricted mode to disable SQL*Plus commands
                   that interact with the file system.  The level can
                   be 1, 2 or 3.  The most restrictive is -R 3 which
                   disables all user commands interacting with the
                   file system.
   -S              Sets silent mode which suppresses the display of
                   the SQL*Plus banner, prompts, and echoing of
                   commands.

  <logon> is: (<username>[/<password>][@<connect_identifier>] | /)
              [AS SYSDBA | AS SYSOPER | AS SYSASM] | /NOLOG | [EDITION=value]

    Specifies the database account username, password and connect
    identifier for the database connection.  Without a connect
    identifier, SQL*Plus connects to the default database.

    The AS SYSDBA, AS SYSOPER and AS SYSASM  options are database
    administration privileges.
```

        <connect_identifier> can be in the form of Net Service Name
    or Easy Connect.

      @[<net_service_name> | [//]Host[:Port]/<service_name>]

        <net_service_name> is a simple name for a service that resolves
        to a connect descriptor.

        Example: Connect to database using Net Service Name and the
          database net service name is ORCL.

          sqlplus myusername/mypassword@ORCL

        Host specifies the host name or IP address of the database
    server computer.

        Port specifies the listening port on the database server.

        <service_name> specifies the service name of the database you
        want to access.

        Example: Connect to database using Easy Connect and the
          Service name is ORCL.

          sqlplus myusername/mypassword@Host/ORCL

    The /NOLOG option starts SQL*Plus without connecting to a
    database.

    The EDITION specifies the value for Application
    Edition

  <start> is: @<URL>|<filename>[.<ext>] [<parameter> ...]

    Runs the specified SQL*Plus script from a web server (URL) or the
    local file system (filename.ext) with specified parameters that
    will be assigned to substitution variables in the script.

When SQL*Plus starts, and after CONNECT commands, the site profile
(e.g. $ORACLE_HOME/sqlplus/admin/glogin.sql) and the user profile
(e.g. login.sql in the working directory) are run. The files may
contain SQL*Plus commands.

Refer to the SQL*Plus User's Guide and Reference for more information.
$

■**Tip** In Oracle Database 11*g*, the `login.sql` file is executed at SQL*Plus startup time as well as when you use
the CONNECT command to connect from within the SQL*Plus session.

    Here are brief explanations of the most important command-line options you can use when you
start a SQL*Plus session:

- *The silent option* (-S): If you invoke SQL*Plus with the -S option, the session will run silently; there won't be any output on the screen. When you're running batch jobs and you have no need to see the output of the SQL*Plus session, you can start the session in silent mode. The silent mode is very useful when you're producing reports, because the banner, version, and other information is suppressed.

- *The no-prompt logon option* (-L): If you invoke SQL*Plus with the -L option, it won't prompt you for a new username and password if you fail to log in the first time. Again, this is an option that's handy during the execution of SQL batch jobs through the operating system.

- *The restrict option* (-R): You've already seen how you can use the SQL*Plus -R option (at three different levels) to disable certain operating system commands in SQL*Plus. Refer to the "Using the RESTRICT Command to Disable Commands" section, earlier in this chapter, for more information.

- *The markup option* (-M): You can generate complete web pages from your SQL*Plus sessions by invoking SQL*Plus with the -M option. There is more on the markup command in the "Creating Web Pages Using SQL*Plus" section of this chapter.

SQL*Plus Administrative Commands

SQL*Plus offers a set of database administration and management commands that help you perform administrative chores. I briefly explain these commands in the following sections.

CLEAR Command

The CLEAR command removes several current settings, including settings for columns and the SQL*Plus buffer. You use the CLEAR command to make sure that settings no longer needed are not in force in the current session of SQL*Plus. Listing 4-7 shows sample output of the CLEAR command.

Listing 4-7. *Using the CLEAR Command*

```
SQL> CLEAR BREAKS
breaks cleared
SQL> CLEAR BUFFER
buffer cleared
SQL> CLEAR COLUMNS
columns cleared
SQL> CLEAR SQL
sql cleared
SQL> CLEAR TIMING
SQL> CLEAR SCREEN
```

The CLEAR command by itself clears your screen without affecting any of the settings of SQL*Plus. The CLEAR BUFFER and CLEAR SQL commands achieve the same effect: they remove the SQL in the memory buffer of SQL*Plus. The CLEAR COLUMNS and the CLEAR BREAKS commands remove any column definitions and breaks. The CLEAR TIMING command deactivates all timers. You use the CLEAR SCR (or CLEAR SCREEN) command to clear the screen.

STORE Command

During a given SQL*Plus session, it's likely that you'll need to change your environment settings in order to run a specific SQL script or command. If you want to preserve these settings for future use, you can do so with the help of the STORE command. Once you store the values in a script, you can run that script anytime to restore the original values of all variables. Thus, if you run a report that requires changing some variable values, just run the script that contains the original values after you finish the report to restore the original values of the variables.

The following example shows how to use the STORE command to save your SQL*Plus environment settings:

```
SQL> STORE SET mysqlplus.sql
Created file  mysqlplus.sql
SQL>
```

Executing the previous command will result in the storing of all the current environmental values in the file named sqlplus.sql. Once you store your favorite environment variables in a file, you can easily reuse them anytime you want by simply executing the script. (I explain the execution of SQL scripts in the following sections.) In order to restore the stored values of all system variables, enter

```
SQL> START mysqlplus.sql
```

If you wish, you can just enter @mysqlplus.sql or @@mysqlplus.sql to run the script. You can also add the script to the user profile script so each time you start SQL*Plus, all variables will have the desired values. The STORE command can be used with three options: CREATE, REPLACE, or APPEND. The default is CREATE, which creates a new file. If you wish to replace an existing file and store your SQL*Plus commands there, use the REPLACE option. If you wish to add the commands to an existing file, use the APPEND option.

SHOW Command

You can use the SHOW command to display variable values. To find out the individual values, you type in the specific variable's name, as shown in the following example:

```
SQL> SHOW TTITLE
ttitle ON and is the following 49 characters:
Annual Financial Report for the Women's Club, 2005
SQL>
```

The SHOW ALL command will show you the current settings for all the SQL*Plus environment variables. I briefly explain some of the most important options for the SHOW command in the following sections.

SHOW RECYCLEBIN Command

One of the most useful SQL*Plus commands is the SHOW RECYCLEBIN command. This command will let you see if there are any tables that are eligible for a recovery using the FLASHBACK TO BEFORE DROP command. If you drop a table, that table doesn't go away immediately—it stays in the Recycle Bin until you either get rid of it permanently with the DROP TABLE PURGE command or the database faces space pressure.

I discuss the Flashback Table feature in detail in Chapter 8, but here's what you'll see if there is an eligible table stored in the Recycle Bin:

```
SQL> CREATE TABLE test (name varchar2(30));
Table created.

SQL> DROP TABLE test;
Table dropped.

SQL> SHOW RECYCLEBIN
```

```
ORIGINAL NAME        RECYCLEBIN NAME           OBJECT TYPE     DROP TIME
-------------------------------------------------------------------------
TEST         BIN$oGZbms6pRa6xlbFglGjgUw==$0    TABLE       2008-06-27:13:13:58

SQL>
```

As you can see, the TEST table, after it's dropped with the DROP TABLE command, is automatically renamed by the database and stored in the Recycle Bin.

SHOW USER Command

The SHOW USER command shows the currently logged in username.

```
SQL> SHO USER
USER is "SYSTEM"
SQL>
```

SHOW SGA Command

The SHOW SGA command shows the current allocations of the SGA memory.

```
SQL> SHO SGA

Total System Global Area  452984832 bytes
Fixed Size                  1309568 bytes
Variable Size             237765760 bytes
Database Buffers          209715200 bytes
Redo Buffers                4194304 bytes
SQL>
```

SHOW PARAMETERS Command

The SHOW PARAMETERS command lists all the current default and nondefault values of the initialization parameters.

```
SQL> SHO PARAMETERS

NAME                           TYPE        VALUE
---------------------------    --------    ------
07_DICTIONARY_ACCESSIBILITY    boolean     FALSE
. . .
SQL>
```

You can also issue the SHOW PARAMETERS command to view a specific type of initialization parameter, as shown here:

```
SQL> SHOW PARAMETERS MEMORY

NAME                           TYPE        VALUE
-----------------------------  ----------- ------
hi_shared_memory_address       integer     0
memory_max_target              big integer 820M
memory_target                  big integer 820M
shared_memory_address          integer     0
SQL>
```

You can use the SHOW SPPARAMETER command to view all initialization parameters listed in the SPFILE, as shown in the following example:

```
SQL> SHOW SPPARAMETER db_name

SID      NAME                              TYPE         VALUE
-------- --------------------------------- ------------ ------------
*        db_name                           string       orcl
SQL>
```

SHOW ERRORS Command

The SHOW ERRORS command is useful for seeing the compilation errors associated with a procedure or function. You run the command immediately after you compile the PL/SQL unit. If there are no errors, you'll see the following:

```
SQL> SHO ERRORS PROCEDURE TEST_PROC

NO ERRORS.
SQL>
```

Key SQL*Plus "Working" Commands

All the work you do in SQL*Plus, whether you are issuing simple commands or elaborate scripts to gather information from the database, involves knowing how to use two basic kinds of SQL*Plus commands. The commands in the first group are those that actually *do* something and can be called the group of "working" commands—for example, the RECOVER command recovers a database. The commands in the second group are *formatting* commands, and they will help you get clean output from your queries.

You'll learn about the most important of both kinds of commands in this chapter. In this section you'll look at the commands that do something, and the formatting commands will be covered in the "Commands for Formatting Output and Reporting" section, later in the chapter.

SQLPROMPT Command

As a DBA, you'll more than likely be working on several databases. When you're performing multiple tasks during the day, it's very easy to forget which database you're connected to from a particular SQL*Plus session. To avoid committing blunders (such as dropping production tables instead of development or testing tables), you should always set your environment so that the instance name shows up on your prompt every time, reminding you exactly where you are.

You can use the following command, which uses the special CONNECT_IDENTIFIER predefined variable to help you set your SQL*Plus prompt to show the database name (predefined variables are discussed in the "Predefined SQL*Plus Variables" section, later in this chapter):

```
SQL> SET SQLPROMPT '_CONNECT_IDENTIFIER > '
nick >
```

Notice how the SET command changes your prompt immediately in the SQL*Plus interface. When you use this command, your prompt will no longer be the generic SQL> prompt—it will instead be the more meaningful DBNAME > prompt, which will always remind you which database you are in without you having to make any dangerous guesses. In this example, the database name is nick.

You can use other special predefined variables to set your SQL*Plus prompt. For example, you can make the prompt display the username, as shown here:

```
SQL> SET SQLPROMPT "_USER > "
APPOWNER >
```

If you wish to see both the database name as well as the current user's name, you can do so with the following command, which uses the _USER and _CONNECT_IDENTIFIER variables:

```
SQL> SET SQLPROMPT "_USER'@'_CONNECT_IDENTIFIER > "
APPOWNER@nick >
```

The following prompt uses the _PRIVILEGE and _USER predefined variables to show the current user's name and the privilege the user logged in with:

```
SQL> SET SQLPROMPT "_USER _PRIVILEGE> "
SYS AS SYSDBA>
```

The following formulation shows the username, current date, and the database name (nick), using the three predefined variables _USER, _DATE, and _CONNECT_IDENTIFIER, respectively:

```
SQL> SET SQLPROMPT "_USER 'on' _DATE 'at' _CONNECT_IDENTIFIER > "
SYS on 20-JUN-05 at nick>
```

If you wish, you can incorporate the preceding line in your login.sql file, which will set your session values every time you log in, instead of having to reset them manually each time.

DESCRIBE Command

The DESCRIBE command describes or lists the columns and the column specifications of a table. It also enables you to describe an Oracle package or procedure. The DESCRIBE command is immensely useful when you're performing routine DBA activities. If, for example, you aren't sure what column to select in a particular table, but you're sure what table you should be querying, the DESCRIBE command helps out by giving you all the column names. Because you can describe even the metadata (the data dictionary), it's very easy to get familiar with and use table and column information that is critical for the database.

Listing 4-8 shows how the DESCRIBE command enables you to display the columns and column types for a table.

Listing 4-8. *Using the DESCRIBE Command*

```
SQL> DESCRIBE employees
 Name                          Null?                        Type
 ----------------------------- -------- ---------------------
 EMPLOYEE_ID                   NOT NULL              NUMBER(6)
 FIRST_NAME                                       VARCHAR2(20)
 LAST_NAME                     NOT NULL           VARCHAR2(25)
 EMAIL                         NOT NULL           VARCHAR2(25)
 PHONE_NUMBER                                     VARCHAR2(20)
 HIRE_DATE                     NOT NULL                   DATE
 JOB_ID                        NOT NULL           VARCHAR2(10)
 SALARY                                             NUMBER(8,2)
 COMMISSION_PCT                                     NUMBER(2,2)
 MANAGER_ID                                         NUMBER(6)
 DEPARTMENT_ID                                      NUMBER(4)
SQL>
```

HOST Command

The HOST command enables you to use operating system commands from within SQL*Plus. You may, for example, want to see if a file exists in a certain directory, or you may want to use the cp or tar commands at the UNIX level and return to your SQL*Plus session to resume interacting with the Oracle database.

Here is an example showing how to use the HOST command:

```
SQL> HOST cp /u01/app/oracle/new.sql  /tmp
```

The HOST command in the preceding example will help you copy the new.sql file from the specified directory to the tmp directory.

Just about any command you can use at the operating system level can be executed using the HOST command. You can replace the HOST command with ! (bang, or exclamation point) to run operating system commands from within SQL*Plus, as in the following example:

```
SQL> ! cp /u01/app/oracle/new.sql  /tmp
```

■ Note If you just type the command by itself, as in HOST or !, you'll be transported to the operating system directory from which you logged into the SQL*Plus session.

When you're done with your operating system task, just type **exit** on the command line, and you'll return to the SQL*Plus session you just left. Here's an example:

```
SQL> HOST
$ exit
SQL>
```

SPOOL Command

The SPOOL command enables you to save the output of one or more SQL statements to an operating system file in both UNIX and Windows:

```
SQL> SET LINESIZE 180
SQL> SPOOL employee.lst
SQL> SELECT emp_id, last_name, salary, manager FROM employee;
SQL> SPOOL OFF;
```

By default, spooled text files are saved as filename.lst. Although the default behavior is to save the output in a file, you can also send the output to a printer. Spooling files is very useful when you use SQL to help write SQL scripts, and you can see examples in the Appendix of this book.

You can append to, or replace, an existing spool file (replacing is the default). Here is the full syntax of the command:

```
SPOOL { file_name[.ext] [CRE[ATE]|REP[LACE]|APP[END]]| OFF | OUT }
```

This is what the various options stand for:

- FILE_NAME: Specifies the name of the spool file. The file extension is optional, and .lst is the default extension in most cases.

- CREATE: Creates a new file.

- REPLACE: Replaces the contents of an existing file and creates a new file if the file doesn't exist. This is the default behavior.

- APPEND: Adds the contents of the buffer to the end of a file you specify.

- OFF: Stops spooling.

- OUT: Stops spooling and sends the file to your default printer. This option is not available on some operating systems.

The SPOOL command can be put to a lot of uses. For example, you can easily export the SPOOL command to capture the results of a SELECT statement. First, control the output format by specifying the HEADING, FEEDBACK, and LINESIZE variables. Here's an example:

```
SQL> SPOOL /u01/app/oracle/data/employees.txt;
SQL> SELECT * FROM hr.employees;
SQL> SPOOL OFF;
```

The employees.txt file captures all the data in the HR.EMPLOYEES table. You can then employ the SQL*Loader utility to load the data into a different table.

ACCEPT and PROMPT Commands

The ACCEPT command is used to read user input from the screen and save it in a variable. You can either specify the variable or let SQL*Plus create one. The ACCEPT command is typically used to read user input in response to prompts from the SQL*Plus interface.

The PROMPT command comes in handy when you're creating interactive scripts. The command sends a message or just a blank line from SQL*Plus to the screen, and it's commonly used to elicit user input or to display comments. For example, including the line PROMPT "Testing" in a script will result in the following output:

```
SQL> "Testing"
```

The ACCEPT and PROMPT commands are usually used together in a SQL script, typically to request user input and save the input in variables that can be used later in the program. The following example illustrates the use of these commands:

```
SQL> PROMPT 'Please enter your last name'
SQL> ACCEPT lastname CHAR FORMAT a20 alapati
```

EXECUTE Command

When you use scripts that invoke PL/SQL code in the form of procedures and packages, you need to use the EXECUTE command to actually fire off the individual procedures in a package. Here is an example of using this command:

```
SQL> EXECUTE add_data

PL/SQL procedure successfully completed
SQL>
```

Note that you can specify either the keyword EXEC or EXECUTE to execute a procedure or function.

PAUSE Command

Often, you'll be executing scripts that generate output that doesn't fit on one screen. The output just zips past you on the screen, and it's gone before you can actually read it. You can use the SPOOL command to capture the entire output, but it's a waste to do this constantly, because you'll be creating files all day long just so you can look at the output of your scripts. SQL*Plus provides the PAUSE command so you can pause after every full screen of output. You just press the Enter key to see the next full screen.

The following example shows how to use the PAUSE command to slow down the output displayed on your terminal:

```
SQL> SHOW PAUSE
PAUSE is OFF
SQL> SET PAUSE ON
SQL> SHOW PAUSE
PAUSE is ON and set to ""
```

After you set the PAUSE command, the output won't flash by on the screen whenever you issue a SQL command. SQL*Plus will display a screen of output and wait for you to press Enter. When you run your queries with the PAUSE command set on, you need to press the Enter key in order to view the first screen of output.

Commands for Formatting Output and Reporting

Using the regular SQL*Plus commands, coupled with some formatting commands, you can add structure to the output of your queries and create rudimentary reports. Although your firm may have sophisticated software that will keep you from having to use SQL*Plus's formatting and reporting capabilities much of the time, chances are that you'll sometimes want to use SQL*Plus's formatting features to make your output pretty, or perhaps just legible! The formatting capabilities are somewhat primitive, but they get the job done in most cases, because most of your reports will be for database-management purposes.

BREAK Command

The BREAK command specifies where a formatting change occurs, as well as specifying the type of change. You can use the BREAK command on a column, a row, an action, or the whole report. For example, you can use the BREAK command to skip a line each time a specified column's value changes. Or you can specify that certain computed figures be printed at the end of a report.

Here's an example of the BREAK command:

```
BREAK ON DEPT_ID SKIP PAGE ON JOB_ID SKIP 1 ON SALARY SKIP 1
```

In the preceding example, there are three break columns, since each ON clause specifies a break—there is a break on the DEPT_ID, JOB_ID, and SALARY columns. Thus, each time there is a value in any one of these three break columns, SQL*Plus will perform the action specified by the particular break on that column. The actions are executed by SQL*Plus starting from the innermost break (on SALARY) and moving to the outermost break (on DEPT_ID).

When you use the ON clause in a BREAK command, it should be accompanied by an ORDER BY clause in the SQL statement that follows the formatting commands. In the following example, the BREAK command (the same one as in the previous example) is used along with a SQL statement, to produce meaningful output.

```
SQL> BREAK ON DEPT_ID SKIP PAGE ON JOB_ID SKIP 1 ON SALARY SKIP 1
SQL> SELECT dept_id, job_id, salary, emp_name
     FROM employees
     WHERE salary > 50000
     ORDER BY dept_id, job_id, salary, emp_name;
```

Using this BREAK command on the three columns will give us output in the following format:

- All rows with identical DEPT_ID values will be printed on the same page, and all rows with identical JOB_ID values will be printed in groups.

- In each group of jobs, jobs with identical SALARY values will be printed as separate groups.

- Changes in the emp_name column don't matter, since there is no break on the emp_name column.

COLUMN Command

The COLUMN command shows various properties of any specified column in a table. Once this command is issued, the settings for column format put in place by this command can be used by all the SQL commands in this session. Therefore, if you're running similar reports all the time, you may find it beneficial to include the COLUMN command specifications in a file using the STORE SET command.

You can use a number of options for the COLUMN command, but here's a simple example of how to use it:

```
SQL> COLUMN dept FORMAT a15 HEADING 'Department'
SQL> COLUMN cost FORMAT $9999
```

In the first COLUMN command, the DEPT column is specified to be up to 15 characters in length. Longer names will be truncated. It further specifies a meaningful heading under which the department names should be listed. The second COLUMN command specifies that the cost column will display a leading dollar sign.

COMPUTE Command

As its name indicates, the COMPUTE command is used for several types of computations, including averages, standard deviations, and so on. Here's an example of how to use this command. The SELECT collates the data for the COMPUTE command to work on:

```
SQL> COMPUTE AVG OF sales ON district
SQL> SELECT region, district, sales
     FROM total_sales
     WHERE district = 'NORTH';
SQL>
```

REPFOOTER Command

The REPFOOTER command prints specified footer text at the bottom of a report. Here's an example:

```
SQL> REPFOOTER PAGE RIGHT 'END OF THE 1st QUARTER RESULTS REPORT'
```

REPHEADER Command

The REPHEADER command is similar to the REPFOOTER command, but instead of placing a footer at the bottom of your report, it places a header at the top of your report, formatted as you specify. The following example prints the report header in the top center of the first page of the report:

```
SQL> REPHEADER PAGE CENTER '1st QUARTER RESULTS REPORT FOR 2008'
```

BTITLE and TTITLE Commands

The TTITLE command places a title at the top of each page of your report, and the BTITLE command does the same at the bottom of each page. Here are some examples to illustrate their use:

```
SQL> TTITLE 'Annual Financial Report for the Women's Club, 2008'
SQL> BTITLE '2005 Report'
```

■**Caution** After you use the BTITLE and TTITLE commands, as well as many other SQL*Plus commands, you have to manually turn them off to prevent all the ensuing SQL commands in that session from inheriting those settings. For example, if you don't turn the title off after you create a report, all the subsequent output for any command will be printed with the same title.

Creating Command Files in SQL*Plus

Instead of using a single command each time, you can use a set of commands together by writing them to a file and then running the file. When you do this, all the SQL commands included in the file will be executed sequentially.

Typing **edit** (or **ed**) at the SQL prompt will bring up your default editor (generally vi in UNIX and Notepad in Windows). Then you can type your commands, and name and save your file so you can execute the commands later on.

You can set the default editor's name in either your glogin.sql or login.sql file. Of course, you can also set the default editor after you log into SQL*Plus.

Saving the SQL Buffer Contents to a File

Often when you're writing fairly complex scripts, it is useful to take the contents of the SQL buffer and save them to a file. You can then retrieve the file for use later or use it for an automated execution. The SAVE command helps you save the SQL buffer contents. Here's a simple example:

```
SQL> SELECT username,process,sid,serial#
     FROM v$session
     WHERE status = 'ACTIVE'
     .
SQL> SAVE status.sql
Created file status.sql
SQL>
```

After you've typed some SQL, you can just type the dot (.) character on a new line. This indicates that you're finished writing the block of SQL. When you type the SAVE filename command, the contents stored in the SQL memory buffer are saved as a file with the specified filename—in this case, status.sql.

Note that the SAVE command, as shown in the preceding example, uses the default CREATE option, meaning it will create a new file called status.sql. However, if you already have a file called status.sql, you must use the SAVE command with the REPLACE option. If you wish to add on to an existing file, specify the APPEND option with the SAVE command. Here are some examples:

```
SQL> SAVE REPLACE status.sql
SQL> SAVE APPEND status.sql
```

Executing SQL Scripts in SQL*Plus

If you want to execute a SQL script, you have two choices:

- If you don't intend to make any changes before execution, just invoke the script by using the *at* sign (@).

- If the file containing the script is in the directory from which you started SQL*Plus, all you have to do is type the name of the file. If the command file is in a different directory, you have to give the full path for the file in order to run it in SQL*Plus.

On UNIX systems, you can configure an environment variable called ORACLE_PATH to tell SQL*Plus where to look for a script. This way, you can put all your routine SQL scripts in one location, and you don't need to specify the complete path for the file each time you want to execute an existing script. On my UNIX servers, for example, this is how I set the variable:

```
$ export $ORACLE_PATH=/u01/app/oracle/admin/dba/sql
```

On Windows systems, you can edit the Windows registry to specify the ORACLE_PATH variable.

Listing 4-9 shows a script called status.sql being run—it is in the directory from which SQL*Plus was invoked.

Listing 4-9. *Using the at (@) Command to Execute a Script*

```
SQL> @status.sql
USERNAME        STATUS    PROCESS     SID     SERIAL#
------------------------------------------------------------
                ACTIVE    2076          1        1
                ACTIVE    2080          2        1
                ACTIVE    2084          3        1
                ACTIVE    2088          4        1
                ACTIVE    2092          5        1
                ACTIVE    2096          6        1
SYSTEM          ACTIVE    1856:444      8       58
7 rows selected.
SQL>
```

The status.sql script is run in Listing 4-9 without any path information, because it is located in the same directory from which you logged into SQL*Plus. You can run a script located in a different directory by entering the complete path of the script's location, as in @/u01/app/oracle/admin/dba/sql/status.sql.

You can also execute the status.sql script by just typing the command **run status.sql**. The RUN command will execute the contents of the specified file. Or, if your SQL commands are actually listed on the screen (that is, stored in the SQL*Plus buffer), you can use the / command to execute the SQL code. Listing 4-10 shows the use of the / command. Note that when you use the / command to execute a script, the commands aren't listed again. Instead, the / command executes the contents of the SQL*Plus buffer.

Listing 4-10. *Using the / Command to Execute a Script*

```
SQL> /
USERNAME        STATUS    PROCESS     SID     SERIAL#
------------------------------------------------------------
                ACTIVE    2076          1        1
. . .
7 rows selected.
SQL>
```

You could also have used the RUN command instead of the / command, and your SQL would have been executed the same way. The RUN command lists the contents of the script it just executed, unlike the / command, which doesn't show the code in the SQL*Plus buffer that it's executing. The RUN command is shown in Listing 4-11.

Listing 4-11. *Using the RUN Command to Execute a Script*

```
SQL> RUN status.sql
  1  SELECT username,status
  2* FROM v$session
USERNAME                         STATUS
-----------------------------    --------
                                 ACTIVE
                                 ACTIVE
                                 ACTIVE
                                 ACTIVE
                                 ACTIVE
                                 ACTIVE
SYSTEM                           ACTIVE
7 rows selected.
SQL>
```

■**Caution** When you invoke a script with the RUN command, the SQL is shown on the screen before it's executed. The / command won't show the SQL, but executes it right away. Because of this, you have to exercise extreme caution when you use the / command. The script in the buffer might not be what you intended to run.

Creating a Windows Batch Script

You can easily create a batch script in a Windows system to run your SQL*Plus commands. For instance, say you have a script file called testscript.sql that provides information about the users in your database. If you want to schedule this script to run at a specified time, you must first create a Windows batch file that invokes the testscript.sql script file. You can then use the Windows *at* scheduling utility, if you wish, to schedule the batch script.

Here's a simple example. First create a batch file, named testbatch.bat, containing the following (the testscript.sql script writes its output to the output.txt file):

```
sqlplus username/password@connect_identifier @C:\temp\testscript.sql
notepad.exe C:\temp\output.txt
```

The preceding batch file will start a SQL*Plus session, run the testscript.sql script, and output the results of the testscript.sql file into the output.txt file using the notepad executable.

DEFINE and UNDEFINE Commands

During the course of writing and using SQL scripts, you sometimes need to specify variables and their values. The DEFINE command enables you to create your own variables (user variables) that continue to hold the values you specify for the duration of the SQL*Plus session or until you use the UNDEFINE command and unset the variables. Here is an example demonstrating the use of the DEFINE and UNDEFINE commands:

```
SQL> DEFINE dept = finance
SQL> UNDEFINE dept
```

The preceding example is straightforward. In SQL*Plus, however, you'll often use the DEFINE command in scripts to substitute values for variables. You typically do this by using the DEFINE command with a substitution variable instead of a user variable. A substitution variable is specified by adding an ampersand (&) to the user variable, as in &VARIABLE.

Listing 4-12 presents a simple example of the use of the DEFINE command with a substitution variable.

Listing 4-12. *Using the DEFINE Command*

```
SQL> col segment_name for a27
DEFINE owner = '&1'
SELECT segment_name,segment_type,extents
FROM dba_segments
WHERE owner = upper ('&owner')
AND extents > 10
AND segment_name NOT LIKE 'TMP%'
ORDER BY segment_type,extents desc
SQL> @extents.sql
Enter value for 1: system
SEGMENT_NAME                  SEGMENT_TYPE       EXTENTS
HELP_TOPIC_SEQ                       INDEX            18
PRODUCT_PROFILE                      TABLE            22
SQL>
```

In the extents.sql script in Listing 4-12, the owner variable was defined, but instead of it being given a hard-coded single value, it takes on any substituted value provided by the user. Thus, this same script can be run for any user in the database. All you need to do is plug in a different name for the schema owner each time you run the script.

Predefined SQL*Plus Variables

SQL*Plus provides a set of predefined variables, which you can use in the same way as the other substitution variables that you may create. Listing 4-13 shows the list of the predefined SQL*Plus variables, which you can see by using the DEFINE command without any arguments.

Listing 4-13. *Predefined SQL*Plus Variables Shown by the DEFINE Command*

```
SQL> DEFINE
DEFINE _DATE              = "23-DEC-07" (CHAR)
DEFINE _CONNECT_IDENTIFIER = "orcl2" (CHAR)
DEFINE _USER              = "SYS" (CHAR)
DEFINE _PRIVILEGE          = "AS SYSDBA" (CHAR)
DEFINE _SQLPLUS_RELEASE    = "1101000600" (CHAR)
DEFINE _EDITOR            = "ed" (CHAR)
DEFINE _O_VERSION          = "Oracle Database 11g Enterprise Edition Release
11.1.0.6.0 - Production
With the Partitioning, OLAP, Data Mining and Real Application Testing options"
(CHAR)
DEFINE _O_RELEASE          = "1101000600" (CHAR)
SQL> exit
SQL>
```

Here's what the variables stand for:

- DATE: Contains the current date or a user-defined fixed string

- CONNECT_IDENTIFIER: Contains the name of the database you are connected to

- USER: Contains the username as supplied by the user to make the current connection (this is the same as the output from the SHOW USER command)

- PRIVILEGE: Contains the privilege level of the current connect (can be AS SYSDBA, AS SYSOPER, or blank to indicate a normal connection)

- SQLPLUS_RELEASE: Shows the SQL*Plus release number

- EDITOR: Shows the editor that is being used

- O_VERSION: Shows the Oracle Database version (Enterprise Edition, for example), along with the database options

- O_RELEASE: Shows the Oracle Database release number

Using Comments in SQL*Plus

Often, you'll need to use nonexecutable comments in your SQL*Plus scripts and reports. Here's a brief description of the commenting features available in SQL*Plus:

- *The /* ... */ delimiters*: You can enclose one or more lines in your script with these delimiters to indicate that those lines are comments.

- *The -- notation*: You can preface the lines you want commented by a pair of hyphens. Developers often use these at the end of a code line to place comments.

- *The* REMARK *(or just* REM) *command*: The REMARK command before the beginning of a line indicates that the line is not to be executed.

Listing SQL Commands

SQL*Plus stores your most recently issued SQL statement in an area of memory called the *SQL buffer*. Unfortunately, SQL*Plus lets you save only the last command you issued in the buffer. Every new statement that you enter replaces the previous statement in the buffer. If you want to see the previous command you issued, type the word **LIST** or just the letter l.

```
SQL> l
  1  SELECT username, status, process, sid, serial#
  2  FROM v$session
  3* WHERE status = 'ACTIVE'
SQL>
```

If you want to see what's in your SQL script before you execute it, load it from the operating system into the SQL buffer by using the GET command, as follows:

```
SQL> GET status.sql
  1  SELECT username,status,process,sid,serial#
  2  FROM v$session
  3* WHERE status = 'ACTIVE'
SQL>
```

■**Caution** If you just enter the slash (/) command in your SQL*Plus session, you'll execute the last command you entered, which is always stored in the SQL buffer. It's a very good idea to always use the LIST command to first see what you're actually executing.

Sometimes you may want to execute several SQL command scripts consecutively. You can specify all the scripts you want to run in one main script and just run that main script—all the included scripts will run consecutively. Here's an example of how you can embed several SQL scripts into one main file:

```
SQL> GET one_script.sql
  1   @check.sql
  2   @create_table.sql
  3   @insert_table.sql
  4*  @create_constraint.sql
SQL>
```

When you run the `one_script.sql` script, its four constituent scripts will run one after the other. This is an efficient way to execute scripts, especially when you're creating and populating a new database, provided you have already tested the individual scripts.

■**Note** You can also use the @@*commandfile* notation, as in @@one_script.sql, to run command files that include several command files. The use of the @@ notation ensures that Oracle looks for the individual files in the same path as the command file.

Editing Within SQL*Plus

Often you'll want to make minor changes in the SQL code you're using. It isn't necessary to resort to your editor for minor changes, though, because SQL*Plus comes with its own change command, aptly called CHANGE. Simple pattern-matching techniques are used to modify SQL*Plus command lines. Therefore, you can add or modify a word or a part of a word by just replacing an existing pattern in a word with a new one.

The general pattern for changing SQL text is C/OLD/NEW, where C is the shortened form of the CHANGE command, which lets you change the first occurrence of the specified text on the current line, OLD stands for the actual SQL you intend to change, and NEW stands for the SQL text that is replacing the old text. Listing 4-14 shows how to use pattern matching to replace text in a SQL*Plus session.

Listing 4-14. *Changing Text Using Pattern Matching*

```
 SQL> SELECT username,status,process,sid,serial
  2    FROM v$session
  3*   WHERE status = 'ACTIVE';
select username,status,process,sid,serial
                                 *
ERROR at line 1:
ORA-00904: invalid column name
SQL> 1
  1* SELECT username,status,process,sid,serial
SQL> c/serial/serial#
  1* SELECT username,status,process,sid,serial#
SQL> l
  1  SELECT username,status,process,sid,serial#
  2  FROM v$session
  3* WHERE status = 'ACTIVE'
SQL> /
```

```
USERNAME              STATUS    PROCESS    SID    SERIAL#
----------------      -------   -------    ---    --------
                      ACTIVE    2076       1      1
                      ACTIVE    2080       2      1
                      ACTIVE    2084       3      1
                      ACTIVE    2088       4      1
                      ACTIVE    2092       5      1
                      ACTIVE    2096       6      1
SYSTEM                ACTIVE    1856:444   8      58
7 rows selected.
SQL>
```

If you have a complicated script, making changes using pattern matching as shown in Listing 4-14 can quickly get hairy! Use the runtime editor instead to make your changes conveniently. Saving the changes will bring you into the SQL*Plus interface automatically, and you can execute your edited SQL there.

■**Note** In UNIX, the usual editor is the vi editor, and in Windows, the usual editor is Notepad. You invoke them by typing **ed** at the SQL*Plus command line.

Inserting and Deleting Lines

You can always remove a line from or add one to your SQL text by merely invoking the editor and making the changes there. The SQL*Plus interface also offers you easy ways to add and delete lines. Using the INPUT command, you can easily add one or more lines to the SQL text already in the SQL buffer.

To use the INPUT command, just type the letter **i**. Listing 4-15 shows how you can insert text on a new line at the end of a SQL script. When you're done inserting new lines, you can type a period (.) to get the SQL prompt back.

■**Note** The semicolon (;) normally acts as the terminator for SQL statements. The period (.) is the default value for the BLOCKTERMINATOR variable, and it indicates the end of the statement inputting.

Listing 4-15. *Using the INPUT Command (i) to Insert a New Line at the End of a Script*

```
SQL> SELECT username, status, process, sid, serial#
  2  FROM v$session
  3* WHERE status = 'ACTIVE'

SQL> i
  4  and username = 'HR';

USERNAME     STATUS     PROCESS      SID       SERIAL#
---------    -------    --------     ----      --------
HR           ACTIVE     1856:444     8         64
SQL>
```

Listing 4-16 shows how to insert a line in the middle of a SQL script. You just print the line on the screen by using the LIST command and then add the new line afterward using the INPUT command.

Listing 4-16. *Using the INPUT Command to Insert a Line in the Middle of a Script*

```
SQL> SELECT username, status, process, sid, serial#
  2  FROM v$session
  3  WHERE status='ACTIVE'

 SQL> 1
 1* SELECT username, status, process, sid, serial#
SQL> i
  2i ,logon_time,terminal
  3i .

SQL> l
  1  SELECT username, status, process, sid, serial#,
  2  logon_time,terminal
  3  FROM v$session
  4* WHERE status='ACTIVE'
SQL>
```

Similarly, you can delete one or more lines of the SQL buffer by using the delete command DEL (or just D), accompanied by the line number, as shown in Listing 4-17.

Listing 4-17. *Deleting Text in SQL*Plus*

```
SQL> SELECT username, status, process, sid, serial#
  2  FROM v$session
  3  WHERE status = 'ACTIVE'
  4* AND username='HR'
SQL> del4
SQL> l
  1  SELECT username, status, process, sid, serial#
  2  FROM v$session
  3* WHERE status = 'ACTIVE'
SQL>
```

The DEL command will delete the specified line. Using the DEL command without a line number will remove the last line of the SQL you have in the buffer.

Adding to Text

Sometimes you need to add a word or two to a particular line. Instead of invoking the editor, you can just use the APPEND command to accomplish this, as shown in Listing 4-18.

Listing 4-18. *Using the APPEND Command*

```
SQL> SELECT username, profile
  2  FROM dba_users
  3  .
SQL> l
  1* SELECT username, profile
SQL> APPEND , created_date
  1* select username, profile, created_date
SQL> l
  1  SELECT username, profile, created_date
  2* FROM dba_users
SQL>
```

Sometimes, you may have a semicolon inside one of your statements, which will be interpreted as a statement terminator by SQL*Plus, leading to an error. Here's an example:

```
SQL> INSERT INTO EMPLOYEES VALUES ('BEGIN
  2  LOAD_PROCEDURE);
  3* END');
```

The semicolon in line 2 is not the end of the statement, and therefore you'll get the following error when you enter the preceding statement:

```
ERROR:
        ORA-01756: quoted string not properly terminated
```

The default value of the SQLTERMINATOR variable is a semicolon (;). You can resolve the problem here by simply turning off the use of the semicolon as a statement terminator, by using the SQLTERMINATOR variable, as shown here:

```
SET SQLTERMINATOR OFF
SQL> INSERT INTO EMPLOYEES VALUES ('BEGIN
  2  LOAD_PROCEDURE);
  3* END')
    /
```

Note that since you turned off the use of the semicolon as a statement terminator, you should use the slash (/) to execute the statement. You can also use the BLOCKTERMINATOR variable, whose default value is a period (.), to signify the end of the statement.

Incorporating Comments with the REMARK Command

The REMARK command is straightforward. It enables you to incorporate comments in your SQL scripts. Here it's shortened to REM.

```
SQL> GET user_report.sql
1 REM This script gives you the usernames and their profiles
2 REM Author: sam alapati
3 REM Date: JUNE 20,2005
4 SELECT username, profile FROM dba_users;
SQL>
```

Copying Tables with the COPY Command

On large tables, you tend to get into trouble using the CREATE TABLE AS SELECT (CTAS) technique because Oracle does not commit between the inserts, and in the meantime, the undo segments may run out of space. You are also limited to non-LONG data types when you use this technique. By using the COPY command, you can copy data from a query into a table in the same or a remote database. The COPY command gives you a way to easily copy all types of tables, and it avoids many of the problems of using the CTAS technique, because it does commit while it's copying the data from the source table.

Here's the syntax of the SQL COPY command:

```
SQL> COPY
usage: COPY FROM <db> TO <db> <opt> <table> { (<cols>) } USING <sel>
  <db>   : database string, e.g., hr/your_password@d:chicago-mktg
  <opt>  : ONE of the keywords: APPEND, CREATE, INSERT or REPLACE
  <table>: name of the destination table
  <cols> : a comma-separated list of destination column aliases
  <sel>  : any valid SQL SELECT statement
SQL>
```

If the FROM or TO clause is missing, the current SQL*Plus connection is used. The key parameter is opt, which lets you specify one of the following:

- APPEND: Inserts records into the target table and creates the table if it doesn't exist
- CREATE: Creates the target table and inserts rows into it
- INSERT: Inserts rows into an existing table
- REPLACE: Drops the existing table, re-creates it, and loads data into it

The USING <sel> clause lets you specify the query that determines the rows and columns you want to copy from the target table.

■**Tip** If a table consists of a LONG column, you can't use the CTAS method to make a copy of the table. You can, however, use the COPY command to copy this table.

Listing 4-19 shows how to use the COPY command. Note that the hyphen (-) is the "continue" character, and it lets you break up long SQL statements over multiple lines. Make sure you use the continue character and don't hit Enter after the first line!

Listing 4-19. *Using the COPY Command*

```
SQL> COPY FROM sysadm/sysadm1@finance1-
  >    CREATE test01 -
  >    USING SELECT * FROM employee;

Array fetch/bind size is 15. (arraysize is 15)
Will commit when done. (copycommit is 0)
Maximum long size is 80. (long is 80)
Table TEST01 created.

    4954 rows selected from sysadm@finance1
    4954 rows inserted into TEST01.
    4954 rows committed into TEST01 at DEFAULT HOST connection.
SQL>
```

You can make the COPY command's execution faster by increasing the size of the SQL*Plus parameters ARRAYSIZE, COPYCOMMIT, and LONG, if necessary.

Using the CREATE TABLE AS SELECT method is usually faster than using the COPY command when you're copying data from one table to another on the same server—using the COPY command involves copying data from the server to the client SQL*Plus interface before copying it back to the database again. Obviously this will increase the overhead and take longer to process than directly copying from the server to the same server.

Making DML Changes Permanent with SQL*Plus

When you use SQL*Plus, you can enter DML statements either separately or as part of a named or an anonymous block of PL/SQL code. Here are the different ways in which DML changes are made permanent:

- You can commit the results of a transaction by using the COMMIT keyword at the end of the transaction.
- You can set the AUTOCOMMIT setting to ON in your SQL*Plus session, which results in an automatic COMMIT statement being appended to every SQL statement you issue in that session.

- You can issue a DDL command, such as DROP INDEX, that will also automatically ensure that any pending transaction is followed with either a COMMIT or ROLLBACK statement.

- You can exit gracefully from SQL*Plus by typing in **EXIT** or **QUIT**, which are identical in their effects. When you issue the EXIT command, Oracle will automatically commit all changes you made in that session, even if you never issued a commit request, or even if the AUTOCOMMIT setting has been set to OFF. When you use either the EXIT or QUIT command, the following will happen:

  - All pending changes are rolled back or committed.
  - The user is logged out of Oracle.
  - The SQL*Plus session is terminated.
  - Control is returned to the operating system.

Creating Web Pages Using SQL*Plus

When you embed SQL*Plus in program scripts, you can use the MARKUP command in the following way to produce HTML output:

```
SQLPLUS -MARKUP "HTML ON"
```

Before executing any SQL commands, this command outputs the HTML and BODY tags.

If you want to output an HTML page that can be embedded in an existing web page, you can use the MARKUP command as follows:

```
SQL> SET MARKUP HTML ON SPOOL ON
SQL> commands here . . .
SQL> SET MARKUP HTML OFF SPOOL OFF
```

Key SQL*Plus Database Administration Commands

Although you may use every SQL*Plus command in the course of database administration, some specific commands in SQL*Plus exist for the sole use of the Oracle DBA. There are four powerful database administration commands that you can use from SQL*Plus—the RECOVER command, the STARTUP and SHUTDOWN commands, and the ARCHIVE LOG command.

RECOVER Command

The RECOVER command, as you can imagine, is used to recover a database or one of its files or tablespaces after a database failure. To be able to run this command, you need to have the OSOPER or the OSDBA role. You can perform manual or automatic recovery, and in either case, you're responsible for first restoring all the necessary datafiles so you can recover your database.

The RECOVER command is complex and critical, and you'll examine it in great detail in Chapter 16, which deals with database recovery.

STARTUP and SHUTDOWN Commands

The STARTUP and SHUTDOWN commands are used to start up and shut down your Oracle instance. For details about both of these commands, see Chapter 10.

ARCHIVE LOG Command

Archive logs are the archived or stored redo logs, and they play a critical role in database recovery. Any user with the OSDBA or OSOPER privilege can issue the ARCHIVE LOG command. It enables you to start and stop the archiving of redo log files, as shown here:

```
SQL> ARCHIVE LOG START
Statement processed.
SQL> ARCHIVE LOG STOP
Statement processed.
SQL>
```

You can use the ARCHIVE LOG LIST command to view details about the archive logs being archived, as shown here:

```
SQL> ARCHIVE LOG LIST
Database log mode              Archive Mode
Automatic archival             Enabled
Archive destination            /a03/app/oracle/admin/NICKO/arch/
Oldest online log sequence     933
Next log sequence to archive   937
Current log sequence           937
SQL>
```

The preceding command shows that the database is in the archive mode and also that automatic archiving is enabled.

Using SQL to Generate SQL

There will be occasions when you have to write a SQL script that involves a number of similar lines. A good example would be a script in which you are assigning a set of privileges to several users. You can, of course, execute separate SQL statements for each user, but it is a waste of time to do so, besides being a mind-numbing exercise. Fortunately, you can use SQL to generate a script with all the SQL statements that need to be executed. Using SQL to generate SQL essentially involves using the output of one SQL statement as input for another SQL statement.

It is very easy to write SQL code that generates more SQL code as output. First, you write the SQL to generate the SQL. Next, you start spooling a file, where the output of the first SQL script will be captured. Then you execute the SQL code that will actually generate SQL code as its output. The spooled script will contain the final set of commands you are interested in. Finally, you execute this spooled script that contains the generated SQL code.

■**Caution** Always make sure you set the heading off, echo off, and feedback off. This will give you a clean, spooled output script, which you can execute directly without any changes.

Here is an example that you are likely to be familiar with:

1. Set the environment variables:

   ```
   SQL> SET ECHO OFF HEADING OFF FEEDBACK OFF
   ```

2. Name a spool file, to which the output of the first script will be written:

   ```
   SQL> SPOOL test.txt
   ```

3. Execute the SQL that creates more SQL:

```
SQL> SELECT 'grant connect, resource to '||username||';' FROM dba_users;
```

This is part of the output of the preceding command:

```
GRANT CONNECT, RESOURCE TO DBA1;
GRANT CONNECT, RESOURCE TO MAMIDI;
GRANT CONNECT, RESOURCE TO JEFFRESS;
GRANT CONNECT, RESOURCE TO CAMPBELL;
GRANT CONNECT, RESOURCE TO ALAPATI;
GRANT CONNECT, RESOURCE TO BOLLU;
GRANT CONNECT, RESOURCE TO BOGAVELLI;
SQL> SPOOL OFF
```

4. The spooled script will have captured the preceding commands. Now run that script (test.txt in this example):

```
SQL> @test.txt
Grant succeeded.
Grant succeeded.
Grant succeeded.
Grant succeeded.
Grant succeeded.
Grant succeeded.
Grant succeeded.
SQL>
```

As you can see, if you had to run this GRANT command for a hundred users, the effort would be the same as for one user. You can easily adapt the preceding technique when you are performing a task that applies to a number of objects or users in your database at the same time. This is a very useful little technique to have in your arsenal. You'll find many uses for it in performing your routine administrative tasks.

Oracle SQL Developer

Oracle offers a free graphical tool called *Oracle SQL Developer* for use in database development. You can use Oracle SQL Developer to run SQL statements and scripts, and create and modify PL/SQL programs; the tool comes with built-in versioning and source control system capabilities, as well as reporting capabilities. You can use this tool on Windows, Linux, and Mac OS X. You can use Oracle SQL Developer's Migration Workbench to browse objects and data in third-party databases and migrate to Oracle from these databases. This tool is well integrated with Oracle Application Express.

Oracle Enterprise Manager

Oracle Enterprise Manager (OEM), Oracle's GUI-based comprehensive database-management toolset, has been a part of the Oracle server software for many years, and Oracle has substantially improved it over time. It provides a wide array of services, including reporting features and event notification through e-mail and pagers.

It's possible to manage a database with homegrown SQL and PL/SQL scripts, but OEM provides an attractive console-based client framework to help you perform almost all of your day-to-day management activities, including tasks such as backup, recovery, export, import, and data loading. Although you can use Oracle-supplied packages to perform these tasks, OEM makes it a lot easier to use new Oracle Database 11*g* DBA tools like the Segment Advisor, SQL Access Advisor, and SQL

Tuning Advisor. While the installation of various OEM components was substantially more complex in previous versions, the latest versions of OEM are quite user friendly.

Starting with the Oracle Database 10g release, there are two versions of the OEM—a single-database version called the Database Control, and a systemwide version that lets you manage your entire system, called the Grid Control. With the Grid Control, you can manage your enterprise-wide database, application servers, hosts, and other services. This section shows you how to configure and use both versions of the OEM. If you aren't comfortable writing scripts, OEM is ideal for you because it comes with all the essential scripts to manage a database and other services. Modern Oracle DBAs should strive to master the OEM and use its powerful functionality to enhance the depth and breadth of their database management.

■**Note** If you're using Oracle Application Server 10g, you can use the Application Server Control to manage the application server instance.

Traditionally, Oracle DBAs have used a variety of scripts to manage their databases. You can either write a script yourself or obtain just about any script you want at one of the many fine Oracle DBA sites on the Internet (I listed some of these sites in the Introduction). Scripts are either SQL-based or a combination of SQL*Plus and UNIX shell scripts. You can manually monitor the system or schedule the scripts to provide automated monitoring and notification through pagers or e-mail. Most DBAs also use operating system–based tools, such as HP's GlancePlus, sar, vmstat, and iostat.

If you have a single database with few users, you can probably manage it with a few automated scripts and some occasional manual monitoring. However, using the single-instance Database Control tool makes day-to-day management a snap. If you have to manage several databases, you'll need a tool to help you perform such tasks as object creation, security maintenance, database monitoring and notification, event management, backing up, recovering, and data loading. A number of excellent management tools are also available from third-party sources such as Quest Software (http://www.quest.com) and Embarcadero Technologies (http://www.embarcadero.com). However, you get the Database Control tool as part of your Oracle Server software, so it's the logical choice for managing your Oracle database.

Monitoring database performance is not the only benefit of using OEM. Proactive event management lets you set thresholds for various database parameters for event notification. Job scheduling makes the traditional crontab seem antiquated. You can even perform application tuning and some reverse-engineering of the schema with OEM. Finally, you can perform many DBA tasks, such as backup, recovery, data loading, and online table reorganization, much more easily using OEM. You can even publish trend charts about the database performance, uptime, and capacity planning.

Your DBA skill level will increase as you explore the various areas of OEM. You'll be much more effective as a DBA, and you'll significantly reduce the time you need to complete important but tedious tasks such as checking logs and monitoring various components of the database.

Benefits of Using OEM to Manage Databases

OEM offers several features that make it an attractive tool for managing Oracle databases. The complete toolset of OEM allows you to monitor databases, manage physical storage and the various database objects, and analyze database performance. Let's look at the various benefits OEM provides.

Out-of-the-Box Management

OEM offers a true out-of-the-box solution for complete systems monitoring and management. While I do cover the configuration of the various components of OEM in the section "Configuring and Using the Database Control" later in this chapter, but there really isn't any heavy-duty configu-ration necessary to get started with OEM, even for the Grid Control version. In fact, the OEM Database Control doesn't need any configuration at all, if you create a new Oracle database with the Database Configuration Assistant (DBCA), or you choose to create a new database when you install Oracle Database Server software.

Web-Based Management

You can view the OEM console on your workstation or access it through your web server. OEM uses Secure Sockets Layer (SSL), so database security isn't compromised when you access your databases through the Internet. All tiers of OEM communicate via HTTP, so they can go through any firewall that HTTP communications are allowed to go through. In some situations, the management server has to make a direct Oracle net connection to the managed instance. The web-based OEM console has all the features of the regular console, so all you need is a web browser to access your databases from anywhere, at any time.

Real-Time Monitoring

OEM provides excellent real-time monitoring in addition to its capability to provide reports on the database. Without OEM, you're forced to use SQL scripts, and the information isn't always quick in coming. For example, SQL scripts that can detect users locking an object are notoriously slow in finishing. By using OEM, on the other hand, you can immediately see all the locks in the database. Similarly, OEM helps you identify the waits in the system and find out what's causing them while they're occurring.

Complete Environment Monitoring

As you already know, a poorly performing (or unavailable) database could be the result of a problem anywhere in the application stack—in the database, in the web servers, or in the server that's hosting any of the components of the application. OEM monitors the performance of all the components of this stack, not just the Oracle database. As a result, you can quickly figure out why the database is performing poorly all of a sudden. Maybe you have a web server that isn't able to process the connect requests efficiently for some reason, while your database is performing just fine.

This is a sampling of the items that OEM can monitor and report on:

- The entire platform
- End-user experience
- Systems and web application availability
- The extended network components
- Business transactions
- Historical data analysis and change tracking

Application Performance Monitoring

OEM provides Application Performance Monitoring (APM) tools, which provide you with an easy way to diagnose system problems and monitor database performance. APM tools gather and report not only on the status, but also the response times of all the databases in your system. This informa-tion helps you proactively manage your databases and prevent problems from happening.

When DBAs use OEM's alert systems and notifications, they can quickly inform managers about poorly performing system components. These alerts thus help you resolve bottlenecks before the database becomes completely unavailable to users.

APM performs the following functions:

- Monitors the performance and availability of the system

- Indicates outages and bottlenecks throughout the application system

- Analyzes the root causes of performance problems

- Diagnoses performance with drill-downs

- Minimizes application downtime through the use of efficient problem-resolution tools

Scalable Management Capability

OEM is a highly scalable tool, and you don't need additional resources to monitor an ever-growing enterprise. To add new servers to your system, all you need to do is start up a Management Agent on the new node. The agent will help you gather all pertinent information about servers and databases.

Consolidated Database Management

OEM provides you with a quick top-level view of the entire environment—servers, databases, application servers, and so forth—through its home pages. Each managed target has a home page that provides a concise overall view of system health and performance. By summarizing key information on the home pages, OEM helps you quickly identify the root cause of any system problems.

OEM also enables you to efficiently query for the latest code patches for all the Oracle products installed in your enterprise. If new patches are available, you can download and install them easily with OEM.

Integrated Systems Management

You can easily integrate OEM with a systemwide monitoring tool such as HP OpenView. This integration of the database and server management tools lets you view both the database and system events from a single browser. The two products essentially act like a single integrated management suite. OEM uses the Smart Plug-In (SPI) to provide the integration of OEM and OpenView operations.

OEM Architecture and Components

Oracle Enterprise Manager comes in two flavors—Database Control and Grid Control. To monitor and manage just a single database, OEM Database Control is all you need. You don't have to configure anything to use the OEM Database Control—it's ready to use the moment you create a new Oracle Database 11g database, if you do so using the DBCA or the Oracle Universal Installer. If you create a database from scratch using the CREATE DATABASE statement, on the other hand, you have to configure Database Control using the emca (Enterprise Manager Configuration Assistant) utility.

To manage large-scale, complex environments, you must use the OEM Grid Control, which you install separately from the Oracle database.

You can consider the Database Control to be a subset of the Grid Control, since the Grid Control can do everything that the Database Control can do, besides helping you manage systemwide nondatabase targets as well.

■**Note** In addition to the Database Control and Grid Control, the OEM product also includes the Oracle Enterprise Manager Application Server Control, which helps you manage individual Oracle Application Server instances. An Oracle Application Server instance is automatically installed as part of the Grid Control installation. The Grid Control Management Server is run by this Oracle Application Server.

Configuring and Using the Database Control

Database Control can come already configured for your use if you choose to use the DBCA to create a new database. For a database you create with manual commands, however, you must configure the Database Control using a special utility. In this section, I explain both the automatic and manual configuration of the Database Control. The OEM Database Control uses an HTTP server, and you can view the Database Control console with an Internet browser. The default URL for the Database Control is http://*hostname*:*portnumber*/em. For example, on my Linux server, I access the Database Control using the following URL:

```
http://localhost:5500/em
```

■**Note** If the default port for OEM is already in use, Database Control will use a different port number. To see which port your database is using, examine the $ORACLE_HOME/install/portlist.ini file.

Automatically Configuring the Database Control

If you select the option of creating a new database when you install the Oracle Database Server software, or if you use the DBCA to create a new database, then Database Control is automatically installed and configured for you. When you choose the option of creating a new database during Oracle Server software installation, you are given a choice between the Database Control and Grid Control, as shown in Figure 4-1.

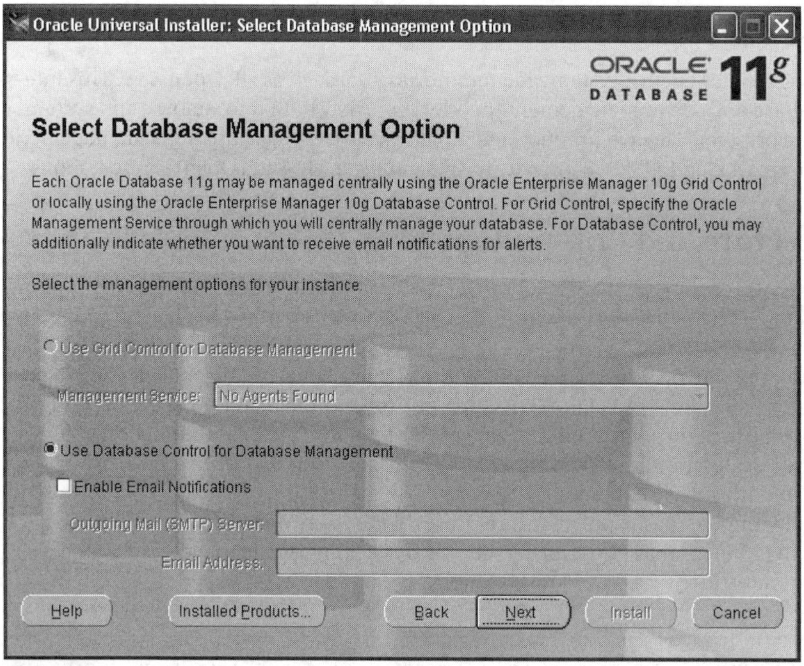

Figure 4-1. *Selecting the database management option*

■Note If you choose to create your database manually or to upgrade your database to Oracle Database 11*g*, you must configure the Database Control using the dbconsole build script ($ORACLE_HOME/bin/emca for UNIX/Linux systems and $ORACLE_HOME\bin\emca.bat for Windows). This script configures the Database Control and starts up the dbconsole process. This is discussed next in the "Manually Configuring the Database Control" section of this chapter.

Manually Configuring the Database Control

If you manually create a new Oracle Database 11*g* database or upgrade one to Oracle Database 11*g*, you must configure the Database Control using the emca utility, found in the $ORACLE_HOME/bin directory in UNIX/Linux and Windows systems. You can use the emca utility for several purposes besides configuring the Database Control, and it can be run with the options shown here:

$ emca [*operation*] [*mode*] [*dbType*] [*flags*] [*parameters*]

To configure the Database Control for your database, issue the emca command and provide values for things such as the port number and the database name, when the emca utility prompts you to do. Listing 4-20 shows the output from the emca configuration command that I ran on my server.

Listing 4-20. *Running emca to Configure the Database Control*

```
$ emca -config dbcontrol db

STARTED EMCA at Dec 3, 2007 3:02:48 PM
EM Configuration Assistant, Version 11.1.0.5.0 Production
Copyright (c) 2003, 2005, Oracle.  All rights reserved.

Enter the following information:
Database SID: orcl
Database Control is already configured for the database orcl
You have chosen to configure Database Control for managing the database orcl
This will remove the existing configuration and the default settings and perform a
fresh configuration
Do you wish to continue? [yes(Y)/no(N)]: y
Listener port number: 1521

Password for SYS user:
Password for DBSNMP user:
Password for SYSMAN user:
Password for SYS user:
Email address for notifications (optional): salapati@netbsa.org
Outgoing Mail (SMTP) server for notifications (optional): netbsa.org
-----------------------------------------------------------------

You have specified the following settings

Database ORACLE_HOME ................ /u01/app/oracle/product/11.1.0.6/db_1

Local hostname ............... localhost.localdomain
Listener port number ............... 1521
Database SID ............... orcl2
```

```
Email address for notifications ............... salapati@netbsa.org
Outgoing Mail (SMTP) server for notifications ............... netbsa.org

-------------------------------------------------------------------
Do you wish to continue? [yes(Y)/no(N)]: y
Dec 3, 2007 3:08:58 PM oracle.sysman.emcp.EMConfig perform
INFO: This operation is being logged at
/u01/app/oracle/cfgtoollogs/emca/orcl2/emca_2007_12_03_15_08_28.log.
Dec 3, 2007 3:08:59 PM oracle.sysman.emcp.util.DBControlUtil stopOMS
INFO: Stopping Database Control (this may take a while) ...
Dec 3, 2007 3:09:06 PM oracle.sysman.emcp.EMReposConfig uploadConfigDataToRepository
INFO: Uploading configuration data to EM repository (this may take a while) ...
Dec 3, 2007 3:12:13 PM oracle.sysman.emcp.EMReposConfig invoke
INFO: Uploaded configuration data successfully
Dec 3, 2007 3:12:42 PM oracle.sysman.emcp.util.DBControlUtil configureSoftwareLib
INFO: Software library is already configured.
Dec 3, 2007 3:12:42 PM oracle.sysman.emcp.util.DBControlUtil configureSoftwareLib
INFO:  EM_SWLIB_STAGE_LOC (value) will be ignored.
Dec 3, 2007 3:12:42 PM oracle.sysman.emcp.util.DBControlUtil secureDBConsole
INFO: Securing Database Control (this may take a while) ...
Dec 3, 2007 3:13:00 PM oracle.sysman.emcp.util.DBControlUtil secureDBConsole
INFO: Database Control secured successfully.
Dec 3, 2007 3:13:01 PM oracle.sysman.emcp.util.DBControlUtil startOMS
INFO: Starting Database Control (this may take a while) ...
Dec 3, 2007 3:17:20 PM oracle.sysman.emcp.EMDBPostConfig performConfiguration
INFO: Database Control started successfully
Dec 3, 2007 3:17:21 PM oracle.sysman.emcp.EMDBPostConfig performConfiguration
INFO: >>>>>>>>>> The Database Control URL is https://localhost.localdomain:5502/em
<<<<<<<<<<<
Dec 3, 2007 3:18:41 PM oracle.sysman.emcp.EMDBPostConfig invoke
WARNING:
************************  WARNING  ************************

Management Repository has been placed in secure mode wherein Enterprise Manager
data will be encrypted.  The encryption key has been placed in the file:
/u01/app/oracle/product/11.1.0.6/db_1/localhost.localdomain_orcl2/sysman/config
/emkey.ora.   Please ensure this file is backed up as the encrypted data will
become unusable if this file is lost.

**********************************************************
Enterprise Manager configuration completed successfully
FINISHED EMCA at Dec 3, 2007 3:18:41 PM
$
```

You can test the new Database Control connection by using the URL shown in the Database Control configuration output (toward the end of Listing 4-20). Here is the URL from Listing 4-20:

```
http://localhost:localdomain:1158/em
```

Make sure you specify em after the last slash—otherwise, you'll merely succeed in getting to the Oracle Containers for J2EE home page!

The Database Control login screen in Figure 4-2 shows that the Database Control configuration was successful.

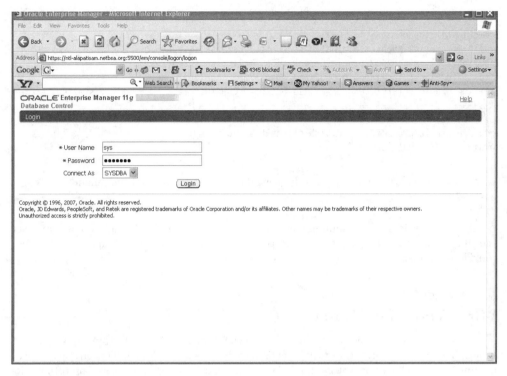

Figure 4-2. *The Database Control login screen*

Accessing the Database Control

Before you can manage a database with the help of the Database Control, you must first make sure that the target database is running. In addition, you must make sure the Oracle listener service is running. If the listener service hasn't been started, and you try connecting to the Database Control, you may see errors like the following:

```
The Network Adapter could not establish connection
ORA-12541:TNS:no listener
```

Once you've made sure that the database and the listener service are running, you have to make sure that the dbconsole process is running on your system—it is needed in order to access the Database Control as a web application. You can use the START, STOP, and STATUS options of the emctl utility to work with dbconsole, and you can also use the SETPASSWD option (EMCTL SETPASSWD DBCONSOLE) to establish a password for dbconsole.

To check the status of dbconsole, use the emctl status dbconsole command as shown here:

```
$ emctl status dbconsole
Oracle Enterprise Manager 11g Database Control Release 11.1.0.6.0
Copyright (c) 1996, 2007 Oracle Corporation.  All rights reserved.
https://localhost.localdomain:5502/em/console/aboutApplication
Oracle Enterprise Manager 11g is not running.
------------------------------------------------------------------
Logs are generated in directory
/u01/app/oracle/product/11.1.0.6/db_1/localhost.localdomain
_orcl2/sysman/log
$
```

You start the dbconsole process with the `emctl start dbconsole` command:

```
$ emctl start dbconsole
Oracle Enterprise Manager 11g Database Control Release 11.1.0.6.0
Copyright (c) 1996, 2007 Oracle Corporation.  All rights reserved.
https://localhost.localdomain:5502/em/console/aboutApplication
Starting Oracle Enterprise Manager 11g Database Control ................ started.
------------------------------------------------------------------
Logs are generated in directory
/u01/app/oracle/product/11.1.0.6/db_1/localhost.local
domain_orcl2/sysman/log
$
```

You can stop the dbconsole process by using the `emctl stop dbconsole` command:

```
$ emctl stop dbconsole
```

Once dbconsole is up and running, you can access Database Control through your web browser using the following URL: `http://host.domain:port/em`. As shown earlier in the chapter, a typical URL would look like this:

```
http://localhost:5500/em
```

A Brief Tour of the Database Control

The Database Control interface is very intuitive, so I won't spend a whole lot of time walking you through the various Database Control links or list all of its capabilities. You don't need a special user account (like SYSMAN, which you use for the Grid Control) to log into the Database Control console. Use one of the privileged database accounts like SYS so you can log in with the SYSDBA privileges. When you log in, you'll be in the Database Control home page, shown in Figure 4-3. The Oracle Database Control home page provides a launching point for performance tuning and other management activities.

The Database Control home page allows you to do the following:

- Start up and shut down your database.

- Assess the current health of the database by checking the alerts.

- Drill down into various management tasks via the Performance, Availability, Server, Schema, Data Movement, and Software and Support tabs (discussed in the following sections).

The database refreshes the home page every minute by default, and it contains the following sections:

- Performance

- Availability

- Server

- Schema

- Data Movement

- Software and Support

Let's quickly review each of the main sections or pages of Database Control in the following sections.

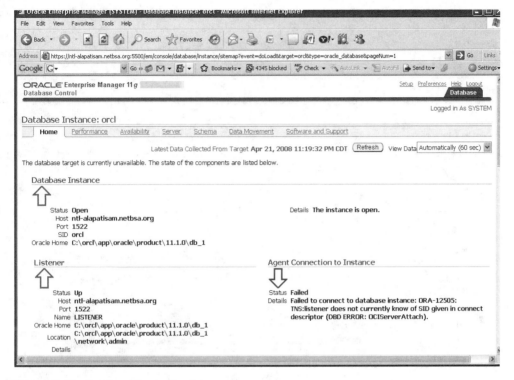

Figure 4-3. *The Database Control home page*

Performance

The Performance page shows you the overall status of the database and helps you quickly identify causes of performance bottlenecks. Figure 4-4 shows the top part of the Performance page, which contains three important charts that tell you at a quick glance how the instance is performing currently: Host CPU, Active Sessions, and SQL Response Time. The middle of the home page contains a Diagnostic Summary section that shows any current problems in the database alert log. The Space Summary section shows any tablespaces or segments under space pressure. The High Availability section shows the usable free space in the flash recovery area.

The bottom of the Performance page is probably more important on a day-to-day basis for you, since it contains a useful alert table. The table shows the various alerts issued recently by the database. You can view the brief message for the various errors and drill down to an alert that's critical, to get the details about that alert.

■**Tip** Oracle recommends that you start investigating waits if the level of waits is at twice the Maximum CPU line in the sessions graph. If your instance throughput is decreasing, and there is an increasing amount of contention within the database, you should start looking into tuning your database.

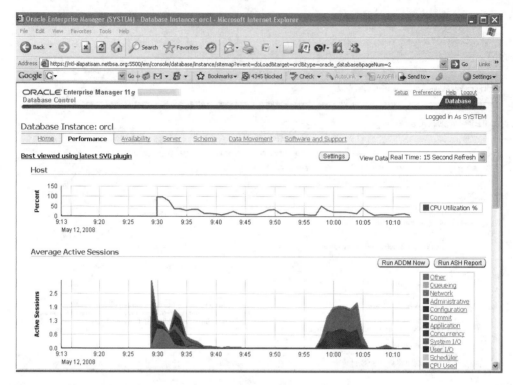

Figure 4-4. *The Database Control Performance page*

Using the Performance page, you can do the following:

- View instance performance.

- Identify the SQL statements, sessions, and users that are using the most resources in the database (top SQL, top sessions, and top users).

- Run the Automatic Database Diagnostic Monitor (ADDM).

Availability

The Availability page contains the Backup/Recovery and the Oracle Secure Backup sections. You can manage RMAN and its recovery catalog from the Backup/Recovery link.

Server

The Server page is your jumping off point for several key Oracle database management activities:

- *Storage*: Lets you manage tablespaces, datafiles, and control files, redo log groups, and archive logs. You can also migrate to ASM from this section.

- *Database Configuration*: Lets you access the various memory advisors and view the database feature usage charts. You can also manage automatic undo management from here. You can check the current initialization parameters in use and modify them.

- *Oracle Scheduler*: Helps you manage all aspects of the Oracle Scheduler, as well as the automated maintenance tasks.
- *Statistics Management*: Lets you manage the Automatic Workload Repository (AWR) and the AWR baselines.
- *Resource Manager*: Helps you manage the Oracle Resource Manager.
- *Security*: Helps manage users, roles, and privileges. You can also configure audit policies, implement the Transparent Data Encryption (TDE) feature, and create virtual private database policies from this section.

Figure 4-5 shows the Database Control Server page.

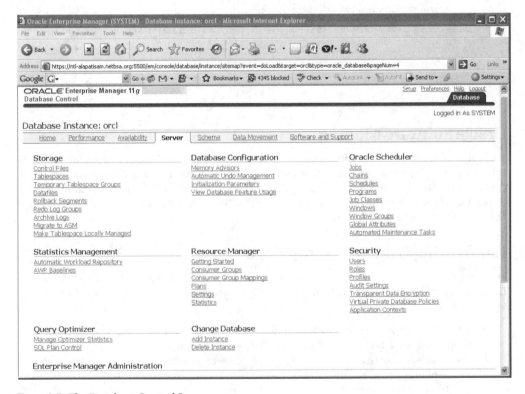

Figure 4-5. *The Database Control Server page*

Schema

The Schema page lets you manage various database objects such as tables, indexes, views, synonyms, database links, and materialized views. You can also manage stored code such as functions, procedures, and packages from here, in addition to triggers. Under the Change Management section, there's an interesting link to the Dictionary Comparisons page. Here, you can perform a comparison of database objects in different databases.

Data Movement

The Data Movement page has links that let you perform an export and import of data and transport tablespaces. You can also clone databases by clicking the Clone Database link under the Move Database Fields section. You can set up and manage both Oracle Streams and Replication from the Data Movement page.

Software and Support

The Software and Support page lets you access several important database tools and features, as I summarize here:

- *Configuration*: Lets you clone Oracle homes

- *Database Software Patching*: Lets you access the Patch Advisor and stage and apply code patches

- *Deployment Procedure Manager*: Provides access to the Deployment Procedure Manager and the Deployment and Provisioning Software Library

- *Real Application Testing*: Lets you work with the Database Replay feature and the SQL Performance Analyzer

Oracle Software Cloning

The Database Control enables you to clone an Oracle home. You can also clone Oracle homes from a master installation to one or more servers using the Grid Control. The Grid Control will automatically adjust host names, IP addresses, and other related settings. If you want to create multiple new installations at once, you can do so. In addition, you can also save a selection of master installations to use repeatedly in cloning operations.

Configuring Using the Setup Page

You can gain access to the Database Control Setup page by clicking the Setup link at the top of the Database Control home page. On the Setup page, there are options for configuring the following things:

- *Administrators*: By default, a super-administrator account with the name SYSMAN is created during the installation of the OEM Database Control. The super administrator can create other administrators as well as create roles in the system. You should use the SYSMAN account only to perform general configuration tasks and to create other administrative accounts for your daily database administration.

- *Notification Methods*: You can use this page to set up e-mail notifications from the Database Control. You need to provide your SMTP mail server information and your e-mail address to do this. Figure 4-6 shows the Notification Methods page.

- *Patching Setup*: You can directly download various patches for your Oracle software from MetaLink using the Database Control. From the Patching Setup page, you can enter your MetaLink credentials to search for new patches in Oracle MetaLink and download them.

- *Blackouts*: You can suspend monitoring for a specified target for any reason, including maintenance activity on that target. This way, you don't get notifications indicating false problems in the database.

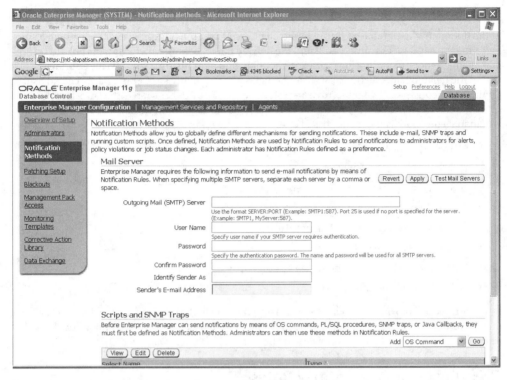

Figure 4-6. *The Database Control Notification Methods page*

- *Management Pack Access*: Premium functionality is included in four Management Packs—the Oracle Diagnostics Pack, the Oracle Tuning Pack, the Oracle Configuration Management Pack, and the Oracle Change Management Pack—and they are subject to additional Oracle licensing. The Management Pack Access page lets you grant or remove access to these packages, based on your Oracle licensing agreement. Here's what they offer:

  - The Oracle Diagnostics Pack includes performance-monitoring abilities (database and host), the ADDM, the AWR, a system for event notification and notification blackouts, and a history of events and metrics (database and host).

  - The Oracle Tuning Pack includes SQL Access Advisor, SQL Tuning Advisor, SQL Tuning Sets, and database-object reorganization help.

  - The Oracle Configuration Management Pack facilitates database and host configuration, management of deployments, cloning of databases and Oracle homes, and searching and comparing of configuration policies.

  - The Oracle Change Management Pack allows you to make changes in database schemas. You can track changes, compare and synchronize objects and schemas, modify schema objects, and evaluate and undo the changes, should this be necessary.

■**Caution** You will violate your Oracle license if you use the four Management Packs described here without additional licensing from Oracle Corporation.

The Related Links Section and the Advisor Central Page

At the bottom of the Database Control home page and also at the bottom of every page such as the Performance page, for example, you'll find the Related Links section, which contains links to several management tools, including jobs, Oracle Scheduler, and alert history. The Advisor Central link is part of the Related Links section as well, and it takes you to the Advisor Central page. The Advisor Central page consists of two tabs: Advisors and Checkers. The Advisors tab is the launch pad for using the various specialized tools for the management advisory framework. Each of these important management advisors are discussed elsewhere in the book:

- ADDM (see Chapter 17)
  - SQL Performance Analyzer
  - SQL Tuning Advisor (see Chapter 18)
- Segment Advisor (see Chapter 17)
- Data Recovery Advisor (see Chapter 16)
- Memory Advisors (see Chapter 17)
- Automatic Undo Management (see Chapter 8)
- MTTR Advisor (see Chapter 18)

The Checkers tab on the Advisor Central page takes you to the Checkers page, where you can see the results of various checks performed by the database, such as a DB Structure Integrity Check, for example. Chapter 18 explains the concept of checkers in the Oracle Database 11*g* release.

Creating Database Control Roles

A role is a collection of predefined target privileges created by the privileged administrators. By default, only the SYS, SYSTEM, and SYSMAN users can log into the Database Control console. After logging in as one of these three users, you can assign management privileges to other user accounts in the database. Here's how you create roles:

1. Log into the Database Control as SYS, SYSTEM, or SYSMAN.
2. Click the Setup link and click the Create button.
3. In the Create Role Properties page, enter a name for the role and enter a description. Click Next.
4. In the System Privileges page, select View Any Target and click Next.
5. Under Available Targets, select the Database type. Choose the databases you want from the drop-down list. Click Next.
6. Under Available Targets, choose Listener and select the appropriate listener. Click Next.
7. Under Target Privileges, choose Full (under Batch Assignment). Click Next.
8. Click the Administrators button to get to the Create Role Administrators page. Here, you'll see the list of available administrators to whom you can grant the newly created OEM role. Select the administrators and click Finish.

Linking to MetaLink

Oracle Database 11*g* allows you to link directly from the OEM to the Oracle MetaLink service, which means that OEM can automatically track patches. If you want to receive an alert when the OEM detects a new patch, you can easily set it up. If you'd like, the OEM can even notify you when a system needs one of the new patches. Once you have applied a patch, Oracle will update the Oracle Universal Installer inventory to ensure that it knows your latest patch level.

Here's how to download and apply software patches manually:

1. Click Setup on the Database Control home page.

2. Click the Patching Setup link on the Setup page.

3. In the Patching Setup page, specify the MetaLink username and password. The Patch Search URL has the default MetaLink login page address (`http://updates.oracle.com`).

Oracle will use the MetaLink credentials you specified to run the RefreshFromMetalink job at regular intervals. This job will collect the Oracle critical-path information and the latest patch collection criteria from MetaLink, and it will update the OEM repository with the data.

■**Note** Alternatively, you can access Oracle MetaLink by going to `http://metalink.oracle.com`. Once you have logged in, you can search for and download patches.

Policy-Based Configuration Framework

Oracle Database 11*g* contains a policy-based framework to help you easily track targets that may be violating established configuration policies. OEM provides a set of policies based on Oracle's best-practice configuration to ensure that your database performs at an optimal level, and Oracle Database 11*g* enables you to monitor all of your databases to see if there are any violations of the predetermined configuration policies. Oracle collects these configuration metrics for databases, host machines, and listener services.

On the Database Control home page, there is a section called Diagnostic Summary, which shows you whether there are any policy violations anywhere. If you drill down, using the All Policy Violations button, you can get to the Policy Violations page, which summarizes all policy violations in your databases and hosts. If you wish, you can disable a policy by going to the Manage Policy Library page.

Here are some typical policy rules:

• The "critical patch advisories for Oracle Homes" policy rule checks for missing Oracle patches.

• The "insufficient number of control files" policy rule checks for the use of a single control file.

• The "listener password" policy rule checks for password-protected listeners.

Tracking Database Feature-Usage Statistics

In Oracle Database 11*g*, you can track database usage metrics, which enable you to understand two important phenomena:

• How you are using the various features of your Oracle database, including whether the database is currently using a given feature, and the first and last times a given feature was used.

• The high-water mark (HWM) statistics for important database attributes. The HWM is simply the highest usage point a feature has attained to that time.

The database features that you can track include advanced replication, Oracle Streams, virtual private database (VPD), and various auditing features.

The database collects HWM statistics for items such as the following:

- Maximum size of tables
- Maximum number of Oracle datafiles
- Maximum number of user sessions
- Size of the largest data and index segments

Examining Database Feature-Usage Statistics

To view database usage statistics in the Database Control, follow these steps:

1. On the Database Control home page, click the Administration link and go to the Database Configuration group. Click the Database Feature Usage link.

2. You'll now be in the Database Usage Statistics property sheet, which shows the database feature-usage statistics in the form of a table. The table lists all the available database features by name and lets you see if the database is currently using each one, as well as providing the first usage and last usage times. To view details about the usage statistics of any feature, just click the associated link. Figure 4-7 shows the Feature Usage portion of the Database Usage Statistics property sheet.

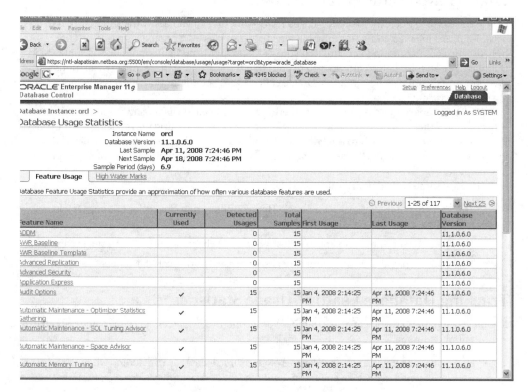

Figure 4-7. *The Feature Usage portion of the Database Usage Statistics property sheet*

3. To view the database HWMs, click the High Water Marks tab in the Database Usage Statistics property sheet. In the High Water Marks page, you can see the HWMs for all database objects, as well as the last sampled value for each feature, and the version of the database feature. Figure 4-8 shows the High Water Marks page.

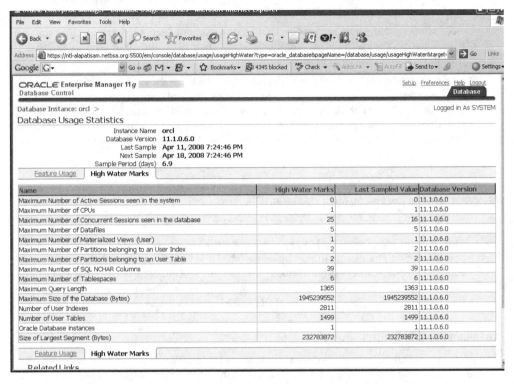

Figure 4-8. *The High Water Marks page of the Database Usage Statistics property sheet*

OEM Grid Control

The purpose of the OEM Grid Control is to facilitate the management of entire systems, including hosts, databases, web servers, listeners, and other services. It provides you with a powerful and convenient centralized means of managing your entire infrastructure, not just your Oracle databases. You can manage your systems from just about anywhere, including from mobile devices.

When you click the Databases tab on the Grid Control home page, you'll see a list of all the databases that are under the purview of the Grid Control. Just click the database you want to examine in detail. The Grid Control Database page provides the same functionality as the single-instance Database Control console.

The Grid Control Framework Components

The Grid Control consists of the following four components:

- *OEM Grid Control*: This is the main OEM web-based interface for monitoring your enterprise. You can manage hosts, databases, listeners, application servers, HTTP servers, and web applications from this centralized Grid Control.

- *OEM Management Agent*: You install an OEM Management Agent on every host that you wish to manage. It's the agent's job to monitor the host, databases, and other services and to send the information to the OEM Management Service.

- *Oracle Management Service (OMS)*: This is the middle tier of the Grid Control stack. The Management Service provides the user interface for the Grid Control and interacts with the Management Agent and the Management Repository, which contains the data for the OEM Grid Control. The Management Service receives all data from the Management Agents, and it then sends the data to be stored in the Management Repository.

■**Note** In order to install the Management Service, the Grid Control installation process first installs the Oracle Application Server on your system, which includes an HTTP server.

- *Management Repository*: The Management Repository contains all pertinent information about hosts, databases, and other targets that the OEM Grid Control needs. The repository consists of two tablespaces in the database hosting the OEM Grid Control. Note that the Database Control doesn't require the creation of any extra tablespaces for hosting the Management Repository—only the Grid Control version of OEM needs the repository.

Installing the Grid Control

As you know, the Database Control doesn't need any additional software, since it's a part of the Oracle database software. You must, however, install the OEM Grid Control separately, either by downloading the software from Oracle's web site or by using the appropriate CD. Installing Grid Control consists of two steps: installing the OEM Grid Control software on the host from which you intend to use the Grid Control console, and installing a Management Agent on each of the hosts you want to monitor.

In the following sections, I first show how to install the Grid Control software and then the Management Agent. Here are the steps in the installation process:

1. Log into the host as the Oracle software owner and mount the Oracle Database 11*g* CD. Change the directory to the CD, and execute the runInstaller script:

   ```
   $ ./runInstaller
   ```

2. At the Welcome window, click Next.

3. Accept the default Operating System Group Name and click Next.

4. A separate window asking you to run the root.sh UNIX script will appear. Leave this window open, and open a new terminal window.

5. Execute `orainstRoot.sh` as the root user in the terminal window, as shown here:

```
$ cd $ORACLE_BASE/oraInventory
$ su
$ <rootpassword>
$ ./orainstRoot.sh
$ exit
```

6. Once you run the `orainstRoot.sh` script, go back to the Oracle Universal Installer window and click Continue.

7. In the Specify File Locations window, choose the directory for the OEM files, and click Next.

8. In the Select a Product to Install window, you can install the OEM Grid Control in an existing Oracle database or you can create a new database. You can also choose to install a Management Service or Management Agent from this window. In this example, I chose the option that creates a new Oracle database. Click Next.

■**Note** When you choose to install the Grid Control using a new database, Oracle will create a new Oracle Database 11*g* database on your server. If you want to install using an existing Oracle database, your database must be version 9.2 or higher.

---

9. The Oracle Universal Installer will make the necessary prerequisite checks, after which you click Next.

10. Choose a password for the default SYSMAN user, and click Next.

11. Select passwords for the SYS, SYSTEM, and DBSMNP users in the new database, and click Next.

12. In the next window, you have the option of setting up MetaLink and Proxy information. These are optional and have no bearing on the functioning of the Grid Control. Once you make your choice, click Next.

13. In the Database Identification window that appears next, choose the SID and the Global Database Name for the database. Click Next.

14. In the Database File Location window, specify the location for all the database files, and click Next.

15. Review the list of components that are going to be installed in the Summary screen that appears, and click Install.

16. You'll now see a series of windows indicating the progress of the installation. You'll be asked to run the `root.sh` script again as the root user. Log in as the root user in a separate window and run the `root.sh` script. Then go back to the installation window, and click OK.

17. The Configuration Assistants window will show the status of the various configuration assistants, such as the Oracle Database Configuration Assistant. On my system, there were 16 configuration assistants. After the new Oracle database is created, you'll see the following message:

```
The Oracle Agent will now be installed on the same machine as the database
that was just created. This database will then be available through
Grid Control to manage its environment.
```

Click OK.

18. When the Setup Privileges window appears, open a new terminal window and run the orainstRoot.sh script yet again. Once the script completes, go back to the installer window, and click Next. The Configuration Assistants window will appear again and the Agent Configuration Assistant will install the Oracle Agent.

19. You'll see an End of Installation message from the installer, along with a list of the port numbers you can use to access the Grid Control, the Oracle Application Server that's installed as part of the Grid Control installation, and the Oracle database that was created to host the Grid Control.

20. Click Exit to end the installation.

Installing and Deploying the OEM Management Agent

Use the following steps to install the OEM Management Agent on each server you want to monitor:

1. Start the Oracle Universal Installer and perform the first seven steps in the preceding "Installing the Grid Control" section.

2. In the Select a Product window, choose the Additional Management Agent installation type, and click Next.

3. Specify the name of your host server in the next page, and click Next.

4. Click Next after reading the security warning (regarding secure HTTP mode), and then click OK.

5. Review the Summary window, and click Next to start the actual agent installation process.

6. Once your installation completes, click Yes to exit the Oracle Universal Installer.

7. Verify that your databases and hosts can be seen by the newly installed Management Agent. You can do this by logging into the Grid Control and clicking the Targets tab. You will see all the discovered hosts. Click any host and then click Databases. You should now be able to view all the Oracle databases that are running on that host.

Once you successfully install the agents on your servers, you can use the information they collect to monitor all your Oracle databases, hosts, web servers, and listeners.

Managing the Management Agent

The emctl utility is used to configure agents and consoles for not only the Grid Control, but also the Database Control and Oracle Application Server. You can check the status of the agent and stop and start the agent service with the following commands:

- `emctl status agent`
- `emctl start agent`
- `emctl stop agent`

Tip The emctl executable is common to both UNIX/Linux and Windows systems. However, remember that there is a separate emctl executable for the Database Control and the Management Agent. You'll find the appropriate emctl executable by using the full path for it, under the right home directory. In this case, since we're using the emctl executable to manage the OEM agent, we'd go to the directory where the agent software was installed. If you just type in **emctl**, you may be looking at the wrong executable.

The Oracle Management Service

Before you can start using the Grid Control interface, you must first make sure that the middle tier, the Oracle Management Service, is running. At the end of the Grid Control software installation, the OMS should be automatically started by the installer. You can use the following command to check whether the OMS is running:

```
$ emctl status oms
Oracle Enterprise Manager 10g Release 10.1.0.3.0.
Copyright (c) 1996, 2004 Oracle Corporation.  All rights reserved.
Oracle Management Server is Up
$
```

If the OMS isn't running, start it up this way:

```
$ emctl start oms
Oracle Enterprise Manager 10g Release 10.1.0.3.0.
Copyright (c) 1996, 2004 Oracle Corporation.  All rights reserved.
Starting HTTP Server ...
Starting Oracle Management Server ...
Checking Oracle Management Server Status ...
Oracle Management Server is Up
$
```

Connecting to the Grid Control

Once you know OMS is running, as discussed in the previous section, you're ready to log into the Grid Control console. In order to do this, you must know the port number for the Grid Control, which you can get from the portlist.ini file, located in the $ORACLE_HOME/install directory.

The first item in the setupinfo file shows the port number of the Grid Control. You connect to the Grid Control interface by typing a URL with the following format into your web browser:

```
http://your_servername:port_number/em
```

The Grid Control installation includes an Oracle Application Server instance, which is administered using a special ias_admin user account. This is the default information for the embedded Application Server instance on my server:

```
Instance Name:    EnterpriseManager0.ntl-alapatisam.netbsa.org
ias_admin password: This password is the same the SYSMAN account.
```

These are the connection details for the Management Repository on my server:

```
Host: ntl-alapatisam.netbsa.org
Port: 1521
SID: emrep
```

Logging Into the Grid Control

When you install the Grid Control, a super-administrator account, SYSMAN, is automatically installed, and you provide the password for it at that time. You use this SYSMAN account to log into OEM for the first time.

You can't rename or delete this account, but you can later set up administrator accounts for various users who need to use the Grid Control to manage databases. You can limit the privileges of each administrator to control which databases they can access, and you can set up customized notification rules for them.

■**Note** You must log into the Grid Control using the SYSMAN account, not your database accounts like sys or system.

Once you successfully log into the Grid Control, you'll be in its home page. From the home page, you can manage databases either by choosing Databases from the drop-down list of targets or by clicking the Targets tab and clicking the Databases link.

Features of the Grid Control

The Grid Control is an enormously powerful monitoring and management tool. I devote the following sections to explaining the important features, but I make no attempt to cover the various database management features, which are identical to those in the Database Control.

Enterprise Configuration Management

You can perform the following two enterprise-wide configuration-related tasks through the Grid Control:

- Obtaining host and database configuration information
- Changing the configuration

Obtaining Host and Database Configuration Information

Management Agents, which run on the database hosts, collect configuration information about their hosts and send it back to the OEM's Management Repository every 24 hours. Here's what they send:

- Memory, CPU, and I/O configuration on the host
- Details about the operating system, such as vendor, version, installed software components, patches, and database patch information
- Properties associated with the database and its instances
- Information about tablespaces and datafiles
- Information about control files and redo logs

Monitoring and Managing Enterprise Configuration

You can use the Grid Control to monitor and manage the configuration once it has the relevant details. Here's what the Grid Control allows you to do with respect to managing your configuration:

- Look at and contrast the hardware and software configurations of different hosts and databases.
- Monitor any changes to host configurations.
- Summarize your configuration.
- Search for configurations.
- Carry out cloning operations on Oracle homes and database instances.
- Look at violations of host and database policies.
- Patch Oracle and manage warnings about critical patches.

Grouping Targets

To facilitate the management of a large number of targets, the Grid Control lets you organize large numbers of systems into groups. For example, you can grant a Grid Control user access only to certain groups. You can group targets into homogeneous groups (databases only, for example) or heterogeneous groups (such as a database, listener, application server, and host server).

Using the Grid Control Home Page

The Grid Control home page provides an overall view of the entire enterprise. Use this as your starting point when you're evaluating the health of your database, since it provides information about the entire Oracle environment, not just the database.

The home page shows you the following things:

- *Status*: Provides the status of the monitored Oracle targets, including the availability and open alerts for each target. Targets include hosts, databases, web servers, and listeners.

- *Critical Patch Advisories*: Displays a visual summary of any patch advisories and the affected Oracle homes.

- *Deployments Summary*: Provides a summary of your entire system configuration, including hardware and software.

- *Resource Center*: Provides links to Oracle documentation, release notes, support, and the Oracle Technology Network (OTN).

The Grid Control home page contains tabs that offer links to the following entities:

- *Targets*: Targets include the host servers, databases, application servers, web applications, and groups.

- *Deployments*: The Deployments home page has sections for critical patch advisories, deployments, configuration, patching, cloning, and policies (managing policy violations).

- *Alerts*: This page will tell you if any of your targets are down.

- *Jobs*: The Job Activity page contains information on all scheduled, running, and finished jobs in your database.

- *Management System*: This page contains information about the Management Service and the Management Repository. It provides details about the general health of OEM, availability, backlogs, and alerts about the OEM itself and all the targets.

At the top (and the bottom) of the Grid Control home page, you'll find additional links to the following pages:

- *Setup*: The Setup page is similar to the Setup page in the Database Control.

- *Preferences*: The Preferences page is where you can change preferred credentials, including the password of the SYSMAN account.

- *Help*: This page provides details about each of the pages in the Grid Control.

- *Logout*: This link will log you out of the Grid Control.

Monitoring Your Entire System with the Grid Control

You can use the Grid Control to monitor not only Oracle databases, but also web applications, host performance, application servers, and database groups. In the following sections, I briefly summarize the Grid Control capabilities in the nondatabase areas. The Grid Control has all the features of the Database Control, as regards the management of databases; in addition, you can manage all the other parts of your system.

Monitoring Web Applications

In order to view your web applications through the Grid Control, select Web Applications from the View drop-down list on the home page. You can perform the following tasks from the Web Applications home page:

- *Review web application alerts*: You can use the Grid Control to view alerts regarding your web applications. Whenever an application fails to perform according to a preset performance-policy threshold, Grid Control will alert you. You specify the alerts when you create your web applications. In order for the Grid Control to monitor the application, you must, of course, add the target to OEM.

- *Monitor transaction performance*: The Grid Control will monitor your web applications to see if they are conforming to availability and service-level requirements. You can monitor and track key transaction-performance indicators like average page response, slowest page, and the response time (in milliseconds).

  You can go to the Transaction Playback page and view the summary and breakdown of the time spent on each web page in your application.

- *Analyze page performance*: Using the Grid Control, you can track the web server response time and correlate this information with the response times of URLs from various users. You can also perform end-user performance review of the slow URLs.

Monitoring Host Performance

You can monitor the performance of your hosts and track configuration changes through the Grid Control. You can reach the Host home page by clicking the Targets tab and then selecting the host you want to investigate. The Host home page summarizes the availability and status of the host. From the Host home page, you can navigate to the performance and configuration areas:

- *Performance*: You can use the Grid Control to view host performance, including CPU usage, memory, disk I/O, etc. You can view current CPU load and swap utilization on your system without using operating system tools like sar and top.

- *Configuration*: You can view the hardware and software configuration on the host. If you wish, you can perform a side-by-side comparison of any two hosts on your system. This enables you to identify the differences between a development and production server, for example. You will see the differences in operating system patches, packages, and Oracle software versions.

Monitoring Application Servers

You can monitor the application servers in your environment by clicking the Targets tab and then clicking the Web Applications link. You'll see a list of all the web applications in your system here, and you can click a specific application to examine its performance. In addition to monitoring your web applications, you can also monitor the web servers used by your applications, including the Oracle Application Server instances.

Managing Groups

The Groups subtab under the Targets tab lists all the groups defined in the Grid Control. The Grid Control's Groups capability lets you organize your databases and hosts into related groups. For example, you can collect all your production databases into a group called Production Databases. Groups let you run a job in all related targets with a single command. In addition, you can view all alerts and configuration policy violations in your production databases separately from the development and test databases.

You can perform the following tasks from the Groups page:

- Add, remove, and configure groups.
- Access a group's home page.
- View alerts and policy violations for a group.

Oracle Database 11*g* Architecture, Schema, and Transaction Management

CHAPTER 5

■ ■ ■

Oracle Database 11*g* Architecture

In the first four chapters, I set the stage for working with Oracle. It's time now to learn about the fundamental structures of Oracle Database 11g. Oracle uses a set of logical structures called data blocks, extents, segments, and tablespaces as its building blocks. Oracle's physical database structure consists of datafiles and related files. Oracle memory structures and a set of database processes constitute the Oracle instance, and are responsible for actually performing all the work for you in the database.

To understand how the Oracle database works, you need to understand several concepts, including transaction processing, backup and recovery, undo and redo data, the optimization of SQL queries, and the importance of the data dictionary. This chapter provides an outline of the important Oracle automatic management features, as well as the sophisticated built-in performance tuning features, including the Automatic Workload Repository (AWR) and the Automatic Database Diagnostic Monitor (ADDM); a brand new diagnostic framework introduced in this release; and the new Data Recovery Advisor, which helps you easily recover from several types of data disasters and errors. I also outline Oracle's advisor-based Management Framework.

Oracle Database Structures

In discussing the Oracle database architecture, you can make a distinction between the physical and logical structures. You don't take all the data from the tables of an Oracle database and just put it on disk somewhere on the operating system storage system. Oracle uses a sophisticated logical view of the internal database structures that helps in storing and managing data properly in the physical datafiles. By organizing space into logical structures and assigning these logical entities to users of the database, Oracle databases logically separate the database users (who own the database objects, such as tables) from the physical manifestations of the database (datafiles and so forth).

The following sections discuss the various logical and physical data structures.

Logical Database Structures

Oracle databases use a set of logical database storage structures in order to manage the physical storage that is allocated in the form of operating system files. These logical structures, which primarily include tablespaces, segments, extents, and blocks, allow Oracle to control the use of the physical space allocated to the Oracle database.

Taken together, a set of related logical objects in a database is called a *schema*. Remember that Oracle database objects, such as tables, indexes, and packaged SQL code, are actually logical entities. Dividing a database's objects among various schemas promotes ease of management and a higher level of security.

Let's look at the logical composition of an Oracle database from the bottom up, starting with the smallest logical components and moving up to the largest entities:

- *Data blocks*: A *data block* is the smallest building block of the Oracle database and consists of a specific number of bytes on the disk.

- *Extents*: An *extent* is two or more consecutive Oracle data blocks, and this is the unit of space allocation.

- *Segments*: A *segment* is a set of extents that you allocate to a logical structure like a table or an index (or some other object).

- *Tablespaces*: A *tablespace* is a set of one or more datafiles, and usually consists of related segments. The datafiles contain the data of all the logical structures that are part of a tablespace, like tables and indexes.

The following sections explore each of these logical database structures in detail.

Data Blocks

The Oracle *data block* is at the foundation of the database storage hierarchy and is the basis of all database storage in an Oracle database. A data block consists of a specific number of bytes of disk space in the operating system's storage system. An Oracle database allocates free database space in terms of Oracle data blocks.

A data block is the smallest logical component of an Oracle database. For example, you can size an Oracle data block in units of 2KB, 4KB, 8KB, 16KB, or 32KB (or even larger chunks), and it is common to refer to the data blocks as *Oracle blocks*. The storage disks on which the Oracle blocks reside are themselves divided into *disk blocks*, which are areas of contiguous storage containing a certain number of bytes—for example, 4,096 or 32,768 bytes (4KB or 32KB; each kilobyte has 1,024 bytes).

How Big Should the Oracle Block Size Be?

You, as the DBA, have to decide how big your Oracle blocks should be and set the `DB_BLOCK_SIZE` parameter in your Oracle initialization file (the `init.ora` file). Think of the block size as the minimum unit for conducting Oracle's business of updating, selecting, or inserting data. When a user selects data from a table, the select operation will "read," or fetch, data from the database files in units of Oracle blocks.

If you choose the common Oracle block size of 8KB, your data block will have exactly 8,192 bytes. If you use an Oracle block size of 64KB (65,536 bytes), even if you just want to retrieve a name that's only four characters long, you'll have to read in the entire block of 64KB that happens to contain the four characters you're interested in.

■**Tip** If you're coming to Oracle from SQL Server, you can think of the Oracle block size as being the same as the SQL Server page size.

As was mentioned earlier, the operating system also has a disk block size, and the operating system reads and writes information in whole blocks. Ideally, the Oracle block size should be a multiple of the disk block size; if not, you may be wasting time reading and writing whole disk blocks while only making use of part of the data on each I/O. On an HP-UX system, for example, if you set your Oracle block size to a multiple of the operating system block size, you gain 5 percent in performance.

Oracle offers the following guidelines for choosing the database block size:

- Choose a smaller block size if your rows are small and access is predominantly random.

- Choose a larger block size if the rows are small and access is mostly sequential (or random and sequential), or if you have large rows.

In Chapter 10, which discusses the creation of Oracle databases, you'll learn a lot more about Oracle database block size and the criteria for choosing an appropriate block size.

■**Note** The Oracle block size that you should choose depends on what you're going to do with your database. For example, a small block size is useful if you're working with small rows and you're doing a lot of index lookups. Larger block sizes are useful in report applications when you're doing large table scans. If you are unsure about what block size to use, remember that Oracle recommends that you choose a block size of 8KB for systems that process a large number of transactions.

Multiple Oracle Data Block Sizes

The DB_BLOCK_SIZE initialization parameter determines the standard block size in your Oracle database, and it can range from 2KB to 32KB. The system tablespace is always created with the standard block size, and Oracle lets you specify up to four additional nonstandard block sizes. For example, you can have 2KB, 4KB, 8KB, 16KB, and 32KB block sizes all within the same database—I discuss the reasons you might wish to do this shortly, in the "Tablespaces" section. If you choose to configure multiple Oracle block sizes, you must also configure corresponding subcaches in the buffer cache of the system global area (SGA), which is Oracle's memory allocation, as you'll learn in the "Understanding Main Memory" section of this chapter.

Multiple data block sizes aren't always necessary, and you'll do just fine in most cases with one standard Oracle block size. Multiple block sizes are useful primarily when transporting tablespaces between databases with different database block sizes.

What's Inside a Data Block?

All data blocks can be divided into two main parts: the row data portion and the free space portion. (There are also other smaller areas, such as overhead and header space for maintenance purposes.) The *row data* section of data blocks contains the data stored in the tables or their indexes. The *free space* section is the space left in the Oracle block for new data to be inserted or for existing rows in the block to be extended.

Sometimes it may be useful to find out exactly what data is in a particular block or to find out which block contains a particular piece of data. You can actually "see" what's inside a data block by "dumping" the block contents. Oracle blocks can be dumped at the operating system level (referred to as *binary dumps*), and you can also perform Oracle-formatted block dumps.

The most common reason for performing a block dump is to investigate *block corruption*, which may be caused by operating system or Oracle software errors, hardware defects, or memory or I/O caching problems. The Recovery Manager (RMAN) provides ways to recover from block corruption, and you can also use the Data Recovery Advisor to adopt other strategies to recover from data block corruption, as I explain in Chapter 16.

Let's look at what's actually in an Oracle data block. First, before you do a data dump, you need to find out which datafile and data block you want to dump. Listing 5-1 shows a query that enables you to determine the file and block IDs.

Listing 5-1. *Query to Identify File and Block IDs*

```
SQL> SELECT segment_name,
     file_id,
     block_id
     FROM dba_extents
     WHERE owner = 'OE'
     AND segment_name LIKE 'ORDERS%';

SEGMENT_NAME            FILE_ID      BLOCK_ID
------------------      --------     ---------
ORDERS                  397          32811
SQL>
```

You can alternatively use the following query to get the same information:

```
SQL> SELECT header_file,header_block FROM dba_segments
     WHERE segment_name = 'PERSONS';

HEADER_FILE     HEADER_BLOCK
-----------     ------------
        397     32811
SQL>
```

Next, you issue the following command, using the appropriate file and block numbers, to get a dump of the block you need:

```
SQL> ALTER SYSTEM DUMP DATAFILE 397 BLOCK 32811;

System altered.
SQL>
```

The preceding command will produce a block dump in the default trace directory (UDUMP) of the Oracle database. Listing 5-2 shows part of the output of this command.

Listing 5-2. *A Sample Block Dump*

```
Dump file /a03/app/oracle/admin/pasu/udump/pasu_ora_29673.trc
...
Start dump data blocks tsn: 110 file#: 397 minblk 32811 maxblk 32811
buffer tsn: 110 rdba: 0x6340802b (397/32811)
scn: 0x0001.610ac43d seq: 0x01 flg: 0x04 tail: 0xc43d2301
frmt: 0x02 chkval: 0x882e type: 0x23=PAGETABLE SEGMENT HEADER
  Extent Control Header
  -----------------------------------------------------------------
Extent Header:: spare1: 0  spare2: 0  #extents: 59  #blocks: 483328
              last map  0x00000000  #maps: 0      offset: 2720
Highwater::  0x63826009  ext#: 58     blk#: 8192   ext size: 8192
#blocks in seg. hdr's freelists: 0
  #blocks below: 479093
  mapblk  0x00000000  offset: 58
                Unlocked
```

```
-----------------------------------------------------------
Low HighWater Mark :
Highwater:: 0x6381ef7e  ext#: 4   blk#: 3957 ext size: 8192
  #blocks in seg. hdr's freelists: 0
  #blocks below: 36725
  mapblk  0x00000000  offset: 4
  Level 1 BMB for High HWM block: 0x63824028
  Level 1 BMB for Low HWM block: 0x6381e018
-----------------------------------------------------------
  Segment Type: 1 nl2: 0       blksz: 8192   fbsz: 0
  L2 Array start offset:  0x00001438
  First Level 3 BMB:  0x6340802a
  L2 Hint for inserts:  0x63408029
  Last Level 1 BMB:  0x63824028
  Last Level II BMB:  0x63412029
  Last Level III BMB:  0x6341202a
Map Header:: next 0x00000000 #extents:59 obj#:4916681 flag: 0x10000000
. . .
End dump data blocks tsn: 110 file#: 397 minblk 32811 maxblk 32811
```

It is possible to interpret and read dump data to find details about the information in a table or an index. Let's look at a simple example that shows how you can get the table name from the preceding block dump information. Take the `obj#` shown in second-to-last line, and run the following query:

```
SQL> SELECT name
  2 FROM sys.obj$
  3*WHERE  obj#='4916681';

NAME
---------------
PERSONS
SQL>
```

The previous example is trivial, but it demonstrates how you can derive information straight from a database block dump. Of course, if you need more significant data from the dumps, you'd have to employ more rigorous techniques.

Extents

When several contiguous data blocks are combined, they are called an *extent*. When you create a database object like a table or an index, you allocate it an initial amount of space, called the *initial extent*, and you also specify the size of the next extent. Once allocated to a table or an index, the extents remain allocated to that particular object, unless you drop the object from the database, in which case the space will revert to the pool of allocatable free space in the database.

Segments

A set of extents forms the next higher unit of data storage, the *segment*. Oracle calls all the space allocated to any particular database object a segment. So if you have a table called Customer, you simply refer to the space allocated to it as the "Customer segment." When you create an index, it will have its own segment named after the index name. Data and index segments are the most common type of Oracle segments. There are also temporary segments that the database uses for transactions involving sorting, for example, and undo segments, which the database uses to store undo information.

When all extents of a segment fill up, Oracle automatically allocates additional extents as necessary, and these extents may not be contiguous.

Tablespaces

Oracle databases are logically divided into one or more *tablespaces*. An Oracle tablespace is a logical entity that contains the physical datafiles. Tablespaces store all the usable data of the database, and the data in the tablespaces is physically stored in one or more datafiles. Datafiles are Oracle-formatted operating system files. The tablespace is a purely logical construct and is the primary logical storage structure of an Oracle database. You usually should keep related tables together in the same tablespace, since the tablespace also acts as the logical container for logical segments such as tables.

How big you make your tablespaces depends on the size of your tables and indexes and the total amount of data in the database—there are no rules about the minimum or maximum size of tablespaces (the maximum size is too large to be of any practical consequence). It is quite common to have tablespaces that are 100GB in size coexisting in the same database with tablespaces as small as 1GB or even much smaller.

The datafiles that contain the data for the tablespaces in a database together constitute the total amount of physical space assigned to a particular database. (The size of a tablespace is the sum of the sizes of the datafiles that contain its data, and if you add up the sizes of the tablespaces or the sizes of all the datafiles, you will get the size of the database itself.) If you're running out of space in your database because you're adding new data, you need to create more tablespaces with new datafiles, add new datafiles to existing tablespaces, or make the existing datafiles of a tablespace larger. You'll learn how to perform each of these tasks in Chapter 6.

There is no hard and fast rule regarding the number of tablespaces you can have in an Oracle database. The following five tablespaces are generally the default tablespaces that all databases must have, even though it's possible to create and use a database with just the first two:

- System tablespace

- Sysaux tablespace

- Undo tablespace

- Temporary tablespace

- Default permanent tablespace

Traditionally, Oracle DBAs have used dozens and sometimes even hundreds of tablespaces to store all their application tables and indexes, and if you really think you need a large number of tablespaces to group all related application tables and indexes together, that's okay. However, you aren't required to use a large number of tablespaces. Today, most organizations use Logical Volume Managers (which were discussed in Chapter 3) to stripe the logical volumes and the datafiles over a number of physical disks. Thus, a large tablespace could span several physical disks. Previously, it was necessary to create tablespaces on different physical disks to avoid I/O contention, but with today's disk organization structures you don't have that problem, and you can make do with fewer tablespaces if you wish. You can use just one tablespace for all your application data if you wish, since the datafiles that are part of the tablespace are going to be spread out over several disks anyway. This is also why the traditional requirement to separate tables and index data in different tablespaces isn't really valid anymore.

WHY TABLESPACES?

Tablespaces perform a number of key functions in an Oracle database, but the concept of a tablespace is not common to all relational databases. For instance, the Microsoft SQL Server database doesn't use this concept at all. Here's a brief list of the benefits of using tablespaces:

- Tablespaces make it easier to allocate space quotas to various users in the database.

- Tablespaces enable you to perform partial backups and recoveries based on the tablespace as a unit.

- Because a large object like a data warehouse partitioned table can be spread over several tablespaces, you can increase performance by spanning the tablespace over several disks and controllers.

- You can take a tablespace offline without having to bring down the entire database.

- Tablespaces are an easy way to allocate database space.

- You can import or export specific application data by using the import and export utilities at the tablespace level.

Tablespaces are now used mainly to separate related groups of tables and indexes. This may be important for you if you need to transport tablespaces across different databases and platforms using the Oracle Data Pump utility, or if you use different database block sizes for different tablespaces. If you don't think you'll be performing these administrative tasks using tablespaces, you can conceivably use just a couple of tablespaces to store all the data in your database.

Block Sizes and Tablespaces

Each tablespace uses the default block size for the database, unless you create a tablespace with a different nonstandard block size. As you've already seen, Oracle lets you have multiple block sizes in addition to the default block size. Because tablespaces ultimately consist of Oracle data blocks, this means that you can have tablespaces with different Oracle block sizes in the same database. This is a great feature, and it gives you the opportunity to pick the right block size for a tablespace based on the data structure of the tables it contains.

The customization of the block size for a tablespace provides several benefits:

- *Optimal disk I/O*: Remember that the Oracle server has to read the table data from mechanical disks into the buffer cache area for processing. One of your primary goals as a DBA is to optimize the expensive I/O involved in reading from and writing to disk. If you have tables with very long rows, you are better off with a larger block size—each read will fetch more data than you'd get with a smaller block size, and you'll need fewer read operations to get the same amount of data. Tables with large object (LOB) data will also benefit from a very large block size. On the other hand, tables with small row lengths can use a small block size as the building block for the tablespace. If you have large indexes in your database, you will need a large block size for their tablespace, so that each read will fetch a larger number of index pointers.

- *Optimal caching of data*: Oracle provides separate pools for the various block sizes, and this leads to a better use of Oracle's memory. I discuss this in the following sections.

- *Easier transport of tablespaces*: If you have tablespaces with multiple block sizes, it's easier to use Oracle's "transport tablespaces" feature. In Chapter 13, you'll find examples showing you how to transport tablespaces between databases.

■**Note** Each Oracle tablespace consists of one or more operating system datafiles, and a datafile can only belong to one tablespace. At database creation time, the only two tablespaces you *must* have are the System tablespace (the key Oracle tablespace, which contains Oracle's data dictionary), and the Sysaux tablespace (which is auxiliary to the System tablespace and contains data used by various Oracle products and features). Oracle will automatically create the System tablespace first, followed by the Sysaux tablespace, but you provide a datafile for each. Later on, you can add and drop tablespaces as you wish, but you can't drop or rename the System and Sysaux tablespaces.

Of course, you must ultimately also create separate application tablespaces to store your data and indexes. It is these tablespaces that will constitute the bulk of the total database size.

Locally managed tablespaces keep the space-management information in the datafiles themselves, and the tablespaces automatically track the free or used status of blocks in each datafile. The information about the free and used space in the datafiles is kept in bitmaps within the datafile headers—*bitmaps* are maps that use bits to keep track of the space in a block or a group of blocks. Remember that when an object needs to grow, Oracle will assign new space in units of extents, not in terms of individual data blocks. So when a new extent needs to be allocated to an object, Oracle will select the first free datafile and look up its bitmap to see if it has enough free contiguous data blocks. If so, Oracle will allocate the extent and then change the bitmap in that datafile to show the new used status of the blocks in the extent.

During this process, the data dictionary isn't used in any way, so recursive SQL operations are significantly reduced. Rollback information is not generated during this updating of the bitmaps in the datafiles. The benefits are especially significant if your database is an OLTP database with numerous inserts, deletes, and updates taking place on a continuous basis.

Types of Tablespaces

Besides the System and Sysaux tablespaces, you'll most likely also have undo and temporary tablespaces. You'll also use several other "permanent" tablespaces to hold your data and indexes.

Here's a summary of the key types of tablespaces you're likely to encounter:

- Bigfile tablespaces are tablespaces with a single large datafile, whose maximum size can range from 8 to 128 terabytes, depending on the database block size. Thus, your database could conceivably be stored in just one bigfile tablespace.

- Smallfile tablespaces can contain multiple datafiles, but the files cannot be as large as a bigfile datafile. Smallfile tablespaces, which are the traditional tablespaces, are the default in Oracle Database 11g, and Oracle creates both System and Sysaux tablespaces as smallfile tablespaces.

- Temporary tablespaces contain data that persists only for the duration of a user's session. Usually Oracle uses these tablespaces for sorting and similar activities for users.

- Permanent tablespaces include all the tablespaces that aren't designated as temporary tablespaces.

- Undo tablespaces contain undo records, which Oracle uses to roll back, or undo, changes to the database.

- Read-only tablespaces don't allow write operations on the datafiles in the tablespace. You can convert any normal (read/write) tablespace to a read-only tablespace in order to protect data or to eliminate the need to perform backup and recovery of large datafiles that don't change.

DATABASE VS. INSTANCE

Before you delve deeply into the logical and physical structures that make up an Oracle database, you need to be clear about a fundamental concept—the difference between an Oracle *instance* and an Oracle *database*. It is very common for people to use the terms interchangeably, but they refer to different things altogether.

An *Oracle database* consists of files, both datafiles and Oracle system files. These files by themselves are useless unless you can interact with them somehow, and this requires the help of the operating system, which provides processing capabilities and resources, such as memory, to enable you to manipulate the data on the disk drives. When you combine the specific set of processes created by Oracle on the server with the memory allocated to it by the operating system, you get the *Oracle instance*.

You'll often hear people remarking that the "database is up," though what they really mean is that the "instance is up." The database itself, in the form of the set of physical files it's composed of, is of no use if the instance is not up and running. The instance performs all the necessary work for the database. Normally, there is a one-to-one relationship between a database and an instance, unlike in Microsoft SQL Server, where each instance could support multiple databases. However, multiple computers can share access to data by setting up clusters known as Oracle Real Application Clusters (Oracle RAC). Oracle RAC consists of multiple instances running on multiple clustered computers that communicate with each other through an interconnect. The cluster setup uses Oracle Clusterware to access the database that runs on a shared disk system.

By harnessing the computing power of multiple servers, Oracle RAC provides redundancy, scalability, and high availability. You can easily handle increasing data processing demands by simply adding additional nodes to access the database.

Physical Database Structures

Physical database structures refer to the actual Oracle database files at the operating system level. The Oracle database consists of the following three main types of files:

- *Datafiles*: These files store the table and index data.
- *Control files*: These files record changes to all database structures.
- *Redo log files*: These online files contain the changes made to table data.

In addition to these three types of files, an Oracle database makes use of several other operating system files to manage its operations. These include initialization files (like init.ora and the server parameter file [SPFILE]), network administration files (like tnsnames.ora and listener.ora), alert log files, trace files, and the password file. In addition, you also have backup files, which you must restore in case of a media failure.

Datafiles

Oracle datafiles make up the largest part of the physical storage of your database. A datafile can belong to only one database, and one or more datafiles constitute the logical entity called the tablespace, which I described earlier in this chapter. Oracle datafiles constitute most of a database's total space.

When the database instance needs to read table or index data, it reads that from the datafiles on disk, unless that data is already cached in Oracle's memory. Similarly, the database writes new table or index data or updates to existing data to the datafiles on disk for permanent storage.

To be able to use the disk for storing your data, directories and a file system must be created for you by the system administrator. You also need all the proper rights to read from and write to these directories and files. Then, when you create a tablespace, you assign it these datafiles. Before you create a database, your system administrator will assign a certain amount of disk space for the database based on your initial sizing estimates. All the administrator gives you are the assigned mount points for the various disks (for example, /prod01, /prod02, /prod03, and so on). You then need to create your directory structure under the mount points. After you install your software and create the Oracle administrative directories, you can use the remaining file system space for storing database objects, such as tables and indexes.

Oracle-managed files, which were introduced in Oracle8i (and which we'll discuss shortly), simplify the administration of Oracle databases. The Oracle Managed Files (OMF) feature eliminates the need for you to manage operating system files. You simply specify your database operations in terms of database objects, without using filenames.

The OMF feature aims at relieving DBAs of their traditional file-management tasks. When you use the OMF feature, you don't have to worry about the names and locations of the physical files. Instead, you can focus on the objects you're creating. Oracle will automatically create and delete files on the operating system as needed.

The OMF-based files are ideal for test and small databases, but if you have a terabyte-sized database with a large number of archived logs and redo logs, you need flexibility, which the OMF file system can't provide.

OMF drastically simplifies both the initial database creation as well as the management tasks. If you want to use OMF with your database, read the discussion of OMF in Chapter 17, where you'll learn how to create and manage OMF-based files.

For example, suppose you create a tablespace called customer01 with a 500MB datafile. As you load more data into your database, Oracle will allocate new extents to the database tables by allocating space from the datafile. When the table uses up almost all of the initial 500MB space allocation, you need to enlarge the tablespace by adding a new datafile to it. You may alternatively increase the size of the existing datafile by resizing it as well. If you don't, the table can't increase in size, and any attempts to add data to it will result in an error.

Although the database places the data in actual datafiles, there is no direct link between the tables and indexes and the datafiles they are placed in. These objects are only linked to the logical tablespace; it is the tablespace that is linked to the datafiles. Thus, Oracle maintains a separation between the logical objects (such as tables) and the physical datafiles. In other words, there is no direct connection during object creation or growth between the object and the datafiles it resides in. You can create or move an existing table or index by specifically declaring the tablespace, but you can't specify a datafile directly.

The Control File

The *control file* is a file that the Oracle DBMS maintains to manage the state of the database, and it is probably the single most important file in the Oracle database. Every database has one control file, but due to the file's importance, multiple identical copies (usually three) are maintained—when the database writes to the control file, all copies of the file get written to. The control file is critical to the functioning of the database, and recovery is difficult without access to an up-to-date control file. Oracle creates the control file (and the copies) during the initial database creation process.

The control file contains the names and locations of the datafiles, redo log files, current log sequence numbers, backup set details, and the all-important *system change number* (SCN), which indicates the most recent version of committed changes in the database—information that is not accessible by users even for reading purposes. Only Oracle can write information to the control file, and the Oracle server process continually updates the control file during the operation of the database.

Control files are vital when the Oracle instance is operating. When you turn the instance on, Oracle reads the control file for the location of the data and log files. During the normal operation of the database, the database consults the control file periodically for necessary information regarding virtually every structure of the database.

The control file is also important in verifying the integrity of the database and when recovering the database. The checkpoint process instructs the database writer to write data to the disk when some specific conditions are met, and the control file notes all checkpoint information from the online redo log files. This information comes in handy during a recovery—the checkpoint information in the control file enables Oracle to decide how far back it needs to go in recovering data from the online redo log files. The checkpoint indicates the SCN up to which the datafiles are already written to the datafiles, so the recovery process will disregard all the information in the online redo log files before the checkpoint noted in the control file.

When you start an Oracle instance, it consults the control file first, to identify all the datafiles and the redo log files that must be opened for database operations.

■**Note** The checkpoint process is discussed in more detail in the "Checkpoint" section later in this chapter.

Due to its obvious importance, Oracle recommends that you keep multiple copies of the control file.

The V$CONTROLFILE dynamic view gives you the names of all the control files. The STATUS column will be NULL if the name can be determined, which is the case always. If the name can't be determined (which shouldn't happen), you'll see the value INVALID in the STATUS column. The IS_RECOVER_DEST_FILE column shows YES if the control file was created in the flash recovery area and a value of NO otherwise. Here's the output of a query on the V$CONTROLFILE view:

```
SQL> SELECT status, name, is_recovery_dest_file FROM V$CONTROLFILE;

STATUS        NAME                                     IS_RECOVERY_DEST
-----------   --------------------------------------   ----------------
              C:\ORACLE\ORADATA\MARK1\CONTROL01.CTL          NO
              C:\ORACLE\ORADATA\MARK1\CONTROL02.CTL          NO
              C:\ORACLE\ORADATA\MARK1\CONTROL03.CTL          NO
SQL>
```

Redo Log Files

The *redo log files* record all the changes made to the database, and they are vital during the recovery of a database. If you need to restore your database from a backup, you can recover the latest changes made to the database from the redo log files. The set of redo log files that are currently being used to record the changes to the database are called *online redo log files*. These logs can be archived (copied) to a different location before being reused, and the saved logs are called *archived redo logs*.

Oracle writes all final changes made to data (committed data) first to the redo log files, before applying those changes to the actual datafiles themselves. Thus, if a system failure prevents these data changes from being written to the permanent datafiles, Oracle will use the redo logs to recover all transactions that committed but couldn't be applied to the datafiles. Thus, redo log files guarantee that no committed data is ever lost. If you have all the archived redo logs since the last database backup, and a set of the current redo logs as well, you can always bring a database up to date.

■**Note** Current redo log files are often referred to as *online redo logs* to distinguish them from the older saved or archived redo log files.

Redo log files consist of *redo records*, which are groups of *change vectors*, each referring to a specific change made to a data block in the Oracle database. A single transaction may involve multiple changes to data blocks, so it may have more than one redo record. Initially, the contents of the log are kept in the *redo log buffer* (a memory area), but they are transferred to disk very quickly. If your database comes down without warning, the redo log can help you determine whether all transactions were committed before the crash or if some were still incomplete.

Oracle redo log files contain the following information about database changes made by transactions:

- Indicators specifying when the transaction started
- The name of the transaction
- The name of the data object that was being updated (e.g., an application table)
- The "before image" of the transaction (the data as it was before the changes were made)
- The "after image" of the transaction (the data as it was after the transaction made the changes)
- Commit indicators that indicate whether and when the transaction completed

When a database crashes, all transactions, both uncommitted as well as committed, have to be applied to the datafiles on disk, using the information in the redo log files. All redo log transactions that have both a begin and a commit entry must be redone, and all transactions that have a begin entry but no commit entry must be undone. (Redoing a transaction in this context simply means that you apply the information in the redo log files to the database; you do not rerun the transaction itself.) Committed transactions are thus re-created by applying the "after image" records in the redo log files to the database, and incomplete transactions are undone by using the "before image" records in the undo tablespace. Redo log files are an essential part of database management, and they are one of the main ways you enforce database consistency.

Oracle requires that every database have at least two redo log groups, each group consisting of at least one individual log file member. Oracle writes to one redo log file until it gets to the end of the redo log file, at which point it performs a log switch and starts writing to the second log file (and then to the third, if it exists).

By default, Oracle will write over the contents of a redo log file, unless you choose to archive your redo files. Oracle recommends that you archive the filled-up redo log files, so you can maintain a complete record of all the changes made to the database since the last backup. If you archive your redo log files, you are said to be running your database in the *archivelog* mode. Otherwise, you're running in the *noarchivelog* mode.

Because of the critical importance of the redo log files in helping recover from database crashes, Oracle recommends *multiplexing* (maintaining multiple copies of) the redo log files. Multiplexing the online redo log files by placing two or more copies of the redo logs on different disk drives will ensure that you won't easily lose data changes that haven't been recorded in your datafiles.

Other Files

Although an Oracle database consists of datafiles, redo log files, and the control files, the database also requires other files in order to operate. These files include the SPFILE, the password file, the alert log file, as well as various trace file and the backup files. I explain these other files briefly in the following sections.

The SPFILE

When you create a new database, you specify the initialization parameters for the Oracle instance in a special configuration file called the *server parameter file*, or SPFILE. You can also use an older version of the configuration file called the init.ora file, but Oracle recommends the use of the more sophisticated SPFILE. In the SPFILE, you specify the memory limits for the instance, the locations of the control files, whether and where the archived logs are stored, and other settings that determine the behavior of the Oracle database server. You can't, however, edit the SPFILE manually, as you could the init.ora file, since the SPFILE is a binary file.

The SPFILE is always stored on the database server, thus preventing the proliferation of parameter files that sometimes occurs with the use of the init.ora file. By default, the SPFILE (and the init.ora file) is placed in the ORACLE_HOME/dbs directory in UNIX systems and the ORACLE_HOME\database directory in Windows systems. The ORACLE_HOME directory is the standard location for the Oracle executables.

■**Note** You'll find a detailed discussion of the SPFILE, including how to create one from your init.ora file, in Chapter 10, where you will learn about creating Oracle databases.

Oracle allows you to change a number of the initialization parameters after you start up the instance; these are called *dynamic initialization parameters*. Unlike the traditional init.ora initialization file, the SPFILE can automatically and dynamically record the new values of dynamic parameters after you change them, ensuring that you don't forget to incorporate the changes. You can't change the rest of the parameters, referred to as static initialization parameters, dynamically. That is, you must restart your instance if you need to modify any of those parameters.

You can use the V$SPPARAMETER data dictionary view to look at the initialization parameter values you have explicitly set in the SPFILE for your database. (The analogous view, if you are using the init.ora file, is the V$PARAMETER view.) In addition to the parameter values you set explicitly in the SPFILE, the V$SPPARAMETER view shows all the default values for all database configuration parameters (the values in effect in the instance right now).

■**Caution** Sometimes you'll see references to undocumented or hidden Oracle parameters. These parameters usually have an underscore (_) prefix. Don't use them unless you're requested to do so by Oracle support experts or other trustworthy sources.

The Password File

The *password* file is an optional file in which you can specify the names of database users who were granted the special SYSDBA or SYSOPER administrative privileges, which enable them to perform privileged operations, such as starting, stopping, backing up, and recovering databases. Chapter 12 shows you how to create and maintain the password file.

The Alert Log File

Every Oracle database has an *alert log* named alertdb_name.log (where *db_name* is the name of the database). The alert log captures major changes and events that occur during the running of the Oracle instance, including log switches, any Oracle-related errors, warnings, and other messages. In addition, every time you start up the Oracle instance, Oracle will list all your initialization parameters in the alert log, along with the complete sequence of the startup process. You can also use the alert log to automatically keep track of tablespaces that are created and datafiles that are added or resized.

The alert log can come in handy during troubleshooting—it is usually the first place you should check to get an idea about what was happening inside the database when a problem occurred. In fact, Oracle support may ask you for a copy of the pertinent sections of the alert log during their analysis of database problems.

In Oracle Database 11g, the recommended procedure is to create a diagnostic repository called the Automatic Diagnostic Repository (ADR), which is a one-stop location for storing all database-related errors, trace files, and dump files. If you set up the ADR by specifying the new initialization parameter DIAGNOSTIC_DEST, Oracle will create and maintain two alert log files, one in text format and the other in an XML format. Otherwise, Oracle puts the alert log in the location specified for the BACKGROUND_DUMP_DEST initialization parameter. If you don't specify a value for this parameter, Oracle places the alert log in a default location.

To see if there are any Oracle-related errors in your alert log, simply issue the following command (finance is the database name in this example):

```
$ grep ORA- alert_finance.log
ORA-1503 signalled during: CREATE CONTROLFILE SET DATABASE "FINANCE" RESETLOGS...
ORA-1109 signalled during: ALTER DATABASE CLOSE NORMAL...
ORA-00600: internal error code, arguments:[12333], [0], [0], [0], [], [], [], []
```

As you can see, several Oracle errors are listed in the alert log for the database finance. A regular scan of your database for all kinds of Oracle errors should be one of your daily database management tasks. You can easily schedule a script to scan the alert log and then e-mail you the results. You can also use the Oracle Enterprise Manager (OEM) Database Control (or the Grid Control) interface to quickly review any errors in your alert log files.

Trace Files

All diagnostic files, including the trace files, are stored under the directory you specify for the DIAGNOSTIC_DEST initialization parameter. The trace directory under the ADR home directory holds the various trace files such as the debugging trace files for the background processes (log writer, database writer, and so on) that Oracle writes during instance operation. The alert directory under the ADR home directory contains the alert log file for the database instance (discussed in the previous section).

The core directory under the ADR home directory holds any core files generated during major errors such as the ORA-600 internal Oracle software errors.

The Oracle server will write all debugging trace files on behalf of a user process to the trace directory. All trace files you generate using Oracle's SQL tracing features (explained in Chapters 19 and 20) will show up here.

Backup Files

You can use backup files made either by yourself or by the RMAN backup and recovery tool to restore database files following a media failure or user error. The media failure may consist of an erroneously deleted database file or a damaged datafile. Regardless of the reason, the backup files help you restore the database and recover it to the present time with the help of the archived redo logs.

■**Note** An Oracle directory object is an alias for a file system directory. You use directory objects mainly when you use the external tables feature, which I explain in Chapter 14. Directory objects offer management flexibility by letting you reference operating system directories through a database object name. Directories aren't owned by any particular schema. You must grant users privileges on a particular directory before they can use it.

Oracle Processes

Oracle server processes running under the operating system perform all the database operations, such as inserting and deleting data. These Oracle processes, together with the memory structures allocated to Oracle by the operating system, form the working Oracle instance. There is a set of mandatory Oracle processes that need to be up and running for the database to function at all. Other Oracle processes are necessary only if you are using certain specialized features of Oracle (such as replicated databases).

A *process* is essentially a connection or thread to the operating system that performs a task or job. The Oracle processes you'll encounter in this section are continuous, which means that they come up when the instance starts, and they stay up for the duration of the instance's life. Thus, they act like Oracle's hooks into the operating system's resources. A *process* on a UNIX system is analogous to a *thread* on a Windows system.

Oracle processes are divided into two general types both for efficiency and to keep client processes separate from the database server's tasks:

- *User processes*: These processes are responsible for running the application that connects the user to the database instance.

- *Oracle processes*: These processes perform the Oracle server's tasks, and you can divide them into two major categories: *server processes* and *background processes*. Together, these processes perform all the actual work of the database, from managing connections to writing to log files and datafiles to monitoring the user processes.

Interaction Between the User and Oracle Processes

User processes run application programs and Oracle tools, such as SQL*Plus. The user processes communicate with the server processes through the user interface and request that the Oracle server processes perform work on their behalf. Oracle responds by having its server processes service the user processes' requests. It's the job of the server processes to monitor user connections, accept requests for data, and return the results to the users. All SELECT requests, for example, involve reading data from the database, and it's the server processes that return the output of the SELECT statement back to the users.

You'll examine the two types of Oracle processes—the server processes and the background processes—in detail in the following sections.

The Server Process

When you run an Oracle tool, such as the OEM Database Control or the SQL*Plus interface, you do so through a user process. An Oracle session is a specific connection of a user to the Oracle instance through the Oracle user process. The session duration lasts from the time you connect to the database by providing a username/password combination until you log out.

The *server process* is the process that services an individual user process. Each user connected to the database has a separate server process created for the duration of the session. The server process is created to service the user's process and is used by the user process to communicate with the Oracle database server. When the user submits a request to select data, for example, the server process created for that user's application checks the syntax of the code and executes the SQL code. It then reads the data from the datafiles into the memory blocks. (If another user intends to read the same data, the second user's server process will read it not from disk again, but from Oracle's memory, where the data usually remains for a while.) Finally, the server process returns the requested data to the user process.

The number of user processes for each server process depends on the type of server configuration. You can have three types of server configuration, as explained here:

Dedicated server configuration: The most common configuration for the server process is to assign each user a *dedicated* server process. Under the dedicated server process approach, each user has a one-to-one connection to the database through a dedicated server process.

Shared server configuration: Multiple user processes share a server process. When you use the shared server architecture, several users connect through a *dispatcher* and use a shared server process. Even though the dedicated server approach is most commonly used, is easier to set up and tune, and is fine in most cases, it's better under some circumstances to use a shared server process, which helps conserve critical system resources, such as memory. When you use a shared server configuration, you can also configure shared server *connection pooling*. Connection pooling lets you reuse existing timed-out connections to service other active sessions. You can also configure shared server *session multiplexing*, which combines multiple sessions for transmission over the same network connection.

Database resident connection pooling (DRCP): This connection method, introduced in the Oracle Database 11g release, is useful for applications that must maintain persistent connection to the database, which leads to an increased demand on server resources. DRCP lets you set up pooled dedicated connections across applications and processes. When a client requires a connection to the database, a connection broker, instead of the dedicated server, will connect the client to the database. The connection broker is in charge of managing client connections, by allocating servers from a pool of dedicated servers. The connection broker hooks up the client connection to a dedicated server, and once the client's request is fulfilled, the dedicated server is returned to the pool of available servers.

I explain the important Oracle connection methods, including the new DRCP method, in Chapter 11.

The Background Processes

The *background processes* are the real workhorses of the Oracle instance—they enable large numbers of users to concurrently and efficiently use information stored in database files. Oracle creates these processes automatically when you start an instance, and by being continuously hooked into the operating system, these processes relieve the Oracle software from having to repeatedly start numerous, separate processes for the various tasks that need to be done on the operating system's server. Each of the Oracle background processes is in charge of a separate task, thus increasing the efficiency of the database instance. These processes are automatically created by Oracle when you start the database instance, and they terminate when the database is shut down.

Table 5-1 lists the key Oracle background processes. There are other specialized background processes that you'll need to use only if you're implementing certain advanced Oracle features.

Table 5-1. *Key Oracle Background Processes*

Background Process	Function
Database writer (DBW*n*)	Writes modified data from the buffer cache to disk (datafiles)
Log writer (LGWR)	Writes redo log buffer contents to the online redo log files

Table 5-1. *Key Oracle Background Processes*

Background Process	Function
Checkpoint (CKPT)	Updates the headers of all datafiles to record the checkpoint details
Process monitor (PMON)	Cleans up after finished and failed processes
System monitor (SMON)	Performs crash recovery and coalesces extents
Archiver (ARC*n*)	Archives filled online redo log files
Manageability monitor (MMON)	Performs database-manageability-related tasks
Manageability monitor light (MMNL)	Performs tasks like capturing session history and metrics
Memory manager (MMAN)	Coordinates the sizing of the SGA components
Job queue coordination process (CJQO)	Coordinates job queues to expedite job processes

I briefly discuss the main Oracle background processes in the following sections.

Database Writer

Oracle doesn't modify data directly on the disks—all modifications of data take place in Oracle memory. The *database writer* process is then responsible for writing the "dirty" (modified) data from the memory areas known as *database buffers* to the actual datafiles on disk.

It is the DBW*n* process's job to monitor the use of the database buffer cache, and if the free space in the database buffers is getting low, the database writer process makes room available by writing some of the data in the buffers to the disk files. The database writer process uses the *least recently used* (LRU) algorithm (or a modified version of it), which retains data in the memory buffers based on how long it has been since someone asked for that data. If a piece of data has been requested very recently, it's more likely to be retained in the memory buffers.

The database writer process writes dirty buffers to disk under the following conditions:

1. When the database issues a checkpoint

2. When a server process can't find a clean reusable buffer after checking a threshold number of buffers

3. Every 3 seconds

■**Note** When a user commits a transaction, it is not immediately made permanent by the database writer process with an immediate write to the database files. Oracle conserves physical I/O by waiting to perform a more efficient write of batches of committed transactions at once.

For very large databases or for databases performing intensive operations, a single database writer process may be inadequate to perform all the writing to the database files. Oracle provides for the use of multiple database writer processes to share heavy data modification workloads. You can have a maximum of 20 database writer processes (DBW0 through DBW9, and DBWa through DBWj). Oracle recommends using multiple database writer processes, provided you have multiple processors.

You can specify the additional database writer processes by using the DB_WRITER_PROCESSES initialization parameter in the SPFILE Oracle configuration file. If you don't specify this parameter, Oracle allocates the number of database writer processes based on the number of CPUs and processor groups on your server. For example, on my 32-processor HP-UX server, the default is four database writers (one database writer per eight processors), and in another 16-processor server, the default is two database writers.

Oracle further recommends that you first ensure that your system is using asynchronous I/O before deploying additional database writer processes beyond the default number—you may not need multiple database writer processes if so. (Even when a system is capable of asynchronous I/O, that feature may not be enabled.) If your database writer can't keep up with the amount of work even after asynchronous I/O is enabled, you should consider increasing the number of database writers.

Log Writer

The job of the *log writer* process is to transfer the contents of the redo log buffer to disk. Whenever you make a change to a database table (whether an insertion, update, or deletion), Oracle writes the committed and uncommitted changes to a redo log buffer (memory buffer). The LGWR process then transfers these changes from the redo log buffer to the redo log files on disk. The log writer writes a commit record to the redo log buffer and writes it to the redo log on disk immediately, whenever a user commits a transaction.

If you've multiplexed the redo log (as you're supposed to!), the log writer will write the contents of the redo log buffer to all members of the redo log group. If one or more members are damaged or otherwise unavailable, the log writer will just write to the available members of a group. If it can't write to even one member of a redo log group, the log writer signals an error. Each time the log writer writes to the redo log on disk, it transfers all the new redo log entries that arrived in the buffer since the log writer last copied the buffer contents to the redo log.

The log writer writes all redo log buffer entries to the redo logs under the following circumstances:

- Every 3 seconds.

- When the redo log buffer is one-third full.

- When the database writer signals that redo records need to be written to disk. Under Oracle's write-ahead protocol, all redo records associated with changes in the block buffers must be written to disk (that is, to the redo log files on disk) before the datafiles on disk can be modified. While writing dirty buffers from the buffer cache to the storage disks, if the database writer discovers that certain redo information has not been written to the redo log files, it signals the log writer to first write that information, so it can write its own data to disk.

- In addition, as mentioned earlier, the log writer writes a commit record to the redo log following the committing of each transaction. The redo log files, as you learned earlier, are vital during the recovery of an Oracle database from a lost or damaged disk.

Before the database writer writes the changed data to disk, it ensures that the log writer has already completed writing all redo records for the changed data from the log buffer to the redo logs on disk. This is called the *write-ahead protocol*.

When you issue a commit statement to make your changes permanent, the log writer first places a commit record in the redo log buffer and immediately writes that record to the redo log, along with the redo entries pertaining to the committed transaction. The writing of the transaction's commit record to the redo log is the critical event that marks the committing of the transaction. Each committed transaction is assigned a system change number, which the log writer records in the redo log. The database makes use of these SCNs during a database recovery. The database waits to change the data blocks on disk until a more opportune time and returns a success code indicating the successful committing of the transaction, although the changed data buffers haven't yet been copied to the datafiles on disk. This technique of indicating a successful commit ahead of the actual writing of the changed data blocks to disk is called the *fast commit* mechanism.

The redo log files may contain both committed as well as uncommitted transaction records, because of the way the log writer records redo records in the redo logs on disk. If the database needs buffer space, the log writer may also write the redo log entries to the redo log files from the redo log buffer even before it commits a transaction. Of course, the database ensures that these entries are written to the datafiles only if the transaction is committed later on.

Checkpoint

The *checkpoint* process is charged with telling the database writer process when to write the dirty data in the memory buffers to disk. After telling the database writer process to write the changed data, the CKPT process updates the datafile headers and the control file to record the checkpoint details, including the time when the checkpoint was performed. The purpose of the checkpoint process is to synchronize the buffer cache information with the information on the database disks.

Each checkpoint record consists of a list of all active transactions and the address of the most recent log record for those transactions. A checkpointing process involves the following steps:

1. Flushing the contents of the redo log buffers to the redo log files

2. Writing a checkpoint record to the redo log file

3. Flushing the contents of the database buffer cache to disk

4. Updating the datafile headers and the control files after the checkpoint completes

There is a close connection between how often Oracle performs the checkpointing operation and the recovery time after a database crash. Because database writer processes write all modified blocks to disk at checkpoints, the more frequent the checkpoints, the less data will need to be recovered when the instance crashes. However, checkpointing involves an overhead cost. Oracle lets you configure the database for *automatic checkpoint tuning*, whereby the database server tries to write out the dirty buffers in the most efficient way possible, with the least amount of adverse impact on throughput and performance. If you use automatic checkpoint tuning, you don't have to set any checkpoint-related parameters.

Process Monitor

When user processes fail, the *process monitor* process cleans up after them, ensuring that the database frees up the resources that the dead processes were using. For example, when a user process dies while holding certain table locks, the PMON process releases those locks so other users can use the tables without any interference from the dead process. In addition, the PMON process restarts failed server processes (in a shared server architecture) and dispatcher processes. The PMON process sleeps most of the time, waking up at regular intervals to see if it is needed. Other processes will also wake up the PMON process if necessary.

The PMON process automatically performs dynamic service registration. When you create a new database instance, the PMON process registers the instance information with the listener, which is the entity that manages requests for database connections (Chapter 11 discusses the listener in detail). This *dynamic service registration* eliminates the need to register the new service information in the listener.ora file, which is the configuration file for the listener.

System Monitor

The *system monitor* process, as its name indicates, performs system-monitoring tasks for the Oracle instance, such as these:

- Upon restarting an instance that crashed, SMON determines whether the database is consistent.

- SMON coalesces free extents if you use locally managed tablespaces, which enables you to assign larger contiguous free areas on disk to your database objects.

- SMON cleans up unnecessary temporary segments.

Like the PMON process, the SMON process sleeps most of the time, waking up to see if it is needed. Other processes will also wake up the SMON process if they detect a need for it.

Archiver

The *archiver* process is used when the system is being operated in an *archivelog mode*—that is, the changes logged to the redo log files are being saved and not being overwritten by new changes. If you run your database in the *no archivelog mode*, Oracle will overwrite the redo log files with new redo log records. When you choose to run the instance in an archivelog mode, no such overwriting can take place—each filled log will be saved or archived in a special location.

The database makes available a filled redo log group for archiving as soon as it completes a redo log switch. The ARC*n* process's job is to copy one of the filled members of a redo log group to an archived redo log file. Thus, if you've multiplexed the redo log, and if group 1 contains the members a_log1 and b_log1, the archiver background process will copy either of the two members. This archived redo log file will include the redo entries from the redo log group member.

The archiver process will archive the redo log files to the location you specify in the SPFILE or the init.ora file. The archived redo log encompasses all the copies of every group created since you enabled archiving for a database. You usually copy these archived logs to tape and send them to an offsite storage location to ensure you have a complete set of backups and archived redo logs so that you can perform a database recovery if the need arises. Archived redo logs are also useful for updating a standby database as well as for mining old data using the LogMiner utility.

If a huge number of changes are being made to your database, and your logs are consequently filling up very quickly, you can use multiple archiver processes up to a maximum of 30 (ARC0 through ARC*n*). The LOG_ARCHIVE_MAX_PROCESSES parameter in the initialization file will determine how many archiver processes Oracle will initially start. If the log writer process is writing logs faster than the default single archiver process can archive them, the LGWR process automatically starts a new ARC*n* process, thus raising the number of processes from the default of 2. Since the database automatically starts additional processes to make sure that it keeps up with the storing of the redo logs being generated, you don't really need to set the LOG_ARCHIVE_MAX_PROCESSES parameter. Since it is a dynamic parameter, you can alter the number of archiver processes while the database is running, as shown here:

```
SQL> ALTER SYSTEM SET LOG_ARCHIVE_MAX_PROCESSES=8;
```

■**Tip** If you aren't sure what new background processes are actually running in your database, just check the processes by issuing the ps -eaf | grep ora command in UNIX and Linux systems. For each active process, the process name and database name will be listed. For example, the log writer process will show up as ora_lgwr_ *pasprod*, where *pasprod* is the name of the database. You can get a complete list of all the background processes (running and not running) by querying the V$BGPROCESS view.

ASM-Related Processes

A few background processes are present only if you're using an Automatic Storage Management (ASM) storage system. Here's a summary of the ASM-related background processes:

- The *rebalance master* (RBAL) process coordinates disk rebalancing activity when you use an ASM-based storage system.

- The *ASM rebalance* (ARB*n*) processes perform the disk rebalancing activity in an ASM instance.

- The *ASM background* (ASMB) process is present in all Oracle databases that use an ASM storage system. The ASMB process communicates with the ASM instance by logging into the ASM instance as a foreground process.

■**Note** The RBAL and ARB*n* processes are used only if you use Oracle's Automatic Storage Management. When you use ASM, you must create an ASM instance, and that instance will use these processes to perform disk storage management. The ASMB process acts as the mediator between your database (when you're using ASM-based disk storage) and the ASM instance. I discuss ASM in detail in Chapter 17.

Miscellaneous Background Processes

The database writer, log writer, archiver, and checkpoint background processes are the most commonly referenced background processes. However, Oracle Database 11*g* can have many more background processes running to support an instance. I describe the most important of these background processes briefly here.

- The *manageability monitor* process collects several types of statistics to help the database manage itself, such as, for example, the AWR snapshot information, which is the basis for the performance diagnostics capability of the database. In addition, MMON issues alerts when database metrics violate their threshold values.

- The *manageability monitor light* process shows up as Manageability Monitor Process 2 when you query the V$BGPROCESS view. The process flushes data from the Active Session History (ASH) to disk whenever the buffer is full. The MMNL process also performs other manageability-related tasks, such as capturing session history data and computing database metrics.

- The *memory manager* process coordinates the sizing of the memory components.

- Oracle uses the *job queue coordination* process to schedule and run user jobs. The CJQO process dynamically spawns job queue slave processes (J000 through J999), which run the user jobs. When you enable the flashback database feature (which I explain in Chapter 16), Oracle starts the *recovery writer* (RVWR) process to write the flashback data from the flashback buffer to the flashback logs. In a sense, the RVWR'S job is analogous to that of the LGWR background process.

- Oracle tracks the physical location of database changes in a new file called the change-tracking file. Oracle's backup utility, the Recovery Manager, uses the change-tracking file to determine which data blocks to read during an incremental backup, making the incremental backups faster by avoiding reading entire datafiles. The *change-tracking writer* (CTWR) process is the new Oracle background process that writes change information to the change-tracking file. You'll learn more about the CTWR process in Chapter 15, which discusses database backups.

- The *recoverer* (RECO) process is used to coordinate distributed databases and other specialized processes.

■**Note** Besides the processes discussed here, other Oracle background processes that perform specialized tasks may be running in your system. For example, if you use Oracle Real Application Clusters, you'll see a background process called the *lock* (LCK*n*) process, which is responsible for performing interinstance locking.

- The *flashback data archiver* (FBDA) process is in charge of writing changes to tables that are enabled for the flashback data archive into the history tables.
- The *result cache background* (RCBG) process is in charge of the result cache management.

You can view all available Oracle background processes by querying the V$BGPROCESS view.

Oracle Memory Structures

Oracle uses a part of its memory allocation to hold both program code and data, which makes processing much faster than if it had to fetch data from the disks constantly. These memory structures enable Oracle to share executable code among several users without having to go through all the preexecution processing every time a user invokes a piece of code.

The Oracle server doesn't always write changes to disk directly. It writes database changes to the memory area, and when it's convenient, it writes the changes to disk. Because accessing memory is many times faster than accessing physical disks (memory access is measured in nanoseconds, whereas disk access is measured in milliseconds), Oracle is able to overcome the I/O limitations of the disk system. The more your database performs its work in memory rather than in the physical disk storage system, the faster the response will be. Of course, as physical I/O decreases, CPU usage will also decrease, thus leading to a more efficient system.

THE HIGH COST OF DISK I/O

Although secondary storage (usually magnetic disks) is significantly larger than main memory, it's also significantly slower. A disk I/O involves either moving a data block from disk to memory (a disk read) or writing a data block to disk from memory (a disk write). Typically, it takes about 10–40 milliseconds (0.01–0.04 seconds) to perform a single disk I/O.

Suppose your update transaction involves 25 I/Os—you could spend up to 1 second just waiting to read or write data. In that same second, your CPUs could have performed millions of instructions—the update takes a negligible amount of time compared to the disk reads and disk writes. If you already have the necessary data in Oracle's memory, the retrieval time would be much faster, as memory read/writes take only a few nanoseconds. This is why avoiding or minimizing disk I/Os plays such a big role in providing high performance in Oracle databases.

Understanding Main Memory

All computers use memory, which actually consists of a hierarchy of different levels of memory. The heart of this hierarchy is *main memory*, which contains all the instruction executions and data manipulations. All main memories are random access memory (RAM), which means that you can read any byte in memory in the same amount of time. Typically, you can access main memory data in the 10–100 nanosecond range.

An important part of the information Oracle stores in the RAM allocated to it is the program code that is executing currently or that has been executed recently. If a new user process needs to use the same code, it's available in memory in a compiled form, making the processing time a whole lot faster. The memory areas also hold information about which users are locking a certain table, thereby helping different sessions communicate effectively. Most important, perhaps, the memory areas help in processing data that's stored in permanent disk storage. Oracle doesn't make changes directly to the data on disk: data is always read from the disks, held in memory, and changed there before being transferred back to disk.

It's common to use the term *buffers* to refer to units of memory. Memory buffers are page-sized areas of memory into which Oracle transfers the contents of the disk blocks. If the database wants to read (select) or update data, it copies the relevant blocks from disk to the memory buffers. After it makes any necessary changes, Oracle transfers the contents of the memory buffers to disk.

Oracle uses two kinds of memory structures, one shared and the other process-specific. The *system global area* is the part of total memory that all server processes (including background processes) share. The process-specific part of the memory is known as the *program global area* (PGA), or *process-private memory*. The following sections examine these two components of Oracle's memory in more detail.

The System Global Area

The SGA is the most important memory component in an Oracle instance. In large OLTP databases, especially, the SGA is a much larger and more important memory area than the PGA. In data warehousing environments, on the other hand, the PGA can be the more important Oracle memory area, because it critically influences the efficiency of large data sorts and hashes, which are commonly part of analytic computations in data warehouses.

The SGA's purpose is to speed up query performance and to enable a high amount of concurrent database activity. Because processing in memory is much faster than disk I/O, the size of the SGA is one of the more important configuration issues when you're tuning the database for optimal performance. When you start an instance in Oracle, the instance takes a certain amount of memory from the operating system's RAM—the amount is based on the size of the SGA component in the initialization file. When the instance is shut down, the memory used by the SGA goes back to the host system.

The SGA isn't a homogeneous entity; rather, it's a combination of several memory structures. The following are the main components of the SGA:

- *Database buffer cache*: Holds copies of data blocks read from datafiles.
- *Shared pool*: Contains the library cache for storing SQL and PL/SQL parsed code in order to share it among users. It also contains the data dictionary cache, which holds key data dictionary information.
- *Redo log buffer*: Contains the information necessary to reconstruct changes made to the database by DML operations. This information is then recorded in the redo logs by the log writer.
- *Java pool*: Represents the heap space for instantiating your java objects.
- *Large pool*: Stores large memory allocations, such as RMAN backup buffers.
- *Streams pool*: Supports the Oracle Streams feature.

When you start the Oracle instance, Oracle allocates memory as needed until it reaches the size set in the MEMORY_TARGET initialization parameter, which sets the limit for the total memory allocation. If your total memory allocation is already at the MEMORY_TARGET limit, you can't dynamically increase memory to any memory component without decreasing some other component's memory allocation. Oracle does allow you to exchange the memory from one dynamically sizable memory component to another.

For example, you can increase the memory assigned to the buffer cache by taking it from the shared pool. If you have certain jobs run only at specified times of the day, you can write a simple script that runs before the job executes and modifies the allocation of memory among the various components. After the job completes, you can have another script run that changes the memory allocation back to the original settings.

The next few sections discuss the various components of the SGA. You can manage the SGA yourself, by calibrating the memory you make available to the Oracle instance with the changing memory requirements of the running instance. However, the best way to manage the SGA (as well as the PGA) is simply by adopting automatic memory management, which I explain later in this chapter, in the section titled "Automatic Memory Management."

The Database Buffer Cache

The *database buffer cache* consists of the memory buffers that Oracle uses to hold the data read by the server process from datafiles on disk in response to user requests. Buffer cache access is, of course, much faster than reading the data from disk storage. When the users modify data, those changes are made in the database buffer cache as well. The buffer cache thus contains both the original blocks read from disk and the changed blocks that have to be written back to disk.

You can group the memory buffers in the database buffer cache into three components:

- *Free buffers*: These are buffers that do not contain any useful data, and, thus, the database can reuse them to hold new data it reads from disk.

- *Dirty buffers*: These contain data that was read from disk and then modified, but hasn't yet been written to the datafiles on disk.

- *Pinned buffers*: These are data buffers that are currently in active use by user sessions.

When a user process requests data, Oracle will first check whether the data is already available in the buffer cache. If it is, the server process will read the data from the SGA directly and send it to the user. If the data isn't found in the buffer cache, the server process will read the relevant data from the datafiles on disk and cache it in the database buffer cache. Of course, there must be free buffers available in the buffer cache for the data to be read into them. If the server process can't find a free buffer after searching through a threshold number of buffers, it asks the database writer process to write some of the dirty buffers to disk, thus freeing them up for writing the new data it wants to read into the buffer cache.

Oracle maintains an LRU list of all free, pinned, and dirty buffers in memory. It's the database writer process's job to write the dirty buffers back to disk to make sure there are free buffers available in the database buffer cache at all times. To determine which dirty blocks get written to disk, Oracle uses a modified LRU algorithm, which ensures that only the most recently accessed data is retained in the buffer cache. Writing data that isn't being currently requested to disk enhances the performance of the database.

The larger the buffer cache, the fewer the disk reads and writes needed and the better the performance of the database. Therefore, properly sizing the buffer cache is very important for the proper performance of your database. Of course, simply assigning an extremely large buffer cache can hurt performance, because you may end up taking more memory than necessary and causing paging and swapping on your server.

Using Multiple Database Buffer Cache Pools

Generally, a single default buffer cache is sufficient to serve the instance's memory needs. Assigning the same database buffer cache for all the database objects may not be very efficient at times, because different objects and various types of data may have different requirements as to how long they should be retained in the data cache. For example, table A may be accessed a hundred thousand times during a day, whereas table B may be accessed only twice during the same day. Clearly, it makes sense here to retain table A in the buffer cache throughout the day, so as to increase the speed of access, while table B can be removed after each use, to conserve space in the cache.

Oracle gives you flexibility in the use of the buffer cache by allowing you to configure the database buffer cache into multiple *buffer pools*. A buffer pool in this context is simply a part of the total buffer cache that is subject to different retention criteria for database objects like tables. For example, you can take a total buffer cache of 500MB and divide it into three pools, with 200MB in the first two pools and 100MB in the third. Once you have created separate buffer pools, you can assign a table exclusively to that buffer pool when you create that table. You can also use the ALTER TABLE or ALTER INDEX command to modify the type of buffer pool that a table or an index should use. Table 5-2 lists the main types of buffer pools that you can configure.

Note that any database objects that you haven't assigned to the keep or the recycle buffer pool will be assigned to the default buffer pool, which is sized according to the value you provide for the DB_CACHE_SIZE initialization parameter. The keep and the recycle buffer pools are purely optional, while the default buffer pool is mandatory.

Remember that the main goal in assigning objects to multiple buffer pools is to minimize the misses in the data cache and thus minimize your disk I/O. In fact, all buffer-caching strategies have this as their main goal. If you aren't sure which objects in your database belong to the different types of buffer caches, just let the database run for a while with some best-guess multiple cache sizes and query the data dictionary view V$DB_CACHE_ADVICE to get some advice from Oracle itself.

Table 5-2. *Main Buffer Pool Types*

Buffer Pool	Initialization Parameter	Description
Keep buffer pool	DB_KEEP_CACHE_SIZE	Keeps the data blocks always in memory. You may have small tables that are frequently accessed, so to prevent them from being aged out of the database buffer cache, you can assign the tables to the keep buffer cache when they are created.
Recycle buffer pool	DB_RECYCLE_CACHE_SIZE	Removes the data from the cache immediately after use. You need to use this buffer pool carefully, if you decide to use it at all. The recycle buffer pool will cycle out the object from the cache as soon as the transaction is over. Obviously, you would use the recycle buffer pool only for large tables that are infrequently accessed and that do not need to be retained in the buffer cache indefinitely.
Default buffer pool	DB_CACHE_SIZE	Contains all data and objects that are not assigned to the keep and recycle buffer pools.

Multiple Database Block Sizes and the Buffer Cache

As was mentioned earlier, you can have multiple block sizes for your database. You have to choose a standard block size first, and then you can choose up to four other nonstandard cache sizes.

The DB_BLOCK_SIZE parameter in your initialization parameter file determines your *standard* block size in the database and frequently is the only block size for the entire database. The DB_CACHE_SIZE parameter in your initialization parameter file specifies the size (in bytes) of the cache of the standard block sized buffers. Notice that you don't set the *number* of database buffers; rather, you specify the *size* of the buffer cache itself in the DB_CACHE_SIZE parameter.

You can have up to five different database block sizes in your databases. That is, you can create your tablespaces with any one of the five allowable database block sizes. Although most databases use only a single standard block size (such as 4KB, 8KB, or 16KB), you can choose to use some or all of the four nonstandard block sizes as well. For example, you may have some data warehouse–type tables that will benefit from a high database block size, such as 32KB. However, most of the other tables in the database may serve online processing needs, and should use the standard block size of 4KB. If you happen to be using all four of the allowable nonstandard block sizes besides the standard block size buffers, you can create tablespaces with all five block sizes. However, before you can create these nonstandard block size tablespaces, you must configure nonstandard subcaches in the buffer caches for each nonstandard block size you wish to use. You can specify the nonstandard buffer cache subcaches by using the DB_*n*K_CACHE_SIZE initialization parameter, where *n* is the block size in kilobytes—it can take a value of 2, 4, 8, 16, or 32.

As you've seen, the database buffer cache can be divided into three pools: the default, keep, and recycle buffer pools. The total size of the buffer cache is the sum of memory blocks assigned to all the components of the database buffer cache. The keep and recycle buffer pools can only be created with the standard block size, but you can use up to five different block sizes to configure the default buffer pool.

Here's an example that shows how you can specify different values for each of the buffer cache's subcaches in your initialization parameter file. In the example, the numbers on the right show the memory allocated to a particular type of buffer cache.

```
DB_KEEP_CACHE_SIZE  = 48MB
DB_RECYCLE_CACHE_SIZE = 24MB
DB_CACHE_SIZE = 128MB /* standard 4KB block size */
DB_2k_CACHE_SIZE =48MB /* 2KB nonstandard block size */
DB_8k_CACHE_SIZE =192MB /* 8KB nonstandard block size */
DB_16k_CACHE_SIZE = 384MB /* 16KB nonstandard block size */
```

The total buffer cache size in this example will be the sum of all the preceding subcaches, which comes to about 824MB.

The Buffer Cache Hit Ratio

Buffer reads are much faster than reads from disk. The all-important principle in appropriately sizing the buffer cache is summarized in the phrase "touch as few blocks as possible," since disk I/Os necessary for reading data from Oracle blocks on disk are more time consuming than reading the data from the SGA. This is why the buffer cache *hit ratio*, which measures the percentage of time users accessed the data they needed from the buffer cache (rather than requiring a disk read), is such an important indicator of performance of the Oracle instance.

You derive the buffer cache hit ratio as follows:

```
hit rate = (1 - (physical reads)/(logical reads)) * 100
```

In this calculation, the physical and logical reads (reads from disk and from memory, respectively) are accumulated from the start of the Oracle instance. So if you calculate the ratio on Monday morning after a restart on Sunday night, it will show a very low hit ratio. As the week progresses, the hit ratio could increase dramatically, because as more read requests come in, Oracle satisfies them with the data that is already in memory.

Unfortunately, Oracle does not give you any reliable rules or guidelines to indicate how much memory you should allocate for your buffer cache ratio or the SGA. Some trial and error with data loads should give you a good idea about the right size.

In Chapter 20, I present much more information on the tuning of the database buffer cache. A high buffer cache hit ratio doesn't always correlate with superior database performance. It is entirely possible for your database to have a very high hit ratio—say, in the high 90s—and still have a performance problem. For example, even if your total logical reads and hit ratio are high, your SQL queries could still be inefficient.

The Shared Pool

The shared pool is a very important part of the Oracle SGA, and sizing it appropriately for your instance will help avoid several types of Oracle instance bottlenecks. Unlike the database buffer cache, which holds actual data blocks, the shared pool holds executable PL/SQL code and SQL statements, as well as information regarding the data dictionary tables. The *data dictionary* is a set of key tables that Oracle maintains, and it contains crucial metadata about the database tables, users, privileges, and so forth.

Proper sizing of the shared pool area benefits you in a couple of ways. First, your response times will be better because you're reducing processing time—if you don't have to recompile the same Oracle code each time a user executes a query, you save time. Oracle will reuse the previously compiled code if it encounters the same code again. Second, more users can use the system because the reuse of code makes it possible for the database to serve more users with the same resources. Both the I/O rates and the CPU usage will diminish when your database uses its shared pool memory effectively.

The following sections discuss the library cache and the data dictionary cache, both of which are components of the shared pool.

The Library Cache

All application code, whether it is pure SQL code or code embedded in the form of PL/SQL program units, such as procedures and packages, is parsed first and executed later. Oracle stores all compiled SQL statements in the *library cache* component of the shared pool. The library cache component of the shared pool memory is shared by all users of the database. Each time you issue a SQL statement, Oracle first checks the library cache to see if there is an already parsed and ready-to-execute form of the statement in there. If there is, Oracle uses the library cache version, reducing the processing time considerably—this is called a *soft parse*.

If Oracle doesn't find an execution-ready version of the SQL code in the library cache, the executable has to be built fresh—this is called a *hard parse*. Oracle uses the library cache part of the shared pool memory for storing newly parsed code. If there isn't enough free memory in the shared pool, Oracle will jettison older code from the shared pool to make room for your new code.

All hard parses involve the use of critical system resources, such as processing power, and internal Oracle structures, such as latches; you must make every attempt to reduce their occurrence. High hard-parse counts will lead to resource contention and a consequent slowdown of the database when responding to user requests.

You should make decisions about the library cache size based on hit and miss ratios on the library cache as I explain in Chapter 20. If your system is showing more than the normal amount of misses (meaning that code is being reparsed or reexecuted often), it is time to increase the library cache memory. The way to do this is to increase the total memory allocated to the shared pool.

The Data Dictionary Cache

The *data dictionary cache* component of the shared pool primarily contains object definitions, user-names, roles, privileges, and other such information. When you run a segment of SQL code, Oracle first has to ascertain whether you have the privileges to perform the planned operation. It checks the data dictionary cache to see whether the pertinent information is there, and if not, Oracle has to read the information from the data dictionary into the data dictionary cache. Obviously, the more often you find the necessary information in the cache, the shorter the processing time. In general, a data dictionary cache miss, which occurs when Oracle doesn't find the information it needs in the cache, tends to be more expensive than a library cache miss.

There is no direct way to adjust the data dictionary cache size. You can only increase or decrease the entire shared pool size. Therefore, the solution to a low data dictionary cache hit ratio or a low library cache hit ratio is the same: increase the shared pool size.

Tip A cache miss on either the data dictionary cache or the library cache component of the shared pool has more impact on database performance than a miss on the buffer pool cache. For example, a decrease in the data dictionary cache hit ratio from 99 percent to 89 percent leads to a much more substantial deterioration in performance than a similar drop in the buffer cache hit ratio.

Result Cache

In Oracle Database 11*g*, there is a brand new component of the SGA called the *result cache*. The result cache is an area of the SGA where the database stores the results of both SQL queries and PL/SQL functions, so long as you enable these caches. You can cache the results of queries and query fragments in memory in the SQL query result cache. When the database executes the same SQL query again, it can simply retrieve the results from the result cache instead of reexecuting the query, thus enhancing performance significantly. PL/SQL function result caching works very similarly to the SQL query result cache. When a cached function is reexecuted, the database doesn't execute the function body, merely returning the cached result immediately instead.

You use the RESULT_CACHE_MODE initialization parameter to control whether the database caches a SQL query or a PL/SQL function's results. You can also utilize the new result cache hint to override the settings of the RESULT_CACHE_MODE parameter. You manage both caches through the PL/SQL package DBMS_RESULT_CACHE or through the Enterprise Manager. Chapter 20 discusses the SQL query result cache and the PL/SQL function result cache.

The Redo Log Buffer

The *redo log buffer*, usually less than a couple of megabytes in size, and thus nowhere near the size of the database buffer cache and the shared pool cache, is nonetheless a crucial component of the SGA. When a server process changes data in the data buffer cache (via an insert, a delete, or an update), it generates redo data, which is recorded in the redo log buffer. The log writer process writes redo information from the redo log buffer in memory to the redo log files on disk.

You use the LOG_BUFFER initialization parameter to set the size of the redo log buffer, and it stays fixed for the duration of the instance. That is, you can't adjust the redo log buffer size dynamically, unlike the other components of the SGA.

The log writer process writes the contents of the redo log buffer to disk under any of the following circumstances:

- The redo log buffer is one-third full.
- Users commit a transaction.
- The database buffer cache is running low on free space and needs to write changed data to the redo log. The database writer instructs the log writer process to flush the log buffer's contents to disk to make room for the new data.

The redo log buffer is a circular buffer—the log writer process writes the redo entries from the redo log buffer to the redo log files, and server processes write new redo log entries over the entries that have been written to the redo log files. The database allocates a small amount of memory, such as 5MB or so, for the redo log buffer. In most cases, you can leave the size of this buffer at its default value allocated by the database. Large redo log buffers will reduce your log file I/O (especially if you have large or many transactions), but your commits will take longer as well.

The log writer process usually writes to the redo log files very quickly, even when its workload is quite heavy. You'll run into more problems if your redo log buffer size is too small than if it is too large. A redo log buffer that is too small will keep the log writer process excessively busy—it will be constantly writing to disk. Furthermore, if the log buffer is too small, it will frequently run out of space to accommodate new redo entries.

Oracle provides an option called *nologging* that lets you bypass the redo logs almost completely and thus avoid contention during certain operations (such as a large data load). You can also batch the commits in a long job, thus enabling the log writer process to more efficiently write the redo log entries.

The Large Pool and the Java Pool

The large pool is a purely optional memory pool, and Oracle manages it quite differently from the shared pool. You only need to configure the large pool if you're using parallel queries in your data-base. Oracle also recommends configuring this pool if you're using RMAN or the shared server configuration instead of the default dedicated server configuration. You set the size of this pool in the initialization file by using the LARGE_POOL_SIZE parameter. The large pool memory component is important if you're using the shared server architecture.

The Java pool (set by using the JAVA_POOL_SIZE parameter) is designed for databases that contain a lot of Java code, so that the regular SGA doesn't have to be allocated to components using Java-based objects. Java pool memory is reserved for the Java Virtual Machine (JVM) and for your Java-based applications. If you're deploying Enterprise JavaBeans or using CORBA, you could potentially need a Java pool size greater than 1GB.

The Streams Pool

Oracle Streams is a technology for enabling data sharing among different databases and among different application environments. The Streams pool is the memory allocated to support Streams activity in your instance. If you manually set the Streams pool component by using the STREAMS_POOL_SIZE initialization parameter, memory for this pool is transferred from the buffer cache after the first use of Streams. If you use automatic shared memory management (discussed next), the memory for the Streams pool comes from the global SGA pool. The amount transferred is up to 10 percent of the shared pool size.

The Program Global Area

Oracle creates a program global area for each user when the user starts a session. This area holds data and control information for the dedicated server process that Oracle creates for each individual user. Unlike the SGA, the PGA is for the exclusive use of each server process and can't be shared by multiple processes. A session's logon information and persistent information, such as bind variable information and data type conversions, are still a part of the SGA, unless you're using a shared server configuration, but the runtime area used while SQL statements are executing is located in the PGA.

For example, a user's process may have some cursors (which are handles to memory areas where you store the values for variables) associated with it. Because these are the user's cursors, they are not automatically shared with other users and so the PGA is a good place to save those private values. Another major use of the PGA is for performing memory-intensive SQL operations that involve sorting, such as queries involving ORDER BY and GROUP BY clauses. These sort operations need a working area, and the PGA provides that memory area.

■Note For most OLTP databases, where transactions are very short, the PGA use is quite low. On the other hand, complex, long-running queries, which are more typical of DSS environments, require larger amounts of PGA memory.

You can classify the PGA memory into the following types:

- *Private SQL area*: This area of memory holds SQL variable bind information and runtime memory structures. Each session that executes a SQL statement will have its own private SQL area.

- *Runtime area*: The runtime area is created for a user session when the session issues a SELECT, INSERT, UPDATE, or DELETE statement. After an INSERT, DELETE, or UPDATE statement is run, or after the output of a SELECT statement is fetched, the runtime area is freed by Oracle.

If a user's session uses complex joins or heavy sorting (grouping and ordering) operations, the session uses the runtime area to perform all those memory-intensive operations.

■**Note** A cursor is a handle to a private SQL area in memory, and the OPEN_CURSORS initialization parameter determines the maximum number of cursors in a session.

To reduce response time, all the sorts that are performed in the PGA should be performed completely in the cache of the work area—this is known as an *optimal mode operation*, since all work is done in memory, with no disk I/O whatsoever. If the sort operation spills onto the disk because the memory areas aren't adequate, that will slow down the sort operation. A SQL operation that is forced to use the disk area in a limited fashion is a *single-pass operation*, and it leads to slower performance than when the operation executes entirely in the memory cache. However, if your runtime memory area is too small relative to the sort operation, Oracle will have to conduct multiple passes over the data being sorted, which is very disk intensive, and will result in extremely slow response times for the user. Thus, there is a direct correlation between the PGA size and query performance.

■**Caution** Many Oracle manuals suggest that you can allocate up to half of the total system memory for the Oracle SGA. This guideline assumes that the PGA memory will be fairly small. However, if the number of users is very large and the queries are complex, your PGA component may end up being even larger than the SGA. You should estimate the total memory requirements by projecting both SGA and PGA needs.

You can tune the size of these private work areas, but this is a hit-or-miss approach that involves weighing a number of complex Oracle configuration parameters related to the work areas. The parameters that you need to manually configure include the SORT_AREA_SIZE, HASH_AREA_SIZE, and BITMAP_AREA_SIZE parameters.

The sum of all the PGA memory used by all sessions makes up the PGA used by the instance. Oracle recommends that you use *automatic PGA management*, which automates the allocation of PGA memory. This helps you use the memory allocated to your database more efficiently. The feature performs especially well when you have varying workloads, because it dynamically adjusts its available memory bounds and the work profiles on a continuous basis. Manual management of PGA could easily lead to either too little or too much memory being allocated, which causes severe performance problems.

You automate PGA memory allocation by ensuring that the WORKAREA_SIZE_POLICY initialization parameter is set to its default value of auto. If you set the parameter value to manual, you'll have to specify all the PGA work area–related parameters mentioned previously. The WORKAREA_SIZE_POLICY parameter ensures the automation of PGA memory. However, you must also set the size of the total PGA memory allocation by specifying a value for the PGA_AGGREGATE_TARGET initialization parameter. For example, if you set PGA_AGGREGATE_TARGET=5000000000 in your initialization parameter file, Oracle uses the 5GB PGA allocation as a global target for the instance. Oracle will try to keep the total PGA memory used by all server processes attached to the instance under this target value.

If you don't set a value for the PGA_AGGREGATE_TARGET parameter, you'll be using the manual mode to manage the work areas. Alternatively, you can activate the manual mode by setting the WORKAREA_SIZE_POLICY parameter to manual. Oracle strongly recommends using automatic PGA management because it enables much more efficient use of memory. For users, this means better throughput and faster response time for queries in general.

■ **Note** In a manual management mode, any PGA memory that isn't being used isn't automatically returned to the system. Every session that logs into the database is allocated a specific amount of PGA memory, which it holds until it logs off, no matter whether it's performing SQL operations or not. Under automatic PGA management, the Oracle server returns all unused PGA memory to the operating system. On a busy system, this makes a huge difference in database and system performance. Suppose you set the PGA_AGGREGATE_TARGET parameter to 5GB. Oracle will not immediately grab all of the 5GB when you start the instance, as it does in the case of the SGA_TARGET parameter. It will only take the memory as necessary from the system, subject to the limit of 5GB. As soon as a session releases the run-area memory, the memory is automatically released to the operating system.

When you use automatic PGA memory management by setting the PGA_AGGREGATE_TARGET parameter, Oracle will do its best to assign enough memory to all work areas so they work in an optimal manner, executing all memory-intensive SQL operations in the cache memory. At worst, some work areas will use the disk areas in a single-pass mode. However, if you set the PGA_AGGREGATE_TARGET parameter too low relative to the work area needs of your instance, Oracle will be forced to conduct multipass executions of the sort- or hash-intensive SQL operations, with disastrous results for your instance performance.

Automatic Memory Management

In previous versions of Oracle, DBAs spent quite a bit of time pondering the sizing of the SGA. It wasn't uncommon for them to recalibrate the SGA size quite often as part of their instance-tuning efforts. In Oracle Database 11g, you can configure *automatic memory management* by using the new MEMORY_TARGET initialization parameter. All you need to do is assign a certain value for the MEMORY_TARGET parameter, and Oracle will automatically manage the distribution of this memory between the SGA and the PGA components. Oracle's allocation of the SGA memory to the various components isn't static, but changes with the changing workload of the database. Oracle can automatically manage the following five components of the SGA (the relevant Oracle initialization parameter is in parentheses):

- Database buffer cache (DB_CACHE_SIZE)
- Shared pool (SHARED_POOL_SIZE)
- Large pool (LARGE_POOL_SIZE)
- Java pool (JAVA_POOL_SIZE)
- Streams pool (STREAMS_POOL_SIZE)

As you can see, Oracle automatically tunes five components of the SGA, which are referred to as the automatically sized SGA parameters. You must still manage the rest of the SGA components yourself, even under automatic shared memory management. The following are the manually tunable components of the SGA:

- Keep buffer cache (DB_KEEP_CACHE_SIZE)
- Recycle buffer cache (DB_RECYCLE_CACHE_SIZE)

- Any nonstandard block size buffer caches (DB_nK_CACHE_SIZE)
- Redo log buffer (LOG_BUFFER)

Note that the first three components in this list are optional. As the DBA, you must set the value for each of the manual SGA components.

Memory Management Options and Defaults for Database Installation

When you create a database with the Database Configuration Assistant (DBCA), if you choose the basic installation option, automatic memory management is enabled by default. If you choose the advanced installation option instead, you'll get to choose from the following three memory management configurations:

- Automatic memory management
- Automatic shared memory management + automatic PGA memory management
- Manual shared memory management + automatic PGA memory management

If you create a database with the CREATE DATABASE statement and don't provide any memory management–related initialization parameters, manual shared memory management is the default. For the PGA, automatic PGA memory management will be the default configuration.

■**Note** If the SGA_TARGET parameter is set to zero (the default), the auto-tuned SGA parameters behave as in previous versions of Oracle.

You can learn more about automatic memory management configuration in Chapter 17.

A Simple Oracle Database Transaction

So far in this chapter, you've seen the components of the Oracle database system: the necessary files and memory allocations and how you can adjust them. It's time now to look into how Oracle processes users' queries and how it makes changes to data. It's important to understand the mechanics of SQL transaction processing because all interaction with an Oracle database occurs either in the form of SQL queries that read data or SQL (or PL/SQL) operations that modify, insert, or delete data.

A transaction is a logical unit of work in an Oracle database, and consists of one or more SQL statements. A transaction begins with the first executable SQL statement and terminates when you commit or roll back the transaction. Committing a transaction will make your changes permanent, and rolling back the changes will, of course, undo them. Once you commit the transaction, all other users' transactions that start subsequently will be able to see the changes made by your transactions.

When a transaction fails to execute completely (say, due to a power failure), the entire transaction must be undone. Oracle will roll back any changes made by earlier SQL statements in the transaction, leaving the data in its original (pretransaction) state. The whole process is designed to maintain *data consistency*—a transaction is an all-or-nothing concept.

The following simple example of a row being inserted outlines how Oracle processes transactions:

1. A user requests a connection to the Oracle server through a 3-tier or an *n*-tier web-based client using Oracle Net Services.

2. Upon validating the request, the server starts a new dedicated server process for that user.

3. The user executes a statement to insert a new row into a table.

4. Oracle checks the user's privileges to make sure the user has the necessary rights to perform the insertion. If the user's privilege information isn't already in the library cache, it will have to be read from disk into that cache.

5. If the user has the requisite privileges, Oracle checks whether a previously executed SQL statement that's similar to the one the user just issued is already in the shared pool. If there is, Oracle executes this version of the SQL; otherwise Oracle parses and executes the user's SQL statement. Oracle then creates a private SQL area in the user session's PGA.

6. Oracle first checks whether the necessary data is already in the data buffer cache. If not, the server process reads the necessary table data from the datafiles on disk.

7. Oracle immediately applies row-level locks, where needed, to prevent other processes from trying to change the same data simultaneously.

8. The server writes the change vectors to the redo log buffer.

9. The server modifies the table data (inserts the new row) in the data buffer cache.

10. The user commits the transaction, making the insertion permanent. Oracle releases the row locks after the commit is issued.

11. The log writer process immediately writes out the changed data in the redo log buffers to the online redo log file.

12. The server process sends a message to the client process to indicate the successful completion of the INSERT operation. The message would be "COMMIT COMPLETE" in this case. (If it couldn't complete the request successfully, it sends a message indicating the failure of the operation.)

13. Changes made to the table by the insertion may not be written to disk right away. The database writer process writes the changes in batches, so it may be some time before the inserted information is actually written permanently to the database files on disk.

Note In the previous example, since a new row is being inserted, there's no undo information to record in the undo tablespace. (The ROWID of the new row goes to the undo segment, so you can use a DELETE...WHERE ROWID=... statement to roll back the insert if necessary. If the user had updated a row instead, Oracle would have had to record the before-update row in the undo records. Until the original transaction commits the update, all other users will see the original data values of the row.

Committing and Rolling Back

You must be clear about two fundamental transaction-related terms: committing and rolling back transactions. I briefly explain these terms here. Chapter 8 contains additional discussion of these two key concepts.

Committing a Transaction

When you commit a transaction, say by issuing the COMMIT statement, Oracle makes all the changes performed by all the SQL statements in that transaction a permanent part of the database. Before Oracle commits the results of a transaction, it does the following:

- It generates undo information that essentially consists of the before-change values of the data that are going to be modified. The undo data is stored in the undo segments, which are located in the undo tablespace.

- It also generates redo log data containing changes to the data blocks and to the rollback blocks, in the redo log buffer. The database may write the redo log buffer contents to disk before it commits the transaction.

- It makes changes to the database buffers in the SGA. The database may write the modified buffers to disk before it commits the transaction.

The database may write the transaction changes that are made first in the database buffers in the SGA to the datafiles immediately or sometime after the transaction commits or even before the transaction commits. Once the database commits a transaction, it does the following things:

- The database assigns and records an SCN for the committed transaction.

- The log writer writes the redo log entries to the redo log on disk, from the redo log buffer in the SGA; the log writer also records the transaction SCN in the redo log file, marking the official committing of the transaction.

- The database releases all table and row locks.

- The database marks the transaction as being completed.

Rolling Back a Transaction

You can undo changes made by a transaction that hasn't yet been committed, by issuing the ROLLBACK command. While a redo log contains all changes made to the transaction, the undo segments contain all the old values that existed before you made the changes. You can either roll back the changes made by the entire transaction or just go back to a marker you placed in the transaction, called a *savepoint*. There are many types of rollbacks, such as the following:

- A rollback requested by a user

- A rollback due to a process or an instance terminating in an abnormal fashion

- A rollback of an uncommitted transaction during a recovery

- A statement-level rollback due to a statement execution error

Regardless of the reason for the rollback, the procedure is the same:

- The database uses the before-change data in the undo tablespace to undo all changes made during the transaction.

- The database releases all the transaction and table locks.

- The database ends the transaction.

Data Consistency and Data Concurrency

Databases aren't very useful if a large number of users can't access and modify data simultaneously. *Data concurrency* refers to the capability of the database to handle this concurrent use by many users. To provide consistent results, the database also needs a mechanism within it that ensures users don't step on each other's changes. *Data consistency* refers to the ability of a user to get a meaningful and consistent view of the data, including all the changes made to it by other users.

Oracle uses special structures called *undo segments* to ensure data consistency. For example, when you're reading a set of data for a transaction, Oracle ensures that the data you read is *transaction-set consistent*; that is, it guarantees that the data you see reflects a single set of committed transactions. Oracle also provides *read consistency* of data, meaning that all the data selected by your queries comes from a single point in time. Oracle's undo segments are part of the undo tablespace mentioned earlier in this chapter.

Oracle uses locking mechanisms to ensure data concurrency. By allowing one user to lock individual rows or entire tables, that user is guaranteed exclusive use of the table for updating purposes. An important feature of the Oracle locking mechanisms is that they are, for the most part, automatic. You don't need to concern yourself with the details of how to lock the objects you want to modify—Oracle will take care of it for you behind the scenes.

Oracle uses two basic modes of locking. The *exclusive lock mode* is used for updates, and the *share lock mode* is used for SELECT operations on tables. The share lock mode enables several users to simultaneously read the same rows in a table. The exclusive lock mode, because it involves updates to the table, can only be used by one user at any given time. Exclusive locks are almost always applied to the specific rows being updated, permitting simultaneous use of the database by several users. Oracle releases the locks it holds on the tables and other internal resources automatically after the issue of a COMMIT or ROLLBACK command.

Oracle locking is complex, and you'll learn about it in detail in Chapter 8, along with how Oracle ensures data consistency and concurrency.

The Database Writer and the Write Ahead Protocol

The database writer, as you saw earlier, is responsible for writing all modified buffers in the database buffer cache to the datafiles. Further, it has the responsibility of ensuring there is free space in the buffer cache so the server process can read in new data from the datafiles when necessary. The (log) *write ahead protocol* also requires that the redo records in the redo log buffer associated with the changed data in the data buffer cache are written to the redo logs before the changes are recorded in the datafiles. The importance of the redo log contents makes it imperative that Oracle write the contents of the redo log file to permanent storage before it writes the changes to the datafiles on disk.

When users commit their transactions, the log writer process immediately writes only a single commit record to the redo log files. The entire set of records affected by the committed transaction may not be written simultaneously to the datafiles. This *fast commit mechanism*, along with the write ahead protocol, ensures that the database is not kept waiting for all the physical writes to be completed after each transaction. As you can well imagine, a huge OLTP database with numerous changes throughout the day cannot function optimally if it has to write to disk after every committed data change.

■**Note** If there are a large number of transactions and, therefore, a large number of commit requests, the log writer process may not write each committed transaction's redo entries to the redo log immediately. It may batch multiple commit requests if it is busy writing previously issued commit records. This batched writing of redo entries from multiple committed transactions is known as *group commits*.

The System Change Number

The system change number, or SCN, is an important quantifier that the Oracle database uses to keep track of its state at any given point in time. When you read (SELECT) the data in the tables, you don't affect the state of the database, but when you modify, insert, or delete a row, the state of the database is different from what it was before. Oracle uses the SCN to keep track of all the changes made to the database over time. The SCN is a *logical time stamp* that is used by Oracle to order events that occur within the database. The SCN is very important for several reasons, not the least of which is the recovery of the database after a crash.

SCNs are like increasing sequence numbers, and Oracle increments them in the SGA. When a transaction modifies or inserts data, Oracle first writes a new SCN to the rollback segment. The log writer process then writes the commit record of the transaction immediately to the redo log, and this commit record will have the unique SCN of the new transaction. In fact, the writing of this SCN to the redo log file denotes a committed transaction in an Oracle database.

The SCN helps Oracle determine whether crash recovery is needed after a sudden termination of the database instance or after a SHUTDOWN ABORT command is issued. Every time the database performs a checkpoint operation, Oracle writes a START SCN command to the datafile headers. The control file maintains an SCN value for each datafile, called the STOP SCN, which is usually set to infinity, and every time the instance is stopped normally (with the SHUTDOWN NORMAL or SHUTDOWN IMMEDIATE command), Oracle copies the START SCN number in the datafile headers to the STOP SCN numbers for the datafiles in the control file. When you restart the database after a graceful shutdown, there is no need for any kind of recovery because the SCNs in the datafiles and the control files match. On the other hand, abrupt instance termination does not leave time for this matching of SCNs, and Oracle recognizes that instance recovery is required because of the varying SCN numbers in the datafiles on the one hand and the control file on the other. As you'll learn in Chapter 16, they play a critical role during database recovery. Oracle determines how far back you should apply the archived redo logs during a recovery based on the SCN.

Undo Management

When you make a change to a table, you should be able to undo or roll back the change if necessary. The information needed to undo or roll back changes in transactions, which mostly consists of the prechange table row information, is called *undo data* (the change vectors), and it is stored in *undo records*. When you issue a ROLLBACK command, Oracle uses these undo records to replace the changed data with the original versions. As Chapter 8 explains, the undo records are vital during database recovery when all unfinished or uncommitted transactions must be discarded to make the database consistent.

Oracle strongly recommends the use of the *Automatic Undo Management* (AUM) feature, where the Oracle server itself will maintain and manage the undo (rollback) segments. All you need to do is provide a dedicated undo tablespace and set the initialization parameter UNDO_MANAGEMENT to auto. Oracle will create the necessary number of undo segments, which are structurally similar to the traditional rollback segments, and it'll size and extend them as necessary. It's not uncommon for new undo segments to be created and old ones to be deactivated based on the number of transactions going on in the database. Chapter 8 provides further information about the AUM feature.

Because Oracle will do the sizing of the individual undo segments for you, the two decisions you have to make are the size of the undo tablespace and the setting for the UNDO_RETENTION initialization parameter (which determines how long Oracle will try to retain undo records in the undo tablespace). Remember that your undo tablespace should not only be able to accommodate all the long-running transactions, but also has to be big enough to accommodate any *flashback* features you may implement in your database—Oracle's flashback features let you undo changes to data at various levels. Several flashback features, such as Flashback Query, Flashback Versions Query, and Flashback Table, utilize undo data. I discuss the undo-related Flashback features in Chapter 8.

You can use Oracle's Undo Advisor through the OEM to figure out the ideal size for your undo tablespaces and the ideal duration to specify for the UNDO_RETENTION parameter. Using the current undo space consumption statistics, you can estimate future undo generation rates for the instance.

Backup and Recovery Architecture

You must perform regular backups of any database that contains useful information. All databases depend on mechanical components like disk drives, and they are also subject to unexpected events like power failures and natural catastrophes. Programmatic and user errors also necessitate protecting data through a strong backup system. Recovery involves two main objectives: first, you must return the database to a normal operating state with as little downtime as possible. Second, you mustn't lose any useful data.

It's important to understand the basics of how Oracle manages its backup and recovery operations. You've seen some of the components previously, but I put it all together here. The following Oracle structures ensure that you can recover your databases after a problem:

- *The control file*: The control file contains datafile and redo log information, as well as the latest system change number, which is key to the recovery process.

- *Database backups*: These are file or tape backups of the database datafiles. Since these backups are made periodically, they most likely won't contain all the data needed to bring the database up to date. The backup files include both backups of the datafiles as well as the archived redo log files.

- *The redo logs*: The redo logs, as you've seen earlier in this chapter, contain all changes made to the database, including uncommitted and committed changes.

- *The undo records*: These records contain the before images of blocks changed in uncommitted transactions.

Recovery involves restoring all backups first. Since the backups can't bring you up to date, you apply the redo logs next, to bring the database up to date. Since the redo logs may contain some uncommitted data that shouldn't really be in the database, however, Oracle uses the undo records to roll back all the uncommitted changes. When the recovery process is complete, your database will not have lost any committed or permanent data.

User-Managed Backup and Recovery

You can perform all backup and recovery procedures by issuing direct commands through SQL*Plus and operating system commands. However, Oracle strongly recommends that you use the Oracle-provided Recovery Manager to perform your backup and restore work.

RMAN

RMAN is Oracle's main backup and recovery tool. You can use RMAN from the command line as well as through a GUI interface. RMAN enables various types of backup and recovery techniques, and several of these techniques are unique to the tool. For example, a big benefit of using RMAN is that it automatically maintains all records of existing database backups, without you having to maintain that information somewhere.

The Automatic Disk-Based Backup and Recovery feature uses a flash recovery area to help you automate the management of backup-related files. Oracle recommends that you use such a flash recovery area, which is a location on disk where the database stores and manages all recovery-related files, like archived redo logs and other files for your database. Files no longer needed in the flash recovery area are deleted automatically when RMAN needs to reclaim space for new files. If you don't use a flash recovery area, you must manually manage disk space for your backup-related files.

Oracle Secure Backup

RMAN can't back up files directly to tape devices, and therefore, you need to use another tool to perform tape backups when working with RMAN. There are several excellent third-party tools for this purpose, but you can also use Oracle's own Oracle Secure Backup feature, which is an out-of-the-box backup and recovery solution for Oracle customers. Oracle Secure Backup copies datafiles directly to tape and manages the archiving of those tapes as well. Chapter 15 provides an introduction to Oracle Secure Backup.

You can easily configure the Backup Manager through OEM. By using OEM and Oracle Secure Backup together, you can easily back up and recover databases enterprise-wide.

Flashback Recovery Techniques

Quite often, you may be called upon to help recover from a logical corruption of the database, rather than from a hardware failure. You can use the following flashback techniques in Oracle Database 11*g* to recover from logical errors:

- *Flashback Database*: Takes the entire database back to a specific point in time
- *Flashback Table*: Returns individual tables to a past state
- *Flashback Drop*: Undoes a DROP TABLE command and recovers the dropped table
- *Flashback Query, Flashback Version Query, and Flashback Transaction Query*: Retrieve data from a time (or an interval) in the past
- *Flashback Transaction Backout*: Lets you undo a transaction, together with all its dependent transactions as well, with just a single click in the Database Control
- *Flashback Data Archive*: Stores history of the changes made to a table, which you can use to make queries using older versions of data and for auditing purposes as well

I discuss the Flashback Database, Flashback Drop, and the Flashback Data Archive features in Chapter 16, which deals with recovery techniques. I discuss the Flashback Table, Flashback Query, Flashback Version Query, Flashback Transaction Query, and the new Flashback Transaction Backout features that rely on undo data, and are discussed in Chapter 8.

■**Note** The new Oracle Database 11*g* feature, Flashback Data Archive, lets you automatically store, retrieve, and purge historical data for any length of time you wish. I discuss this exciting feature in Chapter 16.

The Oracle Data Dictionary and the Dynamic Performance Views

Oracle provides a huge number of internal tables to aid you in tracking changes to database objects and to fix problems that will occur from time to time. Mastering these key internal tables is vital if you want to become a savvy Oracle DBA. All the GUI tools, such as OEM, depend on these key internal tables (and views) to gather information for monitoring Oracle databases. Although you may want to rely on GUI tools to perform your database administration tasks, it is important to learn as much as you can about these internal tables. Knowledge of these tables helps you understand what is actually happening within the database.

You can divide the internal tables into two broad types: the static data dictionary tables and the dynamic performance tables. You won't access these tables directly; rather, you'll access the information through views based on these tables. Chapter 23 is dedicated to a discussion of these views, and you can get a complete list of all the data dictionary views by issuing the following simple query:

```
SQL> SELECT * FROM dict;
```

The following sections examine the role of these two important types of tables (and views).

The Oracle Data Dictionary

Every Oracle database contains a set of read-only tables, known as the *data dictionary*, which contain *metadata* (information about the various components of the database). The Oracle data dictionary is the heart of the database management system, and mastery of it will take you far in your quest to become an expert DBA. If you understand the data dictionary well, you can easily perform database management tasks. You access the read-only data dictionary tables through views built on them. Views are like logical tables built on underlying Oracle tables, and I discuss them in detail in Chapter 7. DBAs and developers depend heavily on the data dictionary for information about the various components of the database—these tables contain information such as the list of tables, table columns, users, user privileges, file and tablespace names, and so on. A simple query, such as the following, necessitates several calls to the data dictionary before Oracle can execute it:

```
SQL> SELECT employee_name
     FROM emp
     WHERE city = 'NEW YORK';
```

It's important to note that the data dictionary tables don't report on aspects of the running instance. The data dictionary holds only information about the database, such as the database files, tables, functions, and procedures, as well as user-related information. Another set of views, called the *dynamic performance views*, records information about the currently running instance.

■**Tip** The data dictionary tables describe the entire database: its logical and physical structure, its space usage, its objects and their constraints, and user information. You can't access the data dictionary tables directly; instead, you're given access to views built on them. You also can't change any of the information in the data dictionary tables yourself. Only Oracle has the capability to change data in the data dictionary tables. When you issue a query involving the CITIES column in a table named EMPLOYEES, for example, the database will consult various data dictionary tables to verify that the table and the column exist, and to confirm that the user has the rights to execute that statement. As you can imagine, a heavily used OLTP database will require numerous queries on its data dictionary tables during the course of a day.

The Oracle super user SYS owns most of the data dictionary tables (though some are created under the system username), and they are stored in the System tablespace.

■**Tip** Oracle recommends that you analyze both the data dictionary and the dynamic performance tables (also referred to as fixed tables) on a regular basis to improve performance. Chapter 19 shows you how to analyze these tables.

The Dynamic Performance (V$) Views

In addition to the data dictionary, Oracle maintains an important set of *dynamic performance tables*. These tables maintain information about the current instance, and Oracle continuously updates these tables.

The set of virtual dynamic tables is referred to as the *X$ tables*. Oracle doesn't allow you to access the X$ tables directly; rather, Oracle creates views on all these tables and then creates synonyms for these views. You'll be accessing these views, called the *V$ views*, to get information about various aspects of a running instance. The V$ views are the foundation of all Oracle database performance tuning. If you wish to master the Oracle database, you must master the V$ dynamic views, because they are the wellspring of so much knowledge about the Oracle instance.

The dynamic performance views, like the data dictionary views, are based on read-only tables that only Oracle can update. Some of the tables capture sessionwide information, and some of them capture systemwide information. You'll find the dynamic views extremely useful in session management, backup operations, and, most important, performance tuning. Remember, though, that the dynamic performance tables are only populated for the duration of the instance and are cleaned out when you shut down the instance.

The Three Sets of Data Dictionary Views

Oracle doesn't allow you to access the internal data dictionary tables directly. It creates views on the base dictionary tables and creates public synonyms for these views so users can access them. There are three sets of data dictionary views—USER, ALL, and DBA—with each set of views pertaining to a similar item containing similar columns. The views in each category are prefixed by the keywords USER, ALL, or DBA. Each of these sets of views shows only the information the user is granted privileges to access, as follows:

- *USER*: The USER views show a user only those objects that the user owns. These views are useful to users, especially developers, for viewing the owner's objects, grants, and so on.

- *ALL*: The ALL views show you information about objects for which you have been granted privileges. The views with the prefix ALL include information on the user's objects, and all other objects on which privileges have been granted, directly or through a role.

- *DBA*: The DBA views are the most powerful in their range. Users who have been assigned the DBA role can access information about any object or any user in the database. The DBA-prefixed dictionary views are the ones you use to monitor and administer the database.

How Is the Data Dictionary Created?

The data dictionary is created automatically when you create the database. Well, almost automatically, because you do have to run the `catalog.sql` script manually (located in the `$ORACLE_HOME/rdbms/admin` directory) if you aren't using the Database Configuration Assistant. The `catalog.sql` script creates the data dictionary tables, views, and synonyms, and they're the first set of objects to populate the database. The data dictionary, once created, has to remain in the System tablespace.

In the rest of the chapter, you'll see detailed references to the DBA data dictionary tables only, because the focus here is on database management. There are many data dictionary tables and views. You'll examine the most useful of the data dictionary views in the next few sections.

Using the Static Data Dictionary Views

The data dictionary contains metadata about your database. The data dictionary tables and the views based on them are called static, because the running database instance doesn't modify data in these tables and views. The tables and views are modified only if you make a change to the data dictionary itself, for example, by creating a table or a new user. No matter whether you manage the database manually or use sophisticated GUI-based management tools, the data dictionary (along with the dynamic performance tables) is the source for all information about the database.

The Oracle Optimizer

In most cases, when users issue a query against the database, there's more than one way to access the tables and retrieve the data. Because there are many ways to execute the same statement, Oracle uses a *Cost-Based Optimizer* (CBO) to choose the best execution plan for queries, based on the cost of the query in terms of resource use.

Query optimizing is at the heart of modern relational databases and is an essential part of how Oracle conducts its operations. The query optimizer is transparent to users, and Oracle will automatically apply the best access and join methods to your queries before it starts processing.

■**Note** To choose the best execution plans, Oracle uses statistics on tables and indexes, which include counts of the number of rows and the data distribution of "data skew" in the tables within the database. (The physical storage statistics and the data distribution statistics for all database tables and indexes, columns, and partitions are stored in various data dictionary tables.) Armed with this information, the optimizer usually succeeds in finding the best path to access the necessary data for executing a SQL statement. Oracle also lets you use *hints* to override the optimizer's choice of an execution path. This is because in some instances the application developer's knowledge of the data enables the use of more efficient execution plans than the optimizer can come up.

I discuss the Oracle optimizer in detail in Chapter 19, in the context of performance tuning.

■**Tip** You can also use the Oracle optimizer in an enhanced tuning mode, as shown in Chapter 19. The Oracle optimizer in the tuning mode is the basis of the SQL Tuning Advisor feature, also explained in Chapter 19.

Talking to the Database

In order for a user to communicate with the database, he or she must first connect to the database by creating a user session. The user communication with the database is done through one of several interfaces. This section will quickly review Oracle database connectivity aspects and the main communication interfaces, including SQL*Plus, SQL Developer, and the OEM Database Control and Grid Control interfaces, which serve as the main DBA management consoles.

Connecting to Oracle

You can connect to the Oracle database from the server on which the Oracle RDBMS is running. However, DBAs as well as application developers and users generally connect to the database through the network using Oracle Net, a component of Oracle Net Services. Oracle Net enables network sessions from a client application to an Oracle database server. It acts as the data courier for the clients and the database server, and it is in charge of establishing and maintaining the connection as well as transmitting messages between client and server. Oracle Net is installed on each computer in the network.

■**Note** Oracle Net Services is Oracle's mechanism for interfacing with the communication protocols (TCP/IP for example) that define the way data is transmitted on a network.

Since a connection to a database and a user session are closely related to a user process but are actually quite different from each other, let me take a minute to explain the differences between a connection and a session.

An Oracle connection represents a communication link between a user's process and an Oracle Database instance. This communication link, or pathway, can be located on the same server as both the user process and the database server process run. The communication pathway can also be established using network software, as is the case when the client runs on one computer and the Oracle database on another, with both of them communicating via the network.

A session represents a specific user connection to a running Oracle instance via a user process. A session starts when, for example, you start SQL*Plus and log into the database, and it lasts until you disconnect or exit. You can create multiple simultaneous sessions under the same Oracle username and password credentials. Under the common dedicated server approach, as you saw earlier, the database creates a dedicated server process to serve each user session. When you use a shared server approach, multiple user sessions share a single server process.

For a connection to succeed, the client application must specify the location of the database. On the database side, the Oracle Net listener, known simply as the *listener*, is the process that listens for incoming client connection requests. You configure the listener in the listener.ora file, where you provide the database address. The listener.ora file also defines the protocol the listener is listening on and related information. On the client side, you can either use the tnsnames.ora file to list the database server connection details, which include the database name, server name, and connection protocol, or use the much simpler *easy connect method*.

Oracle Enterprise Manager

Oracle Enterprise Manager is Oracle's GUI-based management tool that lets you manage one or more databases efficiently. OEM enables security management, backups, and routine user and object management. Because OEM is GUI-based, you don't have to know a lot of SQL to use the tool. However, understanding the V$ and dynamic performance views will enhance your knowledge of how the database works—OEM will be an even more powerful tool in your hands after you master the management of the database using the data dictionary–based and dynamic performance table–based SQL queries. Oracle has really improved OEM in its most recent versions, and all serious practitioners of the trade should master the use of the tool for both daily database management and scheduling routine database administration tasks and troubleshooting. Chapter 4 explains the configuration and use of the OEM tool set.

In Oracle Database 11g, you have the option of using either the Database Control or Grid Control version of Enterprise Manager. The Enterprise Manager Database Control is automatically installed along with the Oracle software and is designed to run as a stand-alone application. In order to manage several databases, however, you need to separately install the Enterprise Manager Grid Control software on your server and the OEM Agent software on all the targets you wish to monitor.

The Oracle Enterprise Manager tool always looked promising in previous versions, but it delivered inconsistent performance. This hard reality, plus the fact that many DBAs are comfortable with manual commands and scripts based on the database dictionary and the dynamic (V$) views, led to a low acceptance rate of the tool. Since the Oracle Database 10g release, the OEM tool has gone through a sea change and delivers high-level performance. I strongly recommend using the Database Control or the Grid Control tool to monitor and manage your databases. You can invoke all the new management advisors and tools, like the ADDM from the OEM toolset, without having to use complex Oracle PL/SQL packages. I show OEM examples throughout this book.

■Note Traditionally, all GUI tools relied on the same V$ performance views that are used in database queries. However, OEM can access key performance data directly from the SGA, without making any SQL queries. This is done by attaching directly to the SGA and reading the statistics from the shared memory. When your database is performing extremely slowly or hangs, you can't rely on the dynamic V$ views to troubleshoot the problem—doing so may actually end up making matters worse! This is one more reason why you should make the OEM your main means of monitoring and managing the Oracle instance.

SQL*Plus

SQL*Plus is an Oracle tool that lets you enter and run SQL statements and PL/SQL (a procedural extension to the Oracle SQL language) blocks. As a DBA, you can perform all your tasks right from the SQL*Plus interface itself. However, as I explain in the previous section, you may want to make the SQL*Plus interface your secondary, rather than primary, tool for accessing the Oracle RDBMS. I discuss SQL*Plus in detail in Chapter 4.

Oracle Utilities

Oracle provides several powerful tools to help with loading and unloading of data and similar activities. The following sections describe the main ones.

Data Pump Export and Import

The Data Pump Export and Import utilities are the successors to the traditional export and import utilities; they help with fast data loading and unloading operations. The original export and import utilities are still available, but Oracle recommends the use of the newer and more sophisticated tools. Chapter 13 discusses the Data Pump utilities in detail.

SQL*Loader

The SQL*Loader is a powerful and fast utility that loads data from external files into tables of an Oracle database. Chapter 14 discusses SQL*Loader in detail.

■Note You use the SQL*Loader to load external data into an Oracle table. Sometimes, though, you need to use some external data but don't want to go to the trouble of loading the data into a table. The *external tables* feature offers some of the SQL*Loader utility's functionality.

External tables let you use data that resides in external text files as if it were in a table in an Oracle database. You can write to external tables as well as read from them. I describe the external tables in detail in Chapter 13.

LogMiner

The LogMiner utility lets you query online and archived redo log files through a SQL interface. As you know, redo log files hold the history of all changes made to the database. Thus, you can use the LogMiner to see exactly which transaction and what SQL statement caused a change, and if necessary, undo it. Chapter 16 shows you how to use the LogMiner tool for precision recovery.

Automatic Diagnostic Repository Control Interface

The automatic diagnostic repository control interface (ADRCI) is a command-line tool that helps you manage the brand-new Oracle Database 11g diagnosability infrastructure. Through the ADRCI, you can view diagnostic data and health monitor reports besides managing incident packaging and transmission (to Oracle Support). You can access all types of diagnostic data, including incident descriptions, trace and dump files, alert log contents, and the new health monitor reports through the ADRCI interface.

Scheduling and Resource Management

Oracle Database 11g provides several utilitarian tools for scheduling jobs and managing database and server resource usage, and they're outlined in the following sections.

The Oracle Scheduler

The Oracle Scheduler facility lets DBAs schedule tasks from within the Oracle database, without having to write shell scripts and scheduling them through the operating system. You can even schedule operating system jobs on remote servers, without installing Oracle software on the remote server.

The basic components of the Oracle Scheduler are jobs, programs, and schedules. The Oracle Scheduler offers much more functionality than using the old DBMS_JOBS package. You can now create common jobs and schedules that you can share across users. You can also group similar jobs into job classes and use resource plans to prioritize resources among resource consumer groups. You can schedule PL/SQL and Java programs as well as operating system shell scripts through the Scheduler.

You'll find a complete treatment of the Oracle Scheduler in Chapter 18.

Database Resource Manager

The Database Resource Manager lets you exercise control over how the server resources, especially CPU resources, are allocated among your users. You first group the users according to common resource requirements, and you then create directives that dictate how resources are to be allocated to these groups. The Database Resource Manager controls how long the sessions run, thus ensuring that resource usage matches the stated objectives. I discuss the Database Resource Manager in detail in Chapter 12.

Automatic Database Management

Traditionally, Oracle DBAs had to exercise great care in setting numerous initialization parameters, and they would spend quite a bit of their time tweaking those parameters, trying to achieve an ideal database configuration. Oracle started a major push toward a self-managing database with the 9i version, and in Oracle Database 10g and Oracle Database 11g, Oracle has taken that effort further, offering a more complete set of self-managing features, especially in the performance-tuning area. In the long run, the goal is to automate all routine tasks and free up the DBAs and other professionals to use their time to further the strategic interests of their businesses.

The following sections summarize the main automatic management features in Oracle Database 11g.

Automatic Database Diagnostic Monitor

The Automatic Database Diagnostic Monitor, or ADDM, is probably the most revolutionary aspect of the new self-managing Oracle database. The ADDM is a diagnostic engine built right into the database kernel—it is a rule-based expert system that encapsulates decades of Oracle's performance-tuning expertise. It analyzes performance data frequently and either makes a recommendation by itself or suggests that you invoke one of the other Oracle advisory components, such as the SQL Tuning Advisor.

The ADDM proactively performs automatic monitoring of the database at regular intervals throughout the day, performs a top-down analysis of performance data and bottlenecks, and presents a set of findings that include the root causes of problems and the recommendations to fix them. In addition, it provides the rationale behind its recommendations. Because the ADDM quantifies the identified problems in terms of their impact on overall performance, you can focus on fixing problems that will give you the biggest performance gains.

You can also run the ADDM manually through the Enterprise Manager or the command line. The ADDM's diagnostic abilities can be used during the development phase of applications, reducing potential problems in production. The ADDM will enable developers to perform "what-if" tests very easily.

Chapter 17 explains the ADDM in detail.

Automatic Undo Retention Tuning

Setting the UNDO_RETENTION parameter to zero or just leaving it out of your SPFILE will instruct Oracle to perform proactive automatic undo retention tuning, thus reducing the occurrence of the well-known "snapshot too old" errors that lead to the failure of many an overnight production batch job. Under automatic undo retention tuning, Oracle will figure out the ideal retention period for undo data, based on the length of the transactions and other related factors. I discuss automatic undo retention tuning in Chapter 8.

Automatic Optimizer Statistics Collection

Oracle Database 11g a automatically gathers statistics for the cost-based optimizer through a regularly scheduled job. The job gathers statistics on all objects in the database that have missing or stale statistics. Oracle creates this job automatically at database creation time, and the Scheduler automatically manages it. Chapter 19 discusses the automatic collection of optimizer statistics.

Automatic Storage Management

Automatic Storage Management is a way of organizing your storage that integrates your file system with a volume manager that's designed for Oracle files. ASM divides Oracle datafiles into extents, which it distributes evenly across the disk system. ASM automatically redistributes I/O load across all available disks whenever storage configuration changes, avoiding manual disk tuning. ASM also provides mirroring and striping, thus enhancing protection and performance, as in RAID systems. I discuss ASM in detail in Chapter 17.

Automatic SQL Tuning

In Oracle Database 11g, the database runs the SQL Tuning Advisor as part of its nightly maintenance tasks. The Automatic SQL Tuning Advisor makes recommendations to improve poorly performing SQL queries. I discuss automatic SQL tuning in Chapter 19.

Common Manageability Infrastructure

In order to be self-tuning and self-managing, a database must have the ability to automatically "learn" how it is being used. To this end, Oracle provides a common manageability infrastructure, which captures workload information and uses it to make sophisticated self-management decisions. The heart of the manageability infrastructure is the new *Automatic Workload Repository*, or AWR, which serves as a repository for all the other server components that aid automatic management of the database.

Oracle has built instrumentation into the various layers of its technology stack to capture the metadata that helps in diagnosing performance. It stores this data in the AWR and utilizes a comprehensive suite of management advisors to provide guidance on optimizing database operations. In the following sections, I briefly explain the various components of the common manageability infrastructure of Oracle Database 10*g*. You'll fully explore all of these in later chapters.

Automatic Workload Repository

The AWR plays the role of the "data warehouse of the database," and it is the basis for most of Oracle's self-management functionality. The AWR collects and maintains performance statistics for problem-detection and self-tuning purposes. By default, every 60 minutes the database collects statistical information from the SGA and stores it in the AWR, in the form of snapshots.

Several database components, such as the ADDM and other management advisors, use the AWR data to detect problems and for tuning the database. Like the ADDM, the AWR is automatically active upon starting the instance. You'll learn more about the AWR in Chapter 17.

Active Session History

The database samples all active sessions every second, and the session information is stored in a circular buffer in SGA. A session that's either waiting for a nonidle event or was on the CPU is considered an active session.

Even though the ADDM provides you with detailed instance information by periodically analyzing the AWR data, you are at a loss if you want to know what's happened in the database in a recent time period (such as in the past five minutes). Active Session History and its related historical views provide you with insight into current activity in the database. Chapter 19 discusses ASH in detail.

Fault Diagnosability Infrastructure

Occasionally, a database might encounter problems due to database code bugs or data corruption of some kind. Oracle Database 11*g* contains a *fault diagnosability infrastructure* for detecting, diagnosing, and resolving problems. The infrastructure may even help you prevent some types of problems by detecting them before they can do any damage to your database. You reap the following benefits from the advanced fault diagnosability infrastructure:

- Proactive detection of database problems
- Containment of the damage that could be caused by problems, by detecting them early and fixing them
- Reduction in problem diagnosis and resolution time
- Simplification of your communications with Oracle Support in the resolution of major problems, by enabling the easy transmission of problem data to the support personnel

The fault diagnosability infrastructure makes use of the following components to help the proactive monitoring, diagnosis, and resolution of problems and errors in the database:

- The health monitor performs proactive health checks to scope out problems in the database. When a critical error first occurs, the health monitor automatically captures what is called *first-failure data* and analyzes it. It creates a health check report and makes it part of the diagnostic data for that error. You can also manually invoke a health check if you suspect there might be a problem of some type in the database.

- Incident packaging service (IPS) lets you automatically package all diagnostic data concerning a critical error into a zipped file for transmitting to Oracle Support. Oracle Database 11*g* tags every trace file and other diagnostic data with the error's incident number. Thus, you don't have to go rummaging through various diagnostic directories for the relevant files for a database incident. IPS automatically gathers necessary files and adds them to the incident package for transmitting to Oracle.

- The Data Recovery Advisor shows you problems such as data corruption or a missing datafile and recommends repair options. You can accept the Data Recovery Advisor's recommendations or use the scripts it creates to manually repair the problem yourself.

- The Support Workbench lets you capture critical error diagnostics and transmit them to Oracle Support. You can set up things so you can directly transmit the incident file to Oracle Support from the Support Workbench, which you can access through the Enterprise Manager.

- The SQL Test Case Builder can reproduce problems caused by a SQL statement failure, so Oracle Support can resolve the problem for you.

- The Automatic Diagnostic Repository is a file-based repository for storing database diagnostic data such as the alert log, trace files, health monitor reports, and so on. This is a new feature of Oracle Database 11*g*. There is an ADR base under which each database instance as well as other Oracle product instances store their diagnostic data in a separate dedicated ADR home directory. The use of a consistent directory structure and diagnostic data format across products and instances lets Oracle Support easily analyze diagnostic data across instances.

- ADRCI is a command-line tool new in Oracle Database 11*g* that helps you view diagnostic data as well as package incident and problem information into zip files for transmission to Oracle Support. You can also incorporate ADRCI commands in script files.

Server-Generated Alerts

Oracle now sends out proactive server-generated alerts to warn you about problems like a tablespace running out of space. You can configure server-generated alerts by setting warning and critical thresholds on database metrics. The Oracle server automatically alerts you, for example, when the physical database reads per second cross a preset threshold value, or when a tablespace is low on free space. I discuss server-generated alerts in Chapter 18.

Automated Tasks Feature

Oracle automatically performs certain maintenance tasks, such as collecting optimizer statistics, by scheduling these jobs through the Oracle Scheduler. Oracle keeps track of which database objects don't have statistics or have stale statistics, and automatically refreshes statistics for these objects. In previous versions of Oracle, the DBA was responsible for collecting up-to-date statistics on all objects in the database. Now the database itself manages the collection of these statistics. I discuss automated tasks in Chapter 18.

Following are the three automated maintenance tasks that are run in the database on a nightly basis, during the maintenance window:

- *Automatic Optimizer Statistics Collection*: Collects statistics for the cost optimizer
- *Automatic Segment Advisor*: Identifies segments that have space you can reclaim
- *Automatic SQL Tuning Advisor*: Examines high-load SQL statements and makes recommendations for tuning them

You can, if you want, disable these jobs or modify the times when the database runs them.

■**Note** The manageability infrastructure, as well as all the automatic management features, are installed when you install the Oracle Database 11*g* software.

Advisory Framework

Oracle Database 11*g* comes with several management advisors, which help tune your SQL queries, size your memory and undo configuration parameters, and figure out the right indexes and materialized views for your database. The advisors use a uniform interface—the Advisor Central in the OEM, or the DBMS_ADVISOR package, when you invoke them manually. All the advisors use the Automatic Workload Repository as the source of their data and as a repository for their reports. Chapter 18 introduces the advisory framework in detail. Here's a brief description of the main management advisors, which you'll see in detail in later chapters.

SQL Tuning Advisor

The SQL Tuning Advisor provides recommendations for running SQL statements faster, by replacing manual tuning with tuning suggested by the Automatic Tuning Optimizer , which is the Cost-Based Optimizer in a tuning mode. The SQL Tuning Advisor calls the Automatic Tuning Optimizer to perform optimizer statistics analysis, SQL profiling, access-path analysis, and SQL structure analysis. I discuss the SQL Tuning Advisor in Chapter 19.

SQL Access Advisor

The SQL Access Advisor provides advice on materialized views, indexes, and materialized view logs, in order to design the most appropriate access structures to optimize SQL queries. Chapter 7 shows you how to use the SQL Access Advisor.

Segment Advisor

Often, table segments become fragmented over time. The Segment Advisor checks database object space usage and helps you regain excess space in segments by performing segment-shrinking operations. The Segment Advisor also helps in predicting the size of new tables and indexes and analyzing database-object growth trends. Chapter 17 shows you how to use the Segment Advisor.

Change Management

When you're making system changes such as upgrading your database to a new release or modifying the server configuration, you ideally would test and validate before making the changes in the production system. The difficulty, however, lies in the fact that it's not easy to simulate the production system on a test system, thus introducing a serious element of uncertainly when undertaking major system changes.

Oracle Database 11g has introduced two key features, called Database Replay and SQL Performance Analyzer, to help you manage change confidently. I briefly review these two interesting features in the following sections. Chapter 20 contains a detailed discussion of these two change management features.

Database Replay

Database Replay lets you test the impact of system changes by replaying and testing a production workload on a test system first. You first capture the production workload of the production database over a representative period of time such as a peak period. You then move this captured data over to a test system and replay the workload on that system, which you configure in an identical fashion to the production system. The replay of the production workload on the test system shows you the errors, data and performance divergence, and other statistics that help you determine whether you can safely make the change on the production system.

SQL Performance Analyzer

The SQL Performance Analyzer helps you assess the impact of a system change on the SQL statements that are part of your database workload. This analyzer gives you detailed information about the performance of the SQL statements, including before- and after-change exertion statistics. You can use the analysis to make a decision as to whether the system changes (such as a database upgrade) that you're planning will lead to an improvement in performance.

Efficient Managing and Monitoring

You've seen a bewildering number of tools and components of management infrastructure for monitoring and managing your Oracle databases. Traditionally, DBAs used a variety of methods to manage and monitor their databases, and complaints about frequent midnight pages and weekend work were common. You can avoid all that by taking a proactive approach and by automating management as much as you can—and with Oracle Database 11g, you can automate quite a bit!

My advice is not to reinvent the wheel by using outmoded monitoring scripts and management techniques. Here's a suggested way to use Oracle's variety of tools to maximum benefit:

- Make the OEM Database Control or Grid Control your main DBA tool. You can access all the monitoring and performance tools through the OEM. Configure the OEM to send you event-based pages or e-mails.

- Use RMAN as your main database backup and recovery solution.

- Configure the flash recovery area so you can automate backup and recovery.

- Use the Scheduler to automate your job system.

- Change your export and import scripts to the new Data Pump technology, both to save time and to take advantage of the new features.

- Wherever possible, use the Database Configuration Assistant to create new databases and the Database Upgrade Assistant (DBUA) to upgrade to Oracle Database 11g from earlier versions.

- Let Oracle automatically collect statistics—don't bother using the DBMS_STATS package or the ANALYZE command to manually collect optimizer statistics.

- Make sure you collect system statistics in addition to the automatic optimizer statistics collected by Oracle.

- Let Oracle manage the SGA and the PGA automatically with the new automatic memory management feature using the `MEMORY_TARGET` initialization parameter.

- Use Oracle's alert system to prevent space-related problems.

- Make use of the SQL Access Advisor to recommend new indexes, materialized views, and table and index partitioning.

- Let the Segment Advisor, which runs automatically, recommend objects to shrink. Shrinking objects will reclaim unused and fragmented space, as well as decrease query response time.

- Use the SQL Tuning Advisor to proactively tune problem SQL code.

I explain each of these topics in detail in this book.

CHAPTER 6

■ ■ ■

Managing Tablespaces

In the next chapter, you'll learn how Oracle DBAs create and manage the schema objects, which include tables, indexes, views, materialized views, synonyms, triggers, database links, and so on. Before we look at the various schema objects, though, you need to learn how to manage the all-important Oracle tablespaces. As you learned in Chapter 5, *tablespaces* are logical entities—each of an application's tables and indexes are stored as a segment, and the segments are stored in the data-files that are parts of tablespaces. A tablespace is thus a logical allocation of space for Oracle schema objects. There is, however, no one-to-one correspondence between a schema object like a table or index and a tablespace.

When you use the word *tablespace*, you're actually referring to a permanent tablespace, which is where you store your schema objects. (If you're migrating from a pre–Oracle Database 10*g* release database, you must first create the Sysaux tablespace before upgrading.) All permanent tablespaces are created by using Oracle datafiles. In addition to permanent tablespaces, you have the following important types of Oracle tablespaces:

- Temporary tablespaces are used to store objects for the duration of a user's session only. You use tempfiles to create a temporary tablespace, instead of datafiles.

- Undo tablespaces are a type of permanent tablespace that are used to store undo data, which is used to undo changes to data.

Every Oracle tablespace must have the mandatory System and Sysaux tablespaces. The System tablespace is permanent and contains vital data dictionary information that helps the database function. The System tablespace is the first tablespace you create when you create a new database. The Sysaux tablespace is auxiliary to the System tablespace, and it stores the metadata for various Oracle applications, as well as operational data for internal performance tools like the Automatic Workload Repository. Both the System and Sysaux tablespaces are treated differently from the other tablespaces. You can't rename or drop either of these tablespaces.

Before you can create tables or indexes, you should create the tablespaces to hold the data. Tablespaces consist of one or more datafiles (or tempfiles, if you are creating a temporary tablespace). Although your data and objects reside in operating system files, the organization of these files into Oracle tablespaces makes it easy for you to group related information.

You must first ensure that you have the necessary directory structure created on the host system, so you can create datafiles. Oracle will format the operating system files and allocate them to the tablespaces when you specify a datafile size and a fully specified filename during tablespace creation.

■**Note** Tablespaces are not unique to Oracle. DB2 databases also have tablespaces, although Microsoft SQL Server databases don't use them. The tempdb database in a SQL Server database corresponds to the temporary tablespace in an Oracle database.

Tablespace Extent Sizing and Space Management

Before you actually create a tablespace, you must be aware of two other important concepts: *extent sizing* and *segment space management*. I discuss these concepts in the two subsequent sections.

Allocating the Extent Size: Autoallocate vs. Uniform

Any time an Oracle object needs to grow in size, space is added to the object in terms of extents. When you create locally managed tablespaces, you have two options for managing the extent sizes: you can let the database automatically choose the extent size (by selecting the AUTOALLOCATE option) or you can specify that the tablespace be managed with uniform-sized extents (the UNIFORM option).

If you choose the UNIFORM option, you specify the actual size of the extents by using the SIZE clause. If you omit the SIZE clause, Oracle will create all extents with a uniform size of 1MB, but you can choose a much larger uniform extent size if you wish.

You can't change the extent size once you create the tablespace. If you think that all the segments in a tablespace are approximately of the same size, and that they'll grow in a similar fashion, you can choose the UNIFORM extent size option. If you do this, you can select a few extent sizes, create all your tablespaces with one of these uniform extent sizes, and allocate objects to the tablespaces based on their size.

Traditionally, Oracle DBAs worried about the number of extents in a segment. You should be more concerned about the size of the extents, though, since extent size has a bearing on the read and write performance of a segment. For example, if you choose a very small UNIFORM extent size, the database can't prefetch data or do multiblock reads, thus adversely impacting performance. Oracle suggests the following extent size guidelines, if you wish to set the extent sizes yourself:

- 64KB for small segments

- 1MB or medium segments

- 64MB for large segments

Under the AUTOALLOCATE option, Oracle will manage the extent size automatically. The extent size starts at 64KB and is progressively increased to 64MB by the database. The database automatically decides what size the new extent for an object should be, based on the segment's growth pattern. Interestingly, Oracle will *increase* the extent size for an object automatically as the object grows! Autoallocate is especially useful if you aren't sure about the growth rate of an object and you would like Oracle to deal with it.

■**Note** The default for tablespace extent management is the AUTOALLOCATE option.

If you know the exact space requirements for your objects, you can choose the UNIFORM extents option, which leads to efficient use of all available space. For example, say you know that your largest tables will consume a lot of space and will therefore need a very high extent size. Create a tablespace with a very large uniform size for such tables.

If you aren't sure what extent size will be best, AUTOALLOCATE will let the database determine the extent size but it may waste some space due to the varying size of extents.

■**Tip** Oracle recommends that unless all the objects in a tablespace are of the same size, you should use the AUTOALLOCATE feature. In addition to the simplicity of management, the AUTOALLOCATE option for extent sizing can potentially save you a significant amount of disk space, compared to the UNIFORM extent size option.

Automatic vs. Manual Segment Space Management

You can use the space in an Oracle block for two purposes: inserting fresh data or updating existing data in the blocks. When you delete data from a block, or an update statement changes the existing data length to a smaller size, there will be an increase in free space in the block. Segment space management is how Oracle manages this free space within the individual Oracle data blocks.

If you specify manual segment space management (by using the keyword MANUAL), the database manages the free space of segments in the tablespace using entities known as *freelists* and a pair of storage parameters, PCTFREE and PCTUSED. Oracle keeps track of how much free space is in its data blocks by maintaining freelists. Every table and index maintains a list of all its data blocks with free space greater than PCTUSED. That is, freelists contain the list of all blocks eligible for data insertion. Oracle first checks the appropriate freelist before making any insertions into tables or indexes. The Oracle database has to do a lot of work to maintain the freelists, as blocks reach their PCTUSED threshold after insertions and fall below the threshold due to deletions.

The PCTFREE parameter lets you reserve a percentage of space in each data block for future updates to existing data. For example, you may have some data on a person's address in a certain block. If you update that address later, so that it is larger, there should ideally be room in the existing block for the enlarged address. This is exactly what the PCTFREE parameter provides: room for the existing rows to grow. The PCTUSED parameter, on the other hand, deals with the threshold below which the used space must fall before new data can be placed in the blocks. For example, if the PCTUSED parameter is set at 40 percent, Oracle can't insert new data into the block until the amount of used space falls below this threshold level.

You can see easily how the PCTFREE and PCTUSED parameters together optimize the use of space within an Oracle block. Suppose 80 percent of the space in a block is filled with data. This will be the maximum amount of data that you can insert inside the block if the PCTFREE parameter is set to 20 percent. If some deletes take place in this block, there will be potential room to insert new rows, but Oracle uses the PCTUSED parameter in a clever way to keep any newly available free space from automatically being used for new inserts. Oracle incurs an overhead when it tries to use newly available free space in data blocks, so Oracle waits until the used space falls below the PCTUSED setting before using that free space. Until then, although there may be free spaces in partially used blocks, Oracle ignores them and goes to new data blocks to insert data.

The PCTFREE and PCTUSED parameters and the freelists comprise a manual way of checking for space, because you are making Oracle continually check for blocks with the right amount of free space. In a database with heavy updates, inserts, and deletes, this could lead to a slowdown of your transactions.

If you choose automatic segment space management when creating a tablespace (by specifying AUTO), the database will use *bitmaps* to track free space availability in a segment. A bitmap, which is contained in a bitmap block, indicates whether free space in a data block is below 25 percent, between 25 and 50 percent, between 50 and 75 percent, or above 75 percent. For an index block, the bitmaps can tell you whether the blocks are empty or formatted.

MIGRATING FROM DICTIONARY-MANAGED TO LOCALLY MANAGED TABLESPACES

Although locally managed tablespaces are the default in the Oracle Database 11*g* release, if you are upgrading an older database to the Oracle Database 11*g* release, you may want to migrate your tablespaces from being dictionary managed to locally managed. You can simply create new tablespaces, which will be locally managed by default, and then migrate all your tables to the new tablespaces using the ALTER TABLE command, as shown here:

```
SQL> ALTER TABLE emp MOVE TABLESPACE tbsp_new;
```

In order to move your indexes, use the ALTER INDEX REBUILD command, as shown here:

```
SQL> ALTER INDEX emp_pk_idx REBUILD
     TABLESPACE tbsp_idx_new
```

Once you finish migrating all your objects to the new locally managed tablespaces, drop your old tablespaces to reclaim the space.

If you don't want to create new tablespaces and go through the trouble of migrating all tables and indexes, you can use the PL/SQL package DBMS_SPACE_ADMIN, which enables you to perform the tablespace migration. You first need to migrate all the other tablespaces to a local management mode before you migrate the System tablespace. If you migrate your System tablespace from dictionary managed to locally managed first, all other tablespaces become read-only. Make sure that you first take a cold backup of the database before performing the tablespace migration. Here's an example of how you can migrate a dictionary-managed tablespace (USERS) to a locally managed tablespace:

```
SQL> EXECUTE dbms_space_admin.tablespace_migrate_to_local ('USERS');
```

The TABLESPACE_MIGRATE_TO_LOCAL procedure can be used online, while users are selecting and modifying data. However, if the DML operations need a new extent to be allocated, the operations will be blocked until the migration is completed.

Once you've migrated all your other tablespaces to locally managed tablespaces, you can move the System tablespace. Here's the command (you'll have to perform a few housekeeping chores beforehand, like making other tablespaces read only, etc.):

```
SQL> EXECUTE dbms_space_admin.tablespace_migrate_to_local ('SYSTEM');
```

Note that if you use the DBMS_SPACE_ADMIN package to migrate from dictionary-managed to locally managed tablespaces, you won't have the option of switching to the new Automatic Segment Space Management feature. All dictionary-managed tablespaces use the older manual segment space management by default, and you can't change to Automatic Segment Space Management when you migrate to locally managed tablespaces. Since Automatic Segment Space Management offers so many benefits (such as the ability to use the Online Segment Shrink capability of the Segment Advisor), you probably are better off biting the bullet and planning the migration of all your objects to newly created locally managed tablespaces. By default, Oracle creates all new tablespaces as locally managed with automatic segment space management.

In addition, if your current dictionary-managed tablespaces have a space fragmentation problem, the problem won't disappear when you convert to locally managed tablespaces by using an in-place migration with the DBMS_SPACE_ADMIN package. Again, you're better off creating a new locally managed tablespace and moving your objects into it. Chapter 17 shows how to perform such migrations easily, using Oracle's online table reorganization features.

Oracle recommends using automatic segment management and notes that it is scalable as well as efficient when it comes to space management. The performance gains are particularly striking if the database objects have varying row sizes. Maintenance of these bitmaps will consume space, but it is less than 1 percent for most large objects.

■Note The segment space management that you specify at tablespace creation time applies to all segments you later create in the tablespace.

Creating Tablespaces

You create tablespaces by using the CREATE TABLESPACE statement. To create a temporary tablespace, you must use the CREATE TEMPORARY TABLESPACE statement, and to create an undo tablespace, the CREATE UNDO TABLESPACE statement. The first step in creating a tablespace is to create a directory structure to which the database allocates the datafiles in the tablespace. Let's therefore look at datafiles first in the following section.

Data Files and Tablespaces

A tablespace can have one or more datafiles, and a datafile can belong to only one tablespace. Oracle creates a datafile for a tablespace when you specify the keyword DATAFILE during tablespace creation. The datafile that is created will be allocated a certain amount of physical disk space from the operating system disks. When Oracle first creates a datafile, it's empty but is allocated exclusively for Oracle's use, and the free space shown by the df -k command shows it as used space from the operating system's point of view.

As a segment grows in size, Oracle allocates extents to it from the free space in its datafiles. When the tablespace starts to fill up, you can either add new datafiles to it or extend the size of the existing datafiles by using the RESIZE command.

In light of the benefits they offer, you should always create locally managed tablespaces with the *default* AUTOALLOCATE option, unless you expect the tablespace to contain objects of the same size requiring same-sized extents. Similarly, choose the *default* automatic segment space management (by specifying SEGMENT SPACE MANAGEMENT AUTO when creating a tablespace) for managing segments, because it gives better performance and space utilization than manual segment space management. As mentioned previously, AUTOALLOCATE is the default for extent management, and automatic segment space management is the default for segment space management.

Let's create a (permanent) tablespace by using the CREATE TABLESPACE command. Note that you must use a DATAFILE clause before the file specification, since this is a permanent tablespace. For a temporary tablespace, you must use the clause TEMPFILE instead.

```
SQL> CREATE TABLESPACE test01
  2  DATAFILE '/pasx02/oradata/pasx/test01.dbf'
  3* SIZE 500M;
Tablespace created.
SQL>
```

■**Note** Non-DBA users must have the CREATE TABLESPACE system privilege granted in order to be able to create a tablespace.

In the previous tablespace creation statement, I didn't specify any choices for extent management (local or dictionary), extent size (uniform or autoallocate), or segment space management (auto or manual).

Now, let's execute the following query to determine the defaults for extent management, extent allocation type, and segment space management:

```
SQL> SELECT extent_management,
  2  allocation_type,
  3  segment_space_management
  4  FROM dba_tablespaces
  5* WHERE tablespace_name='TEST01';

EXTENT_MAN  ALLOCATIO  SEGMEN
----------  ---------  -------
LOCAL       SYSTEM     AUTO
SQL>
```

Note the defaults in Oracle Database 11*g* Release 1:

- *Extent management*: LOCAL
- *Allocation of extent sizes*: AUTOALLOCATE (shows up as SYSTEM in the preceding output)
- *Segment space management*: AUTO

I could create an identical tablespace by explicitly specifying all of these choices, as shown here:

```
SQL> CREATE TABLESPACE test02
  2  DATAFILE '/pasx02/oradata/pasx/test02.dbf' size 500M
  3  EXTENT MANAGEMENT local
  4  AUTOALLOCATE 500M
  5* SEGMENT SPACE MANAGEMENT auto;

Tablespace created.
SQL>
```

Although by default extent management is local for all permanent tablespaces, you specify the EXTENT MANAGEMENT LOCAL clause in the CREATE TABLESPACE statement if you want to specify the autoallocate or the uniform clause for extent allocation. You can use the same query that I used in the case of the test01 tablespace to verify that the two tablespaces, test01 and test02, have identical extent management (LOCAL), allocation type (AUTOALLOCATE), and segment space management (AUTO).

■**Note** By default, Oracle Database 11*g* tablespaces are locally managed, with automatic segment space management. When you create this type of tablespace, you can specify default storage parameters, like INITIAL, NEXT, PCTINCREASE, MINEXTENTS, or MAXEXTENTS, but the database will ignore the settings.

Extent Allocation and Deallocation

An Oracle extent consists of a set of contiguous data blocks, which are the smallest unit of space allocation in Oracle. Each Oracle data block corresponds to a specific number of bytes of disk space. Each of your database tables and indexes is called a *segment*, which is a set of extents allocated for a specific data structure. Note that extents are always contiguous in an operating system file, but not necessarily so on the disk itself. Extents help performance by enhancing Oracle's ability to prefetch data required for queries. Each partition of a table or index has its own segment (and besides table and index segments, you also have rollback, temporary, and undo segments in an Oracle database).

When Oracle needs to allocate an extent to a segment, it first selects a candidate datafile and searches the datafile's bitmap for the required number of adjacent free blocks. If it can't find the necessary free space in that datafile, Oracle will look in another datafile, or if there are no more, it will issue an error stating that it is out of free space.

Once Oracle allocates space to a segment by allocating a certain number of extents to it, that space will remain with the extent unless you make an effort to deallocate it. If you truncate a table with the DROP STORAGE option (TRUNCATE TABLE table_name DROP STORAGE), for example, Oracle deallocates the allocated extents. You can also manually deallocate unused extents using the following command:

```
SQL> ALTER TABLE table_name DEALLOCATE UNUSED;
```

When Oracle frees extents, it automatically modifies the bitmap in the datafile where the extents are located, to indicate that they are free and available again.

Storage Parameters

Remember that extents are the units of space allocation when you create tables and indexes in tablespaces. Here is how Oracle determines extent sizing and extent allocation when you create tablespaces:

- The default number of extents is 1. You can override it by specifying MINEXTENTS during tablespace creation.
- You don't have to provide a value to the MAXEXTENTS parameter when you use locally managed tablespaces. Under locally managed tablespaces, the MAXEXTENTS parameter is set to UNLIMITED, and you don't have to configure it at all.
- If you choose UNIFORM extent size, the size of all extents, including the first, will be determined by the extent size you choose.

Three examples of tablespace creation with various specifications for extent management are shown in Listings 6-1 through 6-3, and in the queries that follow the creation statements, you'll see the following headings:

- *Initial extent*: This storage parameter determines the initial amount of space that is allocated to any object you create in this tablespace. For example, if you specify a UNIFORM extent size of 10MB and specify an INITIAL_EXTENT value of 20MB, Oracle will create two 10MB-sized extents, to start with, for a new object. The example in Listing 6-1 shows an initial extent size of 5,242,880 bytes, based on the UNIFORM SIZE value, which is 5MB for this tablespace.
- *Next extent*: The NEXT_EXTENT storage parameter determines the size of the subsequent extents after the initial extent is created.
- *Extent management*: This column can show a value of LOCAL or DICTIONARY, for locally managed and dictionary-managed tablespaces, respectively.
- *Allocation type*: This column refers to the extent allocation, which can have a value of UNIFORM for uniform extent allocation, or SYSTEM for the AUTOALLOCATE option for sizing extents.
- *Segment space management*: This column shows the segment space management for the tablespace, which can be AUTO (the default) or MANUAL.

Listing 6-1. *Creating a Tablespace with Uniform Extents Using the UNIFORM SIZE Clause*

```
SQL> CREATE TABLESPACE test01
     DATAFILE '/pasx02/oradata/pasx/test01_01.dbf' SIZE 100M
     UNIFORM SIZE 5M;

Tablespace created.
SQL>

SQL> SELECT initial_extent,next_extent,
     extent_management, allocation_type,segment_space_management
     FROM dba_tablespaces;

INITIAL_EXTENT   NEXT_EXTENT   EXTENT_MAN   ALLOCATION_TYPE   SEGMENT_MAN
--------------   -----------   ----------   ---------------   -----------
 5242880          5242880       LOCAL        UNIFORM           AUTO
SQL>
```

If you choose to use the UNIFORM option for extent allocation but don't specify the additional SIZE clause, Oracle will create uniform extents of size 1MB by default, as shown in Listing 6-2.

Listing 6-2. *Creating a Tablespace with Uniform Extents*

```
SQL> CREATE TABLESPACE test01
     DATAFILE '/u09/oradata/test/test01.dbf' SIZE 100M
     UNIFORM;
```

```
Tablespace created.
SQL>

SQL> SELECT initial_extent,next_extent,
     extent_management,allocation_type,segment_space_management
     FROM dba_tablespaces;

INITIAL_EXTENT   NEXT_EXTENT   EXTENT_MAN   ALLOCATION_TYPE   SEGMENT_MAN
--------------   -----------   ----------   ---------------   -----------
1048576          1048576       LOCAL        UNIFORM           AUTO
SQL>
```

If you choose the AUTOALLOCATE method of sizing extents, Oracle will size the extents starting with a 64KB (65536 bytes) minimum extent size. Note that you can specify the autoallocate method for extent sizing either by explicitly specifying it with the AUTOALLOCATE keyword, or by simply leaving out the keyword altogether, since by default, Oracle uses the AUTOALLOCATE method anyway. Listing 6-3 shows an example that creates a tablespace with system-managed (automatically allocated) extents.

Listing 6-3. *Creating a Tablespace with Automatically Allocated Extents*

```
SQL> CREATE TABLESPACE test01
     DATAFILE '/pasx02/oradata/pasx/test01_01.dbf' SIZE 100M;

Tablespace created.
SQL>

SQL> SELECT initial_extent,next_extent,
     extent_management,allocation_type,segment_space_management
     FROM dba_tablespaces;

INITIAL_EXTENT    NEXT_EXTENT    EXTENT_MAN    ALLOCATION_TYPE    SEGMENT_MAN
--------------    -----------    ----------    ---------------    ----------
65536                            LOCAL         SYSTEM             AUTO
SQL>
```

Note that there is no value for the autoallocated tablespace for NEXT_EXTENT in Listing 6-3. When you choose the AUTOALLOCATE option (here it is chosen by default) rather than UNIFORM, Oracle allocates extent sizes starting with 64KB for the first extent. The next extent size will depend entirely upon the requirements of the segment (table, index, etc.) that you create in this tablespace.

Storage Allocation to Database Objects

You create tablespaces so that you can create various types of objects, such as tables and indexes, in them. When you create a new table or index segment, Oracle will use certain storage parameters to allocate the initial space and to alter allocations of space as the object grows in size.

You can omit the specification of storage parameters, such as INITIAL, NEXT, MINEXTENTS, MAXEX-TENTS, and PCTINCREASE, when you create objects like tables and indexes in the tablespaces. For locally managed tablespaces, Oracle will manage the storage extents, so there is very little for you to specify in terms of storage allocation parameters. Oracle retains the storage parameters for backward compatibility only.

You don't have to set the PCTUSED parameter if you're using locally managed tablespaces. If you set it, your object creation statement won't error out, but Oracle ignores the parameter. However, you can use the PCTFREE parameter to specify how much free space Oracle should leave in each block for future updates to data. The default is 10, which is okay if you don't expect the existing rows to get longer with time. If you do, you can change the PCTFREE parameter upward, say to 20 or 30 percent.

Of course, there is a price to pay for this—the higher the PCTFREE parameter, the more space you will "waste" in your database.

CREATING TABLESPACES WITH NONSTANDARD BLOCK SIZES

The default block size for all tablespaces is determined by the DB_BLOCK_SIZE initialization parameter for your database. You have the option of creating tablespaces with block sizes that are different from the standard database block size. In order to create a tablespace with a nonstandard block size, you must have already set the DB_CACHE_SIZE initialization parameter, and at least one DB_nK_CACHE_SIZE initialization parameter. For example, you must set the DB_16K_CACHE_SIZE parameter, if you wish to create tablespaces with a 16KB block size.

By using a nonstandard block size, you can customize a tablespace for the types of objects it contains. For example, you can allocate a large table that requires a large number of reads and writes to a tablespace with a large block size. Similarly, you can place smaller tables in tablespaces with a smaller block size.

Here are some points to keep in mind if you're considering using the multiple block size feature for tablespaces:

- Multiple buffer pools enable you to configure up to a total of five different pools in the buffer cache, each with a different block size. (This is discussed in Chapter 4.)

- The System tablespace always has to be created with the standard block size specified by the DB_BLOCK_SIZE parameter in the init.ora file.

- You can have up to four nonstandard block sizes.

- You specify the block size for tablespaces in the CREATE TABLESPACE statement by using the BLOCKSIZE clause.

- The nonstandard block sizes must be 2KB, 4KB, 8KB, 16KB, or 32KB. One of these sizes, of course, will have to be chosen as the standard block size by using the DB_BLOCK_SIZE parameter in the init.ora file.

- If you're transporting tablespaces between databases, using tablespaces with multiple block sizes makes it easier to transport tablespaces of different block sizes.

You use the BLOCKSIZE keyword when you create a tablespace, to specify a nonstandard block size. The following statement creates a tablespace with a nonstandard block size of 16KB (the standard block size, which is determined by the value you specify for the DB_BLOCK_SIZE initialization parameter, is 8 KB):

```
SQL> CREATE TABLESPACE test01 datafile '/u09/oradata/testdb/test01.dbf'
     BLOCKSIZE 16K;
```

Adding Space to a Tablespace

When your tablespace is filling up with table and index data, you need to expand its size. You do this by adding more physical file space with the ALTER TABLESPACE command:

```
SQL> ALTER TABLESPACE test01
     ADD DATAFILE '/finance10/app/oracle/finance/test01.dbf'
     SIZE 1000M;
```

You can also increase or decrease the size of the tablespace by increasing or decreasing the size of the tablespace's datafiles with the RESIZE option. You usually use the RESIZE option to correct data-file sizing errors. Note that you can't decrease a datafile's size beyond the space that is already occupied by objects in the datafile.

The following example shows how you can manually resize a datafile. Originally, the file was 250MB, and the following command doubles the size of the file to 500MB. Note that you need to use the ALTER DATABASE command, not the ALTER TABLESPACE command, to resize a datafile.

```
SQL> ALTER DATABASE DATAFILE '/finance10/oradata/data_09.dbf'
     RESIZE 500m;
```

You can use the AUTOEXTEND provision when you create a tablespace or when you add datafiles to a tablespace to tell Oracle to automatically extend the size of the datafiles in the tablespace to a specified maximum. Here's the syntax for using the AUTOEXTEND feature:

```
SQL> ALTER TABLESPACE data01
     ADD DATAFILE '/finance10/oradata/data01.dbf' SIZE 200M
     AUTOEXTEND ON
     NEXT 10M
     MAXSIZE 1000M;
SQL>
```

In the preceding example, 10MB extents will be added to the tablespace when space is required, as specified by the AUTOEXTEND parameter. The MAXSIZE parameter limits the tablespace to 1,000MB. If you wish, you can also specify MAXSIZE UNLIMITED, in which case there is no set maximum size for this datafile and hence for the tablespace. However, you must ensure that you have enough operating system disk space to accommodate this.

Oracle also offers the *Resumable Space Allocation* feature, which temporarily suspends operations that might otherwise fail for lack of space, and then resumes the operations after you add space to the database object. This makes the use of the AUTOEXTEND feature less attractive. The Resumable Space Allocation feature is discussed in detail in Chapter 8.

Removing Tablespaces

Sometimes you may want to get rid of a tablespace. You can remove a tablespace from the database by issuing this simple command:

```
SQL> DROP TABLESPACE test01;
```

If the test01 tablespace includes tables or indexes when you issue a DROP TABLESPACE command, you'll get an error. You can either move the objects to a different tablespace or, if the objects are dispensable, you can use the following command, which will drop the tablespace and all the objects that are part of the tablespace:

```
SQL> DROP TABLESPACE test01 INCLUDING CONTENTS;
```

■**Caution** In Oracle Database 10*g*, database objects such as tables aren't dropped right away when you issue a DROP TABLE command. Instead, they go to the Recycle Bin (discussed in Chapter 16), from which you can reclaim the table you "dropped."

When you use the DROP TABLESPACE . . . INCLUDING CONTENTS command, the objects in the tablespace are dropped right away, bypassing the Recycle Bin! Any objects belonging to this tablespace that are in the Recycle Bin are also purged permanently when you issue this command. If you omit the INCLUDING CONTENTS clause and the tablespace contains objects, the statement will fail, but any objects in the Recycle Bin will be dropped.

The DROP TABLESPACE . . . INCLUDING CONTENTS statement will not release the datafiles back to the operating system's file system. To do so, you have to either manually remove the datafiles that were a part of the tablespace or issue the following command to remove both the objects and the physical datafiles at once:

```
SQL> DROP TABLESPACE test01 INCLUDING CONTENTS AND DATAFILES;
```

The preceding statement will automatically drop the datafiles along with the tablespace.

If there are referential integrity constraints in other tables that refer to the tables in the tablespace you intend to drop, you need to use the following command:

```
SQL> DROP TABLESPACE test01 CASCADE CONSTRAINTS;
```

The one tablespace you *can't* drop, of course, is the System tablespace. You also can't drop the Sysaux tablespace during normal database operation. However, provided you have the SYSDBA privilege and you have started the database in the MIGRATE mode, you'll be able to drop the Sysaux tablespace.

Of course, there aren't many reasons why you would want to drop your Sysaux tablespace. If you simply want to move certain users out of this tablespace, you can always use the appropriate move procedure specified in the V$SYSAUX_OCCUPANTS view.

The V$SYSAUX_OCCUPANTS view shows you details about the space usage by each occupant of the Sysaux tablespace. It also provides you with the move procedure to use for a given occupant, if you want to move the occupant to a different tablespace. Here's a sample query using this view:

```
SQL> SELECT  occupant_name, schema_name, space_usage_kbytes,
  2* move_procedureFROM V$SYSAUX_OCCUPANTS;
```

OCCUPANT_NAME	SCHEMA_NAME	SPACE_USG_KB	MOVE_PROCEDURE
LOGMNR	SYSTEM	7488	SYS.DBMS_LOGMNR_D.SET_TABLESPACE
. . .			
ULTRASEARCH	WKSYS	7296	MOVE_WK

```
20 rows selected.
SQL>
```

If you wish to move the Sysaux occupant ULTRASEARCH to a new tablespace called ULTRA1, you can do so using the MOVE_WK procedure owned by the WKSYS schema, as shown here:

```
SQL> EXECUTE WKSYS.MOVE_WK('ULTRA1');
```

This section introduced you to several useful data dictionary views that help you manage the database. Although using the OEM Database Control reduces the need to use most of these views on a frequent basis, it's important to master the contents of these views, so you know where the database stores important information.

Number of User Tablespaces

Oracle DBAs have traditionally used a large number of tablespaces for managing database objects. Unfortunately, the larger the number of tablespaces in your database, the more time you'll have to spend on mundane tasks, such as monitoring space and allocating space to the tablespaces. Disk contention between indexes and tables and other objects were pointed out as the reason for creating large numbers of tablespaces, but with the types of disk management used today in most places, where Logical Volume Managers stripe operating system files over several disk spindles, traditional tablespace-creation rules don't apply. You're better off using a very small number of tablespaces—perhaps just four or five—to hold all your data.

Tablespace Quotas

You can assign a user a tablespace quota, thus limiting the user to a certain amount of storage space in the tablespace. You can do this when you create the user, or by using the ALTER USER statement at a later time. Chapter 11 shows you how to assign tablespace quotas to users.

In Chapter 9, I discuss Oracle's Resumable Space Allocation feature. User-quota-exceeded errors are an important type of resumable statement. When a user exceeds the assigned quota, Oracle will automatically raise a space-quota-exceeded error.

Proactive Tablespace Space Alerts

If a segment needs to be extended to accommodate the insertion of new data, there must be free space available in the tablespace that the segment belongs to. If not, the new data can't be inserted, and you'll get an Oracle error indicating that the operation failed due to the lack of space in the tablespace.

You can write scripts to alert you that a tablespace is about to run out of space, but the database itself can send you proactive space alerts for all locally managed tablespaces, including the undo tablespace. The Oracle database stores information on tablespace space usage in its system global area (SGA). The new Oracle background process MMON checks tablespace usage every ten minutes and raises alerts when necessary.

The database will send out two types of tablespace out-of-space alerts: a warning alert and a critical alert. The warning alert cautions you that a tablespace's free space is running low, and the critical alert tells you that you should immediately take care of the free space problem so the database doesn't issue "out of space" errors. Both of these alerts are based on threshold values called warning and critical thresholds, which you can modify.

■**Tip** When you *upgrade* to Oracle Database 11*g*, by default, both the percent full and the bytes remaining alerts are disabled. You must explicitly set both alerts yourself. For a given tablespace, you can use either or both types of alerts.

Types of Alert Thresholds

There are two ways to set alert thresholds: you can specify that the database alert be based on the *percent of space used* or on the *number of free bytes left in the tablespace*:

- *Percent full*: The database issues an alert when the space used in a tablespace reaches or crosses a preset percentage of total space. For a *new* database, 85 percent full is the threshold for the warning alerts, and 97 percent full is the threshold for the critical alerts. You can, if you wish, change these values and set, for example, 90 and 98 percent as the warning and critical thresholds.

- *Bytes remaining*: When the free space falls below a certain amount (specified in KB), Oracle issues an alert. For example, you can use a warning threshold of 10,240KB and a critical threshold of 4,096KB for a tablespace. By default, the "bytes remaining alerts" (both warning and critical) in a *new* database are disabled, since the defaults for both types of bytes-remaining thresholds are set to zero. You can set them to a size you consider appropriate for each tablespace.

■**Tip** You can disable the warning or critical threshold tablespace alerts by setting the threshold values to zero.

Setting the Alert Thresholds

The easiest way to set and modify tablespace space alerts is by using the Oracle Enterprise Manager (OEM). Just go to the OEM Home Page and select Administration ➤ Related Links ➤ Manage Metrics ➤ Edit Thresholds. From the Edit Thresholds page, you can set warning and critical thresholds for your tablespaces. You can also specify a response action when an alert is received, in the form of a command or script that is made accessible to the Management Agent.

You can also use the Oracle-provided PL/SQL package DBMS_SERVER_ALERT to set warning and critical space alerts. Listing 6-4 shows how you can set a "bytes remaining" alert threshold using the warning value and the critical value attributes.

Listing 6-4. *Setting a Tablespace Alert Threshold*

```
SQL> BEGIN
       DBMS_SERVER_ALERT.SET_THRESHOLD(
       metrics_id              => DBMS_SERVER_ALERT.TABLESPACE_BYT_FREE,
       warning_operator        => DBMS_SERVER_ALERT.OPERATOR_LE,
       warning_value           => '10240',
       critical_operator       => DBMS_SERVER_ALERT.OPERATOR_LE,
       critical_value          => '2048',
       observation_period      => 1,
       consecutive_occurrences => 1,
       instance_name           => NULL,
       object_type             => DBMS_SERVER_ALERT.OBJECT_TYPE_TABLESPACE,
       object_name             => 'USERS');
     END;
SQL>
```

In Listing 6-4, note that the warning_value attribute sets the bytes-remaining alert warning threshold at 10MB and the critical_value attribute sets the critical threshold at 2MB.

You can always add a datafile to a tablespace to get it out of the low-free-space situation. However, one easy way to avoid this problem altogether, in most cases, is to use autoextensible tablespaces. Autoextensible tablespaces will automatically grow in size when table or index data grows over time. For a new database, this may prove to be an excellent solution, saving you from out-of-space errors if you create tablespaces that are too small and from wasting space if you create too large a tablespace. It's very easy to create an autoextensible tablespace—all you have to do is include the AUTOEXTEND clause for the datafile when you create or alter a tablespace. Just make sure that you have enough free storage to accommodate the autoextensible datafile.

Managing Logging of Redo Data

When you perform an insert, update, or delete operation, the database produces redo records to protect the changed data. The database makes use of the redo records when it has to recover a database following a media or an instance failure. However, the recording of the redo data creates an overhead. When you perform an operation such as a create table as select . . . (CTAS) operation, you really don't need the redo data, because you can rerun the statement if it fails midway. You can't switch off the production of redo data for normal DML activity in your database. However, you can do so for a direct load operation, as I explain in Chapter 14.

You can specify the NOLOGGING clause when you create a tablespace, so the database doesn't produce any redo records for any of the objects in that tablespace. When you specify the NOLOGGGING option in a CREATE TABLESPACE statement, all database objects that you create in that tablespace will inherit that attribute. However, you can specify the LOGGING clause in a CREATE TABLE or ALTER TABLE statement to override the NOLOGGING clause that you specified for the tablespace.

Managing the Availability of a Tablespace

You can change the status of a tablespace to offline, to make a tablespace or a set of tablespaces unavailable to the users of the database. When you make a tablespace offline, all tables and indexes in that tablespace become out of reach of the users. You normally take tablespaces offline when you want to make an application unavailable to users by or when you want to perform management operations such as renaming or relocation the datafiles that are part of a tablespace. When you take a tablespace offline, the database automatically takes all datafiles that are part of that tablespace offline.

You can't take the System or the temporary tablespaces offline. You can specify either the NORMAL1, TEMPORARY, or IMMEDIATE parameters as options to the tablespace offline statement. Here's how you choose among the three options:

- If there are no error conditions for any of the datafiles of tablespace, use the OFFLINE NORMAL clause, which is the default when you offline a tablespace.

- Using the OFFLINE NORMAL clause is considered taking a tablespace offline cleanly, which means the database won't have to perform a media recovery on the tablespace before bringing it back online. If you can't take the tablespace offline with the OFFLINE NORMAL clause, specify the OFFLINE TEMPORARY clause. If the NORMAL and TEMPORARY settings don't work, specify the OFFLINE IMMEDIATE clause, as shown here:

```
SQL> ALTER TABLESPACE users OFFLINE IMMEDIATE;
```

When you specify the OFFLINE IMMEDIATE clause, the database requires media recovery of the tablespace before it can bring the tablespace online.

When you are ready to bring a tablespace online, issue the following statement:

```
SQL> ALTER TABLESPACE <tablespace_name> ONLINE;
```

Renaming Tablespaces

You can rename tablespaces by using the ALTER TABLESPACE statement, as shown here:

```
SQL> ALTER TABLESPACE test01 RENAME TO test02;

Tablespace altered.
SQL>
```

You can rename both permanent and temporary tablespaces, but there are a few restrictions:

- You can't rename the System and Sysaux tablespaces.
- The tablespace being renamed must have all its datafiles online.
- If the tablespace is read-only, renaming it doesn't update the file headers of its datafiles.

Sometimes, you may need to rename a datafile. The process for this is straightforward:

1. Take the datafile offline by taking its tablespace offline. Use the following command:

   ```
   SQL> ALTER TABLESPACE test01 OFFLINE NORMAL;

    Tablespace altered.
   SQL>
   ```

2. Rename the file using an operating system utility such as cp or mv in UNIX, or copy in Windows.

   ```
   $ cp /u01/app/oracle/test01.dbf    /u02/app/oracle/test01.dbf
   ```

3. Rename the datafile before bringing it online by using the following command:

```
SQL> ALTER TABLESPACE test01
  2  RENAME DATAFILE
  3  '/u01/app/oracle/test01.dbf'
  4  TO
  5* '/u02/app/oracle/test01.dbf';

Tablespace altered.
SQL>
```

Read-Only Tablespaces

By default, all Oracle tablespaces are both readable and writable when created. However, you can specify that a tablespace cannot be written to by making it a read-only tablespace. The command to do so is simple:

```
SQL> ALTER TABLESPACE test01 READ ONLY;
```

If you want to make this read-only tablespace writable again, you can use the following command:

```
SQL> ALTER TABLESPACE test01 READ WRITE;
```

Taking Tablespaces Offline

Except for the System tablespace, you can take any or all of the tablespaces *offline*—that is, you can make them temporarily unavailable to users. You usually need to take tablespaces offline when a datafile within a tablespace contains errors or you are changing code in an application that accesses one of the tablespaces being taken offline.

Four modes of offlining are possible with Oracle tablespaces: *normal, temporary, immediate*, and *for recovery*. Except for the normal mode, which is the default mode of taking tablespaces offline, all the other modes can involve recovery of the included datafiles or the tablespace itself. You can take any tablespace offline with no harm by using the following command:

```
SQL> ALTER TABLESPACE index_01 OFFLINE NORMAL;
```

Oracle will ensure the checkpointing of all the datafiles in the tablespace (index_01 in this example) before it takes the tablespace offline. Thus, there is no need for recovery when you later bring the tablespace back online.

To bring the tablespace online, use the following command:

```
SQL> ALTER TABLESPACE index_01 ONLINE;
```

Temporary Tablespaces

A temporary tablespace, contrary to what the name might indicate, does exist on a permanent basis as do other tablespaces, such as the System and Sysaux tablespaces. However, the data in a temporary tablespace is of a temporary nature, which persists only for the length of a user session. Oracle uses temporary tablespaces as work areas for tasks such as sort operations for users and sorting during index creation. Oracle doesn't allow users to create objects in a temporary tablespace. By definition, the temporary tablespace holds data only for the duration of a user's session, and the data can be shared by all users. The performance of temporary tablespaces is extremely critical when your application uses sort- and hash-intensive queries, which need to store transient data in the temporary tablespace.

■**Note** Oracle writes data in the program global area (PGA) in 64KB chunks. Therefore, Oracle advises you to create temporary tablespaces with extent sizes that are multiples of 64KB. For large data warehousing and decision-support system databases, which make extensive use of temporary tablespaces, the recommended extent size is 1MB.

The very first statement after starting up an instance that uses the temporary tablespace creates a sort segment, which is shared by all sort operations in the instance. When you shut down the database, the database releases this sort segment. You can query the V$SORT_SEGMENT view to review the allocation and deallocation of space to this sort segment. You can see who's currently using the sort segment by querying the V$SORT_USAGE view. Use the V$TEMPFILE and DBA_TEMP_FILES views to find out details about the tempfiles currently allocated to a temporary tablespace.

As mentioned earlier, you must use the TEMPFILE clause when specifying the files that are part of any temporary tablespace. There is really no difference, as far as you are concerned, between a DATA-FILE clause that you specify for permanent tablespaces and the TEMPFILE clause you specify for temporary tablespaces. However, Oracle distinguishes between the two types of files. Tempfiles have little or no redo data associated with them.

Creating a Temporary Tablespace

You create a temporary tablespace the same way as you do a permanent tablespace, with the difference being that you specify the TEMPORARY clause in the CREATE TABLESPACE statement and substitute the TEMPFILE clause for the DATAFILE clause. Here's an example:

```
SQL> CREATE TEMPORARY TABLESPACE temp_demo
     TEMPFILE 'temp01.dbf' SIZE 500M
     AUTOEXTEND ON;
```

The SIZE clause in the second line specifies the size of the datafile and hence the size of the temporary tablespace, as 500MB. In the preceding statement, the AUTOEXTEND ON clause will automatically extend the size of the temporary file, and thus the size of the temporary tablespace. By default, all temporary tablespaces are created with uniformly sized extents, with each extent sized at 1MB. You can, however, specify the UNIFORM SIZE clause to specify a nondefault extent size, as shown in the following statement:

```
SQL> CREATE TEMPORARY TABLESPACE temp_demo
     TEMPFILE 'temp01.dbf' SIZE 500M
     EXTENT MANAGEMENT LOCAL UNIFORM SIZE 16M;
```

In the previous statement, the EXTENT MANAGEMENT clause is optional. The UNIFORM SIZE clause specifies a custom extent size of 16MB instead of the default extent size of 1MB.

■**Tip** You use the TEMPFILE clause, not the DATAFILE clause, when you allocate space to a temporary tablespace.

It's common to create a single temporary tablespace (usually named Temp) for each database, but you can have multiple temporary tablespaces, which are part of a temporary tablespace group, if your database needs them to support heavy sorting operations.

In order to *drop* a default temporary tablespace, you must first use the ALTER TABLESPACE command to create a new default tablespace for the database. You can then drop the previous default temporary tablespace like any other tablespace.

■**Note** Oracle recommends that you use a locally managed temporary tablespace with a 1MB uniform extent size as your default temporary tablespace.

Altering a Temporary Tablespace

You can issue the `ALTER TEMPORARY TABLESPACE` statement to perform various temporary tablespace management tasks, including adding a tempfile to grow a temporary tablespace. Here's an example showing how you can make the temporary tablespace larger:

```
SQL> ALTER TABLESPACE temp
    ADD TEMPFILE '/u01/app/oracle/tempfile/tempo3.dbf' size 1000M reuse;
```

You can similarly use the following `ALTER TABLESPACE` command to resize a tempfile:

```
SQL> ALTER DATABASE TEMPFILE '/u01/app/oracle/tempfile/temp03.dbf'
    RESIZE 200M;
```

And you can use the following statement to drop a tempfile and remove the operating system file:

```
SQL> ALTER DATABASE TEMPFILE '/u01/app/oracle/tempfile/temp03.dbf'
    DROP INCLUDING DATAFILES;
```

When you drop a tempfile belonging to a temporary tablespace, the tablespace itself will remain in use.

You can shrink a temporary tablespace, just as you can a normal tablespace. The following example shows how to issue the `ALTER TABLESPACE` statement to shrink a temporary tablespace:

```
SQL> ALTER TABLESPACE temp SHRINK SPACE KEEP 500m;
```

Shrinking Temporary Tablespaces

You may have to increase the size of a temporary tablespace to accommodate an unusually large job that makes use of the temporary tablespace. After the completion of the job, you can shrink the temporary tablespace using the clause `SHRINK SPACE` in an `ALTER TABLESPACE` statement. Here's an example:

```
SQL> ALTER TABLESPACE temp SHRINK SPACE;

Tablespace altered.
SQL>
```

The `SHRINK SPACE` clause will shrink all tempfiles to a minimum size, which is about 1MB. You can employ the `KEEP` clause to specify a minimum size for the tempfiles, as shown here:

```
SQL> ALTER tablespace temp SHRINK SPACE
    KEEP 250m;
```

Oracle uses a peculiar logic when shrinking tempfiles in a temporary tablespace. Let's say you have a temporary tablespace that contains two 1GB tempfiles. You issue a command to shrink the tablespace to 1GB, a shown here:

```
SQL> ALTER TABLESPACE temp SHRINK SPACE KEEP 1000M;

Tablespace altered.
SQL>
```

If you query the V$TEMPFILE view, you'll see this:

```
SQL> SELECT file#, name, bytes/1024/1024 mb FROM v$tempfile;

FILE#    NAME                                      MB
-----    -------------------------------------     ---------
1        /u01/app/oracle/tempfile/temp01.dbf       999.9375
2        /u01/app/oracle/tempfile/temp02.dbf'      1.0625
```

The database shrinks one of the two tempfiles all the way down to 1MB and the other only by 1MB, leaving 999MB of space intact in that tempfile. If your goal is to shrink a particular tempfile down to a certain minimum, you can do so by specifying the name of the particular tempfile you want to shrink, as shown here:

```
SQL> ALTER TABLESPACE temp SHRINK SPACE
     TEMPFILE tempfile '/u01/app/oracle/oradata/prod1/temp02.dbf'
     KEEP 100m;


Tablespace altered.
SQL>
```

The ALTER TABLESPACE statement shown here shrinks just the tempfile you list by the amount you specify with the KEEP clause. It leaves the other tempfiles in the TEMP tablespace alone. The KEEP clause in the previous statement ensures that the tempfile I specify retains 500MB of space. The following example shows how to shrink a single tempfile without any specific retained space:

```
SQL> ALTER TABLESPACE temp
     SHRINK tempfile '/u01/app/oracle/tempfile/temp03.dbf';
```

Since I didn't specify the KEEP clause in the previous statement, the database shrinks the tempfile I specified to the minimum possible size, which is about 1MB.

Default Temporary Tablespace

When you create database users, you must assign a default temporary tablespace in which they can perform their temporary work, such as sorting. If you neglect to explicitly assign a temporary tablespace, the users will use the critical System tablespace as their temporary tablespace, which could lead to fragmentation of that tablespace, besides filling it up and freezing database activity. You can avoid these undesirable situations by creating a *default* temporary tablespace for the database when creating a database by using the DEFAULT TEMPORARY TABLESPACE clause. Oracle will then use this as the temporary tablespace for all users for whom you don't explicitly assign a temporary tablespace. I show the creation of the default temporary tablespace in Chapter 10, where I explain how to create a new Oracle database.

Note that if you didn't create a *default* temporary tablespace while creating your database, it isn't too late to do so later. You can just create a temporary tablespace, as shown in the preceding example, and make it the default temporary tablespace for the database, with a statement like this:

```
SQL> ALTER DATABASE DEFAULT TEMPORARY TABLESPACE temptbs02;
```

You can find out the name of the current default temporary tablespace for your database by executing the following query:

```
SQL> SELECT PROPERTY_NAME, PROPERTY_VALUE
     FROM database_properties
     WHERE property_name='DEFAULT_TEMP_TABLESPACE';


PROPERTY_NAME                     PROPERTY_VALUE
----------------------            ------------------
DEFAULT_TEMP_TABLESPACE           TEMP
```

Note You can't use the AUTOALLOCATE clause for temporary tablespaces. By default, all temporary tablespaces are created with locally managed extents of a uniform size. The default extent size is 1MB, as for all other tablespaces, but you can use a different extent size if you wish when creating the temporary tablespace.

Temporary Tablespace Groups

Large transactions can sometimes run out of temporary space. Large sort jobs, especially those involving tables with many partitions, lead to heavy use of the temporary tablespaces, thus potentially leading to a performance hit. Oracle Database 10*g* introduced the concept of a *temporary tablespace group*, which allows a user to utilize multiple temporary tablespaces simultaneously in different sessions.

Here are some of the main characteristics of a temporary tablespace group:

- A temporary tablespace group must consist of at least one tablespace. There is no explicit maximum number of tablespaces.

- If you delete all members from a temporary tablespace group, the group is automatically deleted as well.

- A temporary tablespace group has the same namespace as the temporary tablespaces that are part of the group.

- The name of a temporary tablespace cannot be the same as the name of any tablespace group.

- When you assign a temporary tablespace to a user, you can use the temporary tablespace group name instead of the actual temporary tablespace name. You can also use the temporary tablespace group name when you assign the default temporary tablespace for the database.

Benefits of Temporary Tablespace Groups

Using a temporary tablespace group, rather than the usual single temporary tablespace, provides several benefits:

- SQL queries are less likely to run out of sort space because the query can now simultaneously use several temporary tablespaces for sorting.

- You can specify multiple default temporary tablespaces at the database level.

- Parallel execution servers in a parallel operation will efficiently utilize multiple temporary tablespaces.

- A single user can simultaneously use multiple temporary tablespaces in different sessions.

Creating a Temporary Tablespace Group

When you assign the first temporary tablespace to a tablespace group, you automatically create the temporary tablespace group. To create a tablespace group, simply specify the TABLESPACE GROUP clause in the CREATE TABLESPACE statement, as shown here:

```
SQL> CREATE TEMPORARY TABLESPACE temp01
     TEMPFILE '/u01/oracle/oradata/temp01_01.dbf'
     SIZE 500M TABLESPACE GROUP tmpgrp1;
```

The preceding SQL statement will create a new temporary tablespace, temp01, along with the new tablespace group named tmpgrp1. Oracle creates the new tablespace group because the key clause TABLESPACE GROUP was used while creating the new temporary tablespace.

You can also create a temporary tablespace group by specifying the same TABLESPACE GROUP clause in an ALTER TABLESPACE command, as shown here:

```
SQL> ALTER TABLESPACE temp02
     TABLESPACE GROUP tmpgrp1

Tablespace altered.
SQL>
```

The preceding statement will cause Oracle to create a new group named tmpgrp1, since there wasn't a prior temporary tablespace group with that name.

If you specify a pair of quotes (' ') for the tablespace group name, you are implicitly telling Oracle not to allocate that temporary tablespace to a tablespace group. Here's an example:

```
SQL> CREATE TEMPORARY TABLESPACE temp02
     TEMPFILE '/u01/oracle/oradata/temp02_01.dbf'  SIZE 500M
     TABLESPACE GROUP '';
```

The preceding statement creates a temporary tablespace called temp02, which is a regular temporary tablespace and doesn't belong to a temporary tablespace group.

If you completely omit the TABLESPACE GROUP clause, you'll create a regular temporary tablespace, which is not part of any temporary tablespace group:

```
SQL> CREATE TEMPORARY TABLESPACE temp03
     TEMPFILE '/u01/oracle/oradata/temp03_01.dbf' SIZE 500M;
  Tablespace created.
SQL>
```

Adding a Tablespace to a Temporary Tablespace Group

As shown in the preceding section, you can add a temporary tablespace to a group by using the ALTER TABLESPACE command. You can also change which group a temporary tablespace belongs to by using the ALTER TABLESPACE command. For example, you can specify that the tablespace temp02 belongs to the tmpgrp2 group by issuing the following statement:

```
SQL> ALTER TABLESPACE temp02 TABLESPACE GROUP tmpgrp2;
```

The database will create a new group with the name tmpgrp2 if there is no such group already.

Setting a Group as the Default Temporary Tablespace for the Database

You can use a temporary tablespace group as your default temporary tablespace for the database. If you issue the following statement, all users without a default tablespace can use any temporary tablespace in the tmpgrp1 group as their default temporary tablespaces:

```
SQL> ALTER DATABASE DEFAULT TEMPORARY TABLESPACE tmpgrp1;
```

The preceding ALTER DATABASE statement assigns *all the tablespaces* in tmpgrp1 as the default temporary tablespaces for the database.

Assigning Temporary Tablespace Groups When Creating and Altering Users

When you create new users, you can assign them to a temporary tablespace group instead of to the usual single temporary tablespace. Here's an example:

```
SQL> CREATE USER salapati IDENTIFIED BY sammyy1
     DEFAULT TABLESPACE users
     TEMPORARY TABLESPACE tmpgrp1;
User created.
```

```
SQL>
```

Once you create a user, you can also use the ALTER USER statement to change the temporary tablespace group of the user. Here's a SQL statement that does this:

```
SQL> ALTER USER salapati TEMPORARY TABLESPACE tmpgrp2;
```

Viewing Temporary Tablespace Group Information

You can use the new DBA_TABLESPACE_GROUPS data dictionary view to manage the temporary tablespace groups in your database. Here is a simple query on the view that shows the names of all tablespace groups:

```
SQL> SELECT group_name, tablespace_name
     FROM dba_tablespace_groups;

GROUP_NAME          TABLESPACE_NAME
----------          ---------------
TMPGRP1             TEMP01
SQL>
```

You can also use the DBA_USERS view to find out which temporary tablespaces or temporary tablespace groups are assigned to each user. Here's an example:

```
SQL> SELECT username, temporary_tablespace
     FROM dba_users;

USERNAME            TEMPORARY_TABLESPACE
--------            --------------------
SYS                 TEMP
SYSTEM              TEMP
SAM                 TMPGRP1
SCOTT               TEMP
. . .
SQL>
```

Default Permanent Tablespaces

Prior to the Oracle Database 10*g* release, the System tablespace was the default *permanent* tablespace for any users you created if you neglected to assign the user to a default tablespace. As of Oracle Database 10*g*, you can create a *default permanent tablespace* to which a new user will be assigned if you don't assign a specific default tablespace when you create the user.

■**Note** You can't drop a default permanent tablespace without first creating and assigning another tablespace as the new default tablespace.

To find out what the current permanent tablespace for your database is, use the following query:

```
SQL> SELECT property_value FROM database_properties
     WHERE property_name='DEFAULT_PERMANENT_TABLESPACE';

PROPERTY_VALUE
--------------
```

```
USERS
SQL>
```

You can create a default permanent tablespace when you first create a database, as shown here:

```
CREATE DATABASE
DATAFILE '/u01/app/oracle/test/system01.dbf' SIZE 500M
SYSAUX DATAFILE '/u01/app/oracle/syaux01.dbf' SIZE 500M
DEFAULT TABLESPACE users
DATAFILE '/u01/app/oracle/users01.dbf' SIZE 250M
. . .
```

The previous CREATE DATABASE statement results in the creation of a default permanent tablespace named users, created by using the DEFAULT TABLESPACE clause (shown in the last two lines of the statement).

Note The database creation process is explained in detail in Chapter 10.

You can also create or reassign a default permanent tablespace after database creation, by using the ALTER DATABASE statement, as shown here:

```
SQL> ALTER DATABASE DEFAULT TABLESPACE users;
```

Bigfile Tablespaces

Oracle Database 11g can contain up to 8 exabytes (8 million terabytes) of data. Don't panic, however, thinking how many millions of datafiles you'd need to manage in order to hold this much data. You have the option of creating really big tablespaces called, appropriately, *bigfile tablespaces*. A bigfile tablespace (BFT) contains only one very large datafile. If you're creating a bigfile-based permanent tablespace, it'll be a single datafile, and if it's a temporary tablespace, it will be a single temporary file. The maximum number of datafiles in Oracle is limited to 64,000 files. So, if you're dealing with an extremely large database, using bigfile tablespaces ensures you don't bump against the ceiling for the number of datafiles in your database.

Depending on the block size, a bigfile tablespace can be as large as 128 terabytes. In previous versions of Oracle, you always had to keep in mind the distinction between datafiles and tablespaces. Now, using the bigfile concept, Oracle has made a tablespace logically equal to a datafile by creating the new one-to-one relationship between tablespaces and datafiles. With Oracle Managed Files (OMF), datafiles are completely transparent to you when you use a BFT, and you can directly deal with the tablespace in many kinds of operations.

Note The traditional tablespaces are now referred to as *smallfile* tablespaces. Smallfile tablespaces are the default tablespaces in Oracle Database 11g. You can have both smallfile and bigfile tablespaces in the same database.

Here's a summary of the benefits offered by using BFTs:

- You only need to create as many datafiles as there are tablespaces.
- You don't have to constantly add datafiles to your tablespaces.
- Datafile management in large databases is simplified—you deal with a few tablespaces directly, not many datafiles.

- Storage capacity is significantly increased because you don't reach the maximum-files limitation quickly when you use BFTs.

Restrictions on Using Bigfile Tablespaces

There are few restrictions on using BFTs. You can use them only if you use a locally managed tablespace with automatic segment space management. By now, you know that locally managed tablespaces with automatic segment space management are the default in Oracle Database 11g Release 1. Oracle also recommends that you use BFTs along with a Logical Volume Manager or Automated Storage Management feature that supports striping and mirroring. Otherwise, you can't really support the massive datafiles that underlie the BFT concept. Both parallel query execution and RMAN backup parallelization would be adversely impacted if you used BFTs without striping.

To avoid creating millions of extents when you use a BFT in a very large (greater than one terabyte) database, Oracle recommends that you change the extent allocation policy from AUTOALLOCATE, which is the default, to UNIFORM and set a very high extent size. In databases that aren't very large, Oracle recommends that you stick to the default AUTOALLOCATE policy and simply let Oracle take care of the extent sizing.

Creating Bigfile Tablespaces

You can create bigfile tablespaces in three different ways: you can specify them at database creation time and thus make them the default tablespace type, you can use the CREATE BIGFILE statement, or you can use the ALTER DATABASE statement to set the default type to a BFT tablespace. Let's look into each of these methods in the following sections.

You can specify BFTs as the default tablespace type during database creation. If you don't explicitly specify BFT as your default tablespace type, your database will have the traditional smallfile tablespace as the default.

Here's a portion of the CREATE DATABASE statement, showing how you specify a BFT:

```
SQL> CREATE DATABASE
     SET DEFAULT BIGFILE tablespace
     . . .
```

Once you set the default tablespace type to bigfile tablespaces, all tablespaces you create subsequently will be BFTs unless you manually override the default setting, as shown shortly.

Irrespective of which default tablespace type you choose—bigfile or smallfile—you can always create a bigfile tablespace by specifying the type explicitly in the CREATE TABLESPACE statement, as shown here:

```
SQL> CREATE BIGFILE TABLESPACE bigtbs_01
     DATAFILE '/u01/oracle/data/bigtbs_01.dbf' SIZE 100G
     . . .
```

In the preceding statement, the explicit specification of the BIGFILE clause will override the default tablespace type, if it was a smallfile type. Conversely, if your default tablespace type is BIGFILE, you can use the SMALLFILE keyword to override the default type when you create a tablespace.

When you specify the CREATE BIGFILE TABLESPACE clause, Oracle will automatically create a locally managed tablespace with automatic segment space management. You can specify the datafile size in kilobytes, megabytes, gigabytes, or terabytes.

■**Tip** On operating systems that don't support large files, the bigfile size will be limited by the maximum file size that the operating system can support.

You can dynamically change the default tablespace type to bigfile or smallfile, thus making all tablespaces you subsequently create either bigfile or smallfile type tablespaces. Here's an example that shows how to set the default tablespace type in your database to bigfile:

```
SQL> ALTER TABLESPACE SET DEFAULT BIGFILE TABLESPACE;
```

You can also migrate database objects from a smallfile tablespace to a bigfile tablespace, or vice versa, after changing a tablespace's type. You can migrate the objects using the ALTER TABLE . . . MOVE or the CREATE TABLE AS SELECT commands. Or you can use the Data Pump Export and Import tools to move the objects between the two types of tablespaces.

Altering a Bigfile Tablespace

You can use the RESIZE and AUTOEXTEND clauses in the ALTER TABLESPACE statement to modify the size of a BFT. Note that both these space-extension clauses can be used directly at the tablespace, not the file, level. Thus, both of these clauses provide datafile transparency—you deal directly with the tablespaces and ignore the underlying datafiles.

Here are more details about the two clauses:

- RESIZE: The RESIZE clause lets you resize a BFT directly, without using the DATAFILE clause, as shown here:

  ```
  SQL> ALTER TABLESPACE bigtbs RESIZE 120G;
  ```

- AUTOEXTEND: The AUTOEXTEND clause enables automatic file extension, again without referring to the datafile. Here's an example:

  ```
  SQL> ALTER TABLESPACE bigtbs AUTOEXTEND ON NEXT 20G;
  ```

Viewing Bigfile Tablespace Information

You can gather information about the BFTs in your database by using the following data dictionary views:

- DBA_TABLESPACES
- USER_TABLESPACES
- V$TABLESPACE

All three views have the new BIGFILE column, whose value indicates whether a tablespace is of the BFT type (YES) or smallfile type (NO).

You can also use the DATABASE_PROPERTIES data dictionary view, as shown in the following query, to find out what the default tablespace type for your database is:

```
SQL> SELECT property_value
     FROM database_properties
     WHERE property_name='DEFAULT_TBS_TYPE';

PROPERTY_VALUE
--------------
SMALLFILE
SQL>
```

Managing the Sysaux Tablespace

Oracle Database 10g mandates the creation of the Sysaux tablespace, which serves as an auxiliary tablespace to the System tablespace. Until now, the System tablespace was the default location for storing objects belonging to components like the Workspace Manager, Logical Standby, Oracle Spatial, LogMiner, and so on. The more features the database offered, the greater was the demand for space in the System tablespace. In addition, several features had to be accommodated in their own repositories, like the Enterprise Manager and its Repository. On top of all this, you had to create a special tablespace for the Statspack Repository.

To alleviate this pressure on the System tablespace and to consolidate all the repositories for the various Oracle features, Oracle Database 10*g* offers the Sysaux tablespace as a centralized single storage location for various database components. Using the Sysaux tablespace offers the following benefits:

- There are fewer tablespaces to manage because you don't have to create a separate tablespace for many database components. You just assign the Sysaux tablespace as the default location for all the components.

- There is reduced pressure on the System tablespace.

The size of the Sysaux tablespace depends on the size of the database components that you'll store in it. Therefore, you should base your Sysaux tablespace sizing on the components and features that your database will use. Oracle recommends that you create the Sysaux tablespace with a minimum size of 240MB. Generally, the OEM repository tends to be the largest user of the Sysaux tablespace.

Creating the Sysaux Tablespace

If you use the Oracle Database Configuration Assistant (DBCA), you can automatically create the Sysaux tablespace when you create a new database, whether it is based on the seed database or a completely new, built-from-scratch, user-defined database. During the course of creating a database, the DBCA asks you to select the file location for the Sysaux tablespace. When you upgrade a database to Oracle Database 10*g*, the Database Upgrade Assistant will similarly prompt you for the file information for creating the new Sysaux tablespace.

■**Tip** The Sysaux tablespace is mandatory, whether you create a new Oracle Database or migrate from a release prior to Oracle Database 10*g*.

You can create the Sysaux tablespace manually at database creation time. Here is the syntax for creating the Sysaux tablespace:

```
CREATE DATABASE mydb
USER sys IDENTIFIED BY abc1def
USER system IDENTIFIED BY uvw2xyz
. . .
SYSAUX DATAFILE '/u01/oracle/oradata/mydb/sysaux01.dbf' SIZE 500M REUSE
. . .
```

If you omit the SYSAUX creation clause from the CREATE DATABASE statement, Oracle will create both the System and Sysaux tablespaces automatically, with their datafiles being placed in system-determined default locations. If you are using Oracle Managed Files, the datafile location will be dependent on the OMF initialization parameters. If you include the DATAFILE clause for the System tablespace, you must use the DATAFILE clause for the Sysaux tablespace as well, unless you are using OMF.

You can only set the datafile location when you create the Sysaux tablespace during database creation, as shown in the preceding example. Oracle sets all the other attributes, which are mandatory and not changeable, with the ALTER TABLESPACE command. Once you provide the datafile location and size, Oracle creates the Sysaux tablespace with the following attributes:

- Permanent
- Read/write
- Locally managed
- Automatic segment space management

You can alter the Sysaux tablespace using the same ALTER TABLESPACE command that you use for other tablespaces. Here's an example:

```
SQL> ALTER TABLESPACE sysaux ADD DATAFILE
     '/u01/app/oracle/prod1/oradata/sysaux02.dbf' SIZE 500M;
```

Usage Restrictions for the Sysaux Tablespace

Although using the ALTER TABLESPACE command to change the Sysaux tablespace may make it seem as if the Sysaux tablespace is similar to the other tablespaces in your database, several usage features set the Sysaux tablespace apart. Here are the restrictions:

- You can't drop the Sysaux tablespace by using the DROP TABLESPACE command during normal database operation.
- You can't rename the Sysaux tablespace during normal database operation.
- You can't transport a Sysaux tablespace like other tablespaces.

Encrypting Tablespaces

Oracle has been gradually improving its encryption capabilities over the years. In Oracle8*i*, Oracle introduced the DBMS_OBFUSCATION_TOOLKIT package, and in the Oracle 10.1 release, Oracle introduced the DBMS_CRYPTO package to facilitate encryption. Both the toolkit and the DBMS_CRYPTO package required the application to manage the encryption keys and call the API to perform the necessary encryption/decryption operations.

Why You Need Encrypted Tablespaces

In Oracle Database, Oracle introduced the new Transparent Data Encryption (TDE) feature, which let you easily encrypt a column's data in a table. The encryption is called transparent because the Oracle database takes care of all the encryption and decryption details, with no need for you to manage any tables or triggers to decrypt data. Now, in Oracle Database 11*g*, you can encrypt an entire tablespace by simply using a pair of special clauses during tablespace creation. Encrypting a tablespace keeps the data in the tablespaces from being accessed by unauthorized users directly from the operating system file system. Encryption lets you safely send backup media to offsite storage or other locations.

When you encrypt a column(s) for a table, there are limitations on certain queries. By encrypting the entire tablespace, some of these restrictions are removed. For example, in Oracle Database 10*g*, you can't encrypt a column if that column is part of a foreign key or used in another database constraint. By encrypting the tablespace, this restriction is lifted. Following are additional considerations to using tablespace-level encryption:

- Function-based indexes
- Index range scans
- Data type restrictions
- Partitioned/subpartitioned tables

Tablespace encryption depends on the transparent data encryption feature of the Oracle database, which requires you to create and maintain a secure credentials repository called an *Oracle Wallet* to store the master encryption key for the database.

Creating the Oracle Wallet

An Oracle Wallet is a container to store authentication and signing credentials. The tablespace encryption feature relies on the Oracle Wallet to store and protect the master key used in the encryption. There are two kinds of Oracle Wallets—encryption wallets and auto-open wallets. You must manually open an encryption wallet after database startup, whereas the auto-open wallet automatically opens upon database startup. The encryption wallet is commonly recommended for tablespace encryption, unless you're dealing with unattended Oracle Data Guard environments, in which case the automatic opening of the wallet comes in handy.

> ▪**Note** Although you can't create an encrypted undo tablespace or temporary tablespace, when the database writes data from any encrypted tablespace to the undo tablespace or the temporary tablespace (or the redo log files), it automatically encrypts the data. Thus, you don't have to encrypt the undo or the temporary tablespace.

The Oracle Wallet, which is actually a file in your directory system, is named `ewallet.p12` under both Windows and UNIX/Linux based systems. The location where Oracle stores this file is operating system specific. However, you can specify a nondefault location by using the parameter `ENCRYPTION_WALLET_LOCATION` in the `sqlnet.ora` file, as shown here:

```
ENCRYPTION_WALLET_LOCATION =
 (SOURCE=
    (METHOD=file)
    (METHOD_DATA=
       (DIRECTORY=/apps/oracle/general/wallet)    )  )
```

In order to use TDE, you must have the `ALTER SYSTEM` privilege as well as have a password for an Oracle Wallet. If you don't have an Oracle Wallet, you must create one and then add a master key to it. You can create the Oracle Wallet in several ways:

- By invoking the Oracle Wallet Manager through a GUI interface
- By invoking the Oracle Wallet Manager by issuing the command `owm` at the command line
- By using the `mkstore` command from the operating system command line

> ▪**Tip** Use the following syntax to create a wallet from the OS:
>
> ```
> mkstore -wrl $ORACLE_BASE/admin/$ORACLE_SID/wallet –create
> Enter password:
> Enter
> ```

However, the simplest way to create the Oracle Wallet is by using a SQL statement, which is the method we use here. Before you create the Oracle Wallet, you must first create a directory named `wallet` under the directory `$ORACLE_BASE/admin/$ORACLE_SID`. If you don't do this, you'll get the error ORA-28368: "Cannot auto-create wallet." The most straightforward way to create the wallet is to use the following command in SQL*Plus:

```
SQL> ALTER SYSTEM SET ENCRYPTION KEY IDENTIFIED BY  "password"
```

```
System altered.
```

```
SQL>
```

The ALTER SYSTEM statement shown here both creates the wallet, if it doesn't already exist, and adds a master key to it. You must, of course, replace the word "password" with your own password for the wallet.

The ALTER SYSTEM statement you issued in the previous example works in the following way:

- If you already have an Oracle Wallet, it opens that wallet and creates (or re-creates) the master encryption key.

- If you don't have an Oracle Wallet already, it creates a new wallet, opens the wallet, and creates a new master encryption key.

Now that you've successfully created the Oracle Wallet, you're ready to encrypt tablespaces using the new tablespace encryption feature.

Creating an Encrypted Tablespace

Once you create the Oracle Wallet, creating an encrypted tablespace is a breeze. The tablespace creation statement for an encrypted tablespace has the following syntax:

```
SQL> CREATE TABLESPACE <tbsp_name>
     ENCRYPTION
     DEFAULT STORAGE(encrypt)
```

The ENCRYPTION clause in the second line doesn't actually encrypt the tablespace. You merely provide the encryption properties by setting values for the keyword ENCRYPTION. You may specify the USING clause to specify the name of the encryption algorithm you want to use, such as 3DES168, AES128, AES192, and AES256, unless you want to use the default algorithm of AES128, in which case you can omit the USING clause altogether.

It's the ENCRYPT keyword passed to the STORAGE clause in the third line that performs the actual encryption of the tablespace. In the following text, let's review how to encrypt a tablespace.

Following is an example showing how to create a simple encrypted tablespace that uses the default DES128 encryption. Since you don't have to specify the default encryption level, you don't specify the USING clause for the encryption clause in line 3.

```
SQL> CREATE TABLESPACE encrypt1
  2  DATAFILE 'c:\orcl11\app\oracle\oradata\eleven\encrypt_01.dbf'
  3  SIZE 100m
  4  ENCRYPTION
  5* DEFAULT STORAGE (encrypt);
```

```
Tablespace created.
SQL>
```

The new column encrypted in the DBA_TABLESPACES table lets you check the encryption status of a tablespace:

```
SQL> SELECT tablespace_name,encrypted
     FROM dba_tablespaces;
```

```
TABLESPACE_NAME          ENC
---------------          ------
SYSTEM                   NO
SYSAUX                   NO
UNDOTBS1                 NO
TEMP                     NO
```

```
USERS                 NO
ENCRYPT1              YES

6 rows selected.

SQL>
```

The query reveals that the encrypt1 tablespace is encrypted.

You can query the V$ENCRYPTED_TABLESPACES view to see the name and encryption algorithm of all encrypted tablespaces in the database, as shown here:

```
SQL> SELECT t.name, e.encryptionalg_algorithm
     FROM v$tablespace t, v$encrypted_tablespace e
     WHERE t.ts# = e.ts#;
```

Data Dictionary Views for Managing Tablespaces

In order to manage tablespaces in an Oracle database, you'll want to get familiar with a few key dictionary views:

- DBA_TABLESPACES
- DBA_FREE_SPACE
- DBA_SEGMENTS
- DBA_DATA_FILES
- DBA_TABLESPACE_GROUPS

In addition to these views, the dynamic performance views V$DATAFILE and V$FILESTAT are also very useful in managing and monitoring the use of tablespaces in your database. I explain the key dictionary views briefly in the following sections.

DBA_TABLESPACES

The DBA_TABLESPACES view is a very important dictionary view for managing tablespaces. Using this view, you can find out various things about tablespaces, such as whether they are offline or online; whether they are undo, permanent, or temporary; what the extent management type, the allocation type, and the segment space management type are; and whether they are made up of smallfiles or a bigfile. You've already seen how to use this view in the "Creating Tablespaces" section of this chapter. You can use the DBA_TABLESPACES dictionary view to find out important information about a tablespace, including the following:

- Initial extent size
- Next extent size
- Default maximum number of extents
- Status (online, offline, or read-only)
- Contents (permanent, temporary, or undo)
- Type of extent management (DICTIONARY or LOCAL)
- Segment space management (AUTO or MANUAL)

DBA_FREE_SPACE

The DBA_FREE_SPACE view tells you how much free space you have in the database at any given moment. You can use the query in Listing 6-5 to find out how much free space you have in your tablespaces. Note that space belonging to a table that you dropped and is in the Recycle Bin shows up as free space in this view. However, you can't use it for any other object. You get the space back only after you permanently remove the item with the ALTER TABLE . . . PURGE statement.

Listing 6-5. *Querying the DBA_FREE_SPACE View*

```
SQL> SELECT tablespace_name, SUM(bytes)
  2  FROM DBA_FREE_SPACE
  3* GROUP BY tablespace_name;

TABLESPACE_NAME          SUM(BYTES)
---------------          ----------
CWMLITE                    11141120
DRSYS                      10813440
EXAMPLE                      262144
INDX                       26148864
ODM                        11206656
SYSTEM                      4325376
TOOLS                       4128768
UNDOTBS1                  202047488
USERS                      26148864
XDB                          196608
10 rows selected.
SQL>
```

DBA_SEGMENTS

As you're aware, the Oracle database contains several kinds of segments: table, index, undo, and so on. The DBA_SEGMENTS data dictionary view shows the segment name and type and the tablespace the segment belongs to, among other things. The view provides you with detailed information on the various segments in the database, as seen in the example in Listing 6-6.

Listing 6-6. *Querying the DBA_SEGMENTS View*

```
SQL> SELECT
  2  tablespace_name,
  3  segment_name,
  4  segment_type,
  5  extents,          /*Number of extents in the segment*/
  6  blocks,           /*Number of db blocks in the segment*/
  7  bytes             /*Number of bytes in the segment*/
  8  FROM dba_segments
  9* WHERE owner = 'HR';
```

TABLESPACE_NAME	SEGMENT_NAME	SEGMENT_TYPE	EXTENTS	BLOCKS	BYTES
EXAMPLE	REGIONS	TABLE	1	8	65,536
EXAMPLE	LOCATIONS	TABLE	1	8	65,536
EXAMPLE	DEPARTMENTS	TABLE	1	8	65,536
EXAMPLE	JOBS	TABLE	1	8	65,536
EXAMPLE	EMPLOYEES	TABLE	1	8	65,536
EXAMPLE	JOB_HISTORY	TABLE	1	8	65,536
EXAMPLE	REG_ID_PK	INDEX	1	8	65,536
EXAMPLE	COUNTRY_PK	INDEX	1	8	65,536

```
EXAMPLE        LOC_ID_PK      INDEX        1     8     65,536
EXAMPLE        DEPT_ID_PK     INDEX        1     8     65,536
EXAMPLE        DEPT_LOC_IX    INDEX        1     8     65,536
. . .
25 rows selected.
SQL>
```

DBA_DATA_FILES

The DBA_DATA_FILES data dictionary view is yet another extremely useful view that you'll refer to often while managing the space in your database. You can query the view to find out the names of all the datafiles, the tablespaces they belong to, and datafile information such as the number of bytes and blocks and the relative file number. A simple query on the DBA_DATA_FILES view shows all your datafiles, as shown in Listing 6-7.

Listing 6-7. *Querying the DBA_DATA_FILES View*

```
SQL> SELECT file_name, tablespace_name FROM DBA_DATA_FILES;

FILE_NAME                                   TABLESPACE_NAME
------------------------------------------- -------------
C:\ORACLENT\ORADATA\MANAGER\SYSTEM01.DBF    SYSTEM
C:\ORACLENT\ORADATA\MANAGER\UNDOTBS01.DBF   UNDOTBS
C:\ORACLENT\ORADATA\MANAGER\CWMLITE01.DBF   CWMLITE
C:\ORACLENT\ORADATA\MANAGER\DRSYS01.DBF     DRSYS
C:\ORACLENT\ORADATA\MANAGER\EXAMPLE01.DBF   EXAMPLE
C:\ORACLENT\ORADATA\MANAGER\INDX01.DBF      INDX
C:\ORACLENT\ORADATA\MANAGER\TOOLS01.DBF     TOOLS
C:\ORACLENT\ORADATA\MANAGER\USERS01.DBF     USERS
8 rows selected.
SQL>
```

The DBA_DATA_FILES view is especially useful when you join it with another data dictionary view, as the example in Listing 6-8 illustrates. The query produces a report showing you the tablespace sizes, free and used space, and the percentage of used space in each tablespace. At the end, you also get the sum of total space allocated to all the tablespaces, and the breakdown of free and used space in the database.

Listing 6-8. *Joining Multiple Data Dictionary Views*

```
BREAK ON REPORT
COMPUTE SUM OF tbsp_size ON REPORT
compute SUM OF used      ON REPORT
compute SUM OF free      ON REPORT

COL tbspname      FORMAT a20        HEADING 'Tablespace Name'
COL tbsp_size     FORMAT 999,999    HEADING 'Size|(MB)'
COL used          FORMAT 999,999    HEADING 'Used|(MB)'
COL free          FORMAT 999,999    HEADING 'Free|(MB)'
COL pct_used      FORMAT 999        HEADING'% Used'

SQL> SELECT df.tablespace_name              tbspname
  2  sum(df.bytes)/1024/1024               tbsp_size,
  3  nvl(sum(e.used_bytes)/1024/1024,0)    used,
  4  nvl(sum(f.free_bytes)/1024/1024,0)    free,
```

```
 5  nvl((sum(e.used_bytes)*100)/sum(df.bytes),0) pct_used,
 6  FROM DBA_DATA_FILES df
 7  (SELECT file_id
 8  SUM(nvl(bytes,0)) used_bytes
 9  FROM dba_extents
10  GROUP BY file_id) e,
11  (SELECT  MAX(bytes) free_bytes, file_id
12  FROM dba_free_space
14  GROUP BY file_id) f
15  WHERE e.file_id(+) = df.file_id
16  AND df.file_id = f.file_id(+)
17  GROUP BY df.tablespace_name
18* ORDER BY 5 DESC
```

Tablespace Name	Size (MB)	Used (MB)	Free (MB)	% Used
---------------	------	------	-----	-------
PERSON_INFO_I	2,299	2,245	54	98
PERSONS_I	26348	6,185	162	97
LABELS_I	2,038	1,980	58	97
. . .				
CBC_I	501	7	490	1
QUEST	10	0	10	1
TEST2	10	0	1	0
	--------	-------	-------	
Grand Total	291,528	224,473	43,602	
SQL>				

The DBA_TEMP_FILES view is analogous to the DBA_DATA_FILES view, and shows the temporary tablespace temp file information.

DBA_TABLESPACE_GROUPS

You can group a set of temporary tablespaces together into a temporary tablespace group. The DBA_TABLESPACE_GROUPS view shows you all the tablespace groups in your database. You can also find out the individual tablespace name in each group by using this view.

V$DATAFILE

The V$DATAFILE view contains information about the datafile name, the tablespace number, the status, the time stamp of the last change, and so on. The V$TEMPFILE view shows you particulars about the temporary tablespace files. The V$DATAFILE view provides important information when you join it to the V$FILESTAT view.

V$FILESTAT

The V$FILESTAT view provides you with detailed data on file read/write statistics, including the number of physical reads and writes, the time taken for that I/O, and the average read and write times in milliseconds. The V$TABLESPACE view provides information about the tablespaces. Listing 6-9 shows how you can join the V$DATAFILE, V$TABLESPACE, and V$FILESTAT views to obtain useful disk I/O information.

Listing 6-9. *Getting Disk I/O Information*

```
SQL> SELECT d.name, t.name, f.phyrds, f.phywrts,
  2  f.readtim, f.writetim
  3  FROM V$DATAFILE d,
  4  V$FILESTAT f,
  5  V$TABLESPACE t
  6  WHERE f.file# = d.file#
  7* AND d.ts# = t.ts#;
```

NAME	T.NAME	PHYRDS	PHYWRTS	READTIM	WRITETIM
C:\ORACLEN T\ORADATA\ MANAGER\SY STEM01.DBF	SYSTEM	46180	98697	29637	473716
C:\ORACLEN T\ORADATA\ MANAGER\UN DOTBS01.DBF	UNDOTBS	330	140887	801	165629
C:\ORACLEN T\ORADATA\ MANAGER\DR SYS01.DBF	DRSYS	649	23	515	0
C:\ORACLEN T\ORADATA\ MANAGER\IN DX01.DBF	INDX	34	23	4	0

```
SQL>
```

Easy File Management with Oracle Managed Files

The previous sections have dealt with operating system file management, where you, the DBA, manually create, delete, and manage the datafiles. Oracle Managed Files enable you to bypass dealing with operating system files directly.

As you learned in Chapter 5, in an Oracle database, you deal with various types of database files, including datafiles, control files, and online redo log files. In addition, you also have to manage tempfiles for use with temporary tablespaces, archived redo logs, RMAN backup files, and files for storing flashback logs. Normally, you'd have to set the complete file specification for each of these files when you create one of them. Under an OMF setup, however, you specify the file system directory for all the previously mentioned types of Oracle files by specifying three initialization parameters: DB_CREATE_FILE_DEST, DB_CREATE_ONLINE_LOG_DEST_n, and DB_RECOVERY_FILE_DEST. Oracle will then automatically create the files in the specified locations without your having to provide the actual location for it.

OMF offers a simpler way of managing the file system—you don't have to worry about specifying long file specifications when you're creating tablespaces or redo log groups or control files. When you want to create a tablespace or add datafiles when using OMF, you don't have to give a location for the datafiles. Oracle will automatically create the file or add the datafile in the location you specified in the init.ora file for datafiles. Note that you don't have to use a DATAFILE or TEMPFILE clause when creating a tablespace when you use the OMF-based file system.

Here are a couple of examples showing how simple it is to create a tablespace and add space to it under an OMF system:

```
SQL> CREATE TABLESPACE finance01;
SQL> ALTER TABLESPACE finance01 ADD DATAFILE 500M;
```

Similarly, when you want to drop a tablespace, you just need to issue the DROP TABLESPACE command and the OMF datafiles are automatically removed by Oracle, along with the tablespace definition:

```
SQL> DROP TABLESPACE finance01;
```

OMF files are definitely easier to manage than the traditional manually created operating system files. However, there are some limitations:

- OMF files can't be used on raw devices, which offer superior performance to operating system files for certain applications (such as Oracle Real Application Clusters).

- All the OMF datafiles have to be created in one directory. It's hard to envision a large database fitting into this one file system.

- You can't choose your own names for the datafiles created under OMF. Oracle will use a naming convention that includes the database name and unique character strings to name the datafiles.

Oracle recommends using OMF for small and test databases. Normally, if you drop a datafile, the database won't have any references to the datafile, but the physical file still exists in the old location—you have to explicitly remove the physical file yourself. If you use OMF, Oracle will remove the file for you when you drop it from the database. According to Oracle, OMF file systems are most useful for databases using Logical Volume Managers that support RAID and extensible file systems. Smaller databases benefit the most from OMF, because of the reduced file-management tasks. Test databases are another area where an OMF file system will cut down on management time.

You have to use operating system–based files if you want to use the OMF feature; you can't use raw files. You do lose some control over the placement of data in your storage system when you use OMF files, but even with these limitations, the benefits of OMF file management can outweigh its limitations in some circumstances.

Benefits of Using OMF

You can create tablespaces with OMF-based files. You can also specify that your online redo log files and your control files are in the OMF format. OMF files offer several advantages over user-managed files:

- Oracle automatically creates and deletes OMF files.

- You don't have to worry about coming up with a naming convention for the files.

- It's easy to drop datafiles by mistake when you're managing them. With OMF files, you don't run the risk of accidentally deleting database files.

- Oracle automatically deletes a file when it's no longer needed.

- You can have a mix of traditional files and OMF files in the same database.

In the following sections, we'll look at the OMF feature in some detail.

Creating Oracle Managed Files

You can create OMF files when you create the database, or you can add them to a database that you created with traditional datafiles later on. Either way, you need to set some initialization parameters to enable OMF file creation.

Initialization Parameters for OMF

You need to set three initialization parameters to enable the use of OMF files. You can set these four parameters in your parameter file, and you can change them online with the ALTER SYSTEM or ALTER

SESSION statement. You can use each of these parameters to specify the file destination for different types of OMF files, such as datafiles, control files, and online redo log files:

- DB_CREATE_FILE_DEST: This parameter specifies the default location of datafiles, online redo log files, control files, block-change tracking files, and tempfiles. You can also specify a control file location if you wish. Unfortunately, the DB_CREATE_FILE_DEST parameter can take only a single directory as its value; you can't specify multiple file systems for the parameter. If the assigned directory for file creation fills up, you can always specify a new directory, because the DB_CREATE_FILE_DEST parameter is dynamic. This enables you to place Oracle datafiles anywhere in the file system without any limits whatsoever.

- DB_CREATE_ONLINE_LOG_DEST_n: You can use this parameter to specify the default location of online redo log files and control files. In this parameter, n refers to the number of redo log files or control files that you want Oracle to create. If you want to multiplex your online redo log files as Oracle recommends, you should set n to 2.

- DB_RECOVERY_FILE_DEST: This parameter defines the default location for control files, archived redo log files, RMAN backups, and flashback logs. If you omit the DB_CREATE_ONLINE_LOG_DEST_n parameter, this parameter will determine the location of the online redo log files and control files. The directory location you specify using this parameter is also known as the *flash recovery area*, which I explain it in detail in Chapter 10.

In addition to the preceding three initialization parameters, the DB_RECOVERY_FILE_DEST_SIZE parameter specifies the size of your flash recovery area.

If you don't specify any of these initialization parameters in your init.ora file or SPFILE, you can still use the ALTER SYSTEM command to dynamically enable the creation of OMF files, as shown in the following example:

```
SQL> ALTER SYSTEM SET DB_CREATE_FILE_DEST =
  2  '/test01/app/oracle/oradata/finance1';
System altered.
SQL>
```

As long as you specify the DB_CREATE_FILE_DEST parameter, you can have Oracle create OMF files for you, and you can use both the user-managed and OMF files simultaneously without a problem.

File-Naming Conventions

Oracle uses the OFA standards in creating filenames, so filenames are unique and datafiles are easily identifiable as belonging to a certain tablespace. Table 6-1 shows the naming conventions for various kinds of OMF files and an example of each type. Note that the letter t stands for a unique tablespace name, g stands for an online redo group, and u is an 8-character string.

Table 6-1. *OMF File-Naming Conventions*

OMF File Type	Naming Convention	Example
Datafile	ora_*t*%_*u*.dbf	ora_data_Y2ZV8P00.dbf
Temp file (default size is 100MB)	ora_%*t*_*u*.tmp	ora_temp_Y2ZWGD00.tmp
Online redo log file (default size is 100MB)	ora_%*g*_%*u*.log	ora_4_Y2ZSQK00.log
Control file	ora_*u*%.ctl	ora_Y2ZROW00.ctl

Different Types of Oracle Managed Files

You can use OMF to create all three types of files that the Oracle database requires: control files, redo log files, and, of course, datafiles. However, there are interesting differences in the way OMF requires you to specify (or not specify) each of these types of files. The following sections cover how Oracle creates different types of files.

Control Files

As you have probably noticed already, there is no specific parameter that you need to include in your init.ora file to specify the OMF format. If you specify the CONTROL_FILES initialization parameter, you will, of course, have to specify a complete file location for those files, and obviously they will not be OMF files—they are managed by you. If you don't specify the CONTROL_FILES parameter, and you use the DB_CREATE_FILE_DEST or the DB_CREATE_ONLINE_LOG_DEST_n parameter, your control files will be OMF files.

If you are using a traditional init.ora file, you need to add the control file locations to it. If you are using an SPFILE, Oracle automatically adds the control file information to it.

Redo Log Files

OMF redo log file creation is similar to control file creation. If you don't specify a location for the redo log files, and you set either the DB_CREATE_FILE_DEST or the DB_CREATE_ONLINE_LOG_DEST_n parameter in the init.ora file, Oracle automatically creates OMF-based redo log files.

Datafiles

If you don't specify a datafile location in the CREATE or ALTER statements for a regular datafile, or a tempfile for a temporary tablespace, tempfile, or an undo tablespace datafile, but instead specify the DB_CREATE_FILE_DEST parameter, all these files will be OMF files.

Simple Database Creation Using OMF

Let's look at a small example to see how OMF files can really simplify database creation. When you create a new database, you need to provide the control file, redo log file, and datafile locations to Oracle. You specify some file locations in the initialization file (control file locations) and some file locations at database creation (such as redo log locations). However, if you use OMF-based files, database creation can be a snap, as you'll see in the sections that follow.

Setting Up File Location Parameters

For the new OMF-based database, named nicko, let's use the following initialization parameters:

```
db_name=nicko
DB_CREATE_FILE_DEST = '/u01/app/oracle/oradata'
DB_RECOVERY_FILE_DEST_SIZE = 100M
DB_RECOVERY_FILE_DEST = '/u04/app/oracle/oradata'
LOG_ARCHIVE_DEST_1 = 'LOCATION = USE_DB_RECOVERY_FILE_DEST'
```

Note that of the four OMF-related initialization parameters, I chose to use only the DB_CREATE_FILE_DEST, DB_RECOVERY_FILE_DEST_SIZE, and DB_RECOVERY_FILE_DEST parameters. I didn't have to use the fourth parameter, DB_CREATE_ONLINE_LOG_DEST_n, in this example. When this parameter is left out, Oracle creates a copy of the log file and the redo log file in the locations specified for the DB_CREATE_FILE_DEST and the DB_RECOVERY_FILE_DEST parameters. I thus have two copies of the control file and the online redo log files.

The setting for the last parameter, LOG_ARCHIVE_DEST_1, tells Oracle to send the archived redo logs for storage in the flash recovery area specified by the DB_RECOVERY_FILE_DEST parameter.

Starting the Instance

Using the simple `init.ora` file shown in the preceding section, you can start an instance as shown in Listing 6-10.

Listing 6-10. *Creating the OMF-Based Instance*

```
SQL> connect sys/sys_passwd as sysdba
Connected to an idle instance.
SQL> STARTUP NOMOUNT PFILE='initnicko.ora';
ORACLE instance started.
Total System Global Area    188743680 bytes
Fixed Size                    1308048 bytes
Variable Size               116132464 bytes
Database Buffers             67108864 bytes
Redo Buffers                  4194304 bytes
SQL>
```

Creating the Database

Now that you've successfully created the new Oracle instance, you can create the new database nicko with this simple command:

```
SQL> CREATE DATABASE nicko;

  Database created.
SQL>
```

That's it! Just those two simple lines are all you need to create a functional database with the following structures:

- A System tablespace created in the default file system specified by the `DB_CREATE_FILE_DEST` parameter (`/u01/app/oracle/oradata`)
- A Sysaux tablespace created in the default file system (`/u01/app/oracle/oradata`)
- Two duplexed redo log groups
- Two copies of the control file
- A default temporary tablespace
- An undo tablespace automatically managed by the Oracle database

Where Are the OMF Files?

You can see the various files within the database by looking in the alert log for the new database, `alert_nicko.log`, which you'll find in the `$ORACLE_HOME/rdbms/log` directory, since we didn't specify the `BACKGROUND_DUMP_DIR` directory in the `init.ora` file.

In the following segment from the alert log file for the database, you can see how the various files necessary for the new database were created. First, Oracle creates the control files and places them in the location you specified for the `DB_CREATE_ONLINE_LOG_DEST_n` parameter.

```
Sun Jan  13 17:44:51 2008
create database nicko
default  temporary tablespace temp
Sun Jan  13 17:44:51 2008
WARNING: Default passwords for SYS and SYSTEM will be used.
         Please change the passwords.
Created Oracle managed file /u01/app/oracle/oradata/NICKO/controlfile/o1_mf_150w
. . .
```

```
Sun Jan  13 17:46:37 2008
Completed: create database nicko
default  temporary tablespace
MMNL started with pid=13, OS id=28939
```

Here's what the alert log shows regarding the creation of the control files:

```
Created Oracle managed file /u01/app/oracle/oradata/NICKO/controlfile/o1_mf_150w
h3r1_.ctl
Created Oracle managed file /u04/app/oracle/oradata/NICKO/controlfile/o1_mf_150w
h3_.ctl
```

Next, the Oracle server creates the duplexed online redo log files. Oracle creates the minimum number of groups necessary and duplexes them by creating a set of online log files (two) in the locations specified by the DB_CREATE_ONLINE_LOG_DEST and the DB_RECOVERY_FILE_DEST parameters:

```
Created Oracle managed file /u01/app/oracle/oradata/NICKO/onlinelog/o1_mf_1_150w
h48m_.log
Created Oracle managed file /u04/app/oracle/oradata/NICKO/onlinelog/o1_mf_1_150w
hf07_.log
Created Oracle managed file /u01/app/oracle/oradata/NICKO/onlinelog/o1_mf_2_150w
honc_.log
Created Oracle managed file /u04/app/oracle/oradata/NICKO/onlinelog/o1_mf_2_150w
hwh0_.log
```

The System tablespace is created next, in the location you specified for the DB_CREATE_FILE_DEST parameter:

```
create tablespace SYSTEM datafile /* OMF datafile */
  default storage (initial 10K next 10K) EXTENT MANAGEMENT DICTIONARY online
Created Oracle managed file /u01/app/oracle/oradata/NICKO/datafile/o1_mf_system_
150wj4c3_.dbf
Completed: create tablespace SYSTEM datafile /* OMF datafile
```

The default Sysaux tablespace is created next, as shown here:

```
create tablespace SYSAUX datafile /* OMF datafile */
  EXTENT MANAGEMENT LOCAL SEGMENT SPACE MANAGEMENT AUTO online
Sun Jan 33 17:46:16 2008
Created Oracle managed file /u01/app/oracle/oradata/NICKO/datafile/o1_mf_sysaux_
150wkk9n_.dbf
Completed: create tablespace SYSAUX datafile /* OMF datafile
```

The undo tablespace is created next, with the default name of SYS_UNDOTS in the location specified by the DB_CREATE_FILE_DEST parameter. A temporary tablespace named TEMP is also created in the same directory:

```
CREATE UNDO TABLESPACE SYS_UNDOTS DATAFILE SIZE 10M AUTOEXTEND ON
Created Oracle managed file
/test01/app/oracle/oradata/ora_omf/finDATA/ora_sys_undo_yj5mg123.dbf
...
Successfully onlined Undo Tablespace 1.
Completed: CREATE UNDO TABLESPACE SYS_UNDOTS DATAFILE  SIZE 1
CREATE TEMPORARY TABLESPACE TEMP TEMPFILE
Created Oracle managed file
/test01/app/oracle/oradata/ora_omf/finDATA/ora_temp_yj5mg592.tmp
Completed: CREATE TEMPORARY TABLESPACE TEMP TEMPFILE
```

Adding Tablespaces

Adding other tablespaces and datafiles within an OMF file system is easy. All you have to do is invoke the CREATE TABLESPACE command without the DATAFILE keyword. Oracle will automatically create the datafiles for the tablespace in the location specified in the DB_CREATE_FILE_DEST parameter. The example that follows shows how to create the tablespace:

```
SQL> ALTER SYSTEM SET DB_CREATE_FILE_DEST =
  2 '/test01/app/oracle/ora_omf/finance1';
System altered.
SQL> CREATE TABLESPACE omftest;
Tablespace created.
SQL> SELECT file_name FROM dba_data_files
  2  WHERE tablespace_name='OMFTEST';
FILE_NAME
-----------------------------------------------------------
/test01/app/oracle/oradata/ora_omf/ora_omftest_yj7590bm.dbf
SQL>
```

Compare the OMF tablespace-creation statement shown previously with the typical tablespace-creation statement, and you'll see how OMF simplifies database administration. Adding datafiles is also simple with OMF, as shown by the following example:

```
SQL> ALTER TABLESPACE omftest ADD DATAFILE;
```

OMF files, as you can see, simplify file administration chores and let you create and manage databases with a small number of initialization parameters. You can easily set up the necessary number of locations for your online redo log files, control files, and archive log files by specifying the appropriate value for the various OMF parameters. Oracle's ASM-based file system relies on the OMF file system.

Copying Files Between Two Databases

You can copy files directly between databases over Oracle Net, without using either OS commands or utilities such as the FTP protocol. You can use the DBMS_FILE_TRANSFER package to copy binary files within the same server or to transfer a binary file between servers. You use the COPY_FILE procedure to copy files on the local system, The GET_FILE procedure to copy files from a remote server to the local server and the PUT_FILE procedure to read and copy a local file to a remote file system. Here's a brief explanation of the key procedures of this new package.

COPY_FILE

The COPY_FILE procedure enables you to copy binary files from one location to another on the same or different servers. Before you can copy the files, you must first create the source and destination directory objects, as follows:

```
SQL> CREATE OR REPLACE DIRECTORY source_dir as '/u01/app/oracle/source';
SQL> CREATE OR REPLACE DIRECTORY dest_dir as '/u01/app/oracle/dest';
```

Once you create your source and destination directories, you can use the COPY_FILE procedure to copy files, as shown here:

```
SQL> BEGIN
    DBMS_FILE_TRANSFER.COPY_FILE(
    source_directory_object      => 'SOURCE_DIR',
    source_file_name             => 'test01.dbf',
    destination_directory_object => 'DEST_DIR',
```

```
      destination_file_name        => 'test01_copy.dbf');
      END;
      /
SQL>
```

Ensure that the copy was correctly copied by checking the destination directory.

GET_FILE

You use the GET_FILE procedure to copy binary files from a remote server to the local server. First, log into the remote server and create the source directory object, as shown here:

```
SQL> CONNECT system/system_passwd@remote_db
Connected.
SQL> CREATE OR REPLACE DIRECTORY source_dir as '/u01/app/oracle/source';
```

Next, you log into the local server and create a destination directory object, as shown here:

```
SQL> CONNECT system/system_passwd@local_db
Connected.
SQL> CREATE OR REPLACE DIRECTORY dest_dir as /'u01/app/oracle/dest';
```

Once you create the source and destination directories, ensure that you have a database link between the two databases, or create one if one doesn't exist:

```
SQL> CREATE DATABASE LINK prod1
      CONNECT TO system IDENTIFIED BY system_passwd
      USING 'prod1';
SQL>
```

You must make sure that you've set up the connection to the prod1 database using a tnsnames.ora file, for example, before you can create the database link.

Now you execute the GET_FILE procedure to transfer the file from the remote server to the local server, as shown here:

```
SQL> BEGIN
      DBMS_FILE_TRANSFER.GET_FILE(
      source_directory_object      => 'SOURCE_DIR',
      source_file_name             => 'test01.dbf',
      source_database              => 'remote_db',
      destination_directory_object => 'DEST_DIR',
      destination_file_name        => 'test01.dbf');
      END;
      /
SQL>
```

Note that for the SOURCE_DATABASE attribute, you provide the name of the database link to the remote database.

PUT_FILE

You use the PUT_FILE procedure to transfer a binary file from the local server to a remote server. As in the case of the previous two procedures, you must first create the source and destination directory objects, as shown here (in addition, you must ensure the existence of a database link from the local to the remote database):

```
SQL> CONNECT system/system_passwd@remote_db
Connected.
SQL> CREATE OR REPLACE DIRECTORY source_dir as '/u01/app/oracle/source';
```

```
SQL> connect system/system_passwd@local_db
Connected.
SQL> CREATE OR REPLACE DIRECTORY dest_dir as /'u01/app/oracle/dest';
```

You can now use the PUT_FILE procedure to put a local file on the remote server, as shown here:

```
SQL> BEGIN
    DBMS_FILE_TRANSFER.PUT_FILE(
    source_directory_object       => 'SOURCE_DIR',
    source_file_name              => 'test01.dbf',
    destination_directory_object  => 'DEST_DIR',
    destination_file_name         => 'test01.dbf',
    destination_database          => 'remote_db');
    END;
    /
SQL>
```

Finding Out How Much Free Space Is Left

The DBMS_SPACE package is useful for finding out how much space is used and how much free space is left in various segments such as table, index, and cluster segments. Recall that the DBA_FREE_SPACE dictionary view lets you find out free space information in tablespaces and datafiles, but not in the database objects. Unless you use the DBMS_SPACE package, it's hard to find out how much free space is in the segments allocated to various objects in the database. The DBMS_SPACE package enables you to answer questions such as the following:

- How much free space can I use before a new extent is thrown?
- How many data blocks are above the high-water mark (HWM)?

The DBA_EXTENTS and the DBA_SEGMENTS dictionary views do give you a lot of information about the size *allocated* to objects such as tables and indexes, but you can't tell what the used and free space usage is from looking at those views. If you've been analyzing the tables, the BLOCKS column will give you the HWM—the highest point in terms of size that the table has ever reached. However, if your tables are undergoing a large number of inserts and deletes, the HWM isn't an accurate indictor of the real space used by the tables. The DBMS_SPACE package is ideal for finding out the used and free space left in objects.

The DBMS_SPACE package has three main procedures: the UNUSED_SPACE procedure gives you information about the unused space in an object segment, the FREE_BLOCKS procedure gives you information about the number of free blocks in a segment, and the SPACE_USAGE procedure gives you details about space usage in the blocks.

Let's look at the UNUSED_SPACE procedure closely and see how you can use it to get detailed unused space information. The procedure has three IN parameters (a fourth one is a default parameter) and seven OUT parameters. Listing 6-11 shows the output from the execution of the UNUSED_SPACE procedure.

Listing 6-11. *Using the DBMS_SPACE.FREE_SPACE Procedure*

```
SQL> DECLARE
  2  v_total_blocks         NUMBER;
  3  v_total_bytes          NUMBER;
  4  v_unused_blocks        NUMBER;
  5  v_unused_bytes         NUMBER;
  6  v_last_used_extent_file_id   NUMBER;
  7  v_last_used_extent_block_id  NUMBER;
  8  v_last_used_block            NUMBER;
```

```
 9  BEGIN
10  dbms_space.unused_space (segment_owner => 'OE',
11    segment_name      => 'PRODUCT_DESCRIPTIONS',
12    segment_type      => 'TABLE',
13    total_blocks      => v_total_blocks,
14    total_bytes       => v_total_bytes,
15    unused_blocks     => v_unused_blocks,
16    unused_bytes      => v_unused_bytes,
17    last_used_extent_file_id   => v_last_used_extent_file_id,
18    last_used_extent_block_id  => v_last_used_extent_block_id,
19    last_used_block            => v_last_used_block,
20    partition_name             => NULL);
21    dbms_output.put_line ('Number of Total Blocks  :
      '||v_total_blocks);
22    dbms_output.put_line ('Number of Bytes         :
      '||v_total_bytes);
23    dbms_output.put_line ('Number of Unused Blocks :
      '||v_unused_blocks);
24    dbms_output.put_line ('Number of unused Bytes  :
      '||v_unused_bytes );
25    END;
Number of Total Blocks  : 384
Number of Bytes         : 3145728
Number of Unused Blocks : 0
Number of unused Bytes  : 0
PL/SQL procedure successfully completed.
SQL>
```

Working with Operating System Files

The wonderful UTL_FILE package enables you to write to and read from operating system files easily. The UTL_FILE package provides you with a restricted version of standard operating-system stream file I/O. The procedures and functions in the UTL_FILE package let you open, read from, write to, and close the operating system files. Oracle also uses a client-side text I/O package, the TEXT_IO package, as part of the Oracle Procedure Builder.

Using the UTL_FILE Package

It's easy to use the UTL_FILE package to read from and write to the operating system files. In many cases, when you need to create reports, the UTL_FILE package is ideal for creating the file, which you can then send to external sources using the FTP utility. The following sections take you through a simple example that illustrates the use of this package.

Creating the File Directory

The first step in using the UTL_FILE package is to create the directory where you want to place the operating system files. You need to create a special directory for this purpose, using the following command:

```
SQL> CREATE DIRECTORY utl_dir AS '/u50/oradata/archive_data';
            /*the directory could be named anything you want - utl_dir
            is just an example*/
```

```
Directory created.
SQL>
```

■**Tip** The UTL_FILE_DIR initialization parameter is still valid, but Oracle doesn't recommend using it anymore. Oracle recommends that you use the new CREATE DIRECTORY command instead. Using the CREATE DIRECTORY approach is better because you don't have to restart the database (when you want to add the UTL_FILE_DIR parameter).

Granting Privileges to Users

You must grant your users privileges to read and write files in the utl_dir directory that you just created. You can do this by executing the following command:

```
SQL> GRANT READ, WRITE ON DIRECTORY utl_dir to public;

Grant succeeded.
SQL>
```

Key UTL_FILE Procedures and Functions

The UTL_FILE package uses its many procedures and functions to perform file manipulation and text writing and reading activities. The next sections briefly cover the key procedures and functions in the UTL_FILE package.

■**Note** UTL_FILE.FILE_TYPE is a file-handling data type, and you use it for all the procedures and functions of the UTL_FILE package. Any time you use the UTL_FILE package within a PL/SQL anonymous code block or a procedure, you must first declare a file handle of UTL_FILE.FILE_TYPE, as you'll see later.

Opening an Operating System File

You use the FOPEN function to open an operating system file for input and output. You can open a file in three modes: read (r), write (w), or append (a).

Reading from a File

To read from a file, you first specify the read (r) mode when you open a file using the FOPEN function. The GET_LINE procedure enables you to read one line of text at a time from the specified operating system file.

Writing to a File

To write to a file, you must open the file in the write (w) or append (a) mode. The append (a) mode just adds to the file, and the write (w) mode overwrites the file if it already exists. If the file doesn't already exist in the UTL_FILE directory, the UTL_FILE utility will first create the file and then write to it. Note that you don't have to create the file manually—the FOPEN function takes care of that for you.

When you want to write a line to the file, you can use the PUT procedure. After the package writes a line, you can ask it to go to a new line by using the NEW_LINE procedure. Better yet, you can just use the PUT_LINE procedure, which is like a combination of the PUT and NEW_LINE procedures, to write to the text file.

Closing a File

When you finish reading from or writing to the file, you need to use the FCLOSE procedure to close the operating system file. If you have more than one file open, you may use the FCLOSE_ALL procedure to close all the open files at once.

Exceptions

Whenever you use the UTL_FILE package in a PL/SQL procedure or block, make sure you have an exception block at the end to account for all the possible errors that may occur while you're using the package. For example, your directory location may be wrong, or a "no data found" error may be raised within the procedure. You may have a read or write error due to a number of reasons. The UTL_FILE package comes with a large number of predefined exceptions, and I recommend using all the exceptions at the end of your procedure or code block to facilitate debugging. If you use RAISE_APPLICATION_ERROR to assign an error number and a message with the exceptions, you'll have an easier time debugging the code.

A Simple Example Using the UTL_FILE Package

The following anonymous PL/SQL code uses the UTL_FILE package to write password-related information using the DBA_USERS and the DBA_PROFILES dictionary views. Your goal is to produce an operating system file listing user names, their maximum allowable login attempts, their password lifetime, and their password lock time. Listing 6-12 shows the code block.

Listing 6-12. *Using the UTL_FILE Package to Perform Text Input and Output*

```
SQL> DECLARE
     v_failed dba_profiles.limit%TYPE;
     v_lock   dba_profiles.limit%TYPE;
     v_reuse  dba_profiles.limit%TYPE;
     /* the fHandle declared here is used every time
     the OS file is opened /*
     fHandle UTL_FILE.FILE_TYPE;
     vText VARCHAR2(10);
     v_username dba_users.username%TYPE;
     CURSOR users IS
     SELECT username FROM dba_users;
     BEGIN
     /* Open  utlfile.txt file for writing, and get its file handle */
     fHandle :=  UTL_FILE.FOPEN('/a01/pas/pasp/import','utlfile.txt','w');
/* Write a line of text to the file utlfile.txt */
UTL_FILE.PUT_LINE(fHandle,'USERNAME'||'ATTEMPTS'||'LIFE'||'LOCK'||);
/* Close the utlfile.txt file */
UTL_FILE.FCLOSE(fHandle);
/* Open the utlfile.txt file for writing, and get its file handle */
     fHandle := UTL_FILE.FOPEN('/a01/pas/pasp/import','utlfile.txt','a');
     OPEN users;
        LOOP
        FETCH users INTO v_username;
        EXIT when users%NOTFOUND;
SELECT p.limit
```

```
       INTO v_failed
       FROM dba_profiles p, dba_users u
       WHERE p.resource_name='FAILED_LOGIN_ATTEMPTS'
       AND p.profile=u.profile
       AND u.username=v_username;
SELECT p.limit
       INTO v_life
       FROM dba_profiles p, dba_users u
       WHERE p.resource_name='PASSWORD_LIFE_TIME'
       AND p.profile=u.profile
       AND u.username=v_username;
SELECT p.limit
       INTO v_lock
       FROM dba_profiles p, dba_users u
       WHERE p.resource_name='PASSWORD_LOCK_TIME'
       AND p.profile=u.profile
       AND u.username=v_username;
       vtext :='TEST';
       /* Write a line of text to the file utlfile.txt */
       UTL_FILE.PUT_LINE(fHandle,v_username||v_failed||_life||v_lock);
       /* Read a line from the file utltext.txt */
       UTL_FILE.GET_LINE(fHandle,v_username||v_failed||v_life||v_lock);
       /* Write a line of text to the screen */
       UTL_FILE.PUT_LINE(v_username||_failed||v_life||v_lock);
    END LOOP;
    CLOSE users;
      /* Close the utlfile.txt file */
      UTL_FILE.FCLOSE(fHandle);
     /* this is the exception block for the UTL_File errors */
     EXCEPTION
       WHEN UTL_FILE.INVALID_PATH THEN
RAISE_APPLICATION_ERROR(-20100,'Invalid Path');
WHEN UTL_FILE.INVALID_MODE THEN
        RAISE_APPLICATION_ERROR(-20101,'Invalid Mode');
WHEN UTL_FILE.INVALID_OPERATION then
        RAISE_APPLICATION_ERROR(-20102,'Invalid Operation');
      WHEN UTL_FILE.INVALID_FILEHANDLE then
        RAISE_APPLICATION_ERROR(-20103,'Invalid Filehandle');
      WHEN UTL_FILE.WRITE_ERROR then
        RAISE_APPLICATION_ERROR(-20104,'Write Error');
      WHEN UTL_FILE.READ_ERROR then
        RAISE_APPLICATION_ERROR(-20105,'Read Error');
      WHEN UTL_FILE.INTERNAL_ERROR then
        RAISE_APPLICATION_ERROR(-20106,'Internal Error');
      WHEN OTHERS THEN
        UTL_FILE.FCLOSE(fHandle);
END;
```

Schema Management

An important part of the Oracle DBA's job is to support developers in creating database objects and, later on, to manage these objects in production systems. This chapter will give you a thorough understanding of objects such as tables, indexes, views, sequences, and triggers, which will help in the development process and also in troubleshooting problems during data loads and other situations.

To create a table, index, or other object, you first need to create tablespaces in your databases. Several special types of tables, such as the temporary tables and external tables, are very useful to the DBA in performing specialized tasks. I discuss both of these special tables, as well as index-organized tables and clusters, in this chapter. I also introduce the topic of table partitioning, which is useful when dealing with large amounts of data. I follow this discussion with coverage of index creation and management. Indexes have a significant bearing on the performance of database queries, and I provide basic guidelines for creating good Oracle indexes in this chapter. You'll find more information on index management in Chapter 19, which deals with performance tuning.

When loading data into tables, an important part of an Oracle DBA's job is managing database constraints and troubleshooting problems caused by table constraints. In this chapter, I also provide a summary of all the major types of constraints, constraint states, and their implications.

Managing other database objects, such as views, sequences, and synonyms, is another important part of the Oracle DBA's skill set. I explore these topics in detail before concluding the chapter with a discussion of creating and managing materialized views, which are a powerful feature of the Oracle database. You'll also learn how to use the new SQL Access Advisor to figure out the proper materialized views for your database.

You use a particular type of SQL statement called a data definition language (DDL) statement to create and manage Oracle database objects, including tables and indexes. As an Oracle DBA, you'll be using DDL SQL statements quite frequently to manage your database. However, there are other important types of Oracle SQL statements as well, and I start the chapter by introducing these main types of Oracle SQL statements.

Types of SQL Statements

Relational database principles underlie SQL. You need only instruct the language what to do, not how to do it. In addition to working with traditional relational data, Oracle's new XML-centric extensions to its SQL language enable you to manage XML, full text, multimedia, and objects. Oracle Database 11g integrates XML query, storage, and update functionality in the database engine. No matter which tool you use to access the Oracle database, ultimately you'll be using Oracle SQL to perform your transactions. Your application program or the Oracle tool you use may allow you access to the database without your using SQL, but the tools and applications themselves have to use SQL to process your requests.

SQL includes commands for data modeling, data definition, data access, data security, and data administration. SQL statements used by Oracle can be broadly divided into several groups based on whether they change the table data, the table structures, or some other session or instance characteristic. The SQL statement types are as follows:

- System control
- Session control
- Embedded SQL
- Data manipulation
- Transaction control
- Data definition

The following sections examine each of these broad types of SQL statements in detail.

System-Control Statements

You can use the system-control statement ALTER SYSTEM to alter the properties of a running database instance. For example, you can use ALTER SYSTEM to modify certain initialization parameters, such as the shared pool component of the system global area (SGA). At present, the ALTER SYSTEM command is the only system-control SQL statement in Oracle.

Here's an example of the ALTER SYSTEM command:

```
SQL> ALTER SYSTEM KILL SESSION '25,9192';

Session killed
SQL>
```

Session-Control Statements

Session-control statements dynamically alter the properties of an individual user's session. For example, if you intend to trace what your SQL session is doing in the database, you can use the ALTER SESSION SET SQL_TRACE=TRUE SQL statement to trace your session alone. The session-control statements also come in handy when you're changing several initialization parameters just for your session.

■**Note** PL/SQL (Oracle's procedural extension of the SQL language) doesn't support session-control statements.

Common session-control statements include the ALTER SESSION and SET ROLE commands. Here's an example of the use of the ALTER SESSION statement, wherein the ALTER SESSION command is used to set the data format for the duration of the session:

```
SQL> ALTER SESSION SET NLS_DATE_FORMAT = 'MM-DD-YYYY HH:MI:SS';

Session altered.
SQL>
```

Embedded SQL Statements

Embedded SQL statements are data definition language, data manipulation language (DML), and transaction-control statements (such as OPEN, CLOSE, FETCH, and EXECUTE) used in a procedural language program, such as the statements used with the Oracle precompilers.

Data Manipulation Language Statements

The data manipulation language statements are statements that either query (retrieve) or manipulate (change) data in a table. For the most part, DML statements modify the data in the schema objects. In most online transaction processing (OLTP) systems, the bulk of Oracle's work consists of accepting requests from users that contain DML statements and returning the results of those statements.

You'll deal with four important DML statements most of the time: SELECT, INSERT, UPDATE, and DELETE. Note that in addition to these four common DML statements, there are others that facilitate the execution of the four basic DML statements. For example, the MERGE statement deals with conditional inserts and deletes, and you use the LOCK TABLE statement to modify the default Oracle locking mechanism.

SELECT Statements

SELECT statements are queries that retrieve data from a table or a set of tables (or views). Oracle provides set operators, such as UNION, MINUS, and INTERSECT, that enable you to combine the results of several queries to get one final result set of data. You can use the ORDER BY command to sort the results provided by Oracle; otherwise, the results will not be in any particular order. When you need data from several tables, you need to join the tables in your SELECT statements. You can limit the result set when you join tables by providing a join condition.

You can also use subqueries as part of the main or top query. A subquery in the WHERE clause of a SELECT statement is called a *nested subquery*. A subquery that is part of the FROM clause of a SELECT statement is called an *inline view*. The Appendix provides examples of subqueries, nested subqueries, and inline views.

INSERT, DELETE, and UPDATE Statements

The INSERT statement inserts new rows into existing tables, and the DELETE statement removes entire rows from tables. The UPDATE command modifies one or more columns of a single row, or multiple rows within a table. Although optimizing the writing of SELECT statements that address large tables is an important part of performance tuning, it's the SQL statements that modify, delete, or add data that cause more frustration for the DBA when dealing with an OLTP database. Designing proper tables and indexes is important if the database is to efficiently process a large number of concurrent inserts, deletes, and updates to tables. In addition, the DBA needs to properly size the undo tablespace and the online redo logs to efficiently process these types of statements.

Transaction-Control Statements

Transaction-control statements are used to control the changes made by data-manipulation SQL statements, such as INSERT, UPDATE, and DELETE. These are the four transaction-control statements:

- COMMIT: When this statement follows a set of DML statements, the changes will be made permanent.

- ROLLBACK: When this statement follows one or more DML statements, the changes made by the preceding statement or statements will be undone. If there are no save points, all statements from the beginning of the transaction will be rolled back.

- SAVEPOINT: This statement allows flexibility in your transactions, helping you set intermediate points in the transaction to which you can roll back (undo) your transactions.

- SET TRANSACTION: This rarely used statement denotes the start of a transaction and is used in statements like SET TRANSACTION READ ONLY.

Data Definition Language Statements

Data definition language statements enable you to *define* the structure of the various schema objects in the Oracle database. DDL statements enable you to create, alter, and remove database objects, such as tables and indexes. These are some of the main uses of DDL statements:

- Creating tables, indexes, and other schema objects
- Creating and modifying procedures, functions, and packages
- Dropping and modifying database objects
- Creating and managing users of the database
- Granting and revoking privileges on objects
- Creating and altering tablespaces
- Creating and modifying database links

Oracle Schemas

In Oracle, a *schema* is defined as a collection of logical structures of data, or schema objects, although it is used mostly as a synonym for the database user (specifically, the application owner) that owns the schema pertaining to a specific application. Thus, the accounting schema within a company database would own all the tables and code pertaining to the accounting department. In addition to containing tables, a schema contains other database objects, such as PL/SQL procedures, functions and packages, views, sequences, synonyms, and clusters. This logical separation of the objects within the database allows you considerable flexibility in managing and securing your Oracle databases.

Although the DBA can use the CREATE SCHEMA statement to populate a schema with database objects such as tables and views, more often the application owner creates the database objects and is referred to as the *schema owner*. The user who creates the objects owns database objects such as tables, views, procedures, functions, and triggers. The owner of the object has to explicitly assign specific rights to other users, such as SELECT or UPDATE, if those other users are to use the objects.

USER-DEFINED OBJECT TYPES

Oracle Database 11*g* is an object-relational database and, as such, it allows users to define several types of data other than the standard relational data types. These user-defined data types include the following:

- *Object types*: These complex types are an abstraction of real-world entities.
- *Array types*: These types are used to create ordered sets of data elements of the same type.
- *Table types*: These types are used to create an unordered set of data elements of the same data type.
- *XML schema*: This is a new object type that is used to create types and storage elements for XML documents based on the XML schema.

The Appendix provides examples of how to create various kinds of user-defined object types. In this chapter, the focus is on the traditional relational objects.

In addition, the owner may also create synonyms, which are aliases for the various objects for other users in the database. Synonyms, which are explained in the "Using Synonyms" section, later in this chapter, serve multiple purposes, including masking the ownership of data objects and simplifying SQL statements for users by eliminating the need for them to specify the schema owner's name each time they access a database object not owned by themselves.

There are two basic ways to create a schema in an Oracle database. The common way is to log in as the schema owner and create all the tables, indexes, and other objects that you plan to include in your schema. Since the objects are all created by the same schema owner, they'll automatically be part of the schema.

The second way to create a schema is to explicitly create it by using the CREATE SCHEMA statement. The CREATE SCHEMA statement lets you create multiple tables and views, as well as grant users privileges on those tables and views, all in a *single* SQL statement.

Oracle Tables

Tables are the basic units of data storage in an Oracle database. A table is a logical entity that makes the reading and manipulation of data intuitive to users. A table consists of columns and rows, and a table row corresponds to a single record. When you create a table, you give it a name and define the set of columns that belong to it. Each column has a name and a specific data type (such as VARCHAR2 or DATE). You may have to specify the width or the precision and scale for certain columns, and some of the table columns can be set to contain default values.

■**Note** You can create either relational tables or object tables in Oracle databases. Relational tables are the basic table structures with rows and columns to hold data. Object tables use object types for their column definitions and are used to hold object instances of a particular type. In this chapter, we exclusively use relational tables.

WHAT'S THE DUAL TABLE?

The *dual table* belongs to the sys schema and is created automatically when the data dictionary is created. The dual table has one column called "dummy" and one row, and it enables you to use the Oracle SELECT command to compute a constant expression. As you have seen, everything in Oracle has to be in a table somewhere. Even if something isn't in a table, such as the evaluation of an arithmetical expression, a query that retrieves those results needs to use a table, and the dual table serves as a catchall table for those expressions. For example, to compute the product of 9 and 24,567, you can issue the following SQL command: SELECT 9*24567 FROM dual.

There are four basic ways in which you can organize tables in an Oracle database:

- *Heap-organized tables*: A heap-organized table is nothing but the normal Oracle table, where data is stored in no particular order.

- *Index-organized tables*: An index-organized table stores data sorted in a B-tree indexed structure.

- *Clustered tables*: A clustered table is part of a group of tables that shares the same data blocks, because data from the clustered tables are often requested together.

- *Partitioned tables*: A partitioned table lets you divide a large amount of data into subtables, called *partitions*, according to various criteria. Partitioning is especially useful in a data warehouse environment.

This section of the chapter will discuss the standard (heap-organized) Oracle tables. I'll discuss the other types of tables in the "Special Oracle Tables" section, later in the chapter.

Estimating the Table Size

Before you create a new table, it's a good idea to estimate the size of the table you'll need now and the size you expect in the future. Knowing the size of the table allows you to make the right decisions about space allocation.

Algorithms are available for figuring out the potential size of tables and indexes—they take the row size in bytes and multiply it by the estimated number of rows in the table. Estimation of table size is more an art than a precise science, and you don't need to agonize over coming up with "accurate" figures. Just use common sense and make sure you are not wildly off the mark.

You can simplify table-size estimation by using the OEM Database Control or by using the CREATE_TABLE_COST procedure of the DBMS_SPACE package. The following sections illustrate both approaches to sizing a new table.

Using Database Control to Estimate Table Size

Let's look at the steps you need to follow to derive size estimates for a new table using the Database Control interface:

1. From the Database Control home page, click the Administration tab.
2. Click Tables in the Schema list.
3. Click the Create button at the bottom-right corner.
4. Select Standard or the Index Organized type.
5. On the Create Table page, enter the new table name and the column data types in the columns section. Click the Estimate Table Size button.
6. In the Estimate Table Size page, enter the estimated number of rows in your table (see Figure 7-1).

Once you finish all the steps, OEM will quickly tell you how much space you'll need to accommodate the new table. It will also tell you how much space you need to allocate to the tablespace in which you're going to create your new table.

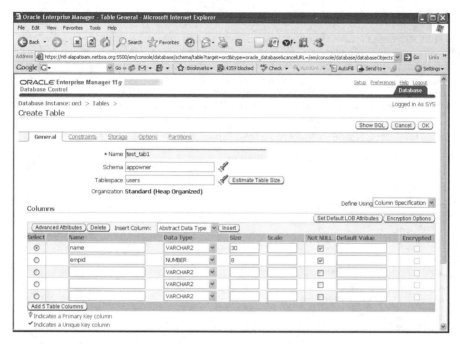

Figure 7-1. *Using the OEM Database Control to estimate table size*

■**Note** The following discussion of table operations deals with the "normal" or "regular" heap-organized Oracle tables, whose rows aren't stored in any particular order into the table. Most of the table operations discussed are common to all types of Oracle tables, but with some syntax modifications or limitations.

ORACLE ROW FORMAT AND SIZE

The Oracle database stores each row of a table as one or more row pieces. If a table row is longer than the row piece, the database may store the row using multiple row pieces, by chaining the row across the multiple blocks. Of course, if the table row is small, a data block can contain multiple table rows. The database uses the ROWIDs of the row pieces to chain the pieces together. Each of the row pieces contains a row header and the data for all or part of a row's columns.

Using the DBMS_SPACE Package to Estimate Space Requirements

The DBMS_SPACE package enables you to analyze segment growth and space requirements. You can use a procedure from this package to estimate size requirements for table indexes. If you know the approximate length of a new table's rows and the estimated number of rows, the DBMS_SPACE package will tell you the estimated space you need to create the table, given the storage attributes of the tablespace in which you plan to create it. You can use either the column information of the table or its row size to output the estimated table size. Listing 7-1 shows a simple example.

Listing 7-1. *Using the DBMS_SPACE Package to Estimate Space Requirements*

```
SQL> SET SERVEROUTPUT ON
SQL> DECLARE
  2    l_used_bytes NUMBER;
  3    l_allocated_bytes NUMBER;
  4    BEGIN
  5    DBMS_SPACE.CREATE_TABLE_COST (
  6    tablespace_name     => 'PERSON_D',
  7    avg_row_size        => 120,
  8    row_count           => 1000000,
  9    pct_free            => 10,
 10    used_bytes          => l_used_bytes,
 11    alloc_bytes         => l_allocated_bytes);
 12    DBMS_OUTPUT.PUT_LINE ('used = ' || l_used_bytes || ' bytes'
 13    ||   'allocated = ' || l_allocated_bytes || ' bytes');
 14*END;
SQL> /
used = 138854400 bytes    allocated = 167772160 bytes
PL/SQL procedure successfully completed.
SQL>
```

Note that the DBMS_SPACE package also contains the SPACE_USAGE procedure, which helps you deallocate unused space (actually unused extents) allocated to tables, indexes, and other objects. Here's the syntax for using this procedure to deallocate space allocated to a table:

```
SQL> ALTER TABLE persons DEALLOCATE UNUSED;
Table altered.
SQL>
```

Creating a Simple Table

To create a table in your own schema, you must have the CREATE TABLE system privilege; to create a table in another user's schema, you must have the CREATE ANY TABLE system privilege. Always specify a tablespace for the table creation—if you don't, the table will be created in the user's default tablespace. You must have either enough space quota in the tablespace where you are going to create your tables, or you must have the UNLIMITED TABLESPACE system privilege. Listing 7-2 gives the *syntax* for creating a simple table.

■**Tip** If your database consists of large read-only tables, consider using the Oracle table compression feature to save storage space.

Listing 7-2. *Creating a Simple Table*

```
SQL> CREATE TABLE emp (
        empno       NUMBER(5) PRIMARY KEY,
        ename       VARCHAR2(15) NOT NULL,
        ssn         NUMBER(9),
        job         VARCHAR2(10),
        mgr         NUMBER(5),
        hiredate    DATE DEFAULT (SYSDATE),
        sal         NUMBER(7,2),
        comm        NUMBER(7,2),
        deptno      NUMBER(3) NOT NULL
                    CONSTRAINT dept_fkey REFERENCES hr.dept(dept_id))
        TABLESPACE admin_tbs01

SQL>
```

In the CREATE TABLE statement in Listing 7-2, there are several integrity constraints, including a primary key and a foreign key defined on various columns of the table. Constraints are discussed in the "Managing Database Integrity Constraints" section, later in this chapter.

■**Note** You can use the ENCRYPT clause to transparently encrypt column data. You can encrypt columns of type CHAR, NCHAR, VARCHAR2, NVARCHAR2, NUMBER, DATE, and RAW. The user who encrypts the column will see the data in its unencrypted format. Encryption involves setting an encryption key and some other details—see the Oracle manual titled *Oracle Advanced Security Administrator's Guide,* accessible through http://tahiti.oracle.com, for additional information on encryption.

Here's how you would encrypt the ssn column in the previous table creation statement:

```
ssn       NUMBER(9) ENCRYPT
```

Once you create a new table, you can populate the table with data in several ways: you can use an INSERT command to insert data or use SQL*Loader (see Chapter 14) to load data. Or, you may decide to create a new table and have data come from an existing table in the same or a different database. This uses the well-known CREATE TABLE AS SELECT (CTAS) technique, which I explain shortly, in the "Creating a New Table with the CTAS Option" section. You can also use the SQL MERGE command to insert data from another table based on specific conditions. The use of the MERGE command is explained in the Appendix.

■**Note** If you are creating your database objects in a locally managed tablespace, you don't have to set storage parameters for any objects you create in that tablespace.

What Is a Null Value?

A null value means you simply leave a column blank in a row. A null value for a column in a certain row doesn't indicate a zero value for that column. Rather, the null indicates there is no value for that column in that row. If you have missing, inapplicable, or unknown data for a column, you use a null to indicate that. You can't leave any column in a table as a null value. A column will allow null values only if you don't specify the NOT NULL constraint for that column. In addition, when you designate a column as the primary key for that table, the column will not allow null values. Try to include all null values toward the end of the table, to conserve disk space. This is so because of the way Oracle stores null values. Any comparison between a null and other values can't be true or false, since the null signifies an unknown value.

Default Values for Columns

You can assign default values to columns. When you insert a new row, you can omit a value for any column with a default value. The database will automatically supply the default value for that column. If you don't explicitly define a default value for a column, the column value defaults to null. For example, if you set the 20 as the default value of the DEPT_NO column in the employees table, Oracle will insert the value 20 for the DEPT_NO column, even though that column doesn't have a value when new data in inserted.

Virtual Columns

In an Oracle Database 11g release database, you can use virtual columns in a table. A *virtual column* is a column that is derived by evaluating an expression based on one or more of the actual columns of the table or by evaluating a SQL or PL/SQL function. Unlike normal columns, the virtual column data is not stored permanently on disk. The database computes the virtual column values when you query it, by dynamically evaluating an expression on other columns or by computing a function.

You can use virtual columns in both DDL and DML statements. You can defined indexes on them and collect statistics on them as well.

Creating a Virtual Column

You use the clause GENERATED ALWAYS AS when you specify a virtual column as part of a CREATE TABLE statement, as the following example illustrates:

```
SQL>  CREATE TABLE emp (
  2    empno      NUMBER(5) PRIMARY KEY,
  3    ename      VARCHAR2(15) NOT NULL,
  4    ssn        NUMBER(9),
  5    sal        NUMBER(7,2),
  6*   hrly_rate  NUMBER(7,2) generated always as (sal/2080));

Table created.
SQL>
```

The last line in the previous example shows the specification of the virtual column. If you want, you can also specify the optional keyword VIRTUAL, as shown here:

```
SQL>  CREATE TABLE emp3
  2    (sal number (7,2),
  3    hrly_rate number (7,2) generated always as (sal/2080)
  4    VIRTUAL
  5*   CONSTRAINT HourlyRate CHECK (hrly_rate > 8.00));

Table created.
SQL>
```

In both of the examples shown here, hrly_rate is a virtual column generated by evaluating the expression sal/2800 for each row. You can also add a virtual column to an existing table by executing the ALTER TABLE statement, as shown in this example:

```
SQL> ALTER TABLE employees ADD (income AS (salary*commission_pct));
Table altered.
SQL>
```

Since I didn't specify a data type for the virtual column income, Oracle will automatically assign a default data type based on the data type for the two columns (salary and commission_pct) from which the database computes the virtual column.

Limitations of Virtual Columns

Some limitations exist on the use of virtual columns in a table, which I summarize here:

- You can't create virtual columns on an index-organized table, external table, temporary table, object, or a cluster.
- You can't create a virtual column as a user-defined type, large object (LOB), or RAW.
- All columns in the column expression must belong to the same table.
- The column expression must result in a scalar value.
- The column expression in the AS clause can't refer to another virtual column.
- You can't update a virtual column by using it in the SET clause of an update statement.
- You can't perform a delete or insert operation on a virtual column

Adding a Column to a Table

Adding a column to a table is a very straightforward operation. You simply use the ALTER TABLE command to add a column to a table, as shown here:

```
SQL> ALTER TABLE emp
     ADD (retired char(1));

Table altered.
SQL>
```

Dropping a Column from a Table

You can drop an existing column from a table by using the following command:

```
SQL> ALTER TABLE emp
     DROP (retired);

Table altered.
SQL>
```

If the table from which you're dropping the column contains a large amount of data, you can ask Oracle to merely mark the column as unused, without trying to remove the data at all. You won't see the column in any queries or views, and all dependent objects, such as constraints and indexes, defined on the column are removed. For all practical purposes, you can "drop" a large column this way very quickly.

Here's an example that marks as unused the hiredate and mgr columns in the emp table:

```
SQL> ALTER TABLE emp SET UNUSED (hiredate, mgr);
```

During a maintenance window, you can then permanently drop the two columns by using the following command:

```
SQL> ALTER TABLE emp DROP UNUSED COLUMNS;
```

If you think that the large number of rows in a table could potentially exhaust the undo space, you can drop a column with the optional CHECKPOINT clause. This will reduce the generation of undo data while dropping the column by applying checkpoints after a certain number of rows. Here's an example that makes the database apply a checkpoint each time it removes 10,000 rows in the emp table:

```
SQL> ALTER TABLE emp DROP UNUSED COLUMNS CHECKPOINT 10000;
```

Renaming a Table Column

You can easily rename table columns using the rename column command. For example, the following command will rename the retired column in the emp table to non_active. Note that you can also rename the column constraints, if you wish.

```
SQL> ALTER TABLE emp
     RENAME COLUMN retired TO non_active;
Table altered.
SQL>
```

■**Tip** You can rename tempfiles, as well as datafiles and the redo log files, using the ALTER DATABASE command.

Renaming a Table

On occasion, an application developer may want to rename a table. Renaming a table is straightforward:

```
SQL> ALTER TABLE emp
     RENAME TO emp;
Table altered.
SQL>
```

Removing All Data from a Table

To remove all the rows from a table, you can use the TRUNCATE command, which, contrary to its name, doesn't abbreviate or shorten anything—it summarily removes all the rows very quickly. TRUNCATE is a DDL command, so it can't be undone by using the ROLLBACK command.

You can also remove all the rows in a table with the DELETE * FROM TABLE . . . command, and because this is a DML command, you can roll back the deletion if you desire. However, because the DELETE command writes all changes to the undo segments, it takes a much longer time to execute. The TRUNCATE command doesn't have to bother with the undo segments, so it executes in a few seconds, even for the largest tables.

Here's an example of the TRUNCATE command in action:

```
SQL> SELECT COUNT(*) FROM test;

  COUNT(*)
-----------
    31

SQL> TRUNCATE TABLE test;

Table truncated.

SQL> SELECT COUNT(*) FROM test;
```

```
COUNT(*)
------------
       0
SQL>
```

Creating a New Table with the CTAS Option

To create a new table that is identical to an existing table, or to create a new table that includes only some rows and columns from another table, you can use the CREATE TABLE AS SELECT * FROM command. With this command, you can load a portion of an existing table into a new table by using where conditions, or you can load all the data of the old table into the newly created table by simply using the SELECT * FROM clause, as shown in the following code snippet:

```
SQL> CREATE TABLE emp_new
     AS
     SELECT * FROM emp;

Table created.
SQL>
```

If the table has millions of rows, and your time is too limited to use the simple CTAS method, there are a couple of ways to speed up the creation of new tables that contain large amounts of data. If the table you're creating is empty, you don't need to be concerned with the speed with which it's created—it's created immediately. But if you're loading the new table from an existing table, you can benefit from using the PARALLEL and NOLOGGING options, which speed up the loading of large tables.

The PARALLEL option enables you to do your data loading in parallel by several processes, and the NOLOGGING option instructs Oracle not to bother logging the changes to the redo log files and roll-back segments (except the very minimum necessary for housekeeping purposes). Here's an example:

```
SQL> CREATE TABLE employee_new
  2 AS SELECT * FROM employees
  3 PARALLEL DEGREE 4
  4*NOLOGGING;

Table created.
SQL>
```

The other method you can use to save time during table creation is to simply move a table from one tablespace to another. You can take advantage of the moving operation to change any storage parameters you wish. Here's an example of the ALTER TABLE . . . MOVE command, which enables you to move tables between tablespaces rapidly. In this example, the employee table is moved from its present tablespace to a new tablespace:

```
SQL> ALTER TABLE employee MOVE new_tablespace;
```

When you move a table, the ROWIDs of the rows change, thus making the indexes on the table unusable. You must either re-create the indexes or rebuild them after you move the table.

Placing a Table in Read-Only Mode

You can make any table in an Oracle database a read-only table, which means that the database will not permit you to add, remove, or alter the data in any way. For example, if you have a configuration table that you want to keep safe from any changes by any users, you can change the status of the table to read-only.

Use the ALTER TABLE statement to place a table in the read-only mode. Here's an example:

```
;
SQL> ALTER TABLE test READ ONLY;
```

Once you place a table in read-only mode, the database won't permit the following operations on that table:

- `TRUNCATE TABLE`
- `SELECT FOR UPDATE`
- Any DML operations
- `ALTER TABLE ADD/MODIFY/RENAME/DROP COLUMN`
- `ALTER TABLE SET COLUMN UNUSED`
- `ALTER TABLE DROP/TRUNCATE/EXCHANGE (SUB)PARTITION`
- `ALTER TABLE UPGRADE INCLUDING DATA` or `ALTER TYPE CASCADE INCLUDING TABLE DATA` for a type with read-only table dependents
- Online redefinition
- `FLASHBACK TABLE`

You can perform the following operations on a read-only table:

- `SELECT`
- `CREATE/ALTER/DROP INDEX`
- `ALTER TABLE ADD/MODIFY/DROP/ENABLE/DISABLE CONSTRAINT`
- `ALTER TABLE` for physical property changes
- `ALTER TABLE MOVE`
- `RENAME TABLE` and `ALTER TABLE RENAME TO`
- `DROP TABLE`

You can return a table to the normal read-write status by specifying the `READ WRITE` clause in the `ALTER TABLE` statement, as shown here:

```
SQL> ALTER TABLE test READ WRITE;
```

Table Compression

You can compress data in a table to save disk space and reduce memory usage, besides speeding up query performance. There is some overhead associated with table compression when you're loading data or performing DML operations, however. You can use table compression for both data warehousing applications, which involve primarily read-only operations, as well as OLTP systems, which include heavy DML operations. You can perform insert, delete, and update operations on compressed tables. To reduce your overhead, try to compress data that is mostly used for read-only operations and that is infrequently updated. Historical data and archival data are good candidates for table compression.

When the database compresses a table, it eliminates all duplicate values in a data block. The database stores all duplicate values in the table at the beginning of the block, in a symbol table for the block. The database replaces multiple occurrences of the duplicate data with a short reference to the symbol table. You can perform all operations that you can perform on a normal table on a compressed table. You can compress tables and materialized views. You can also compress only some of the partitions of a partitioned table.

Oracle offers *tablespace compression* as well. If you compress a tablespace, all tables you create in that tablespace are automatically compressed.

Once you define a table as a compressed table, the compression will occur when the data is undergoing any of the following operations:

- Load through direct-path SQL*Loader operations
- Load through a CTAS statement
- Parallel insert statements
- Serial insert statements with an append hint
- Single-row or array inserts and updates

The biggest hit on performance due to compression of data occurs during the insertion of data using any of the methods shown here. Deleting compressed data, however, is just as fast as deleting uncompressed data. In addition, updating also is slower in a compressed table.

In addition to creating a table with compression enabled, you can also compress existing data in a table by using the ALTER TABLE . . . MOVE statement. When you compress the data in this way, the database needs to acquire an exclusive lock on the table, which prevents all updates and inserts until the compression operation completes. Alternatively, you can use the DBMS_REDEFINITION package to perform an online redefinition of the table to avoid the locking of the table.

Enabling Compression

You can enable compression by specifying the COMPRESS clause either in a CREATE TABLE statement or in an ALTER TABLE . . . COMPRESS statement. If you're altering a table, only new data will be compressed. Thus, the table can have both compressed and uncompressed data in it at the same time. You can disable table compression for a table by using the ALTER TABLE . . . UNCOMPRESS statement. Disabling compression doesn't compress the already compressed data in the table—it makes sure that the new data is uncompressed.

■**Note** You can use table compression in both an OLTP as well as a data warehousing environment. You can get the best results by compressing all read-only or historical data, which rarely changes.

There are a couple of variants of the COMPRESS clause: you must use the COMPRESS FOR ALL OPERATIONS clause to enable compression for all operations. In order to enable it only for direct-path inserts (bulk insert operations), specify the COMPRESS FOR DIRECT_LOAD OPERATIONS clause. The clause COMPRESS by itself is equivalent to the COMPRESS FOR DIRECT_LOAD OPERATIONS clause.

Note that if you enable compression only for direct-path inserts, you can't drop any columns later on. You can add columns only if you don't specify default values for the columns. These restrictions don't apply when you enable compression for all operations on a table.

Examples of Table Compression

The following example shows how to enable compression for all operations on a table, which is what you'd want to do in an OLTP setting:

```
SQL> CREATE TABLE test
        name varchar2(20)
        address varchar2(50))
        COMPRESS FOR ALL OPERATIONS;
```

You can use either of the following statements to enable compression for direct-path inserts only on a table:

```
SQL> CREATE TABLE test
        name varchar2(20)
```

```
        address varchar2(50))
        COMPRESS;
SQL> CREATE TABLE test
        name varchar2(20)
        address varchar2(50))
        COMPRESS FOR DIRECT_LOAD OPERATIONS
```

As you can see from the examples, the COMPRESS FOR ALL OPERATIONS clause is what you must use for compressing OLTP tables. You can use the following query to find out which tables are compressed in your database:

```
SQL> SELECT table_name, compression, compress_for
        FROM dba_tables;
```

```
TABLE_NAME          COMPRESS     COMPRESS_FOR
----------------    --------     --------------------
EMP                 ENABLED      DIRECT LOAD ONLY
DEPT                ENABLED      FOR ALL OPERATIONS
SQL>
```

The COMPRESS_FOR column shows the type of table compression (all operations or direct load only).

Dropping Tables

You can drop a table by using the DROP TABLE *table_name* command. In order to be able to drop a table, the user must own the table (it must be in your schema), or the user must have the DROP ANY TABLE privilege.

When you use the DROP TABLE command, however, the table doesn't go away immediately—Oracle simply renames the table and stores it in the Recycle Bin, which is in reality simply a data dictionary table. Thus, you can bring back a table you dropped accidentally by using the following command:

```
SQL> FLASHBACK TABLE emp TO BEFORE DROP;
```

The ability to bring back a dropped table is known as the *Flashback Drop* feature. Chapter 16 explains this feature in detail and provides information about managing the Recycle Bin.

If you are sure that you'll never need the table, you can get rid of it *permanently* by using the PURGE option with your DROP TABLE command, as shown here:

```
SQL> DROP TABLE emp PURGE;
```

When you use the preceding PURGE command, the emp table is dropped immediately, and you can't get it back! Again, you'll see a lot more about this command in Chapter 16.

■**Note** The DROP TABLE *table_name* PURGE command is equivalent to the old DROP TABLE *table_name* command in pre–Oracle Database 10*g* release databases.

When you drop a table, all indexes you had defined on the table will be dropped as well. If the table you want to drop contains any primary or unique keys referenced by foreign keys of other tables, you must include the CASCADE clause in the DROP TABLE statement, in order to drop those constraints as well:

```
SQL> DROP TABLE emp CASCADE CONSTRAINTS;
```

Special Oracle Tables

The simple tables you saw in the previous sections satisfy most of the data needs of an application, but these aren't the only kind of tables Oracle allows you to create. You can create several kinds of specialized tables, such as temporary tables, external tables, and index-organized tables. In the following sections, you'll examine these important types of tables.

Temporary Tables

Oracle allows you to create temporary tables to hold data just for the duration of a session or even a transaction. After the session or the transaction ends, the table is truncated (the rows are automatically removed). Temporary tables are handy when you are dealing with complex queries or transactions that require transitory row information to be stored briefly before it is written to a permanent table.

The data in temporary tables cannot be backed up like that in other permanent tables. No data or index segments are automatically allotted to temporary tables or indexes upon their creation, as is the case for permanent tables and indexes. Space is allocated in temporary segments for the temporary tables only after the first INSERT command is used for the tables.

Temporary tables increase the performance of transactions that involve complex queries. One of the traditional responses to complex queries is to use a view to make the complex queries simpler to handle, but the view needs to execute each time you access it, thereby negating its benefits in many cases. Temporary tables are an excellent solution for cases like this, because they can be created as the product of complex SELECT statements used for the particular session or transaction, and they are automatically purged of data after the session.

Note Although Oracle doesn't analyze the temporary table data to gather the data distribution, that's not a problem for efficient query processing, because the temporary tables can keep constantly accessed join and other information in one handy location. You can repeatedly access this table rather than having to repeatedly execute complex queries.

Temporary tables are created in the user's temporary tablespace and are assigned temporary segments only after the first INSERT statement is issued for the temporary table. They are deallocated after the completion of the transaction or the end of the session, depending on how the temporary tables were defined.

Here are some attractive features of temporary tables from the Oracle DBA's point of view:

- Temporary tables drastically reduce the amount of redo activity generated by transactions. Redo logs don't fill up as quickly if temporary tables are used extensively during complex transactions.

- Temporary tables can be indexed to improve performance.

- Sessions can update, insert, and delete data in temporary tables just as in normal permanent tables.

- The data is automatically removed from the temporary table after a session or a transaction.

- You can define table constraints on temporary tables.

- Different users can access the same temporary table, with each user seeing only his or her session data.

- Temporary tables provide efficient data access because complex queries need not be executed repeatedly.

- The minimal amount of locking of temporary tables means more efficient query processing.
- The structure of the table persists after the data is removed, so future use is facilitated.

Creating a Session Temporary Table

Here is an example of a temporary table that lasts for an entire session. You use the `ON COMMIT DELETE ROWS` option to ensure that the data remains in the table only for the duration of the session.

```
SQL> CREATE GLOBAL TEMPORARY TABLE flight_status(
     destination VARCHAR2(30),
     startdate DATE,
     return_date DATE,
     ticket_price NUMBER)
     ON COMMIT PRESERVE ROWS;
```

The `ON COMMIT PRESERVE ROWS` option in the preceding example indicates that the table data is saved for the entire session, not just for the length of the transaction.

Creating a Transaction Temporary Table

Unlike session temporary tables, transaction temporary tables are specific to a single transaction. As soon as the transaction is committed or rolled back, the data is deleted from the temporary table. Here's how you create a transaction temporary table:

```
SQL> CREATE GLOBAL TEMPORARY TABLE sales_info
     (customer_name VARCHAR2(30),
     transaction_no NUMBER,
     transaction_date DATE)
     ON COMMIT DELETE ROWS;
```

The `ON COMMIT DELETE ROWS` option makes it clear that the data in this table should be retained only for the duration of the transaction that used this temporary table.

Index-Organized Tables

Index-organized tables (IOTs) are somewhat of a hybrid, because they possess features of both indexes and tables. IOTs are tables in which the data is stored in a B-tree index structure (in a primary key sorted manner), but they are unlike regular or heap-organized tables because regular tables do not order data. They are unlike regular indexes because while indexes consist only of the indexed columns, IOTs include both the key and the non-key columns. Oracle uses the B-tree index structures to store its data by sorting it by the primary key.

When you update an IOT, it is the index structure that really gets updated. Data access is much faster because you only have to perform one I/O to access the index/table. There is no need to access the index and the real table separately, as is the case with traditional indexed tables. The actual row data, and not merely the ROWID, is held in the index leaf block along with the indexed column value. IOTs are especially well suited for cases where you need to issue queries based on the values of the primary key. IOTs are convenient for very large databases (VLDBs) and OLTP applications. You can reorganize IOTs without rebuilding the indexes separately, which means that the reorganization time is less than it would be if you used regular heap-based tables. The major differences between normal tables and IOTs are shown in Table 7-1.

Table 7-1. *Differences Between Regular Oracle Tables and Index-Organized Tables*

Regular Oracle Tables	Index-Organized Tables
Physical ROWIDs	Logical ROWIDs
Uniquely identified by ROWID	Uniquely identified by primary key
Can contain LONG and LOB data	Can't contain LONG data
Allowed in table clusters	Not allowed in table clusters
Larger space requirements	Smaller space requirements
Slower data access	Faster data access

Listing 7-3 shows how to create an IOT.

Listing 7-3. *Creating an Index-Organized Table*

```
SQL> CREATE TABLE employee_new(
       employee_id NUMBER,
       dept_id NUMBER,
       name VARCHAR2(30),
       address VARCHAR2(120),
       CONSTRAINT pk_employee_new PRIMARY KEY (employee_id))
     ORGANIZATION INDEX TABLESPACE empindex_01
     PCTTHRESHOLD 25
     OVERFLOW TABLESPACE overflow_tables;
```

A few keywords in the previous CREATE TABLE statement are worth reviewing carefully. The key phrase ORGANIZATION INDEX indicates that this table is an IOT rather than a regular heap-organized table. The PCTTHRESHOLD keyword indicates the percentage of space reserved in the index blocks for the employee_new IOT. Any part of a row in the table that does not fit the 25 percent threshold value in each data block is saved in an overflow area. The CREATE TABLE statement assigns the overflow_tables tablespace to hold the overflow of data from the index blocks. You can set the threshold value to accommodate both the key columns as well as the frequently accessed first few non-key columns. You can find out which rows exceed the threshold value by executing the ANALYZE TABLE . . . LIST CHAINED ROWS statement.

You can employ the optional INCLUDING clause to specify the non-key columns you want stored with the key columns. As long as the database doesn't exceed the threshold specified by you, it tries to accommodate all non-key columns up to and including the column you specify with the INCLUDING clause in the index leaf block. The database stores the rest of the non-key columns in the overflow segment. The PCTTHRESHOLD clause will override the INCLUDING clause if there is a conflict between the values you specify for the two clauses. Listing 7-4 shows how to employ the INCLUDING clause.

Listing 7-4. *Using the INCLUDING Clause When Creating an Index-Organized Table*

```
SQL> CREATE TABLE employee_new(
       employee_id NUMBER,
       dept_id NUMBER,
```

```
name VARCHAR2(30),
address VARCHAR2(120),
CONSTRAINT pk_employee_new PRIMARY KEY (employee_id))
ORGANIZATION INDEX TABLESPACE empindex_01
PCTTHRESHOLD 25
INCLUDING name
OVERFLOW TABLESPACE overflow_tables;
```

In Listing 7-4, the INCLUDING clause instructs the database to include the employee_id, dept_id, and name columns (all of which are non-key columns) in the index leaf block, along with the key column values, of course.

Remember that index entries in IOTs can be large because they contain not just a key value, but all the row values. So IOTs do not necessarily have all of their data stored in the index blocks. It is quite possible for the key and part of the row to be saved in the index blocks and for the rest to be in some other tablespace. If the PCTTHRESHOLD parameter is too low, there is a risk of a chaining problem in which parts of the row reside in different data blocks, leading to a slowdown of your queries.

External Tables

Databases in general, and data warehouses in particular, need to regularly extract data from various sources and transform it into a more useful form. For example, a data warehouse may collect data from the OLTP data sources and transform it according to some business rules to make it useful for management.

Traditionally, the way to load a data warehouse has been to first load staging tables with the raw data. Sometimes the data would be transformed outside of the database and loaded directly in one pass to the warehouse tables. Either method is usually very cumbersome, even when you use state-of-the-art extraction and transformation tools or custom scripts.

Oracle allows the use of *external tables*—that is, tables that use data that resides in external operating system files. External tables don't need any storage in terms of extents in the Oracle database—the definition of an external table merely makes an entry in the data dictionary, which enables you to load data into other Oracle database tables from the external tables. If you drop an external table in Oracle, you'll only be removing its definition from the data dictionary—the data itself remains safe in the external source files.

External tables are commonly used as intermediate staging tables during data transformations. External tables enable you to view externally stored data as if it were inside a table in the Oracle database. You can perform queries and joins on external tables, but you can't update, insert, or delete from these tables; no DML operations are permissible on external tables.

■**Note** Chapter 14 provides a detailed example of using external tables and discusses them in more depth.

Partitioned Tables

Oracle databases can be quite large, and it's not uncommon to encounter tables that hold several gigabytes (or even several terabytes) worth of data. *Partitioning* is a way of logically dividing a large table into smaller chunks to facilitate query processing, DML operations, and database management. All the partitions share the same logical definition, column definitions, and constraints.

Improvements in query response times are startling when you partition a multibillion-row table into hundreds or thousands of partitions. In some busy environments, new partitions may be created as often as every hour! Partitioning leads directly to better query performance because the database needs to search only the relevant partitions of the table during a query. This avoidance of unneeded partitions when querying is called *partition pruning*; the availability of one partition is independent of the availability of the other partitions.

Data I/O can also be enhanced by using partitions because you can keep the partitions of a heavily accessed table on different disk drives. If you are using the Oracle parallel DML features, partitioned tables provide you with better performance.

Partitioning a table also provides *partition independence*, meaning, among other things, that you can perform your backup and recovery operations, data loading, and index creation on partitions of a large table instead of the whole table. For example, you can copy a single partition's data using the Data Pump Export utility, reducing export and import times dramatically when you only need part of the entire data set. The ability to perform tasks on partitions instead of entire tables means that your database downtime will be reduced drastically.

■**Note** Although partitioned tables generally improve query performance in very large tables, they aren't a panacea for poor coding or other design problems in the application. Partitioning also carries a price in terms of additional work to maintain the partitions and their indexes. Of course, you also have to pay for the partitioning capability, as it's an option that you have to license separately from Oracle Corporation.

Partitioning tables is also an effective way of purging or archiving older data that you don't need right now. It is very common for large data warehouses to archive data that is older than a certain date, and partitioned tables make archiving easy. For example, each quarter you can drop the oldest partition and replace it with a new partition. The partitioned table in this case will end up having roughly the same amount of data, and it will cover the same length of time (a quarterly collection of company data for three years will always have 12 partitions in the table). In addition, large table exports can be performed more quickly when you partition the table into smaller chunks and export each partition separately.

Oracle offers six different ways to partition your table data: *range partitioning, interval partitioning, hash partitioning, list partitioning, reference partitioning,* and *system partitioning*. In addition, you can use *composite partitioning* (combine two partitioning methods to divide the data into smaller subpartitions) strategies, which takes the actual number of partitioning methods to over a dozen types. No matter which partitioning method you use, you must specify the following information when creating a partitioned table:

- *Partitioning method*: This is one of the six types of partitioning.

- *Partitioning column (or columns)*: This is the column or columns on the basis of which you want to partition the table (for example, transaction_date). The range or set of values of the partitioning columns are called the *partitioning keys*.

- *The partition descriptions*: These descriptions specify the criteria for the inclusion of the actual partitioning keys in each partition. You use a partition bound for range partitioning and use the clause VALUES LESS THAN to limit the partitioning key values in each partition. In list partitioning, you specify a list of literal values that tell Oracle what partitioning key values qualify for inclusion in a partition.

The following sections discuss the different types of partitioning and show how to partition a table.

Range Partitioning

Range partitioning is a popular way to partition Oracle tables, and it was the first type of partitioning introduced by Oracle. Range partitioning is used for data that can be separated into ranges based on some criterion. You get the best results from range partitioning if the data falls evenly into the different ranges that you create. Your ranges can be based on a sequence number or a part number, but the range-partitioning technique is usually based on time (monthly or quarterly data, for example).

Let's say you need to create a table to hold three years of quarterly sales data for a major airline. This could easily add up to several hundreds of millions of transactions. If you partition the sales table by a range of quarters and decide to hold no more than three years' worth of data at any given time, you could have 12 partitions in the table, partitioned by quarters. Each time you enter a new quarter, you can archive the oldest quarter's data, thus keeping the number of partitions constant. By partitioning the huge table, which might have a total of 480 million rows, for example, any queries you run would only have to deal with one-twelfth of the table—that is, about 40 million rows—which makes a big difference. Partitioning thus provides you with a divide-and-conquer technique for dealing efficiently with massive amounts of table data.

Listing 7-5 shows the DDL for creating a range-partitioned table, with each year's worth of data divided into four partitions. With each new quarter, you can add another partition. Thus, you'll end up with 12 partitions over a three-year period.

Listing 7-5. *Creating a Range-Partitioned Table*

```
SQL> CREATE TABLE sales_data
  2  (ticket_no NUMBER,
  3  sale_year  INT NOT NULL,
  4  sale_month INT NOT NULL,
  5  sale_day   INT NOT NULL)
  6  PARTITION BY RANGE (sale_year, sale_month, sale_day)
  7  (PARTITION sales_q1 VALUES LESS THAN (2008, 04, 01)
  8  TABLESPACE ts1,
  9  PARTITION sales_q2 VALUES LESS THAN (2008, 07, 01)
 10  TABLESPACE ts2,
 11  PARTITION sales_q3 VALUES LESS THAN (2008, 10, 01)
 12  TABLESPACE ts3,
 13  PARTITION sales_q4 VALUES LESS THAN (2009, 01, 01)
 14* TABLESPACE ts4);

Table created.
SQL>
```

The CREATE TABLE statement in Listing 7-5 will create four partitions, each stored in a separate tablespace. Notice how the partitions are based on date ranges. The first partition, sales_q1, will include all transactions that took place in the first three months (one quarter) of the year 2008. The second quarter, sales_q2, will include transactions that occurred between April and June of 2008(months 4, 5, and 6 of the year), and so on.

It is common in range-partitioned tables to use a catchall partition as the very last one. When this is the case, the last partition will contain values less than a value called *maxvalue*, which is simply any value higher than the values in the second-to-last partition. Note that each partition has a specific name and is stored in a separate tablespace.

In the partitioned sales_data table, the sales data for June 10, 2008 (sale_year=2004, sale_month=6, and sale_day=10) has a partitioning key of (2004, 6, 10) and would be stored in partition sales_q2. When a query requests data for June 10, 2008, the Oracle query zooms in on partition sales_q2 and completely ignores the rest of the table data.

Interval Partitioning

Interval partitioning is an extension of the traditional range-partitioning method. In order to implement interval partitioning for a table, you must first specify a minimum of one range partition for that table. Whether you use the minimum single-range partition or multiple-range partitions, the high value of the range partitioning key is called the *transition point*. The database automatically creates interval partitions after the data in the table crosses the transition point.

If, for example, you use monthly intervals for a table, and the highest value for the range partitions is January 1, 2009, then the transition point will be at January 1, 2009. The first month interval, then, would be January 2008, and its lower boundary would be January 1, 2008. Similarly, the lower boundary for the December 2008 interval would be December 1, 2008. It doesn't matter in this case whether the November 2008 partition already exists.

Here's what you need to know about interval partitioning:

- Use the INTERVAL clause in the CREATE TABLE statement to create an interval-partitioned table.

- Specify at least one range partition using the partition clause, before specifying your interval partitions.

- You can't use a partitioning key that includes more than one column.

- The partitioning key must be of the NUMBER or DATE type.

- You can optionally specify the tablespaces for the partition data by including the STORE IN clause in the CREATE TABLE statement.

In the following example, I create an interval-partitioned table with four range partitions, identified by p0, p1, p2, and p3. The four range partitions are created on the time_id column, with the transition point being the highest value of the range partitions, which is January 1, 2008 (in partition p3). Once the time_id column's value crosses January 1, 2009, the database will automatically spawn interval-based partitions, all with a width of one month.

```
CREATE TABLE interval_sales
    ( prod_id      NUMBER(6)
    , cust_id      NUMBER
    , time_id      DATE
    , channel_id   CHAR(1)
    , promo_id     NUMBER(6)
    , quantity_sold NUMBER(3)
    , amount_sold  NUMBER(10,2)
    )
  PARTITION BY RANGE (time_id)
  INTERVAL(NUMTOYMINTERVAL(1, 'MONTH'))
    ( PARTITION p0 VALUES LESS THAN (TO_DATE('1-1-2006', 'DD-MM-YYYY')),
      PARTITION p1 VALUES LESS THAN (TO_DATE('1-1-2007', 'DD-MM-YYYY')),
      PARTITION p2 VALUES LESS THAN (TO_DATE('1-7-2008', 'DD-MM-YYYY')),
      PARTITION p3 VALUES LESS THAN (TO_DATE('1-1-2009', 'DD-MM-YYYY')) );
```

There is no limit on the number of interval partitions in a table. In our example here, the database will continue to create a new interval partition for each new month.

Hash Partitioning

Suppose the transaction data in the previous example were not evenly distributed among the quarters. What if, due to business and cyclical reasons, an overwhelming number of sales occurred in the last two quarters, with the earlier quarters contributing relatively negligible sales? Range partitioning will be good only in theory, because the last two quarters could end up each having almost half of the original nonpartitioned table's data.

In such cases, it's better to use the *hash-partitioning* scheme. All you have to do is decide on the number of partitions, and Oracle's hashing algorithms will assign a hash value to each row's partitioning key and place it in the appropriate partition. You don't have to know anything about the distribution of the data in the table, other than that the data doesn't fall into some easily determined ranges. All you need to do is provide a partition key, which in the hash-partitioning scheme shown next is the ticket_no column:

```
SQL> CREATE TABLE sales_data
  2  (ticket_no NUMBER,
  3  sale_year  INT NOT NULL,
  4  sale_month INT NOT NULL,
```

```
   5  sale_day    INT NOT NULL)
   6  PARTITION BY HASH (ticket_no)
   7  PARTITIONS 4
   8* STORE IN (ts1,ts2,ts3,ts4);
Table created.
SQL>
```

In the preceding example, four hash partitions are created in four tablespaces. We won't know in which partition the data for, say, June 10, 2008, is stored. Oracle determines the storage based on a hashing algorithm, and you have no control whatsoever over the row-to-partition mapping.

List Partitioning

There may be times when you'll want to partition the data not on the basis of a time range or evenly distributed hashing scheme, but rather by known values, such as city, territory, or some such attribute. *List partitioning* is preferable to range or hash partitioning when your data is distributed among a set number of discrete values. For example, you may want to group a company's sales data according to regions rather than quarters. List partitioning enables you to group your data on the same lines as real-world groupings of data, rather than arbitrary ranges of time or some such criterion.

For example, when you're dealing with statewide totals in the United States, you'll be dealing with 50 different sets of data. It makes more sense in this situation to partition your data into four or five regions, rather than use the range method to partition the data alphabetically. Listing 7-6 shows how to use list partitioning to partition the ticket_sales table. The partitions are made up of groups of flight-originating cities, shown by the start_city column.

Listing 7-6. *Creating a List-Partitioned Table*

```
SQL> CREATE TABLE sales_data
   2  (ticket_no NUMBER,
   3  sale_year   INT NOT NULL,
   4  sale_month INT NOT NULL,
   5  sale_day    INT NOT NULL,
   6  destination_city   CHAR(3),
   7  start_city         CHAR(3))
   8  PARTITION BY LIST (start_city)
   9  (PARTITION northeast_sales  values ('NYC','BOS','PEN') TABLESPACE ts1,
  10  PARTITION southwest_sales values ('DFW','ORL','HOU') TABLESPACE ts2,
  11  PARTITION pacificwest_sales values('SAN','LOS','WAS') TABLESPACE ts3,
  12* PARTITION  southeast_sales values ('MIA','CHA','ATL')  TABLESPACE ts4);

Table created.
SQL>
```

In the previous list-partitioning example, the partition description specifies a list of values for the start_city column. Our table creation statement created four list partitions. Only cities that fall in this list will be included in the partition. A ticket with the information 9999, 2004, 06, 01, DFW, HOU will be stored in the southwest_sales partition.

Reference Partitioning

If two tables are related to one another, you can take advantage of this relationship by partitioning the two tables on the basis of the existing parent-child relationship. The relationship is enforced by primary key and foreign key constraints. If two tables share a parent-child relationship, you only need to formally partition the parent table. Once you do this, you can equipartition the child table, which inherits the partitioning key from the parent table. You thus avoid duplicating key columns.

Any partition maintenance operations on the parent table will automatically cascade to the child table as well.

A simple example will make reference partitioning clear. The tables orders and orderitems are related to each other, on the basis of the orderid column in the two tables. This relationship is captured by the referential constraint orderid_refconstraint. The parent table, orders, is partitioned on the OrderDate column using a range-partitioning scheme, as shown here:

```
CREATE TABLE orders
    ( order_id           NUMBER(12),
      order_date         DATE,
      order_mode         VARCHAR2(8),
      customer_id        NUMBER(6),
      order_status       NUMBER(2),
      order_total        NUMBER(8,2),
      sales_rep_id       NUMBER(6),
      promotion_id       NUMBER(6),
      CONSTRAINT orders_pk PRIMARY KEY(order_id)
    )
  PARTITION BY RANGE(order_date)
    ( PARTITION Q1_2005 VALUES LESS THAN (TO_DATE('01-APR-2005','DD-MON-YYYY')),
      PARTITION Q2_2005 VALUES LESS THAN (TO_DATE('01-JUL-2005','DD-MON-YYYY')),
      PARTITION Q3_2005 VALUES LESS THAN (TO_DATE('01-OCT-2005','DD-MON-YYYY')),
      PARTITION Q4_2005 VALUES LESS THAN (TO_DATE('01-JAN-2006','DD-MON-YYYY'))
    );
```

Since there is a parent-child relationship between the orders and orderitems tables, you use reference partitioning on the constraint orderid_refconstraint for orderitems, to create the partitioned table. The clause FOREIGN KEY (order_id) REFERENCES order (order_id) shows that the orderitems table is created with the reference-partitioning scheme. The orderitems table is equipartitioned with reference to the parent table orders.

```
CREATE TABLE order_items
    ( order_id           NUMBER(12) NOT NULL,
      line_item_id       NUMBER(3)  NOT NULL,
      product_id         NUMBER(6)  NOT NULL,
      unit_price         NUMBER(8,2),
      quantity           NUMBER(8),
      CONSTRAINT order_items_fk
      FOREIGN KEY(order_id) REFERENCES orders(order_id)
    )
PARTITION BY REFERENCE(order_items_fk);
```

You can use all partitioning strategies with reference partitioning, with the exception of interval partitioning.

When creating a reference-partitioned table, the partition by reference clause in the CREATE TABLE statement specifies the name for the reference constraint that is the basis for the reference partition. You must ensure that this referential constraint is both enabled and enforced.

In the example, the child table orderitems has four partitions: Q1_2005, Q2_2005, Q3_2005, and Q4_2005. Each of these four partitions contains the order_items column values that correspond to orders in the parent table's partition

Note the following features about a reference-partitioned table:

- The reference-partitioning example here doesn't use any partition descriptors. If you do provide partition descriptors, they must be the same as the number of partitions or subpartitions in the parent table. That is, the child table will have one partition for each partition or subpartition of the parent table.

- You can name the partitions of a reference-partitioned table.

- If you don't name the partitions, the partitions will derive their names from the corresponding partitions of the parent table.
- You can specify an explicit tablespace for the partitions of a reference-partitioned table.
- If you don't specify a tablespace, the partitions of a reference-partitioned table are stored along with the corresponding partition of the parent table, in the same tablespace.

■**Note** You can't specify partition bounds for the partitions of a reference-partitioned table.

Virtual Column-Based Partitioning

Earlier in this chapter, you learned how to create and use virtual columns in an Oracle database. You can use one or more columns of a table to create a virtual column on that table. You can partition a table on a virtual column. What this means is that you can partition a table on a partition key that doesn't actually exist in the table. Your partitioning key is defined by the same expression that the database uses for the virtual column.

You can use all basic partitioning strategies, including the different combinations of composite partitioning, with virtual column-based partitioning of a table.

In the following example, I partition the sales table using a virtual column for the subpartitioning key. The virtual column total_amount is defined as the product of the amount_sold and quantity_sold columns.

```
CREATE TABLE sales
  ( prod_id      NUMBER(6) NOT NULL
  , cust_id      NUMBER NOT NULL
  , time_id      DATE NOT NULL
  , channel_id   CHAR(1) NOT NULL
  , promo_id     NUMBER(6) NOT NULL
  , quantity_sold NUMBER(3) NOT NULL
  , amount_sold  NUMBER(10,2) NOT NULL
  , total_amount AS (quantity_sold * amount_sold)
  )
PARTITION BY RANGE (time_id) INTERVAL (NUMTOYMINTERVAL(1,'MONTH'))
SUBPARTITION BY RANGE(total_amount)
SUBPARTITION TEMPLATE
  ( SUBPARTITION p_small VALUES LESS THAN (1000)
  , SUBPARTITION p_medium VALUES LESS THAN (5000)
  , SUBPARTITION p_large VALUES LESS THAN (10000)
  , SUBPARTITION p_extreme VALUES LESS THAN (MAXVALUE)
  )
(PARTITION sales_before_2007 VALUES LESS THAN
       (TO_DATE('01-JAN-2007','dd-MON-yyyy'))
)
ENABLE ROW MOVEMENT
PARALLEL NOLOGGING;
```

Notice that the ENABLE ROW MOVEMENT clause ensures that a row can migrate from its current partition to a different partition if the virtual column's value evaluates to a value that doesn't belong in the current partition any longer.

System Partitioning

System partitioning is a unique partitioning method, where the application and not the database controls the placement of the data. The database merely lets you break a table up into partitions, without any idea of what each of the partitions will contain. The application controls what goes into the individual partitions. You must explicitly specify the partition when inserting data into a system-partitioned table. So, if you try to insert data into a system-partitioned table without specifying the specific partition into which the data goes, the insert will fail.

The biggest advantage in using system partitioning is that you can create and maintain tables that are equipartitioned with respect to a base table.

Creating a System-Partitioned Table

The following example shows how to create a system-partitioned table:

```
CREATE TABLE test (c1 integer, c2 integer)
PARTITIONED BY SYSTEM
(
  PARTITION p1 TABLESPACE tbs_1,
  PARTITION p2 TABLESPACE tbs_2,
  PARTITION p3 TABLESPACE tbs_3,
  PARTITION p4 TABLESPACE tbs_4
);
```

The clause PARTITIONED BY SYSTEM, of course, specifies that the table use system partitioning.

Inserting Data

When you're inserting data using an INSERT or MERGE statement, you must specify the partition into which you want the new row to be placed. Here's an example of an insertion into a system-partitioned table:

```
SQL> INSERT INTO test PARTITION (p1) VALUES (4,5);
```

The example specifies the partition p1 for inserting the new data.

Deleting and Updating Data

Unlike the insert operation, deleting and updating data in a system-partitioned table doesn't require you to use a partition-aware syntax, by specifying the partition name in the DELETE or UPDATE command. However, Oracle recommends that you specify the partition, so the database can use partition pruning and avoid scanning the entire table for the data.

Limitations

System partitioning doesn't support the CREATE TABLE AS SELECT and the INSERT INTO TABLE AS statements. The reason in both cases is that system partitioning doesn't make use of a partitioning method, and hence there's no mapping between rows and partitions.

Composite Partitioning

Sometimes, merely partitioning on range, hash, or list schemes may not be enough. You can further break down a large table into *subpartitions* for more control over data placement and performance. Oracle offers several types of composite partitioning. For example, under the range-hash-partitioning method, you first partition the table using range partitioning and then subpartition each of those partitions using a hash scheme. In a range-list-partitioning scheme, you first partition the table using range partitioning and then subpartition those partitions using list partitioning. Similarly, you can use the range-range, list-list, list-hash, and list-range composite partitioning methods.

Range-Hash Partitioning

Sometimes you may partition a table range-wise, but the distribution may not be very equal. You can make this a better partitioning scheme by hash partitioning after the range partitioning is done. This will allow you to store the data more efficiently, although it becomes more complex to manage.

Range-hash partitioning combines the best of the range- and hash-partitioning schemes. Range partitioning, as you've already seen, is easy to implement, and hash partitioning provides you benefits such as striping and parallelism.

Listing 7-7 shows a simple example of how to create a range-hash-partitioned table.

Listing 7-7. *Creating a Range-Hash-Partitioned Table*

```
SQL> CREATE TABLE scout_gear (equipno NUMBER,equipname VARCHAR(32),price NUMBER)
  2  PARTITION BY RANGE (equipno) SUBPARTITION BY HASH(equipname)
  3  SUBPARTITIONS 8 STORE IN (ts1, ts2, ts3, ts4)
  4  (PARTITION p1 VALUES LESS THAN (1000),
  5  PARTITION p2 VALUES LESS THAN (2000),
  6  PARTITION p3 VALUES LESS THAN (3000),
  7* PARTITION p4 VALUES LESS THAN (MAXVALUE));
Table created.
SQL>
```

In this example, the scout_gear table is first partitioned by range on the equipno column—four range-based partitions are created. These four partitions are then subpartitioned on the equipname column using a hash-partitioning scheme, resulting in 32 subpartitions altogether. Note the SUBPARTITIONS clause in line 3.

Range-List Partitioning

In the range-list-partitioning method, you first partition the data based on a range of values. You then use list partitioning to break up the first set of partitions, using a list of discrete values. Listing 7-8 shows an example of how to create a range-list-partitioned table.

Listing 7-8. *Creating a Range-List-Partitioned Table*

```
SQL> CREATE TABLE quarterly_regional_sales
  2  (ticket_no NUMBER,
  3  sale_year INT NOT NULL,
  4  sale_month INT NOT NULL,
  5  sale_day DATE,
  6  destination_city  CHAR(3),
  7  start_city        CHAR(3))
  8  PARTITION BY RANGE(sale_day)
  9  SUBPARTITION BY LIST (start_city)
 10  (PARTITION q1_2004 VALUES LESS THAN (TO_DATE('1-APR-2004','DD-MON-YYYY'))
 11  TABLESPACE t1
 12  (SUBPARTITION  q12004_northeast_sales VALUES  ('NYC','BOS','PEN'),
 13  SUBPARTITION   q12004_southwest_sales VALUES  ('DFW','ORL','HOU'),
 14  SUBPARTITION   q12004_pacificwest_sales VALUES ('SAN','LOS','WAS'),
 15  SUBPARTITION   q12004_southeast_sales VALUES  ('MIA','CHA','ATL')
 16  ),
 17  PARTITION q2_2004 VALUES LESS THAN (TO_DATE('1-JUL-2004','DD-MON-YYYY'))
```

```
18   TABLESPACE t2
19   (SUBPARTITION  q22004_northeast_sales  VALUES  ('NYC','BOS','PEN'),
20   SUBPARTITION    q22004_southwest_sales VALUES    ('DFW','ORL','HOU'),
21   SUBPARTITION    q22004_pacificwest_sales VALUES ('SAN','LOS','WAS'),
22   SUBPARTITION    q22004_southeast_sales VALUES    ('MIA','CHA','ATL')
23   ),
24   PARTITION q3_2004 VALUES LESS THAN (TO_DATE('1-OCT-2004','DD-MON-YYYY'))
25   TABLESPACE t3
26   (SUBPARTITION  q32004_northeast_sales  VALUES  ('NYC','BOS','PEN'),
27   SUBPARTITION    q32004_southwest_sales VALUES    ('DFW','ORL','HOU'),
28   SUBPARTITION    q32004_pacificwest_sales VALUES ('SAN','LOS','WAS'),
39   SUBPARTITION    q32004_southeast_sales VALUES    ('MIA','CHA','ATL')
30   ),
31   PARTITION q4_2004 VALUES LESS THAN (TO_DATE('1-JAN-2005','DD-MON-YYYY'))
32   TABLESPACE  t4
33   (SUBPARTITION  q42004_northeast_sales  VALUES  ('NYC','BOS','PEN'),
34   SUBPARTITION    q42004_southwest_sales VALUES    ('DFW','ORL','HOU'),
35   SUBPARTITION    q42004_pacificwest_sales VALUES ('SAN','LOS','WAS'),
36   SUBPARTITION    q42004_southeast_sales VALUES    ('MIA','CHA','ATL')
37   )
38*  );
Table created.
SQL>
```

The preceding statement will create 16 subpartitions in the range-list-partitioned table with 4 subpartitions in each tablespace (t1, t2, t3, t4). Each time you insert a row of data into the quarterly_regional_sales table, Oracle will first check whether the value of the partitioning column for a row falls within a specific partition range. Oracle will then map the row to a subpartition within that partition, by mapping the subpartition column value to the appropriate subpartition based on the values in that subpartition's list. For example, the row with the column values (9999, 2004, 10, 1, 'DAL', 'HOU') maps to subpartition q32004_southwest_sales.

Composite Interval-List-Partitioned Tables

You must use a subpartition template to create a table with list subpartitions. Otherwise, you'll be able to create only a default subpartition for every interval partition.

In the example shown in Listing 7-9, the sales table is first interval partitioned on the time_id columns, with a daily interval. The table is then subpartitioned by list on the channel_id column.

Listing 7-9. *Creating an Interval-List-Partitioned Table*

```
CREATE TABLE sales
  ( prod_id       NUMBER(6)
  , cust_id       NUMBER
  , time_id       DATE
  , channel_id    CHAR(1)
  , promo_id      NUMBER(6)
  , quantity_sold NUMBER(3)
  , amount_sold   NUMBER(10,2)
  )
 PARTITION BY RANGE (time_id) INTERVAL (NUMTODSINTERVAL(1,'DAY'))
 SUBPARTITION BY RANGE(amount_sold)
    SUBPARTITION TEMPLATE
    ( SUBPARTITION p_low VALUES LESS THAN (1000)
    , SUBPARTITION p_medium VALUES LESS THAN (4000)
```

```
  , SUBPARTITION p_high VALUES LESS THAN (8000)
  , SUBPARTITION p_ultimate VALUES LESS THAN (maxvalue)
  )
( PARTITION before_2000 VALUES LESS THAN (TO_DATE('01-JAN-2000','dd-MON-yyyy')))
PARALLEL;
```

Composite Interval-Range Partitioning

As in the case of the list subpartitioning, you must use a subpartition template if you want to create range subpartitions for the future interval partitions in an interval-range-partitioned table. Without such a template, you'll manage to create only a range subpartition with the MAXVALUE upper boundary for every interval partition.

The example shown in Listing 7-10 illustrates the creation of an interval-range composite partitioned table. The interval partitions are created using daily intervals on the time_id column and the range subpartitions by partitioning on the amount_sold column.

Listing 7-10. *Creating an Interval-Range-Partitioned Table*

```
CREATE TABLE sales
  ( prod_id        NUMBER(6)
  , cust_id        NUMBER
  , time_id        DATE
  , channel_id     CHAR(1)
  , promo_id       NUMBER(6)
  , quantity_sold  NUMBER(3)
  , amount_sold    NUMBER(10,2)
  )
PARTITION BY RANGE (time_id) INTERVAL (NUMTODSINTERVAL(1,'DAY'))
SUBPARTITION BY LIST (channel_id)
  SUBPARTITION TEMPLATE
  ( SUBPARTITION p_catalog VALUES ('C')
  , SUBPARTITION p_internet VALUES ('I')
  , SUBPARTITION p_partners VALUES ('P')
  , SUBPARTITION p_direct_sales VALUES ('S')
  , SUBPARTITION p_tele_sales VALUES ('T')
  )
( PARTITION before_2000 VALUES LESS THAN (TO_DATE('01-JAN-2000','dd-MON-yyyy')))
PARALLEL;
```

Partition Maintenance Operations

After you initially create partitioned tables, you can perform a number of maintenance operations on the partitions. For example, you can add and drop partitions to maintain a fixed number of partitions based on a quarterly time period.

In this section, I illustrate the use of these maintenance operations by assuming a range-partitioning scheme. These maintenance operations apply to all types of partitioning schemes, with a few exceptions, like the following:

- Range and list partitions can't be coalesced.

- Hash partitions can't be dropped, split, or merged.

- Only list partitions allow the modification of partitions by adding and dropping the partition values.

Adding Partitions

You can add a new partition to the ticket_sales table to include a new quarter, as follows:

```
SQL> ALTER TABLE ticket_sales
     ADD PARTITION sales_quarter5 VALUES LESS THAN
     (TO_DATE('1-APR-2005','DD-MON-YYYY'))
     TABLESPACE ticket_sales05;
```

   This example adds a new quarterly partition for the first quarter of the year 2005, which comes after the last quarter in the original table.

Splitting a Partition

The add partition statement will add partitions only to the upper end of the existing table. But what if you need to insert some new data into the middle of a table? What if an existing partition becomes too large, and you would rather have smaller partitions? Splitting a partition takes the data in an existing partition and distributes it between two partitions.
   You can use the split partition clause to break up a partition, as shown here:

```
SQL> ALTER TABLE ticket_sales
     SPLIT PARTITION ticket_sales01 AT (2000) INTO
     (PARTITION ticket_sales01A, ticket_sales01B);
```

Merging Partitions

You can use the MERGE PARTITIONS command to combine the contents of two adjacent partitions. For example, you can merge the first two partitions of the ticket_sales table in the following way:

```
SQL> ALTER TABLE ticket_sales
     MERGE PARTITIONS ticket_sales01, ticket_sales02 INTO PARTITION
     ticket_sales02;
```

Renaming Partitions

You can rename partitions in the same way you rename a table. Here is an example:

```
SQL> ALTER TABLE
     RENAME PARTITION fight_sales01 TO quarterly_sales01;
```

Exchanging Partitions

The EXCHANGE PARTITION command enables you to convert a regular nonpartitioned table into a partition of a partitioned table. Here's an example:

```
SQL> ALTER TABLE ticket_sales
     EXCHANGE PARTITION ticket_sales02 WITH ticket_sales03;
```

   A partition exchange doesn't involve the actual movement of data. Oracle renames the source table as a partition and the target partition as the source table. Thus, the database completes the loading process with no data movement.

Dropping Partitions

Dropping partitions is easy if you don't have any data in the partitions. Here's an example:

```
SQL> ALTER TABLE ticket_sales
     DROP PARTITION ticket_sales01;
```

If you do have data in the partitions that you intend to drop, you need to be careful to use the additional UPDATE GLOBAL INDEXES clause with the preceding drop partition syntax. Otherwise, all globally created indexes will be invalidated. Local indexes will still be okay, because they're mapped directly to the affected partitions only.

Coalescing Partitions

The hash-partitioned and list-partitioned tables enable you to coalesce their partitions. *Coalescing partitions* amounts to shrinking the number of partitions. In a hash-partitioned table, the COALESCE command will reorganize the data of the removed partition into the remaining partitions based on a hash function. The database chooses a specific partition for coalescing, and drops it after reorganizing its data among the remaining partitions. In range-hash partitioning, you can coalesce subpartitions.

Here's an example of coalescing a hash-partitioned table, which will reduce the number of partitions by one:

```
SQL> ALTER TABLE ticket_sales
     COALESCE PARTITION;
```

▪**Note** I've presented only a bare introduction to the vast and complex topic of Oracle table partitioning. Please refer to the Oracle documentation for a complete discussion of this powerful feature, including restrictions on the numerous partition-maintenance operations.

Data Dictionary Views for Managing Tables

Several data dictionary views can help in managing Oracle tables. The most important one is the DBA_TABLES view—it gives you the owner, the number of rows, the tablespace name, space information, and a number of other details about all the tables in the database. Listing 7-11 shows a sample query.

Listing 7-11. *Using the DBA_TABLES Data Dictionary View*

```
SQL> SELECT tablespace_name, table_name, num_rows
     FROM dba_tables
     WHERE owner='HR';
```

TABLESPACE_NAME	TABLE_NAME	NUM_ROWS
EXAMPLE	DEPARTMENTS	27
EXAMPLE	EMPLOYEES	107
EXAMPLE	JOBS	19
EXAMPLE	JOB_HISTORY	10
EXAMPLE	LOCATIONS	23
EXAMPLE	REGIONS	4

```
6 rows selected.
SQL>
```

Use the DBA_TAB_PARTITIONS view to find out detailed information about partitioned tables. Listing 7-12 shows an example of this view that summarizes information about a partitioned table from an earlier example in this chapter.

Listing 7-12. *Using the DBA_TAB_PARTITIONS Data Dictionary View*

```
TABLE_NAME            PARTITION_NAME         SUBPARTITION_COUNT
-----------           -----------------      ------------------
SALES_DATA            SALES_Q1                        0
SALES_DATA            SALES_Q2                        0
SALES_DATA            SALES_Q3                        0
SALES_DATA            SALES_Q4                        0
SALES_HASH            SYS_P3161                       0
SALES_HASH            SYS_P3162                       0
SALES_HASH            SYS_P3163                       0
SALES_HASH            SYS_P3164                       0
SALES_LIST            NORTHEAST_SALES                 0
SALES_LIST            SOUTHWEST_SALES                 0
SALES_LIST            PACIFICWEST_SALES               0
SALES_LIST            SOUTHEAST_SALES                 0
SCOUT_GEAR            P1                              8
SCOUT_GEAR            P2                              8
SCOUT_GEAR            P3                              8
SCOUT_GEAR            P4                              8
QUARTERLY_REGIONAL_SALES  Q1_2009                     4
QUARTERLY_REGIONAL_SALES  Q2_2009                     4
QUARTERLY_REGIONAL_SALES  Q3_2009                     4
QUARTERLY_REGIONAL_SALES  Q4_2009                     4
20 rows selected.
SQL>
```

The DBA_TAB_COLUMNS view is another useful data dictionary view that provides a lot of information about table columns. Listing 7-13 shows a simple query using this view.

Listing 7-13. *Using the DBA_TAB_COLUMNS Data Dictionary View*

```
SQL> SELECT column_name, data_type,
     nullable
     FROM dba_tab_columns
     WHERE owner='HR'
     AND table_name = 'EMPLOYEES';

COLUMN_NAME          DATA_TYPE            NULLABLE
---------------      -----------          ---------
EMPLOYEE_ID          NUMBER               N
FIRST_NAME           VARCHAR2             Y
LAST_NAME            VARCHAR2             N
EMAIL                VARCHAR2             N
PHONE_NUMBER         VARCHAR2             Y
HIRE_DATE            DATE                 N
JOB_ID               VARCHAR2             N
SALARY               NUMBER               Y
8 rows selected.
SQL>
```

Of course, you could have obtained this type of information easily by using the DESCRIBE command. Listing 7-14 shows how to use this command.

Listing 7-14. *Using the DESCRIBE Command*

```
SQL> DESCRIBE new_employees
```

Name	Null?	Type
EMPLOYEE_ID	NOT NULL	NUMBER(6)
FIRST_NAME	NOT NULL	VARCHAR2(20)
LAST_NAME	NOT NULL	VARCHAR2(25)
HIRE_DATE	NOT NULL	DATE
JOB_ID	NOT NULL	VARCHAR2(10)
SALARY		NUMBER(8,2)

```
SQL>
```

EXTRACTING OBJECT DDL USING THE DBMS_METADATA PACKAGE

Often you'll want to re-create a table or create a similar table in a different database, and it would be nice to have the DDL for the original table handy. If you're using a third-party tool, such as the SQL Navigator from Quest Software, all you have to do is click a few buttons, and your table DDL statements will be shown on the screen.

But what commands can you use to get the CREATE TABLE statement that created a table? You could get this information from the DBA_TABLES and DBA_TAB_COLUMNS views, but you would have to write lengthy SQL statements to do so. Alternatively, you can use the Oracle-supplied DBMS_METADATA package to quickly get the DDL statements for your tables and indexes.

As an example, let's get the DDL for the employee table using this package. Here is the output of the package execution:

```
SQL> CONNECT hr/hr
Connected.SQL> SET LONG 100000
SQL> SELECT dbms_metadata.get_ddl('TABLE','EMPLOYEE') from dual;

DBMS_METADATA.GET_DDL('TABLE','EMPLOYEE')
--------------------------------------------------------------------------------
CREATE TABLE "HR"."EMPLOYEES"
 ("EMPLOYEE_ID" NUMBER(6,0),
  "FIRST_NAME" VARCHAR2(20),
  "LAST_NAME" VARCHAR2(25) CONSTRAINT "EMP_LAST_NAME_NN" NOT NULL ENABLE,
  "HIRE_DATE" DATE CONSTRAINT "EMP_HIRE_DATE_NN" NOT NULL ENABLE,
  "SALARY" NUMBER(8,2),
  "COMMISSION_PCT" NUMBER(2,2),
  "MANAGER_ID" NUMBER(6,0),
  "DEPARTMENT_ID" NUMBER(4,0),
  CONSTRAINT "EMP_SALARY_MIN" CHECK (salary > 0) ENABLE NOVALIDATE,
  USING INDEX PCTFREE 10 INITRANS 2 MAXTRANS 255
STORAGE(INITIAL 65536 NEXT 1048576
MINEXTENTS 1  MAXEXTENTS 2147483645 PCTINCREASE 0
  FREELISTS 1 FREELIST GROUPS 1 BUFFER_POOL DEFAULT) TABLESPACE
  "EXAMPLE"  ENABLE,
  CONSTRAINT "EMP_EMP_ID_PK" PRIMARY KEY ("EMPLOYEE_ID")
  USING INDEX PCTFREE 10 INITRANS 2 MAXTRANS 255
  STORAGE(INITIAL 65536 NEXT 1048576 MINEXTENTS 1 MAXEXTENTS
2147483645 PCTINCREASE 0
  FREELISTS 1 FREELIST GROUPS 1 BUFFER_POOL DEFAULT) TABLESPACE
```

```
"EXAMPLE" ENABLE,
 CONSTRAINT "EMP_DEPT_FK" FOREIGN KEY ("DEPARTMENT_ID")
  REFERENCES "HR"."DEPARTMENTS" ("DEPARTMENT_ID") ENABLE NOVALIDATE,
DBMS_METADATA.GET_DDL('TABLE','EMPLOYEES')
  STORAGE(INITIAL 65536 NEXT 1048576 MINEXTENTS 1 MAXEXTENTS
2147483645 PCTINCREASE 0
  FREELISTS 1 FREELIST GROUPS 1 BUFFER_POOL DEFAULT) TABLESPACE "EXAMPLE"
SQL>
```

■**Tip** The output of the get_ddl procedure in the DBMS_METADATA package spits out its DDL text in long format. If you don't have the LONG variable set in your SQL*Plus session, you may not see the entire DDL statement.

This is the most elegant and the easiest way to get the DDL for your tables and indexes using SQL*Plus. If you need the DDL statements for your database objects, you should use the DBMS_METADATA package. Of course, you can always use the OEM Database Control to extract all types of DDL for your database objects.

Clusters

Clusters are two or more tables that are physically stored together to take advantage of similar columns between the tables. If two tables have an identical column and you frequently need to join the two tables, for example, it is advantageous to store the common column values in the same data block. The goal is to reduce disk I/O and thereby increase access speed when you join related tables. However, clusters will reduce the performance of your INSERT statements, because more blocks are needed to store the data of multiple tables.

In order to create clustered tables, you must first create a cluster. The following example creates a cluster named emp_dept that will store the emp and dept tables, clustered by the deptno column:

```
SQL> CREATE CLUSTER emp_dept(deptno NUMBER(3))
  2  TABLESPACE users;

Cluster created.
SQL>
```

You can create the two tables, emp and dept, that are part of the cluster, as shown here:

```
SQL> CREATE TABLE dept(
  2  deptno NUMBER(3) PRIMARY KEY)
  3* CLUSTER emp_dept (deptno);

Table created.
SQL>

SQL> CREATE TABLE emp(
  2  empno NUMBER(5) PRIMARY KEY,
  3  ename VARCHAR2(15) NOT NULL,
  4  deptno NUMBER(3) REFERENCES dept)
  5* CLUSTER emp_dept(deptno);
```

```
Table created.
SQL>
```

Make sure you cluster only those tables that your applications access frequently in join statements.

Hash Clusters

You can create a *hash cluster* and store tables in the cluster. Rows are retrieved according to the results of a hash function. To find any row value, all you need to do is find the hash value for a cluster's key value, which you can get by using the hash function. The hash values point to data blocks in the hash cluster, so a single I/O will get you the row data and lead to more efficient performance. When your application uses equality queries such as, say, a query that returns all rows for region 10, hash clusters are a better choice than using a normal table with indexes. The reason is that the database hashes the specified cluster key, and the hash key value directly points to the area on disk where the database has stored the rows.

Here's a simple example of how you create a hash cluster:

```
SQL> CREATE CLUSTER emp_dept(deptno NUMBER(3))
  2  TABLESPACE users
  3* HASH IS deptno HASHKEYS 200;

Cluster created.
SQL>
```

Once you create the hash cluster, you create the cluster tables just as you would in a regular cluster. The HASHKEYS value specifies the maximum number of unique hash values that can be generated by the hash function.

Oracle Indexes

Oracle indexes provide speedy access to table rows by storing sorted values of specified columns, and using those sorted values to easily look up the associated table rows, much the same way you use a book's index to quickly find a particular item you're interested in. Indexes enable you to find a row with a certain column value without your having to look at more than a small fraction of the total rows in the table. Thus, the proper use of indexes will reduce your expensive disk I/Os to a bare minimum. Indexes are purely optional database structures, and they're maintained completely by Oracle.

Using an index involves a trade-off between speedy retrieval of query results and slower updates and insertions. The first part of the trade-off, the speedy execution of queries, is quite apparent: if you look up a sorted index rather than performing a full table scan, your queries will be faster. But every time you update, insert, or delete a row in a table with indexes, the indexes have to be updated, inserted, or deleted as well. This makes these processes more time consuming on a table with indexes. In addition, don't forget that large tables will have large indexes, and you need a large disk to accommodate these indexes in addition to the table data.

In general, if your tables are mostly used for reading (selecting) data, as in a data warehouse, you are better off with more indexes. If your database is more of an OLTP type, with heavy inserts, updates, and deletes, you are better off with fewer indexes.

Unless you need to access most of the rows of a table, indexed queries often provide results much more quickly than queries that do not use indexes. There is no limit to the number of indexes you can have on a single Oracle table but, as mentioned previously, there are performance implications. An index is completely transparent to the user—that is, the user's SQL statement does not have to be changed when you create indexes. However, it is incumbent upon application developers to be well versed in the subject of indexes and how they work, so that they can build efficient queries.

■**Note** You'll find a detailed discussion on appropriate indexing strategies in Chapter 19.

Oracle indexes can be of several types, the most important of which are listed here:

- *Unique and nonunique indexes*: Unique indexes are those based on a unique column, usually something like the social security number of an employee. Although you can explicitly create unique indexes, Oracle recommends that you not do so. Oracle advises you to use unique constraints instead. When you place a unique constraint on a table's column, Oracle will automatically create unique indexes on those columns.

- *Primary and secondary indexes*: Primary indexes are the unique indexes in a table that must always possess a value; they can't be null. Secondary indexes are other indexes in the same table that may not be unique.

- *Composite indexes*: Composite indexes are indexes that contain two or more columns from the same table. They're also known as *concatenated indexes*. Composite indexes are especially useful for enforcing uniqueness in a table's columns in cases where there's no single column that can uniquely identify a row.

INDEXES AND KEYS

Often, you'll see the terms "index" and "key" being used interchangeably. However, the two things are actually different from each other. An index is a physical structure that's stored in the database. You can create, alter, and drop an index, and you mostly use an index to speed up access to the table data. Keys, on the other hand, are a purely logical concept. Keys represent the integrity constraints that you create to enforce the business rules. The confusion between an index and a key normally arises because often the database uses an index to enforce an integrity constraint. Just remember that the two things are different.

Guidelines for Creating Indexes

Although it is well known that indexes will enhance database performance, you will need to understand how to make them work well for you. Placing unnecessary or inappropriate indexes on your table may prove to be detrimental to performance.

Here are some guidelines for creating efficient indexes for your Oracle tables:

- Index only if you need to access no more than 4 or 5percent of the data in a table. The alternative to using an index to access row data in a table is to read the entire table sequentially from top to bottom, which is called a *full table scan*. Full table scans are better for queries that require a high percentage of the data in a table. Remember that using indexes to retrieve rows requires *two* reads: an index read followed by a table read.

- Avoid indexes on relatively small tables. Full table scans are just fine for small tables. There's no need to store both table and index data for small tables.

- Create primary keys for all tables. When you designate a column as a primary key, Oracle automatically creates an index on the column.

- Index the columns that are involved in multitable join operations.

- Index columns that are used frequently in WHERE clauses.

- Index the columns that are involved in ORDER BY and GROUP BY operations, or other operations, such as UNION and DISTINCT, that involve sorting. Because indexes are already sorted, the sorting necessary to perform the previously mentioned operations will be considerably reduced.

- Columns that consist of long character strings are usually poor candidates for indexing.

- Columns that are frequently updated should ideally not be indexed because of the overhead involved.

- Index tables with high selectivity only. That is, choose to index tables where few rows have similar values.

- Keep the number of indexes small.

- Composite indexes may need to be used where single-column values may not be unique by themselves. In composite indexes, the driving or the first column should be the most selective column.

Always keep in mind the *golden rule* of indexing a table: The index on a table should be based on the types of queries you expect to occur against the table's columns. You can create more than one index on a table; you can choose to create an index on column X, or column Y, or both, and you can also create a composite index on both columns X and Y. You will make the right decisions about which index to create by thinking about the most frequent types of queries involving the table's data.

Oracle Index Schemes

Oracle provides several indexing schemes to suit the requirements of different types of applications. During the design phase, you should select the right index type after you conduct a careful analysis of the particular requirements of your application.

The B-tree index implementation uses the concept of a balanced (which is what the "B" stands for) search tree as the basis of an index's structure. Oracle uses its own variation on the B-tree called the "B*tree" for implementing B-tree indexes. These are the regular default indexes created when you use a CREATE INDEX statement in Oracle. The term "B*tree index" isn't generally used to refer to Oracle regular indexes—they are just called "indexes."

B-tree indexes are structured in the form of an inverse tree, with top-level blocks called *branch blocks* and lower-level blocks called *leaf blocks*. In the hierarchy of nodes, all nodes except the top or root node have one *parent node* and may have zero or more nodes beneath them called *child nodes*. If the depth of the tree structure—that is, the number of levels—is the same from each leaf block to the root node, the tree is called a *balanced tree* or *B-tree*.

B-trees automatically maintain the necessary level of index for the size of the table. B-trees also ensure that the index blocks are always between half used and full. B-trees permit select, insert, update, and delete operations with very few I/Os per statement. Most B-trees have only three or fewer levels. When you use a B-tree, you need to read only the B-tree blocks, so the number of disk I/Os will be the number of B-tree levels (say, three) plus the I/Os for performing an update or delete (two: one to read and one to write). To search through a B-tree, you would only need three or fewer disk I/Os.

Oracle's implementation of the B-tree, the B*tree, always keeps the tree balanced. The leaf blocks contain two items: the indexed column values and the corresponding ROWID for the row that contains the particular column value. The ROWID is a unique Oracle pointer that identifies the physical location of the row in question, and it is the fastest way to access a row in an Oracle database. Scanning the index will quickly get you the ROWID of the row, and from there it's a quick hop to the row itself. If the query just wanted the value of the indexed column itself, of course, the latter step is omitted because you don't have to fetch any more data for the query.

Estimating the Size of an Index

As in the case of tables, you can use the DBMS_SPACE package to estimate the size of a new index. You must provide the DDL statement that creates the index as an attribute to the CREATE_INDEX_COST procedure of the package, as shown in Listing 7-15.

Listing 7-15. *Using the DBMS_SPACE Package to Estimate a New Index's Space Requirements*

```
SQL> SET SERVEROUTPUT ON
SQL> declare
  2   l_index_ddl VARCHAR2(1000);
  3   l_used_bytes NUMBER;
  4   l_allocated_bytes NUMBER;
  5   BEGIN
  6   DBMS_SPACE.create_index_cost (
  7   ddl  => 'create index persons_idx on persons(person_id)',
  8   used_bytes => l_used_bytes,
  9   alloc_bytes => l_allocated_bytes);
 10   DBMS_OUTPUT.PUT_LINE ('used = ' || l_used_bytes || 'bytes'
 11   || '   allocated = ' || l_allocated_bytes || 'bytes');
 12* END;
SQL> /

used = 154414918bytes    allocated = 427720704bytes

PL/SQL procedure successfully completed.
SQL>
```

Note the interesting difference between the two size-related attributes of the CREATE_INDEX_COST procedure:

- used_bytes shows the number of bytes that the index data actually represents.
- alloc_bytes shows the number of bytes the index will take up in the tablespace when you actually create it.

■**Tip** The table on which you are planning to create the new index must, of course, exist, and the database should have the latest statistics on that table, in order to use the DBMS_SPACE package to estimate index sizes.

Creating an Index

You create an index using the CREATE INDEX statement, as follows:

```
SQL> CREATE INDEX employee_id ON employee(employee_id)
     TABLESPACE emp_index_01;
```

If you are creating an index for a large table with data already populated, you can choose to collect optimizer statistics at table creation time by specifying the COMPUTE STATISTICS option as shown in this example:

```
SQL> CREATE INDEX employee_id ON employee(employee_id)
     TABLESPACE emp_index_01
     COMPUTE STATISTICS;
```

If you don't specify any storage settings, the database will use the default storage options of the tablespace you specify for the creation of the index.

By default, Oracle allows duplicate values in the indexed column, also known as the key column. However, you can specify a unique index, which disallows duplicate values for a column in multiple rows. To create a unique index, use the CREATE UNIQUE INDEX statement, as shown here:

```
SQL> CREATE UNIQUE INDEX employee_id ON employee(employee_id)
     TABLESPACE emp_index_01;
```

The examples I showed thus far are all indexes created on a single column. You can also create a composite index on a table, by specifying multiple columns in the CREATE INDEX statement, as shown in this example:

```
SQL> CREATE INDEX employee_id ON employee(employee_id,location_id)
     TABLESPACE emp_index_01;
```

All the examples of index creation thus far showed you how to explicitly create an index on a table's column. However, there is also a different way to create an index on a table, and that is by simply specifying a UNIQUE or PRIMARY KEY integrity constraint on that table. When you do so, Oracle automatically creates a unique index on the unique key or primary key. The database will create the index automatically when the constraint is enabled and by default names the index after the constraint. Here are two examples that demonstrate situations when the database creates an automatic index on a table's columns.

In the first case, I specify a unique constraint on two columns: dept_name and location.

```
SQL> CREATE TABLE dept(
     dept_no   NUMBER(3),
     dept_name   VARCHAR2(15),
     location    VARCHAR2(25),
     CONSTRAINT dept_name_ukey UNIQUE(dept_Name,location);
```

The database automatically creates a unique index on these two columns to enforce the unique constraint named dept_name_ukey.

In the second example, I show how to specify a primary key constraint on a column when creating a table.

```
SQL> CREATE TABLE employee (
     empno NUMBER (5) PRIMARY KEY, age INTEGER)
     ENABLE PRIMARY KEY USING INDEX
     TABLESPACE users;
```

The CREATE TABLE statement shown here enables the primary key constraint, which automatically creates a unique index on the empno column.

You can also specify that the database use an existing index to enforce a new constraint you are creating, as shown in this example:

```
SQL> ALTER TABLE employee ADD CONSTRAINT test_const1
     PRIMARY KEY (pkey1) USING INDEX ind1;
```

In this example, the new primary key I specify uses the existing index ind1, instead of having the database create a new index. Interestingly, you can also specify a CREATE INDEX statement when creating a unique or primary key constraint. The following example creates a primary key on a column:

```
SQL> CREATE TABLE employee (
     emp_id INT  PRIMARY KEY USING INDEX (create index ind1
     ON employee (emp_id)))
```

The use of the CREATE INDEX statement in this example gives you more control over the creation of the index for the primary key constraint you specified.

Special Types of Indexes

The normal or typical index you create in an Oracle database is called a *heap index*. Oracle also offers several special types of index for specific needs. I explain the main types of index in the following sections.

Bitmap Indexes

Bitmap indexes use bitmaps to indicate the value of the column being indexed. This is an ideal index for a column with a low cardinality and a large table size. These indexes are not usually appropriate for tables with heavy updates and are well suited for data warehouse applications.

Bitmap indexes consist of a bit stream (0 or 1) for each column in the index. Bitmap indexes are very compact compared to the normal B-tree indexes. Table 7-2 presents a comparison of B-tree indexes and bitmap indexes.

Table 7-2. *B-tree Indexes vs. Bitmap Indexes*

B-tree Indexes	Bitmap Indexes
Good for high-cardinality data	Good for low-cardinality data
Good for OLTP databases	Good for data warehousing applications
Use a large amount of space	Use relatively little space
Easy to update	Difficult to update

To create a bitmap index, you use the `CREATE INDEX` statement with the `BITMAP` keyword added to it:

```
SQL> CREATE BITMAP INDEX gender_idx ON employee(gender)
     TABLESPACE emp_index_05;
```

I've seen query performance significantly improve when ordinary B*tree indexes were replaced with bitmap indexes in some very large tables. However, each bitmap index entry covers a large number of rows in the table, so when data is updated, inserted, or deleted in the table, the necessary bitmap index updates are very large, and the index can increase substantially in size. The only way around this increase in bitmap index size, and the consequent drop in performance, is to maintain the bitmap index by regularly rebuilding the index. You may decide that a bitmap index is not a smart alternative for tables that involve large numbers of inserts, deletes, and updates.

Reverse-Key Indexes

Reverse-key indexes are fundamentally the same as B-tree indexes, except that the bytes of key column data are reversed during indexing. The column order is kept intact; only the bytes are reversed. The biggest advantage to using reverse-key indexes is that they tend to avoid hot spots when you do sequential insertion of values into the index. Here's how to create one:

```
SQL> CREATE INDEX reverse_idx ON employee(emp_id) REVERSE;
```

When you use a reverse-key index, the database doesn't store the index keys next to each other in a lexical order. Thus, when you use a nonequality predicate in your query, results are going to be slow because the database has to perform a full-table scan. Under reverse-key index, the database can't run an index range scan query.

Key-Compressed Indexes

You can save index storage space as well as improve performance by creating indexes using key compression. Any time the indexed key has a repeatedly occurring component, or you are creating a unique multicolumn index, you'll benefit by using key compression. Here is an example:

```
SQL> CREATE INDEX emp_indx1 ON employees(ename)
     TABLESPACE users
     COMPRESS 1;
```

The previous statement compresses all duplicate occurrences of an indexed key in the index leaf block (level 1) of the index.

Function-Based Indexes

Function-based indexes precompute functions on a given column and store the results in an index. When where clauses include functions, function-based indexes are an ideal way to index the column. Here's how to create a function-based index, using the LOWER function:

```
SQL> CREATE INDEX lastname_idx ON employees(LOWER(l_name));
```

This CREATE INDEX statement will create an index on the l_name (last name) column, which contains the last names of the employees in uppercase. However, this index will be a function-based index, since the database will actually create the index on the l_name column after first using the LOWER function to convert the l_name column values to lowercase.

Partitioned Indexes

Partitioned indexes are used to index partitioned tables. Oracle provides two types of indexes for partitioned tables: *local* and *global*.

The essential difference between the two is that local indexes are based on the underlying table partitions. If the table is partitioned 12 ways using date ranges, the indexes are also distributed over the same 12 partitions. There is a one-to-one correspondence, in other words, between data partitions and index partitions. There is no such one-to-one correspondence between global indexes and the underlying table partitions—a global index is partitioned independently of the base tables.

The following sections cover the important differences between managing globally partitioned indexes and locally partitioned indexes.

Global Indexes

Global indexes on a partitioned table can be either partitioned or nonpartitioned. The globally nonpartitioned indexes are similar to the regular Oracle indexes for nonpartitioned tables. You just use the regular CREATE INDEX syntax to create these globally nonpartitioned indexes.

Here's an example of a global index on the ticket_sales table:

```
SQL> CREATE INDEX  ticketsales_idx ON ticket_sales(month)
     GLOBAL PARTITION BY  range(month)
     (PARTITION ticketsales1_idx VALUES LESS THAN (3)
     PARTITION ticketsales1_idx VALUES LESS THAN (6)
     PARTITION ticketsales2_idx VALUES LESS THAN (9)
     PARTITION ticketsales3_idx VALUES LESS THAN (MAXVALUE);
```

Note that there's substantial maintenance involved in the management of globally partitioned indexes. Whenever there is DDL activity on a partitioned table, its global indexes need to be rebuilt. DDL activity on the underlying table will mark the associated global indexes as unusable. By default, any table maintenance operation on a partitioned table will invalidate (mark as unusable) global indexes.

Let's use the ticket_sales table as an example to see why this is so. Let's assume that you drop the oldest partition each quarter, in order to make room for the new partition for the new quarter. When a partition belonging to the ticket_sales table gets dropped, the global indexes could be invalidated, because some of the data the index is pointing to isn't there anymore. To prevent this invalidation due to the dropping of a partition, you have to use the UPDATE GLOBAL INDEXES option along with the DROP PARTITION statement, as shown here:

```
SQL> ALTER TABLE ticket_sales
     DROP PARTITION sales_quarter01
     UPDATE GLOBAL INDEXES;
```

■**Note** If you don't include the UPDATE GLOBAL INDEXES statement, the entire global index will be invalidated. You can also use the UPDATE GLOBAL INDEX option when you add, coalesce, exchange, merge, move, split, or trun-cate partitioned tables. Of course, you can use the ALTER INDEX . . . REBUILD option to rebuild any index that becomes unusable, but this option also involves additional time and maintenance.

When you have a small number of index leaf blocks leading to high contention, Oracle recommends using hash-partitioned global indexes. The syntax for creating a hash-partitioned global index is similar to that used for a hash-partitioned table. For example, the following statement creates a hash-partitioned global index:

```
SQL> CREATE INDEX hgidx ON tab (c1,c2,c3) GLOBAL
     PARTITION BY HASH (c1,c2)
     (PARTITION p1  TABLESPACE tbs_1,
     PARTITION p2  TABLESPACE tbs_2,
     PARTITION p3  TABLESPACE tbs_3,
     PARTITION p4  TABLESPACE tbs_4);
```

Local Indexes

Locally partitioned indexes, unlike globally partitioned indexes, have a one-to-one correspondence with the table partitions. You can create locally partitioned indexes to match partitions or even subpartitions. The database constructs the index so that it is equipartitioned with the underlying table. Any time you modify the underlying table partition, the database automatically maintains the index partition. This is probably the biggest advantage to using locally partitioned indexes—Oracle will automatically rebuild the locally partitioned indexes whenever a partition gets dropped, or any other DDL activity occurs on a partition.

Here is a simple example of creating a locally partitioned index on a partitioned table:

```
SQL> CREATE INDEX ticket_no_idx ON
     ticket_sales(ticket__no) LOCAL
     TABLESPACE localidx_01;
```

■**Tip** You can use the new SQL Access Advisor tool to get recommendations on which indexes to create. The SQL Access Advisor will also tell you which of your indexes aren't being used and hence are candidates for removal. I show how to use the SQL Access Advisor in the "Using the SQL Access Advisor" section, later in this chapter.

Invisible Indexes

By default, the optimizer "sees" all indexes. However, you can create an index as an invisible index that's not seen by the optimizer and hence isn't taken into account by the optimizer when it's creating the execution plan for a statement. You can use the invisible index as a temporary index for certain special operations or for testing the use of an index before making it "official." In addition, sometimes making an index invisible could be used as an alternative to dropping an index or making it unusable. You can make an index invisible temporarily to test the effects of dropping the index.

The database maintains an invisible index just as it does a normal (visible) index. The only difference will be that that optimizer won't be able to make use of the invisible index. After making an index invisible, you can make it and all other invisible indexes visible to the optimizer again by setting the `optimizer_use_invisible_indexes` parameter to TRUE either at the session or the system level. The default value of this parameter is FALSE, meaning the optimizer can't make use of any invisible indexes by default.

Creating an Invisible Index

You must add the clause `INVISIBLE` to the `CREATE INDEX` statement to make the index invisible, as shown here:

```
SQL> CREATE INDEX test_idx ON test(tname)
     TABLESPACE testdata
     STORAGE (INITIAL 20K
     NEXT 20k
     PCTINCREASE 75)
     INVISIBLE;
```

The previous statement creates the invisible index test_idx for the tname column of the table test.

Altering an Index to Make It Invisible

In addition to creating an invisible index, you can alter an existing index to an invisible status, by issuing the `ALTER INDEX` statement as shown here:

```
SQL> ALTER INDEX test_idx INVISIBLE;
```

To make an invisible index visible again, use the following statement:

```
SQL> ALTER INDEX test_idx VISIBLE;
```

A query on the DBA_INDEXES view indicates whether an index is visible, as shown here:

```
SQL> SELECT INDEX_NAME, VISIBILITY FROM USER_INDEXES
     WHERE INDEX_NAME = 'INDX1';

     INDEX_NAME      VISIBILITY
     ----------      ----------
     INDX1           VISIBLE
SQL>
```

Monitoring Index Usage

Oracle offers the EXPLAIN PLAN and SQL Trace tools to help you see the path followed by your queries on the way to their execution. You can use the EXPLAIN PLAN output or the results of a SQL Trace to see what the execution path of the query looks like and thus determine whether your indexes are being used. I discuss EXPLAIN PLAN and SQL Trace in detail in Chapter 19.

Oracle also provides an easier way to monitor index usage in your database. If you are doubtful as to the usefulness of a particular index, you can ask Oracle to *monitor* the index usage. This way, if the index turns out to be redundant, you can drop it and save the storage space and the overhead during DML operations.

Here's what you have to do to monitor index usage in your database. Assume you're trying to find out whether the p_key_sales index is being used by certain queries on the sales table. Make sure you use a representative time period to gauge index usage. For an OLTP database, this period could be relatively short. For a data warehouse, you may need to run the monitoring test for several days to accurately check index usage.

To start monitoring the index use, log in as the owner of the p_key_sales index and run this command:

```
SQL> ALTER INDEX p_key_sales MONITORING USAGE;

   Index altered.
SQL>
```

Now, run some queries on the sales table. End the monitoring by using the following command:

```
SQL> ALTER INDEX p_key_sales NOMONITORING USAGE;

   Index altered.
SQL>
```

You can now query the V$OBJECT_USAGE dictionary view to find out whether the p_key_sales index is being used. The following results confirm that the index is indeed being used:

```
SQL> SELECT * FROM v$object_usage
     WHERE index_name='P_KEY_SALES';

INDEX_NM      TAB_NM    MON    USED    START_MON             END_MONITORING
-----------   -------   ----   -----   --------------------  --------------------
P_KEY_SALES   SALE      NO     YES     01/23/2008 06:20:45   01/23/2008 06:40:22
```

In the preceding output, Oracle placed a YES value in the USED column, thus indicating that the index in question was being used by the database. If the index had been ignored during the monitoring period, the column would contain NO instead. The reason why you can't actually get an estimate of the number of times an index is used is because the database performs the index usage monitoring only at parse time—if it were done for each execution, there would be a performance hit.

Index Maintenance

Index data constantly changes due to the underlying table's DML activity. Indexes often become too large if there are many deletions, because the space used by the deleted values is not reused automatically by the index. You can use the REBUILD command on a periodic basis to reorganize indexes to make them more compact and thus more efficient. You can also use the REBUILD command to alter the storage parameters you set during the initial creation of the index. Here's an example:

```
SQL> ALTER INDEX sales_idx REBUILD;

Index altered
Sql>
```

Rebuilding indexes is better than dropping and re-creating a bad index, because users will continue to have access to the index while you're rebuilding it. However, indexes in the process of rebuilding do impose many limits on users' actions. An even more efficient way to rebuild indexes is to do them *online*, as shown in the following example. You can perform all DML operations, but not any DDL operations, while the online rebuild of the index is going on.

```
SQL> ALTER INDEX p_key_sales REBUILD ONLINE;

Index altered.
SQL>
```

You can speed up the online index build by adding the ONLINE NOLOGGING clause to the ALTER INDEX statement shown here. When you add this clause, the database doesn't generate redo data for the index rebuild operation.

Managing Database Integrity Constraints

Integrity constraints in relational databases enable easy and automatic enforcement of important business rules in the database tables. For example, in a human resources–related table, you can't have an employee without assigning him or her to a supervisor. When you create the relevant tables, you can declare the necessary integrity constraints, which must be satisfied each time data is entered or modified in the table.

You can also use application logic to enforce business rules, but integrity constraints are usually simpler to enforce than application logic, and they usually do their job by making sure that inserts, updates, and deletes of table data conform to certain rules. Application logic, on the other hand, has the advantage that it can reject or approve data without having to check the entire table's contents. Thus, you have to determine which method you'll use to enforce the business rules—application logic or integrity constraints—based on the needs of your application. In any case, integrity constraints are so fundamental to the operation of relational databases that you are bound to use them in your database.

By default, Oracle allows null values in all columns. If null values are not permissible for some columns in a table, you need to use the NOT NULL constraint when specifying the column. Note that you can impose the database constraints on tables either at table creation time or later by using the ALTER TABLE command. Obviously, however, if you already have null columns or duplicate data, it is not possible to alter the table to impose a NOT NULL or unique constraint on the table.

You can enforce several types of constraints in an Oracle table. For simplicity's sake, you can divide the constraints into five different types:

- Primary key constraints
- NOT NULL constraints
- Check constraints
- Unique constraints
- Referential integrity constraints

I discuss each of these types of constraints in the following sections. In addition, I also present a brief discussion of integrity constraint states.

Primary Key Constraints

The primary key is a very important kind of constraint on a table. When you want a column's values to be identified uniquely, you can do this by creating a primary key on the column value. A column on which a primary key has been defined has to be *unique* as well as *not null*.

A table can have only one primary key. You can create a primary key when creating the table, as shown in the following example:

```
SQL> CREATE TABLE dept
       (dept_id number(9) PRIMARY KEY);
```

You can also add a constraint to an existing table in the following way:

```
SQL> ALTER TABLE dept
       ADD PRIMARY KEY(dept_id);
```

Since the constraint wasn't assigned a name in the preceding example, Oracle will assign a system-generated constraint name. If you want to give your own name to the constraint, you can use the following command, which names the constraint dept_pk:

```
SQL> ALTER TABLE dept
       ADD CONSTRAINT
       dept_pk PRIMARY KEY(dept_id);
```

```
Table altered.
SQL>
```

Note that if the primary key will have more than one column in it (meaning that it will be a composite key), you can't specify the primary key designation against the column name during table creation. You have to specify the primary key columns as a separate item at the end of the CREATE TABLE statement, after listing all the columns.

■**Note** In both of the preceding examples, Oracle automatically creates an index on the column you designate as the primary key.

Not Null Constraints

A table usually has one or more columns that can't be allowed to be left *null*—that is, with no values. A good example is the last_name column in the employee table. You can force users to always put a value in this column at table creation time by using the NOT NULL option for the column you don't want to be null:

```
SQL> CREATE TABLE employee
     (last_name VARCHAR(30) NOT NULL);
```

If the table has already been created and you want to modify a column from a nullable to a non-nullable constraint, you can use the following statement:

```
SQL> ALTER TABLE employee MODIFY last_name NOT NULL;
```

Check Constraints

You use check constraints to ensure that data in a column is within some parameters that you specify. For example, say the salary for an employee in a firm can't be equal to or exceed $100,000 under any circumstances. You can enforce this condition by using the following statement, which uses the CHECK constraint on the SALARY column:

```
SQL> CREATE TABLE employee
     (employee_id     NUMBER,
      last_name       VARCHAR2(30),
      first_name      VARCHAR2(30),
      department_id   NUMBER,
      salary          NUMBER CHECK(salary < 100000));
```

Unique Constraints

Unique constraints are very common in relational databases. These constraints ensure the uniqueness of the rows in a relational table. You may have more than one unique constraint on a table. For example, a unique constraint on the employee_id column ensures that no employee is listed twice in the employee table.

In the following example, the first statement specifies a unique constraint on the combination of the dept_name and location columns:

```
SQL> CREATE TABLE dept(
     dept_no   NUMBER(3),
     dept_name    VARCHAR2(15),
     location     VARCHAR2(25),
     CONSTRAINT dept_name_ukey UNIQUE(dept_Name,location);
```

You can also create a unique constraint on the department table by executing the ALTER TABLE statement:

```
SQL> ALTER TABLE dept
     ADD CONSTRAINT dept_idx UNIQUE(dept_no);

Table altered.
SQL>
```

Referential Integrity Constraints

Referential integrity constraints ensure that values for certain important columns make sense. Suppose you have a parent table that refers to values in another table, as in the case of the dept table and the employee tables. You shouldn't be able to assign an employee to a department in the employee table if the department doesn't exist in the department table.

You can ensure the existence of a valid department by using a referential integrity constraint. In this case, the department_id column is the dept table's primary key, and the dept_id column in the employee table, which refers to the corresponding column in the department table, is called the *foreign key*. The table containing the foreign key is usually referred to as the *child table*, and the table containing the referenced key is called the *parent table*. As with all the other types of constraints, you can create the referential integrity constraint at table creation time or later on, with the help of the ALTER TABLE statement:

```
SQL> CREATE TABLE employee
     (employee_id      NUMBER(7),
      last_name        VARCHAR2(30),
      first name       VARCHAR2(30),
      job              VARCHAR2(15),
      dept_id          NUMBER(3) NOT NULL
      CONSTRAINT dept_fkey REFERENCES dept(dept_id));
```

The database designates the dept_id column of the employee table as a foreign key because it refers to the dept_id column in the dept table. Note that for a column to serve as the referenced column, it must be unique or be a primary key in the reference table.

Integrity Constraint States

As you saw in the previous section, integrity constraints are defined on tables to ensure that data that violates preset rules doesn't enter the tables. However, during times like data loading, you can't keep the integrity constraints in a valid state, as this will lead to certain problems. Oracle lets you disable constraints when necessary and enable them when you want. Let's examine the various ways you can alter the states of table constraints.

During large data loads, using either the SQL*Loader or the Import utility, it may take a considerably longer time to load the data if you have to check for integrity violations for each row inserted into the table. A better strategy would be to disable the constraint, load the data, and worry about any possible insertion of bad data later on. After the load is completed, the constraints are brought into effect again by enabling them. When you disable the constraint as explained here, the database drops the index. It's therefore a better strategy to precreate nonunique indexes for constraints, which the database doesn't have to drop because they can handle duplicates.

■**Note** The *enabled* state is Oracle's default constraint state.

You can disable constraints in two ways: you can specify either the *disable validate* or the *disable no validate* constraint state, using the DISABLE VALIDATE or DISABLE NO VALIDATE command, respectively. Similarly, you can use the ENABLE VALIDATE or the ENABLE NO VALIDATE commands when enabling a constraint. The next sections briefly discuss the different ways to disable and enable constraints.

Disable Validate State

When you use the DISABLE VALIDATE command, you're doing the following two things at once. First, by using the VALIDATE clause, you're ensuring that all the data in the table satisfies the constraint. Second, by using the DISABLE clause, you're doing away with the requirements of maintaining the constraint. Oracle drops the index on the constraint, but keeps it valid. Here's an example:

```
SQL> ALTER TABLE sales_data
     ADD CONSTRAINT quantity_unique
     UNIQUE (prod_id,customer_id) DISABLE VALIDATE;
```

When you issue the preceding SQL statement, Oracle ensures that only unique combinations of the unique key prod_id and customer_id exist in the table, but it will *not* maintain a unique index. Note that because I have chosen to keep the constraint in a *disabled* state, no DML is possible against the table. This option is really ideal for large data warehouse tables, which are normally used only for querying purposes.

Disable No Validate State

Under the disable no validate constraint state, the constraint is disabled and there is no guarantee of the data meeting the constraint requirements, because Oracle does not perform constraint validation. This is essentially the same as a DISABLE constraint command.

Enable Validate State

This constraint state will have an enabled constraint that ensures that all data is checked to ensure compliance with the constraint. This state is exactly the same as the plain enabled state. The following example shows the use of this state:

```
SQL> ALTER TABLE sales_data ADD CONSTRAINT sales_region_fk
     FOREIGN KEY (sales_region) REFERENCES region(region_id)
     ENABLE VALIDATE;
```

Enable No Validate State

Under this constraint state, the database checks all new inserts and updates for compliance with the constraint. Because the existing data won't be checked for compliance, there's no assurance that the data already in the table meets the constraint requirements. You'll usually use this option when you're loading large tables and you have reason to believe that the data will satisfy the constraint. Here's an example:

```
SQL> ALTER TABLE sales ADD CONSTRAINT sales_region_fk
     FOREIGN KEY (sales_region_id) REFERENCES time(time_id)
     ENABLE NOVALIDATE;
```

A better strategy would be to use the DISABLE NOVALIDATE state while you load data, transition to the ENABLE NOVALIDATE state while you clean the data, and then finally, adopt the ENABLE VALIDATE state at the end of the extraction, transformation, loading (ETL) cycle.

Rely Constraints

Data ETL steps are usually undertaken before loading data into data warehouse tables. If you have reason to believe that the data is good, you can save time during loading by disabling and not validating the constraints. You can use the ALTER TABLE command to disable the constraints with the RELY DISABLE NOVALIDATE option, as shown in the following example:

```
SQL> ALTER TABLE sales ADD CONSTRAINT sales_region_fk
     FOREIGN KEY (sales_region_id) REFERENCES time(region_id)
     RELY DISABLE NOVALIDATE;
```

Deferrable and Immediate Constraints

In addition to specifying the type of validation of a constraint, you can specify *when* exactly this constraint is checked during the loading process.

If you want the constraint to be checked immediately after each data modification occurs, choose the *not deferrable* option, which is, in fact, the default behavior in Oracle databases. If you want a one-time check of a constraint after the whole transaction is committed, choose the *deferrable* option. All constraints and foreign keys may be declared *deferrable* or *not deferrable*.

If you choose the *deferrable* option, you have two further options. You can specify that the *deferrable* constraint is either *initially deferred* or *initially immediate*. In the former case, the database will defer checking until the transaction completes. If you choose the *initially immediate* option, the database checks the constraint before any data is changed. Note that if you precreate an index, it must be nonunique to handle duplicate values.

The following example shows how to specify this kind of constraint in the employee table:

```
SQL> CREATE TABLE employee
     employee_id        NUMBER,
     last_name          VARCHAR2(30),
     first_name         VARCHAR2(30),
     dept               VARCHAR2(30) UNIQUE
     REFERENCES department(dept_name)
     DEFERRABLE INITIALLY DEFERRED;
```

Oracle also provides a way of changing a deferrable constraint from *immediate* to *deferred* or vice versa with the following statements:

```
SQL> SET CONSTRAINT constraint_name DEFERRED;
SQL> SET CONSTRAINT constraint_name IMMEDIATE;
```

Constraint- and Index-Related Views

How do you find out what constraints exist on a table's columns? When a process fails with the message "Referential integrity constraint violated," what's the best way to find out what the constraint and the affected tables are? The constraint- and index-related data dictionary views are critical for resolving problems similar to these. In the following sections, you'll examine the key constraint- and index-related views.

DBA_CONSTRAINTS

The DBA_CONSTRAINTS view provides information on all types of table constraints in the database. You can query this view when you need to figure out what type of constraints a table has. The view lists several types of constraints, as shown by the following query:

```
SQL> SELECT DISTINCT constraint_type FROM DBA_CONSTRAINTS;

Constraint_type
--------------------
        C                       /* check constraints */
        P                       /* primary key constraint */
        R                       /* referential integrity (foreign key) constraint */
        U                       /* unique key constraint */
SQL>
```

The following query lets you know what, if any, constraints are in the TESTD table. The response indicates that the table has a single check constraint defined on it. The SYS prefix in the NAME column shows that CONSTRAINT_NAME is a default name, not one that was explicitly named by the owner of the table.

```
SQL> SELECT constraint_name, constraint_type
  2  FROM DBA_CONSTRAINTS
  3* WHHERE table_name='TESTD';

CONSTRAINT_NAME        CONSTRAINT_TYPE
--------------------   ----------------
SYS_C005263            C
SQL>
```

Note that if you want to see the particular referential constraints and the delete rule, you have to use a slight variation on the preceding query:

```
SQL> SELECT constraint_name, constraint_type,
        R_constraint_name, delete_rule
        FROM dba_constraints
        WHERE table_name='ORDERS';

CONSTRAINT_NAME          TYPE    R_CONSTRAINT_NAME    DELETE_RULE
----------------------   ------  ------------------   -----------
ORDER_DATE_NN            C
ORDER_CUSTOMER_ID_NN     C
ORDER_MODE_LOV           C
ORDER_TOTAL_MIN          C
ORDER_PK                 P
ORDERS_SALES_REP_FK      R       EMP_EMP_ID_PK        SET NULL
ORDERS_CUSTOMER_ID_FK    R       CUSTOMERS_PK         SET NULL
7 rows selected.
SQL>
```

DBA_CONS_COLUMNS

The DBA_CONS_COLUMNS view provides the column name and position in the table on which a constraint is defined. Here's the view:

```
SQL> DESC DBA_CONS_COLUMNS

  Name
  ----------------
  OWNER
  CONSTRAINT_NAME
  TABLE_NAME
  COLUMN_NAME
```

```
POSITION
SQL>
```

Using Views

A *view* is a *virtual table*—it's a specific representation of a table or set of tables, and it is defined by using a SELECT statement. A view doesn't physically exist, like regular tables, as part of a tablespace. A view, in effect, creates a virtual table or subtable with only those rows and/or columns that you want the user to access.

A view is the product of a stored query, so only the view definition is stored in the data dictionary. When you export the database, you'll see the statement "exporting views," but that's referring only to the view definitions and not to any physical objects

You can query views and even modify, remove, or add data using UPDATE, DELETE, or INSERT statements, provided the user has the appropriate privileges on the underlying base tables. For example, if you grant a user only the INSERT privilege on the base table underlying a view, that user can only insert new rows into that table but won't be able to select, update, or delete any rows.

Views are used in applications for several reasons, including the following:

- Reduce complexity.

- Improve security.

- Increase convenience.

- Rename table columns.

- Customize the data for users.

- Protect data integrity.

You create views by using a SQL statement that describes the composition of the view. When you invoke the view, the query by which the view is defined is executed, and the results are presented to you. A query on a view looks exactly like a regular query, but the database converts the query on the view into an identical query on the underlying tables. In order to create a view, you must have the CREATE VIEW system privilege, and to create a view in any schema, rather than just in your own, you need the CREATE ANY VIEW system privilege. In addition, you must either own the underlying tables or must be granted the SELECT, INSERT, UPDATE, and DELETE object privileges on all the tables underlying the view. You can use a view to add *column-level* or *value-based* security to a table. Column-level security is provided by creating views that give access to selected columns of base tables. Value-based security involves using a WHERE clause in the view definition, which displays only selected rows of base tables. In order to use a view, a user needs privileges on the view itself, and not on the base tables underlying the view.

The following statement creates a view called MY_EMPLOYEES that gives a specific manager's information only on the employees managed directly by her:

```
SQL> CREATE VIEW my_employees AS
     SELECT employee_id, first_name, last_name, salary
     FROM employees
     WHERE manager_id=122;

View created.
SQL>
```

■**Tip** You can add the WITH READ ONLY clause to a CREATE VIEW statement to ensure that users can only select from the view. This means the users can't modify the view and thus indirectly update, insert, or delete any rows of the underlying base tables. Otherwise, by default, Oracle allows you to update the view.

Now the manager with the ID 122 can query the my_employees view just as he or she would a normal table, but it gives this manager information on his or her employees only. Listing 7-16 shows the output of a query on the view.

Listing 7-16. *Selecting Data from a View*

```
SQL> SELECT * FROM my_employees;

EMPLOYEE_ID FIRST_NAME   LAST_NAME    SALARY
----------- -----------  ---------    ------
        133 Jason        Mallin       3300
        134 Michael      Rogers       2900
        135 Ki           Gee          2400
        136 Hazel        Philtanker   2200
        188 Kelly        Chung        3800
        189 Jennifer     Dilly        3600
        190 Timothy      Gates        2900
        191 Randall      Perkins      2500
8 rows selected
SQL>
```

You can also specify multiple base tables or even views in the FROM clause, when creating a view. The views you create thus are called *join views*, and the following example shows the creation of one such view:

```
SQL> CREATE VIEW view_1 AS
     SELECT ename, empno, job,dname
     FROM employee, dept
     WHERE employee.deptno IN (10, 60)
     AND employee.deptno = DEPT.DEPTNO;
```

Although you use views mostly for querying purposes, under some circumstances you can also use INSERT, DELETE, and UPDATE views. For example, you can perform a DML operation on a view if it doesn't have any GROUP BY, START WITH, or CONNECT BY clauses, or any subqueries in its SELECT clause. However, since a view doesn't really exist, you'll be modifying the underlying table data, and the view will therefore be subject to the same integrity constraints as the underlying base tables. The following example shows how to insert rows into a view named sales_view, which depends on the employees table.

```
SQL> INSERT INTO sales_view
     VALUES (1234, 'ALAPATI', 99);
```

The previous statement inserts the new row into the underlying base table named employees. Updates, deletes, and inserts on a view are subject to a few restrictions. For example, when you use a CHECK constraint when creating a view, you can't insert a row or update the base table with that row, if the view can't select the row from the underlying base table.

You can drop a view by simply using the DROP VIEW command, as shown here:

```
SQL> DROP VIEW my_employees;

View dropped.
```

Instead of dropping and re-creating a view, you can also use the OR REPLACE clause to redefine a view, as shown in the following example:

```
SQL> CREATE OR REPLACE VIEW view1 AS
     SELECT empno, ename,deptno
     FROM employee
     WHERE deptno=50;
```

If there are other views in a database that depend on a replaced view, they'll become unusable. You can recompile an invalidated view by executing the ALTER VIEW statement. If a PL/SQL program unit such as a procedure or function depends on the view, the database may invalidate that program unit if the changes in the new view pertain to the number of view columns or the column names in the view or the data types.

Using Materialized Views

Every time you need to access a view, Oracle must execute the query that defines the view in question and get you the results. This process of populating the view is called *view resolution,* and it must be done afresh each time a user refers to the view. If you're dealing with views with multiple JOIN and GROUP BY clauses, this process of view resolution could take a very long time. If you need to access a view frequently, it is very inefficient to have to constantly resolve the view each time.

Oracle's *materialized views* offer a way out of this predicament. You can think of materialized views as specialized views that have a physical representation, unlike normal views. They occupy space and need storage just like your regular tables. You can even partition materialized views and create indexes on them if necessary.

■**Note** A view is always computed on the fly, and its data isn't stored separately from the tables on which it's defined. Thus, queries using views, by definition, guarantee that up-to-the-minute data will be returned. Any change in the source tables on which the view is defined will be reflected by the view instantaneously. Materialized views, on the other hand, are static objects that derive their data from the underlying base tables. If you refresh your materialized views infrequently, the data in them may be at odds with the data in the underlying tables.

Traditionally, data warehousing and other similar large databases have needed summary tables or aggregate tables to perform their work. Defining these summary tables and constantly maintaining them was a complex task. Any time you added data to the underlying detail table, you had to manually update all the summary tables and their indexes. Oracle's materialized views offer a way to simplify summary management in large databases. Materialized views in these environments are also called *summaries* because they store summarized data.

You can use tables, views, or other materialized views as the source for a materialized view. The source tables are called *master tables,* and it's common to refer to the master tables as *detail tables* in a data warehousing environment. When you create a new materialized view, Oracle will automatically create an internal table to hold the data of this materialized view. Thus, a materialized view will take up physical space in your database, whereas a regular view doesn't, since a view is only the output of a SQL query.

You can do the following with a materialized view:

- Create indexes on a materialized view.

- Create a materialized view on partitioned tables.

- Partition a materialized view.

■**Tip** You can use an index to access a materialized view directly, as you would a table. Similarly, you can also access a materialized view directly in an INSERT, UPDATE, or DELETE statement. However, Oracle recommends that you not do so, and that you let the Oracle Cost Based Optimizer (CBO) make the decision about whether to rewrite your normal queries to take advantage of a materialized view. If the execution plan using the materialized view has a lower cost of accessing it compared to accessing the tables directly, Oracle will automatically do so.

You can use various types of aggregations like SUM, COUNT(*), AVG, MIN, and MAX in a materialized view. You can also use multiple table joins in the materialized view definition.

Creating a materialized view is pretty straightforward, but optimizing it can be tricky. Optimizing a materialized view involves both ensuring that the Oracle cost-based optimizer rewrites users' queries to use the materialized views that you have created, and keeping the data in the materialized views current. Let's briefly look at these two aspects of optimizing materialized views.

Query Rewriting

In large databases with heavy time- and processing power–consuming activity, such as table joins and the use of aggregates like SUM, materialized views speed up queries. Materialized views makes queries faster by recalculating and storing the results of expensive join and aggregate operations. The beauty of Oracle's materialized view facility is that you can specify during their creation that the database must automatically update the materialized views whenever there are changes in the underlying base tables. The materialized views are completely transparent to users. If users write queries using the underlying table, Oracle will automatically rewrite those queries to use the materialized views—this query-optimization technique is known as *query rewrite*. The Oracle CBO will automatically recognize that it should rewrite a user's query to use the materialized view rather than the underlying tables if the estimated query cost of using the materialized views is lower. Query cost here refers to the I/O, CPU, and memory costs involved in processing a SQL query. Complex joins involve a lot of I/O and CPU expense, and the use of materialized views will avoid incurring this cost each time you need to perform such joins. Because the materialized views already have the summary information precomputed in them, your queries will cost much less in terms of resource usage, and hence run much more quickly.

The automatic query rewrite optimization technique is at the heart of materialized view usage. The QUERY_REWRITE_ENABLED initialization parameter allows you to enable or disable query writing at a global level. The parameter can take the following values:

- *FALSE*: The database doesn't rewrite any queries.
- *TRUE*: The database compares the cost of the query with and without a rewrite and chooses the cheaper method.
- *FORCE*: The database always rewrites the query, without evaluating any costs. Use the FORCE setting if you are certain that the query is beneficial and will result in shortening the response time.

The default value for this parameter is TRUE, provided you set the OPTIMIZER_FEATURES_ENABLE parameter to 10.0.0 or higher (it is FALSE if you set the OPTIMIZER_FEATURES_ENABLE parameter to 9.2.0 or lower), which means that Oracle automatically uses the query rewrite feature. When the parameter is set to TRUE, Oracle will estimate the cost of the query both with and without a rewrite and will choose the one with the lesser processing cost. When you enable query rewriting, it's enabled systemwide, for the entire database.

You must specify the FORCE value for the OPTIMIZER_QUERY_REWRITE parameter only if you are sure that it is beneficial to do so. To enable query rewriting for a specific materialized view, you must explicitly specify the ENABLE QUERY REWRITE clause when you create the materialized view.

The Rewrite_or_Error Hint

Let's say you create a new materialized view and find out that the intended queries aren't being rewritten to take advantage of your new materialized view. If the queries take too long to complete without the materialized view, you can force Oracle to stop executing the query without the materialized view. You can use a hint (a user-created directive that provides guidance to the CBO; I discuss hints in detail in Chapter 19) to tell Oracle to issue an error instead of executing the unrewritten query. The hint is called the REWRITE_OR_ERROR hint, and here's how you use it:

```
SQL> SELECT /*+ REWRITE_OR_ERROR */
    prod_id
```

```
        SUM(quantity_sold) AS sum_sales_qty
        FROM sales_data
        GROUP BY prod_id
SQL>
```

If the query fails to rewrite, you'll see the following error:

```
ORA-30393: a query block in the statement did not write.
```

Once you get the preceding error, you can use the DBMS_MVIEW.EXPLAIN_REWRITE procedure to figure out why the query didn't rewrite, and fix the problem so it will rewrite as planned and take advantage of your materialized view.

Rewrite Integrity

When you set up query rewrite, Oracle will use only fresh data from the materialized views by default. Further, it only utilizes ENABLED VALIDATED primary, unique, or foreign key constraints. The QUERY_REWRITE_INTEGRITY initialization parameter determines the optimizer's behavior in this regard. The default behavior is known as the ENFORCED mode. Besides this mode, the QUERY_REWRITE_INTEGRITY parameter can take two other values:

- TRUSTED: In this mode, the optimizer will accept several relationships other than those accepted under the ENFORCED mode. The optimizer will accept, for example, unenforced relationships as well as declared but not ENABLED VALIDATED primary or unique key constraints. Since you are allowing the optimizer to accept relationships on trust (not on an enforced basis), more queries will be eligible for a query rewrite.

- STALE_TOLERATED: The optimizer will accept fresh and stale data, as long as the data is valid. Of course, you'll rewrite more queries in this mode, but you also run a higher risk of getting incorrect results if the stale data doesn't accurately represent the true nature of the current table.

Refreshing Materialized View Data

Since a materialized view is defined on underlying master tables, when the data in the master tables changes, the materialized view becomes outdated. To take care of this problem, materialized views are updated, thus keeping them in sync with the master tables. The following sections present the materialized view refresh options.

Refresh Mode

You can choose between the ON COMMIT and ON DEMAND modes of data refresh.

- ON COMMIT: In this mode, whenever a data change in one of the master tables is committed, the materialized view is refreshed automatically to reflect the change.

- ON DEMAND: In this mode, you must execute a procedure like DBMS_MVIEW.REFRESH to update the materialized view.

The default refresh mode is ON DEMAND.

Refresh Type

You can choose from the following four refresh types:

- COMPLETE: This refresh option will completely recalculate the query underlying the materialized view. Thus, if the materialized view originally took you 12 hours to build, it'll take about the same time to rebuild it. Obviously, you wouldn't want to use this option each time a few rows are modified, dropped, or inserted into your master tables.

- FAST REFRESH: Under the fast refresh mechanism, Oracle will use a *materialized view log* to log all changes to the master tables. It'll then use the materialized view log to update the materialized view. The materialized view log is a table based on the associated materialized view. Each of the tables involved in the join in the materialized view needs its own materialized view log to capture changes to the tables. Oracle can also use data from partition maintenance operation or a data load made by using the SQL*Loader direct-path method to perform the fast refresh of a materialized view.

- FORCE: If you choose this option, Oracle will try to use the fast refresh mechanism. If it isn't able to use it for some reason, it'll use the complete refresh method.

- NEVER: This refresh option never refreshes a materialized view. Obviously, this isn't a viable option for a materialized view whose master tables undergo significant change over time.

The default refresh type is FORCE.

Using the DBMS_MVIEW Package

Even after you specify the query rewrite mechanism, the Oracle cost-based optimizer may not always automatically rewrite a query, accessing the master tables instead of the materialized view. Thus, even though you have a materialized view, the optimizer ignores it, defeating the purpose of creating and maintaining the materialized view. The Oracle optimizer does this because some conditions for query rewrite may not have been met. You can use the Oracle-supplied DBMS_MVIEW package to diagnose this and other materialized view problems.

You can use the DBMS_MVIEW package's procedures in the following way:

- Use the EXPLAIN_MVIEW procedure to see what types of query rewrite are possible.

- Use the EXPLAIN_REWRITE procedure to see why a particular query is not being rewritten to use the materialized view.

- Use the TUNE_MVIEW procedure to enable a query rewrite. This procedure will suggest how you can rewrite a materialized view to make it eligible for a query rewrite. The TUNE_MVIEW procedure also tells you how to satisfy the requirements for a fast refreshable materialized view. The procedure will take your input and produce a materialized view creation script (and any necessary materialized view logs) that is ready to implement.

Creating Materialized Views

In this section, I'll show you how to create a basic materialized view, using some of the options that I described in the previous sections. If you aren't sure about which materialized views to create, you can take advantage of Oracle's SQL Access Advisor, which can make specific recommendations regarding the use of indexes and materialized views. The SQL Access Advisor can design a materialized view and tell you whether it's eligible for a query rewrite. The "Using the SQL Access Advisor" section, later in this chapter, covers the SQL Access Advisor in detail.

There are three steps required to get the materialized views going, although the creation itself is simple:

1. Grant the necessary privileges.

2. Create the materialized view log (assuming you're using the FAST refresh option).

3. Create the materialized view.

Granting the Necessary Privileges

You must first grant the necessary privileges to the user who is creating the materialized views. The main privileges are those that enable the user to create a materialized view. In addition, you must grant the QUERY REWRITE privilege to the user, by using either the GLOBAL QUERY REWRITE privilege or specific QUERY REWRITE privileges on each object that is not part of the user's schema. Here are the grant statements that enable a user to create a materialized view in the user's schema:

```
SQL> GRANT CREATE MATERIALIZED VIEW TO salapati;
SQL> GRANT QUERY REWRITE TO salapati;
```

In addition, if the user doesn't already have it, you must grant the ability to create tables, by using the following GRANT statement:

```
SQL> GRANT CREATE ANY TABLE TO salapati;
```

If the user doesn't own any of the master tables that are part of the materialized view definition, you must grant the user the SELECT privilege on those individual tables, or just make the following grant:

```
SQL> GRANT SELECT ANY TABLE TO salapati
```

Creating the Materialized View Log

Let's use the fast refresh mechanism for our materialized view. In most cases, you must create a materialized view log if you want to use the fast refresh mechanism. This will require the creation of two materialized view logs, of course, to capture the changes to the two master tables that are going to be the basis for our materialized view.

If you want to use the fast refresh mechanism to refresh the materialized view, you must first create materialized view logs for al the tables that are part of the materialized view. In our case, these are the products and the sales tables. In addition, you must also specify the ROWID clause in the CREATE MATERIALIZED VIEW LOG statement when you want to use the fast refresh mechanism. You must also include all columns referenced in the materialized view, and the SEQUENCE and the INCLUDING NEW VALUES clause, as shown in the following example:

```
SQL> CREATE MATERIALIZED VIEW LOG
        ON products WITH SEQUENCE, ROWID
        (prod_id, prod_name, prod_desc, prod_subcategory,
        prod_subcategory_desc,
        prod_category, prod_category_desc, prod_weight_class,
        prod_unit_of_measure, prod_pack_size, supplier_id, prod_status,
        prod_list_price, prod_min_price)
        INCLUDING NEW VALUES;

SQL> CREATE MATERIALIZED VIEW LOG ON sales
        WITH SEQUENCE, ROWID
        (prod_id, cust_id, time_id, channel_id, promo_id,
        quantity_sold, amount_sold)
        INCLUDING NEW VALUES;
```

The example shows how to create two materialized view logs to capture changes in the products and sales master tables, respectively. In the next step, I show how to create the materialized view itself.

Creating the Materialized View

Now you are ready to create your materialized view. The example, shown in Listing 7-17, uses the FAST REFRESH clause to specify the refresh mechanism for the materialized view.

Tip If you already have a table containing some type of aggregates or summary results in your database, you can use the CREATE MATERIALIZED VIEW statement with the ON PREBUILT TABLE clause to register the existing summary table as a materialized view.

Listing 7-17. *Creating a Materialized View*

```
SQL CREATE MATERIALIZED VIEW product_sales_mv
    TABLESPACE test1
    STORAGE (INITIAL 8k NEXT 8k PCTINCREASE 0)
    BUILD IMMEDIATE
    REFRESH FAST
    ENABLE QUERY REWRITE
    AS SELECT p.prod_name, SUM(s.amount_sold) AS dollar_sales,
    COUNT(*) AS cnt, COUNT(s.amount_sold) AS cnt_amt
    FROM sales s, products p
    WHERE s.prod_id = p.prod_id  GROUP BY p.prod_name;GROUP BY p.prod_name;
SQL>
```

Let's look at some of the important clauses of the CREATE MATERIALIZED VIEW statement:

- BUILD IMMEDIATE populates the materialized view right away, and this is the default option. The alternative is to use the build deferred option, which will actually load the materialized view with data later on, at a specified time.

- REFRESH FAST specifies that the materialized view should use the FAST refresh method, which requires using the two materialized logs that you created in the previous step, to capture all changes to the master tables. The ON COMMIT part of the REFRESH clause specifies that all committed changes to the master tables should be propagated to the materialized view immediately upon the committing of the changes.

- ENABLE QUERY REWRITE means that the Oracle optimizer will transparently rewrite your queries to use the newly created materialized views instead of the underlying master tables.

- The AS subquery defines the materialized view. Oracle will store the output of this subquery in the materialized view you're creating. You can use any valid SQL subquery you wish here.

- The last four lines of code contain the actual query defining the materialized view; it retrieves the output from the master tables and makes it part of the materialized view.

Note Due to space limitations, I presented a simple example of creating a materialized view and materialized view log here. In reality, you may have to satisfy additional requirements to be able to create these objects. For example, to enable a fast-refreshable materialized view with materialized view logs, there are specific conditions that you must satisfy. Refer to the Oracle manuals (especially the *Data Warehousing Guide*) for the full requirements.

Note that you can enable query rewrite by specifying ENABLE QUERY REWRITE when you create the materialized view itself (as shown in Listing 7-16) or by specifying the option after the materialized view is created, by using the ALTER MATERIALIZED VIEW statement.

Instead of using the EXPLAIN_REWRITE procedure of the DBMS_MVIEW package, you can use the EXPLAIN PLAN tool to see the proposed execution plan for the query. Your EXPLAIN PLAN should not show any references to the underlying base tables. It should show that the materialized view is being referred to instead, to convince you that the query rewrite is indeed forcing queries to use the new materialized view.

■**Tip** Collect optimizer statistics (see Chapter 19) for a materialized view immediately after you create it. This helps the Oracle optimizer optimize the query rewriting process.

If you think you don't need a materialized view, you can drop it by simply using the DROP MATE-RIALIZED VIEW statement, as shown here:

```
SQL> DROP MATERIALIZED VIEW sales_sum_mv;
```

Using the SQL Access Advisor

As you realize by now, materialized views are very helpful, but creating and maintaining them is no trivial task. It's not easy to figure out the optimal or best materialized views to create. You can use the SQL Access Advisor to help determine which materialized views, materialized view logs, indexes, and partitioned tables you must create in your database. The SQL Access Advisor can also recommend removal of certain indexes to enhance performance.

■**Note** In addition to making recommendations for creating new materialized views (and indexes as well) and helping to implement those recommendations, the SQL Access Advisor also helps you optimize your materialized views by showing you how to ensure query rewriting and to make a materialized view fast-refreshable.

The SQL Access Advisor can use one of the following sources of SQL to determine ideal materialized views and indexes:

- A hypothetical database workload
- An actual workload you provide
- SQL cache

You can also filter the workloads according to criteria such as queries containing only a certain table or tables.

You can use the SQL Access Advisor tool manually, by invoking various procedures that belong to the DBMS_ADVISOR package. Or, you can take a smart shortcut by invoking the SQL Access Advisor wizard through the OEM Database Control (or Grid control) interface.

You can also use the DBMS_ADVISOR's QUICK_TUNE procedure, if you want to get quick recommendations for a single SQL statement. The following sections explain all three methods, with the easiest method, using the OEM Database Control, being first.

Using the OEM Database Control

The SQL Access Advisor works the same way when you invoke it using the OEM Database Control (or Grid Control) as it does when you invoke it directly through the DBMS_ADVISOR package. The reason for this is that the OEM internally relies on the DBMS_ADVISOR package for its functionality. You can provide a SQL workload as input to the SQL Access Advisor, and you can use a user-defined workload, current and recent SQL statements in the database's SQL cache, or a SQL repository as the source for this SQL workload.

When you use the SQL Access Advisor through the OEM, you create tasks and view the recommendations with the help of an intuitive SQL Access Advisor wizard. You provide the SQL statements that are going to use the materialized views during several steps presented by the wizard. You can access this wizard through the Advisor Central link on the Database Control home page (under the

Related Links section at the bottom of the page). You can also access it through links provided on individual alerts or performance pages.

■Tip You can also use the SQL Access Advisor in an evaluation mode, where the advisor evaluates existing indexes and materialized views and tells you which of those are being utilized by the database.

Follow these steps to use the SQL Access Advisor through the Database Control:

1. Clear the SQL cache.
2. Grant the necessary privileges.
3. Create the SQL cache.
4. Get the SQL Access Advisor recommendations.
5. Review the recommendations.
6. Implement the recommendations.

Clearing the Cache

The first step is to flush the shared pool to clear the cache of older SQL statements:

```
SQL> ALTER SYSTEM FLUSH SHARED_POOL;

System altered.
SQL>
```

Granting Necessary Privileges

You must next grant the user sh the ADVISOR privilege in order to use the SQL Access Advisor:

```
SQL> GRANT ADVISOR TO sh;

Grant succeeded.
SQL>
```

Creating the SQL Cache

In order to provide a SQL workload, you can use any one of the methods mentioned previously. In this example, the workload is created by providing three SQL statements that become part of the SQL cache. Connect as the SH user, and run the SQL statements shown in Listing 7-18.

Listing 7-18. *Providing a SQL Workload for the SQL Access Advisor*

```
SQL> SELECT c.cust_last_name, SUM(s.amount_sold),
     SUM(s.quantity_sold)
     FROM sales s, customers c, products p
     WHERE c.cust_id = s.cust_id
     AND s.prod_id = p.prod_id
     AND c.cust_state_province IN ('Texas','New Jersey')

SQL> SELECT c.cust_id, SUM(amount_sold)
     FROM sales s, customers c
     WHERE s.cust_id= c.cust_id GROUP BY c.cust_id;
```

```
SQL> SELECT SUM(unit_cost)
     FROM costs
     GROUP BY prod_id;
```

■**Tip** The SQL Access Advisor can be resource-hungry and thus adversely affect your production database performance. To avoid this, simply collect the necessary workload-related data from the production database and use one
of your test databases to run the SQL Access Advisor's analysis and recommendation steps.

Getting the SQL Access Advisor Recommendations

The previous step created the SQL workload. Using this workload, the SQL Access Advisor will
recommend the necessary materialized views. Log into the OEM Database Control with SYSDBA
privileges, and then follow these steps to use the SQL Access Advisor:

1. Go the OEM home page ➤ Advisor Central (under the Related Links section) ➤ ?SQL Access
   Advisor.

2. The Initial Options page will be displayed. You can choose between the following:

   • *Default options*: Your task will use the Oracle-recommended options.

   • *Inherit options*: Your task will inherit the options from the selected task or template.

   For this example, select Use Default Options and click Next.

3. The Workload Source page is displayed. In this page, you must select one of the following as
   the source for your SQL workload:

   • Current and Recent SQL Activity

   • Import Workload from SQL Repository

   • User-Defined Workload; Import SQL from a Table or View

   • Create a Hypothetical Workload from the Following Schemas and Tables

   You've already executed the three SQL statements you want to use as your workload, so
   select the Current and Recent SQL Activity option.

4. Click Filter Options to fine-tune the scope of the SQL workload. Select Filter Workload under
   Filter Options. Under the USERS section, select the option that states Include Only SQL
   Statements Executed by These Users. Enter **SH** in the Users field.

5. The Recommendation Options page is displayed. There are two sections: Recommendation
   Types and Advisor Mode.

   In the Recommendation Types section, you must select one of the following:

   • Indexes

   • Materialized Views

   • Both Indexes and Materialized Views

   • Partitioned tables

   • Evaluation Only

   Since our goal is to create materialized views, select the second option.

In the Advisor Mode section, choose one of the following two modes for the SQL Access Advisor:

- *Limited*: This mode is quicker and only processes statements with the highest cost.

- *Comprehensive*: This mode takes longer to finish, but it performs an exhaustive analysis. The Comprehensive mode is very resource-intensive, so you may not want to run it during the day in a production database.

Select the Limited mode option.

6. The Schedule page is displayed. This page lets you run the analysis immediately or schedule it for a later time. You can also enter a task name for your SQL Access Advisor job in the Task Name box at the top of the page. Go all the way to the bottom of the page and select Immediately under the Start options. Click Next.

7. The Review page appears next, and you can confirm all your choices before the Advisor starts its run.

8. You'll see the Advisor Central page next, with a confirmation note saying that your SQL Access Advisor job was created successfully.

Reviewing the Recommendations

Once the SQL Access Adviser job successfully completes, you can review the recommendations and decide whether you want to implement them. Follow these steps:

1. On the Advisor Central page (see step 7 in the previous section), navigate to the Results section at the bottom of the page and select your task name. Click View Result.

2. The Results for Task: *Task Number* page appears next. Click Recommendation ID 1 to see the recommendation details.

3. Change the Schema Name for the Create Materialized View to SH, and click OK.

4. On the next page, click Show SQL to view the materialized view generation script, and click OK.

Implementing the Recommendations

To implement the recommendations, follow these steps:

1. Click Schedule Implementation on the Results for Task page.

2. Enter your task name and click Submit.

3. Click View to see if your job is running.

4. Review the summary, click Materialized View, enter **SH** in the schema field, and click Go.

Using the DBMS_ADVISOR Package

Since the OEM Database Control offers such an intuitive interface for using the SQL Access Advisor to generate recommendations regarding indexes and materialized views, I won't discuss the laborious steps you need to use when invoking the SQL Access Advisor through the DBMS_ADVISOR package. I'll merely summarize the approach here:

1. Run some SQL statements so you can use them for your task later on.

2. Create a task using the CREATE_TASK procedure.

3. Create a workload using the CREATE_SQLWKLD procedure.

4. Link your task to the workload by using the ADD_SQLWKLD_REF procedure.

5. Use the appropriate procedure for loading either a hypothetical workload, a SQL cache workload, or a SQL tuning set.

6. Set the task parameters by using the SET_TASK_PARAMETER procedure.

7. Generate recommendations by using the EXECUTE_TASK procedure, using your task name.

8. View the recommendations using the USER_ADVISOR_RECOMMENDATIONS view.

Here's a query using the USER_ADVISOR_ACTIONS view that shows the SQL Access Advisor's recommendations:

```
SQL> SELECT rec_id, action_id, SUBSTR(command,1,30) AS command
     FROM user_advisor_actions WHERE task_name = :task_name
     ORDER BY rec_id, action_id;

     REC_ID       ACTION_ID       COMMAND
------------  ------------  ------------------------------
     1             5          CREATE MATERIALIZED VIEW LOG
     1             8          ALTER MATERIALIZED VIEW LOG
     1             9          CREATE MATERIALIZED VIEW LOG
     1            19          CREATE INDEX
SQL>
```

Using the QUICK_TUNE Procedure

You can use the QUICK_TUNE procedure of the DBMS_ADVISOR package when you have a single SQL statement to tune. You need to supply a task name and a SQL statement as inputs to the procedure. Here's an example:

```
VARIABLE task_name VARCHAR2(255);
VARIABLE sql_stmt VARCHAR2(4000);
EXECUTE :sql_stmt := 'SELECT COUNT(*) FROM customers
                    WHERE cust_state_province=''TX''';
EXECUTE :task_name  := 'MY_QUICKTUNE_TASK';
EXECUTE DBMS_ADVISOR.QUICK_TUNE(DBMS_ADVISOR.SQLACCESS_ADVISOR, -
             :task_name, :sql_stmt);
```

This will produce identical results as when you use all the steps outlined in the "Using the DBMS_ADVISOR Package" section.

Using Synonyms

Synonyms are aliases for objects in the database, and they are used mainly to make it easy for users to access database objects owned by other users, and for security purposes. Synonyms hide the underlying object's identity and can be either private or public. *Public* synonyms are accessible by all the users in the database, and *private* synonyms are part of the individual user's schema—access rights have to be individually granted to specific users before they can use the private synonyms. Oracle synonyms can be created for tables, views, materialized views, and stored code, such as packages and procedures.

Synonyms are very powerful from the point of view of allowing users access to objects that do not lie within their schemas. All synonyms have to be created explicitly with the create synonym command, and the underlying objects can be located in the same database or in other databases that are connected by database links.

There are two major uses of synonyms:

- *Object transparency*: Synonyms can be created to keep the original object transparent to the user.
- *Location transparency*: Synonyms can be created as aliases for tables and other objects that belong to a database other than the local database.

▓**Note** Keep in mind that even if you know the synonym for a schema table, you can't necessarily access it. You must also have been granted the necessary privileges on the table for you to be able to access the table.

When you create a table or procedure, the database creates it in your schema, and other users can access it only by using your schema name as a prefix to the object's name. Listing 7-19 shows a couple of examples that illustrate this point.

Listing 7-19. *Using Schema Names to Access Tables*

```
SQL> SHOW USER

USER is "SYSTEM"

SQL> DESC employees

ERROR:
ORA-04043: object employees does not exist

SQL> DESC hr.employees

Name                 Null?     Type
---------------      --------  --------------
EMPLOYEE_ID          NOT NULL  NUMBER(6)
FIRST_NAME                     VARCHAR2(20)
LAST_NAME            NOT NULL  VARCHAR2(25)
EMAIL                NOT NULL  VARCHAR2(25)
PHONE_NUMBER                   VARCHAR2(20)
HIRE_DATE            NOT NULL  DATE
JOB_ID               NOT NULL  VARCHAR2(10)
SALARY                         NUMBER(8,2)
COMMISSION_PCT                 NUMBER(2,2)
MANAGER_ID                     NUMBER(6)
DEPARTMENT_ID                  NUMBER(4)
SQL>
```

As you can see, when the user SYSTEM tried to describe the table without the schema prefix, Oracle issued an error stating that the table "does not exist." The way around this is for the schema owner to create a synonym with the same name as the table name. Once the user SYSTEM uses the schema.table notation, the table's contents can be seen.

Creating a Public Synonym

Public synonyms are owned by a special schema in the Oracle database called PUBLIC. As mentioned earlier, public synonyms can be referenced by all users in the database. Public synonyms are usually created by the application owner for tables and other objects such as procedures and packages so the users of the application can see the objects.

The following code shows how to create a public synonym for the employees table:

```
SQL> CREATE PUBLIC SYNONYM employees FOR hr.employees;

Synonym created.
SQL>
```

Now any user can see the table by just typing the original table name.

If you wish, you could provide a different name for the table in the CREATE SYNONYM statement. Remember that the DBA must explicitly grant the CREATE PUBLIC SYNONYM privilege to user hr before that user can create any public synonyms.

Just because you can see a table through a public (or private) synonym doesn't mean that you can also perform SELECT, INSERT, UPDATE, or DELETE operations on the table. To be able to perform those operations, a user needs specific privileges for the underlying object, either directly or through roles, from the application owner. The topic of granting privileges and roles is discussed in Chapter 12.

Creating a Private Synonym

Private synonyms, unlike public synonyms, can be referenced only by the schema that owns the table or object. You may want to create private synonyms when you want to refer to the same table by different aliases in different contexts. You create private synonyms the same way you create public synonyms, but you omit the PUBLIC keyword in the CREATE statement.

The following example shows how to create a private synonym called addresses for the locations table. Note that once you create the private synonym, you can refer to the synonym exactly as you would the original table name.

```
SQL> CREATE SYNONYM addresses FOR hr.locations;

Synonym created.
SQL> SELECT * FROM addresses;
```

Dropping a Synonym

You can drop both private and public synonyms with the DROP SYNONYM command, but there is one important difference. If you are dropping a public synonym, you need to add the keyword PUBLIC after the keyword DROP.

Here's an example of dropping a private synonym:

```
SQL> DROP SYNONYM addresses;

Synonym dropped.
SQL>
```

Managing Synonyms

The DBA_SYNONYMS view provides information on all synonyms in your database. Synonyms are based on underlying base tables, and you can find out the names of the base objects by issuing a query such as the following:

```
SQL> SELECT TABLE_NAME, SYNONYM_NAME
    FROM dba_synonyms
    WHERE OWNER = 'SALAPATI';
```

```
TABLE_NAME        SYNONYM_NAME
----------        ------------
DEPT              DEPT
EMP               EMP
SQL>
```

Use the DBA_SYNONYMS view to clarify the names of the base tables underlying synonyms.

Switching to a Different Schema

If you have to constantly use tables owned by a different schema and there aren't any synonyms on the table, you may be forced to use the schema qualifier in front of every table name. For example, you might need to use scott.emp to refer to the emp table owned by the user scott. To avoid this, you can simply use the ALTER SESSION SET SCHEMA statement, as shown here:

```
SQL> CONNECT samalapati/sammyy1
SQL> ALTER SESSION SET CURRENT_SCHEMA = scott;
SQL> SELECT * FROM emp;
```

The use of the ALTER SESSION statement here doesn't confer any automatic object privileges. In order to query the emp table without any schema qualifier, as shown in the preceding example, the user must have SELECT privileges on the emp table.

Using Sequences

Oracle uses a sequence generator to automatically generate a unique sequence of numbers that users can use in their operations. Sequences are commonly used to create a unique number to generate a unique primary key for a column. We'll look at using an Oracle sequence to generate employee numbers during a data insert.

■**Note** If users were to use programmatically created sequence numbers instead, Oracle would have to constantly lock and unlock records holding the maximum value of those sequences to ensure an orderly incrementing of the sequence. This locking would result in users waiting for the next value in the sequence to be issued to their transactions. Oracle's automatic generation of sequences increases database concurrency.

You have several options to choose from to create a sequence. We will use a plain vanilla sequence that starts at 10,000 and is incremented by 1 each time. The sequence is never recycled or reused, because we want distinct sequence numbers for each employee.

■**Note** There are two pseudo-columns called currval and nextval that you can use to query sequence values. The currval pseudo-column provides you with the current value of the sequence, and the nextval pseudo-column gets you the new or next sequence number.

First, create a sequence as shown in the following example. This is usually the way you use a sequence to generate a unique primary key for a column.

```
SQL> CREATE SEQUENCE employee_seq
     START WITH 10000
     INCREMENT BY 1
     NOMAXVALUE
```

```
     NOCYCLE;
Sequence created.
SQL>
```

Second, select the current sequence number by using the following statement:

```
SQL> SELECT employee_seq.currval FROM dual;
```

Third, insert a new row into the employee table using nextval from the employee_seq sequence:

```
SQL> INSERT INTO employees(employee_id, first_name, last_name, email,
  2  phone_number, hire_date)
  3  VALUES
  4* (employee_seq.nextval,'sam','alapati','salapati.tnt.org'
     ,345-555-5555,to_char('21-JUN-2005');
1 row created.

SQL> COMMIT;
Commit complete.
SQL>
```

Finally, check to make sure the employee_id column is being populated by the employee_seq sequence:

```
SQL> SELECT employee_id, first_name, last_name
     FROM employees
     WHERE last_name = 'alapati';
EMPLOYEE_ID     FIRST_NAME          LAST_NAME
-------------   ----------------    ----------
      10011     sam                 alapati
SQL>
```

Note that you can have an Oracle sequence that is incremented continuously, but there may be occasional gaps in the sequence numbers. This is because Oracle always keeps 20 values (by default) in memory, and that's where it gets the nextval from. If there should be a database crash, the numbers stored in memory will be lost, and there will be a gap in that particular sequence.

Using Triggers

Oracle triggers are similar to PL/SQL procedures, but they are automatically fired by the database based on specified events. For DBAs, triggers come in handy in performing audit- and security-related tasks. Besides the standard Oracle triggers, which fire before or after DML statements, there are powerful triggers based on system events, such as database startup and shutdown and the users logging on and logging off. Chapter 11 shows you how to use triggers to enhance database security.

You create a trigger with the CREATE TRIGGER statement. You can choose to have the trigger fire BEFORE, AFTER, or INSTEAD OF the triggering event.

The following example shows the structure of the CREATE TRIGGER statement for a BEFORE event trigger. Before a DML statement can delete, insert, or update a row in the employees table, Oracle automatically fires this trigger:

```
SQL> CREATE TRIGGER scott.emp_permit_changes
     BEFORE DELETE
     OR INSERT
     OR UPDATE
     ON employees
. . .
/* Your SQL or PL/SQL code here
```

When you create a trigger, it is enabled by default. If you want to temporarily disable a trigger for some reason, you use the following statement:

```
SQL> ALTER TRIGGER test DISABLE;
```

You can reenable this trigger by using the following command:

```
SQL> ALTER TRIGGER test ENABLE;
```

Viewing Object Information

There are several important data dictionary views you can use to find out detailed information about any of the database objects discussed in this chapter. DBAs also make heavy use of data dictionary views to manage various schema objects. I provide a brief list of the important views here, some of which were explained earlier in the chapter. To get complete information about the types of information you can glean from each of these views, use the SQL command DESCRIBE (as in DESCRIBE DBA_CATALOG).

Views for Managing Database Objects

In this section, you'll look at the important data dictionary views that help you manage *nondata* objects (that is, objects other than tables and indexes). The following is a list of the important data dictionary views for looking up various database objects:

- *DBA_SYNONYMS*: Information about database synonyms
- *DBA_TRIGGERS*: Information about triggers
- *DBA_SEQUENCES*: Information about user-created sequences
- *DBA_DB_LINKS*: Information about database links

As mentioned earlier, the DBA_OBJECTS view provides important information on the preceding objects, as well as several other types of database objects. However, the preceding views provide detailed information about the object, such as the source text of a trigger, which you won't get from the DBA_OBJECTS view.

You manage objects such as tables and views by referring to the data dictionary views, such as DBA_TABLES and DBA_VIEWS. There are also separate views for partitioned tables. Let's look at the key table- and index-related dictionary views.

DBA_OBJECTS

The DBA_OBJECTS view contains information about all the objects in the database, including tables, indexes, packages, procedures, functions, dimensions, materialized views, resource plans, types, sequences, synonyms, triggers, views, and table partitions. As you can surmise, this view is useful when you need to know general information regarding any database object. Listing 7-20 shows a query designed to find out the created time and the LAST_DDL_TIME (the last time the object was modified). This type of query helps you identify when a certain object was modified, and is often used for auditing purposes.

Listing 7-20. *Querying the DBA_OBJECTS View*

```
SQL> SELECT object_name,
  2  object_type,
  3  created,
  4  last_ddl_time,
  5  FROM DBA_OBJECTS
```

```
    6  WHERE owner ='APPOWNER'
    7* AND object_name LIKE 'YTD%';

OBJECT_NAME            OBJECT_TYPE     CREATED        LAST_DDL_TIME
-----------------      ----------      ----------     -------------
YTD_ADJ2005050603      TABLE           01/23/2008     01/23/2008
SQL>
```

DBA_TABLES

The DBA_TABLES view contains information about all relational tables in your database. The DBA_TABLES view is your main reference for finding out storage information, the number of rows in the table, logging status, buffer pool information, and a host of other things. Here's a simple query on the DBA_TABLES view:

```
SQL> SELECT tablespace_name,table_name
     FROM DBA_TABLES;

TABLESPACE_NAME             TABLE_NAME
---------------             ----------------
EXAMPLE                     DEPARTMENTS
EXAMPLE                     EMPLOYEES_INTERI
EXAMPLE                     EMPLOYEES_NEW
EXAMPLE                     JOBS
EXAMPLE                     JOB_HISTORY
EXAMPLE                     TEST
6 rows selected.
SQL>
```

Note The DBA_ALL_TABLES view contains information about all object tables and relational tables in a database, while the DBA_TABLES view is limited to only relational tables.

You can use the DBA_TABLES view to find out things such as whether table compression and row-level dependency tracking are enabled, and whether the table has been dropped and is in the Recycle Bin.

DBA_EXTERNAL_TABLES

The DBA_EXTERNAL_TABLES view shows details about any external tables in a database, including their access type, access parameters, and directory information.

DBA_TAB_PARTITIONS

The DBA_TAB_PARTITIONS view is similar to the DBA_TABLES view, but it provides detailed information about table partitions. You can get information about the partition name, partition high values, partition storage information, and partition statistics, plus all the other information that's available from the DBA_TABLES view. Listing 7-21 shows a simple query using the DBA_TAB_PARTITIONS view.

Listing 7-21. *Querying the DBA_TAB_PARTITIONS View*

```
SQL> SELECT table_name, partition_name,
  2  high_value,
  3* FROM DBA_TAB_PARTITIONS;
```

TABLE_NAME	PARTITION_NAME	HIGH_VALUE
SALES	SALES_Q2_2004	TO_DATE(' 2007-07-01 00:00:00')
SALES	SALES_Q3_2004	TO_DATE(' 2007-10-01 00:00:00')
SALES	SALES_Q4_2004	TO_DATE(' 2008-01-01 00:00:00')
SALES	SALES_Q1_2005	TO_DATE(' 2008-04-01 00:00:00')
SALES	SALES_Q2_2005	TO_DATE(' 2008-07-01 00:00:00')
SALES	SALES_Q3_2005	TO_DATE(' 2008-10-01 00:00:00')
SALES	SALES_Q4_2005	TO_DATE(' 2009-01-01 00:00:00')
EMPLOYEES	EMPLOYEES1	100
EMPLOYEES	EMPLOYEES2	300

```
SQL>
```

DBA_PART_TABLES

The DBA_PART_TABLES view provides information about the type of partition scheme and other storage parameters for partitions and subpartitions. You can find out the partition type of each partitioned table using the following query:

```
SQL> SELECT table_name, partitioning_type,
  2  def_tablespace_name
  3  FROM DBA_PART_TABLES;
```

TABLE_NAME	PARTITION_TYPE	DEF_TABLESPACE_NAME
EMPLOYEES	RANGE	EXAMPLE
EMPLOYEES_INTERIM	RANGE	EXAMPLE
COSTS	RANGE	EXAMPLE
SALES	RANGE	EXAMPLE

```
SQL>
```

DBA_TAB_MODIFICATIONS

The DBA_TAB_MODIFICATIONS view shows all DML changes in a table since statistics were last collected for that table. Here's a query on this view:

```
SQL> SELECT table_name, inserts, updates, deletes
     FROM DBA_TAB_MODIFICATIONS;
```

TABLE_NAME	INSERTS	UPDATES	DELETES
WRH$ACTIVE_SESSION_HISTORY	1233	0	0
WRH$SERVICE_STAT	5376	0	0
WRH$SERVICE_WAIT_CLASS	1050	0	0

```
. . .
SQL>
```

The database doesn't update the DBA_TAB_MODIFCATIONS view in real time. Consequently, you may not see the changes you make to various tables immediately reflected in this view.

DBA_TAB_COLUMNS

Suppose you want to find out the average length of each row in a table or the default value of each column (if there is one). The DBA_TAB_COLUMNS view is an excellent way to quickly get detailed column-level information on schema tables, as shown in Listing 7-22.

Listing 7-22. *Using the DBA_TAB_COLUMNS View*

```
SQL> SELECT column_name,
  2  avg_col_len,
  3  data_type,
  4  data_length,
  5  nullable,
  6  FROM dba_tab_columns
  7* WHERE owner='OE';
```

COLUMN_NAME	AVG_COL_LEN	DATA_TYPE	DATA_LENGTH	NULL
CUSTOMER_ID	4	NUMBER	22	N
CUST_FIRST_NAME	7	VARCHAR2	20	N
CUST_LAST_NAME	8	VARCHAR2	20	N
TRANSLATED_DESCRIPTION	245	NVARCHAR2	4000	N
PRODUCT_DESCRIPTION	123	VARCHAR2	2000	Y
WARRANTY_PERIOD	5	INTERVAL YEA	5	Y

```
SQL>
```

DBA_VIEWS

As you know, views are the product of a query on some database table(s). The DBA_VIEWS dictionary view provides you with the SQL query that underlies the views. Listing 7-23 shows how to get the text of a view, OC_CUSTOMERS, owned by user oe.

▪Tip To ensure you see the whole text of the view when you use the DBA_VIEWS view, set the long variable to a large number (for example, SET LONG 2000). Otherwise, you'll see only the first line of the view definition.

Listing 7-23. *Getting the Source for a View Using the DBA_VIEWS View*

```
SQL> SET LONG 2000
SQL> SELECT text
  2  FROM DBA_VIEWS
  3  WHERE view_name ='OC_CUSTOMERS'
  4* AND owner = 'OE';

TEXT
--------------------------------------------------
SELECT c.customer_id, c.cust_first_name,
 c.cust_last_name, c.cust_address,
          c.phone_numbers,c.nls_languag
e,c.nls_territory,c.credit_limit, c.cust_email,
  CAST(MULTISET(SELECT o.order_id, o.order_mode,
    MAKE_REF(
oc_customers,o.customer_id),
```

```
      o.order_status,o.order_t
otal,o.sales_rep_id,
   CAST(MULTISET(SELECT l.order_id,l.line_item_id,
      l.unit_price,l.quantity,
         MAKE_REF(oc_product_information,
            l.product_id)
FROM order_items l
WHERE o.order_id = l.order_id)
AS order_item_list_typ)
FROM orders o
WHERE c.customer_id = o.customer_id)
AS order_list_typ)
FROM customers c
SQL>
```

DBA_MVIEWS

The DBA_MVIEWS dictionary view tells you all about the materialized views in your database, including whether the query rewrite feature is enabled or not on the views. Listing 7-24 shows you how to use this view.

Listing 7-24. *Using the DBA_MVIEWS View*

```
SQL> SELECT
  2   mview_name,
  3   query,
  4   updatable,
  5   rewrite_enabled,   /* whether query rewrite is enabled */
  6   refresh_mode,      /* demand,commit, or never */
  7   refresh_method     /* complete,force, fast, or never */
  8* FROM dba_mviews;

MVIEW_NAME        QUERY                          UPD   REW  REFR REFRESH_ME
----------------  -----------------------------  ----  ---- ---------------
MONTH_SALES_MV    SELECT t.calendar_month_desc   N     Y    DEMAND FORCE
PCAT_SALES_MV     SELECT t.week_ending_day       N     Y    DEMAND COMPLETE
SQL>
```

DBA_INDEXES

You can use the DBA_INDEXES dictionary view to find out just about everything you need to know about the indexes in your database, including the index name, index type, and the table and tablespace an index belongs to. Certain columns, such as BLEVEL (tells you the level of the B-tree index) and DISTINCT_KEYS (number of distinct index key values), are populated only if you've collected statistics for the index using the DBMS_STATS package.

DBA_IND_COLUMNS

The DBA_IND_COLUMNS view is similar to the DBA_CONS_COLUMNS view in structure, and it provides information on all the indexed columns in every table. This is important during SQL performance tuning when you notice that the query is using an index, but you aren't sure exactly on which columns the index is defined. The query in Listing 7-25 may reveal that the table has indexes on the wrong columns after all.

Listing 7-25. *Querying the DBA_IND_COLUMNS View*

```
SQL> SELECT index_name,
  2  table_name,
  3  column_name,
  4  column_position
  5  FROM DBA_IND_COLUMNS
  6* WHERE table_owner='OE';


INDEX_NAME                 TABLE_NAME      COLUMN_NAME       COLUMN_POSITION
----------------------     -----------     ----------------  ---------------
CUST_ACCOUNT_MANAGER_IX    CUSTOMERS       ACCOUNT_MGR_ID    1
CUST_LNAME_IX              CUSTOMERS       CUST_LAST_NAME    1
CUST_EMAIL_IX              CUSTOMERS       CUST_EMAIL        1
INVENTORY_PK               INVENTORIES     PRODUCT_ID        1
INVENTORY_PK               INVENTORIES     WAREHOUSE_ID      2
INV_PRODUCT_IX             INVENTORIES     PRODUCT_ID        1
ORDER_PK                   ORDERS          ORDER_ID          1
ORD_SALES_REP_IX           ORDERS          SALES_REP_ID      1
ORD_CUSTOMER_IX            ORDERS          CUSTOMER_ID       1
SQL>
```

■**Tip** You can identify composite keys easily by looking in the INDEX_NAME column. If the same INDEX_NAME entry appears more than once, it's a composite key, and you can see the columns that are part of the key in the COLUMN_NAME column. For example, INVENTORY_PK is the primary key of the INVENTORIES table and is defined on two columns: PRODUCT_ID and WAREHOUSE_ID. You can glean the order of the two columns in a composite key by looking at the COLUMN_POSITION column.

INDEX_STATS

The INDEX_STATS view is useful for seeing how efficiently an index is using its space. Large indexes have a tendency to become unbalanced over time if many deletions are in the table (and therefore index) data. Your goal is to keep an eye on those large indexes with a view to keeping them balanced.

Note that the INDEX_STATS view is populated only if the table has been analyzed by using the ANALYZE command, as follows:

```
SQL> ANALYZE index hr.emp_name_ix VALIDATE STRUCTURE;
Index analyzed.
```

The query in Listing 7-26 using the INDEX_STATS view helps determine whether you need to rebuild the index. In the query, you should focus on the following columns in the INDEX_STATS view to determine if your index is a candidate for a rebuild:

- *HEIGHT*: This column refers to the height of the B-tree index, and it's usually at the 1, 2, or 3 level. If large inserts push the index height beyond a level of 4, it's time to rebuild, which flattens the B-tree.

- *DEL_LF_ROWS*: This is the number of leaf nodes deleted due to the deletion of rows. Oracle doesn't rebuild indexes automatically and, consequently, too many deleted leaf rows can lead to an unbalanced B-tree.

- *BLK_GETS_PER_ACCESS*: You can look at the *BLK_GETS_PER_ACCESS* column to see how much logical I/O it takes to retrieve data from the index. If this row shows a double-digit number, you should probably start rebuilding the index.

Listing 7-26. *Using the INDEX_STATS View to Determine Whether to Rebuild an Index*

```
SQL> SELECT height,         /*Height of the B-Tree*/
  2  blocks,                /* Blocks in the index segment */
  3  name,                  /*index name */
  4  lf_rows,               /* number of leaf rows in the index */
  5  lf_blks,               /* number of leaf blocks in the index */
  6  del_lf_rows,           /* number of deleted leaf rows
                               in the index */
  7  rows_per_key           /* average number of rows
                               per distinct key */
  8  blk_gets_per_access    /* consistent mode block reads (gets)  */
  8  FROM INDEX_STATS
  9* WHERE name='EMP_NAME_IX';

HEIGHT  BLOCK       LF_ROWS  LF_BLKS  DEL_LF_ROWS  ROWS_PER_KEY  BLK_GETS
------  ----------- -------  -------- -----------  ------------  ---------
16      EMP_NAME_IX 107      1        0            1             1
SQL>
```

CHAPTER 8

■■■

Oracle Transaction Management

Transaction management is at the heart of database processing. In order for a large number of users to run concurrent transactions, the DBMS must manage the transactions with the least amount of conflict while ensuring the consistency of the database. Transaction management ensures that a database is accessible to many users simultaneously, and that users can't undo each other's work.

A *transaction* is a logical unit of work consisting of one or more SQL statements. Transactions may encompass all of your program or just a part of it. A transaction may perform one operation or an entire series of operations on the database objects, either interactively or as part of a program. Transactions are begun implicitly whenever data is read or written, and they are ended by a COMMIT or ROLLBACK statement.

In this chapter, I cover the basics of transaction management. I start with an explanation of a transaction in the context of a relational database, I explain the main types of data anomalies, and I explain the standard transaction isolation levels and Oracle's implementation of the read-committed isolation level for maintaining consistency and concurrency.

The concept of *serializability* is crucial in transaction processing. Concurrency of usage gives relational databases their great strength, and serializability conditions ensure the concurrency of database transactions. In this chapter, I explain how Oracle uses the twin techniques of transaction locking and multiversion concurrency control using undo records to enforce serializability in transactions. The other component in Oracle's transaction management is its automatic locking feature, which helps Oracle increase concurrency.

Undo space management is an important part of transaction management, and in this chapter you'll learn about the Automatic Undo Management (AUM) feature. You'll also learn how to use Oracle's powerful flashback features, which help you perform various tasks such as quickly recovering from logical errors, for example. I explain the key Oracle flashback features such as the Flashback Query, Flashback Versions Query, Flash Transaction Query, and the powerful Flashback Table features, which help in auditing and correcting logical data errors. All of these Flashback features rely on the use of undo data in your undo tablespace.

Longer transactions can run the risk of failing to complete due to space errors. You'll learn how to use Oracle's new Resumable Space Allocation feature to resume transactions that are suspended due to a space-related error. You'll also learn how to use autonomous transactions. This chapter also provides an introduction to the Oracle Workspace Manager feature, which offers version control for table data.

Oracle Transactions

DDL statements issued by a DBA usually aren't very complex to process. The DDL commands alter the schema (which means changing the data dictionary), which contains object definitions and other related metadata for the database. DML language (also called *query language*) operations are a different kettle of fish altogether. The majority of DML statements retrieve data from the database, and the rest modify data or insert new data. DML transaction processing involves compiling and executing SQL statements in the most efficient manner with the least contention among multiple transactions, while preserving the consistency of the database.

A transaction starts implicitly when the first executable SQL statement begins, and it continues as the following SQL statements are processed until one of the following events occurs:

- COMMIT: If a transaction encounters a COMMIT statement, all the changes to that point are made permanent in the database.

- Rollback: If a transaction encounters a ROLLBACK statement, all changes made up to that point are cancelled.

- *DDL statement*: If a user issues a DDL statement, such as CREATE, DROP, RENAME, or ALTER, Oracle first commits any current DML statements that are part of the transaction, before executing and committing the results of the DDL statement. This is called an *implicit commit*, since the committing of the DML statements immediately preceding the DDL statements isn't explicitly done by the user.

- *Normal program conclusion*: If a program ends without errors, all changes are implicitly committed by the database. When you make a normal clean exit from SQL*Plus, the database automatically commits all changes you made to data in that session.

- *Abnormal program failure*: If the program crashes or is terminated, all changes made by it are implicitly rolled back by the database.

When a transaction begins, Oracle will assign the transaction an undo segment, where the original data is recorded whenever data is modified by an update or delete. In the case of an insert operation, the undo segments will record the relevant ROWIDs. The first statement after the completion of a transaction will mark the beginning of a new transaction. In the sections that follow, you'll look at the COMMIT and ROLLBACK transaction control statements in detail.

COMMIT Statement

The COMMIT statement ends a transaction successfully. All changes made by all SQL statements since the transaction began are recorded permanently in the database. Before the COMMIT statement is issued, the changes may not be visible to other transactions.

You can commit a transaction by using either of the following statements, which make the changes permanent:

```
SQL> COMMIT;
SQL> COMMIT WORK;
```

Before Oracle can issue a COMMIT statement, the following things happen in the database:

- Oracle generates undo records in the undo segment buffers in the SGA. As you know, the undo records contain the old values of the updated and deleted table rows.

- Oracle generates redo log entries in the redo log buffers in the SGA.

- Oracle modifies the database buffers in the SGA.

Note The modified database buffers may be written to the disk before a COMMIT statement is issued. Similarly, the redo log entries may be written to the redo logs before a COMMIT statement is ever issued.

When an Oracle transaction is committed, the following three things happen:

1. The transaction tables in the redo records are tagged with the unique system change number (SCN) of the committed transaction.

2. The log writer writes the redo log information for the transaction from the redo log buffer to the redo log files on disk, along with the transaction's SCN. This is the point at which a commit is considered complete in Oracle.

3. Any locks that Oracle holds are released, and Oracle marks the transaction as complete.

■ Note If you set the SQL*Plus variable AUTOCOMMIT to on, Oracle will automatically commit transactions, even without an explicit COMMIT statement.

The default behavior for the COMMIT statement, which is generally the only type you'll encounter, is to use the IMMEDIATE and WAIT options:

- IMMEDIATE vs. BATCH: With the IMMEDIATE option, the log writer writes the redo log records for the committing transaction immediately to disk. If you'd rather the log writer write the redo records by buffering them in memory until it's convenient to write them, you can use the alternative BATCH option.

- WAIT vs. NOWAIT: With the WAIT option, the COMMIT statement doesn't return as successful until the redo records are successfully written to the redo logs. If you'd rather have the COMMIT statement return without waiting for the writing of the redo records, you can use the NOWAIT option.

As you can see, the default behavior means that there is a disk I/O after each commit, and consequently, a slight delay in finishing the transaction. For certain types of long transactions, you may want to avoid the delay resulting from frequent writing of redo log records and waiting for the confirmation of those writes.

You can modify this default behavior by using the initialization parameters COMMIT_WAIT and COMMIT_LOGGING. Use the COMMIT_WAIT parameter to control when the database flushes the redo for a commit to the redo logs. Use the COMMIT_LOGGING parameter to control how the log writer batches redo.

ROLLBACK Statement

The ROLLBACK statement undoes, or rolls back, the changes made by SQL statements within a transaction, so long as you didn't already commit the transaction. Once you issue the ROLLBACK statement, none of the changes made to the tables by SQL statements since the transaction began are recorded to the database permanently. You can roll back an entire transaction by rolling back all changes made by all the SQL statements within that transaction by simply using the ROLLBACK command as follows:

```
SQL> ROLLBACK;
```

You can also partially roll back the effects of a transaction by using *save points* in the transaction. Using a save point, you can roll back to the last SAVEPOINT command in the transaction, as follows:

```
SQL> ROLLBACK TO SAVEPOINT POINT A;
```

The SAVEPOINT statement acts like a bookmark for the uncommitted statements in the transaction. In the second of the preceding examples, the rollback is only up to point A in the transaction. Everything before point A is still committed.

Oracle uses the undo records in the undo tablespace to roll back the transactions after a ROLL-BACK command. It also releases any locks that are held, and it marks the transaction as complete. If the rollback is to a save point, the transaction is deemed incomplete, and you can continue the transaction.

If a SQL statement errors out during its execution, all the changes made by it to that point are automatically rolled back. This is known as a statement-level rollback. A deadlock is a condition that occurs when SQL statements from two sessions contend for the same piece of data. In that situation, Oracle automatically rolls back one of the SQL statements to resolve deadlocks.

Transaction Properties

Transactions in RDBMSs must possess four important properties, symbolized by the ACID acronym, which stands for *atomicity, consistency, isolation*, and *durability* of transactions. Transaction management, in general, means supporting database transactions so the ACID properties are maintained.

Let's look at the transaction properties in more detail:

- *Atomicity*: Either a transaction should be performed entirely or none of it should be performed. That is, you can't have the database performing only a part of a transaction. For example, if you issue a SQL statement that should delete 1,000 records, your entire transaction should abort (roll back) if your database crashes after the transaction deletes 999 records.

- *Consistency*: The database is supposed to ensure that it's always in a consistent state. For example, in a banking transaction that involves debits from your savings account and credits to your checking account, the database can't just credit your checking account and stop. This will lead to inconsistent data, and the consistency property of transactions ensures that the database doesn't leave data in an inconsistent state. All transactions must preserve the consistency of the database. For example, if you wish to delete a department ID from the Department table, the database shouldn't permit your action if some employees in the Employees table belong to the department you're planning on eliminating.

- *Isolation*: Isolation means that although there's concurrent access to the database by multiple transactions, each transaction must appear to be executing in isolation. The isolation property of transactions ensures that a transaction is kept from viewing changes made by another transaction before the first transaction commits. This property is upheld by the database's concurrency control mechanisms, as you'll see in the following sections. Although concurrent access is a hallmark of the relational database, isolation techniques make it *appear* as though users are executing transactions *serially*, one after another. This chapter discusses how Oracle implements *concurrency control*—the assurance of atomicity and isolation of individual transactions in a concurrently accessed database.

- *Durability*: The last ACID property, durability, ensures that the database saves commit transactions permanently. Once a transaction completes, the database should ensure that the transaction's changes are not lost. This property is enforced by the database recovery mechanisms, which make sure that all committed transactions are retrieved. As you saw in Chapter 5, Oracle uses the *write-ahead protocol*, which ensures that all changes are first written to the redo logs on disk before they're transferred to the database files on disk.

■**Note** Users can name a transaction to make it easier to monitor it, and there are several advantages to giving a meaningful name to a long-running transaction. For example, using the LogMiner utility, you can look for details of the specific transaction you're interested in. Chapter 16 shows how to use the LogMiner utility to help undo DML changes. Assigning names to transactions also makes it easier for the user to query the transaction details using the name column of the V$TRANSACTION view.

Transaction Concurrency Control

To ensure data consistency, each user must see a consistent set of data that includes all changes made by that user's transactions as well as all the other users' transactions. In a single-user database, it's a trivial matter to achieve data consistency. However, real-life databases need to allow simultaneous operations by numerous users, a requirement that's known as data concurrency. Improper interactions among transactions can cause data to become inconsistent.

Transaction concurrency is achieved by managing various users' simultaneous transactions without permitting any interference among them. If you're the only user of the database, you don't need to worry about concurrency control of transactions. However, in most cases, databases enable thousands of users to perform simultaneous select, update, insert, and delete transactions against the same table.

One solution to concurrency control is to lock the entire table for the duration of each operation, so one user's transactions do not impact another's. Thus, each user would be operating in isolation, thereby sacrificing data concurrency. However, this would mean that access to the table would be severely reduced. As you'll see, Oracle *does use* locking mechanisms to keep the data consistent, but the locking is done in the least restrictive fashion, with the goal of maintaining the maximum amount of concurrency.

Concurrency no doubt increases the throughput of an RDBMS, but it brings along its own special set of problems, which we'll look at next.

Concurrency Problems

Concurrent access to the database by multiple users introduces several problems. Some of the most important problems potentially encountered in concurrent transaction processing are dirty reads, phantom reads, lost updates, and nonrepeatable reads.

The Dirty-Read Problem

A *dirty read* occurs when a transaction reads data that has been updated by an ongoing transaction but has not been committed permanently to the database. For example, say transaction A has just updated the value of a column, and it is now read by transaction B. What if transaction A rolls back its changes, whether intentionally or because it aborts for some reason? The value of the updated column will also be rolled back as a result. Unfortunately, transaction B has already read the new value of the column, which is now incorrect because of the rolling back of transaction A.

■**Tip** The problem described in this section could be avoided by imposing a simple rule: Don't let any transaction read the intermediate results of another transaction before the other transaction is either committed or rolled back. This way, the reads are guaranteed to be consistent.

The Phantom-Read Problem

Say you're reading data from a table (using a SELECT statement). You re-execute your query after some time elapses, and in the meantime, some other user has inserted new data into the table. Because your second query will come up with extra rows that weren't in the first read, they're referred to as "phantom" reads, and the problem is termed a *phantom read*. Phantom-read problems are caused by the appearance of new data in between two database operations in a transaction.

The Lost-Update Problem

The *lost-update* problem is caused by transactions trying to read data while it is being updated by other transactions. Say transaction A is reading a table's data while it is being updated by transaction

B, and transaction *B* completes successfully and is committed. If transaction *A* has read the data before transaction *B* has fully completed, it might end up with intermediate data. The lost update anomaly occurs because two users have updated the same row, and since the second update overwrites the first, the first update is *lost*. Allowing transactions to read and update a table before the completion of another transaction causes the problem in this case.

The Nonrepeatable-Read (Fuzzy-Read) Problem

When a transaction finds that data it has read previously has been modified by some other transaction, you have a *nonrepeatable-read* (or fuzzy-read) problem. Suppose you access a table's data at a certain point in time, and then you try to access the same data a little later, only to find that the data values are different the second time around. This inconsistent data during the same transaction causes a nonrepeatable-read problem.

Schedules and Serializability

As you can see, all the data problems are due to concurrent access—you can safely assume that a transaction executed in *isolation* will always leave the database in a consistent state when the transaction completes. If the database permits concurrent access, then you need to consider the cumulative effect of all the transactions on database consistency.

To do this, the database uses a *schedule*, which is a sequence of operations from one or more transactions. If all the transactions executed serially, one after another, the schedule would also be *serial*. If the database can produce a schedule that is equivalent in its effect to a serial schedule, even though it may be derived from a set of concurrent transactions, it is called a *serializable schedule*. The serializable schedule consists of a series of intermingled database operations drawn from several transactions, the final outcome of which is a consistent database.

As you can surmise, deriving a schedule is not easy in practice. However, users don't have to concern themselves with the mechanics of serialization when they use their transactions. The Oracle database automatically derives serializable schedules through the use of isolation levels and the management of undo data. Let's look at these important concepts next.

Isolation Levels and the ISO Transaction Standard

You know that one way to avoid data anomalies is to prevent more than one user from viewing or changing data at the same time. However, this defeats our main purpose of providing concurrent access to users. To control this trade-off between concurrency and isolation, you specify an isolation level for each transaction.

The ISO (http://www.iso.ch) standard for transactions rests on the two key transaction-ending statements: COMMIT and ROLLBACK. All transactions, according to the ISO standard, begin with a SELECT, UPDATE, INSERT or DELETE statement. No transaction can view another transaction's intermediate results. Results of a second transaction are available to the first transaction only after the second transaction completes.

The ISO transaction standards ensure the compliance of transactions with the atomic and isolation properties, and help avoid the concurrency problems explained in the previous section. All transactions must ensure that they preserve database consistency. A database is consistent before a transaction begins, and it must be left in a consistent state at the end of the transaction. If you can devise a method to avoid the problems mentioned in the previous section, you can ensure a high degree of concurrent interactions among transactions in the database. There is a price to pay for this, however. Attempts to reduce the anomalies will result in reduced concurrency.

You can achieve consistency by enforcing serial use of the database, but it's impractical. Therefore, the practical goal is to find those types of concurrent transactions that don't interfere with each other—in other words, to find transactions that guarantee a serializable schedule. Proper ordering of the transactions becomes very important, unless they're all read-only transactions.

THE MAIN STAGES OF SQL PROCESSING

SQL statements pass through several stages during their processing: parsing, binding, and executing. Oracle uses *cursors*, private SQL areas, to store parsed statements and other information relating to the statements it's currently processing. Oracle automatically opens a cursor for all SQL statements.

Parsing

During the parsing stage, Oracle does several things to check your SQL statements:

- Oracle checks that your statements are syntactically correct. The server consults the data dictionary to check whether the tables and column specifications are correct.

- Oracle ensures that you have the privileges to perform the actions you are attempting through your SQL statements.

- Oracle draws up the *execution plan* for the statement, which involves selecting the best access methods for the objects in the statement.

After it checks the privileges, Oracle assigns a number called the *SQL hash value* to the SQL statement for identification purposes. If the SQL hash value already exists in memory, Oracle will look for an existing execution plan for the statement, which details the ideal way it should access the various database objects, among other things. If the execution plan exists, Oracle will proceed straight to the actual execution of the statement using that execution plan. This is called a *soft parse*, and it is the preferred technique for statement processing. Because it uses previously formed execution plans, soft parsing is fast and efficient.

The opposite of a soft parse is a *hard parse*, and Oracle has to perform this type of parse when it doesn't find the SQL hash value in memory for the statement it wants to execute. Hard parses are tough on system memory and other resources. Oracle has to create a fresh execution plan, which means that it has to evaluate the numerous possibilities and choose the best plan from among them. During this process, Oracle needs to access the library cache and dictionary cache numerous times to check the data dictionary, and each time it accesses these commonly used areas, Oracle needs to use *latches*, which are low-level serialization control mechanisms, to protect shared data structures in the SGA. Thus, hard parsing contributes to an increase in latch contention.

Any time there's a severe contention for resources during statement processing, the execution time will increase. Remember that too many hard parses will lead to a fragmentation of the shared pool, making the contention worse.

After the parsing operation is complete, Oracle allots a shared SQL area for the statement. Other users can access this parsed version as long as it is retained in memory.

Binding

During the binding stage, Oracle retrieves the values for the variables used in the parsing stage. Note that the variables are expanded to literal values only after the parsing stage is over.

Execution

Once Oracle completes the parsing and binding, it executes the statement. Note that Oracle will first check whether there is a parsed representation of the statement in memory already. If there is, the user can execute this parsed representation directly, without going through the parsing process all over again.

It's during the execution phase that the database reads the data from the disk into the memory buffers (if it doesn't find the data there already). The database also takes out all the necessary locks and ensures that it logs any changes made during the SQL execution. After the execution of the SQL statement, Oracle automatically closes the cursors.

■**Note** It's important for you as a DBA to fully understand the nature of transactions in relational databases. A good reference is the book by Jim Gray (a leading expert on database and transaction processing) and Andreas Reuter, *Transaction Processing: Concepts and Techniques* (Morgan Kaufmann, 1993).

Oracle's Isolation Levels

The ISO transaction standards use the term isolation level to indicate the extent to which a database allows interaction among transactions. Isolation defines how and when the changes made by an operation are made visible to other concurrent operations in the database. Isolation of transactions keeps concurrently executing database transactions from viewing incomplete results of other transactions. The main isolation levels are the serializable, repeatable-read, read-uncommitted, and read-committed isolation levels. Here's what the different transaction isolation levels mean:

- *Serializable*: At the serializable isolation level, all transactions are isolated completely from each other, as if the transactions have executed in a serial fashion, one after the other. Under the serializable level of isolation, a transaction that performs an insert, delete, or update places a write lock on the set of data that is affected by the DML operation. The database locks the affected data until the isolating transaction releases its locks, which happens when this transaction is committed or rolled back. Because other transactions involving DML operations have to wait until the locks are cleared, those transactions won't read any "dirty" data. The serializable level of isolation also helps you avoid nonrepeatable reads, because the subsequent transactions can't update or delete the locked data. You also get rid of phantom data because the subsequent transactions can't insert any new rows that fall into the range of data locked by the first transaction.

- *Repeatable read*: The repeatable-read isolation level guarantees read consistency—a transaction that reads the data twice from a table at two different points in time will find the same values each time. You avoid both the dirty-read problem and the nonrepeatable-read problem through this level of isolation.

- *Read uncommitted*: The read-uncommitted level, which allows a transaction to read another transaction's intermediate values before it commits, will result in the occurrence of all the problems of concurrent usage.

- *Read committed*: Oracle's default isolation level is the read-committed level of isolation at the statement level. Oracle queries see only the data that was committed at the beginning of the query. Because the isolation level is at the statement level, each statement is allowed to see only the data that was committed before the commencement of that statement. The read-committed level of isolation guarantees that the row data won't change while you're accessing a particular row in an Oracle table.

■**Note** If you're in the process of updating a row that you fetched into a cursor, you can rest assured that no one else is updating the same row simultaneously. However, if you're executing queries, you may get different values each time if other transactions have updated data successfully in between your queries. Remember that Oracle only guarantees statement-level isolation here, not transaction-level isolation.

Practical real-world databases need a compromise between concurrency access and serializable modes of operation. The key issue here is that by specifying a high degree of isolation, you can keep one transaction from affecting another, but at the cost of significant deterioration in database performance. On the other hand, a low level of transaction isolation will introduce the data problems outlined earlier in the chapter, but it leads to better performance. A transaction running at a serializable isolation level will appear as if it's running in isolation—it's as if all the other concurrent transactions run either before or after this transaction.

Three of the four main ISO isolation levels allow for some deviation from the theoretical concept of serializable transactions. Table 8-1 shows the extent to which each of the four main levels of isolation suffers from the concurrency problems listed earlier. Note that a value of Yes in the table means that the particular problem is possible under that isolation level, and a value of No means that the problem isn't possible for that isolation level.

Table 8-1. *Preventable Concurrency Problems Under Various Isolation Levels*

Isolation Level	Dirty Read	Nonrepeatable Read	Phantom Read
Read uncommitted	Yes	Yes	Yes
Read committed	No	Yes	Yes
Repeatable read	No	No	Yes
Serializable	No	No	No

As you can see, the last isolation level in Table 8-1, serializable, avoids all concurrency problems, but unfortunately, it's not a practical option because it doesn't allow any concurrent use of the database. Oracle's default read-committed isolation level will get rid of the dirty-read and the lost-update problems. You won't have the dirty-read problem because your queries will read only data that was committed at the beginning of the query, thereby avoiding reading data that may later be rolled back by a different transaction. In addition, you'll avoid the lost-update problem because transactions can't read data that's currently being modified until the updates have been completed.

Transaction- and Statement-Level Consistency

Oracle automatically provides *statement-level* read consistency by default. That is, all data that a query sees comes from a single point in time. This means that a query will see consistent data when it begins. The query sees only data committed before it starts, and no data committed during the course of the query is visible to it. Queries in this context don't have to be SELECT statements. An INSERT with a subquery or an UPDATE or DELETE will also involve an implicit query, and they all return consistent data.

Oracle can also provide transaction-level read consistency, though this is not the default. Oracle can use pre-change data images stored in undo segments to provide the transaction- and statement-level read consistency.

Changing the Default Isolation Level

Oracle's read-committed level of isolation provides protection against dirty reads and lost updates because queries read data only after the COMMIT statement is executed. The transactions are all consistent on a per-statement basis. Readers will not block writers of transactions, and vice versa. As you can see, Oracle's default read-committed isolation level doesn't guarantee you'll avoid the nonrepeatable-read and phantom-read problems. Oracle guarantees only statement-level, not transaction-level, read consistency. However, Oracle allows you to explicitly change the default read-committed isolation level by selecting the serializable isolation level as an alternative.

■**Note** The read-committed level of isolation provides a great deal of concurrency and consistency in the database. However, this mode does not provide transaction-level consistency. Because it's a statement-level isolation, changes made in between statements in a transaction may not be seen by a query, and for this reason you'll continue to have the nonrepeatable-read problem; you simply can't be guaranteed the same results if you repeat your queries. The phantom-read problem also still lurks because the model doesn't prevent other transactions from updating tables in between your queries.

The serializable isolation level will treat the database as a single-user database, thus eliminating the data anomalies caused by simultaneous use and modification of the data. By using the ALTER SESSION statement, you can serialize the isolation level, thus avoiding the concurrency problems. You can change the isolation level from the default level of read-committed to a serializable isolation level using the following statement:

```
SQL> ALTER SESSION SET ISOLATION LEVEL SERIALIZABLE;
```

Once you execute this statement, you are shielded from all transactions, committed as well as uncommitted, that have occurred since you set the transaction. Instead of using the serializable isolation level, you can also use the SET TRANSACTION READ ONLY command to give you repeatable reads without phantom reads. A serializable level of isolation is suited for databases where multiple consistent queries are made during an update transaction. However, serialization isn't a simple choice, because it seriously reduces your concurrency. These are some of the problems involved in setting the serializable isolation level:

- Since serialization involves the locking of data for exclusive use by transactions, it thereby slows down transaction concurrency.

- You have to set the INITTRANS parameter for tables at creation time to at least 3 in order for the serialization level of isolation to take effect. The INITTRANS parameter determines the number of concurrent transactions on a table.

- Throughput in the serialization isolation level is much lower than in the read-committed isolation level, especially in high-concurrency databases with many transactions accessing the same tables for updates.

- You must incorporate error-checking code in the application if you want to use the serializable mode of isolation.

- Serializable transactions are more prone to *deadlocks*, a situation in which transactions are stuck waiting for each other to release locks over data objects. Deadlocks lead to costly rollbacks of transactions.

In general, it's safest to stick with Oracle's default read-committed level of transaction isolation, although it isn't perfect. Oracle recommends that you stick with the default read-committed level of isolation, which produces the maximum throughput with only a slight risk of running into the nonrepeatable-read and phantom-read anomalies.

The read-committed transaction level provides a good trade-off between data concurrency and data consistency. Also, the throughput is much higher with this mode of isolation than with the purer serialization mode. If getting a repeatable read is your objective in using a serializable isolation level, you can always use explicit locks in situations where that is necessary.

For standard OLTP applications, in particular, with their high-volume, concurrent, short-lived transactions that are unlikely to conflict with each other, this mode is ideal from a performance point of view. Very few transactions in an OLTP database issue the same query multiple times, so phantom reads and nonrepeatable reads are rare. Serializable modes of concurrency are more appropriate for databases with mostly read-only transactions that run for a long time.

Implementing Oracle's Concurrency Control

A database may use one or more methods to implement concurrency of use. These include locking mechanisms to guarantee exclusive use of a table by a transaction, time-stamping methods that enable serialization of transactions, and the validation-based scheduling of transactions. Locking methods are called pessimistic because they assume that transactions will violate the serializable schedules unless they're prevented explicitly from doing so. The time-stamping and validation methods, on the other hand, are called optimistic because they don't assume that transactions are bound to violate the serializable schedules.

As you might guess, locking methods cause more delays than the optimistic methods because they keep conflicting transactions waiting for access to the locked database objects. On the positive side, however, locking methods don't have to abort transactions because they prevent potentially conflicting transactions from interacting with other transactions. The optimistic methods usually have to abort transactions when they might violate a serializable schedule.

Time-stamping methods assign time stamps to each transaction and enforce serializability by ensuring that the transaction time stamps match the schedule for the transactions. Validation methods maintain a record of transaction activity. Before committing a transaction, the database validates the changed data against the changed items of all currently active transactions to eliminate any unserialized schedules.

Oracle uses a combination of the available methods. It uses locks along with what is called the multiversion concurrency control system (a variation of the time-stamping method) to manage concurrency.

Oracle locks prevent destructive interaction between transactions that are trying to access the same resource. The resource could be an application table or row, or it could be a shared system data structure in memory. It could also be a data dictionary table or row. Locks ensure data consistency while allowing data concurrency by letting multiple users simultaneously access the database.

Oracle does its locking implicitly; you don't have to worry about which table to lock or how to lock it, as Oracle will automatically place locks on your transaction's behalf when necessary. By default, Oracle uses row-level locking, which involves the least restrictive amount of locking, thus guaranteeing the highest amount of concurrency. By default, Oracle stores the locked row information in the data blocks. Also, Oracle never uses lock escalation—that is, it doesn't go from a lower-level granularity like row-level locking to a higher level of granularity like table-level locking.

Oracle's multiversion concurrency control system is a variation of the time-stamp approach to concurrency control; it maintains older versions of table data to ensure that any transaction can read the original data even after it has been changed by other transactions. Unlike locking, no waits are involved here; transactions use different versions of the same table instead of waiting for other transactions to complete. When transactions want to update a row, Oracle first writes the original before-image to an undo record in the undo tablespace. Queries then have a consistent view of the data, which provides read consistency—they only see data from a single point in time. Using the same mechanism, Oracle is also capable of providing transaction-level read consistency, meaning that all the separate statements in a transaction see data from a single point in time. The multiversion concurrency control system used by Oracle enables you to get by with the less-stringent read-committed mode of isolation instead of having to use the slower but safer serializable isolation level.

Here are some important features of Oracle locking:

- Oracle implements locks by setting a bit in the data item being locked. The locking information is stored in the data block where the row lives.

- Locks are held for the entire length of a transaction and are released when a COMMIT or a ROLL-BACK statement is issued.

- Oracle doesn't use lock escalation. Oracle doesn't need to escalate locks, as it stores the locking information in the individual data blocks. Lock escalation—for example, an escalation from the row level to the table level—reduces concurrency.

- Oracle does use *lock conversion*, which involves changing the restrictiveness of a lock while keeping the granularity of the lock the same. For example, a row share table lock is converted into a more restrictive row exclusive table lock when a SELECT FOR UPDATE statement starts updating the previously locked rows in the table. I explain locking granularity and Oracle locking types in more detail in the following sections.

In the next few sections, you'll learn more about the locking methods and lock types used by Oracle's concurrency control mechanism.

Oracle Locking Methods

Oracle uses locks to control access to two broad types of objects: user objects, which include tables, and system objects, which may include shared memory structures and data dictionary objects. Oracle follows a pessimistic locking approach, which anticipates potential conflicts and will block some transactions from interfering with others in order to avoid conflicts between concurrent transactions.

Granularity, in the context of locking, is the size of the data unit locked by the locking mechanism. Oracle uses *row-level* granularity to lock objects, which is the finest level of granularity (exclusive table locking is the most coarse level). Several databases, including Microsoft SQL Server, provide only page-level, not row-level, locking. A *page* is somewhat similar to an Oracle data block, and it can have a bunch of rows, so page-level locking means that during an update, several rows in addition to the rows of interest are locked; if other users need the locked rows that are not part of the update, they have to wait for the lock on the page to be released. For example, if your page size is 8KB, and the average row length in a table is 100 bytes, about 80 rows can fit in that one page. If one of the rows is being updated, a block-level lock limits access to the other 79 rows in the block. Locking at a level larger than the row level would reduce data concurrency.

Note Remember, the coarser the locking granularity, the more serializable the transactions, and thus the fewer the concurrency anomalies. The flip side of this is that the coarser the granularity level, the lower the concurrency level. Oracle locks don't prevent other users from reading a table's data, and by default, queries never place locks on tables.

All locks acquired by statements in a transaction are held by Oracle until the transaction completes. When an explicit or implicit COMMIT or ROLLBACK is issued by a transaction, Oracle releases any locks that the statements within the transaction have been holding. If Oracle rolls back to a save point, it releases any locks acquired after the save point.

Oracle Lock Types

Locks, as you have seen, prevent destructive interaction between transactions by allowing orderly access to resources. These resources could be database objects such as tables, or other shared database structures in memory. Oracle locks can be broadly divided into the following types, according to the type of object that is locked: DML locks, DDL locks, latches, internal locks, and distributed locks. These lock types are described in the following sections.

DML Locks

DML locks are locks placed by Oracle to protect data in tables and indexes. Whenever a DML state-ment seeks to modify data in a table, Oracle automatically places a row-level lock on the rows in the table that are being modified. (This makes it impossible, for example, for a group of booking clerks to sell the "last" ticket to more than one customer.) Row-level DML locks guarantee that readers of data don't wait for writers of data, and vice versa. Writers will only have to wait when they want to update the same rows that are currently being modified by other transactions.

Any Oracle lock mode will permit queries on the table. A query will never block an update, delete, or insert, and vice versa. An *exclusive lock* only permits queries on a table, and prevents users from performing any other activity on it, like updating or deleting data. A *row exclusive lock*, on the other hand, allows concurrent access to a table for updating, deleting, and inserting data, but prevents any user from locking the entire table for exclusive use. There are other lock modes as well, but for our purposes, it's enough to focus on these two basic Oracle lock modes.

Any query that a transaction issues won't interfere with any other transaction, because all they do is read data—they don't modify it. Queries include transactions using the SELECT statement, as well as transactions such as INSERT, UPDATE, and DELETE if they happen to use an implicit SELECT state-ment. Queries never need locks, and they never need to wait for any other locks to be released. So, a SELECT statement that reads data from a table will never have to wait for a lock to be acquired.

Any INSERT, DELETE, UPDATE, or SELECT FOR UPDATE statements will automatically issue an exclu-sive row-level lock on the rows affected by the transaction. This exclusive row-level lock means that other transactions can't modify the affected rows until the original transaction commits or rolls back, thereby releasing the exclusive locks.

A simultaneous DDL table lock is held for operations that include the INSERT, UPDATE, DELETE, and the SELECT FOR UPDATE DML operations. DML operations need DDL table locks to ensure that some other transaction isn't changing the table definition while modifying data. This means that a table can't be altered or dropped while an uncommitted transaction is still holding a table lock on the table.

Table locks can range from being very restrictive to minimally restrictive. Oracle acquires a row exclusive table lock, which indicates that a transaction holding the lock has updated one or more rows in the table. Other transactions are allowed to select, insert, update, delete, or lock rows in the same table concurrently. However, other transactions can't lock the table exclusively for their own reads or writes. All INSERT, UPDATE, and DELETE statements impose row exclusive locks.

Table 8-2 summarizes the row-level and table-level DML locks that are acquired for the most common database operations.

Table 8-2. *DML Row- and Table-Level Locks Held for Common Operations*

Operation	Row-Level Lock	Table-Level Lock
SELECT . . . FROM table	None	None
INSERT INTO table	Exclusive	Row exclusive
UPDATE table	Exclusive	Row exclusive
INSERT INTO table	Exclusive	Row exclusive
DELETE FROM table	Exclusive	Row exclusive

Here's a brief summary of how Oracle's transactions most commonly use the Oracle locking features:

- The transaction that contains a DML statement acquires exclusive row locks on the rows modified by a statement within the transaction. Until this transaction commits or rolls back, other transactions can't update or delete these rows.

- A query in a transaction can see only committed changes made by earlier statements in the same transaction, but won't be able to see data committed by other transactions after it started.

- In addition to the exclusive row locks, a transaction that contains a DML statement acquires at least a row exclusive table lock on the table that contains the rows. If it's already holding a more restrictive table-level DML lock, it retains the more restrictive lock.

Oracle offers other kinds of table locks besides the row exclusive lock described previously, but they are not important for our purposes here. All you need to understand is that Oracle uses row-level locking for updates, inserts, and deletes, and that it also automatically imposes a row exclusive table lock during these operations.

DDL Locks

As you've seen, Oracle automatically places DML locks on tables that are in the process of having some of their rows modified by a transaction. In addition, such a transaction simultaneously holds a table-level DDL lock on the table, which will prevent other transactions from altering or dropping the table while its DML transactions aren't yet completed.

You can also place DDL locks on tables when you are conducting a purely DDL operation, without any accompanying DML transaction.

Allowing DDL Locks to Wait for DML Locks

By default, a DDL lock request won't wait for a DML lock. That is, the DDL lock request will fail automatically if it's unable to acquire an immediate DML lock on the table. You can, however, use the ddl_lock_timeout initialization parameter to specify the duration for which a DDL statement will wait for a DML lock.

Since the default value of the ddl_lock_timeout parameter is zero, DDL statements won't wait at all for a DML lock. You can set the parameter up to the maximum value of 1,000,000 seconds, which is about 11 and a half days. Here's an example that shows how to set the parameter inside a session:

```
SQL> ALTER SESSION SET ddl_lock_timeout = 30;

Session altered.

SQL>
```

Explicit Table Locking

Whenever you add a column to a table, the database needs to acquire an exclusive DML lock on that table. You can specify that a DDL command wait for a specific length of time before it fails, when it's unable to acquire a DML lock. The LOCK TABLE statement lets you specify the maximum length of time a DDL statement can wait for the acquiring of a DML lock on a table. Use this feature when adding a column that is frequently updated by users.

Here's the syntax of the LOCK TABLE statement:

```
LOCK TABLE . . . IN lockmode MODE [NOWAIT | WAIT integer]
```

In the LOCK TABLE statement, the MODE parameter values NOWAIT and WAIT mean the following:

- If you want the database to return control to you immediately upon finding that a necessary table is already locked by other users, specify the NOWAIT option.

- You can use the wait parameter to specify the number of seconds the LOCK TABLE statement can wait in order to acquire a DML lock. You can set the value of this parameter to any integer value you want—there's no limit.

- If you don't specify either WAIT or NOWAIT, the database will wait until the locked table is available and then lock it before returning control to you.

Latches, Internal Locks, and Distributed Locks

Latches are internal mechanisms that protect shared data structures in the SGA. For example, data dictionary entries are accessed in the buffer by many processes, and latches control the processes' access to these memory structures. The data structures that list the blocks currently in memory are also frequently consulted during the running of the Oracle instance, and server and background processes that need to change or read the data in critical data structures such as these would acquire a very short lock (called a latch, in this instance) on the object. The implementation of latches, including the specification of how long a process will wait for it, is usually specific to the operating system.

Data dictionary locks are used by Oracle whenever the dictionary objects are being modified. *Distributed locks* are specialized locking mechanisms used in a distributed database system or in the Oracle Real Application Clusters (RAC) environment. *Internal locks* are used by Oracle to protect access to structures such as datafiles, tablespaces, and rollback segments.

Explicit Locking in Oracle

Oracle automatically applies the necessary locks to the tables and other objects based on the transactions that are coded in the applications. Oracle's locking mechanism works automatically to ensure statement-level read consistency and concurrency. For the most part, Oracle's default, behind-the-scenes locking operations should suffice, but there occasionally may be situations when the application developer will be better off manually locking tables. Sometimes when the transaction needs to see consistent data across many joined tables, the application developer can use explicit locking. In addition, when you don't want the data values changed during long transactions, it may sometimes be necessary for the application developer to apply explicit locks.

Oracle provides explicit locking features to override the implicit locks placed by Oracle on behalf of transactions. You can override Oracle's default (implicit) locking mechanism at the transaction level or the session level. If you want to override all Oracle's default locking mechanisms, you can do so by using the SET TRANSACTION ISOLATION LEVEL SERIALIZABLE statement at the session level. The same statement will also override the default locking modes at the transaction level. In addition, you can manually lock a table by explicitly using a table lock or by using the SELECT FOR UPDATE command.

Blocking Locks

A blocking lock occurs when a lock placed on an object by a user prevents or blocks other users from accessing the same object or objects. The DBA_BLOCKERS table is useful in getting this information—it tells you which sessions are currently holding locks on objects for which some other object is presently waiting. You can combine the information in the DBA_BLOCKERS table with that in the V$SESSION tables, to find out who is holding the blocking session. Here is the SQL statement:

```
SQL> SELECT a.username, a.program, a.sid, a.serial#
  2  FROM v$session a, dba_blockers b
  3  WHERE a.sid = b.holding_session;
SQL>
```

The following is a simple example of a blocking session: user nick alapati issues the following DML statement, but doesn't commit it:

```
SQL> DELETE FROM emp
       WHERE name='samalapati';
1 row deleted.
SQL>
```

User nina alapati, in the meanwhile, issues an identical statement, but when she executes it, it hangs:

```
SQL> DELETE FROM emp
       WHERE name='samalapati';
```

The second user's DML statement will hang because the first user hasn't committed yet, and thus holds a row-level lock on the row the second user is trying to change. When the first user rolls back or commits, the second user's session automatically moves forward and finishes.

You can use the V$SESSION view to find out which sessions are blocking other sessions. Here's a simple query using the view that shows the blocking lock caused by the previous two SQL statements:

```
SQL> SELECT username, blocking_session
       blocking_session_status
       FROM V$SESSION WHERE blocking_session_status='VALID';
```

When you do find a blocking session, and it is blocking another session from doing its job, you may have to terminate the blocking session by using the ALTER SYSTEM KILL SESSION command. If the process or the session still won't go away, go to the operating system level and kill the process or the thread that spawned the Oracle session.

Deadlocks

Deadlocks occur in any RDBMS when two sessions block each other while each waits for a resource that the other session is holding. This is a catch-22 situation, because the stalemate can't be broken by either session unilaterally. In such circumstances, Oracle steps in, terminates one of the sessions, and rolls back its statement. Oracle quickly recognizes that two sessions are deadlocked and terminates the session that issued the most recent request for a lock. This will release the object locks that the other session is waiting for. You don't really need to do anything when there are deadlocks, although you'll see messages in your dump directory that deadlocks are currently in the database.

When Oracle encounters a deadlock between transactions, it records in the trace file the session IDs involved, the SQL statements issued in the transactions, and the specific object name and the rows on which locks are held in each session involved in the deadlock. Oracle further informs you that the deadlock is not an Oracle error, but is due to errors in application design or is a result of issuing ad hoc SQL. Application designers must write exception handlers in the code to roll back the aborted transaction and restart it.

You can avoid deadlocks by paying attention in the design phase and ensuring the proper locking order of the objects. Given that writers block other writers, deadlocks in Oracle are a rare phenomenon.

Managing Oracle Locks

As I mentioned in the previous sections, locking in Oracle is usually done implicitly by Oracle itself, at the least restrictive level. Users can override Oracle's default locking behavior, but you probably won't find too many cases where you're dealing with user-managed locks. Most of your lock management on a live database will involve checking whether any active locks are actually blocking users from conducting their DML operations. You can use either a script-based approach or the Oracle Enterprise Manager to analyze locks in your instance.

Using SQL to Analyze Locks

It's possible to examine the current locking situation in your instance by using SQL scripts. You may have to first run the `catblock.sql` script, located in the `$ORACLE_HOME/rdbms/admin` directory, before executing any locking-related SQL scripts for the first time in a database. This script will create several important locking-related views, such as DBA_LOCKS, DBA_WAITERS, and DBA_BLOCKERS.

Oracle provides a script called `utllockt.sql` that gives you a lock wait-for graph in a tree-structured format showing sessions that are holding locks affecting other sessions. Using this script, you can see what locks a session may be waiting for and which session is holding the lock. The script is located in the `$ORACLE_HOME/rdbms/admin` directory. Here's a sample execution of the `utllockt.sql` script:

```
SQL> @$ORACLE_HOME/rdbmsa/admin/utllockt.sql
Waiting session  Type      Mode requested   Mode Held       Lock Id1
---------------  ----      --------------   -------------   ---------
682              None      None             None            0
363              TX        Share (S)        Exclusive (X)
```

■**Note** The `utllockt.sql` script prints the sessions in the system that are waiting for locks, and the locks that they are waiting for. The printout is tree-structured. If a session ID is printed immediately below and to the right of another session, then it is waiting for that session. The session IDs printed at the left side of the page are the sessions everyone is waiting for.

In the preceding example, the session ID on the left side, 682, is what session 363 is waiting for. The information printed to the right of each session shows information about the lock it's waiting for. Thus, session 682, although it's holding a lock, doesn't show anything (None) in the lock-information columns because it isn't waiting for any lock. Session 363, however, tells you that it has requested a share (S) lock and is waiting for session 682 to release its exclusive (X) lock on the table row.

In the following example from the `utllockt.sql` script, session 9 is waiting for session 8, session 7 is waiting for session 9, and session 10 is waiting for session 9 as well.

```
* WAITING SESSION   TYPE MODE REQUESTED    MODE HELD         LOCK ID1 LOCK ID2
* ----------------- ---- ----------------- ----------------- -------- --------
* 8                 NONE None              None              0        0
*    9              TX   Share (S)         Exclusive (X)     65547    16
*       7           RW   Exclusive (X)     S/Row-X (SSX)     33554440 2
*       10          RW   Exclusive (X)     S/Row-X (SSX)     33554440 2
```

The lock information to the right of the session ID describes the lock that the session is waiting for (not the lock it is holding).

The V$LOCK and the V$LOCK_HOLDERS views are very helpful in analyzing locks in your instance, but sometimes they take a long time to run. The V$SESSION view can provide a quick idea about the blocking sessions in your database. The blocking_session column of the V$SESSION view reveals the identity of the user who is holding the lock. The blocking_session_status column shows whether the blocking_session data is valid or not. For example, if you find the value VALID in the blocking_session_status column, it means that you'll find the SID of the blocking user under the blocking_session column.

Here's a simple query that shows how to use the V$SESSION view to find out who is blocking a certain session:

```
SQL> SELECT sid, blocking_session, username, event
  2  FROM    v$session
  3* WHERE   blocking_session_status = 'VALID';

SID  BLOCKING_SESSION    USERNAME                     EVENT
---  ----------------    --------    ----------------------------------
24         32            SALAPATI         enq: TX - row lock contention
SQL>
```

The previous query shows that the user with the SID 24 is being blocked by user with the SID 32. The event column shows the type of lock that the blocking session holds.

Note The data dictionary tables that you need to look at to find locking information are the DBA_LOCKS, DBA_BLOCKERS, and DBA_WAITERS views. If, for some reason, you don't see the DBA_BLOCKERS view, run the `catblock.sql` script, located in the `$ORACLE_HOME/rdbms/admin` directory, to create it.

Using Database Control to Manage Session Locks

The most efficient way to see what locks currently exist within your instance is to use the Oracle Enterprise Manager (OEM) Database Control (or Grid Control). You can get to this page by going to Database Control Home Page ➤ Performance ➤ Additional Monitoring Links ➤ Instance Locks. The Instance Locks page shows all locks, both blocking and nonblocking. Most of the locks you'll see are harmless; they are routine nonblocking locks Oracle uses to maintain concurrency.

To see locks that are causing contention in your system, choose the Blocking Sessions option from the drop-down list in the Instance Locks page. The Blocking Session page will show you all the sessions that are currently blocking other sessions. You can also go directly to the Blocking Sessions page by going to Database Control Home Page ➤ Performance ➤ Additional Monitoring Links ➤ Blocking Sessions.

The Blocking Sessions page shows the session IDs of both the blocking and the blocked sessions (see Figure 6-1). You can *terminate* a blocking session by selecting the appropriate session and clicking the Kill Session button.

Figure 6-1 shows that the user nick_alapati is holding an exclusive lock (on a certain row in the test01 table, which you can't see in the figure), thereby blocking the user nina_alapati from getting an exclusive lock on the same row. The blocking session is identified by a value of 1 or greater under the Sessions Blocked column on the Blocking Sessions page (see Figure 8-1). The session that's being blocked is indicated by a value of zero.

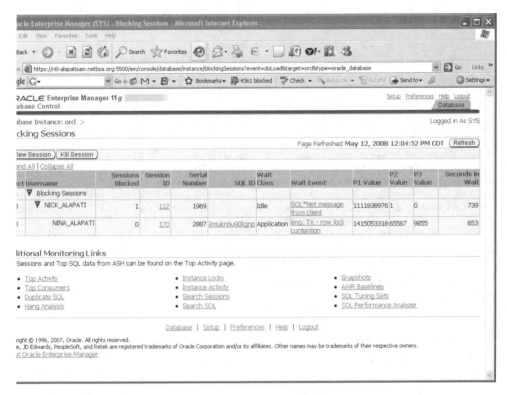

Figure 8-1. *Using the Database Control to identify blocking and waiting sessions*

You can also use OEM's Hang Analysis page (go to Database Control Home Page ➤ Performance ➤ Additional Monitoring Links ➤ Hang Analysis) to find out the exact wait status of the blocking and waiting sessions. The Hang Analysis page will show you the following:

- Instantaneously blocked sessions
- Sessions in a prolonged wait state
- Sessions that are hung

When there is a severe contention for locks in the instance, the Hang Analysis page will help you identify the problems much more quickly than running a SQL script, which might actually worsen the locking problems.

■**Note** Be prepared to wait for a very long time when you run most of the SQL scripts that relate to locking situations. Also, be aware that some of the scripts might sometimes make matters worse. The `utllockt.sql` script, for example, creates a table to store locking information, and it needs to acquire locks to create this table, which might exacerbate the locking problems that you are trying to diagnose in the first place! It's smarter to schedule these scripts using a scheduling tool or the Oracle Enterprise Manager and arrange for database alerts when there are problem locks in the system, so you can take action to fix the problem.

Using Undo Data to Provide Read Consistency

Oracle uses special structures called *undo records* to help provide automatic statement-level read consistency. All data for a single query will come from a single point in time. Only data committed when a query begins will be seen by the query—any changes made by other transactions after a query begins won't be seen by the query once it begins executing.

If a transaction is modifying data, Oracle will write a before-image of the table data to its undo records. For example, if you update the salary of an employee from 10,500 to 11,000, the undo record will store the old salary value of 10,500. When a query begins execution, Oracle will determine the current system change number, which identifies the order in which transactions occurred in the database. When data blocks are read for this query, Oracle will only use data blocks with the SCN that it determined for this query. When it encounters data blocks for the query with a more recent SCN, Oracle will automatically go to the undo segments and reconstruct the data from the undo records stored there. Any changes made by other transactions during the query's execution will have more recent SCNs, and are disregarded, guaranteeing that only consistent data is returned for the query at hand.

Oracle's undo records are stored in the undo tablespace specified at database creation time. The undo tablespace will always hold the before-image of table data for users if other transactions have updated it since a query began. Undo data is used for the following purposes:

- Providing read consistency for SQL queries

- Rolling back unwanted active transactions

- Recovering terminated transactions

- Analyzing older data by using Flashback Query

- Recovering from logical corruptions using the Flashback features

Remember that the undo data remains in the undo tablespace even after a database shutdown. This makes Oracle's undo management valuable for activities beyond providing read consistency and rolling back transactions. By using the Flashback features and undo data together, you can fix logical errors and query past data.

Automatic Undo Management

Automatic Undo Management takes the entire issue of sizing and allocation of undo segments from the DBA's hands and makes it Oracle's responsibility. As the DBA, all you have to do is create an adequately sized tablespace (the undo tablespace) for storing undo information. Oracle will dynamically create undo (rollback) segments and adjust their number to match the instance's workload requirements. The database will automatically allocate and deallocate undo segments to match the transaction throughput in the instance.

■**Tip** Proper undo management means that necessary undo information is not overwritten by newer undo data. By setting the appropriate size for the undo tablespace and the `undo_retention` interval, you can increase the chance that long-running queries can complete without receiving the snapshot-too-old error. It also ensures that critical Flashback features can retrieve the older data they are seeking.

Traditionally, DBAs had to contend with regular ORA_1555 (snapshot-too-old) errors because the rollback segments were being written over with new information too quickly for some transactions. When a DBA uses traditional rollback segments, he or she has the responsibility of monitoring the rollback segments for contention and may also need to change the number and size of the rollback segments. AUM eliminates most of the undo-block and consistent-read contention.

Traditional rollback segments would sometimes be slow to relinquish the space they occupied, even after their transactions completed. Undo segments use space much more efficiently by exchanging space dynamically with other segments. Oracle will create, bring online, and take offline the undo segments automatically as needed. When the undo segments are no longer necessary, Oracle will reclaim the space used by the segments. It is common practice for DBAs to assign a transaction to a specific rollback segment using the SET TRANSACTION command. AUM removes the need to do this manual assignment of rollback segments—Oracle manages all undo space allocation automatically behind the scenes.

Several of the Flashback recovery features, like Flashback Query, Flashback Versions Query, Flashback Transaction Query, and Flashback Table, require the use of undo data.

Setting up AUM

To enable the automatic management of your undo space, you first need to specify the automatic undo mode in the init.ora file or your SPFILE. By default, the database uses AUM in Oracle Database 11g. Second, you need to create a dedicated tablespace to hold the undo information. This will guarantee that you don't end up storing the undo information in the System tablespace, which isn't a great idea. You also must choose an interval for undo retention.

If you want to choose AUM when you create a new database, you need to configure the following three initialization parameters:

- undo_management
- undo_tablespace
- undo_retention

The UNDO_MANAGEMENT Parameter

You specify AUM in your initialization parameter file by adding the following line:

UNDO_MANAGEMENT = auto

The default for undo management in Oracle Database 11g is automatic, which means you can leave out the UNDO_MANAGEMENT initialization parameter if you want.

■**Tip** Use the Database Resource Manager to set up undo quotas for groups of users called consumer resource groups, if you think any users are monopolizing undo tablespace usage.

The UNDO_TABLESPACE Parameter

The UNDO_TABLESPACE parameter isn't mandatory—if you only have a single undo tablespace, you don't have to specify this parameter in your initialization parameter file, because Oracle will use the one available undo tablespace automatically. If you specify AUM and don't have an undo tablespace in your database at all, Oracle will be forced to use the System tablespace (the System rollback segment, to be more specific) for storing the undo data. You should avoid using the System tablespace for storing the undo data, since that tablespace also stores the data dictionary, and you don't want to use up space there and cause problems such as fragmentation. Note that you can't create application tables and indexes in an undo tablespace, since it's exclusively reserved for undo data.

If you have multiple undo tablespaces in your database, however, you must specify which undo tablespace you want the database to use, by specifying the UNDO_TABLESPACE parameter in the initialization parameter file. You can have multiple tablespaces in your database, but only one of them can be active at any given time. You activate an undo tablespace by using the ALTER SYSTEM SET UNDO_TABLESPACE command, which you'll see shortly.

You create an undo tablespace when you create your database. The following database creation statement shows how to create the undo tablespace during database creation:

```
SQL> CREATE DATABASE cust_prod
     . . .
     UNDO TABLESPACE undotbs_01 datafile
     DATAFILE '/u10/orcl/oradata/undotbs01_01.dbf' size 750M;
     . . .
```

■**Note** I also explain the creation of the undo tablespace in Chapter 10, which deals with creating an Oracle database.

You may choose not to create the undo tablespace when you create a new database, and even if you create an undo tablespace at database creation time, you may choose to add another undo tablespace later on. Creating an undo tablespace is like creating any other tablespace, except that you use the keyword UNDO in the CREATE TABLESPACE statement. To create an undo tablespace by itself, in an existing database, use this statement:

```
SQL> CREATE UNDO TABLESPACE undotbs_02
     DATAFILE 'c:\oracle11g\oradata\finance\undotbs01_01.dbf'
     SIZE 500M;

Tablespace created.
SQL>
```

You can add space to an existing undo tablespace by using the ALTER TABLESPACE statement, as shown here:

```
SQL> ALTER TABLESPACE undotbs_01
     ADD DATAFILE '/u09/oradata/test/undo01dbf' 500M;
```

You can create several undo tablespaces for your database, but the instance can only use a single undo tablespace at any given time. Let's say you are using the undo tablespace undotbs_01 as your current undo tablespace. The following alter system SQL statement will dynamically change the undo tablespace for your database:

```
SQL> ALTER SYSTEM SET UNDO_TABLESPACE = undotbs_02;
```

If you want Oracle to continue to use the new undo tablespace you just created, undotbs_02, you need to specify this in the init.ora file. Otherwise, Oracle will always use the default undo tablespace, which is the tablespace you specified for the UNDO TABLESPACE parameter in the database creation statement.

In the preceding example, I used a fixed-size undo tablespace, where there is a hard limit on the undo tablespace size. If the undo data uses up all the assigned space, however, you'll have problems. To avoid this, you should create *auto-extensible* undo tablespaces. Especially when you are creating a new database and implementing it in production, you may not be sure how big you should size your undo tablespace. The best course of action is to let the undo tablespace automatically increase in size, based on the undo requirements. You can enable the automatic growth of the undo tablespace by using the AUTOEXTEND keyword when you create a new undo tablespace, as shown here:

```
SQL> CREATE UNDO TABLESPACE undotbs_01
     DATAFILE '/u10/oradata/prod/undo0101.dbf' SIZE 100M AUTOEXTEND ON;
```

If you've already created the undo tablespace, you can make it auto-extensible by simply adding an auto-extensible data file to the undo tablespace, as shown here:

```
SQL> ALTER TABLESPACE undotbs_01
     ADD DATAFILE '/u01/oradata/prod/undo0102.dbf' AUTOEXTEND ON NEXT 5M
     MAXSIZE UNLIMITED;
```

If, for some reason, you decide that you have to create a fixed-size undo tablespace, you can use the Undo Advisor to get recommendations about the ideal size. The Undo Advisor uses the data collected by the Automatic Workload Repository (AWR) as the basis for its analysis, so you should let the instance run for a good while after you start it, so that the Undo Advisor has enough data to figure out its recommendations. The Undo Advisor takes two inputs—the estimated length of the longest query in the database, and how far you want to go back in time for your Flashback operations that depend on undo data. Using the larger of these as a guide, you can look up the ideal size for your undo tablespace on an Undo Advisor graph. I explain how to use the Undo Advisor later in this chapter, in the "Using the OEM to Manage Undo Data" section.

■**Note** Sometimes when you start an instance or switch an undo tablespace, it takes several minutes for the undo segments to come online. To avoid this problem, the database uses the data in the Automatic Workload Repository to determine the number of undo segments to bring online upon an instance restart or the switching of an undo tablespace. This feature is also known as the *fast ramping up* of undo segments.

The UNDO_RETENTION Parameter

When a transaction commits, the undo data for that transaction isn't needed any more. That undo data will stay in the undo tablespace, however, until space is needed to record undo data for newer transactions. When the newer transactions' undo data comes in, it may overwrite the old undo data (from the committed transactions) if there isn't enough free space left in the undo tablespace. For a long-running query that needs to retain older undo data for consistency purposes, there is a possibility that some of the undo data it needs has been overwritten by other, newer transactions. In this case, you could get an error message ("snapshot too old") from the database indicating that the before-image of the transaction has been overwritten.

To prevent this, Oracle provides the UNDO_RETENTION configuration parameter, which you can set to the interval you wish. Note that in the older manual undo management mode, DBAs don't have the option of determining how long Oracle retains undo information.

Let's briefly review how undo information is managed in an undo segment. Undo information can be classified in two broad types:

- If a transaction that has generated the undo data is still active, the undo data is said to be *active* (uncommitted). Oracle will always retain active undo data to support ongoing uncommitted transactions.

- If the transaction that generated the undo data is inactive (committed), then the undo data is said to be *committed*. The committed undo data can be either *expired* or *unexpired*. Expired data can be overwritten by new transactions. Oracle will try to save the unexpired data as long as it can, subject to undo space limitations. When there is no more room in the undo tablespace for newer transactions, Oracle will finally overwrite the unexpired data, depending on how you configure the UNDO_RETENTION parameter.

The UNDO_RETENTION parameter lets you control the reuse of the committed undo space. By setting the UNDO_RETENTION parameter, you can specify the *lower limit* for how long the database will retain uncommitted undo data as unexpired data, so that it is available for read consistency and Flashback purposes.

Note that setting the UNDO_RETENTION interval is *not* a guarantee that Oracle will always retain undo information for at least that time period. If there is no free space left in the undo tablespace for a new transaction, Oracle will use an unexpired undo extent—a transaction can't be stopped, after all. This is a last-resort event, but you should be aware that it is a possibility. The key is to make the undo tablespace big enough so that it can support your undo retention interval, thus helping Oracle retain undo information for the specified period.

You can set the undo retention size by specifying it in the initialization file as follows:

```
UNDO_RETENTION = 1800
```

The default for the UNDO_RETENTION parameter is 900 seconds.

■**Tip** Your undo tablespace must be able to accommodate any increase in the undo retention period. If the undo tablespace can't keep undo records for the required time, you run the risk of queries failing with the snapshot-too-old error.

If you wish to change the amount of time the database should retain the undo information, you can dynamically change the UNDO_RETENTION parameter as follows:

```
SQL> ALTER SYSTEM SET UNDO_RETENTION = 7200 /* two hours
```

There is no one ideal UNDO_RETENTION time interval. Your retention time interval will depend on how long you estimate your longest transactions may run. Based on the information about the maximum length of transactions in your database, you can arrive at an approximate time to assign for the UNDO_RETENTION parameter.

The V$UNDOSTAT table provides an indicator for helping figure out the undo retention interval. Query the V$UNDOSTAT view as follows:

```
SQL> SELECT MAX(maxquerylen) FROM v$undostat;

MAX(MAXQUERYLEN)
----------------
            210
```

The maxquerylen column of the V$UNDOSTAT view tells you the length of the longest executed query (in seconds) during the past 24 hours. The time set in the UNDO_RETENTION parameter should be at least as long as the time indicated in the maxquerylen column. This, by itself, won't guarantee that a new long-running query will definitely be accommodated, but you'll have a reasonable chance that your longest transactions will have read consistency when using the undo tablespace.

Oracle provides the following guidelines for setting the undo retention interval for a new database:

- *OLTP*: 15 minutes
- *Mixed*: 1 hour
- *DSS*: 3 hours
- *Flashback Query*: 24 hours

If you think all of this undo retention business is too much work, take the easy way out and let Oracle *automatically* tune undo in your database. Oracle automatically tunes the undo retention period for the longest-running query and collects query-duration information every 30 seconds. Depending on your workload characteristics, Oracle will adjust the length of the undo retention period. For example, during the day, shorter transactions may mean a shorter undo retention period, and during the nightly batch jobs, you'd need a much longer undo retention period to avoid the snapshot-too-old errors. If you don't set a value for the UNDO_RETENTION parameter (or if you set a value of 0), Oracle automatically tunes undo with 900 seconds as the minimum value.

Here's a summary of automatic undo retention in Oracle Database 11*g* Release 1:

- If you use an auto-extensible undo tablespace (using an AUTOEXTEND datafile), Oracle will treat any UNDO_RETENTION value you specify as the *low threshold value* and retain undo for at least this time period. If you set an undo retention period of 30 minutes, Oracle will adjust the retention period upward of 30 minutes if needed, but never let it go below 30 minutes (unless faced with a lack of space in the undo tablespace). The database will tune the undo retention to take care of the undo needs of the longest queries in your database. Thus, in the case of auto-extensible undo tablespaces, Oracle will

  - Retain undo data a little longer than the longest query in your database, if space allows it

  - Retain undo data at least as long as the low threshold of undo retention, subject to space limitations

- If you use a fixed-size undo tablespace, Oracle will ignore any UNDO_RETENTION value you may have set. The database will automatically tune undo with the goal of achieving the *maximum possible retention period*, given the undo tablespace size and its usage history. Of course, if you use the guaranteed undo retention feature, as explained later in this chapter, Oracle will have to honor any UNDO_RETENTION period you set. If you've specified any Flashback require-ments, Oracle will satisfy them as well.

- If you're considering a fixed size and an auto-extensible tablespace of the same size, know that the fixed-size tablespace will provide you with a slightly longer undo retention period.

- Even if you do set a value for the UNDO_RETENTION parameter, Oracle will still auto-tune undo, with the value you specified as the minimum value. Note that the value you assign for the UNDO_RETENTION parameter is treated by Oracle as a *requested minimum*. If Oracle determines, through its automatic tuning, that the undo retention period should be longer than this requested minimum to accommodate long transactions, it will retain undo data for the longer retention period.

■**Tip** By default, Oracle Database 11*g* *automatically* tunes the undo retention period. Oracle recommends that you *not* set a value for the UNDO_RETENTION parameter unless your system has Flashback or LOB retention requirements.

In Automatic Undo Management, the database is in charge of creating, allocating, and deallo-cating the undo segments as necessary. You can query the DBA_ROLLBACK_SEGS view to find out which of your undo segments are online, as shown here:

```
SQL> SELECT segment_name, tablespace_name, status
     FROM dba_rollback_segs;
```

The undo segments created under AUM are structurally similar to the traditional rollback segments. The big difference, of course, is that Oracle will automatically create them and drop them as necessary. Oracle creates a predetermined number of undo segments when you create the undo tablespace, and it may bring all or some of them online when you start up the instance. Oracle will always try to assign each transaction its own undo segment, and it will create more undo segments if necessary, based on the transactions in the database. During a day's time, it's common for Oracle to increase and decrease the number of undo segments based on its own internal algorithms and the level of database activity.

If the UNDO_RETENTION parameter is set to AUTO and you fail to create a specific undo tablespace for storing undo information, Oracle will still create undo records in a default tablespace named SYS_UNDOTBS, with a default size of around 200MB.

The following SQL script will tell you the location and size of the undo tablespace in your database:

```
SQL> SELECT file_name, bytes
  2  FROM dba_data_files
  3  WHERE tablespace_name='UNDOTBS';

FILE_NAME                                  BYTES
-----------------------------------        ---------
/u01/orcl/oradata/undotbs01_01.dbf         209715200
SQL>
```

Sizing the Undo Tablespace

Oracle recommends that you size your undo tablespace with the help of the Undo Advisor. However, if you've just created your database, the Undo Advisor won't have enough historical data about undo requirements to help you. Oracle makes the following recommendations for a new database.

Initially, create a small-sized (approximately 500MB) undo tablespace, with the AUTOEXTEND datafile attribute set to ON, thus allowing an automatically extensible tablespace. The tablespace will automatically grow, both to support a growing number of active transactions as well as the growing length of transactions in the database.

After the database has run for a reasonable length of time, use the Undo Advisor to get recommendations for sizing the undo tablespace. Use the maximum time allowed in the Analysis Time Period field. You can use the Longest-Running Query length shown in the OEM Undo Management page for this purpose. You must also specify a value for the New Undo Retention field based on your Flashback requirements. If you wish to be able to flash back your tables, for example, for a period of 24 hours in the past, use 24 hours as the value for this field.

■**Tip** The main reason for fixing the size of the undo tablespace (rather than keeping it auto-extensible) is to prevent a single runaway query from taking up all the free space in the database.

Using these two values (those in the Analysis Time Period field and the New Undo Retention field), the Undo Advisor will recommend the appropriate undo tablespace size. You can then add about 20 percent to the size you arrive at as a safety margin, and make the undo tablespace a fixed-size tablespace by disabling the AUTOEXTEND attribute.

Guaranteed Undo Retention

Under AUM, the Oracle database collects undo data and stores it in the undo segments. Traditionally, Oracle has used data in the undo segments to provide read consistency for queries, to roll back transactions, and to recover terminated transactions. Starting with Oracle9*i*, undo data has been used for even farther-reaching purposes—to query past data and recover from logical errors in the data. Undo data also supports the new Flashback features at the row and table levels.

The UNDO_RETENTION initialization parameter enables you to specify the length of time undo information must be saved in the undo segments. Oracle Database 11*g* automatically tunes undo information by collecting statistics on the longest-running queries and the undo generation rate in your database. If you don't set the UNDO_RETENTION parameter or specify a zero value for the parameter, Oracle automatically tunes undo, using 900 seconds as the default value for the UNDO_RETENTION parameter. By setting a higher value than the default of 900 seconds, you can keep undo records longer and go back further in the past. Since several Flashback features in Oracle Database 11*g* rely on undo data, you should set the UNDO_RETENTION parameter much higher than the default value. (In addition to enabling more effective Flashback features, this will reduce the probability of snapshot-too-old errors.)

Guaranteed undo retention simply means that Oracle will retain undo data for the entire length of the undo retention period you specify, *no matter what*. That is, if you specify half an hour as the undo retention interval, Oracle will retain the undo data for the full 30 minutes, under all circumstances. If you run out of room for recording the undo information generated by new transactions, any new DML transactions will fail, since Oracle won't be able to store the undo information for those changes. Thus, there is a trade-off between guaranteeing undo information and the potential failure of some DML statements.

■**Tip** By default, Oracle doesn't guarantee undo retention; the default retention time is 900 seconds (15 minutes) if you decide to guarantee undo retention.

You can specify guaranteed undo retention for the undo tablespace when you create the database, or by specifying the RETENTION GUARANTEE clause while creating a new undo tablespace, as shown here:

```
SQL> CREATE UNDO TABLESPACE undotbs01
  2  DATAFILE
  3  '/u01/orcl/oradata/undotbs01_01.dbf'
  4  SIZE 10M AUTOEXTEND ON
  5* RETENTION GUARANTEE;
Tablespace created.
SQL>
```

You can also use the ALTER TABLESPACE command to guarantee undo retention in your database, as shown here:

```
SQL> ALTER TABLESPACE undotbs01 RETENTION GUARANTEE;
```

You can use the RETENTION NOGUARANTEE clause to turn off the guaranteed retention of undo information, as shown in the following example:

```
SQL> ALTER TABLESPACE undotbs01 RETENTION NOGUARANTEE;
```

■**Caution** A high value for the UNDO_RETENTION parameter doesn't guarantee the retention of undo data for the duration specified by the UNDO_RETENTION parameter. You must use the RETENTION GUARANTEE clause to guarantee undo retention for a specified time.

Let's say you've configured guaranteed undo retention in your database by using the RETENTION GUARANTEE clause. If your undo tablespace is too small to accommodate all the active transactions that are using it, the following will happen:

- Oracle will issue an automatic tablespace warning alert when the undo tablespace is 85 percent full (if you haven't disabled the automatic tablespace alert feature).

- Oracle will also issue an automatic tablespace critical alert when the undo tablespace is 97 percent full.

- All DML statements will be disallowed and will receive an out-of-space error.

- DDL statements will continue to be allowed.

Managing Undo Tablespaces

Managing undo tablespaces is similar to managing any other tablespaces in your database. You add space to an undo tablespace by adding a datafile, and you decrease the size of an undo tablespace by reducing the size of the datafile(s) in it with the ALTER DATABASE DATAFILE . . . RESIZE command.

You drop an undo tablespace with the normal DROP TABLESPACE command. (If the undo tablespace contains any outstanding transactions, you can't drop it.) The DROP TABLESPACE command, since it removes all contents of the undo tablespace, is similar to using the DROP TABLESPACE . . . WITH CONTENTS command. If you need to switch undo tablespaces for some reason, you can drop the old one after you create a new undo tablespace.

The Snapshot-Too-Old Error

Occasionally, a long-running transaction can't find the undo data it needs, and consequently fails with the well-known Oracle snapshot-too-old error. Here's an example:

```
SQL> BEGIN
  2    purge_data_pkg.main_driver(1502,2005,'N','B','N','N');
  3    END;
  4  /

begin
*
ERROR at line 1:
ORA-01555: snapshot too old: rollback segment number 9 with name "_SYSSMU9$"
too small
ORA-06512: at "APPOWNER.PURGE_DATA_PKG", line 2040
ORA-06512: at "APPOWNER.PURGE_DATA_PKG", line 4318
ORA-06512: at line 2

SQL>
```

Even when you use Automatic Undo Management, as the previous example shows, you can get this error, since the UNDO_RETENTION parameter is set too low. This happens even when there is plenty of free space in the undo tablespace. Your best bet is to raise the value of the UNDO_RETENTION parameter so the necessary undo data isn't overwritten before your long transaction finishes. The only certain way to avoid the snapshot-too-old error is to enable guaranteed undo retention in your database.

Managing Undo Space Information

You can use the SHOW PARAMETER UNDO command in SQL*Plus to see what the configured options are for undo space management, as shown here:

```
SQL> SHOW PARAMETER UNDO

NAME                  TYPE       VALUE
--------------------  -------    -------------
undo_management       string     AUTO
undo_retention        integer    900
undo_tablespace       string     UNDOTBS_01
SQL>
```

■**Note** If you used older versions of Oracle, you are most likely familiar with the SET TRANSACTION USE ROLLBACK SEGMENT . . . statement, which enabled you to assign large rollback segments to a transaction to avoid the snapshot-too-old error. You can use this statement only under manual undo management. If you're using the Oracle-recommended Automatic Undo Management feature, the database will ignore this statement if you use it—however, no errors are generated.

If you use the Database Resource Manager to create consumer groups in your database, which are a convenient way to group your users based on their usage of database resources (see Chapter 12), you can easily prevent a single transaction from taking up most of the undo space, thus hindering new transactions from acquiring undo space. You can set a special parameter called UNDO_POOL to limit the maximum undo space a resource consumer group can use. Once this UNDO_POOL limit is reached, any transactions that need more undo room will error out. Only after some of the currently running transactions in the resource consumer group finish can more undo space be granted to that group.

The following data dictionary views are useful in managing undo space information:

- *V$UNDOSTAT*: This is the view Oracle uses to tune undo space allocation in the database. This view can indicate whether your current allocation of space in the undo tablespace is enough. It also indicates whether you have set the UNDO_RETENTION parameter correctly. The TUNED_UNDORETENTION column in the V$UNDOSTAT view tells you the length of time undo is retained in your undo tablespace.

- *DBA_ROLLBACK_SEGS*: You can use this view to find out the undo segment name, initial, next, and maximum extents, and other related information.

- *DBA_TABLESPACES*: This view will show whether the guaranteed undo retention feature is enabled for a certain undo tablespace.

- *V$TRANSACTION*: You can get transaction information from this view.

- *V$ROLLSTAT*: You can join V$ROLLSTAT and V$ROLLNAME to get a lot of information on the behavior of the undo segments.

- *DBA_UNDO_EXTENTS*: This view provides detailed information on the undo extents within the undo tablespace.

Using the OEM to Manage Undo Data

You can use OEM to help you correctly size your undo tablespace and set the right UNDO_RETENTION parameter value. OEM provides the Undo Advisor to help you determine the space required for your undo tablespace, based on average and peak-level undo generation rates.

To get to the Undo Advisor page, go to the OEM Home Page ➤ Advisor Central ➤ Undo Management and click on the Undo Advisor button. (You can also get to the Undo Advisor by going to the OEM Home Page ➤ Performance Page ➤ Advisor Central ➤ Undo Management and clicking on the Undo Advisor button.)

The Undo Advisor shows you the best undo retention possible for a given undo tablespace size. It can also advise you about the correct size for the undo tablespace, based on an undo retention value that you specify, by analyzing the impact of various hypothetical undo retention values.

You can also use the Undo Management page (OEM Home Page ➤ Administration ➤ Instance ➤ Undo Management) to perform the following tasks:

- Change and edit the undo tablespace.

- View system activity and undo tablespace usage statistics, including the average and maximum undo generation rates and the length (in minutes) of the longest running query.

- Get recommendations for both undo retention length and undo tablespace size.

Figure 8-2 shows the Undo Generation Rate and Tablespace Usage graph from the bottom of the OEM Undo Management page. This graph is color-coded so you can see at a glance how the undo tablespace is handling the amount of undo information generated in your instance.

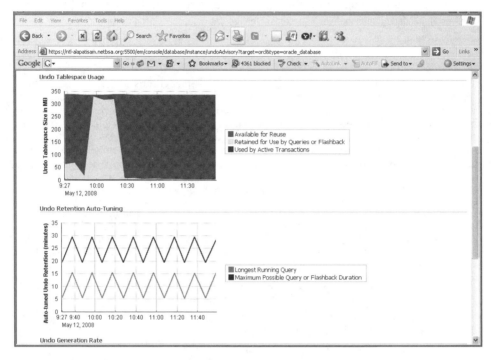

Figure 8-2. *The Undo Generation and Tablespace Usage graph*

Flashback Error Correction Using Undo Data

Up until the Oracle9*i* database version, the only way to correct user errors was to perform point-in-time recovery, which is tedious and somewhat complex. The Oracle9*i* database introduced the first Flashback features in the database. Flashback features enable you to query past versions of data, as well as retrieve the history of changes made to a table's data. You can use the historical information either to query past data or to recover from logical corruption in the data.

Oracle Database 11*g* provides several error-correction techniques that depend on undo data. The following Flashback features in Oracle Database 11*g* depend on undo data:

- *Flashback Query*: Retrieves data from a past point in time.

- *Flashback Versions Query*: Shows you the different versions of table rows, and provides metadata, such as the start and end time of the particular transaction that created the row version.

- *Flashback Transaction Query*: Lets you retrieve historical data for a given transaction, along with the SQL code to undo the changes made to particular rows.

- *Flashback Table*: Recovers a table quickly to its state at a past point in time, without having to perform point-in-time recovery.

- *Flashback Transaction*: Enables you to roll back a transaction, along with all of its dependent transactions.

■**Note** There are other flashback features, like Flashback Drop and Flashback Database, but they don't use undo data. I'll discuss these features in Chapter 16, which deals with database recovery.

In the following sections, we'll look at each of these important Flashback features in detail.

■**Tip** If you want to make serious use of the new Flashback features, make sure that you provide sufficiently sized undo tablespaces. Preferably, you must use auto-extensible undo tablespaces, so that Oracle retains undo data longer than the longest query duration. In addition, you should specify RETENTION GUARANTEE for the undo data. Simply setting a large UNDO_RETENTION value doesn't guarantee that Oracle won't discard unexpired undo data (as was discussed previously).

Querying Old Data with Flashback Query

Using the Flashback Query feature simply involves using the SELECT statement with an AS OF clause. This type of query lets you retrieve committed data as it existed at some time in the past. You can select data from the past based on a time stamp or SCN.

It is common for an application to need older data for analysis purposes. A company's sales force, for example, may need older sales data but may find that it has been modified already. Even more important, sometimes a user error or faulty application code may require the restoration of older data. Right now, the most common way to go back in time is for the DBA to perform a laborious and time-consuming point-in-time database recovery, which may involve some disruption in service and a loss of critical business data. The Flashback Query feature provides you an easy way to query data at a point in time.

Flashback Query with the AS OF Clause

Here's a simple example that shows how to use Flashback Query. Suppose you find that a user was accidentally deleted from your employees table around noon. The only thing you know for sure is that the employee was in the database at 8 AM. You can use a SELECT statement with the AS OF clause to find the lost data.

■**Tip** How far back in time you can go with a Flashback Query depends on your UNDO_RETENTION parameter setting.

First, you must grant the necessary privileges. A user needs to have the privilege to issue a Flashback Query on the table if the user doesn't own the table. Note that you don't need this privilege to execute the DBMS_FLASHBACK package or any of its component procedures.

Here's how the DBA can grant the object privileges to enable a user to issue a Flashback Query:

```
SQL> GRANT FLASHBACK ON employees TO salapati

Grant succeeded.
SQL>
```

Or you could use a statement like this:

```
SQL> GRANT FLASHBACK ANY TABLE TO salapati;

Grant succeeded.
SQL>
```

You can grant the Flashback Query object privilege (GRANT FLASHBACK ANY TABLE) on a table, view, or a materialized view.

Next, use the SELECT . . . AS OF query to retrieve Flashback data from the past.

```
SQL> SELECT * FROM employees AS OF TIMESTAMP
    TO_TIMESTAMP ('2008-09-02 08:00:00', 'YYYY-MM-DD HH:MI:SS')
    WHERE last_name = 'Alapati';
```

Once you confirm the validity of the accidentally deleted data, it's easy to reinsert the data by using the previous query as part of an INSERT statement, as shown here:

```
SQL> INSERT INTO employees
    SELECT * FROM employees AS OF TIMESTAMP
    TO_TIMESTAMP('2008-09-02 08:00:00', 'YYYY-MM-DD HH:MI:SS')
    WHERE last_name = 'Alapati';
```

The previous two examples use a time stamp to pinpoint the exact time the data was accidentally dropped. You could use the SCN for the transaction instead of time stamps. Just note that an SCN will only put you within 3 seconds of the actual occurrence of the event. If you need to be very specific regarding the time point, use the time-stamp method to specify the time.

Flashback Using the DBMS_FLASHBACK Package

Oracle provides a special package called DBMS_FLASHBACK that allows you to see a consistent version of the database at a time (or SCN) that you specify. A big advantage of using the DBMS_FLASHBACK package over the other Flashback features is that you can use existing PL/SQL code with it to retrieve older data without having to add the AS OF and VERSIONS BETWEEN clauses, which you have to do if you wish to use the other types of Flashback features.

You can specify either a time stamp or an SCN number as the starting point for your query. In the simple example that follows, you'll see how you can query for the number of rows that existed in a table before they were deleted permanently from the table.

In the following trivial example that illustrates the use of the DBMS_FLASHBACK package, the following query is first used to get the number of rows that currently exist in the employees table:

```
SQL> SELECT COUNT(*) FROM employees;

  COUNT(*)
-----------
495
```

Suppose you're interested in finding out the number of rows that existed in this table on December 11, 2008. You can call the DBMS_FLASHBACK.ENABLE_AT_TIME procedure, as shown in the following code, to specify the specific past point in time you are interested in:

```
SQL> EXECUTE DBMS_FLASHBACK.ENABLE_AT_TIME (TO_TIMESTAMP '11-DEC-
    2008:10:00:00',
    -'DD-MON-YYYY:hh24:MI:SS');
PL/SQL procedure successfully completed.
SQL>
```

If you'd rather use an SCN instead of a time stamp, you must use the DBMS_FLASHBACK.ENABLE_AT_SYSTEM_CHANGE_NUMBER procedure instead. To get the correct SCN, you can use the DBMS_FLASHBACK.GET_SYSTEM_CHANGE procedure first.

Next, issue the same query as before. Now, the results of the output will reflect the contents of the emp table on December 11, 2004, not the current time. Note that you don't have to use the AS OF formulation in your query, since you're using the DBMS_FLASHBACK package.

Here's the query that gets you the output as of December 11, 2004:

```
SQL> SELECT COUNT(*) FROM emp;

  COUNT(*)
-----------
    525
```

Once you've finished executing your query to fetch the results from a past point in time, disable the DBMS_FLASHBACK package as follows:

```
SQL> EXECUTE DBMS_FLASHBACK.DISABLE ();

PL/SQL procedure successfully completed.
SQL>
```

Enabling the Flashback Query feature in the preceding example allowed you to see how many rows were in a table at a time in the past. You found out from your simple query that the emp table had 525 rows at the time in the recent past that you specified. If you want, you can use cursors to retrieve the past data in order to either compare it to present data in the emp table, or, if necessary, insert it into the emp table. You must open the cursor before you disable the DBMS_FLASHBACK feature, and store the results so you can do the comparisons or inserts.

Use the DBMS_FLASHBACK package in cases where you can't touch the code, as is the case with packaged applications. The package comes in handy when you have to specify the past point in time several times, to retrieve older data. You can recover lost data using other methods, as you will see in Chapter 16, which discusses database recovery. However, the Flashback Query feature gives you a chance to just analyze or verify old data, even in cases where you are not interested in restoring that data.

■**Tip** To ensure data consistency, make sure you issue a COMMIT or a ROLLBACK statement before using a Flashback operation of any kind.

Flashback Versions Query

The Flashback Versions Query feature provides you with row history by letting you retrieve all the versions of a row between either two points in time or two SCNs. Oracle creates a new version of a row each time a COMMIT statement is executed. If you insert a row and subsequently update or delete the row, only the latest version of the row will be preserved in your table. If you wish to find out exactly what changes a row went through over a certain interval of time, you can use the Flashback Versions Query feature. The Flashback Versions Query will return one row for each version of every row in the table. The feature is ideal when you're trying to audit table data or undo erroneous changes to data.

Here are some things to keep in mind about the Flashback Versions query feature:

- You can retrieve only the *committed* versions of a row.
- The query will retrieve all deleted rows as well as current rows.

- The query will retrieve any rows that were deleted and reinserted later on.
- The query result is in the form of a table and contains a row for each version of a row during the time or SCN interval you specify.

By reviewing the history of the rows in a table, you can audit the changes and find out which transactions changed the rows.

Syntax of the Flashback Versions Query

The Flashback Versions Query feature enables you to retrieve all committed versions of a table's data between two time points. If you've updated a table row ten different times, for example, the Flashback Versions Query will get you all ten versions of that row over time.

The complete syntax for the Flashback Versions Query is as follows:

```
SQL> SELECT [pseudocolumns] . . . /* provide details about the row history */
     FROM . . .                   /* table name goes here */
     VERSIONS BETWEEN
     {SCN|TIMESTAMP {expr|MINVALUE} AND
                     {expr|MAXVALUE}}
     [AS OF{SCN|TIMESTAMP expr}]
     WHERE [pseudocolumns . . . ] . . .
```

Using the versions clause in a query will get you multiple versions of the rows returned by the query. In the preceding syntax statement, you can use the VERSIONS clause as a part of your normal SELECT statement, with a BETWEEN clause appended to it. You can also specify an SCN or a TIMESTAMP clause. You must specify the start and end expressions by using MINVALUE and MAXVALUE, which indicate the start time and end time of the interval for which you are seeking the different row versions. The MINVALUE and the MAXVALUE are resolved to the time stamp or the SCN of the oldest and the most recent data that's available in the database, respectively.

Note You must ensure that the beginning and ending interval, framed by either SCNs or time stamps, don't go back beyond the time specified by the UNDO_RETENTION parameter. While you can actually specify a begin or an end time point that lies outside the interval spanned by the UNDO_RETENTION parameter, the query may not work.

Note that the AS OF clause is optional, and when you use it, the database will retrieve all the rows as of that particular SCN or time stamp. If the VERSIONS clause is used by itself, as in VERSIONS BETWEEN SCN MINVALUE and MAXVALUE, without using the optional AS OF clause, the data is retrieved as of the current session. If you add the AS OF clause, as shown next, the data is retrieved as of a specified SCN or clock time:

```
VERSIONS BETWEEN SCN MINVALUE and MAXVALUE AS OF SCN 56789
```

Note You may also use the VERSIONS clause in subqueries of DML and DDL statements.

Flashback Versions Query Pseudo-Columns

The output of a Flashback Versions Query is unlike the output of your typical SELECT statement. The output can show multiple versions of the same row, with a row representing each time the particular row was inserted, updated, or deleted. In addition to the column values you specify in the SELECT statement, Oracle will provide you with values for a set of pseudo-columns for each row version. These pseudo-columns provide metadata about the various row versions, including the type of operation, the begin and end time of the transaction, and so on. It is these pseudo-columns that tell you exactly when a row was modified and what was done to the row at that time.

Here is a brief explanation of each pseudo-column in the Flashback Versions Query output:

- *VERSIONS_STARTSCN and VERSIONS_STARTTIME*: These pseudo-columns tell you the SCN and time stamp when this particular row was first created. If the VERSIONS_STARTTIME is null, the row was created before the lower time boundary of the query.

- *VERSIONS_ENDSCN and VERSIONS_ENDTIME*: These pseudo-columns tell you when this particular row expired. If the VERSIONS_ENDTIME column value is null, it means that the row is either current or that it has been deleted.

- *VERSIONS_OPERATION*: This pseudo-column provides you with information about the type of DML activity that was performed on the particular row. The column has three possible values: I represents an insert, D a delete operation, and U an update operation.

- *VERSIONS_XID*: This pseudo-column displays the unique transaction identifier of the transaction that resulted in this row version.

Note An index-organized table (IOT) will show an update operation as a delete and an insert operation. Your Flashback Versions Query would produce both the deleted and inserted rows as two independent versions. The first version would show a D for the delete operation under the VERSIONS_OPERATION pseudo-column, and the subsequent insert column would show an I for the same pseudo-column.

If the version of a row was created before the MINVALUE or the beginning of the query, you can't capture the value for the starting time stamp or SCN, and your VERSIONS_STARTSCN and VERSIONS_STARTTIME pseudo-columns will be null—there won't be any history for this row in your undo segments.

The VERSIONS_ENDSCN and VERSIONS_ENDTIME pseudo-columns tell you when the row version expired. If the row version is still current at the time of your Flashback Versions Query, the VERSIONS_ENDSCN and VERSIONS_ENDTIME pseudo-columns will be null. Similarly, if the row version has been deleted from the table, you'll see a null value for these two pseudo-columns.

Using Flashback Versions Query

To understand the capabilities and power of the Flashback Versions Query feature, let's look at the simple example shown in Listing 8-1.

Listing 8-1. *Using the Flashback Versions Query Feature*

```
SQL> SELECT versions_xid AS XID, versions_startscn AS START_SCN,
     versions_endscn AS END_SCN,
     versions_operation AS OPERATION,
     empname FROM EMPLOYEES
     VERSIONS BETWEEN SCN MINVALUE AND MAXVALUE
     AS OF SCN 7920
     WHERE emp_id = 222;
```

XID	START_SCN	END_SCN	OPERATION	EMPNAME	SALARY
0003002F00038BA9	2266		I	Nick	19000
0004002D0002B366	0864		D	Sam	20000
000400170002B366	0827	0864	I	Sam	20000

```
SQL>
```

The example in Listing 8-1 retrieves three versions of a row for employee number (emp_id) 222. The AS OF SCN of the query is 7920. That is, we want to know what versions of the row existed at this SCN. Although you see three versions in the output, only one of the row versions is true as of the SCN you're interested in. So, which version is it?

Let's read the query output from top to bottom. Pay particular attention to the START_SCN and the END_SCN columns. All rows will have a START_SCN, but they may have a null value for the END_SCN if the version of the row still exists at the current SCN.

The first row, which inserted (operation I) employee name Nick at SCN 2266, is the latest version of the row. Since the END_SCN is null for the first row, you know that this row still existed at SCN 7920. If you look under the OPERATION column, you see the letter D for the second version (START_SCN 0864), indicating that the middle row was deleted (probably accidentally), and the row didn't exist at SCN 7920. The first row thus reflects the fact that the row was reinserted, with a different employee's name. The bottom or third row has an END_SCN number, so clearly this row expired at SCN 0864. This was the originally inserted version of this row, as indicated by the value I (insert) under the OPERATION column.

■**Note** You must substitute VERSIONS BETWEEN TIMESTAMP . . . for the VERSIONS BETWEEN SCN nn AND nn clause to use time stamps to specify the time interval for retrieving the various versions of a row instead of using SCNs.

Restrictions and Observations on the Flashback Versions Query

Here are the main limitations of the Flashback Versions Query feature:

- You can only use the feature to query actual tables, not views.
- You can't apply the VERSIONS clause across DDL operations.
- The query will ignore purely physical row changes as happen, for example, during a segment shrink operation.
- You can't use this feature if you're dealing with external or temporary tables.

If you want to query past data at a precise time, you must use an SCN, since the actual time might be up to three seconds earlier or later than the time you specify with a time stamp. Oracle Database 11g uses SCNs internally and maps them to time stamps with a granularity of three seconds. This potential gap between an SCN and a time stamp may cause problems when you're trying to flash back to an exact time that immediately follows a DDL operation. Suppose you created a new table. If you use a time stamp, your Flashback Versions Query might start a little before the exact time the table was created and miss the new table entirely. You'll end up with an error in this case instead of the Flashback Version Query results. By using an SCN instead of a time stamp, you can avoid this problem.

Flashback Transaction Query

The FLASHBACK_TRANSACTION_QUERY view lets you identify which transaction or transactions were responsible for a certain change in a table's data during a specified interval. A *Flashback Transaction Query* is simply a query on the FLASHBACK_TRANSACTION_QUERY view, and it can provide transaction information, including the SQL statements needed to undo all the changes made by either a single transaction or a set of transactions during a specified interval of time. This feature enables you not only to correct logical errors, but also to conduct transaction audits in your database.

Flashback Transaction Query gets all its transaction information from the undo segments. Thus, the value you set for the UNDO_RETENTION parameter determines how far back you can go to retrieve undo data.

When you use Oracle's LogMiner tool to undo SQL statements, Oracle has to serially read entire redo log files to get the necessary information. The Flashback Transaction Query feature lets you use an indexed access path to get to the required undo data directly, instead of traversing an entire redo log file. You can also undo a single transaction or a set of bad transactions during an interval of time.

Using the Flashback Transaction Query Feature

You need the SELECT ANY TRANSACTION system privilege to query the FLASHBACK_
TRANSACTION_QUERY view. This view contains columns that let you identify a transaction's time stamp, the identity of the user who made the transaction, the type of operations done during the transaction, and the undo statements necessary to retrieve the original row. Listing 8-2 shows the structure of the FLASHBACK_TRANSACTION_QUERY view.

Listing 8-2. *The Flashback Transaction Query View*

```
SQL> DESC flashback_transaction_query
 Name                     Null?     Type
 ------------------       ------    --------------
 XID                                RAW(8)
 START_SCN                          NUMBER
 START_TIMESTAMP                    DATE
 COMMIT_SCN                         NUMBER
 COMMIT_TIMESTAMP                   DATE
 LOGON_USER                         VARCHAR2(30)
 UNDO_CHANGE#                       NUMBER
 OPERATION                          VARCHAR2(32)
 TABLE_NAME                         VARCHAR2(256)
 TABLE_OWNER                        VARCHAR2(32)
 ROW_ID                             VARCHAR2(19)
 UNDO_SQL                           VARCHAR2(4000)
SQL>
```

The FLASHBACK_TRANSACTION_QUERY view contains the following columns:

- START_SCN and START_TIMESTAMP identify when a certain row was created.

- COMMIT_SCN and COMMIT_TIMESTAMP tell you when a transaction was committed.

- XID, ROW_ID, and UNDO_CHANGE# identify the transaction, the row, and the undo change number, respectively.

- OPERATION tells you whether the DML operation was an insert, update, or delete operation.

■**Note** If you see a value of UNKNOWN under the OPERATION column, it means that there isn't sufficient undo information in your undo tablespace to correctly identify the transaction's exact operation type.

- LOGON_USER, TABLE_NAME, and TABLE_OWNER provide the username, table name, and schema name.

- UNDO_SQL gives you the exact SQL statement required to undo the transaction. Here's an example of the type of data you would find under the UNDO_SQL column:

```
delete from "APPOWNER"."PERSONS" where ROWID =   'AAAP84AAGAAAAA1AAB';
```

Oracle recommends that if any of the tables that are part of the Flashback Transaction Query operation contained chained rows, or if you're using clustered tables, you must turn on supplemental logging in your database before using the Flashback Transaction Query. You can turn supplemental logging on at the database level, using the following SQL statement:

```
SQL> ALTER DATABASE ADD SUPPLEMENTAL LOG DATA;
```

The following query will display all transactions, both committed and active, in all the undo segments:

```
SQL> SELECT operation, undo_sql, table_name
     FROM flashback_transaction_query;
```

The query in Listing 8-3 shows how to determine the operation that will undo a transaction and the specific SQL statement that will undo it.

Listing 8-3. *Identifying SQL Statements to Undo Data Changes*

```
SQL> SELECT operation, undo_sql, table_name
  2  FROM flashback_transaction_query
  3  WHERE start_timestamp >= TO_TIMESTAMP
  4  ('2009-02-15 05:00:00', 'YYYY-MM-DD HH:MI:SS')
  5  AND commit_timestamp <= TO_TIMESTAMP('2009-02-15 06:30:00', 'YYYY-MM-DD
     HH:MI:SS')
  6* AND table_owner='PASOWNER';
```

OPERATION	UNDO_SQL	TABLE_NAME
INSERT	delete from "APPOWNER"."FR_DETAILS" where ROWID = 'AAQXXZAC8AAAB+zAAb';	FR_DETAILS
INSERT	delete from "APPOWNER"."FR_DETAILS" where ROWID = 'AAQXXZAC8AAAB +zAAa';	FR_DETAILS

```
SQL>
```

The OPERATION column in Listing 8-3 indicates that two inserts were made during the time period specified in the query. The UNDO_SQL column shows the exact SQL statement you must run to undo the changes—this is information the query fetched for you from the undo segments. In this simple example, there are only two delete statements that you'll have to execute if you wish to undo the inserts displayed by your query. However, transactions usually contain several DML statements, in which case you'll have to apply the undo changes in the sequence that the query returns them to correctly recover the data to its original state.

■**Tip** Consider using the RETENTION GUARANTEE setting for your undo tablespace if you're going to issue an Oracle Flashback Query or an Oracle Flashback Transaction Query to resolve a critical data error. This will ensure that the database preserves the necessary unexpired undo data in all undo segments.

Flashback Transaction Query Considerations

Keep the following points in mind concerning the Flashback Transaction Query feature:

- Turn on minimal supplemental logging if your operations involve chained rows and special storage structures, such as clustered tables.

- When querying index-organized tables, an update operation is always shown as a two-step delete/insert operation.

- If the query involves a dropped table or a dropped user, it returns object numbers and user IDs instead of the object names and usernames.

Using Flashback Transaction Query and Flashback Versions Query Together

The Flashback Versions Query feature lets you retrieve the various versions of a row, along with their unique version IDs, row version time stamps, SCNs, and so on. It tells you what was in the row and what happened to it. The Flashback Transaction Query feature, on the other hand, not only identifies the type of operations performed on each version of a row, but also provides the necessary undo SQL to put the rows back in their original state. It tells you how to get back to a previous version of the row.

You can combine the capabilities of these two features by using them in sequence, to perform auditing and related activities. Let's look at an example that shows how you can combine the Flashback Versions Query and the Flashback Transaction Query features to undo undesirable changes to your data.

First, use the Flashback Versions Query feature to identify all the row versions in a certain table that have changed in a certain time period, as shown in Listing 8-4 (which is identical to Listing 8-1).

Listing 8-4. *Using the Flashback Versions Query to Identify Changed Row Versions*

```
SQL> SELECT versions_xid AS XID, versions_startscn AS START_SCN,
    versions_endscn AS END_SCN,
    versions_operation AS OPERATION,
    empname FROM EMPLOYEES
    VERSIONS BETWEEN SCN MINVALUE AND MAXVALUE
    AS OF SCN 7920
    WHERE emp_id = 222;


XID                START_SCN    END_SCN    OPERATION    EMPNAME    SALARY
----------------   ---------    --------   ----------   ---------  --------
0003002F00038BA9   2266                    I            Nick       19000
0004002D0002B366   0864                    D            Sam        20000
000400170002B366   0827         0864       I            Sam        20000

SQL>
```

In Listing 8-4, let's say we identified the second row, which indicates a delete operation (D) as the culprit. By mistake, one of our users incorrectly deleted the row. All you need to do in order to extract the correct SQL to undo this delete operation is to take the transaction ID (XID) from this Flashback Versions Query and search for it in the FLASHBACK_TRANSACTION_QUERY view. Listing 8-5 shows the query you'll need to execute.

Listing 8-5. *Selecting Undo SQL Based on a Transaction ID*

```
SQL> SELECT xid, start_scn START, commit_scn COMMIT,
    operation OPERATION, logon_user USER,
    undo_sql
    FROM flashback_transaction_query
    WHERE xid = HEXTORAW('0004002D0002B366');


XID          START     COMMIT    OPERATION    USER   UNDO_SQL
----------   ------    ------    ---------    ----   ----------------------------
00020030D    195243    195244    DELETE       HR     insert into "HR"."EMP"
                                                     ("EMPNO","EMPNAME","SALARY")
```

```
                                          values ('222','Mike','20000');
1 row selected.
SQL>
```

The query in Listing 8-5 gives you the exact undo SQL statement to undo the deletion operation performed by the transaction with XID 0020030002D. As you can see, the Flashback Versions Query and the Flashback Transaction Query provide complementary features. You can use the two together not only to undo logical data errors, but also to audit transactions in your database. By using the two features, you can tell exactly how a certain row came to have a certain set of values and then get the exact SQL statements you need to undo the changes if necessary.

The Flashback Table Feature

Oracle's Flashback Table feature lets you recover a table to a previous point in time. This feature relies on undo information in the database undo segments to perform the point-in-time recovery without restoring any datafiles or applying any archived redo log files, as needed to be done for traditional point-in-time recovery. You can use the Flashback Table feature to roll back changes to a previous point in time defined by either a time stamp or an SCN.

Since you rely on undo data to flash back a table (rather than restoring your backup files), you don't have to take your database or tablespaces offline during a Flashback Table operation. Oracle acquires exclusive DML locks on the table or tables that it is recovering, but the tables continue to remain online.

■**Note** There are two distinct table-related Flashback features in Oracle Database 11*g*. The first, Flashback Table, lets you flash back a table to a past point in time. This feature depends entirely on the availability of the necessary undo data, and is discussed in this chapter. The second feature, Flashback Drop (FLASHBACK TABLE *table_name* TO BEFORE DROP), lets you retrieve a table that has been dropped altogether. This feature is helpful in performing a point-in-time recovery and relies on the Recycle Bin, not undo data. I'll discuss the Flashback Drop feature in Chapter 16, which deals with database recovery.

How the Flashback Table Feature Works

Flashback Table uses undo information to restore data rows in changed blocks of tables with DML statements like INSERT, UPDATE, and DELETE. Let's review the steps in a Flashback Table operation.

■**Note** You can't flash back any of the SYS user's objects.

First, you need to make sure the user performing the Flashback Table operation has all privileges, which could be either FLASHBACK ANY TABLE or the more specific FLASHBACK object privilege on the table to be flashed back. The user must also have SELECT, INSERT, DELETE, and ALTER privileges on the table.

The flashback operation doesn't preserve Oracle ROWIDs when it restores rows in the changed data blocks of the table, since it uses DML operations to perform its work. These DML operations change the ROWIDs of the affected rows, so you must ensure that you have enabled row movement in the tables you are using for the Flashback Table feature, as shown here:

```
SQL> ALTER TABLE emp ENABLE ROW MOVEMENT;

Table altered.
SQL>
```

Once you enable row movement in the table, you are ready to flash back the table to any time or any SCN in the past, providing you have the necessary undo information in your undo tablespace.

Before you use the Flashback Table feature, note its complete syntax:

```
SQL> FLASHBACK TABLE
     [schema.]table
     [,[schema.]table] . . .
     TO {{SCN|TIMESTAMP} expr
     [{ENABLE|DISABLE}TRIGGERS ]
     |BEFORE DROP[RENAME TO table]
     };
```

In this chapter, you'll only see the FLASHBACK TABLE . . . TO SCN|TIMESTAMP part of the FLASH-BACK TABLE statement. In the last line, BEFORE DROP refers to the FLASHBACK DROP feature, which is covered in Chapter 16 in the discussion of database recovery techniques.

Here's an example that shows how to flash back a table to a past SCN:

```
SQL> FLASHBACK TABLE emp TO SCN 5759290864;
Flashback complete.
SQL>
```

■**Tip** When a Flashback Table operation completes, all indexes that belong to the tables in the Flashback Table list will have their indexes reverted to the time to which the tables are flashed back. However, the optimizer statistics will still reflect the current data in the table.

You can also specify a time to flash back to, using a time stamp instead of an SCN, as shown here:

```
SQL> FLASHBACK TABLE persons TO TIMESTAMP TO_TIMESTAMP
     ('2008-01-30  07:00:00', 'YYYY-MM-DD HH24:MI:SS');
```

The preceding FLASHBACK TABLE command restores the persons table to 10:00 AM on April 5, 2005.

You can use the following statement to flash back a table by one day:

```
SQL> FLASHBACK TABLE persons to TIMESTAMP (SYDATE -1);
```

You can flash back more than one table at a time, as shown in the following example (but first make sure you enable row movement for both tables):

```
SQL> FLASHBACK TABLE persons,person_orgs TO TIMESTAMP (SYSDATE -1)
```

The Flashback Table operation is an in-place, online operation and thus doesn't involve taking datafiles or tablespaces offline, unlike traditional point-in-time recovery. Oracle disables all relevant triggers by default and reenables them upon completing the table recovery, though you can override this by appending the ENABLE TRIGGERS clause to your FLASHBACK TABLE statement, as shown here:

```
SQL> FLASHBACK TABLE persons to TIMESTAMP TO_TIMESTAMP
     ('2009-04-05 10:00:00', 'YYYY-MM-DD HH24:MI:SS')
     ENABLE TRIGGERS;
```

If you don't have sufficient undo data to flash back the table, you'll get the error shown in Listing 8-6, which means that part of the undo information was overwritten. Unfortunately, the Flashback Table feature can't help you here, as it relies entirely on the presence of adequate undo information. The only solution is to use a larger undo tablespace or enable the guaranteed undo retention feature as explained in the "The UNDO_RETENTION Parameter" section, earlier in this chapter.

Listing 8-6. *Failure of a Flashback Table Operation*

```
SQL> FLASHBACK TABLE emp,dept to TIMESTAMP (SYSDATE -1);
 flashback table emp, dept to TIMESTAMP (SYSDATE -1)
               *
ERROR at line 1:
ORA-00604: error occurred at recursive SQL level 1
ORA-12801: error signaled in parallel query server P005
ORA-01555: snapshot too old: rollback segment number 108 with name
"_SYSSMU108$" too small
01555, 00000, "snapshot too old: rollback segment number %s with name \"%s\" too
small"
// *Cause: rollback records needed by a reader for consistent read are
//         overwritten by other writers
// *Action: If in Automatic Undo Management mode, increase undo_retention
//          setting.
```

Undoing a Flashback Table Operation

If it turns out that your Flashback Table results aren't to your liking, you can use the FLASHBACK TABLE statement again to go back to just before you first issued the FLASHBACK TABLE statement.

It's important to always note your current SCN before running a Flashback Table operation so that you can undo it with the FLASHBACK TABLE . . . TO SCN statement if necessary. You can find out the current SCN in your database by using the following query:

```
SQL> SELECT current_scn from V$DATABASE;

CURRENT_SCN
--------------------
 5581746576
SQL>
```

Restrictions on the Flashback Table Feature

Several restrictions apply to the Flashback Table feature. Here are the important ones:

- You can't flash back a table owned by SYS, recovered objects, or a remote table.

- You can't flash back a table to a time preceding any DDL operation involving a change in table structure, such as modifying or dropping a column, truncating a table, adding a constraint, or performing any partition-related operations, such as adding or dropping a partition.

- The FLASHBACK statement involves a single transaction, and the Flashback operation succeeds entirely or it fails. If the flashback operation involves multiple tables, all of the tables must be flashed back or none.

- If Oracle discovers any constraint violations during the Flashback operation, it abandons the operation, leaving the tables in their original state.

- If you shrink a table or change any nonstorage attributes of a table (other than attributes such as PCTFREE, INITTRANS, and MAXTRANS), you won't be able to flash back to a time before these changes were made.

Note The entire flashback table operation executes as a single transaction.

Flashback Transaction

You can use the Flashback Transaction feature to back out an unwanted transaction. You can back out not only the unwanted transaction, but also its dependent transactions as well, with a single click. So, if you're using the Database Control to do this instead of a PL/SQL procedure, the Flashback Transaction feature offers a far superior alternative to restoring backups to undo transactions, since the database remains online to users while you're backing out the unwanted transactions. Undo data is the key to the Flashback Transaction feature. The database uses the undo data to create and execute the necessary compensation transactions that'll undo the unwanted transaction.

The TRANSACTION_BACKOUT procedure analyzes all transactional dependencies and performs the necessary DML operations to undo the changes made in a transaction. Execution of the procedure also generates reports of the changes it made. However, the critical thing to know is that the procedure doesn't automatically commit the DML operations that it performs, but waits for you to explicitly commit the transaction and make the backout operation permanent.

Using Flashback Transaction

You can back out transactions either through the Database Control or by executing PL/SQL procedures. To back out a transaction manually, use the DBMS_FLASHBACK.TRANSACTION_BACKOUT procedure. The TRANSACTION_BACKOUT procedure contains the following parameters:

```
PROCEDURE TRANSACTION_BACKOUT
 Argument Name                  Type                In/Out   Default?
 ----------------------------- ------------------- ------   --------

 NUMTXNS                        NUMBER              IN
 XIDS                           XID_ARRAY           IN
 OPTIONS                        BINARY_INTEGER      IN       DEFAULT
 SCNHINT                        NUMBER              IN       DEFAULT
PROCEDURE TRANSACTION_BACKOUT
 Argument Name                  Type                In/Out   Default?
 ----------------------------- ------------------- ------   --------

 NUMTXNS                        NUMBER              IN
 XIDS                           XID_ARRAY           IN
 OPTIONS                        BINARY_INTEGER      IN       DEFAULT
 TIMEHINT                       TIMESTAMP           IN
PROCEDURE TRANSACTION_BACKOUT
 Argument Name                  Type                In/Out   Default?
 ----------------------------- ------------------- ------   --------

 NUMTXNS                        NUMBER              IN
 NAMES                          TXNAME_ARRAY        IN
 OPTIONS                        BINARY_INTEGER      IN       DEFAULT
 SCNHINT                        NUMBER              IN       DEFAULT
PROCEDURE TRANSACTION_BACKOUT
 Argument Name                  Type                In/Out   Default?
 ----------------------------- ------------------- ------   --------

 NUMTXNS                        NUMBER              IN
 NAMES                          TXNAME_ARRAY        IN
 OPTIONS                        BINARY_INTEGER      IN       DEFAULT
 TIMEHINT                       TIMESTAMP           IN
```

As you can see, the procedure is overloaded. Here's what the different parameters stand for:

- NUMTXNS: Indicates the number of transactions to be backed out.

- NAMES: Defines a list of transactions to be backed out, which you can pass out in the form of an array by using XIDs or by passing the names of the transactions.

- TIMEHINT: Lets you specify a time if you're identifying transactions by name.

- SCNHINT: Lets you specify the SCN for identifying transactions.
- OPTIONS: Lets you specify the backout options. You can use the following values for the OPTIONS parameter:
  - *Cascade*: Use this to back out the child transactions before backing out the parent transactions.
  - *Nocascade*: Use this if a transaction isn't supposed to have any dependent transactions.
  - *Nocascade_force*: Use this to back out the transactions and ignore any dependent transactions.
  - *Nonconfict_only*: Use this to back out only the changes made to the nonconflicting rows of a transaction.

Monitoring the Backout of Transactions

You can query the data dictionary views DBA_FLASHBACK_TXN_STATE and DBSA_FLASHBACK_TXN_REPORT to view the reports generated by executing the TRANSACTION_BACKOUT procedure.

Transaction Management

Oracle enables you to use two special types of transactions, discrete transactions and autonomous transactions, to help you manage transactions. I briefly review these two concepts in the following sections.

Discrete Transactions

To enhance the speed of transactions, Oracle enables the explicit use of discrete transactions. When you specify a transaction as a discrete transaction, Oracle skips certain routine processing overhead, such as writing the undo records, thereby speeding up the transaction. Oracle doesn't modify the data blocks until the transaction commits.

You use the BEGIN_DISCRETE_TRANSACTION procedure, which is part of the DBMS_TRANSACTION package, to implement the discrete transaction strategy. Short transactions run faster when you use this procedure, but if discrete transactions occur during the course of long queries, and these queries request data modified by the discrete transactions, there could be problems. Because discrete transactions skip the undo writing process, it isn't possible for a long-running query to get a consistent view of the data. Oracle doesn't generate undo records for discrete transactions because the data blocks aren't modified until the discrete transaction commits.

Autonomous Transactions

A transaction can run as part of another transaction. In such cases, the parent transaction is called the main transaction, and the independent child transaction is called the autonomous transaction. An autonomous transaction is formally defined as an independent transaction that can be called from another transaction. Notice that although the child transaction is called from the parent transaction, it is independent of the parent transaction.

Packages, procedures, functions, and triggers could all include transactions marked as autonomous. You have to include a directive in the main transaction so that Oracle will know you intend to use an autonomous transaction within the main transaction. The autonomous transaction can have its own ROLLBACK and COMMIT statements, just like normal transactions. The main transaction, by using an autonomous transaction, can pause and execute the autonomous transaction, and then continue from where it stopped. In other words, you leave the calling transaction's context, execute SQL statements that are part of the autonomous transaction, either commit or roll back your transaction, and resume the parent transaction upon returning to the calling transaction's context. Note that the autonomous transaction does not share transaction resources, such as locks, with the parent transaction.

Autonomous transactions provide developers with the ability to create more fine-grained transactions, where a transaction will not be an all-or-nothing affair. You can have the nested autonomous transactions commit or roll back their transactions independent of the calling parent transaction.

■Note If you don't use an autonomous transaction, all the changes in your session will be committed or rolled back at once (when you issue a COMMIT or ROLLBACK statement). The autonomous transactions give you the ability to commit or roll back the subprogram's changes independent of the main program. Also note that if you don't commit or roll back an autonomous transaction, Oracle will issue an error message.

Listing 8-7 provides a simple example of an autonomous transaction. Note that the PRAGMA AUTONOMOUS_TRANSACTION (a compiler directive) statement is instructing Oracle to mark the attached piece of code, the loans function, as autonomous.

Listing 8-7. *A Simple Autonomous Transaction*

```
SQL> CREATE OR REPLACE package lending AS function loans
     (user_id integer) return real;
     -- add additional functions and/or packages
     END lending;
     CREATE OR REPLACE PACKAGE BODY lending AS
     function loans (user_id integer) return REAL IS
     PRAGMA AUTONOMOUS_TRANSACTION;
     loan_bal REAL;
     BEGIN
       --the code goes here
     END;
     -- any additional functions and/or packages go here
     END lending;
SQL>
```

Autonomous transactions provide you with a lot of flexibility. You can suspend the main transaction, run the autonomous transaction, and resume the processing of the main transaction. The autonomous transaction's committed changes are visible to the main transaction, because the default isolation level in Oracle is read committed, meaning that a transaction will see all the committed data.

There can be many uses for autonomous transactions. For example, you can use the transactions to send error-logging messages. You can have a single procedure that will write error messages to an error log table and invoke this procedure as an autonomous transaction from a regular transaction. Listing 8-8 shows how to write error messages to a table.

Listing 8-8. *Writing Error Messages to a Table*

```
SQL> CREATE OR REPLACE PROCEDURE error_log(error__msg in varchar2,
     procedure_name IN VARCHAR2 IS
     PRAGMA AUTONOMOUS_TRANSACTION;
     BEGIN
     INSERT INTO log_table (error_msg, procedure_name)
     VALUES (error_msg,procedure_name));
     COMMIT;
```

```
      EXCEPTION
      WHEN OTHERS THEN ROLLBACK;
      END;
SQL>
```

Autonomous transactions can serve other purposes in the Oracle database. For example, they can enable the handling of nonstandard PL/SQL coding issues, such as using DDL statements in triggers. Autonomous transactions also are useful in performing an audit of database queries and failed (unauthorized) database activity.

Listing 8-9 shows an example in which the autonomous transaction feature is used to audit (presumably) unauthorized update activity. Even when a user is unsuccessful in the update attempt, the user's name can be successfully logged into an audit table if you code a simple pair of triggers that use the autonomous transaction feature.

Listing 8-9. *Using an Autonomous Transaction to Audit Database Activity*

```
SQL> CREATE OR REPLACE TRIGGER aud_bef_trig
      BEFORE INSERT ON emp FOR EACH ROW
      DECLARE
      PRAGMA AUTONOMOUS_TRANSACTION
      BEGIN
       INSERT INTO audit_employee VALUES (
       :new.username, 'before insert', sysdate);
       COMMIT;
      END;

SQL> CREATE OR REPLACE TRIGGER aud_aft_trig
      AFTER INSERT ON emp FOR EACH ROW
      DECLARE
      PRAGMA AUTONOMOUS TRANSACTION
      BEGIN
       INSERT INTO audit_emp VALUES (
       :new.username, 'after insert', sysdate);
       COMMIT;
      END;
SQL>
```

Note that you can't always just use a pair of normal triggers to audit database activity because auditing data provided by the triggers won't be recorded if the triggering statement is rolled back.

Resumable Space Allocation

Imagine you're running a very long batch job and it runs out of space for some reason, whether because of an unexpected amount of data or because of a failure to notice that the space was running out for the objects involved in the DML transactions. Or perhaps there was a "maximum number of extents reached" error. What are your options when this sort of thing happens (as it inevitably will)?

Most of the time, you must correct the space problem or other condition that caused the error in the first place, and then restart your transactions. More often than not, you will roll back the whole operation, which will take quite a bit of time. Sometimes you have to restart at the very beginning of the program, which is a waste of time. In any case, your actions as a DBA are limited to playing catchup after the fact to rectify the error and redo the operation. Oracle's Resumable Space Allocation feature will suspend database operations that run into problems due to lack of space, and it restarts those operations automatically when the space problems are fixed. The Resumable Space Allocation feature comes in handy when you're trying to ensure that key batch jobs or data loads run within the window of operation they are allotted when they encounter space-related issues.

■**Tip** To take full advantage of the Resumable Space Allocation feature, you should use locally managed tablespaces coupled with Automatic Undo Management.

You can explicitly make operations run in the Resumable Space Allocation mode by using the ALTER SESSION command. The Resumable Space Allocation feature will just suspend operations until the problem is fixed (such as by your adding a datafile to extend space) and it will resume automatically after that.

Resumable Operations

The following types of database operations are resumable:

- *Queries*: These operations can always be resumed after they run out of temporary sorting space.

- *DML operations*: Insert, update, and delete operations can be resumed after an error is issued.

- *DDL operations*: Index operations involving creating, rebuilding, and altering are resumable, as are CREATE TABLE AS SELECT operations and several other DDL operations.

- *Import and export operations*: SQL*Loader data load jobs that run out of space are resumable. You must use the RESUMABLE parameter when you specify the SQL*Loader job, to make the operation resumable. Two other resumable operation parameters, RESUMABLE_TIMEOUT and RESUMABLE_NAME, can be set only if you set the RESUMABLE parameter.

Common Resumable Errors

You can resume operations after fixing any of the following types of errors during the execution of any operation:

- *Out of space errors*: Typically, operations fail when you can't add extents to your tables or indexes because the tablespace is full. You need to add a datafile to your tablespace to enable the objects to throw a new extent and continue to grow. The typical error message is ORA-01653.

- *Maximum extents errors*: When a table or a rollback segment reaches the maximum extents specified, it can't grow any further, even if you have space in the tablespace. You end up with errors such as ORA-01628.

- *User's space quota errors*: If the user's quota on a tablespace is exceeded, your operations on that tablespace will come to a halt. The typical Oracle error is ORA-01536.

Using the Resumable Space Allocation Feature

To use the Resumable Space Allocation feature, a user must have the appropriate privileges:

```
SQL> GRANT RESUMABLE TO salapati;

Grant succeeded.
SQL>
```

When you wish to revoke the privilege, use the following command:

```
SQL> REVOKE RESUMABLE FROM salapati;

Revoke succeeded.
SQL>
```

You can enable a session for Resumable Space Allocation in one of two ways—set the resumable_timeout initialization parameter, or use the ALTER SESSION command to enable and disable resumable space allocation. The following sections discuss these methods.

Using the RESUMABLE_TIMEOUT Initialization Parameter

Using the RESUMABLE_TIMEOUT initialization parameter, you can enable the resumable space allocation features across the entire system. For example, to enable all database sessions for Resumable Space Allocation for a period of two hours, you'd set the parameter this way:

```
RESUMABLE_TIMEOUT=7200
```

You can change the RESUMABLE_TIMEOUT parameter dynamically using the ALTER SYSTEM command. You can also dynamically disable the feature by setting the parameter to 0.

Using the ALTER SESSION Statement

You can enable Resumable Space Allocation in your session simply by using the following statement, regardless of whether you've set the RESUMABLE_TIMEOUT initialization parameter:

```
SQL> ALTER SESSION ENABLE RESUMABLE;

Session altered.
SQL>
```

Similarly, you can disable the feature by using the ALTER SESSION ENABLE TIMEOUT statement.

Providing a Timeout Interval

You can also use the optional TIMEOUT clause with the ALTER SESSION ENABLE RESUMABLE statement to specify a time interval within which you need to fix the problem that caused the operation to be suspended. If you don't respond within the allotted time interval, the program will error out with the ORA-30032 error ("the statement has timed out"), and you can't resume it from where it stopped.

In the following example, the TIMEOUT parameter is set to 18,000 seconds (5 hours). The Oracle default timeout is set for 7,200 seconds. If you don't want to change the default timeout period, all you have to do is issue the simpler ALTER SESSION ENABLE RESUMABLE command.

```
SQL> ALTER SESSION ENABLE RESUMABLE TIMEOUT 18000;

Session altered.
SQL>
```

■**Note** By default, the Resumable Space Allocation feature is disabled for all sessions unless you've set the RESUMABLE_TIMEOUT initialization parameter to a nonzero value.

You can also set the timeout interval using the DBMS_RESUMABLE package, as follows:

```
SQL> EXECUTE DBMS_RESUMABLE.set_session_timeout(4349,18000);

PL/SQL procedure successfully completed.
SQL>
```

In the preceding example, the first number in the parentheses, 4349, is the SID of the session for which you want the timeout to be enforced. You can omit the SID if you're setting the timeout for the current session. The second number, 18000, is the timeout period.

Naming a Resumable Operation

You may sometimes want to name an operation to help track it later on. The NAME parameter is optional and has no real operational significance.

You can name any resumable operation in the following manner:

```
SQL> ALTER SESSION ENABLE RESUMABLE
    NAME 'resumable_test';

Session altered.
SQL>
```

■**Caution** If an operation is suspended, any locks that are held by Oracle on various database objects will *not* be released automatically. The locks and other resources will be released only after the transaction either completes successfully upon resumption or ends and throws an exception.

A Resumable Operation Example

Let's look at a simple example of the Resumable Space Allocation feature.

First, the alert log showed the following message, indicating that a DML statement was suspended because the undo tablespace ran out of space. Instead of erroring out immediately, the statement is merely suspended.

```
Fri Aug 1 11:15:00 2008
statement in resumable session 'User PASOWNER(11), Session 173, Instance 1' was
suspended due to
    ORA-30036: unable to extend segment by 8 in undo tablespace 'UNDOTBS_01'
```

Once the problem was corrected by adding space to the undo tablespace (UNDOTBS_01), the alert log showed the following message, indicating that the suspended statement was resumed after the problem was cleared:

```
Fri Aug 1 11:21:52 2008
statement in resumable session 'User PASOWNER(11), Session 173, Instance 1' was
resumed
```

If space wasn't added to the undo tablespace within the timeout interval, the suspended statement would be aborted. The following entry from the alert log shows that situation:

```
Fri Aug 1 10:29:34 2008
Errors in file /a03/app/oracle/admin/pasx/bdump/pasx_smon_7091.trc:
ORA-30036: unable to extend segment by 8 in undo tablespace 'UNDOTBS_01'
Fri Aug 1 10:33:07 2008
statement in resumable session 'User PASOWNER(11), Session 184, Instance 1' was
aborted
```

Notification of Suspended Operations

Upon suspending an operation for a space-related problem, Oracle will automatically generate an AFTER SUSPEND system event. If you want automatic notification, you can write a trigger that will be set off by this event, as shown here:

```
SQL> CREATE OR REPLACE TRIGGER page_dba
     AFTER SUSPEND ON DATABASE
     DECLARE
     PRAGMA AUTONOMOUS_TRANSACTION;
     BEGIN
     /* Code here that'll page the DBA */
     COMMIT;
     END;
Trigger created.
SQL>
```

Note that the trigger must always be declared as an autonomous transaction.

Operation-Suspended Alert

When Oracle suspends a resumable session, it automatically issues an *operation-suspended alert* through the automatic Server Generated Alerts feature. Once you fix the problem by allocating the necessary resources and the operation completes, Oracle will automatically clear this alert.

Monitoring Resumable Space Allocation

You can monitor resumable operations by using the DBA_RESUMABLE view. This view provides the name of the operation, the user's SID, the start time of the statement, the error message encountered, the suspend and resume times, and the text and current status of the SQL statements. The V$SESSION_WAIT view also provides information about suspended resumable statements. The EVENT column of this view shows you that a statement is suspended, pending the clearance of a "wait error."

The DBMS_RESUMABLE package contains procedures to help you manage suspended sessions. The SET_SESSION_TIMEOUT procedure, for example, allows you to specify the time a suspended session will wait before failing.

Managing Long Transactions

Suppose you're running transactions in your database that are extremely long—maybe even as long as a whole day. Oracle primarily uses locks to ensure concurrency and atomicity, but locks on a long-running transaction can reduce concurrency dramatically because other users are forced to wait for the long-running transaction to complete.

Fortunately, Oracle provides the Workspace Manager, a feature you can use to version-enable tables, so different users can maintain different versions of the data. During long-running transactions, changes can be made to the same table in different workspaces, and these versions are finally reconciled and the results are stored permanently in the original table. You can think of a *workspace* as a virtual environment shared by several users making changes to the same data.

In addition to facilitating long transactions, the Workspace Manager enables you to create multiple data scenarios for what-if analyses. It can also help you track the history of all the changes to a set of tables. The feature is especially useful in collaborative projects because it allows teams to share content.

The Workspace Manager enables simultaneous read and write access to production data during long transactions. It uses multiple versioning of tables to enable the simultaneous reading and writing of data. Consistency is guaranteed because the final, permanent version of the table will not have any conflicts within the data. All the users see is their own virtual version of the database—that is, different versions of the rows in the same tables. But the versions each user sees from his or her workspace are guaranteed to be transactionally consistent; the user's versions will have the original data the user started with, plus all the changes he or she made to the original data.

Benefits of Using the Workspace Manager

Among other things, the Workspace Manager enables you to try out various scenarios with your data (such as the effects of different marketing campaigns) before you finally settle on one acceptable version that you can make permanent by merging all the virtual versions of the table data. Merging, in effect, incorporates the child workspace data with the original (parent workspace) data. If, after analysis, you decide to nullify all the child workspace's data, you can do so by rolling it back, just like you would roll back a transaction under normal circumstances.

Note Although the Workspace Manager provides you with the capability to create multiple versions of one table, or even of all the tables in your database, it doesn't impose a severe storage cost because only the changed rows in each workspace are versioned, and these new versions are saved in the original table (and in the original tablespace). In other words, you don't need to make any special storage allocations for the database tables that belong to different versions.

The Workspace Manager offers the following features:

- You can maintain multiple versions of data, which you can keep or discard as necessary.

- Multiple users can simultaneously access and modify the same data.

- The updates made by several users over time are isolated in workspaces until they're merged into the production database.

- Conflicts between multiple versions are resolved automatically by the Workspace Manager.

Table Versioning and Workspaces

The concepts of *table versioning* and *workspaces* are the foundation of the Workspace Manager feature. Table versioning enables you to have different sets of rows sharing the same table name. The amazing thing about table versioning is that users can continue to change data through DML operations on a day-to-day basis. The Workspace Manager maintains the structure of the versioned tables using views based on the original production table. This ability to version-enable even production tables makes the Workspace Manager very powerful in performing what-if analyses.

You can use the WM$VERSIONED_TABLES and WM$VERSION_TABLE tables to find out details about the versioned tables. The WMSYS schema owns both of these tables, so first make sure that you have the WMSYS schema in your database.

Workspaces enable users to make changes to versions of a table, and the workspaces isolate the versioned tables until they're finally discarded or merged with the original table. This ability of the workspaces to save the versioned tables means that access to the original tables isn't impeded. You can assign each workspace to one or several users, and they can see a consistent view of the database, including the rows in their versions of the tables in the workspace, plus all the other tables at the time the workspaces were either created or refreshed, whichever is later.

Note that when versioned tables are created in a database, the original table is renamed *tableName*_LT. Oracle also creates a new table called *tableName*_AUX and a view with an identical name as the original table. When users log in, they are placed, by default, in the LIVE workspace. All other workspaces that exist in the database are children of the LIVE workspace. Whenever you refresh your workspace, you can see the latest changes made in the parent workspace, which also includes any changes merged from other child workspaces. The merging of a workspace with the parent LIVE tablespace makes the changes in the child workspace public. The MERGE statement follows the resolution of any conflicts.

The Workspace Manager feature is provided with the Oracle software, but it won't be automatically installed in a database that you create manually. If you use the DBCA to create a new database, and you let Oracle create a seed database as part of the Oracle software installation, the Workspace Manager feature is automatically installed.

An easy way to find out whether the Workspace Manager is already installed is to look for the WMSYS user using the DBA_USERS view, since WMSYS owns the Workspace Manager tables. If that user is already there, you can go ahead and use the feature. Otherwise you'll need to install the Oracle Workspace Manager in your database.

The easiest way to use the Workspace Manager is by accessing it through OEM. OEM lets you create and manage workspaces, as well as enable and disable table versioning.

PART 3

■■■

Installing Oracle Database 11*g*, Upgrading, and Creating Databases

CHAPTER 9

■ ■ ■

Installing and Upgrading to Oracle Database 11*g*

This chapter will give you a good understanding of the procedure for correctly installing the Oracle Database 11*g* server software, and it includes an example of an installation of Oracle Database 11*g* on a server using the Red Hat Enterprise Linux WS 3 operating system.

There are some variations in the installation procedure for the different flavors of UNIX, such as Sun's Solaris, Hewlett Packard's HP-UX, IBM's AIX, and so on, but the steps are essentially the same. Several steps need to be performed before and after the installation of the Oracle software, both by you and the Linux/UNIX system administrator, and this chapter explains those steps. The software must be installed according to a sensible plan, and this chapter shows you how to install Oracle by following the well-known Optimal Flexible Architecture (OFA) guidelines.

Note that you'll be going through the main features of a generic Oracle installation in this chapter. It's important that you have access to the Oracle installation manuals for your specific operating system before you begin installing the Oracle Database 11*g* software. The installation manuals are all available on the Oracle Technology Network (OTN) web site.

Of course, if you're configuring Oracle Real Application Clusters (RAC) or some such advanced architecture, you'll need more time to finish the installation. Complex as the Oracle database server software is, the actual time you need to install the software is trivial compared to the time you need to spend to ensure that all the preinstallation steps have been completed correctly. If you follow all the recommended steps, the installation process should work the first time around.

Installing Oracle

When it comes to the mechanics of the process, installing the Oracle server software is really a simple affair. Installing all the software will probably not take you more than a couple of hours. All the real effort goes into the proper planning of such things as the physical space and memory allocation, and the operating system configuration you need for your Oracle databases to function optimally.

■Note Installing the Oracle client is a much simpler task. When you invoke the Oracle installer, simply choose the client installation option instead of the server installation option.

I'm assuming that you, or your organization, have bought the necessary software from Oracle Corporation. If that's the case, the software CDs will have been sent to you by Oracle. If you just want to try the Oracle database software, however, you don't have to purchase a thing. You can download the Oracle server software freely from the OTN web site at `http://technet.oracle.com/`. The OTN site has complete enterprise versions of the server software for all UNIX, Linux, and Windows servers. In addition, you can check out the operating system installation and administration manuals at `http://tahiti.oracle.com`.

Reviewing the Documentation

You can save yourself a lot of grief during the installation process by carefully reviewing the Oracle installation manuals for your particular operating system. These manuals are very clear and provide you with a detailed map of the installation process. You'll need to review three sets of installation documents:

- *Oracle Installation Guide for your operating system*: This document will provide you with information about the system requirements, UNIX users and groups, and other require-ments, and it will step you through the installation and post-installation processes.

- *Release Notes and Release Notes Addendums*: The Release Notes and any related Addendums are very important, and they cover the most recent changes to the installation and upgrade procedures for many components of the Oracle database server and client. The last-minute changes that are covered in the Release Notes (and related Addendums) may make the differ-ence between a successful installation of the various components and an error-prone installation.

- *README files*: The README files are usually in the \doc\readmes directory on the first product CD-ROM.

The Release Notes and the README files inform you about any potential restrictions, limita-tions concerning the installation, and the use of new Oracle Database 11g software.

■**Note** The Installation Guide and the Release Notes are available at the OTN site (`http://technet.oracle.com/`), or you can access them by going to `http://docs.oracle.com/` or `http://tahiti.oracle.com/`.

Determining Disk and Memory Requirements

You should focus on two key operating system resources when you are planning a new Oracle instal-lation: disk storage and the amount of memory (RAM) that your systems need on the server machine.

The amount of total physical space (disk storage) will depend on the size of your applications and data. The Oracle software itself takes approximately 1.5–2 gigabytes of disk space, depending on the operating system. You also have to run one or more databases with this software, so the total space you need will depend on the requirements for all the databases considered together. You need to determine the sizes of the tables and indexes and the number of stored procedures you will have in the database. You also need to find out as much as you can about the growth expectations for your data over time. If you have a database that you anticipate will grow quickly, you need to make allow-ances for that. Plan ahead, because disk space is something that needs to be budgeted for, and you may find yourself scrambling for space if you are way off the mark.

■**Tip** For larger databases, the size of the tables and indexes will be the predominant component of total database size. Fortunately, you can easily find out your database's size by using database-sizing spreadsheets. One such sizing spreadsheet is available from Blue Hills Technology Corporation at `http://bhtech.com/`. Although the spreadsheet is for an older version of Oracle, the idea behind it remains the same, and you can derive meaningful estimates of the size of your tables and indexes using this spreadsheet.

The total amount of memory that you need will depend on the size and nature of your applications. Oracle does provide a rule of thumb for memory requirements, and you can follow this rule when you are in the initial stages of planning your system. Later on, you can adjust these initial estimates.

The minimum requirement that Oracle imposes for memory is 256MB, but this is not enough for serious applications. Depending on your application's size and the number of users, your memory requirements may run to several gigabytes of RAM. In addition, Oracle requires that you allocate swap space that is about two to three times your Oracle RAM allocation. The requirements of the applications that your system will be running will determine the total memory you need. At the very least, your system shouldn't be memory-bound, because inadequate memory leads to excessive swapping and paging, and your system could slow to a crawl. In Chapter 20, you'll learn how to monitor memory usage and determine when you may need to increase it.

Optimal Flexible Architecture

Although the Oracle database server software and the databases managed by the server will function even if they're installed on a single disk or a set of disks without any organization, as such, you'll lose performance and endanger the safety of the databases if you don't follow a well-thought-out strategy regarding disk allocation. Oracle strongly recommends a disk layout methodology formally called the *Optimal Flexible Architecture* for efficiency as well as many other reasons.

Before you start any installation of the Oracle software itself, it is absolutely necessary for you to be familiar with the OFA recommendations regarding proper disk layout. The OFA is a set of recommendations from Oracle Corporation aimed at simplifying management of complex software and databases often running under multiple versions of software. The OFA essentially imposes a standardized way of naming the different physical components of Oracle and places them on the file system according to a logical plan.

■Note The OFA guidelines were formulated at Oracle in 1990 in an internal paper by Cary Millsap. Millsap revised them in 1995 and published them under the title "OFA Standard: Oracle for Open Systems." You can find this paper and many other excellent white papers at `http://www.hotsos.com/`.

The OFA guidelines are only Oracle's recommendations, and you do not have to follow them in their entirety, but OFA was designed to minimize disk contention, to provide for operating more than one database without administrative confusion, and to improve database performance. Laying out the UNIX directories according to the OFA guidelines leads to a clear and efficient distribution of Oracle's various files, even with several databases simultaneously running under different Oracle versions. You can consider the OFA guidelines a set of best practices regarding two important issues—disk layout and naming conventions—based on extensive field experience by Oracle professionals. Although originally intended only for internal Oracle use, the OFA is now the standard by which all Oracle installations should be measured.

If you've ever walked into an organization and taken over a database installation that had files stored all over the place, you'll immediately recognize the benefits of the OFA. If the previous DBA has adhered to the OFA guidelines, any new hire can easily go to the standard directories and look for various types of information. If your database is growing and needs more space, following the OFA guidelines will ensure that space will be added in the right directories with the standard naming convention. The standardization of directory and file placement leads to minimal administrative overhead and helps create more efficient databases. When you separate categories of files into independent UNIX subdirectories, files in one category are minimally affected by operations on files in other categories.

The usefulness of the OFA guidelines becomes particularly clear when you are trying to manage multiple databases on the same server. You can simplify administration by using the structured OMF system for maintaining your files. Creating new databases won't pose any problems, because each database is separated into its own directories, simplifying user administration and the creation of new databases. The OFA guidelines contribute to database reliability, because your hard drive failures won't propagate to whole applications—they help in balancing the load efficiently across the disk drives, thereby enhancing performance and minimizing contention. The OFA guidelines also promote the efficient separation of administrative files from several databases by using standard naming conventions. Another big benefit in using the OFA guidelines is that they enable you to simultaneously run multiple versions of Oracle software. You thus can run your production and test databases using different versions of Oracle on the same server.

Before plunging into a detailed discussion of the OFA concepts and the implementation details, you should be familiar with the following terms:

Mount points: These are directories in the UNIX file system that are used to access mounted file systems.

Product files: These are the many sets of configuration and binary executable files that come with the Oracle software.

Versions: These can refer to entirely different releases or to point upgrades (patch upgrades). For example, 9.2.0.1.0 and 10.1.0.2.0 are different versions of the server software.

Oracle datafiles: These are the UNIX files that hold Oracle table and index data.

Oracle administrative files: These include the database log files, error logs, and so forth.

Tablespaces: These refer to the logical allocation of space within Oracle and are discussed in detail in Chapter 6.

■**Tip** If you are using NFS file systems, you should know that these can't guarantee that writes always complete successfully, leaving open the possibility of file corruption. Unless your storage vendor is listed in the Oracle Storage Compatibility Program (OSCP) member list, don't install the software on NFS file systems.

Mount Points

Mount points are the directory names under which file systems are mounted by the UNIX operating system. That is, the mount point refers to the top-level directory of a file system. Oracle recommends that all your Oracle mount points be named according to the convention /*pm*, where *p* is a string constant to distinguish itself from other mount points and *m* is a two-digit number. This means you can name your mount points /u01, /u02, /u03, and so on. Keep the mount point names simple, and don't include any hardware-related information in the mount point name. That way, changing your disk system hardware will not affect the mount point names.

Oracle recommends that you have four mount points to fully comply with the OFA guidelines. The first of these is for locating the Oracle Database 11*g* server binaries, and the other three are for holding the database files. Let's say you're creating mount points for a database named prod. In this case, the three mount points designated for the datafiles can be clearly named as follows: /u01/oradata/prod, /u02/oradata/prod, and /u03/oradata/prod. This nomenclature makes it clear that these file systems are meant for Oracle databases and that the data for different databases is stored on separate mount points.

Directory and File-Naming Conventions

In Linux and UNIX systems, a home directory is the directory that a user lands in when he or she first logs in. All home directories should follow the naming convention /*pm*/*h*/*u*, where *pm* is the mount point name, *h* is a standard directory name, and *u* refers to the directory owner. For example, the /u01/app/oracle directory could be the home directory for the user named oracle. Note that the entire home directory for each user (e.g., /u01/app/oracle) is denoted by the letter *h* for the purposes of the following discussion.

Directory Structure

During the installation, you'll be prompted for the path for several key Oracle directories, and I'll briefly discuss these in this section. You can use any directory structure you wish for these directories, but, as you'll see, following the standard directory structures recommended here makes it easy to administer multiple databases and software versions on the same server.

Oracle Base

At the root of the Oracle directory structure is the directory called Oracle base, denoted by the environmental variable ORACLE_BASE. The Oracle base directory is the top directory for all Oracle software installations. As mentioned previously, Oracle recommends that you use the form */pm/h/u*.

The default owner of the Oracle base directory is usually a user named oracle, and the standard directory is usually named app. Therefore, the Oracle base directory usually has the form of */pm/app/oracle* (for example, /u01/app/oracle).

The Oracle installer will take this as the default Oracle base and install all the software under this base directory. You can create the Oracle base directory by using the following commands (assuming that u01 is your mount point and user oracle is the Oracle software owner):

```
# mkdir -p /u01/app/oracle
# chown -R oracle:oinstall /u01/app/oracle
# chmod -R 775 /u01/app/oracle
```

Oracle Home

The Oracle home directory, denoted by the ORACLE_HOME environment variable, is very important, since the Oracle server software executable files and other configuration files are located under this directory. For example, the $ORACLE_HOME/bin directory holds the executables for the Oracle products, and the $ORACLE_HOME/network directory holds the Oracle Net Services files.

In Oracle Database 11*g*, the OFA-recommended Oracle home directory path has changed. In order to comply with the OFA requirement of enabling the simultaneous running of multiple versions of Oracle software, you need to install Oracle software in a directory with the following path: */pm/h/u*/product/*v*/type_[*n*], where the new variables have the following meanings:

v: The version of the software

type: The type of installation, such as database (db), client (client), or companion (companion)

n: An optional counter, which enables you to install the same product multiple times under the same Oracle base directory

In the preceding syntax for the Oracle home, the first part, */pm/h/u*, is nothing but the Oracle base directory. Thus the Oracle home directory is always located underneath the Oracle base directory, and it can also be specified as $ORACLE_BASE/product/*v*/type_[*n*].

Using the preceding OFA-based Oracle home path, you can install different products—the server and the client with the same release number (Oracle 11.1.0)—in the same Oracle base directory.

■**Note** The formal name for the Oracle database server version in this book is Oracle Database 11*g* Release 2. However, you'll occasionally see references to 11.1, 11.1.0, or Oracle 11.1, all of which are alternative names for the same software.

```
/u01/app/oracle/product/11.1.0/db_1
/u01/app/oracle/product/11.1.0/client_1
```

The db_1 and client_1 at the end,of the paths indicate that these are the Oracle home directories for the *first installation* of the Oracle database and the Oracle client software, respectively.

Oracle supports multiple Oracle homes, but you can't install products from one release of Oracle into an Oracle home directory of a different release. You must install the Oracle Database 10.2 software into a new Oracle home directory. For example, you can't install Release 10.2 software into an existing Oracle9*i* Oracle home directory. You can install this release more than once on the same system, however, as long as you choose a separate Oracle home directory for each release. It's also okay to install the same product multiple times in the Oracle home directory, as shown here:

```
/u01/app/oracle/product/11.1.0/db_1
/u01/app/oracle/product/11.1.0/db_2
```

Once you finish your Oracle software installation, set your ORACLE_HOME environment variable to specify your Oracle home directory.

When you install the Oracle Database 11*g* software, the Oracle Universal Installer prompts you to provide the Oracle base location. Oracle recommends that you share the Oracle base for all Oracle homes that you create on a server. Although the installer will derive the default Oracle home location from the Oracle base location you provide during the installation, you can change this default location.

In the current version, the ORACLE_BASE environment variable is only recommended, but Oracle intends to make it a mandatory variable in future releases. Oracle recommends that you create the flash recovery area and the datafiles under the Oracle base location.

Flash Recovery Area and Datafile Location

The Oracle base is your starting point for the default locations of all datafiles and the flash recovery area. Oracle recommends that you place the Oracle home, the Oracle datafiles, and the flash recovery area on separate mount points, as shown in the following example:

```
$ORACLE_BASE/flash_recovery_area
$ORACLE_BASE/oradata
$ORACLE_BASE/product/11.1.0/db_1
```

Of course, in an Oracle RAC installation, you share the flash recovery area and the datafiles among the different nodes of the RAC.

Automatic Diagnostic Repository

In Oracle Database 11*g*, all diagnostic data is consolidated into the new Automatic Diagnostic Repository (ADR). The database stores the ADR under the ADR base directory. The new initialization parameter DIAGNOSTIC_DEST sets the default location of the ADR base directory. The following is how the database determines the value of the DIAGNOSTIC_DEST parameter, if you don't explicitly set the parameter.

- If you set the ORACLE_BASE environment variable, the default value of the DIAGNOSTIC_DEST parameter is the same as the value of the ORACLE_BASE variable.

- If you haven't set the ORACLE_BASE environment variable, the default value of the DIAGNOSTIC_DEST parameter is set to $ORACLE_HOME/log.

Oracle Inventory Directory

Oracle uses a special directory called the Oracle Inventory directory, also known as OraInventory, to store an inventory of all the Oracle software on a server. Multiple Oracle installations can share the same Oracle Inventory directory. You need to specify the path for this directory only the first time you install an Oracle product on a server. The usual format of this directory is as follows:

```
$ORACLE_BASE/ora_inventory
```

For example, if `/u01/app/oracle` is your `ORACLE_BASE` directory location, then the Oracle Inventory directory will be

```
/u01/app/oracle/ora_inventory
```

The first time you install Oracle software, the installer prompts for the OraInventory directory path, and creates the directory itself.

Administrative Files

Every Oracle database has several administrative files associated with it. Among these files are configuration files, core dump files, trace files, export files, and other related log files. You need to store these files under separate directories for ease of maintenance. Assuming you have about ten or so of these directories for each database, you can see why it's imperative that you have a simple means of organizing them. Oracle recommends the following directory structure for clarity: /h/admin/d/a, where h is the Oracle base directory (e.g., /u01/app/oracle), admin indicates that this directory holds administration-related files, d refers to the specific database, and a refers to the subdirectories for each specific type of administrative files. For example, the /u01/app/oracle/admin/prod1/bdump directory will contain all background process trace files as well as the all-important alert log files for the prod1 database.

Table 9-1 lists some of the standard administrative directories that you'll need in most cases. Of course, you may add to the recommended list or modify it to fit your circumstances.

Table 9-1. *Typical Administrative Directories*

Directory	Contents
adhoc	Contains ad hoc SQL files
arch	Contains archived redo log files
create	Contains SQL scripts that you can use for creating your databases
dpdump	Contains the Data Pump Export files
pfile	Contains instance parameter files (such as init.ora)

Product Files

The whole idea behind properly naming and placing the product files is to be able to implement multiple versions of the Oracle server software simultaneously. This is necessary because when you migrate between versions, it is normal to retain the older software versions until you switch over to the new version. Different applications on the system may have different timeframes within which they want to migrate to the new version. Consequently, in most cases, you'll end up having to support multiple versions of the Oracle server software simultaneously.

Oracle recommends that you keep each version of the software in a separate directory distinguished by the naming convention /h/product/v, where h is the home directory, product indicates that the software versions are under this directory, and v is the version of the product. For example, I have a directory on my system called /u01/app/oracle/product/10.1.0.2.0 under which I save all the Oracle server software subdirectories during installation. If I decide to install the 10.2.0 version, I'll do so under the directory /u01/app/oracle/product/10.2.0. You can see that this type of naming convention makes it very easy to install and manage multiple versions of the Oracle software.

Installing on a Multihomed Computer

A server with multiple IP addresses is called a *multihomed* computer. A multihomed computer uses multiple network cards, with each IP address linked to a distinct host name or an alias.

By default the installer identifies the host name on a multihomed computer by using the `ORACLE_HOSTNAME` environment variable. You can set the `ORACLE_HOSTNAME` environment variable in the following way.

```
Bourne, Bash, or Korn shell:
$ ORACLE_HOSTNAME=myhost.us.example.com
$ export ORACLE_HOSTNAME

C shell:
% setenv ORACLE_HOSTNAME myhost.us.example.com
```

In the previous examples, the fully qualified host name is `myhost.us.example.com`. If you haven't set the `ORACLE_HOSTNAME` environment variable and the server has multiple network cards, the installer finds the host name by looking up the first entry in the `/etc/hosts` file. All clients must be able to access the server by utilizing this host name or an alias for it.

Database Files

The administrative and product files are generic files. Oracle databases contain another set of key files called *database files*. These include the datafiles that contain the table and index data and certain operational files called *control files* and *redo log files*. Control files are crucial to the operation of the database, and redo log files hold information necessary to recover the database during an instance crash and similar situations.

The OFA recommendation for control and redo log files is to follow the naming conventions `/pm/q/d/control`n`.ctl` and `/pm/q/d/redo`n`.log`, respectively. In this notation, *pm* is the mount point; *q* is an indicator, such as `oradata`, denoting that the files contain Oracle-related data; *d* is the database name (provided by the `DB_NAME` initialization parameter, which is the same as the SID for the database); and *n* is a two-digit number.

Since Oracle recommends that you have multiple control files and duplexed online redo log files, it's common to see the following naming structure for redo log files and control files:

```
/u01/oradata/prod1/control01.ctl
/u05/oradata/prod1/control02.ctl
/u02/oradata/prod1/redo01.log
/u04/oradata/prod1/redo02.log
```

Oracle recommends that all tablespaces be named with no more than eight characters, with the format *tn*, where *t* is a descriptive name for the tablespace and *n* is a two-digit number. For datafiles, the recommended notation is `/pm/q/d/tn.dbf`, where *pm* is the mount point; *q* is an indicator, usually `oradata`; *d* is the database name; *t* is the descriptive name for the tablespace that contains this datafile; and *n* is a two-digit number. Thus, a typical datafile under the OFA guidelines would have a name like `/u20/oradata/prod/system01.dbf`, which refers to a datafile in the System tablespace.

OFA file-naming conventions are designed to achieve the following goals:

- Show which tablespace a datafile belongs to.
- Distinguish database files from other files on the system.
- Distinguish between database files belonging to various databases.
- Identify control files, redo log files, and datafiles easily.

Table 9-2 clearly shows how an OFA-compliant database enables you to easily manage files belonging to several database versions. The example also shows two Oracle home directories, one for Oracle 9.2 and the other for Oracle 10.2. There are a total of four mount points. The Oracle software is on mount point /u01, and the database files are distributed across three mount points: /u02, /u03, and /u04.

Table 9-2. *Directory Structure for an OFA-Compliant Oracle Database*

Directory Format	Description
/	Root directory
/u01	User data mount point 1
/u01/app/	Subdirectory for application software
/u01/app/oracle/	Oracle base directory
/u01/app/oracle/admin	Directory for the Oracle administrative files
/u01/app/oracle/admin/ nina/	Admin subdirectory for the nina database
/u01/app/oracle/ flash_recovery_area/	Subdirectory for recovery files
/u01/app/oracle/ flash_recovery_area/nina	Recovery files for the nina database
/u01/app/oracle/product/	Distribution files
/u01/app/oracle/product/ 10.2.0	Oracle home directory for Oracle Database 10g Release 2 (10.2.0)
/u01/app/oracle/product/ 11.1/db_1	Oracle home directory for Oracle Database 11g Release 1 (11.1.0)
/u02	User data mount point 2
/u02/oradata/	Subdirectory for Oracle data
/u02/oradata/nina/	Subdirectory for database files for the nina database
/u03	User data mount point 3
/u03/oradata/	Subdirectory for Oracle data
/u03/oradata/nina/	Subdirectory for database files for the nina database
/u04	User data mount point 4
/u04/oradata/	Subdirectory for Oracle data
/u04/oradata/nina/	Subdirectory for database files for the nina database

Creating Directories for Oracle Database Files

Although our concern in this chapter is with installing Oracle server software, the storage space necessary for database files (which includes the files for tables and indexes, as well as the files for the redo logs and the undo tablespace and so on) will, in most cases, dwarf the space needed for the installation files.

Although nothing prevents you from placing all your database files on one storage device, Oracle recommends that you use a logical volume spread over several disks or use a RAID system. Oracle further recommends that you use the SAME (stripe-and-mirror-everything) technique. For each of the mount points you select for your database files, you need to issue the following commands as root in order to set the owner, group, and permissions:

```
# mkdir /mount_point/oradata
# chown oracle:oinstall /mount_point/oradata
# chmod 775  /mount_point/oradata
```

Using the preceding command structure, you can create as many subdirectories for your data-files as necessary; for example, /u10/oradata, /u11/oradata, and so on.

Creating the Flash Recovery Area

The flash recovery area is a disk area set apart for storing all the recovery-related files. It's a good idea to create it on entirely different storage devices from where you have your datafiles. You also need to set another parameter, DB_RECOVERY_FILE_DEST, to indicate the location of the flash recovery area. You can set the physical size of the flash recovery area by using the DB_RECOVERY_FILE_DEST_SIZE initialization parameter.

Here is how you create the flash recovery area directory:

```
# mkdir /mount_point/flash_recovery_area
# chown oracle:oinstall /mount_point/flash_recovery_area
# chmod 775 /mount_point/flash_recovery_area
```

For example, you can designate /u20/flash_recovery_area as your flash recovery area, and set the DB_RECOVERY_FILE_DEST_SIZE parameter to 5GB.

Performing Preinstallation Tasks

The installation of the Oracle software, as I mentioned earlier, is a straightforward exercise. You do the bulk of your work *before* the installation of the software. Your crucial partner in this process is the Linux/UNIX system administrator.

To estimate the total disk space you need, you have to add the space required for the Oracle Database 11*g* installation to the total space you expect the database files to consume. For example, for an Oracle Database 11*g* installation on the HP UNIX system, Oracle recommends that you allocate around 2GB of space for your software. You must add this 2GB to whatever space estimates you've come up with for your database files in the previous section.

You can also estimate memory requirements by following some basic guidelines. Most small OLTP systems require about 500MB of RAM, medium installations require about 1GB, and larger installations require more RAM. A more important issue at software installation time is that you allocate enough swap space for your system.

■**Note** The Oracle Universal Installer, which comes with the software distribution, will let you install a seed database. This might be a good idea if you are a complete beginner. If you already have some experience, you're better off configuring your own customized database.

Checking the Preinstallation Requirements

The preinstallation tasks depend on your operating system, but the steps are similar. In this discussion, I show you how to install the Oracle software on a Red Hat 3.0 WS Linux operating system. You will need to consult your specific documentation from Oracle for the exact installation procedures for your operating system.

The installation process for Oracle Database 11*g* is much more automated than were previous versions. The installation process automatically checks the following prerequisites:

- *Platform version*: The installation process checks to make sure the operating system is appropriate for the Oracle installation. If you were using an HP-UX system, for example, you would need to have at least the HP-UX-11.11 operating system version. In this chapter, since we're using a Linux-based server for the Oracle installation, we can use one of the following Linux distributions, which are certified for Oracle Database 11g:
  - Oracle Enterprise Linux 4.0
  - Oracle Enterprise Linux 5.0
  - Red Hat Enterprise Linux 4.0
  - Red Hat Enterprise Linux 5.0
  - SUSE Linux Enterprise Server 10.0
- *Operating system patches*: The installation process checks to ensure that you've applied the latest operating system patches.
- *Kernel parameters*: The installation process verifies that your OS kernel settings are adequate. It also verifies that you have installed the necessary OS system packages.
- *Space*: The installation process checks to ensure that you have the minimum amount of temporary space in your /tmp directory before starting the installation. It also checks for adequate swap space.
- ORACLE_HOME *directory*: The installation process checks that you have either a non-empty Oracle home directory or one that qualifies for the installation because it contains a release on top of which Oracle Database 11g can be installed.

Note If you aren't sure whether your operating system is certified for a certain Oracle release, you can check the latest Oracle product and platform certification matrices on the Oracle web site: http://www.oracle.com/technology/support/metalink/content.html.

Although it's true that the Oracle installer software checks to ensure that all the prerequisites are satisfied, you shouldn't wait until installation time to find out. You must diligently check each necessary component, to make sure your installation will be a smooth process, instead of erroring out several times. You can divide the checking of the prerequisites into tasks that fall into the domain of the UNIX or Linux (or Windows) system administrator and those that are the responsibility of the Oracle DBA.

Oracle Products Installed with the 11.1 Release

The following products are installed by default when you install the 11.1 release database server.

- *Oracle Application Express*: Tool for developing and deploying web applications
- *Oracle Warehouse Builder*: Tool to design, deploy, and manage business intelligence systems
- *Oracle Configuration Manager*: Tool that collects and uploads configuration information to the Oracle configuration repository
- *Oracle SQL Developer*: Graphical version of SQL*Plus
- *Oracle Database Vault*: Tool that enables you to secure business data

System Administrator's Preinstallation Tasks

The UNIX/Linux system administrator needs to perform several steps before you can install your Oracle software. First, the system administrator should make sure that the latest operating system patch sets are applied, per Oracle's installation recommendations. The other important tasks are creating separate mount points for the Oracle software, reconfiguring the kernel (if necessary), creating the necessary users and groups on the UNIX/Linux server, and making sure that the Oracle users have the right file and directory permissions.

All these system administrator tasks are covered in some detail in the following sections. The tasks are discussed in general, but the examples are all based on an actual installation on a Red Hat Linux 3 system.

Verifying Operating System Software

The system administrator must check several things regarding the compatibility of the operating system software for the Oracle installation, such as checking the OS and kernel versions and making sure necessary packages are present and patches applied.

Checking Operating System Version

The system administrator must also make sure that the server on which you're installing Oracle is using the correct operating system version for Oracle Database 11g. On a Linux system, for example, the operating system must be one of the following for installing Oracle Database Release 1 for Linux x86 and Linux x86-64.

- Asianux 2.0
- Asianux 3.0
- Oracle Enterprise Linux 4.0
- Oracle Enterprise Linux 5.0
- Red Hat Enterprise Linux 4.0
- Red Hat Enterprise Linux 5.0
- SUSE Linux Enterprise Server 10.0

The correct version of Linux must be installed on a platform certified for it. To find out what OS version is installed on a UNIX or Linux server, use the following command:

```
# cat /etc/issue
Red Hat  Enterprise Linux WS Release 3  (Taroon Update 4)
Kernel \r on an \m
```

Checking Kernel Version

Once the system administrator has ensured that one of the approved operating system versions is indeed being used, the next step is to check to ensure that the OS is using the correct kernel version. The Oracle Universal Installer performs checks on your system to verify that it meets the requirements. If you don't have the necessary OS version, the installation will fail, however, so it is a good idea to verify the requirements before you start the Oracle Universal Installer.

Following are the kernel requirements for Oracle Database 11g Release 1:

- *For Asianux 2.0, Oracle Enterprise Linux 4.0, and Red Hat Enterprise Linux 4.0*: 2.6.9
- *For Asianux 3.0, Oracle Enterprise Linux 5.0, and Red Hat Enterprise Linux 5.0*: 2.6.18
- *For SUSE Linux Enterprise Server 10*: 2.6.16.21

On my Red Hat Linux Enterprise Linux 4.0 system, the kernel version must be at least at the 2.4.21-27 EL level. The system administrator can verify the kernel version by using the following command:

```
# uname -r
2.6.9-55.0.0.0.2.EL
```

The uname command shows that the kernel version is 2.6.9 and the errata level is 55.0.0.0.2.EL.

In this case, the kernel version is exactly what is required. If it turns out that you need kernel updates or a newer OS version, the system administrator will have to download the updates and install them, in most cases. Alternatively, you can use the command /cat /proc/version to find out your kernel version.

Checking for Required Packages

The installation process also requires that certain operating system packages be installed. For example, my Linux 3 OS must have the following packages:

```
make-3.79.1
gcc-3.2.3-34
glibc-2.3.2-95.20
compat-db-4.0.14-5
compat-gcc-7.3-2.96.128
compat-gcc-c++-7.3-2.96.128
compat-libstdc++-7.3-2.96.128
compat-libstdc++-devel-7.3-2.96.128
openmotif21-2.1.30-8
setarch-1.3-1
```

The system administrator can verify whether a particular required package is installed by using the following command:

```
# rpm -q package_name
```

If a package is not installed, the system administrator can copy it from the OS software installation CDs or download it from the Linux vendor.

Applying Necessary OS Patches

The system administrator must ensure that all required operating system patches are installed before performing the Oracle software installation. Oracle's operating system–specific guides will provide you with the required and recommended patches for your operating system.

Checking Physical OS Requirements for Oracle Installation

Check that you have at least the following memory and physical space:

- A minimum of 1024MB of physical RAM.
- 1GB of swap space, or twice the size of the physical RAM if your RAM is between 256MB and 512MB. Oracle provides a matrix that shows the amount of swap space for varying RAM sizes.
- At least 400MB of free space in the /tmp directory.
- From 1.5GB to 3GB of disk space for the Oracle software, depending on the installation type.

The root user should run the following two commands to check the amount of RAM and swap space:

```
# grep MemTotal /proc/meminfo
MemTotal:      1203934 kB
# grep SwapTotal /proc/meminfo
SwapTotal:     2040244 kB
```

To check the available disk space, run the following command:

```
# df -h
Filesystem      Size    Used    Avail    Used%    Mounted on
```

```
/dev/sda3      11G      8.7G      1.7G     85%     /
/dev/sda1      99M       15M       79M     16%     /boot
none          588M         0      588M      0%     /dev/shm
```

To find out how much space you have in your /tmp directory, the system administrator can run the following command:

```
$ df -k /tmp
```

Based on the physical disk storage requirements, the Oracle DBA will need to prepare an installation-requirements document, identifying the resources required and the preferred layout of the disks. Once the DBA's requirements pass through any necessary approvals, the system administrator will allocate the memory and disk space. The system administrator will also provide the location of all your mount points.

Creating Mount Points for the Installation

Oracle *recommends* a minimum of four mount points for an OFA-compatible Oracle installation. You absolutely *must have* at least two mount points: one for the software and the other for the database files. However, you actually need more than that for a database with several large datafiles. A minimum OFA-compatible installation requires four mount points: one for the Oracle software and three for the various database files.

The number of mount points you need depends on your total space requirements. If your computations indicate that you need around 200GB of total space, and each of your mount points supports 7GB, you would need roughly 30 mount points for your applications.

It is important that the UNIX administrator name the mount points in accordance with the OFA guidelines discussed earlier in this chapter.

Reconfiguring the Kernel

Oracle requires huge amounts of shared memory segments, which are usually not configured by default in the Linux (or UNIX) operating system. There is a good possibility that the system administrator will need to change certain kernel parameters, such as the ones dealing with memory and semaphores (structures that control access to the operating system's memory).

■**Note** It is extremely important for the kernel to be reconfigured at the outset. If enough memory resources aren't configured per Oracle's guidelines, either your installation will not succeed or you will encounter an error when you try to create a database after the installation of the Oracle software. The kernel reconfiguration is a very simple task for the administrator. All he or she has to do is change the kernel configuration file and regenerate a new kernel file using the appropriate command. The system administrator then needs to restart the system with the new kernel file replacing the older version.

Each UNIX or Linux operating system may have a different set of kernel requirements for an Oracle installation. Table 9-3 shows the kernel requirements for the Red Hat Linux 3 operating system I am using for the Oracle software installation.

Table 9-3. *Sample Linux Kernel Requirements for an Oracle Installation*

Parameter	Value
semmsl	250
semmns	32000

Table 9-3. *Sample Linux Kernel Requirements for an Oracle Installation (Continued)*

Parameter	Value
semopm	100
semmni	128
shmall	2097152
shmmax	Minimum of half the physical memory or 4GB
shmmni	4096
file-max	65536 (512*processes)
ip_local_port_range	Minimum 1024
ip_local_port_range	Maximum 65000
rmem_default	262144
rmem_max	4194304
wmem_default	262144
wmem_max	262144

To view the current kernel configuration, issue this command:

```
$ cat /etc/sysctl.conf
```

During the operating system prerequisite checks, the Oracle installer might show errors that can be fixed by reconfiguring the UNIX or Linux kernel. If the kernel needs reconfiguring, the system administrator will need to edit to the kernel configuration file.

If the values of any of the kernel parameters are not big enough, the installation will fail; if the values of any parameters are below the minimum values, you must edit the /etc/sysctl.conf file to specify the larger values for the parameters, as shown here:

```
fs.file-max = 512 * PROCESSES
kernel.shmall = 2097152
kernel.shmmax = 2147483648
kernel.shmmni = 4096
kernel.sem = 250 32000 100 128
net.ipv4.ip_local_port_range = 1024 65000
net.core.rmem_default = 262144
net.core.rmem_max = 4194304
net.core.wmem_default = 262144
```

On my Linux server, I modified the /etc/sysctl.conf file, but this may vary depending on your OS. After reconfiguring the kernel parameter settings and generating a new kernel, the system administrator must reboot the system using the new kernel for the new settings to take effect.

The system administrator can also use the following command on Red Hat Linux to dynamically change the current values of the kernel parameters, without a need to reboot the system (this will only change the values temporarily and they'll revert to their original values upon rebooting):

```
# /sbin/sysctl -p
```

After the kernel parameters have been changed, the system administrator can verify the settings by running the following commands as root:

```
/sbin/sysctl -a | grep shm
/sbin/sysctl -a | grep sem
/sbin/sysctl -a | grep file-max
/sbin/sysctl -a | grep ip_local_port_range
```

■**Note** Oracle uses the shared memory segments of the operating system to share data among its various processes.

In addition to modifying the kernel parameters, the system administrator must also check limits on user processes as well as certain user login shell scripts, and change them if necessary. The following sections discuss these additional changes to be made by the system administrator.

Changing Shell Limits

Oracle recommends setting limits on the number of processes and open files each Linux account may use. To improve the performance of Oracle software on Linux systems, the system administrator must increase certain shell limits for the oracle user by adding the following lines to the /etc/security/limits.conf file:

```
oracle      soft   nproc   2047
oracle      hard   nproc   16384
oracle      soft   nofile  1024
oracle      hard   nofile  65536
```

You must also add the following line to the /etc/pam.d/login file:

```
session     required    /lib/security/pam_limits.so
```

Changing Login Scripts

The system administrator must also make changes to the Oracle users' login shell. The changes depend on the default shell type.

For the Bourne, BASH, or Korn shell, add the following lines to the /etc/profile file:

```
if [ $USER = "oracle" ];
then
    if [ $SHELL = "/bin/ksh" ]; then
    ulimit -p 16384
    ulimit -n 65536
else
  ulimit -u 16384 -n 65536
    fi
fi
```

For the C shell (csh or tcsh), add the following lines to the /etc/csh.login file:

```
if ( $USER == "oracle" ) then
  limit maxproc 16384
  limit descriptors 65536
endif
```

Creating Necessary Groups

Operating system groups consist of a set of users who perform related tasks and have similar privileges. Oracle recommends that you create three operating system groups for both Linux and UNIX operating systems: OSDBA, OSOPER, and ORAINVENTORY (Oracle Inventory group). The default name for the OSDBA group is *dba*, for the OSOPER group is *oper*, and for the ORAINVENTORY group is *oinstall*. You can find out whether each of these three groups already exists in your system by checking the /etc/group file.

Members of the OSDBA (dba) group will have the SYSDBA Oracle database privilege, which lets them perform privileged actions such as starting up and shutting down the database. The ORAINVENTORY (oinstall) group is mandatory when you install Oracle software for the first time on any server. The ORAINVENTORY group owns all Oracle inventory, which is a catalog of all the Oracle software installed on a server. All new installations and upgrades are performed by users belonging to the ORAINVENTORY group.

The OSOPER (oper) group is optional, and you need to create it only if you plan to grant any users the OSOPER Oracle privilege to perform a limited set of administrative tasks, such as backing up databases. All database users with the OSOPER privilege will be members of the OSOPER group at the OS level.

■**Note** Users belonging to the ORAINVENTORY group must be given read, write, and execute privileges on the ORAINVENTORY directory only. The group shouldn't be given write permissions for any other directories.

Creating the Oracle Inventory Group

The ORAINVENTORY group needs to be created only if it doesn't already exist in your system. Here's the command to create it, with the default name for the group:

```
# /usr/sbin/groupadd oinstall
```

The Oracle installer creates the oraInst.loc file when you install Oracle software on a server for the first time. This file tells you the name of the ORAINVENTORY group and the path of the Oracle Inventory directory. Use the following command to determine whether the ORAINVENTORY group already exists on your server:

```
# more /etc/oraInst.loc
```

If the oraInst.loc file exists, you'll see the following, which means you don't have to create the ORAINVENTORY group:

```
inventory_loc=/u01/app/oracle/oraInventory
inst_group=oinstall
```

Creating the OSDBA Group

Create this group only if one doesn't exist, or if you want to give a new group of users DBA privileges in a new Oracle installation. Use the following command to create the OSDBA group:

```
# /usr/sbin/groupadd dba
```

Creating the OSOPER Group

The OSOPER group is optional—it should be created only if you're planning to create one or more Oracle users with limited administrative privileges. Here's how you create the OSOPER group:

```
# /usr/sbin/groupadd oper
```

The OSASM Group (asmadmin)

In order to clearly divide the responsibilities between ASM administration and database administration, Oracle 11*g* introduces a new SYSASM privilege. There is a new operating system group called

OSASM, which you use exclusively for ASM administration. Members of the OSASM group can connect as SYSASM using operating system authentication, similar to members using the SYSDBA privilege for database administration.

Create a new OSASM operating system group with the following command:

```
# /usr/sbin/groupadd asadmin
```

The group name in this example is asadmin.

Verifying That an Unprivileged User Exists

An unprivileged user called nobody is necessary to own the external jobs (extjob) executable. Before you install the Oracle software, verify that the user nobody exists in the system. If the user nobody doesn't exist, create the user by executing the following command:

```
$ /usr/sbin/useradd -g nobody
```

Creating the Oracle Software Owner User

After the system administrator has created the necessary groups, he or she needs to create the all-important user that owns the Oracle software, usually named oracle (you can choose any name, but oracle is used by convention). The oracle user is the owner of the Oracle software, and this user's default or primary group will be the newly created ORAINVENTORY group.

You need to install Oracle software as the Oracle software owner (the oracle user), rather than as root. The oracle user's secondary group should be the OSDBA group, and if necessary, the OSOPER group as well. The oracle user will have a home directory like all the other users (usually something like /u01/app/oracle), under which you'll create the rest of the directory structure for holding the Oracle Database 11g server software.

■**Caution** Don't use the root account to install or modify Oracle software. Only the oracle user should perform the Oracle software installation operations.

Under an HP-UX system, you can use the administrative tool SAM to create the users. In any UNIX or Linux system, you can create the users manually, with the following command:

```
# /usr/sbin/useradd –g oinstall –G dba  –d  /home/oracle  -p oracle1  oracle
```

In the preceding command

g denotes the primary group of the user oracle, which is the oinstall group.

G is the secondary group, which is the dba group.

d denotes the home directory for the new user.

p is the password for the oracle user.

You may use the following command to set the password for the oracle user, if you wish:

```
# /usr/bin/passwd oracle
```

Refer to Chapter 3 for more details about the passwd command.

Note that the default home directory of the oracle user should be similar to that of the normal users of the system. The ORACLE_HOME directory is not meant for the oracle user; it's the location for the Oracle software binaries and similar files.

■**Note** The oracle user should be given read, write, and execute privileges on all files and directories that are part of the Oracle Database 11*g* installation.

Setting File Permissions

The next step is to set the default Linux/UNIX file permissions. To do this, the system administrator must first check the existing default permissions by issuing the umask command. If the umask is set to anything but 022, change it to 022 by issuing the umask 022 command. The system administrator can simply open the default login shell (which, for the BASH shell on Red Hat Linux, is .bash_profile) and add this line:

```
umask    022
```

As you saw in Chapter 3, the default permissions for a newly created file system are 666 under the octal notation. That is, everyone is able to read and write any file. By using a default file permission of 644 (by using the umask of 022), you are granting any users other than the oracle user read permission only on the file systems. Of course, the system administrator must make sure the oracle user has write permissions to create files in all the user's directories.

The UNIX administrator must ensure that a local bin directory exists, such as /user/local/bin or /opt/bin. The administrator must further ensure that this directory is included in the PATH environment variable used by the oracle user and that the oracle user has execute permission on this directory.

The system administrator must also create a directory with the name /var/opt/oracle that is owned by the oracle user. This directory will contain files that describe various components of the Oracle server software installation. The following commands will create the directory and assign it the necessary privileges:

```
$ mkdir /var/opt/oracle
$ chown oracle:dba /var/opt/oracle
$ chmod 755 /var/opt/oracle
```

Creating Necessary Directories

The system administrator (root) must also create the Oracle base directory, which acts as a top-level directory for Oracle software installations, and its ownership must be assigned to the oracle user. Assuming you choose the standard /u01/app/oracle directory as your Oracle base directory, you can create it and assign the necessary ownership and file permissions with these commands:

```
$ mkdir -p /u01/app/oracle
$ chown -R oracle:oinstall /u01/app/oracle
$ chmod -R 775 /u01/app/oracle
```

During the installation, you must set the ORACLE_BASE environment variable to specify the full path to this directory (/u01/app/oracle).

Oracle Inventory Directory

The Oracle Inventory directory is usually the /$ORACLE_BASE/oraInventory directory, and it contains an inventory of all Oracle software installed on the system. You don't need to explicitly create this directory. The Oracle Universal Installer will prompt you for its location the first time it installs software on your server. The installer creates the directory and assigns the Oracle user the necessary rights.

Oracle Home Directory

As mentioned earlier in this chapter, the Oracle home directory is the key directory where the installer actually installs all the Oracle executables. The Oracle home directory must be a subdirectory of the Oracle base directory you just created. You don't have to explicitly create the Oracle home directory— the installer prompts you for a symbolic name as well as the direct location for it. The installer will then automatically create this directory and assign the Oracle user the necessary privileges.

This is an example of the correct format for the Oracle home directory (first installation of the database software):

```
$ORACLE_BASE/product/11.1.0/db_1
```

Database Directories (for Data Storage)

Of course, the Oracle home directory is only for the Oracle binaries. The DBA must also create separate database directories for locating the datafiles, control files, redo logs, and other files. The Oracle installer suggests a subdirectory of the Oracle base directory for locating these files.

However, the system administrator must create separate directories for the database-related files. Ideally, these directories must be created on separate physical devices. This way, you can distribute physical I/O as well as have different devices for locating your duplexed control files and redo log files. Although the same drive can be used for creating all the directories, it won't be possible to fully implement the OFA guidelines.

Create multiple database directories using the following format (adjusted for your requirements), and make sure that the oracle user has write permissions on them:

```
$ mkdir -p /prod10/oradata/prod
$ chown -R oracle:oinstall /prod10/oradata/prod
$ chmod -R 775 /prod10/oradata/prod
```

Flash Recovery Area

As I mentioned earlier in this chapter, Oracle strongly recommends that you maintain a flash recovery area for storing all recovery-related files. You must place the recovery files on a different physical disk from the database files, to prevent a disk failure from affecting both the current database files and the recovery files.

Here's an example showing how to create and set the appropriate owner, group, and permissions on the directory for the flash recovery area. I named the subdirectory flash_recovery_area, but it could be anything that you specify using the DB_RECOVERY_FILE_DEST parameter:

```
$ mkdir -p /prod20/oradata/prod/flash_recovery_area
$ chown -R oracle:oinstall /prod20/oradata/prod/flash_recovery_area
$ chmod -R 775 /prod20/oradata/prod/flash_recovery_area
```

Oracle Owner's Preinstallation Tasks

As I mentioned earlier, the system administrator must create an account for the owner of the Oracle software. Usually, this is an account with the name oracle. The Oracle owner—in our case, the oracle user—needs to set the environment variables before the installation of the software.

Setting the Environment Variables

You need to log in as the oracle user and set a number of environment variables. Although all of the environment variables can be set manually, you are better off editing the default shell startup file, which, on my Red Hat Linux server, is the .bash_profile file in the home directory of the oracle user (the /home/oracle directory by default). By editing the shell startup file, you will ensure that the environment will always be set appropriately each time you log in. Here are the main environment variables that you need to set:

- ORACLE_BASE: The ORACLE_BASE variable is the starting directory for all Oracle installations. All the software files and other files are placed in directories underneath the ORACLE_BASE directory. In our example, the directory is /u01/app/oracle.

- ORACLE_HOME: When you're installing the Oracle server, the ORACLE_HOME variable should be set to *oracle_base*/product/10.2.0/db_1. In our case, this will be /u01/app/oracle/product/10.2.0/db_1. The Oracle installer prompts you for the value of the ORACLE_HOME variable during the installation of the software.

■**Caution** Your environment variables may be slightly different from the ones listed here, depending on your operating system and its version. Always check the operating system–specific installation guides—it's well worth the effort to read them. The specifics in this chapter are based on a Red Hat Linux operating system.

■**Note** You can identify existing ORACLE_HOME directories by looking at the contents of the oratab file:

```
# cat /etc/oratab
```

If the oratab file exists, it contains lines similar to the following:

```
prod1:/a03/app/oracle/product/11.1.0:Y
prod2:/a04/app/oracle/product/10.2.0:Y
```

The oratab file's contents reveal that there is one 11.1 and one 10.2 version of Oracle home on this server.

- PATH: The PATH variable should be set to the following:

  ```
  $ export PATH=$ORACLE_HOME/bin:/usr/bin:/usr/ccs/bin:
  /etc:/usr/binx11:/usr/local/bin
  ```

- DISPLAY: You may or may not have to set the DISPLAY environment variable. See the "Setting the DISPLAY Variable" sidebar for details.

■**Note** An easy way to check whether you need to set the DISPLAY variable is to run an x11-base program such as xclock. Simply type the following command in a new xterm, dtterm, or xconsole at the very outset:

```
$ xclock
```

You can also specify the complete path to the xclock program this way:

```
$ /usr/bin/x11/xclock
```

If the DISPLAY variable is set, you'll see a small analog clock displayed on your screen. If the DISPLAY variable isn't set correctly, you'll see the following message:

```
$ xclock
Error: Can't open display:
$
```

- TNS_ADMIN: The TNS_ADMIN variable is used to set the location of the Oracle Net configuration files. By default, the network configuration file, called tnsnames.ora, is located in the $ORACLE_HOME/network/admin directory.

- ORACLE_SID: The important ORACLE_SID variable need not be set if you are not planning to create a database right now.

- ORAENV_ASK: In addition to the environment variables in the .profile file, you need to add another line to source the oraenv file, so all user sessions will automatically read the oraenv file upon logging in as the oracle software user. The oraenv file will prompt the oracle user for the correct SID of the database he or she wants to use. On a system with several database instances, the oraenv file comes in handy in making this choice as soon as you log in. Here's the line you must add to the .profile file:

  . /usr/local/bin/oraenv

- If you set the value of the ORAENV_ASK variable to NO, the current value of ORACLE_SID will be assumed to be the SID you want to use.

SETTING THE DISPLAY VARIABLE

If you're performing the Oracle installation directly from an X Window System workstation or X terminal connected to the server on which you're installing the software, just start an X terminal window. No other changes are necessary. If you're installing the software on a remote system, you must set the DISPLAY environment variable so the X applications will display on your local PC or workstation window.

If you're using the Bourne, BASH, or Korn shell, enter this command:

$ DISPLAY=localhost:0.0; export DISPLAY

If you're using the C shell, enter this command:

% setenv DISPLAY localhost:0.0

In both of the preceding commands, replace *localhost* with the IP address or symbolic name of the host PC or workstation where you want to run the Oracle installer. Here's an example that sets the DISPLAY variable using an IP address of 174:16.14.15:

$ export DISPLAY=174:16:14:15:0.0

If you're getting errors when trying to run the Oracle installer (even after setting your DISPLAY environment variable), you may have to use the xhost program to add your local host name to the list of hosts allowed to make connections to the X server on the host where you're running the Oracle installer. The xhost program is a server access-control program for X windows, and you can add your local host name to the access list for the X Window System as follows:

$ xhost +localhost

Or you can use the following variation, to enable access for anyone, by essentially turning access control off:

$ xhost +
access control disabled, clients can connect from any host
$

Once you finish installing the Oracle software, you can turn access control off again by using the xhost command with the - option (xhost -).

■**Tip** It may be a good idea to incorporate as many of the environment variables as possible in the shell startup file in the oracle user's home directory. This way, when you log in as the oracle user, the variables will already be in force in your shell.

You must also edit the /home/oracle/.bash_profile file as follows, so the environment variables are set correctly each time the user oracle logs in:

```
umask 022
PATH=/bin:/usr/bin:/usr/local/bin:/usr/X11R6/bin
ORACLE_BASE=/u01/app/oracle
ORACLE_HOME=$ORACLE_BASE/product/11.1.0/db_1
PATH=$ORACLE_HOME/bin:$PATH
LD_LIBRARY_PATH=$ORACLE_HOME/lib
export ORACLE_BASE ORACLE_HOME
export PATH LD_LIBRARY_PATH
```

■**Tip** If you're installing the Oracle 11.1.0 software on a server where you already have other Oracle databases, make sure you back up those databases first. Delete the ORACLE_HOME environment variable that you're currently using, and stop all running services if you're installing software in an already existing Oracle Database 11*g* release 1 (11.1) home.

A Final Checklist for the Installation

To ensure that your Oracle installation won't abort in the middle, make sure you satisfy the following requirements:

- Make sure you have enough temporary space. There is usually only a small amount of tempo-rary space on most UNIX servers—something like 100MB or so. If this is the case on your system, your Oracle installation will fail midway through, because Oracle uses the temporary directory on the server heavily during the installation process. You have two ways to get around this problem. You can either ask your system administrator to increase the size of the temporary directory on the server, or you can change the environment variable for the temporary directory. Usually, you do this by setting the TMPDIR environment variable to something other than /tmp and making sure that there is at least 400MB of space under this temporary directory. Here's how I changed my temporary space during the Oracle installation:

  ```
  $ export TMPDIR=/test01/app/oracle/tmp
  $ export TMP=/test01/app/oracle/tmp
  ```

- Set the swap space to a high amount, at least satisfying Oracle's requirements specified in the operating system–specific installation guide. Oracle provides a matrix recommending varying swap space requirements based on the size of the available RAM. Make sure you allo-cate about 500MB to avoid any swapping or paging problems on the server.

- Modify the UNIX kernel to meet your installation requirements. Even if you install the server software correctly, if kernel parameters such as SHMMAX and SEMMNS are not set high enough and you have a large number of processes in your initialization file, your database creation will fail.

- Set the DISPLAY variable properly so the Oracle installer will come up correctly. If you're installing the Oracle software directly on the server, you need to change the DISPLAY variable on the server; if you're installing remotely from a client, you need to set the variable on the client. In most cases, a command such as the following will set up your display correctly:

```
$ export DISPLAY=<Your IP address or hostname>:0.0
```

- Sometimes when you are working on a workstation, you will be unable to use the X Window System emulation on the machine, which means the Oracle Universal Installer cannot function in the GUI mode. In these circumstances, use the xhost command in a window on the workstation. Here's an example:

```
$ xhost +localhost
```

- Mount the installation CD correctly, if you've chosen to use it to install the software. Just follow your operating system–specific installation guide for the correct CD installation commands.

Accessing the Installation Software

Once you have finished all the preinstallation work, you are ready to install the Oracle Database 11*g* software. In this chapter, I install Oracle Database 11*g* Release 1 software on a Linux server as an example. You can install directly from the Oracle software distribution available on CD or DVD. You can also download the software for free, from the Oracle Technology Network web site (http://technet.oracle.com).

Using Oracle Software Packages

The following are the important CDs that are part of the Oracle Enterprise Edition software CD pack:

- *Oracle Database 11g CD*: This is the only CD you'll need to install the Oracle Database 11*g* server software.

- *Companion CD*: This CD contains additional software that you may want to install for products like Oracle JVM, Oracle Multimedia, and Oracle Text.

- *Oracle Database 11g Client CD*: This CD contains the client software you may need to install on your users' or developers' servers.

- *Oracle Enterprise Manager CD*: This CD contains the Enterprise Manager Grid Control software, which lets you manage all the databases, servers, and other components from a centralized location. The local OEM Database Control is automatically installed when you create a new Oracle database.

■**Caution** Make sure you are logged in as the Oracle software owner, oracle, and not as root, when you perform the various installation procedures. Otherwise, your installation process will fail. There are only a couple of times during the installation process when you'll need to log in as root to perform certain tasks.

In several versions of Linux and UNIX, the Oracle CDs load automatically, but sometimes you may have to use an explicit command, such as the following to mount the CD (make sure you log in as the root user to run these commands):

```
$ umount /dev/cdrom
$ mount /dev/cdrom      /mnt/cdrom
mount:  block device /dev/cdrom is write-protected, mounting read-only
$
```

Your Oracle software CD is now mounted for your use, and you should see its files under the CD mount point, which is /mnt/cdrom in our case.

You can move to the /mnt/cdrom directory to view the files on the CD, as shown here:

```
$ cd /mnt/cdrom
$ ls
doc   install   response   runInstaller   stage   welcome.htm
```

The runInstaller file is the executable you must run to invoke the Oracle Universal Installer, which helps you install the Oracle server software.

■**Note** In the installation example that follows, I used the Linux x86–specific Oracle Database 11*g* version 11.1 software.

Downloading Oracle Software

The Oracle software download site (http://technet.oracle.com) gives clear instructions on how to download and install the software on various operating systems. Once you download the software, you usually need to use either the gunzip (gzip) utility on UNIX and Linux systems or the WinZip utility on Windows to unzip the compressed installation files before you can install the software.

Here's a brief summary of the Oracle software downloading process: First download the zipped Linux x86 file by FTP. The file name is ship.db.cpio.gz. Once the file is downloaded, the following two steps will extract the software files. The following command unzips the original ship.db.cpio.gz file that I downloaded:

```
$ gunzip ship.db.cpio.gz
```

The next command extracts the installation files:

```
$ cpio -idmv < ship.db.cpio
```

Once you have extracted the zipped file, you'll see a new directory named Disk1, which is created as a subdirectory in the directory from which you extracted the zipped file. The Disk1 directory contains several directories and one binary file, runInstaller, which is the executable for invoking the Oracle Universal Installer.

You can use the runInstaller script and invoke the Oracle Universal Installer not just for the initial installation of the Oracle Database 11*g* software, but also for modifications and additions to the initial software configuration. Ensure your system administrator is nearby, because you may need help with setting the DISPLAY variable for the installer GUI, or you may run into unforeseen space or file privilege problems. You'll also need the administrator to run the root.sh script (discussed in the next section) as the root user, toward the end of the installation process.

■**Tip** Make sure you have enough space in the temporary directory, as the Oracle installer creates a lot of files in this directory. Your installation may stop in the middle, and you'll have to restart it if this happens. About 400MB to 500MB of space in the /tmp directory should be available for the Oracle installer's use during the installation process.

You can install the Oracle software in the following ways:

- Install directly from the Oracle product CDs.
- Install from software downloaded from the OTN site.
- Copy the software from the product CDs to disk, and install it from disk.

In the next section, I show you how to copy the software from the Oracle product CDs to disk, and to install from there.

Installing the Software

You can install the Oracle server software from the software CD or the downloaded files directly, but Oracle recommends that you perform the installation from a staging directory on your system. If you're installing Oracle from the CD, first create a staging directory, such as /staging. You can then copy the contents of the CD to your staging directory, as shown here:

```
$ cp -r /mnt/cdrom  /staging
```

The previous command will recursively copy all the directories on the installation CD to the /staging directory. Installing from disk is slightly faster than installing from the CD. Saving the installation files on disk in this manner will also help you down the road, when you need to invoke the Oracle installer to perform installation-related tasks—you won't need to locate the CD.

In this section, I detail the interactive installation method, which involves you responding to the installer's prompts from the command line. I also briefly discuss the less frequently employed automated installation method using response files in the section "Using Response Files to Install Oracle Software" later in this chapter.

To begin the installation process, switch to the appropriate directory and execute the runInstaller script as the oracle user. (If you're using the extracted files, you'll start from the Disk1 directory. If you're using the CD staging area, it'll be the /staging directory.)

To start from the /staging directory, first go to the directory:

```
$ cd /staging
```

Check to make sure the runInstaller executable script is there:

```
$ ls
doc   install  response  runInstaller  stage  welcome.htm
```

Invoke the Oracle Universal Installer by executing the runInstaller script:

```
$ ./runInstaller
[pasu] $ ./runInstaller
Starting Oracle Universal Installer . . .
Checking Installer requirements . . .
Checking operating system version: must be redhat 2.1, UnitedLinux-1.0 or redhat-3
                                                        Passed
Preparing to launch Oracle Universal Installer from /tmp/OraInstall . . .
 Please wait . . .
```

At this point, assuming there are no problems with the DISPLAY variable settings, the GUI version of the Oracle Universal Installer should show up. (If the GUI doesn't show up on your screen, you probably have to adjust your DISPLAY variable or use the xhost command, as explained earlier.) The following series of windows and prompts will be displayed during the Oracle Database 11*g* Release 1 server software installation:

1. You'll see the Welcome to the Oracle Database 11*g* Installation window, as shown in Figure 9-1. In Oracle Database 11*g* Release 1, you can choose between the options Basic Installation and Advanced Installation. Basic Installation is the default method, and it quickly installs the Oracle software and, optionally, also creates a general-purpose database for you. The Advanced Installation option will let you upgrade databases to the 11*g* version, use raw devices or the Automatic Storage Management options for storage, specify different passwords for administrators (like SYS and SYSTEM schemas), configure automatic database backups and Oracle Enterprise Manager (OEM) notifications, and other options.

   Choose Advanced Installation and click Next, which will start up the installer in the advanced mode.

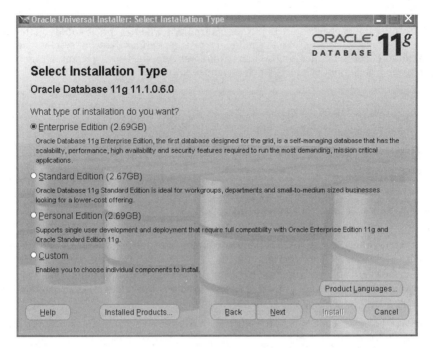

Figure 9-1. *The Oracle Universal Installer's welcome window*

2. Oracle offers you a choice of installation types in the Select Installation Type window. You can choose one of the following installation types when installing Oracle Database 11*g*:

   • *Enterprise Edition*: Installs the Oracle database with all of its performance, high availability, and security features to enable the running of mission-critical applications

   • *Standard Edition*: Installs a scaled-down offering suitable for small businesses and departments within a large organization

   • *Custom*: Allows you to choose individual components to install

   Choose the Enterprise Edition option (1.28GB) and click Next.

3. The Specify Home Details window is next. You specify the Oracle home name and provide the complete path to the Oracle home directory. If this is the first installation of Oracle Database 11*g* software on this server, I recommend the following path:

   `/u01/app/oracle/product/11.1.0/db_1`

   Click Next after you specify the Oracle home path.

▌Caution Oracle recommends that you specify an empty or nonexistent directory for the Oracle home location. Otherwise, Oracle will warn you before letting you proceed further.

---

4. Oracle will perform product-specific prerequisite checks at this point. Note that the earlier OS-compatibility checks were purely for determining whether Oracle could run the Universal Installer successfully. At this point, the installer verifies that your system meets the minimum necessary operating system requirements for the Oracle Database 11*g* server software installation. The installer checks the following:

- Operating system

- Operating system packages

- Operating system kernel

- Physical memory

- Swap space

- Network configuration

- Oracle home setting (for compatibility and space)

The installer may simply issue a warning if some minor requirements aren't met, or it may ask you to bring the system up to par before proceeding further. If your kernel parameters or OS level aren't correct, for example, there will be a warning that the particular component failed the check and that you need to cancel the installation at this point. Once you fix the kernel parameters or whatever it was that the installer objected to, you can restart the installation process by running the `runInstaller` script once again.

5. Once you pass the checks without getting any error messages from the installer, as shown in Figure 9-2, click Next.

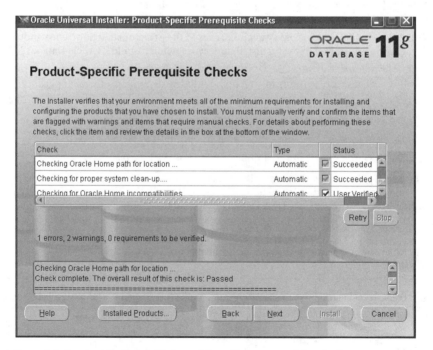

Figure 9-2. *Passing the Oracle Universal Installer's prerequisite checks*

6. The installer displays the Select Configuration Options window. Here, you're presented with three options, as shown in Figure 9-3:

- Create a Database

- Configure Automatic Storage Management (ASM)

- Install Software Only

Choose the last option to just install the database software, and click Next.

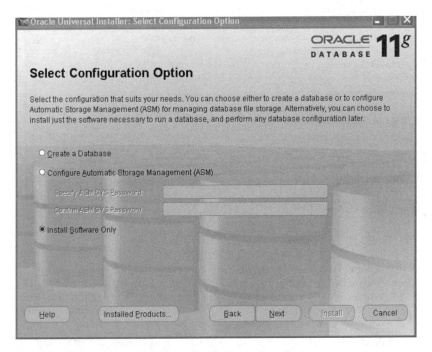

Figure 9-3. *Selecting a configuration for the Oracle installation*

7. You'll be shown a Summary window as a final confirmation (see Figure 9-4). Click Install to begin the actual installation of the Oracle binaries.

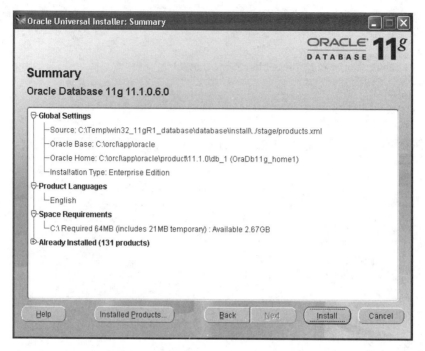

Figure 9-4. *Summary of installation settings*

8. The Install window appears and shows the components as they are installed on your server. At the bottom of this screen, you'll also see the directory name to which the installation log is being written. It can sometimes be nerve-wracking to watch the installer seemingly stall on some action, but you can monitor what the installer is doing on the server by using the `tail` command and monitoring the installation log file in a separate window.

9. The install process will pause briefly to ask you to run a privileges script named `root.sh` as the system administrator (root). Open a different window and run the `/u01/app/oracle/ product/11.1/db_1/root.sh` script as root. The `root.sh` script sets the values for the `ORACLE_OWNER` and `ORACLE_HOME` environment variables. The script adds the appropriate values to the `/etc/oratab` file.

   In addition, if you're installing Oracle software for the first time on this server, the installer also asks the root user to run `orainstRoot.sh`, located in the `/u01/app/oracle/oraInventory` directory.

10. Once you've run one or both scripts as required, click OK. You'll immediately see the End of Installation window, which signifies the successful end of the Oracle Database 11*g* software installation.

11. Click Exit and confirm the choice to end the Oracle Universal Installer session.

   Your Oracle Database 11*g* server installation is now complete.

■**Note** Oracle Database 11*g* supports multiple Oracle homes, meaning that you can install the server software in different Oracle directories.

Using Response Files to Install Oracle Software

By creating a response file and specifying this file when you start the Oracle Universal Installer, you can automate some or all of the Oracle Database installation. When you use a response file, you can run the Oracle Universal Installer in one of the following modes, depending on whether you specify all of the required information or not:

- *Silent mode*: Oracle Universal Installer runs in silent mode if you use a response file that specifies all the required information. None of the Oracle Universal Installer windows are displayed.

- *Suppressed mode*: Oracle Universal Installer runs in suppressed mode if you do not specify all the required information in the response file. Oracle Universal Installer displays only the windows that prompt you for the information that you did not specify.

The silent mode is useful when you can't be physically present for an installation—the response file will contain the responses to the questions asked by the installer. This method can be very useful for client installations when you can't physically visit and install the software on all the different client servers. It is also particularly useful when you need to perform multiple installations on similarly configured systems, because the response file will ensure uniformity and consistency in the product installation. For example, suppose you're working in an organization that has multiple geographical locations and client installations are required, but there are no skilled database personnel at some of the locations—the silent mode is the simplest way to install Oracle in such as situation. The silent mode is also useful if your server doesn't have the X Window System software.

Oracle supplies different response files for the installation of various types of software. I provide a list of the important response files Oracle provides, later in this section.

Before you can run the Oracle installation in either silent or suppressed mode, you need to create the oraInst.loc file, which lists the Oracle products on your server, and then create the response files themselves.

Creating the oraInst.loc File

If you have never had an Oracle installation on your server, you must create the oraInst.loc file in the /etc directory as the root user. If you had an older Oracle installation (even one that has been uninstalled), you'll have this file already. The file provides the installer with the location of the inventory of Oracle products installed on your server.

To create the oraInst.loc file, follow these steps:

1. Log in as the root user and change to the /etc directory:

   ```
   # cd /etc
   ```

2. Create the oraInst.loc file with the following two lines:

   ```
   inventory_loc=ORACLE_BASE/oraInventory
   inst_group= oinstall
   ```

3. Enter the following commands to set the appropriate owner, group, and permissions on the oraInst.loc file:

   ```
   # chown oracle:oinstall oraInst.loc
   # chmod 664 oraInst.loc
   ```

Creating the Response Files

The easiest way to create a response file is to edit one of the Oracle-provided response file templates, located in the /db/response directory on the CD. If you create a staging directory, the response files will be in the /staging/response directory. If you don't create a staging directory, they'll be in the

/Disk1/response directory. These are the response file templates provided by Oracle, with each one meant for a specific purpose:

- enterprise.rsp: Oracle Database 11*g* Enterprise version
- standard.rsp: Oracle Database 11*g* Standard version
- netca.rsp: Oracle Net Configuration Assistant
- custom.rsp: Custom installation of Oracle Database 11*g*
- emca.rsp: Enterprise Manager Configuration Assistant
- dbca.rsp: Database Configuration Assistant

The response file for the Enterprise Edition installation is copied from the CD during installation, along with the other files and scripts. It's located in a separate directory called response, which is located in the same directory as the runInstaller executable file. You need to copy the response file to a directory on your own system and edit it according to your needs. The editing of the response file may take some time, but it's well worth it if you're planning multiple installations.

Once you've edited the response file, you can start the automatic silent installation. Make sure you set your DISPLAY variable correctly before using the silent mode for installation. When you're ready to start, run this command:

```
$ cd $CDROM_mount_directory
$ ./runInstaller  -silent  -response[Response File Name]
```

The preceding command will run the Oracle Universal Installer in the silent mode. You must include responses for all the prompts in the response file in order to specify the -silent option. You won't see any installer screens—only the progress information in the terminal.

If you include responses for some of the prompts in the response file, and just use the runInstaller command without the -silent option, the Oracle Universal Installer will run in suppressed mode. During this type of installation, the installer displays only those screens for which you didn't specify any information.

When Oracle finishes a silent installation, it will display the following message on the screen:

```
The installation of Oracle Database 11g was successful.
Please check /u01/app/oracle/oraInventory/logs
/silentInstall.log for more details.
```

At this point, you need to manually run the root.sh script, just as you would in the normal manual installation procedure. You'll find the root.sh script in the /u01/app/oracle/product/ 10.2.0.0.0 directory. After the root.sh script runs successfully, you're done with the silent installation of Oracle. Of course, you still have to create your database and configure the networking components.

Oracle provides a whole set of response files for several types of installations, including server and client installations. You'll probably use the Oracle client response file more frequently, because it makes it unnecessary for you to physically visit all the client stations for a new installation.

After the Installation

After you've installed the Oracle Database 11*g* server software, you still have some chores left to do. You need to perform several post-installation steps carefully to make sure that the software functions correctly. As with the installation procedures, the system administrator and the oracle user are responsible for specific tasks. Let's look at the important tasks that the system administrator and the Oracle software owner (user oracle here) must perform after the server software installation is finished.

System Administrator's Post-Installation Tasks

The UNIX/Linux administrator has to perform the following tasks after the installation of Oracle software is complete:

- Update the database shutdown and startup scripts.
- Create additional operating system accounts.

Updating Shutdown and Startup Scripts

The Oracle software comes with sample scripts that automatically start up and shut down the database, and the system administrator must add them to the system startup and shutdown scripts. When installed, these scripts will start up and shut down the Oracle database whenever the server is booted up or shut down, ensuring that the database is always closed cleanly and that you don't have to manually bring up the database after system crashes. These sample scripts are located in the $ORACLE_HOME/bin directory. To start a database automatically upon system reboot, use the dbstart.sh script. To stop a database upon system shutdown, use the dbshut.sh script. Both these files are designed to be run as part of the system boot procedure.

In most versions of UNIX and Linux, the contents of the /etc/oratab file will determine whether your database will automatically start up or shut down each time the server starts up and shuts down. The /etc/oratab file is simply a list of the databases running on a server, each with a yes or no indicator for automatic startup and shutdown. If you're creating a new database named finance1, and you want to automate the startup and shutdown process for it, here's what you would need to add to the oratab file:

```
finance1:/u01/app/oracle/product/11.1/db_1:Y
```

The entry in the /etc/oratab file has three components separated by colons: the database name, the Oracle home location, and a Y or N indicating whether the database should automatically start and stop when the host starts up or shuts down. If you want automatic startup and shutdown, specify Y at the end of the line; otherwise specify N.

The UNIX or Linux administrator must add the database startup and shutdown scripts to the system startup and shutdown scripts. For example, on an HP UNIX system, the rc scripts (in the /sbin directory) are run automatically whenever the system moves from one run level to the other. When the system moves to run level 0 (shutdown), the rc script halts the UNIX system by stopping certain daemons and server processes. Similarly, when the run level changes from 0 to 1, the rc script starts the system by starting the necessary daemons and server processes. The system administrator has to include Oracle-related information in the /sbin/rc script to automate the shutdown and startup of the Oracle databases whenever the UNIX server stops and starts for any reason.

Following is an example of the startup information that the system administrator needs to add to the rc script (you must modify the generic dbstart.sh and dbshut.sh scripts to reflect particular database names):

```
/u01/app/oracle/product/11.1.0/bin/dbstart_finance
/u01/app/oracle/product/11.1.0/bin/lsnrctl start
```

And here is an example of the shutdown information:

```
/u01/app/oracle/product/11.1.0/bin/dbshut_finance
/u01/app/oracle/product/11.1.0/bin/lsnrctl stop
```

The script will determine whether to use the startup or shutdown scripts after testing the system run level. The first lines in the preceding startup and shutdown information will start and stop the database (named finance in our example). The second lines will start and stop the Oracle listener process, which helps you establish communication with the database server (the Oracle listener is discussed in detail in Chapter 11).

Creating Additional Operating System Accounts

After the installation is complete, the system administrator must create any other necessary user accounts. All the DBA users must be part of the OSDBA group.

Oracle Owner's Post-Installation Tasks

The oracle user has a set of tasks to perform after the Oracle server software is installed. These include setting the correct environment, applying any necessary Oracle patches, and setting the initialization parameters.

Setting the Environment

Before you can create a database on your system, you need to set some environment variables. The most important of these are the ORACLE_HOME, ORACLE_SID, TNS_ADMIN, CLASS_PATH, TWO_TASK, and LD_LIBRARY_PATH variables. Please refer to your operating system–specific guidelines before you set these and other environment variables.

As the oracle user, you also need to initialize the oraenv script (the coraenv script if you're using the C shell). This script lets you ensure a common environment for all Oracle users. The oraenv script is initialized by including it in the .login or .profile file. For example, for a single-instance database in the Korn shell, this is what you'd need to add to your .login or .profile file:

```
ORAENV_ASK=NO
. /usr/local/bin/oraenv
```

Miscellaneous Tasks

You need to perform some additional tasks as the oracle user. Make sure you check the patch directory on your CD and apply any available patches. You also need to ensure that your databases are a part of the /etc/oratab file, so they can be automatically started up and shut down.

■**Tip** Back up the root.sh script, as it may be overwritten during additional Oracle product installations.

Setting Initialization Parameters

You also have to edit the sample initialization file and modify it for your needs. After you create the database, make sure you create an SPFILE, which is a more sophisticated way of managing your initialization parameters than the traditional init.ora file. Creating SPFILEs is discussed in detail in Chapter 10.

THE ORATAB FILE

The oratab file, which is usually located in the /etc directory on UNIX systems, is useful for several reasons. First, you can use this file to specify whether you want automatic start/stop procedures in place for your databases. Second, oraenv reads the contents of the /etc/oratab file during the setting of the environment variables. If you want to back up all the databases on the server in sequence, you can use the oratab file to provide a list of all the databases the backup script must include.

Configuring Oracle Net Services

To enable connectivity to the database, you must configure Oracle Net Services. The configuration tasks include starting the listener process or, if the listener is already running on the server, making sure your databases are registered with it. All databases automatically register with the listener when they are created.

We haven't covered creating databases yet, so you probably won't have to configure the network connections at this point. You'll learn all about connectivity in Chapter 11, which discusses Oracle Net Services.

Uninstalling Oracle

Sometimes, your installation process may get messed up in the middle, or a lack of disk space may force you to abort the installation abruptly. In this case, the best thing is to simply uninstall all the components that you have already installed. You can install again from scratch when you are ready. There may also be times when you need to remove Oracle software from your server. Before you remove the software, make sure you remove the databases from the server.

During an installation

- Oracle automatically removes all files, including files that belong to configuration assistants and patch sets, during the uninstallation process.

- The installer automatically cleans up all the Windows registry entries.

The following two sections list the simple steps you need to follow to uninstall first the Oracle databases and then the Oracle software.

Removing All Oracle Databases Running on Your Server

Before you remove the Oracle software, first remove all databases from the server, using the Database Configuration Assistant (DBCA). Log in as the oracle user, and get the list of databases from a file such as /etc/oratab. Here's an example:

```
$ cat /etc/oratab
prod1:/a03/app/oracle/product/10.2.:N
prod2:/a03/app/oracle/product/10.2:Y
test1:/a03/app/oracle/product/11.1:N
test2:/a03/app/oracle/product/11.1:Y
$
```

For each database listed in the /etc/oratab file, follow these steps:

1. Use the oraenv or the coraenv script to set up the environment correctly for the particular database you want to remove. Here's an example that removes the database named prod1 from the server:

   ```
    $ . oraenv
   ORACLE_SID = [prod2] ? prod1
   $
   ```

2. Start the DBCA by issuing the following command:

   ```
    $ dbca
   ```

3. Click Next when you see the Welcome window.

4. Select Delete a Database in the Operations window that appears. Click Next.

5. Select the database you want to remove, click Finish, and confirm your choice in the next window.

6. After the database is removed, you are prompted to click Yes to go back to the Operations window and delete more databases or No to exit the DBCA session.

Removing the Oracle Software

To remove the Oracle software, log in as the oracle user and follow these steps:

1. Set the ORACLE_HOME environment variable to specify the path of your Oracle home directory, as shown here:

   ```
   $ export ORACLE_HOME=/u01/app/oracle/product/11.1.0/db_1
   ```

2. Stop all Oracle processes that may be running, using the appropriate commands, as shown here:

   • *Database Control*: $ORACLE_HOME/bin/emctl stop dbconsole

   • *Oracle Net Listener*: $ORACLE_HOME/bin/lsnrctl stop

3. Start the Oracle installer by using the following command:

   ```
   $ /staging/runInstaller
   ```

4. Click Installed Products in the Welcome window.

5. The Inventory Contents tab is displayed, showing you all Oracle homes in your database. Select the Oracle home you wish to remove, and click the Remove button. If there are any dependencies, the installer may not allow you to uninstall the products right away. Click Yes in the Confirmation dialog that appears next.

When the uninstallation is over, click Cancel to exit, and click Yes. Note that no files will remain in the Oracle home directory after a complete uninstallation of the software.

Upgrading to Oracle Database 11*g*

In the previous section of this chapter, you've learned how to install the Oracle Database 11*g* server software. Of course, the next step is to run a database with this software. In most cases, you already have Oracle databases running with older release server software. You must therefore upgrade your current databases to the Oracle Database 11*g* release. Chapter 10 shows you how to create an Oracle database from scratch. This chapter shows you how to upgrade a pre–Oracle Database 11*g* release database to the Oracle Database 11*g* release. The chapter first reviews the available methods of upgrading to the new version and then explains how to use the new Database Upgrade Assistant (DBUA) tool as well as how to upgrade manually, which includes the use of Oracle's new Pre-Upgrade Information Tool and the Post-Upgrade Status Tool.

Routes to Oracle Database 11*g*

Oracle has made the process of upgrading from Oracle9*i* (or even older releases) or an Oracle Database 10*g* database simple by automating a large portion of the upgrade process. I discuss the different upgrade paths to migrate to Oracle Database 11*g* in this section.

Depending on your current database release, you may or may not be able to directly upgrade to the Oracle Database 11*g* Release 1 (11.1) version. You can directly upgrade to Oracle Database 11*g* Release 1 if your current database is based on an Oracle 9.2.0.4 or newer release. For Oracle database releases older than Oracle 9.2.0.4, you have to migrate via one or two intermediate releases, as shown by the following upgrade paths:

- 7.3.3 (or lower) => 7.3.4 => 9.2.0.8 => 11.1
- 8.0.5 (or lower) => 8.0.6 => 9.2.0.8 => 11.1
- 8.1.7 (or lower) => 8.1.7.4 => 9.2.0.8 => 11.1
- 9.0.1.3 (or lower) => 9.0.1.4 => 9.2.0.8 => 11.1
- 9.2.0.3 (or lower) => 9.2.0.8 => 11.1

For example, if you want to upgrade a database from Release 8.1.6, the following would be your game plan: upgrade Release 8.1.6 to 8.1.7; upgrade 8.1.7 to Release 9.2.0.8; upgrade Release 9.2.0.8 to Release 11.1.

Upgrade Methods and Tools

There are two ways for you to upgrade: the traditional manual method or the Database Upgrade Assistant method, which automates the upgrade process. The DBUA is an improved version of the Oracle Data Migration Assistant, which was a tool provided in previous versions of the database.

■**Note** The Oracle Database 11*g* upgrade process is somewhat automatic even if you do it manually. The following sections will show how the manual process uses the STARTUP UPGRADE command. After running this command, you have to run the main upgrade script, which upgrades your installation without causing dependency problems. The database determines the order in which it should upgrade components by querying the DBA_SERVER_REGISTRY data dictionary view. It will also query this view for the upgrade status of each component after the conclusion of the database upgrade. The new Post-Upgrade Status Tool, which I discuss later in this chapter, also uses the DBA_SERVER_REGISTRY view.

The DBA_REGISTRY or the DBA_SERVER_REGISTRY view both contain the upgrade status of individual database components. These views are almost identical, except that the DBA_REGISTRY view has the extra namespace column. If you set the namespace to SERVER, you get identical results using either data dictionary view.

In the past, the upgrade process required you to run various scripts throughout the process, but the Oracle Database 11*g* upgrade process only requires a single upgrade script (there's an example of the use of this script in the "Upgrading Manually" section later).

The Manual Upgrade Process

If you use the manual upgrade process, you must perform due diligence: this means removing or changing all your obsolete initialization parameters and running all the Oracle-provided database upgrade scripts. This method's advantage is that you control the whole upgrade process. There are drawbacks to the manual method, however: you must back up the database yourself, you must use the correct initialization parameters, and you must give the System tablespace adequate free space.

■**Note** The old Export and Import utilities are still available, should you wish to use them, though they've been supplanted by the Data Pump Export and Import utilities. They are still pretty useful if you have a very small database.

The Database Upgrade Assistant

If you use the DBUA, it does the preinstallation checks for you and automatically manages the upgrade process by performing the following tasks:

- Performs initialization checks, including for invalid data types, unsupported character sets, invalid user accounts, and sufficient free space in the tablespaces
- Backs up the database
- Creates any necessary objects
- Invokes the correct upgrade script
- Shows the progress of the upgrade process
- Creates the parameter and listener files in the new Oracle home

■**Tip** The DBUA uses a GUI, but you can also use it in the silent mode.

The Pre-Upgrade Information Tool

Before you start an upgrade, you have to check your system for any necessary changes. Luckily, we have the Pre-Upgrade Information Tool, which does this for us. The Pre-Upgrade Information Tool, which is implemented by executing an Oracle-supplied script, helps you collect various critical pieces of information before the upgrade process begins. Too often in the past, DBAs have needed to restart the upgrade process because of initialization features that were incompatible or tablespace sizes that were too small, and this new tool helps avoid that situation.

■**Note** The manual process and the DBUA both use the same Pre-Upgrade Information Tool. The DBUA automatically runs it as part of this initial check.

The Pre-Upgrade Information Tool provides information about the following:

- *The Sysaux tablespace*: Before you run the upgrade script, you have to create the Sysaux tablespace. The Pre-Upgrade Information Tool will recommend the correct settings for this.
- *Log files*: The new version of Oracle needs redo log files to be at least 4MB. If your existing log files are smaller than this, the Pre-Upgrade Information Tool will tell you to increase their size.
- *Tablespace sizes*: If your existing tablespaces lack the free space required, the Pre-Upgrade Information Tool will tell you so you can increase their size.
- *Initialization parameters*: The Pre-Upgrade Information Tool tells you which initialization parameters you should remove (because they are deprecated and obsolete) and which you should add before you can upgrade.
- *Database versions and compatibility level*: The Pre-Upgrade Information Tool lets you know whether you need to change the compatibility level of your database with the COMPATIBLE initialization parameter.
- *Time estimates*: The Pre-Upgrade Information Tool will give you an estimate of how long the upgrade will take.

The Pre-Upgrade Information Tool will do a lot of the work for you. Just make sure that you implement the recommended changes, and you will be ready to upgrade to Oracle Database 11g.

The Pre-Upgrade Information Tool is actually a SQL script, called `utlu111i.sql` (in `$ORACLE_HOME/rdbms/admin`). Here's how you invoke the Pre-Upgrade Information Tool:

```
SQL> @$ORACLE_HOME/rdbms/admin/utlu111i.sql
```

The Post-Upgrade Status Tool

The new Post-Upgrade Status Tool gives you an accurate summary of the upgrade process and lists any necessary corrective steps that need to be taken. No error messages during the upgrade process doesn't guarantee that you upgraded successfully—the Post-Upgrade Status Tool looks in DBA_SERVER_REGISTRY to ascertain the status of every database component. If one or more components didn't upgrade correctly, the Post-Upgrade Status Tool will show the details.

■**Tip** The Post-Upgrade Status Tool runs automatically when you use the DBUA. You have to run it yourself if you are doing a manual upgrade.

DATABASE COMPATIBILITY

The database compatibility level is set by the value of the COMPATIBLE initialization parameter—the compatibility level specifies the release with which the database must remain compatible. This is important because the COMPAT-IBLE parameter helps you guarantee backward compatibility with an earlier release. The parameter's default value in Oracle Database 11*g* Release 1 is 11.0.0.0, and the minimum value is 10.0.0. When you are upgrading to Oracle Database 11*g*, and you set the COMPATIBLE parameter to 10.0.0, it means that you can undo the changes made by the upgrade process and go back to the older release if the upgrade doesn't pan out. Otherwise, the only way to go back to the older release is to restore from a backup.

Oracle recommends that you set the COMPATIBLE parameter to 10.0.0 before you upgrade to Oracle Database 11*g*, which ensures that you can always revert to the Oracle Database 10*g* release if necessary. However, the price you pay for this convenience is that you can only use a limited subset of the new Oracle Database 11*g* features. After you've upgraded your database and are sure that you want to continue further, you can set the COMPATIBLE initial-ization parameter in your SPFILE to match the new release number (11.1.0).

The Post-Upgrade Status Tool provides you with the following information:

- The name and status (VALID or INVALID) of each database component
- The version compatibility of the component with the current database version
- Suggestions for corrective action if it finds invalid components (such as the names of appro-priate scripts to run)

The Post-Upgrade Status Tool is also a SQL script, called `utlu111s.sql` and located in the `$ORACLE_HOME/rdbms/admin` directory.

While manual upgrades are easy, the burden of due diligence is on you, and you can lose a lot of time if you make any mistakes.

■**Tip** Which of the two upgrade methods (DBUA or manual upgrade) is superior? The underlying scripts and upgrade procedures are identical for both methods—choose the method you're most comfortable with.

Preparing the Database for the Upgrade

Before you upgrade to Oracle Database 11*g*, you must be aware of the following changes concerning privileges, timestamps, and the Oracle Database Vault.

Deprecated CONNECT Role

In Oracle Database 11*g*, the CONNECT role has only the CREATE SESSION privilege and nothing else. In previous versions, the CONNECT role had other privileges, which are automatically revoked during an upgrade to Oracle Database 10*g*. If you think any of the users with the CONNECT role in the previous release need the privileges that used to be a part of the CONNECT role, you must grant the specific required privileges prior to upgrading to Oracle Database 11*g*.

Timestamp with Time Zone Data Type

If the time zone versions used by the Oracle Database 11*g* server and the database that's being upgraded are different, the upgrade will fail. To avoid this, you must first update the existing database to time zone file version 4 (path 5632264—TZ v4 FILE).

Disable Oracle Database Vault

You must disable the Oracle Database Vault before upgrading the database, in case you've enabled it.

Upgrading with the DBUA

The DBUA combines the work of the Pre-Upgrade Information Tool and the manual upgrade process. The DBUA performs the following pre-upgrade steps automatically:

- Sets ORACLE_HOME to the new Oracle Database 11*g* locations.
- Changes the oratab file entries to the new location.
- Copies your current init.ora file to the new Oracle Database 11*g* default init.ora location ($ORACLE_HOME/dbs in UNIX and Linux systems).
- Checks that your tablespaces have adequate space before the upgrade process begins. These checks also cover the undo tablespace and the rollback segments.
- Checks for unsupported character sets and invalid data types and usernames, and so on.
- Performs backups, if you choose.
- Updates obsolete initialization parameters.
- Configures the database with the Enterprise Manager, if you choose.
- Writes detailed trace and log files, as well as showing the upgrade progress.

The DBUA can upgrade not only a single instance configuration, but also Oracle Real Application Clusters and standby database configurations as well.

Starting the DBUA

Start the DBUA by simply typing **dbua** at the operating system prompt. You have to log in as the oracle user first. On a Windows server, you start the DBUA tool by going to Start ➤ All Programs ➤ Oracle ➤ Configuration and Migration Tools ➤ Database Upgrade Assistant.

As mentioned previously, you can do a *silent upgrade* using the DBUA if you don't want to use the GUI. This means you won't see any prompts when you invoke the DBUA.

Here's how you would invoke the DBUA in the silent mode for a database called nina:

```
$ dbua -silent -dbName nina
```

That's it. Your current database will be migrated to the Oracle Database 11g release.

Running the DBUA

Let's take a look at the steps in the automatic upgrade process using the DBUA from the command line.

1. Invoke the DBUA with this command:

   ```
   $ dbua
   ```

2. The DBUA GUI Welcome window is displayed, as shown in Figure 9-5. Click Next.

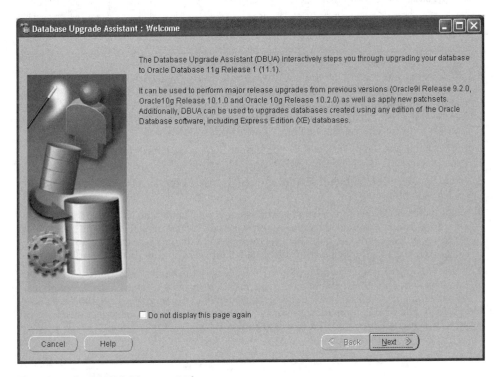

Figure 9-5. *The DBUA Welcome window*

3. In the Selecting a Database Instance window, first ensure that the database you want to upgrade is running. Then select the instance you want to upgrade, and click Next.

4. In the Recompile Invalid Objects window, select the option to recompile invalid objects. The upgrade process always invalidates several database objects, and you have the option of letting the DBUA automatically recompile invalid database objects as soon as the upgrade is over.

■**Tip** Telling Oracle to recompile invalid objects as part of the upgrade process is the same as running the `utlrp.sql` script as part of a manual upgrade.

5. In the next window, Choosing a Database Backup Procedure, you can select the option to do a cold backup of your database. If you have already made backups, choose the I Have Already Backed Up My Database option.

■**Tip** If the upgrade process doesn't go well, and you need to go back to the pre-upgrade database, the DBUA-created database backup makes it easy to do so. You can also make a backup manually, prior to starting the upgrade process. If you choose the option to let the DBUA do the backup, it will back up the database files to the file location you specify in the Backup Directory field before it starts the upgrade of the database to the 11.1.0 release. The DBUA will also create a file called `db_name_restore.sh` (`db_name_restore.bat` in a Windows system), which enables you to easily restore the current database files if necessary.

6. In the Management Options window, you can choose to configure the OEM. The options for database control are the Grid Control or Database Control version of the OEM. The Database Control component is bundled with the installation package, and Oracle automatically installs it; the Grid Control must be installed separately. If you haven't installed the Grid Control software, choose the Database Control option at this point.

7. In the Database Credentials window, you have to choose passwords for the default Oracle users, such as SYSMAN and DBSNMP.

8. In the Recovery Configuration window, you can choose to specify a flash recovery area as well as to enable archiving.

9. In the Network Configuration window, you can use the Listener tab to choose whether you want to register the upgraded database with selected listeners or all the listeners. If you have directory services configured in the new Oracle home, you must use the Directory Service tab and choose to either register the upgraded database with your directory service or not.

10. In the Upgrade Summary window, shown in Figure 9-6, the names of the source and target databases and the database versions are displayed, along with a list of all obsolete and new initialization parameters. An estimate of the time it'll take to upgrade the database is also provided. The DBUA automatically shuts down the database that is being upgraded before it starts the upgrade process. Click Finish to begin.

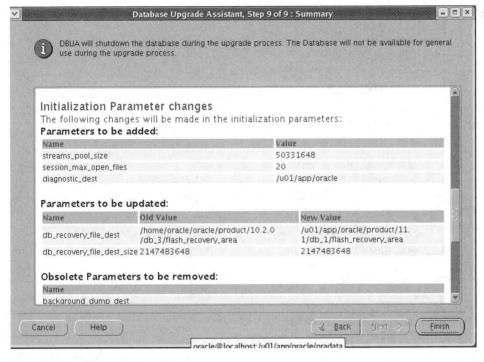

Figure 9-6. *The Upgrade Results window*

11. When the database upgrade is finished, you'll see the results in the Upgrade Results window for you to review. You have three options at this point:

- Configure database passwords.

- Restore the database to what it was before the upgrade and revert all changes made to the database.

- Close the window to finish the installation.

Restoring the Pre-Upgrade Database

If you aren't sure you want to upgrade to the new version at the conclusion of the DBUA upgrade process, you can simply click the Restore button to revert to the previous database version. If the DBUA backed up your database, then Oracle will automatically restore the original database and the original database settings. If the DBUA didn't do the backup, the DBUA can't automatically revert the database to the previous version. You'll have to use your backups to manually restore the database from the earlier version.

You can also run an Oracle-provided script at a later time to go back to the previous database. Oracle automatically creates this script when you select to back up the database during the beginning of the upgrade process.

Upgrading Manually

Let's step through the manual database upgrade process in this section so you understand what happens during a database upgrade. Recall that the DBUA does a lot of the following steps for you.

Upgrade and Downgrade Scripts

Following are the various scripts you use for upgrading to Oracle Database 11g. You'll find all these scripts in the $ORACLE_HOME/rdbms/admin directory.

- catdwgrd.sql enables a direct downgrade from the Oracle Database 11g release to the Oracle Database 11g release from which you upgraded.
- catupgrd.sql enables a direct upgrading to the Oracle Database 11g release.
- utlu111i.sql analyzes the database you're upgrading and shows the requirements and issues for upgrading to Oracle Database 11g.
- utlu111s.sql shows the component upgrade status after upgrading to Release 11.1.
- utlrp.sql recompiles PL/SQL modules such as packages, procedures, and types that are in an invalid state.
- utluppset.sq performs upgrade actions that don't require you to keep the database in upgrade mode.

Following is the list of steps to manually upgrade to Oracle Database 11g:

1. Create a spool file.
2. Log in as a user with the SYSDBA privilege, and run the Pre-Upgrade Information Tool. Make any changes it recommends.
3. Back up the database you're going to upgrade.
4. Copy the current init.ora file to the new Oracle Database 11g init.ora file location.
5. Shut down the database and restart it under the new Oracle 11g home in the STARTUP UPGRADE mode.
6. Create the required Sysaux tablespace.
7. Run the catupgrd.sql upgrade script.
8. Check to see if any objects became invalidated during the database upgrade.
9. Run the utlrp.sql script to recompile any objects that became invalid during the database upgrade.
10. Run the Post-Upgrade Status Tool.
11. End the spool file.
12. Shut down and start up the new database.

In the following sections, I explain each of the upgrade actions I listed.

Creating a Spool File

Create a spool file to record the upgrade process so that you can easily review it later.

```
SQL> SPOOL upgrade.log
```

Running the Pre-Upgrade Information Tool

First, copy the Pre-Upgrade Information Tool (utlu11i.sql script) from the Oracle Database 11g $ORACLE_HOME/rdbms/admin directory to a temporary directory such as /u01/app/oracle/upgrade, for example. Log into SQL*Plus as the user SYS. To start the Pre-Upgrade Information Tool, run the following:

```
SQL> @/u01/app/oracle/upgrade/utlu11i.sql
```

To see the results of the pre-upgrade check, turn spooling off with the following command:

```
SQL> spool off
```

Check the upgrade.log spool file to see if you meet all upgrade requirements. Listing 9-1 shows part of the output from a sample run.

Listing 9-1. *Partial Output of the Pre-Upgrade Information Tool*

```
SQL> @utlu111i.sql
Oracle Database 11.1 Pre-Upgrade Information Tool    01-30-2008 05:33:22
.
************************************************************************
Database:
************************************************************************
--> name:         ORCL10
--> version:      10.2.0.1.0
--> compatible:   10.2.0.1.0
--> blocksize:    8192
--> platform:     Linux IA (32-bit)
--> timezone file: V2
.
************************************************************************
Tablespaces: [make adjustments in the current environment]
************************************************************************
--> SYSTEM tablespace is adequate for the upgrade.
.... minimum required size: 723 MB
.... AUTOEXTEND additional space required: 243 MB
--> UNDOTBS1 tablespace is adequate for the upgrade.
.... minimum required size: 471 MB
.... AUTOEXTEND additional space required: 441 MB
--> SYSAUX tablespace is adequate for the upgrade.
.... minimum required size: 412 MB
.... AUTOEXTEND additional space required: 182 MB
--> TEMP tablespace is adequate for the upgrade.
.... minimum required size: 61 MB
.... AUTOEXTEND additional space required: 41 MB
--> EXAMPLE tablespace is adequate for the upgrade.
.... minimum required size: 69 MB
.
************************************************************************
Update Parameters: [Update Oracle Database 11.1 init.ora or spfile]
************************************************************************
WARNING: --> "sga_target" needs to be increased to at least 336 MB
.
************************************************************************
Renamed Parameters: [Update Oracle Database 11.1 init.ora or spfile]
```

```
****************************************************************************
-- No renamed parameters found. No changes are required.
.
****************************************************************************
Obsolete/Deprecated Parameters: [Update Oracle Database 11.1 init.ora or spfile]
****************************************************************************
--> "background_dump_dest" replaced by  "diagnostic_dest"
--> "user_dump_dest" replaced by  "diagnostic_dest"
--> "core_dump_dest" replaced by  "diagnostic_dest"
.
****************************************************************************
Components: [The following database components will be upgraded or installed]
****************************************************************************
--> Oracle Catalog Views          [upgrade]  VALID
--> Oracle Packages and Types      [upgrade]  VALID
--> JServer JAVA Virtual Machine   [upgrade]  VALID
--> Oracle XDK for Java            [upgrade]  VALID
--> Oracle Workspace Manager       [upgrade]  VALID
--> OLAP Analytic Workspace        [upgrade]  VALID
--> OLAP Catalog                   [upgrade]  VALID
--> EM Repository                  [upgrade]  VALID
--> Oracle Text                    [upgrade]  VALID
--> Oracle XML Database            [upgrade]  VALID
--> Oracle Java Packages           [upgrade]  VALID
--> Oracle interMedia              [upgrade]  VALID
--> Spatial                        [upgrade]  VALID
--> Data Mining                    [upgrade]  VALID
--> Expression Filter              [upgrade]  VALID
--> Rule Manager                   [upgrade]  VALID
--> Oracle OLAP API                [upgrade]  VALID
.
****************************************************************************
Miscellaneous Warnings
****************************************************************************
WARNING: --> Database is using an old timezone file version.
.... Patch the 10.2.0.1.0 database to timezone file version 4
.... BEFORE upgrading the database.  Re-run utlu111i.sql after
.... patching the database to record the new timezone file version.
WARNING: --> Database contains stale optimizer statistics.
.... Refer to the 11g Upgrade Guide for instructions to update
.... statistics prior to upgrading the database.
.... Component Schemas with stale statistics:
....    SYS
....    OLAPSYS
....    SYSMAN
....    CTXSYS
....    XDB
WARNING: --> Database contains schemas with objects dependent on network
packages.
.... Refer to the 11g Upgrade Guide for instructions to configure Network ACLs.
.... USER SYSMAN has dependent objects.
WARNING: --> EM Database Control Repository exists in the database.
.... Direct downgrade of EM Database Control is not supported. Refer to the
.... 11g Upgrade Guide for instructions to save the EM data prior to upgrade.
```

```
.
PL/SQL procedure successfully completed.
SQL> spool off
```

Make all the changes pointed out by the Pre-Upgrade Information Tool before proceeding with the upgrade.

Backing up the Database

Back up the database you are upgrading, either by using RMAN or by using your own backup techniques.

■**Tip** At this point, make sure you've set your ORACLE_HOME variable to the new Oracle home using the format $ORACLE_BASE/product/11.1/db_name.

Copying the Parameter File

Copy your current init.ora file to its default location in the new Oracle Database 11g home ($ORACLE_HOME/dbs). You should also make the changes that the Pre-Upgrade Information Tool recommended. Remove all obsolete and deprecated parameters and add the new parameters, such as MEMORY_TARGET, which automates memory management.

If you're using a password file, move or copy that password file to the Oracle Database 11g Release 1 (11.1) Oracle home.

Starting Up the New Database

Shut down the current database if it's running, and start it up again with the updated init.ora parameter file under the new Oracle Database 11g home. Make sure the ORACLE_HOME and the PATH variables point to the new Oracle Database 11g Release 1 (11.1) directories. You must use the STARTUP UPGRADE command to start up your database under the Oracle 11.1 version, which tells Oracle to modify those initialization parameters that would otherwise cause errors during the upgrade (for example, the new startup mode will set the job_que_processes parameter to 0). The startup upgrade mode starts a restricted session and prepares the environment for the upgrade.

Listing 9-2 shows how to start the database using the STARTUP UPGRADE command. Note that if you're storing your initialization parameter in the default location ($ORACLE_HOME/dbs), you don't need to specify its path when you use the STARTUP UPGRADE command.

Listing 9-2. *Starting the Database with the STARTUP UPGRADE Command*

```
SQL> CONNECT sys/sammyy1 AS SYSDBA
Connected to an idle instance.
SQL> STARTUP UPGRADE
ORACLE instance started.

Total System Global Area   314572800 bytes
Fixed Size                     1236756 bytes
Variable Size                 99164396 bytes
Database Buffers             213909504 bytes
Redo Buffers                    524288 bytes
Database mounted.
Database opened.
SQL>
```

If you're upgrading from the Oracle Database 9*i* Release 2 (9.2) database, you must create a Sysaux tablespace, which is mandatory for the Oracle 10*g* and 11*g* releases. Here's the code for creating the Sysaux tablespace.

```
SQL> CREATE TABLESPACE sysaux DATAFILE '/u01/app/oracle/sysaux01.dbf'
     SIZE 1000m
     EXTENT MANAGEMENT LOCAL
     SEGMENT SPACE MANAGEMENT AUTO
     ONLINE;
```

The database is now technically converted into an Oracle Database 11*g* version database, as the following query shows:

```
SQL> SELECT * FROM V$VERSION;

BANNER
Oracle Database 11g Enterprise Edition Release 11.1.0.6.0 - Production
PL/SQL Release 11.1.0.6.0 - Production
CORE    11.1.0.6.0 - Production
TNS for Linux: Version 11.1.0.6.0 - Production
NLSRTL Version 11.1.0.6.0 - Production

SQL>
```

In the next step, you actually upgrade the current database to the 11.1 version.

Running the Upgrade Script

From the Oracle Database 11*g* Release 1 (11.1) environment, run the catupgrd.sql script (found in the $ORACLE_HOME/rdbms/admin directory). This script automatically runs the appropriate upgrade script for the database version you're upgrading and uses procedures from the DBMS_REGISTRY package to execute various component upgrades.

Make sure you're logged in as a user with SYSDBA privileges, and run the upgrade script from the new environment:

```
SQL> @$ORACLE_HOME/rdbms/admin/catupgrd.sql
```

The catupgrd.sql script creates and alters certain data dictionary tables and upgrades or installs several database components in the new database.

Running the Upgrade Actions Script

After the catupgd.sql script finishes executing, you must run the new upgrade script called catuppset.sql to perform upgrade actions that don't require the database to be in upgrade mode.

```
SQL> @$ORACLE_HOME/rdbms/admin/catuppst.sql
```

You can run the catuppst.sql script simultaneously with the catupgd.sql script in a different SQL*Plus session.

Restarting the Instance

Restart the instance to reinitialize the system parameters. The restart ensures that all caches and buffers are cleared and ensures the integrity and consistency of the newly upgraded database.

Running the Post Upgrade Actions Script

Execute the new upgrade script `catuppset.sql` to perform the remaining upgrade actions that don't require you to run the database in upgrade mode.

```
SQL> @catuppset.sql
```

You can run the `catuppset.sql` script simultaneously with the `catupgd.sql` script to save time.

Checking for Invalid Objects

Oracle will create, drop, and alter some database objects as the upgrade process progresses, thus invalidating some internal Oracle packages and procedures. After the upgrade script has finished, you need to check for invalid objects:

```
SQL> SELECT count(*) FROM DBA_OBJECTS
     WHERE status = 'INVALID';
```

Recompiling and Validating Objects

By running the Oracle-provided `utlrp.sql` script, you can do a recompilation and validation of all the objects invalidated during the upgrade process. During this process, `utlrp.sql` calls `utlprp.sql` (a wrapper based on the UTL_RECOMP package). Note that Oracle will dynamically compile each of the invalidated objects when they are accessed if you don't do it now. However, this runtime compilation of invalidated objects could slow down your database's performance.

You can recompile all invalidated Oracle database objects using the `utlrp.sql` script:

```
SQL> @$ORACLE_HOME/rdbms/admin/utlrp.sql
. . .
PL/SQL procedure successfully completed.

TIMESTAMP
-----------------------------------------------
COMP_TIMESTAMP UTLRP_END  2008-2-21    15:20:49
PL/SQL procedure successfully completed.
SQL>
```

To check that there aren't any invalid objects left, you should run the check again:

```
SQL> SELECT count(*) FROM dba_objects
     WHERE status = 'INVALID';


  COUNT(*)
---------------
        0
1 row selected.
SQL>
```

Once it has validated all the invalid objects, the `utlrp.sql` script validates each individual component in the database and updates the DBMS_SERVER_REGISTRY view.

■**Note** You can revert to the older database as long as you have a backup of the database made before starting the upgrade process. It's vital to have a backup, since the upgrade process may fail before it's completed, leaving you with a database that won't be functional under the pre- or post-upgrade version of Oracle.

Running the Post-Upgrade Status Tool

After the upgrade process completes, you must run the Post-Upgrade Status Tool, using the following script:

```
SQL> @$ORACLE_HOME/rdbms/admin/utlu1111s.sql
```

The Post-Upgrade Status Tool summarizes the upgrade process, which should look similar to Listing 9-3, if everything went okay during the database upgrade.

Listing 9-3. *Partial Output from the Post-Upgrade Status Tool*

```
Oracle Database 11.1 Upgrade Status Utility
01-30-2008  22:05:04
.
Component                          Status    Version      HH:MM:SS
.
Oracle Server                      VALID     11.1.0.1.0   00:14:01
JServer JAVA Virtual Machine       VALID     11.1.0.1.0   00:11:08
Oracle Workspace Manager           VALID     11.1.0.1.0   00:00:40
OLAP Analytic Workspace            VALID     11.1.0.0.0   00:00:25
OLAP Catalog .                     VALID     11.1.0.1.0   00:00:50
Oracle OLAP API                    VALID     11.1.0.1.0   00:00:31
Oracle Enterprise Manager          VALID     11.1.0.1.0   00:08:06
Oracle XDK                         VALID     11.1.0.1.0   00:00:58
Oracle Text                        VALID     11.1.0.1.0   00:00:45
Oracle XML Database                VALID     11.1.0.1.0   00:09:29
Oracle Database Java Packages      VALID     11.1.0.1.0   00:01:00
Oracle interMedia                  VALID     11.1.0.1.0   00:16:11
Spatial                            VALID     11.1.0.1.0   00:04:43
Oracle Expression Filter           VALID     11.1.0.1.0   00:00:13
Oracle Rules Manager               VALID     11.1.0.1.0   00:00:11
.
Total Upgrade Time: 01:13:55
PL/SQL procedure successfully completed.
SQL>
```

The utlu111s.sql script shows that the database components have been upgraded correctly. If you see the INVALID status for any component, that'll most likely be taken care of when you run the utlrp.sql script next. If that fails, you may have to rerun the catupgrd.sql.

The Post-Upgrade Status Tool determines the upgrade status of each database component by querying the DBA_SERVER_REGISTRY view. You can also query the DBA_SERVER_REGISTRY view, as shown in Listing 9-4.

Listing 9-4. *Querying the DBA_SERVER_REGISTRY View for Post-Upgrade Information*

```
SQL> SELECT comp_id, comp_name, version, status
     FROM DBA_SERVER_REGISTRY;

COMP_ID     COMP_NAME                         VERSION     STATUS
---------   -------------------------------   ---------   ------
CATALOG     Oracle Database Catalog           1.1.1.0.6   VALID
CATPROC     Oracle Database Packages          11.1.0.6    VALID
JAVAVM      JServer JAVA Virtual Machine       11.1.0.6    VALID
```

```
CATJAVA        Oracle Database Java Packages        11.1.0.6    VALID
CONTEXT        Oracle Text                          11.1.0.6    VALID
SQL>
```

The Post-Upgrade Status Tool will tell you how the upgrade went. If you didn't cleanly upgrade a component, the Post-Upgrade Status Tool will tell you what you have to do to fix the problem.

■**Caution** Don't start the newly upgraded database under the old Oracle home—this corrupts your database.

Ending the Spool File

After the upgrade script had finished, you can turn off the spooling of the upgrade process:

```
SQL> SPOOL OFF
```

Restarting the New Database

You can now shut down and restart the instance so you're ready for normal database operations:

```
SQL> SHUTDOWN IMMEDIATE
SQL> STARTUP
```

After the Upgrade

After the upgrade, you have a brand-new Oracle Database 11g (11.1.0) instance. Of course, at this point, all your old application code continues to remain at the Oracle 9.2, Oracle Database 10g, or whatever release level you upgraded from. You may want to test the new database features as well as your old applications, to see that they run in the upgraded database without problems.

It's a good idea to promptly back up the new database. You must also change the passwords for the Oracle-supplied user accounts if you manually upgraded the database. You may also need to modify the listener.ora file, as well as migrate to the SPFILE from your init.ora file.

Resetting Passwords for Stronger Password Protection

After the upgrade is completed, you may want to reset the user passwords to take advantage of the case sensitivity new to Oracle Database 11g. If you create a brand-new Oracle Database 11g release database, passwords are automatically case sensitive. If you're upgrading to Oracle Database 11g, however, you must reset each user's password with the ALTER USER statement. Chapter 12 explains the new password case-sensitivity feature in Oracle Database 11g.

You can also start migrating database jobs to the new Oracle Scheduler and check out the Automatic Jobs feature, the Automatic Database Diagnostic Monitor, and many other goodies you have available in your new Oracle Database 11g Release 1 database.

Downgrading to an Old Version

Oracle supports downgrades to the 10.1 and 10.2 releases. You can downgrade only to the exact release from which you upgraded. If you upgraded to 11.1 from 10.1, you can't downgrade to 10.2. If you've set the COMPATIBLE parameter to 11.0.0 or higher, you won't be able to downgrade, however. You can downgrade to Oracle Database 10g Release 2 (10.2) if the COMPATIBLE parameter is set to 10.2.0 or lower. Similarly, you can downgrade to Oracle Database 10g Release 1 (10.1) if the COMPATIBLE parameter is set to 10.1.0.

Here's a summary of the steps you must take to downgrade your Oracle Database 11g Release 1 (11.1) database to a lower release:

1. Log into the database as the owner of the Oracle Database 11g Release 1 (11.1) Oracle home directory.

2. Go the $ORACLE_HOME/rdbms/admin directory and start SQL*Plus from there.

3. Connect to the database as the user SYS.

   ```
   SQL> CONNECT ssys/sammyy1 AS sysdba
   ```

4. Start up the instance in downgrade mode.

   ```
   SQL> STARTUP DOWNGRADE
   ```

5. Drop the user sysman from the database.

   ```
   SQL>DROP USER sysman CASCADE;
   ```

6. Turn spooling on to capture the downgrade effects.

   ```
   SQL> SPOOL downgrade.log
   ```

7. Issue the command to run the downgrade.

   ```
   SQL> @catdwgrd.sql
   ```

8. The catdowngrd.sql script downgrades the database to the major release from which you upgraded to Oracle Database 11g Release 1. Once the script stops running, turn spooling off as shown here:

   ```
   SQL> SPOOL OFF
   ```

9. Shut down the instance.

   ```
   SQL> SHUTDOWN IMMEDIATE
   ```

10. Change the ORACLE_HOME and PATH variables to point to the correct release to which you've just downgraded the database.

CHAPTER 10

■■■

Creating a Database

You can create an Oracle database as part of the Oracle software installation process in both Windows and UNIX versions. The Oracle Universal Installer provides several templates for database creation, including the decision-support system (DSS) and online transaction processing (OLTP) templates. You can also invoke the Oracle Database Configuration Assistant (DBCA), a GUI tool, which will guide you through the installation process.

Until you become very well versed in the creation of databases, however, you may be better off using the tedious but more flexible manual mode to create databases. I recommend that you manually type in the database creation SQL statements line by line from SQL*Plus; this will give you insight into the various steps involved in creating a database and the potential problems at every stage. Later on, when you're more comfortable with the process, you can just enter all the commands into a script and run the whole script to create other databases, or just use the DBCA.

Before you start creating an Oracle database, there are some steps you need to take: ensuring that you have the right permissions, checking that the file structures are in place, and determining whether you have sufficient resources to start up your new database. Next you need to set up the initialization parameters for the database. This chapter covers all of these topics and provides a summary of the important Oracle configuration (initialization) parameters, with guidelines for their use in your database.

After you create a new database, there are additional tasks you must perform, which I discuss in this chapter: running the necessary post–database creation scripts, changing the passwords, and configuring the database for archive logging. You'll need to know the various modes in which you can start an Oracle instance, as well as how to stop it in different modes and how to restrict access to just the DBAs when necessary. To round out your basic knowledge, we'll look at how to quiesce and suspend a database, which you'll need to know to efficiently manage your databases, and how to drop an Oracle database with the DROP DATABASE command.

Getting Ready to Create the Database

You can create a new database either manually (using scripts) or by using the Oracle Database Configuration Assistant. The DBCA is configured to appear immediately after the installation of the Oracle software to assist you in creating a database, and you can also invoke the DBCA later on to help you create a database.

Whether you create a database manually or let Oracle create one for you at software installation time, a configuration file called init.ora, or its newer equivalent, SPFILE, holds all the database configuration details. After the initial creation of the database, you can always change the behavior of the database by changing the initialization parameters. You can also change the behavior of the database for brief periods or during some sessions by using the ALTER SYSTEM and ALTER SESSION commands to change certain initialization parameter values.

Before you create a database, however, you need to make sure you have the necessary software and appropriate memory and storage resources. The next few sections run through the brief list of things to check.

Installing the Oracle Software

Before you can create a database, you must first install the Oracle Database 11*g* software. If you haven't already done so, see Chapter 9, which covers the installation of the Oracle server software on UNIX and Linux systems.

Creating the File System for the Database

Planning your file systems is an important task, and you need to complete it before you start creating the database. You have to plan the location of the various database files, such as the redo log files and archivelog files, before you create the database, and the placement of the files can have serious effects on performance down the road. Let's look at the sizing and location issues in some detail.

Sizing the File System

The amount of file system space you need depends primarily upon the total space you need to allocate for Oracle datafiles. You use datafiles to create the System and Sysaux tablespaces, as well as the undo tablespace, default permanent tablespace, redo logs, and files to hold application data (tables and indexes). Your overall space estimate should include space for the following:

- *Tables and indexes*: Table and index data is the biggest component of the physical database. You first need to estimate the size of all the tables, which you can base on the number and width of columns and the expected number of rows in each table. You don't need accurate numbers here; rough figures should suffice. You must know what indexes are needed by your application. You also need to know the type of indexes you're going to create, as this has a major bearing on the physical size of the indexes. You can use formulas to determine the space required for the indexes.

- *Undo tablespace*: How much space needs to be allocated to the undo tablespace depends on the size of your database and the nature of your transactions. If you anticipate a lot of large transactions, or you need to plan for large batch jobs, you will require a fairly large undo tablespace. You can always enlarge the undo tablespace later on by adding datafiles to the undo tablespace.

- *Temporary tablespace*: The temporary tablespace size also depends on the nature of your application and the transaction pattern. If the queries involve a lot of sorting operations, you're better off with a larger temporary tablespace in general. Note that you'll be creating the temporary tablespace explicitly during creation of the database and assigning it to be the *default temporary tablespace* for the users in the database.

- *Default permanent tablespace*: As I explained in Chapter 6, it's a good idea to assign a default permanent tablespace for the database. All database users are automatically assigned the default permanent tablespace.

- *System and Sysaux tablespaces*: The System and Sysaux tablespaces are both mandatory tablespaces used by the database to store data dictionary information and objects pertaining to various Oracle schemas.

- *Redo log files*: Redo log files are critical for the functioning of a database, and they're key components when you're trying to recover the database without any loss of committed data. Oracle recommends that you have a minimum of two redo log groups (with each group having one or more members). Redo log files need to be *multiplexed*—that is, you should have more than a single redo log file in each group, because they're a critical part of the database and they're a single point of failure. With multiplexed redo logs, the instance will continue to run even if one copy of the redo log file is removed by error or is corrupted.

The appropriate size for the redo log file will depend on how quickly your database is writing to the log. If you have a lot of DML operations in your database, and the redo logs seem to be filling up very quickly, you may want to increase the size of the log files. (You can't increase the size of an existing redo log file, but you can create larger redo log files and drop the smaller files.) The redo log files are written in a circular fashion, and your goal should be to size the log files such that no more than two or three redo log files are filled up every hour. The fundamental conflict here is between performance and recovery time. A very large redo log file will be efficient because there won't be many log switches and associated checkpoints, all of which impose a performance overhead on the database. However, when you need to perform recovery, larger redo logs take more time to recover from, because you have more data to recover.

You can figure out the optimal redo log file size by looking at the OPTIMAL_LOGFILE_SIZE column of the V$INSTANCE_RECOVERY view, after your database has been running for a while. An easier way to get recommendations for the redo log file size is to view the Redo Log Groups page of the Oracle Enterprise Manager (OEM) Database Control.

Note Oracle recommends that you have four redo log groups, to keep the log writer from having to wait for an available group after each log switch. The members of the redo log groups (the redo log files) should be the same size. Oracle suggests sizing the redo log files such that they switch about every 20 minutes during a busy workload and about once an hour during normal workloads.

- *Flash recovery area*: Oracle recommends that you create a flash recovery area to hold all database backup- and recovery-related files needed for a recovery from a media failure. The flash recovery area holds all datafile backups, Recovery Manager (RMAN) backups, flashback logs, archived redo log files, and control file backups. The size of the flashback area depends on the size and frequency of your backups and on how long you want to retain backups on disk. For example, if you plan on taking weekly backups, you must allocate enough space in the flash recovery area to hold one week's full backups as well as the archived redo logs. If you plan on taking incremental backups in between the weekly full backups, you must also allocate space for those backups in the flash recovery area.

Choosing the Location for the Files

You should place the database files, such as the system, redo log, and archivelog files, in locations that allow you to benefit from the Optimal Flexible Architecture (OFA) guidelines, which I discussed in Chapter 5. Following the OFA guidelines for file placement in your database offers the following benefits:

- Makes it easy for you to locate and identify the various files, such as database files, control files, and redo log files

- Makes it easy to administer multiple Oracle databases and multiple Oracle software versions

- Improves database performance by minimizing contention among the different types of files

If you followed the OFA guidelines while installing your software, you should be in good shape regarding the way your files are physically laid out.

Ensuring Sufficient Memory Allocation

If you don't have enough memory in the system to satisfy the requirements of your database, your database instance will fail to start. Even if it does start, there will be a lot of memory paging and swapping that will slow your database down. The cost of memory is such a small component of enterprise computing costs these days that you're better off getting a large amount of memory for the server on which you plan to install the Oracle database. In Oracle Database 11g, you can use the new MEMORY_TARGET initialization parameter to completely automate the allocation of memory to the Oracle instance.

Getting Necessary Authorizations

You will need authorization to be granted by the UNIX/Linux system administrator for you to be able to create file systems on the server. Your Oracle username should be included in the DBA group by the system administrator, if you are working on a UNIX or a Linux server.

Setting the OS Environment Variables

Before you proceed to create the database, you must set all the necessary operating system environment variables. In UNIX and Linux environments, you must set the following environment variables:

- ORACLE_SID: This is your database's name and is the same as the value of the DB_NAME initialization parameter.

- ORACLE_BASE: This is the top directory for the Oracle software, which for our purposes, is /u01/app/oracle. ORACLE_BASE is currently a recommended variable, but Oracle intends to make it a required variable in a future release.

- ORACLE_HOME: This is the directory in which you installed the Oracle software. Oracle recommends you use the following format for this variable: $ORACLE_BASE/product/release/db_n. For this chapter's purposes, this directory is /u01/app/oracle/product/11.1.0.0/db_1.

- PATH: This is the directory in which Oracle's executable files are located. Oracle's executables are always located in the $ORACLE_HOME/bin directory. You can add the location of Oracle's executable files to the existing PATH value in the following way:

  export PATH=$PATH:$ORACLE_HOME/bin

- LD_LIBRARY_PATH: This variable points out where the Oracle libraries are located. The usual location is the $ORACLE_HOME/lib directory.

Creating the Parameter File

Every Oracle instance makes use of a set of initialization parameters that dictate database limits such as the number of users, specify the names and locations of key files and directories, and optimize performance by setting the size of key resources such as memory. Before you jump into the details of Oracle database creation, it's important to familiarize yourself with the important Oracle initialization parameters and how Oracle uses them.

Types of Database Parameter Files

Oracle uses a *parameter file* to store the initialization parameters and their settings for an instance. You can use either of the following two types of parameter files:

- *Server parameter file* (SPFILE): A binary file that contains the initialization parameters

- *Initialization parameter file* (PFILE): A text file that contains a list of all initialization parameters

The key difference between these two types of files is that with an SPFILE, you have the option of making any changes to the initialization parameters while an instance is running persist across an instance shutdown. You can't do this using the PFILE, since any dynamic changes that are also not recorded in that file will not persist after you restart your instance.

Note that I use the filename init.ora to refer to the PFILE, as the standard name for the PFILE is init*db_name*.ora. After I create the database, I'll show you how to create the SPFILE from the init.ora file.

The initialization parameter file was traditionally the only type of file in which you could store these initialization parameter values. An initialization parameter file is a text file that you can edit like any other text file. By default, this file is located in the $ORACLE_HOME/dbs directory (though you can store it in any place that's helpful to you). If you store the configuration file in a location other than the default, you must specify the complete location when you start the instance. If the initialization parameter filename and the location follow the default conventions, you don't have to specify the name or location of the file at startup.

■**Note** The initialization files are used not only to create the database itself, but also each time you start an Oracle instance. You can tune several aspects of a database's performance by modifying parameter values. You can change some of these parameters dynamically while the instance is running, but for other changes to take effect, you'll have to restart the instance.

The initialization parameter file includes parameters that will help tune the instance, that set limits on certain database resources, and that specify the names and locations of important files. It also contains parameters that affect database performance, such as those specifying the amount of memory allocated to Oracle. Once you create the initialization file, you can start the instance by using the file in your database startup commands.

You can dynamically modify several important configuration parameters while the instance is running. The dynamic changes are made in a SQL*Plus session, without changing the init.ora file itself. You can make an instance-wide change by using the ALTER SYSTEM statement and a session-wide change by using the ALTER SESSION statement. These modifications won't be permanent, however; as soon as you shut down the database, the changes are gone and you're back to the values hard-coded in the init.ora file. To make any configuration parameter changes permanent, you must edit the initialization parameter (init.ora) file.

If you want to make the dynamic changes permanent, so that the parameter is automatically updated and the database uses these new values upon restarting, you should use a server parameter file. The SPFILE is also an initialization file, but you can't make changes to it directly because it's a binary file, not a text file. Using the SPFILE to manage your instance provides several benefits, as you'll see in the "Using a Server Parameter File" section later in the chapter. Oracle recommends that you use the SPFILE because of the advantages it offers.

The Initialization Parameter File

In the database creation example I show later, I use the traditional init.ora file to create the database. Once I create my database, I'll create an SPFILE from this init.ora file. Oracle provides a template to make it easy for you to create your own initialization parameter file. This template is located in the $ORACLE_HOME/dbs directory in UNIX/Linux systems and in the $ORACLE_HOME/database directory in Windows systems. Copy this init.ora template, rename it init*db_name*.ora, and then edit it to meet your own site's requirements. Don't be too nervous about trying to make "correct" estimates for the various configuration parameters, because most of the configuration parameters are easily modifiable throughout the life of the database. Just make sure you're careful about the handful of parameters that you can't change without redoing the entire database from scratch. I point out these parameters in the "Important Oracle Database 11*g* Initialization Parameters" section later in this chapter.

The interesting thing about the initialization parameter file is that it contains the configuration parameters for memory and some I/O parameters, but not for the database filenames or the tablespaces that the datafiles belong to. The control file holds all that information. The initialization file, though, has the locations of the control files and the dump directories for error messages. It also specifies the modes chosen for undo management, the optimizer, and archiving for the redo logs.

With the exception of DB_NAME, all Oracle initialization parameters are optional. Oracle will simply use the default values for all the initialization parameters you leave out of the initialization parameter file.

Of course, when you let Oracle use default values for a parameter, you relinquish control over that parameter. You should leave parameters out of the init.ora file only if you determine that their default values are okay for your database. In general, it's a good idea to use approximate sizes for the important configuration parameters and use a trial-and-error method to determine whether you need to use parameters that are new or that you haven't used before.

Oracle Database 11g is highly configurable, but that benefit also carries with it the need for DBAs to learn not only how the large number of parameters work, but also how they may interact with one another to produce results at variance with your original plans. For example, an increase in the SGA size may increase database performance up to a point, but too big an increase might actually slow the database down, because the operating system might be induced to swap the higher SGA in and out of real memory. Be cautious about making configuration changes; always think through the implications of tinkering with initialization parameters.

Changing the Initialization Parameter Values

You can change the value of any initialization parameter by simply editing the init.ora file. However, for the changes to actually take effect, you have to *bounce* the database—stop it and start it again. As you can imagine, this is not always possible, especially if you are managing a production database. However, you can change several of the parameters on the fly—these are called *dynamic* parameters for that reason. The parameters you can change only by changing the init.ora file and then restarting the database are called *static* parameters.

You have three ways to change the value of dynamic parameters: the ALTER SESSION, ALTER SYSTEM, and ALTER SYSTEM . . . DEFERRED commands.

Using the ALTER SESSION Command

The ALTER SESSION command enables you to change dynamic parameter values for the duration of the session that issues the command. The ALTER SESSION command is used only to change a parameter's value temporarily.

Here is the general syntax for the command:

```
ALTER SESSION SET parameter_name=value;
```

Using the ALTER SYSTEM Statement

The ALTER SYSTEM statement changes the parameter's value for all sessions. However, these changes will be in force only for the duration of the instance; when the database is restarted, these changes will go away, unless you modify the init.ora file accordingly or you use the SPFILE.

Here is the syntax for this command:

```
ALTER SYSTEM SET parameter_name=value;
```

Using the ALTER SYSTEM . . . DEFERRED Statement

The ALTER SYSTEM . . . DEFERRED statement will make the new values for a parameter effective for all sessions, but not immediately. Only sessions started after the statement is executed are affected. All currently open sessions will continue to use the old parameter values.

Here is the syntax for this command:

```
ALTER SYSTEM SET parameter_name DEFERRED;
```

The ALTER SYSTEM . . . DEFERRED statement works only for only a few initialization parameters. Therefore, you must use the ALTER SYSTEM statement instead for systemwide initialization parameter changes. Any parameter value change you make through the ALTER SYSTEM statement, of course, applies immediately to all sessions.

When you change the value of a parameter by using the ALTER SESSION or ALTER SYSTEM statement, the change in the parameter's value will last only for the duration of the instance. When you have to restart the instance, the parameter values will revert to their old values, unless you record the changes in the init.ora file or you use (started up your instance with) the SPFILE.

Important Oracle Database 11g Initialization Parameters

The following sections present the most important Oracle initialization parameters you need to be familiar with. For the sake of clarity, I've divided the parameters into various groups, such as audit-related parameters, process and session parameters, memory configuration parameters, and so on. My parameter groupings are arbitrary and are designed simply to make it easier to understand the configuration of a new database.

Although this list looks long and formidable, it isn't a complete list of the initialization parameters for Oracle Database 11g—it's a list of only the most commonly used parameters. Oracle Database 11g has over 250 documented initialization parameters that DBAs can configure (if you add the undocumented or hidden initialization parameters, the total comes to well over a thousand parameters). Don't be disheartened, though. The basic list of parameters that you need in order to start your new database can be fairly small and easy to understand. Oracle has, for the first time, grouped together the most common initialization parameters, and according to Oracle, most databases should only need these basic parameters set. Oracle advises you to become familiar with these basic parameters and to use other parameters only when directed to do so by the documentation or in special circumstances. Later on, as you study various topics such as backup and recovery, performance tuning, networking, and so on, you'll have a chance to really understand how to use the more esoteric initialization parameters.

DIAGNOSTIC_DEST

Oracle Database 11g uses a new infrastructure for storing diagnostic information, called the Automatic Diagnostic Repository (ADR). You specify the location of this directory with the initialization parameter DIAGNOSTIC_DEST. The DIAGNOSTIC_DEST parameter specifies the structure of the ADR in the following way:

<diagnostic_dest>/diag/rdbms/*<dbname>*/*<instname>*

If your database name is orcl1 and the instance name is also orcl1, the ADR home directory will be

<diagnostic_dest>/diag/rdbms/orcl1/orcl1

The ADR home directory contains alert logs, trace files, core files, and incident files, as I explain in Chapter 5. If you set the ORACLE_BASE directory, the location of the ADR is derived from that. Otherwise, the default location of the diagnostic directory is $ORACLE_HOME/log.

FIXED_DATE

This is a new initialization parameter in Oracle Database 11g that enables you to set a constant date that SYSDATE will return instead of the current date. You can undo the FIXED_DATE setting with a value of NONE. Here is the syntax of the parameter:

Example: FIXED_DATE = YYYY-MM-DD-HH24:MI:SS (or the default Oracle date format)

Default value: None

Parameter type: Dynamic

Audit-Related Parameters

An Oracle database can be configured to audit actions by its users, and you can configure this auditing feature according to several criteria, although the default behavior of the database is not to audit actions. The following parameters let you configure how you audit your database usage.

AUDIT_TRAIL

The AUDIT_TRAIL parameter turns auditing on or off for the database. If you don't want auditing to be turned on, do nothing, since the default value for this parameter is none, or false, which disables database auditing. If you want auditing turned on, you can set the AUDIT_TRAIL parameter to any of the following values:

- *os*: Oracle writes the audit records to an operating system audit trail, which is an operating system file, including audit records from the OS, audit records for the SYS user, and those database actions that are always automatically audited.

- *db*: Oracle records the same type of auditing as with the os setting, but it directs all audit records to the database audit trail, which is the AUD$ table owned by SYS.

- *db,extended*: This is similar to the db setting, but also provides extended audit information like the SQLBIND and SQLTEXT columns of the SYS.AUD$ table.

- *none*: This value disables auditing.

In addition, you have two XML-related AUDIT_TRAIL values:

- *XML*: This value for audit trail enables database auditing and writes audit details to OS files in XML format.

- *XML,EXTENDED*: This value prints all database audit records plus the SQLTEXT and SQLBIND values to OS files in the XML format.

The parameter is set as follows:

Example: AUDIT_TRAIL=db

Default value: None

Parameter type: Static

Chapter 12 provides more information about auditing actions within an Oracle database.

■**Tip** Even if you don't set the AUDIT_TRAIL parameter to any value, Oracle will still write audit information to an operating system file for all database actions that are audited by default. On a UNIX system, the default location for this file is the $ORACLE_HOME/rdbms/audit directory. Of course, you can specify a different directory if you wish.

AUDIT_FILE_DEST

The AUDIT_FILE_DEST parameter specifies the directory in which the database will write the audit records, when you choose the operating system as the destination with the AUDIT_TRAIL parameter by specifying AUDIT_TRAIL=os. You can also specify this parameter if you choose the XML or XML,EXTENDED options for the AUDIT_TRAIL option, since the audit records are written to operating system files in both cases.

Example: AUDIT_FILE_DEST=/u01/app/oracle/audit

Default value: $ORACLE_HOME/rdbms/audit

Parameter type: Dynamic. You can modify this parameter with the ALTER SYSTEM . . . DEFERRED command.

AUDIT_SYS_OPERATIONS

If set to a value of true, AUDIT_SYS_OPERATIONS will audit all actions of the SYS user and any other user with a SYSDBA or SYSOPER role and will write the details to the operating system audit trail specified by the AUDIT_TRAIL parameter. By writing the audit information to a secure operating system location, you remove any possibility of the SYS user tampering with an audit trail that is located within the database. The possible values are true and false.

Example: AUDIT_SYS_OPERATIONS=true

Default value: false

Parameter type: Static

LDAP_DIRECTORY_SYSAUTH

LDAP_DIRECTORY_SYSAUTH is a new initialization parameter in Oracle Database 11g that enables or disables directory authentication for the SYSDBA and SYSOPER privileges. Possible values are yes and no.

Example: LDAP_DIRECTORY_SYSAUTH=yes

Default value: None

Parameter type: Static

Database Name and Other General Parameters

The most important of the general parameters is the parameter that sets the name of the database. Let's look at this set of parameters in detail.

DB_NAME and DB_UNIQUE_NAME

The DB_NAME parameter sets the name of the database. This is a mandatory parameter, and the value is the same as the database name you used to create the database. The DB_NAME value should be the same as the value of the ORACLE_SID environment variable. This parameter can't be changed after the database is created. You can have a DB_NAME value of up to eight characters.

Example: DB_NAME=orcl11

Default value: false

Parameter type: Static

The DB_UNIQUE_NAME parameter lets you specify a globally unique name for the database.

DB_DOMAIN

The DB_DOMAIN parameter specifies a fully qualified name (in Internet dot notation) for the database, and this is typically the same as the name of the organization that owns the database. The DB_DOMAIN parameter specifies the logical location of the database within the network structure, and you should set this parameter if your database is part of a distributed system.

Example: DB_DOMAIN=world

Default value: Null

Parameter type: Static

INSTANCE_NAME

The INSTANCE_NAME parameter will have the same value as the DB_NAME parameter in a single instance environment. You can associate multiple instances to a single database service (DB_NAME) in a Real Application Clusters environment.

Example: INSTANCE NAME=orcl11

Default value: The instance SID

Parameter type: Static

SERVICE_NAME

The SERVICE_NAME parameter provides a name for the database service, and it can be anything you want it to be. Usually, it is a combination of the database name and your database domain.

Example: SERVICE_NAME=orcl11

Default value: DB_NAME.DB_DOMAIN

Parameter type: Dynamic. This parameter can be changed with the ALTER SYSTEM command.

COMPATIBLE

The COMPATIBLE parameter allows you to use the latest Oracle database release, while making sure that the database is compatible with an earlier release.

Suppose you upgrade to the Oracle Database 11g Release 1 version, but your application developers haven't made any changes to their Oracle 10.2 application. In this case, you could set the COMPATIBLE parameter equal to 10.2 so the untested features of the new Oracle version won't hurt your application. Later on, after the application has been suitably upgraded, you can reset the COMPATIBLE initialization parameter to 11.1.0, which is the default value for Oracle Database 11g Release 1.

If, instead, you immediately raise the compatible value to 10.2, you can use all the new 10.2 features, but you won't be able to downgrade your database to 9.2 or any other lower versions. You must understand this irreversible compatibility clearly, before you set the value for this parameter.

Example: COMPATIBLE=11.1.0.6

Default value: 10.2.0

Parameter type: Static

INSTANCE_TYPE

The INSTANCE_TYPE parameter specifies whether your instance is a database instance or an Automatic Storage Management instance. You specify ASM if the instance is an Automatic Storage Management instance. A setting of RDBMS denotes a normal database instance.

Example: INSTANCE_TYPE=asm

Default value: RDBMS

Parameter type: Static

■**Note** A set of parameter values is specific to an Oracle database using ASM, and some parameters pertain only to the special ASM instances. You'll review these initialization parameters in Chapter 17, where I discuss ASM in detail.

NLS_DATE_FORMAT

The NLS_DATE_FORMAT parameter specifies the default date format Oracle will use. Oracle uses this date format when using the TO_CHAR or TO_DATE functions in SQL. There is a default value, which is derived from the NLS_TERRITORY parameter. For example, if the NLS_TERRITORY format is America, the NLS_DATE_FORMAT parameter is automatically set to the DD-MON-YY format.

Example: NLS_DATE_FORMAT=DD-MM-YYYY HH:MI:SS

Default value: Depends on the NLS_TERRITORY variable and the operating system

Parameter type: Dynamic. This parameter can be altered by using the ALTER SESSION command.

File-Related Parameters

You can specify several file-related parameters in your init.ora file. Oracle requires you to specify several destination locations for trace files and error messages. In addition, you need to specify the UTL_FILE_DIR parameter in order to use the UTL_FILE package. The following sections cover the key file-related parameters.

IFILE

You can use the IFILE parameter to embed another initialization file in it. For example, you can have a line in your init.ora file such as this:

```
ifile=config.ora
```

In the config.ora file, you could then have some common initialization parameters for several instances. You can have up to three levels of nesting.

Default value: No default value

Parameter type: Static

CONTROL_FILES

Control files are key files that hold datafile names and locations and a lot of other important information. The database needs only one control file, but because this is such an important file, you always save multiple copies of it. The way to multiplex the control file is to simply specify multiple locations (up to a maximum of eight) in the CONTROL_FILES parameter. The minimum number of control files is one, but Oracle recommends you have at least two control files per instance, and most DBAs usually use three. If one of the control files is damaged or accidentally deleted, the instance will fail when it tries to access that control file. When this happens with multiple copies of the control file, you can always restart the database after first copying the undamaged control file to a different location.

When you use the CREATE DATABASE statement, Oracle creates the control files listed in the CONTROL_FILES parameter. If you don't include this parameter in your initialization file when creating the database, Oracle will create a control file using a default operating system–dependent filename or, if you have enabled Oracle Managed Files, it will create Oracle-managed control files. You must have a minimum of one control file and may have up to eight control files per database.

Example: CONTROL_FILES=('/u01/app/oracle/orcl11/control/ctl01.ora', ' /u01/app/oracle/orcl11/control/ctl02.ora',/ u01/app/oracle/orcl11/control/ctl03.ora'

Default value: Depends on the operating system

Parameter type: Static

CONTROL_FILE_RECORD_KEEP_TIME

The CONTROL_FILE_RECORD_KEEP_TIME parameter specifies how many days Oracle will retain records in the control file before overwriting them. Oracle recommends that you set this parameter to a high value, to ensure that all online disk backup information remains in the control file. For example, if you maintain a flash recovery area that holds two full weekly backups and daily incremental backups, you must set CONTROL_FILE_RECORD_KEEP_TIME to at least 21 days.

Example: CONTROL_FILE_RECORD_KEEP_TIME=14

Default value: Seven days

Parameter type: Modifiable dynamically, with the ALTER SYSTEM statement

UTL_FILE_DIR

You can use the UTL_FILE_DIR parameter to specify the directory (or directories) Oracle will use to process I/O when you use the Oracle UTL_FILE package to read from or write to the operating system files. You can set UTL_FILE_DIR to any OS directory you want. If you just specify an asterisk (*) instead of any specific directory name, the UTL_FILE package will read and write to and from all the OS directories; Oracle recommends against this practice.

Example: UTL_FILE_DIR=/u01/app/oracle/utl_dir

Default value: None; you can't use the UTL_FILE package to do any I/O with this setting.

Parameter type: Static

■**Caution** You'll need to use some directory on the server where you have read/write privileges as the setting for UTL_FILE_DIR; otherwise the package can't process I/O to the operating system. If you use * as the value for the UTL_FILE_DIR parameter, however, users can write to and read from *all* directories for which you have read/write privileges. Obviously, you don't want this to happen!

Oracle Managed Files Parameters

You'll need to use three parameters to specify the format of the Oracle Managed Files (OMF) when you decide to use the feature: DB_CREATE_FILE_DEST, DB_CREATE_ONLINE_LOG_DEST_*n*, and DB_RECOVERY_FILE_DEST. I describe the first two parameters in the sections that follow and the third under the "Recovery-Related Parameters" section. Chapter 6 discusses in more detail how to use the initialization parameters dealing with OMF.

DB_CREATE_FILE_DEST

The DB_CREATE_FILE_DEST parameter specifies the default location for Oracle-managed datafiles. It's also the directory where Oracle will create datafiles and temporary files when you don't specify an explicit location for them. The directory must already exist with the correct read/write permissions for Oracle.

Example: DB_CREATE_FILE_DEST=/u01/app/oracle/orcl11/dbfile/

Default value: None

Parameter type: Dynamic. It can be changed using either the ALTER SYSTEM or ALTER SESSION command.

DB_CREATE_ONLINE_LOG_DEST_n

The DB_CREATE_ONLINE_LOG_DEST_*n* parameter specifies the default location for OMF online redo log files and control files. To multiplex the online redo log files or the control file, specify more than one value for the parameter. Oracle creates one member of each online redo log and one control file in each location when you specify a value of *n* greater than one. You can have a maximum of five separate directory locations. Please see Chapter 17 for examples of how to use this parameter.

Example: DB_CREATE_ONLINE_LOG_DEST_1=/u01/app/oracle/orcl11/log

Default value: None

Parameter type: Dynamic. This parameter can be changed using either the ALTER SYSTEM or ALTER SESSION command.

Process and Session Parameters

Several initialization parameters relate to the number of processes and the number of sessions that your database can handle. The following sections explore the important process and session parameters.

PROCESSES

The value of the PROCESSES parameter will set the upper limit for the number of operating system processes that can connect to your database concurrently. Both the SESSIONS and TRANSACTIONS parameters derive their default values from this parameter.

Example: PROCESSES=200

Default value: At least 6, but varies according to the operating system

Parameter type: Static

DB_WRITER_PROCESSES

The DB_WRITER_PROCESSES parameter specifies the initial number of database writer processes for your instance. Instances with very heavy data modification may opt for more than the default, which is one process or the number of CPUs divided by 8, whichever is greater. You can have up to 20 processes per instance.

Example: DB_WRITER_PROCESSES=12

Default value: 1 or the number of CPUs divided by 8, whichever is greater

Parameter type: Static

OPEN_CURSORS

The OPEN_CURSORS parameter sets the limit on the number of open cursors a single session can have at any given time.

Example: OPEN_CURSORS=300

Default value: 50

Parameter type: Modifiable with the ALTER SYSTEM statement

Memory-Configuration Parameters

The memory-configuration parameters determine the memory allocated to key components of the SGA. There are two major areas of memory you allocate to Oracle from the operating system's memory: the system global area (SGA) and the program global area (PGA). Oracle Database 11g takes the guessing and fine-tuning out of both SGA and PGA memory allocations. You can simply set the MEMORY_TARGET parameter to completely automate Oracle's memory management.

■**Note** Oracle's guidelines regarding the ideal settings for the various components of memory, such as the DB_CACHE_SIZE and shared pool, are often vague and not really helpful to a beginner. For example, Oracle states that the DB_CACHE_SIZE should be from 20 to 80 percent of the available memory for a data warehouse database. The shared pool recommendation for the same database is between 5 and 10 percent. The wide ranges make the DB_CACHE_SIZE recommendations useless. If your total memory is 2GB, you're supposed to allocate from 100MB to 200MB of memory for the shared pool. If your total memory allocation is 32GB, your allocation for the shared pool would be between 1.6GB and 3.2GB, according to the "standard" recommendations. The best thing to do is use a trial-and-error method to see whether the various memory settings are appropriate for your database.

Let's briefly review the key Oracle Database 11g parameters concerning memory allocation. The buffer cache is the area of Oracle's memory where it keeps data blocks that have been read in from disk, and the data blocks may be modified here before being written back to disk again. Having a big enough buffer cache will improve performance by avoiding too many disk accesses, which are much slower than accessing data in memory.

You can set up the buffer cache for your database in units of the standard or primary block size you chose for the database (using the DB_BLOCK_SIZE parameter), or you can use nonstandard-block-sized buffer caches. If you want to base your buffer cache on the standard block size, you use the DB_CACHE_SIZE parameter to size your cache.

MEMORY_MAX_TARGET

The MEMORY_MAX_TARGET parameter defines the maximum value to which you can set the MEMORY_TARGET initialization parameter. The value can range from 0 to the maximum physical memory available to the Oracle instance. You can set the value in KB, MB, or GB.

Example: MEMORY_MAX_TARGET=1800m

Default value: 0

Parameter type: Static

If you omit the MEMORY_MAX_TARGET parameter but set the MEMORY_TARGET parameter, the MEMORY_MAX_TARGET parameter's value defaults to that of the MEMORY_TARGET parameter's value.

MEMORY_TARGET

The MEMORY_TARGET parameter specifies the memory allocated to Oracle when you use automatic memory management to allocate memory to the Oracle instance. The database will raise or lower the values of the SGA and the PGA components so the combined value is equal to the MEMORY_TARGET parameter setting. You can set the value in KB, MB, or GB.

Example: MEMORY_TARGET=1000m

Default value: 0

Parameter type: Dynamic

DB_CACHE_SIZE

The DB_CACHE_SIZE parameter sets the size of the default buffer pool for those buffers that have the primary block size (this is the block size defined by DB_BLOCK_SIZE). For example, you can use a number like 1024MB.

Example: DB_CACHE_SIZE = 750MB

Default value: If you're using the MEMORY_TARGET parameter, the default is 0. If you aren't using MEMORY_TARGET, it's the greater of 48MB or 4MB.

Parameter type: Dynamic. It can be modified with the ALTER SYSTEM command.

If you're using automatic memory management, of course, you don't have any specific memory-related initialization parameters, including the DB_CACHE_SIZE parameters. The database assigns a default value of 0 for this parameter if you choose automatic memory management and ignore this parameter. However, you can assign a specific value for this parameter even when you choose to implement automatic memory management. When you do so, Oracle will treat the value you assign for the DB_CACHE_SIZE parameter as the minimum value for the memory pool.

DB_KEEP_CACHE_SIZE

The normal behavior of the buffer pool is to treat all the objects placed in it equally. That is, any object will remain in the pool as long as free memory is available in the buffer cache. Objects are removed (aged out) only when there is no free space. When this happens, the oldest unused objects sitting in memory are removed to make space for new objects.

The use of two specialized buffer pools—the keep pool and the recycle pool—allows you to specify at object-creation time how you want the buffer pool to treat certain objects. For example, if you know that certain objects don't really need to be in memory for a long time, you can assign them to a *recycle pool*, which removes the objects right after they're used. In contrast, the *keep pool* always retains an object in memory if it's created with the KEEP option.

The DB_KEEP_CACHE_SIZE parameter specifies the size of the keep pool, and it's set as follows:

Example: DB_KEEP_CACHE_SIZE = 500MB

Default value: 0; by default, this parameter is not configured.

Parameter type: Dynamic. It can be changed by using the ALTER SYSTEM command.

DB_RECYCLE_CACHE_SIZE

The DB_RECYCLE_CACHE_SIZE parameter specifies the size of the recycle pool in the buffer cache. Oracle removes objects from this pool as soon as the objects are used. The parameter is set as follows:

Example: DB_RECYCLE_CACHE_SIZE = 200MB

Default value: 0; by default, this parameter is not configured.

Parameter type: Dynamic. It can be changed by using the ALTER SYSTEM command.

DB_nK_CACHE_SIZE

If you prefer to use nonstandard-sized buffer caches, you need to specify the DB_*n*K_CACHE_SIZE parameter for each. You can use 2, 4, 8, 16, or 32 as the value for the variable *n*.

Example: DB_8K_CACHE_SIZE=4096MB

Default value: 0

Parameter type: Dynamic. You can change the value of this parameter's value with the ALTER SYSTEM command.

AUDIT_SYS_OPERATIONS

The AUDIT_SYS_OPERATIONS parameter enables and disables the auditing of actions by the user SYS as well as any users connecting with the SYSDBA or the SYSOPER privileges. The database writes the audit records to the operating system audit trail. Possible values are true and false.

Example: AUDIT_SYS_OPERATIONS=true

Default value: false

Parameter type: Static

CLIENT_RESULT_CACHE_LAG

The CLIENT_RESULT_CACHE_LAG initialization parameter specifies the maximum time that can elapse before the OCI client query makes another round-trip to retrieve database changes pertaining to queries cached on the client. The range of values is 0 to a system-dependent maximum value.

Example: CLIENT_RESULT_CACHE_LAG = 10000

Default value: 5000 (seconds)

Parameter type: Static

CLIENT_RESULT_CACHE_SIZE

The CLIENT_RESULT_CACHE_SIZE parameter specifies the maximum memory allocated to the client per process result set cache (in bytes). You must set a nonzero value for this parameter to enable the client query cache feature. You can override this parameter by setting the client configuration parameter OCI_RESULT_CACHE_MAX_SIZE. The range of values is 0 to an operating system–dependent value.

Example: CLIENT_RESULT_CACHE_SIZE = 50M

Default value: 0

Parameter type: Static

CONTROL_MANAGEMENT_PACK_ACCESS

The `CONTROL_MANAGEMENT_PACK_ACCESS` parameter specifies which of the two Server Manageability Packs should be active in the database. You can use the following two packs:

- *Diagnostic pack*: Includes AWR, ADDM, and so on
- *Tuning pack*: Includes the SQL Tuning Advisor, SQL Access Advisor, and so on

You'll need a separate license for the diagnostic pack in order to enable the tuning pack. Possible values are `diagnostic`, `none`, and `diagnostic+tuning`.

Example: `CONTROL_MANAGEMENT_PACK=diagnostic`

Default value: `diagnostic+tuning`

Parameter type: Dynamic. Modifiable with the `ALTER SYSTEM` statement

LARGE_POOL_SIZE

The shared pool can normally take care of the memory needs of shared servers as well as Oracle backup and restore operations, and a few other operations. Sometimes, though, this may place a heavy burden on the shared pool, causing a lot of fragmentation and the premature aging-out of important objects from the shared pool due to lack of space.

To avoid these problems, you can use the `LARGE_POOL_SIZE` parameter to mostly free up the shared pool for caching SQL queries and data dictionary information. If the `PARALLEL_AUTOMATIC_TUNING` parameter is set, the large pool is also used for parallel-execution message buffers. The amount of memory required for the large pool in this case depends on the number of parallel threads per CPU and the number of CPUs.

Example: `LARGE_POOL_SIZE=800M`

Default value: 0 (if the pool is not required for parallel execution and `DBWR_IO_SLAVES` is not set)

Parameter type: Dynamic. The `ALTER SYSTEM` command can be used to modify this parameter.

Archivelog Parameters

Oracle gives you the option of archiving your filled redo logs. When you configure your database to archive its redo logs, the database is said to be in an *archivelog mode*. You should always archivelog your production databases unless there are exceptional reasons for not doing so. If you decide to archive the redo logs, you have to specify that in the initialization file using the three parameters described next.

LOG_ARCHIVE_DEST_n

The `LOG_ARCHIVE_DEST_`*n* parameters (where *n* = 1, 2, 3, . . . 10) define up to ten archivelog destinations. This parameter enables you to specify the location (or locations) of the archived logs.

You should set this parameter only if you are running the database in archivelog mode. You can set the database to run in archivelog mode when you create the database by specifying the `ARCHIVELOG` keyword in your `CREATE DATABASE` statement.

This is how you specify the `LOG_ARCHIVE_DEST_`*n* parameter (*n*=1):

Example: `LOG_ARCHIVE_DEST_1='LOCATION=/u02/app/oracle/arch/'`

Default value: None

Parameter type: Dynamic. You can use the `ALTER SESSION` or the `ALTER SYSTEM` command to make changes.

LOG_ARCHIVE_FORMAT

The LOG_ARCHIVE_FORMAT parameter specifies the default filename format for the archived redo log files. In this example, %t stands for the thread number, %s for the log sequence number, and %r for the resetlog's ID that ensures a unique name for archived redo logs across multiple incarnations of the database (the multiple incarnations are created after using a resetlogs operation).

Example: LOG_ARCHIVE_FORMAT = 'log%t_%s_%r.arc'

Default value: Operating-system dependent

Parameter type: Static

Undo Space Parameters

The main undo-related parameters are the UNDO_MANAGEMENT, UNDO_TABLESPACE, and UNDO_RETENTION parameters. Note that you can specify the undo-retention guarantee when you create the database by using the RETENTION GUARANTEE clause in the CREATE UNDO TABLESPACE statement.

UNDO_MANAGEMENT

If the UNDO_MANAGEMENT parameter is set to auto, the undo tablespace is used for storing the undo records, and Oracle will automatically manage the undo segments.

Example: UNDO_MANAGEMENT = auto

Default value: auto

Parameter type: Static

UNDO_TABLESPACE

The UNDO_TABLESPACE parameter determines the default tablespace for undo records. If you have only a single undo tablespace, you don't need to specify this parameter—Oracle will automatically use your undo tablespace. If you don't have an undo tablespace available, Oracle will use the System rollback segment for undo storage, which isn't a good option. If you don't specify a value for this parameter when you create the database, and you have chosen to use Automatic Undo Management (AUM), Oracle will create a default undo tablespace with the name UNDOTBS. This default tablespace will have a single 10MB datafile that will be automatically extended without a maximum limit.

Example: UNDO_TABLESPACE = undotbs1

Default value: The first undo tablespace available

Parameter type: Dynamic. You can use the ALTER SYSTEM command to change the default undo tablespace.

UNDO_RETENTION

The UNDO_RETENTION parameter specifies the amount of redo information to be saved in the undo tablespace before it can be overwritten. The appropriate value for this parameter depends on the size of the undo tablespace and the nature of the queries in your database. If the queries aren't huge, they don't need to have large snapshots of data, and you could get by with a low undo retention interval. Similarly, if there is plenty of free space available in the undo tablespace, transactions won't be overwritten, and you are less likely to run into the snapshot-too-old problem.

If you plan on using the Flashback Query feature extensively, you will have to figure out how far back in time your Flashback queries will go, and specify the UNDO_RETENTION parameter accordingly.

Example: UNDO_RETENTION = 14400 (4 hours)

Default value: 900 (seconds)

Parameter type: Dynamic. You can use the ALTER SYSTEM command to increase the value to a practically unlimited time period.

Oracle Licensing Parameter

The use of Oracle software is limited by the license agreement between Oracle and the customer. There are two important parameters that control the usage of Oracle licenses, LICENSE_MAX_USERS and LICENSE_MAX_SESSIONS, the first setting a limit on the number of concurrent Oracle users and the second, the maximum number of users you can create in a database.

LICENSE_MAX_SESSIONS

The LICENSE_MAX_SESSIONS parameter sets the maximum number of concurrent sessions you can have at any given time. Once your database reaches this limit, new sessions can't connect, getting a warning about the database reaching its maximum user capacity. If you set a zero value for this parameter, the database doesn't enforce session licensing.

Example: LICENSE_MAX_SESSIONS=250

Default value: 0

Parameter type: Dynamic. You can issue the ALTER SYSTEM command to change the value of this parameter.

■**Note** You must set either the LICENSE_MAX_SESSIONS parameter or the LICENSE_MAX_USERS parameter, but not both. That is, you must set one of the parameters to zero and the other to a positive number.

LICENSE_MAX_USERS

The LICENSE_MAX_USERS parameter specifies the maximum number of users you can create in your database. The value of this parameter can range from zero to the number of user licenses.

Example: LICENSE_MAX_USRS=1200

Default value: 0

Parameter type: Dynamic. You can issue the ALTER SYSTEM command to change the value of the parameter.

Performance- and Diagnostics-Related Parameters

You can configure several performance-related parameters in your parameter file. In addition, you can set several parameters to change the diagnostic capabilities of the database when you're performing activities such as tracing SQL statements.

STATISTICS_LEVEL

You set the STATISTICS_LEVEL parameter to specify the level of statistics collection by Oracle. There are three possible values for this parameter: BASIC, TYPICAL, and ALL. Setting this parameter to the default value of TYPICAL will ensure the collection of all major statistics required for database self-management and will provide the best overall performance. When the STATISTICS_LEVEL parameter is set to ALL, Oracle collects additional statistics, such as timed OS statistics and plan-execution statistics.

Example: STATISTICS_LEVEL = typical

Default value: TYPICAL

Parameter type: Modifiable with either the ALTER SESSION or the ALTER SYSTEM statement

---

■**Caution** Setting the STATISTICS_LEVEL parameter to BASIC disables the collection of many of the important statistics required by Oracle Database 11*g* features and functionality, including these:

- Automatic Workload Repository (AWR) snapshots
- Automatic Database Diagnostic Monitor (ADDM)
- All server-generated alerts
- Automatic Shared Memory Management
- Automatic optimizer statistics collection
- Buffer cache advisory and the mean time to recover (MTTR) advisory
- Timed statistics

OPTIMIZER_CAPTURE_SQL_PLAN_BASELINES

The OPTIMIZER_CAPTURE_SQL_PLAN_BASELINES parameter enables the SQL Plan Management feature by enabling the capturing of repeatable SQL statements and the generation of SQL plan baselines for those statements. Possible values for this parameter are true and false.

Example: OPTIMIZER_CAPTURE_SQL_PLAN_BASELINES=true

Default value: false

Parameter type: Dynamic. Modifiable with the ALTER SESSION or the ALTER SYSTEM statement.

OPTIMIZER_MODE

The OPTIMIZER_MODE parameter dictates the type of optimization you want Oracle's query optimizer to follow. You can set the optimizer mode to the following values:

- all_rows: The query optimizer uses a cost-based approach for all SQL statements and optimizes with a goal of best throughput (minimum resource cost to complete the entire statement).
- first_rows_*n*: The query optimizer uses a cost-based approach and optimizes with a goal of best response time to return the first *n* rows (where *n* = 1, 10, 100, or 1000).
- first_rows: The query optimizer uses a mix of costs and heuristics to find the best plan for quickly returning the first few rows.

■**Note** The first_rows setting is available for backward compatibility—Oracle recommends using the first_rows_*n* setting instead.

Example: OPTIMIZER_MODE = first_rows

Default value: all_rows

Parameter type: Dynamic. You can modify the value by issuing the ALTER SESSION or ALTER SYSTEM statement.

OPTIMIZER_FEATURES_ENABLE

The OPTIMIZER_FEATURES_ENABLE parameter enables the database to retain the behavior of an older Oracle software release after you upgrade it. For example, after upgrading an Oracle 10.2 release database to the Oracle 11.1 release, you can set the OPTIMIZER_FEATURES_ENABLE parameter to 10.2, thus retaining the optimizer behavior of Oracle Database 10*g* Release 2.

Example: OPTIMIZER_FEATURES_ENABLE = 10.2

Default value: 11.1.0.6

Parameter type: Dynamic. You can use the ALTER SESSION or the ALTER SYSTEM command to make changes.

OPTIMIZER_DYNAMIC_SAMPLING

When an object doesn't have any optimizer statistics collected, Oracle dynamically samples the data in order to collect a quick set of statistics. You control the level of dynamic sampling by setting the OPTIMIZER_DYNAMIC_SAMPLING parameter.

Example: OPTIMIZER_DYNAMIC_SAMPLING = 2

Default value: Ranges from 0 to 2, depending upon the value of the OPTIMIZER_FEATURES_ENABLE parameter (if less than 9.0.1, 0; for 9.2.0, 1; and for 10.0.0 or higher, 2).

Parameter type: Dynamic. It can be modified by the ALTER SESSION or ALTER SYSTEM command.

OPTIMIZER_USE_INVISIBLE_INDEXES

The OPTIMIZER_USE_INVISIBLE_INDEXES parameter enables or disables the use of invisible indexes. Possible values are true and false.

Example: OPTIMIZER_USE_INVISIBLE_INDEXES=true

Default value: false

Parameter type: Dynamic. You can modify it with the ALTER SESSION or ALTER SYSTEM command.

OPTIMIZER_USE_PENDING_STATISTICS

The OPTIMIZER_USE_PENDING_STATISTICS parameter specifies whether the cost optimizer can use pending statistics. Possible values are true and false.

Example: OPTIMIZER_USE_PENDING_STATISTICS=true

Default value: false

Parameter type: Dynamic. You can modify it with the ALTER SESSION or ALTER SYSTEM command.

OPTIMIZER_USE_SQL_PLAN_BASELINES

The OPTIMIZER_USE_SQL_PLAN_BASELINES initialization parameter enables or disables the use of SQL plan baselines stored in the database. If you enable SQL Plan Management by enabling this feature, the optimizer will look for a SQL plan baseline and choose the plan with the lowest cost. Possible values are true and false.

Example: OPTIMIZER_USE_SQL_PLAN_BASELINES=true

Default value: true

Parameter type: Dynamic. You can modify it with the ALTER SESSION or ALTER SYSTEM command.

PLSQL_CODE_TYPE

The PLSQL_CODE_TYPE initialization parameter enables you to specify native or interpreted compilation mode for PL/SQL library units. Possible values are interpreted and native.

Example: PLSQL_CODE_TYPE=native

Default value: interpreted

Parameter type: Dynamic. You can modify it with the ALTER SESSION or ALTER SYSTEM statement.

RESULT_CACHE_MAX_RESULT

The RESULT_CACHE_MAX_SIZE parameter specifies the percentage of the result cache that any single result can use. The range of values is from 1 to 100.

Example: RESULT_CACHE_MAX_RESULT=25

Default value: 5 percent

Parameter type: Dynamic. You can modify it with the ALTER SYSTEM command.

RESULT_CACHE_MAX_SIZE

The RESULT_CACHE_MAX_SIZE parameter specifies the maximum amount of the SGA that the result cache can use. Setting this parameter to 0 disables the result cache. The range of values is from 0 to an operating system–dependent value.

Example: RESULT_CACHE_MAX_SIZE=500m

Default value: Depends on the value you assign for the MEMORY_TARGET, SGA_TARGET, and SHARED_POOL parameters

Parameter type: Dynamic. You can modify it with the ALTER SYSTEM command.

RESULT_CACHE_MODE

The RESULT_CACHE_MODE parameter specifies when the database will use the results cache in memory for a SQL statement. Possible values are manual and force.

Example: RESULT_CACHE_MODE=force

Default value: manual

Parameter type: Dynamic. You can modify it with the ALTER SESSION or ALTER SYSTEM statement.

If you set the value of this parameter to manual, you must use a RESULT_CACHE hint in a query for the database to cache its results. If you specify the value force, the database will try to cache the results of all statements whenever it's possible to do so.

SEC_CASE_SENSITIVE_LOGON

The SEC_CASE_SENSITIVE_LOGON parameter enables or disables password case sensitivity. Possible values are true and false.

Example: SEC_CASE_SENSITIVE_LOGON=true

Default: true

Parameter type: Dynamic. You can modify it with the ALTER SYSTEM command.

SEC_MAX_FAILED_LOGIN_ATTEMPTS

You use the SEC_MAX_FAILED_LOGIN_ATTEMPTS parameter to specify the maximum number of unsuccessful authentication attempts a client can make before the server process automatically drops the connection attempt. The minimum value is 1 and maximum value is unlimited.

Example: SEC_MAX_FAILED_LOGIN_ATTEMPTS=3

Default: 10

Parameter type: Dynamic. You can modify it with the ALTER SYSTEM command.

QUERY_REWRITE_ENABLED

The QUERY_REWRITE_ENABLED parameter determines whether query rewriting is enabled or disabled, which is of importance mostly when you use materialized views.

Example: QUERY_REWRITE_ENABLED=false

Default: true if the OPTIMIZER_FEATURES_ENABLE parameter is set to 10.0.0 or higher; false if it is set to 9.2.0 or lower.

Parameter type: Dynamic. You can modify it with the ALTER SESSION or ALTER SYSTEM command.

QUERY_REWRITE_INTEGRITY

The QUERY_REWRITE_INTEGRITY parameter specifies the degree to which Oracle will enforce integrity rules during a query rewrite: trusted, enforced, or stale tolerated.

- trusted: Oracle assumes the materialized view is current and allows rewrites using relationships that are not enforced by Oracle.
- enforced: This is the safest mode; Oracle doesn't use transformations that rely on unenforced relationships. This mode always uses fresh data, guaranteeing consistency and integrity.
- stale_tolerated: Oracle will allow query rewrites using unenforced relationships.

Example: QUERY_WRITE_INTEGRITY = trusted

Default value: enforced

Parameter type: Dynamic. You can modify it with the ALTER SESSION or ALTER SYSTEM command.

CURSOR_SHARING

This crucial initialization parameter specifies how Oracle's SQL statements are supposed to share cursors. The three possible values are forced, exact, and similar. You'll learn more about setting this parameter in Chapters 19 and 20.

Example: CURSOR_SHARING = force

Default value: exact

Parameter type: Dynamic. Both the ALTER SESSION and ALTER SYSTEM commands can be used to change the value.

■**Caution** You have to be extremely careful when using the CURSOR_SHARING parameter. As you'll learn in Chapter 19, using the forced option will force Oracle to use bind variables, and thus will enhance your application performance. However, there are many caveats, and the wrong option for this parameter can hurt performance.

DB_BLOCK_SIZE

The DB_BLOCK_SIZE parameter sets the standard database block size (measured in bytes, such as 4096, which is a 4KB block size). The System tablespace and most other tablespaces use the standard block size. You set the standard block size from 2KB to 32KB (2, 4, 8, 16, or 32) in the DB_BLOCK_SIZE parameter. (Because the size is specified in bytes, the actual range for the DB_BLOCK_SIZE parameter is 2,048–32,768.) You can also specify up to four nonstandard block sizes when creating tablespaces.

You have to carefully evaluate your application's needs before you pick the correct database block size. Whenever you need to read data from or write data to an Oracle database object, you do so in terms of data blocks. Also, you always should make the DB_BLOCK_SIZE value a multiple of your operating system's block size, which you can ascertain from your UNIX or Windows system administrator.

■**Tip** Remember that the data block is the smallest unit in the Oracle physical database structure. When you are querying data, the rows aren't fetched individually; rather, the entire set of blocks in which the rows reside is read into memory in one fell swoop.

If you're supporting data warehouse applications, it makes sense to have a very large DB_BLOCK_SIZE—something between 8KB and 32KB. This will improve database performance when reading huge chunks of data from disk. Large data warehouses perform more full table scans and thus perform more sequential data access than random access I/Os.

However, if you're dealing with a typical OLTP application, where most of your reads and writes consist of relatively short transactions, a large DB_BLOCK_SIZE setting would be overkill and could actually lead to inefficiency in input and output operations. Most OLTP transactions read and write a very small number of rows per transaction, and they conduct numerous transactions with random access I/O (index scans), so you need to have a smaller block size, somewhere from 2KB to 8KB. A larger block size may be too large for most OLTP applications, as the database has to read large amounts of data into memory even when it really needs very small bits of information. Data warehousing applications, on the other hand, will benefit from a large block size, say 32KB.

Example: DB_BLOCK_SIZE=32768

Default value: 8192 (bytes)

Parameter type: Static

■**Note** You can't simply change the DB_BLOCK_SIZE parameter in the init.ora file after the database is created. The block size is more or less permanent. However, you can get around the need to re-create the whole database by creating new tablespaces (all but the System tablespace) with the required block size by using the BLOCKSIZE parameter, which will perform a roundabout change in the block size. Officially, the DB_BLOCK_SIZE parameter will still be set at the original value you specified. You can then use the online redefinition feature to move tables to the newly created tablespaces with the new block size. You can also do this using OEM.

DB_FILE_MULTIBLOCK_READ_COUNT

The DB_FILE_MULTIBLOCK_READ_COUNT parameter specifies the maximum number of blocks Oracle will read during a full table scan. The larger the value, the more efficient your full table scans will be. The general principle is that data warehouse operations need high multiblock read counts because of the heavy amount of data processing involved. If you are using a 16KB block size for your database, and the DB_FILE_MULTIBLOCK_READ_COUNT parameter is also set to 16, Oracle will read 256KB in a single I/O. Depending on the platform, Oracle supports I/Os up to 1MB.

Note that when you stripe your disks, the stripe size should be a multiple of the I/O size for optimum performance. If you are using an OLTP application, a multiblock read count such as 8 or 16 would be ideal. Large data warehouses could go much higher than this.

Example: DB_FILE_MULTIBLOCK_READ_COUNT = 32

Default value: Platform dependent

Parameter type: Dynamic. It is modifiable with either an ALTER SYSTEM or an ALTER SESSION command.

■**Tip** Since Oracle Database has been self-tuning this parameter since Release 10.2, it's probably a good idea not to set this parameter.

SQL_TRACE

The SQL_TRACE parameter will turn the SQL trace utility on or off. You can leave this parameter at its default setting of false (off), setting it to true (on) only when you are tuning a specific query or set of queries. Because of the heavy overhead, you should always use this parameter at the session, not the instance, level. Chapter 20 shows you how to use trace queries and format the trace output to help you in tuning SQL queries.

Example: SQL_TRACE = on

Default value: false

Parameter type: Dynamic. It can be changed with the ALTER SYSTEM or ALTER SESSION command.

PARALLEL_MAX_SERVERS

The PARALLEL_MAX_SERVERS parameter determines the number of parallel execution processes. Oracle recommends two parallel processes per CPU on larger systems, and four processes per CPU on smaller systems.

Default value: Depends on the values of the CPU_COUNT, PARALLEL_AUTOMATIC_TUNING, and PARALLEL_ADAPTIVE_MULTI_USER parameters

Parameter type: Dynamic. It can be changed only at the system level with the ALTER SYSTEM command.

TIMED_STATISTICS

The TIMED_STATISTICS parameter is used to tell Oracle whether it should collect timed statistics during tracing. The possible values are true (timed statistics are collected) and false (timed statistics are not collected). If timed statistics are collected, they are used in some dynamic performance views. If you set the STATISTICS_LEVEL parameter to the recommended level of TYPICAL or to AUTO, the TIMED_STATISTICS parameter is by default set to true.

Example: TIMED_STATISTICS = true

Default value: true if the STATISTICS_LEVEL parameter is set to TYPICAL or ALL, false otherwise

Parameter type: Dynamic. You can change it with the ALTER SYSTEM or ALTER SESSION command.

PLSQL_OPTIMIZE_LEVEL

The PLSQL_OPTIMIZE_LEVEL parameter specifies the optimization level that will be used to compile PL/SQL library units. The higher you set this parameter (in a range from 0 to 2), the more effort the compiler makes to optimize PL/SQL library units. According to Oracle, setting this parameter to 2 pays off in better execution performance, but setting this parameter to 1 will result in almost as good a compilation with less use of compile-time resources.

Example: PL_SQL_OPTIMIZE_LEVEL = 2

Default value: 2

Parameter type: Dynamic. You can use the ALTER SYSTEM or ALTER SESSION command to change the value.

Recovery-Related Parameters

When you create a new database, you'll need to configure several recovery-related parameters. When an instance crash occurs, all the data on disk is safe, but the data stored in the database buffers is wiped out instantaneously. Redo logs are on disk, so they are intact, but the redo log buffers are wiped out. To recover successfully from such a crash, the database needs to be brought to a consistent state by using Oracle's redo logs and the undo records from the undo tablespace. The redo log records are used to write all the committed data to disk, and the undo records are used to roll back any uncommitted data that was stored on disk.

Recovering an instance can take a long time—and can keep the database out of commission for an unacceptable length of time—if you don't configure any thresholds that determine how long an instance recovery can take. You can, for example, specify a precise time target for a complete instance recovery, and the database will automatically adjust the frequency of the checkpoints to make sure that there's only a certain maximum amount of redo information to be rolled back when instance recovery is performed.

Of course, if you set a very low recovery time target, your instance recovery will be quick, but the database will need an excessive number of checkpoints on an ongoing basis, which will affect performance. There's no one magic number for this recovery time target. You have to take into consideration your site's service-level agreement and the tolerance for downtime.

The flash recovery area is an area reserved for all Oracle backup and recovery-related files, and it contains copies of current control files and online redo logs, as well as archived redo logs, flashback logs, and RMAN backups. The flash recovery area is completely separate from the database area, which is the location for the current database files (datafiles, control files, and online redo logs). The flash recovery area isn't mandatory, but Oracle strongly recommends using it to simplify backup and recovery operations. You'll learn more about the flash recovery area in Chapter 16.

The two parameters described next, DB_RECOVERY_FILE_DEST_SIZE and DB_RECOVERY_FILE_DEST, are used to configure the flash recovery area.

DB_RECOVERY_FILE_DEST_SIZE

The DB_RECOVERY_FILE_DEST_SIZE parameter specifies (in bytes) the size of the flash recovery area.

Example: DB_RECOVERY_FILE_DEST_SIZE=2000M

Default value: None

Parameter type: Dynamic. The ALTER SYSTEM command can be used to change the value.

DB_RECOVERY_FILE_DEST

The DB_RECOVERY_FILE_DEST parameter specifies the default location for the flash recovery area. If you don't specify DB_CREATE_ONLINE_LOG_DEST_*n* when using OMF files, Oracle uses the location you specify for the DB_RECOVERY_FILE_DEST parameter as the default location for online redo log files and control files.

Example: DB_RECOVERY_FILE_DEST = /u05/app/oracle/fla

Default value: None

Parameter type: Dynamic. The ALTER SYSTEM command can be used to change the value.

■**Note** You must set the DB_RECOVERY_FILE_DEST_SIZE parameter in order to set the DB_RECOVERY_FILE_ DEST parameter. If you want to use the Flashback Database feature (explained in Chapter 16), you must also use the DB_FLASHBACK_RETENTION_TARGET parameter.

DB_FLASHBACK_RETENTION_TARGET

The DB_FLASHBACK_RETENTION_TARGET parameter specifies how far back (in minutes) you can flash back your database. The Flashback Database feature relies on flashback logs, and the DB_FLASHBACK_ RETENTION_TARGET parameter dictates the length of time the flashback logs are retained. How far back you can flash back your database depends on how much flashback data Oracle has kept in the flash recovery area.

Example: DB_FLASHBACK_RETENTION_TARGET = 2880

Default value: 1440 (minutes)

Parameter type: Dynamic. The ALTER SYSTEM command can be used to change the value.

RESUMABLE_TIMEOUT

The RESUMABLE_TIMEOUT parameter enables or disables the Resumable Space Allocation feature and specifies resumable timeout at the system level. For example, if you set RESUMABLE_TIMEOUT=3600, the database will suspend any resumable space type operation and wait one hour (3,600 seconds) before erroring out. Chapter 8 discusses the Resumable Space Allocation feature in detail.

Example: RESUMABLE_TIMEOUT = 7200

Default value: 0

Parameter type: Dynamic. You can use the ALTER SYSTEM or ALTER SESSION command to change this parameter.

Corruption-Checking Parameters

The Oracle database is equipped with certain features that can automatically check your data blocks on the datafiles for consistency and data corruption. Block checking involves going through the data on the block and checking for consistency. Block checking prevents memory and data corruption, but costs from 1 to 10 percent overhead, so use these parameters with caution during peak production periods.

DB_LOST_WRITE_PROTECT

The DB_WRITE_LOST_PROTECT parameter is mainly for a Data Guard environment, where you have databases in either a standby or a primary role. The parameter enables or disables lost write detection. A database lost write occurs when the I/O subsystem signals the completion of a write before the write is stored on disk. Possible values are none, typical, and full.

Example: DB_LOST_WRITE_PROTECT=full

Default value: none

Parameter type: Dynamic. The ALTER SYSTEM command can be used to change the value.

DB_ULTRA_SAFE

You can use the DB_ULTRA_SAFE initialization parameter to control the default settings for parameters that control database protection levels, such as the DB_BLOCK_CHECKING and DB_BLOCK_CHECKSUM parameters. You may set the DB_ULTRA_SAFE parameter to the following values:

- OFF: The database doesn't make any changes if you set any of the following parameters: DB_BLOCK_CHECKING, DB_BLOCK_CHECKSUM, or DB_LOST_WRITE_PROTECT.
- DATA_ONLY: The database sets the DB_BLOCK_CHECKING parameter to MEDIUM, the DB_LOST_WRITE_PROTECT parameter to TYPICAL, and the DB_BLOCK_CHECKSUM parameter to FULL.
- DATA_AND_INDEX: The database sets the DB_BLOCK_CHECKING parameter to FULL. The other two protection-related parameters will have the same values as you get when you choose the DATA_ONLY value for the DB_ULTRA_SAFE parameter.

Example: DB_ULTRA_SAFE = data_and_index

Default Value: OFF

Parameter type: Static

DB_BLOCK_CHECKSUM

Block checksums enable the detection of corruption caused by disks or the I/O system. Before Oracle writes a data block to disk, it calculates a checksum for that block and stores the value in the block itself. When it subsequently reads data from this block, it computes the checksum again and compares its value to the one it computed when writing to the block. If the checksums are different, Oracle notifies you that the data block is corrupted. You may have to perform a media recovery in this case, as explained in Chapter 16.

Oracle recommends that you turn block checksumming on in your database to catch corruptions in data blocks as well as redo log files. You can set the DB_BLOCK_CHECKSUM parameter to turn on the computing of checksums. You can use either the FULL or TYPICAL mode, or set it to OFF. In the FULL mode, Oracle will trap any in-memory corruption before it is recorded on the disk. However, Oracle recommends that you set this parameter to the alternative value of TYPICAL, since it involves a lower overhead (1 to 2 percent, instead of 4 to 5 percent). If you choose the OFF mode, DBW*n* calculates checksums just for the System tablespace.

Example: DB_BLOCK_CHECKSUM = full

Default value: TYPICAL

Parameter type: Dynamic. The ALTER SYSTEM command can be used to change the value.

DB_BLOCK_CHECKING

Using the DB_BLOCK_CHECKING parameter, you can set the database to check for corrupted data blocks. You can set this parameter to low, medium, or full, with each level involving a progressively higher amount of block checking (or you can set it to off to turn it off). When you enable block checking, Oracle automatically checks a block for consistency each time that block is modified. If a block isn't consistent, Oracle will mark it as corrupt and create a trace file. Depending on your workload, there is a 1 to 10 percent overhead when you turn block checking on. Oracle recommends that you turn block checking on. Note that Oracle checks the blocks in the System tablespace in all settings.

You can set the DB_BLOCK_CHECKING parameter to one of the following:

- OFF or FALSE: The database doesn't perform block checking for tablespaces other than the System tablespace.

- LOW: The database performs only basic block header checks after a change of the block contents in memory.

- MEDIUM: In addition to the checks performed under the LOW setting, the database also performs semantic block checking for all non-index-organized table blocks.

- FULL or TRUE: The database performs all the checks specified under the LOW and MEDIUM settings, and additionally, performs semantic checks for index blocks.

Example: DB_BLOCK_CHECKING = medium

Default value: false

Parameter type: Dynamic. You can use the ALTER SYSTEM or ALTER SESSION command to change this parameter.

DB_SECUREFILE

You use the DB_SECUREFILE parameter to specify whether you want the database to treat large objects as SecureFiles, new in Oracle Database 11g, or traditional BasicFiles. If you set this parameter to the value NEVER, the database will create all LOBS that you specify as SecureFiles as traditional Basic-Files. The value PERMITTED allows the creation of LOBs as SecureFiles. You can also assign the values ALWAYS and NEVER for this parameter.

Example: DB_SECUREFILE = always

Default value: PERMITTED

Parameter type: You can change this parameter with either the ALTER SYSTEM or the ALTER SESSION statement.

Security-Related Parameters

The following initialization parameters concern database security, including password authentication.

OS_AUTHENT_PREFIX

Oracle uses the value of the OS_AUTHENT_PREFIX parameter as a prefix to the operating system–authenticated usernames.

Default value: OPS$

Parameter type: Static

■**Note** The default value of OPS$ is well known to Oracle DBAs. However, Oracle suggests that you set the prefix value to the null string "" (OS_AUTHENT_PREFIX =""), which implies that you mustn't add any prefix to operating system–account names.

REMOTE_LOGIN_PASSWORDFILE

The REMOTE_LOGIN_PASSWORDFILE initialization parameter specifies whether Oracle checks for a password file for authentication purposes, and how many databases can use the password file. If you set the value to NONE, Oracle ignores any password file, and all privileged users must be authenticated by the operating system. If you use the SHARED value, Oracle will look for a password file to authenticate users, and one or more databases can share the same password file and can contain names other than SYS. Chapter 11 shows how to create a password file. The value EXCLUSIVE lets only one database use the password file, and it can include both SYS and non-SYS users.

Example: REMOTE_LOGIN_PASSWORDFILE = shared

Default value: EXCLUSIVE

Parameter type: Static

■**Tip** When you are using Oracle RAC, all instances must have the same value for the REMOTE_LOGIN_PASSWORDFILE parameter.

Undocumented Initialization Parameters

In addition to the initialization parameters listed in this chapter, Oracle has several undocumented initialization parameters. These parameters are not supposed to be altered in any way by regular users, and Oracle will not help you troubleshoot several kinds of problems that may occur if you use these undocumented and unsupported parameters. Once you gain sufficient experience, though, you will be able to make good use of some of these parameters.

Listing 10-1 shows how to query for the list of undocumented initialization parameters.

Listing 10-1. *Query to List the Undocumented Oracle Parameters*

```
SQL> SELECT
        a.ksppinm parameter,
        a.ksppdesc description,
        b.ksppstvl session_value,
        c.ksppstvl instance_value
        FROM x$ksppi a, x$ksppcv b, x$ksppsv c
        WHERE
        a.indx = b.indx
        AND a.indx = c.indx
        AND SUBSTR (a.ksppinm,1,1) = '_'
        ORDER BY a.ksppinm;
```

This query produced a list of 911 undocumented parameters for the Oracle Database 11*g* release.

Viewing the Current Initialization Parameter Values

How do you know what values the numerous initialization parameters are currently set to for your database? The following sections describe several ways.

Reading the init.ora File (or the SPFILE)

You can always use a file editor such as Windows Notepad to examine init.ora files, not only to view the settings for initialization parameters, but also (at your own risk) to change their values. However, there is a major drawback to doing this: you cannot see the default values of all the initialization parameters. Remember that there are about 300 initialization parameters in Oracle Database 11*g*, and you will probably not set the values of more than a quarter of these parameters explicitly by using your init.ora file.

The V$PARAMETER View

A good and quick way to find out the initialization settings for your database is to query the V$PARAMETER view. You can run the following query to find out the values of all the parameters:

```
SQL> SELECT name, value, isdefault FROM v$parameter;
```

The isdefault column has a value of true if the parameter is the default value and false if you actually set it to something other than the default value.

When I ran this command on my NT server, the output showed about 250 parameters. If you want to see only one or a set of related parameters and their values, you can add a WHERE clause to the previous SQL query.

The SHOW PARAMETER Command

Even though it's easy to query the V$PARAMETER view, there's a simpler means of querying the database about your initialization parameters. You can just type SHOW PARAMETER and you'll see all the initialization parameters with their values. You can also limit the vast amount of output by passing a keyword to SHOW PARAMETER. For example, the keywords LOCKS, FILES, LOG, and many others can be passed along to the SHOW PARAMETER command to get the values of a related set of parameters. (Note that the resulting list may not necessarily be a set of related parameters, as the command just uses a pattern search of the NAME column to pull the values from the V$PARAMETER table.)

Listing 10-2 shows an example of the use of the SHOW PARAMETER command. Here, the output shows all initialization parameters that contain the string "lock".

Listing 10-2. *Using the SHOW PARAMETER Command*

```
SQL> SHOW PARAMETER LOCK

NAME                                 TYPE          VALUE
------------------------------       -------       ------
db_block_buffers                     integer           0
db_block_checking                    boolean       FALSE
db_block_checksum                    boolean        TRUE
db_block_size                        integer        8192
db_file_multiblock_read_count        integer           8
ddl_wait_for_locks                   boolean       FALSE
distributed_lock_timeout             integer          60
dml_locks                            integer         400
gc_files_to_locks                    string
lock_name_space                      string
lock_sga                             boolean       FALSE
SQL>
```

Creating a New Database

As I mentioned at the beginning of the chapter, you have several ways to create an Oracle database. One way is to have Oracle create a database for you as part of the server software installation. You simply choose the installation option to create a new database, and Oracle will lead you through the necessary steps to configure a database. Alternatively, you can use the DBCA to create a new database.

Manual Creation

In this section, I show you how to create a new database from scratch, using individual database creation statements. Of course, if you are familiar with the database creation process, you don't have to run these SQL statements one by one—just create a script with all the necessary statements, and simply execute the script from SQL*Plus.

Setting OS Variables

You can use the SQL*Plus interface to create the database, either directly from a workstation or through a terminal connected to the server where you want to create the database. Before you log into the SQL*Plus session, however, you will need to set some environment variables at the operating system level.

First, make sure ORACLE_HOME is set for the session you log into. The ORACLE_HOME environment variable in Oracle Database 11*g* databases is in the following format:

```
$ORACLE_BASE/product/11.1.0/db_1
```

You can thus set your ORACLE_HOME as in the following example:

```
$ export ORACLE_HOME=/u01/app/oracle/product/11.1.0/db_1
```

Second, set the Oracle system identifier (ORACLE_SID) for your database to uniquely identify your database. This value will be the same as your DB_NAME initialization parameter value (which in this example is nina).

```
$ export ORACLE_SID=nina
```

Finally, make sure you set the LD_LIBRARY_PATH variable as shown here:

```
$ export LD_LIBRARY_PATH=$ORACLE_HOME/lib
```

Ensuring You Have the Privileges to Create Databases

Every Oracle database has a set of default administrative users to manage the database or to monitor various components of the database. Of these default users, two are special because their accounts can be used to perform most of the database administrative tasks. They are the SYS and SYSTEM accounts.

The default password for SYS is *change_on_install* and the password for the SYSTEM account is *manager*. You can specify passwords for these two critical accounts as part of your database creation process, as you'll see shortly. In addition to the two administrative user accounts, most types of Oracle databases come with several other default accounts, usually with default passwords. (See the "Changing the Passwords for the Default Users" section later in this chapter to learn how to ensure that you change all the default passwords.) All users except SYS need to be explicitly granted high-level privileges before they can perform special administrative functions, such as creating databases and starting, stopping, and backing them up. The SYSDBA privilege will allow a user to create databases.

The interesting thing about the SYSDBA privilege is that you don't really need to have the database open or even have a database before you can invoke it. Before you create the database, you'll be creating the instance (SGA + Oracle processes), and the SYSDBA privilege is in effect even at the instance level. You'll be connecting to the database as the super user SYS with the SYSDBA privilege, as shown here:

```
SQL> CONNECT sys AS sysdba
```

If the system administrator sets the oracle user to be part of a special group called DBA in the /etc/group file, you can also use the following command to log in as user SYS with the SYSDBA privilege:

```
SQL> CONNECT / AS sysdba
```

Creating the init.ora File

Before you can start the Oracle instance, you first must create the initialization parameter file (init.ora). Once you create the instance, you can create an SPFILE from your init.ora file. As you will recall, an Oracle instance consists of certain Oracle background processes and Oracle memory. Once you have the instance running, you can create the database proper. As most of the parameters in the initialization file are easily modifiable later on, the goal at this point isn't to be precise or exhaustive, but rather to get the instance up and running quickly.

The Oracle instance I created as an example for the database nina (initnina.ora), shown in Listing 10-3, contains the standard parameters to help support an OLTP application. Thus, you won't see data warehouse–oriented parameters in this initialization file. You'll notice that in several cases, I explicitly state the default values for certain parameters—this is purely for pedagogical reasons.

Listing 10-3. *The Initialization Parameter File for the Example Database nina*

```
# first, specify the name of the databasedb_name=nina
\pard\ri144\sl-240\slmult0 #for an ASM instance, use instance_type=ASM.
Following is the default\par
instance_type=RDBMS\par
# you can set the db_name to your organization name as well\par
db_domain=world\par
# following two parameters set the max number of open files and processes\par
db_files=1000\par
processes=600\par
# following is the default block size\par
db_block_size=8192\par
# following is the default value for the statistics_level parameter \par
statistics_level=typical\par
# following is the default audit_trail value\par
audit_trail=none\par
# following three lines set the dump directory destinations\par
background_dump_dest=\rquote /u01/app/oracle/admin/nina/\rquote\par
user_dump_dest=\rquote /u01/app/oracle/admin/nina/\rquote\par
core_dump_dest=\rquote /u01/app/oracle/admin/nina/\rquote\par
# following parameter sets the database compatibility level\par
compatible=10.2.1.0\par
# two control files are specified below\par
control_files=(\lquote /u01/app/oracle/oradata/cont1.ctl\rquote ,\par
 \lquote /u01/app/oracle/oradata/cont2.ctl\rquote )\par
# cursor sharing is set to force, to make the database use bind variables\par
cursor_sharing=force\par
# following two parameters set the SGA and the PGA targets.\par
sga_target=300M\par
pga_aggregate_target=2000M\par
# the multiblock read count is 16\par
db_file_multiblock_read_count=16\par
# the following will ensure that flashback logs \par
# are retained for 2 hours\par
db_flashback_retention_target=7200\par
# Following two parameters configure the optional flash recovery area\par
db_recovery_file_dest=\rquote /u02/app/oracle/flash_recovery_area\rquote\par
db_recovery_file_dest_size=1000M\par
# Following two parameters control the archiving of the redo\par
# log files. For now, I am not archiving the logs, but these two parameters\par
# enable me to turn it on later.\par
log_archive_dest_1=\rquote LOCATION=/u02/app/oracle/arch/\rquote\par
log_archive_format=\rquote log%t_%s_%r.arc\rquote\par
# following is the default optimizer mode\par
optimizer_mode=all_rows\par
# the following line makes it necessary to use a password file\par
#to connect as SYSDBA\par
remote_login_passwordfile=none\par
#Following parameter allows certain operations to resume after a suspension\par
resumable_timeout=1800\par
```

```
# the following two parameters pertain to automatic undo management\par
undo_management=auto\par
undo_retention=7200\par
# The following is optional, since I'm using only
#a single undo tablespace\par
undo_tablespace=undotbs_01\par
\pard\f1\par
}
```

■**Tip** The default value for the STATISTICS_LEVEL initialization parameter is TYPICAL. You need to use this setting if you want to use several of Oracle's features, including the Automatic Shared Memory Management feature.

Once you configure your initialization file, you are ready to create the instance. Make sure you save the initnina.ora file in the $ORACLE_HOME/dbs directory, which is the default location for an init.ora file or an SPFILE on UNIX/Linux systems (on a Windows system, the default location is $ORACLE_HOME\database). This way, Oracle will always find it without you having to specify the complete path of the location.

Starting the Oracle Instance

To create the database, first you must have the instance up and running. Remember, an instance can exist without any database attached to it, and the active instance makes it possible for you to create the database. Follow these steps:

1. Make sure you have specified the correct ORACLE_SID and ORACLE_HOME locations, as explained earlier in the "Setting OS Variables" section in this chapter.

2. Log in to the database through the SQL*Plus interface, as shown here:

```
oracle@localhostdbs]$ sqlplus /nolog
SQL*Plus: Release 11.1.0.6.0 - Production on Fri Mar 7 15:35:32 2008

Copyright (c) 1982, 2007, Oracle.  All rights reserved.

SQL> CONNECT sys AS sysdba
Enter password:
Connected to an idle instance.
SQL>
```

3. Start the instance in the NOMOUNT mode, since you don't have any control files to mount yet. If you use the plain STARTUP command, Oracle will look for the control files. You're probably thinking, "But we haven't created those files yet!" Not to worry—that will come during the creation of the database itself.

   If you saved your init.ora file in the default location ($ORACLE_HOME/dbs), and you correctly specified the ORACLE_SID environment variable (nina) before you started the instance, you don't have to specify the init.ora file explicitly.

```
SQL> STARTUP NOMOUNT
ORACLE instance started.

Total System Global Area    314572800 bytes
Fixed Size                    1236756 bytes
Variable Size                99164396 bytes
```

```
Database Buffers          213909504 bytes
Redo Buffers                5169152 bytes
SQL>
```

If you didn't save your init.ora file in the default location ($ORACLE_HOME/dbs), you must specify the complete path and the name of the file:

```
SQL>    NOMOUNT PFILE='/u01/app/oracle/product/10.2.0/db_1/dbs/initnina.ora'
```

■**Tip** It's common to get a couple of ORA-01078 errors (failure to process system parameters) at this point. Just correct the error shown in the message in the init.ora file, and you should have no problem starting your instance.

---

4. The instance will start using the parameters specified in the initnina.ora file. You can see that all the background processes for your database instance have been started by using the ps -ef command, as shown here:

```
[oracle@localhost]$ ps -ef | grep nina

oracle     5211     1   0 Mar05 ?        00:00:32 ora_pmon_nina
oracle     5213     1   0 Mar05 ?        00:00:06 ora_vktm_nina
oracle     5217     1   0 Mar05 ?        00:00:04 ora_diag_nina
oracle     5219     1   0 Mar05 ?        00:00:06 ora_dbrm_nina
oracle     5221     1   0 Mar05 ?        00:00:11 ora_psp0_nina
oracle     5225     1   0 Mar05 ?        00:04:39 ora_dia0_nina
oracle     5227     1   0 Mar05 ?        00:00:07 ora_mman_nina
oracle     5229     1   0 Mar05 ?        00:00:19 ora_dbw0_nina
oracle     5231     1   0 Mar05 ?        00:00:17 ora_lgwr_nina
oracle     5233     1   0 Mar05 ?        00:01:34 ora_ckpt_nina
oracle     5235     1   0 Mar05 ?        00:00:15 ora_smon_nina
oracle     5237     1   0 Mar05 ?        00:00:01 ora_reco_nina
oracle     5239     1   0 Mar05 ?        00:00:52 ora_mmon_nina
oracle     5241     1   0 Mar05 ?        00:01:22 ora_mmnl_nina
oracle     5249     1   0 Mar05 ?        00:00:04 ora_fbda_nina
oracle     5251     1   0 Mar05 ?        00:00:07 ora_smco_nina
oracle     5257     1   0 Mar05 ?        00:00:03 ora_qmnc_nina
oracle     5273     1   0 Mar05 ?        00:00:00 ora_q000_nina
oracle     5275     1   0 Mar05 ?        00:00:02 ora_q001_nina
(DESCRIPTION=(LOCAL=YES)(ADDRESS=(PROTOCOL=beq)))
oracle    27290     1   0 15:29 ?        00:00:00 ora_w000_ninal11
oracle    27394 27375   0 15:36 pts/2    00:00:00 grep nina
[oracle@localhost] $
```

5. You can execute a simple query at this stage to verify the version of the database, as shown here:

```
SQL> SELECT * FROM v$version;

BANNER
--------------------------------------------------------------------------------
Oracle Database 11g Enterprise Edition Release 11.1.0.6.0 - Production
PL/SQL Release 11.1.0.6.0 - Production
CORE 11.1.0.6.0 Production
TNS for Linux: Version 11.1.0.6.0 - Production
```

```
NLSRTL Version 11.1.0.6.0 - Production
SQL>
```

As you can see in the example in Listing 10-4, Oracle will write all the startup and shutdown information to the alert log, as well as any errors during instance creation and routine database operation. The alert log also lists all the nondefault initialization parameters that you had specified in your init.ora file. Note the starting up of all the Oracle processes: database writer (DBWn), process monitor (PMON), log writer (LGWR), checkpoint (CKPT), system monitor (SMON), and recoverer (RECO). The startup shown in Listing 10-4 is clean so far, as there are no errors either on the screen or in the alert log file.

Listing 10-4. *The Instance Creation Process in the Alert Log*

```
Wed Feb 13 15:05:22 2008
Starting ORACLE instance (normal)
LICENSE_MAX_SESSION = 0
LICENSE_SESSIONS_WARNING = 0
Picked latch-free SCN scheme 2
Autotune of undo retention is turned on.
IMODE=BR
ILAT =73
LICENSE_MAX_USERS = 0
SYS auditing is disabled
Starting up ORACLE RDBMS Version: 11.1.0.6.0.
Using parameter settings in server-side pfile
/u01/app/oracle/product/11.1.0.6/db_1/dbs/initorcl11.ora
System parameters with non-default values:
  processes              = 600
  instance_type          = "RDBMS"
  sga_target             = 300M
  control_files          = "/u01/app/oracle/oradata/orcl11/cont1.ctl"
  control_files          = "/u01/app/oracle/product/11.1.0.6
/db_1/dbs/ /u01/app/oracle/oradata/orcl11/cont2.ctl"
  db_block_size          = 8192
  compatible             = "11.1.0"
  log_archive_dest_1     = "LOCATION=/u02/app/oracle/arch/"
  log_archive_format     = "log%t_%s_%r.arc"
  db_files               = 1000
  db_recovery_file_dest  = "/u02/app/oracle/oradata/orcl11/flash_recovery_area"
  db_recovery_file_dest_size= 1000M
  db_flashback_retention_target= 7200
  undo_management        = "AUTO"
  undo_tablespace        = "undotbs_01"
  undo_retention         = 7200
  resumable_timeout      = 1800
  remote_login_passwordfile= "NONE"
  db_domain              = "world"
  cursor_sharing         = "force"
  audit_trail            = "NONE"
  db_name                = "orcl11"
  optimizer_mode         = "all_rows"
  pga_aggregate_target   = 2000M
  statistics_level       = "typical"
Wed Feb 13 15:05:24 2008
WARNING:Oracle instance running on a system with low open file descriptor
```

```
          limit. Tune your system to increase this limit to avoid
          severe performance degradation.
PMON started with pid=2, OS id=3548
Wed Feb 13 15:05:25 2008
DIAG started with pid=4, OS id=3554
Wed Feb 13 15:05:25 2008
DBRM started with pid=5, OS id=3557
Wed Feb 13 15:05:25 2008
VKTM started with pid=3, OS id=3550
VKTM running at (100ms) precision
Wed Feb 13 15:05:25 2008
PSP0 started with pid=6, OS id=3559
Wed Feb 13 15:05:25 2008
DIA0 started with pid=8, OS id=3563
Wed Feb 13 15:05:25 2008
DSKM started with pid=7, OS id=3561
Wed Feb 13 15:05:25 2008
MMAN started with pid=7, OS id=3565
Wed Feb 13 15:05:26 2008
DBW0 started with pid=9, OS id=3567
Wed Feb 13 15:05:26 2008
LGWR started with pid=10, OS id=3569
Wed Feb 13 15:05:26 2008
SMON started with pid=12, OS id=3573
Wed Feb 13 15:05:26 2008
CKPT started with pid=11, OS id=3571
Wed Feb 13 15:05:26 2008
RECO started with pid=13, OS id=3575
Wed Feb 13 15:05:26 2008
MMON started with pid=14, OS id=3577
Wed Feb 13 15:05:27 2008
MMNL started with pid=15, OS id=3579
ORACLE_BASE not set in environment. It is recommended
that ORACLE_BASE be set in the environment
Wed Feb 13 15:10:24 2008
```

At this point, you have a running Oracle instance, which consists of the Oracle processes and the SGA memory that you allocated for it. You don't have a database yet; you'll create one from scratch in the next section.

Creating the Database

The simplest database you can create will have a System tablespace to hold the data dictionary, a Sysaux tablespace, a pair of control files and redo log files, a default temporary tablespace, and an undo tablespace. Once you have this database going, you can add any number of new tablespaces to it.

Let's create a bare-bones Oracle Database 11g database now. You can create your new database either by entering each line of the database-creation statement individually or by creating a database-creation script with the entire statement, as shown in Listing 10-5, and executing the script.

Listing 10-5. *The CREATE DATABASE Script*

```
SQL> CREATE DATABASE nina
  2  USER SYS IDENTIFIED BY sys_password
  3  USER SYSTEM IDENTIFIED BY system_password
```

```
 4   LOGFILE GROUP 1 ('/u01/app/oracle/oradata/nina/redo01.log') SIZE 100M,
     a.   GROUP 2 ('/u01/app/oracle/oradata/nina/redo02.log') SIZE 100M,
     b.   GROUP 3 ('/u01/app/oracle/oradata/nina/redo03.log') SIZE 100M
 5   MAXLOGFILES 5
 6   MAXLOGMEMBERS 5
 7   MAXLOGHISTORY 1
 8   MAXDATAFILES 300
 9   CHARACTER SET US7ASCII
10   NATIONAL CHARACTER SET AL16UTF16
11   EXTENT MANAGEMENT LOCAL
12   DATAFILE '/u01/app/oracle/oradata/nina/system01.dbf' SIZE 500M REUSE
13   SYSAUX DATAFILE '/u01/app/oracle/oradata/nina/sysaux01.dbf' SIZE 325M REUSE
14   DEFAULT TABLESPACE users
15   DATAFILE '/u01/app/oracle/oradata/nina/users01.dbf'
16   SIZE 500M REUSE AUTOEXTEND ON MAXSIZE UNLIMITED
17   DEFAULT TEMPORARY TABLESPACE tempts1
18   TEMPFILE '/u01/app/oracle/oradata/nina/temp01.dbf'
19   SIZE 200M REUSE
20   UNDO TABLESPACE undotbs
21   DATAFILE '/u01/app/oracle/oradata/nina/undotbs01.dbf'
22   SIZE 200M REUSE AUTOEXTEND ON MAXSIZE UNLIMITED;

Database created.
SQL>
```

Here's a quick review of the CREATE DATABASE statement:

- Line 1 issues the CREATE DATABASE command to Oracle. This command prompts the creation of two control files, and their locations are read from the initnina.ora parameter file. If control files with the same names already exist at the time of database creation (from a prior failed installation), you must specify the CONTROLFILE REUSE clause in the CREATE DATABASE statement.

- Lines 2 and 3 show how you can specify the passwords for the two key users SYS and SYSTEM. These are optional clauses, and if you omit them, users SYS and SYSTEM are assigned the default passwords change_on_install and manager, respectively. Since these are well-known default passwords, Oracle advises you to use these clauses to change the default passwords.

- Line 4 creates the pair of online redo log groups required by Oracle.

- Lines 5 through 8 specify the maximum setting for datafiles, log files and such.

- Lines 9 and 10 specify the character sets used by the database. Just use these character sets for all the databases you'll be creating, unless you have special needs based on languages other than English.

- Line 11 specifies that the System tablespace should be locally managed, rather than dictionary managed.

- Line 12 creates the System tablespace with one datafile of 500MB. The data dictionary is created within this System tablespace. One system rollback segment is also automatically created.

- Line 13 creates the new default tablespace Sysaux. You must create the Sysaux tablespace, or your database creation statement will fail.

- Lines 14 through16 create the *default permanent* tablespace TEMP01 with one 500MB-sized tempfile. All users have to be allotted a temporary tablespace when they are initially created in the database. If you don't do so, the users will be allocated to the default temporary tablespace, TEMP01, automatically. Notice how line 14 specifies that the file used for the temporary tablespace is a *temp file*, not a regular datafile. You can't create the temporary tablespace with a normal datafile specification.

- Lines 17 through 19 create the new *default temporary* tablespace for the database. Any users that aren't explicitly assigned a permanent tablespace will automatically be allocated this tablespace as their default tablespace, instead of the System tablespace.

- Lines 20 through 22 create the undo tablespace for the new database.

Oracle automatically mounts and opens the database after it creates all the files described previously. As you'll see in the last part of this chapter, *mounting* a database involves reading the control files, and *opening* the database enables all users to access the various parts of the new database.

Take a peek at the alert log at this point to see what Oracle actually did when the CREATE DATABASE command was issued. Listing 10-6 shows the relevant portion from the alert log.

Listing 10-6. *The Database Creation Process in the Alert Log*

```
Sun Feb 13 15: 13:00 2008
create database orcl11
   USER SYS IDENTIFIED BY *****
USER SYSTEM IDENTIFIED BY ******
LOGFILE GROUP 1 ('/u01/app/oracle/oradata/orcl11/redo01.log') SIZE 100M,
          GROUP 2 ('/u01/app/oracle/oradata/orcl11/redo02.log') SIZE 100M,
          GROUP 3 ('/u01/app/oracle/oradata/orcl11/redo03.log') SIZE 100M
   MAXLOGFILES 5
   MAXLOGMEMBERS 5
   MAXLOGHISTORY 1
   MAXDATAFILES 100
   CHARACTER SET US7ASCII
   NATIONAL CHARACTER SET AL16UTF16
   EXTENT MANAGEMENT LOCAL
   DATAFILE '/u01/app/oracle/oradata/orcl11/system01.dbf' SIZE 325M REUSE
   SYSAUX DATAFILE '/u01/app/oracle/oradata/orcl11/sysaux01.dbf' SIZE 325M REUSE
   DEFAULT TABLESPACE users
      DATAFILE '/u01/app/oracle/oradata/orcl11/users01.dbf'
      SIZE 500M REUSE AUTOEXTEND ON MAXSIZE UNLIMITED
   DEFAULT TEMPORARY TABLESPACE tempts1
      TEMPFILE '/u01/app/oracle/oradata/orcl11/temp01.dbf'
      SIZE 20M REUSE
UNDO TABLESPACE undotbs
      DATAFILE '/u01/app/oracle/oradata/orcl11/undotbs01.dbf'
      SIZE 200M REUSE AUTOEXTEND ON MAXSIZE UNLIMITED
Database mounted in Exclusive Mode
Lost write protection disabled
Wed Feb 13 15:33:08 2008
Successful mount of redo thread 1, with mount id 3893367911
Assigning activation ID 3893367911 (0xe8101467)
Thread 1 opened at log sequence 1
  Current log# 1 seq# 1 mem# 0: /u01/app/oracle/oradata/orcl11/redo01.log
Successful open of redo thread 1
Wed Feb 13 15:33:08 2008
MTTR advisory is disabled because FAST_START_MTTR_TARGET is not set
```

```
Wed Feb 13 15:33:08 2008
SMON: enabling cache recovery
processing ?/rdbms/admin/dcore.bsq
create tablespace SYSTEM datafile  '/u01/app/oracle/oradata/orcl11/
system01.dbf' SIZE 325M REUSE

   EXTENT MANAGEMENT LOCAL online
Wed Feb 13 15:33:20 2008
Completed: create tablespace SYSTEM datafile
   '/u01/app/oracle/oradata/orcl11/system01.dbf' SIZE 325M REUSE

   EXTENT MANAGEMENT LOCAL online
create rollback segment SYSTEM tablespace SYSTEM
   storage (initial 50K next 50K)
Completed: create rollback segment SYSTEM tablespace SYSTEM
   storage (initial 50K next 50K)
processing ?/rdbms/admin/dsqlddl.bsq
processing ?/rdbms/admin/dmanage.bsq
CREATE TABLESPACE sysaux DATAFILE  '/u01/app/oracle/oradata/orcl11/
sysaux01.dbf' SIZE 325M REUSE

   EXTENT MANAGEMENT LOCAL SEGMENT SPACE MANAGEMENT AUTO ONLINE
Wed Feb 13 15:33:36 2008
Completed: CREATE TABLESPACE sysaux DATAFILE
'/u01/app/oracle/oradata/orcl11/sysaux01.dbf' SIZE 325M REUSE

   EXTENT MANAGEMENT LOCAL SEGMENT SPACE MANAGEMENT AUTO ONLINE
processing ?/rdbms/admin/dplsql.bsq
processing ?/rdbms/admin/dtxnspc.bsq
CREATE UNDO TABLESPACE UNDOTBS DATAFILE
'/u01/app/oracle/oradata/orcl11/undotbs01.dbf'
     SIZE 200M REUSE AUTOEXTEND ON MAXSIZE UNLIMITED
Successfully onlined Undo Tablespace 2.
Completed: CREATE UNDO TABLESPACE UNDOTBS DATAFILE
'/u01/app/oracle/oradata/orcl11/undotbs01.dbf'
     SIZE 200M REUSE AUTOEXTEND ON MAXSIZE UNLIMITED
CREATE TEMPORARY TABLESPACE TEMPTS1 TEMPFILE
'/u01/app/oracle/oradata/orcl11/temp01.dbf'
     SIZE 20M REUSE

Completed: CREATE TEMPORARY TABLESPACE TEMPTS1 TEMPFILE
'/u01/app/oracle/oradata/orcl11/temp01.dbf'
     SIZE 20M REUSE

ALTER DATABASE DEFAULT TEMPORARY TABLESPACE TEMPTS1
Completed: ALTER DATABASE DEFAULT TEMPORARY TABLESPACE TEMPTS1
CREATE  TABLESPACE USERS DATAFILE  '/u01/app/oracle/oradata/orcl11/users01.dbf'
     SIZE 500M REUSE AUTOEXTEND ON MAXSIZE UNLIMITED
   SEGMENT SPACE MANAGEMENT MANUAL
Wed Feb 13 15:34:12 2008
Completed: CREATE  TABLESPACE USERS DATAFLE
'/u01/app/oracle/oradata/orcl11/users01.dbf'
     SIZE 500M REUSE AUTOEXTEND ON MAXSIZE UNLIMITED
   SEGMENT SPACE MANAGEMENT MANUAL
```

```
ALTER DATABASE DEFAULT TABLESPACE USERS
Completed: ALTER DATABASE DEFAULT TABLESPACE USERS
processing ?/rdbms/admin/dfmap.bsq
. . .
Wed Feb 13 15:34:32 2008
SMON: enabling tx recovery
Starting background process SMCO
Wed Feb 13 15:34:33 2008
SMCO started with pid=17, OS id=4055
Wed Feb 13 15:34:38 2008
Starting background process FBDA
Wed Feb 13 15:34:38 2008
FBDA started with pid=19, OS id=4059
replication_dependency_tracking turned off (no async multimaster replication found)
Starting background process QMNC
Wed Feb 13 15:34:40 2008
QMNC started with pid=20, OS id=4063
Completed: create database orcl11
. . .
Wed Feb 13 15:50:43 2008
Sat Feb 16 11:00:18 2008
```

■**Tip** If you want to see exactly what Oracle is doing during the database-creation process, go to the directory where the alert log is located and run the following command:

```
$ tail -f alertnina.log
```

Here are the key steps in the database-creation log shown in Listing 10-6:

- The database mounted statement means that Oracle has opened the control files you specified in the init.ora file.

- The successful open of redo thread 1 statement indicates that the first redo log file has successfully been created and opened for recovery purposes.

- The Sysaux and System tablespaces are successfully created.

- The rollback segment named "system" is created in the System tablespace.

- The undo tablespace, UNDOTBS, is successfully created.

- The TEMP01 tablespace is created as a temporary tablespace, using a temp file instead of the regular datafiles used for permanent tablespaces. *After* the temporary tablespace is created, the ALTER DATABASE DEFAULT TEMPORARY TABLESPACE TEMP01 statement is executed to designate TEMP01 as the default temporary tablespace for this database.

- The USERS tablespace is created and the ALTER DATABASE DEFAULT TABLESPACE USERS statement is executed to designate the USERS tablespace as the default permanent tablespace for the new database.

- The new background processes, QMNC and MMNL, are started.

> ■**Note** When you create the flash recovery area, which is a specialized location for storing recovery-related files, you can't use the traditional LOG_ARCHIVE_DEST and LOG_ARCHIVE_DUPLEX_DEST parameters. You must instead specify the LOG_ARCHIVE_DEST_*n* parameter.

Running Oracle Scripts to Create Data Dictionary Objects

Oracle provides two important scripts, catalog.sql and catproc.sql, that you need to run right after you create your new database:

- catalog.sql populates the database with the data dictionary views, public synonyms, and other objects. The data dictionary base tables, the parents of the V$ views, are the first objects created in the Oracle database.

- catproc.sql creates the Oracle-provided packages and other objects to support the use of PL/SQL code in the database.

When you run these scripts, you'll see a lot of information flow past on the screen, indicating that the necessary database objects are being created, and so on. Just let the two scripts do what they are supposed to do. It should take about an hour or so to run both scripts.

> ■**Note** Ignore any errors that you see during the execution of the catalog.sql and catproc.sql scripts. These errors mostly state that the object that is to be dropped doesn't exist. If it bothers you to see all those errors, you can reassure yourself by running each script twice. You won't see any errors during the second execution if you do this.

Connect as the SYS user with SYSDBA privileges, and run the scripts as follows:

```
SQL> @$ORACLE_HOME/rdbms/admin/catalog.sql
. . .
Grant succeeded

PL/SQL procedure successfully completed.
SQL>
SQL> @$ORACLE_HOME/rdbms/admin/catproc.sql
. . .

PL/SQL procedure successfully completed.
SQL>
```

A Simple Way to Create a Database

You've seen how to create a database by first specifying various initialization parameters in the parameter file to start the instance and then using the CREATE DATABASE statement to create the database itself. Both the initialization parameter file and the CREATE DATABASE statement are pretty detailed, if not complex. However, you don't have to have such an elaborate initialization file and CREATE DATABASE statement each time you create a new database. If you want to create a new Oracle database in a hurry, you can do so by following these steps:

1. Create a new init.ora file with just one parameter, DB_NAME (DB_NAME=orcl11, for example).

2. Start up your new instance as follows:

```
SQL> STARTUP NOMOUNT
ORACLE instance started.
Total System Global Area    188743680 bytes
Fixed Size                    1308048 bytes
Variable Size               116132464 bytes
Database Buffers             67108864 bytes
Redo Buffers                  5169152 bytes
SQL>
```

3. Create your new database with the following simple statement:

```
SQL> CREATE DATABASE;
Database created.
SQL>
```

Oracle will automatically create an OMF System and a Sysaux tablespace. The database will run with manual undo management using rollback segments. Of course, you must still run the two scripts, `catalog.sql` and `catproc.sql`, in order to create the data dictionary and the Oracle packages.

■**Tip** The initialization parameter file will contain the locations for the datafiles, redo log files, and control files. Oracle will automatically create a 100MB auto-extensible system file, a pair of redo logs, control files, an undo tablespace, and a temporary tablespace. Simple as that! Chapter 17 shows you other interesting features of OMF.

Using the DBCA to Create a Database

The simplest way to create an Oracle database is to the use the Oracle database creation wizard, Database Configuration Assistant. The Oracle Universal Installer automatically invokes the DBCA when you choose to create a database as part of the installation of the Oracle Database 11*g* software. You can also launch DBCA anytime after the installation is completed to create an Oracle database.

You can run the DBCA in interactive or silent mode, and it has several benefits, including providing templates for creating DSS, OLTP, or hybrid databases. The biggest benefit to using the DBCA is that for DBAs with little experience, it lets Oracle set all the configuration parameters and start up a new database quickly without errors. Finally, the DBCA also automatically creates all its file systems based on the highly utilitarian Optimal Flexible Architecture standard.

The DBCA is an excellent tool, and it even allows you to register a new database automatically with Oracle Internet Directory (OID). However, I recommend strongly that you use the manual approach initially, so you can get a good idea of what initialization parameters to pick and how the database is created step by step. Once you gain sufficient confidence, of course, the DBCA is, without a doubt, the best way to create an Oracle database of any size and complexity.

You can perform the following tasks with the DBCA:

- Create a database.
- Change the configuration of an existing database.
- Delete a database.
- Configure ASM.

Starting DBCA

On a Windows operating system, click Start and then select Programs ➤ Oraclehome_name ➤ Configuration and Migration Tools ➤ Database Configuration Assistant. You can start DBCA on a UNIX or Linux system by typing **dbca** at the command-line prompt. Since DBCA is a GUI tool, make sure you set the DISPLAY environment variable correctly before you invoke the tool.

Database Creation Steps

Here's a summary of the steps you must follow to create a new database using the DBCA:

1. If you haven't already started DBCA, type **dbca** at the operating system prompt.

2. In the Welcome window, click Next.

3. The DBCA Operations window appears. Select Create a Database, and click OK.

4. In the Database Templates window, the DBCA offers you a choice of the type of database you can create. The three choices are Data Warehouse, General Purpose, and Transaction Processing. You can select the default General Purpose template if you aren't sure which type of database you want to create. You can also select the Custom Database option if you wish, where you'll have to provide more information to DBCA in order to create the database. Click Next.

5. In the Database Identification window, enter the database name in the form database_name.domain name (for example, orcl11.world). In the SID field, enter the system identifier, which defaults to the database name (orcl11). Click Next.

6. In the Management Options window, you can set up management by the Oracle Enterprise Manager. You can choose between the Grid Control and Database Control. If you have already installed the Oracle Management Agent on the host computer, you can select Grid Control. Otherwise, select Configure Database Control for local management. You can also select the Enable Daily Backup to Recovery Area option in this window. Click Next.

7. In the Database Credentials window, specify passwords for the administrative accounts such as SYS and SYSTEM. Click Next.

8. In the Storage Options window, specify the type of storage devices you want to use for the new database. Select File System and click Next.

9. In the Database File Locations window, using the Choose Common Location for All Database Files option, specify the Oracle software home and the directory path where you want DBCA to create the database files. You can choose Oracle Managed Files if you want, making the database completely manage the database files.

10. In the Recovery Configuration window, choose between the default noarchivelog mode and archivelog mode of operating the database. Oracle recommends that you choose the Enable Archiving option to enable the archiving of the redo logs. Oracle recommends that you also enable the Select Flash Recovery Area option so the database will use a flash recovery area to store all backup- and recovery-related files. The flash recovery area is distinct from the storage location of the current database files such as datafiles, control files, and online redo logs.

11. In the Database Content page, select Sample Schemas to include the Sample Schemas tablespace (EXAMPLE tablespace) in your database. Oracle recommends you do this in order to use the examples based on the sample schemas such as HR and OE.

12. In the Initialization Parameters page, you can set the initialization parameters related to the following four areas:

   • Memory

   • Sizing

   • Character Sets

   • Connection Mode

Let's take a closer look at each of these areas before continuing with creating our database.

Memory

The Memory window lets you set initialization parameters that control how the database manages the memory allocated to it. You can choose between the Typical and the Custom options to specify a method of memory management. The easiest way to manage memory is to select Typical and enter a percentage value, such as 40 percent. The instance will then use Automatic Memory Management, a new Oracle Database 11g feature, to automatically tune both the SGA and the PGA.

Sizing

In the Sizing tab, you specify the database block size and the maximum number of user processes that can connect simultaneously to the database. For the block size, accept the default value, which is 8KB. For processes, use a number such as 150, unless you know that you have a larger number of processes.

Character Sets

Use the default value for the database character set, which supports the language used by the operating system for all database users and database applications.

Connection Mode

The Connection Mode tab lets you specify the connection method users will use to connect to the database. Select Dedicated Server Mode to specify the default mode in which the database operates.

13. Once you make your choices for memory allocation, database block sizing, character sets, and connection mode, click Next.

14. In the Security Settings window, select the new enhanced default, which includes the enabling of auditing and default password file settings.

15. In the Automatic Maintenance Tasks page, select the Enable automatic maintenance tasks option so the three automated maintenance tasks can run daily in the database.

16. In the Database Storage window, you can modify the default file locations for the datafiles, control files, and redo logs. Once you've done so, click Next.

17. In the Creation Options window, select Create Database and click Finish. DBCA presents a confirmation page. Review the information and click OK to start the database creation. Once the database creation finishes, click Exit to leave the DBCA.

Changing the Configuration of a Database

You can use DBCA to change certain database configuration options for an existing database. For example, you can change the memory allocation method or the database storage method using the DBCA.

Deleting a Database

You can delete a database easily with the DBCA. Select the Delete a Database option in the Operations window. DBCA will remove all the database files. If you're on the Windows operating system, DBCA also deletes the associated services, thus enabling you to make a clean deletion of the database instead of physically removing the database files yourself.

Creating Additional Tablespaces

Now you have a real Oracle database humming away on your server, although you still can't do a whole lot with it because it's just a bare-bones database. You don't have any application code, application objects, or data stored in it. To be able to create objects and load data, you need physical space, and you assign the space by creating a number of tablespaces.

The first thing you should do is size your planned tables, indexes, and other database objects using standard table-sizing guidelines. This will give you an idea of how many tablespaces you'll need to create. You don't want thousands of small tablespaces, because you'll have a hard time managing all of them. The idea is to have as many tablespaces as are necessary to group related application tables. You can theoretically create everything in just one large tablespace, but that defeats the purpose of having a tablespace in an Oracle database.

Once you've decided on the tablespaces you need, use commands like the following to create the additional tablespaces (by default, Oracle will create a locally managed tablespace):

```
SQL> CREATE TABLESPACE sales01
     DATAFILE '/u02/app/oracle/oradata/nina/sales01_01.dbf' size 500M
     Tablespace created.
SQL>
SQL> CREATE TABLESPACE sales02
     DATAFILE '/u02/app/oracle/oradata/nina/sales02_01.dbf' size 500M
     Tablespace created.
SQL>
```

Now, verify the tablespaces in the new database, as shown in Listing 10-7.

Listing 10-7. *Query Showing Various Characteristics of Tablespaces in the New Database*

```
SQL> SELECT tablespace_name, extent_management,
     allocation_type, segment_space_management
     FROM dba_tablespaces;
```

TABLESPACE_NAME	EXTENT_MAN	ALLOCATIO	SEGMEN
SYSTEM	LOCAL	SYSTEM	MANUAL
UNDOTBS_01	LOCAL	SYSTEM	MANUAL
SYSAUX	LOCAL	SYSTEM	AUTO
TEMP01	LOCAL	UNIFORM	MANUAL
USERS	LOCAL	SYSTEM	MANUAL
SALES01	LOCAL	SYSTEM	AUTO
SALES02	LOCAL	SYSTEM	AUTO

```
7 rows selected.
SQL>
```

The query shows a total of seven tablespaces, five of which were created during the database-creation process (System, Sysaux, undo, temporary, and the default permanent tablespace). The other two are the newly created application tablespaces, sales01 and sales02.

STARTING OEM DATABASE CONTROL

The Oracle Enterprise Manager comes in two versions: the Grid Control and Database Control. You have to install the OEM Grid Control software separately and use it along with agents on remote servers to manage your entire system. The Database Control is part of the Oracle Database 11g server software, and no special installation is necessary.

If you create your new database using the DBCA, Oracle automatically starts up the Database Control service. If you manually create the database, you must run the following command to start up the dbconsole for the Enterprise Manager:

```
$ emctl start dbconsole
```

Once you start up the dbconsole process, you can access OEM Database Control by opening your web browser and entering the following URL:

```
http://hostname:portnumber/em
```

In the URL, *hostname* is your computer name or address, and *portnumber* is the Database Control HTTP port number. The default port is 1158 on my Red Hat Linux server, and you can look up port values by viewing the portlist.ini file, located in the $ORACLE_HOME/install/portlist directory.

Changing the Passwords for the Default Users

One of the first tasks to perform after you create a new database is to change the passwords for all the default users. The names and number of these default users could differ among databases. For example, if you choose to let Oracle create your database using the Oracle Universal Installer, you can pick a database customized for an OLTP, a DSS, or a hybrid database. Each of these databases has a different group of specialized default users associated with it. Nevertheless, all types of databases will have at least a handful of common default users.

The following are some of the common default users in a new Oracle database:

```
SQL> SELECT username FROM dba_users;

USERNAME
--------
DBSNMP
SYSTEM
SYS
OUTLN
. . .
SQL>
```

You don't have to worry about the SYS and SYSTEM passwords, as you've already changed them during the database-creation process. The OUTLN user account is used to provide stored outlines for SQL queries, and the DBSNMP account is for the Oracle Intelligent Agent. There may be other users created in your database, depending on the type of database you create and the options you choose for your database. The default password for each of these accounts is the same as the username. Change these passwords immediately, as they represent a potential security problem. For each of the default users, you must modify the default passwords, as shown in the following examples:

```
SQL> ALTER USER outln IDENTIFIED BY 'new_password';
SQL> ALTER USER dbsnmp IDENTIFIED BY 'new_password';
```

■**Tip** Most default accounts (other than SYS, SYSTEM, DBSNMP, and SYSMAN) are initially locked with their passwords expired. You need to unlock and reset the passwords for these accounts, using the ALTER USER statement. Chapter 12 details how to unlock user passwords.

Case-Sensitive Passwords

In Oracle Database 11*g*, all passwords are case sensitive by default. When you upgrade a database to the Oracle Database 11*g* release, however, passwords will continue to remain case insensitive, and you must use the ALTER USER statement to make these passwords case sensitive.

The initialization parameter SEC_CASE_SENSITIVE_LOGON controls the password case sensitivity. By default, this parameter is set to true, meaning passwords are case sensitive by default. If for some reason you need to alter this default, say because one of your applications requires the use of case-insensitive passwords, you can do so by setting the SEC_CASE_SENSITIVE_LOGON parameter to false.

Changing the Archive Logging Mode

You can configure a database to run in noarchivelog mode or in archivelog mode. In noarchivelog mode, Oracle won't archive or save the redo logs it fills up. Instead, it overwrites them when it needs to write to a new log file. In archivelog mode, Oracle ensures that it first saves the filled-up redo log file before permitting it to be overwritten.

The distinction between archivelog mode and noarchivelog mode is extremely important. If you archive all the filled redo logs, you'll have a complete record of the changes made to the database since the last backup. In the event that you lose a disk, for example, you can use your backups of the database along with the archived redo logs to recover the database without losing any committed data. Chapters 15 and 16 deal with database backup and recovery in detail. Here, I'll show you how to alter the logging mode of a database.

Before you change anything, you should confirm the archivelog mode of the database. Here is one way of doing so:

```
SQL> SELECT log_mode FROM v$database;

LOG_MODE
----------------
NOARCHIVELOG
1 row selected.
SQL>
```

The other method is to use the ARCHIVE LOG LIST command:

```
SQL> ARCHIVE LOG LIST

Database log mode              No Archive Mode
Automatic archival             Disabled
Archive destination            /u02/app/oracle/oradata/arch/
Oldest online log sequence     3
Current log sequence           4
SQL>
```

This command shows the archivelog destination (/u02/app/oracle/arch) and confirms that the database is running in noarchivelog mode (No Archive Mode). Automatic archival is disabled as well.

Now that you've verified that your database is indeed running in the noarchivelog mode, let's see what you need to do to turn archiving on in your new database.

First, make sure that the archivelog-related parameters in your init.ora file (or SPFILE) are set. In my init.ora file, I add (or uncomment) the following parameters:

```
log_archive_dest_n = 'LOCATION=/u02/app/oracle/oradata/nina/arch'
log_archive_format = 'log%t_%s_%r.arc'
```

Second, you need to shut down the database so it can use the new archivelog-related information, which wasn't in the init.ora file or was commented out initially. Note that only the LOG_ARCHIVE_ DEST_n parameter is a dynamically modifiable parameter. The other archivelog-related parameter, LOG_ARCHIVE_FORMAT, is static, meaning you can't use the ALTER SYSTEM command to change the archive logging mode of your database; you have to bounce your database. However, you have a certain amount of room to maneuver around this limitation. You don't really have to set the static parameter for archiving to begin. The LOG_ARCHIVE_FORMAT variable just sets the format for the way your archived log files are named, and if you don't specify a value, they will take Oracle's default archivelog naming convention.

Here's the database shutdown command:

```
SQL> SHUTDOWN IMMEDIATE

Database closed.
Database dismounted.
ORACLE instance shut down.
SQL>
```

Third, start the database in mount mode only, by using the following command:

```
SQL> STARTUP MOUNT
```

Next, use the following command to turn archive logging on:

```
SQL> ALTER DATABASE ARCHIVELOG
Database altered.
SQL>
```

Finally, open the database. Your database will now run in archivelog mode.

```
SQL> ALTER DATABASE OPEN
Database altered.
SQL>
```

You can confirm that the database is running in archivelog mode by using the following command. The results show that the database is in archive mode and that the automatic archival setting is enabled.

```
SQL> ARCHIVE LOG LIST

Database log mode              Archive Mode
Automatic archival             Enabled
Archive destination            /u02/app/oracle/oradata/nina/arch/
Oldest online log sequence     3
Next log sequence to archive   4
Current log sequence           4
SQL>
```

If you decide to turn off archiving for some reason, you can do so by using the ALTER DATABASE NOARCHIVELOG command, as shown in the following extract, after first starting up with the STARTUP MOUNT command:

```
SQL> ALTER DATABASE NOARCHIVELOG;

Database altered.
SQL> archive log list
Database log mode              No Archive Mode
Automatic archival             Disabled
```

Archive destination	/u02/app/oracle/oradata/nina/arch/
Oldest online log sequence	47
Current log sequence	48

```
SQL>
```

■Note With Oracle Database 10*g* Release 10.1, Oracle deprecated the LOG_ARCHIVE_START parameter. When you place the database in the archivelog mode, Oracle automatically starts archiving the redo logs.

Running the pupbld.sql File

You may occasionally see errors like the following when new users you have created try accessing the database through SQL*Plus:

```
Error accessing PRODUCT_USER_PROFILE
Warning:  Product user profile information not loaded!
You may need to run PUPBLD.SQL as SYSTEM
```

The product_user_profile table is a table Oracle maintains to control access to the database through SQL*Plus. Chapter 12 discusses how to use the product_user_profile table to restrict operations by certain users. Make sure you are logged in as the SYSTEM user and run the following script to ensure that this table can be accessed properly by all users, so that their SQL*Plus privileges can be checked properly:

```
SQL> @$ORACLE_HOME/sqlplus/admin/pupbld.sql
DROP SYNONYM PRODUCT_USER_PROFILE
. . .
Synonym created.
SQL>
```

Using a Server Parameter File

The init.ora file is the initialization file where you specify values for all the parameters you intend to use at database-creation time. But what if you need to change some of the parameters later on? You can do so in two ways: You can change the init.ora parameters, and stop and start the database instance. Or, if the parameter is dynamically configurable, you can change its value while the instance is running. Although being able to dynamically reconfigure database parameters is nice, there are inherent problems with this approach. When you restart the database, dynamically changed parameters are gone, because they weren't part of the init.ora file; if you intend to make a change permanent after you dynamically change it, you have to remember to correctly modify the init.ora file so those changes will become permanent the next time the database reads the file when it's restarted. Often, DBAs forget to perform this manual chore.

The server parameter file is an alternative (or a complement) to the init.ora file, and it makes the dynamic parameter changes permanent on an ongoing basis. You can specify that any dynamic parameter changes made by using the ALTER SYSTEM command be saved permanently in the server parameter file, which already consists of all the parameters in the regular init.ora file. After you create the database, you can create the SPFILE from your init.ora file as shown in the next section. If you later use this SPFILE to start your database, all dynamic changes made to the initialization parameters can be permanently saved in the SPFILE. By using the SPFILE, you can ensure that dynamic parameter changes will not be lost in between database shutdowns and restarts.

The file is called a *server* file because it is always maintained on the machine where the Oracle database server is located. Oracle recommends the use of the SPFILE to dynamically maintain the database configuration parameters.

The number of dynamically modifiable parameters in Oracle Database 11g is quite high. More than half of the initialization parameters are dynamically changeable through the ALTER SYSTEM statement, which means that the SPFILE is a smart way to permanently record a dynamically changed parameter value.

When the database is started, unless you specify the type of initialization file and its location explicitly, Oracle will look for the SPFILE first. On UNIX/Linux systems, the default location for the SPFILE is the $ORACLE_HOME/dbs/ directory ($ORACLE_HOME\dbs in Windows). In the default directory, Oracle first looks for a file named spfile$ORACLE_SID.ora (in our case, for the database nina, this would be spfilenina.ora). If it can't find this file, it then looks for a file named spfile.ora. If spfile.ora isn't found, Oracle will next look for the init.ora file in the same default directory. The init.ora file is traditionally named init$ORACLE_SID.ora (in our example, it is initnina.ora).

Note Although the SPFILE is placed in the $ORACLE_HOME/dbs directory by default, you can place it anywhere as long as you specify the location in an initialization parameter file by using the SPFILE parameter.

The V$SPPARAMETER dynamic view is comparable to the V$PARAMETER view and is used to record all the initialization parameter names and their values when using the SPFILE rather than the init.ora file.

Creating a Server Parameter File

Oracle lets you use the traditional init.ora file (or PFILE) as the configuration file. However, Oracle also recommends that you create and use an SPFILE for all databases. You can create the SPFILE from the init.ora file, and the process is very simple.

You must first log in as a user with SYSDBA or SYSOPER privileges. Then run the following command, in which PFILE is the init.ora file for our new nina database (initnina.ora):

```
SQL> CREATE spfile
    FROM
    pfile = '/u03/app/oracle/dbs/initnina.ora';

File created.
SQL>
```

Caution Once you create the SPFILE, a subsequent request to create it from the init.ora file will overwrite the existing SPFILE.

The previous command will create the SPFILE in the default location ($ORACLE_HOME/dbs). The file will be named spfilenina.ora. You can also create an SPFILE by giving it an explicit name, as shown in the following example:

```
SQL> CREATE spfile = '/u03/app/oracle/dbs/nina_spfile.ora'
    FROM
    pfile = '/u03/app/oracle/dbs/initnina.ora';
```

If you want Oracle to create an SPFILE from your init.ora file, and both files are located in their default locations ($ORACLE_HOME/dbs), you can simply issue the following command:

```
SQL> CREATE spfile FROM pfile;

File created.
SQL>
```

You can also create a new init.ora file from the SPFILE in the default location by using the following command:

```
SQL> CREATE pfile FROM spfile;

File created.
SQL>
```

If you bounce the database now, the instance will start up using your new SPFILE. Oracle will look for the initialization parameter lists in their default locations in the following order, and it will use the first one it finds:

1. It looks for the spfile$ORACLE_SID.ora file in the default location.

2. It looks for a file called spfile.ora in the default location.

3. It looks for the traditional init.ora file, with the name init$ORACLE_SID.ora, in the default location.

■**Tip** Although you can change the init.ora text file to your heart's content, don't try modifying the SPFILE directly. You'll end up corrupting it, and your instance may fail to start the next time you try to use the SPFILE!

Creating the SPFILE from the init.ora file doesn't mean that you can't use the init.ora file anymore. If you need to start the instance with the original init.ora file, you can do so as before by specifying it explicitly:

```
SQL> STARTUP PFILE='/u01/app/oracle/product/10.1.0.2.0/dbs/initnina.ora';
```

However, you can't specify the SPFILE instead of the PFILE in the preceding example—Oracle won't allow you to specify the SPFILE directly in a STARTUP command. However, you can do so indirectly by using a PFILE (init.ora) file that includes just one initialization parameter: the SPFILE parameter:

```
spfile = ' /u01/app/oracle/product/10.1.0.2.0/dbs/spfilenina.ora
```

After creating this new init.ora file, you can specify the PFILE variable in the STARTUP command, as shown earlier.

Listing 10-8 shows the contents of the SPFILE (called SPFILEnina.ora) that was created from the initnina.ora file.

Listing 10-8. *A Sample SPFILE*

```
*.compatible='11.1.0.6'
*.control_files='/u01/app/oracle/oradata/nina/control1.ctl',
'/u01/app/oracle/oradata/nina/control2.ctl'
*.cursor_sharing='force'
*.db_block_size=8192
*.db_domain='world'
*.db_file_multiblock_read_count=16
*.db_files=1000
* db_flashback_retention_target=720
*.db_name='nina'
*.db_recovery_file_dest='/u02/app/oracle/flash_recov_area'
*.db_recovery_file_dest_size=1000M
* instance_type='RDBMS'
*.log_archive_dest_1='LOCATION=/u02/app/oracle/arch/'
```

```
*.log_archive_format='log%t_%s_%r.arc'
*.pga_aggregate_target=1000M
*.processes=600
*.remote_login_passwordfile='none'
*.resumable_timeout=1800
*.sga_target=300M
*.statistics_level='typical'
*.undo_management='auto'
*.undo_retention=7200
*.undo_tablespace='undotbs_01'
*.
```

Tip It's customary for DBAs to place comments in the init.ora file, but the SPFILE will not include comment lines from the init.ora file. However, the SPFILE will retain comments placed on the *same line* as the parameter in the init.ora file (for example, CURSOR_SHARING=false # comment).

Setting the Scope of Dynamic Parameter Changes

You now have an SPFILE that contains all your initialization parameters, and you can control whether any changes to the initialization parameters persist by being recorded in the SPFILE or not. Once you create an SPFILE, you can use a special SCOPE clause as part of all your ALTER SYSTEM commands that will determine whether the changes persist or not. The SCOPE clause can take the following three values:

- SPFILE
- MEMORY
- BOTH

When the SCOPE clause is set to MEMORY, changes are merely temporary and they go away after the database is restarted. When the SCOPE clause is set to BOTH, all dynamic changes get recorded in the SPFILE and are operational in the instance immediately. When the SCOPE clause is set to SPFILE, changes aren't applied immediately but only get recorded in the SPFILE; dynamic and static configuration parameters become effective only after the next startup of the database. If the database instance is started with an SPFILE, SCOPE=BOTH is the default option used by Oracle.

Note For static parameters, SCOPE=SPFILE is the only option, because the parameters can't be activated right away by definition.

As you can see, you have enormous flexibility in determining how long a change in a dynamically configurable parameter's value will persist. Here are some examples:

```
SQL> ALTER SYSTEM SET
       log_archive_dest_2='location=/test02/app/oracle/oradata/arch'
       SCOPE=SPFILE;
SQL> ALTER SYSTEM SET log_checkpoint_interval=600
       SCOPE=MEMORY;
SQL> ALTER SYSTEM SET license_max_users=200
       SCOPE=BOTH;
```

RMAN, Oracle's backup and recovery tool, will back up the server parameter file automatically when you back up your database. If you wish to modify several parameters in the SPFILE, the easiest way to do so is to first create an init.ora file from the SPFILE (as discussed in the previous section), make changes in the init.ora file, and create a new SPFILE from it. This process will, however, involve restarting the database.

■**Tip** Always create an SPFILE soon after you create the initial database. You'll be making a lot of initialization parameter changes on a new database, and the SPFILE gives you the chance to make these changes permanent if you so wish. This eliminates a lot of confusion later on, when you're making changes to several initialization parameters at once.

Creating an SPFILE or PFILE from Memory

You can re-create the SPFILE or the PFILE from the current values of the initialization parameters that an instance is currently using. The following command will create an SPFILE from the current values in use:

```
SQL> CREATE spfile FROM MEMORY;
```

The command creates a new SPFILE in the default location, but you can specify an alternative location. You can similarly create a regular initialization parameter file, as shown in this example:

```
SQL> CREATE pfile FROM MEMORY;
```

This command will come in handy when you lose the current parameter file. In a RAC environment, the command will capture the parameter settings being used by each of the instances in the system.

Starting Up and Shutting Down the Database from SQL*Plus

You can start up and shut down your Oracle database from the SQL*Plus interface, the OEM interface, and an RMAN interface. I'll focus on performing these operations using the SQL*Plus interface in this chapter.

Starting the Database

When you issue the STARTUP command to start an Oracle database, Oracle will look for the initialization parameters in the default location, $ORACLE_HOME/dbs (for UNIX/Linux). There, Oracle will look for the correct initialization file to use, in the following order:

- spfile$ORACLE_SID.ora
- spfile.ora
- init$ORACLE_SID.ora

■**Note** Regardless of which file Oracle reads, you don't have to specify the path and location of the file if it's in the default location. If you wish to store your initialization file in a nondefault location, you have to specify the location when you issue the startup commands.

You can start an Oracle database in several modes. Let's take a quick look at the different options you have while starting up a database.

The STARTUP NOMOUNT Command

You can start up the instance in a SQL*Plus session with just the instance running by using the STARTUP NOMOUNT command. The control files aren't read and the datafiles aren't opened when you open a database in this mode. The Oracle background processes are started up, and the SGA is allocated to Oracle by the operating system. In fact, the instance is running by itself, much like the engine of a tractor trailer being started with no trailer attached to the cab (you can't do much with either).

Listing 10-9 shows the use of the STARTUP NOMOUNT command.

Listing 10-9. *Using the STARTUP NOMOUNT Command*

```
SQL> STARTUP NOMOUNT
ORACLE instance started.

Total System Global Area    314572800 bytes
Fixed Size                    1236756 bytes
Variable Size                99164396 bytes
Database Buffers            213909504 bytes
Redo Buffers                  5169152 bytes
SQL>
```

Sometimes during certain maintenance operations and during recovery times, you can't have the database open for public access. That's when this partial opening of the database is necessary. You also use the NOMOUNT startup option during database creation and when you have to re-create control files.

The STARTUP MOUNT Command

The next step in the startup process, after the instance is started, is the mounting of the database. During the mount stage, Oracle associates the instance with the database. Oracle opens and reads the control files and gets the names and locations of the datafiles and the redo log files. You can mount an already started instance with the ALTER DATABASE command, or you can use the STARTUP MOUNT command when you initially start the database.

If you've already started the database in the nomount mode, use this command:

```
SQL> ALTER DATABASE MOUNT;
Database altered.
SQL>
```

To start up in the mount mode directly, use this command:

```
SQL> STARTUP MOUNT
ORACLE instance started.
Total System Global Area    314572800 bytes
Fixed Size                    1236756 bytes
Variable Size                99164396 bytes
Database Buffers            213909504 bytes
Redo Buffers                  5169152 bytes
Database mounted.
SQL>
```

You usually need to start up a database in mount mode when you're doing activities such as performing a full database recovery, changing the archive logging mode of the database, or renaming datafiles. Note that all three of these operations require Oracle to access the datafiles but can't accommodate any user operations in the files.

The STARTUP OPEN Command

The last stage of the startup process is opening the database. When the database is started in the open mode, all valid users can connect to the database and perform database operations. Prior to this stage, the general users can't connect to the database at all. You can bring the database into the open mode by issuing the ALTER DATABASE command as follows:

```
SQL> ALTER DATABASE OPEN;
Database altered.
```

More commonly, you simply use the STARTUP command to mount and open your database all at once:

```
SQL> STARTUP
Oracle instance started.

Total System Global Area     314572800 bytes
Fixed Size                     1236756 bytes
Variable Size                 99164396 bytes
Database Buffers             213909504 bytes
Redo Buffers                   5169152 bytes
Database mounted.
Database opened.
SQL>
```

To open the database, the Oracle server first opens all the datafiles and the online redo log files, and verifies that the database is consistent. If the database isn't consistent—for example, if the SCNs in the control files don't match some of the SCNs in the datafile headers—the background process will automatically perform an instance recovery before opening the database. If media recovery rather than instance recovery is needed, Oracle will signal that a database recovery is called for and won't open the database until you perform the recovery.

■Note When you issue the simple STARTUP command, Oracle will process all the startup steps in sequence and will start the instance and open it for public access all at once. As long as your ORACLE_SID parameter is set to the right database, you don't need to specify the database name in the STARTUP command.

Automatically Starting Databases

You can let all your databases start up automatically each time the operating system restarts by simply using standard operating system scripts. Each operating system will have its own system-specific way of automating Oracle database startups. Here, I'll discuss the startup and shutdown scripts used in UNIX/Linux systems, and I'll specifically use examples for a Red Hat Linux environment. Automatic startup on Windows systems is covered in Chapter 20.

Oracle provides two files, dbstart and dbshut, that use the standard /etc/oratab file contents to determine which Oracle databases are running on the server, and automatically start up and shut down all the databases whenever the system is started up and shut down. In most UNIX/Linux systems, these two scripts are located in the $ORACLE_HOME/bin directory. After I created the new nina database, I added it to the oratab file by adding the following line (which specifies the database name, ORACLE_HOME, and whether the database should be automatically stopped and started):

```
nina:/u01/app/oracle/product/10.2.0/db_1:Y
```

In order to make a database start up and shut down automatically upon a system reboot, you must add a script to the /etc/rc.d/init.d directory. This file will include the Oracle-provided dbstart and dbshut scripts in it, as shown in Listing 10-10. The script uses a case statement to determine whether to start or stop all the Oracle databases and the Oracle Listener service.

Listing 10-10. *A Script to Start and Stop Oracle Database and the Oracle Listener*

```
#!/bin/sh
# /etc/rc.d/init.d/oracle
# Description: The following script
# starts and stops all Oracle databases and listeners
case "$1" in
start)
echo -n "Starting Oracle Databases: "
date +"! %T %a %D : Starting Oracle Databases after
system start up." >> /var/log/oracle
echo "------------------------------" >> /var/log/oracle
su - oracle -c dbstart >> /var/log/oracle
echo "Done."
echo -n "Starting Oracle Listeners: "
su - oracle -c "lsnrctl start" >> /var/log/oracle
echo "Done."
echo ""
echo "-----------------------------------" >> /var/log/oracle
date +"! %T %a %D : Finished." >> /var/log/oracle
echo "-----------------------------------" >> /var/log/oracle
;;
stop)
echo -n "Shutting Down Oracle Listeners: "
echo "-------------------------------------" >> /var/log/oracle
date +"! %T %a %D : Shutting Down All Oracle Databases
as part of system shutdown." >> /var/log/oracle
echo "-------------------------------------" >> /var/log/oracle
su - oracle -c "lsnrctl stop" >> /var/log/oracle
echo "Done."
echo -n "Shutting Down Oracle Databases: "
su - oracle -c dbshut >> /var/log/oracle
echo "Done."
echo ""
echo "---------------------------------------" >> /var/log/oracle
date +"! %T %a %D : Finished." >> /var/log/oracle
echo "---------------------------------------" >> /var/log/oracle
;;
restart)
echo -n "Restarting Oracle Databases: "
echo "---------------------------------------" >> /var/log/oracle
date +"! %T %a %D : Restarting Oracle Databases
 after system startup." >> /var/log/oracle
echo "---------------------------------------" >> /var/log/oracle
su - oracle -c dbshut >> /var/log/oracle
su - oracle -c dbstart >> /var/log/oracle
echo "Done."
echo -n "Restarting the Oracle Listener: "
su - oracle -c "lsnrctl stop" >> /var/log/oracle
```

```
echo "Done."
echo ""
echo "--------------------------------------------------" >> /var/log/oracle
date +"! %T %a %D : Finished." >> /var/log/oracle
echo "--------------------------------------------------" >> /var/log/oracle
;;
*)
echo "Usage: oracle {start|stop|restart}"
exit 1
esac
```

The system administrator needs to create start and kill symbolic links in the appropriate run-level directories /etc/rc.d/rcX.d. The following commands will ensure that the databases will come up in run levels 2, 3, and 4:

```
$ ln -s ../init.d/oracle /etc/rc.d/rc2.d/S99oracle
$ ln -s ../init.d/oracle /etc/rc.d/rc3.d/S99oracle
$ ln -s ../init.d/oracle /etc/rc.d/rc4.d/S99oracle
```

In order to stop the databases on each host reboot or restart, you must also add the following links:

```
$ ln -s ../init.d/oracle /etc/rc.d/rc0.d/K01oracle # Halting
$ ln -s ../init.d/oracle /etc/rc.d/rc6.d/K01oracle # Rebooting
```

Restricting Database Access

Sometimes when you're performing data loads or an export or import of data, or when you're performing other critical maintenance tasks, you'll want the database to be open for you but not for general users. You can do so in a couple of different ways. First, you can bring up the database in a restricted mode, which will provide you with complete access and prevent general users from connecting, as shown in Listing 10-11.

Listing 10-11. *Starting a Database in Restricted Mode*

```
SQL> STARTUP RESTRICT;

ORACLE instance started.
Total System Global Area    314572800 bytes
Fixed Size                    1236756 bytes
Variable Size                99164396 bytes
Database Buffers            213909504 bytes
Redo Buffers                  5169152 bytes
Database mounted.
Database opened.
SQL>
```

When you're done with your maintenance or other tasks and wish to open up the database to the general public, you can simply use the ALTER SYSTEM command, as follows:

```
SQL ALTER SYSTEM DISABLE RESTRICTED SESSION;
System altered.
SQL>
```

You can also change an open and unrestricted database to a restricted state of operation by using the following command:

```
SQL> ALTER SYSTEM ENABLE RESTRICTED SESSION;
System altered.
SQL>
```

When you put a database in a restricted mode using the ALTER SYSTEM command, as shown previously, existing users are not hindered in any way. Only new logins are prevented, unless they have the restricted session privilege. Once you are finished doing whatever you needed to do, you can put the database back in an unrestricted open mode by using the ALTER SYSTEM DISABLE RESTRICT SESSION command. Sometimes you may want to use an open database but prevent any changes to the database for the time being. That is, you want to allow reads (SELECT operations) against the database, but no writes. Listing 10-12 shows how you can put your database in a read-only mode.

Listing 10-12. *Putting a Database in a Read-Only Mode*

```
SQL> STARTUP MOUNT
ORACLE instance started.
Total System Global Area      314572800 bytes
Fixed Size                      1236756 bytes
Variable Size                  99164396 bytes
Database Buffers              213909504 bytes
Redo Buffers                    5169152 bytes

Database mounted.
SQL> ALTER DATABASE OPEN READ ONLY;
Database altered.
SQL>
```

The read-only mode is usually employed by standby databases, which are copies of production databases designed to relieve the querying load on the parent production database.

Shutting Down the Database

You may need to shut down a running database for some types of backups, for upgrades of software, and so on, and there are several ways to do this. The option you choose will affect the time it takes to shut down the database and the potential for needing database instance recovery upon restarting the database. The following sections cover the four available database shutdown command options.

The SHUTDOWN NORMAL Command

When you issue the SHUTDOWN NORMAL command to shut the database down, Oracle will wait for all users to disconnect from the database before shutting it down. If a user goes on vacation for a week after logging in to a database, and you subsequently issue a SHUTDOWN NORMAL command, the database will have to keep running until the user returns and logs out. The normal mode is Oracle's default mode for shutting down the database.

The command is issued as follows:

```
SQL> SHUTDOWN NORMAL
```

or

```
SQL> SHUTDOWN
```

Here are some details about the SHUTDOWN NORMAL command:

- No new user connections can be made to the database once the command is issued.
- Oracle waits for all users to exit their sessions before shutting down the database.

- No instance recovery is needed when you restart the database because Oracle will write all redo log buffers and data block buffers to disk before shutting down. Thus, the database will be consistent when it's shut down in this way.

- Oracle closes the datafiles and terminates the background processes. Oracle's SGA is deallocated.

The SHUTDOWN TRANSACTIONAL Command

If you don't want to wait for a long time for a user to log off, you can use the SHUTDOWN TRANSACTIONAL command. Oracle will wait for all active transactions to complete before disconnecting all users from the database, and then it will shut down the database. The command is issued as follows:

```
SQL> SHUTDOWN TRANSACTIONAL
```

Here are the details about the SHUTDOWN TRANSACTIONAL command:

- No new user connections are permitted once the command is issued.

- Existing users can't start a new transaction and will be disconnected.

- If a user has a transaction in progress, Oracle will wait until the transaction is completed before disconnecting the user.

- After all existing transactions are completed, Oracle shuts down the instance and deallocates memory. Oracle writes all redo log buffers and data block buffers to disk.

- No instance recovery is needed because the database is consistent.

The SHUTDOWN IMMEDIATE Command

Sometimes, a user may be running a very long transaction when you decide to shut down the database. Both of the previously discussed shutdown modes are worthless to you under such circumstances. Under the SHUTDOWN IMMEDIATE mode, Oracle will neither wait indefinitely for users to log off nor wait for any transactions to complete. It simply rolls back all active transactions, disconnects all connected users, and shuts the database down. Here is the command:

```
SQL> SHUTDOWN IMMEDIATE
```

Here are the details about the SHUTDOWN IMMEDIATE command:

- No new user connections are allowed once the command is issued.

- Oracle immediately disconnects all users.

- Oracle terminates all currently executing transactions.

- For all transactions terminated midway, Oracle will perform a rollback so the database ends up consistent. This rollback process is why the SHUTDOWN IMMEDIATE operation is not always *immediate*. This is because Oracle is busy rolling back the transactions it just terminated. However, if there are no active transactions, the SHUTDOWN IMMEDIATE command will shut down the database very quickly. Oracle terminates the background processes and deallocates memory.

- No instance recovery is needed upon starting up the database because it is consistent when shut down.

The SHUTDOWN ABORT Command

The SHUTDOWN ABORT command is a very abrupt shutting down of the database. Currently running transactions are neither allowed to complete nor rolled back. The user connections are just disconnected. This is the command:

```
SQL> SHUTDOWN ABORT
```

These are the details about the SHUTDOWN ABORT command:

- No new connections are permitted once the command is issued.
- Existing sessions are terminated, regardless of whether they have an active transaction or not.
- Oracle doesn't roll back the terminated transactions.
- Oracle doesn't write the redo log buffers and data buffers to disk.
- Oracle terminates the background processes, deallocates memory immediately, and shuts down.
- Upon restarting, Oracle will perform an *automatic* instance recovery, because the database isn't guaranteed to be consistent when shut down.

When you shut down the database using the SHUTDOWN ABORT command, the database has to perform instance recovery upon restarting to make the database transactionally consistent, because there may be uncommitted transactions that need to be rolled back. The critical thing to remember about the SHUTDOWN ABORT command is that the database may be shut down in an inconsistent mode. In most cases, you aren't required to explicitly use a RECOVER command, because the database will perform the instance recovery on its own.

Tip Oracle recommends that you always shut down the database in a consistent mode by using the SHUTDOWN or SHUTDOWN IMMEDIATE command and not the SHUTDOWN ABORT command before backing it up.

Listing 10-13 shows what happens when an attempt is made to put a database in a read-only mode after the SHUTDOWN ABORT command was used to shut it down first. Note that Oracle won't put the datafiles in read-only mode until the database is manually recovered. (You'll find a lot more information on recovery in Chapter 16.)

Listing 10-13. *The SHUTDOWN ABORT Command and the Need for Instance Recovery*

```
SQL> SHUTDOWN ABORT
ORACLE instance shut down.
SQL> STARTUP MOUNT
ORACLE instance started.
Total System Global Area     314572800 bytes
Fixed Size                     1236756 bytes
Variable Size                 99164396 bytes
Database Buffers             213909504 bytes
Redo Buffers                   5169152 bytes
Database mounted.
SQL> ALTER DATABASE OPEN READ ONLY;
alter database open read only
*
ERROR at line 1:
ORA-16005: database requires recovery
SQL> RECOVER DATABASE;
Media recovery complete.
SQL>
```

■**Note** In all shutdown modes, upon the issuing of the SHUTDOWN command, all new user connection attempts will fail. Except for the SHUTDOWN ABORT command, all the other SHUTDOWN commands won't require instance recovery upon database startup.

Quiescing a Database

Suppose you want to put your database in a restricted mode to perform table reorganization or some other administrative task. Schema changes are especially hard to make while users are conducting live transactions in the database. The same goes for when you have to import data into a large table while users are connected to the database. You have to perform these activities during a "maintenance window," or you have to shut down the database and bring it up in a restricted mode.

But what if you don't have a maintenance window in which to shut down and restart the database? Or, as so often happens in practice, the assumed window magically disappears because you encounter some problem in performing your tasks during the allotted time? You are forced to wait for the next weekend, in most cases. To redress this problem, *quiescing* a database gives you the opportunity to put the database in a single-user mode without having to ever shut the database down.

When a database is put in a quiesced state by the DBA, the following conditions apply:

- All inactive sessions are prevented from issuing any database commands until the database is unquiesced.

- All active sessions are allowed to compile.

- All new login attempts will be queued. A user trying to log in during the time the database is in a quiesced state won't get an error message. Rather, his or her login attempts will seem to hang.

- Only DBA queries, transactions, and PL/SQL statements will be allowed in the database. To be more precise, queries and statements issued by all users in the Oracle Resource Manager SYS_GROUP consumer group are allowed.

To place the database into a quiesced state, you use the following ALTER SYSTEM command as the SYS or SYSTEM user:

```
SQL> ALTER SYSTEM QUIESCE RESTRICTED;
System altered.
SQL>
```

Later on, when you've finished your administrative tasks, you can allow regular access to the database by issuing the following command:

```
SQL> ALTER SYSTEM UNQUIESCE;
System altered.
SQL>
```

Once the database is unquiesced, all the queued logins are allowed into the database, and all the inactive transactions are once again allowed to turn active by letting them execute their DML statements.

Suspending a Database

If you want to suspend all I/O operations during some special administrative job, you can suspend the database. All reads from and writes to the datafiles and control files are prohibited while the database is under suspension. The suspension of activity on a database may be necessary when you want to perform an emergency backup of a tablespace, for example, or specialized chores such as splitting a mirror, which you can't do in any other way.

You can suspend and resume a database as follows:

```
SQL> ALTER SYSTEM SUSPEND;
System altered.
SQL> ALTER SYSTEM RESUME;
System altered.
SQL>
```

Dropping a Database

In the past, Oracle DBAs constantly bemoaned their inability to issue a simple DROP DATABASE command to remove a database. Starting with the Oracle Database 10g release, you can drop a database with the help of a simple DROP DATABASE command. When you issue this command, all datafiles, redo log files, and control files are removed automatically. However, it doesn't remove any parameter files, like the init.ora file and the alert.log file.

You must start the database in the RESTRICT MOUNT mode for this operation, as shown in Listing 10-14.

Listing 10-14. *Dropping a Database Using the DROP DATABASE Command*

```
SQL> CONNECT sys/sys_passwd AS SYSDBA
Connected to an idle instance.
SQL> STARTUP RESTRICT MOUNT
ORACLE instance started.
Total System Global Area        314572800 bytes
Fixed Size                        1236756 bytes
Variable Size                    99164396 bytes
Database Buffers                213909504 bytes
Redo Buffers                      5169152 bytes
Database mounted.

SQL> SELECT name FROM v$database;
NAME
---------
NINA

SQL> DROP DATABASE;
Database dropped.
Disconnected from Oracle Database 10g Enterprise Edition Release 10.2.0.0.0 -Beta
With the Partitioning, OLAP and Data Mining options
SQL>
```

The STARTUP RESTRICT MOUNT command ensures that no other users can connect to the database. Make sure you verify the name of the database before using the DROP DATABASE command to drop the database.

■**Caution** Obviously, you can't test the DROP DATABASE command casually! Be careful, since this command is unforgiving—it doesn't give you any chances to recall the command. All your datafiles, log files, and control files will vanish before you can blink!

Using the Data Dictionary to Monitor Database Status

The dynamic view V$INSTANCE is useful in monitoring the current status of an instance. The following query tells you that the database is open and no shutdowns are pending:

```
SQL> SELECT instance_name, status,
  2  shutdown_pending,
  3  active_state
  4* FROM v$instance
SQL> /

INST     STATUS   SHUTDOWN    ACTIVE
NAME              PENDING     STATE
-----    ------   --------    ------
nina     OPEN     NO          NORMAL
SQL>
```

In the preceding output, the active state is *normal*, which means that the database is neither in the process of being quiesced nor is it already in a quiesced state. The database status column indicates *open*, where a suspended database would have a status of *suspended*.

The DATABASE_PROPERTIES view will provide the name of the default temporary tablespaces in your database, in addition to a host of other information regarding NLS parameters.

The V$DATABASE view gives you plenty of details about your database. Here's a typical query, which shows the name of the database, whether archive logging is turned on (yes), and whether the database is in the flashback database mode (no):

```
SQL> SELECT name, log_mode,
     flashback_on
     FROM v$database;

NAME        LOG_MODE      FLASHBACK_ON
-------     ----------    ------------
PASPROD     ARCHIVELOG    NO
SQL>
```

What Next?

You've now created the new database, but you still need to do a few things to make it fully functional (patience—you're almost there!). At this point, you have the instance up and running and you have a first draft of the physical database based on tentative estimates.

To make this database do something useful, you need to create users. And to empower the users and ensure the security of the database, you'll need to grant these users specific roles and privileges.

You have to create objects such as tables, views, indexes, synonyms, sequences, and so on, based on the requests of the application development team. You also have to create the necessary application code in the database, including stored procedures and packages. Because an empty database with no data won't do anyone much good, you need to load data into the database. You also have to establish connectivity between the database you just created, the users, and other systems that need to access your database.

Finally, to secure your database from unexpected failures and malfunctioning systems, you need to back up the database and put a regular backup schema in place before you go off on your long-awaited and well-earned vacation. The remaining chapters of this book address all these important topics in detail.

Connectivity and User Management

CHAPTER 11

■ ■ ■

Connectivity and Networking

One of the DBA's key tasks is to establish and maintain connectivity between the database on the server and the user community. In the traditional client/server model, users connect to databases on separate servers by using a client, and the client/server model is still used in many places to run business functions. However, web-based connection models are much more common today as a means of connecting to databases. Oracle calls its set of connectivity solutions (which encompasses connectivity, manageability, and network security) Oracle Net (previously SQL Net) Services. In this chapter, I show how to use Oracle Net, a component of Oracle Net Services, to make and maintain connections between clients and databases. I also show you how to install the Oracle Client software. You'll also see how to use the new Oracle Instant Client, which lets you connect to an Oracle database without the use of network configuration files.

Oracle Database 11g provides several methods of connecting database servers to end users. For small sets of users, you can use the Oracle tnsnames.ora file, which is a local file containing the connection details. The new easy connect method lets clients connect to your databases without any configuration files. The most sophisticated connection method provided by Oracle is the directory naming method, which makes use of the LDAP-compliant Oracle Internet Directory (OID). You can use OID for security management and other purposes besides facilitating database connectivity. There is also an external naming method, which uses external naming services such as the Network Information Service to configure client connections to the Oracle database.

This chapter will provide you with a quick introduction to Java Database Connectivity (JDBC) as well. You'll learn how to connect to an Oracle database from within a Java program, and you'll step through a small example that illustrates the basic concepts of Oracle JDBC.

Oracle Networking and Database Connectivity

After you create the database and various database objects and load the data, the next big step is to establish connectivity between the database server and the users who will be using it. Oracle Net Services is the set of services that makes this possible. Oracle Net Services components have to "live" on both the client and the server, and they typically use the TCP/IP network protocol to establish network connectivity between clients and the database server.

Oracle Net Services is configured with several important features to make life easier for DBAs:

- *Location transparency*: Clients need not know the network location or any other privileged information about database services, because you can maintain all the information required to make database connections in a centralized repository. Users are given only the database name, and the connection is entirely transparent to them.

- *Centralized configuration*: For large installations, a centralized means of establishing and maintaining connections makes a lot of sense. The LDAP-compliant directory server supported by Oracle provides a very efficient centralized repository for meeting all your networking needs. Network, authentication, and other security information is saved in a central place where numerous users then access this information. Maintenance is extremely easy, because regardless of the number of clients, you only have to maintain the centralized information.

- *Scalability*: Oracle offers a specialized architecture, called the *shared server architecture*, to enhance scalability. This architecture enables several users to share the same connection process through the use of a dispatcher process. A small number of server connections can enable a large number of end users to use the system, thus increasing the scalability of the system. In addition, Oracle offers the Connection Manager feature, which provides connection multiplexing whereby multiple connections are taken care of simultaneously.

SHARED SERVER VS. DEDICATED SERVER ARCHITECTURE

You can set up a connection architecture where the Oracle server starts a separate server process for each client connection, or you can enable several clients to share a single server process. The separate server processes use dedicated connections between each client and the Oracle server, and it is therefore named the *dedicated server architecture*. The *shared server architecture* is the term for connections where several user processes use the same Oracle server connection to perform their work.

Shared Server Architecture

The shared server architecture relies on a dispatcher service to process connection requests from clients. A single dispatcher can service many client connections simultaneously. Dispatchers essentially act as mediators between the clients and the shared servers. Dispatchers are in charge of receiving requests from clients and placing them in a request queue, from which the shared server picks them up.

When you use a dispatcher (that is, when you use the shared server approach), the listener will not hand off a connection request to the database server directly; it hands the request off to the dispatcher. This is referred to as a *direct hand-off* to the dispatcher. The listener can also redirect a client connection to a dispatcher. In this case, the listener will pass the dispatcher's network address to the client connection, and this information enables the client to connect to the dispatcher, whereupon the listener connection is terminated.

You can use the Oracle Connection Manager to configure session multiplexing, which involves pooling multiple client sessions through a network connection to a shared server destination.

Dedicated Server Architecture

Dedicated server processes do not involve any sharing of resources by clients. Each client is assigned a dedicated server connection. The Oracle listener will start up a dedicated server process whenever a client process requests a connection. The listener passes the dedicated server's protocol address back to the client; the client then uses that to connect directly to the database server. The listener connection is terminated as soon as it passes the dedicated server's address to the client.

This chapter deals exclusively with the more commonly used dedicated server architecture. To learn how to set up a shared server configuration, please refer to Oracle's manual for networking, the *Net Services Administrator's Guide*.

Networking Concepts: How Oracle Networking Works

When you want to open a database session from a client, whether it's a traditional client or a browser-based client, you need to connect to the database across a network. Suppose you're establishing a connection over an existing network from your desktop to an Oracle database on a UNIX server across town. You need a method of making a connection between your desktop and the Oracle database (which involves the use of specialized software), you need some kind of interface to conduct the session (which, in this example, will be SQL*Plus), and you need some way of communicating with the industry-standard network protocols, such as TCP/IP.

To make it easier for you to configure and manage network connections, Oracle provides Oracle Net Services, which is a suite of components that provide connectivity solutions in distributed, heterogeneous computing environments. Oracle Net Services consists of Oracle Net, Oracle Net Listener, Oracle Connection Manager, Oracle Net Configuration Assistant, and Oracle Net Manager. The Oracle Net Services software is installed automatically as part of the Oracle Database Server or the Oracle Client software installation.

Oracle Net is a software component that initiates, establishes, and maintains connections between clients and servers. That's why Oracle Net must be installed on both the client and the server. Oracle Net consists mainly of two components:

- *Oracle Network Foundation Layer*: Responsible for establishing and maintaining the connection between the client application and the server, as well as exchanging messages between them

- *Oracle Protocol Support*: Responsible for mapping Transparent Network Substrate (TNS) functionality to industry-standard protocols used in connections

All servers that host an Oracle database also run a service called the Oracle Net Listener (commonly referred to as just the *listener*), whose main function is to listen for requests from client services to log into the Oracle database. The listener, after ensuring that the client service has the matching information for the database (protocol, port, and instance name), passes the client request on to the database. The database will allow the client to log in, provided the username and password are authenticated. Once the listener hands off the user request to the database, the client and the database will be in direct contact, without any help from the listener service.

Oracle provides a number of GUI-based utilities to help configure network connections for your databases. These utilities include the Oracle Connection Manager, Oracle Net Manager, and Oracle Net Configuration Assistant. These tools can help you take care of all your networking needs. After you finish reading this chapter, just click these program icons and start experimenting with test connections.

How a Web Application Connects to Oracle

To make an Internet connection to an Oracle database, the web browser on the client communicates with the web server and makes the connection request using the HTTP protocol. The web server passes the request along to an application, which processes it and communicates with the Oracle database server using Oracle Net (which is configured on both the database server and the client).

In the next sections, you'll look at some important terms that are crucial in Oracle networking.

Database Instance Names

As you know by now, an Oracle instance consists of the SGA and a set of Oracle processes. The *database instance name* is specified in the initialization file (init.ora) as the INSTANCE_NAME parameter. When you talk about the Oracle system identifier (SID), you are simply referring to the Oracle instance.

Normally, each database can have only one instance associated with it. In an Oracle Real Application Clusters (RAC) configuration, however, a single database could be associated with multiple instances.

Global Database Names

The *global database name* uniquely identifies an Oracle database and is of the format *database_name.database_domain*, for example, sales.us.acme.com. In this global database name, "sales" is the database name and "us.acme.com" is the database domain. Since no two databases in the same domain could have the same database name, every global database name is unique.

Database Service Names

To a client, the database logically appears as simply a service. There is a many-to-many relationship between services and databases, since a database can be represented by one or more services, each dedicated to a different set of clients, and a service can cover more than one database instance. You identify each database in your system by its service name, and you specify the service name of a database with the SERVICE_NAMES initialization parameter. The service name parameter's value defaults to the global database name.

Note that a database can be addressed by more than one service name. You may do this when you want different sets of clients to address the database differently to suit their particular needs. For example, you can take the same database and create two service names like the following:

```
sales.us.acme.com
finance.us.acme.com
```

The sales people will use the sales.us.acme.com service name, and the finance.us.acme.com service name will be used by the accounting and finance departments.

Connect Descriptors

To connect to any database service in the world from your desktop, you need to provide two bits of information:

- Name of the database service
- Location of the address

Oracle uses the term *connect descriptor* to refer to the combined specification of the two necessary components for a database connection: a database service name and its address. A connect descriptor address portion contains three components: the communications protocol used for the connection, the host name, and the port number.

Knowing the communication protocol helps ensure that the networking protocols agree, so you can establish a connection. The standard protocol is TCP/IP or TCP/IP with Secure Sockets Layer (SSL). The standard port number for Oracle connections on UNIX servers is either 1521 or 1526. The default port on Windows machines is 1521. Because you can't have more than one database with the same service name on any host, an Oracle database service name and a host name will uniquely identify any Oracle database in the world. Here's an example of a typical connect descriptor:

```
(DESCRIPTION
   (ADDRESS=(PROTOCOL=tcp) (HOST=sales-server) (PORT=1521))
   (CONNECT_DATA=
    (SERVICE_NAME=sales.us.acme.com)))
```

In this connect descriptor, the ADDRESS line specifies that the TCP protocol will be used for network communication. HOST refers to the UNIX (or Windows) server on which the Oracle listener is listening for connection requests at a specific port: 1521. The ADDRESS part of the connect descriptor is also called the *protocol address*.

Clients wishing to connect to the database first connect to the Oracle listener process. The listener receives the incoming connection requests and hands them off to the database server. Once the client and database server hook up through the mediation of the listener, they're in direct communication, and the listener won't involve itself any further in the communication process for this client connection.

Connect Identifiers

A *connect identifier* is closely related to the connect descriptor. You can use the connect descriptor as your connect identifier, or you can simply map a database service name to a connect descriptor. For example, you can take a service name such as "sales" and map it to the connect descriptor you saw in the previous section. Here's an example showing the mapping of the sales connect identifier:

```
sales=
(DESCRIPTION
    (ADDRESS=(PROTOCOL=tcp) (HOST=sales-server) (PORT=1521))
    (CONNECT_DATA=
       (SERVICE_NAME=sales.us.acme.com)))
```

Connect Strings

You connect to a database by providing a *connect string*. A connect string contains a username/password combination and a connect identifier. One of the most common connect identifiers is a net service name, which is a simple name for a database service.

The following example shows a connect string that uses a complete connect descriptor as the connect identifier:

```
CONNECT scott/tiger@(DESCRIPTION=
  (ADDRESS=(PROTOCOL=tcp)
  (HOST=sales_server1)
  (PORT=1521))
  (CONNECT_DATA=(SERVICE_NAME=sales.us.acme.com)))
```

Here's a much easier way to connect to the same database, using the connect identifier *sales*:

```
CONNECT scott/tiger@sales
```

Both of the preceding examples will connect you to the sales database, but obviously the second connect string (using the sales connect identifier) is much simpler.

USING ORACLE NET SERVICES TOOLS

Oracle Net provides you with several GUI and command-line tools to configure connections between clients and database services. The most common command line you'll probably use is the lsnrctl utility, which helps manage the Oracle Net Listener service. The following are the important GUI tools that help you manage Oracle Net Services:

- *Oracle Net Configuration Assistant (NCA)*: This tool is used mostly to configure network components during installation, and it enables you to select one of the available options (I discuss these options later in the chapter) to configure client connectivity. The easy-to-use GUI interface enables you to quickly configure client connections under any naming method you choose. On UNIX/Linux systems, you can start NCA by running netca from the $ORACLE_HOME/bin directory. On Windows, choose Start ➤ Programs ➤ Oracle - HOME_NAME ➤ Configuration and Migration Tools ➤ Net Configuration Assistant.

- *Oracle Net Manager*: Oracle Net Manager can be run on clients and servers, and it allows you to configure various naming methods and listeners. With this tool, you can configure connect descriptors in local tnsnames.ora files or in a centralized OID, and you can easily add and modify connection methods.

  To start Oracle Net Manager from the Oracle Enterprise Manager console, select Tools ➤ Service Management ➤ Oracle Net Manager. To start Oracle Net Manager as a stand-alone application on UNIX, run netmgr from $ORACLE_HOME/bin. On Windows, choose Start ➤ Programs ➤ Oracle - HOME_NAME ➤ Configuration and Migration Tools ➤ Net Manager.

- *Oracle Enterprise Manager*: OEM in Oracle Database 11g can do everything that the Oracle Net Manager can do, but for multiple Oracle homes across multiple file systems. In addition, using the OEM, you can export directory naming entries to a tnsnames.ora file.

- *Oracle Directory Manager*: This powerful tool enables you to create the various domains and contexts necessary for using OID. You can also perform password policy management and many Oracle advanced security tasks with this tool. On UNIX/Linux systems, you can start OID by running oidadmin from the $ORACLE_HOME/bin directory. On Windows, choose Start ➤ Programs ➤ Oracle - HOME_NAME ➤ Integrated Management Tools ➤ Oracle Directory Manager.

Establishing Oracle Connectivity

In order to connect to an Oracle database using the network, you must first establish a network connection between your client and the server. You must have either the Oracle Client or the Oracle Database Server software installed on the machine you're making the connection from. I explain the installation of the Oracle Client software in the following section.

Here are the steps you must take to make a successful connection:

1. Make sure the database server is installed and the Oracle instance is running.

2. Make sure that your Oracle Client software is installed on the client machine.

3. Check that the database server and client are running on the same network. Check this by using the ping command:

```
C:\> ping prod1
Pinging prod1.netbsa.org [172.14.152.1] with 32 bytes of data:
Reply from 172.14.152.1: bytes=32 time<1ms TTL=255
Reply from 172.14.152.1: bytes=32 time<1ms TTL=255
Reply from 172.14.152.1: bytes=32 time<1ms TTL=255
Reply from 172.14.152.1: bytes=32 time<1ms TTL=255
Ping statistics for 172.14.152.1:
    Packets: Sent = 4, Received = 4, Lost = 0 (0% loss),
Approximate round trip times in milli-seconds:
```

```
          Minimum = 0ms, Maximum = 0ms, Average = 0ms
C:\>
```

The results of the `ping` command show that the connection is successful. If the connection can't be made, you'll see a connection request timed out message, and the number of sent packets of data will be more than the number of received packets in the `ping` statistics.

4. The TCP/IP protocol must be installed on both the server and the client; if you install Oracle server and client software, these protocols are automatically installed in the form of the Oracle Net software component.

5. Ensure that the Oracle Net Listener service is running on the server and is listening at the appropriate port for incoming requests for connections.

6. Configure the client for connecting to the database. You can connect to an Oracle database by using one of four available methods: local naming, easy connect naming, directory naming, and external naming. I discuss these methods later in this chapter.

7. Connect to the database with SQL*Plus or a third-party tool. For example, with SQL*Plus you can connect to the database by providing the username/password combination and the database name:

```
C:\> sqlplus system/sammyy1@orcl

SQL*Plus: Release 11.1.0.6.0 - Production on Thu Mar 20 09:25:27 2008
Copyright (c) 1982, 2007, Oracle.  All rights reserved.

Connected to:
Oracle Database 11g Enterprise Edition Release 11.1.0.6.0 - Production
With the Partitioning, OLAP, Data Mining and Real Application Testing options

SQL>
```

In the following sections, I'll discuss the Oracle Client, the listener, and naming methods in more detail.

The Oracle Client

If you wish to access an Oracle database from a PC, you must first install the Oracle Client software on the PC. The Oracle Client software comes with the Oracle Server software, and you can also download the Oracle Client software from the OTN site (http://technet.oracle.com). The Oracle Client software is available for download separately. Although the Oracle Server and Oracle Client software versions need not be the same, Oracle recommends you use matching versions of the types of software so you can take advantage of new features.

You can determine your Oracle Client version by looking at the output when you invoke the SQL*Plus utility, as shown here:

```
$ sqlplus
C:\>sqlplus

SQL*Plus: Release 11.1.0.6.0 - Production on Thu Mar 20 09:27:14 2008

Copyright (c) 1982, 2007, Oracle.  All rights reserved.

Enter user-name:
```

The output of the preceding SQL*Plus command shows that I have Release 11.1.0.6.0 Oracle Client software on my system.

When you install the Oracle Client software, you have four options:

- *Administrator*: Lets applications connect to local or remote Oracle databases and administer them as well

- *Runtime*: Lets you connect to local or remote Oracle databases

- *Custom*: Lets you select individual components from the Administrator and Runtime installation components

- *Instant Client*: Installs only the shared libraries required by Oracle Call Interface (OCI), Oracle C++ Call Interface (OCCI), and Java Database Connectivity OCI applications

---

■**Note** The new Instant Client is discussed shortly in the "The Instant Client" section.

Installing the Oracle Client

Here's how you install the Oracle Client software:

1. Insert the Oracle Database 11*g* Client CD in the CD drive, or run the runInstaller script from your staging directory, as shown in Chapter 9.

2. Select Install/Deinstall Products, and click Next.

3. The Welcome window is displayed. Click Next.

4. In the Specify File Locations page, accept the default file directory or enter an Oracle home name and directory path. Click Next.

5. In the Select Installation Type screen, you're offered four choices—Instant Client, Administrator, Runtime, or Custom. Select Runtime Installation from the list, and click Next.

6. Review the components of the Runtime install, and click Install.

7. After the installation of the Oracle Client software is completed, the Oracle Net Configuration Assistant will appear. Select the "No, I Will Create Service Names Myself" option, and click Next.

8. Under Database SID, enter your database name, and click Next.

9. Select TCP as the protocol, and click Next.

10. Under Host Name, enter your host server name, and select the standard port. Click Next.

11. Click the Yes button to test the connectivity, and click Next.

12. When you see the message, "Connecting . . . Test Successful," click Next.

13. Select No when asked if you would like to configure another service. Click Next.

14. Confirm the completion of the Net Service Name configuration by clicking Next.

15. Click Finish and Exit.

■**Tip** If there are multiple Oracle installations on a PC, there may be several tnsnames.ora files on the system as well. A user may be unable to connect to a new database after adding the network configuration information to a tnsnames.ora file if it's not the one in use. Make sure the correct tnsnames.ora file is in the Oracle Client's path.

Using the TWO_TASK Environment Variable

You can bypass the use of an Oracle Net name by setting the TWO_TASK environment variable (on UNIX/Linux) or the LOCAL environment variable (on Windows).

The TWO_TASK environment variable specifies the connect string for connecting to a remote machine. SQL*Net will check the value of the TWO_TASK environment variable and automatically add it to your connect string, as shown in the following example:

```
$ export TWO_TASK=mydb
```

Once you set the TWO_TASK environment variable, you can connect to the mydb database in the following way:

```
$ sqlplus scott/tiger
```

Note that you didn't have to use the specification sqlplus scott/tiger@mydb, since you're using the TWO_TASK variable.

On a Windows server, the following is the equivalent for setting the TWO_TASK environment variable:

```
$ SET LOCAL=<mydb>
$ sqlplus scott/tiger
```

The Instant Client

The Oracle Client installation described in the previous section requires you to go through all the preparatory steps needed for a regular Oracle Database Server software installation. Fortunately, you may not always need to install the complete Oracle Client software for connecting to an Oracle database. Oracle's new Instant Client software allows you to run your applications without installing the standard Oracle Client or having an ORACLE_HOME. You don't need to install the Oracle Client software on every machine that needs access to the Oracle database. All existing OCI, ODBC, and JDBC applications will work with the Instant Client. If you wish, you can even use SQL*Plus with the Instant Client.

The Instant Client offers the following advantages, as compared to the full-blown Oracle Client software:

- It is free.
- It takes less disk space.
- The installation is faster (five minutes or so).
- No CD is required.
- It has all the features of the regular Oracle Client, including SQL*Plus if necessary.

Installing the Instant Client

Here are the steps to install the new Instant Client software and connect quickly to an Oracle database:

1. Download the Instant Client software from the OTN web site. You must install the Basic client package and you can also include any of the advanced optional packages. The packages contain the following items:

   - *Basic*: Files required to run OCI, OCCI, and JDBC-OCI applications

   - *SQL*Plus*: Additional libraries and executables for running SQL*Plus with Instant Client

   - *JDBC Supplement*: Additional support for XA, Internationalization, and RowSet operations under JDBC

   - *ODBC Supplement*: Additional libraries for enabling ODBC applications with Instant Client (Windows only)

   - *SDK*: Additional files for developing Oracle applications with Instant Client

2. Unzip the selected packages into a single directory, and name it something like "instantclient".

3. In UNIX and Linux systems, set the environment variable LD_LIBRARY_PATH to instantclient (thus making sure the setting for the parameter matches the name of the directory that contains the packages). On Windows systems, set the environment variable PATH to instantclient.

4. Test your connection to the Oracle server.

The Listener and Connectivity

The Oracle Net Listener is a service that runs only on the server and listens for incoming connection requests. Oracle provides a utility called *lsnrctl* to manage the listener process. Here's a summary of how the listener fits into Oracle networking:

- The database registers information about the services, instances, and service handlers with the listener.

- The client makes the initial connection with the listener.

- The listener receives and verifies the client connection request and forwards it to the service handler for the database service. Once the listener hands off the client request, the listener is out of the picture for that connection.

The listener.ora file, whose default location is the $ORACLE_HOME/network/admin directory on UNIX systems and the $ORACLE_HOME\network\admin directory on Windows systems, contains the configuration information for the listener. Because the listener service is run only on the server, there is no listener.ora file on the client machines. Listing 11-1 shows a typical listener.ora file.

All the configuration parameters in listener.ora have default values, and you don't have to configure a listener service manually anymore. After the first database on the server is created, the listener service automatically starts, and the listener configuration file, listener.ora, is placed in the default directory. Upon the creation of a new database, the database's network and service information is automatically added to the listener's configuration file. Upon instance startup, the database registers itself automatically with the listener, and the listener starts listening for connection requests to this database.

Listing 11-1. *A Typical Listener Configuration File*

```
# LISTENER.ORA Network Configuration File:
/u01/app/oracle/product/11.1.0.6.0 /db_1/network/admin/listener.ora
# Generated by Oracle configuration tools.
SID_LIST_LISTENER =
  (DESCRIPTION_LIST =
    (DESCRIPTION =
```

```
      (ADDRESS_LIST =
        (ADDRESS = (PROTOCOL = IPC)(KEY = EXTPROC4))
      )
      (ADDRESS_LIST =
        (ADDRESS = (PROTOCOL = TCP)(HOST = NTL-ALAPATISAM)(PORT = 1521))
      )
    )
  )

SID_LIST_LISTENER =
  (SID_LIST =
    (SID_DESC =
      (SID_NAME = PLSExtProc)
      (ORACLE_HOME = /u01/app/oracle/product/11.1.0/db_1)
      (PROGRAM = extproc)
    )
    (SID_DESC =
      (GLOBAL_DBNAME = remorse.world)
      (ORACLE_HOME = /u01/app/oracle/product/11.1.0/db_1)
      (SID_NAME = remorse)
    )
    (SID_DESC =
      (GLOBAL_DBNAME = finance.world)
      (ORACLE_HOME = /u01/app/oracle/product/11.1.0/db_1)
      (SID_NAME = finance)
    )  )
```

Automatic Service Registration

The Oracle PMON process is in charge of the dynamic service registration of new Oracle database service names with the listener—when you create new Oracle databases, they'll automatically register themselves with the listener service. The PMON process will update the listener.ora file after each new database is created on a server.

For automatic service registration, the init.ora file or the SPFILE should contain the following parameters:

- SERVICE_NAMES (for example, sales.us.oracle.com)
- INSTANCE_NAME (for example, sales)

If you don't specify a value for the SERVICE_NAMES parameter, it defaults to the global database name, which is a combination of the DB_NAME and DB_DOMAIN parameters. The INSTANCE_NAME parameter's value defaults to the SID entered during Oracle installation or database creation.

You can check the status of the listener on the server by using the lsnrctl utility, as shown in Listing 11-2. The output shows how long the listener has been up and where the configuration file for the listener service is located. It also tells you the names of the databases for which the listener is "listening" for connect requests.

Listing 11-2. *Using the lsnrctl Utility to Check the Status of the Listener*

```
 $ lsnrctl status
C:\>lsnrctl status

LSNRCTL for 32-bit Windows: Version 11.1.0.6.0 - Production on 20-MAR-2008

Copyright (c) 1991, 2007, Oracle.  All rights reserved.
```

```
Connecting to (DESCRIPTION=(ADDRESS=(PROTOCOL=TCP)(HOST=ntl-alapatisam.netbsa.or
g)(PORT=1522)))
STATUS of the LISTENER
------------------------
Alias                     LISTENER
Version                   TNSLSNR for 32-bit Windows: Version 11.1.0.6.0 - Produ
ction
Start Date                03-MAR-2008 11:15:53
Uptime                    16 days 21 hr. 14 min. 27 sec
Trace Level               off
Security                  ON: Local OS Authentication
SNMP                      OFF
Listener Parameter File   c:\orcl\app\oracle\product\11.1.0\db_1\network\admin\l
istener.ora
Listener Log File         c:\orcl11\app\oracle\diag\tnslsnr\ntl-alapatisam\liste
ner\alert\log.xml
Listening Endpoints Summary...
  (DESCRIPTION=(ADDRESS=(PROTOCOL=tcp)(HOST=ntl-alapatisam.netbsa.org)(PORT=1522
)))
  (DESCRIPTION=(ADDRESS=(PROTOCOL=ipc)(PIPENAME=\\.\pipe\EXTPROC1522ipc)))
Services Summary...
Service "orcl" has 1 instance(s).
  Instance "orcl", status READY, has 1 handler(s) for this service...
Service "orclXDB" has 1 instance(s).
  Instance "orcl", status READY, has 1 handler(s) for this service...
Service "orcl_XPT" has 1 instance(s).
  Instance "orcl", status READY, has 1 handler(s) for this service...
The command completed successfully
C:\>
```

In the Services Summary section of Listing 11-2, the status can have one of the following values:

- READY: The instance can accept connections.

- BLOCKED: The instance cannot accept connections.

- UNKNOWN: The instance is registered in the listener.ora file rather than through dynamic service registration. The status is thus unknown.

Listener Commands

You can run other important commands besides the status command after invoking the lsnrctl utility. For example, the services command will let you see what services the listener is monitoring for connection requests.

■Note You can also check the status of the listener service from the Net Services Administration page in Oracle Enterprise Manager.

You can see the various lsnrctl commands available by using the help command in the lsnrctl interface, as shown in Listing 11-3.

Listing 11-3. *Using lsnrctl Help to List the lsnrctl Commands*

```
$ lsnrctl help

LSNRCTL for 32-bit Windows: Version 11.1.0.6.0 - Production on 20-MAR-2008
Copyright (c) 1991, 2007, Oracle.  All rights reserved.

The following operations are available
An asterisk (*) denotes a modifier or extended command:

start               stop               status
services            version            reload
save_config         trace              change_password
quit                exit               set*
show*$
```

You can start the listener by using the start command, and you can stop the listener by using the stop command after invoking the lsnrctl utility. If you want to issue these commands from the operating system command line, you can use the commands lsnrctl start and lsnrctl stop to perform the two tasks.

If you make changes to the listener.ora file, one way to put the changes into effect is to restart your listener. The other and safer method is to merely reload the listener information, which includes the newly made changes to the listener configuration file. The lsnrctl reload command lets you reload the listener on the fly, without your having to bounce it. Currently connected clients will continue to be connected while the listener is being reloaded (or even bounced) because the listener has already "handed off" the connections to the database and isn't involved between the client and the database service.

■**Caution** I advise not modifying the listener.ora file unless you absolutely have to, and with dynamic automatic service registration, there is less need for you to modify the file. Nevertheless, there may be times when you have to change some part of the listener file, which consists of network configuration information for all the services the listener is monitoring for connection requests.

Listener Management

Although it's quite easy to set up the listener service, you can do several things afterward to tune up your connection process and to make the listener service secure. I'll cover some of these options in the following sections.

Multiple Listeners

You can have more than one listener service running on the same server, but you'll usually do this when you're using Oracle Real Application Clusters (RAC). If you do use multiple listener services, you can configure the CONNECT_TIME_FAILOVER parameter, which determines how long a client connection waits for a connection through one listener before attempting a connection through another.

Setting a Queue Size

Sometimes a large volume of simultaneous connection requests from clients may overwhelm a listener service. To keep the listener from failing, you can use the QUEUESIZE parameter in the listener.ora configuration file to specify how many concurrent connection requests can be made.

For most operating systems, the default value for QUEUESIZE is a small number, such as 5. Here's an example showing how to set the QUEUESIZE parameter:

```
LISTENER=
 (DESCRIPTION=
  (ADDRESS=(PROTOCOL=tcp)(HOST=sales-server)(PORT=1521)(QUEUESIZE=10)))
```

Setting a Password for the Listener

When the listener is first set up, there's no password protection set for the utility. Any user who can get into the operating system can easily stop the listener and prevent clients from making new connections just by typing **lsnrctl stop** at the command prompt.

■**Note** The default password for the listener service is "listener," and you don't have to specify this password when you use the listener.

You can set your own password for the listener utility as shown in Listing 11-4.

Listing 11-4. *Setting a Password for the Listener*

```
LSNRCTL> set password
Password:
The command completed successfully
LSNRCTL> change_password
Old password:
New password:
Reenter new password:
Connecting to (DESCRIPTION=(ADDRESS=(PROTOCOL=TCP)(HOST=ntl-alapatisam.netbsa.org
)(PORT=1521)))
Password changed for LISTENER
The command completed successfully
LSNRCTL> save_config
Connecting to (DESCRIPTION=(ADDRESS=(PROTOCOL=TCP)(HOST=ntl-alapatisam.netbsa.org
)(PORT=1521)))
Saved LISTENER configuration parameters.
Listener Parameter File
/u01/app/oracle/product/11.1.0/db_1/network/admin/listener.ora
Old Parameter File  /u01/app/oracle/product/11.1.0/db_1/network/admin/listener.bak
```

After you change the password successfully, you can't stop or start the listener service as before—you need to use your password to do so. You need to use the set password clause at the lsnrctl prompt to provide the listener with your (new) password, and then you can start and stop the listener service once again. Note that set password doesn't set a new password; it merely causes the listener to ask you for the listener password so you can perform administrative tasks.

Listing 11-5 shows an attempt to stop the listener, which was refused because the password wasn't provided. The listener is then stopped properly with the set password command.

Listing 11-5. *Stopping a Listener with Password Protection*

```
$ lsnrctl stop
LSNRCTL for 32-bit Windows: Version 11.1.0.6.0 - Production on 20-MAR-2008

Copyright (c) 1991, 2001, Oracle Corporation.  All rights reserved.
```

```
Connecting to (DESCRIPTION=(ADDRESS=(PROTOCOL=TCP)(HOST=ntl-alaptisam.netbsa.org
)(PORT=1521)))
TNS-01169: The listener has not recognized the password
$ lsnrctl set password
Password:
The command completed successfully
LSNRCTL> stop
Connecting to (DESCRIPTION=(ADDRESS=(PROTOCOL=IPC)(KEY=EXTPROC0)))
The command completed successfully
```

Naming and Connectivity

In the previous examples of connect descriptors and connect identifiers, the "sales" connect identifier was used to connect to the sales service. A connect identifier can be the connect descriptor itself or a simpler name (like "sales") that resolves into a connect descriptor. A commonly used simple connect identifier is called a *net service name*. Thus, the sales connect identifier in those earlier examples is a net service name.

Because providing the complete connect descriptor each time you want to make a connection is very tedious, the use of net service names makes more sense. In order to do so, however, you need to maintain a central repository of all the mappings between net service names and the connect descriptor information so that Oracle can validate the net service names. Thus, when a user starts the connection process by using the net service name "sales", the central repository is searched for the connect descriptor for "sales." Once the connect descriptor is found, a connection is initiated by Oracle Net to the database on the specified server.

Oracle allows you to have several types of naming repositories, and you can access the mapping information stored in these locations with one of the following four naming methods:

- *Local naming*: Uses a file called tnsnames.ora stored on each client to connect to the database server
- *Easy connect naming*: Enables connections without any service name configuration
- *External naming*: Uses a third-party naming service to resolve service names
- *Directory naming*: Uses a centralized LDAP-compliant directory server to resolve service names

No matter which naming method you use, the name-resolving process is the same. The following steps are followed under each naming method to resolve a connect descriptor to a net service name:

1. Select the naming method—local, easy connect, external naming, or directory service naming.
2. Map the connect descriptors to the service names.
3. Configure clients to use the naming method chosen in step 1.

The Local Naming Method

Local naming is the simplest and easiest way to establish Oracle connectivity. Using this method, you store service names and their connect descriptors in a localized configuration file named tnsnames.ora. By default, this file is always stored in the $ORACLE_HOME/network/admin directory. Oracle provides a sample tnsnames.ora file for your use, and you can find it in the default directory. (You can think of the tnsnames.ora file as being similar to the /etc/hosts file, which contains the networking information for UNIX/Linux systems.) The tnsnames.ora file is always present on the client machine; if the database server is also used for client-type connections, there will be a tnsnames.ora file on the server for the other databases you need to connect to from that server.

When you initiate a connection by using either the SQL*Plus interface or some other means, you need to provide your username and password for the database you are connecting to. Once you do so, Oracle Net has to figure out which server the database is running on, so it consults the tnsnames.ora file to resolve the network address, the protocol, and the port for the database server. When it successfully resolves these, it initiates contact with the listener on the machine where the database server is located. Once the listener hands off the connection to the database server, the database authenticates your username and password.

Once you configure connections using the local naming method, all database connections, whether they are made directly through SQL*Plus or through an application's logon page, will use the tnsnames.ora file to resolve service names.

In addition to the tnsnames.ora file, client machines make use of another file called sqlnet.ora when they use the local naming method. The sqlnet.ora file is located on each client and contains import network configuration parameters. (Of course, if a server is used as a client as well, there will be a sqlnet.ora file on the server.) Chapter 11 shows how to use the SQLNET.AUTHENTICATION_SERVICES parameter to configure operating system authentication. Here's a typical sqlnet.ora file:

```
# SQLNET.ORA Network Configuration File:
/u01/app/oracle/product/10.1.0/db_1/network/admin/sqlnet.ora
# Generated by Oracle configuration tools.
NAMES.DEFAULT_DOMAIN = wowcompany.com
SQLNET.AUTHENTICATION_SERVICES= (NTS)
NAMES.DIRECTORY_PATH= (TNSNAMES)
```

The tnsnames.ora and sqlnet.ora configuration files are usually located in the $ORACLE_HOME/ network/admin directory on UNIX/Linux systems and in the $ORACLE_HOME\network\admin directory on Windows systems. However, you can place these files anywhere you like. If you place them in a nondefault location, you have to use the TNS_ADMIN environment variable to tell Oracle where the files are. Oracle will search for the two files in the following locations, and it will use the first of each it finds:

1. Oracle looks in the directory specified by the TNS_ADMIN environment variable.

2. For the tnsnames.ora file, Oracle will look in the global configuration directory. For a UNIX/ Linux system, this is usually the /var/opt/oracle directory.

3. Oracle will look in the standard network directories: $ORACLE_HOME/network/admin on UNIX/ Linux systems and $ORACLE_HOME\network\admin on Windows systems.

Modifying tnsnames.ora Manually

To configure local naming, you have to edit the tnsnames.ora file provided by Oracle when you create a database. All you need to do is go to the default tnsnames.ora location, $ORACLE_HOME/ network/admin, and edit this file to reflect your network and database service name information. When you add a new database to your system, you also need to physically add the new database service name mapping to each user's tnsnames.ora file or send all your users a new, updated tnsnames.ora file to replace the old one. Listing 11-6 shows a typical tnsnames.ora file.

Listing 11-6. *A Typical tnsnames.ora File*

```
# TNSNAMES.ORA Network Configuration File:
/u01/app/oracle/product/10.1.0/db_1/network/admin/tnsnames.ora
# Generated by Oracle configuration tools.
finance =
  (DESCRIPTION =
    (ADDRESS_LIST =
      (ADDRESS = (PROTOCOL = TCP)(HOST = localhost)(PORT = 1521))
    )
    (CONNECT_DATA =
```

```
        (SERVICE_NAME = finance.world)
    )
  )
salesprod =
  (DESCRIPTION =
    (ADDRESS_LIST =
      (ADDRESS = (PROTOCOL = TCP)(HOST = 172.11.150.1)(PORT = 1521))
    )
    (CONNECT_DATA =
      (SERVICE_NAME = salesprod.world)
    )
  )
custprod =
  (DESCRIPTION =
    (ADDRESS_LIST =
      (ADDRESS = (PROTOCOL = TCP)(HOST = custprod)(PORT = 1521))
    )
    (CONNECT_DATA =
      (SERVICE_NAME = custprod.world)
    )
  )
```

Three databases are listed in the tnsnames.ora file in Listing 11-6, and all three have different features that distinguish them. The first entry is for the finance database, which is on the desktop computer, NTL-ALAPATISAM. The salesprod database is located on the UNIX server, whose IP address is 172.11.150.1, and Oracle Net can connect to it using port 1521 and the TCP protocol. The last database uses a symbolic name, custprod, instead of the IP address, to denote the host server.

If you were to add a fourth database, orderprod, located on the host with IP address 172.16.11.151, to this tnsnames.ora file, you would need to add the appropriate connect identifier to the tnsnames.ora file, as shown here:

```
orderprod =
  (DESCRIPTION =
    (ADDRESS_LIST =
      (ADDRESS = (PROTOCOL = TCP)(HOST = 172.16.11.151)(PORT = 1521))
    )
    (CONNECT_DATA =
      (SERVICE_NAME =orderprod.world)
    )
```

Once you configure a net service name and modify the tnsnames.ora file, here's how you connect to the database:

1. Distribute the new service name configuration to your clients. You may do so by copying the tnsnames.ora and sqlnet.ora files to your clients, who must have the Oracle Client software installed. Alternatively, you can use the Oracle Net8 Assistant or Net8 Configuration Assistant to configure the net service names on the client itself.

2. Make sure the listener on the server where the database is running is started. Check that the listener is using the same protocol and address as that you configured for the net service name in the tnsnames.ora file. Also make sure that the listener is using the TCP/IP protocol and is listening on the default port 1521.

3. Make sure that the target database you're trying to connect to is running.

4. Test the new connection by using the following syntax:

```
CONNECT username/password@net_service_name
```

Although local naming is quite easy to implement, it is a cumbersome method to use if you have a large number of client installations that need to access the database server directly because you need to maintain a local copy of the tnsnames.ora file on all your local clients. Furthermore, when you change hosts or add databases to your system, you need to ensure that you make the changes in all your client tnsnames.ora files. Of course, if you have a small client base, the maintenance of the tnsnames.ora files shouldn't be a problem.

Modifying tnsnames.ora with the Net Configuration Assistant

I prefer using the Oracle Net Configuration Assistant (NCA) to add a new service to my tnsnames.ora file, rather than manually adding it to the file. Like the listener.ora file, the tnsnames.ora file is somewhat tricky, with all its parentheses, and it's easy to make a mistake when you're manually editing it. Creating new services using the GUI is very easy, with the NCA prompting you for the server name, database name, network address, and protocol type. Once you're done configuring the connection, there will be a new or an updated tnsnames.ora file in the default location that includes the database services you just added.

To use the NCA, you must first install the Oracle Client software on the client machine by using the Oracle Client CD. The NCA comes bundled with both the server and the client versions of the software. You can create a connection and test it, all in under a minute.

Here are the steps involved in using the NCA to configure a new service name in your tnsnames.ora file:

1. Start the Oracle Net Configuration Assistant on a UNIX/Linux server with the netca command, as shown here:

   ```
   $ export DISPLAY=172.16.14.15:0.0
   $ netca
   ```

■**Note** You can start the NCA on a Windows system by selecting Start ➤ Programs ➤ Oracle ➤ Configuration and Migration Tools.

---

2. The Welcome page is displayed next. Select Local Net Service Name Configuration, and click Next.

3. On the Net Service Name Configuration page, select Add and click Next.

4. In the Service Name Configuration page, enter the service name you want to configure. In this example, it is the database named emrep.netbsa.org. Note that the database service name is generally the same as the global database name. Click Next.

5. In the Select Protocol page, select TCP and click Next.

6. In the TCP/IP Protocol page, enter the name of the host on which the database is running. Select the standard port number, 1521. Click Next.

7. In the Test Page, click the "Yes, Perform a Test" button, and click Next.

8. The NCA will try to connect to the database using the new configuration and will show you the results. If the connection fails, make sure the listener for the target database is up and that the default username and password combination the test process uses (system/ manager) is changed to a valid username/password combination. Also, make sure that you've provided the correct database name and domain name.

9. The NCA will then ask you to confirm the net service name in the Net Service Name page. Click Next.

10. In the Another Service Name page, you can choose to configure more service names.

11. On the Net Service Name Configuration Done page, click Next. Click Finish on the Welcome page when it reappears.

■**Note** You can also configure net service names using the Net Services Administration page in Oracle Enterprise Manager, or the Oracle Net Manager GUI.

The Easy Connect Naming Method

Oracle DBAs can simplify client configuration by using the *easy connect naming* method. Using this method, your database clients can connect to the database without using the tnsnames.ora configuration file for TCP/IP environments. All that your clients need is the host name and the optional port number and service name of the database. You thus have configuration-free, out-of-the-box TCP/IP connectivity to any database in your system.

The only condition for using the easy connect naming method is that you must have support for the TCP/IP protocol on both the client and the server. However, you don't have to configure a tnsnames.ora file. You can look at this new connection method as an extension of the host naming method introduced in Oracle9*i*.

Here's the general syntax of this new connecting method:

```
$ CONNECT username/password@[//]host[:port][/service_name]
```

In this easy connect syntax statement, there are four things you need to focus on:

- *// (double slash)*: This is optional.

- *Host*: This is a mandatory parameter. You can specify either a symbolic host name or the IP address of the server hosting your target database.

- *Port*: This is an optional parameter. If you don't specify a port, the default port, 1521, is used.

- *Service_name*: This specifies the service name of the database (the default is the host name), and it is optional. You can leave this parameter out if your host name and database server name are identical. If they aren't, you must provide a valid service name to identify your database.

The following example shows a connection being made to the dev1 database located on the hp50 server. The connection is being made directly from the operating system prompt, so the SQLPLUS keyword is used instead of CONNECT:

```
$ sqlplus system/system_passwd@ntl-alapatisam.netbsa.org:1521/emrep.netbsa.org
-
SQL*Plus: Release 11.1.0.6.0 - Production on Thu Mar 20 09:38:15 2008

Copyright (c) 1982, 2007, Oracle.  All rights reserved.


Connected to:
Oracle Database 11g Enterprise Edition Release 11.1.0.6.0 - Production
With the Partitioning, OLAP, Data Mining and Real Application Testing options

SQL>
```

Note that you can also connect without using the optional port number, as shown here:

```
$ sqlplus system/system_passwd@ntl-alaptisam.netbsa.org/emrep.netbsa.org
```

Note that the main parameters of the easy connect method are the same as the connection information the local naming method requires in the `tnsnames.ora` file. The information provided in the preceding example would be configured in the `tnsnames.ora` file as follows:

```
(DESCRIPTION=
  (ADDRESS=(PROTOCOL=tcp)(HOST=ntl_alapatisam.netbsa.org)(PORT=1521))
  (CONNECT_DATA=
    (SERVICE_NAME=emrep.netbsa.org)))
```

If I am connecting from within SQL*Plus, I can use the following syntax:

```
$ sqlplus /nolog

SQL*Plus: Release 11.1.0.6.0 - Production on Thu Mar 20 09:38:15 2008

Copyright (c) 1982, 2007, Oracle.  All rights reserved.
SQL> connect system/system_passwd@ntl-alaptisam.netbsa.org:1521/emrep.netbsa.org

Connected.
SQL>
```

■**Note** Of the four items you need to specify in the easy connect naming method, only the host name is mandatory.

Configuring Easy Connect Naming

As the name indicates, the easy connect naming method needs very little in the way of configuration. You specify the easy connect method by using the `EZCONNECT` keyword as a value for the `NAMES.DIRECTORY_PATH` variable in the `sqlnet.ora` file. Consider the following `sqlnet.ora` file:

```
# sqlnet.ora Network Configuration File:
/u01/app/oracle/10.1.0/db_1/network/admin/sqlnet.ora
# Generated by Oracle configuration tools.
NAMES.DEFAULT_DOMAIN = netbsa.org
SQLNET.AUTHENTICATION_SERVICES = (NTS)
NAMES.DIRECTORY_PATH = (TNSNAMES,EZCONNECT)
```

The last line shows the connect methods that Oracle Net will use to resolve connect identifiers to connect descriptors. The `NAMES.DIRECTORY_PATH` parameter specifies the order of the naming methods Oracle Net will use to resolve connect identifiers to connect descriptors. In this example, TNSNAMES is the first setting, so Oracle Net will use the `tnsnames.ora` file by default. If it fails to connect using the `tnsnames.ora` file, it will try connecting through the `EZCONNECT` method.

If you want `EZCONNECT` to be the default method, you can manually edit your `sqlnet.ora` file so that `EZCONNECT` comes first in your `NAMES.DIRECTORY_PATH` parameter, as shown here:

```
NAMES.DIRECTORY_PATH = (EZCONNECT, TNSNAMES)
```

Restrictions on the Easy Connect Naming Method

There are a few restrictions to using the easy connect naming method:

- You must install the Oracle Database 11*g* Net Services software on the client.
- TCP/IP protocol support must be provided on the client and the database server.
- You can't use any advanced features of Oracle networking such as connection pooling, external procedure calls, or Heterogeneous Services.

Database Resident Connection Pooling

Up until the Oracle Database 11g release, you could use two ways to connect user sessions to the database: a dedicated server process, which handles one user process at a time, or a shared server process, which serves multiple user processes. In Oracle Database 11g, you can use a third way to connect sessions to the database, which is a variation on the dedicated server approach and relies on the concept of using a pool of servers to serve connection requests.

Web-based applications typically acquire a connection, use it briefly, and relinquish it quickly. It's common for these applications to share or reuse sessions. Web applications don't usually maintain a continuous active connection to the database, but use the database occasionally over a period of time, and usually don't maintain state while they're connected to the database. Database connection pooling helps service thousands of end users through a small number of database sessions, thus enhancing database scalability. Technologies such as PHP can't avail themselves of connection pooling through the application server, since each Web server process requires a dedicated database connection.

Oracle's brand-new *database resident connection pooling* (DRCP) connection method uses pools of servers for serving a large number of user sessions. DRCP makes fewer demands for memory when compared to the dedicated server and the shared server configurations. DRCP is especially designed to help architectures such as PHP with the Apache server, that can't take advantage of middle-tier connection pooling because they used multiprocess single-threaded application servers. DRCP enables applications such as these to easily scale up to server connections in the tens of thousands.

DRCP is quite similar to the dedicated server in the sense that it works like a dedicated server configuration, but each user connection doesn't have to retain an exclusive dedicated server for the lifetime of a connection. Each database connection acquires a server from the pool of servers, for a brief period. When the user session completes its work, it releases the server connection back to the server pool.

How DRCP Works

DRCP uses a connection broker that assigns each new client session to an available pooled server. Once the client connection's request is served by the database, the connection releases the pooled server back to the server pool. Thus, the sessions use memory and other resources only while the database is actually performing tasks for the sessions and release those resources when they release the pooled server back to the pool of servers.

As long as the database doesn't reach the maximum number of pooled servers, the connection broker will create a pooled server to assign to a new client connection, if it can't find a free pooled server. Once the maximum number of pooled servers is reached, the connection broker can't create a new pooled server. It sends the client connections to a wait queue until some pooled servers are freed up. Unlike in a dedicated server approach where the amount of (PGA) memory used is proportional to the number of user sessions, under DRCP, the amount of memory is proportional to the number of active pooled servers. The following example shows how you can make significant gains in memory usage by switching to DRCP from a dedicated server configuration.

In the example, I assume that there are a total of 5,000 client connections, and that each client session requires 200KB of memory and each server process requires 5MB of memory. Also, let's assume that you need a maximum of 200 server connections. You can compute the total memory requirements for the dedicated server configuration and the DRCP method as shown:

```
Dedicated server
Total memory required = 5000 X (200KB + 5MB) = 260GB

Database Resident Connection Pooling

Total Memory Required = 200 X (200KB + 5MB) =  502 MB

Shared Server
500 X 200KB + 200 X 5MB =  11GB
```

You can see that while a dedicated server configuration requires a total of 260GB, you'll need only a little over a half gigabyte under the DRCP configuration.

Enabling and Disabling DRCP

By default, the database comes preconfigured with a default connection pool named SYS_DEFAULT_CONNECTION_POOL. You must, however, start the default connection pool in order to take advantage of the DRCP feature. You start the connection pool by executing the START_POOL procedure of the DBMS_CONNECTION_POOL package, as shown here:

```
SQL> connect sys/sammyy1 as sysdba
SQL> exec dbms_connection_pool.start_pool();

PL/SQL procedure successfully completed.
SQL>
```

You can check the status of the connection pool with the following query:

```
SQL> select connection_pool, status, maxsize from dba_cpool_info;

CONNECTION_POOL                 STATUS    MAXSIZE
---------------------------     ------    --------
SYS_DEFAULT_CONNECTION_POOL     ACTIVE    80
SQL>
```

Once you start the connection pool, it will remain open even if you stop the database and start it back up again. You can stop the connection pool by executing the STOP_POOL procedure, as shown here:

```
SQL> exec dbms_connection_pool.stop_pool();

PL/SQL procedure successfully completed.
SQL>
```

The background process Connection Monitor (CMON) manages the connection pool. Applications hand back dedicated server processes to the CMON process, which returns the process back to the connection pool.

You can specify the DRCP connection in the following way:

If you're using an EZ Connect string, specify POOLED in the string, as shown here:

```
myhost.comany.com:1521/mydb.company.com:POOLED
```

If you're using a tnsnames.ora file, specify SERVER=POOLED in the TNS connect string, as shown here:

```
mydb = (DESCRIPTION=(ADDRESS=(PROTOCOL=tcp) (HOST=myhost.company.com)
        (SERVER=POOLED)))
```

Configuring DRCP

You use the following parameters to configure DRCP in your database:

You can configure the connection pool based on your database's usage requirements. Here are the main DRCP configuration parameters:

- INACTIVITY_TIMEOUT: Maximum idle time allowable for a pooled server before it is terminated

- MAX_LIFETIME_PER_SESSION: The time to live (TTL) duration for a pooled session

- MAX_USES_PER_SESSION: The maximum number of times a pooled server can be released to the connection pool

- `MAX_SIZE` and `MIN_SIZE`: The maximum and minimum number of pooled servers in the connection pool

- `MAX_THINK_TIME`: The maximum time a client can remain inactive after obtaining a pooled server from the connection pool

You can execute the CONFIGURE_POOL procedure of the DBMS_CONNECTION_POOL package to configure several connection pool configuration parameters at once. You can execute the ALTER_PARAM procedure of the DBMS_CONNECTION_POOL package to modify the value of a single connection pool configuration parameter, as shown here:

```
SQL> exec dbms_connection_pool.alter_param(' ','INACTIVITY_TIMEOUT','2400')
```

The previous example shows how you can configure the `INACTIVITY_TIMEOUT` parameter. The database allows a pooled server to remain idle for up to one hour before terminating the connection based on the value of 2400 for the `INACTIVITY_TIMEOUT` parameter.

You can restore the connection pool configuration to its default values by executing the RESTORE_DEFAULTS procedure, as shown here:

```
SQL> exec dbms_connection_pool.restore_defaults()
```

The RESTORE_DEFAULTS procedure helps restore all connection pool configuration parameters to their default values.

Monitoring DRCP

Use the following views to monitor DRCP:

- *DB_CPOOL_INFO*: Shows the name of the connection pool, its status, the maximum and minimum number of connections, and the timeout for idle sessions

- *V$CPOOL_STAT*: Shows pool statistics such as the number of session requests and wait times for a session request

- *V$CPOOL_CC_STATS*: Shows details about the connection class-level statistics

The External Naming Method

The external naming method uses external naming services such as the Network Information Service (NIS), originally developed by Sun Microsystems, to resolve net service names. NIS systems keep a central database of host names and use a flat namespace based on a master server.

Here are the steps you need to perform to use the external naming method for name resolution:

1. Have your system administrator configure NIS if it isn't already in place.

2. Create a `tnsnames.ora` file as you would in the local naming method.

3. Convert the `tnsnames.ora` file to a tnsnames map, which you'll need for the NIS server later on. You can derive the tnsnames map from the `tnsnames.ora` file by having your system administrator use the `tns2nis` command, as shown here:

   ```
   # tns2nis tnsnames.ora
   ```

4. Copy the tnsnames map file to the server on which the NIS is running.

5. Install the tnsnames map file on the NIS server using the makedbm NIS program, as shown here:

   ```
   # makedbm tnsnames /var/yp/'domainname'/tnsnames
   ```

6. Test the NIS installation of the tnsnames map by using the following command:

```
# ypmatch net_service_name tnsnames
```

You should get a confirmation back in the following form:

```
description=(address=(protocol=tcp)
 (host=host_name)(port=port_number)))
 (connect_data=(service_name=service_name)))
```

7. Edit the sqlnet.ora file as follows:

```
NAMES_DIRECTORY_PATH=(nis, hostname, tnsnames)
```

The nis method should be listed first inside the brackets so that Oracle Net will attempt to resolve the service name using NIS first. Apart from that, the order of the items in the brackets doesn't matter.

The Directory Naming Method

Traditionally, network information was stored on multiple servers, often in different formats, but today's Internet-based applications leave many organizations open to huge security risks. Decentralized systems are a constant source of worry for most security professionals. Centralized directory services for authenticating users and enforcing security policies enhance an organization's power to safeguard its networked resources.

Directory services are huge centralized repositories that contain all the metadata pertaining to databases, networks, users, security policies, and so forth. The directory behind these services can replace a large number of localized files, such as the tnsnames.ora file, and can provide a single point of name resolution and authentication. These directories are relatively low-update databases with substantial numbers of reads against them. Retrieval performance is a key factor in the success of a directory service.

Here are some examples of the kinds of data that such directories can manage efficiently:

- Usernames and passwords
- User profiles
- Authorization policies
- Network configuration and Net Services information

Many kinds of commercial directory services are available, including Microsoft's Active Directory and Oracle Internet Directory, and they can be employed to perform a host of functions for an organization.

The *directory naming method* stores database connection information in a Lightweight Directory Access Protocol (LDAP)–compliant directory server. The connect identifiers are stored under an Oracle context that contains entries for use with OID.

Although a centralized setup may seem daunting at first, it is quite easy to set up. The initial cost may be higher, but the cost of managing the information over time is minimal. In addition to helping clients connect to central networks and databases, directories such as OID are valuable for providing enterprise-wide security.

Oracle Internet Directory

OID is an LDAP-compliant directory service that stores connect identifiers, among other things. LDAP is a popular protocol for accessing online services, and it is an Internet standard for storage and directory access. OID is very scalable because it is implemented on the highly scalable Oracle database. Thus, a potentially huge amount of directory information can be stored and easily accessed. The data is secure because it is stored in the database, and OID is a high-availability service, just like the Oracle database. The LDAP specification is also attractive because of the minimal client software it needs.

You can use OID for many applications, such as address books, security credential repositories, and corporate directory services. Oracle strongly recommends moving to OID as a way of configuring database connectivity. By deemphasizing Oracle Names, a connection method offered in the past, Oracle is positioning OID as the main alternative to the traditional local naming method, which involves the use of the `tnsnames.ora` network configuration file. The Oracle database can use OID to store usernames and passwords and to store a password verifier along with the entry of each user. Other Oracle components use OID for various purposes:

- *Oracle Application Server Single Sign-On*: Uses OID to store user entries
- *Oracle Collaboration Suite*: Uses OID for centralized management of information about users and groups
- *Oracle Net Services*: Uses OID to store and resolve database services and net service names
- *Oracle Advanced Security*: Uses OID for central management of user authentication credentials, authorizations, mappings to shared schema, single password authentication, Enterprise user security, and the central storage of Public Key Infrastructure (PKI) credentials

OID includes the following elements:

- *Oracle directory server*: Provides service names and other information by using a multitiered architecture over TCP/IP
- *Oracle directory replication server*: Replicates LDAP data between Oracle directory servers
- *Directory administration tools, including the following*:

  - Oracle Directory Manager, a GUI that helps you administer OID and other command-line administration tools

  - Directory server management tools within Oracle Enterprise Manager 10*g* Application Server Control console, which enable you to monitor real-time events from a web browser

The basic idea behind the use of OID is straightforward. Users connect to OID, which is an application running on an Oracle database. Users provide OID with an Oracle service identifier (a database name). The directory returns the complete connection information—host name, connection protocol, port number, and database instance name—to the client, which then connects to the database server. The connect identifiers are stored in the Oracle context, which contains entries such as database names and service names, for use with Oracle software such as OID.

Oracle's Advanced Security option uses OID to centrally manage user-related information. If you are using Oracle's replicated database technology, OID will come in very handy in managing the complexity of multiple servers and network protocols.

Although Oracle would like you to convert all your network configurations to OID, it is not clear that OID is worth the extra administrative overhead for most small to medium-sized enterprises. Remember that OID is not a product meant exclusively for network configuration. Networking database connections is only a small part of the capabilities of OID. The local naming approach (or the new easy connect naming method) is still useful for most organizations because of its simplicity.

How OID Makes Database Connections

When you use OID to resolve names, remember that the client doesn't have a file, such as `tnsnames.ora`, with the name-resolution information. When using directory naming, Net Services clients connect to a database as follows:

1. The person wanting to connect types his or her usual username/password combination into the client computer, along with a connect identifier.

2. The `sqlnet.ora` file on the client specifies that it's using OID to resolve names, so the Net Services client hands its request to the OID listener/dispatcher process.

3. The OID listener/dispatcher relays the LDAP request to the Oracle directory server.

4. The directory server connects to the OID database and resolves the connect identifier to the underlying connect descriptor, which contains the network, server, and protocol information. It sends this detailed connect descriptor information to the Net Services client.

5. The client sends the connect descriptor it receives to the Oracle Net Listener (or to the dispatcher, if shared servers are being used).

6. The listener service receives the connection request and, after verifying it, sends it to the database.

The Organization of OID

A directory contains a set of information about various objects, such as employee names and addresses or database service name information (as is discussed in this chapter). The information in a directory is arranged in a hierarchical structure called the Directory Information Tree (DIT).

Every directory entry is made up of various object classes and attributes, as follows:

- Directories are made up of object classes.

- Object classes are groups of attributes.

- Attributes are the containers that hold the data.

A directory consists of *entries*, which are collections of information about an object. To identify an entry unambiguously, you need something to tell you where it is located in the directory structure. This unambiguous address locator is the *distinguished name* (DN) of the entry. A DN is like an address that exactly locates an entry in the directory—it gives you the complete path from the top of the hierarchy to where an entry is located.

Here's an example of a DN:

```
cn=nina
ou=finance
c=us
o= wowcompany
```

This DN for the nina entry has the following nodes:

- cn: Common name

- ou: Organizational unit

- c: Country

- o: Organization

Thus, the DN nina.finance.us.wowcompany *uniquely identifies* the person with the name Nina working in the finance department of the US branch of Wowcompany. Note that each of the various nodes are called *relative distinguished names* (RDNs), so in essence a DN is nothing more than a string of RDNs.

A *naming context* is a contiguous subtree on a single directory server. An *Oracle context* contains relevant entries for use with Oracle features, such as Oracle Net Service directory naming and enterprise user security. You can have multiple Oracle contexts in one directory server. OID will create a default Oracle context at the root of the directory information tree. In the DIT, the Oracle context RDN (cn=OracleContext) is the default location a client uses to look up matching connect descriptors for a connect identifier in the directory.

An Oracle context in a directory tree would have all the service names underneath it, including complete network- and server-connection information. In addition to subentries that support directory naming, an Oracle context contains other entries to support enterprise security. Therefore, if you're trying to connect to a database on a server, the OID server doesn't have to search the directory tree all the way from the root entry to the last node. You merely have to provide it with a partial DN from the top root node to the Oracle context. The Oracle context will contain the net service names underneath it, and the net service names will contain the detailed connect information.

The *administrative context*, also known as the *directory naming context*, is a directory entry that contains an Oracle context. The following simple example demonstrates these sometimes confusing concepts.

The complete DN for the database orcl is the following:

```
dc=com,dc=wowcompany
cn=orcl,
cn=description,
cn=address,
cn=port,
cn=service_name
```

In the DN, dc stands for *domain component* and is usually used to describe domain elements in the directory.

The important point to note is that because all the connect descriptor information is under the Oracle context RDN, you don't have to provide the full DN each time you want to look up the connection information for the database. You can replace the preceding lengthy DN with the following generic-looking DN:

```
dc=com,dc=wowcompany,cn=OracleContext
```

Note that dc identifies a domain component and cn stands for a common name. In this example, com and wowcompany are both domain components and are therefore at the top of the directory tree.

Installing OID

You can install OID using the Oracle Application Server 10*g* Release 2 (10.1.2.0.0) software. You must choose the OracleAS Infrastructure 10*g* option in the Select a Product to Install window when using the Oracle Universal Installer. This option lets you install a new OID on your server. In the next page of the Oracle Universal Installer—the Select Installation Type page—select the Identify Management and Metadata Repository option; this creates a Metadata Repository, which is a requirement for installing OID.

Coverage of the installation and management of OID is beyond the scope of this book. Please refer to the Oracle Application Server Release 2 documentation on the http://technet.oracle.com web site for details.

Once you've configured OID, you're ready to enter Oracle net service names into it. You can use several methods to do so. The easiest ways are to add service names using Oracle Net Manager, if you're adding entries individually, or to import your entire tnsnames.ora file into OID using Oracle Enterprise Manager.

Oracle and Java Database Connectivity

Frequently, Java programs need to connect to a database to perform data manipulation tasks. JDBC is an interface that permits a Java program to connect to a database and issue DML and DDL SQL statements. JDBC allows the use of dynamic SQL statements, for situations where you may not know the number and types of columns until run time. (If you're going to write static SQL, you can use SQLJ, which lets you embed SQL statements in Java.) JDBC provides a rich library of routines that help you open and close connections to databases and process data.

In the following sections, you'll see how you can use JDBC to connect to and work with Oracle databases from Java.

Establishing Database Connectivity

Before you can connect to a database, you have to select the appropriate drivers. Oracle provides four major kinds of JDBC drivers:

- *JDBC thin driver.* This pure Java client–based driver provides a direct connection to the database using the TCP/IP protocol. The driver requires a listener and uses sockets for making connections to databases.

- *JDBC OCI driver.* This driver needs a client installation of Oracle, so it is specific to Oracle. This driver is highly scalable and can use connection pooling to serve large numbers of users.

- *JDBC server-side thin driver.* Running on the server, this driver connects to remote databases and provides the same functionality as the client-based thin driver.

- *JDBC server-side internal driver.* As its name indicates, this driver resides on the server and is used by the Java Virtual Machine (JVM) to talk to the Oracle database server.

Once you choose a specific type of JDBC driver, you must specify the JDBC driver in one of two ways: use the static `registerDriver()` method of the JDBC `DriverManager` class, or use the `forName()` method of the `java.lang` class. Here are the two methods of specifying the JDBC driver:

```
DriverManager.registerDriver ("new oracle.jdbc.OracleDriver()");
```

and

```
Class.forName("oracle.jdbc.driver.OracleDriver")
```

Once you've loaded the JDBC driver, it's time to make the connection to the database by using the static `getConnection()` method of the `DriverManager` class. This will create an instance of the JDBC connection class. Listing 11-7 shows the code for doing this.

Listing 11-7. *Making the Database Connection*

```
connection conn=DriverManager.getConnection(
"jdbc:oracle:thin:@prod1:1521:finprod", username, passwd);
/* Here's what the different parts of the connection object stand for: */
jdbc=protocol
oracle=vendor
thin=driver
prod1=server
1521=port number
finprod=Oracle database
username=database username
password=database password
```

If all your information is valid, you are connected to the database from your Java application.

Working with the Database

Now that you've learned how to connect to the database using JDBC, it's time to find out how you can process SQL statements in the database through the JDBC connection.

You can't execute SQL directly from your Java program. First you need to create JDBC statements, and then you need to execute your SQL statements. Let's look at these two steps in detail.

Creating the Statement Object

To relay your SQL statements to the database, you need to create a JDBC Statement object. This object will associate itself with an open connection and henceforth act as the conduit through which SQL statements are transferred from the Java program to the database for execution.

Here's how you create the JDBC Statement object:

```
statement stmt = conn.createStatement();
```

No SQL statements are associated with the stmt object. However, under the Statement class, there is another object called PreparedStatement that always contains a SQL statement in addition to being the channel for the statement's execution. This SQL statement is compiled immediately, and it can be compiled just once and used many times thereafter, which is a great benefit.

For simplicity, however, I'll just use the Statement object in this discussion. Let's now turn to the execution of SQL statements.

Executing SQL Statements

You can understand JDBC SQL statements if you separate the SELECT statements that query the database from all the other statements. Unlike the others, SELECT statements don't change the state of the database.

Let's first look at how to deal with query statements.

Handling Queries

SELECT statements use the executeQuery() method to get the query results. The method returns the results in the ResultSet object. Listing 11-8 shows an example.

Listing 11-8. *Getting the Query Results*

```
string first_name,last_name,manager;
number salary;
resultSet rs = stmt.executeQuery("SELECT * FROM Employees");
 while (rs.next()) {
  first_name = rs.getString("first_name");
  last_name = rs.getString("last_name");
  manager = rs.getString("manager");
  salary = rs.getNumber("salary");
  system.out.println(first_name + last_name "works for"
  Manager "salary is:" salary.");
```

Note that rs is an instance of the resultSet object, and it holds the query results. The resultSet object also provides a cursor, so you can access the results one by one. Each time you invoke the resultSet method, the cursor moves to the next row in the result set.

Handling DDL and Nonquery DML Statements

Any statement that changes the state of the database—be it a DDL statement or a DML statement such as INSERT, UPDATE, or DELETE—is executed using the executeUpdate() method. Note that the word "update" in the method name indicates that the SQL statement will change something in the database.

Here are some examples of executeUpdate() statements:

```
statement stmt = conn.createStatement();
   stmt.executeUpdate("CREATE TABLE Employees" +
```

```
    "(last_name VARCHAR2(30), first_name VARCHAR2(20),
      manager VARCHAR2(30), salary(number");
  stmt.executeUpdate("INSERT INTO Employees " +
    "VALUES ('Alapati', 'Valerie', 'Shannon', salary)");
```

The preceding statements create the `Statement` object, and then they create a table and insert some data into it.

All your normal SQL transaction properties, such as consistency and durability, are maintained when you use JDBC to execute SQL statements. By default, each statement commits after its execution because the value of `conn.setAutoCommit()` is set to `true`, as you can see in the following example. You can ensure that there is a commit after every statement in either of the following ways (and if you wish, you can also use the `conn.rollback()` method to roll back a statement):

```
conn.setAutoCommit(false);
```

or

```
conn.commit();
```

Here's a simple example that shows how to use the `commit()` and `rollback()` statements:

```
conn.setAutoCommit(false);
    Statement stmt = conn.createStatement();
stmt.executeUpdate("INSERT INTO employees
VALUES('Alapati','Valerie','Nicholas',50000 )");
    conn.rollback();
stmt.executeUpdate("INSERT INTO employees
VALUES('Alapati','Nina','Nicholas',50000)");
    conn.commit();
```

Error Handling

All programs must have an exception handler built in; especially those DML statements that change the database state. One way to do this is to use the `rollback()` statement when you run into an error, so your partial changes are all undone.

You can use the `SQLException()` method to catch errors. In Java programs, you use a `try` code block to generate (or throw) an exception, and the `catch` block will "catch" the exception thus thrown. Listing 11-9 shows a sample Java code block that illustrates these concepts.

Listing 11-9. *Handling Errors in Java*

```
try { conn.setAutoCommit(false);
    stmt.executeUpdate(" " +
    "(Disney World', 'MickeyMouse', 2.00)");
     conn.commit();
     conn.setAutoCommit(true);
    }
catch(SQLException ex) {
     system.err.println("SQLException: " + ex.getMessage());
     conn.rollback();
    conn.setAutoCommit(true);
    }
```

A Complete Program

Listing 11-10 shows a sample program that puts together all the concepts of the preceding sections. The example first registers the Oracle thin driver and connects to the database using it. The program updates some rows in a table and uses the result set to print the data.

Listing 11-10. *A Complete Java Program Using JDBC*

```
/* import java packages */
import java.sql.*;
public class accessDatabase{
    public static void main(String[] args)
        throws SQLException {
        stringfirst_name,last_name ;
        number salary ;
        connection c = null;
/* register the Oracle Driver */
        try {
            class.forName("oracle.jdbc.driver.OracleDriver");
            c = DriverManager.getConnection(
                "jdbc:oracle:thin:@prod1:1521:finprod",
                "user", "user_passwd");
/* create the statement object */
            statement s = c.createStatement();
            c.setAutoCommit(false);
            s.executeUpdate("CREATE TABLE employees " +
                "(first_name VARCHAR2(30), last_name VARCHAR2(20),salary NUMBER)");
            s.executeUpdate("INSERT INTO employee VALUES " +
                "('nicholas', 'Alapati', 50000 )");
            c.commit();
            c.setAutoCommit(true);
/* the result set */
            resultSet rs = s.executeQuery("SELECT * FROM Employees");
            while( rs.next() ){
                first_name = rs.getString("first_name");
                last_name = rs.getString("last_name");
                salary = rs.getFloat("salary");
                System.out.println(first_name + last_name + " works for " +
    Manager + " salary is:"  + salary");
            }
/* exception handler */
        } catch (ClassNotFoundException ex){
            system.out.println(ex);
        } catch (SQLException ex){
            if ( c != null ){
                c.rollback();
                c.setAutoCommit(true);
            }
            system.out.println("SQLException caught");
            system.out.println("---");
            while (ex != null){
                system.out.println("Message    : " + ex.getMessage());
                system.out.println("SQLState   : " + ex.getSQLState());
                system.out.println("ErrorCode : " + ex.getErrorCode());
```

```
                     system.out.println("---");
                     ex = ex.getNextException();
                 }
             }
         }
}
```

As our focus is on Oracle database administration and not on programming, I presented the simple Java program here mainly to draw your attention to aspects of Oracle database connectivity.

CHAPTER 12

■■■

User Management and Database Security

Database security means different things to different people. The essential thing to remember, though, is that the underlying goal of database security is to prevent unauthorized use of the database or its components. Database security depends on system and network security as well, but this chapter mostly focuses on how you can provide solid security at the database level.

The first thing you'll learn in this chapter is how to create and manage users in an Oracle database. Everything users can do within an Oracle database is based on explicit privileges granted to them. You can grant users system and object privileges directly, but it's far more common to grant these privileges to roles, and to then grant roles to users, so this chapter shows you how to work with roles.

You'll also learn about Oracle profiles and how to manage them. Profiles let you set limits on the resources used by each user in the database and enforce a password policy for security purposes. The Oracle Resource Manager enables you to allocate scarce database and server resources among groups of users according to a resource plan. This chapter provides you with an introduction to this tool.

While controlling database access through the use of grants and privileges is fairly common, you must also consider using Oracle's powerful fine-grained access control feature, which lets you control access at the row level. This chapter discusses Oracle's fine-grained access control feature, also known as a virtual private database, in detail.

In a production database, it's *always* a good idea to audit database usage. You can audit both changes made to the data and database events, such as unsuccessful attempts to log into the database. Triggers based on system events can provide your database with a strong security layer, and this chapter explains how to use these special triggers. I also show how you can use Oracle's fine-grained auditing polices.

Data encryption is an important tool for most organizations today. Oracle offers several ways to encrypt your data, including special PL/SQL encryption packages, the capability to encrypt a table's columns with the transparent data-encryption feature, and the ability to encrypt an entire tablespace. I cover these encryption features in this chapter.

In short, these are the main aspects of Oracle database security management:

- Controlling access to data (authorization)
- Restricting access to legitimate users (authentication)
- Ensuring accountability on the part of the users (auditing)
- Safeguarding key data in the database (encryption)
- Managing the security of the entire organizational information structure (enterprise security)

Users are, of course, why a database exists, so let's look at how to manage users in an Oracle database before covering the various Oracle security management techniques.

Managing Users

User management is a pretty complex topic because not only does it deal with authorizing users to use the database, but it also touches on vital topics such as security and resource management. The DBA creates the users in the database and sets limits on their access to the various components. The DBA also limits the physical space and system resources that the users can use, generally by assigning database roles and setting privileges. You'll see later on how to make sure that the default passwords associated with various database users are changed soon after creating a new database.

When you create a new database, the only users at first will be the application or schema owners. Later on, you'll create the actual end users who will be using the database on a day-to-day basis. For the first set of users, the application owners, you will be more concerned with allocating sufficient space and other privileges to create objects in the database. For the end users, your primary concern will be their access rights to various objects and the limits on their use of resources while accessing the database.

Temporary and Default Tablespaces

All users need a *temporary tablespace* where they can perform work such as sorting data during SQL execution. Users also need to have a *default tablespace*, where their objects will be created if they don't explicitly assign a different tablespace during object creation.

You can create a default temporary tablespace and a default permanent tablespace for all users during the database-creation process (Chapter 10 explains how to create these two tablespaces). Once you have created these two tablespaces, you don't have to specify them again when you create a new database user.

■**Caution** If you don't assign a specific tablespace as the default tablespace, the System tablespace becomes your default tablespace. If a user creates a very large object in the System tablespace, he or she might take up all the space in it and make it impossible for the SYS super user to create any new objects in it, causing the database to come to a grinding halt. This is the main reason why you should always create a default tablespace for every user.

Creating a New User

You use the CREATE USER statement to create a user. It's good practice to assign each new user both a default temporary and a default permanent tablespace. Since I'm assuming that you've already created both of these tablespaces when you created the database, the CREATE USER statement can be very simple, as shown here:

```
SQL> CREATE USER salapati IDENTIFIED BY sammyy1;
User created.
SQL>
```

This statement creates a new user, salapati, with sammyy1 as the password. You don't have to assign a default temporary or permanent tablespace to the user (assuming that you created a default temporary and permanent tablespace for the database while creating your database). You can use the ALTER TABLESPACE DEFAULT TEMPORARY TABLESPACE statement to set up a default temporary tablespace after creating a database. Query the DATABASE_PROPERTIES view to see the current values for the default tablespace.

The following query shows the new user's default (permanent) and temporary tablespaces:

```
SQL> SELECT default_tablespace, temporary_tablespace
  2  FROM dba_users
  3* WHERE username='SALAPATI';

DEFAULT_TABLESPACE      TEMPORARY_TABLESPACE
-------------------     ------------------------
USERS                   TEMPTBS_01

SQL>
```

The new user can't connect to the database, however, because the user doesn't have any *privileges* to do so. This is what happens when the user salapati tries to connect using SQL*Plus:

```
$ sqlplus salapati/sammyy1

SQL*Plus: Release 11.1.0.6.0 - Production on Fri Mar 21 11:55:38 2008

Copyright (c) 1982, 2007, Oracle.  All rights reserved.ERROR:
Ora-01045: user SALAPATI lacks CREATE SESSION privilege; logon denied

Enter user-name:
```

In order for the salapati user to connect and start communicating with the database, you must grant the CREATE SESSION system privilege to the new user, as shown here:

```
SQL> GRANT CREATE SESSION TO salapati;
Grant succeeded.
SQL>
```

If you've followed the Oracle-recommended practice and have created default temporary and permanent tablespaces when creating the database, any new user you create will be able to use them instead of using the System tablespace as the temporary and default tablespace by default. In any case, after you create a user, the new user can't create new objects, such as tables and indexes, right away. In the following example, USERS is the default permanent tablespace for the database, and you can see what happens when the user tries to create a table:

```
SQL> CONNECT salapati/sammyy1
Connected.
SQL> CREATE TABLE xyz (name VARCHAR2(30));
create table xyz (name varchar2(30))
*
ERROR at line 1:
ORA-01950: no privileges on tablespace 'USERS'
SQL>
```

Let's say you assigned the default permanent tablespace USERS to all users. Since user salapati didn't specify a tablespace for creating the new xyz table, Oracle tries to create it in the default permanent tablespace, USERS. However, the user wasn't granted any *quota* on the tablespace. By default, users aren't given any space quotas on any tablespaces. Since the user is assigned the USERS tablespace but isn't allocated a quota of space in that tablespace, the user can't create any objects in the USERS tablespace. You must explicitly allocate tablespace quotas to a user.

It's common to assign specific tablespace quotas at user creation time. Here's how you grant a space quota on a tablespace to a user:

```
SQL> ALTER USER salapati
  2  QUOTA 100M ON users;
User altered.
SQL>
```

■**Tip** If you don't want a user to create any objects at all in the database, don't assign a quota on any tablespace. If it's an existing user with a specific quota on a tablespace, you can use the ALTER USER statement to set this quota to 0. When you use the ALTER USER statement to assign a quota of 0 on all tablespaces, any objects already created by the user will remain, but the user won't be able to create any new objects. The existing objects also cannot grow in size, since you revoked the tablespace quotas.

Once the new user is given a space quota on a tablespace, the user can create database objects such as tables and indexes. By default, any objects a user creates will be placed in the user's default permanent tablespace (USERS in our example). The user can choose to create the objects in any tablespace, however, as long as the user has a space quota on that tablespace. If you want a user to have unlimited space usage rights in all tablespaces, you need to grant the user the UNLIMITED TABLESPACE privilege, as shown here:

```
SQL> GRANT UNLIMITED TABLESPACE TO salapati;
Grant succeeded.
SQL>
```

If you want a user to create his or her own tablespaces, you must enable the user to create a tablespace by using the GRANT CREATE TABLESPACE TO *username* command. Similarly, you must grant the DROP TABLESPACE privilege. If a user wishes to subsequently create database objects in a tablespace that he or she has created, the user won't need any space quotas on those tablespaces. You can see the individual tablespace quotas allocated to a user by using the DBA_TS_QUOTAS view, as shown here:

```
SQL> SELECT tablespace_name, username, bytes FROM DBA_TS_QUOTAS;
```

TABLESPACE	USERNAME	BYTES
SYSAUX	DMSYS	196608
SYSAUX	OLAPSYS	16252928
SYSAUX	WK_TEST	12582912
SYSAUX	SYSMAN	78577664
RMAN_TBSP	RMAN	8585216

```
SQL>
```

As you can see, four different users, all owners of various Oracle components, have quotas in the Sysaux tablespace, and the user RMAN has a quota on a tablespace created exclusively for the Recovery Manager's use.

Since they aren't mandatory, you can create a database without a default temporary tablespace or a default (permanent) tablespace. In such a case, you can assign both tablespaces explicitly when you create a new user. You can also assign a quota on the default permanent tablespace. Here's an example showing how to create a user by explicitly specifying the default tablespaces (temporary and permanent). The GRANT QUOTA clause gives the user a 500MB space allocation in the USERS tablespace so the user can create objects there:

```
SQL> CREATE USER salapati IDENTIFIED BY sammyy1
     TEMPORARY TABLESPACE TEMPTBS01
     DEFAULT TABLESPACE USERS
     QUOTA 500M ON USERS;

User created.
SQL>
```

If you omit the QUOTA clause, the new user can't use any space in the tablespace USERS, which is the default tablespace for the user. If you have created a permanent default tablespace, as recommended by Oracle, you can omit the DEFAULT TABLESPACE clause. If you haven't, you should specify the DEFAULT TABLESPACE clause; otherwise, the new user will be assigned the System tablespace as the default tablespace and that's not a good idea, since you don't want users possibly creating objects in the System tablespace.

Altering a User

You use the ALTER USER statement to alter a user in the database. Using this statement, you can do the following:

- Change a user's password.
- Assign tablespace quotas.
- Set and alter default and temporary tablespaces.
- Assign a profile and default roles.

Here's an example showing how a DBA (or the user being altered) can use the ALTER USER command to change a user's password:

```
SQL> SHOW USER

USER is "SALAPATI"

SQL> ALTER USER salapati IDENTIFIED BY sammyy1;

User altered.
SQL>
```

Only a DBA or another user to whom you've granted the ALTER USER privilege can change passwords with the ALTER USER statement. Users can also change their own passwords with the PASSWORD command in SQL*Plus, as shown here:

```
SQL> PASSWORD

Changing password for SALAPATI
Old password: *********
New password: *********
Retype new password: *********
Password changed
SQL>
```

Whether users assign their own passwords or a DBA creates their passwords, a DBA won't ever be able to find out what any user's password is, since all passwords are stored in the encrypted form. However, I'll show you later in this chapter how to log in as another user by making use of the encrypted password.

Dropping a User

To drop a user, you use the DROP USER statement, as shown here:

```
SQL> DROP USER salapati;

User Dropped.
SQL>
```

The DROP USER statement will remove just the user from the database, but all the objects owned by the user will remain intact. If other objects in the database depend on this user, you won't be able to use the simple DROP USER command—you must use the DROP USER . . . CASCADE statement, which drops the user, the user's schema objects, and any dependent objects as well. Here's an example:

```
SQL> DROP USER salapati CASCADE;

User Dropped.
SQL>
```

In Chapter 16, you'll learn about Oracle's new Recycle Bin, which keeps the database from dropping a table permanently when you issue a DROP TABLE statement. This gives you the chance to revive a "dropped" table if necessary. When you drop a user, however, all tables and other objects in the user's schema will be dropped permanently, without using the Recycle Bin! Therefore, if you aren't sure whether you will need a user's objects later, but you want to deny access, simply leave the user and the user's schema intact, but deny the user access to the database by using the following statement:

```
SQL> REVOKE CREATE SESSION FROM salapati;

Revoke succeeded.
SQL>
```

Since a user can have the CREATE SESSION privilege through another role such as CONNECT, for example, Oracle recommends that you use the ALTER USER *username* ACCOUNT LOCK statement to ensure that a user is locked out of the database.

Creating and Using User Profiles

We have so far created a new user, assigned the user a set of default and temporary tablespaces, and granted the user the privileges to connect to the database. What is the limit on the amount of database resources this person can use? What if he or she unwittingly starts a SQL program that guzzles CPU resources like crazy and brings your system to its knees?

You can set the individual resource limits in Oracle by using what are known as *profiles*. A profile is a collection of resource-usage and password-related attributes that you can assign to a user. Multiple users can share the same profile, and you can have an unlimited number of profiles in an Oracle database. Profiles set hard limits on resource consumption by the various users in the database and help you limit the number of sessions a user can simultaneously keep open, the length of time these sessions can be maintained, and the usage of CPU and other resources. Here, for example, is a profile called "miser" (because it limits resource usage to a minimum):

```
SQL> CREATE PROFILE miser
  2  LIMIT
  3  connect_time 120
  4  failed_login_attempts 3
  5  idle_time 60
  6* sessions_per_user 2;
Profile created.
SQL>
```

When a user with the miser profile connects, the database will allow the connection to be maintained for a maximum of 120 seconds and will log the user out if he or she is idle for more than 60 seconds. The user is limited to two sessions at any one time. If the user fails to log in within three attempts, the user's accounts will be locked for a specified period or until the DBA manually unlocks them.

■**Note** Besides user profiles, you can also use some third-party tools that include query governs, which limit the types of queries that users can use within the database, thus ensuring that the database is not loaded down by inefficient queries.

Profile Parameters and Limits

Oracle databases enable you to set limits on several parameters within a profile. The following sections provide brief explanations of these parameters, which can be divided into two broad types: *resource parameters*, which are concerned purely with limiting resource usage, and *password parameters*, used for enforcing password-related security policies.

Resource Parameters

The main reason for using resource parameters is to ensure that a single user or a set of users doesn't monopolize the database and server resources. Here are the most important resource parameters that you can set within an Oracle Database 11*g* database:

- CONNECT_TIME: Specifies the total time (in minutes) a session may remain connected to the database.

- CPU_PER_CALL: Limits the CPU time used per each call within a transaction (for the parse, execute, and fetch operations).

- CPU_PER_SESSION: Limits the total CPU time used during a session.

- SESSIONS_PER_USER: Specifies the maximum number of concurrent sessions that can be opened by the user.

- IDLE_TIME: Limits the amount of time a session is idle (which is when nothing is running on its behalf).

- LOGICAL_READS_PER_SESSION: Limits the total number of data blocks read (from the SGA memory area plus disk reads).

- LOGICAL_READS_PER_CALL: Limits the total logical reads per each session call (parse, execute, and fetch).

- PRIVATE_SGA: Specifies a session's limits on the space it allocated in the shared pool component of the SGA (applicable only to shared server architecture systems).

- COMPOSITE_LIMIT: Sets an overall limit on resource use. A composite limit is a limit on the sum of several of the previously described resource parameters, measured in service units. These resources are weighted by their importance. Oracle takes into account four parameters to compute a weighted COMPOSITE_LIMIT: CPU_PER_SESSION, CONNECT_TIME, LOGICAL_READS_PER_SESSION, and PRIVATE_SGA. You can set a weight for each of these four parameters by using the ALTER RESOURCE COST statement, as shown in the following example:

```
SQL> ALTER RESOURCE COST
  2  cpu_per_session 200
  3  connect_time 2;
Resource cost altered.
SQL>
```

■**Tip** If you don't use a weight for any of these four parameters, the parameters will be ignored in the computation of the COMPOSITE_LIMIT parameter.

Password Parameters

Oracle provides you with a wide variety of parameters to manage user passwords. You can set the following password-related profile parameters to enforce your security policies:

- FAILED_LOGIN_ATTEMPTS: Specifies the number of consecutive login attempts a user can make before being locked out.

- PASSWORD_LIFE_TIME: Sets the time limit for using a particular password. If you don't change the password within this specified time, the password expires.

- PASSWORD_GRACE_TIME: Sets the time period during which you'll be warned that your password has expired. After the grace period is exhausted, you can't connect to the database with that password.

- PASSWORD_LOCK_TIME: Specifies the number of days a user will be locked out after reaching the maximum number of unsuccessful login attempts.

- PASSWORD_REUSE_TIME: Specifies the number of days that must pass before you can reuse the same password.

- PASSWORD_REUSE_MAX: Determines how many times you need to change your password before you can reuse a particular password.

- PASSWORD_VERIFY_FUNCTION: Lets you specify an Oracle-provided password-verification function to set up an automatic password-verification mechanism.

The Default Profile

As you can see, you can set a number of resource- and password-related attributes to control access to the database and resource usage. If you create a user and don't explicitly assign any profile to the user, the user will inherit the *default* profile, as shown here:

```
SQL> SELECT profile FROM dba_users
     WHERE username = 'SALAPATI'
PROFILE
-----------
DEFAULT
```

The default profile, unfortunately, isn't very limiting at all—virtually all the resource limits are set to UNLIMITED, meaning there's no limit on resource usage whatsoever.

Listing 12-1 shows the results of querying the DBA_PROFILES table regarding the attributes for the profile named default.

Listing 12-1. *Resource Limits for the Default Profile*

```
SQL> SELECT DISTINCT resource_name, limit
  2  FROM dba_profiles
  3* WHERE profile='DEFAULT';

RESOURCE_NAME                    LIMIT
-------------------------------- ----------
PASSWORD_LOCK_TIME               1
IDLE_TIME                        UNLIMITED
CONNECT_TIME                     UNLIMITED
PASSWORD_GRACE_TIME              7
```

```
LOGICAL_READS_PER_SESSION        UNLIMITED
PRIVATE_SGA                      UNLIMITED
LOGICAL_READS_PER_CALL           UNLIMITED
SESSIONS_PER_USER                UNLIMITED
CPU_PER_SESSION                  UNLIMITED
FAILED_LOGIN_ATTEMPTS            10
PASSWORD_LIFE_TIME               180
PASSWORD_VERIFY_FUNCTION         NULL
PASSWORD_REUSE_TIME              UNLIMITED
PASSWORD_REUSE_MAX               UNLIMITED
COMPOSITE_LIMIT                  UNLIMITED
CPU_PER_CALL                     UNLIMITED

16 rows selected.
SQL>
```

■**Caution** If you don't assign a profile to a user, Oracle assigns that user the default profile. Because the default profile uses a value of UNLIMITED for several parameters, you could end up with resource usage problems if users are assigned the default profile.

By default, the default password profile is enabled when you create a database.

Assigning a User Profile

You can assign a user a profile when you create the user. Here's an example:

```
SQL> CREATE USER salapati IDENTIFIED BY sammyy1
     TEMPORARY TABLESPACE TEMPTBS01
     DEFAULT TABLESPACE USERS
     GRANT QUOTA 500M ON USERS;
     PROFILE 'prod_user';

User created.
SQL>
```

You can also assign a profile to a user any time by using the ALTER USER statement, as shown here:

```
SQL> ALTER USER salapati
  2  PROFILE test;

User altered.
SQL>
```

You can use the ALTER USER statement to assign an initial profile or to replace the current profile with another.

Altering a User Profile

You can alter a profile by using the ALTER PROFILE statement, as follows:

```
SQL> ALTER PROFILE test
  2  LIMIT
  3  sessions_per_user 4
  4* failed_login_attempts 4;

Profile altered.
SQL>
```

The previous ALTER PROFILE statement limits the sessions a user can create as well as the maximum login attempts (before locking the user's account) to four.

Password Management Function

You can use the Oracle provided script named utlpwdmg.sql (from the $ORACLE_HOME/rdbms/admin directory) to implement various password management features such as setting the default password resource limits. This script lets you create a password verification function named verify_function_11g. The verify_function_11g function helps you implement password complexity in your database and lets you customize it for ensuring complex password checking.

The verify_function_11g function lets you implement password protection features such as the following:

- Ensuring that all passwords are at least eight characters long

- Ensuring that every password contains at least one number and one alphabetic character

- Ensuring that a password differs from the previous password by at least three characters

- Checking to make sure that passwords aren't simply a reverse of the usernames

- Checking to make sure the passwords aren't the same as or similar to the name of the server

- Checking to make sure that a password isn't in a set of well-known and common passwords such as "welcome1" or "database1"

Here's how you can execute the ALTER PROFILE statement in the utlpwdmg.sql script to create the verify_function_11g function first and, immediately after that, alter the DEFAULT profile that comes with the database and is automatically assigned to all users for whom you haven't assigned a profile.

```
ALTER PROFILE DEFAULT LIMITPASSWORD_LIFE_TIME 180
PASSWORD_GRACE_TIME 7
PASSWORD_REUSE_TIME UNLIMITED
PASSWORD_REUSE_MAX UNLIMITED
FAILED_LOGIN_ATTEMPTS 10
PASSWORD_LOCK_TIME 1
PASSWORD_VERIFY_FUNCTION verify_function_11G;
```

Once you create the verify_function_11g function as shown here, the database will automatically execute the function every time the DBA or a user creates or modifies a password. The function ensures that the passwords meet the requirements specified by the function. Of course, you may alter the function to create more stringent password checks in your database.

When Do Profile Changes Go into Effect?

Unless you change the setting of the RESOURCE_LIMIT initialization parameter from its default value of false, the profile changes you make will never be applied. The RESOURCE_LIMIT parameter determines whether the resource limits are enforced in database profiles. You need to set this parameter to true in the init.ora file and restart the database, or use the ALTER SYSTEM command, as shown here:

```
SQL> ALTER SYSTEM SET resource_limit=true;

System altered.
SQL>
```

■**Tip** Make sure you have the RESOURCE_LIMIT initialization parameter set to true so that the resource limits set by the profiles will be enforced. Otherwise, Oracle will ignore the limits set in the CREATE or ALTER PROFILE statement. The password-related profile attributes don't depend on the RESOURCE_LIMIT parameter—they are enabled automatically when you create the profile.

Dropping a User Profile

Dropping a profile is straightforward. Here's how you would drop the test profile:

```
SQL> DROP PROFILE test CASCADE;

Profile dropped.
SQL>
```

The test profile is assigned to several users in the database, and to drop the profile for all of them, you must use the CASCADE keyword. Note that the users who were assigned the test profile will now be automatically assigned the default profile.

What Happens When Profile Limits Are Reached?

When a user hits either a session-level or a call-level resource limit, Oracle rolls back the user's state-ment that is in progress and returns an error message. If it's a call-level limit (such as CPU_PER_CALL), the user's session remains intact, and other statements belonging to the current transaction remain valid. If a session-level limit is reached, the user can't go any further in that session.

How Do You Know What the Profile Limits Should Be?

You have several ways to gather the statistics to determine the optimal values for several critical resource limits, such as LOGICAL_READS_PER_SESSION. If you're too liberal with the value, some users may hog resources, and if you're too conservative, you'll be fielding many calls from irate users who are prevented from completing their jobs.

By using the IDLE_TIME profile attribute, you can limit the amount of time a user's session can remain idle. However, using the DBMS_RESOURCE_MANAGER package may be a better way to control a user's idle connection time, and I explain this package in the "Using the Database Resource Manager" section of this chapter. Using this package, you can set a maximum idle limit for a session as well as limit the length of time an idle session can block other sessions.

Try to get some information from test runs that you've made of certain jobs. If you don't have reliable historical data, use the AUDIT SESSION statement to acquire baseline data for several param-eters, such as connect time and logical reads. You can also use Oracle Enterprise Manager (OEM) to gather the data. In addition, you may have feedback (or complaints!) from the users themselves about programs that are failing due to limits on resource use or that need longer connect times to the database server.

Managing Resources

With large numbers of database users, resource management becomes an important issue. Server resources are ultimately limited, and you must have some means of apportioning the scarce resources among the users. Oracle provides a powerful tool, the Database Resource Manager, which allows you to control database resource usage in a sophisticated manner.

You can use either the user profiles I discussed in the previous section or the Database Resource Manager to control resource usage in your database. User profiles are effective in controlling the resource usage of individual users, but Oracle prefers that you use profiles mainly for password management. Oracle recommends using the Database Resource Manager to control resource usage.

The Database Resource Manager

Suppose you're managing a production database with the following problems:

- Batch jobs are taking up most of the available resources, which is hurting other, more critical jobs that need to run at the same time.

- Excessive loads at peak times are causing critical processes to run for an unacceptably long time.

- You schedule large jobs and really can't predict when they might be launched.

- Some users are using an excessive amount of CPU time, causing you to kill their sessions abruptly.

- Some users are using a very high degree of parallelism in their operations, which is hurting the performance of the system as a whole.

- You can't manage active sessions.

- You want to prioritize jobs according to some scheme, but you can't do so using operating system resources.

As you can see, all these problems stem from the inability of the DBA to allocate the limited resources efficiently among competing operations, which leads to lopsided resource allocation and very long response times for critical jobs. The Oracle Resource Manager is the answer—it allows you to create resource plans, which specify how much of your resources should go to the various consumer groups. You can group users based on their resource requirements, and you can have the Database Resource Manager allocate a preset amount of resources to these groups. You can distribute the available CPU resources by allocating a set percentage of CPU time to various users. Thus, you can easily prioritize your users and jobs. Your higher-priority online users will be served faster, while your lower-priority batch jobs may take longer.

Using the Database Resource Manager, it's possible for you to ensure that your critical user groups (formally referred to as *resource consumer groups*) are always guaranteed enough resources to perform their tasks.

The Database Resource Manager also enables you to limit the length of time a user session can stay idle and to automatically terminate long-running SQL statements and user sessions. Using the Database Resource Manager, you can set initial login priorities for various consumer groups. By using the concept of the active session pool, you can also specify the maximum number of concurrently active sessions for a consumer group—the Database Resource Manager will automatically queue all subsequent requests until the currently running sessions complete. The DBA can also automatically switch users from one resource group to another, based on preset resource usage criteria, and can limit the amount of undo space a resource group can use.

The following four elements are integral to the Database Resource Manager:

- *Resource consumer group*: A resource consumer group is used to group together similar users based on their resource needs.

- *Resource plan*: The resource plan lays out how resource consumer groups are allocated resources. Each resource plan contains a set of resource consumer groups that belong to this plan, together with instructions as to how resources are to be allocated among these groups. For example, a resource plan may dictate that the CPU resource be allocated among three resource consumer groups so that the first group gets 60 percent and the remaining two groups 20 percent of the total CPU time. A resource plan can also have subplans, which enable the allocation of resources in greater detail among resource consumer groups.

- *Resource allocation method*: The resource allocation method dictates the specific method you choose to use to allocate resources like the CPU. These are the available methods of allocating database resources:

    - *CPU method*: Oracle uses multiple levels of CPU allocation to prioritize and allocate CPU usage among the competing user sessions.

    - *Idle time*: You can direct that a user's session be terminated after it has been idle for a specified period of time. You can also specify that only idle sessions blocking other sessions be terminated.

    - *Execution time limit*: You can control resource usage by setting a limit on the maximum execution time of an operation.

    - *Undo pool*: By setting an undo pool directive, you can limit the total amount of undos that can be generated by a consumer resource group.

    - *Active session pool*: You can set a maximum allowable number of active sessions within any consumer resource group. All sessions that are beyond the maximum limit are queued for execution after the freeing up of current active sessions.

    - *Automatic consumer group switching*: Using this method, you can specify that a user session be automatically switched to a different group after it runs more than a specified number of seconds. The group the session should switch to is called the switch group, and the time limit is the switch time. The session can revert to its original consumer group after the end of the top call, which is defined as an entire PL/SQL block or a separate SQL statement.

    - *Canceling SQL and terminating sessions*: By using `CANCEL_SQL` or `KILL_SESSION` as the switch group, you can direct a long-running SQL statement or even an entire session to be canceled or terminated.

    - *Parallel degree limit*: You can use this method to specify the limit of the degree of parallelism for an operation.

- *Resource plan directive*: The resource plan directive links a resource plan to a specific resource consumer group.

Using the Database Resource Manager

You manage the Database Resource Manager by executing procedures in the Oracle-supplied DBMS_RESOURCE_MANAGER package. It enables you to create a resource plan for the various consumer groups and to assign the plans to the consumer groups. As a DBA, you'll already have privileges to execute any procedure in the DBMS_RESOURCE_MANAGER package, but for any other users that need to use the Database Resource Manager, you'll need to grant a special system privilege called ADMINISTER_RESOURCE_MANAGER so they can use the Database Resource Manager, as shown here:

```
SQL> EXEC DBMS_RESOURCE_MANAGER_PRIVS.GRANT_SYSTEM_PRIVILEGE -
    (GRANTEE_NAME => 'scott', PRIVILEGE_NAME => 'ADMINISTER_RESOURCE_MANAGER');
```

The DBMS_RESOURCE_MANAGER package has several procedures, but we'll focus on a few important ones that will let you use the package to control resource allocation among database users.

■Note The following discussion of the Database Resource Manager is meant to familiarize you with the various steps involved in creating resource plans and enforcing them. The Resource Plan Wizard in the OEM toolset is really the best way to quickly create resource plans in your database once you get the hang of the various steps involved in creating and maintaining the plans.

Here are the steps you need to follow to start using the Database Resource Manager:

1. Create a pending area. This is the work area where you create and validate resource consumer groups, resource plans, and plan directives.

2. Create a resource consumer group. This is a grouping of users who will receive the same amount of resources.

3. Create a resource plan. This is a collection of directives that specify how Oracle should allocate resources to resource consumer groups.

4. Create a plan directive. This associates resource consumer groups with resource plans and allocates resources among resource consumer groups.

5. Validate the pending area. This process validates the resource consumer group, the resource plan, and the plan directive.

6. Submit the pending area. This creates the resource consumer group, the resource plan, and the plan directives, and makes them active.

Once this is all done, you can assign users to resource consumer groups, and they'll get the resources that have been assigned to that group.

Creating a Pending Area

Before you can use the Database Resource Manager to allocate resources, modify an old plan, or create a new plan, you need to create what is called a *pending area* to validate changes before their implementation. The pending area serves as a work area for your changes. All the resource plans you'll create will be stored in the data dictionary, and the pending area is the staging area where you work with resource plans before they are implemented.

Here's how you create the pending area:

```
SQL> EXECUTE dbms_resource_manager.create_pending_area;
PL/SQL procedure successfully completed.
SQL>
```

You can also clear the pending area by using the following procedure if you think you've made errors while creating the various components of the Database Resource Manager:

```
SQL> EXECUTE dbms_resource_manager.clear_pending_area;
PL/SQL procedure successfully completed.
SQL>
```

Creating Resource Consumer Groups

Once the pending area is active, you can create the resource consumer groups to which you'll allocate your users. You can assign users initially to one group and switch them to another group later, if necessary. You use three parameters to create a resource consumer group: consumer group name (CONSUMER_GROUP), a comment (COMMENT), and the method for distributing CPU resources among the resource consumer group's active sessions (CPU_MTH). There are two choices you can use for the CPU_MTH parameter—the RUN_TO_COMPLETION method schedules sessions that will take the most time ahead of other, less time-intensive sessions, and the default ROUND_ROBIN method, which uses a round-robin scheduling system.

The example in Listing 12-2 shows how to create three consumer groups in the database: local, regional, and national. Note that I'm not using the CPU_MTH parameter, since I plan to use the default ROUND_ROBIN method.

Listing 12-2. *Creating the Resource Consumer Groups*

```
SQL> EXECUTE dbms_resource_manager.create_consumer_group -
  > (consumer_group => 'local', comment => 'local councils');
PL/SQL procedure successfully completed.
SQL> EXECUTE dbms_resource_manager.create_consumer_group -
  > (consumer_group => 'regional', comment => 'regional councils');
PL/SQL procedure successfully completed.
SQL>
SQL> EXECUTE dbms_resource_manager.create_consumer_group -
  > (consumer_group => 'national', comment => 'national office');
PL/SQL procedure successfully completed.
SQL>
```

Determining What Groups Exist in Your Database

You can query the DBA_RSRC_CONSUMER_GROUPS view for information about what groups currently exist in your database (before validating and submitting the pending area), as shown in Listing 12-3.

Listing 12-3. *Querying the DBA_RSRC_CONSUMER_GROUPS View*

```
SQL> SELECT consumer_group, status
  2* FROM dba_rsrc_consumer_groups;

CONSUMER_GROUP                  STATUS
------------------------------- -------
AUTO_TASK_CONSUMER_GROUP        PENDING
DEFAULT_CONSUMER_GROUP          PENDING
SYS_GROUP                       PENDING
OTHER_GROUPS                    PENDING
LOW_GROUP                        ACTIVE
AUTO_TASK_CONSUMER_GROUP         ACTIVE
DEFAULT_CONSUMER_GROUP           ACTIVE
SYS_GROUP                        ACTIVE
LOW_GROUP                       PENDING
OTHER_GROUPS                     ACTIVE
LOCAL                           PENDING
REGIONAL                        PENDING
NATIONAL                        PENDING
13 rows selected.
SQL>
```

Three new groups were created in the previous section—national, regional, and local—but Listing 12-3 shows eight distinct consumer groups. The same query would have given you the following output before you created the three new groups in the pending area:

```
SQL> SELECT consumer_group,status
  2  FROM dba_rsrc_consumer_groups;

CONSUMER_GROUP                 STATUS
-------------------------- ------
ORA$AUTOTASK_URGENT_GROUP
BATCH_GROUP
ORA$DIAGNOSTICS
ORA$AUTOTASK_HEALTH_GROUP
ORA$AUTOTASK_SQL_GROUP
ORA$AUTOTASK_SPACE_GROUP
ORA$AUTOTASK_STATS_GROUP
ORA$AUTOTASK_MEDIUM_GROUP
INTERACTIVE_GROUP
OTHER_GROUPS
DEFAULT_CONSUMER_GROUP
SYS_GROUP
LOW_GROUP
AUTO_TASK_CONSUMER_GROUP

14 rows selected.
SQL>
```

The five resource consumer groups that you see in the preceding output are default groups that exist in every Oracle database:

- *OTHER_GROUPS*: This isn't really a group, because you can't assign users to it. When a resource plan is active, OTHER_GROUPS is the catchall term for all sessions that don't belong to this active resource plan.

- *DEFAULT_CONSUMER_GROUP*: If you don't assign users to any group, they will, by default, become members of the default group.

- *SYS_GROUP and LOW_GROUP*: These are part of the default plan, named system_plan, that exists in every database.

- *BATCH_GROUP*: This is a default group intended for use with batch operations.

- *AUTO_TASK_CONSUMER_GROUP*: This is a default resource consumer group used for automatically executed tasks, such as the gathering of statistics. The priority for jobs such as statistics collection will remain below jobs in the default consumer group. Oracle supplies seven default resource plans for each database, as shown by the output of the following query:

```
SQL> SELECT plan, comments FROM dba_rsrc_plans;

      PLAN                COMMENTS
-------------------    -------------------------------------------------------
MIXED_WORKLOAD_PLAN    Example plan for a mixed workload that prioritizes
                       interactive operations over batch operations.
ORA$AUTOTASK_SUB_PLAN  Default sub-plan for automated maintenance tasks.  A
                       directive to this sub-plan should be included in
                       every top-level plan to manage the resources consumed
                       by the automated maintenance tasks.
```

ORA$AUTOTASK_HIGH_SUB_PLAN
                              Default sub-plan for high-priority, automated
                              maintenance tasks. This sub-plan is referenced by
                              ORA$AUTOTASK_SUB_PLAN and should not be referenced
                              directly.

INTERNAL_PLAN   Internally-used plan for disabling the resource
                              manager.

DEFAULT_PLAN   Default, basic, pre-defined plan that
                              prioritizes SYS_GROUP operations and
                              allocates minimal resources for automated
                              maintenance and diagnostics operations.

INTERNAL_QUIESCE   Plan for quiescing the database. This plan
                              cannot be activated directly. To activate, use
                              the quiesce command.

DEFAULT_MAINTENANCE_PLAN   Default plan for maintenance windows that
                              prioritizes SYS_GROUP operations and allocates
                              the remaining 5% to diagnostic operations and 25%
                              to automated maintenance operations.

```
7 rows selected.
SQL>
```

If you query the DBA_RSRC_CONSUMER_GROUPS view after you validate the pending area,
you'll see the five default groups and the three groups you just created. In Listing 12-4, you can see
that the STATUS shows ACTIVE instead of PENDING for the three new resource consumer groups that I
created.

Listing 12-4. *Listing the Resource Consumer Groups*

```
SQL> SELECT consumer_group, status
     FROM dba_rsrc_consumer_groups;

CONSUMER_GROUP                  STATUS
------------------------------  --------
AUTO_TASK_CONSUMER_GROUP        ACTIVE
DEFAULT_CONSUMER_GROUP          ACTIVE
SYS_GROUP                       ACTIVE
OTHER_GROUPS                    ACTIVE
LOW_GROUP                       ACTIVE
LOCAL                           ACTIVE
REGIONAL                        ACTIVE
NATIONAL                        ACTIVE
8 rows selected.
SQL>
```

Creating Resource Plans

A resource plan contains directives that control the allocation of resources among various resource
consumer groups. Resource plans enable you to set limits on resource use by specifying limits on
four variables: CPU, number of active sessions, degree of parallelism, and the order in which queued
sessions will execute. Let's look at the five parameters that control these resources in more detail:

- CPU_MTH: You use this resource allocation method to specify how you wish to allocate the CPU resource among the resource consumer groups. The default method is called EMPHASIS, and it uses percentages to allocate CPU among the various groups. The alternative method, RATIO, uses ratios instead.

- ACTIVE_SESS_POOL_MTH: This parameter determines the limit on the number of active sessions in a resource consumer group. The only method available is the ACTIVE_SESS_POOL_ABSOLUTE method, which is the default.

- PARALLEL_DEGREE_LIMIT_MTH: This is the parameter that determines the degree of parallelism used by a specific operation. The only option is PARALLEL_DEGREE_LIMIT_ABSOLUTE (which is the default).

- SUB_PLAN: If this is TRUE, you can't use the plan as the top plan (you can use it as a subplan only). The default value is FALSE.

- QUEUEING_MTH: This parameter determines the order in which queued sessions will execute. Only the default FIFO_TIMEOUT option is currently available.

You can also create subplans (plans within plans), which let you subdivide resources among different users.

Create your resource plan by invoking the DBMS_RESOURCE_MANAGER package again:

```
SQL> DBMS_RESOURCE_MANAGER.CREATE_PLAN
     (PLAN => 'membership_plan',
     CPU_MTH -> 'RATIO',
     COMMENT => 'New Membership Recruitment');
PL/SQL procedure successfully completed.
SQL>
```

Creating Plan Directives

You now have a resource plan, but the plan still doesn't have any resource limits assigned to it. You need to create a *resource plan directive* to assign resources to the various resource consumer groups in the database. You can allocate resources according to the following criteria:

- *CPU*: Using the CPU method, you can allocate resources among consumer groups or subplans. You can use multiple levels of CPU resource allocation to prioritize CPU usage. For example, you could specify that level 2 gets CPU resources only if any CPU resources are left after level 1 is taken care of.

- *Sessions*: You can control the maximum number of active sessions open at any time by using the ACTIVE_SESSION_POOL parameter. You can also allow for the termination of long-running SQL queries and user sessions.

- *Degree of parallelism*: You can set a limit on the degree of parallelism during any operation.

- *Automatic consumer group switching*: You can specify that, under some conditions, the database will automatically switch sessions to another consumer group.

- *Undo usage*: You can set limits on the number of undo operations a resource consumer group can generate. The database automatically terminates SQL statements that cause the undo generated by a consumer group to exceed its undo limit. This will prevent new members of the consumer group from issuing DML statements.

- *Idle time limit*: The idle-time-limit resource directive, set by using the MAX_IDLE_TIME parameter, helps you control resource use by various sessions in a busy database. You can use it to set the maximum idle time for a single session. In addition, you can also limit the amount of time a user session can block another session by setting the MAX_IDLE_BLOCKER_TIME parameter.

- *Session switching*: You can use the SWITCH_GROUP parameter to specify the consumer group to which a session can be switched upon meeting specific switching criteria. The two switch group names are CANCEL_SQL and KILL_SESSION. Assigning a session to the former will result in canceling the current call, and assigning a session to the latter will terminate the session. The SWITCH_GROUP parameter can also specify values for the following switching-related parameters:

  - SWITCH_IO_MEGABYTES: This parameter specifies the number of megabytes of I/O a session can transfer before the database takes an action.

  - SWITCH_IO_REQS: This parameter specifies the number of I/O requests a session can execute before the database takes an action.

  - SWITCH_FOR_CALL: If you set this parameter to TRUE, the database returns a session that was switched to its original group after the top call completes.

Here's an example that shows how you can limit a session in a resource plan to a maximum idle time of 600 seconds and a maximum idle time of only 300 seconds if it happens to be blocking another session:

```
SQL> EXECUTE dbms_resource_manager.create_plan_directive -
    (plan                  => 'prod_plan',
    group_or_subplan       => 'dss_group',
    comment                => 'Limit idle time',
    max_idle_time          => 900,
    max_idle_blocker_time  => 300);
```

In the preceding example, when a session exceeds 900 seconds (or 300 seconds if it's blocking another session), the PMON background process will automatically kill the offending session.

Listing 12-5 shows how to create a plan directive using the CPU method. The plan directive assigns 70 percent of the available CPU time at the first level to the local group, and the rest, 30 percent, to the regional group. It allocates 100 percent of the CPU at the second level to the national group. Note that this example uses the default *emphasis* method of CPU allocation, which allocates CPU in terms of percentages. There also is an alternative allocation method called *ratio*, which allocates CPU resources by using ratios.

Listing 12-5. *Creating Plan Directives Using the CPU Method*

```
SQL> EXECUTE dbms_resource_manager.create_plan -
    directive (plan  => 'membership_plan', -
    GROUP_OR_SUBPLAN => 'local', COMMENT => 'LOCAL GROUP',-
    CPU_P1 => 70);
PL/SQL procedure successfully completed.
SQL> EXECUTE dbms_resource_manager.create_plan -
    directive (plan  => 'membership_plan', -
    GROUP_OR_SUBPLAN => 'REGIONAL',COMMENT=> 'regional group',-
    CPU_P1 => 30);
PL/SQL procedure successfully completed.
SQL> EXECUTE dbms_resource_manager.create_plan
    directive (plan  => 'membership_plan', -
    GROUP_OR_SUBPLAN => 'national',comment => 'national group',-
    CPU_P2 => 100);
PL/SQL procedure successfully completed.
SQL>
```

■**Tip** If you don't include a resource directive for OTHER_GROUPS, and the plan directive is for a primary or top plan, Oracle won't let you use your directives for the other groups in OTHER_GROUPS.

Validating the Pending Area

After you've created the resource consumer groups, the resource plans, and the plan directives, you are ready to validate the changes you made. Here's how you do it:

```
SQL> EXEC DBMS_RESOURCE_MANAGER.VALIDATE_PENDING_AREA();
PL/SQL procedure successfully completed.
```

Submitting the Pending Area

By submitting the pending area, you actually create all the necessary entities, such as the resource consumer group, the resource plan, and the plan directives, and make them active. You submit the pending area as follows:

```
SQL> EXEC DBMS_RESOURCE_MANAGER.SUBMIT_PENDING_AREA();
PL/SQL procedure successfully completed.
```

You can use the query in Listing 12-6 to determine resource plan directives that are currently in force for various groups.

Listing 12-6. *Determining the Status of the Resource Plans*

```
SQL> SELECT plan,group_or_subplan,cpu_p1,cpu_p2,cpu_p3, status
  2* FROM dba_rsrc_plan_directives;
```

PLAN	GROUP	CPU_P1	CPU_P2	CPU_P3	STATUS
SYSTEM_PLAN	SYS_GROUP	100	0	0	ACTIVE
SYSTEM_PLAN	OTHER_GROUPS	0	100	0	ACTIVE
SYSTEM_PLAN	LOW_GROUP	0	0	100	ACTIVE
INTERNAL_QUIESCE	SYS_GROUP	0	0	0	ACTIVE
INTERNAL_QUIESCE	OTHER_GROUPS	0	0	0	ACTIVE
INTERNAL_PLAN	OTHER_GROUPS	0	0	0	ACTIVE
MEMBERSHIP_PLAN	REGIONAL	30	0	0	ACTIVE
MEMBERSHIP_PLAN	NATIONAL	0	100	0	ACTIVE
MEMBERSHIP_PLAN	OTHER_GROUPS	0	0	100	ACTIVE
MEMBERSHIP_PLAN	LOCAL	70	0	0	ACTIVE

```
10 rows selected.
SQL>
```

Assigning Users to Consumer Groups

After you create your resource consumer groups and validate your pending area, you can assign some of your users to the consumer groups you've created. Let's say you want to assign three users named local_user, regional_user, and national_user to the three resource groups as follows: assign local_user to the *local* consumer group, regional_user to the *regional* consumer group, and national_user to the *national* consumer group.

Remember that the three users are already members of a default group, the default_consumer_ group. Therefore, you need to first grant the three users privileges to switch their groups before you

can actually switch them to your new groups. Listing 12-7 shows how you can use the DBMS_
RESOURCE_MANAGER package to assign and switch users' consumer groups.

■**Tip** If you grant the PUBLIC user the privilege to switch groups, you won't have to grant the privilege to all the
users in the group individually. If you have a large number of users in each group, this is a better approach.

Listing 12-7. *Assigning Users to Consumer Groups*

```
SQL> EXECUTE dbms_resource_manager_privs.grant_switch_
    consumer_group ('local_user','local', true);
PL/SQL procedure successfully completed.
SQL> EXECUTE dbms_resource_manager.set_
    initial_consumer_group ('local_user','local');
PL/SQL procedure successfully completed.
SQL> EXECUTE dbms_resource_manager_privs.grant_
    switch_consumer_group('regional_user','regional', true);
PL/SQL procedure successfully completed.
SQL> EXECUTE dbms_resource_manager.set_initial_
    consumer_group ('regional_user','regional');
PL/SQL procedure successfully completed.
SQL> EXECUTE dbms_resource_manager_privs.grant_
    switch_consumer_group('national_user','national',true);
PL/SQL procedure successfully completed.
SQL> EXECUTE dbms_resource_manager.set_
    initial_consumer_group ('national_user','national');
PL/SQL procedure successfully completed.
SQL>
```

You can verify that the three users have been assigned to the appropriate consumer groups by
using the query in Listing 12-8.

Listing 12-8. *Verifying Resource Consumer Group Membership of Users*

```
SQL> SELECT username, initial_rsrc_consumer_group
  2  FROM dba_users;

USERNAME                 INITIAL_RSRC_CONSUMER_GROUP
----------------         ---------------------------
SYS                      SYS_GROUP
SYSTEM                   SYS_GROUP
SALAPATI                 DEFAULT_CONSUMER_GROUP
NATIONAL_USER            NATIONAL
REGIONAL_USER            REGIONAL
LOCAL_USER               LOCAL
6 rows selected.
SQL>
```

Note that super users SYS and SYSTEM are default members of the SYS_GROUP. User salapati
is a member of the DEFAULT_CONSUMER_GROUP, to which all users in the database are automatically
assigned when they are first created. Your three new users, local_user, regional_user, and national_
user, are correctly assigned to their new consumer groups, LOCAL, REGIONAL, and NATIONAL,
respectively.

Automatic Assignment of a Resource Consumer Group to a Session

You can have the Database Resource Manager automatically assign a user session to a particular consumer group, based on certain session attributes. You map the session attributes to various consumer groups, and when the user logs in, the relevant consumer group is automatically assigned to the user based on the user's attributes. If there is a conflict, it can be resolved by a prioritizing of the mapping between session attributes and resource consumer groups.

You use two DBMS_RESOURCE_MANAGER packages, SET_CONSUMER_GROUP_MAPPING and SET_CONSUMER_MAPPING_PRI, to map session attributes and consumer resource groups and set the priorities in the mappings. There are two distinct types of session attributes. The first set encompasses login attributes, which help the Database Resource Manager determine the user's initial consumer group. The other set of session attributes consists of runtime attributes.

The following are some of the session attributes that are considered when mapping a user session to a particular consumer resource group:

```
ORACLE_USER

SERVICE_NAME

CLIENT_OS_USER

CLIENT_PROGRAM

CLIENT_MACHINE

MODULE_NAME
```

You map each of these session attributes to a particular resource consumer group using the SET_CONSUMER_GROUP_MAPPING procedure. In the following example, the hr user is mapped to the HUMAN_RESOURCES_GROUP at login time:

```
SQL> EXECUTE DBMS_RESOURCE_MANAGER.SET_CONSUMER_GROUP_MAPPING
     (DBMS_RESOURCE_MANAGER.ORACLE_USER, 'HR', 'HUMAN_RESOURCES_GROUP');
```

After login time, as the user's session attributes change, so does the user's resource consumer group, based on the mapping between session attributes and resource groups.

At times, there can be a conflict between two mappings, and to resolve these conflicts, you use the SET_CONSUMER_MAPPING_PRI procedure to set priorities for the various session attributes, ranging from 1 to 10, with 1 being the least important and 10 being the most important priority value. Here's an example:

```
SQL> EXECUTE DBMS_RESOURCE_MANAGER. SET_CONSUMER_GROUP_MAPPING_PRI (
     EXPLICIT => 1, CLIENT_MACHINE => 2, MODULE_NAME => 3, ORACLE_USER => 4,
     SERVICE_NAME => 5, CLIENT_OS_USER => 6, CLIENT_PROGRAM => 7,
     MODULE_NAME_ACTION => 8, SERVICE_MODULE=>9, SERVICE_MODULE_ACTION=>10);
```

When a session attribute changes, the user is automatically switched to the relevant resource consumer group.

Enforcing Per-Session CPU and I/O Limits

The database can also automatically switch sessions based on the session's CPU and I/O usage, thus letting you enforce CPU and I/O usage per session. If a user is using excessive CPU, say, instead of killing that user's session, you can have the database automatically switch the user to another resource group that has a lower CPU allocation. You can specify that the database take one of the following actions when a session exceeds its preset resource limits:

- Switch the session to a resource group with lower resource allocation.
- Terminate the session.
- Abort the SQL statement that issued the database call.

Specify the values for the session within parameters such as SWITCH_IO_MEGABYTES, SWITCH_GROUP, and SWITCH_TIME when you create a plan. I present a couple of examples to show how you can set up automatic session switching to alternate resource consumer groups based on a session's resource usage.

The following example shows how to specify session switching to a low-priority group if a session exceeds a specified limit on CPU usage:

```
SQL> BEGIN
        dbms_resource_manager.create_plan_directive (
        plan                    => 'peaktime',
        group_or_subplan        => 'oltp',
        mgmt_p1                 =>   75,
        switch_group            => 'low_Group',
        switch_time             => 10
        switch_for_call         => true);
    END;
```

When a session exceeds a preset CPU usage limit, the session is automatically switched to the resource consumer group LOW_GROUP, which is a lower- priority resource consumer group. Since I specified the SWITCH_FOR_CALL parameter, the database switches the session back to its original resource consumer group after the high-resource call is completed.

The following example shows how to specify that the database terminate a session if it exceeds a preset CPU usage limit:

```
SQL> BEGIN
        dbms_resource_manager.create_plan_directive (
        plan                => 'peaktime',
        group_or_subplan   =>  'oltp',
        mgmt_p1            =>    75,
        switch_group       => 'kill_session',
        switch_time        =>  60);

    END;
```

The previous code specifies that the database must kill a session (SWITCH_GROUP=> 'kill_session') when the session exceeds 60 seconds of CPU usage time.

Enabling the Database Resource Manager

Just because you created a new plan and plan directives and submitted your pending area doesn't mean that Oracle will automatically enforce the resource plans. It's your job to explicitly activate the Database Resource Manager, either by specifying the RESOURCE_MANAGER_PLAN initialization parameter in the init.ora file or by using the ALTER SYSTEM command as follows:

```
SQL> ALTER SYSTEM SET resource_manager_plan=MEMBERSHIP_PLAN;
System altered.
SQL> SELECT * FROM v$rsrc_plan;
NAME
--------------------------------
MEMBERSHIP_PLAN
SQL>
```

If you decide to deactivate the Database Resource Manager, you can use the following command:

```
SQL> ALTER SYSTEM SET resource_manager_plan='';
System altered.
SQL> SELECT * FROM v$rsrc_plan;
no rows selected
SQL>
```

At any given time, you can query V$RSRC_CONSUMER_GROUP to see what the resource usage among the consumer groups looks like:

```
SQL> SELECT name,active_sessions,cpu_wait_time, consumed_cpu_time,
     current_undo_consumption
     FROM v$rsrc_consumer_group;
```

NAME	ACTIVE SESSIONS	CPU_ WAIT	CONSUMED_ CPU_TIME	CURRENT UNDO_CONS
REGIONAL	0	0	0	0
NATIONAL	0	0	0	0
OTHER_GROUPS	1	0	74	0
LOCAL	0	0	18017	0

```
SQL>
```

Data Dictionary Views

The following data dictionary views help you manage the Database Resource Manager:

- The V$SESSION view shows which resource consumer groups the sessions are currently assigned to.

- The DBA_RSRC_CONSUMER_GROUP_PRIVS view shows all resource consumer groups granted to users or roles.

- The DBA_RSRC_PLANS view shows all resource plans in the database.

- The V$RSRC_PLAN view shows all currently active resource plans.

Using OEM to Administer the Database Resource Manager

Now that you've sweated through all the error-prone, time-consuming work of creating and enabling resource plans, let me remind you that using the Oracle Enterprise Manager to manage the Database Resource Manager is a far easier alternative. Here's a brief introduction to using OEM to administer the Database Resource Manager.

Using the Resource Monitors Page

You can use the Resource Monitors page to display the current state of the active resource plan. You can view statistics for the currently active plan, and you can select a plan from the list and activate it. The Consumer Group Statistics table lists a series of statistics for the consumer groups that are part of the current resource plan.

■**Tip** When you activate a plan using the Resource Monitors page, you must exit the page and then choose Resource Monitors to update the page.

Creating, Editing, and Deleting Resource Plans

You can manage the list of resource plans through the Resource Plans property sheet. As you know by now, you can use resource plans to allocate resources among consumer groups. The Resource Plans property sheet lets you create, delete, and modify the settings of a resource plan.

To manage a resource plan, go to Database Control Home Page ➤Administration ➤ Consumer Groups. From the Object_Type drop-down window, select Resource Plans. The Resource Plans page appears, with a listing of all the current resource plans. You can either create a new resource plan or select a resource plan from the list.

Managing Resource Consumer Groups

You can manage resource groups through the Resource Consumer Groups property sheet. You can use the property sheet to create, delete, and modify the settings of a resource consumer group.

To manage a resource consumer group, go to Database Control Home Page ➤ Administration ➤ Consumer Groups. The Resource Consumer Groups page appears, showing all resource consumer groups for the current database. You can create, edit, and delete resource consumer groups from here.

Controlling Database Access

Once you create users in the database, you need to control their access to the various data objects. To take a simple example, a clerk in the human resources department of an organization may be able to see the salary data of employees, but he or she should not have the authority to change salaries. Oracle uses several means to control data access, and the most elementary way to do so is by assigning database *privileges* and *roles* to database users.

Privileges in an Oracle Database

A *privilege* is the right to execute a particular type of SQL statement or to access a database object owned by another user. In an Oracle database, you must explicitly grant a user privileges to perform any activity, including connecting to a database or selecting, modifying, and updating data in a table other than their own.

There are two basic types of Oracle privileges: *system privileges* and *object privileges*. You use the GRANT statement to grant specific system privileges as well as object privileges to users. The following sections cover these two types of Oracle privileges in detail.

■**Note** You can manage your users through Database Control by going to Database Control Home Page ➤ Administration ➤ Users (under the Users and Privileges Section).

System Privileges

You grant a system privilege to a user so the user can perform either a particular action within the database or an action on any schema object of a particular type. A good example of the first type of system privilege is the privilege that lets you connect to a database, called the CONNECT privilege. Other such system privileges include the CREATE TABLESPACE, CREATE USER, DROP USER, and ALTER USER privileges. The second class of system privileges grants users the right to perform operations that affect objects in any schema. Examples of this type of system privilege include ANALYZE ANY TABLE, GRANT ANY PRIVILEGE, INSERT ANY TABLE, GRANT ANY PRIVILEGE, INSERT ANY

TABLE, DELETE ANY TABLE, and so on. As you can see, system privileges are very powerful, and granting them to the wrong user could have a devastating impact on your database.

Here are some common system privileges in an Oracle database:

- ADVISOR
- ALTER DATABASE
- ALTER SYSTEM
- AUDIT SYSTEM
- CREATE DATABASE LINK
- CREATE TABLE
- CREATE ANY INDEX
- CREATE SESSION
- CREATE TABLESPACE
- CREATE USER
- DROP USER
- INSERT ANY TABLE

Granting System Privileges

You use the GRANT statement to grant system privileges to users. When you grant a system privilege to a user, the user can immediately use that privilege. Thus, privileges work in a dynamic fashion.

■Tip You can use either Oracle Enterprise Manager Database Control or SQL statements to GRANT and REVOKE system privileges.

For example, to grant the CREATE SESSION system privilege to the sample user, hr, allowing hr to log onto an Oracle database, issue the following statement:

```
SQL> GRANT CREATE SESSION TO hr;
Grant succeeded.
SQL>
```

The CREATE SESSION privilege enables a user to log onto an Oracle database.

■Tip You can grant all system privileges to a user (except the SELECT ANY DICTIONARY privilege), by specifying ALL PRIVILEGES in the GRANT statement, as shown here:

```
SQL> GRANT ALL PRIVILEGES TO salapati;
Grant succeeded.
SQL>
```

ALL PRIVILEGES itself isn't a system privilege—it's a convenient way to grant all privileges in one step. You can revoke all system privileges similarly, by using the REVOKE ALL PRIVILEGES statement.

As a DBA, you can also grant a system privilege to PUBLIC, in which case all users in the database can perform the actions authorized by the privilege. Here's an example:

```
SQL> GRANT CREATE SESSION TO public;
Grant succeeded.
SQL>
```

Once you grant the CREATE SESSION privilege to PUBLIC, all users can log into the database without being granted the CREATE SESSION privilege on an individual basis. As you can see, granting a privilege to PUBLIC is fraught with danger, since all users will have that privilege.

You can grant a system privilege to a user, provided one of the following is true:

- You have been granted the system privilege with the WITH ADMIN OPTION clause.

- You have been granted the GRANT ANY PRIVILEGE system privilege.

Here's an example of the use of the WITH ADMIN OPTION clause when granting a system privilege:

```
SQL> GRANT CREATE SESSION TO salapati WITH ADMIN OPTION;
Grant succeeded.
SQL>
```

The GRANT ANY OBJECT privilege is a special system privilege that lets the grantee grant (and revoke) object privileges for objects in any schema. The interesting thing is that when the grantee of this privilege grants any privileges on any object, it appears as if the schema owner granted the privilege (the DBA_TAB_PRIVS view shows this). However, if you're auditing the use of the GRANT statement, you'll see the real user who issued this statement. All users with the SYSDBA privilege automatically have the GRANT ANY OBJECT privilege.

Revoking System Privileges

You use the REVOKE statement to revoke system privileges. The revoking of the privileges takes place immediately. Here's an example:

```
SQL> REVOKE DELETE ANY TABLE FROM pasowner;
Revoke  succeeded.
SQL>
```

You can use the REVOKE statement to revoke only those privileges that were previously granted to the user with a GRANT statement.

Only users with the SYSDBA privilege or those who have been explicitly granted object privileges can access objects in the SYS schema. You can also enable other users' access to SYS-owned objects by granting one of the following three *roles* to those users. (Roles are named sets of privileges, and I discuss them in the "Roles" section of this chapter.)

- SELECT_CATALOG_ROLE: This role grants SELECT privileges on the data dictionary views.

- EXECUTE_CATALOG_ROLE: This role grants EXECUTE privileges on the data dictionary packages.

- DELETE_CATALOG_ROLE: This role enables users to delete records from the audit table, called SYS.AUD$. (This table is discussed in the "Auditing Database Usage" section later in this chapter.)

You can also use the SELECT ANY DICTIONARY system privilege to grant a user (usually developers) the privilege to select data from any object in the SYS schema.

The SYSDBA and SYSOPER SYSASM System Privileges

There are two powerful administrative system privileges, known as SYSDBA and SYSOPER. Because of the powerful nature of these privileges, some restrictions apply to their administration. You can't use WITH ADMIN OPTION when granting these roles; only a user connected as SYSDBA can grant (or revoke) these privileges to other users; and you can't grant this system privilege to a role.

The SYSDBA system privilege includes the RESTRICTED SESSION privilege and has all system privileges with WITH ADMIN OPTION, including the SYSOPER system privilege. The SYSDBA privilege lets you do the following:

- Perform STARTUP and SHUTDOWN operations.
- Use the ALTER DATABASE command to open, mount, back up, or change a character set.
- Use the CREATE DATABASE command.
- Perform ARCHIVELOG and RECOVERY operations.
- Create an SPFILE.

The SYSOPER privilege similarly includes the RESTRICTED SESSION privilege, and it lets you do the following:

- Perform STARTUP and SHUTDOWN operations.
- Use the ALTER DATABASE command to open, mount, or back up.
- Perform ARCHIVELOG and RECOVERY operations.
- Create an SPFILE.

■**Tip** Several normal database operations require users to query some data dictionary tables routinely. Therefore, it's a good idea to grant your developers on the development databases a set of basic system privileges by granting these users the SELECT_CATALOG_ROLE. This role gives the developers select privileges on all data dictionary views.

In addition to the SYSDBA and the SYSOPER privileges, there's also a SYSASM privilege, which you can use to administer Automatic Storage Management (ASM) instances. Although you can work with ASM instances using your SYSDBA privileges, Oracle prefers you to separate database administration and ASM administration. In Chapter 17, I discuss the SYSASM privilege in more detail in the section "Automatic Storage Management."

Object Privileges

Object privileges are privileges on the various types of database objects. An object privilege allows a user to perform actions on a specific table, view, materialized view, sequence, procedure, function, or package. Thus, all users of the database will need object privileges, even if they may not need any system privileges. There are some common object privileges that apply to all database objects and some that apply to only certain objects.

You can use the following SQL statements when you grant object privileges:

- ALTER
- SELECT
- DELETE
- EXECUTE

- INSERT
- REFERENCES
- INDEX

The following list identifies the different types of object privileges in an Oracle database, the main object privileges of each type, and an example for each object type:

- *Table privileges*: SELECT, ALTER, DELETE, INSERT, and UPDATE

  GRANT DELETE ON bonuses TO hr

■**Tip** You can grant INSERT and UPDATE privileges at a column level. Here is an example that shows how you grant the INSERT privilege on the column salary in the persons table:

SQL> GRANT INSERT (salary) ON persons to salapati;

In order to grant privileges at the row level, you can use Oracle's virtual private database (which I discuss in the "Fine-Grained Data Access" section of this chapter) or the Oracle Label Security feature.

- *View privileges*: SELECT, DELETE, INSERT, and UPDATE

  GRANT SELECT, UPDATE
  ON emp_view TO PUBLIC;

- *Sequence privileges*: ALTER and SELECT

  GRANT SELECT
  ON oe.customers_seq TO hr;

- *Procedure, function, and package privileges*: EXECUTE and DEBUG

  GRANT EXECUTE ON employee_pkg TO hr;

- *Materialized view privileges*: SELECT and QUERY REWRITE

  GRANT QUERY REWRITE TO hr

- *Directory privileges*: READ and WRITE

  GRANT READ ON DIRECTORY bfile_dir TO hr

If you grant a user an object privilege with an additional GRANT OPTION clause, the user can in turn grant that privilege to other users in the database. Here's an example:

SQL> GRANT DELETE ON bonuses TO hr WITH GRANT OPTION;

Once you grant the user hr the DELETE privilege on the bonuses table in the preceding manner, hr can turn around and grant that privilege to any other users.

The owner of any object has all rights on the object and can grant privileges on that object to any other user in the database. The schema owner has the right to grant these privileges—not the DBA or the SYSTEM or SYS users. You can grant an *object privilege* to a user, provided one of the following is true:

- You are the owner of the object.
- The object's owner gave you the object privileges with the GRANT OPTION.
- You have been granted the GRANT ANY OBJECT system privilege.

■**Note** You can't grant object privileges on some schema objects, such as clusters, indexes, triggers, and database links. You control the use of these types of objects with a system privilege instead. For example, to alter a cluster, a user must own the cluster or have the ALTER ANY CLUSTER system privilege.

An object owner can add the additional ALL clause to a GRANT statement in order to grant all possible privileges on an object. For example, both the following GRANT statements are equivalent:

```
SQL> GRANT SELECT,INSERT,UPDATE,DELETE on EMPLOYEES TO oe;
SQL> GRANT ALL ON EMPLOYEES TO oe;
```

The schema owner can grant one type or all types of privileges at once on any given object. Here are some examples that illustrate the granting of object privileges:

```
SQL> GRANT SELECT ON ods_process TO tester;
Grant succeeded.
SQL> GRANT INSERT ON ods_process TO tester;
Grant succeeded.
SQL> GRANT ALL ON ods_servers TO tester;
Grant succeeded.
SQL> GRANT INSERT ANY TABLE TO tester;
grant insert any table to tester
*
ERROR at line 1:
ORA-01031: insufficient privileges
SQL>
```

The ODS user is able to grant all privileges (SELECT, INSERT, UPDATE, and DELETE) on the ods_servers table to the tester user by using the GRANT ALL command. But ODS fails to successfully grant the INSERT ANY TABLE privilege to tester, because this requires a *system privilege* (INSERT ANY TABLE) that ODS does not have. Note, however, that the system user can successfully make this grant, as shown here:

```
SQL> CONNECT system/manager@finance1
Connected.
SQL> SHOW USER
USER is "SYSTEM"
SQL> GRANT INSERT ANY TABLE TO tester;
Grant succeeded.
SQL>
```

If the owner of an object grants an object privilege to a user with the WITH GRANT clause, the grantee of the privilege is given the right to grant that same object privilege to other users. Here's an example:

```
SQL> GRANT INSERT ANY TABLE TO tester WITH GRANT OPTION
```

Column-Level Object Privileges

In the previous discussion, object privileges always implied a right to perform a DML action on an entire table. However, a user can also be granted privileges on only certain columns of a table, as shown in the following examples:

```
SQL> GRANT UPDATE (product_id) ON sales01 TO salapati;
Grant succeeded.
SQL>
```

Revoking Object Privileges

Revoking object privileges is analogous to granting privileges. You simply issue the REVOKE statement for each object privilege you want to revoke:

```
SQL> CONNECT ods/ods@finance1;
Connected.
SQL> REVOKE SELECT, INSERT ON ods_process FROM tester;
Revoke succeeded.
SQL>
```

Note that you can't revoke privileges at a column level, even though the privilege may have been granted at that level. You'll have to use the table level for the revocation of a privilege, regardless of the level at which it was granted, as you can see in the following example:

```
SQL> REVOKE UPDATE (hostname) ON ods_process FROM tester;
revoke update(hostname) on ods_process from tester
                  *
ERROR at line 1:
ORA-01750: UPDATE/REFERENCES may only
be revoked from the whole table, not by column
SQL> REVOKE UPDATE ON ods_process FROM tester;
Revoke succeeded.
SQL>
```

The GRANT ANY OBJECT Privilege

A user with the GRANT ANY OBJECT system privilege can grant and revoke any object privilege as if he or she were the actual object owner. When you connect as SYSDBA (user SYS), you are automatically granted this role with the WITH ADMIN OPTION clause.

Invoker Rights and Definer Rights

When you create a stored procedure in Oracle, it is executed by using the creator's privileges. This is the default behavior, and the stored procedure is said to have been created with *definer's rights*. When a user executes the procedure, it executes with the creator's (definer's) object privileges, not the particular user's, but there may be several situations where you don't want all users to be able to execute a procedure with the same rights. You can customize the accessibility of a procedure by creating it with *invoker's rights*, meaning the procedure will execute with the privileges of the user, not the creator, of the procedure.

When you create a procedure with invoker's rights, the procedure will execute under the user's security context, not the owner's security context. Thus, any user who intends to execute a procedure from a different schema will need to have the object privileges on all the tables that are part of the procedure. All DML privileges on those tables should be granted directly, not through any role, to the user.

The AUTHID clause in a CREATE PROCEDURE statement indicates that this procedure is being created with user's or invoker's rights, not with the default owner's or definer's rights. Here is an example:

```
SQL> CREATE OR REPLACE PROCEDURE delete_emp
  2  (p_emp_id number)
  3  AUTHID current_user IS
  4  BEGIN
  5  DELETE FROM emp WHERE
  6  emp_id = p_emp_id;
  7  COMMIT;
  8* END;

Procedure created.
SQL>
```

In line 3, the AUTHID clause specifies that the procedure will execute with the privileges of the current_user, the invoker of the procedure. Obviously, the user must have the explicit object privilege on the table, DELETE on emp, for the procedure to execute successfully.

Roles

Although you can fairly easily manage user privileges by directly granting and revoking them, the job can quickly become overwhelming when you add more users and the number of objects keeps increasing. It's very difficult, after a while, to keep track of each user's current privileges. Oracle addresses this problem by using *roles*, which are named sets of privileges that can be assigned to users.

Think of roles as a set of privileges that you can grant and revoke with a single GRANT or REVOKE command. A role can contain both a set of privileges and other roles as well. Roles make it easy for you to assign multiple privileges to a user. A default role is a role that's automatically operative when a user creates a session, and you can assign more than one default role to a user.

■**Tip** The DBA role, which is predefined in Oracle databases, is a set of system privileges WITH ADMIN OPTION, meaning that the user with this role can grant these privileges to other users as well. In most cases, you grant this role to a handful of users who perform database administration.

There are several predefined roles in an Oracle database, including the EXP_FULL_DATABASE, IMP_FULL_DATABASE, and RECOVERY_CATALOG_OWNER roles. In addition, every Oracle database contains the following three important roles, which have listed privileges:

- *The CONNECT role*: CREATE SESSION (earlier, the CONNECT role had several other privileges, but now it has only the single CREATE SESSION privilege)

- *The RESOURCE role*: CREATE CLUSTER, CREATE INDEXTYPE, CREATE OPERATOR, CREATE PROCEDURE, CREATE SEQUENCE, CREATE TABLE, CREATE TRIGGER, CREATE TYPE

- *The DBA role*: All system privileges with the WITH ADMIN OPTION clause

There are also two other predefined roles, EXP_FULL_DATABASE and IMP_FULL_DATABASE, which enable a user to perform a Data Pump Export and Import at the database level.

The DBA role is traditionally assigned to all individuals in an organization who perform database administration tasks. Oracle has indicated, however, that it may drop the DBA, CONNECT, and RESOURCE roles in future versions, and it recommends that you create your own roles to replace these three.

■**Note** By default, no user is granted any system privileges except those who have been granted the DBA role.

Creating a Role

Assuming you have either been granted the DBA role or you have a specific system privilege called CREATE ROLE, you can create a role in the following manner:

```
SQL> CREATE ROLE new_dba;
Role created.
SQL>
```

The new_dba role just created doesn't have any privileges attached to it, so you must now grant privileges to this role. You may even grant other preexisting roles to the new_dba role. Roles are empty vessels into which you can pour any number of system and object privileges.

Once the role has been created, you simply assign the role to a user, and the user will inherit all the privileges contained in the role. Listing 12-9 shows how to grant various database privileges to a new role.

Listing 12-9. *Granting Privileges to a Role*

```
SQL> GRANT CONNECT TO new_dba;
Grant succeeded.
SQL> GRANT SELECT ANY TABLE TO new_dba;
Grant succeeded.
SQL> GRANT UPDATE ANY TABLE TO new_dba;
Grant succeeded.
SQL> GRANT select_catalog_role TO new_dba;
Grant succeeded.
SQL> GRANT exp_full_database TO new_dba;
Grant succeeded.
SQL> GRANT imp_full_database TO new_dba;
Grant succeeded.
SQL>
```

To grant user salapati all the preceding privileges, all you need to do is this:

```
SQL> GRANT new_dba TO salapati;
Grant succeeded.
SQL>
```

A user can be assigned more than one role, and all of the roles that are granted to that user will be active when the user logs into the database.

Role Authorization

In the example in the previous section, a password wasn't needed to use the role. However, you can specify that a role must be authorized before it can be used. You can specify role authorization in several ways:

- *Database authorization*: You use a password when a role is authorized by the database, as shown in this example:

  ```
  CREATE ROLE clerk IDENTIFIED BY password;
  ```

- *Database authorization with a PL/SQL package*: A developer can create a role and specify that a PL/SQL package be used to authorize that role. In the following example, the admin_role role is enabled by a module defined inside the hr.admin PL/SQL package:

  ```
  CREATE ROLE admin_role IDENTIFIED USING hr.admin;
  ```

- *Externally, by the operating system, network, or other external source*: You can require that a role be authorized by an external source before it can be enabled, as shown here:

  ```
  CREATE ROLE accts_rec IDENTIFIED EXTERNALLY;
  ```

- *Globally, by an enterprise directory service*: You can also define a role as a global role, which means that a user can only be authorized to use the role by an enterprise directory service. The following statement creates a global role that can be authorized by a directory service:

  ```
  CREATE ROLE supervisor IDENTIFIED GLOBALLY;
  ```

Granting a Role Using WITH ADMIN OPTION

If you grant a user a role using the WITH ADMIN OPTION clause, the grantee can do the following:

- Grant the role to or revoke it from any user or other role in the database.
- Grant the role with the WITH ADMIN OPTION.
- Alter or drop the role.

Granting a Role to Another Role

You normally grant a role to a user. The user then can immediately exercise all the privileges encompassed by the role. However, you can grant a role to another role. In this case, the database will add all the privileges of the role being granted to the privilege domain of the grantee role.

The PUBLIC User Group and Roles

If you grant a role to PUBLIC, the database makes the role available to all the users in your database. If you wish to give a certain privilege or role to all the users in the database, you simply grant this privilege or role to the PUBLIC user group, which exists in every database by default. This is not a recommended way to grant privileges, however, for obvious reasons.

Disabling and Enabling a Role

You can disable a user's role by inserting the appropriate row into the Product_User_Profile table in the SYSTEM schema. Listing 12-10 shows you how to insert a row into this table to disable the TEST123 role, which has been assigned to the user TESTER.

Listing 12-10. *Disabling a Role Using the Product_User_Profile Table*

```
SQL> INSERT INTO PRODUCT_USER_PROFILE(PRODUCT,userid,attribute,char_value)
  2* VALUES('SQL*Plus','TESTER','ROLES','TEST123');

1 row created.
SQL> COMMIT;
Commit complete.
SQL> CONNECT tester/tester@finance1
Connected.
SQL> SELECT * FROM hr.regions;;
select * from hr.regions
               *ERROR at line 1:
ORA-00942: table or view does not exist
```

As you can see, once the TEST123 role is disabled, the TESTER user can't select from the database tables, and an error is issued when the SELECT is attempted.

When you want to reenable the TEST123 role, all you need to do is delete the appropriate row from the Product_User_Profile table, as shown here:

```
SQL> DELETE FROM product_user_profile
  2  WHERE userid='TESTER'
  3* AND char_value = 'TEST123';
1 row deleted.
SQL> commit;
Commit complete.
```

Dropping a Role

Dropping a role is simple. Just use the DROP ROLE command:

```
SQL> DROP ROLE admin_user;
Role dropped.
SQL>
```

Using Views and Stored Procedures to Manage Privileges

In addition to using roles and privileges, Oracle also enables data security through the use of views and stored procedures. You've already seen in Chapter 5 how views on key tables or even table joins can not only hide the complexity of queries, but also provide significant data security.

DBA Views for Managing Users, Roles, and Privileges

The OEM is very handy when managing users in the database. However, you may wish to use a SQL script from time to time to glean information about the users. Specific data dictionary views can help you see who has what role, and what privileges a certain role has. You can also see what system- and object-level privileges have been granted to a certain user. Table 12-1 presents the key data dictionary views you can use to manage users, privileges, and roles in the database.

Table 12-1. *Data Dictionary Views for Managing Users*

Data Dictionary View	Description
DBA_USERS	Provides information about users
DBA_ROLES	Shows all the roles in the database
DBA_COL_PRIVS	Shows column-level object grants
DBA_ROLE_PRIVS	Shows users and their roles
DBA_SYS_PRIVS	Shows users who have been granted system privileges
DBA_TAB_PRIVS	Shows users and their privileges on tables
ROLE_ROLE_PRIVS	Shows roles granted to roles
ROLE_SYS_PRIVS	Shows system privileges granted to roles
ROLE_TAB_PRIVS	Shows table privileges granted to roles
SESSION_PRIVS	Shows privileges currently enabled for the current session
SESSION_ROLES	Shows roles currently enabled for the current session

Fine-Grained Data Access

The traditional means of ensuring data security (using privileges, roles, views, etc.) works pretty well, but it has certain limitations. Chief among these is the fact that most security measures are too broad-based, with the result that you end up unnecessarily restricting users when your primary goal is to ensure that users can freely access information they need. In addition to the traditional concepts of roles and privileges, Oracle provides more fine-grained, lower-level data security techniques. For example, you can allow all users to access a central table, such as a payroll table, but you can institute security policies that limit an individual user's access to only those rows in the table that pertain to his or her department. Such limitations are transparent to the database users.

Oracle uses two related mechanisms to enforce fine-grained security within the database: an *application context* and a *fine-grained access control (FGAC) policy*. Oracle uses the term *virtual private database* to refer to the implementation of fine-grained access control policies using application contexts. Often, you'll find the terms fine-grained access control, virtual private database, and row-level security used interchangeably to refer to Oracle's capability to ensure security at the individual row level instead of the table level.

By using Oracle's fine-grained access control, you can fine-tune security policies in a very sophisticated manner. You can use the fine-grained access control for the following purposes:

- Enforce row-level access control through SELECT, INSERT, UPDATE, and DELETE statements.

- Create a security policy that controls access based on a certain value of a column.

- Create policies that are applied the same way always as well as policies that dynamically change during the execution of the query.

- Create sets of security policies, called policy groups.

Oracle lets you control row-level access to database objects through the virtual private database (VPD) feature. Each user of an application can be limited to seeing only a part of a table's data by using the VPD concept. This row-level security is enforced by attaching a security policy directly to a database object, such as a table, view, or synonym. No matter which tool the user uses to access the database (SQL*Plus, an ad hoc query tool, or a report writer), the user can't elude this row-level security, which is enforced by the database server. Since the database enforces VPD, it provides much stronger security than application-based security.

VPD uses a type of query rewrite to restrict users to certain rows of tables and views. A security policy is attached to the table or tables to which you want to control access, and stored procedures are written to modify any relevant SQL statements made against the tables in question. When a user issues an UPDATE statement against a table with such a security policy, Oracle will dynamically append a predicate (a WHERE clause) to the user's statement to modify it and limit the user's access to that table.

For example, if a user belonging to the sales department issues the statement UPDATE EMPLOYEE SET salary=salary*1.10, the security policies attached to the employees table will cause Oracle to add the fine-grained security function to the clause WHERE dept='SALES' to ensure that only employees in sales are affected. Here is the original query:

```
UPDATE EMPLOYEE SET salary=salary*1.10
```

And here is the modified statement:

```
UPDATE EMPLOYEE SET salary=salary*1.10 WHERE dept='SALES'
```

To create a VPD, you have to create what is known as an *application context* and then implement fine-grained access control to enforce the row-level security for database tables and views. The application context helps you create security policies that draw upon certain aspects of a user's session information. To take a simple example, when a user logs into the database, the user's ID identifies the user, and based on that piece of information, the application's security policy sets limits on what the user can do within the database. VPD is simply the implementation of an application context with fine-grained access control.

■**Note** VPD policies can be applied to `SELECT`, `INSERT`, `UPDATE`, `INDEX`, and `DELETE` statements.

Application Context

An application context allows you to define a set of application attributes, usually a set of session environmental variables, that you can use to control an application's access to the database. Using application attributes, you can supply relevant predicate values for fine-grained access control policies. Oracle uses a built-in application context namespace called USERENV, which has a set of predefined session attributes attached to it. These predefined attributes are then used by Oracle to control access. When a user logs in, the database automatically captures key session attributes such as the username, machine name, and IP address from the USERENV application context.

You can find out session-related information about any user by using the USERENV application context, as shown by the examples in Listing 12-11. In the first example, the TERMINAL attribute shows the name of the terminal from which the user is accessing the database. The second example uses the OS_USER attribute to show the name of the operating system account name of the database user. The third example gets the username by which the current user is authenticated from the SESSION_USER attribute.

Listing 12-11. *Using sys_context to Discover Session Information*

```
SQL> CONNECT system/system_passwd;
Connected.
SQL>

SQL> SELECT sys_context ('USERENV', 'TERMINAL')
  2   FROM DUAL;
SYS_CONTEXT('USERENV','TERMINAL')
---------------------------------
NTL-ALAPATISAM
SQL>

SQL> SELECT sys_context ('USERENV', 'OS_USER') FROM DUAL;
SYS_CONTEXT('_USERENV','CURRENT_USER')
-------
oracle
SQL>

SQL> CONNECT fay/fay1;
Connected.
SQL>

SQL> SELECT first_name,last_name,employee_id FROM employees
  2   WHERE UPPER(last_name)=sys_context('USERENV', 'SESSION_USER');
  3
FIRST_NAME      LAST_NAME    EMPLOYEE_ID
---------------  ---------    ------------
Pat             Fay          202
1 row selected.
SQL>
```

Besides the TERMINAL, CURRENT_USER, and SESSION_USER attributes shown in the examples in Listing 12-11, several other important predefined attributes belong to the USERENV namespace. Table 12-2 lists some of the common predefined attributes.

Table 12-2. *Common Predefined Attributes in the USERENV Namespace*

Attribute	Description
instance	Instance ID
entryID	Auditing entry identifier
current_user	Name of the user who started the session
session_user	Database username by which the current user is authenticated
db_name	Name of the database
host	Name of the machine on which the database is running
os_user	Operating system account name
terminal	Client terminal through which the database is being accessed
ip_address	IP address of the client machine
external_name	External name of the database user

When a user logs in, it's useful to identify the type of the user and to capture certain key user attributes. You can later use this information in the security policies that are attached to the database objects. The built-in USERENV namespace is ideal for capturing these kinds of information.

The USERENV namespace, of course, is just one of the application context namespaces that you can use. You'll have to create your own application context so you can define which attributes you want to use in setting your security policies. To define your own application context, you need to do the following:

1. Create a PL/SQL package that sets the context with the help of functions.

2. Create an application context that uses the package you created.

Creating a Package to Set the Context

To set the application context for the hr user, you need to create a PL/SQL package. Listing 12-12 shows you how to create a simple package called HR_CONTEXT to set the application context. The package includes a single procedure that selects the value of the employee_id column into the empnum variable. Since this SELECT statement is based on a WHERE clause that determines the last_name of the employee based on the value of the SESSION_USER attribute, the employee_id will be that of the username by which the current user is authenticated by the database.

Listing 12-12. *Creating a Package to Set the Application Context*

```
SQL> CONNECT hr/hr
Connected.

SQL> CREATE OR REPLACE PACKAGE hr_context AS
  2  PROCEDURE select_emp_no ;
  3* END;
```

```
SQL> /
Package created.

SQL> CREATE OR REPLACE PACKAGE BODY hr_context as
  2   PROCEDURE select_emp_no IS
  3   empnum number;
  4   BEGIN
  5   SELECT employee_id INTO empnum FROM employees WHERE
  6   UPPER(last_name) =
  7   sys_context('USERENV', 'SESSION_USER');
  8   dbms_session.set_context('employee_info', 'emp_num', empnum);
  9   END select_emp_no;
 10* END;
SQL> /
Package body created.
SQL>
```

Creating the Application Context

You can think of an application context as a named set of variable=value pairs that are specific to a session. Once you create the package (HR_CONTEXT) that helps set the application context, you can go ahead and create the application context itself as follows. Note that the hr user uses the package just created in the previous section to create the employee_info application context.

```
SQL> CONNECT system/system_passwd;
Connected.
SQL> GRANT CREATE ANY CONTEXT TO hr;
Grant succeeded.

SQL> CONNECT hr/hr;
Connected.
SQL> CREATE CONTEXT employee_info USING hr.context;
Context created.
SQL>
```

You can set the application context for a user in two ways. The first is to implement an application context by itself, without fine-grained access control. To do this, you just create an event trigger on a user's logon so the user will invoke the SELECT_EMP_NO procedure belonging to the HR_CONTEXT package upon logging into the database. Here's how you create the logon trigger to set the initial context for a user:

```
SQL> CREATE OR REPLACE TRIGGER hr.security_context
  2   AFTER LOGON ON DATABASE
  3   BEGIN
  4   hr_context.select_emp_no;
  5* END;
SQL> /
Trigger created.
SQL>
```

The preceding logon trigger uses the SELECT_EMP_NO procedure of the HR_CONTEXT package you created to grab the user's employee_id and store it in the emp_num variable.

The second way to set or reference an application context is to do so as an integral part of VPD, using a policy function implementing fine-grained access control. The following section discusses this in detail.

Fine-Grained Access Control

Traditionally, security policies were applied to entire applications. Users were given roles or privileges, based on which they could access the tables in the application. This always left open the possibility of users using tools such as SQL*Plus to go around the application's security protocols and modify data in the database tables. Furthermore, application-level security enforcement meant you had to manage a grant/revoke policy for each user in the system for access to all the tables in the database.

There are situations where you might want to limit access to an application's data to certain segments of users. Of course, you could create views to such a thing, but managing views poses several problems, such as maintenance and auditing usage.

Fine-grained access control enables you to restrict Oracle users so that they can only use the data you want them to access and modify. FGAC is facilitated through the use of *policy functions,* which you attach to the tables or views you want to secure. It uses dynamically modifiable statements to restrict or limit users to certain portions of a table, view, or synonym. When a user's SQL statements are parsed, FGAC makes Oracle automatically evaluate the policy functions (you can attach more than one policy to a table). Oracle will execute the user's query after dynamically modifying the query if necessary.

■**Note** FGAC enables you to implement fine-grained data security. You can enforce a row-level security policy using this feature.

FGAC involves the following steps:

1. You create a policy function that will dynamically add a predicate to a user's DML statement. A predicate is the WHERE clause based on an operator (=, !=, IS, IS NOT, >, >=, EXIST, BETWEEN, IN, NOT IN, and so on). Here's an example of such a function:

```
cust_no = (SELECT custno FROM orders
WHERE
custname = SYS_CONTEXT ('USERENV','SESSION_USER'))
```

The package that implements your security policy will dynamically append a predicate to all SELECT statements on the ORDERS table, returning only those orders that pertain to the user's customer number (cust_no).

2. A user enters a statement such as the following:

```
SELECT * FROM orders;
```

3. Oracle will use the policy function you created to dynamically modify the user's statement. For example, the statement in step 2 would be modified by the policy function in step 1 as follows:

```
SELECT * FROM orders WHERE custno = (
   SELECT custno FROM customers
   WHERE custname = SYS_CONTEXT('USERENV', 'SESSION_USER'))
```

4. Oracle uses the username returned by SYS_CONTEXT('USERENV', 'SESSION_USER') and executes the modified original query, thus limiting the data returned from the ORDERS table to that customer's data only.

Creating a Package That Will Access the Context

Let's look at a simple example of FGAC. This FGAC implementation will use a policy that limits an employee to only seeing appropriate data in the employees table.

First, we will create the hr_security package, which we will use later to access the application context. This package is the key to row-level security, since it generates the dynamic-access predicates for a table. Listing 12-13 shows how to create the hr_security package.

Listing 12-13. *Creating the hr_security Package*

```
SQL> CREATE OR REPLACE PACKAGE hr_security AS
  2  FUNCTION empnum_sec (A1 VARCHAR2, A2 VARCHAR2)
  3  RETURN varchar2;
  4  END;
  5*/
Package created.
SQL> CREATE OR REPLACE PACKAGE BODY hr_security AS
  2  FUNCTION empnum_sec (A1 VARCHAR2, A2 VARCHAR2)
  3  RETURN varchar2
  4  IS
  5  d_predicate varchar2 (2000);
  6  BEGIN
  7  d_predicate:= 'employee_id =
  8  SYS_CONTEXT("EMPLOYEE_INFO","EMP_NUM")';
  9  RETURN d_predicate;
 10  END empnum_sec;
 11  END hr_security;
 12* /
Package body created.
SQL>
```

The package created in Listing 12-13, hr_security, will use the employee_info context (created earlier in the "Creating the Application Context" section) to get the emp_num variable. As you recall from the previous section, the employee_info application context gets the emp_num variable from the USERENV namespace (the SESSION_USER attribute of the USERENV namespace).

The d_predicate predicate in the hr_security package indicates the transformation that should be applied to any queries made by any employee whose employee_id matches the emp_num variable obtained from the employee_info context. For example, if user salapati issues the following command:

```
SQL> SELECT * FROM employees;
```

it will be modified by our predicate (d_predicate) as follows:

```
SQL> SELECT * FROM employees
  2* WHERE employee_id = SYS_CONTEXT ('EMPLOYEE_INFO', 'EMP_NUM');
```

Creating the Security Policy

The hr_security package created in the previous section lets you attach a dynamic predicate (WHERE employee_id = SYS_CONTEXT ('EMPLOYEE_INFO', 'EMP_NUM')) to any SQL statements that can be used by employees whose employee_id matches the emp_num derived by using the employee_info application context. But we still haven't attached a *security policy* to the employees table. That is, we now have to specify what kinds of SQL statements, and precisely what tables, the hr_security package would be applied to.

In previous releases of the Oracle database, all security polices were dynamic, meaning the database had to execute the policy function for each DML statement. Of course, repeated execution of the policy functions costs system resources and could hurt performance in a busy OLTP database. Oracle now offers several choices regarding the type of policy you can use. You can specify the following five types of security policies by using the POLICY_TYPE parameter of the DBMS_RLS.ADD_ POLICY procedure:

- *Dynamic*: Each time a statement is parsed or executed, the security policy function is executed afresh. This is the default policy type, and you can specify it either by setting the POLICY_TYPE parameter to DBMS_RLS.DYNAMIC or by just leaving the parameter out altogether.

- *Static*: This type of policy function needs to be executed only once, when a user first accesses a database object. Thereafter, the value of the policy function is cached in the SGA, and all users accessing the object will get the same predicate. You can choose this type by setting the POLICY_TYPE parameter to DBMS_RLS.STATIC. The function must be deterministic so that the predicate returned is always the same: if you have a branch in the function that can return different predicates, you must specify a dynamic security policy instead.

- *Shared static*: This is identical to a static policy, and it is applied to multiple objects. Shared policies reduce your administrative burden by letting a single security policy cover several database objects. You can enable it by setting the POLICY_TYPE parameter to DBMS_RLS.SHARED_STATIC.

- *Context sensitive*: Under this type of security policy, the policy predicate can be modified based on changes in certain context attributes within a user's session. The database caches the policy predicate in the SGA. You choose this type by setting the POLICY_TYPE parameter to DBMS_RLS.CONTEXT_SENSITIVE.

- *Shared context sensitive*: This policy type is similar to context-sensitive policies, but it is shared across multiple objects. You choose this type by setting the POLICY_TYPE parameter to DBMS_RLS.SHARED_CONTEXT_SENSITIVE.

You can add a security policy to a database by using the DBMS_RLS package (*RLS* stands for *row-level security*) provided by Oracle. This package enables you to administer security policies, which means you can add and drop policies, policy groups, or application contexts. You provide the name of the table, view, or synonym for which you want the security policy to apply, as well as the security policy for implementing the FGAC. You also specify the particular types of SQL statements the policy applies to, such as a SELECT, INSERT, UPDATE, DELETE, CREATE INDEX, or ALTER INDEX statement.

Here are the main procedures of the DBMS_RLS package:

- *DBMS_RLS.ADD_POLICY*: Adds a policy to a table, view, or synonym

- *DBMS_RLS.CREATE_POLICY_GROUP*: Creates a policy group

- *DBMS_RLS.ADD_POLICY_CONTEXT*: Adds the context for the application

You create the security policy using the DBMS_RLS.ADD_POLICY procedure, as shown here:

```
SQL> CONNECT system/system_passwd
Connected.

SQL> EXECUTE dbms_rls.add_policy('hr','employees','manager_policy','hr',-
    'hr_security.empnum_sec','select');
PL/SQL procedure successfully completed.
```

Note that you could also have executed the preceding statement in the following equivalent manner:

```
SQL> BEGIN
  2  dbms_rls.add_policy
  3  (object_schema => 'hr',
  4  object_name      => 'employees',
  5  policy_name      => 'manager_policy',
  6  function_schema => 'hr',
  7  policy_function => 'hr_security.empnum_sec',
```

```
 8   statement_types => 'select');
 9*  END;
SQL> /
```

The DBMS_RLS.ADD_POLICY procedure in the preceding statements creates a policy called manager_policy in the hr schema. This security policy is actually implemented by the function empnum_sec, which is part of the hr_security package that you created earlier. The security policy specifies that it applies to all SELECT operations against the employees table.

To put it simply, the new security policy you created (manager_policy) will limit all SELECT statements against the hr.employees table to information that pertains to the employee_id of the user who issued the query.

You can check that the new policy was indeed created successfully by making the following query:

```
SQL> SELECT object_name, policy_name, sel, ins, upd, del, enable
       FROM all_policies;
```

OBJECT_NAME	POLICY_NAME	SEL	INS	UPD	DEL	ENABLED
EMPLOYEES	MANAGER_POLICY	YES	NO	NO	NO	YES

```
SQL>
```

The output of the query indicates that all SELECT statements against the employees table are now controlled by the manager_policy security policy.

To make the security policy functions accessible to the public so that all users accessing the database will use it, you can make the following grant:

```
SQL> GRANT EXECUTE ON hr_security TO public;
Grant succeeded.
```

Column-Level VPD

You've seen how you can enforce row-level security anytime you access a table. Oracle also lets you use a column-level VPD to enforce row-level security whenever a query references a certain *column or columns* only. You can apply column-level VPD to a table or a view.

Creating a column-level security policy is almost identical to creating regular security policies—you just add the additional SEC_RELEVANT_COLS parameter in the DBMS_RLS.ADD_POLICY procedure to specify the relevant columns for security. Here's how you use the DBMS_RLS.ADD_POLICY procedure to create a column-level security policy.

```
SQL> BEGIN
  2   dbms_rls.add_policy
  3   (object_schema       => 'hr',
  4    object_name         => 'employees',
  5    policy_name         => 'manager_policy',
  6    function_schema     => 'hr',
  7    policy_function     => 'hr_security.empnum_sec',
  8    statement_types     => 'select,insert',
  9    sec_relevant_cols   => 'salary');
 10*END;
SQL> /
```

The column-level policy created in the preceding example would come into effect only if the salary column of the employees table is accessed. Suppose a user subsequently issues the following query:

```
SQL> SELECT fname, lname, salary FROM employees;
```

The column-level VPD policy kicks into action when it sees that the `salary` column is referenced in a query, and the policy function implementing the column-level security policy returns the predicate `WHERE salary ='my_salary'`, thus transforming the query as follows:

```
SQL> SELECT fname, lname, salary FROM employees WHERE salary = 'my_salary';
```

Policy Groups

When you access a table, Oracle looks up the application context (the policy context) to determine which policy group, and therefore which security policy, should be enforced. There is one default policy group called SYS_DEFAULT that can never be dropped from the database, and every policy belongs to this group by default.

Using Oracle Policy Manager

You can use the Oracle Policy Manager GUI, an extension to Oracle Enterprise Manager, to administer Oracle Label Security (discussed next) as well as to create VPD security policies. Oracle Policy Manager will help you effortlessly create application contexts and complex security policies to enforce fine-grained data security. This definitely beats creating application contexts and security policies manually.

When you use OEM to create a VPD policy, you create an application context and provide the table (or view or synonym) name, the policy name, the function name that generates the predicate, and the statement types to which the policy applies (`SELECT`, `INSERT`, `UPDATE`, or `DELETE`). Oracle Policy Manager executes the `DBMS_RLS.ADD_POLICY` function to create the FGAC policy to support your VPD.

Label-Based Access Control

Oracle allows you to label parts of your data, and users can be granted privileges to access data with certain labels. Security policies are implemented on a single column, which represents the label. The Oracle Label Security feature (based on the older Trusted Oracle security product) is built on the same components that help you create a VPD. You can easily construct labels to limit access to rows in a certain table, and use label authorizations and privileges to set up a label-based security policy. The Oracle Policy Manager GUI is mainly designed to create and administer Oracle Label Security policies.

Auditing Database Usage

Just because you have set up a sophisticated system of access controls using privileges, roles, views, and even fine-grained security policies doesn't guarantee that database security won't be breached. Auditing database usage lets you know whether your access control mechanisms are indeed working as designed. Auditing involves monitoring and recording (selected) users' database activity.

Oracle's built-in auditing features allow you to track the changes made to database objects. You can audit the granting of privileges within the database, as well as non-DML and non-DDL changes, such as database startup and shutdown events. Auditing user activity can potentially lead to a large amount of data to keep track of, but fortunately, Oracle offers you a lot of control over what type of activities you want to audit. You can audit just at the session level or at the entire database level.

Oracle makes a broad distinction between *standard auditing* and *fine-grained auditing*. Standard auditing is based on statement-, privilege-, and object-level auditing. Fine-grained auditing deals with data access at a granular level, with actions based on content, such as value > 100,000. I discuss standard auditing first, and then fine-grained auditing.

Standard Auditing

Oracle Database 11g lets you audit database use at three different levels: statement, privilege, and object. A *statement-level audit* specifies the auditing of all actions on any type of object. For example, you can specify that the database audit all actions on tables by using the AUDIT TABLE statement. A *privilege-level audit* tracks actions that stem from system privileges. You can audit all actions that involve the use of a granted privilege, such as auditing all CREATE ANY PROCEDURE statements. Finally, an *object-level audit* monitors actions such as UPDATE, DELETE, and INSERT statements on a specific table, so you could audit all DELETEs on the hr_employees table.

For each of the three levels of auditing, you can choose to audit either by *session* or by *access*. If you audit by session, Oracle will log just one record for all similar statements that fall under the purview of auditing. If you audit by access, Oracle writes a record for each access. You can also decide to log only whether a certain action failed or succeeded by using the WHENEVER SUCCESSFUL and the WHENEVER NOT SUCCESSFUL auditing options. When the operation is unsuccessful, it's usually an indication that the user doesn't have privileges to perform the operation. You'll want to know who is attempting such unauthorized operations.

■**Tip** One of the common arguments against the use of Oracle database auditing is that it will consume a lot of space in the database. If you spend time analyzing *why* you are auditing, you can limit the amount of data written to the audit trail. By using a focused auditing policy that targets only vital data, rather than systemwide auditing, you can limit the auditing output to a manageable amount. You may also decide to turn on auditing only if you encounter questionable activity in the database.

Enabling Auditing

In order for you to audit any user activity within the database, and even attempt to log into the database, you need to enable auditing by specifying the AUDIT_TRAIL parameter in your init.ora file. Audit records contain the audit information, such as the audited user, the type of operation, and the date and time of the operation, and the AUDIT_TRAIL parameter specifies what is done with these records. The parameter can take the following values:

- NONE: Disables database auditing. NONE is the default value for this parameter.

- OS: Specifies that Oracle will write the audit records to an operating system file (operating system audit trail).

- DB: Specifies that Oracle will write the audit records to the database audit trail, viewable as DBA_AUDIT_TRAIL (stored in the SYS.AUD$ table).

- DB, EXTENDED: Specifies that Oracle will send all audit records to the database audit trail (SYS.AUD$), and in addition, populates the SQLBIND and SQLTEXT CLOB columns.

- XML: Specifies database auditing, with the XML-format audit records going to the OS files.

- XML, EXTENDED: Same as the XML setting, but also records all audit-trail columns, including SQLTEXT and SQLBIND.

There is a default location in which Oracle will place the audit file, and you can easily change the location of this file by using the AUDIT_FILE_DEST parameter in the init.ora file, as shown here:

```
AUDIT_TRAIL=DB
AUDIT_FILE_DEST=/a10/app/oracle/oradata/audit_data
```

If you specify `AUDIT_TRAIL=OS`, the audit trail won't store the audit information in the database. It will instead store that information in the location specified by the `AUDIT_FILE_DEST` parameter. If you specify `AUDIT_TRAIL=OS` and omit the `AUDIT_FILE_DEST` parameter, by default the audit information will be written to the `$ORACLE_HOME/rdbms/audit/` directory.

■Tip If you specify `AUDIT_TRAIL=DB`, the audit records will be logged to a special table owned by SYS called SYS.AUD$, located in the System tablespace. If you want to do any kind of serious auditing on your database, the tablespace will quickly run out of space. Make sure you change the storage parameters of the SYS.AUD$ table and add more space to the System tablespace before you turn auditing on. Otherwise, you run the risk of filling up your System tablespace while auditing the database.

You can use the DBA_AUDIT_TRAIL view to make use of the information in the database audit trail table (SYS.AUD$). Depending on the event you are auditing and the options you select for auditing, you may see the following types of data in the audit trail:

- Operating system login
- Database username
- Terminal and session identifiers
- Operation performed or attempted
- Date and time stamp
- SQL text that triggered the auditing

You don't need to be overly concerned with the filling up of the SYS.AUD$ table when auditing is turned on. You can always truncate the table after exporting the contents to a different location or when you deem it isn't necessary to store the contents of the audit table any longer.

Oracle's Default Auditing

Even when you don't set up database auditing by specifying the `AUDIT_TRAIL` parameter at all, by default Oracle will log three types of database actions to the `$ORACLE_HOME/rdbms/audit` directory:

- Connections as SYSOPER or SYSDBA
- Database startup
- Database shutdown

Typically, the audit file captures the `CONNECT`, `SHUTDOWN`, and `STARTUP` events undertaken by the user SYS, who, of course has the SYSDBA privileges.

You can audit all actions of the user SYS, including all users connecting with the SYSDBA or SYSOPER privileges, by setting the `AUDIT_SYS_OPERATIONS` init.ora parameter to `true`.

`AUDIT_SYS_OPERATIONS=TRUE`

Note that if this parameter is set, all actions of the SYS user will be audited, *whether you set the* `AUDIT_TRAIL` *parameter or not.* The parameter has a default value of `false`.

Turning Auditing On

Once you have set the `AUDIT_TRAIL` parameter, you will have enabled auditing in your database. However, for the actual auditing to begin, you must also specify which tables and what actions you want the database to audit.

You can start auditing actions at any level by using the appropriate command. Listing 12-14 shows a sampling of commands that specify auditing at various levels, with different options.

Listing 12-14. *Turning Auditing On in the Database*

```
SQL> AUDIT SELECT ON employees;
Audit succeeded.
SQL> AUDIT DELETE ANY TABLE BY salapati WHENEVER NOT SUCCESSFUL;
Audit succeeded.
SQL> AUDIT UPDATE ANY TABLE;
Audit succeeded.
SQL> AUDIT SESSION BY SALAPATI;
Audit succeeded.
SQL> AUDIT SELECT,INSERT,UPDATE,DELETE
  2  ON employees BY ACCESS WHENEVER SUCCESSFUL;
Audit succeeded.
SQL>
```

Here is a more powerful audit option that ensures the auditing of all privileges:

```
SQL> AUDIT ALL PRIVILEGES;
Audit succeeded.
SQL>
```

Obviously, the audit trail for this auditing choice will be large if you have many users who have been granted object privileges in the database.

■Note The AUDIT SESSION statement does not audit the statements executed during an entire session—it logs the session start time, the end time, and the logical and physical I/O resources consumed by this session, among other things.

Turning Auditing Off

To turn auditing off, you use a statement that is almost identical to the one you used to turn auditing on. The big difference, of course, is that you use the NOAUDIT keyword in place of AUDIT. Here are some examples:

```
SQL> NOAUDIT SESSION;
Noaudit succeeded.
SQL> NOAUDIT DELETE ANY TABLE BY salapati WHENEVER NOT SUCCESSFUL;
Noaudit succeeded.
SQL> NOAUDIT DELETE ANY TABLE BY salapati;
Noaudit succeeded.
```

■Note You can use either of the last two statements to turn DELETE ANY TABLE BY salapati WHENEVER NOT SUCCESSFUL off. That is, the NOAUDIT keyword, when applied to a more general statement, will turn off lower-level auditing that is subsumed by the general privilege.

If you want to turn off all the levels of auditing—statement, privilege, and object—you can do so by using the following three SQL statements:

```
SQL> NOAUDIT ALL;               /* turns off all statement auditing */
SQL> NOAUDIT ALL PRIVILEGES;    /* turns off all privilege auditing */
SQL> NOAUDIT ALL ON DEFAULT;    /* turns off all object auditing    */
```

Customizing Database Auditing with Triggers

Oracle *triggers* are special blocks of code that are triggered or fired off by certain events in the database. Most applications use triggers to update one table based on an action in another table. A trigger could fire off based on DML or DDL statements, and they can be used to help enforce business rules within the database. You can audit specific user actions by simply writing triggers or other stored procedures that will log user information to a table when the user performs a specific database operation.

You can create several types of triggers in Oracle, including DML and DDL triggers, which are based on actions performed by users on tables and views, and system-level triggers, which are more broad-based. In the following sections you'll learn about these types of triggers.

■**Tip** You don't have to necessarily turn database-wide auditing on if you're solely interested in a specific user's actions or want to audit limited actions in the database. You can write triggers that will insert information into a log table upon the occurrence of specified events.

Using DML-Based Triggers for Auditing

The most commonly used triggers in Oracle databases are DML triggers; applications routinely use them to maintain business rules within the database. Oracle triggers are easy to implement, and you can employ them if you're interested in a modest range of auditing activity. Listing 12-15 shows a small example of how to use a trigger to audit insert operations by users on a certain table.

Listing 12-15. *A Typical DML Trigger*

```
SQL> CONNECT tester/tester1
Connected.

SQL> CREATE OR REPLACE TRIGGER audit_insert
  2   AFTER INSERT ON tester.xyz
  3   FOR EACH ROW
  4   INSERT INTO xyz_audit
  5* VALUES(user, sysdate);
Trigger created.
SQL>

SQL> CONNECT tester/tester1
Connected.

SQL> INSERT INTO xyz
  2   VALUES
  3   ('sam alapati');
1 row created.

SQL> COMMIT;
Commit complete.
```

```
SQL> CONNECT system/system_passwd
Connected.
SQL> SELECT * FROM xyz_audit;
USER_NAME      ACTION_DATE
--------------------------
TESTER         24-MAR-08
SQL>
```

The more actions you want to audit, the larger the space required to hold the audit trail. You have to understand why you are auditing and only audit those activities that are of true significance to your organization.

Note There are no rules regarding the operations you should audit. In some organizations, all DML changes (INSERT, UPDATE, and DELETE) may have to be audited to ensure that you can track down any unauthorized changes. In other organizations, simply auditing failed logins might suffice.

Using System-Level Triggers for Auditing

Triggers that fire after DML operations, such as an INSERT or a DELETE, are the most commonly used triggers in Oracle databases, but they aren't the only types of triggers you can use. Oracle provides powerful system-level triggers, such as those set to fire after database startup and before database shutdown. Login and logoff triggers are especially useful for database auditing.

The following are the main types of system-level triggers that Oracle Database 11g offers:

- *Database startup triggers*: You can use these triggers mostly to execute code that you want to execute immediately after database startup.

- *Logon triggers*: These triggers provide you with information regarding the logon times of a user and details about the user's session.

- *Logoff triggers*: These triggers are similar to the logon triggers, but they execute right before the user's session logs off.

- *DDL triggers*: You can capture all database object changes with these triggers.

- *Server error triggers*: These triggers capture all major PL/SQL code errors into a special table.

Let's look at a simple example that shows the potential of the special Oracle triggers for auditing users. This example first creates a simple table to hold logon data. Whenever a user logs in, the table captures several pieces of information about the user. By auditing the logoff items with another trigger, it is easy to find out how long the user was inside the database on a given day.

Here are the steps involved in creating a logon/logoff auditing system using system-level triggers:

1. Create a test table called logon_audit:

```
SQL> CREATE TABLE logon_audit(
  2  user_id   VARCHAR2(30),
  3  sess_id   NUMBER(10),
  4  logon_time  DATE,
  5  logoff_time DATE,
  6* host      VARCHAR2(20));
Table created.
SQL>
```

2. Create a pair of logon and logoff triggers:

```
SQL> CREATE OR REPLACE TRIGGER logon_audit_trig
  2  AFTER LOGON
  3  ON DATABASE
  4  BEGIN
  5  INSERT INTO logon_audit
  6  VALUES
  7  (user,
  8  sys_context('userenv', 'sessionid'),
  9  sysdate,
 10  null,
 11  sys_context('userenv', 'host'));
 12* END;
Trigger created.

SQL> CREATE OR REPLACE TRIGGER logoff_audit_trig
  2  AFTER LOGOFF
  3  ON DATABASE
  4  BEGIN
  5  INSERT INTO logon_audit
  6   VALUES
  7  (user,
  8  sys_context('userenv', 'sessionid'),
  9  null,
 10  sysdate,
 11  sys_context('userenv', 'host'));
 12* END;
Trigger created.
SQL>
```

3. Review your users' login/logout details:

```
SQL> SELECT * FROM logon_audit;
USER_NAME  SESS_ID  LOGON_TIME          LOGOFF_TIME  HOST_NAME
---------  -------  ------------------- -----------  ----------

SYSTEM     347      24-MAR-085 07:00:30              NTL-ALAPATI
HR         348      24-MAR-08  07:10:31              NTL-ALAPATI
HR         348      24-MAR-08 07:32:17               NTL-ALAPATI
SQL>
```

You could also use a DDL trigger to capture changes made to objects by users, including modification, creation, and deletion of various types of objects. You can capture a large number of attributes about the event and the user that sets off a DDL trigger.

To capture some of the important attributes of a user event, you first need to create a table to log DDL changes. Once you have done that, you can create a DDL trigger like the one shown in Listing 12-16. In this example, the table is named DDL_LOG and the trigger is DDL_LOG_TRIG.

Listing 12-16. *Using DDL Triggers to Audit Users*

```
SQL> CREATE OR REPLACE TRIGGER
  2  ddl_log_trig
  3  AFTER DDL ON DATABASE
  4  BEGIN
  5  INSERT INTO ddl_log
  6  (username,
```

```
 7  change_date,
 8  object_type,
 9  object_owner,
10  database
11  )
12  VALUES
13  (ora_login_user,
14  sysdate,
15  ora_dict_obj_type,
16  ora_dict_obj_owner,
17  ora_database_name)
16* END;
Trigger created.
SQL>
```

Once the trigger is in use, you can query the DDL_LOG table to see the changes. As you can see here, users HR and SYSTEM have made several DDL-based changes to the database:

```
SQL> SELECT * FROM ddl_log;
USERNAME   CHANGE_DATE   OBJECT_TYPE       OBJECT_OWNER   DATABASE_NAME
--------   -----------   ---------------   ------------   -------------
HR         24-MAR-08     SYNONYM           HR             NINA
SYSTEM     24-MAR-08     OBJECTPRIVILEGE   SYSTEM         NINA
HR         24-MAR-08     TRIGGER           HR             NINA
SQL>
```

Using Flashback Features for Auditing

In addition to using the standard Oracle auditing features described in the previous sections, you can also take advantage of Oracle's Flashback capabilities to audit changes made to a table's rows. For example, you can use the Flashback Query feature to examine a table's data at a past point in time. Using the Flashback Transaction Query, you can find out all the changes made to a row since a past point in time or an SCN.

The Flashback Versions Query will return each version of a row that existed in the specified period. You can easily identify the user and the specific operation that resulted in any inappropriate or unauthorized modifications to data. Using the transaction details from this query, you can go ahead and identify the entire transaction(s) with the help of another flashback feature, Flashback Transaction Query.

The Flashback Query, Flashback Versions Query, and Flashback Transaction Query features rely on undo data and are discussed in detail in Chapter 8.

Fine-Grained Auditing

Suppose you're interested in using auditing to find out whether users are viewing data in a table they're not really supposed to access. For example, say a manager is supposed to be able to see salary-related information for employees working for him. Can you tell whether the manager is also looking at the salary information of his superiors? Do you need to audit all the SELECT statements done by the manager?

Auditing all SELECT statements would lead to a colossal amount of audit data, but fortunately there's an easy out. Oracle lets you audit actions in the database on the basis of *content*. That is, you can specify that the audit records be written not for all SELECT, INSERT, UPDATE, and DELETE statements, but only for statements that meet certain criteria. Instead of trying to determine policy violations based on what is being done to any data, you apply fine-grained auditing (FGA) policies to individual tables or specific operations that you wish to monitor.

Enabling Fine-Grained Auditing

You use the DBMS_FGA Oracle package to enable fine-grained auditing. With FGA, you can audit only specific rows within a table. You can simulate a trigger for statements by executing a user-written procedure when an audit condition is met. You can catch employee misuse of data. You can also use FGA as an intrusion-detection device.

You don't need to turn on database-wide auditing to use FGA, and since the auditing is based on table access, it is virtually impossible to bypass FGA policies. FGA records are accessible through the DBA_FGA_AUDIT_TRAIL and DBA_COMMON_AUDIT_TRAIL views, with the latter view combining both standard and fine-grained audit log records.

You use the DBMS_FGA package's ADD_POLICY procedure to add a fine-grained audit policy. Listing 12-17 shows the structure of the ADD_POLICY procedure.

Listing 12-17. *The ADD_POLICY Procedure*

```
SQL> EXECUTE DBMS_FGA.ADD_POLICY(
        object_schema        VARCHAR2,
        object_name          VARCHAR2,
        policy_name          VARCHAR2,
        audit_condition      VARCHAR2,
        audit_column         VARCHAR2,
        handler_schema       VARCHAR2,
        handler_module       VARCHAR2,
        enable               BOOLEAN,
        statement_types      VARCHAR2,
        audit_trail          BINARY_INTEGER IN DEFAULT,
        audit_column_opts    BINARY_INTEGER IN DEFAULT);
```

These are the parameters of the ADD_POLICY procedure:

- object_schema: The schema of the object you want to audit. The default is NULL meaning the logon user schema.

- object_name: The name of the object you want to audit.

- policy_name: A user-given name for the audit policy.

- audit_condition: A condition in a row that indicates a monitoring condition. The default value is NULL, which acts as TRUE.

- audit_column: The columns you want to audit for access. The default is NULL, which means that all column access will be audited. The audit_column_opts parameter works in conjunction with this parameter.

- handler_schema: The schema that contains the event handler. The default is NULL, meaning that the current schema will be used.

- enable: The parameter that enables or disables the policy. The default value is TRUE, which enables the policy.

- statement_types: The SQL statement types to which this policy is applicable: INSERT, UPDATE, DELETE, or SELECT. The default is SELECT.

- audit_trail: The parameter that says whether to populate LSQLTEXT and LSQLBIND in the fga_log$ table. A setting of DB does not populate the columns. The default value is DB_EXTENDED, which populates the columns.

- audit_column_opts: Determines whether auditing should be enforced when the query references any column or all columns specified in the audit_column parameter. Set to DBMS_FGA.ALL_COLUMNS, the statement will be audited only if it references all columns specified in the audit_column parameter. The default is DBMS_FGA.ANY_COLUMNS, which means the statement will be audited if it references any column specified in the audit_column parameter.

Using Fine-Grained Auditing

It's time to see how you can use the DBMS_FGA package to enforce fine-grained auditing. The following FGA example audits any DML statement (INSERT, UPDATE, DELETE, and SELECT) on the hr.emp table that accesses the salary column for any employee belonging to the SALES department:

```
SQL> EXECUTE DBMS_FGA.ADD_POLICY(
     object_schema    => 'hr',
     object_name      => 'emp',
     policy_name      => 'chk_hr_emp',
     audit_condition  => 'dept = ''SALES'' ',
     audit_column     => 'salary',
     statement_types  => 'insert,update,delete,select',
     handler_schema   => 'sec',
     handler_module   => 'log_id',
     enable           =>  TRUE);
```

Once the preceding ADD_POLICY procedure is executed, all subsequent SELECT statements that query the emp table for salary information where the employee belongs to the SALES department will be logged in the SYS.FGA_LOG$ table in the System tablespace; DBA_FGA_AUDIT_TRAIL is a view built on this table. You can also capture the SQL text, policy name, and other information through the LSQLTEXT and LSQLBIND columns of fga_log$, providing you specify audit_trail = DBMS_FGA.DB_EXTENDED.

The handler_module and the handler_schema parameters are used to take a predetermined set of actions whenever an audit event occurs, and you can create a trigger-like mechanism called the audit event handler that handles the audit event when it occurs.

Here are what the two event handler–related parameters stand for:

- handler_schema: The schema that owns the data procedure
- handler_module: The procedure or package name

In our example, the handler module is denoted by sec_id, which is the following procedure:

```
SQL> CREATE PROCEDURE sec.log_id (schema1 varchar2, table1 varchar2,
     policy1 varchar2)
     AS
     BEGIN
     UTIL_ALERT_PAGER(schema1, table1, policy1); /*send an alert to my pager*/
     END;
```

■**Tip** You only need the execute privilege on the DBMS_FGA package in order to use FGA. When you use the DBMS_FGA package, the audit records don't go into the standard audit table, the SYS.AUD$ table, even when you turn on the database audit trail. The audit records go into a special table called sys.fga_aud$.

Viewing the Audit Trail

The DBA_FGA_AUDIT_TRAIL view shows you the audit trail (stored in the sys.fga_aud$ table) when you use FGA in your database. It provides fine-grained audit information, such as the time stamp, database user ID, object name, and actual SQL text used in the statement flagged by your FGA policy. Here's an example:

```
SQL> SELECT timestamp,
         db_user,
         os_user,
         object_schema,
         object_name,
         sql_text
     FROM dba_fga_audit_trail;
```

The standard audit trail in Oracle databases is also called DBA_AUDIT_TRAIL and the FGA audit trail is called DBA_FGA_AUDIT_TRAIL. If you wish, you can view both types of auditing in the new DBA_COMMON_AUDIT_TRAIL view, which combines both regular and FGA audit trails.

■**Note** Always try to keep your audit options to the minimum necessary to meet your auditing objectives. As a DBA, you should keep a close watch on the System tablespace and the SYS.AUD$ table when auditing is turned on. If the SYS.AUD$ table gets full, further connections and DML activity in the database might come to a standstill. You may want to archive and purge the records from the SYS.AUD$ table periodically.

Authenticating Users

Database authentication refers to the authentication of the user account and password directly by Oracle. However, although database authentication is easy to set up, it isn't the only or the best means of authenticating Oracle users. You have a choice of several ways of authenticating database users—ways that aren't dependent on the database.

The following section covers the most common means of Oracle user authentication, which is to authenticate users through the database. After this, I briefly discuss some other means of user authentication—external, proxy, and centralized user authentication.

Database Authentication

Database authentication is the standard verification of a user's access privileges by using database passwords. If you're relying on the database to authenticate your users, you should have a strong password-management policy.

Here's an example of database authentication:

```
SQL> CREATE USER scott IDENTIFIED BY tiger;
```

Managing Passwords

Depending on how you create a database (manually or using the DBCA), Oracle will have several accounts with default passwords. If you create a tablespace manually, you may only have SYS, SYSTEM, DBSNMP (the Oracle Intelligent Agent account), and OUTLN (the username for managing the outlines feature). In some cases, the user scott (owner of the old Oracle demo database schema) is also created with the default password of "tiger." A standard database created by the DBCA may have up to 32 default user accounts.

As part of securing the database, you must use all the standard password-management techniques, including changing passwords at set intervals, checking passwords for complexity, and preventing reuse of old passwords.

Let's see how Oracle creates the default user accounts in a new database. The query in Listing 12-18 lists all the usernames and their status. An account may be open or it may be locked or expired. An *open* account is one you can log into, as long as you have a valid password. A *locked* account must be explicitly unlocked by the DBA. A locked regular account usually results from the user trying to enter the database with an incorrect password more times than the specified limit allows. An *expired* account is one whose password has to be changed, which ensures that the same passwords aren't used forever.

Listing 12-18. *Displaying the Account Status of All Users*

```
SQL> SELECT username, account_status
  2  FROM dba_users;

USERNAME                  ACCOUNT_STATUS
----------                ---------------
MGMT_VIEW                            OPEN
SYS                                  OPEN
SYSTEM                               OPEN
DBSNMP                               OPEN
SYSMAN                               OPEN
SCOTT                                OPEN
OUTLN                     EXPIRED & LOCKED
HR                        EXPIRED & LOCKED
. . .
32 rows selected
SQL>
```

The DBA must change the passwords for all default user accounts immediately after the database has been created. Any unnecessary default accounts must be locked and expired.

Password Case Sensitivity

By default, all passwords are case sensitive in Oracle Database 11*g*. The initialization parameter SEC_CASE_SENSITIVE_LOGON controls whether passwords are case sensitive or not. The default value of this parameter is true, which means all passwords are case sensitive by default. If, for some reason, say because some of your applications use hard-coded passwords that require that passwords not be case insensitive, you can instruct the database to disregard case when evaluating passwords, by setting the SEC_CASE_SENSITIVE_LOGON parameter to false, as shown here:

```
sec_case_sensitive_logon=false
```

When you upgrade a pre–Oracle Database 11*g* release database to Oracle Database 11*g*, the passwords remain case insensitive, because that was the behavior in those releases. You must use the ALTER USER statement to change the password of each user, in order to make them case sensitive.

When you upgrade to Oracle Database 11*g*, passwords remain case insensitive until you change the passwords, If you leave the SEC_CASE_SENSITIVE_LOGON parameter at its default value of true, all new passwords will be case sensitive, just as in a newly created Oracle Database 11*g* release database. You can execute the following query in a newly upgraded database to find out in which release a user's password was set or changed.

```
SQL> SELECT username, password, password_versions
     FROM dba_users;

USERNAME                PASSWORD    PASSWORD
-------------------     ---------   --------
MGMT_VIEW                           10G 11G
SYS                                 10G 11G
SYSTEM                              10G 11G
DBSNMP                              10G 11G
SYSMAN                              10G 11G
RMAN                                10G 11G
SH                                  10G 11G
. . .
39 rows selected.
SQL>
```

The column PASSWORD_VERSIONS reveals the database version in which a password was initially set or modified. The output of the query shows that all passwords were either created or changed in the Oracle Database 11g release database. You can't see the (encrypted) passwords in this query as you could in prior releases, but the encrypted passwords are available through the USER$ view.

When a user tries and fails to connect with a wrong password, the database will increase the time between successive attempts after the third failed attempt, for a maximum of 10 seconds.

Secure Password Support

In addition to making all passwords case sensitive by default, Oracle also provides other features to provide secure password support. These features include the passing of all passwords entered by users through the strong hash algorithm (SHA-1, which uses a 160-bit key) and comparing it with the stored credentials for that user, as well as making all passwords use salt, which is a unique random value that's added to the passwords to ensure that the output credentials are unique.

Locking Accounts

Any user account that is locked can be unlocked for free access with the following statement:

```
SQL> ALTER USER hr ACCOUNT UNLOCK;
User altered.
SQL>
```

You can make Oracle lock any account after a certain number of failed login attempts with the CREATE or ALTER PROFILE statement. Oracle lets you specify how long you want the account to be locked after making the specified login attempts to enter the database; after that time is reached, Oracle will *automatically* unlock the account. To close this loophole, simply set the locked time period to UNLIMITED.

Here's an example of creating a profile with the time period for locking the account:

```
SQL> CREATE PROFILE test_profile
  2  LIMIT FAILED_LOGIN_ATTEMPTS 5
  3* PASSWORD_LOCK_TIME UNLIMITED
Profile created.
SQL>
```

The database will lock an account once the `FAILED_LOGIN_ATTEMPTS` limit is reached. However, the DBA can unlock a user's account at any time by using the following command:

```
SQL> ALTER USER hr ACCOUNT UNLOCK;
User altered.
SQL>
```

Password Expiration

Password aging policies, which ensure that users don't hang onto the same password for a long time, are a standard part of database security. Once a password expires, the user is forced to change it.

You can make a password expire with the `ALTER USER` command, as shown here:

```
SQL> ALTER USER hr IDENTIFIED BY hr PASSWORD EXPIRE;
User altered.
SQL>
```

You can also make a password expire with the `ALTER PROFILE` command:

```
SQL> ALTER PROFILE test_profile
  2* LIMIT PASSWORD_LIFE_TIME 30;
Profile altered.

SQL> ALTER USER hr PROFILE test_profile;
User altered.
SQL>
```

The preceding `ALTER PROFILE` statement limits the password life to 30 days, and you can gently remind the user about this by using another clause in your `ALTER PROFILE` statement, `PASSWORD_GRACE_TIME`. Once you set the `PASSWORD_GRACE_TIME` clause as shown here, the first time the user logs in after the end of the password lifetime, the user will receive a warning that the password is about to expire in three days. If the user doesn't change the password within the grace period of three days, the password will expire. After the user's password expires, the password must be changed:

```
SQL> CONNECT hr/hr
ERROR:
ORA-28001: the password has expired
Changing password for hr
New password: **
Retype new password: **
Password changed
Connected.
SQL>
```

The Password File

Oracle will let you choose how you want your privileged users to connect to the database. *Privileged users* are those users who can perform tasks such as starting up and shutting down the database. By default, only the SYS user has the SYSDBA and SYSOPER privileges, both of which are considered high-level privileges. The SYS user can grant these privileges to other users.

Of course, any DBA who knows the SYS password can log in as SYS and perform the privileged tasks. However, by granting the critical privileges SYSDBA and SYSOPER explicitly to users, you force them to provide their username and password, which makes it easy to track the actions of privileged users. The `REMOTE_LOGIN_PASSWORDFILE` initialization parameter specifies whether Oracle checks for a password file.

The REMOTE_LOGIN_PASSWORDFILE parameter can take the following values:

- none: No password file is used, and the database permits only operating system–authenticated users to perform privileged database administration tasks.

- exclusive: Only a single database can use the password file. The file can contain both SYS and non-SYS users.

- shared: A password file is created that can be used by multiple databases. The password file includes both SYS and non-SYS users.

Oracle recommends that you use the REMOTE_LOGIN_PASSWORDFILE=SHARED option for the highest degree of security. There is a way to manually create a password file and specify which users can have the SYSDBA and SYSOPER privileges, but if you use the EXCLUSIVE option, Oracle will automatically add users to the password file upon their being granted the SYSDBA and SYSOPER privileges. You can use the V$PWFILE_USERS view to see who has been granted these privileges besides the default SYS user by using the following query:

```
SQL> CONNECT sys/life1 AS SYSDBA;
Connected.

SQL> GRANT sysoper, sysdba TO tester;
Grant succeeded.

SQL> SELECT * FROM v$pwfile_users;
USERNAME      SYSDB      SYSOP
--------      -----      -----
SYS           TRUE       TRUE
TESTER        TRUE       TRUE
SQL>
```

You use the orapwd command to create a new password file. The following output shows the possible values you can supply with the orapwd command and also which of them are required and which are optional.

```
$ orapwd
Usage: orapwd file=<fname> password=<password> entries=<users> force=<y/n>
ignorecase=<y/n> nosysdba=<y/n>

  where
    file - name of password file (required),
    password - password for SYS (optional),
    entries - maximum number of distinct DBA (required),
    force - whether to overwrite existing file (optional),
    ignorecase - passwords are case-insensitive (optional),
    nosysdba - whether to shut out the SYSDBA logon (optional Database Vault onl
y).

  There must be no spaces around the equal-to (=) character.
S
```

The following command creates a new password file called testpwd:

```
$ orapwd FILE=testpwd PASSWORD=remorse1 ENTRIES=20
```

Encrypted Passwords

By default, Oracle user passwords aren't encrypted, and this leaves them vulnerable to unauthorized use. By setting the following environment variables, one on the client and the other on the server, you can ensure that Oracle will always encrypt a password when it's sending it across a network.

Set this one on the client:

```
ora_encrypt_login=true
```

And set this one on the server:

```
dblink_encrypt_login=true
```

■**Note** All passwords are always automatically encrypted during network connections, using a modified Data Encryption Standard (DES) algorithm.

External Authentication

Another method of authenticating database users is the external authentication method, under which you match the user accounts at the operating system level with the usernames in the database. Oracle manages the user's privileges in the database itself, but the user authentication is performed by the operating system, which is external to the database. The advantage to this method is that you'll need only a single username for both the operating system and database connections. This can also help in auditing user actions, as the database names and operating system accounts correspond.

To use operating system authentication, you first have to set the OS_AUTHENT_PREFIX configuration parameter in the init.ora file as follows:

```
OS_AUTHENT_PREFIX = ""
```

There shouldn't be a space between the pair of quotes.

■**Note** The default value for the OS_AUTHENT_PREFIX parameter is "OPS$", but that is only for maintaining backward compatibility.

When you start the database again, you can start using external authentication based on the underlying operating system. To enable operating system authentication, this is how you need to create your users:

```
SQL> CREATE USER salapati IDENTIFIED EXTERNALLY;
User created.
SQL>
```

Note that the new user isn't given a password—the user doesn't need one. As long as the user can log into the operating system, all he or she will have to do is type the following command to log into the database:

```
$ sqlplus /
```

■Note The well-known Oracle OPS$ORACLE database account is a simple variation on the preceding example of external authentication. OPS$ is a prefix Oracle has used since the Oracle 5 version. You can use any prefix or no prefix at all for operating system external authentication.

The external operating system authentication described in this section doesn't allow users to connect over Oracle Net, because that authentication method isn't considered very secure. Therefore, shared server configurations that use Oracle Net can't, by default, use operating system external authentication. To override this default behavior, you have to set the following parameter in your init.ora file:

```
REMOTE_OS_AUTHENT=TRUE
```

Proxy Authentication

You can use proxy authentication to allow a single, persistent database session to switch identity to other users without having to logon/logoff all the time. You can use several middle-tier products to facilitate user interaction with the Oracle database. A web server is often used as the middle or application layer connecting the clients to the database. You can choose to have the middle tier authenticate your users, or you can have the middle tier pass the username and password to the database for authentication.

Here is an example showing how to authorize connections by a database user logging on from a middle-tier node, using password authentication.

```
SQL> ALTER USER salapati
  2   GRANT CONNECT THROUGH appserv
  3*  AUTHENTICATED USING PASSWORD;
User altered.
SQL>
```

The following example shows how you can allow a persistent session logged on as appserv to take on temporarily the identity of salapati, if the persistent session provides user salapati's password.

```
SQL> ALTER USER salapati
  2*  GRANT CONNECT THROUGH appserv;
User altered.
SQL>
```

Centralized User Authorization

If you use the Oracle Advanced Security option, you can use a Lightweight Directory Access Protocol (LDAP)–based directory service, such as Oracle Internet Directory (OID), to perform user authentication. The directory-based service lets you create enterprise users who can be granted global roles. Centralized user management enables the use of a *single sign-on*—that is, users need only sign in once to access all the databases they need to use.

Because Oracle Advanced Security isn't used by every database, I don't provide a detailed explanation of the implementation of centralized user authorization. Please refer to the Oracle manual *Oracle Advanced Security Administrator's Guide*, available on the http://tahiti.oracle.com web site, for a detailed explanation of this feature.

Enterprise User Security

Large organizations these days have both internal and Web-based applications to manage. It quickly becomes an administrative nightmare to manage users and their privileges on all these different applications. Centralized directories are increasingly being seen as the best way to manage multiple systems within an organization.

LDAP is a popular industry standard, and Oracle has its own implementation of it. Information that has been managed in multiple systems and formats can be brought under one umbrella using a directory service like LDAP. You can replace all your `tnsnames.ora` files on clients and manage user connectivity, authorization, and security with the help of the LDAP directory services. The LDAP directory can provide solid password policy management, data privacy, data integrity, and strong authentication and authorization protocols.

Shared Schemas

When users are registered and maintained in an LDAP repository, they are referred to as *shared schemas* or *schema-independent users*. When an LDAP-registered user connects to a specific database, the database will ask the LDAP server for confirmation of the user's identity and the roles that should be assigned to the user upon connection. Thus, in a database with several hundred users for a certain application, you need to create only one schema to manage the application. The individual user will be registered in the centralized directory, and when the user connects to the database, he or she will be assigned this common schema.

Single Sign-On

If you use the Oracle Application Server, you can take advantage of the Single Sign-On feature, so a user need only log into the system once. Once the user is authenticated, he or she can access all the other applications on the system without having to enter a name and password repeatedly. This automatic authentication is very helpful to system administrators and other key users of systems in an organization.

Data Encryption

Sometimes you may want to *encrypt* data (encode it so only users who are authorized can understand it). Oracle supports encryption of network data through its Advanced Security option. For encryption of data, Oracle provides two PL/SQL packages, the older of which is the DBMS_OBFUSCATION_TOOLKIT package. This package enables data encryption by using the DES algorithm. The toolkit supports triple DES encryption for the highest level of security. It also supports the use of the MD5 secure cryptographic hash.

You can also use the newer PL/SQL encryption package called DBMS_CRYPTO to encrypt and decrypt data. Compared to DBMS_OBFUSCATION_TOOLKIT, DBMS_CRYPTO provides a wider range of advanced security encryption and cryptographic algorithms and is easier to use. Oracle intends this package to replace the older DBMS_OBFUSCATION_TOOLKIT package. Whichever Oracle PL/SQL package you use, you have to manage the data encryption keys, which isn't a trivial task. You often have to create views to help you decrypt the encrypted data, which adds to the management tasks. In addition, you can't index the encrypted data according to Oracle's recommendations, which reduces the value of both of these encryption packages in several cases.

There is also a third, easier option: encrypting data with the transparent data encryption feature. The next section shows you how to easily encrypt Oracle table data using an Oracle Wallet to store encryption keys. You can index the encrypted table's columns as well, thus overcoming one of the biggest drawbacks in using the Oracle encryption packages.

Transparent Data Encryption

Even with all kinds of access control mechanisms in place, you may ultimately come to the realization that your data is physically stored on a disk drive or tape somewhere, making it vulnerable to unauthorized access. You often come across situations where certain key column values in a table need to be encrypted to provide security. You can use the *transparent data encryption* feature to encrypt a column. Transparent data encryption means that the database will handle encryption and decryption automatically, without the user or the application having to manage the encryption key. This means the application no longer needs to handle the cumbersome process of managing the encryption key.

For example, when you create a table, you can simply specify the ENCRYPT keyword along with the column name, as shown in the following example. This statement creates a table that converts the ssn column values into an encrypted data format when they are stored on disk:

```
SQL> CREATE TABLE employees (
     empno      NUMBER(5) PRIMARY KEY
     ename      VARCHAR2(15) NOT NULL,
     ssn        NUMBER(9) ENCRYPT,
. . .
```

The ENCRYPT keyword in the preceding example specifies that the ssn (Social Security number) be encrypted. Once you do this, even if unauthorized users gain access to the data on your storage devices, they can't read the data, since it's encrypted. When authorized users access data, however, the encrypted data is automatically decrypted, and the decryption process is transparent to the user.

An Oracle Wallet is used to store authentication and signing credentials, including private keys and certificates. Before you can start encrypting or decrypting a table, the encryption key is retrieved from the Oracle Wallet and stored in the SGA.

■**Note** In addition to regular database tables, you can also encrypt external tables using the transparent data encryption feature.

In the following sections, I provide a brief introduction to this new Oracle feature, which lets you encrypt one or more of a table's columns when you create the table, or even later on. Here are the steps you need to follow in order to use the transparent data encryption feature:

1. Create an Oracle Wallet.

2. Open the Oracle Wallet.

3. Generate the master encryption key that will be used to encrypt the column's encryption key.

4. Specify exactly how you want the encrypted column to be encrypted.

■**Note** Data decryption is automatic when an authorized user accesses an encrypted column. You don't need to create any views to decrypt the data. As with encryption, the database will load the master and the data encryption keys into the SGA from the Oracle Wallet prior to decrypting data.

Creating the Oracle Wallet with OWM

You create the Oracle Wallet using the Oracle Wallet Manager (OWM). Follow these steps:

1. Start up the Oracle Wallet Manager by typing **owm** at the operating system prompt in a UNIX/Linux system. On a Windows server, select Start ➤ Programs ➤ Oracle ➤ Configuration and Management Tools ➤ Integration Management Tools ➤ Oracle Wallet Manager. Figure 12-1 shows the opening window of the Oracle Wallet Manager.

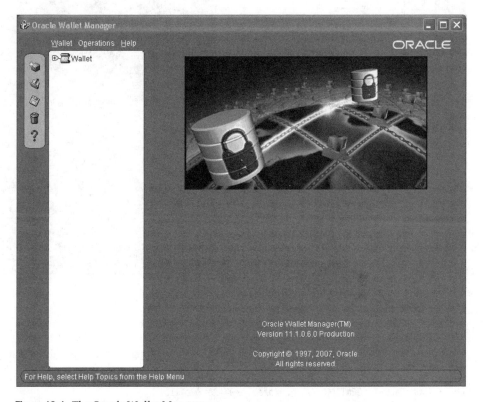

Figure 12-1. *The Oracle Wallet Manager*

2. At the top left of the Oracle Wallet Manager window, click the Wallet menu and choose the New option. If you don't already have a default directory enabled to create the wallet in, the Oracle Wallet Manager will ask if you want to create one. You can choose to create the Oracle Wallet in the default directory, or choose any other directory you wish.

3. A box will open in which you can enter a password for wallet management. This is the same password that you'll use later in SQL*Plus to open the Oracle Wallet and to create and alter the master encryption key. You can also select the wallet type; to keep things simple for now, just choose the default wallet type, which is STANDARD. Click OK.

4. A new empty Oracle Wallet is created, and you're asked if you wish to create a certificate at this time. Click No.

Figure 12-2 shows that your Oracle Wallet is created, without any certificates. You can add Trusted Certificates later on, if you wish. For our examples, you won't need them.

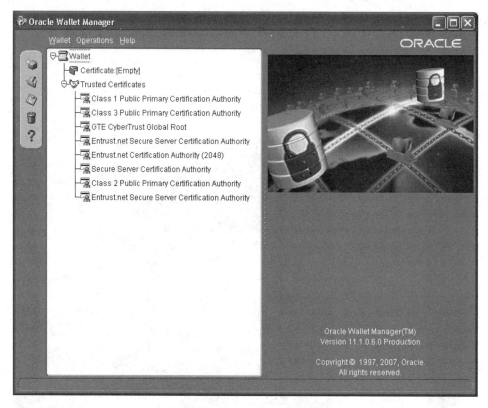

Figure 12-2. *A newly created Oracle Wallet*

The encryption keys are stored in the Oracle Wallet, whose location is specified in the `sqlnet.ora` configuration file. Once you successfully create your new Oracle Wallet, go the `$ORACLE_HOME/network/admin` directory and add the following line to the `sqlnet.ora` file (making sure it points to the directory you chose previously):

```
ENCRYPTION_WALLET_LOCATION = '/etc/oracle/wallet/oracle'
```

Now you're ready to use your Oracle Wallet to encrypt your table columns.

Opening and Closing the Oracle Wallet

Before you can use the transparent data encryption feature to encrypt a column, you must open the Oracle Wallet, since it is closed after you create it. Here's how you open the Oracle Wallet:

```
SQL> ALTER SYSTEM SET ENCRYPTION WALLET OPEN IDENTIFIED BY "password";
System altered.
SQL>
```

Note that the password is whatever you specified when you created the Oracle Wallet. Make sure you enclose it in double quotes.

The Oracle Wallet you opened can be closed in two ways:

- Use the `ALTER SYSTEM SET ENCRYPTION WALLET CLOSE` statement.

- Shut down the database—the wallet will be closed automatically.

Once a wallet is closed, you have to open it again before you use it by using the ALTER SYSTEM SET ENCRYPTION WALLET OPEN statement again. You don't have to open the wallet manually every time, if you use an auto-login wallet (set in the Oracle Wallet Manager). The auto-login wallet is opened when the user that created it logs in. It stays in effect until that user logs off.

Generating the Master Encryption Key

Even if an unauthorized user gains access to the stored table data, the encrypted data in the key columns you encrypted will thwart the user from understanding what's there. Regardless of the number of columns you encrypt in your database, you use a single encryption key for each table. You can change this key if you wish, and the keys for each encrypted table are stored in the data dictionary after they are encrypted by the master key of the database.

The master key's function is to protect the data encryption keys. The data encryption keys are automatically generated when you use the transparent data encryption feature (by using the ENCRYPT keyword), but you have to manually generate the master key to actually encrypt the table columns. Here's how you create the master encryption key:

```
SQL> ALTER SYSTEM SET ENCRYPTION KEY IDENTIFIED BY "password";
System altered.
SQL>
```

Again, you provide your Oracle Wallet password, as in the previous example.

If you ever think the master key has been compromised, you can regenerate a new key by using the same statement. Each time you do so, a new master key is generated by the database.

Encrypting the Table Columns

Now that you've created the master encryption key, you can start encrypting your table data by using the ENCRYPT keyword after the name of the column you want to encrypt.

First, let's look at how to encrypt a column while creating the table. In the following example, the ssn column in the employees table is encrypted:

```
SQL> CREATE TABLE EMPLOYEES
     first_name      VARCHAR2(30),
     last_name       VARCHAR2(30),
     emp_id          NUMBER (9),
     salary          NUMBER(6),
     ssn             NUMBER(9) ENCRYPT;

Table created.
SQL>
```

Table creation is not the only time you can encrypt a table's columns. You can also encrypt a column in an existing table by using the ALTER TABLE statement. Let's add a new column, ENCRYPT_ID, to the employees table:

```
SQL> ALTER TABLE EMPLOYEES ADD (ENCRYPT_ID NUMBER(9) ENCRYPT);
Table altered.
SQL>
```

You can also encrypt an existing column in a table, as shown here:

```
SQL> ALTER TABLE EMPLOYEES MODIFY (EMP_ID ENCRYPT);
Table altered.
SQL>
```

If you check the employees table now, you'll find that the ssn, encrypt_id, and emp_id columns are all encrypted:

```
SQL> DESCRIBE employees

NAME              NULL?         TYPE
------------      -------       -----------------
FIRST_NAME                      VARCHAR2(30)
LAST_NAME                       VARCHAR2(30)
EMP_ID                          NUMBER(9) ENCRYPT
SALARY                          NUMBER(6)
SSN                             NUMBER(9) ENCRYPT
ENCRYPT_ID                      NUMBER(9) ENCRYPT
SQL>
```

Note that encrypting data will result in a performance hit, especially when users are selecting or inserting data. If you decide you want to turn off encryption for any reason, you can do so by using the DECRYPT keyword, as shown here:

```
SQL> ALTER TABLE employees MODIFY (ssn DECRYPT);
```

Encryption Algorithms

The encrypted columns in the employees table use the default encryption algorithm. This default encryption algorithm uses *salt*, which involves adding a random string to data before it's encrypted, thus making it harder for someone to match patterns in the text.

As mentioned earlier, you can index transparently encrypted columns, but Oracle recommends that you not use salt if you plan on using indexes on the encrypted columns. If you don't wish to use salt, specify the ENCRYPT NO SALT option when you encrypt a column. Similarly, if you wish to use a nondefault encryption algorithm, you can do so by specifying the algorithm when you encrypt the column, as shown in the following example, where the 3DES168 algorithm is used:

```
ssn NUMBER(9) ENCRYPT USING '3DES168'
```

Tablespace Encryption

You can use the DBMS_OBFUSCATION_TOOLKIT and the DBMS_CRYPTO packages provided by Oracle to implement encryption of data. Both these packages, however, impose a burden on you in the sense that your application must manage the encryption keys as well as call the APIs to encrypt and decrypt the data. To overcome these drawbacks, Oracle Database 10*g* introduced Transparent Data Encryption (TDE), which enabled you to encrypt columns in a table. The feature is called "transparent" because the database takes care of all the encryption and decryption details.

In Oracle Database 11*g*, you can also encrypt an entire tablespace. In fact, tablespace encryption helps you get around some of the restrictions imposed on encrypting a column in a table through the TDE feature. For example, you can get around the restriction that makes it impossible for you to encrypt a column that's part of a foreign key or that's used in another constraint, by using tablespace encryption.

Restrictions on Tablespace Encryption

You must be aware of the following restrictions on encrypting tablespaces. You

- Can't encrypt a temporary or an undo tablespace.
- Can't change the security key of an encrypted tablespace.
- Can't encrypt an external table.

As with TDE, you need to create an Oracle Wallet to implement tablespace encryption. Therefore, let's first create an Oracle Wallet before exploring how to encrypt a tablespace.

Creating the Oracle Wallet

Tablespace encryption uses Oracle Wallets to store the encryption master keys. Oracle Wallets could be either encryption wallets or auto-open wallets. When you start the database, the auto-open wallet opens automatically, but you must open the encryption wallet yourself. Oracle recommends that you use an encryption wallet for tablespace encryption, unless you're dealing with a Data Guard setup, where it's better to use the auto-open wallet.

Earlier in this chapter, I showed you how to create an Oracle Wallet by using the OWM. However, you can also create an Oracle Wallet through the `mkstore` command at the operating system level or through executing a special SQL*Plus command.

Here's an example showing how to use the `mkstore` command from the operating system command line to create an Oracle Wallet:

```
$ mkstore -wrl $ORACLE_BASE/admin/$ORACLE_SID/wallet -create
Enter password:******
Enter password again:******
```

You can also create the wallet easily by executing the following command in SQL*Plus:

```
SQL> alter system set encryption key identified by "password"
```

The previous command creates an Oracle Wallet if there isn't one already and adds a master key to that wallet.

By default, Oracle stores the Oracle Wallet, which is simply an operating system file named `ewallet.p12`, in an operating system–determined location. You can, however, specify a location for the file by setting the parameter `encryption_wallet_location` in the `sqlnet.ora` file, as shown here:

```
ENCRYPTION_WALLET_LOCATION =
 (SOURCE=
   (METHOD=file)
   (METHOD_DATA=
      (DIRECTORY=/apps/oracle/general/wallet)     )  )
```

You must first create a directory named `wallet` under the `$ORACLE_BASE/admin/$ORACLE_SID` directory. Otherwise, you'll get an error when creating the wallet:

```
ORA-28368: cannot auto-create wallet
```

Once you create the directory named `wallet`, issue the following command to create the Oracle Wallet:

```
SQL> ALTER SYSTEM SET ENCRYPTION KEY IDENTIFIED BY "sammyy11";

System altered.
SQL>
```

The `ALTER SYSTEM` command shown here will create a new Oracle Wallet if you don't have one. It also opens the wallet and creates a master encryption key. If you have an Oracle Wallet, the command opens the wallet and re-creates the master encryption key.

Once you've created the Oracle Wallet, you can encrypt your tablespaces, as I explain in the following section.

Creating an Encrypted Tablespace

The following example shows how to encrypt a tablespace:

```
SQL> CREATE TABLESPACE tbsp1
     DATAFILE '/u01/app/oracle/test/tbsp1_01.dbf' SIZE 500m
     ENCRYPTION
     DEFAULT STORAGE (ENCRYPT);

Tablespace created.
SQL>
```

The storage clause ENCRYPT tells the database to encrypt the new tablespace. The clause ENCRYPTION tells the database to use the default encryption algorithm, DES128. You can specify an alternate algorithm such as 3DES168, AES128, or AES256 through the clause USING, which you specify right after the ENCRYPTION clause. Since I chose the default encryption algorithm, I didn't use the USING clause here.

The following example shows how to specify the optional USING clause, to define a nondefault encryption algorithm.

```
SQL> CREATE TABLESPACE mytbsp2
     DATAFILE '/u01/app/oracle/test/mytbsp2_01.dbf' size 500m
     ENCRYPTION USING '3DES168'
     DEFAULT STORAGE (ENCRYPT);

Tablespace created.

SQL>
```

The example shown here creates an encrypted tablespace, MYTBSP2, that uses the 3DES168 encryption algorithm instead of the default algorithm.

You can check whether a tablespace is encrypted by querying the DBA_TABLESPACES view, as shown here:

```
SQL> SELECT tablespace_name, encrypted
  2  FROM dba_tablespaces;

TABLESPACE_NAME                      ENC
---------------                      ----
SYSTEM                               NO
SYSAUX                               NO
UNDOTBS1                             NO
TEMP                                 NO
USERS                                NO
MYTBSP1                              YES
MYTBSP2                              YES
7 rows selected.

SQL>
```

The database automatically encrypts data during the writes and decrypts it during reads. Since both encryption and decryption aren't performed in memory, there's no additional memory requirement. There is, however, a small additional I/O overhead. The data in the undo segments and the redo log will keep the encrypted data in the encrypted form. When you perform operations such as a sort or a join operation that use the temporary tablespace, the encrypted data remains encrypted in the temporary tablespace.

Oracle Internet Directory

In Chapter 11, I briefly explained the Oracle Internet Directory (OID). Using the OID, you can perform effective security management, including enforcing strict password policies for security management. OID also helps you maintain a single, global identity for each user across the application environment, and helps you centrally store user credentials.

Database Security Dos and Don'ts

A common misunderstanding among DBAs is that once the database is behind a firewall, it's immune to security attacks. This presupposes, of course, that your security threats are always external, when real-life statistics point out that the majority of security violations are from insiders. That's why you have to follow a rock-solid authentication policy and sound data-access policies.

You can take several basic steps to enhance the security of your Oracle database. Most of these steps are based on common sense and prohibit easy entry into the database through well-known backdoor access points. Let's quickly review these security guidelines.

Automatic Secure Configuration

As I mentioned in Chapter 6, when you create a new database using the DBCA, you can choose to implement automatic secure configuration for your database. By making the choice to use the new Oracle Database 11g secure configuration settings, you enable the following security-related features in your new database:

- *Password-specific security settings*: The database will enforce password expiration and other password-related security policies that enforce built-in complexity checking in the default password profile that you assign to users.

- *Auditing*: The database enables auditing for certain privileges by default. These privileges are considered crucial to database security, such as connecting to a database. The database stores the audit records in the AUD$ table by default and sets the audit_trail initialization parameter to the value db.

Adoption of the automatic secure configuration feature ensures that your database conforms to the security features recommended by the Center for Internet Security (CIS) benchmarks.

User Accounts

Oracle recommends that you lock *and* expire all default user accounts except, of course, the SYS and SYSTEM accounts, and other user accounts that you'll need, like DBSNMP, SYSMAN, and MGMT_VIEW. The number of default accounts depends on the number of database features and components you use and how you create your database. For example, creating a database with the help of the DBCA usually results in the creation of a larger number of default accounts than you'll find in a manually created database.

Passwords

You mustn't hard-code Oracle user passwords in shell scripts. Otherwise, your user passwords can be gleaned by using a simple ps -ef | grep command while the process is running.

Change the passwords for all default user accounts immediately after creating the database. You should set passwords for the SYS and SYSTEM users while creating the database, although this isn't mandatory.

Use strict password aging and expiration policies, and force users to change passwords in a timely fashion. Use the FAILED_LOGIN_ATTEMPTS option when setting user profiles to limit unsuccessful login attempts to a reasonable number. Accounts should be locked indefinitely (which is the default behavior) if they hit the FAILED_LOGIN_ATTEMPTS ceiling. This way, the DBA will be the only one who can unlock these accounts. You can also use Oracle's password-complexity verification routine to make sure your users' passwords meet standard password-complexity requirements.

Operating System Authentication

Two initialization parameters enable access to an Oracle database through authentication at the operating system level. One is the well-known OS_AUTHENT_PREFIX parameter, which many people use to create the OPS$ account for use in shell scripts and other places. Of course, using the OPS$ account implies that you're relying on operating system authentication and security.

The other initialization parameter affecting operating system authentication of users is the REMOTE_OS_AUTHENT parameter, which enables users who authenticate themselves not on the server, but on a remote workstation, to gain access to your database. There may be an exceptional circumstance when you want to use this feature. In general, though, you should leave this parameter at its default value of false. Otherwise, a user from a remote system can log in using nonsecure protocols through the remote operating system authorization, and that's a serious violation of security standards. Perhaps more importantly, any user can create an account on his or her own computer with the same name as your externally identified database user.

Database Auditing

Check the audit trail for logins as SYSDBA to make sure that only authorized people are logging in as SYSDBA users. The audit trail also lets you see whether the database was brought up at any time with the auditing feature *disabled*.

You should audit all unsuccessful attempts to log into the database. In addition, you can audit all actions by any user connected as SYSDBA or SYSOPER. To enable auditing of all SYSDBA and SYSOPER operations, you need to set the following initialization parameter:

```
AUDIT_SYS_OPERATIONS=TRUE
```

Note Setting AUDIT_SYS_OPERATIONS=TRUE logs all SYSDBA and SYSOPER activity to an operating system audit trail, not a database audit trail. Thus, the audit trail can't be tampered with by users with powerful privileges within the database.

Granting Privileges

Oracle recommends strongly that you avoid granting ANY privileges, as in delete ANY table, to reduce your vulnerability. You can avoid this problem generally by refraining from (carelessly) granting object privileges *directly* to users. In addition, avoid granting privileges with the ADMIN privilege. The ADMIN privilege means that the user to whom you granted a privilege can grant the same privilege to other users in turn. This means that you, the DBA, can very quickly lose control over who is being granted privileges in your database.

Use *roles* rather than granting privileges directly to users. This will help you a lot on databases with a large user base, where it is hard to check which user has been granted which privilege if you have been granting them directly to the users.

PUBLIC is a *default role* for every user created in the database. Make sure you don't grant any unnecessary roles or privileges to PUBLIC, because every user will automatically inherit those roles and privileges, including default users such as DBSNMP and OUTLN.

The following query shows that PUBLIC has over 12,000 object-level privileges:

```
SQL> SELECT COUNT(*) FROM dba_tab_privs
  2  WHERE grantee='PUBLIC';

  COUNT(*)
  --------
   12814
SQL>
```

Of the more than 12,000 object privileges that have been granted to PUBLIC, over 100 are privileges to execute DBMS packages, such as DBMS_JOB, DBMS_METADATA, DBMS_SNAPSHOT, DBMS_DDL, DBMS_SPACE, and DBMS_OBFUSCATION_TOOLKIT. Revoke all important execution privileges from PUBLIC. Grant important privileges to users through the judicious use of roles.

The SYSDBA privilege gives a user very powerful privileges, including the ability to drop database objects and alter data dictionary tables. It goes without saying that you must hand out the SYSDBA privilege very sparingly.

Dealing with Environments with Multiple DBAs

If you're the only Oracle DBA in your organization, you must have all the system privileges to manage the database. However, if you have a group of Oracle DBAs managing a large number of databases, it's smart not to give everyone the same type of privileges (such as SYSDBA) and the same type of roles (such as DBA). You should create your own specialized roles, with each role containing a specific set of privileges for performing certain database tasks. Thus, a DBA in charge of helping the developers create new objects won't be able to perform certain recovery-related tasks, and vice versa. You can then assign these roles to the DBAs, ensuring that there is a clear demarcation of job duties.

Protecting the Data Dictionary

Users that are granted the ANY system privilege can drop data dictionary tables. To protect your data dictionary, you must set the 07_DICTIONARY_ACCESSIBILITY configuration parameter to FALSE in your parameter file. This will limit the ANY privilege to only those users who log in with the SYSDBA privilege.

Setting Permissions

Set the proper file permissions at the operating system level, as there often can be a security loophole at this level. The default permissions on a newly created file in most UNIX systems are rw-rw-rw. This means that any users who gain admission to the UNIX server can read or copy all files, including your database files. You should set the UMASK variable to 022, so only the Oracle username can read from and write to database files.

Ensure that you remove the SETUID on all Oracle files immediately. Some of the SETUID files may allow the execution of scripts as the root user in UNIX systems.

The UTL_FILE package enables writing to operating system files from within an Oracle PL/SQL program. When you use the UTL_FILE_DIR initialization parameter, never use the * value for the parameter, which means that the package could output files to any directory in the operating system's file system. Restrict the directories to some well-known locations that are exclusively set apart from the UTL_FILE output files.

Remove the PL/SQL EXTPROC functionality unless it is needed. First remove mentions to EXTPROC in both the listener.ora file on the server and the tnsnames.ora file on the client. You then can remove all EXTPROC executables from your $ORACLE_HOME/bin directory. There is usually a pair of executables called extproc and extproc0. The EXTPROC facility gives hackers a way to break into the operating system without any authentication. If you do need to use the EXTPROC functionality, refer to Note 175429.1 on Oracle's MetaLink site (http://metalink.oracle.com).

Make sure you don't allow ordinary users access to your export and import control files, because your passwords may appear in those files.

■**Note**   Peter Finnegan's Oracle security web site (http://www.petefinnigan.com) provides several interesting and useful Oracle security-related articles and scripts, including discussion about the detection of SQL injection and numerous other Oracle security issues. The comprehensive "Oracle Database Checklist" that's available on Finnegan's web site is used to audit Oracle database installations and pretty much covers all Oracle database security issues.

The Network and the Listener

The network and the listener service are vulnerable points of Oracle security—there are many ways you can inadvertently leave avenues open for attacks on your database. Let's first look at how you can strengthen the listener service.

Securing the Listener

As you learned in Chapter 11, you should always use a password for the listener to prevent unauthorized users from preventing connections to the database. Once you set a password for the listener, privileged actions such as shutting down or starting up the listener can't be performed unless you provide the right password.

You can also prevent a user from using the SET command to interfere with listener functions. To do this, you need to add the following line to your listener.ora configuration file:

```
ADMIN_RESTRICTIONS=ON
```

By default, this parameter is set to false. You should also avoid remote management of the listener service, as its password isn't encrypted over the network. The listener password is stored in the listener.ora file, so you must safeguard this file.

Securing the Network

One of the basic security requirements for today's Internet-based database applications is that you must have a firewall protecting your system from the external world. Once you have a firewall in place, keep it secure by not poking holes in it for any reason, such as by using the ports used by the listener to connect to the Internet.

In addition to having a normal firewall, you can use a feature of Oracle Net to add an additional layer of protection called *server-side access controls*. Server-side access controls limit the capability of an address to connect to your database using the listener service. There are two ways to limit the addresses through which connections can be made. You can list either the *invited* (accepted) address or the *excluded* addresses in the sqlnet.ora file. All network addresses in the invited list are allowed to connect, and all addresses in the excluded nodes list are denied access.

When the listener service starts, it reads the sqlnet.ora file and provides access according to the access controls you specified. Here are the additions that you need to make to your sqlnet.ora file to enforce server-side access controls if you are specifying the invited addresses:

```
tcp.validnode_checking = yes
tcp.invited_nodes = (server1.us.wowcompany.com,
172.14.16.152)
```

Here is what you need to add if you are excluding addresses:

```
tcp.excluded_nodes = (server1.us.wowcompany.com,
                      172.14.16.152)
```

■**Note** In general, because it's more likely that you know the addresses that are going to connect to your database, using the `TCP_INVITED_NODES` parameter may be the best way to limit access to your system.

Denying Remote Client Authentication

As you learned earlier in this chapter, letting remote clients authenticate logins is unsafe, and you should always let the server authenticate clients connecting to your database. You can turn client-based operating system authentication off by setting the following parameter in your `init.ora` file:

```
REMOTE_OS_AUTHENT=FALSE
```

The preceding setting will force server authentication of users, which is more secure than trusting the clients to perform operating system authentication.

Setting Security-Related Initialization Parameters

In addition to the `SEC_CASE_SENSITIVE_LOGON` initialization parameter, you can also use the following parameters to enforce database security:

- `sec_protocol_error_further_action`: Enables you to specify what the database must do (drop the connection or continue) when it receives bad network packets from clients, with the underlying presumption that those packets are being sent with malicious intent.

- `sec_protocal_error_trace_action`: Enables you to specify the kind of action to take in order to trace an error. For example, you may want to trace an error or send out an alert following an error.

- `sec_max_failed_login_attempts`: Lets you specify the maximum number of consecutive unsuccessful attempts a user can make and remains in force even if you choose not to enable a password profile for the user.

- `ldap_directory_sysauth`: Enables strong authentication (authentication that uses Kerberos tickets or certificates over a Secure Sockets Layer).

Fine-Grained Network Access Control

Network-related packages such as UTL_TCP, UTL_SMTP, UTL_MAIL, UTL_HTTP, and UTL_INADDR can create a security loophole, because the user PUBLIC has execute privileges on all these packages. A malicious user can easily break into a database through one of these packages. You can use Oracle's find-grained network access control feature to control a user's access to the database through external network services. For example, you can limit a user to access to databases from specific hosts.

You can use the DBMS_NETWORK_ACL_ADMIN and the DBMS_NETWORK_ACL_UTILITY packages to create what are called access control lists (ACLs). An access control list is a list of users and the privileges you grant to those users. You can manage ACLs through Oracle XML DB. The database stores the ACLs in the form of an XML document in the /sys/acl folder in Oracle XML DB.

Creating an Access Control List

Use the CREATE_ACL procedure of the DBMS_NETWORK_ADMIN package to create an ACL, as shown here:

```
SQL> begin
        dbms_network_acl_admin.create_acl (
        acl =>  'my_xml',
        description  => 'Permissions for my network',
        principal => 'APPOWNER',
        is_grant  => 'TRUE',
        privilege  =>  'connect');
      end;
SQL>
```

The following list describes the create_acl procedure parameters:

- acl: Specifies the name of the XML file holding the usernames and privileges in the ACL.

- prinicpal: Indicates the username and must match the username of the session.

- is_grant: Shows whether a privilege is granted or denied.

- privilege: Specifies the network privilege you want to grant or deny. You can specify either CONNECT or RESOLVE as the values for the privilege parameter. You must grant a user the CONNECT privilege if that user needs to connect to the database through any of the network-related PL/SQL packages such as UTL_MAIL, for example. The RESOLVE privilege helps resolve the host name when given the host IP address or vice versa, when using the UTL_INADDR package.

Once you create an ACL, you can add users or privileges to that ACL by executing the ADD_PRIVILEGE procedure as shown here:

```
SQL> begin
        dbms_network_acl_admin.add_privilege (
        acl            => 'test.xml',
        prinicpal      => 'test_users',
        is_grant       =>  true,
        privilege      => 'connect')
      end;
SQL>
```

If an ACL that you reference in the add_privilege procedure doesn't exist, the database creates it.

Assigning the Access Control List to a Host

Use the ASSIGN_ACL procedure to associate the ACL you just created with a network host, as shown here.

```
SQL> begin
        dbms_network_acl_admin.assign_acl (
        acl        => 'test.xml',
        host       => '*.us.mycompany.com',
        lower_port => 80,
        upper_port => null);
      end;
SQL>
```

You can assign ACLs to a host, domain, or IP subnet and optionally specify the TCP port range. When you execute the ASSIGN-ACL procedure, note the following:

- You may assign only a single ACL to each host, domain, or IP subnet.
- The database doesn't automatically drop an older ACL when you replace it with a new ACL. You have to execute the DROP_ACL procedure to drop the ACL.
- You may unassign a control list by executing the UNASSIGN_ACL procedure.

Precedence Order for a Host Computer

If you specify a wildcard character for the host name such as a *, the database assigns the control list to all hosts in the domain you specify. ACLs use the following order of precedence for evaluating host names:

- Fully qualified host names with ports
- Fully qualified host names
- Subdomains under a domain

In the same way, ACLs that you assign to an individual IP address are accorded precedence over ACLs assigned to subnets.

Checking the Privileges and Host Assignments

Use the CHECK_PRIVIELGE function to examine which privileges have been granted to a user in an ACL, as shown in the following example:

```
SQL> SELECT DECODE(dbms_network_acl_admin.check_privilege (
     test.xml', 'hr','resolve'),
     1, 'granted', 0, 'denied', null) privilege
     FROM DUAL;
```

The previous function execution will return 0 if a privilege was denied and 1 if the privilege was granted. It returns NULL if a privilege was neither granted nor denied.

MetaLink and Critical Patch Updates

An important part of security management is keeping up with the latest news about security vulnerabilities and the patches or workarounds to overcome them. Oracle has a policy of quickly issuing fixes for new security problems, so you should check for the latest security patches on the Oracle MetaLink web site (http://metalink.oracle.com).

   You can find regular Oracle security alerts at the following location: http://technet.oracle.com/ deploy/security/alerts.htm. You can also find news about security breaches on the MetaLink site in the "News & Notes" section. If you wish, Oracle will send you e-mail security alerts about new issues. You can sign up for this free service by registering at http://otn.oracle.com/deploy/ security/alerts.htm.

   Oracle provides Critical Patch Updates on a quarterly schedule, and Oracle's customers are notified of these updates via MetaLink, the OTN Security Alerts page, and the Oracle Security RSS newsfeed. If you're already a MetaLink subscriber, you are automatically signed up for the Critical Patch Updates. If a patch addresses a severe threat, Oracle will not wait for the quarterly Critical Patch Update to send the patch to you. In such cases, Oracle will issue an unscheduled Security Alert through MetaLink and will let you immediately download the patch. The patch will also be included in the next quarterly Critical Patch Update. For the most part, though, Critical Patch Updates will be the process by which most patches will be released by Oracle from now on.

   Critical Patch Updates are comprehensive patches that address significant security vulnerabilities and include fixes you can apply, prerequisites for the security fixes, or both. You can thus have a regular, planned quarterly schedule for patching your system. A single patch on a quarterly basis is better than a number of patches that need extensive testing and may conflict with each other.

Oracle has also introduced a new Risk Matrix along with its quarterly Critical Patch Updates. The Risk Matrix enables customers to estimate the scope and severity of the vulnerabilities addressed by each Critical Patch Update. The Risk Matrix tells you the threat you face to confidentiality, integrity, and availability, and the conditions under which your system is most exploitable. You can thus assess the risk to your system and prioritize patching on those systems.

Oracle's Advanced Security Option

Oracle doesn't require or recommend that you use its Advanced Security option to secure your Oracle databases. However, the Advanced Security option provides so many strong security features that you may want to consider using it if your business needs warrant the highest degree of data and network security. Here are some of the additional security features available when you use Oracle's Advanced Security option:

- Encryption of network traffic among clients, application servers, and databases
- Sophisticated authentication methods for users
- Centralized user management
- Support for Public Key Infrastructure (PKI)

Application Security

Although the security guidelines thus far have mostly dealt with preventing unauthorized access to your network and the database, it's extremely important that you review the application security policies to ensure no vulnerabilities exist there. There are some commonsense policies involving roles and SQL*Plus use that your organization must enforce to provide strong application security.

Granting Privileges Through Roles

You've already seen how you can use roles to encapsulate privileges rather than granting privileges directly to various users. You should minimize the number of direct object privileges by letting stored code such as procedures and packages be the means through which users can issue DML statements. Then you can just grant the user the privilege to execute a certain package or procedure to perform any DML actions. Once the package or procedure completes executing, the user will not have the privilege to perform the DML activity from outside the stored code.

Disabling Roles

All application roles should use the SET ROLE statement to enable the roles granted to users. Application users should be granted roles only for specific purposes, and the roles should be revoked from them when they aren't needed any longer.

Application owners should consider creating *secure application roles*, which are enabled by PL/SQL packages. Once you create and assign a secure application role to a user, it automatically gets assigned to the user when the user logs into the database.

Restricting SQL*Plus Usage

One of the first things you should do when opening your database to the public is to tightly restrict the ability of users to use the SQL*Plus interface. You can restrict the SQL*Plus capabilities of a user by using the product_user_profile table.

Useful Techniques for Managing Users

In this section you'll examine some simple scripts that can help you manage your users. You'll also learn about some typical problems that you might encounter in this area.

Altering Profiles

The following code shows how to alter a user's profile:

```
SQL> ALTER PROFILE fin_user
  2   LIMIT
  3   FAILED_LOGIN_ATTEMPTS 5
  4   PASSWORD_LOCK_TIME 1;

Profile altered.
SQL>
```

Listing User Information

You can use the DBA_USERS view to get quite a bit of information about the user population in your database. Here's a typical query using the DBA_USERS view:

```
SQL> SELECT username, profile, account, status
       FROM dba_users;
```

USERNAME	PROFILE	ACCOUNT_STATUS
SYS	DEFAULT	OPEN
SYSTEM	DEFAULT	OPEN
OUTLN	DEFAULT	OPEN
DBSNMP	DEFAULT	OPEN
HARTSTEIN	DEFAULT	OPEN
FINANCE	DEFAULT	OPEN

```
SQL>
```

Determining What SQL a User Is Currently Executing

You can use the query shown in Listing 12-19, which joins the V$SESSION and the V$SQLTEXT tables, to give you the text of the SQL currently being used by a user.

Listing 12-19. *Finding Out the SQL Being Executed by a User*

```
SQL> SELECT a.sid,a.username,
  2   s.sql_text
  3   FROM v$session a,v$sqltext s
  4   WHERE a.sql_address = s.address
  5   AND a.sql_hash_value = s.hash_value
  6   AND a.username LIKE 'HR%'
  7* ORDER BY a.username,a.sid,s.piece;
```

SID	USERNAME	SQL_TEXT
8	HR	BEGIN dbms_stats.gather_table_stats ('HR','REGIONS'); END;

```
SQL>
```

Logging In As a Different User

You may need to sometimes log in as another DBA to perform certain actions. However, even the Oracle DBA doesn't have access to users' passwords, which are stored in an encrypted form. You could use the ALTER USER statement to change the user's password, but you might not want to inconvenience the user by changing the password for good.

In a case like this, you can change the password of a user temporarily and use the new password to get in as that user. Before you change a user's password, get the original encrypted password, which you can use to reset the user's password back after you're done. You can get the encrypted password for all users from the USER$ view. Here's an example:

```
SQL> SELECT 'alter user tester identified by values '||password||';'
  2   FROM user$
  3* WHERE username='TESTER';

'ALTERUSERTESTERIDENTIFIEDBYVALUES'||';'
-------------------------------------------------------
alter user tester identified by values 1825ACAA229030F1;
SQL>
```

Now change the password of user tester so you can log in as that user:

```
SQL> ALTER USER tester IDENTIFIED BY newpassword;
```

When you're done using the tester user account, use the ALTER USER statement again to change user tester's password back to its original value. Make sure you enclose the encrypted password in single quotes.

```
SQL> ALTER USER tester IDENTIFIED BY VALUES '1825ACAA229030F1';
User altered.
SQL>
```

Killing a User's Session

You can use the ALTER SYSTEM command to kill any user's session. You need to first query the V$SESSION view for the values of the SID and serial number of the user. Then using the SID and serial number, you can kill the user's session. Here's an example:

```
SQL> SELECT sid, serial# FROM v$session
  2* WHERE username='SALAPATI';

       SID    SERIAL#
    ----------------
        10        32

SQL> ALTER SYSTEM KILL SESSION '10,32';

System altered.
SQL>
```

If the session you want to kill is involved in a long operation, such as a lengthy rollback, Oracle will inform you that the session is marked to be killed and kills the session once the operation completes. When Oracle kills a session, it rolls back all ongoing transactions and releases all session locks.

If the UNIX process of the user is killed, the Oracle session will most likely be killed also, but that isn't the most graceful way to end a session. If you think you must kill a user's UNIX session, and the Oracle KILL SESSION command isn't working, or it's taking a long time, you can terminate the session rather abruptly by using the UNIX `kill` command as follows. Note that you can use either the `kill` command by itself or with the -9 switch, but in most cases the simple `kill` command will be enough to terminate the UNIX session of your Oracle users:

```
$ kill 345678
```

or

```
$ kill -9 345678
```

You can use the following script to derive the process number from the V$SESSION dynamic view (and the SID and serial number as well):

```
SQL> SELECT process, sid, serial# FROM v$session
     WHERE username='&user';

Enter value for user: SALAPATI
old   2: username='&user'
new   2: username='SALAPATI'

PROCESS      SID    SERIAL#
---------    ----   -------
2920:2836    10     34
SQL>
```

Windows systems don't use the concept of processes, of course, but all user processes are threads of the same Oracle `.exe` process. In order to terminate an Oracle user's session on Windows, you can use the ORAKILL utility, which will kill a specific thread under the Oracle `.exe` process.

Suppose you wish to kill a user's session. How do you find out what that user's thread is? Listing 12-20 shows how you can use a simple query to identify any user's thread in a Windows system.

Listing 12-20. *Identifying a User's Thread in a Windows System*

```
SQL> SELECT sid, spid as thread, osuser, s.program
  2  FROM v$process p, v$session s
  3* WHERE p.addr = s.paddr;

        SID  THREAD   OSUSER           PROGRAM
-----------  ------   ------           -------------
          1  1192     SYSTEM           ORACLE.EXE
          2  1420     SYSTEM           ORACLE.EXE
          3  1524     SYSTEM           ORACLE.EXE
          4  1552     SYSTEM           ORACLE.EXE
          5  1528     SYSTEM           ORACLE.EXE
          6  1540     SYSTEM           ORACLE.EXE
          7  1580     SYSTEM           ORACLE.EXE
          8  1680     SYSTEM           ORACLE.EXE
          9  2948     NETBSA\SAlapati  sqlplusw.exe
         10  4072     NETBSA\SAlapati  sqlplusw.exe
10 rows selected.
SQL>
```

The script in Listing 12-20 will give you the thread numbers associated with each Oracle user. Once you have the thread numbers, you can kill the user's session by using the following command. Here's an example, assuming that the thread number is 2948:

```
C:> orakill 2948
```

This chapter covered a vast terrain, including creating users, granting privileges and roles, auditing the Oracle database, security mechanisms (including the virtual private database concept), authentication methods, and data encryption. For more details about Oracle's user management and security mechanisms, please refer to the *Oracle Database Security Guide* manual.

Data Loading, Backup, and Recovery

CHAPTER 13

■■■

Loading and Transforming Data

One of your most common tasks as a DBA is loading data from external sources. Although you normally do this when you first populate a database, you frequently need to load data into various tables throughout the life of a production database. Traditionally, DBAs have used the SQL*Loader utility to load data from flat files into the Oracle database tables.

Although SQL*Loader has always been an important tool for loading data into Oracle databases, Oracle also provides another way to load tables: using the external tables feature. External tables use SQL*Loader functionality and let you perform complex transformations on data before loading it into the database. Not only can you load data into your database, but you can also unload data into external files. You can then use these files to load data into other Oracle databases.

In many cases, especially in data warehouses, you need to transform the data you load. Oracle provides several means of performing data transformation within the database, including SQL and PL/SQL techniques. For example, the powerful MODEL clause enables you to create sophisticated multidimensional arrays and conduct complex interrow and interarray calculations using simple SQL.

Oracle provides a useful data replication feature called *Oracle Streams*, which lets you propagate changes from one database to another. You can use the Streams feature for various purposes, including the maintenance of a standby database.

This chapter covers all of these topics related to loading and transforming data. First, I'll give you an overview of the extraction, transformation, and loading process.

An Overview of Extraction, Transformation, and Loading

Before you can run your application on an Oracle database, you need to populate your database. One of the most common sources of database data is a set of flat files from legacy systems or some other source.

Traditionally, using the conventional or direct data load method with SQL*Loader was the only way to load this data from the external files into database tables. SQL*Loader is still technically the main Oracle-supplied utility to load data from external files, but you can also use the external tables feature, which employs the SQL*Loader tool to help you access data located in external datafiles.

Because the raw data may contain extraneous information or data in a different format from what your application needs, you frequently need to transform the data in some way before the database can use it. Transforming data is an especially common requirement for data warehouses, which extract their data from multiple sources. It's possible to do some preliminary or basic transformation of the raw data during the SQL*Loader run itself. However, more complex data transformation requires separate steps, and you have a choice of several techniques to manage the transformation process. Most warehouse data goes through three major steps before you can analyze the data: *extraction, transformation, loading* (ETL). These steps are defined as follows:

- *Extraction* is the identification and extraction of raw data, possibly in multiple formats, from several sources, not all of which may be relational databases.

- *Transformation* of data is the most challenging and time consuming of the three processes. Transformation of data may involve the application of complex rules to data. It may also include performing operations such as data aggregation and the application of functions to the raw data.

- *Loading* is the process of placing the data in the database tables. This may also include the task of maintaining indexes and constraints on the tables.

Traditionally, organizations have used two different methods of performing the ETL process: the *transform-then-load* method and the *load-then-transform* method. In the former method, the data is cleaned or transformed before it's loaded into Oracle tables. Custom-made ETL processes are usually used for the transformation of data. In the latter method of data cleansing, you aren't fully taking advantage of Oracle's built-in transformation capabilities in most cases. In the load-then-transform method, the raw data is first loaded into staging tables and moved to the final tables after the data transformation process is performed within the database itself. Intermediate staging tables are the key to the load-then-transform method. The drawback to this technique is that you must maintain multiple types of data in the table, some in a raw and original state and some in a finished state.

Oracle Database 11*g* offers terrific ETL capabilities that enable a newer way to load data into a database: the *transform-while-loading* method. By using the Oracle database to perform all the ETL steps, you can efficiently perform the typically laborious ETL processes. Oracle provides you with a whole set of complementary tools and techniques aimed at reducing the time needed to load data into the database while simplifying the work involved. Oracle's ETL solution includes the following components:

- *External tables*: External tables provide a way to merge the loading and transformation processes. Using external tables will enable you to eliminate cumbersome and time-consuming intermediate staging tables during data loading. External tables are discussed in the "Using External Tables to Load Data" section in this chapter.

- *Multitable inserts*: Using the multitable insert feature, you can insert data into more than one table at the same time, using different criteria for the various tables. This capability eliminates the additional step of first dividing data into separate groupings and then performing data loading. Multitable inserts are discussed in the "Using Multitable Inserts" section in this chapter.

- *Upserts*: This is simply a made-up name indicating the technique by which you can either insert data into a table or just update the rows with a single SQL statement: MERGE. The MERGE statement will insert new data and update data if the rows already exist in the table. This simplifies your loading process because you don't need to worry about whether a table already contains the data. Upserts are discussed in the "Using the MERGE Statement" section in this chapter.

- *Table functions*: Table functions produce a set of rows as output. Table functions return a collection type instance (nested table and VARRAY data types). Table functions are similar to views, but, instead of defining the transform declaratively in SQL, you define it procedurally in PL/SQL. Table functions are a great help when you're doing large and complex transformations, because you can perform the transformations before loading data into a data warehouse. Table functions are discussed in the "Using Table Functions for Data Transformation" section in this chapter.

- *Transportable tablespaces*: These tablespaces provide you with an efficient and speedy way to move data from one database to another. For example, you can migrate data between an OLTP database and a data warehouse using transportable tablespaces. I discuss transportable tablespaces in Chapter 14.

Note You can also use Oracle Warehouse Builder (OWB) to efficiently load data. OWB offers you a wizard-driven facility to load data into the database through SQL*Loader. OWB can load data from an Oracle database or from flat files. In addition, OWB can extract data from other databases such as Sybase, Informix, and Microsoft SQL Server via Oracle Transparent Gateways. OWB combines ETL and design functions in an easy-to-use format.

In the next section, you'll learn how to use the SQL*Loader utility to load data from external files. This will also help you understand how to use external tables to perform data loading. After examining the external tables feature, you'll review the various methods of data transformation offered by Oracle Database 11g.

Using the SQL*Loader Utility

The SQL*Loader utility, which comes with the Oracle database server, is commonly used by DBAs to load external data into an Oracle database. SQL*Loader is an immensely powerful tool that's capable of performing more than just a data load from text files. Here's a quick list of the SQL*Loader utility's capabilities:

- You can use SQL*Loader to transform data before it's loaded into the database or during the data load itself (limited capabilities).

- You can load data from multiple sources: disk, tape, and named pipes. You can also use multiple datafiles in the same loading session.

- You can load data across a network.

- You can selectively load from the input file based on conditions.

- You can load all or part of a table. You can also load data into several tables simultaneously.

- You can perform simultaneous data loads.

- You can automate the load process, so it runs at scheduled times.

- You can load complex object-relational data.

You can use the SQL*Loader utility to perform several types of data loading:

- *Conventional data loading*: Under conventional data loading, SQL*Loader reads multiple rows at a time and stores them in a bind array. SQL*Loader subsequently inserts this whole array at once into the database and commits the operation.

- *Direct-path loading*: The direct-path loading method doesn't use the SQL INSERT statement to load the data into Oracle tables. Column array structures are built from the data to be loaded, and these structures are used to format Oracle data blocks that are then written directly to the database tables.

- *External data loading*: The new external tables feature of Oracle relies on the functionality of SQL*Loader to access data in external files as if it were part of the database tables. When you use the ORACLE_LOADER access driver to create an external table, you are basically using the SQL*Loader's functionality. In Oracle Database 11g, you can also use the new ORACLE_DATAPUMP access driver, which provides the ability to write to external tables.

The conventional and direct-path loading methods offer their own benefits and drawbacks. Because the direct-path loading method bypasses the Oracle SQL mechanism, it is much faster than the conventional loading method. However, when it comes to the data transformation capabilities, the conventional loading method is much more powerful than direct-path loading, because it allows a full range of functions to be applied to the table columns during the load. The direct-path loading method supports a far more limited number of transformations during the load. Oracle recommends that you use the conventional loading method for small data loads and the direct-path loading method for larger loads. You'll learn the specifics of direct-path loading after examining the main SQL*Loader features and using the conventional loading method. External data loading is covered in the "Using External Tables to Load Data" section later in this chapter.

Loading data using the SQL*Loader utility involves two main steps:

1. Select the datafile that contains the data you want to load. The datafile usually ends with the extension .dat and contains the data you want to load. The data could be in several formats.

2. Create a control file. The control file tells SQL*Loader how to map the data fields to an Oracle table and specifies whether the data needs to be transformed in some way. The control file usually ends with the extension .ctl.

The control file will provide the mapping of the table columns to the data fields in the input file. There is no requirement that you have a separate datafile for the load. If you wish, you can include the data in the control file itself, after you specify the load control information such as the field specification and so on. The data can be supplied in fixed-length fields or in free format, separated by a character such as a comma (,) or a pipe (|). Let's begin by studying the all-important SQL*Loader control file.

Exploring the SQL*Loader Control File

The SQL*Loader control file is a simple text file in which you specify important details about the data load job, such as the location of the source datafile. The control file is also the place where you map the datafiles to the table columns. You can also specify any transformation during the load process within the control file. The control file contains the names of the log files for the load and files for catching bad and rejected data. The control file instructs SQL*Loader regarding the following aspects of the SQL*Loader session:

- The source of the data to be loaded into the database
- The column specification of the target table
- The nature of the input file formatting
- The mapping of the input file fields to the table columns
- Data transformation rules (applying SQL functions)
- The locations for the log files and error files

Listing 13-1 shows a typical SQL*Loader control file. SQL*Loader considers data rows in the source datafiles to be records, and you can specify the record formats in the control file. Note that you can also use a separate file for the data. In this example, you see the control information followed by in-line data, as shown by the use of the INFILE * specification in the control file. This specification indicates that the data for the load will follow the control information for the load. If you are doing a onetime data load, it is probably better to keep things simple and place the data in the control file itself. The keyword BEGINDATA tells SQL*Loader where the data portion of the control file starts.

Listing 13-1. *A Typical SQL*Loader Control File*

```
LOAD DATA
INFILE *
BADFILE test.bad
DISCARDFILE test.dsc
```

```
INSERT
INTO TABLE tablename
FIELDS TERMINATED BY ',' OPTIONALLY ENCLOSED BY""
(column1   POSITION (1:2) CHAR,
column2    POSITION (3:9) INTEGER EXTERNAL,
column3    POSITION (10:15) INTEGER EXTERNAL,
column4    POSITION (16:16) CHAR
)
BEGINDATA
AY3456789111111Y
/*   Rest of the data here . . .*/
```

The portion of the control file that describes the data fields is called the *field list*. In the control file in Listing 13-1, the field list is the following section:

```
(column1   POSITION (1:2) char,
 column2   POSITION (3:9) integer external,
 column3   POSITION (10:15) integer external,
 column4   POSITION (16:16) char
)
```

The field list shows the field names, position, data type, delimiters, and any applicable conditions.

You can specify numerous variables in the control file, and you can informally sort them into the following groups:

- Loading-related clauses
- Datafile-related clauses
- Table- and field-mapping clauses
- Command-line parameters in the control file

The following sections describe the parameters you can specify in the control file to configure your data loads.

■**Tip** If you aren't sure which parameters you can use for your SQL*Loader run, just type sqlldr at the operating system prompt to view all the available options. You will see a complete list of all the parameters and their operating system-specific default values (if any exist).

Loading-Related Clauses

The keywords LOAD DATA start off a control file. This simply means that the data is to be loaded from the input datafile to the Oracle tables using the SQL*Loader utility.

The INTO TABLE clause indicates into which table the data will be loaded. If you're loading into multiple tables simultaneously, you'll need an INTO TABLE statement for each table. The keywords INSERT, REPLACE, and APPEND instruct the database how the load will be done. If it is an INSERT, the table is assumed to be empty; otherwise, the loading process will generate an error and stop. The REPLACE clause will truncate the table and start loading new data. You'll often see that a load job using the REPLACE option seems to hang initially. This is because Oracle is busy truncating the table before it starts the load process. The APPEND clause will add the new rows to existing table data.

Datafile-Related Clauses

You can use several clauses to specify the locations and other characteristics of the datafile(s) from which you're going to load data using SQL*Loader. The following sections cover the important data-file-related clauses.

Datafile Specification

You specify the name and location of the input datafile by using the INFILE parameter:

```
INFILE='/a01/app/oracle/oradata/load/consumer.dat'
```

If you don't want to use the INFILE specification, you can include the data in the control file itself. When you include the data in the control file instead of a separate input file, you omit the file location and use the * notation, as follows:

```
INFILE = *
```

If you choose to have the data in the control file itself, you must use the BEGINDATA clause before your data starts:

```
BEGINDATA
Nicholas Alapati,243 New Highway,Irving,TX,75078
. . .
```

Physical and Logical Records

Every physical record in the source datafile is equivalent to a logical record by default, but the control file can specify that more than one physical record be combined into a single logical record. For example, in the following input file, three physical records are also considered three logical records:

```
Nicholas Alapati,243 New Highway,Irving,TX,75078
Shannon Wilson,1234 Elm Street,Fort Worth,TX,98765
Nina Alapati,2629 Skinner Drive,Flower Mound,TX,75028
```

You can transform these three physical records by using either of two parameters in the control file: the CONCATENATE clause or the CONTINUEIF clause.

If your input is in the fixed format, you can specify the number of rows of data to be read for each logical record in the following way:

```
CONCATENATE 4
```

This CONCATENATE clause will combine four rows of data. If each row of data has 80 characters, then the total number of characters in the new logical record that is created will be 320. Therefore, when you use the CONCATENATE clause, you should also specify a record length (RECLEN) clause along with it. In this case, the record length clause is as follows:

```
RECLEN 320
```

The CONTINUEIF clause lets you combine physical records into logical records by specifying one or more characters in a specified location. Here's an example:

```
CONTINUEIF THIS (1:4) = 'next'
```

In this line, the CONTINUEIF clause means that if SQL*Loader finds the four letters next at the beginning of a line, it should treat the data that follows as a continuation of the previous line (the four characters and the word next are arbitrary—continuation indicators can be any arbitrary characters).

If you are using fixed-format data, the CONTINUEIF character may be placed in the very last column, as shown in the following example:

```
CONTINUEIF LAST = '&'
```

This line means that if SQL*Loader encounters the ampersand (&) character at the end of a line, it will treat the following line as a continuation of the preceding line.

■Note Using either CONTINUEIF or CONCATENATE will slow down SQL*Loader, so map physical and logical records one to one. You should do this because when you join more than one physical record to make a single logical record, SQL*Loader must perform additional scanning of the input data, which takes more time.

Record Format

You may specify a record format in one of three ways:

- *Stream record format*: This is the most common record format, which uses a record terminator to indicate the end of a record. When SQL*Loader scans the input file, it knows it has reached the end of a record when it encounters the terminator string. If no terminator string is specified, the last character defaults to a newline character or a linefeed (carriage return followed by a linefeed on Windows) character. The set of three records in the previous example uses this record format.

- *Variable record format*: In this format, you explicitly specify the length at the beginning of the each record, as shown in the following example:

  ```
  INFILE 'example1.dat'  "var 2"
  06sammyy12johnson,1234
  ```

  This line contains two records: the first with six characters (sammyy) and the second with twelve characters (johnson,1234). var 2 indicates that the data records are of variable size, with record size indicators specified as a field of length 2, before every new record.

- *Fixed record format*: In this format, you specify that all records are a specific fixed size. Here's an example, which specifies that every record is 12 bytes long:

  ```
  INFILE 'example1.dat'  "fix 12"
  sammyy,1234, johnso,1234
  ```

  Although at first glance in this example, the record seems to include the entire line (sammyy,1234, johnso,1234), the fix 12 specification means that there are actually two 12-byte records in this line. Thus, when you use the fixed record format, you may have several loader records on each line in your source datafile.

Table- and Field-Mapping Clauses

During a load session, SQL*Loader takes the data fields in the data records and converts them into table columns. The table- and field-mapping clauses pertain to the mapping process between data fields and table columns. The control file provides details about fields, including the column name, position, input record data types, delimiters, and data transformation parameters.

Table Column Name

Each column in the table is specified clearly, with the position and data type of the matching field value in the input file. You don't need to load all the columns in the table. If you omit any columns in the control file, they're set to null.

Position

SQL*Loader must have a way of knowing the location of the various fields in the input file. Oracle calls the individual items in the datafile *fields*, and there is no direct correspondence between these fields and the columns in the table in which you are loading the data. The process of mapping fields in the input datafile to the table columns in the database is called *field setting*, and it is the biggest contributor to CPU time taken during the load. The POSITION clause specifies exactly where in the data record the various fields are. You have two ways to specify the location of the fields: relative and absolute.

Relative position implies that you specify the position of a field with respect to the position of the preceding field, as shown in the following example:

```
employee_id  POSITION(*) NUMBER EXTERNAL 6
employee_name  POSITION(*) CHAR 30
```

In this example, the load starts with the first field, employee_id. SQL*Loader then expects employee_name to start in position 7 and continue for 30 characters. It will look for the next field starting at position 37, and so on.

When you use the POSITION clause in an *absolute position* sense, you just specify the position at which each field starts and ends, as follows:

```
employee_id POSITION(1:6) INTEGER EXTERNAL
employee_name POSITION(7:36) CHAR
```

Data Types

The *data types* used in the control file refer to the input records only and aren't the same as the column data types within the database tables. The following are the main data types used in SQL*Loader control files:

- INTEGER(n)—binary integer, where n can be 1, 2, 4, or 8
- SMALLINT
- CHAR
- INTEGER EXTERNAL
- FLOAT EXTERNAL
- DECIMAL EXTERNAL

Delimiters

After each column's data type is specified, you can specify a *delimiter*, which indicates how the field should be delimited. You can delimit data by using one of the following two clauses: TERMINATED BY or ENCLOSED BY.

TERMINATED BY limits the field to the character specified and denotes the end of a field. Here are a couple of examples:

```
TERMINATED BY WHITESPACE
TERMINATED BY ","
```

The first example indicates that the field is terminated by the first blank that is encountered. The second example simply indicates that the fields are separated by commas.

The ENCLOSED BY " " delimiter specifies that the field is enclosed by a pair of quotation marks. Here is an example:

```
FIELDS TERMINATED BY ',' OPTIONALLY ENCLOSED BY '"'
```

■**Tip** Oracle recommends that you avoid delimited fields and choose positional fields (using the POSITION parameter) where possible. Choosing positional fields means that the database avoids scanning the datafile to find the delimiters you chose, thus reducing processing time.

Data Transformation Parameters

You can apply SQL functions to the field data before loading it into table columns. Only SQL functions that return single values can be used for transforming field values in general. The field should be denoted inside the SQL string as field_name. You specify the SQL function(s) after you specify the data type for the field, and you enclose the SQL string in double quotation marks, as shown in the following examples:

```
field_name  CHAR TERMINATED BY "," "SUBSTR(:field_name, 1, 10)"
employee_name POSITION 32-62 CHAR  "UPPER(:ename)"
salary position 75 CHAR "TO_NUMBER(:sal,'$99,999.99')"
commission INTEGER EXTERNAL "":commission * 100"
```

As you can see, the application of SQL operators and functions to field values before they are loaded into tables helps you transform the data at the same time you are loading it. This is a handy feature.

Command-Line Parameters in the Control File

SQL*Loader allows you to specify a number of runtime parameters at the command line when you invoke the SQL*Loader executable. Usually, you specify in the parameter file those parameters whose values remain the same across jobs. You can then use the command line to start the SQL*Loader job, either interactively or as part of a scheduled batch job. On the command line, you specify runtime-specific parameters, along with the control filename and location.

As an alternative, you may use the OPTIONS clause of the control file to specify runtime parameters inside the control file itself. You can always specify a number of runtime parameters while invoking SQL*Loader, but you're better off using the OPTIONS clause to specify them in the control file, if those parameters are something you'll repeat often. Using the OPTIONS clause comes in handy particularly if your SQL*Loader command-line specification is so long that it exceeds your operating system's maximum command-line size.

■**Note** Specifying a parameter on the command line will override the parameter's values inside a control file.

The following sections cover some of the important parameters you can control using the OPTIONS clause in the control file.

USERID

The USERID parameter specifies both the username and the password of the user in the database who has the privileges for the data load:

```
USERID = samalapati/sammyy1
```

CONTROL

The CONTROL parameter specifies the name of the control file for the SQL*Loader session. The control file may include the specifications for all the load parameters. Of course, you can load data using manual commands, but using a control file gives you more flexibility and enables the automation of the load process.

```
CONTROL = '/test01/app/oracle/oradata/load/finance.ctl'
```

DATA

The DATA parameter simply refers to the input datafile. The default filename extension is .dat. Note that the data doesn't necessarily need to be inside a separate datafile. If you wish, you can include the data at the end of the control file load specifications.

```
DATA = '/test02/app/oracle/oradata/load/finance.dat'
```

BINDSIZE and ROWS

You can use the two parameters BINDSIZE and ROWS to specify a conventional path bind array. SQL*Loader in the conventional path mode doesn't insert data into the table row by row. Rather, it inserts a set of rows at a time, and that set of rows, called the *bind array*, is sized based on either the BINDSIZE or ROWS parameter.

The BINDSIZE parameter sets the bind array size in bytes. On my system, the default bind size is 256,000 bytes.

```
BINDSIZE = 512000
```

The ROWS parameter does not set any limit on the number of bytes in the bind array. It imposes a limit on the number of rows in each bind array, and SQL*Loader multiplies this value in the ROWS parameter with its estimate of the size of each row in the table. The default number of rows under the conventional method on my system is 64.

```
ROWS = 64000
```

■ **Note** If you specify both the BINDSIZE and ROWS parameters, SQL*Loader uses the smaller of the two values for the bind array.

DIRECT

If you specify DIRECT=true, SQL*Loader loads using the direct-path method instead of the conventional method. The default for this parameter is DIRECT=false, meaning the conventional method is the default method used.

ERRORS

The ERRORS parameter specifies the maximum number of errors that can occur before the SQL*Loader job is terminated. The default on most systems is 50. If you don't want to tolerate any errors, set this parameter to 0:

```
ERRORS = 0
```

LOAD

Using the LOAD parameter, you can set the maximum number of logical records to be loaded into the table. The default is to load all the records in the input datafile.

```
LOAD = 10000
```

LOG

The LOG parameter specifies the name of the *log file*. The SQL*Loader log file, as you'll see shortly, provides a lot of information about your SQL*Loader session.

```
LOG = '/u01/app/oracle/admin/finance/logs/financeload.log'
```

BAD

The BAD parameter specifies the name and location of the *bad file*. If any records are rejected due to data formatting errors, SQL*Loader will write the record to the bad file. For example, a field could exceed its specified length and be rejected by SQL*Loader. Note that besides the records rejected by SQL*Loader, other records may be rejected by the database. For example, if you try to insert rows with duplicate primary key values, the database will reject the insert. These records will be part of the bad file as well. If you don't explicitly name a bad file, Oracle will create one and use a default name with the control filename as a prefix.

```
BAD = '/u01/app/oracle/load/financeload.bad'
```

SILENT

By default, SQL*Loader displays feedback messages on the screen showing the load job's progress. You can turn off the display with the SILENT parameter. You can use several options with the SILENT parameter. For example, you can turn off all types of messages with the ALL option, as shown here:

```
SILENT = ALL
```

DISCARD and DISCARDMAX

The *discard file* contains all records rejected during the load because they didn't meet the record selection criteria you specified in the control file. The default is to not have a discard file. Oracle will create this file only if there are discarded records, and, even then, only if you explicitly specify the discard file in the control file. You use the DISCARD parameter to specify the name and location of the discard file.

```
DISCARD = 'test01/app/oracle/oradata/load/finance.dsc'
```

By default, SQL*Loader doesn't impose any limit on the number of records; therefore, all the logical records can be discarded. Using the DISCARDMAX parameter, you can set a limit on the number of records that can be discarded.

■**Tip** Both the bad and discard files contain records in the original format. Therefore, it's easy, especially during large loads, to just edit these files and use them for loading the data that was left out during the first load run.

PARALLEL

The PARALLEL parameter specifies whether SQL*Loader can run multiple sessions when you're employing the direct-path loading method.

```
sqlldr USERID=salapati/sammyy1 CONTROL=load1.ctl DIRECT=true PARALLEL=true
```

RESUMABLE

Using the RESUMABLE parameter, you can turn on Oracle's Resumable Space Allocation feature. This way, if a job encounters a space problem while loading the data, the load job is merely suspended.

You can arrange for a notification about the job suspension and allocate more space so the job can continue without failing. The Resumable Space Allocation feature is discussed in Chapter 8. The default for the RESUMABLE parameter is false, meaning Resumable Space Allocation is disabled. Set RESUMABLE=true to enable this feature.

RESUMABLE_NAME

The RESUMABLE_NAME parameter enables you to identify a specific resumable load job when you use the Resumable Space Allocation feature. The default name is the combination of the username, session ID, and instance ID.

```
RESUMABLE_NAME = finance1_load
```

RESUMABLE_TIMEOUT

The RESUMABLE_TIMEOUT parameter can be set only when the RESUMABLE parameter is set to true. The timeout is the maximum length of time for which an operation can be suspended when it runs into a space-related problem. If the space-related problem is not fixed within this interval, the operation will be aborted. The default is 7,200 seconds.

```
RESUMABLE_TIMEOUT = 3600
```

SKIP

The SKIP parameter is very useful in situations where your SQL*Loader job fails to complete its run due to some errors, but it has already committed some rows. The SKIP parameter lets you skip a specified number of records in the input file when you run the SQL*Loader job the second time. The alternative is to truncate the table and restart the SQL*Loader job from the beginning—not a great idea if a large number of rows have already been loaded into the database tables.

```
SKIP = 235550
```

This example assumes the first job failed after loading 235,549 records successfully. You can find out this information from the log file for the load, or query the table directly.

Generating Data During the Load

The SQL*Loader utility enables you to generate data to load columns. This means that you can do a load without ever using a datafile. More commonly, however, you generate data for one or more columns of the data when you are loading from a datafile. The following types of data can be generated by SQL*Loader:

- *Constant value*: You can set a column to a constant value by using the CONSTANT specification. For example, with the following specification, all the rows populated during this run will have the value sysadm in the loaded_by column:

  ```
  loaded_by     CONSTANT  "sysadm"
  ```

- *Expression value*: You can set a column to the value specified by a SQL operator or a PL/SQL function. You specify the expression value using the EXPRESSION parameter, as shown here:

  ```
  column_name EXPRESSION "SQL string"
  ```

- *Datafile record number*: You can set a column's value to the record number that loaded that row by using the RECNUM column specification:

  ```
  record_num RECNUM
  ```

- *System date*: You can use the `sysdate` variable to set a column to the date you're loading the data:

```
loaded_date    sysdate
```

- *Sequence*: You can generate unique values to load a column by using the `SEQUENCE` function. In the following example, the current maximum value of the `loadseq` sequence is incremented by one each time a row is inserted:

```
loadseq  SEQUENCE(max,1)
```

Invoking SQL*Loader

You can invoke the SQL*Loader utility in a number of ways. The standard syntax for invoking the SQL*Loader is as follows:

```
SQLLDR keyword=value [,keyword=value,. . .]
```

Here's an example showing how to invoke the SQL*Loader:

```
$ sqlldr USERID=nicholas/nicholas1 CONTROL=/u01/app/oracle/finance/finance.ctl \
DATA=/u01/app/oracle/oradata/load/finance.dat \
LOG=/u01/aapp/oracle/finance/log/finance.log \
ERRORS=0 DIRECT=true SKIP=235550 RESUMABLE=true RESUMABLE_TIMEOUT=7200
```

> ■**Note** In the command-line invocation of the SQL*Loader utility, the backslash (\) at the end of each line simply indicates that the command continues on the next line. You can specify a command-line parameter with the parameter name itself or by position. For example, the username/password specification always follows the keyword `sqlldr`. If you ignore a parameter, Oracle will use the default value for that parameter. You can optionally use a comma after each parameter.

As you can see, the more parameters you want to use, the more information you need to provide at the command line. This approach presents two problems. First, if you make typing or other errors, you'll have a mess on your hands. Second, there may be a limit on some operating systems regarding how many characters you can input at the command prompt. Fortunately, you can run the same SQL*Loader job with the following command, which is a lot less complicated:

```
$ sqlldr PARFILE=/u01/app/oracle/admin/finance/load/finance.par
```

The command-line parameter `PARFILE` stands for *parameter file*, which is a file in which you can specify values for all your command parameters. For example, for the load specifications shown in this chapter, the parameter file looks like this:

```
USERID=nicholas/nicholas1
CONTROL='/u01/app/oracle/admin/finance/finance.ctl'
DATA='/app/oracle/oradata/load/finance.dat'
LOG='/u01/aapp/oracle/admin/finance/log/finance.log'
ERRORS=0
DIRECT=true
SKIP=235550
RESUMABLE=true
RESUMABLE_TIMEOUT=7200
```

Using the parameter file is more elegant than typing all the parameters at the command line, and it is a logical approach when you need to regularly run jobs that use the same options. Any option that you specify at the command line will override the value specified for that parameter inside a parameter file.

If you want to use the command line, but you don't want to type the password where someone can easily see it, you can invoke SQL*Loader in the following manner:

```
$ sqlldr CONTROL=control.ctl
```

SQL*Loader will then prompt you for your username/password combination.

Exploring the Loader Log File

The SQL*Loader log file offers a host of information regarding a SQL*Loader run. It tells you how many records were supposed to be loaded and how many actually were loaded. It tells you which records failed to get loaded and why. It also describes the field columns provided in the SQL*Loader control file. Listing 13-2 shows a typical SQL*Loader log file.

Listing 13-2. *A Typical SQL*Loader Log File*

```
SQL*Loader: Release 11.1.0.0.0 - Production on Sun Aug 24 14:04:26 2008
Control File:   /u01/app/oracle/admin/fnfactsp/load/test.ctl
 Data File:      /u01/app/oracle/admin/fnfactsp/load/test.ctl
 Bad File:       /u01/app/oracle/admin/fnfactsp/load/test.badl
Discard File:  none specified
  (Allow all discards)
Number to load: ALL
Number to skip: 0
Errors allowed: 0
Bind array:     64 rows, maximum of 65536 bytes
Continuation:    none specified
Path used:      Conventional
Table TBLSTAGE1, loaded when ACTIVITY_TYPE != 0X48(character 'H')
                 and ACTIVITY_TYPE != 0X54(character 'T')
Insert option in effect for this table: APPEND
TRAILING NULLCOLS option in effect
    Column Name             Position   Len  Term Encl Datatype
------------------------------ ---------- ----- ---- ---- -----
COUNCIL_NUMBER                  FIRST     *   ,        CHARACTER
COMPANY                         NEXT      *   ,        CHARACTER
ACTIVITY_TYPE                   NEXT      *   ,        CHARACTER
RECORD_NUMBER                   NEXT      *   ,        CHARACTER
FUND_NUMBER                     NEXT      *   ,        CHARACTER
BASE_ACCOUNT_NUMBER             NEXT      *   ,        CHARACTER
FUNCTIONAL_CODE                 NEXT      *   ,        CHARACTER
DEFERRED_STATUS                 NEXT      *   ,        CHARACTER
CLASS                           NEXT      *   ,        CHARACTER
UPDATE_DATE                                            SYSDATE
UPDATED_BY                                             CONSTANT
    Value is 'sysadm'
BATCH_LOADED_BY                                        CONSTANT
    Value is 'sysadm'
/*Discarded Records Section: Gives the complete list of discarded
records, including reasons why they were discarded.*/
```

```
Record 1: Discarded - failed all WHEN clauses.
Record 1527: Discarded - failed all WHEN clauses.
Table TBLSTAGE1:
/*Number of Rows: Gives the number of rows
 successfully loaded and the number of rows not
 loaded due to errors or because they failed the
 WHEN conditions, if any. Here, two records failed the WHEN condition*/
  1525 Rows successfully loaded.
  0 Rows not loaded due to data errors.
  2 Rows not loaded because all WHEN clauses were failed.
  0 Rows not loaded because all fields were null.

/* Memory Section: Gives the bind array size chosen for the data load*/
Space allocated for bind array:                99072 bytes(64 rows)
Read    buffer bytes: 1048576
/* Logical Records Section: Gives the total records, number of rejected
 and discarded records.*/
Total logical records skipped:          0
Total logical records read:          1527
Total logical records rejected:          0
Total logical records discarded:       2
/*Date Section: Gives the day and date of the data load.*/
Run began on Sun Mar 06 14:04:26 2009
Run ended on Sun Mar 06 14:04:27 2009
/*Time section: Gives the time taken for completing the data load.*/
Elapsed time was:       00:00:01.01
CPU time was:           00:00:00.27
```

When you examine the log file, focus on the total logical records read and the records that are skipped, rejected, and discarded. When you encounter difficulty running a job, the log file is the first place you should look to see whether or not the data records are being loaded.

Using Return Codes

The log file provides a wealth of information about the load, but Oracle also allows you to trap the exit code after each load run. This enables you to check the results of the load when you run it through a cron job or a shell script. For a Windows server, you may use the at command to schedule the load job. Here are the key exit codes for the UNIX/Linux operating systems:

- EX_SUCC 0 indicates that all the rows were loaded successfully.
- EX_FAIL 1 indicates that there were command-line or syntax errors.
- EX_WARN 2 indicates that some or all rows were rejected.
- EX_FTL 3 indicates operating system errors.

Using the Direct-Path Loading Method

So far, you have looked at the SQL*Loader utility from the point of view of a *conventional load*. As you recall, the conventional loading method uses SQL INSERT statements to insert data into tables one bind array size at a time. The *direct-path loading* option doesn't use the SQL INSERT statement to put data into tables; rather, it formats Oracle data blocks and writes them directly to the database files. This direct-write process eliminates much of the overhead involved in executing SQL statements to load tables. Since the direct-path loading method doesn't contend for database resources, it will load data much faster than a conventional data load. For larger data loads, the direct-path loading method works best, and it may be the only viable method of loading data into tables for the simple reason that a conventional load may require more time than is available.

Besides the obvious advantages of a shorter load time, direct loading also helps you rebuild indexes and presort table data. Using the direct-path loading method as opposed to the conventional loading method has the following advantages:

- The load is much faster than in the conventional loading method because you aren't using SQL INSERT statements for the load.

- The direct load uses multiblock asynchronous I/O for database writes, so the writing is fast.

- You have the option of presorting data using efficient sorting routines with the direct load.

- By setting the UNRECOVERABLE=Y parameter, you can avoid the writing of any redo data during a direct load.

- By using temporary storage, you can build indexes more efficiently during a direct load than when you're using the conventional load method.

■**Note** A conventional load will always generate redo entries, whereas the direct-path loading method will generate such entries only under specific conditions. A direct load also won't fire any insert triggers, unlike the conventional load, which fires the triggers during the load. Users can't make any changes when a table is being loaded using a direct load, unlike in a conventional load.

However, direct-path loads have some serious limitations. You can't use this method under the following conditions:

- You're using clustered tables.

- You're loading parent and child tables together.

- You're loading VARRAY or BFILE columns.

- You're loading across heterogeneous platforms using Oracle Net.

- You want to apply SQL functions during the load.

■**Note** In a direct load, you can't use any SQL functions. If you need to perform a large data load and also transform the data during the load, you have a problem. The conventional data load will let you use SQL functions to transform data, but the method is very slow compared to the direct load. Thus, for large data loads, you may want to consider using one of the newer load/transform techniques, such as external tables or table functions.

Direct Load Options

Several SQL*Loader options are intended especially for use with the direct load option or are more significant for direct loads than conventional loads. The following options are relevant to the direct-path loading method:

- DIRECT: The DIRECT clause must be set to true in order for you to use the direct-path loading method (DIRECT=true).

- DATA_CACHE: The DATA_CACHE parameter comes in handy if you're loading the same data or time-stamp values several times during a direct load. SQL*Loader has to convert the date and timestamp data each time it encounters them. If you have duplicate data and timestamp values in your data, you can reduce unnecessary data conversions, and thus processing time, by specifying the DATA_CACHE parameter. By default, the DATA_CACHE parameter is enabled for 1,000 values. If you don't have duplicate date and timestamp values in your data, or if there are few such duplicates, you can disable the DATA_CACHE parameter by setting it to zero (DATA_CACHE=0).

- ROWS: The ROWS parameter is crucial because you can use it to specify how many rows SQL*Loader will read from the input datafile before saving the insertions to the tables. You use the ROWS parameter to set the ceiling on the amount of data lost if the instance fails during a long SQL*Loader run. When SQL*Loader reads the number of rows specified in the ROWS parameter, it will stop loading data until all of the data buffers are successfully written to the datafiles. This process is called a *data save*. For example, if SQL*Loader can load about 10,000 rows per minute, setting ROWS=150000 saves the data every 15 minutes.

- UNRECOVERABLE: If you want to minimize the use of the redo log, you can do so by using the UNRECOVERABLE parameter during a direct load (specify UNRECOVERABLE in the control file).

- SKIP_INDEX_MAINTENANCE: The SKIP_INDEX_MAINTENANCE parameter, when turned on (SKIP_INDEX_MAINTENANCE=true), instructs SQL*Loader not to bother maintaining the indexes during the load. The default for SKIP_INDEX_MAINTENANCE is false.

- SKIP_UNUSABLE_INDEXES: Setting a value of true for the SKIP_UNUSABLE_INDEXES parameter will ensure that SQL*Loader will load tables with indexes in an unusable state. These indexes won't be maintained by SQL*Loader, however. The default for this parameter is based on the setting for the SKIP_UNUSABLE_INDEXES initialization parameter, whose default value is true.

- SORTED_INDEXES: The SORTED_INDEXES parameter signals SQL*Loader that data is sorted on a specified index, which helps improve load performance.

- COLUMNARRAYROWS: This parameter determines the number of rows loaded before the building of the stream buffer. For example, COLUMNARRAYROWS=100000 loads 100,000 rows first. The size of the direct-path column array is thus determined by this parameter. The default value for this parameter on my UNIX server is 5,000.

- STREAMSIZE: The STREAMSIZE parameter lets you set the size of the stream buffer. The default on my server, for example, is 256,000, and I can increase it using the STREAMSIZE parameter; for example, STREAMSIZE=512000.

- MULTITHREADING: Under MULTITHREADING, the conversion of column arrays to stream buffers and stream buffer loading are performed in parallel. On machines with multiple CPUs, by default, multithreading is turned on (true). If you wish, you can turn it off by setting MULTITHREADING=false.

Direct Loads and Constraint/Trigger Management

The direct-path loading method inserts data directly into the datafiles by formatting the data blocks. By bypassing the INSERT statement mechanism, the table constraints and triggers aren't systematically applied during a direct load. All triggers are disabled, as are several integrity constraints. SQL*Loader automatically disables all foreign keys and check constraints, but the not null, unique, and primary key constraints are still maintained by SQL*Loader. Upon completion of the SQL*Loader run, the disabled constraints are automatically enabled by SQL*Loader if the REENABLE clause has been specified. Otherwise, the disabled constraints must be manually reenabled. The disabled triggers are automatically enabled after the load is completed.

TIPS FOR OPTIMAL USE OF SQL*LOADER

The following tips will help you optimize SQL*Loader during data loads, especially when the data loads are large and/or you have multiple indexes and constraints on the tables in your database.

- Try to use the direct-path loading method as much as possible. It's much faster than conventional data loading.

- Use the UNRECOVERABLE=true option wherever possible (in direct loads). This will save you considerable time, because the newly loaded data doesn't need to be logged in the redo log file. Media recovery is still in force for all the other users of the database, and you can always start a new SQL*Loader run if there's a problem.

- Keep the use of the NULLIF and DEFAULTIF parameters to a minimum. These clauses must be tested for every single row on which they're used.

- Minimize the number of data type and character set conversions, as they slow down processing.

- Wherever possible, use positional fields rather than delimited fields. SQL*Loader can move from field to field much faster if it's given the position of the field.

- Map physical and logical records on a one-to-one basis.

- Disable constraints before the load, as the constraints will slow down the loading. Of course, you may sometimes end up with errors while enabling the constraints, but it's a small price to pay for a much faster data load, especially for large tables.

- If you're using the direct-path loading method, specify the SORTED_INDEXES clause to optimize the load performance.

- If you're doing large data loads, it's smart to drop the indexes on the tables before the load. Index maintenance will slow down your SQL*Loader session. If it isn't possible to drop the indexes, you can make them unusable and use the SKIP_UNUSABLE_INDEXES clause during the load. If it's a direct load, use the SKIP_INDEX_MAINTENANCE clause.

Some Useful SQL*Loader Data-Loading Techniques

Using SQL*Loader is efficient, but it's not without its share of headaches. This section describes how to perform some special types of operations during data loads.

Using the WHEN Clause During Loads

You can use WHEN clauses during data loads to limit the load to only those rows that match certain conditions. For example, in a datafile, you can pick up only those records that have a field matching certain criteria. Here's an example that shows how to use the WHEN clause in a SQL*Loader control file:

```
LOAD DATA
INFILE *
INTO TABLE stagetbl
APPEND
 WHEN (activity_type <>'H') and (activity_type <>'T')
FIELDS TERMINATED BY ','
```

```
TRAILING NULLCOLS
/* Table columns here . . .*/
BEGINDATA
/* Data here . . .*/
```

The WHEN condition will reject all records where the data record field matching the activity_type column in the stagetbl table is neither H nor T.

Loading the Username into a Table

You can use the user pseudo-variable to load the username into a table during the load. The following example illustrates the use of this variable. Note that the target table stagetbl should have a column called loaded_by so SQL*Loader can insert the username into that column.

```
LOAD DATA
INFILE *
INTO TABLE stagetbl
INSERT
(loaded_by    "USER")
/* Table columns and the data follow . . .*/
```

Loading Large Data Fields into a Table

If you try to load any field larger than 255 bytes into a table, even if the table column is defined as VARCHAR2(2000) or a CLOB, SQL*Loader won't be able to load the data. You'll get an error informing you that the "Field in datafile exceeds maximum length." To manage the load of the large field, you need to specify the size of the table column in the control file when you're matching table columns to the data fields, as in this example (for a table column called text):

```
LOAD DATA
INFILE '/u01/app/oracle/oradata/load/testload.txt'
INSERT INTO TABLE test123
FIELDS TERMINATED BY ','
(text CHAR(2000))
```

Loading a Sequence Number into a Table

Suppose you have a sequence named test_seq, and you want this sequence to be incremented each time you load a data record into your table. Here's how to do it:

```
LOAD DATA
INFILE '/u01/app/oracle/oradata/load/testload.txt'
INSERT INTO TABLE test123
   (test_seq.nextval,. . .)
```

Loading Data from a Table into an ASCII File

You may sometimes want to get data out of the database table into flat files; for example, to later use this data to load data into Oracle tables in a different location. You can write complex scripts to do the job if there are a number of tables, but if there are few tables to load, you can use the following simple method of extracting data using SQL*Plus commands:

```
SET TERMOUT OFF
SET PAGESIZE 0
SET ECHO OFF
SET FEED OFF
```

```
SET HEAD OFF
SET LINESIZE 100
COLUMN  customer_id FORMAT 999,999
COLUMN first_name FORMAT a15
COLUMN last_name FORMAT a25
SPOOL test.txt
SELECT customer_id,first_name,last_name FROM customer;
SPOOL OFF
```

You may also use the UTL_FILE package to load data into text files.

Dropping Indexes Before Bulk Data Loads

There are two major reasons why you should seriously consider dropping indexes on a large table before performing a direct-path load using the NOLOGGING option. First, it may take you a longer time to do the load with the indexes included with the table data. Second, if you leave indexes on, there will be redo records generated by the changes that will be made to the index structure during the load.

■**Tip** Even if you choose to load data using the NOLOGGING option, there will be considerable redo generated to mark the changes being made to the indexes. In addition, there will always be some redo to support the data dictionary, even during a NOLOGGING data load operation. The best strategy here is to drop the indexes and rebuild them after the tables are created.

While you're performing a direct load, the instance may fail halfway through, SQL*Loader may run out of space that it needs to update the index, or SQL*Loader may encounter duplicate values for the index keys. This situation is referred to as the *indexes left unusable* condition, as the indexes will be unusable upon instance recovery. In such cases, it may be better to create the indexes after the load is complete.

Loading into Multiple Tables

You can use the same SQL*Loader run to load into multiple tables. Here's an example that shows how to load data into two tables simultaneously:

```
LOAD DATA
INFILE *
INSERT
INTO TABLE dept
 WHEN recid = 1
 (recid  FILLER POSITION(1:1) INTEGER EXTERNAL,
 deptno POSITION(3:4) INTEGER EXTERNAL,
 dname  POSITION(8:21) CHAR)
INTO TABLE emp
 WHEN recid <> 1
 (recid  FILLER POSITION(1:1) INTEGER EXTERNAL,
 empno  POSITION(3:6) INTEGER EXTERNAL,
 ename  POSITION(8:17) CHAR,
 deptno POSITION(19:20) INTEGER EXTERNAL)
```

In the preceding example, data from the same datafile is simultaneously loaded into two tables, dept and emp, based on whether or not the recid field value is 1.

Trapping Error Codes from SQL*Loader

Here's a simple example of how you can trap the process error codes issued by SQL*Loader:

```
$ sqlldr PARFILE=test.par
retcode=$?
if [[retcode !=2 ]]
 then
 mv ${ImpDir}/${Fil} ${InvalidLoadDir}/.${Dstamp}.${Fil}
 writeLog $func "Load Error" "load error:${retcode} on file ${Fil}"
 else
 sqlplus / ___EOF
 /* You can place any SQL statements to process the successfully loaded data */
 ___EOF
```

Loading XML Data into an Oracle XML Database

SQL*Loader supports the XML data type for columns. If a column is of this type, you can use SQL*Loader to load the XML data into a table. SQL*Loader treats the XML columns as CLOBs. Oracle also lets you load the XML data either from a primary datafile or from an external LOB file. You can use fixed-length fields or delimited fields. The contents of the entire file could also be read into a single LOB field.

Using External Tables to Load Data

For many years, Oracle DBAs used SQL*Loader almost exclusively for loading data into Oracle database tables from outside sources, employing either the conventional loading method or the direct-path loading method. Oracle's external tables feature goes one step further and enables you to use the SQL*Loader functionality to access data stored in operating system files without ever loading the data into a real Oracle table.

If your source data doesn't need any transformations when loading into the database, using the SQL*Loader to perform a conventional or a direct load is sufficient. External tables complement the functionality of the SQL*Loader. If you want to perform major data transformations before the load, then external tables are the recommended way to go.

Using the external tables feature, you can visualize external data as if it were stored in an Oracle table. When you create an external table, the columns are listed the same way as they are when you create a regular table. However, the data fields in the external file are merely mapped to the external table columns, not actually loaded into them.

External tables don't actually exist anywhere, inside or outside the database. The term *external table* implies that a given table structure is mapped to a datafile that's located in an operating system file. When you create an external table, the only thing that happens in the database is the creation of new metadata entries in the data dictionary for the new table. You can't change the datafile's contents in any way while you're accessing its contents from within the database. In other words, you can only use the SELECT command when you're dealing with external tables, not the INSERT, UPDATE, or DELETE command.

In reality, an external table is an interface to an external datafile. However, you may query this external table like a virtual table, just as you would query any regular Oracle table, which makes it a very powerful tool for data warehouse ETL activities. You can query external tables or join them with regular tables, without ever loading the external data into your database. In addition, you may create other regular tables or views from the external tables, so this feature comes in handy during the population of data warehouses.

SQL*Loader and the external tables feature perform similarly in terms of data-loading speed, in most cases. The two techniques offer you alternative methods of loading data into your database tables from external sources. The following are the general advantages that the external table method of loading offers in comparison with the SQL*Loader method:

- You can query data in the external files *before* it's loaded into the tables.

- You can perform an extensive range of transformations on the data during the load process itself. SQL*Loader is limited in the number of data transformations you can perform.

- You may choose to perform data transformation at the same time you're loading data into the tables. This is called the *pipelining* of the two phases. When you use SQL*Loader to load directly into the tables, you can't perform anything other than the most minimal data transformation at load time. Consequently, major transformations must be done in a separate step from that of data loading.

- External tables are suitable for large data loads that may have a onetime use in your database.

- External tables save the time involved in creating real database tables and then aggregating the data dimensions for loading into other tables.

- External tables eliminate the need to create staging or temporary tables, which are almost a must if you're using SQL*Loader to load the data from external sources.

- You don't need any physical space even for the largest external table. Once the datafiles are loaded into the operating system, you can create your external tables and start executing SQL queries against them.

If you need to load data remotely, or if your data doesn't need major transformations, SQL*Loader is the best way to go. External tables are in no way as versatile as regular database tables, because they're read-only tables. Furthermore, external tables suffer from the limitation that you can't index them. Therefore, high-powered query work with these tables is impractical. If the data in your staging tables needs to be indexed for some reason, then SQL*Loader is the only viable alternative. The real benefit of the external tables feature is primarily realized in data warehousing environments or in situations where you need to load and transform huge amounts of data when you first load an application.

■Caution If you want to create indexes on a staging table, you're better off using the SQL*Loader utility to load data into the table. You can't index an external table!

For example, suppose you have an external datafile named `sales_data` that contains detailed information about your firm's sales data for the last year. Your firm wants to perform product and time cost analysis based on this raw data. You create a cost table to do this analysis. Now, the `sales_data` datafile contains a lot of detailed information on costs, but your company wants the data to be aggregated, say on the basis of regions. External tables are excellent for this kind of analysis, where you have large amounts of raw data available, but you need only certain transformed parts of this data.

Traditionally, data warehousing DBAs had to create staging tables to first transform data, before loading it into the data warehouse. Using just the SQL*Loader, you would need to load the raw data into your database first, and then apply the necessary transformations to it. Using an external table, you can perform the loading and transform operations in one step!

Now, let's look at how to create and populate external tables.

Creating the External Table Layer

The external table description is also called the *external table layer*, and it is basically a description of the columns in your external table. This external table layer, along with the access driver, maps the data in the external file to the external table definition.

Listing 13-3 shows how to create an external table.

Listing 13-3. *Creating an External Table*

```
SQL> CREATE TABLE sales_ext(
  2  product_id NUMBER(6),
  3  sale_date DATE,
  4  store_id  NUMBER(8),
  5  quantity_sold NUMBER(8),
  6  unit_cost NUMBER(10,2),
  7  unit_price NUMBER(10,2))
  8  ORGANIZATION EXTERNAL (
  9  TYPE ORACLE_LOADER
 10  DEFAULT DIRECTORY ext_data_dir
 11  ACCESS PARAMETERS
 12  (RECORDS DELIMITED BY NEWLINE
 13  BADFILE log_file_dir:'sales.bad_xt'
 14  LOGFILE log_file_dir:'sales.log_xt'
 15  FIELDS TERMINATED BY  "|" LDRTRIM
 16  MISSING FIELD VALUES ARE NULL)
 17  LOCATION ('sales.data'))
 18* REJECT LIMIT UNLIMITED;
Table created.
SQL>
```

Let's analyze this statement in detail, in order to understand the various components of an external table.

CREATE TABLE . . . ORGANIZATION EXTERNAL

The statement CREATE TABLE sales_ext (. . .) describes the external table structure, with the ORGANIZATION EXTERNAL clause that follows it indicating that this isn't going to be a regular Oracle table, but an external table.

The CREATE statement for an external table is very similar to that of a regular table, except that in addition to the column definitions, you must provide the mapping for the columns to the data fields in the external datafile. In addition, the external table creation statement must provide the operating system location of the external datafile.

Access Parameters

The ACCESS PARAMETERS clause, somewhat similar to the OPTIONS clause in a SQL*Loader control file, indicates the various options chosen, as well as the location of the bad file and log file. Several external table parameters are available to specify the format of the data. Important among them are the following:

- RECORD_FORMAT_INFO: This is an optional clause. The default is RECORDS DELIMITED BY NEWLINE.

- FIXED: When you specify a fixed length by using the FIXED clause, you're indicating that all records in the external file are of the same length.

  ```
  ACCESS PARAMETERS (RECORD FIXED 20 FIELDS (. . .))
  ```

- VARIABLE: The VARIABLE clause indicates that each record may be a different size, indicated by a number of digits before the beginning of each record.

  ```
  ACCESS PARAMETERS (RECORDS VARIABLE 2)
  ```

- When you use the VARIABLE clause, every record in this data set will have the following format, with the first two bytes indicating the length of the record:

  22samalapati1999dallastx

- DELIMITED BY: This clause indicates the character that terminates each record. The most common delimiters are the pipe (|) and the comma (,).

- LOAD WHEN: This clause indicates the conditions that must be satisfied before a record can be loaded into a table.

  LOAD WHEN (job != MANAGER)

- LOG FILE, BAD FILE, and DISCARD FILE: These are optional parameters, but a log file is always created by default. The bad file and the discard file are created only if data is rejected or data fails to meet a LOAD WHEN condition.

- Condition: This variable compares all or part of a field against an arbitrarily chosen constant string.

Access Driver

The access parameters describe the external data in the datafiles. The *access driver* ensures that the external data processing matches the description of the external table.

Two types of access drivers are available, and you specify each of them by using the attribute TYPE in the external table creation statement. The first is the ORACLE_LOADER access driver, which is the default. Listing 13-3 creates an external table using the ORACLE_LOADER access driver. Using this access driver, you can *only load data* into a table from an external text file.

The new ORACLE_DATAPUMP access driver lets you both *load and unload data* using external dump files. You can read data into database tables from an external dump file. You can also extract data from an Oracle table into an external table's dump file.

Directory Objects and Their Locations

The clause DEFAULT DIRECTORY indicates the default location for all files that external tables need to read from or write to. You can't place the external datafiles in a random operating system directory for obvious security reasons. For an external table creation statement to succeed, you must first create a *directory object*, and then grant rights to specific users on this directory object.

The LOCATION parameter toward the end of the external table creation statement shown in Listing 13-3 indicates where the datafiles for the external table creation are located. The LOCATION parameter could indicate both a directory object and a filename. The format of the LOCATION parameter is *directory: file*, where *directory* is a directory object you've created in the database, not an actual directory path on your system. If you omit the directory part of the specification, then it's assumed that the datafile(s) is located in the directory specified by the DEFAULT DIRECTORY clause. You can also use the *directory: file* notation to specify the datafiles directly under the ACCESS PARAMETERS clause, if you wish.

SQL*Loader uses the directory object(s) to indicate where the datafiles are located, as well as to store its output files, such as the bad and discard files. A user must have read privileges on the directory object containing the datafiles and write privilege on the directory object containing the output files. If you wish to place both the datafiles and the output files in the same directory object, you may grant both read and write privileges on that directory object to the user. Here's one such example:

```
SQL> CREATE DIRECTORY ext_data_dir AS '/u01/oradata/ext_data';
Directory created.
SQL> GRANT READ, WRITE ON DIRECTORY ext_data_dir TO samalapati;
Grant succeeded.
SQL>
```

Once you create the directory object ext_data_dir and grant the proper rights, you can then use this as the default directory for placing all the external datafiles as well as output files. The LOCATION parameter in the external table creation statement shown in Listing 13-3 simply names the *external datafile*, which will be located in the default directory specified by ext_data_dir.

For demonstration purposes, let's create a new table named costs, into which you'll eventually load the aggregate data (the totals of the unit_cost and unit_price columns) from the external datafile (external table):

```
SQL> CREATE TABLE costs
  2  (sale_date DATE,
  3  product_id NUMBER(6),
  4  unit_cost NUMBER (10,2),
  5  unit_price NUMBER(10,2));
Table created.
```

Now you're ready to insert the necessary aggregate data from the external table (external file, actually) sales_ext into the new costs table. This process of first reading data from an external table and then loading it into a normal database table is called *loading data*. Listing 13-4 shows how to insert data into a normal table from an external table. The Oracle table is named costs, and sales_ext is the external table.

Listing 13-4. *Loading Data into a Normal Table from an External Table*

```
SQL> INSERT INTO costs
     (sale_date,
     product_id, unit_cost, unit_price)
     SELECT
     sale_date,
     product_id,
     sum(unit_cost),
     sum(unit_price)
     FROM sales_ext
     GROUP BY time_id, prod_id;
SQL>
```

Note that you can insert only some of the columns in the external table if you choose, and you can transform the data *before* it's even loaded into your tables. This is the key difference between using external tables and SQL*Loader to load data into Oracle tables. The SQL*Loader tool permits you to perform data transformation, but its capabilities in that area are extremely limited, as you saw earlier in this chapter. You can use just about any arbitrary SQL transformations when creating an external table.

Populating External Tables

The terms *loading* and *unloading* in the context of external tables can be confusing, so let's pause and make sure you understand these terms without any ambiguity. When you deal with external tables, this is what these terms mean:

- *Loading* data means reading data from an external table and loading it into a regular Oracle table. Oracle first reads the data stream from the files you specify. Oracle will then convert the data from its external representation to an Oracle internal data type and pass it along to the external table interface.

- *Unloading* data means reading data from a regular Oracle table and putting it into an external table. Actually, you'll be loading table data into an external file. In Oracle Database 11*g*, you can load and transform large volumes of data into platform-independent, Oracle proprietary flat files for data propagation or storage.

The ORACLE_DATAPUMP access driver can load as well extract data; that is, it can both load an external table from a flat file and extract data from a regular database table to an external flat file. This external flat file data is written in a proprietary format, which only the ORACLE_DATAPUMP access driver can read. You can then use this newly created file to create an external table in the same database or a different database.

When you *load* an Oracle table from an external table (data loading), you use the INSERT INTO . . . SELECT clause, as shown in Listing 13-4. When you populate an external table using Oracle table data (data *unloading*), you use the CREATE TABLE . . . AS SELECT clause (CTAS), as shown later in Listing 13-6.

Following are some of the benefits of being able to populate tables with external tables:

- Loading table data into flat files means that you can now store data or move it to different databases easily. External tables help move large volumes of data across platforms, since they are platform-independent.

- In data warehousing environments, there are many situations where you need to perform complex ETL jobs. You can use SQL transformations to manipulate the data in the external tables before reloading them into the same or other databases.

Note that when you talk about writing to external tables, you are really referring to writing to an external file. You use a SELECT statement to extract table data to this operating system file. The ORACLE_DATAPUMP access driver writes data to this file in a binary Oracle-internal Data Pump format, and you can then use this file to load another external table in a different database.

Creating an External Table with the ORACLE_DATAPUMP Access Driver

The example in Listing 13-5 shows how you can create an external table and populate it with data from an external flat file using the ORACLE_DATAPUMP access driver rather than the ORACLE_LOADER driver.

Listing 13-5. *Creating an External Table with the ORACLE_DATAPUMP Access Driver*

```
SQL> CREATE TABLE test_xt(
  2  product_id          NUMBER(6),
  3  warehouse_id        NUMBER(3),
  4  quantity_on_hand    NUMBER(8))
  5  ORGANIZATION EXTERNAL(
  6  TYPE ORACLE_DATAPUMP
  7  DEFAULT DIRECTORY ext_data_dir
  8  LOCATION  ('test_xt.dmp'));
Table created.
SQL>
```

To load data from this external table into an existing database table, you can use the INSERT INTO . . . SELECT clause, as shown earlier in Listing 13-4.

Writing to an External Table

The example in Listing 13-6 shows how to write to an external table.

Listing 13-6. *Populating an External Table*

```
SQL> CREATE TABLE test_xt
     ORGANIZATION EXTERNAL(
     TYPE ORACLE_DATAPUMP
     DEFAULT DIRECTORY ext_data_dir
     LOCATION ('test_xt.dmp'))
     AS
     SELECT * FROM scott.dept;
```

Note how the external table creation statement uses the SELECT * FROM clause to write data from the scott.dept table to the external table (file). If your new external table contains some but not all of the columns of the table scott.dept, you use the appropriate SELECT statement instead of the SELECT * FROM statement.

■**Note** Remember that when you load an Oracle table from an external table (data loading), you use the INSERT INTO . . . SELECT clause. When you populate an external table using Oracle table data (data unloading), you use the CREATE TABLE . . . AS SELECT clause.

If you now go look in the location specified for the default directory (ext_data_dir), you'll see the following:

```
SQL> ls -altr
Total 24
drwxr-xr-x     5  root    root       4096  March 4   14:08  ..
-rw-r--r--     1  oracle  oinstall     41  March 5   10:08  TEST_XT_28637.log
-rw-r-------   1  oracle  oinstall  12288  March 5   10:08  test_xt.dmp
```

The first file, test_xt_28637.log, logs the creation of this external table. The dump file test_xt.dmp contains the data from the table. You are creating the external table test_xt as an external table. The table structure and data both come from the regular Oracle table scott.dept. If you wish, you can then use this dump file in the same database or a different database to load other tables. Note that you must create the default directory (ext_data_dir) beforehand for this external table creation statement to succeed. The CTAS method of table creation will load the data from the scott.dept table into the new external table dept_xt. The CTAS command simply stores the table data in the external file called dept_xt_dmp. Thus, the external table is really composed of proprietary format, operating system–independent flat files.

You can also use the ORACLE_DATAPUMP access loader to extract Oracle table data into multiple files, as shown here:

```
SQL> CREATE TABLE extract_cust
     ORGANIZATION EXTERNAL
     (TYPE ORACLE_DATAPUMP DEFAULT DIRECTORY ext_data_dir ACCESS PARAMETERS
     (NOBADFILE NOLOGFILE)
     LOCATION ('extract_cust1.exp', 'extract_cust2.exp', 'extract_cust3.exp',
         'extract_cust4.exp'))
     PARALLEL 4 REJECT LIMIT UNLIMITED AS
     SELECT c.*, co.country_name, co.country_subregion, co.country_region
     FROM customers c, countries co where co.country_id=c.country_id;
```

The PARALLEL parameter will speed up the data unloading to the four datafiles. Note that the number of files you specify sets a limit on the degree of parallelization. For example, if you specify PARALLEL=8 and specify only four files, the degree of parallelism would be four, not eight.

Compressing and Encrypting Data

You can specify the COMPRESSION and the ENCRYPTION parameters to ensure that the data is compressed and encrypted when it's written out to the dump file set. By default, the database doesn't compress or encrypt the data. Following is a description of the two parameters.

COMPRESSION

The COMPRESSION parameter specifies whether data is compressed before it is written to a dump file set. By default, compression is disabled (COMPRESSION DISABLED). You can enable compression of the data for the entire upload operation by specifying COMPRESSION ENABLED.

The following example shows how you specify compression:

```
SQL> CREATE TABLE table TEST
     ORGANIZATION EXTERNAL (TYPE ORACLE_DATAPUMP DEFAULT DIRECTORY def_dir1
     ACCESS PARAMETERS (COMPRESSION ENABLED) LOCATION ('test.dmp'));
```

The previous command will ensure that all data written to the test.dmp file is in a compressed format.

ENCRYPTION

You can use the ENCRYPTION parameter to specify whether the database should encrypt data before writing the data to the dump file set. By default, encryption is disabled and you can enable it by using the ENCRYPTIUON ENABLED clause, as shown in the following example:

```
SQL> CREATE TABLE TEST
     ORGANIZATION EXTERNAL (TYPE ORACLE_DATAPUMP DEFAULT DIRECTORY test_dir1
     ACCESS PARAMETERS (ENCRYPTION ENABLED) LOCATION ('test.dmp'));
```

The ENCRYPTION ENABLED clause ensures that the data is encrypted when it's written to the test.dmp dump file.

Using an External Table

Once you create a new external table by populating an external file with data from an Oracle table, you can query the new table as you would any normal Oracle table. For example, the external table you created, test_xt, would show you the same data as a query on the original table (scott.dept). Here's the query:

```
SQL> SELECT * FROM test_xt;
```

The user samalapati is listed as the owner for this new table test_xt, as shown here:

```
SQL> SELECT owner FROM dba_tables
     WHERE table_name='TEST_XT';
     OWNER
-----------
SAMALAPATI
```

Note that as in the case of the original external tables in Oracle9*i*, you can only *select* from an external table. You also cannot insert, delete, or update data in an external table. Therefore, the term *writable external tables* applies in only a limited sense—you can write to the external tables only when you initially create them. Here is an example of what would happen if you attempted to insert into your new external table:

```
SQL> INSERT INTO test_xt (product_id) VALUES (222222);
INSERT INTO test_xt
                        *
ERROR at line 1:
ORA-30657: operation not supported on external organized table
SQL>
```

You would get similar error messages if you tried a DELETE or an UPDATE operation.

Also note that when you use the external tables feature to extract table data to a file, you export only the data. You can't export metadata using external tables. If you wish to extract the metadata for any object, just use DBMS_METADATA, as shown here:

```
SET LONG 2000
SELECT DBMS_METADATA.GET_DDL('TABLE','EXTRACT_CUST') FROM DUAL;
```

Using SQL*Loader to Generate External Table Creation Statements

As you saw in the previous sections, creating external tables correctly and choosing the appropriate access parameters can be a tedious task. Fortunately, there is an easier way to do all this: you can have SQL*Loader *generate* the entire DDL for creating the external tables and all the SQL statements to load the tables directly.

The SQL*Loader command-line parameter EXTERNAL_TABLE will allow you to generate the DDL for creating all your external tables. The default value for the EXTERNAL_TABLE parameter is NOT_USED, which means SQL*Loader will perform a normal data load in using either conventional or direct-path loading. When you use this parameter with the value GENERATE_ONLY, the SQL*Loader utility does not load any data; rather, SQL*Loader generates all SQL statements necessary to load the external tables described in the control file and places these statements in the SQL*Loader log file. If you use the EXTERNAL_TABLE parameter with the EXECUTE option, SQL*Loader will try to execute the SQL statements to create the external tables and perform the load.

The EXTERNAL_TABLE=GENERATE_ONLY option outputs the following information in the SQL*Loader log file:

- A CREATE DIRECTORY statement
- A complete CREATE TABLE statement for the external table, with all necessary access parameters
- All INSERT statements needed for loading the internal tables
- The DELETE statements for the directory and the external table

Let's look at an example that illustrates how to generate the external table creation statements with the help of the SQL*Loader utility. In this example, the internal table name is test_emp. This table must already exist, or you must create it before you can use SQL*Loader. The SQL*Loader-generated external table name is sys_sqlldr_x_ext_test_emp. The control file for SQL*Loader is called `test.ctl`, and it looks like this:

```
LOAD DATA
INFILE *
INTO TABLE test_emp
FIELDS TERMINATED BY ',' OPTIONALLY ENCLOSED BY '"'
(employee_id,first_name,last_name,hire_date,salary,manager_id)
BEGINDATA
12345,"sam","alapati",sysdate,50000,99999
23456,"mark","potts",sysdate,50000,99999
```

Invoke the SQL*Loader utility with test.ctl as your control file. Note that you're generating only the CREATE TABLE and INSERT statements; you aren't actually loading the tables.

```
$ sqlldr USERID=system/sammyy1 CONTROL=test.ctl \
    EXTERNAL_TABLE=GENERATE_ONLY
SQL*Loader: Release 10.2.0.0.0 - Beta on Sun Mar 6 13:49:39 2009
Copyright (c) 1982, 2008, Oracle.  All rights reserved.
oracle@hp50.netbsa.org   [/u01/app/oracle/dba]
$
```

Since no directory was specified for the log file, it will be created in the same directory where you ran SQL*Loader. The log file for the preceding run, test.log, will have all the information in it, including the external directory and table creation statements, and the actual INSERT statements to load the data into those tables. You can create the external table and then load the data directly using SQL without needing to use the SQL*Loader utility again. Listing 13-7 shows the log file generated using the EXTERNAL_TABLE=GENERATE_ONLY parameter.

Listing 13-7. *Using SQL*Loader to Generate the External Table Creation Statements*

```
SQL*Loader: Release 10.2.0.0.0 - Beta on Sun Mar 9 13:49:39 2008


Copyright (c) 1982, 2008, Oracle.  All rights reserved.
Control File:   test.ctl
Data File:      test.ctl
Bad File:     test.bad
Discard File:  none specified
(Allow all discards)
Number to load: ALL
Number to skip: 0
Errors allowed: 50
Continuation:    none specified
Path used:      External Table
Table TEST_EMP, loaded from every logical record.
Insert option in effect for this table: INSERT

    Column Name                      Position  Len  Term Encl Datatype
------------------------------- ---------- ----- ---- ---- ---------
EMPLOYEE_ID                         FIRST     *    ,   O(") CHARACTER
FIRST_NAME                          NEXT      *    ,   O(") CHARACTER
LAST_NAME                           NEXT      *    ,   O(") CHARACTER
HIRE_DATE                           NEXT      *    ,   O(") CHARACTER
SALARY                              NEXT      *    ,   O(") CHARACTER
MANAGER_ID                          NEXT      *    ,   O(") CHARACTER
CREATE DIRECTORY statements needed for files
---------------------------------------------------------------------
CREATE DIRECTORY SYS_SQLLDR_XT_TMPDIR_00000 AS '/u01/app/oracle/dba'
```

```
CREATE TABLE statement for external table:
-------------------------------------------------------------------------
CREATE TABLE "SYS_SQLLDR_X_EXT_TEST_EMP"
(
  "EMPLOYEE_ID" NUMBER,
  "FIRST_NAME" VARCHAR2(20),
  "LAST_NAME" VARCHAR2(20),
  "HIRE_DATE" DATE,
  "SALARY" NUMBER,
  "MANAGER_ID" NUMBER
)
ORGANIZATION external
(
  TYPE oracle_loader
  DEFAULT DIRECTORY SYS_SQLLDR_XT_TMPDIR_00000
ACCESS PARAMETERS
  (
    RECORDS DELIMITED BY NEWLINE CHARACTERSET US7ASCII
    BADFILE 'SYS_SQLLDR_XT_TMPDIR_00000':'test.bad'
    LOGFILE 'test.log_xt'
    READSIZE 1048576
    SKIP 6
    FIELDS TERMINATED BY "," OPTIONALLY ENCLOSED BY '"' LDRTRIM
    REJECT ROWS WITH ALL NULL FIELDS
    (
      "EMPLOYEE_ID" CHAR(255)
        TERMINATED BY "," OPTIONALLY ENCLOSED BY '"',
      "FIRST_NAME" CHAR(255)
        TERMINATED BY "," OPTIONALLY ENCLOSED BY '"',
      "LAST_NAME" CHAR(255)
        TERMINATED BY "," OPTIONALLY ENCLOSED BY '"',
      "HIRE_DATE" CHAR(255)
        TERMINATED BY "," OPTIONALLY ENCLOSED BY '"',
      "SALARY" CHAR(255)
        TERMINATED BY "," OPTIONALLY ENCLOSED BY '"',
      "MANAGER_ID" CHAR(255)
        TERMINATED BY "," OPTIONALLY ENCLOSED BY '"'
    )
  )
  location
  (
    'test.ctl'
  )
)REJECT LIMIT UNLIMITED
INSERT statements used to load internal tables:
----------------------------------------------------------------
INSERT /*+ append */ INTO TEST_EMP
(
  EMPLOYEE_ID,
  FIRST_NAME,
  LAST_NAME,
  HIRE_DATE,
  SALARY,
  MANAGER_ID
```

```
)
SELECT
  "EMPLOYEE_ID",
  "FIRST_NAME",
  "LAST_NAME",
  "HIRE_DATE",
  "SALARY",
  "MANAGER_ID"
FROM "SYS_SQLLDR_X_EXT_TEST_EMP"
Run began on Sun Mar 06 13:49:39 2009
Run ended on Sun Mar 06 13:49:40 2009
Elapsed time was:      00:00:01.22
CPU time was:          00:00:00.27
```

You can see that it's a lot easier to generate the CREATE TABLE statements for the external tables this way, rather than creating them from scratch.

Transforming Data

In most cases, especially in data warehouse environments, the data you're loading needs to be transformed to make it more meaningful for analysis. Oracle Database 11g can help you perform sophisticated and efficient data transformation within the database itself, so you don't need to rely on external processes or tools. You have several ways of performing data transformations in Oracle Database 11g. The following are the most commonly used techniques:

- Derive the data from existing tables. You can use joins or aggregations of data from tables in the same database, or you can gather the data from tables located in external Oracle or non-Oracle databases.

- Use SQL to transform data. SQL techniques including the MERGE statement, multiple-table inserts, and table functions to transform data during the loading process.

- Use the MODEL statement, which helps you perform highly expressive computations using sets of interrelated formulas. Using the MODEL clause, you can now treat an Oracle table as an n-dimensional array and specify interrow references without SQL joins and unions.

■Note You can also use PL/SQL procedural techniques to perform complex data transformations. The real issue here is whether you have the time and expertise at your disposal to code the transformation. In addition, when you're dealing with very large data sets, the use of PL/SQL is not very efficient when you compare it to some of the alternatives.

You'll examine the main Oracle data transformation techniques in more detail in the following sections.

Deriving the Data from Existing Tables

It's common to derive your new transformed data from existing tables in your database or other databases. You have two basic methods you can use to derive data from another table. If you're creating the table for the very first time, you can use the CTAS method to create new tables that meet your specifications. If the table already exists in your database or another database, you can use the INSERT /* APPEND */ INTO . . . SELECT method.

If the tables are in external databases, you can still use the CTAS method by using database links. Using the CTAS method simply means that you create a new table from an existing table. While you're creating the new table, you can apply certain SQL functions to the source table's columns, thereby transforming the data in the process. The following is a simple example showing the use of the CTAS method:

```
SQL> CREATE TABLE new_employees
     AS
     SELECT e.empno, INITCAP(e.ename), e.sal*1.1,
     e.mgr, d.deptno, d.loc, d.dname
     FROM emp e, dept d
     WHERE e.deptno=d.deptno;
Table created.
SQL>
```

The data transformations in this example state that the employee names will all start with a capital letter (INITCAP) and the salary column will be raised by a uniform 10 percent (sal * 1.1).

The next example shows how to load data into an existing table from another table. The use of the NOLOGGING and PARALLEL options in the example make the bulk insert run extremely fast.

```
SQL> INSERT /*APPEND NOLOGGING PARALLEL */
     INTO sales_data
     SELECT product_id, customer_id, TRUNC(sales_date),
     discount_rate, sales_quantity, sale_price
     FROM sales_history;
SQL>
```

Note that even though you used the PARALLEL hint in the preceding INSERT statement, Oracle may not execute your INSERT statement in parallel because, by default, parallel mode is disabled. You first must use the following statement so any DML statements you issue can be considered for parallel execution:

```
SQL> ALTER SESSION ENABLE PARALLEL DML;
Session altered.
SQL>
```

Once you have enabled parallel DML in your session, you can use the PARALLEL hint in your DML statements, and Oracle will parallelize its execution.

■**Caution** There are several restrictions on the use of parallel DML. For example, you can't use parallel DML on a table that has triggers. Refer to Oracle's documentation for more information about conditions that may preclude the use of the parallel DML feature.

Using SQL to Transform Data

It's common to use SQL statements to perform various kinds of data transformations. You can transform data by using simple UPDATE statements, although they could take a considerable time to execute in large tables. For smaller transactions in OLTP databases, the UPDATE statement is adequate when you need to transform data in a column based on some criteria. In the following sections, you'll explore some of the other common ways of using SQL to transform your data before loading: the MERGE statement, multitable inserts, and table functions.

Using the MERGE Statement

The MERGE statement is a powerful means of transforming data because it provides the functionality of checking the data to see whether an update is indeed required for a given row. Suppose you're loading data from a data source into your table. You want to insert customer data only if the customer is a new customer. If the customer's data is already present in your table, you don't want to reload the data, but you may want to update the customer's information based on the new data you just received.

The MERGE statement is actually an UPDATE-ELSE-INSERT operation performed by a single SQL statement. You could do the same thing without using the MERGE statement by performing a two-pass operation. In the first pass, you *update* all rows that have matching customer IDs in the table. In the second pass, you *insert* all rows that don't have a matching customer ID in your table. The following listings show the traditional two-pass update/insert method using separate UPDATE and INSERT statements. First, the update:

```
SQL> UPDATE catalog c SET
     (catalog_name, catalog_desc, catalog_category, catalog_price) =
     SELECT (catalog_name, catalog_desc, catalog_category, catalog_price)
     FROM catalog_data d
     WHERE c.catalog_id=d.catalog_id;
```

Second, the insert:

```
SQL> INSERT INTO catalog c
     SELECT * FROM catalog_data d
     WHERE c.catalog_id NOT IN
     (select catalog_id from catalog_data);
```

You could do the preceding work using a lengthy PL/SQL code piece. The PL/SQL procedures must match each input row against the table to see whether it already exists. Based on the results of the checks, code that either inserts or updates rows is executed.

Whether you use SQL or PL/SQL, you can't avoid the inefficient multiple processing of the same data to complete your update/insert processing. Both methods are fairly tedious and take a long time.

The MERGE statement, sometimes referred to as the *upsert* statement (because it does *both* an update and an insert using a single SQL statement), is a much more efficient way of performing traditionally multiple-pass operations. It's almost like using if-then-else logic. Listing 13-8 shows an update and insert process using the MERGE statement. The MERGE statement in Listing 13-8 instructs that if a certain row exists, update it; otherwise, insert the new row.

Listing 13-8. *Using the MERGE Statement to Perform an Update/Insert*

```
SQL> MERGE INTO target t
        USING source s
        ON (t.product_id=s.product_id)
        WHEN MATCHED THEN UPDATE SET
        t.price=s.price,
        t.discount=s.discount
        WHEN NOT MATCHED THEN INSERT
        (product_id, product_code, product_desc,
        product_price, product_discount)
        VALUES
        (s.product_id, s.product_code, s.product_desc,
        s.product_price, s.product_discount);
```

The WHEN MATCHED THEN UPDATE SET clause determines whether an UPDATE or an INSERT operation will take place. The previous statement will update a row in the table target if that row already exists. If there is no such row, Oracle will insert a new row in the table.

In addition to a straightforward insert/delete operation, you may perform conditional updates/inserts and optionally delete some rows, as shown in the following sections.

Conditional UPDATE and INSERT Statements

Rather than unconditionally inserting or updating all the table rows, you may want to insert or update data only when certain conditions are met. The MERGE statement allows you to conditionally insert or delete data. Now, Oracle allows you to use a WHERE clause in a MERGE statement's UPDATE or INSERT clause to conditionally update or insert data, as shown in Listing 13-9 (note the USING clause in the MERGE statement).

Listing 13-9. *Using UPDATE and INSERT Clauses in a MERGE Statement*

```
SQL> MERGE INTO products p                  /* Destination table
        USING product_changes s             /* Source table
        ON (p.prod_id = s.prod_id)          /* Search/join condition
        WHEN MATCHED THEN UPDATE            /* Update if join
        SET p.prod_list_price = s.prod_new_price
        WHERE p.prod_status <> 'EXPIRED'    /* Conditional update
        WHEN NOT MATCHED THEN
        INSERT                              /* Insert if not join
        SET p.prod_list_price = s.prod_new_price
        WHERE s.prod_status <> 'EXPIRED'    /* Conditional insert
```

Note that Oracle will skip the INSERT or UPDATE operation if the statement doesn't satisfy the WHERE condition. Both the INSERT and UPDATE operations would occur only if the product is *not* an *expired* item (WHERE s.prod_status <> "EXPIRED").

The DELETE Clause with the MERGE Statement

You can now use the MERGE statement with an optional DELETE clause. However, you can't use the DELETE clause independently in a MERGE statement, as with the UPDATE or INSERT clause. You must embed the DELETE statement inside the UPDATE statement. This means that the DELETE statement isn't a global clause, but rather works in the confines of the data affected by the UPDATE clause of the MERGE statement. Listing 13-10 shows how the DELETE clause is embedded within the UPDATE clause.

Listing 13-10. *Using the DELETE Clause in a MERGE Statement*

```
SQL> MERGE INTO products p
     USING product_changes s ON (p.prod_id = s.prod_id)
     WHEN MATCHED THEN UPDATE
     SET p.prod_list_price = s.prod_new_price,
     p.prod_status = s.prod_new_status
     DELETE WHERE (p.prod_status = 'OLD_ITEM')
     WHEN NOT MATCHED THEN INSERT
     (prod_id, prod_list_price, prod_status)
     VALUES (s.prod_id, s.prod_new_price, s.prod_new_status);
```

This MERGE statement will first update the prod_list_price and the prod_status columns of the products table wherever the join condition is true. The join condition (p.prod_id = s.prod_id) joins the two tables: product (the source table) and product_changes (the destination table).

Here are a couple of considerations when using the DELETE statement:

- The DELETE clause affects only the rows that were updated by the MERGE statement.

- The MERGE statement will delete only the rows included in the join condition specified by the ON clause.

In the example, when you use this MERGE statement, the UPDATE clause fires first, and it may set some of the prod_new_status values to expired. The DELETE clause will then remove all the rows whose prod_new_status value was set to expired by the UPDATE clause. The DELETE clause will not remove any other rows with the expired status, unless they are part of the join defined in the ON clause.

Using Multitable Inserts

Suppose you need to insert data from the source table into several target tables. Additionally, you want this loading to be based on various conditions: if condition A, then load into table X; if condition B, then load into table Y; and so on. Normally, you're forced to write several INSERT statements for inserting from the source into the target tables. If the data were very large, this would slow down the data loading. Alternatively, you could write PL/SQL-based code to do the same thing, but that would also slow down the process.

A type of SQL statement called a *multitable insert* enables you to do fast conditional loads of data from one source into multiple tables simultaneously. Because it's still a normal SQL statement, you can parallelize the operation to make the operation even faster. Multitable inserts can be either *unconditional* or *conditional*. You can also have a multitable insert that is a mix of conditional and unconditional inserts. The structure of the multitable insert varies depending on whether all or only some of the source table's rows are being loaded into the target tables.

■**Note** The performance gain from using a multitable insert is directly proportional to the complexity of the data and the number of target tables. Oracle claims that you can achieve a processing speed gain of 400 percent or more.

Loading All the Rows from the Source Table

When you load all rows of a table, you can use either an *unconditional all row insert* or a *conditional all row insert.* In the following example, the source table is called sales_activity, whose data is loaded at the same time into two destination tables: sales and cost. The unconditional insert uses the keywords INSERT ALL, meaning that all the source rows (sales_activity) are loaded into the sales and cost tables.

```
SQL> INSERT ALL
     INTO target1 VALUES (product_id, customer_id, sysdate, product_quantity)
     INTO target2 VALUES
     (product_id,sysdate,product_price,product_discount)
     SELECT s.product_id, s.customer_id, sysdate, s.product_quantity,
     s.product_price, s.product_discount
     FROM source s;
```

After the INSERT ALL keywords, there are two INTO statements, each denoting an insert into a separate table. Notice that the SELECT statement contains all the necessary columns required by both INTO statements for inserting into the two tables.

The conditional insert of all rows from the source table is similar to the unconditional version, except that the keyword WHEN indicates the conditions under which the inserts will be made. The following example shows how to perform a conditional all-row insert:

```
SQL> INSERT ALL
     WHEN product_id IN(SELECT product_id FROM primary) THEN
     INTO target1 VALUES (product_id, customer_id, sysdate, product_quantity)
     WHEN product_id IN (SELECT product_id FROM secondary) THEN
     INTO target2 VALUES
     (product_id, sysdate, product_price, product_discount)
     SELECT s.product_id, s.customer_id, sysdate, s.product_quantity,
     s.product_price, s.product_discount
     FROM source s;
```

This example still inserts all the rows from sales_data, because it uses the key phrase INSERT ALL.

Loading Selected Rows from the Source Table

Sometimes, you're interested in loading only some rows from a table, either based on a condition or unconditionally. You can do this in a multitable insert by using the keywords INSERT FIRST. Listing 13-11 shows how only some of the source table's rows are loaded into each target table, based on a separate condition for each table.

Listing 13-11. *Partial Loading of Rows from the Source Table*

```
SQL> INSERT FIRST
        WHEN (quantity_sold > 10 AND product_id <1000)
          THEN  INTO targetA VALUES
          (sysdate,product_id, customer_id, quantity_sold))
        WHEN quantity_sold <= 10 and product_id >10000
          THEN INTO targetB VALUES
           (sysdate,product_id, customer_id, quantity_sold)
        ELSE
        INTO targetC VALUES
         (time_id, cust_id, prod_id, sum_quantity_sold)
        SELECT s.time_id, s.cust_id, s.prod_id, p.prod_weight_class,
        SUM(amount_sold) AS sum_amount_sold,
        SUM(quantity_sold) AS sum_quantity_sold
        FROM sales s, products p
        WHERE s.prod_id = p.prod_id
        AND s.time_id = TRUNC(sysdate)
        GROUP BY  s.time_id, s.cust_id, s.prod_id, p.prod_weight_class;
```

Using Table Functions for Data Transformation

You can use Oracle's table functions to perform efficient data transformations. Table functions produce a collection of transformed rows that can be queried just like a regular table's data. Oracle table functions are an excellent example of Oracle's sophisticated transform-while-loading paradigm. Table functions can take a set of rows as input and return a transformed set of rows. When you query a table function in a statement, the function returns a collection type instance representing the rows in a table. The collection types can be either a VARRAY or a nested table. Table functions allow you to use PL/SQL, C, or Java with SQL without any problems.

　　Table functions make the traditional use of staging tables redundant. You don't need to create any intermediate tables to perform data transformations before loading data into the final data warehouse tables. Three features make table functions a powerful means of performing fast transformation of data sets:

- *Streaming*: This refers to the direct transmission of results from one process to the other without any intermediate steps. The way in which a table function orders or clusters rows that it fetches from cursor arguments is called *data streaming*.

- *Parallel execution*: This refers to the concurrent execution of the functions on multiprocessor systems.

- *Pipelining*: This technique lets you see the results of a query iteratively, instead of waiting for the entire result set to be batched and returned. Pipelining can thus help table functions reduce the response time by sending results as soon as they are produced in batches. You also have the option of having the table function immediately return rows from a collection by using pipelining. The elimination of (sometimes multiple) staging tables and the lack of need for any manual coding of parallel processing makes the pipelined parallel processing provided by table functions very attractive during large-scale data loading and transformation.

Here's a brief summary of the tasks that table functions can help you perform:

- Return a set of rows

- Return a result set incrementally, so you can process the results gradually

- Accept a cursor as an input

- Return results continuously while the transformation is taking place

- Be parallelized

It's easy to understand what a table function is when you think about a regular Oracle function. An Oracle function such as SUBSTR or TRANSLATE transforms data. For example, you can use the SUBSTR function to cut out a portion of a string, as shown in the following example:

```
SQL> SELECT sysdate FROM dual;
SYSDATE
========
20-MAY-08
SQL> SELECT SUBSTR(sysdate,4,3) FROM dual;
SUBSTRING(SYSDATE)
==================
MAY
SQL>
```

Table functions work the same way as regular Oracle functions that transform data. The only difference is that the table functions can be much more complex, and they can take cursors as inputs and return multiple rows after transforming them.

Suppose you need to load data from a table using an INSERT statement, and suppose that you don't need the data to be in the same format as the data in the source table. You can easily use the INSERT statement with one additional (automatic) step: use a table function to transform the data after it extracts the rows from the source and before the data gets inserted into your target table. Instead of the normal statement:

```
INSERT INTO target_table
SELECT * FROM source_table;
```

you use the following INSERT statement:

```
INSERT INTO target_table
SELECT * FROM (table function(source_table));
```

The previous INSERT statement will take the rows from the source table and insert them into the target table, with the twist that the inserted data will be of a different format from the original data in the target table. The table function will modify the data format before the INSERT operation can insert the data into the target table.

As an example, suppose you have an original table named sales_data, which shows a holding company's stores and sales figures for the two years 2001 and 2002:

```
SQL> SELECT * FROM sales_data;
STORE_NAME                SALES_2001 SALES_2002
------------------------- ---------- --------------------------------
shoe city                            500000
trinkets galore             1400000  1500000
modern tools                1000000  1200000
toys and toys                        800000
SQL>
```

Your goal is to extract data from this table to a target table with a different format. The new table is named yearly_store_sales, and it lists the company sales figures differently—each company's sales figure is listed by year. For example, in the original table, the store modern tools showed two yearly sales numbers in the same row: 1000000 and 1200000. In the new transformed table, these numbers should appear in different rows—that is, the data should show the store/sales year combinations. To do this, the company name may appear more than once in this table:

```
SQL> CREATE TABLE yearly_store_sales
  2  (store_name    VARCHAR2(25),
  3  sales_year     NUMBER,
  4* total_sales    NUMBER);
Table created.
SQL>
```

Because table functions return *sets* of records, you need to create some special object structures to use table functions to transform data. The first object you need to create is an *object type* called yearly_store_sales_row, which reflects the records. Note that the structure of this type is the same as your target table, yearly_store_sales.

```
SQL> CREATE TYPE yearly_store_sales_row AS
  2  OBJECT(
  3  store_name    varchar2(25),
  4  sales_year number,
  5* total_sales number);
Type created.
SQL>
```

The next step is to create a *table type* named yearly_store_sales_table. This table type is based on the object type you just created.

```
SQL> CREATE TYPE yearly_store_sales_table
  2  AS
  3  TABLE OF yearly_store_sales_row;
Type created.
SQL>
```

The package creation statement shown in Listing 13-12 is somewhat complex, and it is the heart of the table function feature. The table function uses a REF CURSOR to fetch the input rows. It then transforms the data and sends it out interactively (that is, it pipelines the data).

Listing 13-12. *Creating the Table Function*

```
SQL> CREATE OR REPLACE PACKAGE sales_package
  2  AS
  3  TYPE sales_cursor_type IS REF CURSOR
  4  RETURN sales_data%ROWTYPE;
  5  FUNCTION modify_sales_data
  6  (INPUTDATA IN sales_cursor_type)
  7  RETURN yearly_store_sales_table
  8  PIPELINED;
  9* END;
SQL> /
Package created.

SQL>
  1   CREATE OR REPLACE PACKAGE BODY sales_package
  2   AS
  3   FUNCTION modify_sales_data(
  4   inputdata IN sales_cursor_type)
  5   RETURN yearly_store_sales_table
  6   PIPELINED IS
  7   inputrec sales_data%ROWTYPE;
  8   outputrow_2001 yearly_store_sales_row :=
       yearly_store_sales_row(NULL,NULL,NULL);
  9   outputrow_2002 yearly_store_sales_row :=
       yearly_store_sales_row(NULL,NULL,NULL);
 10   BEGIN
 11     LOOP
 12       FETCH inputdata INTO inputrec;
 13       EXIT WHEN inputdata%NOTFOUND;
 14       IF INPUTREC.SALES_2001 IS NOT NULL THEN
 15        outputrow_2001.store_name := inputrec.store_name;
 16        outputrow_2001.sales_year := 2001;
 17        outputrow_2001.total_sales:= inputrec.sales_2001;
 18        pipe row (outputrow_2001);
 19       END IF;
 20       IF INPUTREC.SALES_2002 IS NOT NULL THEN
 21         outputrow_2002.store_name := inputrec.store_name;
 22         outputrow_2002.sales_year := 2002;
 23         outputrow_2002.total_sales:= inputrec.sales_2002;
 24         pipe row (outputrow_2002);
 25       END IF;
 26     END LOOP;
 27     RETURN;
 28   END;
 29*  END;
SQL> /
Package body created.
SQL>
```

Let's look at each part of the package carefully:

- In order to return sets of rows from the source table as inputs to the table function, you need to create a REF CURSOR based on the source table rows. The REF CURSOR in the example is named sales_cursor.

- The function modify_sales_data is the table function. It has one input parameter, the REF CURSOR sales_cursor. The function returns data in the format of the source table, yearly_store_sales.

- The keyword PIPELINED at the end means that data flows through the data transformation process. As the input data is processed, the transformed results are continuously fed into the target table.

- The package body shows the details of the function modify_sales_data. The function will transform the original structure of data in the source table into the desired format and insert it into the target table.

In the following INSERT statement, the function modify_sales_data is used. Note how the function is applied to the row data from the original table sales_data. The data is transformed before it is inserted into the yearly_store_sales table.

```
SQL> INSERT INTO yearly_store_sales t
  2    SELECT *
  3    FROM TABLE(sales_package.modify_sales_data(
  4    CURSOR(select store_name,sales_2001,sales_2002
  5    FROM sales_data)));
6 rows created.
SQL> COMMIT;
Commit complete.
SQL>
```

USING TABLE FUNCTIONS TO MINE WEB SERVICES DATA

Web services are self-contained, modular applications that can be published and invoked on the Web. Web services can perform complex business processes or serve as information providers. For example, you will find weather information services and stock market ticker services. Table functions can help you mine web services data.

Here's an outline of how you might use a table function to mine the stock market information that is published on the Web to provide a stock price alert system:

1. A private web service run by a stock market information service is accessed to collect the stock price information.

2. A table function, using a REF CURSOR of stock symbols as inputs, calls a Java stored procedure to gather the stock information from the web service. The table function converts the necessary stock price information into relational table data. The table function processes the information in the REF CURSOR one row at a time, and loads it into the table in a streamed fashion. You can have this information updated at regular intervals.

3. You can then use SQL and PL/SQL code to mine the stock data you collected in step 2. For example, the following is a typical SQL statement that uses the web services data you downloaded into your database table(s):

```
SQL> SELECT AVG(price), MIN(price), MAX(price)
     FROM
     table(stock_service_pack.to_table
     (cursor(select stock_symbol from stocks )));
```

Listing 13-13 shows the data in the new table. Note how the original data in the sales_data table has been transformed into a different format by the table function.

Listing 13-13. *The Transformed Table*

```
SQL> SELECT * FROM yearly_store_sales;
STORE_NAME        SALES_YEAR   TOTAL_SALES
----------------  ----------   ----------
shoe city         2002            500000
trinkets galore   2001           1400000
trinkets galore   2002           1500000
modern tools      2001           1000000
modern tools      2002           1200000
toys and toys     2002            800000
6 rows selected.
SQL>
```

The final SELECT statement from the yearly_store_sales table shows a different layout of data from that of the original table, sales_data. Now each store has a new column and year, and the yearly sales data is in separate rows. This makes it easier to compare the yearly sales figures of the various stores.

This example is rather trivial, but it clearly illustrates how you can use table functions to easily transform data during the process of loading it into another table.

Using the SQL MODEL Clause

It is common for Oracle users to process data using third-party tools, since Oracle SQL has traditionally lacked sophisticated modeling capabilities to produce complex reports. A basic example is the use of spreadsheets, which apply formulas to transform data into new forms. In previous versions of Oracle, in order to produce these spreadsheet-like reports, you needed to either download data into spreadsheet programs like Microsoft Excel or use dedicated multidimensional online analytical processing (OLAP) servers such as Oracle Express. For example, you might use Excel to convert your business data into rule-based business models, with the help of various macros. But third-party spreadsheet tools are cumbersome to use, and you need to expend considerable effort and time to constantly import updated Oracle data into the spreadsheet programs.

Oracle professionals commonly make heavy use of multiple table joins and unions when dealing with complex data warehousing. These techniques help you perform very complex computations, but they are usually slow and computationally expensive.

Oracle offers the powerful MODEL clause, which allows you to use SQL statements to categorize data and apply sophisticated formulas to produce fancy reports directly from within the database itself. You can now produce highly useful Oracle analytical queries, overcoming several drawbacks of Oracle SQL. With the new MODEL clause, you can use normal SQL statements to create multidimensional arrays and conduct complex interrow and interarray calculations on the array cells.

The MODEL clause provides interrow calculation functionality by enabling you to create multidimensional arrays of your query data and letting you randomly access the cells within the arrays. The way the MODEL clause addresses individual cells is called *symbolic cell addressing*. The MODEL clause also performs *symbolic array computation*, by transforming the individual cells using formulas, which it calls *rules*.

The MODEL clause enables you to apply business models to your existing data. When you use the MODEL clause as part of a query, Oracle feeds the data retrieved by the query to the MODEL clause. The MODEL clause rearranges the data into a multidimensional array and applies your business rules to the individual elements of the array. From the application of various user-specified business rules, Oracle derives updated as well as newly created data. However, you won't actually *see* an array as your final form of the output, since Oracle will format the new and updated data into a row format when it delivers the MODEL clause's output to you.

The first step in a MODEL-based query is the creation of the multidimensional array. The following section explains the basis of the arrays created by the MODEL clause.

Creating the Multidimensional Arrays

The MODEL clause creates the multidimensional arrays that are at the heart of its functionality by mapping all the columns of the query that contains a MODEL clause into the following three groups.

- *Partitions*: Basically, a partition is a result handed to the MODEL clause by previous grouping operations. The MODEL clause is always separately applied to the data within each partition.

- *Dimensions*: A dimension is a layer of metadata you can apply to a table to define hierarchical relationships among the table's columns. For example, a dimension named REGION could contain the hierarchy of STATE, COUNTY, and CITY. You may define several dimensions on a table, such as region, time, and product.

- *Measures*: Measures are the fact table data on which you are modeling your report, such as sales or inventories. You can look at the aggregate measure as consisting of a bunch of measure *cells*, with each of the cells identified by a unique combination of dimensions. For example, if sales is your measure, then the sales of detergents for the third quarter of 2008 in the New York region is one cell of the measure, since you can have only one such unique combination of your three dimensions: product (detergents), time (third quarter of 2008), and region (New York region).

The next section looks at how the MODEL feature uses rules to modify your multidimensional array data.

Transforming Array Data with Rules

A *rule* in the context of the MODEL clause is any business rule or formula you want to apply to the array data created by the MODEL clause. You may, for example, use a formula to forecast next year's sales on the basis of the preceding two years' sales data. You create a simple forecasting formula that expresses your business reasoning, and then pass it along to the MODEL clause as a rule.

You use the keyword RULES to indicate that you are specifying the rules that the MODEL clause must apply to its multidimensional array data. For example, you could specify a simple rule as follows:

```
MODEL
. . .
RULES
. . .
(sales['ProductA', 2009] = sales['ProductA', 2007] + sales['ProductA', 2008]
. . .
```

This rule specifies that the sales of ProductA for the year 2009 would be the sum of the sales of ProductA in the years 2007 and 2008.

When you specify the RULES keyword, you may also want to indicate whether the rules you are specifying will be transforming existing data or inserting new rows of data. By default, the RULES keyword operates with the UPSERT specification. That is, if the measure cell on the left side of a rule exists, Oracle will update it. Otherwise, Oracle will create a new row with the measure cell values. Here's an example:

```
MODEL
. . .
RULES UPSERT
sales ('ProductA', 2009) = sales ('ProductA', 2007) + sales ('ProductA', 2009)
. . .
/* MORE RULES HERE */)
```

In this rules specification, if there is already a table or view row that shows the sales for ProductA in the year 2009, Oracle will update that row with the values derived from applying the rule formula. If there is no such row, Oracle will create a new row to show the forecasted sales of ProductA for the year 2009.

If you don't want Oracle to insert any new rows, but just update the existing rows, you can change the default behavior of the RULES clause by specifying the UPDATE option for all the rules, as shown here:

```
MODEL
. . .
RULES UPDATE
Sales ('ProductA', 2009) = sales ('ProductA', 2007) + sales ('ProductA', 2008)
. . .
/* MORE RULES HERE */
```

The previous two examples demonstrated how to apply different rule options at the MODEL clause level. You may also specify rule options at the individual rule level, as shown here:

```
RULES
(UPDATE sales ('ProductA', 2009) = sales ('ProductA', 2007) +
sales ('ProductA', 2008)
```

When you specify a rule option at the individual rule level as shown in this example, the use of the RULES keyword is optional.

■Note If you specify a rule option at the *rule level*, it will override the RULES specification at the MODEL clause level. If you don't specify a rule option at the rule level, the MODEL level option applies to all the rules. If you don't specify an option at the MODEL level, the default UPSERT option will prevail.

You can specify that Oracle should evaluate the rules in either of the following two ways:

- SEQUENTIAL_ORDER: Oracle will evaluate a rule in the order it appears in the MODEL clause. SEQUENTIAL_ORDER is the *default* order of processing rules in a MODEL clause.

- AUTOMATIC_ORDER: Rather than evaluating a rule based on its order of appearance in a list of several rules, Oracle will evaluate the rule on the basis of the dependencies between the various rules in the MODEL clause. If rule A depends on rule B, Oracle will evaluate rule B first, even though rule A appears before rule B in the list of rules under the RULES keyword.

Producing the Final Output

As its output, the MODEL clause will give the results of applying your rules to the multidimensional arrays it created from your table data. A MODEL-based SQL analytical query typically uses an ORDER BY clause at the very end of the query to precisely order its output.

You can use the optional RETURN UPDATED ROWS clause after the MODEL keyword to specify that only the new values created by the MODEL statement should be returned. These new values may be either updated values of a column or newly created rows.

Note that when I say that the MODEL clause will create or update rows, I strictly mean that the changes are shown in the MODEL clause *output*. The MODEL clause doesn't update or insert rows into the table or views. To change the base table data, you must use the traditional INSERT, UPDATE, or MERGE statement.

Using the MODEL Clause

Let's look at a simple SQL example that demonstrates the capabilities of the MODEL clause. Here's the query:

```
SQL> SELECT country, product, year, sales
     FROM sales_view
     WHERE country IN ('Mexico', 'Canada')
     MODEL
     PARTITION BY (country) DIMENSION BY (product, year)
     MEASURES (sale sales)
     RULES
       (sales['ProductA', 2009] = sales['ProductA', 2008] +
       sales['ProductA',2007],
       sales['ProductB', 2009]  = sales['ProductB', 2008],
       sales['All_Products', 2009] = sales['ProductA', 2009] +
       sales['ProductB',2009])
     ORDER BY country, product, year;
```

Sales units are the measure in this example. The query partitions the data by country and forms the measure cells consisting of product and year combinations. The three rules specify the following:

- Total sales of ProductA in 2009 are forecast as the sum of ProductA sales in the years 2007 and 2008.

- Total sales of ProductB in the year 2009 are forecast to be the same as the sales in 2008.

- Total product sales in 2009 are computed as the sum of the ProductA and ProductB sales in 2009.

Here's the output generated by using the preceding SQL statement with the MODEL clause:

```
COUNTRY         PRODUCT         YEAR    SALES
--------        ------------    -----   ---------
Mexico          ProductA        2006    2474.78
Mexico          ProductA        2007    4333.69
Mexico          ProductA        2008    4846.3
Mexico          ProductA        2009    9179.99
Mexico          ProductB        2006    15215.16
Mexico          ProductB        2007    29322.89
Mexico          ProductB        2008    81207.55
Mexico          ProductB        2009    81207.55
Mexico          All_Products    2009    90387.54
Canada          ProductA        2006    2961.3
Canada          ProductA        2007    5133.53
Canada          ProductA        2008    6303.6
Canada          ProductA        2009    11437.13
Canada          ProductB        2006    22161.91
Canada          ProductB        2007    45690.66
Canada          ProductB        2008    89634.83
Canada          ProductB        2009    89634.83
Canada          All_Products    2009    101071.96
```

The SELECT clause first retrieves the product, year, and sales data for the two countries (Mexico and Canada) and feeds it into the MODEL clause. The MODEL clause takes this raw data and rearranges it into a multidimensional array, based on the values of the PARTITION BY (country) and DIMENSION BY (product and year) clauses. After the MODEL clause creates the array, it applies the three formulas listed under the RULES clause to the data. It finally produces the resulting row data, after ordering it by country, product, and year. Note that the MODEL clause shows the original table or view data, as well as the new data that the MODEL clause has calculated.

Using Oracle Streams for Replication and Information Sharing

As companies grow, it becomes important to be able to share information among multiple databases and applications. Disparate information-sharing technologies add to the burden of effectively replicating data. The Oracle Streams feature provides a single unified solution for information sharing across the enterprise.

When you use Oracle Streams, each unit of information is called an *event*, and you share these events in a stream. A stream routes specified information to specified destinations. The Oracle Streams feature captures changes occurring in the database, using both the active and archived redo logs. Streams capture these changes and store them in queues, after proper formatting. Streams then propagate these changes to other databases and apply them to the target databases. Using the Oracle Streams feature, you can capture, propagate, and apply information within an Oracle database, between two Oracle databases, among multiple Oracle databases, or between an Oracle database and a non-Oracle database.

Using Streams, you can transform the streams of data at any of the three points: during capture of data, during propagation to the target, and during application at the destination site. The events may include messages queued into a database queue by applications as well as DML and DDL changes. You can use Oracle Streams for the following applications:

- *Data replication*: You can use Oracle Streams to capture changes from a source database, stage and propagate these changes to a target databases, and consume or apply the changes to the target database.

- *Advanced message queuing*: The Oracle Streams Advanced Queuing (AQ) feature lets you enqueue messages into a queue, propagate messages to subscribing queues, notify user applications that messages are ready for consumption, and dequeue messages at their destination.

- *Event management and notification*: The ability to capture events and propagate them based on rules lets you use Oracle Streams for event notification. Events staged in a queue may be dequeued explicitly by a messaging client or an application, and actions can be taken based on these events, including e-mail notification and cell phone transmission.

- *Data warehouse loading*: Streams can capture changes made to a production database and send those changes over to a data warehouse. During the apply process, you can apply transformations to the data before you load it in the target database.

- *Data protection*: You can use the streams technology to maintain a logical standby database. The logical standby database can remain open for read/write operations, and you can query it as updates are applied. Standby databases are a good solution for offloading queries from your production database.

Note You can use Oracle Streams at multiple levels of granularity: database, schema, and table. Oracle Streams can use rules to configure the capture of changes for the entire database, a specific schema, or a set of tables.

Exploring the Streams Architecture

The three basic elements of Oracle Streams technology are capture, staging, and consumption of events within the Oracle database.

The *capture* process captures change information from the source database, at the table, schema, or database level. Streams capture events in one of two ways: explicitly or implicitly. *Explicit capture* is when users and applications manually enqueue events into a queue. These user-enqueued events can be redo log change records or messages of a user-defined type called user messages. In the *implicit* capture process, the server captures DML and DDL changes from the source database by mining the redo logs and archived redo logs. The implicit capture process, which is an Oracle background process, consists of the following components:

- A reader server, which reads redo logs and divides them into regions
- One or more prepare servers, which scan the regions in parallel and perform prefiltering of changes
- A builder server, which merges redo records it receives from the prepare servers and hands them to the capture process

The capture process formats the merged redo records into a logical change record (LCR) and enqueues them into the staging area for further processing. An LCR describes changes made to a single row with a DML statement. A single DML statement can produce several LCRs. An LCR, which is a set of captured changes, is also called an *event*. LCRs containing information about table data are known as *row LCRs*, and those containing information about DDL changes are called *DDL LCRs*. Rules used by the capture process determine which changes it captures. Note that you can set up Streams such that the database can extract changes from the redo stream at the source and then transmit the LCRs to the target or transmit the entire redo stream the target. The target can then extract the LCRs.

In the *staging* element, the Oracle Streams process stores events in a queue. These events could include both explicit and implicit changes.

In the final stage, *consumption*, the queued events are consumed in the target database. An event is consumed when you dequeue it from an event queue. Users and applications can dequeue events explicitly. However, most of the dequeueing is through an implicit *apply* process. The dequeueing and processing of the captured data is done according to rules. The apply process may apply the captured data directly or transform it using PL/SQL code.

Setting Up Oracle Streams

Following are the steps you must take in order to configure and administer the Oracle Streams feature to propagate changes between multiple databases. Note that this is a very brief overview of the Streams configuration process designed to give you a flavor of the process. You must refer to the appropriate guidelines in the Oracle manuals for setting up Streams in your environment.

1. Make the necessary changes to your `init.ora` or `SPFILE` file to make sure the following are true:

   - The `COMPATIBLE` parameter should be set to 10.2.0 or higher in both databases (you can actually set it to 9.2 or higher).

   - The `JOB_QUEUE_PROCESSES` parameter on the source database should be at least 2.

   - The `GLOBAL_NAMES` parameter should be set to `true` in both the source and target databases.

   - Set `LOG_ARCHIVE_DEST_n`. You must have at least one log archive destination at the site running the downstream capture process.

   - Make sure you allocate at least 200MB to the `STREAMS_POOL_SIZE` memory component of the SGA.

   - Ensure that the undo tablespace is large enough to accommodate the `UNDO_RETENTION` setting.

   - Make sure your source database is in archivelog mode.

2. Create a new user to manage the streams. Before you create the user, you may want to create a new tablespace for the use of this new Streams user.

```
SQL> CREATE TABLESPACE streams_tbs
     DATAFILE '/u01/app/oracle/oradata/
     streams_tbs.dbf' SIZE 100M;
```

Now create the Streams administrator user in the database, as follows:

```
SQL> CREATE USER strmadmin
        IDENTIFIED BY strmadmin
        DEFAULT TABLESPACE streams_tbs
        TEMPORARY TABLESPACE temp
        QUOTA UNLIMITED ON streams_tbs;
```

3. Grant the CONNECT, RESOURCE, and DBA roles to the Streams administrator:

```
SQL> GRANT DBA TO strmadmin;
```

4. Use the GRANT_ADMIN_PRIVILEGE procedure in the DBMS_STREAMS_AUTH package to grant necessary privileges to the Streams administrator:

```
SQL> BEGIN
        DBMS_STREAMS_AUTH.GRANT_ADMIN_PRIVILEGE(
        GRANTEE          => 'strmadmin',
        GRANT_PRIVILEGES => true);
        END;
        /
```

5. Create a database link between the source and target databases, as shown here:

```
SQL> CREATE DATABASE LINK targetdb
        CONNECT TO strmadmin
        IDENTIFIED BY strmadmin
        USING 'target.db.world';
```

6. Oracle Streams moves data between the source and destination databases using queues. You need to create a queue on both the source and destination databases. To do this, you must run the following procedure on both the source and the target databases. This will create both queues with their default names.

```
EXEC DBMS_STREAMS_ADM.SET_UP_QUEUE();
```

7. You need to enable supplemental logging for all the tables on the source databases for which you intend to capture changes. You set up supplemental logging in the following manner:

```
SQL> ALTER TABLE emp ADD SUPPLEMENTAL LOG DATA
        (PRIMARY KEY, UNIQUE) COLUMNS;
```

8. Configure the capture process in the source database, using the ADD_TABLE_RULES procedure of the DBMS_STREAMS_ADM package, as shown here:

```
SQL> BEGIN
        DBMS_STREAMS_ADM.ADD_TABLE_RULES(
        table_name     => 'scott.emp',
        streams_type   => 'capture',
        streams_name   => 'capture_stream',
        queue_name     => 'strmadmin.streams_queue',
        include_dml    => true,
        include_ddl    => true,
        inclusion_rule => true);
        END;
        /
```

Now that you've configured your Oracle Streams setup, you can test the setup by starting a capture process and using an apply process to replicate the emp table from the source database to the emp table in the target database. First, capture the changes using the following procedure:

```
SQL> BEGIN
     DBMS_CAPTURE_ADM.START_CAPTURE(
     capture_name => 'capture_stream');
     END;
     /
```

To migrate the captured changes to the destination database, run the following procedure:

```
SQL> BEGIN
     DBMS_APPLY_ADM.START_APPLY(
     apply_name  => 'apply_stream');
     END;
     /
```

The Oracle Streams feature was discussed very briefly here. However, it's a very powerful feature useful for database replication, migration, and upgrades. The primary interface to Streams is this collection of Oracle-supplied PL/SQL packages. You saw how to use various Oracle-supplied PL/SQL packages to set up and manage the Streams feature, so you know exactly what's happening during the change capture and propagation phases. To help users configure, administer, and monitor their Streams environments, Oracle provides a Streams tool in the OEM Console. I recommend using the Streams feature with the help of the OEM Database Control interface, for convenience.

Using Data Pump Export and Import

Almost all Oracle DBAs are familiar with Oracle's export and import utilities, which help in loading data into and unloading data from databases. In both the Oracle Database 10*g* and Oracle Database 11*g* releases, you must use the more versatile and powerful Data Pump Export and Import utilities to export and import data.

The old export and import utilities continue to be available under Oracle Database 11*g*, but Oracle would prefer you to use the Data Pump technology because it offers more sophisticated features. For example, you can now interrupt export/import jobs in the middle and then resume them. You can restart failed export and import jobs. You can remap object attributes to modify the objects. You can easily monitor your Data Pump jobs from a different session, and you can even modify job attributes on the fly during the course of a job. It's easy to move massive amounts of data quickly using parallelization techniques. Because Oracle provides you the APIs for the Data Pump technology, you can easily incorporate export/import jobs within PL/SQL programs.

You can also use the powerful transportable tablespaces feature to transport large amounts of data quickly, even across disparate operating system platforms.

This chapter provides in-depth coverage of the Data Pump technology, as well as transportable tablespaces.

Introduction to the Data Pump Technology

The Data Pump technology, which was new to Oracle Database 10*g*, is a server-side infrastructure for fast data movement between Oracle databases. The Data Pump technology enables DBAs to transfer large amounts of data and metadata at very high speeds compared with the older export/import technology. Data Pump manages multiple parallel streams of data to achieve maximum throughput. Oracle claims that Data Pump enables you to decrease total export time by more than two orders of magnitude in most data-intensive export jobs. Imports are supposed to run 15 to 45 times faster than with the original import utility (the estimates are for single-thread operations; parallel threads will make the operations even faster). Much of the higher speed comes from using parallelism to read and write export dump files.

Data Pump is a superset of the original export and import utilities, offering several different capabilities. Data Pump lets you estimate job times, perform fine-grained object selection, monitor jobs effectively, and directly load a database from a remote instance via the network.

For compatibility purposes, Oracle still includes the old export and import utilities in Oracle Database 11*g*. Thus, you can continue to use older export and import scripts as usual, without any changes. Once you see how and why the newer Data Pump utilities are better than the older ones, you probably will choose the newer utilities, however. Oracle will eventually deprecate the original export utility, but it will support the original import utility forever. This means that you'll always have a way of importing dump files from earlier versions of Oracle. However, Data Pump Import will not work with databases that are older than the Oracle Database 10*g* Release 1 (10.1) version. Also note that the new Data Pump technology lets you export data only to disk. You cannot use a tape drive when performing a Data Pump export.

Oracle Data Pump technology consists of two components: the Data Pump Export utility, to unload data objects from a database, and the Data Pump Import utility, to load data objects into a database. You access the two Data Pump utilities through a pair of clients called expdp and impdp. As their names indicate, the first of these corresponds to the Data Pump Export utility and the latter to the Data Pump Import utility. You can control both Data Pump Export and Import jobs with the help of several parameters. Here's how you invoke the two utilities:

```
$ expdp username/password (various parameters here)
$ impdp username/password (various parameters here)
```

Unlike the old export and import utilities, the Data Pump utilities have a set of parameters you can use at the command line and a set of special commands you can use only in an interactive mode. I'll explain the main parameters, commands, and other important features of the Data Pump tool set in the "Performing Data Pump Exports and Imports" section later in this chapter. You can also get a quick summary of all Data Pump parameters and commands (including the interactive commands) by simply typing **expdp help=y** or **impdp help=y** at the command line.

The Data Pump Export utility unloads data into operating system files known as *dump files* in a proprietary format that only the Data Pump Import utility can understand. You can take Data Pump Export dump files from an operating system and import them into a database running on a different platform, as you could with the older export/import utilities.

■**Caution** The original export and Data Pump dump files aren't compatible. You can't read the older export dump files with Data Pump Import, and the older import utility can't read Data Pump Export dump files.

In addition to expdp and impdp, you can have other clients perform Data Pump export and import by using the Data Pump API. The database uses the Oracle-supplied package DBMS_DATA PUMP to implement the API, through which you can programmatically access the Data Pump Export and Import utilities. This means that you can create powerful custom data-movement utilities using the Data Pump technology.

The traditional export utility is a normal user process that writes data to its local disks. The old export utility fetches this data from a server process as part of a regular session. In contrast, the Data Pump expdp user process launches a server-side process that writes data to disks on the server node, and this process runs independent of the session established by the expdp client.

Benefits of the Data Pump Technology

The older export/import technology was client-based. The Data Pump technology is purely server-based. All dump, log, and other files are created on the server by default.

Data Pump technology offers several benefits over the traditional export and import data utilities. The following are the main benefits of the Data Pump technology:

- *Improved performance*: The performance benefits are significant if you are transferring huge amounts of data.

- *Ability to restart jobs*: You can easily restart jobs that have stalled due to lack of space or have failed for other reasons. You may also manually stop and restart jobs.

- *Parallel execution capabilities*: By specifying a value for the PARALLEL parameter, you can choose the number of active execution threads for a Data Pump Export or Data Pump Import job.

- *Ability to attach to running jobs*: You can *attach* to a running Data Pump job and interact with it from a different screen or location. This enables you to monitor jobs, as well as to modify certain parameters interactively. Data Pump is an integral part of the Oracle database server, and as such, it doesn't need a client to run once it starts a job.

- *Ability to estimate space requirements*: You can easily estimate the space requirements for your export jobs by using the default BLOCKS method or the ESTIMATES method, before running an actual export job (see the "Data Pump Export Parameters" section later in this chapter for details).

- *Network mode of operation*: Once you create database links between two databases, you can perform exports from a remote database straight to a dump file set. You can also perform direct imports via the network using database links, without using any dump files. The network mode is a means of transferring data from one database directly into another database with the help of database links and without the need to stage it on disk.

- *Fine-grained data import capability*: Oracle9*i* offered only the QUERY parameter, which enabled you to specify that the export utility extract a specified portion of a table's rows. With Data Pump, you have access to a vastly improved fine-grained options arsenal, thanks to new parameters like INCLUDE and EXCLUDE.

- *Remapping capabilities*: During a Data Pump import, you can remap schemas and tablespaces, as well as filenames, by using the new REMAP_ * parameters. Remapping capabilities enable you to modify objects during the process of importing data by changing old attributes to new values. For example, the REMAP_SCHEMA parameter enables you to map all of user HR's schema to a new user, OE. The REMAP_SCHEMA parameter is similar to the TOUSER parameter in the old import utility.

Uses for Data Pump Export and Import

The SQL*Loader tool discussed in the previous chapter is primarily designed to move data into one or more tables from flat files. For exporting or importing entire schemas and even databases, you must use the Data Pump Export and Import utilities. Here are some of the main uses of the Data Pump tools:

- Migrating databases from development to test or production

- Copying test data from development/testing databases to production or vice versa

- Transferring data between Oracle databases on different operating system platforms

- Backing up important tables before you make any changes to them

- Backing up databases

- Moving database objects from one tablespace to another

- Transporting tablespaces between databases

- Reorganizing fragmented table data

- Extracting the DDL for tables and other objects such as stored procedures and packages

---

■**Note** Data Pump doesn't create a perfect backup, because you won't have up-to-the-minute data in the export file when a disaster occurs. However, for smaller databases and individual tablespace exports, data exports are still viable as a backup tool.

As you'll see, the Data Pump Export and Import utilities are extremely versatile and easy to use. You can export just the DDL for objects if you wish, or you can export and import the objects with the data. You also have the choice of exporting and importing a single table (or even a part of a single table), all the tables in a tablespace, an entire schema, or an entire database.

Data Pump Components

On the surface, expdp and impdp are quite similar to the traditional export and import utilities. However, while they are syntactically similar to the Data Pump clients, exp and imp are ordinary user processes that use SQL statements like SELECT, INSERT, and CREATE. In contrast, the new Data Pump utilities are more like control processes that initiate jobs. In Data Pump Export and Import, the database instance handles the Data Pump utilities.

The Data Pump technology consists of three major components:

- *DBMS_DATAPUMP package*: This is the main engine for driving data dictionary metadata loading and unloading. The DBMS_DATAPUMP package (Data Pump API) contains the guts of the Data Pump technology in the form of procedures that actually drive the data loading and unloading jobs. The contents of this package perform the work of both the Data Pump Export and Import utilities.

- *DBMS_METADATA package*: To extract and modify metadata, Oracle provides the DBMS_METADATA package (Metadata API), which has been available since Oracle9*i*. In the traditional export and import utilities, the metadata of the objects is included in the export dump file. In Data Pump technology, you need to use the DBMS_METADATA package to extract the appropriate metadata.

- *Command-line clients*: The two command-line utilities—expdp and impdp—correspond to the old exp and imp utilities. The expdp utility invokes the Data Pump Export utility, and the impdp utility invokes the Data Pump Import utility. The dump files you create with these new utilities aren't compatible with the older export/import utilities.

Note that both packages—DBMS_DATAPUMP and DBMS_METADATA—act as APIs (the Data Pump API and the Metadata API), in the sense that you can use either of them directly in your programs to load and unload data without accessing the expdp and impdp clients.

Data-Access Methods

A Data Pump Import or Export job can access table data in either of two ways:

- *Direct path*: This access uses the Direct Path API. Direct-path exports and imports lead to improved performance, since the direct-path internal stream format is the same format as the data stored in Oracle dump files. This leads to a reduced need for data conversions. The big advantage of the direct-path mode is that it bypasses the database buffer cache and doesn't generate any undo data.

- *External tables*: The external tables feature lets Oracle read data from and write data to operating system files that lie outside the database. Chapter 13 explains external tables in detail.

It is up to Oracle to decide which access method it will employ for a given job. Oracle always tries to use the direct-path method to load or unload data, but under some conditions, it may not be able to employ that method. In the following cases, the structure of the table and/or the indexes precludes the use of direct-path access, so Data Pump will use external tables:

- Clustered tables

- Active triggers in the tables

- A single partition in a table with a global index

- Referential integrity constraints

- Domain indexes on LOB columns

- Tables with fine-grained access control enabled in the insert mode

- Tables with BFILE or opaque type columns

■**Note** The datafile format is identical in external tables and the direct-access method. Therefore, you can easily export data with one method and import it with the other method, if you wish.

Data Pump Files

As in the case of the traditional export and import utilities, Data Pump uses dump files and other log files, but there are significant differences. You'll use three types of files for Data Pump operations:

- *Dump files*: These hold the table data as well as the metadata that's being loaded or unloaded.

- *Log files*: These are the standard files for logging the messages and results of Data Pump operations.

- *SQL files*: Data Pump Import uses a special parameter called SQLFILE, which will write all the DDL statements it will execute during the import job to a file. Data Pump doesn't actually execute the SQL, but merely writes the DDL statements to the file specified by the SQLFILE parameter. You use SQL files only to hold the output of the SQLFILE command during a Data Pump Import job. This parameter is discussed in the "Data Pump Import Parameters" section later in this chapter.

As in the case of the older export/import utilities, all new log files (and SQL files) will overwrite any older files with the same name. If an older dump file of the same name already exists, you'll get an error.

Unlike with the traditional export and import utilities, you use directories and directory objects to store the Data Pump files. The following section explains how to use directory objects.

Using Directory Objects

A Data Pump job creates all its dump files on the server, not on the client machine where a job may have originated. Oracle background processes are responsible for all dump file set I/O, on behalf of the Oracle software owner (usually, the user oracle). This means that for security reasons, you can't let any user specify an absolute file path on the server. In addition to a possible violation of security, there is the matter of safety, as you can unwittingly overwrite a server file if you are given the power to write dump files anywhere on the system. Similarly, you'll be able to read all files that the server has access to, even though you may not have been granted specific privileges to do so. To avoid these types of problems, Data Pump uses directory objects.

■**Caution** Your Data Pump Export and Import jobs will not run unless you create a directory object first. Subsequently, you must also ensure that the user has the necessary file and directory access privileges on that file system.

Directory objects are named objects that Data Pump maps to a specific operating system directory. For example, a directory object named dpump_dir1 can point to the /u01/app/oracle/admin/
export directory on the server. You can then access this directory by simply using the dpump_dir1
directory object name. Oracle creates a *default directory object*, DATA_PUMP_DIR, when you create a
new database or if you upgrade a database to that version. This default DATA_PUMP_DIR directory
object points to a directory named dpdump. The default Data Pump directory is automatically created
by Oracle in one of the following locations:

- ORACLE_BASE/admin/SID

- ORACLE_HOME/admin/SID

If you have defined the ORACLE_BASE directory, Oracle uses the location based on it. Otherwise,
Oracle will create the default directory under the ORACLE_HOME directory. Data Pump will write all
dump files, SQL files, and log files to the directory specified for the default DATA_PUMP_DIR object. To
see exactly where your default DATA_PUMP_DIR directory object is located, you can use the following
query, based on the DBA_DIRECTORIES view:

```
SQL> SELECT * FROM dba_directories;

OWNER   DIRECTORY_NAME   DIRECTORY_PATH
--------------------------------------------------------------------------
SYS     DATA_PUMP_DIR    /u01/app/oracle/product/10.2.0/db_1/admin/orcl/dpdump/
SQL>
```

Only privileged users like SYS and SYSTEM can use the default directory object DATA_PUMP_DIR.
Thus, user SYSTEM can start a Data Pump Export job without providing a directory name. Listing 14-1
shows the output of the Data Pump Export job.

Listing 14-1. *A Data Pump Export Run by the User SYSTEM*

```
C:\>expdp system/sammyy1
Export: Release 11.1.0.6.0 - Production on Saturday, 22 March, 2008 11:10:36

Copyright (c) 2003, 2007, Oracle.  All rights reserved.

Connected to: Oracle Database 11g Enterprise Edition Release 11.1.0.6.0 - Produc
tion
With the Partitioning, OLAP, Data Mining and Real Application Testing options
FLASHBACK automatically enabled to preserve database integrity.
Starting "SYSTEM"."SYS_EXPORT_SCHEMA_01":  system/********
Estimate in progress using BLOCKS method . . .
Processing object type SCHEMA_EXPORT/TABLE/TABLE_DATA
Total estimation using BLOCKS method: 320 KB
Processing object type SCHEMA_EXPORT/USER
. . .
Processing object type SCHEMA_EXPORT/POST_SCHEMA/PROCACT_SCHEMA
. . exported "SYSTEM"."REPCAT$_AUDIT_ATTRIBUTE"          6.398 KB       2 rows
. . .
. . exported "SYSTEM"."SQLPLUS_PRODUCT_PROFILE"            0 KB       0 rows
Master table "SYSTEM"."SYS_EXPORT_SCHEMA_01" successfully loaded/unloaded
********************************************************************************
Dump file set for SYSTEM.SYS_EXPORT_SCHEMA_01 is:
  C:\ORCL\APP\ORACLE\ADMIN\ORCL\DPDUMP\EXPDAT.DMP
Job "SYSTEM"."SYS_EXPORT_SCHEMA_01" successfully completed at 11:11:52

C:\>
```

However, before a nonprivileged user can use Data Pump Export or Import, the DBA must create a directory object or grant privileges to use an existing directory. In addition to the DBA, any user with the CREATE ANY DIRECTORY privilege can create a directory object. Here's how you create a directory object:

```
SQL> CREATE DIRECTORY dpump_dir1 AS '/u01/finance/oradata/dump_dir';
```

In order for a user to use a specific directory, the user must have access privileges to the directory object. For example, in order to let the database read and write files on behalf of user salapati in the new directory object dpump_dir1, you need to grant the following privileges:

```
SQL> GRANT READ, WRITE ON DIRECTORY dpump_dir1 TO salapati
Grant succeeded.
SQL>
```

This command will permit the Oracle database to read and write files in the dpump_dir1 directory object on behalf of the user, but won't give the user any direct privileges on that directory. You'll need the write privilege on all files for a Data Pump Export job. During an import, you'll need read access to the export dump file. You'll also need write privileges on the directory for an import job, so that you can write to the log file. Here's what happens when you are given the read/write privileges on a directory object:

- You can read/write files mapped to that directory object only through Oracle.
- The Oracle database must have privileges to read/write files in that directory.

Once you create a directory and grant the necessary rights, all Data Pump Export and Import jobs can use the DIRECTORY parameter (described shortly) to specify the name of the directory object (DIRECTORY=dpump_dir1). This way, the DIRECTORY parameter will indirectly point to the actual operating system directories and files. Here's an example:

```
$ expdp salapati/password  DIRECTORY=dpump_dir1 dumpfile=testexp01.dmp
```

If a user tries to use the expdp or impdp utility without a DBA creating and granting privileges on a directory beforehand, that user will get an error, which means that Oracle isn't able to find a directory object and, hence, can't start the Data Pump job, as shown in Listing 14-2.

Listing 14-2. *Data Pump Error Caused by Nonspecification of a Directory Object*

```
C:\> expdp hr/hr

Export: Release 11.1.0.6.0 - Production on Saturday, 22 March, 2008 11:13:29

Copyright (c) 2003, 2007, Oracle.  All rights reserved.

Connected to: Oracle Database 11g Enterprise
Edition Release 11.1.0.6.0 - Prodution
With the Partitioning, OLAP, Data Mining and Real Application Testing options

ORA-39002: invalid operation
ORA-39070: Unable to open the log file.
ORA-39145: directory object parameter must be specified and non-null

C:\>
```

In order for the Data Pump utilities to know where to place or get data for their export and import jobs, you need to specify location information when you use the expdp and impdp clients.

As you know by now, you can't use an absolute directory path location for Data Pump jobs; you must always use a directory object. However, you can specify this directory object name during an actual job in several ways:

- DIRECTORY *parameter*: During a Data Pump Export job, you can specify the directory object by using the DIRECTORY parameter:

  ```
  $ expdp hr/hr DIRECTORY=dpump_dir1 . . .
  ```

- DIRECTORY:FILE *notation*: Instead of using the DIRECTORY parameter, you can specify the directory object's name as part of the value for a specific Data Pump file (the dump file, log file, or SQL file). Use a colon (:) to separate the directory and the individual filenames in the file specification. In the following example, dpump_dir2 is the name of the directory object, and the Data Pump filename is salapati.log:

  ```
  $ expdp LOGFILE=dpump_dir2:salapati.log . . .
  ```

- DATA_DUMP_DIR *environment variable*: You can also use the environment variable DATA_DUMP_DIR to point to the directory object on the server. In order to use the DATA_DUMP_DIR environment, you must have first created a specific directory object on the server.

For example, you could first create a new directory object on the server with the variable DATA_DUMP_DIR, and then use the export command to save the value of the DATA_DUMP_DIR variable in the operating system environment. Once you have made the DATA_DUMP_DIR variable part of your operating system environment, you don't need to specify the actual directory name (data_dump_dir2, in this example) explicitly (by using the DIRECTORY parameter) when you perform a Data Pump export. As shown in the following example, you merely need to specify the *name*, not the *location*, for the DUMPFILE parameter.

First, create the directory data_dump_dir2 object, as follows:

```
SQL> CREATE DIRECTORY data_dump_dir2 AS '/u01/app/oracle/datapump/dumpfiles_02';
```

Next, export the environment variable DATA_PUMP_DIR, with the value data_dump_dir2.

```
$ export DATA_PUMP_DIR data_dump_dir2
```

Now, you can perform the export without explicitly using the DIRECTORY parameter, since its value is saved in the DATA_PUMP_DIR environment variable. You merely use the DUMPFILE parameter, and the employees.dmp file will be located in the directory /u01/app/oracle/datapump/dumpfiles_02.

```
$ expdp salapati/password TABLES=employees DUMPFILE=employees.dmp
```

Understanding the Order of Precedence for File Locations

Now that we have reviewed the various ways you can specify a directory object for a Data Pump job, you may wonder how Oracle knows which location to use in case there is a conflict. You can have a situation where you specified a DATA_DUMP_DIR environment variable, but you then also specify a DIRECTORY parameter for the export job. Here's the order of precedence for directory objects:

1. Oracle looks to see if you specified a directory name as part of a file-related parameter (for example, the LOGFILE parameter). Remember that, in these cases, the directory object is separated from the filename by a colon (:).

2. Oracle's second choice is to see whether you specified a directory object during the export or import job by using the DIRECTORY parameter (DIRECTORY=dpump_dir1 . . .). If you explicitly specify the DIRECTORY parameter, you don't need to use the directory name as part of a file-related parameter.

3. If you aren't using an explicit directory object or using the DIRECTORY parameter, Oracle checks whether the Data Pump Export and Import clients are using the environment variable DATA_PUMP_DIR.

4. Finally, Oracle looks to see whether there is a default server-based directory object named DATA_PUMP_DIR. As noted earlier, Oracle automatically creates this directory when you create a new database, or when you upgrade to this version. Note that the default DATA_DUMP_DIR object is available only to DBAs and other privileged users.

The directory object name resolution simply means that Oracle knows which directory it should be using to read or write datafiles. However, you must have already granted the database read/write privileges at the operating system level in order to enable the database to actually use the operating system files.

Data Pump Privileges

All Oracle users can use the Data Pump utilities by default. However, you must have the special privileges EXP_FULL_DATABASE and IMP_FULL_DATABASE to perform advanced tasks. The granting of these roles will make you a privileged user, with the capability to perform the following tasks:

- Export and import database objects owned by any user.
- Attach to and modify jobs started by other users.
- Use all the new remapping capabilities during a Data Pump Import job.

The Mechanics of a Data Pump Job

The Data Pump Export and Import utilities use several processes to perform their jobs, including the key master and worker processes, as well as the shadow process and client processes. Let's look at these important Data Pump processes in detail.

The Master Process

The *master process*, or more accurately, the Master Control Process (MCP), has a process name of DM*nn*. The full master process name is in the format <instance>_DM*nn*_<pid>. There is only one master process for each job. The master process controls the execution and sequencing of the entire Data Pump job. More specifically, the master process performs the following tasks:

- Creates jobs and controls them
- Creates and manages the worker processes
- Monitors the jobs and logs the progress
- Maintains the job state and restart information in the master table
- Manages the necessary files, including the dump file set

The master process uses a special table called the *master table* to log the location of the various database objects in the export dump file. The master table is like any Oracle table and is at the heart of every Data Pump Export and Import job. The master process maintains the job state and restart information in the master table. Oracle creates the master table in the schema of the user who is running the Data Pump job at the *beginning* of every export job. The master table contains various types of information pertaining to the current job, such as the state of the objects in the export/import job, the location of the objects in the dump file set, the parameters of the job, and the status of all worker processes. The master table has the same name as the export job, such as SYS_EXPORT_SCHEMA_01.

The master process uses the master table only for the duration of the export. At the end of the export, as the last step in the export job, it writes the contents of the master table to the export dump file and automatically deletes the master table from the database. The deletion of the master table will occur automatically, as long as the export completed successfully (or if you issue the KILL_JOB command). However, if you use the STOP_JOB command to stop a job or the export fails for some reason, the master table isn't deleted from the database. (Data Pump job commands are described in the "Data Pump Export Parameters" section later in this chapter.) When you restart the export job, it then uses the same master table. Since the master table tracks the status of all the objects, Data Pump can easily tell which objects are in the middle of an export and which have been successfully exported to the dump files.

The master process re-creates the master table saved by the export utility (in the dump file) in the schema of the user who is performing the import. This is the *first step* in any Data Pump Import job. The Data Pump Import utility reads the contents of the master table to verify the correct sequence in which it should import the various exported database objects. As in the case of a Data Pump export, if the import job finishes successfully, Oracle will automatically delete the master table.

■**Note** The master table contains all the necessary information to restart a stopped job. It is thus the key to Data Pump's job restart capability, regardless of whether you stopped the job intentionally or it died unexpectedly.

The Worker Process

The *worker process* is named <instance>_DWnn_<pid>. It is the process that actually performs the heavy-duty work of loading and unloading data. The master process (DMnn) creates the worker process. The degree of parallelism determines the number of worker processes that the master process will create.

The worker processes maintain the rows of the master table. As they export or import various objects, they update the master table with information about the status of the various jobs: completed, pending, or failed.

Shadow Process

When a client logs in to an Oracle server, the database creates an Oracle process to service Data Pump API requests. This *shadow process* creates the job consisting of the master table and the master process. Once a client detaches, the shadow process automatically disappears.

Client Processes

The *client processes* call the Data Pump API. You perform export and import with the two clients, expdp and impdp. In the next section, you'll learn about the various parameters you can specify when you invoke these clients.

Performing Data Pump Exports and Imports

The Data Pump Export utility loads row data from database tables, as well as object metadata, into dump file sets in a proprietary format that only the Data Pump Import utility can read. The dump file sets, which are operating system files, contain data, metadata, and control information. *Dump file sets* usually refer to a single file, such as the default export dump file expdat.dmp.

Quite a few of the Data Pump Import utility's features are mirror images of the Data Pump Export utility features. However, some features are exclusive to the Data Pump Import utility.

In the following sections, we'll look at Data Pump types, modes, and parameters, as well as some examples.

Data Pump Export Methods

You can interface with the Data Pump Export and Import utilities through the command line, using a parameter file, or interactively. Let's now examine the various methods.

■Note Performing a Data Pump export or import of data using manual methods is tedious and error-prone. OEM provides excellent export and import wizards that let you quickly perform an export or import. You can also schedule these jobs using OEM. Before you use the OEM's wizards, however, it's good to go through the manual processes to understand what's involved in using the Data Pump Export and Import utilities.

Using the Command Line

You can use the Data Pump Export utility from the command line in a manner similar to the traditional export utility. Note that by default, you specify the username/password combination after the keyword expdp. Here's a simple example:

```
$ expdp system/manager DIRECTORY=dpump_dir1 DUMPFILE=expdat1.dmp
```

As you can see, the command-line option would quickly get tiring if you were doing anything but the simplest type of exports.

Using a Parameter File

Rather than specifying the export parameters on the command line, you can put them in a parameter file. You then simply invoke the parameter file during the actual export. Here's an example of a parameter file:

```
SCHEMAS=HR
DIRECTORY=dpump_dir1
DUMPFILE=system1.dmp
SCHEMAS=hr
```

Once you create the parameter file, all you need to do in order to export the HR schema is invoke expdp with just the PARFILE parameter:

```
$ expdp PARFILE=myfile.txt
```

■Note You can use all command-line export parameters in an export parameter file. The only exception is the parameter PARFILE itself.

Using Interactive Data Pump Export

Several of you are probably familiar with the interactive feature of the old export and import utilities. All you needed to do during an interactive export or import was type **exp** or **imp** at the command line, and Oracle would prompt you for the rest of the information. Interactive Data Pump is quite different from the interactive mode of the older utilities. As you'll see in the following sections, Data Pump's interactive mode isn't meant to be used in the same way as the exp/imp interactive mode—you can't *start* an interactive job using the Data Pump Export (or Import) utility. You can use the interactive mode only to *intervene* during a running job.

In Data Pump Export, you use the interactive method for one purpose only: to change some export parameters midstream while the job is still running. There are two ways to get into the interactive mode. The first is by pressing the Ctrl+C combination on your keyboard, which interrupts the running job and displays the export prompt (export>) on your screen. At this point, you can deal interactively with the Export utility, with the help of a special set of interesting commands, which I'll explain later in this chapter in the "Interactive Mode Export Parameters (Commands)" section.

The second way to enter the interactive mode of operation is by using the ATTACH command. If you are at a terminal other than the one where you started the job, you can attach to the running job by specifying the ATTACH parameter.

■**Note** In Data Pump, the interactive mode means that the export or import job stops logging its progress on the screen and displays the export> (or import>) prompt. You can enter the special interactive commands at this point. Note that the export or import job keeps running throughout, without any interruption.

You can also perform Data Pump Export and Import operations easily through the OEM Database Control interface. To use this feature, start the Database Control, select Maintenance, and then choose Utilities. On the Utilities page, you can see the various choices for exporting and importing data.

Data Pump Export Modes

As in the case of the regular export utilities, you can perform Data Pump Export jobs in several modes:

- *Full export mode*: You use the FULL parameter when you want to export the entire database in one export session. You need the EXPORT_FULL_DATABASE role to use this mode.

- *Schema mode*: If you want to export a single user's data and/or objects only, you must use the SCHEMAS parameter.

- *Tablespace mode*: By using the TABLESPACES parameter, you can export all the tables in one or more tablespaces. If you use the TRANSPORT_TABLESPACES parameter, you can export just the metadata of the objects contained in one or more tablespaces. You may recall that you can export tablespaces between databases by first exporting the metadata, copying the files of the tablespace to the target server, and then importing the metadata into the target database.

- *Table mode*: By using the TABLES parameter, you can export one or more tables. The TABLES parameter is identical to the TABLES parameter in the old export utility.

Schema mode is the default mode for Data Pump Export and Import jobs. If you log in as follows, for example, Data Pump will automatically perform a full export of all of SYSTEM's objects:

```
$ expdp system/sammyy1
```

If you are the SYSTEM user, you can export another schema's objects by explicitly using the SCHEMAS parameter, as shown in Listing 14-3.

Listing 14-3. *A Data Pump Export Using the Schema Mode*

```
$ expdp system/sammyy1 DUMPFILE=scott.dmp SCHEMAS=SCOTT
Export: Release 11.1.0.6.0 - Production on Tuesday, 25 March, 2008 12:19:31

Copyright (c) 2003, 2007, Oracle.  All rights reserved.

Connected to: Oracle Database 11g Enterprise Edition Release 11.1.0.6.0 -
Production
With the Partitioning, OLAP, Data Mining and Real Application Testing options
FLASHBACK automatically enabled to preserve database integrity.
Master table "SCOTT"."SYS_SQL_FILE_SCHEMA_01" successfully loaded/unloaded
Starting "SYSTEM"."SYS_EXPORT_SCHEMA_01": system/******** dumpfile=scott.dmp
 schemas=SCOTT
total estimation using BLOCKS method:  192  KB
Processing object type SCHEMA_EXPORT/USER
Processing object type SCHEMA_EXPORT/SYSTEM_GRANT
Processing object type SCHEMA_EXPORT/ROLE_GRANT
Processing object type SCHEMA_EXPORT/DEFAULT_ROLE
Processing object type SCHEMA_EXPORT/PRE_SCHEMA/PROCACT_SCHEMA
Processing object type SCHEMA_EXPORT/TABLE/TABLE
Processing object type SCHEMA_EXPORT/TABLE/INDEX/INDEX
Processing object type SCHEMA_EXPORT/TABLE/CONSTRAINT/CONSTRAINT
Processing object type SCHEMA_EXPORT/TABLE/INDEX/STATISTICS/INDEX_STATISTICS
Processing object type SCHEMA_EXPORT/CONSTRAINT/REF_CONSTRAINT
Processing object type SCHEMA_EXPORT/TABLE/STATISTICS/TABLE_STATISTICS
. . exported  "SCOTT"."DEPT"
. . exported  "SCOTT"."EMP"
. . exported  "SCOTT"."SALGRADE"
. . exported  "SCOTT"."BONUS"
Dump file set for SYSTEM.SYS_EXPORT_SCHEMA_01 is:
    /u01/app/oracle/product/10.2.0/db_1/admin/orcl/dpdump/scott.dmp
Job "SYSTEM"."SYS-EXPORT_SCHEMA_01"  successfully completed AT 18:25:16
```

Data Pump Export Parameters

Some of the Data Pump Export utility parameters will be familiar to you from the traditional export utility. Others are quite new. Here, I'll briefly run through the parameters, providing detailed explanations for the most important parameters. For this discussion, I've grouped the parameters into the following categories:

- File- and directory-related parameters

- Export mode-related parameters

- Export filtering parameters

- Encryption-related parameters

- Estimation parameters

- The network link parameter

- Interactive mode export parameters

- Job-related parameters

Note that you can use all the export parameters at the command line or in parameter files, except for those listed in the "Interactive Mode Export Parameters (Commands)" section.

File- and Directory-Related Parameters

You can specify several file- and directory-related parameters during a Data Pump Export job. These include the DIRECTORY, DUMPFILE, FILESIZE, PARFILE, LOGFILE, NOLOGFILE, and COMPRESSION parameters.

DIRECTORY

The DIRECTORY parameter refers to the directory object to be used for dump files and log files. See the "Using Directory Objects" section earlier in this chapter for details.

DUMPFILE

The DUMPFILE parameter provides the name (or list) of the dump file(s) to which the export dump should be written. The DUMPFILE parameter replaces the FILE parameter in the old export utility. You can provide multiple dump filenames in several ways:

- Create multiple dump files by specifying the %U substitution variable. The substitution variable will start at 01 and can go up to 99. For example, a specification like exp%U.dmp can be expanded into filenames such as exp01.dmp, exp02.dmp, exp03.dmp, and so on.

- Provide multiple files in a comma-separated list.

- Specify the DUMPFILE parameter multiple times for a single export job.

Note If you specify the %U notation to indicate multiple dump files, the number of files you can create is equal to the value of the PARALLEL parameter.

If you don't specify the DUMPFILE parameter, Oracle will use the default name expdat.dmp for the export dump file, just as it did with the traditional export utility.

FILESIZE

The FILESIZE parameter is purely optional, and it specifies the size of the dump file in bytes by default. You may use bytes, kilobytes, megabytes, and gigabytes to specify the FILESIZE parameter. If you don't specify this parameter, the dump file has no limits on its size. If you use the FILESIZE parameter by specifying, say 10MB, as the maximum dump file size, your export will stop if your dump file reaches its size limit, and you can restart it after correcting the problem.

PARFILE

The PARFILE parameter stands for the same thing it did in the traditional export utility: the parameter file. As explained earlier in this chapter, you can specify export parameters in a parameter file, instead of entering them directly from the command line.

LOGFILE and NOLOGFILE

You can use the LOGFILE parameter to specify a log file for your export jobs. Here's what you need to remember regarding this parameter:

- If you just specify the LOGFILE parameter without the DIRECTORY parameter, Oracle automatically creates the log file in the location you specified for the DIRECTORY parameter.

- If you don't specify this parameter, Oracle creates a log file named export.log.

If you specify the parameter NOLOGFILE, Oracle does not create its log file (export.log). You still see the progress of the export job on the screen, but Oracle suppresses the writing of a separate log file for the job.

REUSE_DUMPFILES

You can specify the REUSE_DUMPFILE parameter to overwrite an export dump file. By default, the database doesn't overwrite dump files. You can specify the value Y to overwrite a dump file and the value N for the default behavior, which is not to use older dump files. Here's an example showing how to specify this parameter during an export job:

```
$ expdp hr DIRECTORY=dpump_dir1 DUMPFILE=hr.dmp
TABLES=employees REUSE_DUMPFILES=y
```

Of course, you must make sure that you don't need the contents of the preexisting dump file, hr.dmp.

COMPRESSION

The COMPRESSION parameter enables the user to specify which data to compress before writing the export data to a dump file. By default, all metadata is compressed before it's written out to an export dump file. You can disable compression by specifying a value of NONE for the COMPRESSION parameter, as shown here:

```
$ expdp hr/hr DIRECTORY=dpump_dir1 DUMPFILE=hr_comp.dmp COMPRESSION=NONE
```

The COMPRESSION parameter can take any of the following four values:

- ALL: Enables compression for the entire operation.
- DATA_ONLY: Specifies that all data should be written to the dump file in a compressed format.
- METADATA_ONLY: Specifies all metadata be written to the dump file in a compressed format. This is the default value.
- NONE: Disables compression of all types.

Export Mode-Related Parameters

The export mode-related parameters are FULL, SCHEMAS, TABLES, TABLESPACES, TRANSPORT_TABLESPACES, and TRANSPORT_FULL_CHECK. You've already seen all these parameters except the last one, TRANSPORT_FULL_CHECK, in the "Data Pump Export Modes" section earlier in this chapter.

The TRANSPORT_FULL_CHECK parameter checks to make sure that the tablespaces you are trying to transport meet all the conditions to qualify for the transportable tablespaces job. Using this parameter, you can specify whether to check for dependencies between objects inside the transportable set and the other objects in the database. For example, an index is entirely dependent on the table, since it doesn't have any meaning without the table. However, a table isn't dependent on an index, since the table can exist without an index.

You can set the TRANSPORT_FULL_CHECK parameter to a value of Y or N. If you set TRANSPORT_FULL_CHECK=Y, the Data Pump Export job will check for two-way dependencies. If you have a table in the transportable tablespace but not its indexes, or your tablespace contains indexes without their tables, the export job will fail. If you set TRANSPORT_FULL_CHECK=N, the Data Pump Export job will check for one-way dependencies. If your transportable tablespace set contains tables without their indexes, the export will succeed. However, if the set contains indexes without their tables, the export job will fail.

Export Filtering Parameters

Data Pump contains several parameters related to export filtering. Some of them are substitutes for old export parameters; others offer new functionality. Let's look at these important parameters in detail.

CONTENT

By using the CONTENT parameter, you can filter what goes into the export dump file. The CONTENT parameter can take three values:

- ALL exports both table data and table and other object definitions (metadata).
- DATA_ONLY exports only table rows.
- METADATA_ONLY exports only metadata.

Here's an example:

```
$ expdp system/manager DUMPFILE=expdat1.dmp CONTENT=DATA_ONLY
```

■**Note** The CONTENT=METADATA_ONLY option is equivalent to the ROWS=N option in the original export utility.

EXCLUDE and INCLUDE

The EXCLUDE and INCLUDE parameters are two mutually exclusive parameters that you can use to perform what is known as *metadata filtering*. Metadata filtering enables you to selectively leave out or include certain types of objects during a Data Pump Export or Import job. In the old export utility, you used the CONSTRAINTS, GRANTS, and INDEXES parameters to specify whether you wanted to export those objects. Using the EXCLUDE and INCLUDE parameters, you now can include or exclude many other kinds of objects besides the four objects you could filter previously. For example, if you don't wish to export any packages during the export, you can specify this with the help of the EXCLUDE parameter.

■**Note** If you use the CONTENT=DATA_ONLY option (same as the old ROWS=Y parameter), you aren't exporting any objects—just table row data. Naturally, in this case, you can't use either the EXCLUDE or INCLUDE parameter.

Simply put, the EXCLUDE parameter helps you *omit* specific database object types from an export or import operation. The INCLUDE parameter, on the other hand, enables you to *include* only a specific set of objects. Following is the format of the EXCLUDE and INCLUDE parameters:

```
EXCLUDE=object_type[:name_clause]
INCLUDE=object_type[:name_clause]
```

For both the EXCLUDE and INCLUDE parameters, the name clause is optional. As you know, several objects in a database—such as tables, indexes, packages, and procedures—have names. Other objects, such as grants, don't. The name clause in an EXCLUDE or an INCLUDE parameter lets you apply a SQL function to filter named objects.

Here's a simple example that excludes all tables that start with *EMP*:

```
EXCLUDE=TABLE:"LIKE 'EMP%'"
```

In this example, "LIKE 'EMP%'" is the name clause.

The name clause in an EXCLUDE or INCLUDE parameter is optional. It's purely a filtering device, allowing you finer selectivity within an object type (index, table, and so on). If you leave out the name clause component, all objects of the specified type will be excluded or included.

In the following example, Oracle excludes all indexes from the export job, since there is no name clause to filter out only some of the indexes:

```
EXCLUDE=INDEX
```

You can also use the EXCLUDE parameter to exclude an entire schema, as shown in the following example:

```
EXCLUDE=SCHEMA:"='HR'"
```

The INCLUDE parameter is the precise opposite of the EXCLUDE parameter: it forces the *inclusion* of only a set of specified objects in an export. As in the case of the EXCLUDE parameter, you can use a name clause to qualify exactly which objects you want to export. Thus, you have the ability to selectively choose objects at a fine-grained level.

The following three examples show how you can use the name clause to limit the selection of objects:

```
INCLUDE=TABLE:"IN ('EMPLOYEES', 'DEPARTMENTS')"
INCLUDE=PROCEDURE
INCLUDE=INDEX:"LIKE 'EMP%'"
```

The first example is telling the Data Pump job to include only two tables: employees and departments. In the second example, the INCLUDE parameter specifies that only procedures should be included in this export job. The third example shows how you can specify that only those indexes that start with *EMP* should be part of the export job.

The following example shows how you must use slashes (\) to escape the double quotation marks:

```
$ expdp scott/tiger DUMPFILE=dumphere:file%U.dmp
schemas=SCOTT EXCLUDE=TABLE:\"='EMP'\", EXCLUDE=FUNCTION:\"='MY_FUNCTION''\",
```

■**Note** The EXCLUDE and INCLUDE parameters are mutually exclusive. You can use one or the other, not both simultaneously in the same job.

When you filter metadata by using the EXCLUDE or INCLUDE parameters, remember that all objects that depend on any of the filtered objects are processed in the same fashion as the filtered object. For example, when you use the EXCLUDE parameter to exclude a table, you'll also be automatically excluding the indexes, constraints, triggers, and so on that are dependent on the table.

REMAP_DATA

The REMAP_DATA parameter enables you to replace the values in a column with a new value. The new values for a column are specified by a *remap function*. You can use this parameter when you're moving data from a production system to a test system and would like some columns containing sensitive information to be changed for privacy reasons. You can use the same remapping function to remap both child and parent columns in a referential constraint.

The following example shows how to apply remapping functions to two columns in a table:

```
$ expdp hr DIRECTORY=dpump_dir1 DUMPFILE=remap1.dmp TABLES=employees
REMAP_DATA=hr.employees.employee_id:hr.remap.minus10
REMAP_DATA=hr.employees.first_name:hr.remap.plusx
```

In the example, the EMPLOYEE_ID and FIRST_NAME columns from the employees table are remapped using the two functions REMAP10 and PLUSX that belong to the package named REMAP.

DATA_OPTIONS

The DATA_OPTIONS parameter lets you specify options on handling specific types of data during an export. You can only specify the value XML_CLOBS for this parameter (DATA_OPTIONS=XML_CLOBS).

QUERY

The QUERY parameter serves the same function as it does in the traditional export utility: it lets you selectively export table row data with the help of a SQL statement. The QUERY parameter permits you to qualify the SQL statement with a table name, so that it applies only to a particular table. Here's an example:

```
QUERY=OE.ORDERS: "WHERE order_id > 100000"
```

In this example, only those rows in the orders table (owned by user OE) where the order_id is greater than 100,000 are exported.

SAMPLE

Using the SAMPLE parameter, which was brand new in Oracle Database 10g Release 2, you have the capability to export only a subset of data from a table. The SAMPLE parameter lets you specify a percentage value ranging from .000001 to 100. This parameter has the following syntax:

```
SAMPLE=[[schema_name.]table_name:]sample_percent
```

Here's an example:

```
SAMPLE="HR"."EMPLOYEES":50
```

You specify the sample size by providing a value for the SAMPLE_PERCENT clause. The schema name and table name are optional. If you don't provide the schema name, the current schema is assumed. You must provide a table name if you do provide a schema name. Otherwise, the sample percent value will be used for all the tables in the export job. In the following example, the sample size is 70 percent for all tables in the export job because it doesn't specify a table name:

```
$ expdp hr/hr DIRECTORY=dpump_dir1 DUMPFILE=sample.dmp SAMPLE=70
```

TRANSPORTABLE

The TRANSPORTABLE parameter enables you to specify whether you want the database to export the metadata for specific tables (and partitions and subpartitions) when doing a table mode export. You can specify either ALWAYS or NEVER as values for the TRANSPORTABLE parameter. Here's an example:

```
$ expdp sh DIRECTORY=dpump_dir1 DUMPFILE=hr.dmp
TABLES=employees TRANSPORTABLE=always
```

There's no default value of this parameter.

Enforcing Encryption of the Export Data

You can use one or more of the following encryption-related parameters to specify whether data must be encrypted before it's written to a dump set: ENCRYPTION, ENCRYPTION_ALGORITHM, ENCRYPTION_MODE, and ENCRYPTION_PASSWORD. Let's take a closer look at each of these parameters.

ENCRYPTION

Use the ENCRYPTION parameter to specify whether or not to encrypt data before it's written to a dump file. You can assign the following values to the ENCRYPTION parameter:

ALL: Encrypts all data and metadata

DATA_ONLY: Encrypts only data written to the dump file set

ENCRYPTED_COLUMNS_ONLY: Specifies encryption for only encrypted columns using the TDE feature

METADATA_ONLY: Specifies the encryption of just the metadata

NONE: Specifies that no data will be encrypted

■**Note** You can enforce encryption by specifying either the ENCRYPTION or the ENCRYPTION_PASSWORD parameter or both. If you specify the ENCRYPTION_PASSWORD parameter only, the ENCRYPTION parameter will default to the value of ALL.

If you don't specify the ENCRYPTION or the ENCRYPTION_PASSWORD parameter, the ENCRYPTION parameter defaults to NULL. If you omit the ENCRYPTION parameter but specify the ENCRYPTION_PASSWORD parameter, the ENCRYPTION parameter defaults to ALL.

The following example shows how to specify just the data and nothing else:

```
$ expdp hr DIRECTORY=dpump_dir1 DUMPFILE=hr.dmp JOB_NAME=test1
ENCRYPTION=data_only ENCRYPTION_PASSWORD=foobar
```

ENCRYPTION_ALGORITHM

The ENCRYPTION_ALGORITHM parameter specifies the encryption algorithm to use in the encryption of data. The default value is AES128, and you can also specify AE192 and AES256. The following example shows how to specify this parameter:

```
$ expdp hr DIRECTORY=dpump_dir1 DUMPFILE=hr.dmp
ENCRYPTION_PASSWORD=foobar ENCRYPTION_ALGORITHM=AES128
```

ENCRYPTION_MODE

The ENCRYPTION_MODE parameter specifies the type of security to be performed by the database when you choose to encrypt data during an export. The parameter can take three values: DUAL, PASSWORD, and TRANSPARENT. The default value for this parameter depends on whether you specify the other encryption-related parameters, as shown here:

- If you specify only the ENCRYPTION parameter, the default mode is TRANSPARENT.
- If you specify the ENCRYPTION_PASSWORD parameter and the Oracle Encryption Wallet is open, the default is DUAL.
- If you specify the ENCRYPTION_PASSWORD parameter and the Oracle Encryption Wallet is closed, the default is PASSWORD.

DUAL mode enables you to create a dump set that you can import later using either the Oracle Encryption Wallet or the password you specified with the ENCRYPTION_PASSWORD parameter. You can use DUAL mode when you want to import the data into a site that doesn't use the Oracle Encryption Wallet.

PASSWORD mode enables you to secure a dump file set when you transmit it to a remote database, but requires you to provide a password using the ENCRYPTION_PASSWORD parameter during the export. The database will require you to provide the same password during the import of the dump file set.

TRANSPARENT mode enables you to create a dump file set without using the ENCRYPTION_PASSWORD parameter. You use this parameter when you're importing the same database from which you exported the dump file set.

Here's an example that shows how to specify the dual value for the ENCRYPTION_MODE parameter.

```
$ expdp hr DIRECTORY=dpump_dir1 DUMPFILE=hr.dmp
ENCRYPTION=all ENCRYPTION_PASSWORD=encrypt_pwd
ENCRYPTION_ALGORITHM=AES256 ENCRYPTION_MODE=dual
```

ENCRYPTION_PASSWORD

You can use the ENCRYPTION_PASSWORD parameter to encrypt table data or metadata in the export dump file to prevent unauthorized users from reading data from the dump set. Note that if you specify ENCRYPTION_PASSWORD and omit the ENCRYPTION parameter, the database encrypts all data written to the export dump set.

■**Note** If you export a table with encrypted columns but don't specify the ENCRYPTION_PASSWORD parameter, the database stores the encrypted table column or columns as clear text in the export dump file when you do this. The database issues a warning when this happens.

You can supply any password you want when you export a table, even if the table has encrypted columns. The password you supply doesn't have to be the same as the password you use when encrypting a table column. If you set the ENCRYPTION_MODE parameter to PASSWORD or DUAL, the database requires that you also specify the ENCRYPTION_PASSWORD parameter.

The following example shows how to pass a value of testpass for the ENCRYPTION_PASSWORD parameter:

```
$ expdp hr TABLES=employee_s_encrypt DIRECTORY=dpump_dir
        DUMPFILE=hr.dmp ENCRYPTION=ENCRYPTED_COLUMNS_ONLY
        ENCRYPTION_PASSWORD=testpass
```

The dump file for the export will encrypt the encrypted columns in the employees table.

Estimation Parameters

Two interesting parameters enable you to estimate how much physical space your export job will consume: ESTIMATE and ESTIMATE_ONLY.

ESTIMATE

The ESTIMATE parameter will tell you how much space your new export job is going to consume. The space estimate is always in terms of bytes. You can specify that the database provide you the space estimates using either the number of database blocks (BLOCKS option) in the objects that are going to be exported or the optimizer statistics (STATISTICS option) for the tables. The following is the syntax of the ESTIMATE parameter specification:

```
ESTIMATE={BLOCKS | STATISTICS}
```

By default, Oracle estimates the export job space requirements in terms of *blocks*. It simply takes your database block size and multiplies it by the number of blocks all the objects together will need. Here is an example of what you'll see in your log file (and on the screen):

```
Estimate in progress using BLOCKS method . . .
Processing object type SCHEMA_EXPORT/TABLE/TABLE_DATA
Total estimation using BLOCKS method: 654 KB
```

Since the space estimation in terms of blocks is the default behavior, you don't need to specify the ESTIMATE parameter during the export. However, if you have analyzed all your tables recently, you can ask the Data Pump Export utility to estimate the space requirements by using the statistics the database has already calculated for each of the tables. In order to tell the database to use the database statistics (rather than use the default BLOCKS method), you need to specify the ESTIMATE parameter in the following manner:

```
ESTIMATE=STATISTICS
```

Here's what you'll see in your log file when you use the ESTIMATE=STATISTICS parameter:

```
Estimate in progress using STATISTICS method . . .
Processing object type SCHEMA_EXPORT/TABLE/TABLE_DATA
.  estimated "SYSTEM"."HELP"                              35.32 KB
Total estimation using STATISTICS method: 65.72 KB
```

ESTIMATE_ONLY

While the ESTIMATE parameter is operative only during an actual export job, you can use the ESTIMATE_ONLY parameter *without* starting an export job. Listing 14-4 shows one such example.

Listing 14-4. *Using the ESTIMATE_ONLY Parameter*

```
$ expdp system/sammyy1 estimate_only=y

Export: Release 11.1.0.6.0 - Production on Saturday, 22 March, 2008 11:19:4

Copyright (c) 2003, 2007, Oracle.  All rights reserved.

Connected to: Oracle Database 11g Enterprise Edition Release 11.1.0.6.0 - P
tion
With the Partitioning, OLAP, Data Mining and Real Application Testing optio
FLASHBACK automatically enabled to preserve database integrity.
Starting "SYSTEM"."SYS_EXPORT_SCHEMA_01":  system/******** estimate_only=y
Estimate in progress using BLOCKS method . . .
Processing object type SCHEMA_EXPORT/TABLE/TABLE_DATA
.  estimated "SYSTEM"."REPCAT$_AUDIT_ATTRIBUTE"            64 KB
. . .
.  estimated "SYSTEM"."SQLPLUS_PRODUCT_PROFILE"            0 KB
Total estimation using BLOCKS method: 320 KB
Job "SYSTEM"."SYS_EXPORT_SCHEMA_01" successfully completed at 11:20:16

C:\>
```

Although the log indicates that the export job "successfully completed," all the previous job really did was to estimate the space that you will need for the actual export job.

The Network Link Parameter

The Data Pump Export utility provides a way to initiate a *network export*. Using the NETWORK_LINK parameter, you can initiate an export job from your server and have Data Pump export data from a remote database to dump files located on the instance from which you initiate the Data Pump Export job.

Here's an example that shows you how to perform a network export:

```
$ expdp hr/hr DIRECTORY=dpump_dir1 NETWORK_LINK=finance
DUMPFILE=network_export.dmp LOGFILE=network_export.log
```

In the example, the NETWORK_LINK parameter must have a valid database link as its value. This means that you must have created the database link ahead of time. This example is exporting data from the finance database on the prod1 server.

Let's say you have two databases, called local and remote. In order to use the NETWORK_LINK parameter and pass data directly over the network, follow these steps:

1. Create a database link to the remote database, which is named remote in this example:

   ```
   SQL> CREATE DATABASE LINK remote
     2  CONNECT TO scott IDENTIFIED BY tiger
     3  USING 'remote.world';
   ```

2. If there isn't one already, create a Data Pump directory object:

   ```
   SQL> CREATE DIRECTORY remote_dir1 AS '/u01/app/oracle/dp_dir';
   ```

3. Set the new directory as your default directory, by exporting the directory value:

   ```
   $ export DATA_PUMP_DIR=remote_dir1
   ```

4. Perform the network export from the database named remote:

   ```
   $ expdp system/sammyy1 SCHEMAS=SCOTT FILE_NAME=network.dmp NETWORK_LINK=finance
   ```

You'll see that the Data Pump Export job will create the dump file network.dmp (in the directory location specified by remote_dir1) on the server hosting the database named local. However, the data within the dump file is extracted from the user scott's schema in the remote database (named remote in our example). You can see that the NETWORK_LINK parameter carries the dump files over the network from a remote location to the local server. All you need is a database link from a database on the local server to the source database on the remote server.

■**Caution** You can't use Data Pump in the normal way to export data from a read-only database. This is because Data Pump can't create the necessary master table or create external tables on a read-only tablespace. Using the *network mode*, however, you can export data from a read-only database on server A to dump files on server B, where Data Pump is running.

The Encryption Parameter

If your export data dump file includes encrypted column data columns, you can use the new ENCRYPTION_ PASSWORD parameter to supply a password, to prevent the writing of the encrypted column data as clear text in the dump file set. When you import a dump file that was created using an encryption password this way, you'll need to supply the password. Here's an example of using the ENCRYPTION_ PASSWORD parameter:

```
$ expdp hr/hr TABLES=employees DUMPFILE=test.dmp ENCRYPTION_PASSWORD=123456
```

Job-Related Parameters

Several of the Data Pump Export parameters can be classified as job-related parameters. I'll briefly discuss the important ones here.

JOB_NAME

The JOB_NAME parameter is purely optional. You can use this parameter to give an explicit name to the export job, instead of letting Oracle assign a default name. Remember that Oracle gives the master table, which holds critical information about your export job, the same name as the name of the job.

STATUS

The STATUS parameter is useful while you're running long jobs, as it provides you with an updated status at intervals that you can specify. The parameter takes integer values that stand for seconds. The default is 0 and will show new status when it's available. If you want to reassure yourself with minute-by-minute updates concerning a Data Pump job you're currently running, use the STATUS parameter, as shown in Listing 14-5.

Listing 14-5. *Using the STATUS Parameter*

```
$ expdp system/manager STATUS=60 . . .
. . .
Worker 1 Status:
State: EXECUTING
..Object Schema: SYSTEM
..Object Name: SYS_EXPORT_SCHEMA_01
  Object Type: SCHEMA_EXPORT/TABLE/TABLE_DATA
  Completed Objects: 1
  Total Objects: 65
. . exported "SYSTEM"."REPCAT$_SITES_NEW"
Job: SYS_EXPORT_SCHEMA_01
  Operation: EXPORT
  Mode: SCHEMA
  State: EXECUTING
  Bytes Processed: 69,312
  Percent Done: 99
  Current Parallelism: 1
  Job Error Count: 0
  Dump File: C:\ORACLE\PRODUCT\11.1.0\ADMIN\EXPORT\EXPDAT6.DMP
    bytes written: 1,748,992
. . .
```

The STATUS parameter shows the overall percentage of the job that is completed, the status of the worker processes, and the status of the current data objects being processed. Note that the Data Pump log file will show the completion status of the job, whereas the STATUS parameter gives you the status of an ongoing Data Pump job.

FLASHBACK_SCN

The FLASHBACK_SCN parameter specifies the system change number (SCN) that Data Pump Export will use to enable the Flashback utility. If you specify this parameter, the export will be consistent as of this SCN.

The following example shows how you can export the user HR's schema up to the SCN 150222:

```
$ expdp hr/hr DIRECTORY=dpump_dir1 DUMPFILE=hr_exp.dmp FLASHBACK_SCN=150222
```

FLASHBACK_TIME

The FLASHBACK_TIME parameter is similar to the FLASHBACK_SCN parameter. The only difference is that here you use a time, instead of an SCN, to limit the export. Oracle finds the SCN that most closely matches the time you specify, and uses this SCN to enable the Flashback utility. The Data Pump Export operation will be consistent as of this SCN. Here's an example:

```
$ expdp system/sammyy1 DIRECTORY=dpump_dir1 DUMPFILE=hr_time.dmp
FLASHBACK_TIME="TO_TIMESTAMP('25-05-2008 17:22:00', 'DD-MM-YYYY HH24:MI:SS')"
```

■**Note** FLASHBACK_SCN and FLASHBACK_TIME are mutually exclusive.

PARALLEL

PARALLEL is the mighty parameter that lets you specify more than a single active execution thread (worker process) for your export job. Using the PARALLEL parameter means that your jobs will use multiple threads for their execution. You can change the degree of parallelism on the fly by using the ATTACH command. Note that the Data Pump PARALLEL parameter has nothing to do with the Oracle parallel execution features, but they can work together.

The default value of the PARALLEL parameter is 1, meaning a single-thread export operation writing to a single dump file. If you specify anything more than 1 as the value for the PARALLEL parameter, you also should remember to specify the same number of dump files, so the multiple execution threads can simultaneously write to the multiple dump files. Here's an example that shows how you can set the level of parallelism to 3, forcing the export job to write in parallel to three dump files:

```
$ expdp system/manager DIRECTORY=dpump_dir1 DUMPFILE=par_exp%U.dmp PARALLEL=3
```

In this example, the DUMPFILE parameter uses the substitution variable %U to indicate that multiple files should be generated, of the format par_exp*NN*.dmp, where *NN* is a two-character integer starting with 01. Since the PARALLEL parameter is set to 3, the substitution variable will create three files with the following names: par_exp01.dmp, par_exp02.dmp, and par_exp03.dmp.

Note that you don't need to use the %U substitution variable to generate multiple dump files when you choose a value greater than 1 for the PARALLEL parameter. You could simply use a comma-separated list of values, as follows:

```
$ expdp system/manager DIRECTORY=dpump_dir1
  DUMPFILE=(par_exp01.dmp,par_exp02.dmp,par_exp03.dmp)
```

Be aware that if you don't have sufficient I/O bandwidth, you may actually experience a degradation in Data Pump performance with the PARALLEL parameter.

■**Caution** If you specify the PARALLEL parameter, make sure you allocate the same number of dump files as the degree of parallelism. You must also remember that the higher the degree of parallelism, the higher the memory, CPU, and network bandwidth usage as well.

ATTACH

The ATTACH parameter attaches your Data Pump client session to a running job and places you in an interactive mode. You can use this parameter only in conjunction with the username/password combination; you can't use any other export parameters along with it. Here's an example:

```
$ expdp hr/hr ATTACH=hr.export_job
```

The ATTACH parameter is very important, as it's one of the two ways to open an interactive Data Pump job, as explained in the following section.

Interactive Mode Export Parameters (Commands)

As I mentioned earlier in this chapter, the interactive mode of Data Pump is quite different from the interactive export and import mode in the older utilities. Traditionally, the interactive mode gave you the chance to enter a limited set of export/import parameters at the command line in response to the queries made by the export or import utility. You use the interactive mode in the new Data Pump technology only to intervene in the middle of a running job, to either suspend the job or modify some aspects of it. You can enter the interactive mode of Data Pump Export in either of two ways:

- Use the Ctrl+C keyboard combination during a Data Pump Export job, if you want to enter the interactive mode from the same session where you are running the Data Pump job.

- Use a separate session or even a separate server to attach yourself to a running session by using—what else?—the ATTACH command. (You can also attach to a stopped job.) When you successfully attach yourself to a job, you'll be able to use specific export parameters in an interactive mode. I use the word *parameters*, but you may also refer to these as interactive export *commands*.

■**Note** In the Data Pump Export (and Import) utility, the only way to get into an interactive mode of operation is by using the Ctrl+C sequence or by opening another session and "attaching" yourself to that session. You cannot start an interactive Data Pump session from the command line.

Let's examine when you might use the interactive mode in a Data Pump Export job. Suppose that you started a job in the evening at work and left for home. At midnight, you check the status of the job and find that it's barely moving. You can easily start another session, and then connect to the running job and monitor it by using the ATTACH command. When you do this, the running job does not pause. Instead, it opens an interactive window into the running session so you can change some parameters to hasten the crawling export job via a special set of interactive Data Pump Export commands. Using the ATTACH parameter, you can restart jobs that are stalled because of a lack of space in the file system, instead of having to start a new job from the beginning. This feature comes in especially handy when dealing with exports and imports of large amounts of data.

Listing 14-6 shows an example of using the ATTACH command.

Listing 14-6. *Using the ATTACH Command to Attach to a Stopped Job*

```
[orcl] $ expdp system/sammyy1 ATTACH=system.sys_export_schema_01
Export: Release 11.1.0.6.0 - Production on Tuesday, 25 March, 2008 11:58:08

Copyright (c) 2003, 2007, Oracle.  All rights reserved.
Job: SYS_EXPORT_SCHEMA_01
  Owner: SYSTEM
  Operation: EXPORT
  Creator Privs: FALSE
  GUID: F24953A52C006A63E0340060B0B2C268
  Start Time: Monday, 14 March, 2005 11:03:03
  Mode: SCHEMA
  Instance: orcl
  Max Parallelism: 1
```

```
EXPORT Job Parameters:
Parameter Name      Parameter Value:
   CLIENT_COMMAND        system/********
State: EXECUTING
Bytes Processed: 0
Current Parallelism: 1
Job Error Count: 0
Dump File: /u01/app/oracle/product/10.2.0/db_1/admin/orcl/dpdump/expdat.dmp
  bytes written: 4,096

Worker 1 Status:
  State: EXECUTING
```

■**Note** You may attach multiple clients to a single job.

You can attach to a running job by using the ATTACH command as just shown, or by simply using the Ctrl+C (^C) sequence on the server where the job is actually running. When you use the Ctrl+C sequence, you get the interactive export prompt (export>), indicating that Data Pump is awaiting your interactive commands. Here's an example:

```
Starting "SYSTEM"."SYS_EXPORT_SCHEMA_01":  system/********
Estimate in progress using BLOCKS method . . .
(You stop the export job by using the ^C sequence)
export>
```

Note that when you use the ATTACH command or the Ctrl+C sequence to interactively attach to a job, you don't stop the running job itself. The commands will merely stop the display of the job messages on the screen and present you with the prompt (export>).

From the interactive prompt, you can use several options to influence the progress of the currently executing Data Pump job. You may intervene during a running export or import job, not only when you issue the ATTACH command or Ctrl+C sequence, but also when the jobs temporarily fail. For example, your export job may run out of dump file space, as shown by the following set of entries in your export log file:

```
Processing object type SCHEMA_EXPORT/TABLE/COMMENT
Processing object type SCHEMA_EXPORT/VIEW/VIEW
Processing object type SCHEMA_EXPORT/TABLE/CONSTRAINT/REF_CONSTRAINT
ORA-39095: Dump file space has been exhausted: Unable to allocate 524288 bytes
Job "SYSTEM"."SYS_EXPORT_SCHEMA_01" stopped due to fatal error at 18:40
. . .
```

One option is to end this idle export job with the following interactive command:

```
export> KILL_JOB
```

More likely, you would want the job to resume by adding more space to your directory. Here's how you can use the ADD_FILE command to add files to your export directory:

```
export> ADD_FILE=data_dump_dir:expdat02.dmp
```

Once you finish adding space to the export directory, you use the interactive command START_JOB to continue the stopped export job, as shown here:

```
export> START_JOB
```

To resume the logging of the output on your screen, you issue the `CONTINUE_CLIENT` command, as shown here:

```
export> CONTINUE_CLIENT
Job SYS_EXPORT_SCHEMA_01 has been reopened at Sunday, 20 March, 2005 19:15
Restarting "SYSTEM"."SYS_EXPORT_SCHEMA_01":  system/********
parfile=test_export.par
. . .
```

In a Data Pump Import job, your space-related problems are most likely to be caused by running out of room in the tablespaces that contain the tables into which you are importing. In such a case, the import job will stop in the middle. You can add space to the relevant tablespaces, and then use the `ATTACH` command to attach to the held-up job, followed by the `START_JOB` and `CONTINUE_CLIENT` commands as shown in the preceding example.

■**Note** You must be a DBA, or have the EXP_FULL_DATABASE or IMP_FULL_DATABASE role, in order to attach and control Data Pump jobs of other users.

Table 14-1 provides a summary of the interactive Data Pump Export commands.

Table 14-1. *Interactive Data Pump Export Commands*

Command	Description
ADD_FILE	Adds a dump file to the dump file set.
CONTINUE_CLIENT	Returns to logging mode. The job will be restarted if it was idle.
EXIT_CLIENT	Quits the client session and leaves the job running.
HELP	Provides summaries of the usage of the interactive commands.
KILL_JOB	Detaches and deletes the job.
PARALLEL	Changes the number of active workers for the current job.
START_JOB	Starts or resumes the current job.
STATUS	Sets the frequency of job monitoring (in seconds). The default (0) will show the new status when available.
STOP_JOB	Performs an orderly shutdown of the job execution and exits the client.

■**Tip** STOP_JOB=IMMEDIATE performs an immediate shutdown of the Data Pump job.

I'll explain the important interactive Data Pump parameters in the following sections, grouped in the categories of client-related parameters, job-related parameters, and other parameters.

Client-Related Interactive Parameters

The `CONTINUE_CLIENT` parameter will take you out of interactive mode and resume the running export job. Your client connection will still be intact, and you'll continue to see the export messages on your screen. However, the EXIT_CLIENT parameter will stop the interactive session, as well as terminate the client session. In both of these cases, the actual Data Pump Export job will continue to run unhindered.

Job-Related Interactive Parameters

You can use several job-related parameters from any interactive session you open with an export session using the ATTACH command. You can use the STOP_JOB command to stop the export job in an orderly fashion. To stop it immediately, use the STOP_JOB=IMMEDIATE command. You can choose to resume any export jobs you've stopped in this manner with the START_JOB command.

If you decide that you don't really want to continue the job you've just attached to, you can terminate it by using the KILL_JOB parameter. Unlike the EXIT_CLIENT parameter, the KILL_JOB parameter terminates *both the client as well as the export job itself.*

To summarize, the job-related interactive parameters work as follows:

- STOP_JOB stops running Data Pump jobs.
- START_JOB resumes stopped jobs.
- KILL_JOB kills both the client and the Data Pump job.

■**Note** You can *restart* any job that is stopped, whether it's stopped because you issued a STOP_JOB command or due to a system crash, as long as you have access to the master table and an uncorrupted dump file set.

Other Interactive Parameters

From the interactive prompt, you can use the ADD_FILE parameter to add a dump file to your job, if you find that the dump file is filling rapidly and may not have any more free space left. You can also use the HELP and STATUS parameters interactively, and both of these parameters function the same way as their command-line counterparts.

Data Pump Export Examples

Let's look at a few simple Data Pump Export job specifications that demonstrate some of the concepts you've learned in this chapter. The first example creates an export dump file of just two tables: employees and jobs.

```
$ expdp hr/hr TABLES=employees,jobs DUMPFILE=dpump_dir1:table.dmp NOLOGFILE=Y
```

The following example shows how to use a parameter file, as well as how to use the CONTENT and EXCLUDE parameters. The CONTENT=DATA_ONLY specification means you are exporting just rows of data and excluding all object definitions (metadata). The EXCLUDE parameter requires that the countries, locations, and regions tables be omitted from the export. The QUERY parameter stipulates that all the data in the employees table, except that belonging to department_id 20, be exported. The parameter file, exp.par, has the following information:

```
DIRECTORY=dpump_dir1
DUMPFILE=dataonly.dmp
CONTENT=DATA_ONLY
EXCLUDE=TABLE:"IN ('COUNTRIES', 'LOCATIONS', 'REGIONS')"
QUERY=employees:"WHERE department_id !=20 ORDER BY employee_id"
```

You can then issue the following command to execute the exp.par parameter file:

```
$ expdp hr/hr PARFILE=exp.par
```

The following example illustrates a schema mode export. You don't see any mention of the SCHEMA parameter, because Data Pump will export a schema (of the exporting user) by default.

```
$ expdp hr/hr DUMPFILE=dpump_dir1:expschema.dmp
LOGFILE=dpump_dir1:expschema.log
```

■**Note** By default, the Data Pump Export utility will run the export in schema mode.

The following example shows how you can export specific tables from a specific schema:

```
$ expdp hr/hr TABLES=employees,jobs DUMPFILE=dpump_dir1:hrtable.dmp NOLOGFILE=Y
```

Here's an interesting Data Pump Export example, showing how to use the PARALLEL, FILESIZE, and JOB_NAME parameters. It also illustrates the use of the DUMPFILE parameter when there are multiple dump files.

```
$ expdp hr/hr FULL=Y DUMPFILE=dpump_dir1:full1%U.dmp, dpump_dir2:full2%U.dmp
FILESIZE=2G PARALLEL=3 LOGFILE=dpump_dir1:expfull.log JOB_NAME=expfull
```

Now that you've seen how the Data Pump Export utility works, you're ready to look at the Data Pump Import utility features.

Data Pump Import Types and Modes

As in the case of a Data Pump Export job, you can perform a Data Pump Import job from the command line or use a parameter file. Interactive access to the Import utility is available, but it is different from what you are used to when working with the traditional import utilities. The interactive framework is analogous to the interactive access to the Data Pump Export utility, as you'll see shortly.

You can use Data Pump Import in the same modes as Data Pump Export: table, schema, tablespace, and full modes. In addition, you can employ the TRANSPORTABLE_TABLESPACES parameter to import the metadata necessary for implementing the transportable tablespaces feature.

You must have the IMPORT_FULL_DATABASE role in order to perform one of the following:

- Full database import
- Import of a schema other than your own
- Import of a table that you don't own

■**Note** You'll need the IMPORT_FULL_DATABASE role to perform an import if the dump file for the import was created using the EXPORT_FULL_DATABASE role.

Data Pump Import Parameters

As in the case of the Data Pump Export utility, you control a Data Pump Import job with the help of several parameters when you invoke the impdp utility. For this discussion, I've grouped the parameters into the following categories:

- File- and directory-related parameters
- Filtering parameters
- Job-related parameters

- Import mode-related parameters
- Remapping parameters
- The TRANSFORM parameter
- The NETWORK_LINK parameter
- The Flashback parameters

File- and Directory-Related Parameters

The Data Pump Import utility uses the PARFILE, DIRECTORY, DUMPFILE, LOGFILE, and NOLOGFILE commands in the same way as the Data Pump Export utility does. However, SQLFILE is a file-related parameter unique to the Import utility.

The SQLFILE parameter is similar to the old import utility's INDEXFILE parameter. When you perform a Data Pump Import job, you may sometimes wish to extract the DDL from the export dump file. The SQLFILE parameter enables you to do this easily, as shown in the following example:

```
$ impdp system/sammyy1 DIRECTORY=dpump_dir1 DUMPFILE=scott.dmp
  SQLFILE=dpump_dir2:finance.sql SCHEMAS=scott
```

In this example, the SQLFILE parameter instructs the Data Pump Import job to write all the DDL pertaining to the scott schema to the scott.dmp file, located in the directory dpump_dir2. Of course, you must have created dpump_dir2 prior to issuing this command, using the CREATE DIRECTORY AS command. The DIRECTORY=dpump_dir1 parameter value tells the Data Pump Import utility where to find the dump file scott.dmp, from which the Data Pump Import job will extract the DDL for user scott's schema. This example also shows how you can use multiple directories in a single Data Pump job.

Listing 14-7 shows the output from running the previously specified Data Pump Import job.

Listing 14-7. *Running a Data Pump Import Job*

```
[oracle@localhost ] $ impdp system/sammyy1 DIRECTORY=dpump_dir1
DUMPFILE=scott.dmp SQLFILE=dpump_dir2:finance.sql SCHEMAS=scott

Import: Release 11.1.0.6.0 - Production on Tuesday, 25 March, 2008 12:23:07

Copyright (c) 2003, 2007, Oracle.  All rights reserved.

Connected to: Oracle Database 11g Enterprise Edition Release 11.1.0.6.0 -
Production
With the Partitioning, OLAP, Data Mining and Real Application Testing options
Master table "SYSTEM"."SYS_SQL_FILE_SCHEMA_01" successfully loaded/unloaded
Starting "SCOTT"."SYS_SQL_FILE_SCHEMA_01": system/******** dumpfile=scott.dmp
  sqlfile=scott.sql schemas=scott
Processing object type SCHEMA_EXPORT/USER
Processing object type SCHEMA_EXPORT/SYSTEM_GRANT
Processing object type SCHEMA_EXPORT/ROLE_GRANT
Processing object type SCHEMA_EXPORT/DEFAULT_ROLE
Processing object type SCHEMA_EXPORT/PRE_SCHEMA/PROCACT_SCHEMA
Processing object type SCHEMA_EXPORT/TABLE/TABLE
Processing object type SCHEMA_EXPORT/TABLE/INDEX/INDEX
Processing object type SCHEMA_EXPORT/TABLE/CONSTRAINT/CONSTRAINT
Processing object type SCHEMA_EXPORT/TABLE/INDEX/STATISTICS/INDEX_STATISTICS
Processing object type SCHEMA_EXPORT/CONSTRAINT/REF_CONSTRAINT
Processing object type SCHEMA_EXPORT/TABLE/STATISTICS/TABLE_STATISTICS
Job "SYSTEM"."SYS_SQL_FILE_SCHEMA_01" successfully completed at 18:42:20
[oracle@localhost] $
```

It's important to remember that the SQLFILE parameter just *extracts* the SQL DDL to the specified file—no actual data import takes place. By using this parameter, you can extract a SQL script with all the DDL from your export dump file. The DDL in SQLFILE lets you peek at what the import job will execute.

If you edit the finance.sql file, you'll see uncommented, ready-to-use SQL DDL statements to re-create user scott's schema. Listing 14-8 shows the first few lines of the script obtained by using the SQLFILE parameter.

Listing 14-8. *Partial Output Obtained Using the SQLFILE Parameter*

```
-- CONNECT SYSTEM
-- new object type path is: SCHEMA_EXPORT/USER
 CREATE USER "SCOTT" IDENTIFIED BY VALUES 'F894844C34402B67'
     DEFAULT TABLESPACE "USERS"
     TEMPORARY TABLESPACE "TEMP"
     PASSWORD EXPIRE
     ACCOUNT UNLOCK;

-- new object type path is: SCHEMA_EXPORT/SYSTEM_GRANT
GRANT UNLIMITED TABLESPACE TO "SCOTT";

-- new object type path is: SCHEMA_EXPORT/ROLE_GRANT
 GRANT "CONNECT" TO "SCOTT";
 GRANT "RESOURCE" TO "SCOTT";
-- new object type path is: SCHEMA_EXPORT/DEFAULT_ROLE
 ALTER USER "SCOTT" DEFAULT ROLE ALL;
-- new object type path is: DATABASE_EXPORT/SCHEMA/PROCACT_SCHEMA
-- CONNECT SCOTT
BEGIN
sys.dbms_logrep_imp.instantiate_schema(schema_name=>'SCOTT',
export_db_name=>'SALES', inst_scn=>'643491');
COMMIT;
END;
/
new object type path is: SCHEMA_EXPORT/TABLE/TABLE
--CONNECT SYSTEM
CREATE TABLE "SCOTT"."DEPT"
   (  "DEPTNO" NUMBER(2,0),
      "DNAME" VARCHAR2(14),
      "LOC" VARCHAR2(13)
   ) PCTFREE 10 PCTUSED 40 INITRANS 1 MAXTRANS 255 NOCOMPRESS LOGGING
   STORAGE(INITIAL 65536 NEXT 1048576 MINEXTENTS 1 MAXEXTENTS 2147483645
   PCTINCREASE 0 FREELISTS 1 FREELIST GROUPS 1 BUFFER_POOL DEFAULT)
   TABLESPACE "USERS" ;
. . .
```

Note that you'll get the SQL to re-create not only tables and indexes, but all objects, including any functions and procedures in user scott's schema.

The other important file-related Data Pump Import parameter is the new REUSE_DATAFILES parameter. This parameter tells Data Pump whether it should use existing datafiles for creating tablespaces during an import. If you specify REUSE_DATAFILES=Y, the Data Pump Import utility will write over your existing datafiles.

Filtering Parameters

You use the CONTENT parameter, as in the case of a Data Pump export, to determine whether you'll load just rows (CONTENT=DATA_ONLY), rows and metadata (CONTENT=ALL), or just metadata (CONTENT=METADATA_ONLY).

The EXCLUDE and INCLUDE parameters have the same meaning as in an export, and they are mutually exclusive:

- Use the INCLUDE parameter to list the objects that you wish to import.
- Use the EXCLUDE parameter to list the objects you don't want to import.

Here's a simple example of using the INCLUDE parameter. The specification restricts the import to only table objects. Only the persons table will be imported.

```
INCLUDE=TABLE:"= 'persons'"
```

You can use the clause INCLUDE=TABLE:"LIKE 'PER%'" to export only those tables whose name start with *PER*. You can also use the INCLUDE parameter in a negative fashion, by specifying that all objects with a certain syntax be ignored, as shown here:

```
INCLUDE=TABLE:"NOT LIKE 'PER%'"
```

Note that if you use the CONTENT=DATA_ONLY option, you cannot use either the EXCLUDE or INCLUDE parameter during an import.

You can use the QUERY parameter as well to filter data during an import. (In the older export and import utilities, you could use the QUERY parameter only during an export.) You can use the QUERY parameter to specify an entire schema or a single table. Note that if you use the QUERY parameter during import, Data Pump will use only the external tables data method, rather than the direct-path method, to access the data.

You can use the TABLE_EXISTS_ACTION parameter to tell Data Pump import what to do when a table already exists. You can provide four different values to the TABLE_EXISTS_ACTION parameter:

- With SKIP (the default), Data Pump will skip a table if it exists.
- The APPEND value appends rows to the table.
- The TRUNCATE value truncates the table and reloads the data from the export dump file.
- The REPLACE value drops the table if it exists, re-creates it, and reloads it.

Job-Related Parameters

The JOB_NAME, STATUS, and PARALLEL parameters carry identical meanings as their Data Pump Export counterparts. Note that if you have multiple dump files, you should specify them either explicitly or by using the %U notation, as shown earlier in the coverage of Data Pump Export parameters.

Import Mode-Related Parameters

You can perform a Data Pump import in various modes, using the TABLE, SCHEMAS, TABLESPACES, and FULL parameters, just as with the Data Pump Export utility. You can use the TRANSPORTABLE_TABLESPACES parameter when you wish to transport tablespaces between databases.

You use the TRANSPORT_FULL_CHECK parameter in a manner analogous to its use under Data Pump Export, when you're performing a transportable tablespaces operation. The TRANSPORT_FULL_CHECK parameter is applicable to a tablespace transport only if you're using the NETWORK_LINK parameter.

The TRANSPORT_DATAFILES import parameter is used during a transportable tablespaces operation, to specify the list of datafiles the job should import into the target database. You must first copy these files from the source system to the target server. Here's a simple example that illustrates how to use the transport tablespaces-related import parameters:

```
$ impdp salapati/sammyy1 DIRECTORY=dpump_dir1 \
> NETWORK_LINK=source_database_link \
> TRANSPORT_TABLESPACES=users TRANSPORT_FULL_CHECK=Y \
> TRANSPORT_DATAFILES='/wkdir/data/tbs6.f'
```

Remapping Parameters

The remapping parameters clearly mark the superiority of this utility over the older import utility by expanding Oracle's ability to remap objects during the data import process. The remapping parameters are REMAP_TABLES, REMAP_SCHEMA, REMAP_DATAFILE, and REMAP_TABLESPACE. While you did have the ability to remap schemas in the old export and import utilities (by using the FROMUSER/TOUSER specification), you couldn't remap datafiles and tablespaces. I explain the remapping parameters briefly in the following sections.

REMAP_TABLE

The REMAP_TABLE parameter enables you to rename a table during an import operation that uses the transportable method. In addition to renaming regular tables, you can also specify the REMAP_TABLE parameter to provide your own name for the individual partitions of a portioned table that you have exported using the transportable method. This way, you can prevent Oracle from giving default names to the partitions and subpartitions imported by the Data Pump Import utility. Following is an example that shows how to specify the REMAP_TABLE parameter to rename a table:

```
$ impdp hr/HR DIRECTORY=dpump_dir1 DUMPFILE=newdump.dmp -
  TABLES=hr.employees REMAP_TABLE=hr.employees:emp
```

The REMAP_TABLE parameter changes the hr.employees table to the hr.emp table during the import operation.

REMAP_SCHEMA

Using the REMAP_SCHEMA parameter, you can move objects from one schema to another. You need to specify this parameter in the following manner:

```
$ impdp system/manager DUMPFILE=newdump.dmp REMAP_SCHEMA=hr:oe
```

In this example, HR is the source schema, and Data Pump Import will import all of user HR's objects into the target schema OE. The Import utility can even create the OE schema if it doesn't already exist in the target database. Of course, if you want to just import one or more tables from the HR schema and then into the OE schema, you can do that as well, by using the TABLES parameter.

REMAP_DATAFILE

When you are moving databases between two different platforms, each with a separate file-naming convention, the REMAP_DATAFILE parameter comes in handy to change file system names. The following is an example that shows how you can change the file system from the old Windows platform to the new UNIX platform. Whenever there is any reference to the Windows file system in the export dump file, the Import utility will automatically remap the filename to the UNIX file system.

```
$ impdp hr/hr FULL=Y DIRECTORY=dpump_dir1 DUMPFILE=db_full.dmp \
  REMAP_DATAFILE='DB1$:[HRDATA.PAYROLL]tbs6.f':'/db1/hrdata/payroll/tbs6.f'
```

REMAP_TABLESPACE

Sometimes, you may want the tablespace into which you are importing data to be different from the tablespace in the source database. The REMAP_TABLESPACE parameter enables you to move objects from one tablespace into a different tablespace during an import, as shown in the following example. Here, Data Pump Import is transferring all objects from the tablespace example_tbs to the tablespace new_tbs.

```
$ impdp hr/hr REMAP_TABLESPACE='example_tbs':'new_tbs' DIRECTORY=dpump_dir1 \
  PARALLEL=2 JOB_NAME=TESTJOB_01 DUMPFILE=employees.dmp NOLOGFILE=Y
```

REMAP_DATA

You can specify the REMAP_DATA parameter to remap data while importing it into tables. You may want to use it, for example, when you're regenerating primary keys to avoid conflict with existing data. You must create the remap function that determines the remapped values of the columns you want to change.

Here's an example that shows how to specify the REMAP_DATA parameter during import:

```
$ impdp hr DIRECTORY=dpump_dir1 DUMPFILE=expschema.dmp
TABLES=hr.employees REMAP_DATA=hr.employees.first_name:hr.remap.plusx
```

The PLUSX function from the REMAP package remaps the FIRST_NAME column in this example.

TRANSPORTABLE

The TRANSPORTABLE parameter lets you tell the database whether it should use the transportable option during a table-mode import. The two possible values are ALWAYS and NEVER, the latter being the default value.

Note that you can use the TRANSPORTABLE parameter only if you also specify the NETWORK_LINK parameter. Here's an example:

```
$ impdp system TABLES=hr.sales TRANSPORTABLE=always
    DIRECTORY=dpump_dir1 NETWORK_LINK=dbs1
    PARTITION_OPTIONS=departition
    TRANSPORT_DATAFILES=datafile_name
```

If you don't specify the TRANSPORTABLE parameter, by default, the import job uses the direct path or external table method during the import.

DATA_OPTIONS

The DATA_OPTIONS parameter is the counterpart to the DATA_OPTIONS parameter during export operations. You can specify only the SKIP_CONSTRAINT_ERRORS value for this parameter during an import (DATA_OPTIONS=SKIP_CONSTRAINT_ERRORS). The SKIP_CONSTRAINT_ERRORS option lets the import operation continue even if the database encounters any nondeferred constraint violations.

The TRANSFORM Parameter

Suppose you are importing a table from a different schema or even a different database. Let's say you want to make sure that you don't also import the objects' storage attributes during the import—you just want to bring in the data that the table contains. The TRANSFORM parameter lets you specify that your Data Pump Import job should not import certain storage and other attributes. Using the TRANSFORM parameter, you can exclude the STORAGE and TABLESPACE clauses, or just the STORAGE clause, from a table or an index.

During a Data Pump (or traditional) import, Oracle creates objects using the DDL that it finds in the export dump files. The `TRANSFORM` parameter instructs Data Pump Import to modify the DDL that creates the objects during the import job.

The `TRANSFORM` parameter has the following syntax:

```
TRANSFORM = transform_name:value[:object_type]
```

where the syntax elements represent the following:

- *Transform name*: You can modify four basic types of an object's characteristics using four possible options for the `TRANSFORM_NAME` component. Here are the options and what they stand for:

  - `SEGMENT ATTRIBUTES`: Segment attributes include physical attributes, storage attributes, tablespaces, and logging. You can instruct the import job to include the previous attributes by specifying `SEGMENT_ATTRIBUTES=Y` (the default for this parameter) as the transform name. When you do this, the import job will include all four of the segment attributes, along with their DDL.

  - `STORAGE`: You can use the `STORAGE=Y` (default) specification to get just the storage attributes of the objects that are part of the import job.

  - `OID`: If you specify `OID=Y` (the default value), a new OID is assigned to object tables during the import.

  - `PCTSPACE`: By supplying a positive number as the value for this transform, you can increase the extent allocation size of objects and the datafile size by a percentage equal to the value of `PCTSPACE`.

- *Value*: The value of the `TRANSFORM` parameter can be `Y` (yes) or `N` (no). You've already seen that the default value for the first three transform names is `Y`. This means that, by default, Data Pump imports an object's segment attributes and storage features. Alternatively, you can set the value for these parameters to `N`. If you assign a value of `N`, you specify not to import the original segment attributes and/or the storage attributes. The `PCTSPACE` transform name takes a number as its value.

- *Object type*: The object type specifies which types of objects should be transformed. You can choose from tables, indexes, tablespaces, types, clusters, constraints, and so on, depending on the type of transform you're employing for the `TRANSFORM` parameter. If you don't specify an object type when using the `SEGMENT_ATTRIBUTES` and `STORAGE` transforms, the transforms are applied to all tables and indexes that are part of the import.

Here's an example of using the `TRANSFORM` parameter:

```
$ impdp hr/hr TABLES=hr.employees \
  DIRECTORY=dpump_dir1 DUMPFILE=hr_emp.dmp \
  TRANSFORM=SEGMENT_ATTRIBUTES:N:table
```

In this example, the `SEGMENT_ATTRIBUTES` transform is applied with the value of `N`. The object type is table. This specification of the `TRANSFORM` parameter means that the import job will not import the existing storage attributes for any table.

The NETWORK_LINK Parameter

Using the `NETWORK_LINK` parameter, you can perform an import across the network *without using dump files*. The `NETWORK_LINK` parameter enables the Data Pump Import utility to connect directly to the source database and transfer data to the target database. Here's an example:

```
$ impdp hr/hr TABLES=employees DIRECTORY=dpump_dir1 SCHEMAS=SCOTT \
  EXCLUDE=CONSTRAINT NETWORK_LINK=finance
```

In this example, finance is the network link. It is a valid database link, created by you before-hand using the CREATE DATABASE LINK command. Thus, the database shown in the database link is your source for the import job. Data Pump will import the table employees from the remote database finance to your instance where you run the Data Pump Import job. In a network import, the Metadata API executes on the remote instance, extracts object definitions, and re-creates necessary objects in your local instance. It then fetches data from the remote database tables and loads them in your local instance, using the INSERT INTO . . . SELECT SQL statement, as follows:

```
SQL> INSERT INTO employees(emp_name,emp_id) . . . SELECT (emp_name,emp_id) FROM
     finance
```

Note that a Data Pump network import doesn't involve a dump file, as Data Pump will import the table from the source to the target database directly.

Here's an example showing how to use the NETWORK_LINK parameter to perform a direct import from a remote database into a local database:

1. Create a database link in the remote database:

   ```
   SQL> CREATE DATABASE LINK remote
        CONNECT TO system IDENTIFIED BY sammyy1
        USING 'remote.world';
   ```

2. If there isn't one already, create a Data Pump directory object:

   ```
   SQL> CREATE DIRECTORY remote_dir1 AS '/u01/app/oracle/dp_dir';
   ```

3. Set the new directory as your default directory, by exporting the directory value:

   ```
   $ export DATA_PUMP_DIR=remote_dir1
   ```

4. Perform the network import from the database named remote, using the following Data Pump Import command:

   ```
   [local] $ impdp system/sammyy1 SCHEMAS=scott NETWORK_LINK=remote
   ```

Listing 14-9 shows the output of the Data Pump job specification in this example, using the NETWORK_LINK parameter.

Listing 14-9. *Using the NETWORK_LINK Parameter in Data Pump Import*

```
Import: Release 11.1.0.6.0 - Production on Tuesday, 25 March, 2008 12:00:32

Copyright (c) 2003, 2007, Oracle.  All rights reserved.


Connected to: Oracle Database 10g Enterprise Edition Release 10.2.0.0.0 - Beta
With the Partitioning, OLAP and Data Mining options
FLASHBACK automatically enabled to preserve database integrity.
Starting "SYSTEM"."SYS_IMPORT_SCHEMA_01":  system/******** schemas=SCOTT
NETWORK_LINK=remote
Estimate in progress using BLOCKS method . . .
Processing object type SCHEMA_EXPORT/TABLE/TABLE_DATA
Total estimation using BLOCKS method: 32 KB
Processing object type SCHEMA_EXPORT/USER
```

```
Processing object type SCHEMA_EXPORT/SYSTEM_GRANT
Processing object type SCHEMA_EXPORT/ROLE_GRANT
Processing object type SCHEMA_EXPORT/DEFAULT_ROLE
Processing object type SCHEMA_EXPORT/TABLESPACE_QUOTA
Processing object type SCHEMA_EXPORT/TABLE/TABLE
. . imported "SCOTT"."TEST"                                    96 rows
Job "SYSTEM"."SYS_IMPORT_SCHEMA_01" successfully completed at 06:59
[local] $
```

The Flashback Parameters

The FLASHBACK_TIME parameter enables you to import data consistent as of the flashback time you specify in your import job. Oracle finds the SCN closest to the time you specify, and enables the Flashback utility using this SCN. For example, look at the following import statement:

```
$ impdp system/manager FLASHBACK_TIME="TO_TIMESTAMP('01-06-2005 07:00:00;',
'DD-MM-YYYY HH24:MI:SS')"
```

Note that the FLASHBACK_TIME parameter does the same thing as the old CONSISTENT parameter in the traditional import utility.

The FLASHBACK_SCN parameter is similar to the FLASHBACK_TIME parameter, except that you directly specify the SCN.

Whether you use the FLASHBACK_TIME or the FLASHBACK_SCN parameter, it is the SCN that plays the key role in determining the flashback time with which your imported data will be consistent.

Interactive Import Parameters

All the interactive export parameters shown in Table 14-1 are valid for interactive import as well, with one exception: the ADD_FILE command is valid only for Data Pump Export jobs. As with Data Pump Export jobs, when you use the Ctrl+C sequence, the import job will pause, and you'll see the import> prompt, enabling you to enter any of the interactive import commands from there.

Monitoring a Data Pump Job

Two new views—DBA_DATA PUMP_JOBS and DBA_DATA PUMP_SESSIONS—are crucial for monitoring Data Pump jobs. In addition, you can use the V$SESSION_LONGOPS view and the old standby V$SESSION to obtain session information. In most cases, you can join two or more of these views to gain the necessary information about job progress. Let's look at some of the important data dictionary views that help you manage Data Pump jobs.

Viewing Data Pump Jobs

The DBA_DATAPUMP_JOBS view shows summary information of all currently running Data Pump jobs. Here's an example:

```
SQL> SELECT * FROM dba_datapump_jobs;

OWNER_NAME   JOB_NAME    OPERATION JOB_MODE   STATE      DEGREE ATTACHED_SESSIONS
-----------  ----------  --------  --------   ---------  ------ -------- ----------
SYSTEM       SYS_EXPORT  EXPORT    FULL       EXECUTING 1      1
             _FULL_01
SQL>
```

Since the dynamic DBA_DATA PUMP_JOBS view shows only the active jobs, a query on this view will reveal the value of the important JOB_NAME column for any job that is running right now. You'll need to know the job name for a job if you want to attach to a running job in midstream. Because the name of the master table is the same as the JOB_NAME value, you can thus determine the name of the master table through this view.

The JOB_MODE column can take the values FULL, TABLE, SCHEMA, or TABLESPACE, reflecting the mode of the currently executing export or import job.

The STATE column can take the values UNDEFINED, DEFINING, EXECUTING, and NOT RUNNING, depending on which stage of the export or import you execute your query. Of course, when there aren't any active jobs running, the view DBA_DATAPUMP_JOBS returns no rows whatsoever.

Viewing Data Pump Sessions

The DBA_DATAPUMP_SESSIONS view identifies the user sessions currently attached to a Data Pump Export or Import job. You can join the SADDR column in this view with the SADDR column in the V$SESSION view to gain useful information about user sessions that are currently attached to a job. The following query shows this information:

```
SQL> SELECT sid, serial#
     FROM v$session s, dba_datapump_sessions d
     WHERE s.saddr = d.saddr;
```

Viewing Data Pump Job Progress

The V$SESSION_LONGOPS dynamic performance view is not new to Oracle Database 11g. In Oracle9i, you could use this view to monitor long-running sessions.

In the V$SESSION_LONGOPS view, you can use the following four columns to monitor the progress of an export or import job:

- TOTALWORK shows the total estimated number of megabytes in the job.

- SOFAR shows the megabytes transferred thus far in the job.

- UNITS stands for megabytes.

- OPNAME shows the Data Pump job name.

Here's a typical SQL script that you can run to show how much longer it will take for your Data Pump job to finish:

```
SQL> SELECT opname, target_desc, sofar, totalwork
  2  FROM v$session_longops;

OPNAME                  TARGET_DES  SOFAR      TOTALWORK
----------------------  ----------  ---------  ------------
SYS_EXPORT_FULL_01      EXPORT      244        244
SYS_EXPORT_FULL_02      EXPORT      55         244
SQL>
```

In this example, the first row shows that the job is already complete, since the TOTALWORK and SOFAR columns are equal in value. In the second row, the SOFAR value is only 55MB, and TOTALWORK is 244MB. Thus, only about a quarter of the second export job has been completed thus far.

Using the Data Pump API

You can use the Data Pump API to write PL/SQL scripts that export and import data. The Data Pump API is in the DBMS_DATAPUMP package, which you can use for the following tasks:

- Starting a job

- Monitoring a job

- Detaching from a job

- Stopping a job

- Restarting a job

Listing 14-10 presents a simple PL/SQL script that shows how to export a simple schema export of a user. Make sure you create a directory object first and grant the user the appropriate rights to it.

Listing 14-10. *Using the Data Pump API to Create a Data Pump Export Job*

```
DECLARE
  d1 NUMBER;                  -- Data Pump job handle
BEGIN
-- first create a Data Pump job for the export.
  d1 := DBMS_DATAPUMP.OPEN('EXPORT','SCHEMA',NULL,'TEST1','LATEST');
-- Specify a single dump file for the job
  DBMS_DATAPUMP.ADD_FILE(d1,'test1.dmp','DMPDIR');
-- Specify the schema.
  DBMS_DATAPUMP.METADATA_FILTER(d1,'SCHEMA_EXPR','IN (''OE'')');
-- Start the export job.
  DBMS_DATAPUMP.START_JOB(d1);
-- Indicate that the job finished and detach from it.
  dbms_output.put_line('Job has completed');
  dbms_datapump.detach(d1);
END;
/
```

Listing 14-11 shows how to import the dump file you just created. The example uses the remapping parameter to remap OE's objects into the user HR's schema.

Listing 14-11. *Using the Data Pump API to Create a Data Pump Import Job*

```
DECLARE
    d1 NUMBER;                  -- Data Pump job handle
BEGIN
-- Create a Data Pump job to do a "full" import.
  d1 := DBMS_DATAPUMP.OPEN('IMPORT','FULL',NULL,'TEST2');
-- Specify the dump file for the job
  DBMS_DATAPUMP.ADD_FILE(d1,'example1.dmp','DMPDIR');
-- The following will remap schema objects from oe to hr.
  DBMS_DATAPUMP.METADATA_REMAP(d1,'REMAP_SCHEMA','oe','hr');
-- Start the job.
  DBMS_DATAPUMP.START_JOB(h1);
-- Indicate that the job finished and gracefully detach from it.
  dbms_output.put_line('Job has completed');
  dbms_datapump.detach(h1);
END;
/
```

Transportable Tablespaces

Oracle's transportable tablespaces feature offers you an easy way to move large amounts of data between databases efficiently by simply moving datafiles from one database to the other. Instead of re-creating the objects, transportable tablespaces enable you to move large objects effortlessly in a fraction of the time it takes to re-create them manually in a database. Oracle strongly recommends that you use the transportable tablespaces feature wherever applicable because of its superiority to other methods of moving data between databases.

Transporting tablespaces involves copying all the datafiles belonging to the source database to the target database and importing the data dictionary information about the tablespaces from the source database to the target database. Thus, the Data Pump Export and Import utilities, described in the preceding sections of this chapter, are essential players in the transportable tablespaces feature. You can also transport the index tablespaces pertaining to the tables, which makes the entire data transfer extremely fast. The whole operation will take only a little longer than the time it takes for you to copy the datafiles belonging to the tablespace to the new location, by using FTP, remote copy, or some other method such as a tape copy.

Uses for Transportable Tablespaces

You use transportable tablespaces mainly in the context of a data warehouse, but you can employ them in any kind of database. The following are some of the important uses of the transportable tablespaces feature:

- Moving data from a source database (usually OLTP) to a data warehouse
- Moving data from a staging database into a data warehouse
- Moving data from a data warehouse to a data mart
- Performing tablespace point-in-time recovery (PITR)
- Archiving historical data

Transporting a Tablespace

Transporting a tablespace between two databases involves the following main steps:

1. Select the tablespace to be transported (and make sure there are no dependencies with objects in other tablespaces).
2. Generate the transportable tablespace set.
3. Perform the tablespace import. This involves copying datafiles to the target server and importing related metadata into the target database.

Let's go through each of these steps. Note that the tablespace you're transporting must not already exist in the target database.

Selecting the Tablespaces to Be Transported

The primary condition you must meet for transporting tablespaces is that the set of candidate tablespaces must be *self-contained*. For example, if the tables in the tablespaces have any indexes, they should be contained in one of the tablespaces in the set you're transporting. Referential integrity constraints for objects inside the tablespace being transported must not refer to objects outside the tablespace.

You must meet a few other conditions when you're importing tablespaces containing partitioned tables (refer to the Oracle manual "Database Administrator's Guide" for the complete set of conditions). One way to verify that your set of tablespaces meets the self-contained criteria is by using the DBMS_TTS package, as follows:

```
SQL> EXECUTE sys.dbms_tts.transport_set_check('sales01,sales02',true);
PL/SQL procedure successfully completed.
SQL>
```

You must have the EXECUTE_CATALOG_ROLE role to execute the TRANSPORT_SET_CHECK procedure. The procedure TRANSPORT_SET_CHECK returns no errors, indicating that the two tablespaces in your transportable tablespaces set, sales01 and sales02, are self-contained and therefore eligible candidates for transporting. You can further confirm this by querying the transport_set_violations table, which lists all the partially contained tables in a tablespace and any references between objects belonging to different tablespaces.

```
SQL> SELECT * FROM sys.transport_set_violations
no rows selected
SQL>
```

Note Instead of using the TRANSPORT_SET_CHECK procedure, you can simply use the `TRANSPORT_FULL_ CHECK` parameter during Data Pump export and import to specify that a certain tablespace set has no dependencies. However, during the import, you must be using the `NETWORK_LINK` parameter in order to use the `TRANSPORT_FULL_ CHECK` parameter.

Generating the Transportable Tablespace Set

Before you can transport your tablespaces to the target database, you must generate a *transportable tablespace set*. The transportable tablespace set consists of all the datafiles in the tablespaces plus the export dump file, which contains the structural data dictionary information about the tablespaces.

The first thing you need to do before transporting a tablespace is to put the tablespaces in a *read-only* mode. If there are active transactions modifying the tables, you can't transport the tablespace. If your objective is to export a very large table or a part of a very large table, then create a new tablespace where you can put a new table that holds the data of interest. You can then transport this new tablespace to a different database.

```
SQL> ALTER TABLESPACE sales01 READ ONLY;
Tablespace altered.
SQL> ALTER TABLESPACE sales02 READ ONLY;
Tablespace altered.
SQL>
```

Note You can transport a tablespace without first putting it into a read-only mode, but doing so ensures that there aren't any active transactions in that tablespace while you are transporting it.

Once you've put both tablespaces that you want to transport in read-only mode, you have two things left to do to generate your transportable tablespaces set. First, you must use the Data Pump Export utility to generate the data dictionary metadata for the two tablespaces, sales01 and sales02. Second, you must physically copy all the datafiles in the two tablespaces and the export dump file to a directory that the target database can access. The next two sections show you how to perform these steps.

Exporting the Dictionary Information (Metadata) for the Tablespaces

The first step in creating the transportable tablespaces set is to export the metadata that describes the objects that are part of the tablespaces you want to export. Here's the interesting part about the transportable tables feature: no matter how large the tablespace is, this step is done very quickly because all you're exporting is the data dictionary information (metadata) about the objects, not their row data. You also have the option of using the parameter TTS_FULL_CHECK=Y, in which case the export utility will ensure that the tablespaces being exported are fully contained. However, you've already ascertained this in the previous step, so you can leave out this parameter. Listing 14-12 shows the export of the metadata for the pair of tablespaces.

Listing 14-12. *Exporting the Dictionary Metadata for the Tablespaces*

```
[finance] $ expdp oe/oe DIRECTORY=dpump_dir1 DUMPFILE=sales.dmp
              TRANSPORT_TABLESPACES=sales01,sales02 INCLUDE=triggers,constraint,grant

Import: Release 11.1.0.6.0 - Production on Tuesday, 25 March, 2008 12:23:07

Copyright (c) 2003, 2007, Oracle.  All rights reserved.

Connected to: Oracle Database 11g Enterprise Edition Release 11.1.0.6.0 -
Production
With the Partitioning, OLAP, Data Mining and Real Application Testing options
Starting "oe"."SYS_EXPORT_TRANSPORTABLE_01":  oe/********
transport_tablespaces=sales01,sales02
include=triggers,constraint,grant directory=dpump_dir1 dumpfile=sales.dmp
Processing object type TRANSPORTABLE_EXPORT/TYPE/GRANT/OBJECT_GRANT
Master table "OE"."SYS_EXPORT_TRANSPORTABLE_01" successfully loaded/unloaded
******************************************************************************
Dump file set for OE.SYS_EXPORT_TRANSPORTABLE_01 is:
  /u01/app/oracle/dba/sales.dmp
Job "OE"."SYS_EXPORT_TRANSPORTABLE_01" successfully completed at 14:36
oracle@finance.netbsa.org   [/u01/app/oracle]
[finance] $
```

■**Tip** Don't specify the USERID parameter when you use the TRANSPORT_TABLESPACE parameter. When you omit the USERID parameter, the Data Pump Export utility will prompt you for the username. Connect by using the string connect SYS/password as SYSDBA to perform the TRANSPORT_TABLESPACE export.

Note that the export in this example didn't export any *rows* of the tables in the pair of tablespaces you are transporting. The export specifies only which tablespaces are going to be part of your transportable tablespaces set. Only the metadata (table and index definitions) is exported to the export dump file. The export dump file, sales.dmp, will be very small, because it contains just the table definitions, column descriptions, and so forth that will help identify the objects in the tablespace when you export them to the target database.

Copying the Export File and the Tablespace Files to the Target

The next step in generating the transportable tablespaces set is the physical copying of the datafiles contained in the tablespaces and the export dump file containing the metadata about the tablespaces to the target location. Before you can start importing the export dump file to the target database, make sure that the block size of the tablespace is the same as the standard block size of the target tablespace. If it isn't, the target database must have a nonstandard block size specified in its init.ora file of the same size as the block size of the tablespace you want to export.

You must now copy the export dump file, sales.dmp, to the target database using FTP, remote copy (or copy, if you're using Windows), or some other means. You also copy all the datafiles that are part of the two tablespaces sales01 and sales02 to the target location, so they're accessible to the target database for importing.

Performing the Tablespace Import

Next, run the Data Pump Import utility (in the target database), which will plug in the tablespaces and incorporate information about them in the data dictionary of the target database. Because the export dump file doesn't have any data, all you'll be importing is the metadata about the objects. The target database will simply use the copied datafiles from the source database as the datafiles for the transported tablespaces. All you're doing is plugging the tablespaces into the target database.

Listing 14-13 shows the importing of the metadata into the target database from the dump file.

Listing 14-13. *Performing the Transportable Tablespaces Import*

```
C:\>impdp  system/sammyy1 dumpfile=sales.dmp TRANSPORT_DATAFILES='sales01_01.dbf', \
'sales02_01.dbf' directory=dpump_dir1

Import: Release 11.1.0.6.0 - Production on Tuesday, 25 March, 2008 12:23:07

Copyright (c) 2003, 2007, Oracle.  All rights reserved.

Connected to: Oracle Database 11g Enterprise Edition Release 11.1.0.6.0 -
Production
Master table "SYSTEM"."SYS_IMPORT_TRANSPORTABLE_01" successfully loaded/unloaded
Starting "SYSTEM"."SYS_IMPORT_TRANSPORTABLE_01":  system/********
dumpfile=sales.dmp TRANSPORT_DATAFILES='sales01_01.dbf',
'sales02_01.dbf' directory=dpump_dir1
Processing object type TRANSPORTABLE_EXPORT/TYPE/GRANT/OBJECT_GRANT
. . .
C:\>
```

As you can see, there are two parts to the import of the transportable tablespaces. First, the Data Pump Import utility will extract the metadata of the transportable tablespaces from the export dump file. After this, it will extract the various object (tables and indexes) definitions from the dump file into the target database. No data rows are actually imported into the database at this time. The data is already in the datafiles of the tablespaces, and you've already plugged those tablespaces into the target database. The import log will show the tables that are being imported into the target database, but unlike in a normal import process, you don't see the number of rows being imported.

As you can see from the examples, the transportable tablespaces feature is very powerful, because it will let you move entire tablespaces between databases by merely copying the datafiles and exporting the data dictionary information from one database to another. Compared to any of the alternatives, this is a much a faster and more efficient means of transferring very large objects.

■**Tip** You can transport a tablespace to a database with the same or higher compatibility setting. The two databases could be on different platforms.

Transporting Tablespaces Across Platforms with Different Endian Formats

The transportable tablespaces feature applies regardless of the platform of the source and target databases; that is, you can transport tablespaces from a Windows platform, for example, to a UNIX platform and vice versa. However, there is one requirement you must meet in order to perform cross-platform transport of tablespaces: the *endian* format of the datafiles in the source and target databases must be identical.

■**Note** *Endian format* refers to the byte ordering of file systems. Endian format could be one of two types: big or little. If the endian formats of the source and target database are identical, everything you've seen up to now is all you'll need to do to transport the tablespaces. However, if the endian formats are different, you must convert the endian format of the source datafiles, either before or after transporting the datafiles to the target server.

Determining the Endian Format of a Platform

You need to join the well-known V$DATABASE view with the new V$TRANSPORTABLE_PLATFORM view to determine whether the source and target endian formats are identical. For example, the following query reveals that the endian format of a Linux platform is little endian:

```
SQL> SELECT t.endian_format
  2  FROM v$transportable_platform t, v$database d
  4* WHERE t.platform_name = d.platform_name;

ENDIAN_FORMAT
--------------------

Little
SQL>
```

Then run the same query on the other server (target or source) to see what the endian format is. If the endian formats are the same in the source and target platforms, you can transport the tablespaces using the standard method described in the previous section. However, if the endian formats on the two platforms are different (one is little endian and the other is big endian), you need to perform a conversion of the tablespaces either at the source or the target database. Here are the steps:

1. Ensure the tablespaces are self-contained.

2. Make the tablespaces read-only.

3. Export the metadata using Data Pump Export.

4. Convert the datafiles to match the endian format.

5. Copy the files to the target system.

6. Use the Data Pump Import utility to import the metadata.

Let's look at what's involved in each of these steps.

Ensuring Tablespaces Are Self-Contained and Making Them Read-Only

Ensure that the tables you want to transport are all placed in their own separate tablespaces. To ensure that your tablespaces are self-contained, you need to use the TRANSPORT_SET_CHECK procedure in the Oracle-supplied DBMS_TTS package. As of Oracle Database 10g Release 2, you can also use the TRANSPORT_FULL_CHECK parameter while performing the export, to ensure that the tablespaces don't contain dependent objects. For example, setting the TRANSPORT_FULL_CHECK=Y specification ensures that the tablespaces you are exporting won't contain tables without their indexes or any indexes without the parent tables.

Also, alter the tablespace to make it read-only. Once you complete the export of the metadata in the next step, you can make the tablespace read/write again.

Exporting the Metadata Using Data Pump Export

Export the metadata describing the objects in the tablespace(s), by using the TRANSPORTABLE_TABLESPACES parameter, as described earlier in this chapter.

Converting the Datafiles to Match the Endian Format

If your platforms are compatible, but the endian formats are different, you need to convert the datafiles. You may perform the conversion before transporting the tablespace set or after finishing the transport. You can convert the datafiles before transporting the tablespaces, using the CONVERT TABLESPACE command in the Recovery Manager (RMAN) utility, as shown in Listing 14-14.

Listing 14-14. *Using the RMAN CONVERT TABLESPACE Command to Convert Datafiles*

```
RMAN> CONVERT TABLESPACE finance_tbs01
    2> TO PLATFORM 'HP-UX (64-bit)'
    3> FORMAT '/temp/%U';

Starting backup at 09-MAY-08
using channel ORA_DISK_1
channel ORA_DISK_1: starting datafile conversion
input datafile fno=00011 name=C:\ORACLE\TEST02.DBF
converted datafile=C:\TEMP\DATA_D-FINANCE_I-2343065311_TS-TODAY_FNO-11_05FLAUM6
channel ORA_DISK_1: datafile conversion complete, elapsed time: 00:00:17
Finished backup at 09-MAY-08
RMAN> exit
Recovery Manager complete.
```

This example shows how you can use the FORMAT parameter to tell Oracle what format the newly converted file should be and in which directory to put it. But as you can see, Oracle gives the file a name. If you want to specify the name of the datafile yourself, perform the conversion using the DB_FILE_NAME_CONVERT clause. Listing 14-15 shows the results of using the CONVERT TABLESPACE command with the DB_FILE_NAME_CONVERT clause.

Listing 14-15. *Converting Filenames with the DB_FILE_NAME_CONVERT Clause*

```
RMAN> CONVERT TABLESPACE test
    2> TO PLATFORM 'HP-UX (64-bit)'
    3> DB_FILE_NAME_CONVERT = 'c:\oracle\test.dbf','c:\temp\test.dbf';
```

```
Starting backup at 10-MAY-08
using target database controlfile instead of recovery catalog
allocated channel: ORA_DISK_1
channel ORA_DISK_1: sid=151 devtype=DISK
channel ORA_DISK_1: starting datafile conversion
input datafile fno=00011 name=C:\ORACLE\TEST.DBF
converted datafile=C:\TEMP\TEST.DBF
channel ORA_DISK_1: datafile conversion complete, elapsed time: 00:00:16
Finished backup at 10-MAY-08
RMAN>
```

The DB_FILE_NAME_CONVERT clause performs the following functions for you:

- Takes a given filename and converts it to any filename you specify
- Places the converted file in the location you specify

Note that you use the DB_FILE_NAME_CONVERT command when you convert the files directly on the source system, *before* transporting them.

Copying the Files to the Target System

At this point, you need to copy both the *converted* datafile that is part of the tablespace (finance_tbs01 in this example) as well as the expdp dump file, which was named sales.dmp in the earlier transportable tablespaces example, over to the target server where your target database is running.

If you chose to transport the tablespaces (the datafiles that constitute the tablespaces) first instead, you must convert the datafiles on the target platform at this point, before trying to perform the import of the metadata in the tablespace. Here's an example that shows how you can take a datafile that belongs to the HP-UX operating system platform and convert it into a Windows platform:

```
RMAN> CONVERT DATAFILE 'c:\audit_d01_01.dbf'
   2> TO PLATFORM 'Microsoft Windows IA (32-bit)'
   3> FROM platform='HP-UX (64-bit)'
   4> FORMAT '\u01\oradata\finance\export';
```

As in the previous example, where you performed the file conversion on the source system, you may use the DB_FILE_NAME_CONVERT clause when performing the datafile conversion on the target system. Your datafile conversion statement would then have the following format:

```
CONVERT DATAFILE . . . FROM PLATFORM . . . DB_FILE_NAME_CONVERT . . .
```

Here's an example that shows the use of the DB_FILE_NAME_CONVERT clause:

```
RMAN> CONVERT DATAFILE
   2> '/hq/finance/work/tru/tbs_31.f',
   3> '/hq/finance/work/tru/tbs_32.f',
   4> '/hq/finance/work/tru/tbs_41.f'
   5> TO PLATFORM="Solaris[tm] OE (32-bit)"
   6> FROM PLATFORM="HP TRu64 UNIX"
   7> DB_FILE_NAME_CONVERT=
   8> "/hq/finance/work/tru/", "/hq/finance/dbs/tru"
   9> PARALLELISM=5;
```

■Tip By default, Oracle places the converted files in the flash recovery area, without changing the datafile names.

Using Data Pump Import to Import the Metadata

Once you move the converted files over to the target system (or move the files over first and convert them later), use the Data Pump Import utility as follows to import the metadata into the target database:

```
$ impdp system/password DUMPFILE=sales.dmp DIRECTORY=dpump_dir
  TRANSPORT_DATAFILES=/salesdb/sales_101.dbf, /salesdb/sales_201.dbf
```

As you can see, you just plug in the tablespaces and use the Data Pump Import utility to integrate the datafiles and their metadata (found in the `test.dmp` file).

As you've seen in this chapter, the Data Pump Export and Import utilities are valuable assets to a DBA and help you perform numerous tasks. The transportable tablespaces feature is of great help, especially when you're dealing with very large tables. Instead of performing a laborious and long export and import job, all you need to do is copy data fields at the operating system level, and then export and import the metadata.

Time and again, you'll find yourself relying on the wonderful set of tools that are part of the Data Pump technology. It isn't an exaggeration to say that in many databases, the Data Pump utilities will be among the most frequently used of all DBA tools.

CHAPTER 15

■■■

Backing Up Databases

As an Oracle DBA, one of your fundamental tasks is to regularly back up databases. Backups involve making copies of your database to re-create the database if necessary. They provide the basis of all database recoveries—no backup, no recovery. One of the best things you can do to help yourself as a DBA is to focus on a tried-and-tested strategy for backing up the database, because the more time you spend planning backups, the less time you'll spend recovering the database from a mishap.

You can perform database backups in two different ways: use Oracle's Recovery Manager (RMAN) interface or use operating system utilities. I give RMAN-based backups much more attention in this chapter because of the many benefits they offer compared with operating system-based, user-created backups.

Database administrators frequently use tape devices for Oracle backups, because of their convenience and also because tape backups are easy to archive for safekeeping. If you want to use RMAN with tape devices, you need to use a media management layer (MML). Oracle Corporation offers its own media management tool, called Oracle Secure Backup, free with the Oracle server. In this chapter, you'll learn how to install, configure, and integrate Oracle Secure Backup with RMAN to perform sophisticated backups.

You need to consistently check and verify backups to make sure they're correct and usable during a recovery. The latter part of this chapter is devoted to a review of database corruption and the many ways to test for it. I'll also briefly review Oracle Data Guard and the concept of standby databases.

Let's begin with an overview of Oracle database backups.

Backing Up Oracle Databases

Database backups are used to avoid the loss of data, so it's essential to have a backup system in place. Backups involve keeping copies of the key Oracle database files: datafiles, the control file, and the archived redo log files.

Physical backups involve the copying of database files. You can perform physical backups in two main ways:

- Use operating system utilities like cp and dd to back up files to perform user-managed backups. You use a combination of operating system backup commands and SQL*Plus commands to back up the database files.

- Use the Oracle-provided utility Recovery Manager to perform the backups. RMAN can be used in the command-line mode, as well as through the OEM Database Control interface.

RMAN can do everything that user-managed backups can, and it provides several additional capabilities. You also don't need to keep track of the backed-up datafiles and archived redo log files with RMAN, since RMAN itself manages all that information.

In this chapter, I introduce you to using RMAN through the command line so you understand the concepts behind it. Once you gain proficiency in using the tool, feel free to use the Database Control interface to manage RMAN-based backups. Although I'll focus on using RMAN in this chapter, I briefly discuss user-managed backups toward the end of the chapter.

Although disk storage prices keep dropping, tape storage is still the cheaper way to store large amounts of data offsite. If you're using RMAN, you need a third-party media manager to make a backup to a tape device.

Before you start dealing with the mechanics of backups, you need to understand certain terms associated with backups.

Important Backup Terms

A clear understanding of the types of backups and backup concepts is extremely important for a successful recovery. Here, I'll review some terminology related to Oracle database backups.

Archivelog and Noarchivelog Modes

Oracle writes all changes to the data blocks in memory to the online redo logs, usually before they are written to the database files. During a recovery process, Oracle uses the changes recorded in the redo log files to bring the database up-to-date. Oracle can manage the redo log files in two ways:

- *Archivelog mode*: In this mode, Oracle saves (archives) the filled redo logs. Thus, no matter how old the database backup is, if you are running in archivelog mode, you can recover the database to any point in time using the archived logs.

- *Noarchivelog mode*: In this mode, the filled redo logs are overwritten and not saved. The noarchivelog mode thus implies that you can restore only the backup, and you'll lose all the changes made to the database after the backup was performed. The noarchivelog mode of operation means that you can recover from a crash of only the database instance. If there is a media failure (for example, a loss of a disk), a database in noarchivelog mode may be restored from a backup, but it will lose all changes made to the database since the backup was made.

Production systems are usually run in archivelog mode, for the following reasons:

- You can recover completely from an instance failure as well as a media failure.

- You can completely recover all your data in the event of a damaged disk drive.

- You can maintain high availability because a database run in archivelog mode doesn't need to be shut down in order to be backed up. You can perform online backups in this mode, thus keeping the database open for any length of time you wish.

- You can perform open backups—that is, backups while the database is running—only if the database is operating in archivelog mode.

- You need to run your database in archivelog mode to carry out a tablespace point-in-time recovery (PITR).

I can't think of any organization that doesn't care if it loses valuable business data, so just about all production databases are run in archivelog mode. If you're running in noarchivelog mode, the implication is that the data can be restored from other sources, or it's just a test or development database and you don't need to have up-to-the-minute recoverability. Although I do discuss backing up noarchivelog mode databases in this chapter, I concentrate on backing up databases operating in archivelog mode.

■Note If the database is being backed up very frequently (using incremental backups, for example), or you're using a snapshot technology based on a tool such as Hewlett-Packard's Business Copy, you may be able to get away with running in noarchivelog mode for certain types of databases.

Whole and Partial Database Backups

You can back up either an entire database or part of it, such as a tablespace or a datafile. Note that you can't back up a partial database if the database is running in noarchivelog mode, unless all the tablespaces and files in the partial backup are read-only. You can make a whole database backup in either archivelog or noarchivelog mode.

The most commonly performed backup is the whole database backup, and it consists of all the datafiles and one other important file: the control file. Without the control file, Oracle will not open the database, so you need the latest backup of the control file along with all the datafile backups for recovery.

Consistent and Inconsistent Backups

The difference between consistent and inconsistent backups is simple. A *consistent backup* doesn't need to go through a recovery process. When a backup is used to recover a database or a part of a database (such as a tablespace or a datafile), first you need to restore the backup, and then you recover the database. In the case of a consistent backup, you don't have to perform any recovery steps. An *inconsistent backup,* on the other hand, always needs to undergo a recovery.

Oracle assigns every transaction a unique system change number (SCN). Each commit, for example, will advance the SCN forward. Each time Oracle performs a checkpoint, all the changed data in the online datafiles is written to disk. And each time there is a checkpoint, the thread checkpoint in the control file is updated by Oracle. During this thread checkpoint, Oracle makes all the read/write datafiles and the control files consistent to the same SCN. A consistent database means that the SCNs stored in all the datafile headers are identical and are also the same as the datafile header information held in the control files. The important thing is that *the same SCN number must appear in all the datafiles and the control file(s).* The identical SCN means that the datafiles contain data taken from the same point in time. Since the data is consistent, you don't need to perform any recovery steps after you restore (or copy back) a set of backup files.

To make a consistent backup, either the database needs to be closed (with a normal SHUTDOWN or SHUTDOWN TRANSACTIONAL command, not a SHUTDOWN ABORT command) or it needs to be in a mount position after being started (again, after a clean shutdown).

An inconsistent backup is a backup in which the files contain data from different points in time. Most production systems can't be shut down for a consistent backup. Instead, you need to operate those databases on a 24/7 basis. You thus must back up the datafiles of these databases online; that is, while the database is open for transactions. Since the datafiles are being modified by users while you are backing them up, you end up with an inconsistent backup. Inconsistent backups don't mean there is anything wrong with your backups. However, during a recovery process, it isn't sufficient to merely restore these backups. In addition to restoring these backups, you must also supply all archived and online redo logs from the time of the backup to the time to which you want to recover the database. Oracle will read these log files and apply all necessary changes to the restored backup files.

Since you can make an inconsistent backup of a database while it's open, most production databases use inconsistent backups as the foundation of their backup strategy.

Open and Closed Backups

Online or *open* (or *hot/warm*) backups are backups you make while the database is open and accessible to users. You can make an online backup of the entire database (or a tablespace or datafile) as long as the database is being run in archivelog mode. You can't make an online backup if the database is running in noarchivelog mode.

A *closed* backup of a database, also called a *cold* backup, is made while the database is shut down. A closed backup is always consistent, as long as the database wasn't shut down with the SHUTDOWN ABORT command.

■**Note** Remember that if the backup is open (online), or if it is closed (offline) but inconsistent, you may need to use archived redo logs to make the database consistent.

The decision about whether you should make a closed backup or an open backup depends on business requirements. Business requirements dictate the uptime levels, which are then encapsulated in the service-level agreement (SLA). If your SLA requires that your database be up 24/7, you must make online backups. On the other hand, if your organization allows you a backup window that will enable you to bring the database down, you can schedule closed backups. The frequency of closed backups and the number of redo logs produced by the database are both factors in the time it takes to recover the database. If you are performing closed backups on a weekly basis, you may have up to six days' worth of archived logs to apply to the database backup during recovery (in the worst case).

Physical and Logical Backups

Technically speaking, you can divide Oracle backups into logical and physical backups. *Logical backups* are backups made using the Data Pump Export utility, and they contain logical objects like tables and procedures. These backups are in proprietary binary form, and their data can be extracted only by using Oracle's own Data Pump Import utility.

Physical backups refer to the backing up of the key Oracle database files: datafiles, archived redo logs, and control files. Physical backups are made on disk or on tape drives.

This chapter discusses physical backups, which are the cornerstone of Oracle's recovery strategy when confronted with a major loss of data. Logical files are an adjunct, not an alternative, to physical backups.

Backup Levels

Following are the levels at which you can perform Oracle database backups:

- *Whole database*: You back up all files including the control file. This level is applicable to both archivelog and noarchivelog modes of operation.

- *Tablespace backups*: You back up all the datafiles belonging to a tablespace. Tablespace backups are applicable only in archivelog mode.

- *Datafile backups*: You back up a single datafile. Datafile backups are valid in archivelog mode only.

Backup Guidelines

Regardless of your SLA and your recovery requirements, some general guidelines regarding backup processes will help you *avoid* a recovery in most cases. After all, the best strategy for recovery is to avoid having to do one by having an ironclad backup and data protection system in place. The guide-lines are as follows:

- Build redundancy into your systems by using RAID-based storage systems, which will let you mask individual disk failures.

- Perform backups at frequent intervals to reduce your recovery time.

- Maintain offsite storage of your backups with a reliable vendor. The tapes that you store offsite should be part of a regular recovery testing program.

- Run any database deemed to contain useful data for the organization in archivelog mode. You would run a database in noarchivelog mode only when you don't care about the up-to-the-minute recoverability of the data.

- Multiplex the control files on separate disk drives managed by different disk controllers. *Multiplexing* means that Oracle will automatically maintain more than one copy of a file. For example, when you specify two copies of the Oracle control file, Oracle will write to both the control files. Mirror the control files in addition to using the multiplexing offered by Oracle.

■**Note** Unlike in the case of the online redo log file, the Oracle instance will shut down if one of the multiplexed control files can't be written to due to a disk failure, or if the disk on which the control file is located runs out of space.

- A loss of an active redo log file could be a *single point of failure*, which will result in the loss of data. To avoid such an event, Oracle strongly recommends that you multiplex the redo log file. When you multiplex the redo log file, even if one of the files is corrupted or lost, Oracle will continue writing to its copy. A mirrored strategy may not be appropriate here, as both copies might be corrupted at the same time, thus making the extra copy just as useless as the original. Even when the database files are mirrored, it's important to use Oracle multiplexing for both archivelogs and control files.

- Take advantage of the archivelog multiplexing option and set the LOG_ARCHIVE_MIN_SUCCEED_DEST parameter to at least 2 to ensure you have multiple sets of good archived logs.

- After every major structural change, back up the control file. The control file backup takes so little space that you can schedule a job that will back up the control file every hour or so on a busy production machine without affecting its performance.

- Always make more than one copy of the database when it's being backed up to tape, because the tapes can be defective and you may not be aware of it.

- Make at least two copies of the archived redo logs, and keep one on disk for a short recovery time if there's a media problem.

- Though the datafiles, log files, and control files are indeed the key files needed for recovery, you should back up other Oracle database files on a routine basis and put them away safely. These include the server parameter file (SPFILE) or the init.ora file, the sqlnet.ora file, the tnsnames.ora file, and the password file. You can always reconfigure each of these files in case you lose them, but this wastes a lot of critical time, and you could end up making mistakes in the process. These auxiliary files take very little space to store, and you may sometimes need these other files to restore and recover a damaged database.

- Keep the use of the UNRECOVERABLE and NOLOGGING options to a minimum, for obvious reasons. If there's a problem, you won't have those objects in the redo logs, and you won't be able to recover them.

- Use the RMAN tool, which is provided free of cost from Oracle, to perform your backups and recovery. RMAN maintains a log of all the backup and recovery actions performed, so it's easy to keep track of those operations.

- Keep older copies of backups for added protection. It's not a good idea to overwrite your tapes too soon to save a little money. If the current backups turn out to be unusable for some reason (which is a real possibility), you end up losing all of your data. Always know how many archived backups you have and where they are, and safeguard them.

- Your backup scripts should write to a log file or a log table, which should be examined for any problems that might have occurred during the backups.

- Ensure that your applications are separated into independent tablespaces, so you needn't take more than one application offline if you have a major media problem.

- Consider using snapshot technology-based storage system backup techniques for fast backups of large databases.

- Use the Data Pump Export utility (discussed in Chapter 14) to provide supplemental protection.

Testing Your Backups

Too often, the first encounter a DBA has with a defective backup strategy occurs during a frustrating recovery session of a production database. You can attribute the vast majority of problems encountered during recovery to inadequate or even nonexistent planning and testing of the backup and recovery strategy. The time to find out whether your database is recoverable is most definitely not when you are trying to recover a production database in the dead of night. To avoid a catastrophic recovery experience, every DBA should have established and tested backup and disaster recovery plans.

Always validate your backups and make sure that the backups are actually readable. Check for corrupted blocks in the backed-up files, so recovery doesn't become impossible due to bad files. The RMAN utility and user-managed backups both offer ways to check for data block corruption. I discuss these features in the "Database Corruption Detection" section later in this chapter.

You should also make periodic restoration tests mandatory for all key databases.

Maintaining a Redundancy Set

Always keep a redundancy set online so you can recover faster. A *redundancy set* is defined as the following:

- Last backup of all datafiles

- Last backup of the control file

- Multiplexed copies of the current redo log files

- Copies of the current control file that's being used

- All the archived redo logs since the last backup

You may also include the SPFILE or the init.ora, listener.ora, and tnsnames.ora files in your redundancy set.

If you have such a redundancy set, you can recover from a media failure that results in any of the possible losses: a datafile, control file, or online redo log. Make sure you save the redundancy set on completely separate physical volumes and RAID systems than those on which the datafiles, online redo log files, and control files are located. This separation of the redundancy set and the active database files guarantees that you'll never lose any uncommitted data due to media failure.

The ideal way to maintain a redundancy set is to use the flash recovery area, as described in the section "The Flash Recovery Area" later in this chapter. This way, you can maintain the redundancy set in one location on disk and automatically manage this space. Your recovery time will be reduced, as all the necessary backups that are part of your redundancy set are maintained on the disk itself.

Backup Strategies

You can take it for granted that there will be some kind of storage media–related problems over time. You need to have a strategy so you can be ready for this eventuality. Your backup strategy will depend heavily on the type of SLA you have in place, the size of your databases, the amount of changes made to your data, the disk space available, and other factors.

Service-Level Agreements

It is common for most IT departments today to draw up formal SLAs with their clients. SLAs are ways to formalize expectations regarding the availability and performance of the database, as well as other components such as the network. SLAs usually include factors such as the following:

- Maintenance windows
- Upgrade schedules
- Backup and recovery procedures
- Response times for certain key database operations
- Database and server downtime parameters

SLAs specify the uptime for the databases in clear terms. They also specify maintenance windows and the planned recovery time under several identifiable downtimes (for example, downtime due to a disk failure). The concept of *uptime* is pretty tricky—with a 99 percent uptime, you are still down almost four entire days during the year. Whether your organization can handle this or would like a 99.999 percent uptime, which implies only five minutes of downtime, is something you need to nail down in clear terms.

A typical SLA for database operations may look like the following (a partial agreement is shown here):

Standard Processing Services. The Provider shall furnish and allow access to the processing environments listed below:

a. *Mid-tier processing.*

    (1) *Applications to be processed:*

        Financial Information Systems (FIS) to include:

        LIST OF FIS APPLICATIONS

        Other Departmental Applications

    (2) *Hours of Availability.*

        Interactive: Monday-Friday* 07:00-17:00*

        Saturday, Sunday and Holidays Not Applicable

        *Application will be a web-based 24×7×365 system WITH the exception of the scheduled maintenance periods (see below)

        Batch: Not applicable

        Maintenance: Monthly, Fourth Weekend of Every Month

(3) *Standard Processing/Service Requirements.*

> *All of the systems/applications listed in paragraph (1) above are required to be operational 98% of the total time listed in paragraph (2) above. The Information Systems Department will provide a method for the Department of Finance to monitor operational percentages.*

(4) *Processing of data will be limited to the functionality/processing that was being conducted at the time of handing over the operations to the Information Services Department.*

b.   . . .

■Note SLAs also specify the cause of possible service interruptions and the expectations regarding the resumption of normal service. If the disruption of service is not due to a database failure, obviously other factors come into play, such as the network and the servers. You should, however, list the potential reasons for a database failure and the time it will take to recover from each of those failures. The total time taken for any recovery, of course, will include the time taken to restore the lost or damaged files and the time to recover the database. Chapter 16 covers the recovery process.

The type of backup and recovery strategy you want to adopt depends very much on the level of uptime specified in your SLA. The uptime level reflects how quickly you must recover from a failure. If the SLA states that you can take a whole day to restore and recover your database, then you may not need to do a nightly online backup.

You can get by with a once-a-week cold backup (if you're allowed the downtime for it). If your SLA specifies a 99.999 percent uptime, you may want to invest in Oracle Real Application Clusters (RAC), for example.

Usually, you'll find that uptime and cost are directly proportional to each other. What happens if you find out you can't make your main production server function for a very long time? Maybe you should have a standby database in place to take over for the main database in such a case.

Planning a Backup Strategy

There is no "one size fits all" type backup strategy that works for all organizations. Plan on using the flash recovery area, described in the next section, as it will eliminate the need to restore from tape in many cases, saving you valuable time. You also don't need to manually remove the obsolete backup files.

Planning an efficient backup strategy will mean two important things:

- You have all required backup files preferably on disk for a quick restoration and recovery.

- You minimize the space requirements by deleting obsolete backups and keeping only the required backup files on hand.

If you expect few changes in data, you are better off using incremental backups, since they won't consume a lot of space. Incremental backups, as part of your backup strategy, will reduce the time required to apply redo during recovery. However, if most of your database blocks change frequently, your incremental backups will be quite large. In such a case, you are better off making a complete image copy of the database at regular intervals.

Your frequency of backups and whether and how you should use incremental backups depends on the acceptable mean time to recover (MTTR). For example, you can implement a three-level backup scheme where you take a full or level 0 monthly backup, a weekly cumulative level 1 backup, and a daily differential level 1 backup. (See the "Incremental Backups" section in the discussion of RMAN commands later in this chapter for a description of these levels and cumulative and differential backups.) Using this strategy, you most likely can completely recover your database without needing to apply more than a day's worth of redo logs.

You could use the *incrementally updated backups* feature to minimize the MTTR. If on a daily basis, you run the script that appears in the "Incrementally Updated Backups" section later in this chapter, in essence, you can perform any PITR within 24 hours.

A Suggested Backup Schedule for Databases with Few Changes

In this example, you size the flash recovery area so it holds three days' worth of incremental backups. In this and the next example, assume that the retention policy is REDUNDANCY 1; that is, you keep only one set of backups on hand. Use the following commands to make your incremental backups. As explained later in this chapter, the RECOVER COPY command will produce a level 0 whole database backup. Use the following script to save archived logs and incremental backups created *after* SYSDATE-3:

```
RECOVER COPY OF DATABASE TAG "whole_db_copy" UNTIL TIME 'SYSDATE-3';
BACKUP INCREMENTAL LEVEL 1
  FOR RECOVER OF COPY WITH TAG "whole_db_copy" DATABASE;
```

Let's say you start running the script on Sunday, July 20, 2008. You decide that you want to keep only three days' worth of backups in the flash recovery area, including datafiles and archived redo logs. Any backups and archived redo logs older than three days are automatically deleted when the flash recovery area needs additional space for new files. This is what you'll have in the flash recovery area after each of the following days:

- Sunday, July 20: Level 0 backup

- Monday, July 21: Level 0 backup from July 20, level 1 incremental backup from July 21, and the archived logs from July 20 onward

- Tuesday, July 22: Level 0 backup, level 1 incremental backups from July 21 to July 22, archived logs from July 20 onward

- Wednesday, July 23: Level 0 backup, level 1 backups from July 20 to July 23, archived logs from July 20 onward

- Thursday, July 24: Level 0 backup rolled forward to July 21, level 1 backups from July 21 to July 24, and archived logs from July 23 through July 24

- Every day from Friday, July 25, on: Level 0 backup rolled forward to level 1 backup and archived logs from the day of the new level 0 backup until the current day

A Suggested Backup Schedule for Databases with Many Changes

If your database undergoes numerous changes, incremental backups won't be very helpful. You are better off with a full backup of your database at regular intervals. The following example shows how to make a weekly full backup:

```
RMAN> BACKUP DATABASE TAG "weekly_full_bkup";
```

You schedule this backup command to run once a week on Sunday night. Let's say you use the backup command for the first time on Sunday, March 20. This is what the flash recovery area will contain over time:

- Sunday, March 20: Full backup of the database

- Sunday, March 27: Full backup from March 27 and the archived logs from March 20 to March 27 (The full backup from the previous week; March 20 will be deleted, if space requirements dictate it.)

- Sunday, April 3, and every Sunday thereafter: Full backup from that day and archived logs from the previous Sunday to this Sunday

Now that you've had an overview of backing up an Oracle database and reviewed some basic backup strategies, you'll learn about the nuts and bolts of Oracle backups next, beginning with the flash recovery area.

The Flash Recovery Area

Oracle Corporation recommends that you designate the *flash recovery area* as the default area for storing every file related to backup and restore operations. One of the first steps in setting up your backup/recovery strategy is to configure a flash recovery area.

Traditionally, Oracle DBAs had to manage the areas of backup storage, ensuring that there was sufficient space to save their backup-related files. However, you should now allow the database to take care of these chores by using Automatic Disk-Based Backup and Recovery. Using a disk-based backup and recovery strategy minimizes the response time for a database recovery and increases database availability.

Note The flash recovery area isn't mandatory, but it's highly recommended. Some features of Oracle database backup and recovery, such as Oracle Flashback Database, require the use of a flash recovery area. You don't need to store *all* your backup-related files here, although that's what Oracle recommends.

To enable Automatic Disk-Based Backup and Recovery, you have to designate enough disk space for the flash recovery area, set the maximum size for the area, and tell Oracle how long you want to keep backup-related information. Oracle then manages the backup, including archivelog files, control files, and other files (your redundancy set will be part of this set of files). Oracle also deletes any files not needed by your database. Therefore, all you have to do is provide enough space for the flash recovery area and select an appropriate length of time for keeping files.

To delete unwanted files automatically, the Oracle database relies on the Oracle Managed Files (OMF) system. The OMF system automates Oracle database file management by creating and managing the database files that are part of the operating system. To set up an OMF file system, set the following OMF-related initialization parameters: DB_CREATE_FILE_DEST and DB_CREATE_ONLINE_LOG_DEST_*n*. OMF has the ability to create and delete Oracle files without the DBA's intervention. RMAN uses this OMF capability in its backup- and recovery-related functions in conjunction with the flash recovery area. If you want, you can use a flash recovery area with an ASM file system. Chapter 17 provides details on OMF and ASM file systems.

Tip You can share a flash recovery area among multiple databases.

Benefits of the Flash Recovery Area

Following are the key benefits of using the flash recovery area:

- It acts as a central storage area.
- It allows you to automatically manage recovery-related disk space.
- It allows you to carry out backup and restore operations more quickly.
- Backups have an increased reliability, because disks are safer storage devices than tapes.

Because you are no longer restoring tape backups, backup and restore operations are quicker. Even the backups moved to tape from the flash recovery area are retained on disk as long as there is room in the flash recovery area. Backup files that become obsolete per your recoverability goals will be automatically deleted when space is needed for new files.

Ideally, the flash recovery area holds a full backup of every datafile, your incremental backups, control file backups, and every archived redo log that is required for media recovery. In addition, you can use the flash recovery area as a disk cache for tape.

If you configure a flash recovery area, RMAN will store all the backup-related files in it by default. In this case, Oracle will use OMF files and generate the filenames.

The flash recovery area can contain the following:

- *Datafile copies*: The RMAN BACKUP AS COPY command creates image copies of every datafile. The RMAN will in turn store these in the flash recovery area. You can also store RMAN backup pieces in the flash recovery area. (An RMAN backup piece is an operating system file containing the backup of a datafile, a control file, or archived redo log files.)

- *Incremental backups*: If your backup strategy includes any incremental backups, they can be stored here.

- *Control file auto-backups*: The flash recovery area is the default area for all control file auto-backups made by RMAN.

- *Archived redo log files*: Oracle automatically deletes every obsolete file and every file that has been transferred to tape, so the flash recovery area is the ideal place to store archived redo log files.

- *Online redo log files*: Oracle recommends that you save multiplexed copies of the online redo log files in the flash recovery area. Oracle generates its own names for these files.

- *Current control files*: You should also store a multiplexed copy of your current control file in the flash recovery area.

- *Flashback logs*: The Oracle Flashback Database feature, which provides a convenient alternative to traditional PITR, generates flashback logs. Oracle stores the flashback logs in the flash recovery area. The Flashback Database feature (discussed in Chapter 16), if enabled, copies images of each altered block in every datafile into the flashback logs in the flash recovery area.

The multiplexed redo log files and control files contained in the flash recovery area are called *permanent* files, since you should never delete them (if you did, your instance will eventually crash as a result). The other files in the flash recovery area (recovery-related files) are transient files, because they'll be deleted after they are obsolete or have been copied to tape. The transient files include archived redo logs, datafile copies, control file copies, control file auto-backups, and backup pieces.

■Note At the very least, you should keep those archived logs that are not saved to tape in the flash recovery area.

The background process archiver (ARC*n*) will automatically create a copy of every archived redo log file in the flash recovery area, if you have specified the flash recovery area as the place to save archivelogs. If you configure a flash recovery area, you won't be able to use the older LOG_ARCHIVE_DEST and LOG_ARCHIVE_DUPLEX_DEST parameters; you must use the LOG_ARCHIVE_DEST_*n* parameter instead. The LOG_ARCHIVE_DEST_10 parameter is implicitly set to the flash recovery area, where the database will save archived redo log files. If you don't set any other local archiving destinations, LOG_ARCHIVE_DEST_10 is, by default, set to USE_DB_RECOVERY_FILE_DEST. This means that the archived redo log files will be automatically sent to the flash recovery area. In addition, if you've configured other archivelog locations with LOG_ARCHIVE_DEST_*n*, copies of archived redo logs will also be placed in those other locations.

For example, if you configured a flash recovery area and turned on archiving for a database without setting an explicit archivelog location, and then issued the ARCHIVE LOG LIST command, you would see something like this:

```
SQL> ARCHIVE LOG LIST
Database log mode              Archive Mode
Automatic archival             Enabled
Archive destination            USE_DB_RECOVERY_FILE_DEST
Oldest online log sequence     825
Next log sequence to archive   827
Current log sequence           827
SQL>
```

The USE_DB_RECOVERY_FILE_DEST setting points to the flash recovery area for the database. This is because you configured a flash recovery area and didn't specify a LOG_ARCHIVE_DEST_n destination. Therefore, the LOG_ARCHIVE_DEST_10 destination is implicitly set to the flash recovery area. (You can override this behavior by explicitly setting LOG_ARCHIVE_DEST_10 to an empty string.)

Setting the Size of the Flash Recovery Area

Oracle recommends that your flash recovery area should be the same size as the sum of the size of the database, any incremental backups, and every archived redo log. Your flash recovery area must be large enough to accommodate the following:

- A copy of all datafiles
- Incremental backups
- Online redo logs
- Archived redo logs that haven't been backed up to tape
- Control files
- Control file auto-backups

You should save both a multiplexed online redo log file and a current control file, in addition to all the other recovery-related files. Since Oracle recommends that you keep at least two copies of the online redo logs and the control file, you can use the flash recovery area to save a pair of redo log and control files.

The size of your database is the main factor when setting the size of the flash recovery area. Other factors that affect the size of the flash recovery area are

- The RMAN backup retention policy
- The type of storage device for backups (tape and disk or a disk device alone)
- The number of data block changes in your database

Ways to Create a Flash Recovery Area

There are a number of ways you can create a flash recovery area:

- Configure the flash recovery area at database-creation time using the Database Configuration Assistant (DBCA).
- Configure two flash recovery area–related dynamic initialization parameters. You can create a flash recovery area with these two parameters while the database is running.
- Use the OEM Database Control to configure a flash recovery area.

Configuring a Flash Recovery Area

You use two initialization parameters to configure a flash recovery area:

- DB_RECOVERY_FILE_DEST_SIZE: This parameter sets the maximum size of the flash recovery area.

- DB_RECOVERY_FILE_DEST: This parameter points to the location on disk of the flash recovery area. You must locate the flash recovery area on a disk separate from the database area, where you store the active database files such as datafiles, control files, and online redo logs.

You have to specify DB_RECOVERY_FILE_DEST_SIZE before you can specify DB_RECOVERY_FILE_DEST. Here's how you would specify the two flash recovery area initialization parameters in your init.ora file:

```
DB_RECOVERY_FILE_DEST_SIZE = 10G
DB_RECOVERY_FILE_DEST = '/u01/oradata/rcv_area'
```

Note that the database doesn't allocate the amount of disk space set in DB_RECOVERY_FILE_DEST_SIZE to the flash recovery area immediately. Oracle will use this space only as the maximum limit on the flash recovery area size. Until new files necessitate the use of more space, the space is controlled by the operating system, although Oracle has assigned it to the flash recovery area.

Dynamically Defining the Flash Recovery Area

Even if you don't specify a flash recovery area in the init.ora file or the SPFILE, you can use the ALTER SYSTEM statement to configure it while the instance is running. You can create and modify the flash recovery area dynamically using DB_RECOVERY_FILE_DEST and DB_RECOVERY_FILE_DEST_SIZE as follows:

```
SQL> ALTER SYSTEM SET
  2* DB_RECOVERY_FILE_DEST_SIZE = 2G;
System altered.
SQL> ALTER SYSTEM SET
  2  DB_RECOVERY_FILE_DEST = '/u01/app/oracle/flashrec_area';
System altered.
SQL>
```

As noted earlier, you must set the DB_RECOVERY_FILE_DEST_SIZE parameter first, before you set DB_RECOVERY_FILE_DEST. Ensure that you have created the flash recovery area directory before you use DB_RECOVERY_FILE_DEST. The SCOPE=BOTH clause makes sure that the changes you made are written permanently to the SPFILE. Use the ALTER SYSTEM command to make any changes to the flash recovery area after you create it.

■**Note** The DB_RECOVERY_FILE_DEST location is really a synonym for the flash recovery area.

Disabling the Current Flash Recovery Area

If you want to disable the current flash recovery area, set DB_RECOVERY_FILE_DEST to blank (' '). This unsets the destination for the flash recovery area files. You can check the V$RECOVERY_FILE_DEST view to see the current location of the flash recovery area.

RMAN will still access the flash recovery area to carry out backup and recovery tasks, even if you have disabled flash recovery. However, RMAN can't access the automatic space management features of flash recovery.

Examining the Default File Location

The flash recovery area requires that you use OMF, which means you can't use the LOG_ARCHIVE_DEST and LOG_ARCHIVE_DUPLEX_DEST parameters to specify redo log archive destinations (if you use these, you can't enable the flash recovery area). Instead, you must use the newer LOG_ARCHIVE_DEST_*n* parameters.

With OMF, Oracle designates the default location for the datafiles, control files, and redo log files based on the values of DB_CREATE_FILE_DEST and DB_CREATE_ONLINE_LOG_DEST_*n*. You use these two initialization parameters, along with DB_RECOVERY_FILE_DEST, which specifies the location of the flash recovery area.

■**Note** The location specified with DB_RECOVERY_FILE_DEST should not be the same as DB_CREATE_FILE_DEST or any setting in DB_CREATE_ONLINE_LOG_DEST_*n*.

Control Files

Setting the CONTROL_FILES parameter before you start the instance and create a new database means that Oracle creates the control files in the locations that you specify. If you don't set the CONTROL_FILES parameter during instance creation, Oracle creates the control files in default locations, following a set of rules:

- Specifying DB_CREATE_ONLINE_LOG_DEST_*n* gets Oracle to create an OMF-based control file in *n* number of locations. The first directory will hold the primary control file.

- If you specify the DB_CREATE_FILE_DEST and DB_RECOVERY_FILE_DEST parameters, Oracle will create an OMF-based control file in both of these locations.

- If you just specify DB_RECOVERY_FILE_DEST, Oracle creates an OMF-based control file only in the flash recovery area.

- If you omit all the initialization parameters, Oracle creates a non-OMF-based control file in the system-specific default location.

Redo Log Files

As I noted earlier, you can't use the LOG_ARCHIVE_DEST and LOG_ARCHIVE_DUPLEX_DEST parameters to specify redo log archive destinations. If you don't specify the LOGFILE clause when you create a database, Oracle creates the redo log files based on the following rules:

- If you specify the DB_CREATE_ONLINE_LOG_DEST_*n* parameter, Oracle creates an online redo log member in *n* number of locations. The maximum number is equal to the MAXLOGMEMBERS limit.

- If you specify the DB_CREATE_FILE_DEST and DB_RECOVERY_FILE_DEST parameters, Oracle creates an online redo log member in these locations.

- If you just specify the DB_RECOVERY_FILE_DEST parameter, Oracle will create an online redo log member in the flash recovery area only. Oracle will also implicitly set LOG_ARCHIVE_DEST_10 to the flash recovery area.

- If you omit all three initialization parameters, Oracle will create a non-OMF online redo log file in the system-specific default location.

Setting Up Flash Recovery Parameters

Let's review the procedure for configuring the flash recovery area and look at an example of how to set up the flash recovery parameters in your initialization file. This example assumes you are using OMF (see Chapter 17). OMF files are automatically named and managed by the Oracle database itself. You just provide a directory for the files, and Oracle will take care of the rest.

When you use OMF files, you use two parameters to tell Oracle where to create your datafiles, online redo log files, and control files. You use the DB_CREATE_FILE_DEST parameter to specify the location for all database files. You use the DB_CREATE_ONLINE_LOG_DEST_n parameter to specify the location of all online redo log and control files. If you don't specify the second parameter, Oracle will create all three types of files in the directory you specified for the DB_CREATE_FILE_DEST parameter.

For example, here is a set of initialization parameters you might use to create a test database:

```
DB_CREATE_FILE_DEST = /u02/test/oradata/dbfiles/
LOG_ARCHIVE_DEST_1 = 'LOCATION=/u03/test/arc_dest1'
LOG_ARCHIVE_DEST_2 = 'LOCATION=USE_DB_RECOVERY_FILE_DEST'
DB_RECOVERY_FILE_DEST = '/u03/test/oradata/rcv_area'
DB_RECOVERY_FILE_DEST_SIZE = 10G
```

This set of initialization parameters will create the following:

- OMF-based datafiles, online redo log files, and control files in the directory specified by the DB_CREATE_FILE_DEST parameter

- One copy of the current control file in the flash recovery area, since you are using both the DB_CREATE_FILE_DEST and DB_RECOVERY_FILE_DEST parameters

- One copy of the online redo log files in the flash recovery area, since you are using both the DB_CREATE_FILE_DEST and DB_RECOVERY_FILE_DEST parameters

- One copy of the archived redo logs in a file system location, indicated by LOG_ARCHIVE_DEST_1 = 'LOCATION=/u03/test/arc_dest1'

- One copy of the archived redo log files in the flash recovery area, indicated by LOG_ARCHIVE_DEST_2 = 'LOCATION=USE_DB_RECOVERY_FILE_DEST'

If you make sure your flash recovery area is physically separated from the other files, you will have ensured the creation of a safe redundancy set by following the example outlined here. By default, RMAN will send all backups of datafiles and control files to the flash recovery area. In addition, you have specified that copies of the online redo log files and control file also should be sent there. You thus have a complete redundancy set.

Backing Up the Flash Recovery Area

You can back up the flash recovery area with RMAN backup commands. You can only back up the flash recovery area to a tape device using these backup commands.

The RMAN command BACKUP RECOVERY AREA allows you to back up every flash recovery file in either the current flash recovery area or the previous flash recovery area. This will only back up those files that haven't been backed up to tape before.

The RMAN command BACKUP RECOVERY FILES allows you to back up every file that the BACKUP RECOVERY AREA command does, but includes files from all areas on the file system.

■**Tip** You can use the RMAN command BACKUP RECOVERY FILES to move disk backups to tape.

Working with the Flash Recovery Area

You need to ensure that the flash recovery area is large enough for your needs.

When you add a new file to the flash recovery area, Oracle does an update on the list of backup files it considers eligible for deletion. This list contains files that you've backed up to tape or that have become obsolete according to the local retention rules. Here's a summary of Oracle's automatic file deletion policy for the flash recovery area:

- Permanent files (multiplexed redo log files and control files) are never deleted.

- Files that are obsolete under the configured retention policy are eligible for deletion.

- Transient files (files other than the redo log and control files) that have been copied to tape are also eligible for deletion.

Even though a file might become eligible for deletion, Oracle removes it only when the flash recovery area is full. Thus, files recently moved to tape might still be available on disk, if there is no space pressure in the flash recovery area.

The V$RECOVERY_FILE_DEST view is the best place to find information on managing the flash recovery area. You can use this view to check the current location, disk quota, space in use, space reclaimable by deleting files, and total number of files in the flash recovery area:

```
SQL> SELECT * FROM V$RECOVERY_FILE_DEST;

      NAME    SPACE_LIMIT  SPACE_USED  SPACE_RECLAIMABLE  NUMBER_OF_FILES
---------- ------------ --------- ------------------ ----------------
u01/app/oracle 2147483648  1545718272         0                100
SQL>
```

In the V$RECOVERY_FILE_DEST view, the SPACE_LIMIT column contains the allocated flash recovery area space. The SPACE_RECLAIMABLE column contains the value that shows how much space you can reclaim by garbage collecting obsolete and redundant files in the flash recovery area.

You can use the V$FLASH_RECOVERY_AREA_USAGE view to check the space being used by different types of files, and how much space for each type of file you can reclaim by deleting files that are obsolete, redundant, or already backed up to tape.

```
SQL> SELECT * FROM V$FLASH_RECOVERY_AREA_USAGE;
```

FILE_TYPE	PERCENT_SPACE_USED	PERCENT_SPACE_RECLAIMABLE	NUMBER_OF_FILES
CONTROLFILE	0	0	0
ONLINELOG	0	0	0
ARCHIVELOG	43.57	0	96
BACKUPPIECE	28.41	0	4
IMAGECOPY	0	0	0
FLASHBACKLOG	0	0	0

Additionally, Oracle has added the IS_RECOVERY_DEST_FILE column to the V$LOGFILE, V$CONTROLFILE, V$ARCHIVED_LOG, V$DATAFILE_COPY, and V$BACKUP_PIECE views. A value of YES means the file is in the flash recovery area; NO means that it is not.

If the flash recovery area runs out of space and it can't remove any files to compensate, you will see one of the following: a *warning* alert at 85 percent full or a *critical* alert at 97 percent full. If this happens, Oracle adds entries to the alert log file and the DBA_OUTSTANDING_ALERTS view. However, Oracle continues placing recovery-related files in the flash recovery area, until it fills 100 percent of the space; at that point, it issues an error that tells you that the flash recovery area is full.

When the flash recovery area fills up, the database issues the following error:

```
ORA-19815: WARNING: db_recovery_file_dest_size of 2147483648  bytes is 100.00% used,
and has 0 remaining bytes available.
```

The following are two other errors you'll most likely see when you run out of space in the flash recovery area:

- ORA-19809 means that the limit set by the DB_RECOVERY_FILE_DEST_SIZE parameter is exceeded.
- ORA-19804 indicates that Oracle is unable to reclaim a specified amount of bytes from the limit set by DB_RECOVERY_FILE_DEST_SIZE.

■**Note** The ORA-00257 error message is "Archiver error. Connect internal only, until freed." This means that your archivelog directory is full and users can't connect to the database anymore. Existing users can continue to query the database, but no DML can be executed because Oracle can't archive the logs. If you quickly move some of the files in the archivelog directory to a different location, the database is free to continue its normal operations. If you have a script monitoring the free space on your archivelog directory, you shouldn't have this problem.

If any of this ever happens, you can do the following:

- Think about changing your policies that cover backup and archivelog retention.
- Increase the size of DB_RECOVERY_FILE_DEST_SIZE.
- Back up the contents of the flash recovery area to a tape device with the RMAN BACKUP RECOVERY AREA command.
- Delete unnecessary backup files with RMAN. You can issue the DELETE OBSOLETE command to delete the backup files.

If you want to move the flash recovery area, use the DB_RECOVERY_FILE_DEST initialization parameter:

```
SQL> ALTER SYSTEM SET DB_RECOVERY_FILE_DEST='/u01/app/oracle/new_area';
```

Oracle creates the flash recovery area files in the new flash recovery area. You can, if you want, leave the permanent files, flashback logs, and transient files where they are. Eventually, as they become eligible for deletion, Oracle will remove all the transient files. However, you can move the permanent files, transient files, and flashback logs with the standard operating system file commands.

Recovery Manager

The traditional user-managed backup method consists simply of using the operating system commands to copy the relevant files to a different location and/or to a tape device. With RMAN, you back up the database files from *within* the database with the help of the database server itself. RMAN can make backups of datafiles and datafile image copies, control files and control file image copies, archived redo logs, the SPFILE, and RMAN backup pieces. Oracle recommends using the RMAN interface to back up your databases.

■**Note** Most "old-school" Oracle DBAs will be familiar with operating system commands, but newer DBAs may want to focus on RMAN, which offers ease of use, safety, and features that the traditional methods don't have. You can use all the RMAN backup and recovery functionality through the OEM interface (Database Control or Grid Control), without needing to remember complex commands.

RMAN simplifies the backup procedures by enabling the use of powerful yet easy-to-write backup and recovery scripts. RMAN also offers features such as corruption detection within the data blocks and the ability to back up only the changed blocks in the database. You can save RMAN's scripts in the database and use them right from there, so you don't need to write operating system-based scripts. RMAN automatically ensures the backup of all the database files, which eliminates the human-error component that is present in operating system-based backups.

Despite its sophistication, RMAN has some limitations. You can't, for example, read from or write directly to a tape device using RMAN; you need to use what's known as a media management layer to make tape backups.

■**Note** RMAN can create and manage backups on disk and on tape devices, also referred to as system backup to tape (SBT) devices, move backups on disk to tape, and restore backups from tape. However, RMAN interacts with SBT devices through an MML, or media manager. Oracle provides its own MML, in the form of Oracle Secure Backup.

Benefits of RMAN

RMAN provides an array of benefits compared to user-managed backup methods, including the following:

- You can perform incremental backups using RMAN. The size of the backups doesn't depend on database size; rather, it depends on the activity level within the database, because unchanged blocks are skipped during incremental backups. You can't perform incremental backups any other way. You can perform incremental exports, but that isn't considered a real backup for all databases.

- You can repair a datafile with a few corrupt data blocks online, without needing to resort to restoring a file from backup. This is called *block media recovery*.

■**Tip** Even if you use user-managed backups, you can perform block media recovery by cataloging your datafile and archiving redo log backups into the RMAN repository.

- Human error is minimized because RMAN, not the individual DBA, keeps track of all the file-names and locations. Once you understand the use of the RMAN utility, it's easy for you to take over the backup and recovery of databases from another DBA.

- A simple command, such as BACKUP DATABASE, can back up an entire database, without the need for complex scripts.

- The unused block compression feature of RMAN lets you skip copying never-used data blocks in a datafile during a backup, thus saving storage space and backup time.

- It's easy to automate the backup and recovery process through RMAN. RMAN can also automatically parallelize your backup and recovery sessions.

- RMAN can perform error checking during backups and recovery, thus ensuring that the backed-up files aren't corrupt. RMAN has the capability to recover any corrupted data blocks without taking the datafile offline.

- During online backups, no redo is generated, unlike when online backups are performed using the operating system utilities. Thus, the overhead is low for online backups.

- The binary compression feature reduces the size of backups saved on disk.

- If you use the recovery catalog, you can store backup and recovery scripts directly in it.

- RMAN can perform simulated backups and restores.

- RMAN enables you to make *image copies*, which are similar to operating system-based backups of files.

- RMAN can be easily integrated with powerful third-party media management products to make tape backups effortless.

- RMAN is integrated well with the OEM backup functionality, so you can schedule backup jobs easily for a large number of databases through a common management framework.

- You can easily clone databases and maintain standby databases using the RMAN functionality.

As the preceding list clearly shows, it's no contest when it comes to the question of whether you should be using operating system-based backup and recovery techniques (user-managed backup and recovery) or RMAN. Therefore, you'll see quite a bit of discussion about RMAN in this chapter and the next, which deals with recovering databases. Oracle maintains that both RMAN and traditional user-managed backup and recovery methods are equally valid and effective, but recommends the use of RMAN.

RMAN Architecture

RMAN operates via server sessions connecting to the target databases, which are the databases you want to back up or recover. The collection of information about the target database—such as its schema information, backup copy information, configuration settings, and backup and recovery scripts—is called the RMAN repository. RMAN uses this metadata about the target databases to perform its backup and recovery activities. RMAN periodically retrieves metadata from the target database control file and saves it in the recovery catalog.

Following is a list of the entities that enable RMAN to perform its backup and recovery functions:

- *Target database*: This is the database that the RMAN needs to back up. RMAN server sessions running in the target database perform the backup and recovery operations.

- *RMAN repository*: This is RMAN's metadata about backups, archived redo logs, and its own activities. The control file of each database is the primary storage for RMAN's repository.

- *Recovery catalog schema*: This is the database schema in the recovery catalog database that owns the RMAN backup and recovery metadata (the RMAN repository).

- *RMAN client*: You manage RMAN operations through RMAN client sessions. The RMAN client is a command-line interface through which you issue commands to perform backup and recovery operations by communicating with the RMAN server process. You can issue special RMAN commands, as well as SQL statements from the RMAN client. The client starts the RMAN server sessions on the target database and directs them to perform the backup and recovery operations. The RMAN client uses Oracle Net to connect to a target database, so it can be located on any host that is connected to the target host through Oracle Net.

- *RMAN executable*: This is the actual program that manages all backup and recovery operations. You can find the RMAN executable (also known simply as rman) in the $ORACLE_HOME/bin directory. You specify the backup or recovery operation, and the RMAN executable performs it for you by interacting with the target database. It records the results in the control file and the optional recovery catalog.

- *Server processes*: These are the background processes that facilitate communication between the RMAN executable and the target database. The server process performs the real work of reading and writing to disk devices and tape drives during backup and recovery.

Note Three entities are optional when you use RMAN: the flash recovery area, the recovery catalog database (and the recovery catalog schema), and media management software.

The RMAN Repository and Recovery Catalog

You have a choice of two locations for storing the RMAN repository: you can let RMAN store it in the target database control file, or you can configure and use the optional recovery catalog to manage the metadata. The RMAN repository contains information about the following items:

- Datafile backup sets and copies

- Archived redo log copies and backup sets

- Tablespaces and datafile information

- Stored scripts and RMAN configuration settings

By default, RMAN stores all metadata in the control file. All RMAN information is first written in the control file, and then to the recovery catalog if one exists. For instance, when RMAN creates a new backup set, you can view the information in the V$BACKUP_SET view. You can also view the same information in the recovery catalog view, RC_BACKUP_SET. Thus, for every change to the RMAN repository, information is recorded in two places: the control file and the optional recovery catalog. The recovery catalog versions of the RMAN repository are stored in database tables. The control file version of the repository is stored as records within the control file.

If you wish, you can manage the RMAN with just the information in the control file. The objections you'll hear regarding using the recovery catalog are that it's too complex to maintain and that it needs another database to manage it. However, there are some RMAN commands you can use only when you use the recovery catalog. You can also use RMAN-stored scripts only if you use the recovery catalog. If you use the control file, you run the risk of some of the historical data being overwritten, but the recovery catalog will safeguard all such data. This is because the control file allocates a finite space for backup-related activities, while the recovery catalog has more room for storing backup history. One recovery catalog in your system can perform backup, restore, and recovery activities for dozens of Oracle databases. Thus, you can centralize and automate backup and recovery operations by using the recovery catalog. Oracle recommends that you use a dedicated database for running the recovery catalog, but it isn't absolutely necessary.

Note You're strongly advised to use the recovery catalog so you can take advantage of the full range of features provided by RMAN. The discussion of RMAN's features in this chapter and the next assumes the existence of the recovery catalog.

The Media Management Layer

You can make backups directly to your operating system disks using RMAN. If you want to make backups to tape, you'll need additional software called an MML or a media manager. RMAN can move backups on disk to tape and restore the tape backups if necessary. Oracle Database 11g contains a proprietary media management product, called Oracle Secure Backup, which I discuss in the "Oracle Secure Backup" section later in this chapter.

Connecting to RMAN

You can connect to RMAN by simply typing **rman** at the operating system prompt. (Make sure you've set the path variables correctly; in some operating systems, such as SUSE Linux, you may get the operating system's utility, named rman, instead of Oracle's RMAN utility.) This will get you the RMAN> prompt, at which point you can type in the various commands. You can also use the RMAN commands in batch mode or through pipes by using Oracle's DBMS_PIPE package.

You don't need to be a SYSDBA privilege holder to just connect to the RMAN catalog; you can do so with the special rman account and password. As you'll see later in the "Creating the Recovery Catalog" section, the user rman is the owner of the catalog. You can connect to RMAN through database password authentication. You can also connect to the database using operating system authentication. The following sections describe each of these methods.

Connecting to RMAN Using Database Authentication

You can log into the RMAN utility using your database credentials. You issue backup/recovery commands after connecting to the target database. To finish your RMAN session, use the exit command. Here is an example of connecting to the database named orcl, which is the target database:

```
$ rman

Recovery Manager: Release 11.1.0.6.0 - Production on Thu Mar 27 11:09:16 2008
Copyright (c) 1982, 2007, Oracle.  All rights reserved.
RMAN> CONNECT TARGET /
connected to target database: ORCL (DBID=1080111806)
RMAN> exit
Recovery Manager complete.
$
```

USING A MEDIA MANAGEMENT LAYER WITH RMAN

It's not uncommon for Oracle databases to be hundreds of gigabytes in size. Backing up large, mission-critical databases poses challenges to the DBA in terms of the complexity of the techniques and the longer durations of the backups. In recent years, several advances in technology have contributed to easing the DBA's burden in this area. Today's leading solutions do provide an array of choices, in terms of both strategy and third-party tools, to make the backup process extremely efficient and safe.

Manually tracking backup files and backup operations also starts hitting the point of diminishing returns after a while. Even if you use RMAN, a large number of databases make it imperative to work with a third-party tool to manage the backup schedules and to automate the media devices. Oracle maintains the Oracle Backup Solutions Program (BSP), which is a team of vendors whose media management products are designed to work with RMAN. Some of the important players in the field are Legato Systems (NetWorker) and VERITAS (NetBackup). For a complete list of BSP media management software vendors, visit http://otn.oracle.com/deploy/availability/htdocs/bsp.htm#MMV.

NetWorker, for example, provides an automated way of performing backups that includes monitoring all the backups in addition to scheduling them. NetWorker also has the capability to perform parallel backups to multiple tape systems simultaneously, thereby cutting down on the time needed for backups of extremely large databases. Dedicated storage servers and autochanger-based tape drives are used by Legato, as well as other similar private-party offerings. NetWorker accepts data through RMAN, saves it on tape, and provides archiving and indexing services for the tapes. Products such as NetWorker provide much better I/O performance than the traditional operating system utilities.

> Another interesting third-party product is Business Copy XP, offered by Hewlett Packard in support of its HP line of UNIX machines. Business Copy XP is an array-based mirroring strategy that enables you to make copies online in a fraction of the time it normally takes. You can even run background processes on the copied data without adversely affecting production. This reduction in the time taken for backups enables more frequent backups.
>
> In the past, Oracle depended exclusively on third-party products for RMAN media management to access sequential media devices like tape libraries. In fact, Oracle even bundled a single-user version of the Legato NetWorker, called the Legato Single Server Version (LSSV), with the Oracle database. However, in Oracle Database 10*g* Release 2, Oracle introduced its own proprietary media management solution named Oracle Secure Backup.

The following way of specifying the credentials at the operating system level is equivalent to the preceding commands:

```
$ rman target system/system_passwd

Recovery Manager: Release 11.1.0.6.0 - Production on Thu Mar 27 11:38:16 2008
Copyright (c) 1982, 2007, Oracle.  All rights reserved.connected to
 target database: ORCL (DBID=1080111806)
RMAN>
```

Connecting to RMAN Using Operating System Authentication

You can also log in to RMAN using operating system authentication, without using a database user account and password. Here's how you do this:

```
$ rman target /

Recovery Manager: Release 11.1.0.6.0 - Production on Thu Mar 27 11:09:16 2008
Copyright (c) 1982, 2007, Oracle.  All rights reserved.
connected to target database: ORCL (DBID=1080111806)
RMAN>
```

Connecting to the Recovery Catalog

The preceding login examples connect directly to the target database without a recovery catalog. Once you configure the optional recovery catalog, you have the option of connecting to the recovery catalog first and performing all your backup/recovery actions through it. This is the option Oracle strongly recommends because of the benefits of using the recovery catalog. In the following, the recovery catalog is in the database nick and the target database is orcl:

```
$ rman target orcl catalog rman/rman@nick

Recovery Manager: Release 11.1.0.6.0 - Production on Thu Mar 27 11:09:16 2008
Copyright (c) 1982, 2007, Oracle.  All rights reserved.target database Password:
connected to target database: ORCL (DBID=1065483535)
connected to recovery catalog database
RMAN>
```

Redirecting Output to a Log File

By default, RMAN outputs everything to the screen, but you can have it redirect the output to a log file by specifying the parameter LOG when starting RMAN. For example:

```
$ rman LOG /u01/app/oracle/rman.log
```

When you specify the LOG parameter, RMAN doesn't display any output to you. To make RMAN log its output as well as send it to standard output, use the Linux or UNIX tee command, as shown here:

```
$ rman  |  tee /u01/app/oracle/rman.log
```

The tee command makes RMAN output visible to you, while sending it simultaneously to a log file.

Scripting with RMAN

As you'll see in upcoming sections of this chapter, you can use simple manual RMAN commands, such as BACKUP DATABASE and LIST OBSOLETE. However, manual commands aren't the only or the best way to give directives to RMAN. RMAN comes with a powerful scripting language that lets you encapsulate common backup tasks easily. You can store RMAN scripts either in the recovery catalog or as text files. You can create scripts designed for a single database or global scripts that can be used in several databases.

RMAN offers two sorts of scripts: *stored scripts* (kept in the RMAN recovery catalog) and *text scripts* (kept in regular text files). Stored scripts have the advantage that any user who logs into RMAN can access them easily. You can use stored scripts as alternatives to command files for any set of RMAN commands that you regularly execute. Unlike command files, which are stored on the file system, stored scripts are stored in the recovery catalog.

When you need to use a large number of configuration parameters for a particular backup, it's much easier to use a script. RMAN scripts thus perform the same function as regular scripts in UNIX or SQL: they make it easier to store and rerun long sets of commands.

Using Command Files

You can create operating system command files for regularly scheduled RMAN backup jobs. Inside a command file, you can use the @*filename* syntax to specify a command file that you want RMAN to execute. For example, you can create a command file named testfile1 with the following RMAN command:

```
BACKUP DATABASE PLUS ARCHIVELOG;
```

You can then run the command file testfile1 from the operating system command line as follows:

```
$ rman target / @testfile1
```

Note that you can also specify the @*filename* syntax at the RMAN prompt to execute a command file, as shown here:

```
RMAN> @testfile1
```

You can also specify the USING clause at the command-line prompt to specify values for use in substitution variables in a command file, thus making a command file dynamic. I provide a simple example that shows how to create and execute a dynamic shell script. The script calls a command file that contains the substitution variables.

1. Create a command file (monthly_backup.cmd) that uses substitution variables, as shown here:

```
#monthly_backup.cmd
CONNECT TARGET /
RUN
{
  ALLOCATE CHANNEL c1
    DEVICE TYPE sbt
    PARMS 'ENV=(OB_MEDIA_FAMILY=&1)';
  BACKUP DATABASE
    TAG &2
    FORMAT '/u02/app/oracle/bck/&1%U.bck'
    RESTORE POINT &3;
}
EXIT;
```

The command file monthly_backup.cmd uses three substitution variables to name the tape set, to provide the FORMAT string specification, and to name the restore point.

2. Next, create a shell script you'll use to run the monthly_backup.cmd file. The shell script mybackup.sh contains three shell variables, and you can pass the values for those variables at the command line when you execute the script.

```
#!/bin/tcsh
# name: mybackup.sh
# usage: use the tag name and number of copies as arguments
set media_family = $argv[1]
set format = $argv[2]set restore_point = $argv[3]
rman @'/u01/app/oracle/scripts/monthly_backup.cmd' USING $media_family $format ➥
$restore_point
```

Now you have a shell script (mybackup.sh) that you can execute by passing arguments at the command line to specify values for our three substitution variables.

3. Execute the mybackup.sh shell script, as shown here:

```
% mybackup.sh archival_backup bck0906 FY06Q3
```

Each time you run the mybackup.sh script, you can specify different values for the three substitution variables, right at the command line.

Creating and Running Stored Scripts

All stored scripts in RMAN are created with the CREATE SCRIPT command, followed by the actual script contents enclosed within a pair of curly brackets, { }. You can use any commands within the brackets of a CREATE SCRIPT command that you can use in a RUN block. The RMAN scripts do look a bit cryptic at first, but they are highly effective and actually easy to write.

Here's a simplified nightly backup script that performs a full database backup. Note that by using the keyword SQL, you can include regular SQL commands within your RMAN backup script.

```
RMAN> CREATE SCRIPT nightly_backup {
2>    ALLOCATE CHANNEL c1 TYPE DISK;
3>    BACKUP DATABASE FORMAT '/u01/app/oracle/%u';
4>    SQL 'ALTER DATABASE BACKUP CONTROLFILE TO TRACE';
5>    }
created script nightly_backup
RMAN>
```

You execute a script with the RUN command and the EXECUTE SCRIPT command. So, now that you have created the script nightly_backup, all you need to do to run the full backup is to execute the script as follows:

```
RMAN> RUN {EXECUTE SCRIPT nightly_backup;}
executing script: nightly_backup
allocated channel: c1
channel c1: sid=19 devtype=DISK
. . .
RMAN>
```

RMAN scripting enables you to perform complex tasks in a few short lines. The following script uses two tape devices to perform a full database backup. The script allocates the two channels (connections to the server), completes the backup in a specified format, and releases the channels.

```
RMAN> RUN {
2>    ALLOCATE CHANNEL c1 TYPE 'sbt_tape';
3>    ALLOCATE CHANNEL c2 TYPE 'sbt_tape';
4>    BACKUP
5>    FORMAT  'full d%d_u%u'
6>    FILESPERSET 10
7>    DATABASE;
8>    RELEASE CHANNEL c1;
9>    RELEASE CHANNEL c2;
10>   }
```

If you wish, you can incorporate RMAN commands in an operating system file, called a *command file*. Here is an example that shows how you can use an operating system file to execute RMAN commands and store the results in a log file (output.txt):

```
$ rman TARGET/CATALOG rman/cat@catdb CMDFILE commandfile.rcv LOG outfile.txt
```

Checking the Syntax of RMAN Scripts

You can use the CHECKSYNTAX parameter to check the syntax of a script (or any RMAN command) you plan to use with RMAN. Here's an example that shows a script contained in the script file testfile that has the correct syntax:

```
$ rman CHECKSYNTAX @/tmp/testfile
Recovery Manager: Release 11.1.0.6.0 - Production on Thu Mar 27 11:09:16 2008
Copyright (c) 1982, 2007, Oracle.  All rights reserved.

RMAN> # command file with correct syntax
2> restore database;
3> recover database;
4>
The cmdfile has no syntax errors
 Recovery Manager complete.
$
```

Creating Global RMAN Scripts

The scripts you've seen so far are local scripts, since you can use them only in the database in which you create them. You can also create and execute an RMAN *global* script against a database registered in the recovery catalog, providing your RMAN client is connected to the recovery catalog and the target database simultaneously. You can get databases to share RMAN scripts if they connect to the database with the RMAN catalog. The following statement shows the syntax for creating a global script:

```
RMAN> CREATE GLOBAL SCRIPT global_full_backup
      {
      BACKUP DATABASE PLUS ARCHIVELOG;
      DELETE OBSOLETE;
      }
created global script global_full_backup
RMAN>
```

You execute a global script in the same way as a local script:

```
RMAN> RUN {EXECUTE GLOBAL SCRIPT global_full_backup};}
```

Printing a Script

The following PRINT SCRIPT command prints out the contents of the global script example:

```
RMAN> PRINT GLOBAL SCRIPT global_full_backup;
printing stored global script:  global_full_backup
  {backup database plus archivelog ;
   delete obsolete;
   }
RMAN>
```

Listing Script Names

The LIST . . . SCRIPT NAMES command lets you view the names of all the scripts you stored in a recovery catalog. Here's an example:

```
RMAN> LIST SCRIPT NAMES;
```

The LIST . . . SCRIPT NAMES command shows all local and global scripts that you can execute for the database you are currently connected to. To view the script names for all the databases registered in the recovery catalog, execute the LIST ALL SCRIPT NAMES command instead.

Deleting Stored Scripts

Use the DELETE SCRIPT command to delete a stored script from the recovery catalog, as shown here:

```
RMAN> DELETE SCRIPT 'my-script';
```

If the script is global, use the DELETE GLOBAL SCRIPT command instead.

Creating Dynamic Stored Scripts

You can create a dynamic stored script by specifying substitution variables while creating a script with the CREATE SCRIPT command. The USING clause lets you specify values for the substitution variables in a command file. Follow these steps to create and use a dynamic stored script:

1. Create a command file that you can use to create a stored script. In our example, the command file is named myscript.rman, and it contains the CREATE SCRIPT command to create the new stored script. Use substitution variables for values that you want to assign dynamically.

```
RMAN> CREATE SCRIPT quarterly {
        ALLOCATE CHANNEL c1
        DEVICE TYPE sbt
        PARMS 'ENV=(OB_MEDIA_FAMILY=&1)';
        BACKUP
         ' TAG &2
          FORMAT '/disk2/bck/&1%U.bck'
          KEEP FOREVER
          RESTORE POINT &3
          DATABASE;
          }
```

The QUARTERLY script (created using the command file myscript.rman) uses three substitution variables: OB_MEDIA_FAMILY to specify the name of the tape set, FORMAT to specify the format string, and RESTORE_POINT to specify the name of the restore point.

2. Connect to the target database and the recovery catalog, specifying initial values for the three substitution variables in the QUARTERLY script. Place the values after the keyword USING, as in the following example:

```
$ rman target / catalog rman@catdb USING arc_backup bck0908 FY08Q3
```

Note that at this point, you're merely logged in to RMAN: specifying the USING clause during the RMAN login enables you to pass values for the three substitution variables in the script. You'll create the script in the next step.

3. Once you log in to RMAN, execute the command file myscript.rman to create the stored script QUARTERLY.

```
RMAN> @catscript.rman
```

RMAN now has a new stored script named QUARTERLY, which can accept different values for its three substitution variables.

Now that you have created the dynamic stored script, you can execute it every quarter by passing the correct values for the three substitution variables. For example, I can assign the following values to the substitution variables: arch_bkp for the media family, bkp1208 as part of the FORMAT string, and FY0804 as the name of the restore point. Here's how to invoke the stored script with those parameter values:

```
RUN
{
  EXECUTE SCRIPT quarterly
    USING arch_bkp
    bkp1208
    FY08Q4;
}
```

As the example shows, it's very easy to pass different runtime values for the variables inside the dynamic stored script.

Converting RMAN Scripts

You can change scripts from the text format to a stored script and vice versa. Here's how an RMAN command can send the contents of a stored script to a text file:

```
RMAN> PRINT script nightly_backup to file 'test.txt';
script nightly_backup written to file test.txt
RMAN>
```

Replacing a Stored Script

You can issue the REPLACE SCRIPT command to update a stored script. Here's an example:

```
RMAN> REPLACE SCRIPT full_backup
      {
        BACKUP DATABASE;
      }
```

If the script full_backup doesn't exist, RMAN creates the script. To replace a global script, execute the REPLACE GLOBAL SCRIPT command.

Important RMAN Terms

RMAN uses some special terminology. To use RMAN effectively, you need a good understanding of the terms discussed in the following sections.

Backup Piece

A *backup piece* is an operating system file containing the backup of a datafile, a control file, or archived redo log files. This backup information is stored in an RMAN-specific format.

Backup Set

A *backup set* is a logical structure that consists of one or more RMAN backup pieces (the default is one backup piece per backup set). You can create a backup set on disk or tape. If you back up a database, datafile, tablespace, or archivelog, RMAN groups the complete set of relevant backup pieces into one backup set. When you issue the backup command, RMAN creates the backup set to hold the output. Remember that a backup set is a file or set of files in a proprietary format that only RMAN can understand. Thus, only RMAN is able to use the backup sets to recover the database.

By default, RMAN creates a backup set when you use a backup command, whether you are copying to disk or tape (through a media manager).

Image Copy

Image copies are similar to the copies you can make of operating system files with the cp command in UNIX or the copy command in DOS. You can make image copies of datafiles, control files, and archived redo log files. RMAN image copies can be made only to disk; they can't be made to tape.

RMAN can also use copies that you make using non-RMAN operating system utilities. These types of copies are called *user-managed copies* or *operating system copies*. Really, there's no difference between RMAN image copies and normal copies made with the cp command, for example, except that image copies made through the RMAN tool have information about them written to the control file or the recovery catalog. If you use an operating system command such as dd to produce image copies, you can then use the RMAN CATALOG command to record these copies in the RMAN repository. Thus, you can use a manually copied datafile during a recovery, if you first use the CATALOG command to register the file with RMAN. You can then use these user-made copies of datafiles in RMAN operations through the RESTORE and SWITCH commands.

You use the RMAN command BACKUP AS COPY to make image copies. You may also direct RMAN to always produce image copies rather than backup sets (thus changing the default behavior of making backup sets) by performing the following configuration change:

```
RMAN> CONFIGURE DEVICE TYPE DISK BACKUP TYPE TO COPY;
new RMAN configuration parameters:
CONFIGURE DEVICE TYPE DISK BACKUP TYPE TO COPY PARALLELISM 1;
new RMAN configuration parameters are successfully stored
released channel: ORA_DISK_1
starting full resync of recovery catalog
full resync complete
RMAN>
```

You can use the image copies produced by the RMAN BACKUP AS COPY command just like any other file copies made with operating system utilities.

Proxy Copy

RMAN can also perform a special kind of backup called the *proxy copy*, where the media manager is given control of the copying process. Proxy copies can't be used with disks. Here's an example of how you specify a proxy copy:

```
RMAN> BACKUP DEVICE TYPE sbt PROXY DATAFILE 2;
```

Channel

An RMAN session must use some kind of a connection to the server to perform backup and recovery work, and *channels* represent those connections. Channels specify the specific device, disk, or tape that will be used for the backup or recovery. You can either have preconfigured channels (somewhat like default channels) or specify the channel manually.

You can use *automatic channel allocation* to configure channels persistently across sessions. In the following examples, the default device is set to an SBT in the first case and to disk in the second case:

```
RMAN> CONFIGURE DEFAULT DEVICE TYPE TO sbt; /* tape device */
RMAN> CONFIGURE DEFAULT DEVICE TYPE TO disk; /* OS file system */
```

These devices are made part of the RMAN configuration, and until they are changed again through the use of the CONFIGURE command, they remain the default device types for all RMAN sessions.

You can *manually* set the channel type by using the ALLOCATE CHANNEL command. The following command sets the device to sbt, which indicates a sequential tape device. Note that the example uses a RUN block for allocating the channel. A RUN block is used in RMAN when you need to set up the environment for the statements within the block:

```
RMAN> RUN
      {ALLOCATE CHANNEL a1 DEVICE TYPE sbt;
      backup database;
      }
RMAN>
```

Specifying Backup Tags and Backup Formats

RMAN lets you use a *tag* for every backup so you can easily identify the backup. Thus, when you perform a restore or recovery operation, you can specify the tag to identify the backups to use. Tags are very useful in identifying various backups, especially those created using incremental backup strategies. Here's a simple example, showing how you can tag a full database backup:

```
RMAN> BACKUP TAG 'weekly_full_db_bkup' DATABASE;
```

You can use the FORMAT option with backup commands to specify a location and name for backup pieces and copies. You use substitution variables to generate unique filenames. Here's an example that shows how you can specify a file format, as well as the location, using the FORMAT option:

```
RMAN> BACKUP FORMAT='AL_%d/%t/%s/%p' ARCHIVELOG LIKE '%arc_dest%';
```

Making Copies of RMAN Backups

You cannot produce multiple copies of an RMAN image copy while performing the backup itself. However, you can make multiple copies of backup sets within a BACKUP command. You may send each backup copy to a different disk or tape location. You can produce up to four copies of each backup piece in a backup set within a single BACKUP command. You can specify multiple copies in one of the following ways:

- Use the CONFIGURE . . . BACKUP COPIES option.
- Use SET BACKUP COPIES in a RUN block.
- Use the COPIES option in the BACKUP command.

The following example demonstrates how to make copies of a backup to multiple disks:

```
RMAN> BACKUP DEVICE TYPE DISK
      COPIES 2 DATAFILE 1
      FORMAT '/disk1/df1_%U', '/disk2/df1_%U';
```

If you already have a previously made backup on a disk and wish to make a copy of it to another disk, use the BACKUP AS BACKUPSET command in the following way:

```
RMAN> BACKUP DEVICE TYPE DISK AS BACKUPSET DATABASE PLUS ARCHIVELOG;
```

If you would rather copy the previously made backup sets on disk to tape, use the following version of the BACKUP BACKUPSET command:

```
RMAN> BACKUP DEVICE TYPE sbt BACKUPSET ALL
```

After making image copies of a datafile, tablespace, or database, you can back up the image copies of the backups, as either image copies or backups sets. Here are some examples:

- Create an image copy of a database:

  ```
  RMAN> BACKUP AS COPY DATABASE;
  ```

- Copy the previous image copy of the database:

  ```
  RMAN> BACKUP AS COPY COPY OF DATABASE;
  ```

- Make an image copy of a single tablespace:

  ```
  RMAN> BACKUP AS COPY TABLESPACE SYSAUX;
  ```

- Create a backup set from the tablespace image copy:

  ```
  RMAN> BACKUP AS BACKUPSET COPY OF TABLESPACE SYSAUX;
  ```

- Copy a datafile:

  ```
  RMAN> BACKUP AS COPY DATAFILE 2;
  ```

- Copy the datafile copy:

  ```
  RMAN> BACKUP AS COPY COPY OF DATAFILE 2;
  ```

RMAN Backup Locations

Let's say you configured DISK as the default device, using the CONFIGURE DEFAULT DEVICE TYPE command. The actual location on disk where RMAN will create its backup files is determined in the following manner:

- As described earlier in the chapter, you can specify a backup location and name using the FORMAT parameter, in which case, this location will override any location you specified for the flash recovery area. Here's an example:

  ```
  RMAN> BACKUP DATABASE FORMAT '/tmp/%U'; /* %U generates a unique filename */
  ```

- If you don't specify the FORMAT parameter in the backup command, RMAN uses the flash recovery area as the default location for storing the backups, as is the case in the following example:

  ```
  RMAN> BACKUP DATABASE;
  ```

- If you have not configured a flash recovery area and also don't specify the FORMAT parameter during the backup, RMAN will store the backups in an operating system-specific directory on disk.

RMAN Commands

You need to be familiar with a limited set of commands to use the RMAN utility for performing backups. You'll encounter the specific commands pertaining to restoring and recovering databases in Chapter 16. The following sections describe the RMAN commands related to backups, grouped into the following types:

- Backup commands
- Job commands
- Copy commands
- Reporting commands
- Listing commands
- Validating commands

Backup Commands

The most important backup command is obviously the BACKUP command. As noted earlier, you can either specify a channel manually at backup time or let RMAN allocate a default channel.

The BACKUP command allows you to back up the entire database, a tablespace, single datafile (current or a copy), control file (current or a copy), SPFILE, archived redo log, and other backup sets. Here are some examples showing how to use the BACKUP command:

```
RMAN> BACKUP DATABASE;
RMAN> BACKUP TABLESPACE users;
RMAN> BACKUP DATAFILE '/u01/app/oracle/oradata/finance/users01.dbf';
```

The use of the simple BACKUP DATABASE command is the same as using the BACKUP AS BACKUPSET DATABASE command. When you use the preceding commands, RMAN generates one or more *backup sets*, which are RMAN-specific logical backup units.

Image Copy Backups

When you use the BACKUP AS COPY version of the command, RMAN generates *image copies* of the files you want to back up. In order to make corresponding image copy backups for the previous examples, use the following commands:

```
RMAN> BACKUP AS COPY DATABASE;
RMAN> BACKUP AS COPY TABLESPACE USERS;
RMAN> BACKUP AS COPY DATAFILE '/u01/app/oracle/oradata/finance/users01.dbf';
```

■**Note** By default, RMAN creates all backups as backup sets, on tape or on disk.

None of the previous examples used names for the backups created by RMAN. In all such cases, RMAN assigns a default tag to the backups it creates. As explained earlier, you can use the TAG parameter to specify a backup tag. Here's an example, showing how to attach the tag weekly_backup to an RMAN backup:

```
RMAN> BACKUP DATABASE TAG = 'weekly_backup';
```

Logical Checking of RMAN Backups

You can use the keyword LOGICAL during a backup to let RMAN perform a *logical check* of the backup files. Here is an example that checks for logical corruption in the copy of a database copy (duptest), which is made from the copy of a database (test):

```
RMAN> BACKUP AS COPY COPY OF DATABASE FROM TAG 'TEST' CHECK LOGICAL TAG 'DUPTEST';
```

Incremental Backups

All the BACKUP commands in the preceding sections are *full backup* commands. You can also perform incremental backups using RMAN, and in fact, this is one of the big advantages of using RMAN. Incremental backups are much faster than backing up the entire database. Incremental backups will back up only those data blocks that changed since a previous backup.

Incremental backups can be either level 0 or level 1. A level 0 incremental backup copies all data blocks just like a full backup, and acts as the base for subsequent incremental backups. To perform a level 1 incremental backup, you must first have a base level 0 backup.

RMAN provides two types of incremental backups:

- *Differential backup*: Backs up all blocks changed after the most recent incremental backup at level 1 or 0.

- *Cumulative backup*: Backs up all blocks changed after the most recent incremental backup at level 0.

The following command gets a level 0 backup to start with:

```
RMAN> BACKUP INCREMENTAL LEVEL 0 DATABASE;
```

Once you have the level 0 backup, you perform a level 1 differential incremental backup:

```
RMAN> BACKUP INCREMENTAL LEVEL 1 DATABASE;
```

A cumulative incremental backup at level *n* will perform a backup of all changed blocks since the last backup at level *n–1* or lower. So, if you perform the cumulative incremental backup at level 2, it will back up all data blocks changed since level 0 or level 1. Although you can perform a level 2 incremental backup, according to Oracle, only level 0 and level 1 are permitted.

The size of your incremental backup file will depend on the number of changed blocks and the incremental level. Cumulative backups will, in general, be larger than differential backups, since they duplicate the data copied by backups at the same level. However, cumulative backups have the advantage that they reduce recovery time, because you apply only one backup. Thus, Oracle recommends using cumulative backups, if space isn't a problem on your server.

Here's an example that shows how you can use a combination of incremental backups to come up with your backup strategy:

- On Sunday, perform an incremental level 0 backup.

- On Monday through Saturday, perform *differential* incremental level 1 backups.

- Repeat the cycle next week.

In this strategy, if you need to recover data on Thursday evening, you apply the incremental backups from Monday, Tuesday, and Wednesday to Sunday's level 0 backup.

Consider an alternative strategy using cumulative backups:

- On Sunday, perform an incremental level 0 backup.

- On Monday through Saturday, perform *cumulative* incremental level 1 backups.

- Repeat the cycle next week.

Note that in this case, the daily cumulative level 1 backup backs up all blocks changed since the Sunday backup. Thus, if you need to recover your database on Thursday, you need to apply only one cumulative backup from the night before to Sunday's incremental level 0 backup.

Job Commands

You can't use the ALLOCATE CHANNEL and SWITCH commands as stand-alone commands. You must use them with the RUN command, as follows:

```
RMAN> RUN
      {ALLOCATE CHANNEL c1 DEVICE TYPE  sbt
      PARMS='ENV=(NSR_GROUP=default)';
      BACKUP DATAFILE 1;
      }
allocated channel: c1
channel c1: sid=11 devtype=SBT_TAPE
channel c1: MMS Version 2.2.0.1
```

The SWITCH command is similar to the ALTER DATABASE RENAME DATAFILE command. It lets you replace a datafile with file copy made by RMAN.

Datafile Copies

The RMAN BACKUP AS COPY command makes a plain copy of a datafile (you can also use the old COPY command to do this, but Oracle deprecated the COPY command in Oracle Database 10*g*). These image copies are identical to the copies made by using operating system utilities. Here's an example:

```
RMAN> BACKUP AS COPY DATAFILE 1;
Starting backup at 05-JUN-08
using channel ORA_DISK_1
channel ORA_DISK_1: starting datafile copy
input datafile fno=00001 name=C:\ORALE\PRODUCT\11.1.0\ORADATA\NEWS\SYSTEM01.DBF
```

```
output filename=C:\ORALE\PRODUCT\11.1.0\FLASH_RECOVERY_AREA\NEWS\DATAFILE\O1_MF_
SYSTEM_OQ2XPZ1Y_.DBF tag=TAG20041016T143037 recid=2 stamp=539706790
channel ORA_DISK_1: datafile copy complete, elapsed time: 00:02:35
channel ORA_DISK_1: starting datafile copy
copying current controlfile
output filename=C:\ORALE\PRODUCT\11.1.0\FLASH_RECOVERY_AREA\NEWS\CONTROLFILE\O1_
MF_TAG20041016T143037_OQ2XVT4T_.CTL tag=TAG20041016T143037 recid=3 stamp=5397067
96
channel ORA_DISK_1: datafile copy complete, elapsed time: 00:00:07
Finished backup at 05-JUN-08
RMAN>
```

The following example illustrates the use of the older COPY command:

```
RMAN> COPY DATAFILE 1 TO 'c:\download\test.copy';
Starting backup at 05-JUN-08
using channel ORA_DISK_1
channel ORA_DISK_1: starting datafile copy
input datafile fno=00001 name=C:\ORALE\PRODUCT\11.1.0\ORADATA\ORCL\SYSTEM01.DBF
output filename=C:\DOWNLOAD\TEST.COPY tag=TAG20041009T124719 recid=2 stamp=53909
channel ORA_DISK_1: datafile copy complete, elapsed time: 00:01:35
Finished backup at 05-JUN-08
RMAN>
```

Backup Deletion

You use the DELETE command to remove physical backups made by RMAN. The DELETE command deletes physical backups, updates control file records to indicate that the backups are deleted, and also removes their records from the recovery catalog (if you use one). You can delete backup sets, archived redo logs, and datafile copies.

■**Caution**   Always use RMAN'S DELETE command, rather than an operating system deletion command, to remove RMAN backups. Otherwise, the RMAN repository will contain records of backups that are no longer available.

The following example deletes all archived redo logs that RMAN has backed up at least twice to tape:

```
RMAN> DELETE ARCHIVELOG ALL BACKED UP 2 TIMES TO DEVICE TYPE sbt;
```

The DELETE OBSOLETE command will remove all backups you no longer need. You can run DELETE OBSOLETE periodically to delete all backups that are obsolete. A backup is obsolete if it's no longer needed for database recovery, according to your retention policy. The DELETE EXPIRED command removes the recovery catalog records for expired backups and marks them as DELETED. This command is handy when you think you might have deleted RMAN backups or archived logs from disk with an operating system utility. You can first run the CROSSCHECK command so RMAN can mark the backups it can't find as *expired*. An expired backup means that the backup file can't be found by RMAN. You can then use the DELETE EXPIRED command to remove the records for these files from the control file and the recovery catalog.

Reporting Commands

RMAN provides useful reporting commands that enable you to check your backup and recovery processes. You can query RMAN to see which files need backup and which files are obsolete and, therefore, removable.

Schema, Obsolete, Need Backup, and Unrecoverable Reports

The REPORT SCHEMA command lists all datafiles that are part of the target database.

The REPORT OBSOLETE command displays all the backups rendered obsolete based on the retention policy you choose:

```
RMAN> REPORT OBSOLETE;
RMAN retention policy will be applied to the command
RMAN retention policy is set to recovery window of 14 days
no obsolete backups found
RMAN>
```

If there are obsolete backups in the repository, you can delete them with the DELETE OBSOLETE command.

If you use the flash recovery area to store your backups, RMAN automatically deletes obsolete backups when it needs to make room for newer backups. Until then, obsolete backups will remain in the flash recovery area. If you aren't using a flash recovery area, you must manually run the DELETE OBSOLETE command periodically to remove the obsolete backup files.

The REPORT NEED BACKUP command lists any datafiles that need backup to conform with the retention policy you originally chose for your backups. The following example shows that no files need a backup:

```
RMAN> REPORT NEED BACKUP;
RMAN retention policy will be applied to the command
RMAN retention policy is set to redundancy 1
Report of files with less than 1 redundant backups
File #bkps          Name
---- -----  -------------------------------------------------------------
1       0    /u01/app/oracle/product/11.1.0/oradata/nicko/system01.dbf
2       0    /u01/app/oracle/product/11.1.0/oradata/nicko/undotbs01.dbf
3       0    /u01/app/oracle/product/11.1.0/oradata/nicko/sysaux01.dbf
4       0    /u01/app/oracle/product/11.1.0/oradata/nicko/users01.dbf
RMAN>
```

The REPORT UNRECOVERABLE command lists all unrecoverable datafiles. An unrecoverable file is a datafile with a segment that has undergone a nologging operation, and should therefore be backed up immediately.

Catalog Reports

The CATALOG command helps you identify and catalog any files that aren't recorded in RMAN's repository and thus are unknown to RMAN. Any one of the following events might cause this:

- You restore a backup control file.
- Your restore a standby control file.
- You re-create the control file.
- You enable the DB_RECOVERY_FILE_DEST parameter and then disable it.

In addition, you may create file backups of both datafiles and archived redo logs that RMAN won't be aware of. For example, you can use the CATALOG command to catalog database file copies you made as a level 0 backup. You can then do an incremental backup later by using the datafile copy as the basis.

You can catalog all datafile copies, backup pieces, or archivelogs on disk using the CATALOG command. Here are a couple of examples:

```
RMAN> CATALOG DATAFILECOPY '/u01/app/oracle/backup/users01.dbf';
RMAN> CATALOG BACKUPPIECE '/disk1/backups/backup_820.bkp';
```

By using the CATALOG START WITH command, you can make RMAN start searching for all uncataloged files in the directory you specify. This command is especially handy when your filenames are cryptic, as when you use an OMF or ASM file system. The following example shows how you can catalog multiple backup files in a directory at once, using the CATALOG START WITH command:

```
RMAN> CATALOG START WITH '/disk1/backups/';
```

RMAN will first list all files in the /disk1/backups directory and add them to its repository, after you confirm the operation.

If you notice a discrepancy between the recovery catalog entries and the actual backups on disk, RMAN will issue an error when you try to perform a backup or recovery. To get rid of invalid entries in the recovery catalog, you use the DELETE command with the FORCE option, as shown here:

```
RMAN> DELETE FORCE NOPROMPT ARCHIVELOG SEQUENCE 40;
```

Listing Commands

Several RMAN commands let you list various items, like backups and stored scripts in the recovery catalog.

The LIST BACKUP command shows you all the completed backups registered by RMAN. The command shows all backup sets and image copies, as well as the individual datafiles, control files, archived redo log files, and SPFILEs in the backup files. You can also list all backups by querying V$BACKUP_FILES and the RC_BACKUP_FILES recovery catalog view. Listing 15-1 shows the output of the LIST BACKUP command.

Listing 15-1. *Using the LIST BACKUP Command*

```
RMAN> LIST BACKUP;
List of Backup Sets
===================
BS Key  Type LV Size       Device Type Elapsed Time Completion Time
------- ---- -- ---------- ----------- ------------ ---------------
892     Full   169M        DISK        00:01:19     06-JUN-08
  List of Datafiles in backup set 892
  File LV Type Ckp SCN    Ckp Time  Name
  ---- -- ---- ---------- --------- ----
  1       Full 81814      06-JUN-08 C:\ORALE\PRODUCT\11.1.0\
ORADATA\NEWS\SYSTEM01.DBF
. . .
    List of Archived Logs in backup set 917


BS Key  Type LV Size       Device Type Elapsed Time Completion Time
------- ---- -- ---------- ----------- ------------ ---------------
928     Full   3M          DISK        00:00:06     06-JUN-08

  BP Key: 930   Status: AVAILABLE  Compressed: NO  Tag: TAG20041016T132630
  Controlfile Included: Ckp SCN: 81959       Ckp time: 06-JUN-08
RMAN>
```

The LIST COPY command is analogous to the LIST BACKUP command and shows you the complete list of all the copies made using RMAN.

```
RMAN> LIST COPY;
```

The LIST ARCHIVELOG ALL command will list all available archived log copies.

Finally, you can use the LIST SCRIPT NAMES command to display the names of all the stored scripts in the recovery catalog. The LIST GLOBAL SCRIPT NAMES command will show all the global scripts.

Validating Commands

You can use the VALIDATE BACKUPSET command to validate backup sets before you use them from a recovery. In the following example, the VALIDATE command shows that backup set 1 can't be found by RMAN:

```
RMAN> VALIDATE BACKUPSET 1;
using channel ORA_DISK_1
RMAN-00571: ===========================================================
RMAN-00569: =============== ERROR MESSAGE STACK FOLLOWS ===============
RMAN-00571: ===========================================================
RMAN-03002: failure of validate command at 06/05/2008 13:14:04
RMAN-06004: ORACLE error from recovery catalog database: RMAN-20215: backup set
not found
RMAN-06159: error while looking up backup set
RMAN>
```

In addition, you can use the CROSSCHECK command to make sure that a backup is indeed present and is usable. You'll see an example of this command in the "Monitoring and Verifying RMAN Jobs" section later in this chapter.

RMAN Configuration Parameters

RMAN has several configuration parameters, which are set to their default values when you first use RMAN. You don't have to configure anything really to start using RMAN or learn how to use the various commands. Of course, as you become proficient with RMAN, you'll want to configure several of the configuration parameters to suit your needs. Use the SHOW ALL command to see the default values, as shown in Listing 15-2.

Listing 15-2. *Using the SHOW ALL Command*

```
RMAN> SHOW ALL;
using target database control file instead of recovery catalog
RMAN configuration parameters for database with db_unique_name ORCL are:
CONFIGURE RETENTION POLICY TO REDUNDANCY 1; # default
CONFIGURE BACKUP OPTIMIZATION OFF; # default
CONFIGURE DEFAULT DEVICE TYPE TO DISK; # default
CONFIGURE CONTROLFILE AUTOBACKUP OFF; # default
CONFIGURE CONTROLFILE AUTOBACKUP FORMAT FOR DEVICE TYPE DISK TO '%F'; # default
CONFIGURE DEVICE TYPE DISK PARALLELISM 1 BACKUP TYPE TO BACKUPSET; # default
CONFIGURE DATAFILE BACKUP COPIES FOR DEVICE TYPE DISK TO 1; # default
CONFIGURE ARCHIVELOG BACKUP COPIES FOR DEVICE TYPE DISK TO 1; # default
CONFIGURE MAXSETSIZE TO UNLIMITED; # default
CONFIGURE ENCRYPTION FOR DATABASE OFF; # default
CONFIGURE ENCRYPTION ALGORITHM 'AES128'; # default
CONFIGURE COMPRESSION ALGORITHM 'BZIP2'; # default
CONFIGURE ARCHIVELOG DELETION POLICY TO NONE; # default
CONFIGURE SNAPSHOT CONTROLFILE NAME TO 'C:\ORCL\APP\ORACLE\PRODUCT\11.1.0\DB_1\D
ATABASE\SNCFORCL.ORA'; # default
```

You can view the current configuration values of all the RMAN parameters that you change from their default values by using the V$RMAN_CONFIGURATION view, as follows:

```
SQL> SELECT * FROM v$rman_configuration;
CONF#    NAME                            VALUE
-----  ----------------------------    ------------------
1        DEFAULT  DEVICE TYPE  TO       'SBT_TAPE'
2        CONTROLFILE AUTOBACKUP         ON
3        BACKUP OPTIMIZATION            ON
4        RETENTION POLICY               TO REDUNDANCY 2
SQL>
```

If you haven't changed any of the configuration parameters from their default values, the previous query will not return any rows. You can use the CONFIGURE command to change the values of these RMAN configuration parameters. Let's take a closer look at some of the important configurable parameters and how you can change them.

Backup Retention Policy

A backup retention policy tells RMAN when to consider backups of datafiles and log files obsolete. Note that when you tell RMAN to consider a backup file obsolete after a certain time period, RMAN only marks the file obsolete—it doesn't delete it. You must go in and delete the obsolete files.

You can set a retention policy by using either of two methods: the default REDUNDANCY option or the RETENTION WINDOW option. In both cases, you use the CONFIGURE RETENTION POLICY command to set the retention policy for all of your database files by default.

The REDUNDANCY Option

The REDUNDANCY option lets you specify how many copies of the backups you want to retain. The default is 1. You set the retention policy this way:

```
RMAN> CONFIGURE RETENTION POLICY TO REDUNDANCY 2;
new RMAN configuration parameters:
CONFIGURE RETENTION POLICY TO REDUNDANCY 2;
new RMAN configuration parameters are successfully stored
starting full resync of recovery catalog
full resync complete
RMAN>
```

Let's say you're backing up your datafiles every day. The previous RMAN command specifies that RMAN keep only two backups of each database file. RMAN will also retain all redo logs required to recover the two days' worth of datafile backups. Any backups that are older than two days are considered obsolete. Of course, you can save to tape and archive a much older set of backups.

Archived backups are useful if you ever want to perform a PITR to a time further back than your recent backup. In addition, if your current backups end up being unusable, you have an alternative set of backups available.

The RECOVERY WINDOW Option

Setting the backup retention policy using the RECOVERY WINDOW option enables you to specify how far back in time you want to recover from when your database is affected by a media failure. RMAN will keep all backups of datafiles and log files one backup older than the recovery window. For example, if the recovery window is seven days, RMAN will save all backups starting from the backups done immediately before the seven-day period. You set the recovery window as follows:

```
RMAN> CONFIGURE RETENTION POLICY TO RECOVERY WINDOW OF 14 DAYS;
old RMAN configuration parameters:
CONFIGURE RETENTION POLICY TO REDUNDANCY 2;
new RMAN configuration parameters:
CONFIGURE RETENTION POLICY TO RECOVERY WINDOW OF 14 DAYS;
new RMAN configuration parameters are successfully stored
starting full resync of recovery catalog
full resync complete
RMAN>
```

As you can see in this example, you can set the redundancy number or a recovery window, but not both. A change in the value of either of the two options will supersede the values of the existing option.

Default Device Type

The default device for backups is a disk; that is, RMAN will automatically make backups to a file system on your server. If you want to back up to tape, you configure the default device type to sbt (all tape destinations are referred to as sbt). Here's an example:

```
RMAN> CONFIGURE DEFAULT DEVICE TYPE TO sbt;
old RMAN configuration parameters:
CONFIGURE DEFAULT DEVICE TYPE TO DISK;
new RMAN configuration parameters:
CONFIGURE DEFAULT DEVICE TYPE TO 'SBT_TAPE';
new RMAN configuration parameters are successfully stored
starting full resync of recovery catalog
full resync complete
RMAN>
```

If you wish to switch the default device back to disk, you can do so with the following command:

```
RMAN> CONFIGURE DEFAULT DEVICE TYPE TO DISK;
old RMAN configuration parameters:
CONFIGURE DEFAULT DEVICE TYPE TO 'SBT_TAPE';
new RMAN configuration parameters:
CONFIGURE DEFAULT DEVICE TYPE TO DISK;
new RMAN configuration parameters are successfully stored
starting full resync of recovery catalog
full resync complete
RMAN>
```

Encryption and Compression Parameters

You must have the Oracle Advanced Security option to create an encrypted RMAN backup on disk. If you want to create encrypted backups on tape, you must use the Oracle Secure Backup SBT interface. You can query the V$RMAN_ENCRYPTION_ALGORITHM view to see the various encryption algorithms that RMAN supports. RMAN provides the following three modes of encryption:

- *Transparent encryption*: Requires Oracle Public Key Infrastructure (PKI).

- *Password-based encryption*: Requires a password during the backup and the restore of the backup.

- *Dual-mode encryption*: Enables the encryption through either of the first two modes. Decryption can be performed either by supplying a password or by using the Oracle Wallet.

You can use the CONFIGURATION ENCRYPTION and the SET ENCRYPTION commands to encrypt RMAN backups.

In addition to encrypting RMAN backups, you can also specify the compression of RMAN backups. You must use the CONFIGURE COMPRESSION command to instruct RMAN to compress the backups it makes. The CONFIGURE COMPRESSION ALGORTIHM command enables you to specify one of two available compression algorithms: BZIP2 and ZLIB. The default compression algorithm is ZLIB, which Oracle claims is significantly faster (by about 40 percent) than the alternative algorithm, BZIP2. You can query the V$RMAN_COMPRESSION_ALGORITHM view to examine Oracle's description of the difference between the two algorithms. For example:

```
SQL> select algorithm_name,algorithm_description, is_default
  2  from v$rman_compression_algorithm;

ALGORITHM    ALGORITHM DESCRIPTION                        IS_DEFAULT
---------    ----------------------------------------     ----------
ZLIB         fast but little worse compression ratio      YES
BZIP2        good compression ratio but little slower     NO
SQL>
```

As you can see, the ZLIB algorithm is faster, but the BZIP2 algorithm provides a superior compression ratio.

Channel Configuration

Channels are the means by which RMAN conducts its backup and recovery operations, and they represent a single stream of data to a particular device (such as a tape). If you have four channels configured, four connections will be made to the target database to open four separate server sessions.

The following example configures two channels, with channel 1 backing up to the backup directory under /test01 and channel 2 backing up to the backup directory under /test02:

```
RMAN> CONFIGURE CHANNEL 1 DEVICE TYPE DISK FORMAT
 '/test01/app/oracle/oradata/backup/%U';
new RMAN configuration parameters:
CONFIGURE CHANNEL 1 DEVICE TYPE DISK FORMAT'/test01/app/oracle/oradata/backup/%U';
new RMAN configuration parameters are successfully stored
RMAN> CONFIGURE CHANNEL 2 DEVICE TYPE DISK FORMAT
'/test02/app/oracle/oradata/backup/%U';
new RMAN configuration parameters:
CONFIGURE CHANNEL 2 DEVICE TYPE DISK
FORMAT'/test02/app/oracle/oradata/backup/%U';
new RMAN configuration parameters are successfully stored
```

▓**Note** The DISK PARALLELISM parameter and the CHANNEL parameter are related to each other. For example, if the degree of parallelism is 4 and you have specified only two or even no channels at all, RMAN will open four generic channels. If, on the other hand, you have manually configured six channels but set the degree of parallelism to 1, RMAN will use only the first channel and ignore the other five.

If you start the backup with multiple channels, the failure of one channel, say, due to the failure of a tape device, won't stop the backup job. RMAN will instead complete the job using the remaining channels, and report the problem in the V$RMAN_OUTPUT view. This is also known as RMAN's Automatic Channel Failover feature.

Degree of Parallelism

The *degree of parallelism* (the default degree is 1) denotes the number of channels that RMAN can open during a backup or recovery. The time taken to complete the backup or recovery will decrease as you increase the degree of parallelism.

```
RMAN> CONFIGURE DEVICE TYPE DISK PARALLELISM 4;
old RMAN configuration parameters:
CONFIGURE DEVICE TYPE DISK BACKUP TYPE TO COPY PARALLELISM 1;
new RMAN configuration parameters:
CONFIGURE DEVICE TYPE DISK PARALLELISM 4 BACKUP TYPE TO COPY;
new RMAN configuration parameters are successfully stored
released channel: ORA_DISK_1
starting full resync of recovery catalog
full resync complete
RMAN>
```

Backup Optimization

The BACKUP OPTIMIZATION option ensures that RMAN doesn't perform a file backup if it has already backed up identical versions of the file. Here is how you turn on this option:

```
RMAN> CONFIGURE BACKUP OPTIMIZATION ON;
new RMAN configuration parameters:
CONFIGURE BACKUP OPTIMIZATION ON;
new RMAN configuration parameters are successfully stored
starting full resync of recovery catalog
full resync complete
RMAN>
```

Control File Parameters

RMAN has several configuration parameters that deal with control file backups. The following sections cover the important control file parameters.

Control File Auto-Backup

If you set the CONTROLFILE AUTOBACKUP option to ON, each time you do a backup of your datafiles, the control file is automatically backed up along with the SPFILE. Here's how you configure this:

```
RMAN> CONFIGURE CONTROLFILE AUTOBACKUP ON;
old RMAN configuration parameters:
CONFIGURE CONTROLFILE AUTOBACKUP OFF;
new RMAN configuration parameters:
CONFIGURE CONTROLFILE AUTOBACKUP ON;
new RMAN configuration parameters are successfully stored
starting full resync of recovery catalog
full resync complete
RMAN>
```

Now, if you use any BACKUP command, the control file and the SPFILE (if there is one) are both automatically backed up, as shown in the following example:

```
RMAN> BACKUP TABLESPACE sysaux;
Starting backup at 06-JUN-08
. . .
```

```
channel ORA_DISK_1: datafile copy complete, elapsed time: 00:01:16
Finished backup at 06-JUN-05
Starting Control File Autobackup at 06-JUN-05
Finished Control File Autobackup at 06-JUN-05
RMAN>
```

Control File Backup Location and Format

You can use the control file AUTOBACKUP FORMAT parameter to specify the location and format of the control file backups. Here's an example:

```
RMAN> CONFIGURE CONTROLFILE AUTOBACKUP FORMAT FOR DEVICE TYPE DISK TO
 '/test01/app/oracle/oradta/backup/cf_%F';
 new RMAN configuration parameters:
 CONFIGURE CONTROLFILE AUTOBACKUP FORMAT FOR
 DEVICE TYPE DISK TO '/test01/app/oracle/oradata
 /backup/cf_%F'; new RMAN configuration parameters
 are successfully stored
RMAN>
```

Archivelog Deletion Policy

You can set up a persistent policy that regulates when archived redo logs become eligible for deletion from disk. The archived redo log deletion policy you configure applies to all archiving destinations, including the flash recovery area.

The database removes all eligible logs from the flash recovery area automatically. You can also manually delete an eligible archived redo log from any location, including the flash recovery area, by issuing either the DELETE ARCHIVELOG or BACKUP . . . DELETE INPUT command.

By default, RMAN's archived redo log deletion policy is configured to NONE. Under this policy of NONE, an archived redo log will be considered for deletion only if the archived redo log has been transferred to the location specified by the LOG_ARCHIVE_DEST_n parameter, and then it must also have been backed up at least once to disk or tape.

You can configure an explicit archived redo log deletion policy. Issue the CONFIGURE ARCHIVELOG DELETION POLICY BACKED command to configure the policy, as shown in the following example:

```
RMAN> CONFIGURE ARCHIVELOG DELETION POLICY
      TO BACKED UP 2 TIMES TO SBT;
```

This command specifies that all archived redo logs are eligible for deletion after they have been backed up to tape twice.

Working with the Recovery Catalog

Using the recovery catalog is purely optional, as Oracle can use the control file to store the RMAN repository data (metadata). However, as explained earlier in this chapter, it's a good idea to spend the little time it takes to create and use the recovery catalog. I assume the use of the recovery catalog in the discussions in this and the next chapter.

■**Tip** Make sure that the database in which the recovery catalog is being created runs in archivelog mode. This ensures that you can always perform a PITR.

To create the recovery catalog, you must first connect to the database in which you want to create the recovery catalog. You need to create a new recovery catalog owner schema (usually named rman), grant the necessary privileges to it, and then create the recovery catalog. Once you create the catalog, you can register databases in it.

Creating the Recovery Catalog Schema

In order to use the recovery catalog, you need to first create a recovery catalog schema. You can create this schema or user in an existing tablespace or in a new tablespace created for this purpose. The recovery catalog itself is stored in the default tablespace of this schema. The following example creates a schema called rman:

```
SQL> CREATE USER RMAN IDENTIFIED BY rman
     TEMPORARY TABLESPACE temp
     DEFAULT TABLESPACE rman_tbsp
     QUOTA UNLIMITED ON rman_tbsp
User created.
SQL>
```

Make sure you first create the rman_tbsp tablespace for the user rman.

Making the Necessary Grants

The new rman schema owner, rman, needs privileges to maintain and query the recovery catalog. You do this by granting the user the RECOVERY_CATALOG_OWNER role. The following code shows how to make the necessary grants to user rman:

```
SQL> GRANT RECOVERY_CATALOG_OWNER TO rman;
Grant succeeded.
SQL>
```

Connecting to RMAN

You can connect to RMAN in one of two ways. One way is to first invoke RMAN, and then use the CONNECT CATALOG command to connect to it, as shown here (nicko is the database containing the recovery catalog in this example):

```
$ rman
Recovery Manager: Release 11.1.0.6.0 - Production on Thu Mar 27 11:36:34 2008
Copyright (c) 1982, 2007, Oracle.  All rights reserved.
RMAN> CONNECT CATALOG rman/rman@nicko
connected to recovery catalog database
RMAN>
```

You can also connect directly from the operating system level, as follows:

```
$ rman CATALOG rman/rman@nicko
connected to recovery catalog database
RMAN>
```

When you connect to the catalog database directly, you still aren't connected to the target database (unless the target and the catalog database are the same). To connect to the target database, you must now use the following command from within the RMAN interface (nina is the target database name):

```
RMAN> connect target nina
Connected to target database: NINA (DBID=1974138212)
RMAN>
```

Instead of first connecting to the recovery catalog and then to the target database, you can use the following method to connect to the recovery catalog and to the target database in one step:

```
$  rman catalog rman/rman@nicko target nina
Recovery Manager: Release 11.1.0.6.0 - Production on Thu Mar 27 11:36:34 2008
Copyright (c) 1982, 2007, Oracle.  All rights reserved.target database password:
connected to target database: NINA (DBID=1974138212)
connected to recovery catalog database
RMAN>
```

■**Tip** Although you can create the recovery catalog schema in the target database itself, Oracle recommends that you use a dedicated recovery catalog database, to secure the recovery catalog. This way, if the target database needs to be recovered, you'll have the necessary recovery data available in the recovery catalog.

Creating the Recovery Catalog

If you want to utilize the recovery catalog (instead of the default method of using the control file) to store the RMAN metadata, you must first create it in the recovery catalog owner's (rman) schema.

First, connect to the catalog database in one of the two ways shown in the previous section. Next, use the CREATE CATALOG command, which will create the recovery catalog:

```
RMAN> CREATE CATALOG;
recovery catalog created
RMAN>
```

The CREATE CATALOG command creates the RMAN recovery catalog in the tablespace rman_tbsp, which you assigned as the default tablespace for the user rman.

The DROP CATALOG command will remove the recovery catalog:

```
RMAN> DROP CATALOG;
Recovery catalog owner is RMAN
Enter DROP CATALOG command again to confirm catalog removal
RMAN> DROP CATALOG;
Recovery catalog dropped
RMAN>.
```

Registering a Database

For RMAN to do its job, you need to register the target database you want to back up and recover. Registration means that a database is enrolled in the recovery catalog. Once you register the database, RMAN will automatically get all the relevant metadata pertaining to the target database and store it in its own schema.

You don't need a separate recovery catalog for each of your Oracle databases; you can register all your databases in a single recovery catalog.

To register a new database in the recovery catalog, first connect to the target database:

```
$ rman catalog rman/rman@nicko target nina
Recovery Manager: Release 11.1.0.6.0 - Production on Thu Mar 27 11:36:34 2008
Copyright (c) 1982, 2007, Oracle.  All rights reserved.
target database Password:
connected to target database: NINA (DBID=1974138212)
connected to recovery catalog database
RMAN>
```

> ■**Caution** Make sure you set the `ORACLE_SID` to the target database SID before you register a database in the recovery catalog. Otherwise, when you specify the target, you'll connect to the database whose instance name matches the `ORACLE_SID` of your UNIX session, not to the target database.

Next, register the database in the recovery catalog:

```
RMAN> REGISTER DATABASE;
database registered in recovery catalog
starting full resync of recovery catalog
full resync complete
RMAN>
```

The target database is now successfully registered in the recovery catalog. At this point, you can use the REPORT SCHEMA command to make sure all the datafiles of the target database show up in the list.

You can also issue the following command to check the incarnation of the database:

```
RMAN> LIST INCARNATION;
List of Database Incarnations
DB Key  Inc Key DB Name     DB ID       STATUS     Reset SCN  Reset Time
------- ------- --------    ----------- ---------- ---------- -----------
1       8       NINA        1974138212  PARENT          1     11-JAN-08
1       2       NINA        1974138212  CURRENT    318842     05-JUN-08
RMAN>
```

Maintaining the Recovery Catalog

If you choose to create and use a recovery catalog, you must know how to maintain it. The following sections explain important recovery catalog maintenance tasks.

Resynchronizing the Recovery Catalog

Changes made to the target database structure aren't automatically propagated to the recovery catalog. The BACKUP and COPY commands automatically perform a resynchronization each time you perform a backup or copy. But you may need to manually resynchronize the recovery catalog under two circumstances: when your target database has just undergone a number of physical changes and when the target database is performing a very large number of log switches in between the backups.

During a resync operation, RMAN reads the target database's control file to update the information it keeps regarding datafiles, log switches, physical schema, and so forth. Oracle recommends that you resynchronize the recovery catalog after making any changes to the physical structure of a target database. You issue the RESYNC CATALOG command as follows, after connecting to the target database:

```
RMAN> RESYNC CATALOG;
starting full resync of recovery catalog
full resync complete
RMAN>
```

Backing Up the Recovery Catalog

You should always back up the recovery catalog database immediately after you back up the target database. Backing up the recovery catalog becomes even more critical if you're using a single recovery catalog to store the metadata of all the databases in your system. You should follow these principles to afford the maximum possible security to the recovery catalog database:

- Back up the recovery catalog on a frequent basis.

- Never store the recovery catalog in the target database. You could end up losing the target database and the recovery catalog at the same time if there's a media failure.

- Always run the database holding the recovery catalog in archivelog mode.

- Make multiple copies of the recovery catalog database backup, preferably to tape, in addition to disk backups.

- Set the retention policy to a value greater than 1.

- Set `CONTROLFILE AUTOBACKUP` to `ON`, thus ensuring that you can always recover the recovery catalog database, provided you have the control file auto-backup on hand.

- Set a very high value for `CONTROL_FILE_RECORD_KEEP_TIME`, so the control file won't be over-written quickly, wiping out your RMAN repository data.

Note that in addition to using RMAN to back up the recovery catalog database, you can use the Data Pump Export utility to create logical backups of the recovery catalog database.

Recovering the Recovery Catalog

In order to restore and recover the recovery catalog database, you must first restore the control file and the server parameter file for the database from the auto-backups you made earlier. You can then restore and recover the database itself.

If you have failed to make backups of your recovery catalog, or if you have made the backups but are unable to use them (perhaps because you have lost parts of them), you must re-create the recovery catalog. You can re-create the recovery catalog in one of the following ways:

- Execute the `RESYNC CATALOG` command to update the recovery catalog with the repository information from the control file of the target database. Of course, any aged out metadata will be lost for good.

- Execute the `CATALOG START WITH . . .` command to recatalog any available backups.

Cataloging Backups

You can issue the `CATALOG` command to catalog older backups in the recovery catalog. By issuing the `CATALOG` command, you can catalog older backups that have aged out of the control file, thus enabling RMAN to use those backups during a file restore operation. Here's an example that shows how to use the `CATALOG` command:

```
RMAN> CATALOG DATAFILECOPY '/u01/old_backups/users01.dbf';
```

You can execute the `CATALOG START WITH` command to catalog multiple files in a directory, as shown here:

```
RMAN> CATALOG START WITH '/u01/old_backups/';
```

RMAN waits for your confirmation after listing each file, before adding the file to the recovery catalog.

Upgrading the Recovery Catalog

If your RMAN client is from the Oracle 11.1 release, but the recovery catalog schema is from an older version, you must upgrade the recovery catalog. You can determine the schema version of the recovery catalog by executing the following query:

```
SQL> SELECT * FROM rcver;

VERSION
---------
10.02.00
```

If the output of this query shows multiple rows, the highest version number is the catalog schema version. In our example, there's only one version number, 10.2.0, meaning that the catalog version is 10.2.0.

In order to upgrade the recovery catalog, follow these steps:

1. If the recovery catalog owner that you created is from a release before 10.1, execute the following GRANT command (assuming that rman is the catalog owner):

   ```
   SQL> GRANT CREATE TYPE TO rman;
   ```

2. Start RMAN and connect to the recovery catalog database.

   ```
   RMAN> connect catalog rman/rman;
   ```

3. Execute the UPGRADE CATALOG command.

   ```
   RMAN> UPGRADE CATALOG;
   ```

4. Confirm the command by rerunning it.

   ```
   RMAN> UPGRADE CATALOG;
   ```

You can now use the recovery catalog with the RMAN client from the Oracle Database 11g release.

Importing Recovery Catalogs

You may have multiple recovery catalogs, each taking care of databases from different versions of the Oracle database. You can consolidate those recovery catalogs into one catalog, by using the IMPORT CATALOG command. By default, the command imports metadata for all databases registered in the source recovery catalog to the destination recovery catalog. You can, however, specify the databases you want to import into the destination catalog. Also by default, RMAN unregisters an imported database from the source recovery catalog, but you can retain the imported databases in the source catalog by adding the NO UNREGISTER clause to the IMPORT CATALOG command.

Your target databases, recovery catalog databases, and the recovery catalog schema can be from different database versions. However, Oracle recommends that you consolidate all your recovery catalogs into a single catalog at the most recent version of the recovery catalog schema. The IMPORT CATALOG command helps you do this.

In the following example, I use the IMPORT CATALOG command to merge two recovery catalogs, one from the 10.2 release and the other from 11g, into a single 11g release catalog schema. Here are the steps:

1. Connect to the destination recovery catalog.

   ```
   $ rman
   RMAN> connect catalog rman/rman@rman11
   ```

2. Issue the IMPORT CATALOG command along with the connection information for the source recovery catalog (rman10) in step 1.

```
RMAN> import catalog rman1/rman1@rman10;
Starting import catalog at 30-MAR-08
connected to source recovery catalog database
import validation complete
database unregistered from the source recovery catalog
Finished import catalog at 30-MAR-08
RMAN>
```

By default, the IMPORT CATALOG command imports all the registered databases from the source catalog into the destination catalog, but you can specify a particular database or databases, as shown here:

```
RMAN> import catalog rman10/rman10@tenner
      dbid = 123456, 1234557;
RMAN> import catalog rman10/rman10@tenner
      db_name = testdb, mydb;
```

The first example shows how you can specify one or more database identifiers (DBIDs), whereas the second example shows how you can give the names of databases to import. In either case, you are able to limit the import to a specific database or databases.

Moving the Recovery Catalog

You can move the recovery catalog to a different database by using the IMPORT CATALOG command. First, create an empty recovery catalog into the destination database and then issue the IMPORT CATALOG command, as shown in the following example:

```
$ rman
RMAN> connect catalog rman/rman@target_db
RMAN> import catalog rman10/rman10@source_db;
```

The IMPORT CATALOG command moves the recovery catalog contents to the destination database. The IMPORT CATALOG command imports the source_db recovery catalog contents to a catalog in the target_db database.

Dropping a Recovery Catalog

Execute the DROP CATALOG command to remove a recovery catalog, as shown here:

```
RMAN> DROP CATALOG;
```

When you drop the recovery catalog, the actual backups made by RMAN will be untouched. The control files of the target database will contain records of the most recent backups made by RMAN. You can re-create the recovery catalog and register the target database to make the existing backups usable by RMAN again.

Virtual Private Catalogs

Once you register various databases in a recovery catalog, as the recovery catalog owner, you must grant permissions for some users to access the recovery catalog. Even if a user needs access to just one or two databases, you are forced to allow the user access to all databases you registered in the catalog. To enhance security, Oracle recommends that you maintain one central recovery catalog called a *base recovery catalog* in which you register all the databases you wish to manage, and then create smaller *virtual private catalogs* that allow access to sets of databases. A virtual private catalog is merely a set of synonyms and views based on the base recovery catalog, but stored in the schema of the virtual private catalog owner. Thus, you will maintain a single recovery catalog as before while also having the ability to grant users access to subsets of your catalog via virtual private catalogs that you define.

In order to create a virtual private catalog, you must first create an owner for the virtual private catalog. After this, you can go ahead and create the virtual private catalog itself. In the following sections, I show you how to first create the virtual private catalog owner and then the virtual private catalog itself.

Creating the Virtual Private Catalog Owner

Follow these steps to create a new virtual private catalog owner:

1. Start SQL*Plus and connect to the recovery catalog database as a user with administrator privileges (SYS). For example:

```
SQL> connect sys/sammyy1 as sysdba
```

2. Execute the following statement to create the virtual private catalog owner:

```
SQL> CREATE USER virtual1 IDENTIFIED BY virtual1
     DEFAULT TABLESPACE virtual_tbsp1
```

3. Grant the new owner the RECOVERY_CATALOG_OWNER role:

```
SQL> GRANT recovery_catalog_owner TO virtual1;
Start RMAN and connect as the base recovery catalog owner:
RMAN> CONNECT CATALOG rman/rman@catdb
```

4. So the new virtual recovery catalog owner can work with databases, grant the privileges necessary:

```
RMAN> GRANT CATALOG FOR DATABASE prod1 to virtual1;
```

The previous command grants rights to the virtual private catalog owner virtual1 to manage the prod1 database. The GRANT CATALOG command grants access to the user virtual1 for just the prod1 database. You can optionally grant the new user the capability to register new databases in the virtual private catalog owned by virtual1 by issuing the REGISTER DATABASE command as shown here:

```
RMAN> GRANT REGISTER DATABASE TO virtual1;
```

Now that the new virtual private catalog owner has been created, it's time to create the virtual private catalog itself.

Creating the Virtual Private Catalog

Once you've created the new virtual recovery catalog owner, create the virtual private catalog using the following steps:

1. Connect to the base recovery catalog database as the new virtual private catalog owner. For example:

```
RMAN> CONNECT CATALOG virtual1/virtual1@catdb;
```

2. Issue the command to create the virtual private catalog:

```
RMAN> CREATE VIRTUAL CATALOG;
```

The user virtual1 is now ready to work with the virtual private catalog, with access to one database, prod1.

Dropping a Virtual Private Catalog

The base recovery catalog owner can drop the virtual private catalog in a similar fashion as the base recovery catalog, by issuing the following command:

```
RMAN> DROP CATALOG;
```

Revoking Access Granted Through a Virtual Private Catalog

To revoke access to any database from the virtual private catalog owner, issue the `REVOKE CATALOG` command as shown here:

```
RMAN> REVOKE CATALOG FOR DATABASE prod1 FROM virtual1;
```

You can provide a database name as shown here or the DBID for the database. You can revoke the right of the virtual private owner to register new databases in the virtual private catalog (and thus in the base recovery catalog) by issuing the following command:

```
RMAN> REVOKE REGISTER DATABASE FROM virtual1;
```

Examples of RMAN Backups

The following sections take you through a few examples of various kinds of backups you can perform using RMAN.

Backing Up an Entire Database

If you want to back up the entire database, you use the `BACKUP DATABASE` command. RMAN will automatically back up all the datafiles that are part of the database, as shown in Listing 15-3.

Listing 15-3. *Backing Up a Database Using RMAN*

```
RMAN> BACKUP DATABASE;
Starting backup at 06-JUN-08
using channel ORA_DISK_1
channel ORA_DISK_1: starting full datafile backupset
channel ORA_DISK_1: specifying datafile(s) in backupset
input datafile fno=00001 name=C:\ORALE\PRODUCT\10.1.0\ORADATA\ORCL\SYSTEM01.DBF
input datafile fno=00003 name=C:\ORALE\PRODUCT\10.1.0\ORADATA\ORCL\SYSAUX01.DBF
input datafile fno=00005 name=C:\ORALE\PRODUCT\10.1.0\ORADATA\ORCL\EXAMPLE01.DBF
input datafile fno=00002 name=C:\ORALE\PRODUCT\10.1.0\ORADATA\ORCL\UNDOTBS01.DBF
input datafile fno=00004 name=C:\ORALE\PRODUCT\10.1.0\ORADATA\ORCL\USERS01.DBF
. . .
Starting Control File Autobackup at 06-JUN-08
piece handle=C:\ORACLE\PRODUCT\10.1.0\FLASH_RECOVERY_AREA\ORCL\AUTOBACKUP\2005_06
_06\01_MF_N_539094997_0PJ8FDBF_.BKP comment=NONE
Finished Control File Autobackup at 06-JUN-08
RMAN>
```

Backing Up the Archived Logs

You use the BACKUP ARCHIVELOG ALL command to back up all archived logs that you haven't backed up before. You can also use the command BACKUP DATABASE PLUS ARCHIVELOG to back up all datafiles as well as any archived redo log files, as shown in Listing 15-4.

Listing 15-4. *Backing Up a Database and Archived Logs Using RMAN*

```
RMAN> BACKUP DATABASE PLUS ARCHIVELOG;
Starting backup at 06-JUN-08
current log archived
allocated channel: ORA_DISK_1
channel ORA_DISK_1: sid=38 devtype=DISK
channel ORA_DISK_1: starting archive log backupset
channel ORA_DISK_1: specifying archive log(s) in backup set
input archive log thread=1 sequence=4 recid=1 stamp=539702327
. . .
16\O1_MF_ANNNN_TAG20041016T132206_OQ2SPK4S_.BKP comment=NONE
channel ORA_DISK_1: backup set complete, elapsed time: 00:00:05
Finished backup at 06-JUN-08
RMAN>
```

■**Note** If you're running in archivelog mode, your redo log files are being archived continuously. Therefore, there's no need to back up your online redo log files. In fact, RMAN doesn't let you back up the online redo log files. The best way to protect the online logs against media failure is to multiplex them, with duplicate online log members on different disks attached to different disk controllers. Losing an online redo log could mean loss of data if you don't have a copy.

Performing an Online Backup with a Script

The RMAN utility performs online backups in a more efficient manner than the normal user-managed backups, besides providing many extra benefits that make the backups far easier and safer. For one thing, you don't need to place the tablespaces into the begin backup and end backup modes. In addition, you back up only the used space in the database, not the entire allocated space. You also take care of any fractured blocks, because RMAN will continue to read the blocks until it gets a consistent read.

■**Caution** You should never back up your online redo log files when performing an online backup, because you'll run the risk of accidentally restoring the backed up log files and thus corrupt your database.

Listing 15-5 shows a typical script that performs online backups using RMAN, assuming you are backing up to disk.

Listing 15-5. *Performing an Online Backup with RMAN*

```
RMAN> RUN {
# backup the database to disk
ALLOCATE CHANNEL d1 TYPE DISK;
ALLOCATE CHANNEL t2 TYPE DISK;
ALLOCATE CHANNEL t3 TYPE DISK;
#backup the whole db
BACKUP
TAG  whole_database_open
FORMAT '/u01/oradata/backups/db_%t_%s_p%p'
DATABASE;
# switch the current log file
SQL 'alter system archive log current';
#backup the archived logs
BACKUP
ARCHIVELOG ALL
FORMAT '/u11/oradata/backups/al_%t_%s_p%p';
# backup a copy of the control file
BACKUP
CURRENT CONTROLFILE
TAG = cf1
FORMAT '/u12/oradata/backups/cf_%t_%s_p%p';
RELEASE channel d1;
RELEASE channel d2;
RELEASE channel d3;
 }
RMAN>
```

Backing Up the Control File

The BACKUP CURRENT CONTROLFILE command backs up the control file, as shown in Listing 15-6.

Listing 15-6. *Backing Up a Control File Using RMAN*

```
RMAN> BACKUP CURRENT CONTROLFILE;
Starting backup at 06-JUN-08
using channel ORA_DISK_1
channel ORA_DISK_1: starting full datafile backupset
channel ORA_DISK_1: specifying datafile(s) in backupset
including current controlfile in backupset
channel ORA_DISK_1: starting piece 1 at 06-JUN-08
channel ORA_DISK_1: finished piece 1 at 06-JUN-08
piece handle=C:\ORALE\PRODUCT\10.1.0\FLASH_RECOVERY_AREA\NEWS\BACKUPSET\2005_06_
06\O1_MF_NCNNF_TAG20041016T132630_OQ2SYTM3_.BKP comment=NONE
channel ORA_DISK_1: backup set complete, elapsed time: 00:00:07
Finished backup at 06-JUN-08
RMAN>
```

If you had already configured the automatic backup of the control file with the CONFIGURE CONTROLFILE AUTOBACKUP ON command, you can back up the entire database—datafiles, log files, and the control file—with the RMAN command BACKUP DATABASE PLUS ARCHIVELOG (see Listing 15-4).

Backing Up a Tablespace

You can back up individual tablespaces if you are operating the database in archivelog mode:

```
RMAN> BACKUP TABLESPACE USERS;
```

Backing Up a Datafile

You can back up a single datafile by simply using the command BACKUP DATAFILE *filename* or, optionally, specifying the destination as well. In the first case, RMAN will store the backup files in the flash recovery area. Here's an example:

```
RMAN> BACKUP DATAFILE  '/u01/orcl/oradata/system01.dbf';
```

Restarting an RMAN Backup

If an RMAN backup fails before it completes, you can resume the backup from the point where it failed, without needing to redo the entire backup. Let's say you perform a daily backup, and the last backup failed midway. After the backup failure, issue the following command:

```
RMAN> BACKUP DATABASE NOT BACKED UP SINCE TIME 'SYSDATE-1';
```

Note that the BACKUP DATABASE NOT BACKED UP SINCE TIME command will back up only those files that you haven't backed up before.

Specifying Limits for Backup Duration

Sometimes, a nightly backup interferes with the performance of a critical database job. To help with this, you can direct the database to take longer to finish the backup. The DURATION option for the RMAN BACKUP command provides this capability. When you use the DURATION option, RMAN will figure out the appropriate backup speed for the job. You can also add your own directives to either minimize the backup time (MINIMIZE TIME) or to minimize the load (MINIMIZE LOAD) on your system.

You can use the DURATION clause with backup commands, such as BACKUP AS COPY, to specify the time (in hours and minutes) Oracle should take when doing a backup job:

```
DURATION <hrs>:<mins>  [PARTIAL]  [MINIMIZE  {TIME|LOAD}]
```

The options are as follows:

- PARTIAL: You can override RMAN's default behavior when the backup job runs past the interval you specify by using the PARTIAL clause. This clause prevents RMAN error messages.

- MINIMIZE TIME: This tells RMAN to finish the backup as fast as it can.

- MINIMIZE LOAD: This option tells RMAN to slow down if it is within its allotted time for backing up.

■**Note** You must use disks if you want to use the MINIMIZE LOAD option, because you will probably want a tape backup to finish as quickly as possible.

Remember that the DURATION clause's PARTIAL option leads to an error if the backup exceeds its time limit. The MINIMIZE TIME option gets the job done the fastest. The MINIMIZE LOAD option minimizes resource use.

Here's an example of this clause:

```
RMAN> BACKUP AS COPY
2>     DURATION 04:00
3>     MINIMIZE TIME DATABASE;
```

This says

- Limit the backup time to four hours (DURATION 04:00).

- Run the backup at full speed, telling it to finish within the four-hour limit (MINIMIZE TIME) if possible.

- Back up the entire database (DATABASE).

Incrementally Updated Backups

Using the incrementally updated backups feature, you can use image file backups and apply incremental backups to them, thus advancing or rolling forward the initial image copy to the time when you took the level 1 incremental backup. When you perform recovery, you can use the incrementally updated image copy as if it were an actual image copy taken at the time of the incremental backup. Using incrementally updated backups truly revolutionizes backup strategies, as you always have an updated image copy available, no matter when you took the first level 0 full backup. The incrementally updated backup command looks like this:

```
RMAN> BACKUP INCREMENTAL LEVEL 1 FOR RECOVER OF COPY
      WITH TAG 'incr-update' LEVEL 0 DATABASE;
```

This command will take the incremental level 1 backup and update the existing level 0 full backup—in effect, updating the previous level 0 backup to the current day's level 0 backup.

You can run the script shown in Listing 15-7 to set up an incrementally updated backup.

Listing 15-7. *Performing Incrementally Updated Backups Using RMAN*

```
RMAN> RUN {
      RECOVER COPY OF DATABASE WITH TAG 'incr_update';
      BACKUP INCREMENTAL LEVEL 1 FOR RECOVER OF COPY WITH TAG 'incr_update'
      DATABASE;
      }
```

In this script, the RECOVER COPY command will make RMAN apply any incremental level 1 backups to a set of datafile copies with the same tag. The BACKUP command will create a level 1 incremental backup. However, the very first time the script runs, if there isn't already a level 0 backup, the command creates a level 0 backup as a starting point for the incremental backup strategy.

This is what happens when you execute the script:

- On the first day, the BACKUP command will create a level 0 backup, since there isn't one already.

- On the second day, the BACKUP command creates a level 1 incremental backup.

- On the third day, and every day forward, the RECOVER COPY command will apply the level 1 backups to the level 0 backup, thus updating it continuously.

Using the script in Listing 15-7 will make it unnecessary for you to apply multiple incremental backups to the initial level 0 backup. Each day, as the incremental backup (level 1) of that day is applied to the level 0 backup, the level 0 backup becomes a full level 0 backup of that day. You don't need another full database backup. If you need to perform a recovery, you use the latest level 0 backup, which is the updated product of all incremental level 1 backups since the first level 0 backup, and then apply the archivelogs to it.

Fast Incremental Backups

During incremental backups, Oracle must scan the entire datafile. This ensures unnecessarily long incremental backup times.

The *change-tracking file*, which was new in Oracle Database 10*g*, is used to track the physical location of all database block changes. RMAN reads this file to discover which data blocks it has to read and copy. RMAN therefore avoids reading entire datafiles, and backup times will be dramatically reduced.

The change-tracking writer (CTWR) background process, another feature that was new in Oracle Database 10*g*, writes the block-change information to the change-tracking file.

Enabling Block-Change Tracking

If you want to track block changes, you must explicitly enable the feature, as shown here:

```
SQL> ALTER DATABASE
  2  ENABLE BLOCK CHANGE TRACKING
  3  USING FILE '/u01/oradata/finance/changetrack.log';
Database altered.
SQL>
```

To rename or relocate a change-tracking file, use the ALTER DATABASE RENAME FILE statement (ensure that the database is in the mount stage before you rename the change-tracking file):

```
SQL> ALTER DATABASE RENAME FILE
       '/u01/app/oracle/finance/changetrack.log'
       TO
       '/u02/app/oracle/finance/changetrack.log';

Database altered.
SQL>
```

You can disable block-change tracking with the following statement:

```
SQL> ALTER DATABASE DISABLE BLOCK CHANGE TRACKING;
Database altered.
SQL>
```

Monitoring Block-Change Tracking

You can monitor block-change tracking with the V$BLOCK_CHANGE_TRACKING and V$BACKUP_DATAFILE views.

The V$BLOCK_CHANGE_TRACKING view shows the name, size, and status of the file, as shown in this example:

```
SQL> SELECT filename,status,bytes
  2  FROM v$block_change_tracking;

FILENAME                                            STATUS      BYTES
--------------------------------------------------- ----------  ---------
/U01/APP/ORACLE/ORADATA/FINANCE/CHANGETRACK.LOG     ENABLED     11599872
SQL>
```

In the V$BACKUP_DATAFILE view, use the ratio between the BLOCKS_READ column and the DATAFILE_BLOCKS column to calculate the percentage of blocks Oracle is reading. If the BLOCKS_READ to DATAFILE_BLOCKS ratio is too high, you may have to take more frequent backups.

RMAN Compressed Backups

You can compress RMAN backups if you need to save space. The compression factor depends on the nature of the data in your datafiles. Oracle recommends that you use RMAN's built-in compression capability instead of an external compression utility. You must take care not to use both RMAN compression and an external compression utility together.

■**Note**   You can't compress an image copy. You can compress a backup only if you are using backup sets.

Here is the RMAN command to compress a backup set:

```
RMAN> BACKUP AS COMPRESSED BACKUPSET DATABASE PLUS ARCHIVELOG;
```

The V$BACKUP_FILES view contains information about backup filenames and file sizes. In addition, it will tell you the compression status. Here's an example query showing how to do this:

```
SQL> SELECT fname, compressed, backup_type
    FROM v$backup_files;
```

Oracle Corporation believes that the RMAN binary compression technique will reduce the space used by the backup file by about 50 to 75 percent.

Archival Backups

Sometimes, you may want to make a backup for long-term storage. Your goal is not to someday use the backup for restoring the database, but to use the backup to restore data as it appeared at the time of the backup. You may also do this to satisfy regulatory requirements. These types of backups are called *archival backups*, or *long-term backups*, which you can make on tape devices and store offsite.

You can use the KEEP option with the BACKUP command to make long-term backups. The KEEP clause exempts a backup from the currently configured backup retention policy. The KEEP clause instructs RMAN to back up the datafiles, the control file, and the SPFILE. RMAN also generates an archived redo log backup automatically to help recover the database to a consistent state. You can also change an existing backup into an archival backup by using the CHANGE command. You can specify that a backup be kept indefinitely by specifying the KEEP FOREVER clause or limit the retention time by specifying the KEEP UNITL TIME clause with the BACKUP or CHANGE command.

In the following example, I use an optional RESTORE POINT clause to indicate the SCN to which the database must be recovered in order for it to be consistent. This SCN is captured right after the datafile backups are made. RMAN will save this restore point as long as you keep the backup. Here are the steps to make a long-term archival backup.

Connect to the target database and a recovery catalog. You'll need the recovery catalog connection only if you specify the KEEP FOREVER clause, but not for the KEEP clause.

```
RUN
{
ALLOCATE CHANNEL ch1
DEVICE TYPE sbt
PARMS 'ENV=(OB_MEDIA_FAMILY=archival_backup)';
BACKUP DATABASE
  TAG quarterly
KEEP FOREVER
RESTORE  POINT FYO8Q2;
}
```

This code generates a backup of all the datafiles and the archived logs and also creates a restore point to which to restore the database. The KEEP FOREVER clause will save the backup indefinitely. If you want to save a backup for a limited amount of time instead, you can do so by specifying the KEEP UNTIL TIME clause instead of the KEEP FOREVER clause, as shown here:

```
RUN
{
ALLOCATE CHANNEL ch1
DEVICE TYPE sbt
PARMS 'ENV=(OB_MEDIA_FAMILY=archival_backup)';
BACKUP DATABASE
  TAG quarterly
KEEP UNTIL TIME 'SYSDATE+365'
RESTORE  POINT FY08Q2;
}
```

This code will keep the backup for 365 days, after which the backup becomes obsolete and thus eligible for deletion.

Limiting the Size of RMAN Backups

You can limit the maximum size of an RMAN backup set by specifying the MAXSETSIZE parameter. An advantage to limiting a backup set to a certain size is that if the RMAN backup fails midway, you can use RMAN's restartable backup capability to backup only those files that weren't backed up before the failure. Here's an example showing how to limit a backup set's size:

```
RMAN> BACKUP DEVICE TYPE sbt
        MAXSETSIZE 250M
        ARCHIVELOG ALL;
```

You can specify the SECTION SIZE parameter to create a multisection backup, which is a backup set in which each backup piece contains blocks from one section of the file that's being backed up. You can use the SECTION SIZE parameter to perform a parallel backup of a very large datafile. Here's an example showing how to specify the SECTION SIZE parameter:

```
RMAN> BACKUP
        SECTION SIZE 250M
        TABLESPACE TEST;
```

Let's say the TEST tablespace is 1GB in size. You can set up four SBT channels, (parallel setting for the SBT device must be set to 4), and thus break up the backup into four parallel streams, thereby enhancing performance.

Encrypting RMAN Backups

You can configure two types of encryption for RMAN backups. First is transparent encryption, which you can configure with the CONFIGURE ENCRYPTION command. The second type of encryption is dual-mode or password-mode encryption. You can use the SET ENCRYPTION command to specify this type of encryption at the RMAN session level. I explain the procedures for setting up the two types of encryption in this section.

To configure transparent-mode encryption for backups, just use the CONFIGURE command as shown earlier in this chapter, Once you set up this persistent configuration parameter, all further backups will be in encrypted format.

Follow these steps to set up password-mode encryption:

1. Connect to the target database through RMAN.

```
RMAN> connect target /

connected to target database: ORCL (DBID=1170903133)
using target database control file instead of recovery catalog

RMAN>
```

2. Issue the SET ENCRYPTION ON IDENTIFIED BY PASSWORD ONLY command as shown here:

```
RMAN> set encryption on identified by sammyy1 only;

executing command: SET encryption

RMAN>
```

The keyword ONLY tells RMAN to use password-enabled encryption even if you've configured transparent configuration with the CONFIGURE ENCRYPTION command. Any backups you make from now on will be encrypted.

■**Tip** Since wallet-based encryption doesn't involve the use of passwords, it's more secure than password-based encryption. Also, wallet-based encryption makes it easier to transport tablespaces.

Dual-mode encryption refers to data that's protected both by transparent encryption as well as with a password. In order to set up dual-mode encryption, you follow the same steps as you did for enabling password-based encryption, but you must leave out the ONLY keyword.

You must be aware that encrypting RMAN backups involves a CPU overhead. To overcome this, you can run an encrypted backup with multiple RMAN channels.

Monitoring and Verifying RMAN Jobs

You can monitor RMAN's backups using several important data dictionary views. The V$BACKUP_CORRUPTION and V$COPY_CORRUPTION views, for example, provide important information about corrupt blocks. (I'll discuss data block corruption in the "Database Corruption Detection" section later in this chapter.) You can use the V$RMAN_OUTPUT view to monitor a running RMAN job.

The V$RMAN_STATUS view shows the status of all completed jobs as well as commands, as shown here:

```
SQL> SELECT operation, status, start_time, end_time
     FROM v$rman_status;

OPERATION      STATUS        START_TIME      END_TIME
---------      ---------     ----------      ---------
LIST           COMPLETED     28-APR-08       28-APR-08
VALIDATE       COMPLETED     28-APR-08       28-APR-08
BACKUP         FAILED        28-APR-08       28-APR-08
BACKUP         COMPLETED     29-APR-08       29-APR-08
. . .
SQL>
```

You can estimate the backup's progress using the following query on the V$SESSION_LONGOPS view:

```
SQL> SELECT TO_CHAR(start_time,'DD-MON-YY HH24:MI') "Start of
     backup",Sofar, totalwork,
     elapsed_seconds/60 "ELAPSED TIME IN MINUTES",
     ROUND(sofar/totalwork*100,2) "Percentage Completed so far"
     FROM v$session_longops
     WHERE opname='prod1_dbbackup';
```

To ensure the backups made using RMAN are useful during a recovery, you can use the CROSSCHECK and VALIDATE commands, as described in the following sections.

Cross-Checking Backups Made with RMAN

RMAN provides the useful CROSSCHECK command to enable you to check that the backup sets and image copies listed in the recovery catalog actually exist in their specified locations and haven't been accidentally deleted or written over. In addition, the command verifies the headers and ensures that RMAN can read the files. The CROSSCHECK command can thus test both the existence and the readability of the backups. Here's an example of the use of the CROSSCHECK command in RMAN:

```
RMAN> CROSSCHECK BACKUPSET 326;
allocated channel: ORA_DISK_1
. . .
channel ORA_DISK_4: sid=21 devtype=DISK
crosschecked backup piece: found to be 'AVAILABLE'
Crosschecked 1 objects
RMAN>
```

As you can see, RMAN has cross-checked the backup piece and found it to be available, which confirms that the backup files exist and are usable.

Using the RMAN VALIDATE Command

RMAN helps detect both physical and logical corruption. When RMAN encounters corrupt blocks of either kind, it logs the information to the control file and the recovery catalog. The VALIDATE command helps you ensure that the backed-up files exist in the proper locations, and that they are readable and free from any logical and physical corruption. You simply issue the following command to test any particular backup set:

```
RMAN> VALIDATE BACKUPSET 9;
```

To test the entire database and archived log backup sets, you issue the following command:

```
RMAN> BACKUP VALIDATE DATABASE ARCHIVELOG ALL;
```

If the backup set does not exist, RMAN will let you know. If the command does not result in any errors, you can assume that the specified backup set exists and can be used in the recovery process.

The following command doesn't restore any datafiles; it merely validates that the contents of the backup sets are restorable.

```
RMAN> RUN {
     ALLOCATE CHANNEL d1 TYPE DISK;
     RESTORE DATABASE VALIDATE;
     {
```

The BACKUP_VALIDATE command checks for both logical and physical corruption in the datafiles and also determines whether RMAN can back up a datafile. By ensuring that RMAN can back up your datafiles, you know that your RMAN backups will be usable and valid.

You can use the BACKUP_VALIDATE command only at the dataset level, whereas you can use the VALIDATE command at the backup set, tablespace, datafile, or even data block level. You can also use the latter command to check the integrity of the flash recovery area. You can proactively run the VALIDATE command to check for missing datafiles or corrupt data blocks. RMAN logs any failures it finds during the validate command execution in the Automatic Diagnostic Repository (ADR). You can then use the Data Recovery Advisor to view the failures and to fix them. Although by default the VALIDATE command checks for physical data block corruption (interblock), you can specify the CHECK LOGICAL clause to include logical intrablock corruption checks.

Here's an example that shows how to execute the VALIDATE DATABASE command to check for data block corruption at the database level:

```
RMAN> VALIDATE DATABASE;

Starting validate at 01-APR-08
using target database control file instead of recovery catalog
allocated channel: ORA_DISK_1
channel ORA_DISK_1: SID=155 device type=DISK
. . .
channel ORA_DISK_1: validation complete, elapsed time: 00:17:07
List of Datafiles
=================
File Status Marked Corrupt Empty Blocks Blocks Examined High SCN
---- ------ -------------- ------------ --------------- ----------
1    OK     0              12542        72960           4351550
  File Name: C:\ORCL11\APP\ORACLE\ORADATA\ORCL11\SYSTEM01.DBF
  Block Type Blocks Failing Blocks Processed
  ---------- -------------- ----------------
  Data       0              48959
  Index      0              9143
  Other      0              2316
. . .
including current control file for validation
including current SPFILE in backup set
channel ORA_DISK_1: validation complete, elapsed time: 00:00:02
List of Control File and SPFILE
===============================
File Type    Status Blocks Failing Blocks Examined
------------ ------ -------------- ---------------
SPFILE       OK     0              2
Control File OK     0              594
Finished validate at 01-APR-08

RMAN>
```

You can parallelize the database validation by specifying the SECTION SIZE parameter, which divides a file into sections.

Backing Up the Control File

The control file is critical for recovery, as it contains crucial information like database checkpoints and the datafile header checkpoints for the datafiles. A recovery is much harder when you lose all copies of your control file. You also need to create a new control file when you want to change the name of a database, clone a database in a different location, or increase the maximum number of files you specified when you first created the control file.

You've seen how you can back up a control file using RMAN's BACKUP CONTROLFILE command. That command will produce a binary copy of the control file. You can also use the SQL statement ALTER DATABASE BACKUP CONTROLFILE from the SQL*Plus interface or from within RMAN to back up your control files.

It's a good practice to back up your control file on a regular basis by using the BACKUP CONTROLFILE TO TRACE command, as shown here:

```
SQL> ALTER DATABASE BACKUP CONTROLFILE TO TRACE;
Database altered.
SQL>
```

You can use the ALTER DATABASE BACKUP CONTROLFILE TO TRACE AS '*filename*' command to achieve the same result as the preceding command. It will produce a text file that has the CREATE CONTROLFILE statement in it.

You should immediately back up your control file after you perform any of the following operations:

- Create or drop a tablespace.

- Add or rename a datafile.

- Add, rename, or drop an online redo log group or member.

Oracle Secure Backup

Oracle Secure Backup is Oracle Corporation's own media manager for tape backups, which simplifies and automates backup and recovery operations. Underlying Oracle Secure Backup is backup software called Reliaty, which Oracle recently acquired. RMAN, Oracle's recommended backup tool, works effectively with Oracle Secure Backup, as do other third-party media managers. However, Oracle claims that Oracle Secure Backup is the fastest and best integrated media manager for backing up Oracle databases. Note that due to the unavailability of the 11.1 version of Oracle Secure Backup at the time of writing, I've used the Oracle Database 10*g* version instead to explain the main concepts of the tool.

Although Oracle Secure Backup is a relatively new product, it's actually based on a fourth-generation of the Reliaty backup engine, which has a fairly long history. Oracle Secure Backup can be used in UNIX, Linux, and Windows environments. It supports all major tape libraries and drives in SAN, Gigabit Ethernet (GbE), and SCSI environments.

You can use the following tools when working with Oracle Secure Backup:

- A GUI tool called the Oracle Backup Web Interface, which allows you to configure administrative domains, manage operations, and back up and restore data

- A command-line interface, which lets you perform many of the same functions as the GUI tool

- OEM's interface to the Oracle Secure Backup tool

Using Oracle Secure Backup, you initiate a backup using one of these tools, and the RMAN server process backs up the data and passes it to the media manager buffer. Then the media management vendor (MMV) library backs up the database to tape.

Benefits of Oracle Secure Backup

Oracle Secure Backup provides the following benefits:

- Out-of-the-box integration with the RMAN tool
- Automated control of tape backups, automatic tape drive cleaning, and automatic tape expiration and recycling
- Ability to back up both the database and operating system files
- Easy configuration
- Ability to share tape libraries across platforms
- Flexible backup strategies, including full, incremental, and differential backups
- Secondary verification of backup data

Oracle Secure Backup Administrative Domain

Oracle Secure Backup uses the concept of an *administrative domain* as the central piece in managing its activities. An administrative domain is a collection of hosts under the direction of an administrative server. All the machines in your network that you want to treat as a common unit for the purpose of backup and restore operations are grouped together as the administrative domain.

An administrative domain consists of three types of servers:

- *Administrative server*: This server maintains the Oracle Secure Backup catalog files, which contain configuration and history information.
- *Media server*: This server has the secondary storage devices, such as tape drives and robotic tape libraries, attached to it. A media server must have at least one tape drive attached to it. The media server transfers data to and from the attached media devices.
- *Client host server*: This server contains the Oracle databases that are backed up by Oracle Secure Backup.

Typically, an administrative domain consists of a single administrative server at the top, one or more media servers, and one or more client hosts.

A single server can play one or more roles; that is, a single server can be the administrative server, media server, and host server, all rolled in one.

Installing Oracle Secure Backup

You can obtain Oracle Secure Backup software from OTN or install the software from an Oracle-supplied CD-ROM. You must install the Oracle Secure Backup software on your administrative server and on each of the media servers and client hosts in your administrative domain.

Here are the steps for installing Oracle Secure Backup on a Linux platform (UNIX platforms have a similar installation process):

1. Log in as root and create a working directory named backup.

   ```
   $ mkdir -p /usr/local/oracle/backup
   ```

2. Move to the working directory and invoke the setup program.

   ```
   $ cd /usr/local/oracle/backup
   $ /mnt/cdrom/setup
   ```

3. The setup program's welcome page appears, with three choices regarding the operating system. Select option 2 for a Linux installation.

4. The setup process loads the Oracle Secure Backup software onto the server and prompts you to choose yes to continue the installation.

5. The installer will then ask, "Have you already reviewed and customized install/obparameters for your Oracle Secure Backup installation?" You can, if you wish, configure the standard Oracle Secure Backup user named oracle, who is in charge of facilitating RMAN backup and restore operations through Oracle Secure Backup. However, the default answer is yes, meaning you accept the default parameters for the installation.

6. In the next step, you're offered a choice between an interactive and a batch mode of installation. Choose the interactive mode (option a).

7. You are now asked to select a host role, as shown here:

```
Oracle Backup is not yet installed on this machine.
Oracle Backup's Web server has been loaded, but is not yet configured.
You can install this host one of three ways:
(a) administrative host
(the host will also be able to act as a media server or client)
(b) media server
(the host will also be able to act as a client)
(c) client
If you are not sure which way to install, please refer to the Oracle
Backup Installation Guide. (a, b or c) [a]?
```

In this example, let's choose to install an administrative server, by choosing (a).

8. The installation process will then ask you the following question:

```
Is localhost connected to any SCSI tape libraries that you'd like to use with ➥
Oracle
Backup [no]?
```

You can answer yes to configure a tape library. You must probe your platform for SCSI bus-related data, such as host bus adapter, bus address (channel), target, and LUN numbers. The following command will let you identify your device information:

```
[root@localhost] $ cat /proc/scsi/scsi
```

You can use the output of this command to provide the installer information regarding the following:

```
Logical Unit Number
Host SCSI adapter number
SCSI bus address
SCSI target ID
SCSI lun
Confirm your choices and click Enter.
```

9. You'll see the following prompt:

```
Is localhost connected to any SCSI tape drives that you'd like to use with
Oracle Backup [no]?
```

If your server is connected to a tape drive, respond yes. If it isn't, answer no. If you choose yes, the installer will then ask you for details about the tape drive, similar to the details you provided for the tape library (in step 8). Provide the information and press Enter.

10. In the final step, the installer will ask you if you want to install Oracle Secure Backup on another machine. Choose no. You'll see the installation summary.

Using the Oracle Backup Web Interface Tool

Oracle provides the Oracle Backup Web Interface tool on UNIX/Linux, as well as Windows systems. The Backup GUI uses the Apache server. In order to use this tool, make sure that the observiced process is running, as shown here:

```
$ ps -ef | grep observice
root    16127    1  0 10:57  pts/3     00:00:00  observiced -s
oracle  22093 1541  0 12:58  pts/0     00:00:00  grep observice
$
```

To bring up the web browser, type the following address in your web server's address bar: **https:/localhost**. When the security alert box appears, click OK (this box appears because the Oracle Backup Web Interface installs a self-signed security certificate, and thus is unknown to the web browser). You'll then see the Oracle Backup Login page.

Since this is the first time you're logging in, use the username admin and leave the password blank. Once you log in successfully, you'll see the Oracle Backup home page.

On this page, you can perform four major activities using the Oracle Backup Web Interface: configure, manage, backup, and restore operations.

Configuring Oracle Secure Backup

When you install Oracle Secure Backup, it creates default users, hosts, devices, classes, and the null media family. You can choose to use the defaults or configure your own entities, as described in the following sections.

Users

You must have separate users with privileges to use the Oracle Secure Backup utility. You can add, modify, and remove users through either the Oracle Backup Web Interface tool or the obtool command-line interface. These users can be the same as some of your Oracle users if you wish. Classes assign a set of access rights or privileges to users who perform backups and restore operations. Oracle Secure Backup uses the following classes:

- admin: For overall administration of a domain
- operator: For standard day-to-day operations
- oracle: For specific database privileges
- reader: For viewing index information
- user: For allowing specific users to interact in a limited way with their domains

Hosts

Hosts are the server machines that host the Oracle Secure Backup tool. You can distinguish between two types of hosts, based on their access mode:

- *Ob host*: These are servers on which Oracle Secure Backup components run in the background as daemons. These daemons participate in managing the backup and restore operations.
- *Network Data Management Protocol (NDMP) host*: This is a storage appliance from a third-party vendor. An NDMP host implements the NDMP protocol and employs NDMP daemons instead of Oracle Secure Backup daemons to back up and restore files.

Devices

Devices include both tape drives and tape libraries. A library is a medium changer that accepts commands to move media between storage locations and tape drives. Following are the basic components of libraries:

- *Storage element (se)*: Contains a volume when it is not in use
- *Import-export element (iee)*: Moves volumes into and out of the library without opening the door and is physically present only on certain libraries
- *Medium transport element (mte)*: Moves a volume from a storage element to a drive
- *Data transfer element (dte)*: Represents a tape drive

Media Families

Media families are a way of grouping together tape volumes with similar write periods and retention policies. You could, for example, create a media family for all of your onsite full backups. Similarly, you can create another media family for your offsite full backups. You could also define a separate media family for all your incremental backups. Oracle Secure Backup lets you classify your backup media using the following criteria:

- *Volume identification sequence*: Each tape volume has a unique identifier attached to it, when it's either written to the first time or overwritten from the beginning of the tape.
- *Write-allowed period*: Oracle Secure Backup can write to a volume set until a predetermined write-allowed period has expired, at which time it closes the volume to further updates.
- *Retention period*: Oracle Secure Backup determines the expiration date and time for each volume set when you first create the set. You can't write to the set past the expiration date.

Oracle Database Objects

You use Oracle database objects to represent backup and restore parameters that describe your Oracle database. RMAN accesses the database, and Oracle Secure Backup manages the media. Database objects act as intermediaries between RMAN and the Oracle Secure Backup software. Oracle database objects provide necessary information for Oracle Secure Backup to interact with RMAN. RMAN provides the database name, content type, and copy number to Oracle Secure Backup. Based on that information, Oracle Secure Backup determines the Oracle database object.

Performing Backups with Oracle Secure Backup

Before you can back up data, you must log into Oracle Secure Backup as a user having the privileges to perform the backup and create a dataset. A *dataset* is a description file that identifies data you want to back up.

You can back up data in two different ways:

- *On demand*: You can create immediate, one-time-use backup jobs and send your requests to the scheduler when you're ready. Oracle Secure Backup then turns it into a dataset job, making it eligible to run.
- *Scheduled jobs*: You can use the Oracle Secure Backup scheduler to schedule jobs. You can specify backups in terms of day, days of the week, month, quarter, or year.

■**Note** Expert users can use the `obtar` command-line tool to work directly with tape drives, bypassing the Oracle Secure Backup's scheduler.

You can also specify backup windows, to minimize the impact on day-to-day operations.

User-Managed Backups

RMAN is the Oracle-recommended method for backing up and recovering databases. RMAN is designed to take advantage of its knowledge of Oracle's block structures to provide excellent performance, including features like compression, resumable backups and recovery, block-change tracking, and integration with the MML. However, you can make completely valid backups yourself, without the use of RMAN or the Oracle Secure Backup tool, by using operating system copy commands such as `cp` and `dd` in UNIX, and the `copy` command in Windows systems. You can also connect to a media manager if you want to make tape backups. If you choose this approach, you must keep track of all the backups, check their validity, and also decide which of the backups you'll need during a recovery session. This is the reason Oracle calls this method *user-managed backups*.

If you have a simple Oracle database and your backup requirements aren't onerous, you may decide that it's not worth the time and effort that you need to invest in ascending the learning curve associated with RMAN. For you, user-managed backups are probably the ideal solution, even if it means that you lose all the special features that Oracle has built into the RMAN tool.

Making Whole Database Backups

You can make a backup of the entire database when the database is closed or when it's open, provided you're operating in archivelog mode. If you're using noarchivelog mode, you can make only a closed database backup.

Whole Closed Backup

To make a closed, or *cold*, backup, the database must have been shut down cleanly through a normal, immediate, or transactional shutdown.

You need to back up the entire set of files necessary to restore the database: the datafiles, online redo log files, and control files. Technically, you need only one control file to restore the database, but because the `init.ora` file or the `SPFILE` refers to multiple control files, you might as well back up all the multiplexed copies of the control files. You first get a list of the files in each category, and you then copy the files to the target. In the following sections, you'll learn how to back up the three main types of files involved in a whole closed backup.

Backing Up the Datafiles

You can get the list of all the datafiles in your database by using the following query:

```
SQL> SELECT file_name FROM dba_data_files;
```

You can then use the UNIX `cp` command (or the Windows `copy` command) to copy these datafiles to whatever location you want. You may first copy them to an operating system file, and later on copy those files to a tape device, so you can store them offsite. For example, in UNIX, you may use the following command to back up the files:

```
$ cp /u01/orcl/oradata/data_01.dbf   /u09/orcl/oradata/data_01.dbf
```

Backing Up the Online Redo Log Files

You can get the list of online redo files by making the following query:

```
SQL> SELECT member FROM v$logfile;
MEMBER
---------------------------------------------------
C:\ORACLENT\ORADATA\HELPME\RED003.LOG
C:\ORACLENT\ORADATA\HELPME\RED002.LOG
C:\ORACLENT\ORADATA\HELPME\RED001.LOG
SQL>
```

Since you are performing a whole closed backup here, the backups are consistent; that is, when you shut down the database, the datafiles are all consistent and don't need recovery on startup. Thus, the restored online backup logs aren't really useful for recovery. So, you don't really need to back up these online redo log files. However, you'll need redo log files to start the restored instance, so you might as well use these copies of the online redo log files to start your instance.

Backing Up the Control Files

You can find the control filenames and their location by querying the V$CONTROLFILE view:

```
SQL> SELECT name FROM v$controlfile;
NAME
---------------------------------------------------
C:\ORACLENT\ORADATA\HELPME\CONTROL01.CTL
C:\ORACLENT\ORADATA\HELPME\CONTROL02.CTL
C:\ORACLENT\ORADATA\HELPME\CONTROL03.CTL
SQL>
```

A Simple Cold Backup Script

Scripts for cold backups are fairly simple. Because you're doing a backup while the database is shut down, the backup process boils down to copying all the necessary files using the operating system copy utilities. Listing 15-8 shows a sample cold backup script.

Listing 15-8. *A User-Managed Cold Backup Script*

```
#!/bin/ksh
ORACLE_SID=$1
export ORACLE_SID
export ORAENV_ASK=NO
BACKUP_DIR=/test01/app/oracle
. oraenv
sqlplus -s  system/remorse1 << EOF
SET HEAD OFF FEED OFF ECHO OFF TRIMSPOOL ON LINESIZE 200
SPOOL /u01/app/oracle/dba/cold_backup.ksh
SELECT 'cp ' ||file_name||     ' ${BACKUP_DIR}' from sys.dba_data_files;
SELECT 'cp ' ||name ||  ' ${BACKUP_DIR}'  from V$controlfile;
SELECT 'cp ' ||member||  ' ${BACKUP_DIR}' from V$logfile;
SPOOL OFF;
EXIT;
EOF
```

When you run the preceding commands, the output will be `cold_backup.ksh`, which you can then make into an executable script and schedule for regular execution.

Making a Whole Open Backup

There's a world of difference between making closed backups and open (or *hot*) backups. Open backups imply that users are changing data while you're backing up files, and this leads to the use of more complex mechanisms on behalf of the Oracle server to perform the backups.

You need to back up all the datafiles, control files, and archived redo logs for a complete online database backup. You use the normal operating system copy commands to achieve this, but because the database is actually running, you need to add some other commands to make the backups valid and consistent. To understand this, it's necessary to understand what happens within the database during an online backup.

When you first prepare the tablespace for the backup by issuing the BEGIN BACKUP command, Oracle notes the SCNs in the datafile headers and freezes them. In other words, the datafile header checkpoint SCNs will remain constant at their old values until the backup is completed and the command END BACKUP is issued. Oracle will continue writing all the changes to the datafiles and to the redo log files, but the redo log files get filled up pretty fast in most cases, because Oracle will be writing the entire data block instead of just the changes made by individual transactions, as is done during normal operation. As users are modifying the data during the online backup, checkpoints will occur as normal, and data blocks will keep being written to disk as usual. Once the backup is completed for the entire tablespace, Oracle will advance the checkpoint SCN for each file to the latest actual SCN value.

The crucial idea in the hot backup process is that should a crash of the database occur before the end of the backup, recovery can be performed based on the checkpoint that was noted when the tablespace was first put in backup mode. The SCN that is frozen in the file headers is placed there right after a checkpoint, which flushes all the modified records in the buffer to the datafiles. There is a considerable amount of redo log activity during hot backups, mostly to handle what is known as the *fractured block* problem. During the online backup of a particular Oracle block, the block could be in the process of being written to. Consequently, a backed-up copy could conceivably end up with *inconsistent* data, with part of the data from before the change was made and the rest from after the change. The inconsistent block thus produced is called a *fractured* block. Oracle copies the entire block to the redo log file to make sure that it can create a consistent version of the block later on if it indeed has been split during the hot backup process.

The following is the basic hot backup process:

1. Issue the following command:

   ```
   SQL> ALTER DATABASE BEGIN BACKUP;
   ```

2. Copy all the datafiles that are part of all the tablespaces in your database.

   ```
   SQL> host cp /u10/app/oracle/oradata/remorse/users01.dbf
        /u01/app/oracle/remorse/backup
   ```

3. After you back up all the datafiles, end the online backup with the following command:

   ```
   SQL> ALTER DATABASE END BACKUP;
   ```

The END BACKUP command instructs Oracle to take all tablespaces out of backup mode.

■**Note** RMAN doesn't put the tablespaces in the begin backup and end backup modes. The Oracle server session checks the data block header and footer to see whether the data block is fractured. If it is, the RMAN server simply reads the data block again to get a consistent view of it.

When you perform an online full backup of an archivelog database, you must back up the control file using the special BACKUP CONTROLFILE TO '*filename*' command, as shown here:

```
SQL> ALTER DATABASE BACKUP CONTROLFILE TO
     '/u01/app/oracle/oradata/backup/cntlbkp.ctl';
```

During a recovery, you must use the backup of the control file derived in the previous manner to avoid problems you may encounter if you try to use the normal operating system copy of the control file.

As you noticed, you don't need to individually place each tablespace into a hot backup mode. Starting with Oracle Database 10g, you can put all datafiles in online backup mode with a single command. You must make sure, however, that the database is in archivelog mode, mounted, and open.

You've seen how the online backup mechanism works. Listing 15-9 shows a complete online backup script that will dynamically pick up all the tablespaces in the databases and back them up to disk; from there, you can copy them to tape later.

Listing 15-9. *A User-Managed Backup Script*

```
#!/bin/ksh
ORACLE_SID=$1
export  ORACLE_SID
export ORACLE_ASK=NO
BACKUP_DIR=/u01/app/oracle/backup
export BACKUP_DIR
sqlplus -s "sys/sys_password as sysdba" << EOF
set linesize 200
set head off
set feed off
SPOOL /u01/app/oracle/dba/hot_backup.ksh
BEGIN
 dbms_output.put_line ('alter database begin backup;');
  for f1 in (select file_name fn from sys.dba_data_files)
   loop
   dbms_output.put_line( 'host cp '||f1.fn||  ' $BACKUP_DIR');
   end loop;
   dbms_output.put_line ('alter database end backup;');
   dbms_output.put_line('alter database backup
   controlfile to '|| ' $BACKUP_DIR/control'|| ';');
   dbms_output.put_line('alter system switch logfile;');
END;
/
SPOOL OFF;
EXIT
EOF
```

The spooled script hot_backup.sh looks like this:

```
ALTER DATABASE BEGIN BACKUP;
HOST cp /u05/oradata/nicko/system01.dbf $BACKUP_DIR
HOST cp /u05/oradata/nicko/undotbs01.dbf $BACKUP_DIR
. . .
ALTER DATABASE END BACKUP;
ALTER DATABASE BACKUP CONTROLFILE TO  $BACKUP_DIR/control;
ALTER SYSTEM SWITCH LOGFILE;
```

As in the case of your cold backup script, you can make the hot backup script a part of a shell script and run it at the specified backup time.

Making Partial Database Backups

You don't need to back up the entire database at one time. You can back up a part of the database—for instance, a tablespace or just a single datafile. Ordinarily, you can do a partial backup of a database only if the database is running in archivelog mode, but there are a couple of exceptions. If a database in noarchivelog mode has some read-only or offline-normal tablespaces, you can back up those tablespaces by themselves.

You can make a tablespace backup with the tablespace either online or in an offline status, depending on your needs. First, let's look at an example of an offline backup of a tablespace. You first take the tablespace offline, and then you back up the files that compose the tablespace.

```
SQL> SELECT file_name FROM dba_data_files
    WHERE tablespace_name = 'USERS';

    /u05/oradata/nicko/users01.dbf
SQL>
```

As you can see, only one datafile belongs to the tablespace USERS. In order to back up the tablespace, you must back up this datafile. But first, take the tablespace offline, in case users are accessing any of the datafiles in that tablespace.

```
SQL> ALTER TABLESPACE users OFFLINE;
```

Now, you can use an operating system utility like cp (or copy on a Windows system) to back up the datafile belonging to the USERS tablespace.

```
SQL> host copy/u05/oradata/nicko /users01/dbf /u10/oradata/nicko/users01.dbf
```

Once you finish copying all the datafiles belonging to the tablespace (only one datafile in this example), bring the tablespace online.

```
SQL> ALTER TABLESPACE users ONLINE;
```

In order to back up a tablespace without taking it offline, first, put the tablespace in backup mode to let the database know that you're starting an online backup:

```
SQL> ALTER TABLESPACE sysaux BEGIN BACKUP;
Tablespace altered.
SQL>
```

Next, copy the datafile(s) belonging to the online tablespace.

```
SQL> HOST copy /u01/oradata/nicko/sysaux01.dbf /u05/oradata/nicko/sysaux01.dbf
SQL>
```

Finally, issue the following command, to let the database know you're finished:

```
SQL> ALTER TABLESPACE sysaux END BACKUP;
Tablespace altered.
SQL>
```

Monitoring User-Managed Online Backups

Several dynamic performance views help you monitor the online backups and troubleshoot the process. Online backups could take a considerable amount of time, depending on the size of the database. It's not unheard of for the backup process to fail or hang up before it completes. As a DBA, you should be aware of the steps you need to take under those circumstances. Table 15-1 lists the critical V$ views that help monitor and diagnose problems in backups.

Table 15-1. *V$ Views for Monitoring Backups*

View	Description
V$BACKUP	This view is of great help in determining whether any of the datafiles are still in backup mode. Hot backups sometimes get hung up, and you can query the status column of this table to find out whether any file shows ACTIVE as the status. If a file does show this status, and the backup is supposed to have been finished based on the schedule, something obviously went wrong, and you need it to get the file(s) out of hot backup mode.
V$DATAFILE	This view lists all the datafiles that belong to all the tablespaces that need to be backed up.
V$LOG	This view displays all the online redo logs for the database.
V$ARCHIVED_LOG	This view displays historical archived log information from the control file.
V$LOG_HISTORY	This view displays the redo logs that have been archived.

Database Corruption Detection

Regular backups of a production database are imperative, but the backups won't help if they are unusable for some reason. Testing of backups is an often-ignored area of backup and recovery. Unfortunately, many administrators realize its necessity under painful circumstances.

Backed-up database files may become useless during recovery for several reasons: corrupt datafiles and redo logs, accidentally overwritten files, defective tapes, or even nonexistent files. You must get into the habit of regularly testing your production backups according to a schedule. This will help you catch any data corruption. I use the term *corruption* to indicate the fact that the data is inconsistent with what it should be. You are concerned here basically with what is known as *block corruption*, which could be logical or physical.

Detecting Media Corruption

Media corruption can be caused by myriad factors, ranging from user error to bugs in the operating system software, to bad disks, to a Logical Volume Manager (LVM) error, to faulty memory chips. Media defects could lead to corruption in the control files, redo logs, data dictionary, table data, and index data.

Your detection of media corruption anywhere in the database involves using scripts to monitor your alert logs on a regular basis and using some Oracle features that enable early detection of problems. You can almost completely prevent redo log and control file corruption by using multiplexing, at both the operating system level and the Oracle level. Owing to the database's sheer size and the fact that its files are not multiplexed as a matter of course, data block corruption is of most concern to DBAs. Try to catch the corruption messages in your alert logs early on and seek Oracle Worldwide Support's help in fixing any type of corruption issues in your database

Detecting Data Block Corruption

Data block corruption occurs when you have inconsistent data in tables or indexes. You usually end up losing a significant amount of data if you can't fix the corrupted blocks of data. Although you may take several steps to prevent corruption, early detection of corrupted datafiles will help you in two ways:

- It will enable you to find quick ways of salvaging all or as much of the affected data as possible.

- It will save you surprises during a recovery from media errors. Early detection of corruption always will minimize the problem, because it will enable you to take the files offline and reduce the potential damage.

You can use several methods to detect data block corruption. First, you can set a few initialization parameters to trap corrupted block information. Also, you can use utilities such as DBVERIFY and DBMS_REPAIR and the ANALYZE command to enable you to detect data block corruption. These methods are not mutually exclusive; rather, you should use them as complements to each other, as each has its own appealing features. The following sections cover the use of each of these techniques.

Setting Initialization Parameters

You can use the initialization parameter DB_BLOCK_CHECKSUM to force Oracle to perform *check-summing*, which involves the computation of checksums for every data block and its storage in the data block header. When the data is read, the checksums are compared and corrupt data blocks are identified. Oracle recommends that you leave the DB_BLOCK_CHECKSUM parameter at its default setting of TYPICAL (same as TRUE in previous versions). According to Oracle, using this feature in the TYPICAL mode causes only an additional 1 to 2 percent overhead. In the alternative FULL mode, it causes a 4 to 5 percent overhead.

The DB_BLOCK_CHECKING parameter is more sophisticated, and it checks data and index blocks only when the blocks are actually changed. It also detects corruption before the data blocks are marked corrupt. The default for this parameter is OFF. The other possible values are LOW, MEDIUM, and FULL. Block checking may cause a 1 to 10 percent overhead; the overhead is directly linked to update and insert operations in your database. Oracle recommends that you set this parameter value to FULL, if you can handle the additional overhead. You can set this feature by including it in the init.ora file, as in this example, which sets it to LOW:

```
DB_BLOCK_CHECKING=LOW
```

You can also set it dynamically using the ALTER SESSION statement:

```
SQL> ALTER SESSION SET DB_BLOCK_CHECKING=LOW;
```

You can specify the DB_ULTRA_SAFE initialization parameter to control the values of the DB_BLOCK_CHECKSUM and the DB_BLOCK_CHECKING initialization parameters. If you leave DB_ULTRA_SAFE at its default value (OFF), the database sets the values for the two corruption-related parameters at TYPICAL, which involves minimal checks and thus a smaller CPU overhead. If you set DB_ULTRA_SAFE to the value DATA_ONLY or DATA_AND_INDEX, the database will set the value of the two corruption-related parameters to FULL, which results in more intensive corruption checking.

Using the ANALYZE Command

You can use the ANALYZE command to catch corrupted data blocks. The following command verifies each data block in the customer table, and if it finds any corrupted blocks, it adds the suspect rows to the invalid_rows table:

```
SQL> ANALYZE TABLE customer VALIDATE STRUCTURE;
```

In addition to checking for block corruption, the command will make sure that the index data corresponds to the table data.

Using the DBVERIFY Utility

When you suspect data block corruption, you can use the Oracle-provided DBVERIFY utility. The DBVERIFY tool is used from the operating system level. It checks the structural integrity of the database files for corruption.

To illustrate the use of DBVERIFY, the following example verifies a file on a Windows platform (the command works in the same way on UNIX platforms). You can easily write a script that will perform the datafile verification and use crontab to schedule it on a regular basis. Listing 15-10 shows the results of using the DBVERIFY utility.

Listing 15-10. *Output of the DBVERIFY Utility*

```
$ dbv file=/u01/orcl/oradata/system01.dbf
DBVERIFY: Release 11.1.0.6.0 - Production on Sun Mar 30 15:53:46 2008
Copyright (c) 1982, 2007, Oracle.  All rights reserved.
DBVERIFY - Verification starting :
FILE = =/u01/orcl/oradata/system01.dbf
DBVERIFY - Verification complete
Total Pages Examined        : 19200
Total Pages Processed (Data) : 4404
Total Pages Failing   (Data) : 0
Total Pages Processed (Index): 1245
Total Pages Failing   (Index): 0
Total Pages Processed (Other): 2663
Total Pages Processed (Seg)  : 0
Total Pages Failing   (Seg)  : 0
Total Pages Empty           : 10888
Total Pages Marked Corrupt  : 0
Total Pages Influx          : 0
Highest block SCN           : 935681  (0.935681)
$
```

This example shows a simplified use of the DBVERIFY utility, which is invoked by the command DBV on both the UNIX and Windows platforms. The keyword FILE indicates the datafile you want to check for corruption. As you can see, the total pages marked as corrupt are 0, which means the datafile is free of any structural integrity problems—it is not corrupted.

Using the DBMS_REPAIR Package

Though using the DBVERIFY utility is simple, it's severely limited by the fact that it can't be used to fix corrupted data. In Oracle8*i*, Oracle introduced the DBMS_REPAIR package, which can detect and fix data block corruption while datafiles are online. To use this utility, you first need to log in as the user SYS and then create a pair of tables: the first needs to be prefixed with repair_, and the second is called the orphan_key table.

Once you have created the table repair_table, you're ready to run the DBMS_REPAIR package. The repair_table table will log all the information about corrupt data. The CHECK_OBJECT procedure of the DBMS_REPAIR package detects corrupted data blocks and recommends fixes. After the execution of the CHECK_OBJECT procedure, the table repair_table is queried on the columns OBJECT_NAME and CORRUPT_DESCRIPTION to identify if and what type of data block corruption exists.

I discuss various ways of fixing data block corruption in the next chapter, because one of the ways to fix the problem involves restoring the database from backups.

> ### ORACLE'S HARD INITIATIVE
>
> RAID ensures only that data storage drives are redundant, so you can withstand the loss of some disks without losing any data. What if you have a mirrored system, but the data that's being written to a mirrored pair is corrupted? Both the disks in the mirrored pair, of course, will hold corrupted data. Oracle has recently instituted a new initiative, Hardware Assisted Resilient Data (HARD), to prevent data corruption before it occurs. Oracle will incorporate special data validation algorithms inside the storage devices sold by participating vendors in the HARD Initiative, thus *preventing* corrupted data from being written permanently to disk. The HARD Initiative is designed to address problems of the following nature:
>
> - Operating system overwrites of Oracle data
>
> - Partially written blocks and lost writes
>
> - Physically and logically corrupt blocks being written
>
> - Blocks being written to the wrong locations

Enhanced Data Protection for Disaster Recovery

The backup techniques you've seen in this chapter will protect your database from unexpected disk and other hardware failures. If you have a well-designed mirroring or a RAID-configured disk system, you'll have built enough redundancy into your system to survive ordinary disasters. However, even the most stringent backup systems are no guarantee that you have a high-availability system in place. A disaster could easily put your organization data resources out of commission, causing severe service interruptions. For events like those, you need more than the ordinary backup systems in place—you need a *high-availability strategy* in place.

High-Availability Systems

A high-availability system will ensure almost continuous data availability in the face of disasters of just about any kind. The key to providing such high availability is to have *multiple* data systems using various architectures. Oracle provides several alternatives, including the following:

- *Oracle Real Application Clusters*: Oracle RAC uses multiple Oracle instances on multiple nodes (servers) to connect to a single database. In the event of a node failure, the surviving nodes recover the failed instance while providing continuous service to the users, who aren't aware that anything went wrong. Oracle RAC provides high availability, and under some circumstances, it can also enhance performance and provide scalability. However, if the single database goes, everything goes with it, the multiple nodes notwithstanding. You can start at http://www.oracle.com/technology/products/database/clustering/index.html to learn more about Oracle RAC.

- *Oracle Streams*: Oracle's Streams provides high availability by maintaining a distributed database system. Changes from the source database are captured and sent to other databases. High availability is ensured because the failure of one site means customers are switched over to a different site, and they can continue selecting and updating data as before.

- *Oracle Data Guard and standby databases*: Oracle provides the standby database concept, where you can have your primary production database update a secondary database in a different location on a continuous basis. Oracle Data Guard helps you administer sophisticated standby database setups so you can quickly failover from the production database to a standby database in the case of a site disaster, for example.

Oracle Data Guard and standby databases are frequently used to provide disaster recovery, data protection, and high availability. Let's take a quick look at how these work.

Oracle Data Guard and Standby Databases

The standby database feature has been provided by Oracle for many years. Oracle Data Guard is the management and monitoring layer through which the standby databases are maintained. The standby databases are kept up-to-date by propagating changes from the primary server continuously.

In the event of a disaster, a standby database is activated and brought online as the primary database. Besides providing you protection against a total destruction of the primary database, the standby database can also be used for reporting purposes.

The databases maintained in an Oracle Data Guard configuration can be in the same LAN-based location, or they can be in a much wider WAN-supported network. LAN-based local standby databases offer faster failure capabilities, and WAN-based databases are a better bet against a catastrophic disaster affecting your data center or local sites. You can configure a primary database and several standby databases. You can reduce downtime to less than a minute by choosing the proper protection level when you set up the standby databases. Here is a brief summary of the many benefits of using the Oracle Data Guard standby database feature:

- High availability

- Protection against disasters

- Protection against physical data corruption

- Protection against user errors

- Failover and switchover capabilities, which can be used for both planned and unplanned switching of production and standby databases

- Geographical separation of primary and secondary servers through Oracle Net

Oracle provides the excellent Oracle Data Guard Broker to help create and manage the Oracle Data Guard configurations. The Oracle Data Guard Broker can support up to ten databases (one primary and nine standby) at a time. The Oracle Data Guard Broker can manage tasks such as log application, log transportation, and switchover or failover from primary to secondary. The Oracle Data Guard Broker offers two interfaces: a command-line interface and a GUI called the Data Guard Manager.

The Oracle Data Guard Broker is a great tool, in that it automates the many tasks involved in managing complex standby database groupings. It also automates the often-complex networking aspects of maintaining standby databases.

Note Oracle Data Guard isn't meant for maintaining a low downtime. It's meant to serve in a disaster-protection capacity and to provide for an alternative database during scheduled maintenance of the production database.

Physical and Logical Standby Databases

Standby databases come in two flavors: physical and logical. Even the logical database, contrary to what its name implies, is a real standby database. Logical and physical standby databases are maintained in the same fashion: by propagating changes from the main production (primary) database to the standby database.

Physical standby databases are updated by applying the primary database's archived redo logs using the arch background process. However, the LGWR process can also be used to transfer the redo log data from the primary to the standby databases. Physical standby databases are identical to the production database. A physical standby database must undergo a constant recovery process for it to be in tune with the production database.

Logical standby databases, on the other hand, use the same archived logs to derive transaction information, which is applied to the standby database using SQL statements.

The big difference between the two standby databases is that you can't use a physical standby database for reporting while you're performing recovery on it. However, you can continuously access a logical database for reporting and querying, even while you're performing recovery on it. You can have a maximum of nine logical and physical standby databases in one Oracle Data Guard configuration.

Both logical and physical standby databases have their own benefits and drawbacks. The physical standby database is the traditional Oracle standby database, and it is based on applying redo logs from the production server to recover. There are no data limitations—all types of DML and DDL can be propagated mechanically with the application of the redo logs.

Protection Modes

You can choose three data protection modes when you use the Oracle Data Guard feature to maintain standby databases. The protection modes are a reflection of the trade-off between availability and performance. The following modes are available:

- *Maximum protection mode*: This mode, also called the *double failure protection mode*, offers the highest level of protection. This mode guarantees that no data loss will occur if your primary database fails. To ensure this protection, the redo data must be written to both the primary database's online redo log and the standby redo log on at least one standby database, before a transaction can commit. The primary database will shut down if it can't write redo data to at least one of the secondary database redo log files.

- *Maximum availability mode*: This mode, also known as *instant protection mode*, offers protection from the failure of the primary production database. You get the highest level of data protection possible while keeping the primary database available. The redo data from the primary server is written asynchronously following the committing of the transactions on the primary server. You could lose your primary database, your standby database, or the network connection connecting the two, without losing any data under this data protection mode. If you lose the connection to the standby database, the primary server stops shipping changes to it, but doesn't shut down.

- *Maximum performance mode*: If you don't need protection against a zero loss of data, but you would like to keep the production database's performance at its peak level, this is the mode of protection you should choose. The primary database doesn't wait for confirmation from the secondary database before committing its changes. If the primary database fails, the standby database might miss some changes that were already committed on the primary.

As you can see, each mode is designed to provide either a greater amount of performance or a greater amount of data protection. It's up to the individual organization to make a choice between them, based on the firm's needs.

■ ■ ■

Database Recovery

A database can be unavailable for use for a number of reasons, including a system crash, a network failure, a media failure, or a natural disaster. The keys to a successful recovery, of course, are solidly tested backups and regular recovery drills using those backups.

Database recovery is a rather complex topic, and practicing the recovery techniques is essential to a successful recovery. The new Flashback recovery techniques are great alternatives to several more drastic traditional recovery techniques, and you should be comfortable with using these tools. This chapter discusses the important Oracle recovery techniques, but you should also review the Oracle manuals concerning backup and recovery, and you should simulate different types of recovery so you're ready for the real thing, should the need arise!

In this chapter, I'll cover the following topics:

- Types of database failures (system failure, media failure, and so on)
- Automatic crash/instance recovery vs. user-initiated media recovery (the latter being the main focus of this chapter)
- Recovery using Recovery Manager (RMAN)
- Oracle Database 11*g*'s new Flashback-related techniques

Besides having to recover from media failure, you may also encounter situations where data blocks are corrupted, leading to a potential loss of data. You can take steps to prevent data corruption, and you can salvage most of the uncorrupted data from the data blocks using special Oracle-provided packages. You'll learn how to use these techniques in the latter part of this chapter.

Recovery is a process in which mistakes can be very expensive in terms of data loss. Your success during a recovery process directly corresponds to your understanding of backup and recovery concepts and your knowledge of which techniques to apply for different kinds of media losses. At the very end of this chapter, a set of recovery scenarios will outline the steps to be followed during these various types of recovery.

Types of Database Failures

As a DBA, your most important task is to safeguard the enterprise data and enable users to access it with as few disruptions as possible. In the previous chapter, you learned how important it is to have a proper backup and recovery process in place. Your database could stop functioning for a number of reasons, some of them mechanical and others due to user errors or natural disasters, as outlined in the next few sections.

System Failures

The most common system failures are hardware-related failures. A disk drive controller may fail, or the disk head could be defective. Some of the system peripherals or controllers can also malfunction. You may have a problem with a CPU on your system, or the memory chips may turn out to be defective. Of course, you could always end up with a power supply–related failure, especially if you aren't using uninterrupted power supplies. Software-related problems could result from problems on either the operating system side or the Oracle server side. The database might crash without any notice upon hitting a server bug. Similarly, the middle-tier software could cause the network to fail or it could generate other problems.

If you have only one instance running and your entire system goes down, there's really not a whole lot you can do. If you have mission-critical systems, you can prevent the downtime by using a cluster of several nodes, thus avoiding a single point of failure. Oracle offers Real Application Clusters (RAC), which involves running several instances from different servers connecting to a single database. When one node or server goes down, the others can take over within seconds, without any noticeable disruption in service. Oracle also offers the Transparent Application Failover feature, which you can use in tandem with RAC to failover clients transparently from one server to the other.

Data Center Disasters

Data center disasters could range from a tornado to a fire to a terrorist attack. I discussed the Oracle Data Guard feature, which makes use of standby databases, in Chapter 15. Standby databases provide good protection against a data center disaster. Your business will continue to run without any interruption, because all the changes made to your operational database are sent to a duplicate standby database over the network. In a disaster recovery situation, you just turn the duplicate database into your main production database, with almost no disruption and no loss of data.

You can also use Oracle Streams to maintain a distributed database system so a remote distributed database can take over from the primary production system if it suffers a total failure.

Human Error

People can and do make mistakes. DBAs or system administrators can make critical errors that might put their databases in jeopardy. For example, you could accidentally run the wrong batch job, producing data that is meaningless or wrong.

If you have entered incorrect data into a table or deleted some data in error, you have several ways to get out of this jam. You can use Oracle's Flashback Query feature to query old data and replace the lost or wrongly entered data without taking the database offline. Chapter 8 dealt with various Flashback features that use undo data. In this chapter, I discuss the Flashback Database and Flashback Drop features, which enable you to perform a database or table recovery without restoring datafiles.

You can also use Oracle's LogMiner tool to read your redo logs and undo changes to the database. You can use Data Pump Export and Import to replace the affected tables, but you may lose some data in the process. Or, you can perform a *point-in-time recovery* (PITR) to recover the database or a tablespace to a point in time before the problem occurred. However, the new Flashback features are a better alternative in most cases, as you'll see later in this chapter.

Media Failures

The most serious recovery issues are those related to media problems. Damage to disks that prevent them from being read from or written to is the most serious scenario, and you'll have to depend on your backup copies of the database and log files to make the database current without any permanent loss of data. If your datafiles or control files are on the inaccessible media, you'll most likely end up doing a recovery.

In some situations, you may perform a recovery even if there's no media damage—for instance, when there's a serious case of user error. If you have to restore a backed-up datafile or you take a file offline using the `OFFLINE IMMEDIATE` option, you'll need to perform a media recovery. Two factors are critical when disasters occur: the amount of data that becomes unavailable and needs to be replaced from backups, and the amount of time it might take to replace the data.

Failures and Data Repair

As I mentioned earlier, an instance failure doesn't require data recovery. Similarly, a network failure or an abnormal shutdown of an Oracle background process or a problem caused by an out-of-space condition may lead to temporary disruption of work in the database, but none of these situations call for a data recovery.

You need to use data repair techniques only when an error is caused by a media failure or a user error. Let's take a closer look at these two types of critical failures:

- *Media failures*: Media failures occur when the database can't read from or write to a file. You could encounter such a media failure because a file was mistakenly deleted, corrupted, or overwritten. Mechanical problems such as head crashes can also cause a disk failure. What happens as a result of a media failure depends on whether you have a duplicate copy of an affected file. For example, if a redo log file is affected, the database will continue operating without a problem if you've multiplexed the redo log file. If, on the other hand, a datafile error that belongs to the System tablespace encounters errors, the database will shut down immediately.

- *User errors*: User errors are errors in data entry or accidental deletion of data or dropping of a table. You can use multiple techniques to undo the effects of a user error.

Oracle offers several methods to repair failures resulting from media failures and user errors. Of course, you are always going to keep the appropriate backups of the database, but restoring and recovering backups isn't the only solution available to you. Depending on the type of problem you are dealing with, you can use of one of the following methods to fix the failures:

- *Data Recovery Advisor*: The Data Recovery Advisor diagnoses failures, presents repair options, and can execute those options once you approve them. The advisor recommends both manual and automated repair options and can determine the best repair option for you. You can access the Data Recovery Advisor either through the RMAN command line or through the Enterprise Manager. The database automatically detects failures and records them in the Automatic Diagnostic Repository. You can also run a proactive data integrity check or check for block corruption by executing the `VALIDATE` command. No matter whether the failure you are dealing with was detected through a proactive or a reactive check, using the Data Recovery Advisor should be your first step to repairing persistent failures in your database.

- *Flashback techniques*: Oracle Flashback features include features that are useful in viewing past states of data as well as backup- and recovery-related features. Except for the Flashback Drop feature, all the Oracle Flashback features rely on undo data. The main Oracle Flashback features that help you with fixing failures relating to user errors or logical data corruption are as follows:

  - Flashback Database
  - Flashback Table
  - Flashback Drop
  - Flashback Transaction Backout

I dealt with the Flashback Table feature in Chapter 8. I discuss the Flashback Database and the Flashback Drop features later in this chapter. In addition, Oracle Database 11g has introduced a brand-new Flashback feature named Flashback Transaction Backout, which I discuss in this chapter as well.

- *Media recovery*: Media recovery is probably the most drastic way of fixing a persistent failure. If you lose a datafile, for example, you must restore a copy of that datafile from the backups. However, restoring the backups only gets you so far, since the backups are from a previous point in time. Depending on the frequency of your backups, they could be several days or even weeks old. To update the restored file, then, you must next recover the database by updating with the archived redo logs and online redo logs, which is generally what is known as media recovery. You can use several types of media recovery, as explained here:

  - Block media recovery
  - Datafile media recovery
  - Complete recovery
  - Point-in-time recovery

In this chapter, I discuss the three major methods of repairing persistent failures in the database. However, before we start discussing the recovery alternatives, you first need to become familiar with the basic concepts of Oracle database recovery.

The Oracle Recovery Process

You can broadly divide Oracle database recoveries into crash and instance recoveries on one hand and media recoveries on the other. Let's clarify the differences between these two types of recoveries.

Crash and Instance Recovery

Oracle automatically performs crash recovery when a single instance suddenly fails, or when all instances of a multiple-instance Oracle RAC fail. Also, if you shut down your database with the SHUTDOWN ABORT command, Oracle has to perform a crash recovery. Instance recovery is very similar to crash recovery, but it applies to cases where a surviving instance recovers the failed instances in an RAC setup. The essential point about crash and instance recoveries is that you don't apply any backed-up datafiles or archived log files during recovery. Oracle uses only the current datafiles and online redo log files to bring the database up to date.

Crash and instance recovery involves the following two-step procedure:

1. *Roll-forward step*: During this step, formally called *cache recovery*, the database applies the committed and uncommitted data in the current online redo log files to the current online datafiles.

2. *Rollback step*: During this step, formally called *transaction recovery*, the database removes the uncommitted transactions applied in the previous step, using the undo data in the undo segments.

As you know, when the database suddenly crashes, not all the committed transactions will have been written to disk. If your database is large, and the redo log files are also large, it can take a long time for the roll-forward and rollback to complete. By using Oracle's *Fast-Start Fault Recovery* functionality, you can substantially reduce the downtime resulting from system-related outages.

The roll-forward phase of a crash recovery uses the redo logs to see what changes need to be applied to disk. Redo application begins at a point in the redo logs known as the *thread checkpoint redo byte address*. This is the time when the last checkpoint was done before the crash. Because all the data in the buffers is written to disk during a checkpoint, only changes after this last checkpoint position will need to be recovered. *Fast-Start Checkpointing* is the frequent writing of the dirty database buffers in the cache to disk by the database writer (DBW*n*). Fast-Start Checkpointing is the basis of Oracle's Fast-Start Fault Recovery feature. You can minimize the time required for crash recovery by frequently advancing the checkpoint position. Oracle uses a two-pass technique to perform a recovery using the checkpoints. In the first pass, it determines which blocks in the redo logs need recovery, and in the second pass the database applies the required changes.

Starting with Oracle Database 10*g*, the database automatically performs checkpoint tuning by deciding when to write out dirty buffers with the least impact on throughput. All you have to do is specify the time (in seconds) that a crash recovery should take by setting the FAST_START_MTTR_TARGET parameter. The maximum value for FAST_START_MTTR_TARGET is 3,600 seconds (1 hour) and the default is 0. (If you set the value to more than 3,600 seconds, Oracle resets it to 3,600 seconds.) Even if you set the parameter to a large value, checkpointing is enabled by default. The goal of automatic checkpoint tuning is to write as many dirty buffers and perform checkpointing as frequently as possible without increasing the overhead and hurting database throughput.

The following example shows how to set FAST_START_MTTR_TARGET so that crash recovery will take no longer than 1 minute :

```
SQL> ALTER DATABASE SET FAST_START_MTTR_TARGET=60;
```

■**Note** You can also set the value of the FAST_START_MTTR_TARGET parameter in the initialization parameter file.

The target of 60 seconds in the preceding example may not be met exactly by Oracle the very first time during a crash recovery because Oracle initially uses an estimate of the I/O rates on your system. Oracle constantly monitors your system to measure the actual I/O rates, and over time it uses this information to estimate the recovery time more precisely. Every 30 seconds, Oracle estimates the current mean time to recover (MTTR) and places this value in the V$INSTANCE_RECOVERY table. You can query this table, as shown next, to see what Oracle's current estimated MTTR is and adjust your FAST_START_MTTR_TARGET value accordingly.

```
SQL> SELECT recovery_estimated_ios, estimated_mttr, target_mttr
     FROM v$instance_recovery;

RECOVERY_ESTIMATED_IOS      ESTIMATED_MTTR      TARGET_MTTR
------------------------------------------------------------
         994                      20                  52
SQL>
```

■**Note** Using Fast-Start Fault Recovery can lower your crash-recovery times to less than a minute. Although there is some concern that more frequent checkpointing has a performance cost, studies have shown that the performance hit is negligible.

Faster Instance Startup

When you have very large SGAs, it can sometimes take a considerable amount of time for the instance to start. Oracle traditionally used to wait for the initialization of the entire buffer cache before starting the instance, which accounted for most of the delay. Oracle initializes only about 10 percent of the buffer cache before starting up the instance and opening the database. The remaining buffer cache is initialized by the checkpoint process after the database is opened.

Media Recovery

Unlike crash and instance recovery, media recovery isn't automatic—the DBA has to initiate the recovery process. You need the following four items to perform a complete media recovery:

- A full backup of all datafiles
- Archived redo logs since the last full backup
- A control file copy
- Current online redo logs

Oracle media recovery ensures the recovery of up-to-the-minute data, provided you have a copy of a recent backup and archived redo logs. The archived logs are transaction journals, and they contain the complete set of changes made to the database since the last backup. By using the archived redo logs and contents of the online redo logs, you can bring your database up to date. You'll see quite a bit of discussion on recovering databases from a media failure in this chapter.

Dropping a Datafile

Before you can begin a complete media recovery, you must take the datafiles to be recovered offline. You can drop a datafile directly from SQL*Plus with the DROP DATAFILE command. When you issue this command, the datafile is removed both from the tablespace and the operating system as well. Here's an example:

```
SQL> ALTER TABLESPACE TEST DROP DATAFILE '/u01/app/oracle/test/test01.dbf';
```

If the datafile you'd like to drop is the only datafile in a tablespace, you must drop the tablespace itself. The tablespace in which the datafile resides must also be online and read-write.

Restoring vs. Recovering

Using backed-up copies of datafiles and control files to replace lost or damaged datafiles and control files is called *restoring*. Bringing the datafiles up to date using backed-up datafiles and archived redo log files is called *recovery*.

The Media Recovery Process

There are two steps in an Oracle media recovery process: first you restore a backup of the datafiles and make them available to Oracle. Then comes the recovery, when you bring the datafiles up to date by applying the archived redo log files and the online redo log files.

The recovery process itself has two steps:

- *Cache recovery (rolling forward)*: The redo log contains both committed and uncommitted changes. As you know, Oracle writes to the redo log first and the datafiles later. When you restore older files from backups to replace lost or damaged datafiles, those files are missing all the changes made since the time of the backup. The process of applying the contents of both the archived and redo log files to bring the datafiles up to date is called *cache recovery* or *rolling forward*. Once you complete cache recovery, you will have gained all your committed changes, but unfortunately, you'll also have all the uncommitted changes that are part of the redo log.

- *Transaction recovery (rolling back)*: During the application of the redo log data to the datafiles, both committed and uncommitted changes get applied. The uncommitted changes must now be removed from the datafiles. Oracle uses the prechange versions of data stored in the undo segments to remove these uncommitted changes. This second step is called *transaction recovery* or *rolling back*. Oracle gets the undo data through cache recovery, which regenerates the undo segments from the redo log.

■**Note** If you use RMAN, you can recover your datafiles with incremental backups, which are backups that contain only the changes after a previous backup. Chapter 15 explains RMAN incremental backups in detail.

Open and Closed Media Recovery

It's important to remember that a database failure or even a disaster need not involve the entire database. Users can continue to work away on most parts of the database while another part is being repaired with the help of backups.

Open recovery is recovery performed while the database is open to users. Only the affected datafiles or tablespaces are taken offline for recovery. You can continue to run the database as usual, with service being interrupted only for those transactions that involve the damaged part of the database.

A *closed recovery* is a recovery for which you need to shut down the database completely. You'll need to use closed recovery when your entire database needs to be recovered or when your system or rollback (undo) datafiles are damaged.

Time Needed for Recovery

The time it will take you to perform a recovery depends on the following factors:

- On what media do you have your archived redo logs? If the logs are all on tape, it will take much longer to perform the recovery than if they're on disk. It's a good idea to keep an extra copy of the logs on disk somewhere.

- Are you using the parallel recovery feature? Parallel recovery, when it can be implemented, will reduce the time needed to recover the database.

- Do you need to replace the disks right away, or can you get away with just moving the datafiles to a different good location?

- What's your service contract for replacement and repair of parts on the server? Some companies have a response time as short as 45 minutes from the initial call. Some may have a 24-hour turnaround. Make sure you know and understand the implications of your company's service contract with the vendor of your system.

- How frequently do you perform backups? The more infrequently you perform backups, the more logs need to be applied, and the longer the recovery time.

Complete and Incomplete Recovery

If you have a disk go bad on you, and you consequently have to restore and recover from backups, naturally your goal will be a full recovery up to the time the problem occurred. On the other hand, if you're recovering your database due to user errors (such as incorrect data entry), your goal may be to remove the errors from your database by recovering only up to the point when the incorrect activity began. This is typically called *incomplete recovery*, and as you'll see later on, you make the decision about exactly when to stop recovering the database based on different criteria.

Complete recovery simply means a recovery with no loss of data. All the changes in the online and archived redo logs are applied to the most recent backup of the database. Thus, the database is brought up to date with the current point in time. You can perform a complete recovery at the database, tablespace, or datafile level.

Incomplete recovery implies data loss, because you recover only part of the data that existed when the database failure occurred. That is, you apply only some of the archived and current log records to the database. Your database after recovery is consistent, but it's not an up-to-date version. You could have several reasons for wanting to do an incomplete recovery, including user error, loss of necessary archived log files, or loss of an online redo log. When you perform an incomplete recovery, you always open the database after resetting your redo logs. This will, in effect, give you a new version or incarnation of the database. You can make an incomplete recovery only at the database level, not at the tablespace or datafile level.

During both complete and incomplete database recovery, you can't open your database to users. When one or more tablespaces have been logically damaged (due to incorrect data entry, for example), you can perform a *tablespace point-in-time recovery* (TSPITR). Since you don't have to perform an incomplete media recovery of the entire database, recovery will be much quicker. In addition, you don't have to make all of your database inaccessible to users during recovery. TSPITR techniques are cumbersome, and you may want to first consider using the Flashback techniques like Flashback Table and Flashback Drop instead.

Block Media Recovery

If only a few data blocks are corrupted, and the rest of the datafile is good, you should consider performing a *block media recovery* instead of a datafile recovery. You can perform a block media recovery only through RMAN. Even if you're using your own backup and restore techniques, you can still perform a block media recovery through RMAN by using the `CATALOG` command to first register the necessary datafiles and archived redo log backups with RMAN.

Media Recovery vs. Nonmedia Recoveries

Most traditional recoveries are file-based media recoveries. Whether you use RMAN or user-managed recovery techniques, recovery traditionally has meant the restoration and recovery of the datafiles, archived redo logs, and control files. If you lost an entire database or entire datafile due to media problems, you had no recourse but to use the file-based recovery techniques. However, if you were trying to undo user errors or to recover an accidentally dropped table, traditional recovery techniques proved to be overkill and were time consuming.

Over the last few years, Oracle has developed several non-file-based recovery techniques. In these techniques, the emphasis isn't on restoring and recovering files, but on using either undo data, redo logs, or the new Flashback logs to restore lost objects. Here's a list of these non-file-based recovery techniques:

- *Flashback*: Flashback techniques enable you to recover dropped tables or restore a table or a database to a past point in time. Chapter 8 dealt with the Flashback Query, Flashback Versions Query, Flashback Transactions, and Flashback Table techniques, since that chapter discussed undo data, which is the basis for these techniques. In this chapter, as I've mentioned before, I'll cover the other two important Flashback techniques—Flashback Drop and Flashback Database.

- *LogMiner*: Oracle's LogMiner utility lets you mine your redo logs, both online and archived, to uncover and undo erroneous changes to your database. I discuss the LogMiner technique later in this chapter.

- *Data Pump*: You may also consider Oracle's Data Pump Export and Import tools as alternative tools for recovering lost objects. Chapter 14 discusses the Data Pump technology in detail.

Although the traditional file-based recovery techniques have been faithful standbys for a long time, you should consider using the alternative techniques wherever you can use them instead of the older techniques. For example, you can use the Flashback Database feature to revert your datafiles to their state at a past time, thus achieving the same end result as a file-based point-in-time recovery, but more quickly, since you don't have to restore backed-up datafiles, and you apply only a limited amount of redo compared to media recovery.

REDUCING YOUR VULNERABILITY

No aspect of an Oracle DBA's job is more dreadful, or even scary, than recovering databases. Recovery techniques aside, the best way to protect yourself is to reduce your vulnerability in the first place.

The most common errors on a day-to-day basis are hardware related. Disks or the controllers that manage them fail on a regular basis. The larger the database (and the larger the number of disk drives), the greater the likelihood that on any given day a service person is fixing or replacing a faulty part. Because it is well known that the entire disk system is a vulnerable point, you must provide redundancy in your database. Either a mirrored system or a RAID 5 disk system, or a combination of both, will give you the redundancy you need.

If your whole site goes down, you recover without a noticeable disruption if you have a distributed replication database or standby database in place. Otherwise, your uptime will be seriously compromised by a major problem at the production data center.

Keep a complete *redundancy set* somewhere on the production server. This redundancy set should consist of the latest database backups, the archived redo logs since that backup, and a multiplexed copy of the online redo log files and the control file. You can also include the other Oracle files, such as the init.ora or SPFILE, tnsnames.ora, and listener.ora.

The key to a successful recovery is adhering to the simple admonition "Be prepared" by having the right backups, which you know have passed a rigorous (and recent) testing process. In addition, your recovery concepts must be crystal clear in your head. Although you can pore over the books and manuals and probably (eventually) figure out the right sequence of actions for any DBA task, I don't recommend that course of action in the case of database recovery for a number of reasons. First, there's enormous psychological pressure to bring the database up as soon as possible. Second, your normal tranquil work circumstances are transformed rather suddenly and rudely, as your cubicle turns into an overcrowded war room of edgy and frustrated managers—not exactly a great time to be hitting the books. Third, you need to conserve as much time as you can by knowing the drill ahead of time for any number of potential problem situations. And fourth, database recovery is one of those areas where the decisions you make and the commands you execute aren't always retractable. You'll be traveling a one-way street during those times, and any errors you make in haste or ignorance tend to cost you dearly.

In this chapter, I explain several techniques for restoring and recovering databases. Many more techniques are enumerated in the Oracle manuals. It's sometimes bewildering to see the types of recovery situations you can encounter. However, if you have a good set of backups and you're running your database in archivelog mode, you can recover from the loss of any datafile or control file. The only situation in which you might have data loss is if your online redo log files are lost. Therefore, if you multiplex your online redo log files and also mirror them, there's very little chance you'll ever lose any data, even with a major problem involving your disk drives. But if all your drives are inaccessible, mirrored or otherwise, you do have a disaster on your hands, and you need to have an alternative database to switch over to, or at least you need to have an offsite disaster recovery system in place.

In the scenarios of database recovery that follow, I deal only with the recovery of a database running in archivelog mode. The reason is obvious: just about all critical databases are run in archivelog mode. If you understand the recovery procedures in the following sections, you can restore a noarchivelog mode database very easily.

Performing Recovery with RMAN

It's critical to have the right log files during a recovery, and RMAN, with its automatic maintenance of the necessary files, can be a big help. RMAN can help you perform all the user-managed types of recovery, and it provides several other benefits discussed in the following section. This chapter focuses on RMAN recovery techniques, although I do discuss user-managed recovery techniques briefly.

As was explained in Chapter 15, you can use RMAN to make either image copies that are similar to operating system file copies or proprietary backup sets. If you have RMAN image copies, you can directly use them to perform a recovery. However, if you have backup sets, you must first extract the backup files using the RESTORE command before you can perform a recovery.

■**Note** You can use the database backups instead of the actual database files to transport tablespaces. Thus, you don't need to make a running database's datafiles read-only in order to transport tablespaces.

RMAN's Advantages for Recovery

RMAN provides undeniable benefits when compared to the traditional user-managed recovery methods. Here's a summary of what RMAN offers during a database recovery:

- RMAN selects and applies the necessary data and log files during recovery.

- RMAN selects the most recent backup sets and image copies to recover with.

- RMAN can perform recovery at the data block level with the block media recovery feature (an option not otherwise available), which dramatically reduces recovery time.

- RMAN provides *restore optimization*, a great time-saving feature that enables you to bypass datafiles that are okay during the recovery process. RMAN can check the files that need to be restored and avoid recovering bad files.

- RMAN allows you to recover by applying incrementally updated backups, which drastically reduces recovery time.

- RMAN provides the DUPLICATE command, which lets you easily create clones of your production database.

RMAN restores datafiles from backups and applies the necessary archived redo logs to bring the database up to date. RMAN knows, by looking into its recovery catalog, which files it needs. You thus avoid the extremely labor-intensive and error-prone manual intervention in a typical user-managed recovery.

■**Note** The recovery catalog, as you learned in Chapter 15, provides so many benefits that you should plan on using it if RMAN is a part of your backup and recovery strategy.

One of the biggest advantages to using RMAN is that you can check whether your backups are valid before performing a recovery. The following section explains how to validate backups taken with RMAN.

Using VALIDATE BACKUP to Validate RMAN Backups

When you use RMAN to perform backup and recovery tasks, it's easy to verify that a certain backup not only exists, but also is usable. The LIST command shows information about backup sets, proxy copies, and image copies recorded in the RMAN repository. You can use the LIST BACKUP command in RMAN to view information about backup sets, backup pieces, and proxy copies. The LIST COPY command shows information about all datafile copies, archived redo logs, and image copies of archived redo logs. The LIST BACKUP SUMMARY command shows a summary of all RMAN backups.

The LIST commands show usable and unusable backups, backups that can and can't be restored, and expired and unavailable backups. You must use the RECOVERABLE option with the LIST command, to list only those backups that can be used for recovery.

The VALIDATE BACKUPSET command checks the usability of RMAN backups. You can get the backup set information by first using the LIST BACKUP command. You can then use the VALIDATE BACKUPSET command to check a backup set's usability.

Here's an example of the use of the VALIDATE BACKUPSET command:

```
RMAN> VALIDATE BACKUPSET 1;
allocated channel: ORA_DISK_1
channel ORA_DISK_1: sid=155 devtype=DISK
channel ORA_DISK_1: starting validation of datafile backupset
channel ORA_DISK_1: reading from backup piece . . .
channel ORA_DISK_1: restored backup piece 1
piece handle=/u01/app/oracle/10.2.0/db_3/flash_recovery_area/NICKO...
channel ORA_DISK_1: validation complete, elapsed time: 00:00:34
RMAN>
```

The "validation complete" message on the last line is confirmation that RMAN considers the specified backup set valid for a restore operation.

Using the RESTORE . . . VALIDATE Command

You can use the RESTORE . . . VALIDATE command to check whether a certain object of interest is among RMAN's backup sets. Here's an example:

```
RMAN> RESTORE TABLESPACE users VALIDATE;
Starting restore at 29-JUN-05
. . .
Finished restore at 29-JUN-05
RMAN>
```

The RESTORE TABLESPACE users VALIDATE command asks RMAN to confirm whether it can restore the users tablespace from its backup sets. The "Finished restore" message indicates only that the users tablespace can be recovered if necessary—RMAN doesn't perform an actual recovery of the tablespace.

Using the RESTORE . . . PREVIEW Command

In order to successfully restore a database or any part of it, RMAN should have access to all the necessary datafiles and archived redo log files. RMAN provides a handy PREVIEW option you can use with the RESTORE command, which lets you identify all the backup files necessary for a specific restore operation. You can then ensure that all the backups are available before issuing the RESTORE command.

Here are some examples of how you can use the RESTORE command with the PREVIEW option:

```
RMAN> RESTORE DATABASE PREVIEW;
RMAN> RESTORE TABLESPACE users PREVIEW;
RMAN> RESTORE DATAFILE 3 PREVIEW;
```

The RESTORE . . . PREVIEW command provides a detailed report of all backups that are necessary for that RESTORE command to succeed. If you want a summary report instead, use the PREVIEW SUMMARY option instead, as shown here:

```
RMAN> RESTORE DATABASE PREVIEW SUMMARY;
. . .
List of Backups
. . .
List of Archived Log Copies
. . .
Finished Restore at 29-JUN-05
RMAN>
```

Identifying Necessary Files for Recovery

You may need to perform a restore and recovery when you lose control files or datafiles. Your database will shut down immediately if even one of the multiplexed control copies becomes inaccessible. You then can take the appropriate action, as outlined in the "Recovering from the Loss of Control Files" section of this chapter.

To identify which datafiles need recovery, you can run the following SQL statement:

```
SQL> SELECT FILE#, ERROR, ONLINE_STATUS, CHANGE#, TIME
    FROM V$RECOVER_FILE;
```

You can join the V$DATAFILE and V$TABLESPACE views, as shown here, to find out more details about the files you may need to restore and recover:

```
SQL> SELECT r.FILE# AS df#, d.NAME AS df_name, t.NAME AS tbsp_name,
    d.STATUS, r.ERROR, r.CHANGE#, r.TIME
    FROM V$RECOVER_FILE r, V$DATAFILE d, V$TABLESPACE t
    WHERE t.TS# = d.TS#
    AND d.FILE# = r.FILE#;
```

RMAN Recovery Procedures

You really don't have to do a whole lot of work during recovery if you're using RMAN, since RMAN automates the entire recovery process. You use the following RMAN commands to recover the database (or a part of it):

- RESTORE: This command restores the entire database, a tablespace or a single datafile by itself, control files, archived redo logs, and server parameter files from RMAN backup sets or from image copies on disk. You don't have to restore archived redo logs, since RMAN automatically restores any necessary archived redo logs.

- RECOVER: This command will perform the actual media recovery by applying necessary archived logs or incremental backups.

Before you use the RESTORE and RECOVER commands, you must place the database in the appropriate state. For example, if you are recovering a single tablespace, you can keep the database open and take the tablespace offline, and once you are done recovering the datafile, you can bring the tablespace online. However, if you're recovering the entire database, you must first shut down the database and then start it up in the mount mode before starting the restore and recovery process. Then, after the RECOVER command executes without errors, you must open the database.

Recovering with Incrementally Updated Backups

There is overhead involved in taking full image copies of the database every night. In addition, it is time consuming to perform media recoveries using archive logs. To reduce this overhead and recovery time, you can use RMAN to roll forward the image copy of a datafile to a point in time simply by applying incremental backups to image copies. For example, a daily incremental backup can be applied to a base level 0 backup, which is taken once a week, say, on a Sunday. From Monday on, a daily incremental backup is applied to this Sunday level 0 backup. On any given day during the week, after the incremental backup for that day is merged with the level 0 backup, you'll end up with an up-to-date backup as of that day.

When you use incremental backups for recovery, you update the image copies with changes up to the system change number (SCN) at which you took the last incremental backup. After you apply the incremental backups, you must apply all archive logs (since the last incremental backup) as usual, to bring the datafiles up to date. If RMAN has a choice between using an archived log or an incremental backup to perform recovery, it chooses an incremental backup.

Chapter 15 explains the RMAN incremental backup feature in detail.

Monitoring RMAN Jobs

You can monitor the status of both an RMAN backup as well as a recovery job by using the V$RMAN_STATUS view. This view shows all finished and ongoing RMAN jobs. Here's a simple example:

```
SQL> SELECT operation, status from V$RMAN_STATUS;

OPERATION          STATUS
----------------   ---------
REPORT             COMPLETED
BACKUP             COMPLETED
LIST               COMPLETED
RESTORE PREVIEW    COMPLETED
. . .
SQL>
```

Another highly useful data dictionary view for monitoring RMAN jobs is the in-memory V$RMAN_OUTPUT view, which displays all the messages being put out by RMAN during a backup or recovery job.

■**Tip** You can use the Database Control interface to perform most of RMAN's backup and recovery tasks, including point-in-time and Flashback tasks. The RMAN command-line client offers you more flexibility in complex recovery situations, but the Database Control interface is far simpler to use in most situations.

User-Managed Recovery Procedures

Just as you can manage your own backups, user-managed techniques can be used to restore and recover a database. It's my firm belief that RMAN is vastly superior to the old-fashioned manual method, but it's a good idea to be familiar with both methods. When you use the user-managed recovery method, you can learn a lot about the recovery process by watching the different steps that Oracle goes through.

You should use the following general procedure during the user-managed recovery of databases running in the archivelog mode. Specific situations demand different recovery strategies, but the essential techniques are the same, no matter what type of file (control file, system tablespace file, datafile, and so forth) you are recovering.

1. Decide whether you're going to let users access your database during recovery. This decision depends on the extent of the media damage—if most of the files are affected, you need to start up the database in mount mode. If only a single datafile is affected, you can merely take the tablespace to which the datafile belongs offline and leave the database itself open.

2. Restore the affected datafiles to their original location if possible or to an alternative location after renaming them. You must also restore any necessary archived redo log files. The V$RECOVERY_LOG and the V$ARCHIVED_LOG views list the names of archive log files. The V$RECOVERY_LOG view lists only those archived redo log files that the database needs to perform media recovery. If you have enough free space, restore the necessary archived redo log files to the location specified by the LOG_ARCHIVE_DEST_1 initialization parameter. The database will automatically locate the correct log during media recovery.

3. Use the RECOVER DATABASE, RECOVER TABLESPACE, or RECOVER DATAFILE command, depending on the situation, to recover the entire database, a tablespace, or a datafile, respectively.

4. If any archive logs are needed to recover the database, tablespace, or datafiles, Oracle will ask you to supply the archived redo logs, and you can recover up until the point of failure for a complete recovery, or choose to recover to a point in time in the past, if you prefer an incomplete recovery.

5. If you did not open the database in step 1, open it now, using the ALTER DATABASE OPEN command.

If you don't want to recover to the point of failure—for instance, due to previous user errors or if some of the necessary archived redo logs are missing—you can perform an incomplete recovery.

Typical Media Recovery Scenarios

The steps you take during a database recovery depend on the extent of the recovery and which of the files (datafiles, control files, online and archived redo logs) are missing due to a media problem. The following sections take you through several common recovery scenarios using RMAN and user-managed recoveries.

Complete Recovery of a Whole Database

You may have to perform a complete recovery of the whole database when you lose several or all of your datafiles. Before you recover the database, you must restore the backup files. Then you need to apply all the available archived redo logs to the database. In the following sections, you'll learn how to do this with RMAN and with user-managed techniques.

Using RMAN for Whole Database Recovery

Assume that all the datafiles in your database are inaccessible due to a media malfunction. If you have all your archived redo logs, you can restore your backups and do a complete recovery without any loss of data.

To recover an entire database, first start the database but leave it in the mount position, as shown in Listing 16-1. Thus, the database is not open to users while you're restoring files and recovering the database. (You can open the database if you are performing a tablespace recovery.)

Listing 16-1. *Using RMAN to Start the Database*

```
C:\> RMAN TARGET / CATALOG RMAN/RMAN1@NICK
Recovery Manager: Release 11.1.0.6.0 - Production on Mon Mar 31 11:25:29 2008
Copyright (c) 1982, 2007, Oracle.  All rights reserved.
connected to target database (not started)
connected to recovery catalog database

RMAN> startup mount
Oracle instance started
database mounted
. . .
RMAN>
```

Next, you need to restore the datafiles that are lost. Because this is the recovery of an entire database, you ask RMAN to restore all the datafiles from backup sets. The command is very simple: RESTORE DATABASE. RMAN knows where the backed-up files are on disk, and it copies them to their original locations. By default, RMAN will direct the server session to restore backups to the default location, overwriting any previous files that are already there. If you wish, you can have RMAN copy files to new locations by using the SET NEWNAME command, as shown here:

```
RMAN> SET NEWNAME FOR DATAFILE '?/oradata/trgt/tools01.dbf' TO '/tmp/tools01.dbf';
RMAN> RESTORE DATAFILE '?/oradata/trgt/tools01.dbf';
```

Listing 16-2 shows the output of the RESTORE DATABASE command.

Listing 16-2. *The RMAN RESTORE DATABASE Command*

```
RMAN> RESTORE DATABASE;

Starting restore at 29-MAR-08
Using channel ORA_DISK_1
channel ORA_DISK_1: sid=50 devtype=DISK
channel ORA_DISK_1: starting datafile backupset restore
channel ORA_DISK_1: specifying datafile(s) to restore from backup set
restoring datafile 00001 to C:\ORACLE\PRODUCT\10.1.0\ORADATA\NICK\SYSTEM01.DBF
. . .
channel ORA_DISK_1: restore complete
Finished restore at 29-MAR-08
RMAN>
```

Once RMAN restores all the datafiles, you need to synchronize them using the archived redo logs. The RECOVER DATABASE command applies the archived logs to the restored files and synchronizes the SCNs for all the datafiles and the control file. Listing 16-3 shows the output of the RECOVER DATABASE command.

Listing 16-3. *The RMAN RECOVER DATABASE Command*

```
RMAN> RECOVER DATABASE;

Starting recover at 29-MAR-08
using channel ORA_DISK_1
starting media recovery
archive log thread 1 sequence 12 is already on disk as file
. . .
media recovery complete
Finished recover at 29-MAR-08
RMAN>
```

■**Tip** When you use RMAN, you don't have to restore the archived redo logs—RMAN automatically applies archived redo logs as necessary during the recovery process.

Finally, you need to bring the database online so users can access it once again:

```
RMAN> ALTER DATABASE OPEN;
Database opened;
RMAN>
```

Note that you can simplify the preceding steps for recovering the whole database by using the following script:

```
RMAN> RUN {
       shutdown immediate;
       startup mount;
       restore database;
       recover database;
       alter database open;
       }
RMAN>
```

As you can see, RMAN makes the recovery of a database a breeze. You don't have to specify the location of any of the files that you need to restore. RMAN knows where to get the files from by looking in the recovery catalog (or the control file).

Performing a Hot Restore with RMAN

In the previous example, I showed how you first had to restore the datafiles before recovering the database. By default, when you use the RESTORE command, RMAN restores a datafile from an image backup or from a backup set if an image copy isn't available. Either way, you have to wait for RMAN to copy the file to its original location.

However, you don't have to copy the file to the original location. When you need to perform a fast recovery, you can save the time it takes to restore the datafiles by using the image copies directly. You use the special SWITCH command to let Oracle know that you are actually using the image copy for the lost datafile. You can thus skip the restore step and directly head to the recovery stage.

The SWITCH command makes the control file point to the copy of the datafile as the current datafile. This is the same as using the SQL statement ALTER DATABASE RENAME FILE. Note that the filename at the operating system level remains unchanged.

Here's how you use the SWITCH command:

```
RMAN> SWITCH DATABASE TO COPY;
```

The preceding command will perform a hot restore of your database.

■**Tip** Use the SWITCH DATABASE rather than the RESTORE DATABASE command if your goal is to restore as quickly as possible.

User-Managed Whole Database Recovery

The user-managed complete database recovery process starts with the restoration of all lost or damaged datafiles from the backup. You then recover the database by using the RECOVER DATABASE command. Oracle will ask for the necessary archived log files and perform the recovery by applying them. It's easier to let Oracle apply the relevant archived log file than to attempt to do it yourself manually.

You can automate the application of the archived redo log files in two ways. Before you use the RECOVER DATABASE command, you can use the SET AUTORECOVERY ON command. The other way is to specify the AUTOMATIC keyword in the RECOVER command, as in RECOVER DATABASE AUTOMATIC.

The following is a summary of steps required for a complete recovery of your database:

1. Restore the datafiles from backup.

2. Start up the database in the mount mode:

   ```
   SQL> STARTUP MOUNT;
   ```

3. Use the RECOVER DATABASE command to start recovering the database. The AUTOMATIC keyword tells Oracle to automate the application of the archived redo logs. In this example, I'm assuming that you're placing the archived redo logs in the default location specified in the init.ora file or SPFILE.

```
SQL> RECOVER AUTOMATIC DATABASE;
```

If you've placed them in a different location, you'll have to supply the location to Oracle by using the LOGSOURCE parameter of the SET statement, or the RECOVER FROM parameter of the ALTER DATABASE statement. Here are examples of each method of specifying an alternative location for the archived redo log files:

```
SQL> SET LOGSOURCE /new_directory;
SQL> ALTER DATABASE RECOVER FROM '/new_directory';
```

4. Open the database once you're sure Oracle has completed media recovery:

```
Media recovery complete.
SQL> ALTER DATABASE OPEN;
```

Recovering a Tablespace

You need to perform a tablespace recovery when you lose one or more datafiles that belong to the tablespace and you don't have a mirrored copy of the files. The recovery may be open or closed, and it may be a full recovery or a point-in-time recovery, as explained at the beginning of this chapter. You can recover using either RMAN or user-managed techniques.

Using RMAN to Recover a Tablespace

Sometimes you may have to recover a tablespace or a set of tablespaces. You can use the RESTORE and RECOVER commands at the tablespace level for these situations. Since only a part of the database is affected, you don't have to shut down the database—you can leave it open instead. If you wish, you can shut down the database in the mount mode, if several tablespaces or a single very large tablespace is affected.

Here are the recovery steps:

1. Take the tablespace you're going to recover offline. The rest of the database will be functioning normally after you do this:

```
RMAN> ALTER TABLESPACE sysaux OFFLINE;
```

2. Restore the tablespace using the RESTORE TABLESPACE command, as follows:

```
RMAN> RESTORE TABLESPACE sysaux;

Starting restore at 29-MAR-08
using channel ORA_DISK_1
. . .
channel ORA_DISK_1: restore complete
Finished restore at 29-MAR-08
RMAN>
```

3. Recover the tablespace, as follows:

```
RMAN> RECOVER TABLESPACE sysaux;

Starting recover at 29-MAR-08
using channel ORA_DISK_1
starting media recovery
archive log thread 1 sequence 12 is already on disk as file
. . .
media recovery complete
Finished recover at 29-MAR-08
RMAN>
```

4. Finally, bring the recovered tablespace online, as follows:

```
RMAN> ALTER TABLESPACE sysaux ONLINE;
```

User-Managed Recovery of a Tablespace

Say your database is online, and one or more files belonging to it are damaged. If the database writer can't write to the damaged files, Oracle will take the files offline automatically. Otherwise, you must first take the tablespace offline. Then you need to restore the damaged datafiles and perform a recovery.

Here's a summary of the recovery process:

1. Take the affected tablespace offline:

```
SQL> ALTER TABLESPACE sales01 OFFLINE IMMEDIATE;
```

2. Restore the damaged files:

```
SQL> HOST cp /u01/app/oracle/backup/shan/sales_01.dbf
              /u01/app/oracle/oradata/shan/sales_01.dbf
```

3. Recover the offline tablespace:

```
SQL> RECOVER TABLESPACE sales01;
```

4. Bring the tablespace you just recovered online:

```
SQL> ALTER TABLESPACE sales01 ONLINE;
```

Recovering a Datafile

The procedures for recovering from the loss of a datafile depend on the type of tablespace the datafile belongs to. You can use the dynamic performance view V$RECOVER_FILE to determine the files you need to recover.

Let's see what happens when your instance encounters media errors, assuming you are operating in the archivelog mode. If your instance encounters a read error and can't read a datafile, you'll see an operating system error stating this fact, but the database will continue to operate. When the database tries writing the file header during a checkpoint, a write error will be issued. If the instance encounters a write error and can't write to a System or undo tablespace datafile, the instance will immediately shut down.

If the write error pertains to any other tablespace, the database will take that datafile offline—the other datafiles in the tablespace containing this datafile will remain online. Your job then is to restore and recover the affected datafile.

The following discussion deals with the loss of a datafile from a non-System tablespace.

Using RMAN to Recover a Datafile

The recovery process using RMAN is much simpler than the user-managed recovery technique. First of all, you don't need to tell RMAN where to get the backup file from—it identifies the correct file from its recovery catalog. All you have to do is tell RMAN to restore and recover the necessary datafile.

RMAN restores the datafile(s) first and then performs the necessary recovery on the datafile(s) using the archived redo logs. RMAN knows what archived logs to apply to the restored datafile(s).

Let's use a RUN block to perform our datafile recovery, as shown in Listing 16-4. Recovering a datafile is a two-step process: to recover a datafile, you must first restore it from the RMAN backup. The RESTORE DATAFILE command asks RMAN to restore the necessary datafile. The RECOVER DATAFILE command that follows tells RMAN to perform recovery on the restored datafile.

Listing 16-4. *Recovering a Datafile Using RMAN*

```
RMAN> RUN {
2> restore datafile 'C:\ORACLE\PRODUCT\10.1.0\ORADATA\NICK\SYSAUX01.DBF';
3> recover datafile 'C:\ORACLE\PRODUCT\10.1.0\ORADATA\NICK\SYSAUX01.DBF';
4> }

starting full resync of recovery catalog
full resync complete
Starting restore at 12-JUL-08
using channel ORA_DISK_1
channel ORA_DISK_1: restore complete
Finished restore at 12-JUL-08
Starting recover at 12-JUL-08
using channel ORA_DISK_1
starting media recovery
. . .
media recovery complete
Finished recover at 12-JUL-08
starting full resync of recovery catalog
full resync complete
RMAN>
```

Note that behind the scenes, RMAN automatically applies any necessary archive logs without prompting from you during the recovery step.

User-Managed Recovery of a Datafile

If the database instance crashes or can't be started without an error, as the result of a missing or damaged datafile, the identity of the datafile is obvious. However, you can lose a datafile and continue to have an open database. You can use the following statement to find out which files may need a recovery:

```
SQL> SELECT file#, status, error, recover, tablespace_name, name
    FROM V$DATAFILE_HEADER
    WHERE RECOVER = 'YES' OR (RECOVER IS NULL AND ERROR IS NOT NULL);
```

The various possibilities that can be shown in the output of the preceding query can be interpreted as follows:

- If the query results in "no rows selected," then none of the datafiles need recovery.
- If the ERROR column shows NULL, and the RECOVER column says YES, you can recover without having to restore a copy of the datafile.

- If the ERROR column is not NULL, there may be a media problem. Similarly, if the RECOVER column doesn't show the value NO, there may be a problem with the disk.

- In all the previous cases, first check whether the problem is temporary and can be fixed without replacing the media. If the problem isn't temporary, you'll have to perform media recovery.

- A NULL value in the RECOVER column indicates a hardware error.

You can also use the following query of the V$RECOVER_FILE view to find out the file number, status, and other error information for datafiles:

```
SQL> SELECT file#, error, online_status, change#, time
       FROM V$RECOVER_FILE;
```

To recover from the loss of a datafile while the database is open, you must first take the affected tablespace offline. You must then restore the datafile from a backup and recover the tablespace. Here's a summary of the commands you need to use:

```
SQL> ALTER TABLESPACE sales01 OFFLINE IMMEDIATE;

SQL> HOST cp /test01/app/oracle/backup/sales01.dbf
       /test01/app/oracle/oradata/finance/sales01.dbf;

SQL> RECOVER TABLESPACE sales01;

SQL> ALTER TABLESPACE sales01 ONLINE;
```

The ALTER TABLESPACE OFFLINE and ONLINE commands ensure that users don't access the tablespace during the recovery process.

Incomplete Recovery

The previous examples dealt with complete-recovery scenarios. The database or the tablespace, as the case may be, are fully recovered, and there's no loss of data. You use incomplete recovery in situations where you want to recover to a previous point in time, perhaps because you made a data entry error or because an online redo log was lost. After recovery, you end up with a database that's not current to the latest point in time, but it is consistent. In the following sections, you'll see how to perform incomplete recovery using RMAN and user-managed recovery procedures.

Using RMAN for Incomplete Recovery

You can perform three types of incomplete recovery using RMAN, provided you are running your database in the archivelog mode. You can specify a time, SCN, or log sequence number with the SET UNTIL command before using the RESTORE and RECOVER commands. Your choice of recovery type depends on the problem that prompts the incomplete recovery.

- *Time-based recovery*: In this type of recovery, RMAN restores and recovers all files in the database up to a point in time. This is helpful if you know that a problem, such as the accidental dropping of a table, occurred at a certain point in time. You use the SET UNTIL command to perform a time-based recovery, as in this example:

  ```
  SET UNTIL TIME 'Mar 21 2005 06:00:00'
  ```

- *Change-based SCN*: You can perform the recovery up to a specific SCN if you know it. You use the keywords SET UNTIL SCN to specify that files up to that SCN be used. Here is an example:

  ```
  SET UNTIL SCN 1000
  ```

- *Log sequence–based recovery*: You can recover until a particular log sequence number. RMAN selects the files to recover up to but not including the specified sequence number. You use the SET UNTIL SEQUENCE command for a log sequence–based recovery:

```
SET UNTIL SEQUENCE 9923
```

Let's look at an example of a time-based recovery within the current incarnation of the database. Assume that table test was accidentally dropped right before 6 p.m. Listing 16-5 shows the time-based recovery process.

Listing 16-5. *A Time-Based Incomplete Recovery Using RMAN*

```
RMAN> STARTUP MOUNT
RMAN> RUN
2> {set until time 'Jun 30 2008 18:00:00';
3> restore database;
4> recover database;
5> }
executing command: SET until clause
restoring datafile 00024 to /test02/app/oracle/oradata/temp_01.dbf
channel ORA_DISK_1: restored backup piece 1
piece handle=/test01/app/oracle/oradata/backup
/2ddp387s_1_1 tag=null params=NULL
channel ORA_DISK_1: restore complete
Finished restore at 30-JUN-08
Starting recover at 30-JUN-08
using channel ORA_DISK_1
starting media recovery
media recovery complete
Finished recover at 30-JUN-08
RMAN> ALTER DATABASE OPEN RESETLOGS;
Database opened.
RMAN>
```

■ **Note** For a point-in-time recovery to succeed, you must have backups of all datafiles from before the target point in time (or SCN). You must also have all archived redo logs for the period between the SCN of the backups and the target SCN.

In Listing 16-5, the database is first mounted but not opened. RMAN is asked to restore the database (meaning that it is asked to get the backed-up datafiles that are necessary for this restore). It then is asked to recover the database. RMAN knows which archived redo logs are needed based on the information about backups stored in its recovery catalog. RMAN applies the archived redo logs and finishes the recovery process. You can then open the database with the ALTER DATABASE OPEN RESETLOGS command. This is a point-in-time recovery, and you need to make sure that the database doesn't apply the old redo logs by mistake. You ensure this by resetting or reinitializing the redo log files.

Here's the entire script for performing a tablespace PITR using RMAN:

```
RMAN> RUN {
Allocate channel s1 type 'sbt_tape';
Allocate channel s2 type 'sbt_tape';
Set until time '28-JUL-08 06:00:00';
Restore database;
```

```
Recover database;
Sql "alter database open reset logs";
Release channel s1;
Release channel s2;
}
```

Once you query the database and verify that you have recovered it to the previous point in time, you can open the database using the following command, which will undo all changes after the point in time you've recovered to:

```
RMAN> ALTER DATABASE OPEN RESETLOGS;
```

The previous command will archive all online redo logs, reset the log sequence numbers, and give the online redo logs a new time stamp and SCN. You thus eliminate the possibility of corrupting your datafiles by mistakenly applying older redo logs.

If you want to use a specific log sequence number instead of a point in time, you modify the script by replacing the SET UNTIL TIME line with the following:

```
RMAN> SET UNTIL SEQUENCE 1234;
```

WHAT IS RESETLOGS?

Note that after you perform any kind of incomplete recovery, the logs are always reset. Essentially, the RESETLOGS option reinitializes the redo log files, erasing all the redo information they currently have, and resets the log sequence number to 1. To apply any archived redo logs to a datafile, the SCNs and time stamps in the database files have to match the SCNs and time stamps in the headers of the archived redo log files, and when you perform a RESETLOGS operation, the datafiles are stamped with new SCN and time stamp information, making it impossible for the older archived redo logs to be applied to them by mistake.

The RESETLOGS option is used under these circumstances:

- When you use a backup control file to recover
- When you perform an incomplete recovery, rather than a complete recovery
- When you recover using a control file created with the RESETLOGS option

If you were to do the incomplete recovery using an SCN, the SET UNTIL command would be modified as SET UNTIL SCN *nnnn*. If you were to use an archived log sequence number, the command would be SET UNTIL LOGSEQ=*nnnn* THREAD=*nnnn*, where LOGSEQ is the log you want to recover to.

Here's a short script that shows how to perform incomplete recovery using RMAN, where you specify an SCN:

```
RMAN> RUN
{
 ALLOCATE CHANNEL ch1 TYPE sbt;
 RESTORE DATABASE;
 RECOVER DATABASE UNTIL SCN 1000;  # recovers through SCN 999
 ALTER DATABASE OPEN RESETLOGS;
}
```

Recovery Through Current and Ancestor Database Incarnations

Anytime you use the OPEN RESETLOGS command, the incarnation of the database changes and a new incarnation begins. The previous incarnation is termed an *ancestor incarnation*, and the latest is the *current incarnation.* RMAN can recover through multiple incarnations of a database. For example, if you have backups from an older incarnation of the database, you can use them to recover your current database incarnation, but you must specify that the backups are coming from a previous incarnation.

The Simplified Recovery Through Resetlogs feature lets you use archived redo logs from an earlier incarnation of the database. The default format for the LOG_ARCHIVE_FORMAT initialization parameter now includes a %r component, which stands for the RESETLOGS identifier. For example, on a UNIX/Linux system, your archived redo logs will use the format log%t_%s_%r.arc. The variable *t* stands for the thread number, and the variable *s* is the log sequence number. The V$LOG_HISTORY view has two columns, RESETLOGS_CHANGE# and RESETLOGS_TIME, that indicate the database incarnation of the archived redo logs.

The point-in-time recovery example in the previous section dealt with recovery using the current incarnation of the database. Let's look at incomplete database recovery using a parent incarnation of the database. Suppose you want to specify an SCN that isn't in the current incarnation, but is in an ancestor incarnation. There are two requirements for this type of a point-in-time recovery:

- You must reset the current incarnation of the database back to the incarnation to which your target SCN belongs.

- You must use the control file from the older incarnation that contains the target SCN.

To perform point-in-time recovery to the older incarnation, use the following steps:

1. Find out the incarnation key for the incarnation that was current at the time you want to recover your database to. You can find it in the incarnation key column of the output of RMAN's LIST INCARNATION command. Let's say our incarnation key value for this example is 2.

2. Start the database in the following way:

   ```
   RMAN> STARTUP FORCE NOMOUNT;
   ```

3. Reset the current incarnation to the incarnation that was current at the point in time that you want to recover to:

   ```
   RMAN> RESET DATABASE TO INCARNATION 2;
   ```

4. Restore the old control file from a backup and mount the database with the following commands:

   ```
   RMAN> RESTORE CONTROLFILE FROM AUTOBACKUP;
   RMAN> ALTER DATABASE MOUNT;
   ```

5. Restore and recover the database until the point in time or the SCN:

   ```
   RMAN> RESTORE DATABASE;
   RMAN> RECOVER DATABASE UNTIL SCN 1000;
   ```

6. Open the database after resetting the online log files:

   ```
   RMAN> ALTER DATABASE OPEN RESETLOGS;
   ```

Oracle calls the preceding type of recovery Simplified Recovery Through Resetlogs. This feature comes in handy when you perform a point-in-time recovery or a recovery using a backup control file and use the RESETLOGS option to open the database. In these cases, you can still use the backup from before the RESETLOGS operation.

User-Managed Incomplete Recovery

You have looked at how to use RMAN for incomplete recovery; let's look now at how to do it manually. Assume that your database is open and you have decided that you have to perform an incomplete recovery—you want to take the database back to a previous point. All changes since then are gone, whether you want it that way (because of user error, for example) or you're forced to do so (such as when you don't have all the archived redo logs needed for up-to-date recovery). Here's a brief summary of the steps you must take to perform an incomplete recovery:

1. Shut down the database immediately:

   ```
   SQL> SHUTDOWN ABORT;
   ```

2. Restore all the datafiles and make sure all of them are online.

3. Choose one of the following three commands to recover the datafiles, depending upon your situation:

   - *Cancel-based recovery*: Here, you let Oracle apply the archived redo logs until you cancel the recovery process. You could use this method, for example, when there is a gap in your archived redo logs. Here is the command you would use:

     ```
     SQL> RECOVER DATABASE UNTIL CANCEL;
     ```

   - *Time-based recovery*: You have to specify the point in time to which you want the database to be recovered. Here is an example:

     ```
     SQL> RECOVER DATABASE UNTIL TIME '2005-06-30:12:00:00';
     ```

     Or, if you're using a backed-up control file, you should use the following command instead of the preceding one:

     ```
     SQL>  RECOVER DATABASE UNTIL TIME
             '2005-06-30:12:00:00' USING BACKUP CONTROLFILE;
     ```

   - *Change-based recovery*: In the change-based method, you need to find out what SCN you want to go back to, and specify it in the command:

     ```
     SQL> RECOVER DATABASE UNTIL CHANGE 27845;
     ```

4. No matter which of the three methods you use to perform your recovery, you must issue the following command when the recovery is complete, because this is an incomplete recovery:

   ```
   SQL> ALTER DATABASE OPEN RESETLOGS;
   ```

Recovering from the Loss of Control Files

Your instance will shut down immediately if one or all of the control files are inaccessible. Here are two possible scenarios:

- If even a single copy of the duplexed control file is lost, your instance will crash immediately. You then simply copy a duplexed control file to the same location as the lost or damaged control file. If you can't place it in the same location, update your parameter file (use the CONTROL_FILES parameter) to indicate the new location. If you can't replace the lost control file for some reason, just edit the initialization parameter file so it doesn't refer to the lost control file any longer. You can successfully start your instance now.

- If you've lost all your control files, you must restore a backup control file or create a new one. If you restore the control file from backup, you must perform media recovery of the whole database and then perform an OPEN RESETLOGS operation.

The following sections show how to recover from a situation where all your control files are lost. You'll have to recover using a backed-up control file.

Using RMAN to Recover from Control-File Loss

In this section, we'll simulate a control-file loss by deleting both the control files. Make sure you have a backup of the database, including the control files, before you do this.

Once you have deleted your control files, follow these steps:

1. Shut down the database and try to start it up. The instance will start and try to mount the database, but when it doesn't find the control files, the database fails to mount:

```
RMAN> SHUTDOWN IMMEDIATE;
database closed
database dismounted
Oracle instance shut down
RMAN>
RMAN> STARTUP
Oracle instance started
RMAN-00571:
RMAN-00569: ERROR MESSAGE STACK FOLLOWS
RMAN-00571:
RMAN-03002: failure of startup command at 07/11/2008 17:18:05
ORA-00205: error in identifying controlfile, check alert log for more info
RMAN>
```

You can avoid the preceding error messages by using the alternative command STARTUP NOMOUNT:

```
RMAN> SHUTDOWN IMMEDIATE;
database closed
database dismounted
Oracle instance shut down
RMAN>
RMAN> STARTUP NOMOUNT;
connected to target database (not started)
Oracle instance started
. . .
RMAN>
```

2. Issue the RESTORE CONTROLFILE command so RMAN can copy the control file backups to their default locations specified in the init.ora file:

```
RMAN> RESTORE CONTROLFILE FROM AUTOBACKUP;
Starting restore at 14-JUL-08
allocated channel: ORA_DISK_1
. . .
output filename=C:\ORACLE\PRODUCT\10.1.0\ORADATA\NICK\CONTROL03.CTL
Finished restore at 14-JUL-08
RMAN>
```

3. After the restore is over, mount the database:

```
RMAN> ALTER DATABASE MOUNT;
database mounted
RMAN>
```

4. Recover the database as shown in Listing 16-6.

Listing 16-6. *Using RMAN to Recover from the Loss of Control Files*

```
RMAN> RECOVER DATABASE;
Starting recover at 14-JUL-08
Starting implicit crosscheck backup at 14-JUL-08
Crosschecked 5 objects
Finished implicit crosscheck backup at 14-JUL-08
Starting implicit crosscheck copy at 14-JUL-08
Finished implicit crosscheck copy at 14-JUL-08
searching for all files in the recovery area
cataloging files...
cataloging done
starting media recovery
media recovery complete
Finished recover at 14-JUL-08
RMAN>
```

Because RMAN restores the control files from its backups, you have to open the database with the RESETLOGS option:

```
RMAN> ALTER DATABASE OPEN RESETLOGS;
database opened
new incarnation of database registered in recovery catalog
starting full resync of recovery catalog
full resync complete
RMAN>
```

User-Managed Recovery from Control-File Loss

If you've lost all your control files, you can create a brand-new control file by using the CREATE CONTROLFILE command. Listing 16-7 shows a typical control file creation statement derived using the output of the ALTER DATABASE BACKUP CONTROLFILE TO TRACE statement. Here's the SQL statement that will get you the output necessary to run the CREATE CONTROLFILE statement later on:

```
SQL> ALTER DATABASE BACKUP CONTROLFILE TO TRACE;
Database altered.
SQL>
```

■**Tip** Even if you don't have a control file backup, you can easily create a new control file provided you have a complete list of all the datafiles and the redo log files that are part of the database.

After you issue the ALTER DATABASE BACKUP CONTROLFILE TO TRACE statement, you can get a trace file as shown in Listing 16-7 from your trace directory, usually the udump directory.

Listing 16-7. *Recovering Lost Control Files with User-Managed Techniques*

```
Dump file c:\oracle\product\10.1.0\admin\NICK\udump\NICK_ora_2452.trc
Sun Jul 10 16:35:47 2008
ORACLE Version 11.1.0.0.0 - Production vsnsta=0
The following commands will create a new control file and use it
-- to open the database.
-- Data used by Recovery Manager will be lost.
-- Additional logs may be required for media recovery of offline
-- Use this only if the current versions of all online logs are
-- available.
STARTUP NOMOUNT
CREATE CONTROLFILE REUSE DATABASE "NICK" NORESETLOGS  ARCHIVELOG
    MAXLOGFILES 5
    MAXLOGMEMBERS 2
    MAXDATAFILES 200
    MAXINSTANCES 1
    MAXLOGHISTORY 454
LOGFILE
  GROUP 1 'C:\ORACLE\PROD\11.1.0\ORADATA\NICK\REDO01.LOG' SIZE 100M,
  GROUP 2 'C:\ORACLE\PROD\11.1.0\ORADATA\NICK\REDO02.LOG' SIZE 100M
-- STANDBY LOGFILE
DATAFILE
  'C:\ORACLE\PRODUCT\11.1.0\ORADATA\NICK\SYSTEM01.DBF',
  'C:\ORACLE\PRODUCT\11.1.0\ORADATA\NICK\UNDOTBS01.DBF',
  'C:\ORACLE\PRODUCT\11.1.0\ORADATA\NICK\SYSAUX01.DBF'
CHARACTER SET US7ASCII;
-- Commands to re-create incarnation table
-- Below log names MUST be changed to existing filenames on
-- disk. Any one log file from each branch can be used to
-- re-create incarnation records.
-- ALTER DATABASE REGISTER LOGFILE 'C:\ORACLE\PRODUCT\11.1.0\
FLASH_RECOVERY_AREA\NICK\ARCHIVELOG\
2008_07_10\O1_MF_1_1_%U_.ARC';
-- ALTER DATABASE REGISTER LOGFILE 'C:\ORACLE\PRODUCT\11.1.0\
FLASH_RECOVERY_AREA\NICK\ARCHIVELOG\
2008_07_10\O1_MF_1_1_%U_.ARC';
-- Recovery is required if any of the datafiles are restored backups,
-- or if the last shutdown was not normal or immediate.
RECOVER DATABASE
-- All logs need archiving and a log switch is needed.
ALTER SYSTEM ARCHIVE LOG ALL;
-- Database can now be opened normally.
ALTER DATABASE OPEN;
-- No tempfile entries found to add.
```

As you can see, you can make up your own CREATE CONTROLFILE statement, with the catch being that you need to have an accurate record of all the component files of your database. Let's take a closer look at the control file creation script.

The script first starts up the database in nomount mode. Obviously, if you don't have the control files, you can't mount the database. The next line, which includes the CREATE CONTROLFILE statement, is the most critical one in the script. If you have all your redo log files intact, you have to specify the NORESETLOGS option so that Oracle can reuse the redo logs. Alternatively, if your redo logs are lost or damaged, you need to specify RESETLOGS in the CREATE CONTROLFILE statement. Oracle will create new redo files in this case, or if they exist, Oracle will reinitialize them, essentially creating a new set of redo log files. The REUSE parameter asks Oracle to overwrite any of the old control files if they exist in their default locations.

Listing 16-8 shows how to use the CREATE CONTROLFILE statement in Listing 16-7.

Listing 16-8. *Creating New Control Files*

```
SQL> STARTUP NOMOUNT
ORACLE instance started.
Total System Global Area  118255568 bytes
Fixed Size                   282576 bytes
Variable Size              83886080 bytes
Database Buffers           33554432 bytes
Redo Buffers                 532480 bytes
SQL>
SQL> CREATE CONTROLFILE REUSE DATABASE "NICK" NORESETLOGS ARCHIVELOG
. . .
Control file created.
SQL>
SQL> RECOVER DATABASE
ORA-00283: recovery session canceled due to errors
ORA-00264: no recovery required
SQL> ALTER SYSTEM ARCHIVE LOG ALL;
System altered.
SQL> ALTER DATABASE OPEN;
Database altered.
SQL>
```

Recovering a Datafile Without a Backup

Suppose you add a new datafile and users consequently create some objects in it. Before you back up your database over the weekend, the new file is damaged and you need to recover the data. The archived redo logs since the last backup will contain the information regarding the lost file and will enable you to recover the data. The following sections illustrate the procedures involved.

Using RMAN to Recover a File Without a Backup

Suppose you first notice the damaged file when you access the lost or damaged file and get the following error:

```
SQL> CREATE TABLE x (name varchar2 (30));
create table x (name varchar2 (30))
*
ERROR at line 1:
ORA-01116: error in opening database file 5
ORA-01110: data file 5: '/test02/app/oracle/oradata/finance1/test01.dbf'
```

Here are the steps you would follow to fix the problem:

1. Take the affected datafile offline:

```
RMAN> SQL "alter database datafile
   2> ''/test01/app/oracle/oradata/remorse/sales_01.dbf'' offline";
       sql statement: alter database datafile
       ''/test01/app/oracle/oradata/remorse/sales_01.dbf'' offline
RMAN>
```

2. Create a new datafile with the same name as the damaged offline datafile:

```
RMAN> sql "alter database create datafile
    2> ''/test02/app/oracle/oradata/remorse/sales01.dbf'' ";
       sql statement: alter database create datafile
      ''/test02/app/oracle/oradata/remorse/sales01.dbf"
RMAN>
```

3. Recover the new datafile. RMAN will retrieve data from the archived redo logs, so the new datafile is identical to the one that was lost:

```
RMAN> RECOVER DATAFILE '/test01/app/oracle/oradata/remorse/sales_01.dbf';
Starting recover at 30-JUN-08
using channel ORA_DISK_1
using channel ORA_DISK_2
using channel ORA_DISK_3
using channel ORA_DISK_4
starting media recovery
media recovery complete
Finished recover at 30-JUN-08
RMAN>
```

4. Bring the new datafile online:

```
RMAN> SQL "alter database datafile
    2> ''/test02/app/oracle/oradata/finance1/test01.dbf'' online";
       sql statement: alter database datafile
      ''/test02/app/oracle/oradata/remorse/sales01.dbf'' online
RMAN> EXIT
```

User-Managed Recovery of a File Without a Backup

The manual procedure for recovering a file without prior backups is very straightforward, again assuming you have all the archived redo logs available. You first create a new file with the same name as the lost file, and then you use the archived logs (if necessary) to recover the data that was in that file.

The Data Recovery Advisor

The Data Recovery Advisor is a tool that helps you fix data failures, which are defined as corruption or loss of data on a disk. The Data Recovery Advisor makes it easy to diagnose and repair data failures and reduces the MTTR. The Data Recovery Advisor helps you proactively detect and repair data failures before the database is put out of commission and provides an assessment of the impact of a failure in the form of a report. It also determines the best repair options and, although it can perform automatic repairs, leaves the decision up to you. The Data Recovery Advisor helps you diagnose the following types of failures:

- Inaccessible data fields and control files
- Datafiles older than other database files
- Physical corruption
- I/O failures such as hardware errors or operating system failures

You can access the Data Recovery Advisor from the Enterprise Manager Database Control or Grid Control. However, I focus on accessing the Data Recovery Advisor through RMAN, since this approach will help you understand how the various Data Recovery Advisor commands work.

Working with the Data Recovery Advisor

The database can detect a failure when it encounters an error such as corrupted data. In a case like this, the database runs automatic data integrity checks that diagnose the data failure and lodge the results in the Data Recovery Advisor. You can also manually invoke these data integrity checks yourself proactively. You can run a diagnostic check through the Health Monitor or execute the VALIDATE and BACKUP VALIDATE commands to check for block corruption. Whether the database reactively runs a check or you run a proactive check, the failure analysis will be stored in the Automatic Diagnostic Repository (ADR). It's only after the ADR records the failure information that you can invoke the Data Recovery Advisor.

You can analyze a failure in terms of its failure properties:

- *Failure status*: The status of a failure is open until you execute the repair action. Once you repair the failure, the status will be set to closed.

- *Failure priority*: A failure can be assigned a priority of high, medium, or low. The database assigns only the high- and critical-priority levels, but you can downgrade a high-priority failure to the low-priority level, if you think that the database can ignore the failure until it fixes other more important failures. This way, you can limit the output of the LIST FAILURE command, which lists all outstanding failures, with a critical or high priority.

- *Failure grouping*: The Data Recovery Advisor groups related subfailures into one failure. If you want, you can get details about the individual subfailures.

Use the Data Recovery Advisor when some alerts, error messages, or data integrity check results indicate there is a failure in the database. As I mentioned earlier, whether you run a database check yourself or RMAN runs one, the database logs the failure assessments in the ADR. Once the failure is recorded in the ADR, you can invoke the Data Recovery Advisor.

The Data Recovery Advisor depends on the diagnosing infrastructure (please see Chapter 17) for problem diagnosis and solution. Use the DRA when you deal with problems such as lost datafiles, data block corruption, or an I/O failure. You can limit damage by detecting problems automatically along with recommendations for the repairing of the problems, thus helping reduce database downtime.

Here's how you execute the main commands of the Data Recovery Advisor to diagnose and repair failures.

Listing the Failures

Execute the LIST FAILURE command to view all the failures the database is encountering, as shown here:

```
RMAN> list failure;

List of Database Failures
Failure ID Priority Status    Time Detected Summary
---------- -------- --------- ------------- ------------------
4          HIGH     OPEN      30-MAR-08     multiple datafiles
                                            are missing

RMAN>
```

The output shows that multiple datafiles are missing. Note that the output of the LIST FAILURE command shows all failures known to the Data Recovery Advisor. You can also execute the LIST FAILURE . . . DETAIL command to list individual failures, as shown here:

```
RMAN> list failure 4 detail;
```

In addition, you can execute any of the following variations of the LIST FAILURE command:

```
RMAN> list failure critical;
RMAN> LIST FAILURE HIGH;
RMAN> LIST FAILURE LOW;
RMAN> list failure open;
RMAN> list failure closed;
RMAN> list failure exclude failure 12345
```

Determining Repair Options

Execute the ADVISE FAILURE command following the LIST FAILURE command to get a list of both manual and automated repairs. A manual option can often avoid a more laborious automatic repair option. For example, it's easier to replace a table or two than to restore and recover entire datafiles. Here's an example showing how to use the ADVISE FAILURE command:

```
RMAN> advise failure;

List of Database Failures
Failure ID Priority Status    Time Detected Summary
---------- -------- --------- ------------- ----------------------
4          HIGH     OPEN      30-MAR-08     multiple datafiles
                                            are missing

analyzing automatic repair options; this may take some time
allocated channel: ORA_DISK_1
channel ORA_DISK_1: SID=152 device type=DISK

analyzing automatic repair options complete

Manual Checklist
==================================================================
if file C:\ORACLE\PRODUCT\11.1.0\ORADATA\NICK\USERS01.DBF was
unintentionally renamed or moved, restore it

if file C:\ORACLE\PRODUCT\11.1.0\ORADATA\NICK\EXAMPLE01.DBF was
unintentionally renamed or moved, restore it

Automated Repair Options
==================================================================
Option Strategy     Repair Description
------ ------------ -------------------
                    no data loss restore and recover datafile 4,
                    Restore and recover datafile
   Repair script: C:\ORCL11\APP\ORACLE\NICK\DIAG\diag\
   rdbms\nick\nick\hm\reco_128942564.hm


RMAN>
```

In this example, the manual and automated repair options are the same: you must restore and recover the missing datafiles.

Repairing Failures

You must first try to fix the failures by using the manual repairs, before trying the automatic repair recommendations. Before issuing the REPAIR FAILURE command, it may be a good idea to issue the REPAIR PREVIEW command as shown here, to preview the repair strategy:

```
RMAN> repair failure preview;

Strategy        Repair script
------------    -------------------------------------
no data loss    C:\ORCL11\APP\ORACLE\NICK\DIAG\diag\
                rdbms\nick\nick\hm\reco_128942564.hm

contents of repair script:
   # restore and recover datafile
   restore check readonly datafile 4, 5;
   recover datafile 4, 5;

RMAN>
```

Once you have previewed the repair strategy, issue the REPAIR FAILURE command, as shown here:

```
RMAN> repair failure;

Strategy      Repair script
------------ ----------------------------------------------
no data loss
C:\ORCL11\APP\ORACLE\NICK\DIAG\diag\rdbms\nick\
nick\hm\reco_128942564.hm

contents of repair script:
   # restore and recover datafile
   restore check readonly datafile 4, 5;
   recover datafile 4, 5;

Do you really want to execute the above repair
(enter YES or NO) ?   yes
executing repair script

Starting restore at 30-MAR-08
using channel ORA_DISK_1

channel ORA_DISK_1: starting datafile backup set restore
channel ORA_DISK_1: specifying datafile(s) to restore
from backup set
Finished restore at 30-MAR-08

Starting recover at 30-MAR-08
starting media recovery
RMAN-08187: WARNING: media recovery until SCN 3212445 complete
```

```
Finished recover at 30-MAR-08
repair failure complete
Do you want to open the database (enter YES or NO)? yes

RMAN>
```

The V$IR_REPAIR view shows the results of the REPAIR FAILURE command. Here's the structure of the V$IR_REPAIR view:

```
SQL> desc v$ir_repair

Name                     Null?    Type
----------------------   ------   --------------
REPAIR_ID                         NUMBER
ADVISE_ID                         NUMBER
SUMMARY                           VARCHAR2(32)
RANK                              NUMBER
TIME_DETECTED                     DATE
EXECUTED                          DATE
ESTIMATED_DATA_LOSS               VARCHAR2(20)
DETAILED_DESCRIPTION              VARCHAR2(1024)
REPAIR_SCRIPT                     VARCHAR2(512)
ESTIMATED_REPAIR_TIME             NUMBER
ACTUAL_REPAIR_TIMENUMBER
STATUS                            VARCHAR2(7)

SQL>
```

You can issue a query such as the following to view details about all the repair recommendations made by the Data Recovery Advisor:

```
SQL> select repair_id,advise_id,summary,rank
        from v$ir_repair;

REPAIR_ID    ADVISE_ID    SUMMARY                 RANK
---------    ----------   --------------------    ------
   23           21        NO DATA LOSS OPTION       1
   69           67        NO DATA LOSS OPTION       1
   82           80        NO DATA LOSS OPTION       1

SQL>
```

The RMAN commands to access and utilize the Data Recovery Advisor are simple enough, but there's an even easier way to access the Data Recovery Advisor, and that's through the Enterprise Manager.

Cloning a Database

DBAs routinely refresh development and test databases, and they will sometimes need to clone databases to test backup and recovery strategies. If you have a small database, a simple Data Pump Export/Import will suffice, but most databases aren't amenable to this procedure. You can clone databases in three different ways:

- By using the RMAN DUPLICATE command
- By using the OEM Database Control
- By manually performing the copy with SQL*Plus

Note The main purpose of cloning databases is not to create a failover database during a crisis—you use standby databases for that purpose.

Using RMAN to Clone a Database

RMAN provides the DUPLICATE command, which uses the RMAN backups of a database to create a new database. The backup files are restored to the target database, after which an incomplete recovery is performed and the new database is opened with the OPEN RESETLOGS command. The good thing about using RMAN is that all the preceding steps are performed automatically, without any user intervention. The duplicate database can be an exact replica of the original, or it can contain only a subset of it.

The following steps are involved in cloning a database:

1. Create a new init.ora file for the auxiliary database. The init.ora file should have the following parameters, with the datafiles and log file parameters changed to ensure that the original database files aren't used for the new database:

   - DB_FILE_NAME_CONVERT: This parameter transforms the target datafile names to the duplicate database datafile names.

   - LOG_FILE_NAME_CONVERT: This parameter converts the target database redo log filenames to the duplicate database redo log filenames.

2. Start the target database instance. You must start the target database instance in the nomount mode.

3. Connect the recovery catalog to the target database and the auxiliary database:

   ```
   RMAN> CONNECT target / catalog rman/rman1@catalog_db auxiliary
           sys/password@auxiliary_db
   ```

4. Issue the RMAN DUPLICATE command, as follows:

   ```
   RMAN> DUPLICATE TARGET DATABASE TO
           auxiliary_db  /* actual name of auxiliary database here */
           pfile =/u01/app/oracle/10.2.0/db_1/dbs/init_auxiliary_db;
   ```

Before you can issue the DUPLICATE DATABASE command, you must make the disk backups available to the duplicate instance by either manually transferring the backups and copies to the destination host or using NFS or shared disks.

The preceding is a simplified presentation of the database duplication process using RMAN, and you should refer to the Oracle documentation for complete details about duplicating a database. When you issue the DUPLICATE TARGET DATABASE TO . . . command, as shown previously, RMAN will shut down the auxiliary database and start it up again. It then performs the following steps:

- Restores all the backed-up files of the target database to the destination auxiliary database, using all available archived redo logs

- Opens the duplicated database with the RESETLOGS option

■**Note** Whether you perform backup-based database duplication or active database duplication, RMAN must perform an incomplete recovery always. The reason is that RMAN doesn't back up the source database's online redo log files. It creates the duplicate datafiles on the auxiliary instance and recovers them with the help of archived redo logs.

The previous example showed how to duplicate a database by using the source database's backup files. However, you can also duplicate a database without any backups by using the new active database duplication technique. Under active database duplication, you can copy the active database files over the network directly to the auxiliary instance. That's the reason active database duplication is also called network-enabled duplication. I summarize the active database duplication technique here.

In the following database duplication example, I assume that the duplicate database is being created on a different host. Thus, you can use the same directory structure as well as identical database filenames for the duplicate database and the source database. You don't have to rename the duplicate database files as a result. However, you must specify the clause NOFILENAMECHECK with the DUPLICATE DATABASE command, to avoid the unnecessary checks to ensure that identical filenames aren't being used on the same host.

In the following example, I duplicate a database on the same server. I must therefore use different filenames for the target and the duplicate database.

Create an Oracle password file for the auxiliary instance, because you need it when you perform active database duplication. You must use the same SYSDBA password in the duplicate database password file as in the source database. If you want, you can specify the PASSWORD FILE option in the DUPLICATE DATABASE command, to make RMAN copy the source database password file to the destination host. Here's how you create the password file:

```
$ orapwd file=orapwtest1 password=<sys_pwd>
  entries=20  ignorecase=n
```

As I mentioned earlier, you can add the PASSWORD FILE clause to the DUPLICATE DATABASE command, to make RMAN copy the source database password file to the destination database.

Even though I am duplicating the target database to the same server, since I'm using active database duplication, I must ensure that both databases use Oracle Net. In the listener.ora file on the host server, add the name of the duplicate database, as shown here:

```
SID_LIST_LISTENER=
(SID_DESC =
(GLOBAL_DBNAME = prod1)
(ORACLE_HOME = /u01/app/oracle/product/10.1g/)
(SID_NAME =prod1)
   )
(SID_DESC =
(GLOBAL_DBNAME = test1)
(ORACLE_HOME = /u01/app/oracle/product/11.1/)
(SID_NAME =test1)
  )
 )
```

Restart the listener after making the change. You must also make the following change to your tnsnames.ora file:

```
test1=
(DESCRIPTION=
(ADDRESS_LIST =
(ADDRESS = (PROTOCOL = TCP)(HOST = prod1)(PORT = 1521))
)
(CONNECT_DATA =
(SERVER = DEDICATED)
(SERVICE_NAME = test1)
 )
 )
```

Create an initialization parameter file for the auxiliary instance. Since I'm using the SPFILE technique for naming the duplicate database's file, I need only one parameter in this parameter file, which is the DB_NAME parameter.

```
db_name=test1
```

You can specify the actual filenames by specifying the DB_FILE_NAME_CONVERT and the LOG_FILE_NAME_CONVERT parameters in the DUPLICATE DATABASE command itself.

Start the auxiliary instance in nomount mode.

```
$ sqlplus /nolog
SQL> connect sys/sammyy1 as sysdba
Connected to an idle instance
SQL> startup nomount
Oracle Instance started.
Total System Global Area        113246208 bytes
Fixed Size                        1218004 bytes
Variable Size                    58722860 bytes
Database Buffers                 50331648 bytes
Redo Buffers                      2973696 bytes
SQL>
```

The auxiliary instance shown here uses the simple initialization parameter with the DB_NAME parameter. However, I use the SPFILE clause in the DUPLICATE DATABASE command later on, which copies the source database's SPFILE to the default location for the auxiliary instance.

Start RMAN and connect to the target database, source database, and recovery catalog, as shown here:

```
$rman target sys/sammyy1@eleven
connected to target database: ELEVEN (DBID=3481681133)

RMAN> connect auxiliary sys/sammyy1@test1
connected to auxiliary database: TEST1 (not mounted)

RMAN> CONNECT CATALOG rman/rman@catdb
    connected to recovery catalog database
RMAN>
```

Issue the DUPLICATE DATABASE command, as shown here, to create the duplicate database using the active database's files over the network:

```
RMAN> duplicate target database
   2> to test1
   3> from active database
   4> spfile
   5> parameter_value_convert
      '/u01/app/oracle/eleven','/u10/app/oracle/test1'
   6> set log_file_name_convert
      '/u05/app/oracle/eleven', '/u10/app/oracle/test1'
   7> db_file_name_convert '/u10/app/oracle/eleven',
      '/u10/app/oracle/test1';

Starting Duplicate Db at 04-APR-08
using target database control file instead of recovery catalog
 contents of Memory Script:
{
  sql "declare worked boolean;
  begin worked := dbms_backup_restore.networkFileTransfer(
  ''auxdb'', null, null,
...
executing Memory Script
...
Starting backup at 04-APR-08
...
Finished backup at 04-APR-08
...
contents of Memory Script:
{
   set until scn 901715;
   recover
   clone database
   delete archivelog
   ;
}
...
starting media recovery
...
media recovery complete, elapsed time: 00:00:01
Finished recover at 04-APR-08
...
database opened
Finished Duplicate Db at 04-APR-08
RMAN>
```

Specifying the SPFILE clause in the DUPLICATE DATABASE command leads RMAN to copy the source database's SPFILE to the server hosting the auxiliary database. RMAN makes changes to the auxiliary instance's SPFILE, based on the settings you specify in the SPFILE clause when duplicating the database. RMAN will then stop and start the auxiliary instance using the newly edited SPFILE.

RMAN first updates the source database's SPFILE using the values you specify for the PARAMETER_NAME_CONVERT and the SET clauses. RMAN shuts down the auxiliary instance and restarts it using the new SPFILE. RMAN then starts copying the source database files over the network. Once the copying is completed, RMAN recovers the duplicate database before opening it. As part of the database duplication process, RMAN does the following:

- Copy the datafiles, but not the flash recovery area files.
- Copy the necessary archived redo log files.
- Since I specified the SPFILE clause, copy the source database SPFILE over to the target database.
- Copy the password file if you specify the PASSWORD FILE clause.
- Re-create the online redo log files.
- Re-create the control files for the target database.
- Re-create the tempfiles in the directory specified by the DB_CREATE_FILE_DEST parameter.

Active database duplication is the easiest way to duplicate a database since you don't need any prior RMAN backups.

Using Database Control to Clone a Database

The Enterprise Manager Clone Database Wizard steps you through the database cloning operation. Here are the main features of the cloning feature:

- You can clone any Oracle database that is release 8.1.7 or higher.
- The source database can be in the archivelog or the noarchivelog mode.
- You can clone a database while it is open. The Database Control uses RMAN internally for the cloning operation.
- The Database Control will back up the datafiles and restore them in the new location. It will then recover them using archived redo logs.
- The Database Control will create the new instance, a password file, any necessary networking files, and the init.ora file and SPFILE.
- The Database Control will automatically start the new instance in the open mode.

Here are the steps for cloning a database using the Database Control:

1. Click the Maintenance Tab on the Database Home Page of the Database Control.
2. Click the Clone Database item in the Data Movement section (under the Move Database files group).
3. In the Source Type page, choose the Clone a Running Database Instance option.
4. In the Source Working Directory page, enter your operating system username and password. Click Next.
5. In the Select Destination page, enter the new database name and the destination host name. Click Next.
6. In the Destination Options page, you can customize database file locations if you wish. Click Next.
7. In the Schedule page, you can choose whether you want to clone the database immediately or to schedule it for later. Click Next.
8. In the Review page, you can review the source and clone database information, as shown in Figure 16-1. Click the Submit Job button to start the cloning operation.

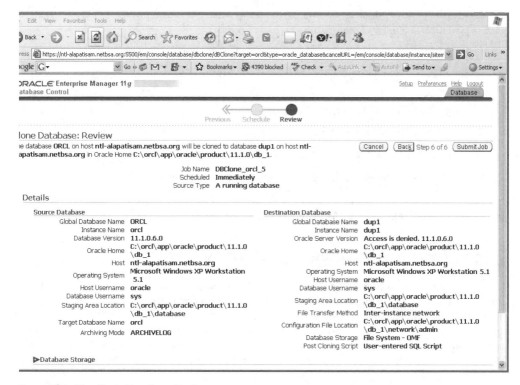

Figure 16-1. *The Clone Database Review page*

Manually Cloning a Database

To clone a database manually, you need to first use the operating system to copy all of the source database files to the target location. If you are on the same server, you also have to change the name of the database; if you are on a different server, you can keep the same name for the databases if you wish. You first back up the source database control file to trace (using the `ALTER DATABASE BACKUP CONTROLFILE TO TRACE` statement) and, using the trace file's contents, create a new control file that will help you create the new clone database.

Here's a summary of the steps involved in manually cloning a database. The procedure is simple, with most of the time being consumed by copying the database files from source to target. Assume that your production database is the *source* database and is named "prod" and your destination (*target*) database is named "test."

1. Copy the prod database files to the target location.

2. Prepare a text file for the creation of a control file for the new database as follows:

   ```
   SQL> ALTER DATABASE BACKUP CONTROLFILE TO TRACE;
   ```

3. On the target location, create all the directories for the various files.

4. Copy the following four sets of files from the production (source) database to the target database: parameter files, control files, datafiles, and redo log files.

5. In all the clone database files, change the database name to test.

6. Run the CREATE DATABASE statement, which was prepared with the ALTER DATABASE BACKUP CONTROLFILE TO TRACE statement.

7. Create the control file for the test database using the following statement:

```
SQL> CREATE CONTROLFILE REUSE SET DATABASE "TEST" RESETLOGS NOARCHIVELOG
```

You'll now have a new database called test that has a new control file pointing to the copied (target) version of the production database.

8. Once you get the prompt back from the previous command, run this command:

```
SQL> ALTER DATABASE OPEN RESETLOGS USING BACKUP CONTROLFILE;
```

9. Finally, change the global name of the database you just created by running the following command:

```
SQL> UPDATE global_name SET global name='test.world';
```

Techniques for Granular Recovery

The techniques you've seen thus far show that both RMAN and user-managed recovery strategies are reliable methods for restoring databases when there's a media-related problem. However, suppose you only need to undo some changes in the database. Even the incomplete recoveries, though they remove unwanted changes, will lead to a loss of data. In addition, sometimes you can't determine exactly when a change was made, so you can't make a precise incomplete recovery. You may also have to close the database to your users during the recovery process if you are recovering the entire database.

Fortunately, you can use several other more granular recovery methods when your needs are more precise. The TSPITR method enables you to recover a tablespace until a specified point in the past. The LogMiner utility, which Oracle provides free of charge, enables you to perform extremely precise recovery based on a reading of the changes recorded in the redo logs. In addition, you can use the Flashback Query feature to identify and recover lost data or wrongly committed incorrect data. Depending on your needs, you may find one of these alternatives a better way to fix data loss problems than having to restore and recover the database every time you have to undo the results of an application error.

Tablespace Point-in-Time Recovery

Suppose you or one of the users of your database has dropped a table by mistake. Or, as it happens sometimes, you truncated the wrong table or you wrongly deleted (or inserted) data into a table. You don't have to recover the entire database when you need to bring back the table's contents. You can use Oracle's TSPITR technique to recover the tablespace containing the lost table to a point in time that's different from the rest of the database.

You can perform TSPITR using RMAN, or you can manage the whole process manually. Essentially, you have to use an auxiliary database so you can recover the tablespace (or tablespaces) to the desired point in time before the damaging action occurred. Once the tablespace is recovered to that clean point, it is brought back to the main database. RMAN makes the TSPITR type of recovery very easy.

Using RMAN for TSPITR

You recover the tablespaces from the database (the *target* database) by first performing the PITR in a temporary instance called the *auxiliary* database, which is created solely to serve as the staging area for the recovery of the tablespaces.

Here's how to use RMAN to perform a TSPITR:

1. Create the auxiliary database. Use a skeleton initialization parameter file for the auxiliary instance along the lines of the following:

```
db_name=help (this is the target database_name)
db_file_name_convert=('/oraclehome/oradata/target/', '/tmp/')
/* Lets you convert the target database datafiles to a different name */
log_file_name_convert=('/oraclehome/oradata/target/redo', '/tmp/redo')
/* Lets you convert the target database redo log files
to a different name. */
instance_name=aux
control_files=/tmp/control1.ctl
compatible=11.1.0
db_block_size=8192
```

2. Start up the auxiliary database in the nomount mode:

```
$ sqlplus /nolog
SQL> CONNECT sys/oracle@aux AS sysdba
SQL> STARTUP NOMOUNT PFILE = /tmp/initaux.ora
```

3. Generate some archived redo logs and back up the target database. You can use the ALTER SYSTEM SWITCH LOGFILE command to produce the archived redo log files.

4. Connect to all three databases—the catalog, target, and auxiliary databases—as follows:

```
$ rman target sys/sys_passwd@nick catalog rman/rman1@nina
    auxiliary system/oracle@aux
```

5. Perform a TSPITR. If you want to recover until a certain time, for example, you can use the following statement (assuming your NLS_DATE format uses the following format mask: *Mon DD YYYY HH24:MI:SS*):

```
RMAN> RECOVER TABLESPACE users UNTIL TIME ('JUN 30 2005 12:00:00');
```

This is a deceptively simple step, but RMAN performs a number of tasks in this step. It restores the datafiles in the users tablespace to the auxiliary database and recovers them to the time you specified. It then exports the metadata about the objects in the tablespaces from the auxiliary to the target database. RMAN also uses the SWITCH command to point the control file to the newly recovered datafiles.

6. Once the recovery is complete, bring the user tablespace online:

```
$ rman target sys/sys_passwd@nick
RMAN> SQL "alter tablespace users online";
RMAN> Exit;
```

7. Shut down the auxiliary instance and remove all the control files, redo log files, and datafiles pertaining to the auxiliary database.

Using LogMiner for Precision Recovery

Oracle provides the excellent LogMiner utility, which helps you perform precision recovery by using the data captured in the redo logs. LogMiner can read the redo logs, which opens the door to a number of possibilities. Remember that redo logs hold the information about the history of the changes made to the database. Although you can use LogMiner's capability to read redo logs for security and auditing purposes, our interest in it in this chapter is solely for database recovery.

When DBAs fix user errors with a PITR, there is a possible loss of valuable data. LogMiner obviates the need for a recovery when you are trying to undo a minor change to the data. In cases where you need to undo a committed change to just one table, LogMiner can help you identify the exact transaction, read the redo log files, and undo the changes that were incorrectly made. If you need to recover from a massive error, LogMiner can still help by pinpointing the time to which you need to recover from backups. You can then perform a time-based or change-based recovery.

LogMiner makes it easy to perform fine-grained recovery by reversing unwanted changes from a table. In addition to serving as a fine-grained recovery tool, the LogMiner utility can help you reconstruct SQL statements to help in auditing and debugging. You can also use this tool to discover the time frame in which a logical corruption occurred.

LogMiner uses the DBMS_LOGMNR and the DBMS_LOGMNR_D packages supplied by Oracle (along with a couple of other, less important packages) to extract the information from the redo logs. In addition, LogMiner uses several dynamic performance views to help analyze the information contained in the redo logs. You can give regular users access to the SYS-owned packages by granting them the EXECUTE_CATALOG_ROLE role. To enable LogMiner to match its object IDs with actual database object names, you have to specify a data dictionary to use, and the easiest thing to do is assign LogMiner the normal data dictionary that belongs to the database.

The V$LOGMNR_CONTENTS view holds a wealth of information that LogMiner uses to help remove unwanted changes in table data. Here is a brief list of the types of information recorded in the V$LOGMNR_CONTENTS view:

- Time stamp
- Username
- Type of action (insert, update, delete, or DDL)
- The transaction numbers and SCNs
- The tables involved in the transaction
- A reconstruction of the SQL that made the changes
- SQL that will undo the change, if necessary

How the LogMiner Utility Works

LogMiner reads redo log files and puts the information it extracts into the V$LOGMNR_CONTENTS view, which you can then query for details about transactions you're interested in. Because the information in the redo logs is in the form of internal object identifiers and data in hex form, Oracle recommends you provide LogMiner with access to the data dictionary so it can translate the contents of the redo log file into a form you can readily understand.

You can provide LogMiner with access to the data dictionary in three different ways:

- You can extract the data dictionary to a flat file.
- You can have a dictionary snapshot placed in the redo logs.
- You can do away with the extraction of the data dictionary and direct LogMiner to just use the online data dictionary.

Note that LogMiner doesn't show you all the SQL statements in the redo log; it just shows the end statement that would need to be applied to the database to undo the unwanted changes.

Supplemental Logging

Before you start using the LogMiner utility, be aware that you must turn on supplemental logging to take full advantage of the LogMiner functionality. As its name indicates, *supplemental logging* logs more information about transactions by logging additional columns in the redo logs. This additional information can be used to undo changes to the database.

Types of Supplemental Logging

There are two *types* of supplemental logging, differing in the set of additional columns logged. The set of additional columns is the *supplemental log group*, the more restrictive supplemental logging uses the conditional supplemental log group, and the more general supplemental logging uses the *unconditional supplemental log group*.

If you want the before-images of these columns to always be logged, even if none of the columns were changed, then you use an unconditional supplemental log group (also known as the *ALWAYS* log group). Here's an example that shows how you create an unconditional supplemental log group:

```
SQL> ALTER TABLE hr.employees
     ADD SUPPLEMENTAL LOG GROUP key_info(empno, ename)
     FROM hr.employees ALWAYS;
```

The *conditional supplemental log group* is a more restricted supplemental log group that logs the before-images of the specified columns in the group only if one of them changes. Here's an example that shows how to create a conditional supplemental log group:

```
SQL> ALTER TABLE hr.employees
     ADD SUPPLEMENTAL LOG GROUP key_info(empno,ename)
     FROM hr.employees;
```

Levels of Supplemental Logging

You also have two *levels* of supplemental logging, one at the database level and the other at the table level. If you turn on supplemental logging for the entire database, keep in mind that it could impose a performance penalty. If you do use supplemental logging at the database level, use the *minimal* supplemental logging, which is an option designed to put the least amount of stress on your database. That said, minimal supplemental logging still provides the information you need to identify and group the operations associated with various DML operations. Oracle strongly recommends you have at least this level of supplemental logging turned on for LogMiner to be effective.

To turn minimal database-wide supplemental logging on, use the following command:

```
SQL> ALTER DATABASE ADD SUPPLEMENTAL LOG DATA;
```

You can specify table-level supplemental logging, which logs only that table's supplemental data in the redo log files. Here's an example showing how you can specify table-level supplemental logging for all columns of a table:

```
SQL> ALTER TABLE HR.EMPLOYEES ADD SUPPLEMENTAL LOG DATA (ALL) COLUMNS;
```

■**Tip** Although supplemental logging is strongly recommended by Oracle if you want to avail yourself of all the features of the LogMiner utility, it does inflict some burden on the system if you choose the more expansive database-wide supplemental logging rather than table-level supplemental logging.

Extracting the Data Dictionary

As mentioned previously, you have three ways to extract the data dictionary information for LogMiner's use: using a flat file, extracting the dictionary to the redo logs, or using the online data dictionary. When you start LogMiner, it builds its own internal data dictionary from the dictionary supplied by one of the preceding three methods.

The easiest method is to use the existing data dictionary, but it isn't valid with the DDL_DICT_ TRACKING option, which means you can't track changes to DDL. Also, you can't track DML operations performed on tables created after the dictionary was extracted.

The problem with the extraction of the dictionary to a flat file is that you can't guarantee it's always consistent, because DDL operations could be changing the database structure while the dictionary is being extracted.

During the extraction of the dictionary to the redo logs, on the other hand, DDL statements aren't allowed, thus ensuring the consistency of the dictionary that's being extracted. Therefore, it is best to extract the data dictionary to the redo logs, because it gives you a consistent version of the data dictionary and enables DDL tracking at the same time.

A LogMiner Session

Before you invoke the LogMiner utility, make sure you create a separate tablespace for LogMiner's data, because the default location for it is the System tablespace. Also, make sure you have minimal database-wide logging turned on, as explained in the previous "Supplemental Logging" section.

Let's look at a simple LogMiner session with minimal supplemental logging already turned on. Note that DBMS_LOGMNR is owned by SYS.

The first step is to extract the data dictionary to the redo logs. The DBMS_LOGMNR_D package builds the data dictionary and stores it in the online redo logs:

```
SQL> EXECUTE sys.DBMS_LOGMNR_D.build( -
> OPTIONS => sys.DBMS_LOGMNR_D.store_in_redo_logs);
PL/SQL procedure successfully completed.
SQL>
```

Next, you need to specify the logs to be included in the LogMiner analysis. Because you chose to use the redo logs to extract the data dictionary, you must specify the redo logs that contain the data dictionary, in addition to the other redo logs you're interested in using in the DBMS_LOGMNR.ADD_ LOGFILE procedure. The first file you add should use the DBMS_LOGMNR.NEWFILE procedure, and all the other ones should use the DBMS_LOGMNR.ADDFILE procedure.

You now can use the V$ARCHIVED_LOG view to find out which of the redo log files the data dictionary was extracted to when you invoked the DBMS_LOGMNR_D.BUILD procedure. The DICTIONARY_BEGIN and DICTIONARY_END columns will tell you in which redo log files your data dictionary is contained. Here's the query:

```
SQL> SELECT SEQUENCE#, DICTIONARY_BEGIN, DICTIONARY_END
  2 FROM V$ARCHIVED_LOG;
```

SEQ#	DIC BEG	DIC END
2	NO	NO
24	YES	YES
25	NO	NO
26	NO	NO
27	NO	NO
28	NO	NO

```
SQL>
```

From the output, you can see that the DICTIONARY_BEGIN and DICTIONARY_END columns are both contained in archived redo log number 24. You must include this in your list of log files, as follows:

```
SQL> EXECUTE DBMS_LOGMNR.ADD_LOGFILE( -
  > LOGFILENAME  => 'C:\ORACLENT\RDBMS\ARC00024.001', -
  > OPTIONS      => DBMS_LOGMNR.NEW);
PL/SQL procedure successfully completed.
SQL>
```

In addition, you need to add the files you're interested in to the ADD_LOGFILE procedure in the DBMS_LOGMNR package:

```
SQL> EXECUTE DBMS_LOGMNR.ADD_LOGFILE( -
  > LOGFILENAME  => 'C:\ORACLENT\RDBMS\ARC00025.001' , -
  > OPTIONS      => DBMS_LOGMNR.ADDFILE);

PL/SQL procedure successfully completed.
SQL>
SQL> EXECUTE DBMS_LOGMNR.ADD_LOGFILE( -
  > LOGFILENAME => 'C:\ORACLENT\RDBMS\ARC00026.001', -
  > OPTIONS      => DBMS_LOGMNR.ADDFILE);

PL/SQL procedure successfully completed.
SQL>
```

Note that you can also add log files without the OPTIONS line, as follows:

```
SQL> EXECUTE DBMS_LOGMNR.ADD_LOGFILE( -
  > LOGFILENAME => 'C:\ORACLENT\RDBMS\ARC00027.001');

PL/SQL procedure successfully completed.
```

Once you've specified the redo log files, it's time to start the LogMiner utility. In this example, in addition to specifying that LogMiner use the redo logs as the source of the data dictionary, you'll also enable DDL tracking, which is turned off by default:

```
SQL> EXECUTE DBMS_LOGMNR.START_LOGMNR(OPTIONS => -
  > DBMS_LOGMNR.DICT_FROM_REDO_LOGS + -
  > DBMS_LOGMNR.DDL_DICT_TRACKING );

PL/SQL procedure successfully completed.
SQL>
```

Using LogMiner to Analyze Redo Logs

Now that you've successfully started LogMiner, you can issue commands against the V$LOGMNR_CONTENTS table to get information about various DML and DDL statements encompassed by the set of redo log files you included earlier. Whenever you query the V$LOGMNR_CONTENTS view, all the redo log files you specified are read sequentially, and the information is loaded into the V$LOGMNR_CONTENTS view. Listing 16-9 shows a simple example.

Listing 16-9. *Analyzing the V$LOGMNR_CONTENTS View*

```
SQL> SELECT SQL_REDO
  2  FROM V$LOGMNR_CONTENTS
  3* WHERE USERNAME='HR';


                                SQL_REDO
----------------------------------------------------------------------------
set transaction read write;
select * from "SYS"."DUAL" where ROWID = 'AAAADdAABAAAANnAAA' for update;
commit;
set transaction read write;
delete from "HR"."REGIONS" where "REGION_ID" = '5'
and "REGION_NAME" =
'northern  europe' and ROWID = 'AAAHrNAAFAAAAESAAE';
delete from "HR"."REGIONS" where "REGION_ID" = '6'
and "REGION_NAME" =
'pacific region' and ROWID = 'AAAHrNAAFAAAAESAAF';
update "HR"."REGIONS" set "REGION_NAME" = 'eastern europe' where
"REGION_NAME" = 'northern africa' and ROWID = 'AAAHrNAAFAAAAESAAG';
commit;
10 rows selected.
SQL>
```

You can see that user HR has deleted two rows and updated one row. You can thus use LogMiner to retrieve DML from a previous period. There's an additional bonus to using LogMiner; it will give you the SQL to undo the preceding DML statements, as shown in Listing 16-10.

Listing 16-10. *Retrieving the SQL to Undo DML Statements*

```
SQL> SELECT SQL_UNDO
  2  FROM V$LOGMNR_CONTENTS
  3* WHERE USERNAME='HR';
                              SQL_UNDO
------------------------------------------------------------------
insert into "HR"."REGIONS"("REGION_ID","REGION_NAME")
values ('5','northern europe');
insert into "HR"."REGIONS"("REGION_ID","REGION_NAME")
values ('6','pacific region');
update "HR"."REGIONS" set "REGION_NAME" = 'northern africa' where
 "REGION_NAME"= 'eastern europe' and ROWID = 'AAAHrNAAFAAAAESAAG';
10 rows selected.
SQL>
```

The INSERT statements replace the deletes, and the UPDATE statement reverses the changes made. Note that SQL*Plus indicates that ten rows were selected in response to your query, although only the three DML operations executed by user HR are displayed.

As you can see, the SQL_UNDO column contains complete statements that are ready to be used in SQL, semicolon and all. However, the statements aren't very easy to read when they're long and complex. LogMiner provides the DBMS_LOGMNR.PRINT_PRETTY_SQL procedure to make the LogMiner output appear less cluttered and enable you to print easy-to-read output.

If you want to continuously analyze data using LogMiner, you don't have to keep adding files manually. You can just add the DBMS_LOGMNR.CONTINUOUS_MINE procedure by using the OPTIONS keyword, and LogMiner will keep adding any redo log files that are archived to the list of files to be analyzed each time you query the V$LOGMNR_CONTENTS view.

Because you started LogMiner with the DDL tracking option turned on, the following query will identify, for example, all the DDL changes made by user SYS:

```
SQL> SELECT sql_undo
  2  FROM v$logmnr_contents
  3  WHERE username='SYS'
  4* AND operation='DDL'
```

When you've finished using LogMiner, end your session with the DBMS_LOGMNR.end_logmnr procedure, as follows:

```
SQL> EXECUTE dbms_logmnr.end_logmnr();
PL/SQL procedure successfully completed.
SQL>
```

Flashback Techniques and Recovery

Oracle's Flashback technology allows you to "rewind" your database, or parts of it, to a previous point in time, without recourse to the traditional, more time-consuming, recovery techniques involving backup files and archived redo logs. It can often provide a quick and effective means of recovering from logical corruptions or user error.

CONVERTING BETWEEN TIME STAMPS AND SCNS

Two SQL functions, SCN_TO_TIMESTAMP and TIMESTAMP_TO_SCN, convert SCNs to a corresponding time-stamp value and vice versa. The SCN_TO_TIMESTAMP SQL function lets you convert an SCN to a calendar time (TIMESTAMP) value. Here's an example:

```
SQL> SELECT current_scn, SCN_TO_TIMESTAMP(current_scn)
  2> FROM v$database;

    CURRENT_SCN          SCN_TO_TIMESTAMP(CURRENT_SCN)
    -------------        ------------------------------------
     5956956             13-JUL-08 09.37.16.000000000 AM
SQL>
```

The TIMESTAMP_TO_SCN function is the inverse of the SCN_TO_TIMESTAMP function. It converts a time stamp to its corresponding SCN.

You can use either a clock time or an SCN to define the exact point to which you wish to restore. If you specify a clock time, Oracle will pick an SCN that's within three seconds of this clock time. Oracle retains the mapping between your clock time and SCNs for a period that is as long as your UNDO_RETENTION initialization parameter.

Flashback Levels

You can use flashback techniques at the row, table, or database levels, as follows:

- *Row level*: You can use Flashback techniques to undo erroneous changes to individual rows. There are four types of row-level Flashback techniques, and all of them rely on undo data stored in the undo tablespace:

    - *Flashback Query*: Allows you to view old row data based on a point in time or an SCN. You can view the older data and, if necessary, retrieve it and undo erroneous changes.

    - *Flashback Versions Query*: Allows you to view all versions of the same row over a period of time so that you can undo logical errors. It can also provide an audit history of changes, effectively allowing you to compare present data against historical data without performing any DML activity.

    - *Flashback Transaction Query*: Lets you view changes made at the transaction level. This technique helps in analysis and auditing of transactions, such as when a batch job runs twice and you want to determine which objects were affected. Using this technique, you can undo changes made by an entire transaction during a specified period.

    - *Flashback Transaction Backout*: Lets you back out a transaction along with all its dependent transactions, with a single click.

- *Table level*: There are two main Flashback features available at the table level:

    - *Flashback Table*: Restores a table to a point in time or to a specified SCN without restoring datafiles. This feature uses DML changes to undo the changes in a table. The Flashback Table feature relies on undo data.

    - *Flashback Drop*: Allows you to reverse the effects of a `DROP TABLE` statement, without resorting to a point-in-time recovery. The Flashback Drop feature uses the Recycle Bin to restore a dropped table.

- *Database level*: The Flashback Database feature allows you to restore an entire database to a point in time, thus undoing all changes since that time. For example, you can restore a dropped schema or an erroneously truncated table. Flashback Database mainly uses flashback logs to retrieve older versions of the data blocks; it also relies, to a much smaller extent, on archived redo logs to completely recover a database without restoring datafiles and performing traditional media recovery.

As you can see, Oracle's Flashback technology employs a variety of techniques. The row-level Flashback techniques and Flashback Table use undo data and are discussed in Chapter 6. In addition, there is also a Flashback Data Archive feature that lets you store and track transactional changes to a table's data. You can use the archive for queries involving historical data or for meeting with regularity compliance requirements. Flashback Drop and Flashback Database rely on the new concept of a Recycle Bin and Flashback log data, respectively, to undo errors at various levels. We will focus on these latter two techniques in this chapter.

Flashback vs. Traditional Recovery Techniques

Unlike traditional recovery techniques, the primary use of Flashback techniques isn't to recover from a media loss, but to recover from human errors. For example, you may accidentally change the wrong set of data or drop a table. Or you may just want to query historical data and perform change analysis. In some extreme cases, you may want to revert the entire database to a previous point in time.

■**Note** If you have a damaged disk drive, or if there is physical corruption (not logical corruption due to application or user errors) in your database, you must still use the traditional methods of restoring backups and using archived redo logs to perform the recovery.

Traditionally, the only way to recover from human error was to employ traditional backup and restore techniques. The process of restoring the database files and then rolling forward through all the redo logs could often involve significant downtime, however, and Flashback technology offers you a much more efficient and much faster way to recover from logical errors, in most cases while the database is still online and available to users. Furthermore, Flashback techniques allow you to selectively restore certain objects. With traditional techniques, you have no choice but to recover the entire database.

Flashback Drop

The Flashback Drop feature provides a means to recover an accidentally dropped table (and its indexes) without the loss of any recent transactions. Most experienced DBAs will have experienced situations where a production table has been accidentally dropped. It takes seconds to issue a DROP TABLE statement; the SQL prompt comes back very quickly—but its consequences can be dire. Unfortunately, you aren't required to confirm your choice to drop a table before the table is gone!

Starting with Oracle Database 10g, when you drop a table, Oracle doesn't get rid of it immediately. It lists the table, and any dependent objects, in the Recycle Bin (more on this shortly) and retains it for as long as possible. If you quickly realize a mistake has been made, you can use the following simple command to immediately restore your lost table:

```
SQL> FLASHBACK TABLE table_name TO BEFORE DROP;
```

■**Tip** One of the best ways to avoid accidentally dropping a table is to use the new prompt variables in SQL*Plus, so your database name and username appear as part of the prompt. I explain this in Chapter 4.

How Flashback Drop Works

Before Oracle Database 10g, executing a DROP TABLE command would result in the immediate removal of the table and all its dependent objects, and all of the related space in that table segment would be released back to the database.

As of Oracle Database 10g, however, the table and dependent objects aren't immediately removed. They are renamed, but they temporarily stay in the same location, and Oracle will retain them for as long as possible, based on space pressure. As noted earlier, these "dropped" objects are listed in the Recycle Bin, which is simply a logical container (a data dictionary table that maintains information about dropped tables, such as their new and original names). You can query it as you would a normal table to view its contents with a simple SELECT * FROM DBA_RECYCLEBIN command. As long as a table is still listed in the Recycle Bin, it can be restored at any time using the Flashback Drop feature.

■**Tip** As of Oracle Database 10g Release 2, you can use the RECYCLEBIN initialization parameter to turn the Flashback Drop capability off. By default, the parameter is set to ON, which means that all dropped tables go into the Recycle Bin and you can recover them using the Flashback Drop feature. By setting the parameter's value to OFF, you turn the Flashback Drop feature off, and tables won't go into the Recycle Bin upon being dropped.

A query on the DBA_FREE_SPACE view will tell you that the space previously occupied by these "dropped" objects is now free. In fact, however, this space is not immediately reclaimable by the database—it is potential free space that is reclaimed later, once the objects have been removed for good. So, despite what the DBA_FREE_SPACE view tells you, these objects will continue to take up their original space allocation in their tablespaces until they are permanently deleted from the Recycle Bin. This deletion can occur in the following circumstances:

- A user can permanently remove the objects from the Recycle Bin using the PURGE command (DROP TABLE *table_name* PURGE).

- Oracle automatically removes the dropped objects in the Recycle Bin due to space pressure—when Oracle doesn't have enough available free space in a tablespace to create a new object or to extend more space to an existing object.

■**Tip** The Flashback Drop feature is automatically enabled in an Oracle Database 11*g* database. You don't have to configure a thing in order to use the feature.

In summary, on issuing a DROP TABLE (or DROP INDEX) command in Oracle Database 11*g*, the objects in question are not truly dropped. Oracle simply hides them, and you can restore them at a later point using Flashback Drop. If you truly do want to permanently remove an object, you can use the PURGE option with the DROP command:

```
SQL> DROP TABLE test PURGE;
```

Let's take a look at all this in a bit more detail.

The Recycle Bin

As mentioned earlier, the Recycle Bin is a logical structure—a data dictionary table named RECYCLEBIN$. You can view the contents of the Recycle Bin for the currently logged in user via the USER_RECYCLEBIN view (RECYCLEBIN is a synonym for USER_RECYCLEBIN). Alternatively, you can view the contents of the Recycle Bin for the entire database via the DBA_RECYCLEBIN view. The following code shows an example of the latter:

```
SQL> SELECT owner, original_name, object_name,
     ts_name, droptime
     FROM dba_recyclebin;

OWNER     ORIGINAL_NAME     OBJECT_NAME                      TS_NAME
------------------------------------------------------------------------
sam       PERSONS      BIN$xTMPjHZ6SG+1xnDIaR9E+g==$0        USERS
```

At the user level, you simply select from the RECYCLEBIN view, instead of the DBA_RECYCLEBIN view. You can also use the SHOW RECYCLEBIN command from SQL*Plus:

```
SQL> SHOW RECYCLEBIN

ORIGINAL NAME     RECYCLEBIN NAME                       OBJECT TYPE  DROP TIME
---------------   -----------------------------------   -----------  -------------------
LOGIN_INFO        BIN$5oAI+vnANcTgNABgsLLCaA==$0        TABLE        2008-06-29:15:48:31
TEST5             BIN$+rRO/h2APITgNABgsLLCaA==$0        TABLE        2008-06-29:15:44:53
SQL>
```

> ■**Tip** The CAN_UNDROP and CAN_PURGE columns of the DBA_RECYCLEBIN view tell you whether you can "undrop" and purge an object, respectively. The SHOW RECYCLEBIN command shows only those objects that you can "undrop."

As you can see, when a table is moved to the Recycle Bin, Oracle assigns it a system-generated name, which is usually 30 characters long. If you wish to query an object in the Recycle Bin, you must use its new system-generated name, enclosed in double quotes:

```
SQL> SELECT * FROM "BIN$xTMPjHZ6SG+1xnDIaR9E+g==$0";

NAME
--------------------
valerie alapati
sam alapati
nina alapati
nicholas alapati
shannon alapati
SQL>
```

> ■**Note** You can only *query* objects in the Recycle Bin. INSERT, UPDATE, and DELETE commands won't work.

Oracle renames all objects in the Recycle Bin, including any dependent objects such as indexes, constraints, and triggers. When you recover a table, Oracle will recover the dependent objects as well, but they'll retain these cryptic system-generated names, so you will need to rename them appropriately.

In order to find out which of your tables are currently in the Recycle Bin, you can simply query the DBA_TABLES view. A table that was dropped and is in the Recycle Bin will show a YES value for the DROPPED column, and NO otherwise.

Restoring a Dropped Table

You can restore any dropped table, as long as it is still listed in the Recycle Bin, by using the FLASHBACK TABLE *table_name* TO BEFORE DROP command (at which point Oracle will also remove it from the Recycle Bin). The following example would restore the previously dropped persons table.

```
SQL> FLASHBACK TABLE persons TO BEFORE DROP;
Flashback complete.
SQL>
```

Alternatively, you can use the system-generated table name:

```
SQL> FLASHBACK TABLE "BIN$xTMPjHZ6SG+1xnDIaR9E+g==$0"
    TO BEFORE DROP;
Flashback complete.
SQL>
```

As part of the Flashback operation, you may want to rename the previously dropped table, as follows (you can use either the system-generated or original table name):

```
SQL> FLASHBACK TABLE "BIN$xTMPjHZ6SG+1xnDIaR9E+g==$0"
    TO BEFORE DROP
    RENAME TO NEW_PERSONS;
```

This is particularly useful when you've already created a new table with the same name as the dropped table.

If you drop a table and then create a new one of the same name, it's possible (if you then drop that new table) that the Recycle Bin will contain several versions of the dropped table, each with a unique system-generated table name. If you then issue a FLASHBACK TABLE . . . TO BEFORE DROP command using the original table name, Oracle will simply recover the latest version of the table. If you want to return to an older version, you can then simply reissue the same command until you recover the required version. Alternatively, you can provide the specific system-generated name of the table you want to recover.

Permanently Removing Tables

As noted previously, if you want to permanently and immediately remove a table, without moving it to the Recycle Bin, you must use the DROP TABLE table_name PURGE command:

```
SQL> DROP TABLE persons PURGE;
Table dropped.
SQL>
```

■**Tip** The new PURGE clause comes in especially handy when you want to drop a sensitive table and don't want it to appear in the Recycle Bin for security reasons.

You can also use the PURGE TABLE or the PURGE INDEX command to permanently erase a previously dropped table or index from the Recycle Bin:

```
SQL> PURGE TABLE persons                .
Table purged.
SQL>
```

Alternatively, you can use the system-generated name:

```
SQL> PURGE TABLE "BIN$Q1qZGCCMRsScbbRn9ivwfA==$0"
Table purged.
SQL>
```

If you have several tables of the same original name in the Recycle Bin, the PURGE command will drop the first table that you originally dropped.

■**Note** Once you remove an object from the Recycle Bin with the PURGE command, or when you drop an object with the PURGE option, you can't apply the Flashback Drop feature to retrieve those objects (or their dependent objects)—the purged objects are gone forever!

You can also use the PURGE TABLESPACE command to remove all objects from the Recycle Bin that are part of that tablespace, as shown here:

```
SQL> PURGE TABLESPACE users;
```

The following command will remove all objects of a single user, scott (along with any dependent objects that live in other tablespaces), from the tablespace named users:

```
SQL> PURGE TABLESPACE users USER scott;
```

To permanently remove all objects from a tablespace, without them moving to the Recycle Bin, you can use the DROP TABLESPACE . . . INCLUDING CONTENTS command. In addition, any objects belonging to the tablespace that are currently in the Recycle Bin are immediately purged. The DROP TABLESPACE command by itself, without the INCLUDING CONTENTS clause, will fail unless the tablespace is empty.

If you wish to permanently remove all of your objects currently in the Recycle Bin, you can use the PURGE RECYCLEBIN command (or PURGE USER_RECYCLEBIN). These will simply remove any objects belonging to the user issuing the command. In order to empty the entire Recycle Bin of all objects, regardless of ownership, you can use PURGE DBA_RECYCLEBIN. However, for obvious reasons, you need the SYSDBA privilege to issue this command.

Note The DROP USER . . . CASCADE command will instruct Oracle to drop the user and all objects owned by the user from the database and will automatically purge any objects in the Recycle Bin that belong to that user.

Finally, remember that Oracle may automatically purge objects from the Recycle Bin if it experiences space pressure. It will start with the oldest objects.

Necessary Privileges

To retrieve a table using the FLASHBACK TABLE *table_name* TO BEFORE DROP command, you must either be the owner or have the drop privileges (DROP TABLE or DROP ANY TABLE) on a table. To use the PURGE command, you need similar privileges. You must have the SELECT privilege and the FLASHBACK privilege on an object in order to query that object in the Recycle Bin.

Flashback Database

Before Oracle Database 10*g*, if you suffered logical database corruption, you would undertake traditional point-in-time recovery techniques, restoring datafile backup copies and then using archived redo logs to advance the database forward. This was often time consuming and cumbersome. No matter how limited the extent of the corruption, you would need to restore entire datafiles and apply the archived redo logs.

Note Oracle can check data block integrity by computing checksums before writing the data blocks to disk. When the block is subsequently read again, the checksum for the data block is computed again, and if the two checksums differ, there is likely corruption in the data block. By setting the DB_BLOCK_CHECKSUM initialization parameter to FULL, you can make the database perform the check in the database buffer cache itself, thus eliminating the possibility of corruption at the physical disk level. The DB_BLOCK_CHECKSUM parameter is FALSE by default.

The Flashback Database feature restores datafiles but without requiring backup datafiles and using just a fraction of the archived redo log information. A Flashback Database operation simply reverts all datafiles of the database to a specified previous point in time. With Flashback Database, the time it takes to recover is directly proportional to the number of changes that you need to undo. Thus, it is the size of the error and not the size of the database that determines the time it takes to recover. This means that you can recover from logical errors in a fraction of the time—perhaps as little as a hundredth of the time, depending on the size of the database—that it would take using traditional methods.

■**Note** Flashing back a database is possible only when there is no media failure. If you lose a datafile or it becomes corrupted, you'll have to recover using a restored datafile from backups.

You can use Flashback Database in the following situations:

- To retrieve a dropped schema
- When a user error affects the entire database
- When you truncate a table in error
- When a batch job performs only partial changes

The Flashback Database feature uses *flashback database logs*, which are stored in the new *flash recovery area*, to undo changes to a point in time just before a specified target time or SCN. Since the specified target time and the actual recovery time may differ slightly, you then use archived redo logs to recover the database over the short period of time between the target time and the actual recovery time.

Once the Flashback Database feature is enabled, you simply use the FLASHBACK DATABASE command to return the database to its state at a previous time, SCN, or log sequence. You can issue the FLASHBACK DATABASE command from either RMAN or SQL*Plus. The only difference is that RMAN will automatically retrieve the necessary archived redo logs, whereas in SQL*Plus you may have to supply the archived redo logs, unless you use the SET AUTORECOVERY ON feature in SQL*Plus.

We'll take a look at the whole Flashback Database process in more detail shortly, but first let's look at how to enable (and disable) the Flashback Database feature.

■**Tip** Since you need the current datafiles in order to apply changes to them, you can't use the Flashback Database feature in cases where a datafile has been damaged or lost.

Configuring Flashback Database

In order to configure the Flashback Database feature, you need to step through a series of operations, as follows:

1. Check that your database is in the archivelog mode by either querying the V$DATABASE view or simply issuing the following command:

```
SQL> ARCHIVE LOG LIST
Database log mode              Archive Mode
Automatic archival             Enabled
Archive destination            /u01/app/oracle/admin/finance/arch/finance
Oldest online log sequence     42035
Next log sequence to archive   42039
Current log sequence           42039
SQL>
```

The preceding output reveals that the database is indeed running in the archivelog mode. If it isn't, you can turn archive logging on with the ALTER DATABASE statement shown in the following code, after first shutting down the database and starting it up initially in the mount mode:

```
SQL> SHUTDOWN IMMEDIATE;
SQL> STARTUP MOUNT;
SQL> ALTER DATABASE ARCHIVELOG;
SQL> ALTER DATABASE OPEN
```

2. Set up a flash recovery area, as described in Chapter 15.

3. Set the DB_FLASHBACK_RETENTION_TARGET initialization parameter to specify how far back you can flash back your database. The following code sets the Flashback target to 1 day (1,440 minutes):

```
SQL> ALTER SYSTEM SET
2    DB_FLASHBACK_RETENTION_TARGET=1440;

System altered.
SQL>
```

4. Shut down and restart the database in the mount exclusive mode. If you are using a single instance, a simple MOUNT command can be used:

```
SQL> SHUTDOWN IMMEDIATE;
    Database closed.
    Database dismounted.
    ORACLE instance shut down.
SQL> STARTUP MOUNT;
```

5. Enable the Flashback Database feature:

```
SQL> ALTER DATABASE FLASHBACK ON;
    Database altered.
SQL>
```

6. Use the ALTER DATABASE OPEN command to open the database and then confirm that the Flashback Database feature is enabled, by querying the V$DATABASE view:

```
SQL> ALTER DATABASE OPEN;
SQL> SELECT FLASHBACK_ON FROM V$DATABASE;
FLA
--------
YES
SQL>
```

If you want to take the easy way out, you can use the OEM Database Control tool to configure Flashback logging in your database using the following steps (assuming you are working in archivelog mode):

1. From the Database Home Page, click the Maintenance tab.

2. Go to the Backup/Recovery section and click Configure Recovery Settings.

3. Under the Flash Recovery Area section, specify the Flash Recovery Area Location and Flash Recovery Area Size settings.

4. Check the box next to the option Enable Flash Database – flashback logging can be used for fast database point-in-time recovery, as shown in Figure 16-2.

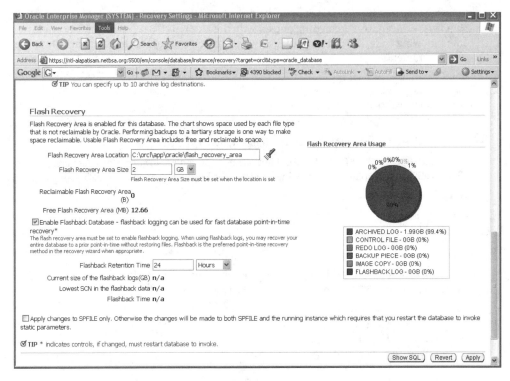

Figure 16-2. *Configuring Flashback Database using the Database Control*

Disabling Flashback Database

You can turn the Flashback Database feature off by issuing the ALTER DATABASE FLASHBACK OFF command. First, though, make sure you shut down the database and restart the database in the mount (or mount exclusive) mode before using this command.

```
SQL> SHUTDOWN IMMEDIATE;
SQL> STARTUP MOUNT;
SQL> ALTER DATABASE FLASHBACK OFF;
```

■**Tip** When you disable the Flashback Database feature, Oracle deletes all Flashback Database logs in the flash recovery area.

If you want to use Flashback Database, but not for certain tablespaces, you can disable it using the ALTER TABLESPACE command:

```
SQL> ALTER TABLESPACE users FLASHBACK OFF;
Tablespace altered.
```

Once disabled, Oracle will not log any Flashback Database data for that tablespace. If you want to switch it back on again, you simply issue this command:

```
SQL> ALTER TABLESPACE users FLASHBACK ON;
Tablespace altered.
SQL>
```

As Chapter 5 explains, you can create a tablespace with the Flashback feature turned off by specifying the FLASHBACK OFF clause when creating the tablespace. By default, of course, Flashback is on.

Flashback Database Concepts

With the Flashback Database feature enabled, a new background process, RVWR (recovery writer), is also enabled. This process copies, at infrequent intervals in order to reduce the I/O and CPU overhead, the before-image of each altered block in the datafiles from the memory buffer (flashback buffer) to the flashback database logs, which are stored in the flash recovery area. This flash recovery area is a dedicated area of disk storage for the retention of recovery-related components, such as these datafile image copies, incremental backups, and archived redo logs.

■**Note** To increase disk throughput, Oracle recommends the use of fast file systems and multiple disk spindles with small stripe sizes (128KB) for flash recovery areas.

The Flashback Database logs are similar to the traditional Oracle redo logs (both logs are written to from a buffer area) but with the big difference that there aren't any *archived* Flashback Database logs! Oracle stores all the Flashback Database logs in the flash recovery area.

■**Note** You need the SYSDBA privilege to perform a Flashback Database operation.

You can use these before-images of data blocks to reconstruct a datafile as it existed at a specific time in the past. In essence, you can back out any changes made after a specified target time. In reality, the Flashback Database logs are used to recover to a time immediately before the target time, and Oracle then uses traditional archive logs to write any changes made during the short gap between the target recovery time and the actual recovery time.

For example, if you want to flash back to 9:00 a.m., it may turn out that the Flashback Database logs nearest to the target time were written at 8:57 a.m. You then apply the changes from archived or online redo log files to cover the three-to-four minute gap. For this reason, although you aren't doing a traditional point-in-time recovery using backup files and archived redo log files, the redo logs must still be available for the entire time period spanned by the Flashback Database logs.

When you actually issue a FLASHBACK DATABASE command, Oracle first checks to see that the required archived and online redo log files are available. If so, it automatically reverts all the currently online datafiles to the SCN or time you specify in the FLASHBACK DATABASE statement.

■**Tip** The time taken to flash back a database depends on how far back you want to go and the number of data block changes in the meantime. If you have a heavily used DML-based database, you'll have more data block changes than if the database were mainly supporting queries.

Flashback Storage Limits

You must bear in mind that Oracle doesn't guarantee that you can flash back your database as far as the time set in the FLASHBACK_RETENTION_TARGET init parameter (one day in our earlier example). If Oracle is running low on free space in the flash recovery area, it will remove some older flashback logs in order to make room for newly arriving datafile backups, archived redo log files, or any other backup-related files that are part of the flash recovery area.

Furthermore, as we noted earlier, the flash recovery area is specifically set aside for the storage of recovery-related files. The database accords priority to storing these recovery-related files over retaining Flashback Database logs. As such, the database will delete Flashback Database logs if it needs the flash recovery area space to accommodate other recovery-related files.

Therefore, it is essential that you monitor the flash recovery area's size to ensure that you have sufficient space so as not to risk losing any of the Flashback Database logs that you need to recover your database.

■**Note** It is possible to create a guaranteed restore point to ensure that Oracle will always keep the Flashback Database logs and redo logs necessary to flash back the database to a specified point in time. I explain restore points and guaranteed restore points in the "Using Restore Points" section, later in this chapter.

The amount of space you need to allocate to the flash recovery area will depend on the value you set for the DB_FLASHBACK_RETENTION_TARGET parameter. After the database has been running for a reasonable length of time with the Flashback Database feature enabled (enough time to make sure that a typical workload is recorded and that the level of data modification activity in your database is adequately captured), you can estimate the space required by querying the V$FLASHBACK_DATABASE_LOG view, as follows:

```
SQL> SELECT estimated_flashback_size, retention_target, flashback_size
     FROM v$flashback_database_log;

ESTIMATED_FLASHBACK_SIZE    RETENTION_TARGET    FLASHBACK_SIZE
------------------------    ----------------    ------------------
        126418944               1440              152600576
SQL>
```

Although this query helps you estimate the required disk space for the Flashback Database logs, there is no guarantee that the space will suffice. In order to find out how far you can flash back your database at any given time, use the following query:

```
SQL> SELECT oldest_flashback_scn,
     oldest_flashback_time
     FROM v$flashback_database_log;

OLDEST_FLASHBACK_SCN    OLDEST_FLASHBACK_
--------------------    ------------------
            5964669     07-03-08 12:22:37
SQL>
```

If the result indicates that you can't wind your database back as far as the time set in the DB_FLASHBACK_RETENTION_TARGET parameter, then you should consider increasing the size of your flash recovery area.

The V$FLASHBACK_DATABASE_STAT view allows you to monitor any modulation in the generation of your Flashback data over the course of a day. You can adjust your retention target or flash recovery area size or both, based on the statistics provided by this view.

Flashback Database in Action

We are now ready to take a look at Flashback Database in action. I use SQL commands in this example, but you can also use RMAN to perform the same steps. For this example, we will first create a table called persons and load it with some test data.

Follow these steps:

1. Create the table:

```
SQL> CREATE TABLE persons AS
     SELECT * FROM persons@prod;

Table created.
SQL>
```

2. Get a count of the total number of rows in the new table:

```
SQL> SELECT COUNT(*) FROM persons;

  COUNT(*)
----------
     32768
```

3. Find out the current SCN of the database:

```
SQL> SELECT current_scn FROM V$DATABASE;

CURRENT_SCN
-----------
    5965123
```

4. Perform an INSERT, doubling the number of rows in our persons table, as shown here:

```
SQL> INSERT INTO persons
     SELECT * FROM persons;

65536 rows created.
SQL>
```

5. Verify the data insertion as follows:

```
SQL> SELECT COUNT(*) FROM persons;

  COUNT(*)
--------------
     65536
```

Our goal is to flash the database back to the point in time when the persons table held 32,768 rows. In effect, this means flashing back to the SCN 5965123. Follow these steps:

1. Shut down the database and start it up again in the mount exclusive mode, as shown here:

```
SQL> SHUTDOWN IMMEDIATE;
SQL> STARTUP MOUNT;
ORACLE instance started.
. . .
Database mounted.
SQL>
```

Note In order to use the Flashback Database feature, the database must be running in mount mode.

---

2. Issue the following simple FLASHBACK DATABASE command:

```
SQL> FLASHBACK DATABASE TO SCN 5964663;
Flashback complete.
SQL>
```

Note that TO SCN takes the database back to its state at that SCN. You can also take a database back to its state just before an SCN by using the TO BEFORE SCN clause. Alternatively, you can use the TO TIMESTAMP or TO BEFORE TIMESTAMP clauses to revert the database to a specified time stamp or to one second before the specified time stamp.

3. In order to query the persons table, you must first open the database, which I try to do here:

```
SQL> ALTER DATABASE OPEN;
alter database open
*
ERROR at line 1:
ORA-01589: must use RESETLOGS or NORESETLOGS option for database open
SQL>
```

As you can see, it didn't work: in order to have write access to the flashed back database, we have to reopen the database with an ALTER DATABASE OPEN RESETLOGS statement. However, you should consider first opening the database using ALTER DATABASE OPEN READ ONLY in order to confirm that you have flashed the database back to the correct point in time or the correct SCN. If, after the initial read-only check, you find that you flashed back too far into the past, you can use redo logs to roll forward. If you haven't gone far enough back, you can reissue the FLASHBACK DATABASE command using an earlier SCN.

Once you are certain you have the right time, finalize the flashback by issuing this command:

```
SQL> ALTER DATABASE OPEN RESETLOGS;
Database altered.
SQL>
```

4. Verify that the database has been flashed back appropriately:

```
SQL> SELECT COUNT(*) FROM persons;
   COUNT(*)
   ---------
   32768
SQL>
```

As an alternative to using an SCN, you may use an archived log sequence, or a prior time, to specify the Flashback point. Here are some examples using time and log sequence numbers:

```
/* will flash back the database to the log sequence 12345 */
SQL> FLASHBACK DATABASE TO SEQUENCE 12345;

/* will flash back the database to an hour ago */
SQL> FLASHBACK DATABASE TO TIMESTAMP(SYSDATE -1/24);
```

No matter whether you use an SCN, a time stamp, or a log sequence number, if you're sure you have recovered your database to the state you wanted, you can make the database available to your users by using the following command:

```
RMAN> ALTER DATABASE OPEN RESETLOGS;
```

Your database will now reflect the state of the database at the past SCN or time stamp you chose. All subsequent changes in the database are removed.

If, on the other hand, you aren't happy with the state of the database after the Flashback Database operation, you can simply undo the results of the entire Flashback operation by issuing the following command:

```
SQL> RECOVER DATABASE;
```

The RECOVER DATABASE command will perform a complete recovery by applying all the changes in the archived redo logs and making the database current again.

If you think you didn't go far back enough the first time when you flashed back your database, you can run the FLASHBACK DATABASE command once again, to take the database further back in time.

If you have flashed back farther than necessary, you can use the RECOVER DATABASE UNTIL command to take the database forward in time.

Flashback Database Considerations

I'll end this section with a few limitations that you must bear in mind when using the Flashback Database feature:

- You must be running the database in the archivelog mode.

- If you've lost a datafile, or you can't use a particular datafile for whatever reason, then you can't use Flashback Database for recovery.

- If a control file has been restored or re-created during the time span you want to flash back over, then you can't use the Flashback Database feature.

- You can't flash back a database to before a RESETLOGS operation.

- You can't flash back a datafile that was shrunk or dropped during the time span covered by the Flashback Table operation.

■**Note** As of Oracle Database 10*g* Release 2, you can use Flashback Database to go back past an OPEN RESETLOGS operation. You can thus return the current database to an ancestor or a sibling incarnation.

Using Restore Points

A *restore point* is an alias for an SCN, which eliminates the need to research and record SCNs or time stamps, which you need to use for Flashback Database and Flashback Table operations. Suppose you're executing a new package or procedure that will modify a large amount of data. You can create a restore point beforehand, just in case you have to reverse the effects of this operation. If you need to ever revert back to the original data, all you need to do is refer to the restore point in a Flashback Database or Flashback Table operation. You can also use restore points in a point-in-time recovery operation.

You can use a restore point when performing the following types of operations:

- Flashback Table
- Flashback Database
- Database recovery operations

■**Note** In order to use restore points, you must be using at least Oracle Database 10*g* Release 2, the database should be running in the archivelog mode, and you must use a flash recovery area.

Here's how you create a restore point:

```
SQL> CREATE RESTORE POINT test;
Restore point created.
SQL>
```

You can drop a restore point by using this command:

```
SQL> DROP RESTORE POINT test;
Restore point dropped.
SQL>
```

Guaranteed Restore Points

The restore point I created in the previous example is known as an *ordinary* restore point. An ordinary restore point merely provides you a convenient way of specifying a prior SCN or a point in time during a Flashback or recovery operation. However, an ordinary restore point doesn't guarantee that the database will retain the Flashback Database logs necessary for a Flashback Database operation to succeed under all circumstances. However, you can also create a *guaranteed* restore point, which guarantees that you can revert your database to the SCN or time specified by the restore point. All you need is enough room in the flash recovery area to store the logs necessary to enforce the guaranteed restore point.

Ordinarily, before undertaking a major operation in the database, you might ensure that you have a backup, just in case you have to revert to the original version of the database if something goes wrong. A guaranteed restore point makes performing a backup unnecessary. With a guaranteed restore point, you are always guaranteed that you can flash back your database to that prior time.

Guaranteed restore points don't depend on the Flashback logs. Thus, you can create a guaranteed restore point even if Flashback logging is turned off. Guaranteed restore points use a logging mechanism that's somewhat similar to the Flashback logs, but it's separate from them.

If you use a guaranteed restore point, Oracle won't delete any Flashback logs that are created after you create the guaranteed restore point. Therefore, you can end up filling up your flash recovery area and causing the database to stop its operations if Flashback logging is enabled when you're using guaranteed restore points. You're better off turning off Flashback logging if you're using guaranteed restore points.

■**Tip** Guaranteed restore points use a separate logging mechanism from the Flashback logging used for a Flashback Database operation. You can use guaranteed restore points with or without Flashback logging enabled—you must, however, configure a flash recovery area.

You create a guaranteed restore point the same way as an ordinary restore point, just adding the GUARANTEE FLASHBACK clause to it, as shown here:

```
SQL> CREATE RESTORE POINT test_guarantee GUARANTEE FLASHBACK DATABASE;
Restore point created.
SQL>
```

You drop a guaranteed restore point in the same way as an ordinary restore point.

Once you create a guaranteed restore point, you can use it to recover your database through a Flashback Database operation in the following manner:

```
RMAN> FLASHBACK DATABASE TO RESTORE POINT test_guarantee;
```

Viewing Restore Points

You use the V$RESTORE_POINT view to view information about restore points in your database. Here's a typical query on that view:

```
SQL> SELECT name, scn, storage_size, time, guarantee_flashback_database
    FROM v$restore_point;
```

```
NAME              SCN         STORAGE_SIZE    TIME                          GUARANTEE
------------------------------------------------------------------------------------
TEST_GUARANTEE    1685977     199409664       09-MAY-08 02.10.55.00 PM      YES
TEST              4039395     0               30-JUN-08 05.49.02.00 AM      NO
SQL>
```

The preceding output shows two restore points, one of which is ordinary and the other being a guaranteed restore point. The SCN column tells you when each of the restore points was created. If you need to perform a recovery now, all you need to do is provide the name of the restore point during the recovery, rather than the actual SCN or calendar time. As you can see, the STORAGE_SIZE column, which shows the space (in bytes) needed for supporting the restore point, is zero for the ordinary restore point and about 200MB for the guaranteed restore point.

As you are aware, you can determine whether a database is running in the Flashback Database mode by using the following query:

```
SQL> SELECT flashback_on FROM v$database;
```

```
FLASHBACK_ON
------------
NO
```

In the preceding example, the NO value for the FLASHBACK_ON column means that the Flashback Database feature is currently not enabled in this database. However, if you've created a restore point, the same query would show this:

```
SQL> SELECT flashback_on FROM v$database;
```

```
FLASHBACK_ON
------------------
RESTORE POINT ONLY
SQL>
```

Even with the Flashback Database feature disabled, you can see that you can use restore points to guarantee your ability to flash back a database. Once you enable the Flashback Database feature, you'll be able to flash back the database to the time or SCN specified by the guaranteed restore point. The logs maintained in the flash recovery area by the guaranteed restore point will enable this flashback of the database, even though there are no Flashback logs during that time period.

Note that a guaranteed restore point guarantees only a Flashback Database operation, not a point-in-time operation or a Flashback Table operation, since they require the necessary backup files and undo data to succeed. However, guaranteed restore points can be used to approximate the SCN or time for a point-in-time or Flashback Table operation.

■**Note** Although you can flash back your database to a guaranteed restore point even if Flashback Database wasn't originally enabled and therefore no Flashback logs were collected, you can only recover exactly to the guaranteed restore point. If you want to recover to any point before that, you must still use a point-in-time recovery technique using backups and archived log files.

Repairing Data Corruption and Trial Recovery

As you saw in Chapter 15, Oracle provides several means of detecting data block corruption. These methods include the use of the ANALYZE command, the DBVERIFY command, and the DB_BLOCK_CHECKING initialization parameter. Oracle also provides the excellent DBMS_REPAIR package, which not only detects corruption, but also helps you fix it. Using this package, you can analyze and repair block corruption in Oracle tables and indexes.

Block Media Recovery

Even if only a few data blocks in a datafile are corrupted, the entire datafile becomes unavailable to users during a normal datafile recovery process whether you use RMAN or user-managed recovery techniques.

RMAN can help you recover from data block corruption by enabling *block media recovery* (BMR). With BMR, your smallest recoverable unit of data is the data block, instead of the datafile. Unlike in datafile recovery, which makes one or more entire datafiles unavailable while you're recovering data, with BMR virtually the entire database continues to be available to users while the corrupted blocks are being recovered. If there's physical corruption involving a known set of data blocks, you can use the block media recovery technique to fix the problem. Only the specific data blocks you are recovering will be unavailable to users. RMAN's BLOCKRECOVER command recovers blocks marked as corrupt in the V$BACKUP_CORRUPTION and V$COPY_CORRUPTION views.

During a block media recovery operation, RMAN restores from backups only those data blocks that need recovery. Redo application time is vastly reduced because you only need to recover certain data blocks, not entire datafiles.

Thus, BMR helps you achieve the following goals:

- Faster recovery time
- Increased database availability

Data block corruption could lead to the following types of messages in your alert log:

```
ORA_11578: ORACLE data block corrupted (file# 9, block# 21)
ORA=01110:  data file 9: /u01/app/oracle/oradata/remorse/users_01.dbf'
```

Once you have the datafile number and the corrupt block number, you can use the following RECOVER . . . BLOCK command to recover the corrupted block:

```
RMAN>  RECOVER
       DATAFILE 9 BLOCK 21;
```

By default, RMAN first searches in the flashback logs for good blocks to replace the corrupted data blocks. After this, it searches the backup files (full and incremental) for the good blocks. Since flashback logs are readily available, as compared to database backups, which may even be stored offsite sometimes, RMAN can quickly find the necessary blocks in the flash recovery area. Of course, in order to use the flashback logs, you must have enabled the Flashback Database feature. RMAN determines the backups from which it needs to get the necessary data blocks to perform recovery.

It then reads the backups and collects the necessary data blocks in memory buffers, and it may use an older backup if it finds that the most recent backup contains corrupt data blocks. RMAN then starts and manages the BMR session, reading any necessary archived redo logs from the backed-up archived logs. The RECOVER . . . BLOCK command always results in a complete recovery; you can't perform a PITR using this command.

Anytime you run a command such as ANALYZE or DBVERIFY (dbv), for example, the database adds rows to the V$DATABASE_BLOCK_CORRUPTION view regarding any blocks that it marks corrupt. There can be two types of corrupt blocks: physical corruption and logical corruption. A physically corrupted block remains unrecognizable to the database, whereas the database can recognize a logically corrupt data block, but the contents of the block are logically inconsistent. Block media recovery can repair only physically corrupted data blocks but not the logically corrupted blocks.

The previous example showed how to use RMAN to recover a single corrupt block. You can also recover multiple corrupt blocks using the same command, but if you have multiple corrupt blocks and need to recover all of them, you can use a slightly different technique. You need to follow these steps to enable RMAN to automatically recover all blocks listed in the V$DATABASE_BLOCK_CORRUPTION view:

1. Issue the following SQL statement to determine how many corrupt blocks exist in the database:

   ```
   SQL> SELECT * FROM V$DATABASE_BLOCK_CORRUPTION;
   ```

2. Next, start RMAN, connect to the target database, and issue the following command:

   ```
   RMAN> RECOVER CORRUPTION LIST;
   ```

RMAN will automatically recover all blocks marked corrupt in the target database and also remove them from the V$DATABASE_BLOCK_CORRUPTION view. You can therefore check the success of the recovery by querying this view after RMAN completes its recovery.

If you think you have extensive database block corruption and you aren't sure whether the preceding method will successfully recover the data, the best course of action is to first get in touch with Oracle Worldwide Support, which has access to specialized tools that can help you extract data from corrupt data blocks. Oracle may charge you extra for these services, but if your data is critical, it may be well worth the expense.

Trial Recovery

While you're recovering databases, the recovery process may encounter corrupt data blocks somewhere along the line. When a situation like this occurs, the recovery process will stop, leaving the database in a consistent state. Although it's possible to recover the database to a point before the corruption occurred, this could be a time-consuming process.

To determine the extent of the damage before you start recovery, you can use a *trial recovery*. Depending on the amount of corruption you find, you can then decide whether you'll use an incomplete recovery or continue recovery beyond the corrupted block by using the ALLOW *n* CORRUPTION recovery option. For example, if you want to ignore a minor amount of corruption, you can use the following command, which can find one corrupt data block yet continue the recovery process:

```
SQL> RECOVER DATABASE ALLOW 1 CORRUPTION;
```

Trial recovery lets you *simulate* the recovery process—it neither performs a real recovery nor fixes data corruption. It lets you know whether there is corruption and, if there is, the extent of the corruption. Trial recovery proceeds in the same way as real data recovery by applying the redo changes. However, trial recovery changes the data blocks only in memory, not permanently on disk. After the test, it rolls back all its changes, leaving only the possible error messages in the alert log file.

Here are the typical trial recovery commands:

```
SQL> RECOVER DATABASE UNTIL CANCEL TEST;
ORA-10574: Test recovery did not corrupt any data block
ORA-10573: Test recovery tested redo from change 9948095 to 9948095
ORA-10570: Test recovery complete
/* The following statement would recover a tablespace */
SQL> RECOVER TABLESPACE users TEST;
```

Troubleshooting Recovery Errors

Recovery management is prone to more errors, and it needs more troubleshooting than any other part of Oracle database administration. If a production recovery is being bogged down by Oracle errors, it gets to be an even more stressful event. You could conceivably run into numerous different problems over the years. This section covers a few common error messages issued during a recovery session.

The ORA-01194 Error

When you're trying to start up a database after a database cloning, you'll usually end up with the ORA-01194 error. Listing 16-11 shows the sequence of Oracle messages and the DBA's responses.

Listing 16-11. *The ORA-01194 Error*

```
SQL> startup
ORACLE instance started.
Total System Global Area  118255568 bytes
Fixed Size                   282576 bytes
Variable Size              83886080 bytes
Database Buffers           33554432 bytes
Redo Buffers                 532480 bytes
Database mounted.
ORA-01589: must use RESETLOGS or NORESETLOGS option for database open
SQL> alter database open noresetlogs;
alter database open noresetlogs
*
ERROR at line 1:
ORA-01588: must use RESETLOGS option for database open
SQL> alter database open resetlogs;
alter database open resetlogs
*
ERROR at line 1:
ORA-01194: file 1 needs more recovery to be consistent
ORA-01110: data file 1: 'C:\ORACLENT\ORADATA\MANAGER\SYSTEM01.DBF'
SQL> recover database until cancel using backup controlfile;
ORA-00279: change 405719 generated at 05/26/2008 15:51:04 needed for thread 1
ORA-00289: suggestion : C:\ORACLENT\RDBMS\ARC00019.001
ORA-00280: change 405719 for thread 1 is in sequence #19
Specify log: {<RET>=suggested | filename | AUTO | CANCEL}
ORA-01547: warning: RECOVER succeeded but OPEN RESETLOGS would get error below
ORA-01194: file 1 needs more recovery to be consistent
ORA-01110: data file 1: 'C:\ORACLENT\ORADATA\MANAGER\SYSTEM01.DBF'
SQL>
```

Oracle keeps issuing the 01194 error message, and even using the RECOVER DATABASE UNTIL CANCEL USING BACKUP CONTROLFILE command (with which you can mimic a recovery) does not succeed in stopping it. The problem is that the changes needed for recovery are in the very last online redo log, not in any archived redo log Oracle might be suggesting to you. When you apply this online redo log, Oracle will finish recovery successfully, as shown in Listing 16-12.

Listing 16-12. *Applying a Redo Log During Recovery*

```
SQL> RECOVER DATABASE UNTIL CANCEL USING BACKUP CONTROLFILE;
ORA-00279: change 405719 generated at 06/30/2008 15:51:04 needed for thread 1
ORA-00289: suggestion : C:\ORACLENT\RDBMS\ARC00019.001
ORA-00280: change 405719 for thread 1 is in sequence #19
Specify log: {<RET>=suggested | filename | AUTO | CANCEL}
C:\ORACLENT\ORADATA\MANAGER\REDO03.LOG
Log applied.
Media recovery complete.
SQL> alter database open resetlogs;
Database altered.
SQL>
```

The ORA-01152 Error

The ORA-01152 error ("File # was not restored from a sufficiently old backup") bedevils quite a few recovery sessions. This is an interesting situation whose solution is similar to the preceding example. You provide all the archived redo logs that Oracle asks for, but you still get errors, as shown in Listing 16-13.

Listing 16-13. *When an Archived Redo Log File Isn't Needed for Recovery*

```
ORA-00289: suggestion :
/u01/app/oracle/admin/finance/arch/finance/_0000012976.arc
ORA-00280: change 962725326 for thread 1 is in sequence #12976
ORA-00278:
logfile'/u01/app/oracle/admin/finance/arch/finance/_0000012975.arc'
no longer needed for this recovery
Specify log: {<RET>=suggested | filename | AUTO | CANCEL}
ORA-01547: warning: RECOVER succeeded but OPEN RESETLOGS would get error below
ORA-01152: file 1 was not restored from a sufficiently old backup
ORA-01110: data file 1: '/pase16/oradata/finance/system_01.dbf'ORA-01112:
media recovery not started
```

In response to the preceding errors, the following recovery command was used:

```
SQL> recover database until cancel using backup controlfile;
ORA-00279: change 962726675 generated at 07/30/2008 04:32:48 needed for thread 1
ORA-00289: suggestion :
/u01/app/oracle/admin/finance/arch/finance/_0000012977.arc
ORA-00280: change 962726675 for thread 1 is in sequence #12977
```

Oracle's response was to ask for an archived redo log file, but because the recovery process has already indicated that it doesn't need any more archived redo logs, you can ignore this misleading request and provide Oracle with the name of your restored online redo log files, starting with the first one. One of those redo log files will have the change number (SCN=962726675) the recovery process is looking for. Just provide Oracle with your redo log files—one member from each redo log group. Listing 16-14 shows the rest of this recovery process.

Listing 16-14. *Using an Online Redo Log File During Recovery*

```
Specify log: {<RET>=suggested | filename | AUTO | CANCEL}
/pase04/oradata/finance/redo01a.rdo
ORA-00279: change 962746677 generated at 07/30/2008 04:33:52 needed for thread 1
ORA-00289: suggestion :
/u01/app/oracle/admin/finance/arch/finance/_0000012978.arc
ORA-00280: change 962746677 for thread 1 is in sequence #12978
ORA-00278: log file '/pase04/oradata/finance/redo01a.rdo'
no longer needed for this recovery
Specify log: {<RET>=suggested | filename | AUTO | CANCEL}
/pase04/oradata/finance/redo02a.rdo
Log applied.
Media recovery complete.
SQL>
```

The ORA-00376 Error

Another common error that you could meet with is the ORA-00376 error, which indicates that your database can't read a certain file or files. The error results in the following messages:

```
ORA-00376: file 10 cannot be read at this time
ORA-01110: data file 10: '/u01/app/oracle/remorse/data_01.dbf'
```

ORA-00376 is usually the result of a datafile or tablespace being offline. By bringing the tablespace or datafile online, you can fix the problem easily. Sometimes the error is the result of the datafile not existing at the tablespace level. In this case, you have to take the tablespace offline, re-create it with the correct datafile name, and bring it online.

The Transaction Backout Feature

You can use Oracle's Flashback Transaction Backout feature to roll back or undo even committed statements. You can roll back a transaction and its dependent transactions as well, without having to take the database offline. The database uses the undo data to create what are called *compensation transactions* to return the data to its before-change state. If a set of related transactions involve complex insert, update, and delete operations, the Flashback Transaction Backout feature lets you undo the entire set of changes with literally a single click (using the Database Control).

Use the TRANSACTION_BACKOUT procedure from the DBMS_FLASHBACK package to perform a transaction backout. Here's the structure of the procedure:

```
PROCEDURE TRANSACTION_BACKOUT
 Argument Name                  Type                    In/Out Default?
 ------------------------------ ----------------------- ------ --------
 NUMTXNS                        NUMBER                  IN
 NAMES                          TXNAME_ARRAY            IN
 OPTIONS                        BINARY_INTEGER          IN     DEFAULT
 TIMEHINT                       TIMESTAMP               IN
```

The transaction backout feature relies primarily on the undo data saved in the undo tablespace. However, the database also needs the redo generated by the undo blocks. Thus, you need both the undo segments and the archived redo logs to perform a Flashback Transaction Backout operation.

Prerequisites

Before you can use the Flashback Transaction Backout feature, you must enable supplemental logging in the database, as shown here:

```
SQL> alter database add supplemental log data;
SQL> alter database add supplemental log data
     (primary key) columns;
```

In order for any user to use the Flashback Transaction Backout feature, grant the following privileges to the user:

```
SQL> grant execute on dbms_flashback to hr;
SQL> grant select any transaction to hr;
```

In addition, if a user wants to back out transactions that use tables in another user's schema, the first user must have the necessary DML privileges on the second user's objects.

Backing Out Transactions

Use the DBMS_FLASHBACK.TRANSACTION_BACKOUT procedure to back out a transaction. The TRANSACTION_BACKOUT procedure contains the following parameters:

```
PROCEDURE TRANSACTION_BACKOUT

Argument Name       Type            In/Out    Default?
----------------    -------------   -------   ----------
NUMBEROFXIDS        NUMBER          IN
XIDS                XID_ARRAY       IN
OPTIONS             BINARY_INTEGER  IN        DEFAULT
SCNHINT             TIMESTAMP       IN
```

In the TRANSACTION_BACKOUT procedure, the parameters stand for the following:

- numberofxids: Number of transactions to be backed out
- xids: List of transaction identifiers that must be passed as an array
- options: Backout options relating to the order in which to back out the parent and child transactions. You can specify the following options:

  - nocascade is the default value and backs out transactions that you don't expect to have any dependent transactions.
  - cascade backs out the dependent transactions first and then the parent transactions.
  - nocascade_force backs out the parent transactions only and ignores the dependent transactions.
  - noconflict_only backs out only the changes to nonconflicting rows of a transaction.

- scnhint: SCN at the beginning of the transaction you are backing out

The TRANSACTION_BACKOUT procedure is an overloaded procedure, and thus there can be multiple variations of the procedure depending on the parameters you specify. Although I can specify the xids parameter, I can also specify the txnames parameter instead, to pass an array of transaction names instead of an array of transaction IDs. Instead of an scnhint parameter, I can also specify the timehint parameter to provide the time at the start of the transaction I am backing out. If you are using transaction names and not transaction IDs, you must specify the timehint parameter instead of the scnhint parameter.

The greater the undo generated by the transaction you're backing out, the longer will it take to undo it. When you execute the TRANSACTION_BACKOUT procedure, the database doesn't automatically back out the transactions. The database performs the necessary DML operations to back out the transactions but stops short of committing them. It holds locks on the rows and the tables involved, thus keeping other transactions from affecting the transaction you want to back out. The database produces a transaction backout report, which you can view before finalizing the transaction backout by committing the changes made by executing the TRANSACTION_BACKOUT procedure. The TRANSACTION_BACKOUT procedure populates the DBA_FLASHBACK_TRANSACTION_STATE and the DBA_FLASHBACK_TRANSACTION_REPORT views. After the database backs out a transaction, it records the transaction in the DBA_FLASHBACK_TRANSACTION_STATE view. Query the DBA_FLASHBACK_TRANSACTION_REPORT view to examine the reports relating to the transaction backout operations.

Using the TRANSACTION_BACKOUT Procedure

The following example shows how to execute the TRANSACTION_BACKOUT procedure to back out a transaction. Before you can execute this procedure, you must first create a variable of an XID_ARRAY type to hold the set of transaction identifiers.

```
declare
    trans_arr xid_array;
begin
    trans_arr := xid_array('030003000D02540','D10001000D02550');
    dbms_flashback.transaction_backout (
        numtxns         => 1,
        xids            => trans_arr,
        options         => dbms_flashback.nocascade
    );
end;
```

The previous code backs out the primary and the dependent transactions in one step. You can also use the Enterprise Manager to back out transactions.

Flashback Data Archive

The undo tablespace can help you out with various flashback-related operations to retrieve older data, but what do you do if the older data is really old, say, from six months or a year ago? Obviously, most databases don't use undo tablespaces that store undo data for that long a period. Of course, the size of the undo tablespace and the amount of undo data generated by the database determines how far back in time can you go. The purpose of the undo tablespace is to help with the rolling back of statements as well as to maintain read consistency in the database, and not to provide a historical record of all changes in data.

A Flashback Data Archive is a mechanism consisting of one or more tablespaces that store transitional changes to a specified table or tables. You can't turn flashback data archiving on for the entire database, but rather must turn it on for specified tables. A Flashback Data Archive is the ideal mechanism to store all transactional changes to any table in the database over a period of time. You may want to save the data for compliance reasons or for other purposes, as I show later in this chapter. I show how to set up and use flashback data archiving in the following sections.

Managing the Flashback Data Archive

You can use the CREATE FLASHBACK ARCHIVE and the DROP FLASHBACK ARCHIVE statements to create and drop a Flashback Data Archive. You use the ALTER FLASHBACK ARCHIVE statement to modify the properties of a Flashback Data Archive, such as the retention period. In the following sections, I explain the various Flashback Data Archive management tasks.

Creating a Flashback Data Archive

Use the CREATE FLASHBACK ARCHIVE statement to create a Flashback Data Archive. Before you execute this statement, make sure that the tablespace you specify in the statement exists. You can specify the following when creating a Flashback Data Archive:

- Name of the archive
- Name of the first tablespace of the archive
- The quota for the archive in the first tablespace
- How far the database must retain the data

Of the four parameters you can specify, only two—the name of the first tablespace for the archive and the retention period for the data—are mandatory. Here's an example that shows how to create a Flashback Data Archive named flash1:

```
SQL> CREATE FLASHBACK ARCHIVE flash1
     TABLESPACE test_tbs
     RETENTION 1 YEAR;
```

The previous statement creates the new flashback archive flash1 and ensures that any tables you enable for archiving will be tracked and the transactional changes to data in the table will be saved for a year. After the year is up, the transactional changes will be automatically deleted, thus keeping only a year's worth of changes at a given time. In the next example, I show how to create a Flashback Data Archive that retains data for three years. In addition, I specify the QUOTA parameter to limit the amount of space that the archive can use in tablespace test_tbs. You can have more than one Flashback Data Archive in a database. In this example, I specify the DEFAULT parameter to mark this flashback archive as the default Flashback Data Archive for the database.

```
SQL> CREATE FLASHBACK ARCHIVE DEFAULT flash1
     TABLESPACE test_tbs
     QUOTA 5g
     RETENTION 3 YEAR;
```

Altering a Flashback Data Archive

You can use the ALTER FLASHBACK ARCHIVE statement to alter the properties of a Flashback Data Archive, such as the size of the archive and changes in the retention time for the archived data. Here are some examples:

- Specify a Flashback Data Archive as the default archive for the database:

  ```
  SQL> ALTER FLASHBACK ARCHIVE flash1 SET DEFAULT;
  ```

- Add a tablespace to the archive:

  ```
  SQL> ALTER FLASHBACK ARCHIVE flash1
       ADD TABLESPACE flash2    QUOTA 10G;
  ```

- Change the retention period:

  ```
  SQL> ALTER FLASHBACK ARCHIVE flash1 MODIFY RETENTION 5 YEAR;
  ```

- Purge all data from an archive:

  ```
  SQL> ALTER FLASHBACK ARCHIVE flash1 PURGE ALL;
  ```

- Purge all data older than a week from an archive:

```
SQL> ALTER FLASHBACK ARCHIVE flash1
        PURGE BEFORE TIMESTAMP (SYSTIMESTAMP - INTERVAL '1' DAY);
```

Dropping a Flashback Data Archive

You can remove a Flashback Data Archive with the following statement:

```
SQL> DROP FLASHBACK ARCHIVE flash1;
```

The previous statement will only remove the Flashback Data Archive. The tablespace that hosts the archive remains intact, since that tablespace may contain other objects besides the Flashback Data Archive.

Viewing the Flashback Data Archive Data

You can use the following views to find out details about the data stored in the Flashback Data Archive:

- *DBA_FLASHBACK_ARCHIVE*: Shows details about the Flashback Data Archive
- *DBA_FLASHBACK_ARCHIVE_TS*: Shows information about the tablespaces hosting the Flashback Data Archive
- *DBA_FLASHBACK_ARCHIVE_TABLES*: Shows information about the tables that are enabled for flashback data archiving

Enabling the Flashback Data Archive

You can only turn archiving on at the table level. You can't turn archiving on for the entire database. By default, the database doesn't archive any changes. You can enable flashback data archiving for a table by specifying the FLASHBACK ARCHIVE clause when you create the table, as shown here:

```
SQL> CREATE TABLE test1
    (name               VARCHAR2(30),
    empno               NUMBER(4) NOT NULL,
    salary              NUMBER)
    FLASHBACK ARCHIVE;
```

In the previous example, I don't specify a name for the Flashback Data Archive. The database stores the historical data in the default Flashback Data Archive as a result. I can specify a particular Flashback Data Archive by adding the name for the archive, as shown in the following example:

```
SQL> CREATE TABLE test1
    (name               VARCHAR2(30),
    empno               NUMBER(4) NOT NULL,
    salary              NUMBER)
    FLASHBACK ARCHIVE flash1;
```

You can also turn flashback data archiving on for an existing table by issuing the ALTER TABLE statement, as shown here:

```
SQL> ALTER TABLE employee FLASHBACK ARCHIVE;
```

To disable flashback data archiving for a table, issue the following statement:

```
SQL> ALTER TABLE employee NO FLASHBACK ARCHIVE;
```

Limitations

Using the Flashback Data Archive imposes certain limitations on the type of DDL statements you can issue. You can't issue the following types of DDL statements on a table that you enabled for a Flashback Data Archive:

- An ALTER TABLE statement that drops, renames, or modifies a table column
- An ALTER TABLE statement that performs partition operations
- A DROP TABLE or a TRUNCATE TABLE statement
- A RENAME TABLE statement

Using Flashback Data Archives: Examples

You can use a Flashback Data Archive for querying historical data, auditing, as well as recovering from data errors. The following examples illustrate how you can utilize the Flashback Data Archive in different situations.

Accessing Historical Data

Using the AS_OF clause in a query, you can access the historical data stored in the Flashback Data Archive, as shown in the following query:

```
SQL> select transaction_number, doctor_name, count
     from patient_info as of
     timestamp to_timestamp ('2009-01-01 00:00:00',
     'YYYY-MM-DD HH23:MI:SS');
```

You can also use the AS_OF clause to recover from logical errors. In the following example, an employee by the name of Zlotkey has a current income of $10,500, as shown by the following query:

```
SQL> SELECT username, salary FROM HR.EMPLOYEES
     WHERE last_name='Zlotkey';

     SALARY
     -------
     10500
SQL>
```

The human resources department makes a wrong update to the EMPLOYEES table, when it raises Zlotkey's salary by $50,000 instead of $500, as shown here:

```
SQL> UPDATE hr.employees SET salary=salary+50000
     WHERE last_name='Zlotkey';

1 row updated.
SQL> commit;

Commit complete.
SQL>
```

Suppose you learn about the wrong update about two hours after it was made. Simply issue the following statement using the AS_OF clause to correct the error:

```
SQL> update hr.employees set salary =
    (select salary from hr.employees
    as of timestamp (systimestamp - interval '120' minute);
    where last_name='Zlotkey')
    where last_name='Zlotkey';

1 row updated.
SQL> commit;

Commit complete.

SQL>
```

Note that at no time do you have to access or query the history table that the database maintains to track the transactional changes to a table's data. The AS_OF clause ensures that the database looks up the relevant information in the history table that supports the Flashback Data Archive. The clause SYSTIMESTAMP - INTERVAL '120' MINUTE will retrieve the values from two hours ago. You can also specify seconds, days, and months in this clause, as shown in the following examples:

```
systimestamp - interval '60' second
systimestamp - interval '7' day
systimestamp - interval '12' month
```

Generating Reports

You can access historical data to create reports that encompass data from the past. Specify the VERSIONS BETWEEN TIMESTAMP clause to retrieve old values of a table's columns, as shown in the following example:

```
SQL> SELECT * FROM patient_info
    VERSIONS BETWEEN TIMESTAMP
    to_timestamp('2009-01-01 00:00:00','YYYY-MM-DD HH23:MI:SS')
    AND MAXVALUE
    WHERE name ='ALAPATI';
```

The query shown here retrieves all versions of the data you selected between January 1, 2009, and today.

Information Lifecycle Management

Information Lifecycle Management (ILM) applications often require multiple versions of a table's rows over time. Specify the VERSIONS BETWEEN TIMESTAMP clause to retrieve all versions of a row or rows over a period of time, as shown in the following example:

```
SQL> SELECT * FROM patient_info
    VERSIONS BETWEEN TIMESTAMP
    to_timestamp ('2009-01-01 00:00:00',
    'YYYY-MM-DD HH24:MI:SS')
    AND
    to_timestamp ('2009-06-30 00:00:00',
    'YYYY-MM-DD HH24:MI:SS')
    WHERE name='ALAPATI';
```

The query shown here retrieves all versions of the rows in the PATIENT_INFO table between January 1, 2009, and June 30, 2009.

PART 6

■■■

Managing the Database

CHAPTER 17

■■■

Automatic Management and Online Capabilities

Oracle has been emphasizing that the Oracle Database 11g server automates management to such an extent that it refers to the database as a *self-managing* database. Well, this is at least partially true, as several traditional time-consuming and error-prone tasks have been replaced with new ways of managing memory, transactions, and resources, and organizing space. In addition, there have been improvements in backup and recovery techniques. However, the DBA is just as essential as ever. If anything, the DBA's role has become even more central because of the new features' added complexity.

This chapter deals with the operational aspects of running an Oracle database. Several components of the database require constant monitoring and modifications, and you'll learn about some important Oracle Database 11g features in detail in this chapter. Earlier chapters introduced several topics that you'll see here, and this chapter will tie together the various aspects of Oracle Database 11g that make the DBA's job easier. The chapter highlights two main operational areas: automatic database management features and online management features.

Oracle Database 10g introduced the revolutionary Automatic Storage Management (ASM) feature, which helps Oracle DBAs manage disk storage with a built-in Logical Volume Manager (LVM) without requiring a system administrator's involvement. Automatic shared memory management is a useful feature that will help you immensely in your day-to-day administration. The online table redefinition feature will help you perform several routine tasks online without reducing database availability. Furthermore, Oracle Managed Files (OMF) will help you reduce database file-management tasks. In the following sections, you'll explore how adopting these new features can make day-to-day database management easier.

The Automatic Database Diagnostic Monitor

Traditionally, organizations have spent considerable amounts of effort on laborious performance-tuning exercises. Oracle Database 11g provides you with powerful and accurate automatic performance-tuning capabilities. The heart of this functionality is the new statistics collection facility, the Automatic Workload Repository (AWR), which automatically collects and saves crucial performance statistics (including those for SQL statements that use the most resources in the database) to help detect performance problems and self-tune the database. AWR saves its data in the Sysaux tablespace. I explain the AWR in detail in Chapter 18.

Instead of running myriad SQL performance-tuning scripts, just go to the Automatic Database Diagnostic Monitor (ADDM, pronounced "adam") as the first source for all your performance troubleshooting work. You'll save a lot of time that you might otherwise spend looking at extraneous issues that really don't have a bearing on performance. Since the ADDM ranks both the problems and its recommendations according to the crucial *DB time* statistic (more on this in a little bit), you have a way of quantitatively estimating the effectiveness of different measures in improving performance.

■**Note** Oracle recommends that you rely on the AWR for all the performance data you need for tuning purposes.

By automatically analyzing performance data for you, the ADDM relieves you of the responsibility of catching a problem at the right time to collect statistics. By default, the AWR collects new performance statistics in the form of an hourly *snapshot* and saves these snapshots for eight days before purging them. An AWR snapshot is a collection of database performance statistics at a single point in time, including statistics for resource-intensive SQL statements. Every time the AWR takes a new snapshot, the ADDM runs automatically, does its top-down system analysis, and reports its findings on the Database Control home page. The ADDM's output consists of a description of each performance problem it identifies, along with the recommended action. The recommendations are ranked by the expected benefit of implementing each of them. You can view the regular ADDM reports from the OEM Database Control or view them from a SQL*Plus session with the help of an Oracle-supplied SQL script.

The ADDM runs automatically, but you can also manually invoke the tool to investigate problems that occur in between the scheduled snapshots. Oracle stores the ADDM analyses in the Sysaux tablespace.

The Purpose of the ADDM

The basic rationale behind the ADDM is to reduce a key database metric called *DB time*, which is the total time (in microseconds) the database spends *actually processing* users' requests.

DB time includes the total amount of time spent on actual database calls (at the user level) and it ignores time spent on background processes. DB time includes both the wait time and processing time (CPU time), but doesn't include the idle time incurred by your processes. For example, if you spend an hour connected to the database and you're idle for 58 of those minutes, the DB time is only 2 minutes.

If a problem contributes to inappropriate or excessive DB time, ADDM automatically flags it as an issue needing attention. If there is a problem in your system, but it doesn't contribute significantly to the DB time, ADDM will simply ignore it. Thus, the ADDM is focused on the single mantra: *reduce DB time*. The ADDM aims to increase the *throughput* of your database, thereby serving more users with the same amount of resources.

Problems That the ADDM Diagnoses

The ADDM analyzes the AWR snapshots every hour by default, comes up with performance recommendations, and ranks them in terms of the expected benefit of implementing the various actions. These are some of the key problems that the ADDM diagnoses:

- Expensive SQL statements
- I/O performance issues
- Locking and concurrency issues
- Excessive parsing
- Resource bottlenecks, including memory and CPU bottlenecks
- Undersized memory allocation
- Connection management issues, such as excessive logon/logoff activity

When you are beset by a severe performance problem, look at the ADDM reports first, to get a good diagnosis of the problem. ADDM ignores the nonproblem areas and focuses on the truly significant causes affecting performance. The ADDM report contains the following:

- Expert problem diagnosis
- Emphasis on the root cause of the problem rather than on the symptoms
- A ranking of the effects of the problems
- Recommendations ranked according to their benefit

Unlike running some complex SQL scripts, the ADDM report has very little overhead associated with it, since its raw material is already saved in the AWR.

The ADDM uses sophisticated time-model statistics in Oracle Database 11*g* that are highly effective in determining where the database spends the most time. These new time-model statistics enable Oracle to focus on only the most critical performance problems. If a problem exceeds the threshold for the key DB time metric, the ADDM tags it as a top performance problem; otherwise, it leaves it alone as a nonproblem area. Let's look at these new time-model statistics in the following section.

Time-Model Statistics

The ADDM bases most of its performance recommendations on *time-model statistics*, the most important of which is the new DB time statistic, explained in the earlier section "The Purpose of the ADDM." Time-model statistics provide a uniform way to quantify various database operations. In addition to DB time, there are other time-model statistics, such as statistics that quantify the time taken by logon statistics and hard and soft parses.

You can use the new V$SESS_TIME_MODEL and V$SYS_TIME_MODEL database views to look at the time-based performance statistics. The V$SYS_TIME_MODEL view provides the accumulated time statistics for various operations in the *entire* database and shows the number of microseconds the database has spent on specific operations. The query in Listing 17-1 demonstrates the kind of operations for which the V$SYS_TIME_MODEL view holds time-based statistics.

Listing 17-1. *A Query Using the V$SYS_TIME_MODEL View*

```
SQL> SELECT stat_name, value FROM v$sys_time_model;
STAT_NAME                                           VALUE
--------------------------------------------------  ----------
DB time                                             3.8422E+13
DB CPU                                              9.2726E+12
background elaps                                    2.7506E+12
background cpu time                                 1.3335E+11
sequence load elapsed ti                            6583934097
parse time elapse                                   3.0984E+11
hard parse elapsed time                             4.7280E+10
sql execute elapsed time                            3.7533E+13
connection management call elapsed time             4.3565E+10
failed parse elapsed time                           3350540297
failed parse (out of shared memory) elapsed time             0
hard parse (sharing criteria) elapsed time          1770964950
hard parse (bind mismatch) elapsed time              706518501
PL/SQL execution elapsed time                       7.0339E+11
inbound PL/SQL rpc elapsed time                     7.3869E+12
PL/SQL compilation elapsed time                     3667675394
```

```
Java execution elapsed time                              1.7993E+11
RMAN cpu time (backup/restore)                                    0
17 rows selected.
SQL>
```

The V$SESS_TIME_MODEL view is similar to the V$SYS_TIME_MODEL view and provides the same types of time statistics, but it shows a session's accumulated time for the various operations rather than information for the entire database.

The AWR collects time-model statistics as part of its hourly snapshots. In addition, the AWR collects object statistics, including the usage statistics for objects, system and session statistics, statistics for high-load SQL statements, and a history of recent session activity, called the Active Session History (ASH). I discuss the AWR statistics, including ASH, in Chapter 18.

ADDM Findings

The ADDM analysis is available in the form of a series of *findings*, of which there are three types: problem, symptom, and informational. Here's an example of a typical ADDM finding:

```
FINDING 1: 45% impact (11223 seconds)
-------------------------------------
SQL statements were not shared due to the usage of literals.
This resulted in additional hard parses which were consuming
 significant database time.
```

This is a *problem finding*, because it's accompanied by an *impact* estimate, which is an estimate of the amount of additional DB time caused by the problem.

The findings are presented in decreasing order of importance (as defined by the impact percentages), and the sum of the impact percentages for all the findings may exceed 100 percent, as you can see in the following example:

```
FINDING 1: 34% impact (289378 seconds)
FINDING 2: 25% impact (214227 seconds)
FINDING 3: 23% impact (193521 seconds)
FINDING 4: 16% impact (134639 seconds)
FINDING 5: 6.1% impact (51563 seconds)
FINDING 6: 2.1% impact (17753 seconds)
```

The sum of the impact percentages can exceed 100 percent of DB time because the performance issues of the various findings might overlap and, therefore, encompass the same portion of DB time.

ADDM Recommendations

ADDM usually proposes one or more *recommendations* for each of the problem findings in its analysis. You may not need to follow all the recommendations to fix the problem. Each recommendation is accompanied by a quantified *benefit* that will result from the adoption of the ADDM recommendation, the benefit being measured in terms of the estimated reduction in DB time.

Here's a typical ADDM recommendation, wherein you're asked to first analyze your application logic:

```
RECOMMENDATION 1: Application Analysis, 45% benefit (11223 seconds)
```

If you see multiple recommendations, which is common, it means that the benefit that accrues from adopting all the recommendations would be equal to the impact percentage noted for the relevant finding. Here's an example:

```
FINDING 1: 34% impact (289378 seconds)
```

The report starts with a finding that has a 34 percent impact on DB time. The finding is accompanied by the following five recommendations, each with a certain benefit. If you sum up the benefit (in percentages) that results from adopting all five recommendations, you'll notice that it's equal to the value of the finding's impact (34 percent):

```
RECOMMENDATION 1: Segment Tuning, 13% benefit (112768 seconds)
RECOMMENDATION 2: Segment Tuning, 6.7% benefit (56805 seconds)
RECOMMENDATION 3: Segment Tuning, 6.1% benefit (51882 seconds)
RECOMMENDATION 4: Segment Tuning, 4.4% benefit (37330 seconds)
RECOMMENDATION 5: Segment Tuning, 3.6% benefit (30594 seconds)
```

ADDM recommendations may include the following:

- *Hardware changes*: The ADDM may recommend that you add more CPUs to your system or change the way you configure your I/O subsystem.

- *Database and application changes*: In some cases, the ADDM may recommend that you change the setting of some of your initialization parameters, instead of rewriting your application code.

- *Space configuration changes*: The ADDM may sometimes make major recommendations, such as using the new Automatic Storage Management feature, in order to fix certain performance problems.

- *Use of performance advisors*: In several cases, the ADDM will recommend that you use a performance advisor, like the SQL Tuning Advisor or the Segment Advisor, to fix your performance problems.

Recommendations may also have *action* and *rationale* components, with actions showing you the various things you need to do to implement the recommendation, while rationales explain the reason for the recommendation. Here's part of an ADDM report that shows an action and the rationale for the recommendation you saw earlier in this section:

```
ACTION: Investigate application logic for possible use of bind variables
    instead of literals. Alternatively, you may set the parameter
    "cursor_sharing" to "force".
RATIONALE: SQL statements with PLAN_HASH_VALUE 2094286255 were found to be
    using literals. Look in V$SQL for examples of such SQL statements.
```

Note that a recommendation may have one or more actions attached to it. Similarly, you may have one or more rationale items.

Managing the ADDM

Oracle manages the ADDM with the help of the new MMON background process. Each time the AWR takes a snapshot (every hour by default), the MMON process tells the ADDM to analyze the interval between the last two AWR snapshots. Thus, by default, the ADDM automatically runs each time the AWR snapshot is taken. As mentioned earlier, you can use the OEM Database Control to view the ADDM's performance analysis and action recommendations.

Configuring the ADDM

Oracle enables the ADDM feature by default, and your only task is to make sure that the STATISTICS_LEVEL initialization parameter is set to TYPICAL or ALL in order for the AWR to gather its performance statistics. If you set STATISTICS_LEVEL to BASIC, you can still use the AWR to collect statistics by using the DBMS_WORKLOAD_REPOSITORY package, but you won't be able to collect several important types of performance statistics.

You can control the volume of statistics collected by the AWR by adjusting either or both of two variables:

- *Snapshot interval*: The default snapshot interval is 60 minutes. Oracle assumes that hourly snapshots are frequent enough for diagnosis and infrequent enough that they won't influence performance.

- *Snapshot retention period*: By default, Oracle retains all snapshots for eight days in the AWR, after which it purges the outdated snapshots.

■**Note** Please refer to Chapter 18 for a detailed discussion of the management of the AWR.

You can change the snapshot interval and snapshot retention periods by using the INTERVAL and the RETENTION parameters of the MODIFY_SNAPSHOT_SETTINGS procedure of the DBMS_WORKLOAD_REPOSITORY package. Chapter 18 shows you how to modify the AWR snapshot interval and retention period.

■**Note** The ADDM runs automatically after each AWR snapshot, and you can run it whenever you choose, such as when an alert recommends that you do so. You can also run it manually when you want an ADDM analysis across multiple snapshots, rather than over the two most recent snapshots, which is the default interval for analysis.

Oracle automatically runs the ADDM following an AWR snapshot, but you can also produce custom ADDM reports by manually running the ADDM if you want to examine, for example, the period between 8 a.m. and 5 p.m., which encompasses multiple AWR snapshots. You just provide the beginning and ending snapshot information, and ADDM will generate a report for the entire period.

Configuring the ADDM Under RAC

If you're using Oracle Real Application Clusters (RAC), you can run the ADDM in multiple modes, as explained here:

- *Database mode*: Analyzes all instances of RAC
- *Instance mode*: Analyzes a single instance of RAC
- *Partial mode*: Analyzes a subset of the instances of RAC

Of course, in a single-instance database, only the instance mode of analysis is available. In the database mode, the ADDM analyzes the performance of all instances of a database. It considers the DB time for the database as the sum of the DB times from all instances. The database analysis report shows you instance-level findings if the findings affect the entire instance. Thus, if a single instance is causing an excessive CPU load, you can find that out with the database analysis report.

Enabling the ADDM

By default, the ADDM is enabled. You can control the running of the ADDM by specifying the initialization parameters CONTROL_MANAGEMENT_PACK_ACCESS and STATISTICS_LEVEL. To enable the ADDM, you must set the CONTROL_MANAGEMENT_PACK_ACCESS parameter to either DIAGNOSTIC or DIAGNOSTIC+TUNING. Since the default value of this parameter is DIAGNOSTIC+TUNING, the ADDM is enabled by default. You can disable the ADDM by setting this parameter in the following way:

```
CONTROL_MANAGEMENT_PACK_ACCESS=NONE
```

You can disable the ADDM by setting the STATISTICS_LEVEL parameter to BASIC.

The Three Modes of the ADDM

In this section, I show how to run the ADDM in the three modes I described earlier. Execute the DBMS_ADDM.ANALYZE_DB procedure to run the ADDM in the database mode, as shown here:

```
BEGIN
DBMS_ADDM.ANALYZE_DB (
    task_name           IN OUT VARCHAR2,
    begin_snapshot      IN     NUMBER,
    end_snapshot        IN     NUMBER,
    db_id               IN     NUMBER := NULL);
END;
/
```

The BEGIN_SNAPSHOT and the END_SNAPSHOT parameter values determine the span of the ADDM analysis. The DB_ID parameter is optional and defaults to the DBID of the database to which you're connected.

The following example shows how to execute a database-wide ADDM analysis for the period between snapshots 99 and 120:

```
VAR tname VARCHAR2(30);
BEGIN
  :tname := 'ADDM for 8 AM to 10 AM'';
  DBMS_ADDM.ANALYZE_DB(:tname, 99,120);
END;
/
```

You can run the ADDM in instance mode by executing the ANALYZE_INST procedure, shown next:

```
BEGIN
DBMS_ADDM.ANALYZE_INST (
    task_name           IN OUT VARCHAR2,
    begin_snapshot      IN     NUMBER,
    end_snapshot        IN     NUMBER,
    instance_number     IN     NUMBER := NULL,
    db_id               IN     NUMBER := NULL);
END;
/
```

Note the INSTANCE_NUMBER parameter, which enables you to specify the instance number. Here's an example that shows how to specify the various mandatory parameters:

```
VAR tname VARCHAR2(30);
BEGIN
  :tname := 'my ADDM for 8 AM to 10 AM';
  DBMS_ADDM.ANALYZE_INST(:tname, 99,120, 1);
END;
/
```

To run the ADDM in partial mode, you must execute the ANALYZE_PARTIAL procedure, which is shown here:

```
BEGIN
DBMS_ADDM.ANALYZE_PARTIAL (
    task_name           IN OUT VARCHAR2,
    instance_numbers    IN     VARCHAR2,
```

```
    begin_snapshot       IN    NUMBER,
    end_snapshot         IN    NUMBER,
    db_id                IN    NUMBER := NULL);
END;
/
```

Here's an example that shows how to run a partial ADDM analysis for four instances of a database:

```
VAR tname VARCHAR2(30);
BEGIN'
  :tname := 'my ADDM for 8 AM to 10 AM';
  DBMS_ADDM.ANALYZE_PARTIAL(:tname, '1,2,3,4', 99, 101);
END;
/
```

The example shown here runs the ADDM analysis for instances 1, 2, 3, and 4 between snapshots 99 and 101.

Displaying an ADDM Report

Execute the GET_REPORT function to view a text report of a completed ADDM task, as shown here:

```
SET LONG 1000000 PAGESIZE 0;
SELECT DBMS_ADDM.GET_REPORT(:tname) FROM DUAL;
```

Determining Optimal I/O Performance

If your I/O system performs at a certain speed, your system can read a database block in a specific number of milliseconds; the DBIO_EXPECTED parameter (which is not an initialization parameter) indicates I/O performance, and the default value for this parameter is 10 milliseconds.

You can find out the current value of the DBIO_EXPECTED parameter by querying the DBA_ADVISOR_DEF_PARAMETERS view as follows:

```
SQL> SELECT parameter_value
     FROM dba_advisor_def_parameters
     WHERE advisor_name='ADDM'
     AND parameter_name='DBIO_EXPECTED';

PARAMETER_VALUE
---------------
10000
SQL>
```

• You can use the SET_DEFAULT_TASK_PARAMETER procedure of the DBMS_ADVISOR package to modify the default value of the DBIO_EXPECTED parameter, as shown here:

```
SQL> SHO USER
USER is "SYS"

SQL> EXECUTE DBMS_ADVISOR.SET_DEFAULT_TASK_PARAMETER(-
   > 'ADDM', 'DBIO_EXPECTED', 6000);

PL/SQL procedure successfully completed.
SQL>
```

Running the ADDM

The Oracle background process MMON schedules the ADDM to run every time the AWR collects its most recent snapshot. Oracle, therefore, automatically generates ADDM reports throughout the day, which you can view through the Database Control.

One of the reasons for invoking the ADDM manually is because an alert might recommend you do it. You can perform an ad hoc ADDM analysis to find out details about a performance problem that's currently occurring in the database. You can create a new AWR snapshot manually and run the ADDM using this and the preceding snapshot.

You can also request that the ADDM analyze past instance performance by examining AWR snapshot data that falls between any two nonadjacent snapshots. The only requirements regarding the selection of the AWR snapshots are these:

- The snapshots must not contain any errors.

- There can't be a database shutdown between the two snapshots. The AWR holds only cumulative database statistics, and once you shut down the database, all the cumulative data will lose its meaning.

■**Note** Although the `addmrpt.sql` script indicates that you can specify the number of days of snapshots, you really aren't given that choice. The script really just lists the last three days of completed snapshots, as you can see here:

```
Specify the number of days of snapshots to choose from
Entering the number of days (n) will result in the most recent
(n) days of snapshots being listed.  Pressing <return> without
specifying a number lists all completed snapshots.
Listing the last 3 days of Completed Snapshots
```

Viewing Detailed ADDM Reports

You can view the ADDM analysis reports in three different ways:

- You can use the Oracle-provided `addmrpt.sql` script (located in the `$ORACLE_HOME/rdbms/admin` directory) to create an ad hoc ADDM report for a time period covered by any pair of snapshots.

- You can use the DBMS_ADVISOR package and create an ADDM report by using the CREATE_REPORT procedure.

- You can use the OEM to view the performance findings of the stored ADDM reports, which are proactively created each hour after the AWR snapshots.

The following sections discuss each of these three methods, but first we'll look at how to read an ADDM report.

Reading an ADDM Report

The ADDM presents the results of its analysis to you in a standard format that consists of the following components:

- The definition of the performance problem

- The root cause of the performance problem

- Recommendation(s) for fixing the problem
- The rationale for the proposed recommendations

Listing 17-2 shows a condensed version of an ADDM report.

Listing 17-2. *An Abbreviated ADDM Report*

```
DETAILED ADDM REPORT FOR TASK 'TASK_4028' WITH ID 4028
                Analysis Period: 01-JUL-2008 from 06:00:11 to 21:00:37
           Database ID/Instance: 866170026/1
        Database/Instance Names: FINANCE/finance
                      Host Name: prod5
               Database Version: 11.1.0.0.0
                 Snapshot Range: from 3068 to 3076
                  Database Time: 687974 seconds
           Average Database Load: 23.9 active sessions


FINDING 1: 42% impact (287205 seconds)
Individual database segments responsible for significant physical I/O were found.


RECOMMENDATION 1: Segment Tuning, 15% benefit (102631 seconds)
   ACTION: Run "Segment Advisor" on TABLE "FIN.UNIT_REGISTR"
           with object id 1817.
     RELEVANT OBJECT: database object with id 1817

   ACTION: Investigate application logic involving I/O
           on TABLE "FIN.UNIT_REGIST" with object id 1817.
     RELEVANT OBJECT: database object with id 1817
     RATIONALE: The SQL statement with SQL_ID "dvycj85pfmb1b" spent
           significant time waiting for User I/O on the hot object.
     RELEVANT OBJECT: SQL statement with SQL_ID dvycj85pfmb1b
     UPDATE UNIT_REGISTR UR SET UR.CARD_PRINTED_FLAG = 'Y'
. . .


RECOMMENDATION 2: Segment Tuning, 6.7% benefit (56805 seconds)
      ACTION: Run "Segment Advisor" on TABLE "APPOWNER.CAMP_POS"
         with object id 1381.
       RELEVANT OBJECT: database object with id 1381
      ACTION: Investigate application logic involving I/O on TABLE
         "APPOWNER.CAMP_POS" with object id 1381.
       RELEVANT OBJECT: database object with id 1381
       RATIONALE: The SQL statement with SQL_ID "gfjfc1g8t2a64" spent
. . .


FINDING 2: 29% impact (202802 seconds)
Individual database segments responsible for significant user I/O wait were found.


RECOMMENDATION 1: Segment Tuning, 12% benefit (84451 seconds)
      ACTION: Run "Segment Advisor" on TABLE "APPOWNER.COM_ORGS" with
         object id 1412.
       RELEVANT OBJECT: database object with id 1412
      ACTION: Investigate application logic involving I/O on TABLE
         "APPOWNER.COM_ORGS" with object id 1412.
       RELEVANT OBJECT: database object with id 1412
```

FINDING 3: 23% impact (160643 seconds)
The buffer cache was undersized causing significant additional read I/O.

RECOMMENDATION 1: DB Configuration, 23% benefit (160643 seconds)
     ACTION: Increase SGA target size by increasing the value of
              parameter "sga_target" by 2128 M.
   SYMPTOMS THAT LED TO THE FINDING: Wait class "User I/O" was consuming
        significant database time.

FINDING 4: 16% impact (134639 seconds)
SQL statements consuming significant database time were found.

RECOMMENDATION 1: SQL Tuning, 4.9% benefit (41134 seconds)
     ACTION: Run SQL Tuning Advisor on the SQL statement with SQL_ID
        "dvycj85pfmb1b".

FINDING 5: 6.1% impact (51563 seconds)
The throughput of the I/O subsystem was significantly lower than expected.

RECOMMENDATION 1: Host Configuration, 6.1% benefit (51563 seconds)
     ACTION: Consider increasing the throughput of the I/O subsystem.
        Oracle's recommended solution is to stripe all data file using the
        SAME methodology. You might also need to increase the number of disks
        for better performance. Alternatively, consider using Oracle's
        Automatic Storage Management solution.

   SYMPTOMS THAT LED TO THE FINDING:
     Wait class "User I/O" was consuming significant database time. (71%
     impact [604143 seconds])

   . . .

~~~~~~

          ADDITIONAL INFORMATION

Wait class "Administrative" was not consuming significant database time.
Wait class "Application" was not consuming significant database time.
Wait class "Cluster" was not consuming significant database time.
Wait class "Commit" was not consuming significant database time.
Wait class "Configuration" was not consuming significant database time.
CPU was not a bottleneck for the instance.
Wait class "Network" was not consuming significant database time.
Wait class "Scheduler" was not consuming significant database time.
Wait class "Other" was not consuming significant database time.

The analysis of I/O performance is based on the default assumption that the
average read time for one database block is 10000 micro-seconds.

An explanation of the terminology used in this report is available when you
run the report with the 'ALL' level of detail.

In an ADDM report, each finding is followed by one or more recommendations. Thus, you might see a Recommendation 1, Recommendation 2, and so on, under each of the findings. For any particular finding, the sum of the benefit that follows the implementation of all recommendations under a finding equals that finding's impact (DB time).

Note the following about the ADDM report shown in Listing 17-2:

- Findings 1 and 2 state that individual database segments responsible for significant physical I/O wait were found. ADDM recommends that you run the Segment Advisor to find out whether you can shrink the problem segments.

- Finding 3 reports an undersized buffer cache and recommends that you increase the SGA_TARGET parameter by 2,128MB.

- For Finding 4, the recommendation is to run the SQL Tuning Advisor on a specific SQL statement.

- For Finding 5, you're asked to look into disk striping and adopting the Automatic Storage Management solution, since the user I/O wait event was taking up considerable DB time.

■**Note** The ADDM'S I/O performance analysis is based on the assumption that the average read time for one database block is 10,000 microseconds.

At the end of the detailed ADDM Report, you'll see a section called Additional Information, which usually shows insignificant wait information.

■**Tip** Oracle enables the ADDM by default, as long as you set the STATISTICS_LEVEL parameter to TYPICAL or ALL. If you set the STATISTICS_LEVEL parameter to BASIC, you'll disable many automatic performance-tuning and statistics-gathering activities, including the AWR and ADDM.

Using the addmrpt.sql Script

You can create an ADDM report by using the addmrpt.sql script, found in the $ORACLE_HOME/rdbms/admin directory. The example in Listing 17-3 shows how to get the ADDM report for the period between 6 a.m. and 2 p.m. To do so, I specified the snapshot numbers corresponding to the 6 a.m. and 2 p.m. snapshot collection times—the addmrpt.sql script makes this easy by displaying a list of snapshot numbers and the corresponding dates and times. (In the script, you can see that snapshot ID 3068 was captured at 6:00 a.m. and 3076 was captured at 2:00 p.m.)

Listing 17-3. *Producing an ADDM Report with the addmrpt.sql Script*

```
$ sqlplus /nolog

SQL*Plus: Release 11.1.0.6.0 - Production on Thu Apr 10 09:21:48 2008
Copyright (c) 1982, 2007, Oracle.  All rights reserved.


SQL> CONNECT sys/syspasswd AS SYSDBA
Connected.
SQL> @/u03/app/oracle/rdbms/admin addmrpt.sql
Current Instance
~~~~~~~~~~~~~~~~~
DB Id        DB Name       Inst Num Instance
```

```
----------- ------------ -------- ------------
877170026     FINANCE               1 finance

Instances in this Workload Repository schema
~~~~~~~~~~~~~~~~~~~~~~~~~~~~~~~~~~~~~~~~~~~~~~
DB Id      Inst Num DB Name      Instance     Host
------------ -------- ------------ ------------ ----
866170026         1 FINANCE         finance     prod5

Using  866170026 for database Id
Using          1 for instance number
Specify the number of days of snapshots to choose from
~~~~~~~~~~~~~~~~~~~~~~~~~~~~~~~~~~~~~~~~~~~~~~~~~~~~~~~~~

Entering the number of days (n) will result in the most recent
(n) days of snapshots being listed.  Pressing <return> without
specifying a number lists all completed snapshots.
Listing the last 3 days of Completed Snapshots
                                                     Snap
Instance     DB Name      Snap Id      Snap Started   Level
------------ ------------ --------- ------------------- -----
finance      FINANCE         3067   22 Jul 2008 05:00     1
                             3068   22 Jul 2008 06:00     1
                             3069   22 Jul 2008 07:01     1
                             3070   22 Jul 2008 08:00     1
                             3071   22 Jul 2008 09:00     1
                             3072   22 Jul 2008 10:00     1
                             3073   22 Jul 2008 11:00     1
                             3074   22 Jul 2008 12:01     1
                             3075   22 Jul 2008 13:00     1
                             3076   22 Jul 2008 14:00     1


Specify the Begin and End Snapshot Ids
~~~~~~~~~~~~~~~~~~~~~~~~~~~~~~~~~~~~~~~~
Enter value for begin_snap: 3068
Begin Snapshot Id specified: 3068
Enter value for end_snap: 3076
End   Snapshot Id specified: 3076


Specify the Report Name
~~~~~~~~~~~~~~~~~~~~~~~~~
The default report file name is addmrpt_1_3068_3076.txt.
To use this name, press <return> to continue, otherwise enter an alternative.
Enter value for report_name:
Using the report name addmrpt_1_3068_3076.txt
Running the ADDM analysis on the specified pair of snapshots . . .
. . .
SQL>
```

You've seen how to get an ADDM report covering a past period, but suppose you are experiencing a performance problem at 2:40 p.m., and the last snapshot is from 2 p.m.—the next snapshot won't be taken until 3 p.m., so your last ADDM report is of no use to you in this case. You can create an ad hoc ADDM report by manually creating a snapshot, as shown here:

```
SQL> EXECUTE dbms_workload_repository.create_snapshot();
PL/SQL procedure successfully completed.
```

Within a few seconds of the creation of this AWR snapshot, Oracle automatically generates an ADDM report (using the period between the snapshot you just executed and the preceding snapshot), which you can view through the OEM Database Control interface.

Using the DBMS_ADVISOR Package

The DBMS_ADVISOR package helps you manage the attributes of the ADDM, as well as perform jobs like creating tasks and retrieving ADDM reports using SQL. ADDM is part of the advisory framework in Oracle Database 11g. A non-DBA user needs the ADVISOR privilege to use the DBMS_ADVISOR package.

The following are the main procedures and functions of the DBMS_ADVISOR package, and they apply not just to the ADDM, but also to all the other database advisors. In this case, of course, we are interested in how to use this package for managing ADDM.

- CREATE_TASK: Creates a new advisor task
- SET_DEFAULT_TASK: Helps you modify default values of parameters within a task
- DELETE_TASK: Deletes a specific task from the repository
- EXECUTE_TASK: Executes a specific task
- GET_TASK_REPORT: Displays the most recent ADDM report
- SET_DEFAULT_TASK_PARAMETER: Modifies a default task parameter

You can get an ADDM report identical to the one we got with the addmrpt.sql script in the previous section by using the GET_TASK_REPORT procedure of the DBMS_ADVISOR package. The GET_TASK_REPORT procedure lets you get an XML, text, or HTML report for a specified task, including an ADDM task. Here's how you get a text report:

```
SQL> SET LONG 1000000
SQL> SELECT dbms_advisor.get_task_report(
  2  task_name, 'TEXT', 'ALL')
  3  FROM dba_advisor_tasks
  4    WHERE task_id=(
  5     SELECT max(t.task_id)
  6     FROM dba_advisor_tasks t, dba_advisor_log l
  7     WHERE t.task_id = l.task_id
  8     AND t.advisor_name='ADDM'
  9*    AND l.status= 'COMPLETED');
SQL>
```

Using the OEM Database Control to View ADDM Reports

You can also view ADDM reports via the OEM interface, using either the Database Control or the Grid Control. Let's look at how to use the Database Control interface to get the ADDM findings.

First, go the ADDM page by following these steps:

1. On the Database Control home page, click the Advisor Central link, which is under the Related Links section at the bottom of the page.

2. On the Advisor Central page, you'll see the Results section at the bottom (see Figure 17-1). The latest ADDM auto-run results (based on the two latest snapshots) are available from this page. From this page you can also get the results of any other advisors you may have run.

Figure 17-1 shows the Advisor Central page with the latest ADDM report shown at the bottom of the page, in the Results section. This automatically run ADDM report was completed just after 10 a.m.

on March 26, 2005, using the most recent pair of consecutive snapshots, 3167 and 3168. Click the report name link to view the detailed ADDM report, as shown in Figure 17-2. You can also save the ADDM results to a file or print the report.

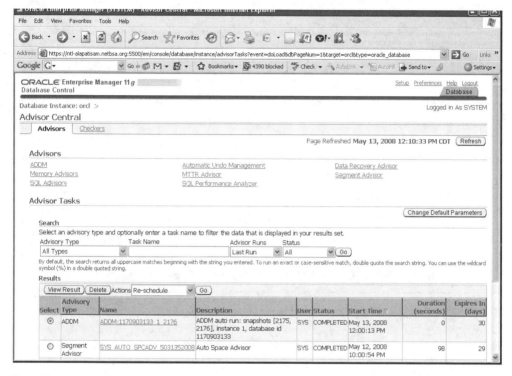

Figure 17-1. *Locating the latest ADDM report on the Advisor Central page of the Grid Control*

■**Tip** Note that you can also view an ADDM report straight from the Database Control home page. Simply go to the Diagnostic Summary section and click the ADDM Findings link, which is a number that shows how many ADDM findings are available for viewing. If your instance doesn't have any ADDM problem findings, this number will be 0.

For each problem identified by the ADDM, its performance findings are displayed in the form of three columns: the Impact column, the Finding column, and the Recommendations column. The Impact column lists the performance problems in the order of their impact on their system. The Impact column is thus very important, because you can start working on fixing the most serious problem that is currently affecting database performance. Even if your guess is that SQL parsing issues are the most pressing issues right now, if the Impact column ranks I/O problems as number one, you should take care of the I/O problems first. The Finding column lists a brief description of the problem, and one or more recommendations are presented in the Recommendations column. For example, the "SQL statements consuming significant database time were found" finding has an impact of 48.33 percent on DB time, and SQL tuning is the recommended action.

In addition to the impact, problem, and recommendations information, the detailed report includes a listing of the symptoms that led to each particular finding. For some problems, the ADDM report also includes a Rationale section that explains the reasoning behind its recommendations. You can drill down the findings to get the rationale and the detailed recommendations. For example, Figure 17-3 shows the rationale behind a certain recommendation.

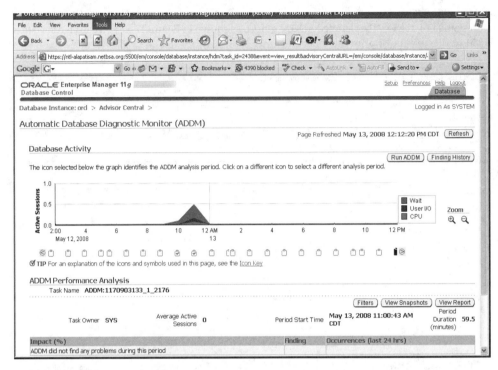

Figure 17-2. *Viewing the latest ADDM report in the OEM Grid Control*

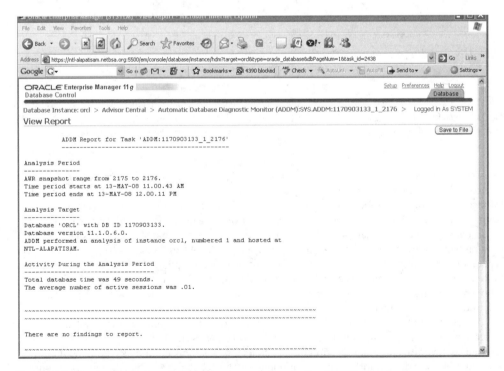

Figure 17-3. *Viewing the rationale for a recommendation in the ADDM report*

Using the Database Control to Run the ADDM

In the previous section, I showed how to use the Database Control to view existing ADDM reports. As explained earlier, ADDM automatically runs by default every hour, immediately after the hourly (default value) AWR snapshot completes. However, you can also manually run the ADDM to produce an ad hoc report if you see a spike in instance activity or you notice excessive waits in the database. Here are the steps to do this:

1. From the Database Control home page, click the Advisor Central link.

2. Click the ADDM link.

3. You will now be in the Run ADDM page, shown in Figure 17-4. You can make one the following choices and then click OK:

   • To analyze current instance performance, create an immediate AWR snapshot and run the ADDM analysis on it and the most recent snapshot.

   • To analyze past instance performance, select either the Period Start Time or the Period End Time option and click one of the snapshot icons under the Active Sessions graph.

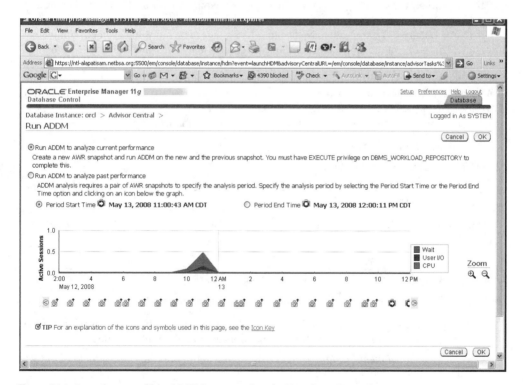

Figure 17-4. *Running an ad hoc ADDM report using the Database Control*

Using ADDM-Related Dictionary Views

The following data dictionary views will help you manage the ADDM:

• The DBA_ADVISOR_RECOMMENDATIONS view shows all the ADDM recommendations in the database.

• The DBA_ADVISOR_FINDINGS view shows the findings of all the advisors in your database.

- The DBA_ADVISOR_RATIONALE view shows the rationale behind all the recommendations.

- The DBA_ADVISOR_ACTIONS view shows all the actions that are necessary to implement the ADDM recommendations.

Automatic Memory Management

It isn't always easy to adjust the system global area (SGA), which is the memory that Oracle assigns to every instance to hold data and control information. You may have a situation where OLTP transactions dominate the database all day, and then you run heavy-duty batch jobs during the night. In such a situation, you'd need a higher allocation for the buffer cache during the day, and an increase in the large pool component of the SGA for the nightly batch jobs.

You can, of course, dynamically change several SGA components, as well as use scripts to change SGA allocations before and after batch jobs, but the fact remains that you are directly responsible for adjusting the SGA components to match instance needs. Problems like the ORA-4031 ("out of shared pool memory") error are all too common when you're manually tuning various parameters. If you try to be extra careful and allocate a lot of SGA memory, you'll run the risk of wasting critical resources and also potentially contributing to paging and other problems, which will affect your database performance.

In Oracle Database 11g, you can make the often-tricky issue of memory management completely automatic. This is one of the more significant improvements in Oracle Database 11g, and it contributes considerably to Oracle's goal of automatic database management. Under automatic memory management, Oracle will automatically allocate and deallocate memory for both the SGA and the PGA based on changing database workloads. Oracle uses internal views and statistics to decide on the best way to allocate memory among the SGA components.

These are some of the benefits of using automatic memory management:

- Reduces the chance of running out of shared pool memory

- Uses available memory optimally

- Improves database performance by constantly matching memory allocations and instance memory needs

You can continue to manually manage the shared memory components in Oracle Database 11g if you wish.

Different Types of Memory Management

Oracle provides several memory management methods, as summarized here:

- *Automatic memory management*: This new option in Oracle Database 11g lets the database manage the SGA and PGA components of memory completely automatically.

- *Automatic shared memory management*: This option automates the management of the SGA but not the PGA.

- *Automatic PGA memory management*: This option automates just the PGA memory.

- *Manual shared memory management*: You set the sizes of the individual components of the SGA such as the shared pool and the buffer cache.

- *Manual PGA memory management*: You set the PGA memory manually.

Oracle recommends that you use automatic memory management, under which the database dynamically adjusts the levels of the individual SGA components as well as the PGA allocations.

The database will redistribute memory from the SGA to the PGA and vice versa, depending on what's needed. Your job is to set the initial level of memory you want to allocate to the database and then let the database handle the day-to-day management of that memory.

Note As of this writing, the Linux, Solaris, Windows, HP-UX, and AIX platforms support automatic memory management.

Enabling Automatic Memory Management

You can enable automatic memory management when creating a database through the Database Configuration Assistant (DBCA). The DBCA offers you a choice of automatic memory management and other types of memory management. You can set the initialization parameters that control automatic memory management by using the Memory tab of the Initialization Parameters page. Select automatic memory management by checking the Use Automatic Memory Management box in the Typical section.

In order to switch to automatic memory management, you must set the MEMORY_TARGET parameter, which sets the target memory for the instance. You can also set the maximum memory size for an instance by specifying a value for the MEMORY_MAX_TARGET initialization parameter.

Before you can allocate the appropriate amount of memory you should assign to the database under the new automatic memory management feature, you must first find out how much memory the database is currently using for its SGA and PGA memory allocations. Your goal is to allocate an amount of memory that's about the same as the sum of the SGA and PGA memory that the database currently consumes. However, this doesn't mean that you can simply sum up the values of the SGA_TARGET and PGA_TARGET parameters to arrive at the total memory requirements of the database. The reason for this is that unlike in the case of the SGA_TARGET parameter, the database doesn't immediately take over the memory you assign for the PGA_TARGET parameter. The database only bases its PGA allocation to each session on the value for the PGA_TARGET parameter. Thus, you can assign a very large value for the PGA_TARGET parameter, but the database might be using only a miniscule portion of this at any given time.

In order to enable automatic memory management for an existing database, follow these simple steps:

1. Find out the current value of the SGA by issuing the following command:

```
SQL> SHOW PARAMETER SGA_TARGET

NAME                    TYPE            VALUE
-------------           -----------     ------
sga_target              big integer     600M
```

You may also query the VSGA_STAT view (SELECT SUM(BYTES) FROM V$SGA_STAT) to get the size of the current SGA.

```
SQL>
```

2. Find out the maximum allocation of PGA at any given time by issuing the following query:

```
SQL> SELECT VALUE FROM V$PGASTAT
  2 WHERE name='maximum PGA allocated';

VALUE
---------
581000192

SQL>
```

3. The query shows that the database allocated about 580MB of memory to the PGA at its maximum level. If you issue the following query, however, you'll get the wrong estimate for the PGA:

```
SQL> SHOW PARAMETER PGA_AGGREGATE_TARGET

NAME                         TYPE             VALUE
----------------------       --------------   ----------
pga_aggregate_target         big integer      5000000000

SQL>
```

About 6GB was allocated to the PGA memory, but the database made use of a maximum of about 580MB at a single time. Therefore, adding the SGA_TARGET and the PGA_AGGREGATE_TARGET parameters is likely to give you an overly large estimate of the memory you need to assign to the database for the automatic allocation of SGA and PGA.

4. Choose the value for the MEMORY_TARGET parameter by adding the values of the SGA_TARGET parameter and the value of the maximum PGA allocated since the instance was started. In our example, this is 600MB (SGA) + 581MB (highest PGA usage in the instance). That is, you'd need about 1200MB or so as the target for the automatic memory allocation to the database.

You can optionally also set the MEMORY_MAX_TARGET parameter if you want. If you don't set a value for this parameter, the database assigns it the same value as that assigned to the MEMORY_TARGET parameter.

After choosing your values, make the necessary changes in the SPFILE, as shown here:

```
SQL> ALTER SYSTEM SET MEMORY_MAX_TARGET=1200M SCOPE=SPFILE;
SQL> ALTER SYSTEM SET MEMORY_TARGET=2000M SCOPE=SPFILE;
SQL> ALTER SYSTEM SET SGA_TARGET=0 SCOPE=SPFILE;
SQL> ALTER SYSTEM SET PGA_AGGREGATE_TARGET=0 SCOPE=SPFILE;
```

By setting the SGA_TARGET and the PGA_AGGREGATE_TARGET parameters to zero, you are giving complete control to the database in adjusting the values of the SGA and the PGA based on the requirements of the database workload.

■**Note** You can also enable automatic memory management by using the Enterprise Manager. Go to the Database Home page ➤ Server ➤ Memory Advisors. Click the Enable button on the Memory Advisor page to enable automatic memory management.

Tuning Automatic Memory Management

You can use the view V$MEMORY_DYNAMIC_COMPONENTS to examine the current sizes of memory components such as the SGA and the PGA. You can get tuning advice for setting the MEMORY_TARGET parameter from the V$MEMORY_TARGET_ADVICE view, as shown in the following example:

```
SQL> SELECT * FROM v$memory_target_advice ORDER BY memory_size;
```

MEMORY_SIZE	MEMORY_SIZE_FACTOR	ESTD_DB_TIME	ESTD_DB_TIME_FACTOR	VERSION
410	.5	34994	1.0085	0
615	.75	34699	1	0
820	1	34699	1	0
1025	1.25	34699	1	0

1230	1.5	34699	1	0
1435	1.75	34699	1	0
1640	2	34699	1	0

7 rows selected.

SQL>

The row where the value of the MEMORY_SIZE_FACTOR is 1 shows the current size of the memory allocation to the instance, made by setting the MEMORY_TARGET parameter. The values for all columns correspond to alternative hypothetical levels of the MEMORY_TARGET parameter. In our example, there is no benefit to increasing the size of the MEMORY_TARGET parameter beyond its current value of 615MB, based on the current database workload.

Automatic Memory Parameter Dependency

Once you set the MEMORY_TARGET parameter, the database will allocate the memory to the SGA and PGA components based on the demands on the database workload. The MEMORY_TARGET parameter is dynamic, and therefore you can change it easily while the database is running. You can set the SGA_TARGET and/or the PGA_AGGREGATE_TARGET parameters even after enabling automatic memory allocation in the database by setting the MEMORY_TARGET parameter.

If you ignore the MEMORY_MAX_TARGET parameter but set the MEMORY_TARGET parameter, the former defaults to the value you set for the latter parameter. If, on the other hand, you just set the MEMORY_MAX_TARGET parameter, the value of the MEMORY_TARGET parameter defaults to zero, meaning automatic memory management is disabled.

Following is the relationship among the various memory sizing parameters when you set the MEMORY_TARGET parameter:

- If you don't set the SGA_TARGET and the PGA_AGGREGATE_TARGET parameters, the database will automatically tune them without setting any minimum values for either the SGA or the PGA.

- If you also set the SGA_TARGET and the PGA_AGGREGATE_TARGET parameters, they are treated as minimum values for the SGA and the PGA.

- If you set only the SGA_TARGET parameter and not the PGA_AGGREGATE_TARGET parameter, you can still auto-tune both SGA and PGA.

- If you set just the PGA_AGGEGATE_TARGET parameter, the database auto-tunes both SGA and PGA.

If you don't set the MEMORY_TARGET parameter, it will default to a value of zero and the following will be true of the SGA and PGA allocations:

- If you set neither the SGA_TARGET nor the PGA_AGGREGATE_TARGET parameters, the database doesn't auto-tune the SGA, meaning that you must set the sizes of the individual components of the SGA. However, the database auto-tunes the PGA.

- If you set only the SGA_TARGET parameter, the database auto-tunes the subcomponents of the SGA.

- The database always auto-tunes the PGA, regardless of whether you set the PGA_AGGREGATE_TARGET parameter or not.

Automatic Optimizer Statistics Collection

In an Oracle database, the query optimizer plays a critical role in executing SQL statements in the most efficient manner. You can execute a given SQL statement in several ways, and it is the query optimizer's job to come up with the fastest and most efficient way to perform each database query.

To arrive at the best plan of execution for any SQL statement, the optimizer first evaluates the available access paths, join orders, and so on, and selects several candidate execution plans. Next, it computes the cost of the alternative plans, based on their use of I/O, CPU, and memory. During this step, the optimizer uses optimizer statistics—crucial statistics that tell the optimizer about data distribution and storage characteristics of tables and indexes, among other things. The optimizer finally compares the costs of the alternative plans and picks the least costly plan.

Note Oracle recommends that you let the database collect optimizer statistics automatically.

Automatically Collecting Optimizer Statistics

Oracle Database 10g introduced the automatic optimizer-statistics collection feature. You thus don't have to deal with questions about the frequency of statistics collection or the objects to include in the collection process, because Oracle will take care of all that for you.

Note There are some situations where manually collecting optimizer statistics still makes sense, and these are discussed in the "Manually Collecting Optimizer Statistics" section of this chapter.

It's very easy to enable automatic statistics collection in Oracle Database 11g—Oracle automatically starts collecting statistics when you create a new Oracle Database 11g database or upgrade to the Oracle Database 11g Release. Oracle uses the DBMS_STATS package to collect optimizer statistics on an automatic basis.

Tip Make sure that the STATISTICS_LEVEL initialization parameter is set to TYPICAL or ALL, in order to ensure the automatic statistics collection feature is enabled.

The Scheduler and the GATHER_STATS_JOB

When you create a new database or upgrade one to the Oracle Database 11g release, Oracle automatically creates a database job called GATHER_STATS_JOB, and Oracle Scheduler automatically schedules the job to run during the maintenance window. Here's how you verify that the automatic statistics-collection job is running:

```
SQL> SELECT job_name
     FROM dba_scheduler_jobs
     WHERE job_name LIKE 'GATHER_STATS%';

JOB_NAME
----------------
GATHER_STATS_JOB
SQL>
```

Oracle schedules the GATHER_STATS_JOB job for automatic execution using the Oracle Scheduler tool. As of Oracle Database 10g, the Scheduler replaces and enhances the old job-scheduling capability that used the DBMS_JOB package (I explain the Scheduler in detail in Chapter 18).

■**Note** I provide more details about automatic optimizer statistics collection, including checking the results of the GATHER_STATS_JOB job, in Chapter 19.

The Oracle Scheduler has two default operation windows:

- The weeknight window covers the time between 10:00 p.m. and 6:00 a.m., Monday through Friday.
- The weekend window covers the time between 12:00 a.m. Saturday and 12:00 a.m. Monday.

Together, the weeknight and the weekend windows are known as the *maintenance* window. Oracle automatically schedules the GATHER_STATS_JOB job to run when the maintenance window opens.

You can disable the automatic collection of statistics in this way:

```
SQL> BEGIN
  2  dbms_scheduler.disable('gather_stats_job');
  3  END;
  4  /
PL/SQL procedure successfully completed.
SQL>
```

The GATHER_STATS_JOB job calls the DBMS_STATS.GATHER_DATABASE_STATS_JOB_PROC procedure to gather the optimizer statistics. The job collects statistics only for objects that fall into one of the following classes:

- *Objects with missing statistics*: Any object without statistics is a candidate for statistics collection.
- *Objects with stale statistics*: Oracle considers an object's statistics stale if 10 percent or more of the object's rows have been modified since the last time statistics were collected for that object.

By default, Oracle monitors the modifications (DML changes) in database objects, so long as you set the STATISTICS_LEVEL initialization parameter to TYPICAL or ALL (TYPICAL is the default value). The GATHER_DATABASE_STATS_JOB_PROC procedure sets priorities among the database objects based on the extent of DML activity in each object. The procedure will analyze the objects that have had the most DML changes first, so that even if it doesn't finish the entire statistics-collection job before the maintenance window closes, it ensures that it collects the most-needed statistics. Note that, by default, the Scheduler will terminate the GATHER_STATS_JOB job if it's still running when the maintenance window closes. The objects for which statistics couldn't be collected before the close of the maintenance window will be processed automatically the next time the job runs. You can, however, use the setting FALSE for the STOP_ON_WINDOW_CLOSE attribute of the GATHER_STATS_JOB job. Chapter 18, which discusses the Oracle Scheduler, explains how to do this.

Using the Database Control to Manage the GATHER_STATS_JOB Schedule

You can always modify the default maintenance window using SQL*Plus. You can also use the OEM Database Control to change the current schedule of the GATHER_STATS_JOB schedule. Here are the steps:

1. From the Database Control home page, click the Administration tab.
2. Go to the Scheduler Group, and click the Windows link.
3. Click the Edit button. You'll then be able to edit the weeknight or the weekend window timings.

Manually Collecting Optimizer Statistics

You can use the DBMS_STATS package to manually collect optimizer statistics at the table, schema, or database level, as well as to gather system statistics, and I show how to do this in Chapter 19. As of Oracle Database 10g, the recommended way to collect optimizer statistics, however, is to let the database automatically do it for you. Under some situations, such as the following, however, you must use the traditional DBMS_STATS package to gather statistics, instead of relying on Oracle's automatic statistics collection:

- When using external tables
- When collecting system statistics
- For collecting statistics on fixed objects, such as the dynamic performance tables
- Immediately after you run a bulk load job, since this will make your existing statistics unrepresentative

Automatic Storage Management

DBAs sometimes maintain thousands of datafiles for each database they manage, so an Oracle storage solution should provide both high-performance I/O and failure-proof storage hardware. In fact, file and I/O management is what usually takes up a large part of an Oracle DBA's time. With Oracle's new ASM feature, you can automate traditional file management tasks. Under an ASM system, the Oracle DBA is in charge of the management of physical storage from within Oracle's framework, instead of relying on the system administrator. Using the ASM disk groups, you can address sets of disks simultaneously, instead of individual disks, and the database can dynamically configure storage based on changing workloads. By allowing the Oracle DBA the flexibility to manage complex storage-management devices across various server and storage platforms, ASM becomes a crucial part of Oracle's grid computing initiative.

ASM is built on OMF, which means you don't have to worry about specifying filenames and locations when creating new databases—all you have to do is identify an ASM disk group, which consists of a set of disks. When you create a database or add a file, you can use familiar CREATE, ALTER, and DROP SQL statements to allocate disk space. ASM acts as Oracle's built-in Logical Volume Manager by handling striping and mirroring functions previously managed by third-party tools. Under ASM, disks are grouped and managed by the database itself and made available for creating tablespaces. You don't have to mount the files as with the normal Linux or UNIX file systems. You also can't use the traditional tools, such as cp and tar, to copy the ASM files, nor can you describe them using the ls command. The database holds all information regarding ASM files. If you use ASM for an Oracle file, the operating system can't see it, but RMAN and Oracle's other tools can.

For example, issue the following command:

```
SQL> ALTER DATABASE BACKUP CONTROLFILE TO TRACE AS <filename>;
```

The file generated by the previous statement will display the names of any ASM files. If ASM uses fully qualified names, you can see datafiles in views such as V$DATAFILE and V$LOGFILE.

When assigning a file to a tablespace or other object in an ASM file system, you don't need to know its name. You can refer to a disk group, and ASM automatically generates the filename.

Instead of learning to utilize a whole set of commands to manage ASM databases, you can just use the OEM Database Control to manage virtually all ASM operations. You can create a new ASM instance with the DBCA or with the Oracle Universal Installer (which uses the DBCA behind the scenes), and you can migrate an existing database to an ASM system with the Database Control.

Benefits of ASM

By using ASM, you can manage data by selecting reliability and performance characteristics for data classes, rather than working with large storage systems on a per-file basis. An ASM file system offers the following benefits:

- ASM provides automatic load balancing over all the available disks, thus reducing hot spots in the file system.

- ASM prevents fragmentation of disks, so you don't need to manually relocate data to tune I/O performance.

- Adding disks is straightforward—ASM automatically performs online disk reorganization when you add or remove storage.

- ASM uses redundancy features available in intelligent storage arrays.

- The ASM storage system stores all types of database files.

- ASM makes your file management tasks easier, because you will be dealing with just a few groups of disks, rather than a multitude of database files. ASM automatically creates the database files and places them in appropriate disk groups.

- ASM does mirroring and striping, which in turn increases reliability and performance. You can select different reliability and performance characteristics for various types of data. For example, you can use fine-grained striping for redo log files and a coarser-grained striping for regular datafiles.

- ASM is free!

■**Tip** ASM and non-ASM files can coexist in the same Oracle database.

Examining the ASM Architecture

The three major components of ASM are the ASM instance, ASM disk groups, and ASM files. Let's look briefly at these important ASM components.

The *ASM instance* is a special Oracle instance—it does not have its own datafiles like a regular Oracle database does. A single ASM instance on a server can manage the ASM file systems for all the Oracle databases on that server. The ASM instance looks after disk groups and gives the database access to the ASM files. The database makes the initial contact with the ASM instance to get information on the datafiles, but it accesses those files directly. The ASM instance must be running for an Oracle database to use the ASM file system, and the ASM instance can't be shut down while the other Oracle databases using ASM file systems are still running, since those databases will crash without the ASM instance.

ASM disk groups are somewhat analogous to logical volumes created by a Logical Volume Manager. Unlike the usual Oracle database files, you don't access ASM files directly. Disks in an ASM context are rather loosely defined and can include a partition of a disk spindle or the entire disk spindle itself. This depends on how the storage system represents the logical unit number (LUN) to the operating system. Any LUN or a disk represented to the operating system is called a disk. Since each operating system could have a different disk-naming system, check your disk-naming system.

ASM files are part of an ASM disk group, which contains all your database files. ASM manages a disk group consisting of several disk drives as a single unit, and it spreads the data evenly among all the disks in the group. You don't have to change the management of your database if you want to switch to an ASM system, because you can use your operating system–based files with the new ASM files. Logical concepts such as extents, segments, and tablespaces work the same way under an ASM system.

Here's a summary of an ASM storage system:

- A database is allowed to have multiple disk groups.

- You can store all of your Oracle database files as ASM files because Oracle sets up a one-to-one mapping between an Oracle database file (datafiles and control files, for example) and an ASM file.

- An ASM disk group comprises a set of disk drives.

- ASM disk groups are permitted to contain files from more than one disk.

- ASM files always spread over every disk in an ASM disk group and belong to one disk group only.

- ASM allocates disk space in *allocation units* of 1MB.

■**Note** You can continue to use your existing operating system file systems, raw devices, or OMF files as usual, along with ASM files, or you can migrate all existing file systems to an ASM-based file system.

In the current release, Oracle recommends that you create the OSASM operating system group and grant the SYSASM system privilege to members of this group. In future releases, Oracle intends to make the OSASM group mandatory. For now, the default operating system group for ASM administrators continues to be the dba group. If a user is part of this group, the user can connect to ASM by issuing the following command:

```
SQL> CONNECT / AS sysasm
```

You can grant the SYSASM privilege to a user in this way:

```
SQL> GRANT SYSASM TO salapati;
```

You can revoke the SYSASM privilege by issuing the REVOKE SYSASM statement. When you log into an ASM instance using the traditional SYSDBA system privilege, the database issues a warning that it records in the alert log.

Installing ASM

If you're creating an ASM instance on a server with just a single Oracle database, you probably don't need a separate Oracle home for the ASM instance. However, if you're running multiple Oracle databases on that server, Oracle recommends that you install ASM in a separate Oracle home. To do so, you use the Oracle Universal Installer and the Database Configuration Assistant to install the Oracle software and configure and create the ASM instance. In the example that follows, we will create an ASM instance in the same home as the existing Oracle database, so we don't have to install anything new.

ASM and Cluster Synchronization Service

An ASM storage system requires the use of an additional specialized instance called ASM, which will actually manage the storage for a set of Oracle databases. In order to use ASM storage for your Oracle databases, you must *first* ensure that you have Oracle's Cluster Synchronization Service (CSS) running on your databases.

CSS is responsible for synchronizing ASM instances and your database instances, and is installed as part of your Oracle software. When you start an ASM instance, it registers itself and the disk groups it manages with the CSS, and when an RDBMS needs to get to a disk group, it relies on the CSS to provide the name of the ASM instance that is managing that disk group.

CSS also synchronizes recovery from an ASM instance failure. You can find out if the CSS service is running by using the following command:

```
$ ps -ef | grep css
  oracle  5506     1  1  Apr 11  ?           630:05 /u03/app/oracle/bin/ocssd.bin
  oracle 12791 10525  2 16:38:39 pts/11    0:00 grep css
$
```

The preceding output of the ps -ef command shows that the CSS service is running. If you get the following result instead, it means that your CSS service hasn't been started:

```
$ ps -ef | grep css
  oracle  2207 19736  0 18:12:39 pts/6      0:00 grep css
$
```

■**Tip** You can't use ASM until the Oracle CSS service is started.

You can also check for the CSS process with the CRSCTL utility, as shown here:

```
$ crsctl check cssd
Failure 1 contacting CSS daemon
$
```

If your CSSD daemon isn't running, as in the preceding example, you must start it by following these steps:

1. Log in as the root user.

2. Make sure you add the Oracle home directory to your path, as shown here:

   ```
   # export PATH=$PATH:/u01/app/oracle/product/11.1.0/bin
   ```

3. Run the following command to start the CSS daemon:

   ```
   # localconfig add
   /etc/oracle does not exist.  Creating it now.
   Successfully accumulated necessary OCR keys.
   Creating OCR keys for user 'root', privgrp 'root'..
   Operation successful.
   Configuration for local CSS has been initialized

   Adding to inittab
   Startup will be queued to init within 30+60 seconds.
   Checking the status of new Oracle init process . . .
   Expecting the CRS daemons to be up within 600 seconds.
   CSS is active on these nodes.
   localhost
   CSS is active on all nodes
   Oracle CSS service is installed and running under init(1M)
   #
   ```

4. Now, check for the CSS daemon again:

   ```
   # crsctl check css
   CSS appears healthy
   #
   ```

You can also check to make sure that the CSS processes are running, as shown here:

```
# ps -ef | grep css
root   24871     1  0   07.59 ?      00:00:00   /bin/su -1   oracle   c   exec
root   24945 24871  0   08.00 ?
00:00:021/app/oracle/product/11.1.0/db_1/bin/ocssd.bin
#
```

The init.cssd script, which acts as the control script for the CSS daemon, starts and stops the CSS service. It is located in the $ORACLE_HOME/css/admin directory. The localconfig add command will automatically add the init.cssd script to your system's /etc/inittab file, as shown here:

```
h1:3:respawn:/sbin/init.d/init.cssd run >/dev/null 2>&1 </dev/null
```

If you create an ASM instance using the DBCA, the CSS daemon is automatically started. The localconfig command and the CRSCTL utility work the same way in a Windows server. However, refer to the documentation for more details on configuring the CSS service on a Windows server.

■**Tip** Since an ASM instance acts as the storage manager for all databases on a server, you'll need a single ASM instance on a node to service all the Oracle databases running there.

Creating an ASM Instance

Before you can create an ASM file system, you must create an ASM instance on your server. To create an ASM instance, you follow the same process you would when creating any other Oracle instance, with the big difference that you use a small number of initialization parameters. It should be noted that the ASM instance won't mount any Oracle database files. The ASM instance's main function is to maintain ASM file metadata, which the regular Oracle databases will use to access the ASM-based database files. An ASM instance usually requires only about 100MB of memory.Unlike normal Oracle databases, ASM instances don't have data dictionaries, so you must connect as an administrator, either using operating system authentication as SYSDBA or SYSOPER, or by using a password file, if you're working over a remote connection. In Oracle Database 11g, you can use the new role, SYSASM, to manage ASM operations. Oracle has introduced the SYSASM role to separate ASM administrative tasks from regular DBA administration. To create the ASM instance, you have to have the SYSDBA privilege. You can perform most management tasks (apart from creating the instance and a few other tasks) with just the SYSOPER privilege, but connecting as SYSDBA means you'll have complete administrative privileges.

■**Note** If you choose to create a new Oracle database during the Oracle Database software installation, or you use the DBCA to create a database, all you have to do to use ASM is choose an ASM storage system from the three storage choices that you're offered (raw devices, OS file systems, and ASM). The DBCA will automatically create the ASM instance for you, along with the Oracle database.

Working with the ASM Instance's Initialization Parameters

You have to create an initialization parameter file with the following parameters before you can create the new instance:

- INSTANCE_TYPE: In an Oracle Database 11*g* database, you have two types of Oracle instances: RDBMS and ASM. RDBMS, of course, refers to the normal Oracle databases, and ASM refers to the new ASM instance. Set the INSTANCE_TYPE parameter to ASM.

- ASM_POWER_LIMIT: The parameter controls the speed of a rebalance operation by controlling the number of ARB processes that can perform the rebalance operation. Rebalancing data redistributes the datafiles evenly and balances I/O load across the disks. The default is 1 and the range is from 1 to 11 (1 is slowest and 11 is fastest).

- ASM_DISKSTRING: This is the location where Oracle should look during a disk-discovery process. The format of the disk string may vary according to your operating system. You can specify a list of values as follows; this example limits the ASM discovery to disks whose names end in c2 and c3 only:

  ```
  ASM_DISKSTRING = '/dev/rdsk/*c2', '/dev/rdsk/*c3'
  ```

- ASM_DISKGROUPS: Here you specify the name of any disk group that you want to mount automatically at instance startup; the default value for this parameter is NULL.

To start an ASM instance off, you first have to create an init.ora file (init+asm.ora) that contains the ASM-related initialization parameters. Here it is:

```
INSTANCE_TYPE=ASM
ASM_POWER_LIMIT =2
ASM_DISKSTRING = '/dev/rdsk/*s1', '/dev/rdsk/*s2'
ASM_DISKGROUPS = dgroupA, dgroupB
```

Oracle will issue an error after the ASM instance is created because we've included the ASM_DISKGROUPS parameter, but no disk groups have yet been created for this new instance. We can create the disk groups after the ASM instance comes up.

Once you have the init.ora file ready, export the new ASM instance's SID just as you would for any regular Oracle database, and start up the new ASM instance, as shown in Listing 17-4.

■Note If your CSS instance wasn't started, you'll see the following error when you try to create your ASM instance:

```
ORA-29701: unable to connect to Cluster Manager
```

If this happens, simply start up the CSS daemon as explained in the "ASM and Cluster Synchronization Service" section earlier in this chapter, and then start up the ASM instance as shown in Listing 17-4.

Listing 17-4. *Starting an ASM Instance*

```
[finance] $ export ORACLE_SID=+ASM
[+ASM] $ sqlplus /nolog
SQL*Plus: Release 11.1.0.6.0 - Production on Thu Apr 10 09:21:48 2008
Copyright (c) 1982, 2007, Oracle.  All rights reserved.


SQL> CONNECT / AS SYSDBA
Connected to an idle instance.
SQL> STARTUP PFILE=initasm+.ora
ASM instance started
```

```
Total System Global Area  79691776 bytes
Fixed Size                 1216820 bytes
Variable Size             53309132 bytes
ASM Cache                 25165824 bytes
ORA-15110: no diskgroups mounted
SQL>
```

Note the new SGA component, ASM Cache, which is sized at about 25MB. In most cases, the total SGA memory allocated to the entire ASM instance remains small, usually less than 100MB.

In the preceding example, we also ended up with the ORA-15110 error, because the disk groups specified in the init.ora file don't exist yet, and the new instance can't mount them. We'll create the disk groups later on and then mount them with the ALTER DISKGROUP . . . MOUNT command. You can avoid the error message by taking out the ASM_DISKGROUPS parameter from the initialization parameter file.

■**Tip** Once you create an ASM instance, you must set the ORACLE_SID environment variable for the ASM instance before you can connect to it, just as you would do for a normal Oracle database instance. The default ASM instance name is +ASM.

You can confirm the name of your new ASM instance with the following query:

```
SQL> SELECT instance_name FROM v$instance;

INSTANCE_NAME
----------------
+ASM
SQL>
```

If you run the LSNRCTL STATUS command from the command line, you'll see that the listener has automatically registered the new ASM instance:

```
Service "+ASM" has one instance(s).
```

You can check the newly created ASM instance processes in the following way:

```
[+ASM] $ ps -ef | grep asm
  oracle  3201    1  0 Jul 3   ?        0:00:00 oracleasm+ (DESCRIPTION =
(LOCAL=YES) (ADDRESS=(PROTOCOL=beq)))
  oracle 11977    1  0 12:56 ?        0:00: 05 asm_pmon_+asm
  oracle 11979    1  0 12:56 ?        0:00: 02 asm_psp0_+asm
  oracle 11981    1  0 12:56 ?        0:00: 02 asm_mman_+asm
  oracle 11985    1  0 12:56 ?        0:00: 02 asm_dbw0_+asm
  oracle 11973    1  1 12:56 ?        0:00: 02 asm_lgwr_+asm
  oracle 11987    1  0 12:56 ?        0:00: 03 asm_ckpt_+asm
  oracle 11989    1  0 12:56 ?        0:00: 02 asm_smon_+asm
  oracle 11991    1  0 12:56 ?        0:00: 02 asm_rbal_+asm
  oracle 11995    1  0 12:56 ?        0:00: 02 asm_gmon_+asm
[+ASM] $
```

All the background processes shown in the preceding output are standard Oracle Database 11*g* processes, with the exception of a couple of background processes specific to an ASM instance. The following section explains the important ASM-specific background processes.

▉**Tip** You don't need to back up an ASM database, since you don't have any physical ASM datafiles to back up! This is also why you can't use the OPEN option while starting an ASM instance. All ASM metadata is either stored in the SGA while the ASM instance is running or stored on the disk groups and mirrored, to provide high availability.

Examining an ASM Instance's Architecture

An ASM instance uses several regular Oracle background processes, such as SMON, PMON, and LGWR. In addition, ASM utilizes two new ones: ASM rebalance master (RBAL) and ASM rebalance (ARB*n*). The RBAL process coordinates disk activity, and the ARB*n* processes perform the rebalancing work, which can include moving data extents.

In addition to ASM's RBAL and ARB*n*, any Oracle database instance that uses ASM will have two ASM-related background processes: RBAL and ASM background (ASMB). RBAL performs global opens of the disks that are part of the ASM disk group, and ASMB connects to the ASM instance as a foreground process and links the ASM instance and your database instance, sending information such as notifications when a datafile is created or deleted, and when statistics are updated.

You can use the OEM Database Control to manage an ASM instance. Its main page shows your ASM instance's status. From here, click the Configuration tab to visit the ASM Configuration page, where you can modify the ASM instance's parameters. You can also go to the ASM main page and check your instance's performance.

Let's review the manual ASM startup and shutdown procedures.

Starting an ASM Instance

The STARTUP command for an ASM instance is quite similar to the STARTUP command for regular Oracle databases, with a couple of interesting differences.

During the mount phase of the normal Oracle STARTUP command, an Oracle database reads the control file and mounts the datafiles specified there. An ASM instance doesn't have any datafiles to mount; it instead mounts the disk groups that you specify in the ASM_DISKGROUPS initialization parameter. The NOMOUNT command is similar to the regular Oracle NOMOUNT command: it starts an ASM instance, but doesn't mount any disk groups. Listing 17-5 shows how the STARTUP NOMOUNT and STARTUP MOUNT commands work in an ASM instance.

Listing 17-5. *The STARTUP NOMOUNT and STARTUP MOUNT Commands in an ASM Instance*

```
SQL> STARTUP NOMOUNT;
ASM instance started

Total System Global Area   79691776 bytes
Fixed Size                  1216820 bytes
Variable Size              53309132 bytes
ASM Cache                  25165824 bytes

SQL> SELECT name FROM v$database;
select name from v$database
                 *
ERROR at line 1:
ORA-01507: database not mounted
SQL> ALTER DATABASE MOUNT;
alter database mount
*
```

```
ERROR at line 1:
ORA-15000: command disallowed by current instance type
SQL>
SQL> ALTER DATABASE OPEN;
alter database open
*
ERROR at line 1:
ORA-15000: command disallowed by current instance type
SQL>
```

To use ASM, you have to have a running ASM instance, and since there aren't any datafiles in an ASM instance, you can't use the STARTUP command's MOUNT or OPEN options. When you issue a STARTUP FORCE command, the ASM instance is first shut down with an internal SHUTDOWN ABORT command and the instance is restarted. You can prevent any client Oracle database instances from connecting to the ASM instance by using the STARTUP RESTRICT command.

The ASM Fast Mirror Resync Feature

If there's a transient disk failure due to a bad cable or a controller, ASM fails to complete writing extents to the failed disk. Traditionally, you fixed the problem by offlining the disk and re-creating the disk's extents on a different disk using redundant extent copies and then dropping the failed disk. Or, you fixed the failed disk and reused it instead of using a different disk. In either case, the migration of extents to the new or the fixed disk took time to complete.

You can use the new ASM fast mirror resync feature in Oracle Database 11g to quickly resynchronize disk groups following a transient disk failure. Under this feature, the database will rewrite only those extents that were modified during the outage, instead of copying the entire disk after offlining it and bringing it back online after repairs. You do take the disk offline but don't drop it under this method. You set the DISK_REPAIR_TIME attribute to control the length of time ASM will wait for you to complete a disk repair and still resynchronize the disk. You save considerable time using the fast mirror resync feature because the database doesn't have to wipe off the contents of the repaired disk before adding it back to the disk group. In addition, ASM doesn't have to perform a lengthy rebalance operation after adding the repaired disk back to the disk group.

Here is an example showing how to set up the fast mirror resync capability by specifying the DISK_REPAIR_TIME attribute in an ALTER DISKGROUP command:

```
SQL> ALTER DISKGROUP dgroupA
     SET ATTRIBUTE 'disk_repair_time'='4h';
```

If you have to take any of the disks that belong to the disk group DGROUPA offline due to failure, you have 4 hours to fix the problem and bring the disk back online. After waiting for 4 hours, ASM drops the disks you took offline to fix. If you bring the disk back online within 4 hours, however, ASM will copy the extents that were on the bad blocks, using the mirrored data from another disk. The point is that ASM avoids the copying of an entire disk's contents whenever there is a transient failure of a disk.

Once you repair the disk, bring the disk online with the following command:

```
SQL> ALTER DISKGROUP dgroupA ONLINE;
```

The default value of the DISK_REPAIR_TIME attribute is 3.6 hours. If you want, you can override the DISK_REPAIR_TIME attribute by specifying the DROP AFTER clause in an ALTER DISKGROUP . . . OFFLINE command:

```
SQL> ALTER DISKGROUP dgroupA
     OFFLINE DISKS IN FAILUREGROUP controller1
     DROP AFTER 4h;
```

You can specify the FORCE option to drop an offlined disk that you are unable to repair, as shown here:

```
SQL> alter diskgroup dgroupA
     drop disks in failuregroup controller1 force;
```

Once you drop the offlined disk group, ASM reconstructs the data in the dropped disk from its redundant copies and stores the same on other disks from the same disk group.

ASM Preferred Mirror Read

ASM provides different levels of mirroring, to support various mirroring strategies. You can create an ASM disk group with the following types of redundancy levels:

- *Normal* provides two-way mirroring.
- *High* provides three-way mirroring.
- *External* bypasses ASM mirroring, and is ideal when you wish to configure hardware RAID to provide redundancy.

The redundancy level you choose determines the amount of disk failure the database will tolerate before it loses data. External redundancy doesn't require any failure groups since it doesn't use mirroring. Normal redundancy requires two failure groups. High redundancy requires at least three failure groups. ASM stores copies of data in different failure groups. In a normal redundancy file, ASM always allocates a primary copy and a secondary copy when it allocates a new extent and stores the two copies in different failure groups

By default, ASM always reads the primary copy of a mirrored extent in both normal and high-redundancy disk groups. However, at times, it may be more efficient to read from a local copy of an extent, even if it isn't in the primary failure group. You can use ASM's preferred mirror read feature to make an ASM instance read from specific failure groups instead of automatically reading from the primary failgroup. This feature is especially useful when dealing with a *stretch cluster*, in which the individual nodes are spread out.

You must set the ASM_PREFERRED_READ_FAILURE_GROUPS initialization parameter to specify a list of preferred mirrored read failure group names, as shown in this example:

```
asm_preferred_read_failure_groups=data.locationA,data.locationB
```

Once you set up a list of preferred failure group names, ASM will prefer to read from disks in those failure groups. The result is that all nodes will read from their local extents, thus leading to improved performance.

You can query the V$ASM_DISK view to find out which disks are in a preferred read failure group:

```
SQL> select preferred_read from v$asm_disk;
```

The value of the PREFERRED_READ column will be Y if a disk belongs to a preferred read failure group.

Changing ASM Disk Group Attributes

You use the ATTRIBUTE clause to specify or change disk group attributes, as I explain in the following sections.

Allocation Unit Size

You can specify multiple allocation unit (AU) sizes such as 1-, 2-, 4-, 8-, 16-, 32-, and 64MB when creating a disk group.

RDBMS Compatibility

Specify the COMPATIBLE.RDBMS parameter for the RDBMS compatibility level. This is the minimum compatible level of the database instance that would allow the instance to mount the ASM disk group.

ASM Compatibility

Specify the COMPATIBLE.ASM parameter to define the format of the ASM metadata. Note that the ASM compatibility level must be at least the same or greater than the RDBMS compatibility level of a disk group.

Disk Repair Time

As you know, the default value of the DISK_REPAIR_TIME attribute is 3.6 hours. You can execute the ALTER DISKGROUP statement to specify an alternative value for this attribute.

Template Redundancy

Specify the TEMPLATE.TNAME.REDUNDANCY attribute to set the template redundancy, which can take the values unprotect, mirror, and high.

Template Striping

You can specify the TEMPLATE.TNAME.STRIPING attribute to specify striping attributes for a template. You can choose either COARSE or FINE as the values for this parameter.

The following example shows how to specify the value for the ASM compatibility level by using the ATTRIBUTE clause in a CREATE DISKGROUP statement:

```
SQL> CREATE DISKGROUP data1 NORMAL REDUNDANCY
    DISK '/dev/raw/raw1', '/dev/raw/raw2'
    ATTRIBUTE 'compatible.asm'='11.1';
```

The default ASM compatibility for an Oracle Database 11g ASM instance is 11.1, and the default database compatibility level is 10.1.

Shutting Down an ASM Instance

To shut down an ASM instance, you run the same commands you would if you were shutting down a normal Oracle database instance:

```
$ sqlplus /nolog
SQL> CONNECT / AS SYSDBA
Connected.
SQL> SHUTDOWN
ASM instance shutdown
SQL>
```

Each Oracle database connected to an ASM instance depends on the status of the ASM instance. If you shut down your ASM instance, every connected Oracle database will also shut down. (This is similar to how all Oracle instances will shut down if you shut down the LVM on the operating system.) When you shut down an ASM instance, it forwards the SHUTDOWN command, in the same mode, to any Oracle databases that are connected to it.

Oracle recommends that you first shut down all database instances (managed by an ASM instance) before shutting down the ASM instance. If you shut down your ASM instance in NORMAL mode, it will wait for every connected Oracle database instance to close their ASM connections before shutting down. If you shut down in IMMEDIATE or TRANSACTIONAL mode, the ASM instance waits until the connected databases have finished all SQL operations before shutting down, but it doesn't wait for them to disconnect. Issuing the SHUTDOWN ABORT command causes the following events to occur:

- The ASM instance terminates immediately.

- All open Oracle connections are automatically terminated.

- All dependent Oracle databases will also terminate immediately. This is why you should be careful about shutting down the ASM instance abruptly.

The asmcmd Command-Line Tool

You can also manage ASM using a command-line tool, which gives you more flexibility than having to use SQL*Plus or the Database Control. The *asmcmd* utility enables you to view and manage files and directories within an ASM disk group. To invoke this command-line administrative tool, enter this command (after the ASM instance is started):

```
$ asmcmd
```

```
ASMCMD>
```

You can issue various asmcmd commands from the ASMCMD> prompt shown here. The asmcmd tool has about a dozen commands you can use to manage ASM file systems, and it includes familiar UNIX/Linux commands such as du, which checks ASM disk usage. To get a complete list of commands, type **help** at the command prompt (ASMCMD>). By typing **help** followed by a command, you can get details about that command.

You can execute asmcmd from the command line by typing in **asmcmd** at the operating system prompt. You can also incorporate asmcmd commands within operating system scripts. Some asmcmd commands such as LSDSK don't require the ASM instance to be running, but most of the commands require a running ASM instance.

You can specify the –a option when executing the asmcmd command to select the type of connection. You can connect either as SYSASM or using the familiar SYSDBA privilege. The default is to connect as SYSASM. The SYSASM privilege is new in Oracle Database 11*g*, and its goal is to demarcate ASM-related administrative tasks from general database administrative tasks. You can continue to connect as SYSDBA, but each time you do so, the database will issue a warning that it records in the alert log file.

■**Note** There is also a new operating system group called OSASM, as mentioned earlier, to which you must assign all users to whom you want to grant ASM-related administrative privileges.

The asmcmd utility implements commands such as cp, which helps you copy files from ASM to the operating system file system and vice versa. The two most important asmcmd commands that you must know about are the md_backup and the md_restore commands, which together form what Oracle calls ASM Backup and Recovery (AMBR). Using the md_backup and the md_restore options of the asmcmd utility, you can re-create ASM disk groups with identical alias directory structures and templates. The ASM backup functionality gathers disk group and failure configuration details and information about templates and alias directory structures. The md_backup command stores this backup-related metadata in a text file. The md_restore option uses the information in the text file to reconstruct disk groups. I discuss the md_backup and the md_restore commands in more detail in the following sections.

md_backup

You can make backups of the ASM metadata for a disk group with the help of the md_backup command. These backups help ASM easily re-create ASM disk groups following the loss of a disk group. Here's the syntax of the md_backup command:

```
md_backup [-b <backup_file>]
[-g '<diskgroup_name>,<diskgroup_name>, . . .']
```

The –b option specifies a name for the backup text file, which is named ambr_backup_ intermediate by default. By default, the md_backup command backs up all ASM disk groups, but you can specify the disk groups you want by using the –g option.

Here's an example showing how to back up a single disk group by executing this command:

```
ASMCMD> md_backup -b /tmp/asmbkp1 -g admdsk1
```

The –g option specifies that a single disk group be backed up, and the –b option specifies the file asmbkp1 as the backup text file.

md_restore

Before you can execute the md_restore command to restore the ASM metadata for a disk group, you must first restore the disk group. Once you do that, you can run the md_restore command, the syntax of which is shown here:

```
md_restore -b <backup_file> [-li]
        [-t (full)|nodg|newdg] [-f <sql_script_file>]
        [-g '<diskgroup_name>,<diskgroup_name>, . . .']
        [-o '<old_diskgroup_name>:<new_diskgroup_name>, . . .']
```

Of the various options you can specify with the md_restore command, the -t option bears some explanation. You can specify the backup type using this option, as explained here:

- full creates the disk group and restores the metadata.

- nodg restores the metadata only.

- newdg creates the disk group with a different name and restores the metadata.

The following example shows how to restore a disk group and create a new disk group by specifying -t newdg:

```
ASMCMD> md_restore -t newdg -o 'DGNAME=asmdsk1:asmdsk2'
        -i backup_file
```

The md_recover command can't restore the actual data stored on the ASM disks. However, it restores the disk groups, modifies templates, and creates the directories. Once you restore the disk group metadata, you can use the RMAN backups to restore the data in the re-created disk groups.

■**Tip** Execute the md_restore command with the -f option regularly, to keep a record of ASM metadata.

Backup and Restore Example

In the following example, I show how to use the md_backup and md_restore commands to restore lost data:

1. Back up the users tablespace:

   ```
   RMAN> BACKUP TABLESPACE users;
   ```

2. Create a directory named test in the disk group DGROUPA. Also create an alias called
   +DGROUPA/test/users.f that points to the ASM datafile that contains the users tablespace:

   ```
   ASMCMD> mkdir +DGROUPA/test
   ASMCMD> mkalias TBSSRA.123.123456789      +DGROUPA/test/users.f
   ```

3. Back up the metadata for the disk group DGROUPA using the md_backup command:

   ```
   ASMCMD> md_backup -g dgroupA
   ```

   The md_backup command stores the backup metadata in the text file named ambr_backup_
   intermediate in the current directory.

4. Simulate a disk failure by dropping the disk group DGROUPA:

   ```
   SQL> ALTER DISKGROUP dgroup1 DISMOUNT FORCE;
   SQL> DROP DIKSGROUP dgroup1 FORCE INCLUDING CONTENTS;
   ```

   The DISMOUNT FORCE clause in the ALTER DISKGROUP command dismounts the disk group and
   force drops it.

5. Execute the md_restore command to restore the ASM metadata for the dropped disk group:

   ```
   ASMCMD> md_restore -b ambr_backup_intermediate_file
           -t full -g data
   ```

6. Using the backup of the users tablespace from step 1, restore the users tablespace:

   ```
   RMAN>RESTORE TABLESAPCE users;
   ```

7. Exit from RMAN once the restore is completed.

Managing ASM Disk Groups

An ASM disk group is a collection of disks analogous to the logical volumes that an LVM creates from
the underlying physical disks. This means that you have to manage the underlying disks indirectly
by managing the disk group.

If you have large numbers of disks, you can group them into a small number of easily managed
disk groups, and if you add storage to your ASM system, you simply add disks to an ASM disk group.
This is good news, because if your database grows quickly, the total storage space increases, but the
number of disk groups remains the same.

Adding Performance and Redundancy with Disk Groups

Two major reasons for using ASM file management are the additional performance and protection,
and the decreased management overhead. Of course, these are the same advantages third-party
vendors claim for their LVM tools, but the major advantage of ASM is that you as an Oracle DBA can
do most of the disk management using ASM. There's no need for you to be an expert in file systems,
RAID, or logical volumes to use ASM; all you need is an understanding of ASM's disk-management
system and Oracle's processes for accessing database files spread over the ASM disks.

ASM gives you performance and redundancy through *striping* and *mirroring*, so let's look at
these two features.

> **■Note** The OEM Database Control is the best way to administer the ASM instance, once you create it. Refer to the Oracle Database 11*g* Release 1 manual *Oracle Database 2 Day DBA* for details about using the Database Control to manage disk groups, as well as all other aspects of an ASM instance.

Examining ASM Striping

ASM systems store your database files on ASM disks. The manner in which you place your database files on ASM disks plays a critical role in the resulting performance. For optimal I/O performance, ASM stripes its files across every disk that is part of its disk group. This means that all the disks in a disk group must be of the same type and performance capacity.

ASM offers two types of striping, with the choice depending on the type of database file. Coarse striping uses a stripe size of 1MB, and you can use coarse striping for every file in your database, except for the control files, online redo log files, and flashback files. Fine striping uses a stripe size of 128KB. You can use fine striping for control files, online redo log files, and flashback files.

Examining ASM Mirroring

Disk mirroring gives us data *redundancy*. This means that, should you lose a disk, you can use the mirror disk to continue operations. This process is not like an OS-level mirroring scheme, but they both provide redundancy for your database. The difference is that OS-based LVMs mirror entire disks, whereas ASM mirrors extents. This means that when ASM allocates an extent (the *primary extent*, in contrast to a *mirrored extent*), it also allocates a mirror copy to one of the disks in the same disk group.

When a disk in a group fails, ASM rebuilds the failed disk using the mirrored extents from other disks in the group. When ASM reconstructs a failed disk, the storage system takes a small performance hit, because ASM requires some extra I/O to reconstruct the failed device.

Failure Groups

Disk failure is not the only way in which you can lose a disk. You can also lose a disk if shared resources, such as SCSI disk controllers, fail. When one of these fails, you cannot access any of the connected disks. A set of disks that fail because they all share a common resource, such as a disk controller, is a *failure group*. You ensure redundancy by mirroring disks on a separate failure group.

To avoid problems, ASM will not place a primary extent and its mirror copy in the same failure group. This means that even if a failure group loses several disks, ASM can survive the disaster and reconstruct the lost disks from the mirror copies that are in a different failure group.

Types of ASM Mirroring

ASM supports three forms of disk mirroring, each with a different level of data redundancy. *External redundancy* doesn't have failure groups, and thus is effectively a no-mirroring strategy. *Normal redundancy* provides two-way mirroring of all fields in a disk group. *High redundancy* provides three-way mirroring, which results in three failure groups, with a disk controller for each.

Creating a Disk Group

The OEM Database Control is the best tool for performing most ASM tasks, including creating a disk group. Using the Disk Group Administration page, you can select redundancy levels, disk-group names, and lists of disks that are members of a disk group. Once you create disk groups, the ASM instance will mount them each time you start the instance, and you won't receive the ORA-15110 error ("No diskgroups mounted") as you did when you first started the ASM instance.

You can also create a disk group with the CREATE DISKGROUP command. Suppose you have three disk controllers and twelve disks. The first four disks are on a separate controller from the second four disks, and so on. You could create three failure groups, each of which has four disks. To start with, you need to start the ASM instance in nomount mode. (If you want to access existing disk groups, you have to use mount mode.) You can then create the disk groups corresponding with the three groups. To do so, you would issue the CREATE DISKGROUP command, as shown in Listing 17-6.

Listing 17-6. *Creating Disk Groups with the CREATE DISKGROUP Command*

```
$ sqlplus /nolog
SQL> CONNECT / AS SYSDBA
Connected to an idle instance.
SQL> STARTUP NOMOUNT
SQL> CREATE DISKGROUP group1 HIGH REDUNDANCY 2
  2 failgroup group1 disk
  3 '/devices/disk1',
  4 '/devices/disk2',
  5 '/devices/disk3',
  6 '/devices/disk4',
  7 failgroup group2 disk
  8 '/devices/disk5',
  9 '/devices/disk6',
 10 '/devices/disk7',
 11 '/devices/disk8',
 12 failgroup group3 disk
 13 '/devices/disk9',
 14 '/devices/disk10',
 15 '/devices/disk11',
 16 '/devices/disk12';
SQL>
```

In order to find the disks, Oracle uses a search string in the following format:

```
/devices/diskname
```

The FAILGROUP and REDUNDANCY keywords are optional, but if you omit FAILGROUP, each disk in the group will be in its own failure group. Specifying the HIGH REDUNDANCY setting creates the following setup:

- There are three failure groups, each defined by FAILGROUP (you must have at least three failure groups to specify HIGH REDUNDANCY).
- Each failure group has four disks.
- Oracle writes data simultaneously to all three disks in the three failure groups.

Adding Disks to a Disk Group

The ALTER DISKGROUP command can be used to add a new disk, as shown here:

```
SQL> ALTER DISKGROUP group1 ADD DISK
     '/devices/disk5' name disk5,
     '/devices/disk6' name disk6,
```

Dropping Disks and Disk Groups

The ALTER DISKGROUP command can be used to drop a disk, as shown here:

```
SQL> ALTER DISKGROUP group1 DROP DISK disk5;
```

You can use the following command to remove a disk group, after putting the database in the MOUNT state:

```
SQL> DROP DISKGROUP group1 INCLUDING CONTENTS
```

The UNDROP clause keeps a pending DROP DISK command from happening. If the disk has already dropped, there is no way for you to retrieve it, even using UNDROP.

The optional FORCE clause means you can't use the UNDROP clause and you can never UNDROP a whole disk group. Here's an example of the UNDROP clause:

```
SQL> ALTER DISKGROUP group1 UNDROP DISKS;
```

This cancels the pending drop of all disks from the group1 disk group.

Rebalancing Disk Groups

When ASM rebalances a disk group, it does so automatically and dynamically. It does this whenever you change the status of a disk in a disk group, whether you are adding or removing a disk from the disk group—it attempts to maintain an I/O balance across all the disks in a disk group. So, when you add or remove disks, you disturb the I/O balance, but ASM sets it right automatically by moving data appropriately for the space you added or removed.

■**Note** Since there will be a performance hit on your system while ASM rebalances a disk group, you should consolidate the times when you add and remove disks so that you reduce the number of times that ASM has to rebalance.

You can also manually rebalance the disk groups if you wish, using the following command; you can assign a value of 1 through 11 for the POWER clause:

```
SQL> ALTER DISKGROUP dgroup1 REBALANCE POWER 5;
```

The POWER clause specifies how fast ASM performs the REBALANCE command. Setting the POWER clause high increases the speed of the rebalancing. The default is 1 (the default value for the ASM_ POWER_LIMIT parameter). Specifying POWER means you are overriding the value you assigned to the ASM_POWER_LIMIT initialization parameter when you started the ASM instance. Of course, it would be nice to rebalance disks quickly rather than slowly, but due to the overhead involved, there's a trade-off between rebalancing speed and database performance.

Managing ASM Files

The datafiles you create in a regular database aren't like the ones in an ASM setup. ASM file management takes over your normal operating system files, which become ASM files and, when you create a new datafile, control file, or redo log, you simply specify an ASM group and not an operating system filename.

So, to create a new tablespace on an ASM disk group, you would run a command like the following:

```
SQL> CREATE TABLESPACE tbsp1 DATAFILE '+group1';
```

In this example, DATAFILE takes a file type (DATAFILE), which indicates that we're going to use the file as a datafile. Here, CREATE TABLESPACE works with a disk group and not with a disk in that group. Note that we don't even refer to a datafile.

The ASM system does indeed create a datafile, though it doesn't compare to regular datafiles. ASM spreads its files across every disk in the disk group, so you can't rely on a backup of a single disk to hold the entire datafile.

It should also be noted that ASM files have a permanent redundancy level and striping policy, which is different from normal datafiles.

ASM files are OMF files, and Oracle will remove them when you don't need them. Note that if you give an ASM file a user alias, Oracle doesn't consider that file an OMF file, so it can't automatically delete it.

■**Note** Administrative files such as trace files, audit files, alert logs, tar files, and core files can't be on an ASM file system. ASM filenames are stored in control files and the RMAN recovery catalog, the same way filenames of regular operating system–based files or OMF-based files are.

Types of ASM Filenames

ASM naming conventions depend on whether you're creating a new file, or referring to an existing file. Here are the usage guidelines for the different file-naming conventions:

- *Fully qualified ASM filenames* are used when referencing existing ASM files (for example, +dgroupA/db2/controlfile/CF.123.456789).

- *Numeric ASM filenames* are also only used when referencing existing ASM files (for example, +dgroupA.123.456789).

- *Alias ASM filenames* employ user-friendly names and are used when you create new files, as well as when you refer to existing files (for example, +dgroupA/myfiles/control_file1).

- *Alias filenames with templates* are strictly for creating new ASM files (for example, +dgroupA/config1(spfile)).

- *Incomplete ASM filenames* consist of a disk group name only and are used only for file creation. Incomplete ASM filenames may be used with or without a template (for example, here is an incomplete filename with a template: +dgroupA(datafile)).

Creating Diskgroup Directories for Alias Filenames

The fully qualified filenames in a disk group are held in a hierarchical directory structure. To use aliases, you have to create a directory structure to support the alias naming conventions. The following example shows how to create a hierarchical directory for a disk group named dgroup1:

```
SQL> ALTER DISKGROUP dgroup1 ADD DIRECTORY '+dgroup1/dir1';
```

After creating the +dgroup1/dir1 directory, you can create alias ASM filenames, such as +dgroup1/dir1/control_file1, for example.

Using Templates with Aliases

Templates are used to apply a set of file attributes, like those referring to file mirroring and striping, to each of the files created in a disk group. There are default templates for each file type (datafile, control file, and so on), and you can create custom file templates.

> ■**Note** Templates are discussed in detail in the "ASM File Templates" section of this chapter.

Using a template, you can create an alias ASM filename when you create a new file. Here's the syntax of a template-based alias ASM filename:

```
diskgroup/alias(template)
```

And here's an example:

```
dgroup1/config1(spfile)
```

Adding and Dropping Aliases

If you create a file and don't use an alias, you can later add an alias with the ADD ALIAS or RENAME ALIAS clauses of the ALTER DISKGROUP statement. The following example replaces a fully qualified ASM filename with an alias:

```
SQL> ALTER DISKGROUP dgroup1 ADD ALIAS '+dgroup1/dir/second.dbf'
     FOR '+dgroup2/ datafile/table.763.1';
```

To delete an alias, use the DROP ALIAS clause.

Dropping Files from a Disk Group

ASM files are often OMF files, but you may sometimes want to use your own aliases for some ASM files. If you use your own aliases, Oracle won't automatically delete the aliases when there is a need to do so. To accomplish this, you have to use ALTER DISKGROUP . . . DROP FILE to delete them:

```
SQL> ALTER DISKGROUP dgroup1 DROP FILE '+dgroup1/payroll/compensation.dbf';
```

Working with ASM Filenames

Here's a brief summary of ASM filename usage:

- When referring to an *existing file*, use a fully qualified name, a numeric name, or an alias. This cannot be an alias with a template, or an incomplete filename with or without a template.

- When *creating a single file*, use any filename, but not a fully qualified filename.

- When *creating multiple files*, only use incomplete filenames or incomplete filenames with templates.

You must avoid using ASM filenames if you can, since one of the main goals in using ASM is to simplify file management by just referring to the disk groups instead.

ASM File Templates

It is easy to specify file attributes in Oracle. You can simply use templates to specify attributes when you create files. Oracle applies templates to individual files, but associates them with the newly created file's disk group.

If you create a disk group, Oracle creates system default templates for that disk group, and these templates contain specific file attributes.

For example, suppose we want to create a new tablespace called tbsp01 in an ASM file system. This tablespace will use datafiles, so we can use the ASM DATAFILE template:

```
SQL> CREATE TABLESPACE tbsp01 DATAFILE '+group1';
```

The tablespace datafile will inherit the attributes such as the striping level of the DATAFILE template.

Creating an ASM-Based Database

To create an ASM-based Oracle database (not an ASM instance, which we created earlier in the chapter), specify the DB_CREATE_FILE_DEST, DB_RECOVERY_FILE_DEST, and the DB_RECOVERY_FILE_DEST_SIZE parameters in your initialization parameter file, as shown here:

```
DB_CREATE_FILE_DEST = '+dgroup1'
DB_RECOVERY_FILE_DEST = '+dgroup2'
DB_RECOVERY_FILE_DEST_SIZE = 100G
```

These three parameters are also used to create an OMF file system, which I discuss in detail in the "Easy File Management with OMF" section, later in this chapter.

Once the preceding parameters have been set up, you simply issue the database creation statement. You don't need to specify datafiles when creating an ASM database, so it's a very straightforward process. Here's how:

```
SQL> CREATE DATABASE;
```

In this example, Oracle will create a System tablespace and a Sysaux tablespace in the disk group dgroup1. In addition, it will create a multiplexed redo log file group and a control file in both dgroup1 and dgroup2. If you configure Automatic Undo Management, an undo tablespace will be created in dgroup1, as well.

Creating new tablespaces and adding various files to the database also become trivial chores, as shown by the next two examples. Here's how you would create a new tablespace:

```
SQL> CREATE TABLESPACE new_tbsp;
```

In order to create a redo log file, use the following statement:

```
SQL> ALTER DATABASE ADD LOGFILE;
```

Migrating Your Database to ASM

You can migrate a database to an ASM system, either by using the OEM Database Control (or the Grid Control) or by using RMAN. You can use RMAN even if you don't use it to back up your current database.

Migrating with RMAN

Here's a brief summary of how to use RMAN to migrate a database to ASM:

1. Shut down the database in a consistent mode by using the SHUTDOWN IMMEDIATE command.

2. Add the DB_CREATE_FILE_DEST and DB_CREATE_ONLINE_LOG_DEST_*n* parameters, as well as the new flash recovery area initialization parameters, DB_RECOVERY_FILE_DEST and DB_RECOVERY_FILE_DEST_SIZE, to your database parameter file so you can use an OMF-based file system. (I explain OMF files shortly in the "Easy File Management with OMF" section of this chapter.) Make sure that the two OMF parameters refer to the disk groups that you want to use in your ASM system.

3. Delete the control file parameter from the SPFILE, since Oracle will create new control files in the OMF file destinations by restoring them from the non-ASM database control files.

4. Start the database with the STARTUP NOMOUNT command:

```
RMAN> CONNECT TARGET;
RMAN> STARTUP NOMOUNT;
```

5. Restore the old control file in the new location, as shown here:

```
RMAN> RESTORE CONTROLFILE from '/u01/orcl/oradata/control1.ctl';
```

6. Mount the database:

```
RMAN> ALTER DATABASE MOUNT;
```

7. Use the following command to copy your database files into an ASM disk group:

```
RMAN> BACKUP AS COPY DATABASE FORMAT +dgroup1;
```

8. Use the SWITCH command (discussed in Chapter 16) to switch all datafiles into the ASM disk group dgroup1:

```
RMAN> SWITCH DATABASE TO COPY;
```

At this point, all datafiles will be converted to the ASM type. You still have your original datafile copies on disk, which you can use to restore your database if necessary.

9. Open the database with the following command:

```
RMAN> ALTER DATABASE OPEN;
```

10. For each redo log member, use the following command to move it to the ASM system:

```
RMAN> SQL "alter database rename '/u01/test/log1' to '+dgroup1' ";
```

11. Archive the current online redo logs, and delete the old non-ASM redo logs. Since RMAN doesn't migrate temp files, you must manually create a temporary tablespace using the CREATE TEMPORARY TABLESPACE statement.

You'll now have an ASM-based file system. You still have your old non-ASM files as backups in the RMAN catalog, and you can delete them if you need the space.

Migrating with Database Control

Instead of going through the cumbersome RMAN migration exercise shown in the previous section, you can simply use the Database Control interface to easily convert your current database to an ASM database. Here are the first few steps:

1. From the Database Control home page, click the Administration tab.

2. In the Change Database group, click the Migrate to ASM link.

3. You'll now be on the Migrate to ASM Database page, as shown Figure 17-5. At this point, make sure you have an ASM instance running on your server. After that, provide the necessary information on the pages that follow to convert your database to ASM.

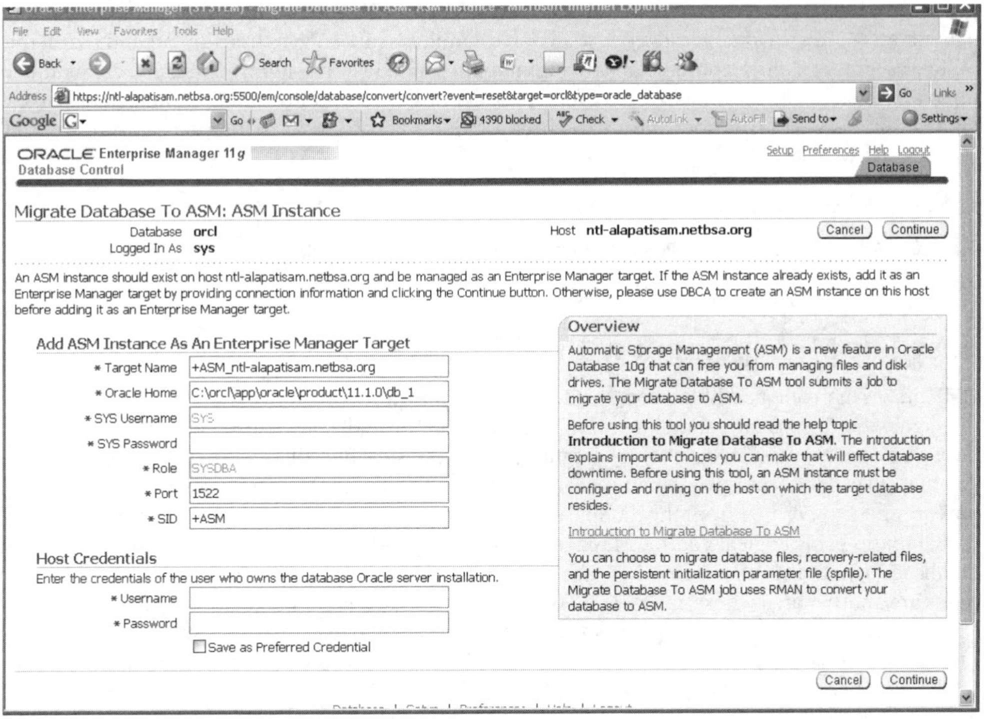

Figure 17-5. *Using the Database Control to migrate to ASM*

Automatic Space Management

Oracle Database 11g provides several automatic space-management features. These features eliminate the need for manually performing several traditional space-management chores. In this section, you'll learn about the following automatic space-management features:

- Automatic Undo Management
- Resumable Space Allocation
- Automatic Online Segment Shrinking

Automatic Undo Management

Undo refers to the before-image of data as it existed before the start of a transaction. All the concurrent transactions running in your database need to be able to fit into the undo space allocated for them, or you're going to have transaction failures. Rollback segment contention and space management used to be big database management issues, but when you use Oracle's recommended Automatic Undo Management (AUM) mode, you don't have to worry about these problems anymore.

Under manual rollback management, you manually manage the rollback segments and have to worry about specifying large segments for large transactions to avoid snapshot-too-old errors. In addition, you have to worry about contention for rollback segments, proper sizing of the segments, and the correct number of segments. When you choose AUM mode, you simply create a dedicated undo tablespace, select the undo retention period, and Oracle will do the rest.

Oracle introduced AUM in the Oracle9*i* release. Under AUM, the rollback segments are internally created and are called *undo segments*. Oracle handles issues such as the number and size of the rollback segments, block contention, and maintenance of read consistency. When you create the undo tablespace during database creation, Oracle creates a set of undo segments, and Oracle automatically increases the number and size of these segments according to an internal algorithm, based on database workload.

■**Note** Chapter 8 discusses the setting up and management of Automatic Undo Management in detail.

Easy File Management with OMF

OMF makes managing datafiles, control files, redo log files, and RMAN backup files a lot easier than managing the various files at the operating system level. Normally, if you drop a datafile, the database won't have any references to the datafile, but the physical file still exists in the old location—you have to explicitly remove the physical file yourself. If you use OMF, Oracle will remove the file for you when you drop it from the database. According to Oracle, OMF file systems are most useful for databases using Logical Volume Managers that support RAID and extensible file systems. Smaller databases benefit the most from OMF, because of the reduced file-management tasks. Test databases are another area where an OMF file system will cut down on management time.

You have to use operating system–based files if you want to use the OMF feature; you can't use raw files. You do lose some control over the placement of data in your storage system when you use OMF files, but even with these limitations, the benefits of OMF file management can outweigh its limitations in some circumstances.

Benefits of Using OMF

You can create tablespaces with OMF-based files. You can also specify that your online redo log files and your control files are in the OMF format. OMF files offer several advantages over user-managed files:

- Oracle automatically creates and deletes OMF files.

- You don't have to worry about coming up with a naming convention for the files.

- It's easy to drop datafiles by mistake when you're managing them. With OMF files, you don't run the risk of accidentally deleting database files.

- Oracle automatically deletes a file when it's no longer needed.

- You can have a mix of traditional files and OMF files in the same database.

In the following sections we'll look at the OMF feature in some detail.

Creating Oracle Managed Files

You can create OMF files when you create the database, or you can add them to your traditionally created database later on. Either way, you need to set some initialization parameters to enable OMF file creation.

Initialization Parameters for OMF

You need to set four initialization parameters to enable the use of OMF files. You can set these three parameters in your parameter file, and you can change them online with the ALTER SYSTEM or ALTER

SESSION statement. You can use each of these parameters to specify the file destination for different types of OMF files:

- DB_CREATE_FILE_DEST: This parameter specifies the default location of datafiles, block-change tracking files, and temporary files. If you don't use any of the DB_CREATE_ONLINE_LOG_DEST_*n* parameters, Oracle uses the DB_CREATE_FILE_DEST parameter value as the default location for all Oracle managed control files and online redo logs. You can also specify a control file location if you wish. Unfortunately, the DB_CREATE_FILE_DEST parameter can take only a single directory as its value; you can't specify multiple file systems for the parameter. If the assigned directory for file creation fills up, you can always specify a new directory, because the DB_CREATE_FILE_DEST parameter is dynamic. This enables you to place Oracle datafiles anywhere in the file system without any limits whatsoever.

- DB_RECOVERY_FILE_DEST_SIZE: This parameter specifies the size of your flash recovery area.

- DB_CREATE_ONLINE_LOG_DEST_*n*: You can use this parameter to specify the default location of online redo log files and control files. In this parameter, *n* refers to the number of redo log files or control files that you want Oracle to create (*n* = 1, 2, 3, . . . 5).

- DB_RECOVERY_FILE_DEST: This parameter defines the default location for RMAN backups, flash-back logs, and archived redo logs. If you omit the DB_CREATE_ONLINE_LOG_DEST_*n* parameter, this parameter will determine the location of the online redo log files and control files. The directory location you specify using this parameter is also known as the *flash recovery area*, and I explain it in detail in Chapter 15.

If you don't specify any of these initialization parameters in your init.ora file or SPFILE, you can still use the ALTER SYSTEM command to dynamically enable the creation of OMF files, as shown in the following example:

```
SQL> ALTER SYSTEM SET DB_CREATE_FILE_DEST =
  2  '/test01/app/oracle/oradata/finance1';
System altered.
SQL>
```

As long as you specify the DB_CREATE_FILE_DEST parameter, you can have Oracle create OMF files for you, and you can use both the user-managed and OMF files simultaneously without a problem.

File-Naming Conventions

Oracle uses the OFA standards in creating filenames, so filenames are unique and datafiles are easily identifiable as belonging to a certain tablespace. Table 17-1 shows the naming convention for various kinds of OMF files and an example of each type. Note that the letter *t* stands for a unique tablespace name, *g* stands for an online redo group, and *u* is an 8-character string.

Table 17-1. *OMF File-Naming Conventions*

OMF File Type	Naming Convention	Example
Datafile	ora_t%_u.dbf	ora_data_Y2ZV8P00.dbf
Temp file (default size is 100MB)	ora_%t_u.tmp	ora_temp_Y2ZWGD00.tmp
Online redo log file (default size is 100MB)	ora_%g_%u.log	ora_4_Y2ZSQK00.log
Control file	ora_u%.ctl	ora_Y2ZROW00.ctl

Different Types of Oracle Managed Files

You can use OMF to create all three types of files that the Oracle database requires: control files, redo log files, and, of course, datafiles. However, there are interesting differences in the way OMF requires you to specify (or not specify) each of these types of files. The following sections cover how Oracle creates the three different types of files.

Control Files

As you have probably noticed already, there is no specific parameter that you need to include in your init.ora file to specify the OMF format. If you specify the CONTROL_FILES parameter, you will, of course, have to specify a complete file location for those files, and obviously they will not be OMF files—they are managed by you. If you don't specify the CONTROL_FILES parameter, and you use the DB_CREATE_
FILE_DEST or the DB_CREATE_ONLINE_LOG_DEST_n parameter, your control files will be OMF files.

If you are using a traditional init.ora file, you need to add the control file locations to it. If you are using an SPFILE, Oracle automatically adds the control file information to it.

Redo Log Files

OMF redo log file creation is similar to control file creation. If you don't specify a location for the redo log files, and you set either of the DB_CREATE_FILE_DEST or the DB_CREATE_ONLINE_LOG_DEST_n parameters in the init.ora file, Oracle automatically creates OMF-based redo log files.

Datafiles

If you don't specify a datafile location in the CREATE or ALTER statements for a regular datafile, or a temp file for a temporary tablespace, temp file, or undo tablespace datafile, but instead specify the DB_CREATE_FILE_DEST parameter, all these files will be OMF files.

Simple Database Creation Using OMF

Let's look at a small example to see how OMF files can really simplify database creation. When you create a new database, you need to provide the control file, redo log file, and datafile locations to Oracle. You specify some file locations in the initialization file (control file locations) and some file locations at database creation (such as redo log locations). However, if you use OMF-based files, database creation can be a snap, as you'll see in the sections that follow.

Setting Up File Location Parameters

For the new OMF-based database, named NICKO, let's use the following initialization parameters:

```
db_name=nicko
DB_CREATE_FILE_DEST = '/u01/app/oracle/oradata'
DB_RECOVERY_FILE_DEST_SIZE = 1000M
DB_RECOVERY_FILE_DEST = '/u04/app/oracle/oradata'
LOG_ARCHIVE_DEST_1 = 'LOCATION = USE_DB_RECOVERY_FILE_DEST'
```

Note that of the four OMF-related initialization parameters, I chose to use only the DB_CREATE_
FILE_DEST, DB_RECOVERY_FILE_DEST_SIZE, and DB_RECOVERY_FILE_DEST parameters. I didn't have to use the fourth parameter, DB_CREATE_ONLINE_LOG_DEST_n, in this example. When this parameter is left

out, Oracle creates a copy of the redo log file in the locations specified for the DB_CREATE_FILE_DEST and the DB_RECOVERY_FILE_DEST parameters. I thus have two copies of the control file and the online redo log files.

The setting for the last parameter, LOG_ARCHIVE_DEST_1, tells Oracle to send the archived redo logs for storage in the flash recovery area specified by the DB_RECOVERY_FILE_DEST parameter.

Starting the Instance

Using the simple init.ora file in the preceding section, you can start an instance as shown in Listing 17-7.

Listing 17-7. *Creating the OMF-Based Instance*

```
$ export ORACLE_SID=nicko
 [nicko] $ sqlplus /nolog
SQL*Plus: Release 11.1.0.6.0 - Production on Thu Apr 10 11:52:13 2008

Copyright (c) 1982, 2007, Oracle.  All rights reserved.
SQL> connect sys/sys_passwd as sysdba
Connected to an idle instance.
SQL> STARTUP NOMOUNT PFILE='initnicko.ora';
ORACLE instance started.
Total System Global Area  188743680 bytes
Fixed Size                  1308048 bytes
Variable Size             116132464 bytes
Database Buffers           67108864 bytes
Redo Buffers                4194304 bytes
SQL>
```

Creating the Database

Now that you've successfully created the new Oracle instance, you can create the new database NICKO with this simple command:

```
SQL> CREATE DATABASE nicko;
  Database created.
SQL>
```

That's it! Just those two simple lines are all you need to create a functional database with the following structures:

- A System tablespace created in the default file system specified by the DB_CREATE_FILE_DEST parameter (/u01/app/oracle/oradata)

- A Sysaux tablespace created in the default file system (/u01/app/oracle/oradata)

- Two duplexed redo log groups

- Two copies of the control file

- A default temporary tablespace

- An undo tablespace automatically managed by the Oracle database

You must remember to update the initialization parameter file (initnicko.ora in our example) with the names and the locations of the control file copies generated by the CREATE DATABASE statement shown here.

Where Are the OMF Files?

You can see the various files within the database by looking in the alert log for the new database, alert_nicko.log, which you'll find in the _$ORACLE_HOME/rdbms/log directory, since we didn't specify the BACKGROUND_DUMP_DEST directory in the init.ora file. If you're using the new Oracle Database 11*g* parameter DIAGNOSTIC_DEST, you'll find the alert log in the <*adr-home*>/alert directory.

In the following segment from the alert log file for the database, you can see how the various files necessary for the new database were created. First, Oracle creates the control files and places them in the location you specified for the DB_CREATE_ONLINE_LOG_DEST_*n* parameter.

```
create database nicko
default  temporary tablespace temp

WARNING: Default passwords for SYS and SYSTEM will be used.
         Please change the passwords.
Created Oracle managed file /u01/app/oracle/oradata/NICKO/controlfile/o1_mf_150w
. . .

Completed: create database nicko
default  temporary tablespace
MMNL started with pid=13, OS id=28939
```

Here's what the alert log shows regarding the creation of the control files:

```
Created Oracle managed file /u01/app/oracle/oradata/NICKO/controlfile/o1_mf_150w
h3r1_.ctl
Created Oracle managed file /u04/app/oracle/oradata/NICKO/controlfile/o1_mf_150w
h3xx_.ctl
```

Next, the Oracle server creates the duplexed online redo log files. Oracle creates the minimum number of groups necessary and duplexes them by creating a set of online log files (two) in the locations specified by the DB_CREATE_ONLINE_LOG_DEST and the DB_RECOVERY_FILE_DEST parameters:

```
Created Oracle managed file /u01/app/oracle/oradata/NICKO/onlinelog/o1_mf_1_150w
h48m_.log
Created Oracle managed file /u04/app/oracle/oradata/NICKO/onlinelog/o1_mf_1_150w
hf07_.log
Created Oracle managed file /u01/app/oracle/oradata/NICKO/onlinelog/o1_mf_2_150w
honc_.log
Created Oracle managed file /u04/app/oracle/oradata/NICKO/onlinelog/o1_mf_2_150w
hwh0_.log
```

The System tablespace is created next, in the location you specified for the DB_CREATE_FILE_DEST parameter:

```
create tablespace SYSTEM datafile /* OMF datafile */
  default storage (initial 10K next 10K) EXTENT MANAGEMENT DICTIONARY online
Created Oracle managed file /u01/app/oracle/oradata/NICKO/datafile/o1_mf_system_
150wj4c3_.dbf
Completed: create tablespace SYSTEM datafile /* OMF datafile
```

The default Sysaux tablespace is created next, as seen here:

```
create tablespace SYSAUX datafile /* OMF datafile */
  EXTENT MANAGEMENT LOCAL SEGMENT SPACE MANAGEMENT AUTO online

Created Oracle managed file /u01/app/oracle/oradata/NICKO/datafile/o1_mf_sysaux_
150wkk9n_.dbf
Completed: create tablespace SYSAUX datafile /* OMF datafile
```

The undo tablespace is created next, with the default name of SYS_UNDOTS in the location specified by the DB_CREATE_FILE_DEST parameter. A temporary tablespace named TEMP is also created in the same directory:

```
CREATE UNDO TABLESPACE SYS_UNDOTS DATAFILE SIZE 10M AUTOEXTEND ON
Created Oracle managed file
/test01/app/oracle/oradata/ora_omf/finDATA/ora_sys_undo_yj5mg123.dbf
. . .
Successfully onlined Undo Tablespace 1.
Completed: CREATE UNDO TABLESPACE SYS_UNDOTS DATAFILE  SIZE 1
CREATE TEMPORARY TABLESPACE TEMP TEMPFILE
Created Oracle managed file
/test01/app/oracle/oradata/ora_omf/finDATA/ora_temp_yj5mg592.tmp
Completed: CREATE TEMPORARY TABLESPACE TEMP TEMPFILE
```

Adding Tablespaces

Adding other tablespaces and datafiles within an OMF file system is easy. All you have to do is invoke the CREATE TABLESPACE command without the DATAFILE keyword. Oracle will automatically create the datafiles for the tablespace in the location specified in the DB_CREATE_FILE_DEST parameter. The example that follows shows how to create the tablespace:

```
SQL> ALTER SYSTEM SET DB_CREATE_FILE_DEST =
  2 '/test01/app/oracle/ora_omf/finance1';
System altered.

SQL> CREATE TABLESPACE omftest;
Tablespace created.

SQL> SELECT file_name FROM dba_data_files
  2  WHERE tablespace_name='OMFTEST';

FILE_NAME
-----------------------------------------------------------
/test01/app/oracle/oradata/ora_omf/ora_omftest_yj7590bm.dbf
SQL>
```

Compare the OMF tablespace-creation statement shown previously with the typical tablespace-creation statement, and you'll see how OMF simplifies database administration. Adding datafiles is also simple with OMF, as shown by the following example:

```
SQL> ALTER TABLESPACE omftest ADD DATAFILE;
```

OMF files, as you can see, simplify file administration chores and let you create and manage databases with a small number of initialization parameters. You can easily set up the necessary number of locations for your online redo log files, control files, and archive log files by specifying the appropriate value for the various OMF parameters. Oracle's ASM-based file system relies on the OMF file system.

Online Segment Shrinking and the Segment Advisor

Oracle recommends that you use *online segment shrinking* to compact segments that become fragmented over time due to the update and delete operations. A segment's high-water mark (HWM) shows the highest point of space usage ever reached by that segment. If you have unused space above the HWM, that means that this space has *never* been used by a table or an index segment.

You can use the DBMS_SPACE package, as shown in Chapter 5, to find out the amount of unused space in a segment. You can then deallocate the unused space in a segment by using the ALTER TABLE (or ALTER INDEX) . . . DEALLOCATE . . . statement, as shown here:

```
SQL> ALTER TABLE persons DEALLOCATE UNUSED KEEP 1000M;
```

Once you execute the preceding statement, Oracle will take everything over 1,000MB from the persons segment and makes the newly free space available for other segments in the tablespace.

For example, if you have used 80 percent of a table segment's space by inserting rows into that segment, the HWM for that segment will be at 80 percent. Later on, even if you delete half the rows, the table's HWM remains at 80 percent. This has a detrimental effect on full-table scans and index scans, because Oracle will scan the table all the way to the HWM, even if there is currently very little data in the table.

A table segment with a large number of deletions will lead to fragmentation, leaving several gaps below its HWM. You can, of course, reclaim the space you allotted to a table by creating a new table, copying all the existing data into it, and dropping the old table. In previous versions of Oracle, you could also compact the unused pockets of space in table or index segments by reorganizing the object, which usually involved the MOVE command. These reorganizations, which basically re-create the object in the same or a different tablespace, are sometimes very time consuming, and they also require additional space. Also, contrary to Oracle's assurances, online availability for DML operations is sometimes diminished.

As of Oracle Database 10g, you can use the *segment-shrinking* capability to make sparsely populated segments give their space back to their parent tablespace. You can reduce the HWM, thereby compacting the data within the segments. Also as of Oracle Database 10g, you can shrink tables (including index-organized tables), partitions and subpartitions of a table, indexes, and materialized views (and materialized view logs).

■**Note** The segment-shrinking capability is termed an *online and in-place* operation. It's online because users can continue to access the tables during the shrinking operation. The operation is in-place because you don't need any duplicate or temporary database space during the segment-shrinking operations.

Oracle handles the shrinking operation internally as an insert/delete operation. Since you are only moving data and not modifying it, triggers on the tables will not fire when you perform the shrink operations. When you shrink a table to compact space, the indexes on the table remain usable after the shrinking operation.

■**Tip** A tablespace must both be locally managed as well as use Automatic Segment Space Management for its segments to be eligible for segment-shrinking operations.

Manual Segment Shrinking

You can use simple SQL commands to shrink segments. The segment-shrinking operation compacts fragmented space in the segments and *optionally* frees the space.

Before shrinking the segments, you must first enable row movement for any segment that you want to shrink. You can enable row movement by using the ENABLE ROW MOVEMENT clause of the ALTER TABLE command, as shown here:

```
SQL> ALTER TABLE test ENABLE ROW MOVEMENT;
```

Of course, if you've already specified the ENABLE ROW MOVEMENT clause at table-creation time, you won't need to issue any commands to enable row movement before starting the segment-shrinking operation. By default, row movement is disabled at the segment level.

There are two phases in a segment-shrinking operation:

- *Compaction phase*: During the compaction phase, the rows in a table are compacted and moved toward the left side of the segment. You thus make the segment dense, but the HWM remains where it was. The recovered space isn't immediately released back as free space. You can continue to issue DML statements and queries on a segment while it is being shrunk. Oracle holds locks only on the packets of the rows involved in the DML operations. If you have any long-running queries, Oracle can read from all the blocks that have technically been reclaimed during the shrinking operation. Of course, this capability is dependent on the time interval you specified for your undo retention parameter.

- *Adjustment of the HWM/releasing-space phase*: In the second phase, which lasts for a very short period of time, Oracle lowers the HWM and releases the recovered free space under the old HWM back to the parent tablespace. Oracle locks the object in an exclusive mode while the HWM is being lowered, meaning that you can't issue any INSERT, UPDATE, or DELETE DML statements against the segment.

■**Caution** During the compacting phase, the object is online and available, but during the second phase, the object becomes briefly unavailable, due to Oracle's exclusive locking of the segment.

The basic statement for shrinking segments performs *both phases* of the segment-shrinking operation (first compacting, then resetting the HWM and releasing the space) in sequence. Here's the statement (the name of the table being shrunk is test):

```
SQL> ALTER TABLE test SHRINK SPACE;
```

Once you issue this command, Oracle will first compact the segment and then reset the HWM level and yield the freed space to the tablespace.

Since the second phase, the resetting of the HWM, will affect DML operations, you may not want to use it when a large number of users are connected to the database. Instead, you may want to issue the following command, which only compacts the space in the segment:

```
SQL> ALTER TABLE test SHRINK SPACE COMPACT;
```

This way, during peak hours, the database will merely compact the space in the segment. During off-peak hours, you can issue the ALTER TABLE *table_name* SHRINK SPACE command, and this will finish the shrinking process by performing the second phase.

If you use the CASCADE option during a segment-shrinking operation, all the dependent segments will be shrunk as well. For example, if you shrink a table, all the dependent index segments will be automatically shrunk. Here's how you specify the CASCADE option:

```
SQL> ALTER TABLE test SHRINK SPACE CASCADE;
```

Using the Segment Advisor to Shrink Segments

Using the new Segment Advisor, you can easily identify the segments that are good candidates for shrinking. The Segment Advisor bases its recommendations on the amount of fragmentation within an object. It determines whether objects have enough space to be reclaimed, taking into account the future space requirements. It bases its estimates of the future space requirements of an object on historical trends. Besides helping you select candidates for shrinking, the Segment Advisor is also helpful in sizing new database objects. The following sections describe how to use the advisor for both purposes.

■**Note** You can use the Segment Advisor only for Oracle Database 10.1 and 10.2, and Oracle Database 11*g* Release 1 and later versions. In order to run the Segment Advisor, you must have the ADVISOR privilege in addition to the CREATE ANY JOB (or CREATE JOB) privilege.

Choosing Candidate Objects for Shrinking

You can invoke the Segment Advisor at either the individual segment level or the tablespace level. You can call the Segment Advisor from the Database Control's Advisor Central page (which you can get to from the Database Control home page by clicking Advisor Central in the Related Links section, and then clicking Segment Advisor). Figure 17-6 shows the main Segment Advisor page.

The Segment Advisor can generate advice at three levels: *object*, *segment*, and *tablespace*. The Segment Advisor's recommendations can be to either a shrink or a reorganization operation, based on the following criteria:

- If you created the objects in the default locally managed tablespaces with Automatic Segment Space Management, the Segment Advisor recommends shrinking the segments.

- If you used manual segment space management, or the object isn't eligible for a shrink operation, the Segment Advisor will recommend an object reorganization.

You can run the Segment Advisor in two modes:

- *Comprehensive analysis*: The Segment Advisor will perform an analysis regardless of whether there are prior statistics or not. If there aren't any prior statistics, the Segment Advisor will sample the objects before generating its recommendations. This analysis is more time consuming.

- *Limited analysis*: This analysis is based strictly on the statistics collected on the segment. If there aren't any statistics for an object, the advisor won't perform any analysis.

The AWR collects all space-usage statistics during its regular snapshot collection. The Segment Advisor, to estimate future segment-space needs, uses the growth-trend report based on the AWR space-usage data. You can view the Segment Advisor recommendations through OEM by clicking the Segment Advisor Recommendations link on the Segment Advisor page.

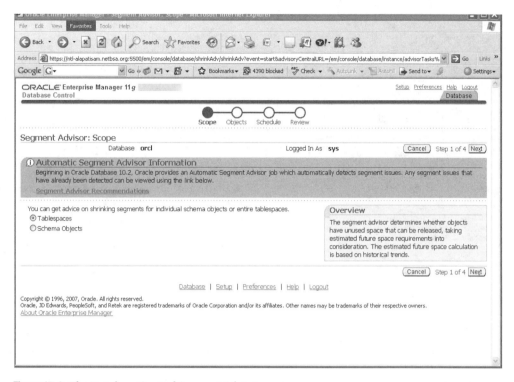

Figure 17-6. *The Database Control Segment Advisor page*

Automatic Segment Advisor Job

In Oracle Database 10.2 and later, Oracle provides an automatic Segment Advisor job called AUTO_SPACE_ADVISOR_JOB, which automatically detects segment-space related issues. Here are the job details, which you can see using the DBA_SCHEDULER_JOBS view:

- JOB_NAME: AUTO_SPACE_ADVISOR_JOB

- PROGRAM_NAME: AUTO_SPACE_ADVISOR_JOB

- SCHEDULER_NAME: MAINTENANCE_WINDOW_GROUP

The Segment Advisor job automatically runs during the maintenance window, identifying candidates for a segment-shrinking operation based on the amount of space fragmentation within an object. You can view the automatic Segment Advisor job recommendations in the same way as any other manually invoked Segment Advisor recommendations, as shown in the previous section. You'll see a list of the Segment Advisor recommendations, from the last time it ran, by clicking the Segment Advisor Recommendations link on the Segment Advisor page. Figure 17-7 shows the Recommendations page.

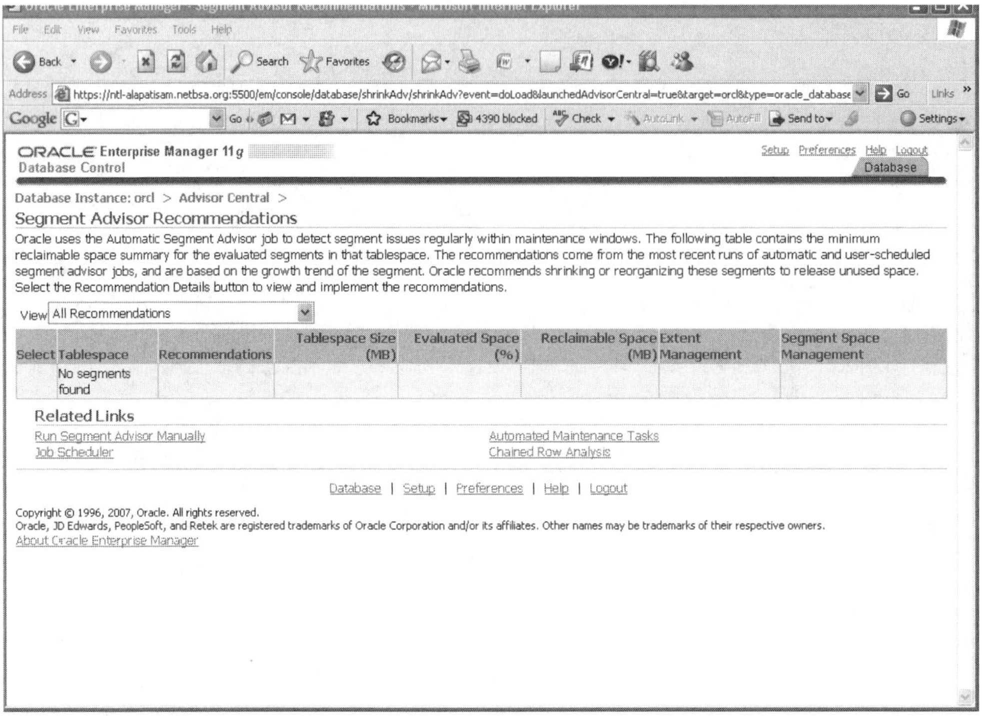

Figure 17-7. *The Segment Advisor Recommendations page*

Automatic Checkpoint Tuning

Oracle is capable of recovering from an unexpected database crash without losing any data. Remember that when the database crashes, there are two phases to the ensuing recovery:

- *Redo or roll-forward phase*: In the first phase, the database applies to the datafiles all changes, including both committed as well as uncommitted changes, that haven't yet been made a part of the datafiles. These transactions are recovered from the redo log.

- *Undo or rollback phase*: In the second phase, all uncommitted transactions that are written to the datafiles in the previous step are undone.

After a crash, the database can't be opened unless it performs recovery. However, here's the interesting part: Oracle lets you open the database before the second phase is completed. As soon as the redo or roll-forward phase is over, the database is opened for the users, while the SMON process performs the undo in the background. When a user's process runs into a transaction locked for rollback, it rolls back the transaction quickly. These intermittent rollbacks don't have a discernible impact on the user's query performance. This means that the database is open far more quickly after a crash than if you waited for both phases of recovery to complete.

■**Note** The time it takes for the second phase (the rollback) to complete depends on how much undo information you have to roll back.

As of Oracle Database 10g, you can automate checkpoint tuning by completely avoiding the setting of any checkpoint-related initialization parameters and by setting the FAST_START_MTTR_ TARGET parameter to a nonzero value. By default, the value of this parameter is 0. Oracle will automatically tune database checkpointing, balancing recovery needs with the overhead on database throughput.

Online Capabilities of Oracle Database 11*g*

In addition to the automatic database management features, Oracle Database 11g offers you opportunities to perform many common tasks online, thus reducing the work that you would otherwise perform only after the database was shut down or an object was taken offline. In some cases (such as the MOVE command), DML operations are prevented until the table is moved. These features offer you continuous online availability, making it easier for you to perform the reorganization tasks. In the sections that follow, you'll examine some of the important online capabilities of the Oracle Database 11g database.

Online Data Reorganization

Oracle provided several online reorganization features, such as the ability to create partitions, move tables, and add constraints, in older versions of its software. The Oracle Database 11g version goes much further and provides more online options for DBAs, including online database reorganization, object validation, and index rebuilding.

Online Database Reorganization with OEM Database Control

You can easily perform offline or online reorganization of database objects using the OEM Database Control. Often you'll see a need to change the storage attributes of a table or an index, and the Database Control makes it easy to perform these reorganizations.

To perform database reorganization with the Database Control, go to the Database Control home page and choose Administration ➤ Reorganize Objects. Figure 17-8 shows the main page of the Database Control Data Reorganization feature. You can choose either offline or online reorganization. Online reorganization is slower, but it provides access to the objects being reorganized.

Once you choose the online reorganization method, OEM will ask you for the list of objects to be reorganized. It then generates an impact report and job summary, which is a summary of the actual reorganization script. In the next step, you decide whether to perform the online reorganization right away or to schedule it for some other time.

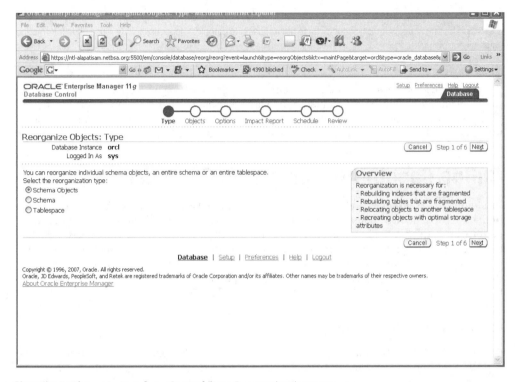

Figure 17-8. *The main Database Control Data Reorganization page*

Using SQL Commands to Perform Online Data Reorganization

In addition to the online data redefinition feature, which I explain shortly in the "Online Data Redefinition" section, you can reorganize data in tables and indexes online, using various SQL commands. Let's briefly look at the important data reorganization methods, first looking at an object validation command.

Validating an Object Online

You can validate the structure of an object while users are making changes to the table, by using the `ANALYZE TABLE . . . VALIDATE STRUCTURE` statement, as shown in the following example:

```
SQL> ANALYZE TABLE persons
  2  VALIDATE STRUCTURE ONLINE;

Table analyzed.
SQL>
```

Rebuilding an Index Online

You can rebuild indexes online, thus improving the availability of large database tables. Note that while users can change the table data, they can't use the parallel DML options during an online index rebuild. Users can, however, perform normal DML operations against the base table.

You can rebuild many kinds of indexes, including function-based indexes and reverse-key indexes, online. Here's an online index rebuilding example:

```
SQL> ALTER INDEX test_idx REBUILD ONLINE;
```

Creating an Index Online

You can also create indexes online, with the following statement:

```
SQL> CREATE INDEX test_idx ON persons(person_id) ONLINE;
```

Coalescing an Index Online

You can coalesce an index online with this statement:

```
SQL> ALTER INDEX test_idx COALESCE;
```

Moving a Table Online

You can move a table from one tablespace to another, with this command:

```
SQL> ALTER TABLE test MOVE TABLESPACE new_tbsp
```

Online Data Redefinition

Oracle offers the *online table redefinition* feature, which lets you redefine objects like database tables online while users continue reading from and writing to them. You can use online data redefinition to create new tables with more efficient physical storage parameters, move tables to different tablespaces, reduce fragmentation in tables, and change a heap table into an index-organized table and vice versa, all while maintaining database availability and performance.

The online data redefinition feature can enhance both data availability and disk usage. Both the newly redefined table and the original table continue to exist together until the DBA decides to switch over to the newly redefined table. The length of the switching process is extremely brief and doesn't depend on table or index size or the complexity of the object redefinition.

If you have materialized views and materialized logs defined on a table, you can't redefine them online. During the redefinition process, local materialized logs are maintained and changes to the master table are tracked using snapshot logs.

■**Note** Whenever possible, use the Segment Advisor for shrinking segments and reclaiming unused space below the HWM. However, if a segment doesn't qualify for the use of the Segment Advisor, as is the case when you use dictionary-managed tablespaces or manual segment space management, use the online table redefinition technique to reorganize segment data. You also use online table redefinition if you plan on making logical or physical changes to any table attributes during the reorganization.

What Can Online Redefinition Do?

You can use online redefinition to perform a number of tasks that would have necessitated taking tables offline in early versions of Oracle. Using the online table redefinition feature, you can do the following:

- Add, drop, or rename columns.
- Transform table data.

- Change data types of the columns.

- Rename table constraints.

- Change the original storage parameters.

- Reduce fragmentation in tables.

- Create a partitioned table out of a regular table online.

- Create an index-organized table (IOT) out of a regular table.

- Move a table to a different tablespace.

The list of tasks you can perform using online redefinition is truly impressive, because you don't have to keep users from accessing the tables while you're performing these common tasks.

The online table redefinition involves a simple sequence of steps:

1. Determine whether a table is a candidate for redefinition.

2. Decide on the structure of the new table, and create a new image of the table.

3. Start the redefinition process by using the DBMS_REDEFINITION package.

4. Create necessary constraints and triggers on the new table.

5. Perform periodic synchronization and validation of data in the new table.

6. Complete the redefinition of the table.

You can perform online table redefinition using one of two methods: a primary key method and a ROWID method. The ROWID method is more complex, and Oracle recommends you use the easier primary key method, which requires that the original and the redefined tables have the same primary key columns. In the following sections, you'll see how to perform online table redefinition using the default primary key method.

An Online Table Redefinition Example

In this example, we'll reorganize the employees table in the HR schema, which has the structure shown in Listing 17-8. For this example, our goal is to drop the salary column in the employees table.

Listing 17-8. *The Structure of the employees Table*

```
Name                        Null?           Type
---------------             --------        ------------
EMPLOYEE_ID                 NOT NULL        NUMBER(6)
FIRST_NAME                                  VARCHAR2(20)
LAST_NAME                   NOT NULL        VARCHAR2(25)
EMAIL                       NOT NULL        VARCHAR2(25)
PHONE_NUMBER                                VARCHAR2(20)
HIRE_DATE                   NOT NULL        DATE
JOB_ID                      NOT NULL        VARCHAR2(10)
SALARY                                      NUMBER(8,2)
COMMISSION_PCT                              NUMBER(2,2)
MANAGER_ID                                  NUMBER(6)
DEPARTMENT_ID                               NUMBER(4)
```

The goal is to remove the salary column in the employees table and partition the table using a range scheme based on the employee_id column. Once we have completed the online redefinition, we can drop the temporary table. The new table will have all the attributes of the temporary table.

Verifying the Eligibility of the Table

The first step in the online redefinition process is to ensure that the employees table is a candidate for the process by using the DBMS_REDEFINITION package. If your table is not eligible, Oracle will issue an error message. The following example shows the use of the package for verifying the employees table:

```
SQL> BEGIN
  2   DBMS_REDEFINITION.CAN_REDEF_TABLE('hr','employees');
  3   END;
  4   /
PL/SQL procedure successfully completed.
SQL>
```

In the DBMS_REDEFINITION.CAN_REDEF_TABLE procedure, you can specify the method of online redefinition as the third parameter, in addition to the schema owner name (hr) and the table name (employees). This third parameter is called the options_flag, and it can take two possible values: DBMS_REDEFINITION.CONS_USE_PK if you want to use the primary key method or DBMS_REDEFINITION. CONS_USE_ROWID if you want to use ROWIDs to do the redefinition. Because you're using the default primary key method, you don't have to specify this third parameter for your procedure.

■**Note** A table doesn't need a primary key for it to be eligible for online redefinition.

Now that the employees table has indeed been verified as an eligible candidate for redefinition, we'll move to the next step, where we'll create an interim table.

Creating the Temporary Table

When you're redefining a production table, you don't want to change the table directly. It's a lot less risky if you can view the results and check the redefinition first. Then you can swap the interim table for the existing production table. In our example, the interim table, hr.employees_temp, will not have the salary column. It will also be partitioned on the employee_id column, as shown in Listing 17-9. These two things—removing the salary column and partitioning the table—are the goals of our redefinition exercise.

Listing 17-9. *Creating the Temporary Table for Online Redefinition*

```
SQL> CREATE TABLE hr.employees_temp
  2   (employee_id       number(6),
  3   first_name         varchar2(20) not null,
  4   last_name          varchar2(25) not null,
  5   email              varchar2(25) not null,
  6   phone_number       varchar2(20),
  7   hire_date          date not null,
  8   job_id             varchar2(10) not null,
  9   commission_pct     number(2,2),
 10   manager_id         number(6),
 11   department_id      number(4))
 12   PARTITION BY RANGE(employee_id)
 13   (PARTITION employees1
     VALUES LESS THAN (100) tablespace TEST01,
```

```
14* PARTITION employees2
    VALUES LESS THAN (300) tablespace TEST02);
```

```
Table created.
SQL>
```

Redefining the Table

You can now start the redefinition process by using the DBMS_REDEFINITION.START_REDIF_TABLE procedure, as shown in Listing 17-10. The START_REDIF_TABLE procedure has the following parameters:

- UNAME: This is the schema name (hr).
- ORIG_TABLE: This is the table you're redefining (employees).
- INT_TABLE: This is the name of the interim table.
- COL_MAPPING: This specifies the mapping between the interim and the original table's columns. If you don't supply any values for this column-mapping parameter, all the columns of the original table will be included in the interim table.
- OPTIONS_FLAG: This specifies the method of redefinition. In this example, because we're using the default primary key method, we can omit this parameter.

■**Tip** When you perform table redefinition, you should be logged in as the schema owner. Make sure the schema owner is granted execute privileges on the DBMS_REDEFINITION package. The schema owner should also be granted the privileges to select, create, alter, drop, and lock any table. Otherwise, you'll encounter the ORA-01031 "Insufficient privileges" error.

Listing 17-10. *Starting the Online Redefinition Process*

```
SQL> BEGIN
  2  dbms_redefinition.start_redef_table('hr','employees',
  3  'employees_temp',
  4  'employee_id employee_id,
  5  first_name first_name,
  6  last_name last_name,
  7  email email,
  8  phone_number phone_number,
  9  hire_date hire_date,
 10  job_id job_id,
 11  commission_pct commission_pct,
 12  manager_id manager_id,
 13  department_id department_id');
 14  END;
 15  /
```

```
PL/SQL procedure successfully completed.
SQL>
```

Make sure the interim and master tables have the same number of rows by running the following queries:

```
SQL> SELECT COUNT(*) FROM employees_temp;

  COUNT(*)
-----------
      107
SQL> SELECT COUNT(*) FROM employees;

  COUNT(*)
----------
      107
SQL>
```

Copying the Dependent Objects

You need to execute the DBMS_REDEFINITION.COPY_TABLE_DEPENDENTS procedure next, to automatically create any existing triggers, indexes, grants, and constraints on the HR.EMPLOYEES_TEMP table. Here's how you do it:

```
SQL> DECLARE
SQL> num_errors PLS_INTEGER;
SQL> BEGIN
      DBMS_REDEFINITION.COPY_TABLE_DEPENDENTS('hr', 'employees',
      'employees_temp',
      DBMS_RE
DEFINITION.CONS_ORIG_PARAMS, TRUE, TRUE, TRUE, TRUE, num_errors);
      END;
```

■**Tip** You can improve the performance of the redefinition process by running the redefinition job in parallel. To do this, you must first execute the following statements before executing the START_REDEF_TABLE procedure to start the table redefinition process:

```
SQL> alter session force parallel dml parallel 8;
SQL> alter session force parallel query parallel 8;
```

What Happens During the Redefinition Process?

Using the DBMS_REDEFINITION package is easy, but a lot is going on behind the scenes. When you execute the DBMS_REDEFINITION.START_REDEF_TABLE procedure, two new tables are created: a temporary table and a permanent table. The temporary table is called RUPD$_Employee, and it lasts for the duration of the session. The permanent table is a snapshot table that holds all the changes made to the master employees table once you execute the START_REDEF_TABLE procedure. The master table's rows are copied to the interim table, and users will be able to update the master table during this process. The changes made by the users are logged in the materialized log during this process.

Listing 17-11 shows a query on DBA_OBJECTS that indicates our new table has been partitioned based on our redefinition. The query also shows the two new tables created during the online redefinition process.

Listing 17-11. *Checking That the New Table Has Been Partitioned Based on Our Redefinition*

```
SQL> SELECT object_type, object_name
  2  FROM dba_objects
  3  WHERE object_name LIKE '%EMPLOYEES%';

OBJECT_TYPE              OBJECT_NAME
----------------         ----------------
TABLE                        EMPLOYEES
TABLE PARTITION          EMPLOYEES_TEMP
TABLE PARTITION          EMPLOYEES_TEMP
TABLE                    EMPLOYEES_TEMP
TABLE                     EMPLOYEES_NEW
SEQUENCE                  EMPLOYEES_SEQ
TABLE                    MLOG$_EMPLOYEES
TABLE                    RUPD$_EMPLOYEES
TRIGGER                  SECURE_EMPLOYEES
9 rows selected.
SQL>
```

Checking for Errors

You can use the DBA_REDEFINITION_ERRORS view to check for any errors during the redefinition process, as shown here:

```
SQL> SELECT OBJECT_NAME, BASE_TABLE_NAME, DDL_TXT
     FROM DBA_REDEFINITION_ERRORS;
```

Synchronizing the Interim and Source Tables

You can use the SYNC_INTERIM_TABLE procedure to synchronize the data in the interim and the source table. This is an optional step. Here's how you execute the procedure:

```
SQL> EXECUTE dbms_redefinition.sync_interim_table ('hr', -
  > 'employees','employees_temp');
PL/SQL procedure successfully completed.
SQL>
```

You should use this procedure only if you have reason to believe that a large number of updates have taken place in the source table after you started the redefinition process (by executing the START_REDEF_TABLE procedure). By using the SYNC_INTERIM_TABLE procedure, you save time in the last phase of the redefinition process if a large number of updates have taken place. Otherwise, you can safely ignore this step, because the last procedure you run, the FINISH_REDEF_TABLE procedure, will perform the synchronization anyway.

Completing the Redefinition Process

Once you're done creating triggers and constraints, and granting privileges on the interim table, it's time to complete the process by running the FINISH_REDEF_TABLE procedure. The interim table at this point has all the data of the source table, but the source table still has its old structure. In our example, the employees table is still not partitioned, and it still contains the salary column.

```
SQL> EXECUTE DBMS_REDEFINITION.FINISH_REDEF_TABLE ('hr', -
  > 'employees', 'employees_temp');

PL/SQL procedure successfully completed.
SQL>
```

When you run the FINISH_REDEF_TABLE procedure, the following things happen:

- Oracle reads the materialized log on the master table so the contents can be added to the interim table.

- The employees table is redefined so it has all the attributes, indexes, constraints, and grants of the interim table, employees_temp.

- Any referential constraints involving the employees_temp table are enabled.

- Any new triggers that you defined on the employees_temp table are also on the newly redefined table and are enabled now.

- The two tables are briefly locked in exclusive mode to make the necessary changes in the data dictionary.

- The materialized view and the log are dropped.

You can confirm that your original table, employees, has indeed been partitioned, by running this query:

```
SQL> SELECT object_type, object_name
  2  FROM dba_objects
  3* WHERE object_name ='EMPLOYEES';

OBJECT_TYPE        OBJECT_NAME
---------------    -----------
TABLE PARTITION      EMPLOYEES
TABLE PARTITION      EMPLOYEES
TABLE                EMPLOYEES
SQL>
```

If you look at the structure of the employees table (say, by issuing the DESCRIBE command), you'll notice that it doesn't have the salary column.

Once you finish the table redefinition, you can drop the employees_temp table. When you drop the interim table, all the indexes, triggers, and constraints on the original table are dropped also, because the original table has become the interim table. The new table has all the necessary triggers, grants, indexes, and (referential) constraints of the interim table.

If you see any significant errors during the preceding process, it is easy to abort the redefinition by using the DBMS_REDEFINITION.ABORT_REDEF_TABLE procedure. This procedure drops the temporary table and logs created during the redefinition process. You can then manually drop the interim table.

Dynamic Resource Management

Traditionally, once any user started a transaction in the database, he or she had to be given the same priority as all the other sessions in the database. This would sometimes lead to a single user monopolizing the database resources and consequently slowing down the database. In Chapter 12, you saw how the Database Resource Manager can help you control resource use within the database by using resource groups and resource plans to allocate critical resources.

In addition to its resource-allocation capabilities, the Database Resource Manager has the following features that help in online management of transactions:

- You can automatically move a long-running operation from a high-priority consumer group to a low-priority group.

- You can limit the number of concurrent long transactions.

- You can prevent any transaction from running if its estimated time for completion exceeds a preset execution limit set by the DBA.

The following sections cover how you can perform each of these tasks using the Database Resource Manager.

Switching Long-Running Transactions

The Database Resource Manager lets you use *plan directives*, which can specify limits on resource usage. Plan directives include the following parameters, which you can use to shift the priority of consumer groups:

- SWITCH_TIME
- SWITCH_GROUP
- SWITCH_ESTIMATE
- SWITCH_IO_MEGABYTES
- SWITCH_IO_REQS
- SWITCH_FOR_CALL

A user will be assigned to a certain consumer group at the beginning of a transaction. If the user's transaction is active for more than the number of seconds specified by the SWITCH_TIME parameter, the transaction is automatically switched to a lower priority group specified by the SWITCH_GROUP parameter.

You can have the Database Resource Manager determine whether it should switch a user session even *before* an operation starts by setting the SWITCH_ESTIMATE parameter to true. In this case, the Database Resource Manager will *estimate* the time it will take for the operation to complete, and based on that time estimate, the Database Resource Manager will determine whether it should switch the user's consumer group right away.

The SWITCH_IO_MEGABYTES attribute in a resource plan directive lets you specify the amount of I/O (in megabytes) that a session can issue before the database takes an action such as switching the session to a different resource group or terminating it. The SWITCH_IO_REQS parameter lets you specify the number of I/O requests that a session can issue before the database takes an action to limit the I/O usage. By setting the SWITCH_FOR_CALL parameter to TRUE, you can make the database return a session that was switched to its original group after the top call completes. Chapter 12 shows examples of how to control user sessions by specifying values for the various parameters I described in this section.

Limiting the Number of Long Transactions with Operation Queuing

When you create resource consumer groups using the Database Resource Manager, you can set the active session pool for each group. An *active session* is one where a transaction or a select operation is currently active. Once the consumer group's active session pool limit is reached, new sessions belonging to the group can't become active. They're queued by the Database Resource Manager and allowed to become active as the current active sessions complete.

You can set an optional time-out period for the queued sessions in each group. If a session is queued past this time-out period, it will abort with an error message. The user then has the choice of resubmitting the job or ignoring it.

Limiting the Maximum Execution Times for Transactions

All DBAs dread the possibility of a very large job that could take up most of the database's resources and bring it to its knees. Most times, you're left to decide whether you should kill the long-running job. The Database Resource Manager helps you avoid such stressful situations by allowing you to set limits on the execution times of operations—it allows you to run only those jobs that fall within a maximum run-time limit that you set.

You have two ways to limit the execution times of a transaction in the database: using the `MAX_ESTIMATED_EXEC_TIME` resource plan directive or the `UNDO_POOL` resource plan directive.

■**Note** You can use the DBMS_APPLICATION.SET_SESSION_LONGOPS procedure to track long-running operations. The procedure will populate the V$SESSION_LONGOPS view.

Using the MAX_ESTIMATED_EXEC_TIME Resource Plan Directive

You can limit the maximum execution times for transactions by using the `MAX_ESTIMATED_EXEC_TIME` resource plan directive. When you set this parameter, the Database Resource Manager will estimate the operation's execution time and will abort the operation if it exceeds the maximum estimated execution time you set.

Using the UNDO_POOL Resource Plan Directive

You can control long-running transactions by limiting the amount of undo space that a resource consumer group can use. Long-running transactions in general tend to need a large amount of undo space to maintain a consistent image of the old data and to enable the session to roll back the transaction.

By default, an active session can use an unlimited amount of undo space, but you can specify a limit to the undo space for a consumer group by using the `UNDO_POOL` resource plan directive. Once all the sessions in a consumer group use up the allotted undo space specified by the `UNDO_POOL` parameter, all insert, update, and delete transactions on behalf of any session transaction within that group will abort with an error.

Online Database Block-Size Changes

Suppose you have a tablespace that has a block size of 8KB, as shown in the following example:

```
SQL> SELECT NAME, VALUE FROM V$SPPARAMETER
  2  WHERE NAME='db_block_size';


NAME                  VALUE
--------------        -----
db_block_size         8192
SQL>
```

Because the block size is 8KB and you have only a single block size, all your tablespaces are created with this default size. Suppose that you now want to create a tablespace with a higher block size—for example, 16KB. Creating a database consisting of tablespaces with different block sizes is easy—each of the tablespace block sizes in the database should correspond to a `DB_nK_CACHE_SIZE` parameter value. Thus, if you want five tablespaces with different sized blocks, you must have all five of the buffer cache sizes configured.

In Listing 17-12, which shows the results of a query in my test database, you don't see any values under any of the five possible `DB_nK_CACHE_SIZE` parameters. This is because I chose only one block size, the standard block size of 8KB, and none of the other optional cache sizes. My total `DB_CACHE_SIZE` value is shown as 25MB (25,165,824 bytes) in the listing, and it's composed of the standard 8KB blocks.

Listing 17-12. *The Buffer Cache nK Size Components*

```
SQL> SELECT NAME, VALUE FROM V$PARAMETER
  2  WHERE NAME LIKE '%cache_size%';

    NAME                           VALUE
    ----------------------    ----------
db_keep_cache_size                    0
db_recycle_cache_size                 0
db_2k_cache_size                      0
db_4k_cache_size                      0
db_8k_cache_size                      0
db_16k_cache_size                     0
db_32k_cache_size                     0
db_cache_size                  25165824
8 rows selected.
SQL>
```

You can easily create a new buffer cache size of 16KB online and create a new tablespace with that block size. You can then create your objects in this new tablespace or move any existing objects into this tablespace, all online.

Here's what you have to do. First, create a new 16KB buffer cache, so you can create a tablespace with a 16KB block size.

```
SQL> ALTER SYSTEM SET DB_16K_CACHE_SIZE =1024M;
System altered.
SQL>
```

Now you can create your new tablespace with the 16KB block size, because you have a matching 16KB buffer cache size. Here's the CREATE TABLESPACE statement:

```
SQL> CREATE TABLESPACE big_block
  3  DATAFILE '/test01/app/oracle/big_block_01.dbf' SIZE 1000M
  4* BLOCKSIZE 16K;
Tablespace created.
SQL>
```

If you have a table that you want to move to the new big_block tablespace with the 16KB block size, all you have to do is use the MOVE command:

```
SQL> ALTER TABLE test MOVE TABLESPACE big_block;
Table altered.
SQL>
```

Of course, you can also use the online table redefinition method to move your table to the new tablespace.

Using Database Quiescing for Online Maintenance

Suppose you want to change the schema of a table. If a transaction is currently using this table, you can't perform this task. If a PL/SQL procedure is later updated to reflect the change in the schema, users currently trying to execute the procedure will receive an error. Fortunately, Oracle has a great *quiescing* feature, whereby you don't have to shut down the database and open it in restricted mode.

You can use this feature when you need to perform actions that require that no active transactions are running in the database. Users will remain logged in, and they can continue to execute their requests that are in progress, while the database is in the quiesced state. The database, however, will block all new transactional requests except those made by the users SYS and SYSTEM. Since current queries in progress are allowed to complete, the database is more available than a database in restricted mode. Quiescing thus puts the database in a partially available state. When you take the database out of the quiesced state, any user requests that were blocked are processed automatically.

The following commands perform the quiescing and unquiescing of the database:

```
SQL> ALTER SYSTEM QUIESCE RESTRICTED;
SQL> ALTER SYSTEM UNQUIESCE;
```

■ **Note** Not every user with DBA privileges can quiesce the database. Only the SYS and SYSTEM users can use this feature.

Users can continue to log into the system unless you're using the shared server architecture. Typical maintenance operations that can require the use of the quiesce database feature are those that need the exclusive use of an object, such as an ALTER TABLE, DROP TABLE, or CREATE PROCEDURE operation. Any DDL statement that a DBA might want to execute in a live database will need exclusive locks, and it will fail if other transactions are using the table.

While the database is in the quiesced state, users other than SYS and SYSTEM won't be able to start any new transactions or queries. Any inactive sessions will be prevented from becoming active. While it is quiesced, Oracle waits for all transactions and queries to commit or roll back, and the database waits for the release of all shared resources, such as enqueues. Upon unquiescing the database, all the blocked actions are allowed to proceed to execution.

Users won't get any error messages during this process. When they try to execute a transaction on a quiesced database, their transaction simply hangs until the database is put into a normal mode again.

Suspending the Database

In addition to the restricted start-up and database quiesce modes, you can run the database in the *suspend* mode to perform certain tasks (such as a backup) without any user activity. You use the following commands to suspend the database and, later, resume it so all users can access the database:

```
SQL> ALTER SYSTEM SUSPEND;
System altered.
SQL> ALTER SYSTEM RESUME;
System altered.
```

When you suspend a database, all transactions will be suspended until the database resumes normal operation mode.

The ability to suspend a database comes in handy when you need to back up a database using a mirrored set of disks. You can suspend the database, split the mirror, and back up the database. You don't have to contend with I/O during the online backup of the split mirror.

CHAPTER 18

■■■

Managing and Monitoring the Operational Database

This chapter deals primarily with the day-to-day management of Oracle databases and covers several major features that help you manage your database:

- Server-generated alerts are automatically raised by the database to let you know when problems occur.

- The Automatic Workload Repository (AWR) is the new infrastructure that automatically collects and maintains numerous performance statistics for self-tuning purposes. The Automatic Database Diagnostic Monitor (ADDM) that you saw in Chapter 17 uses the AWR data for its analyses.

- The Active Session History (ASH) deals with recent session activity, and the database uses it to tune its own performance.

- The advisory framework provides a common framework for various database advisors that supply information about resource utilization and performance. You've seen several of these advisors in other chapters, such as the ADDM, the SQL Access Advisor, and the SQL Tuning Advisor. I explain the common infrastructure of the advisory framework in this chapter.

- The DBMS_FILE_TRANSFER package lets you transfer operating system files directly through the database.

- The Oracle Scheduler provides a very powerful way to schedule complex database jobs.

- Automatic maintenance tasks take care of routine DBA tasks such as collecting optimizer statistics.

- The new diagnostic framework includes several tools, such as the Automatic Diagnostic Repository (ADR), the Support Workbench, incident packaging service (IPS), and the SQL Repair Advisor, that help you diagnose and repair database failures.

In this chapter, I also discuss the management of redo logs as well as the creation of database links to connect to remote databases from your database.

The preceding topics cover most of the Oracle DBA's daily management tasks, and familiarity with them is essential to performing typical data movement, space organization, performance tuning, and other database management tasks.

Types of Oracle Performance Statistics

Oracle DBAs regularly collect several types of performance statistics in order to analyze database bottlenecks and other performance issues. In Oracle Database 11*g*, DBAs now have access to several new types of performance statistics. Besides database statistics at the system and session levels (such as wait statistics, segment usage statistics, and so on), there are also operating system statistics (such as CPU statistics, disk usage statistics, and memory usage statistics) and network statistics. Based on how the various performance statistics are collected and aggregated, you can divide these statistics into two groups: cumulative statistics and database metrics. While cumulative statistics show the accumulated values of key database statistics, metrics measure the rate of change in the cumulative performance statistics.

Cumulative Statistics

Cumulative statistics are the accumulated *total* value of particular statistics since the start of an Oracle instance. The total logons statistic, for example, is a cumulative statistic. Oracle collects several types of cumulative statistics, including statistics for segments and SQL statements, as well as session-wide and system-wide statistics. By comparing the *delta values*—the change in the value of the cumulative statistics between a beginning and an ending period—Oracle analyzes database performance during a specific interval of time.

The Automatic Workload Repository stores important cumulative statistics. I discuss the AWR in the "The Automatic Workload Repository" section of this chapter.

Sample Data

Sample data represents a sample of the total amount of data available. The Active Session History feature automatically collects *session sample data*, which represents a sample of the current state of all active sessions. ASH collects the data in memory, where you can view it with the help of V$ views. The AWR helps save the ASH data permanently by collecting it as part of its regular snapshots.

I discuss the ASH feature in detail in the "Active Session History" section of this chapter.

Baseline Data

A good way to evaluate database performance is by comparing database performance statistics from two periods, where the first period reflects "good" performance. The statistics from the period when the database performed well are called *baseline data*. By comparing current performance with the base period's performance, you can check whether the database is doing better or worse.

ORACLE DATABASE PREMIUM FUNCTIONALITY LICENSING

Several important Oracle performance tools need separate licensing from Oracle Corporation, in addition to the licensing you purchased for the Oracle Database server software. Oracle divides most of its performance functionality into sets of products called Oracle Management Packs, each of which covers several key diagnostic and other management tools. So be aware that while the tools are enabled with the installation of the Oracle Database server software, their production use requires additional licensing.

You can purchase the Management Packs only with the Enterprise Edition, and you can access their features through the OEM Database Control, Grid Control, and API provided by Oracle. You can purchase licensing for just one or for all of these Management Packs. I summarize the functionality of the Management Packs as follows:

Oracle Diagnostics Pack

The Oracle Diagnostics Pack allows you to set up automatic processes to monitor performance and system functionality. It contains a number of features:

- An Automatic Workload Repository
- An Automatic Database Diagnostic Monitor
- An event-notification system
- A history of events and metrics on the database and the host
- Performance monitoring for the database and the host

Oracle Tuning Pack

The Oracle Tuning Pack is only available if you have the Oracle Diagnostic Pack, and it helps you tune the performance of your database. It includes the following features:

- The SQL Access Advisor
- The SQL Tuning Advisor
- SQL tuning sets
- Database object reorganization help

Oracle Configuration Management Pack

The Oracle Configuration Management Pack automates software configuration, software and hardware inventory tracking, patching, and policy management. The Configuration Management Pack facilitates the following:

- Configuring databases and hosts
- Managing deployments
- Staging and viewing of database patches
- Cloning databases and cloning Oracle home
- Searching and comparing configuration
- Managing security and other enterprise policies

Oracle Change Management Pack

The Oracle Change Management Pack lets you evaluate and implement database schema changes. You can track changes, compare and synchronize objects and schemas, modify schema objects and evaluate the changes, and even undo the changes. The Change Management Pack lets you do the following things:

- Reverse-engineer database capability
- Compare databases and schemas, or baselines
- Copy database objects
- Update database object definitions
- Synchronize objects and schemas
- Evaluate the impact of changes
- Clone application schemas

Database Metrics

Database *metrics,* statistics that measure the *rate of change* in a cumulative performance statistic, are also important Oracle performance statistics. In previous Oracle versions, you needed to collect data at various periods to calculate the rate of change of various statistics. Now, Oracle places precomputed metrics at your fingertips. For example, you may be interested in a metric like the number of transactions per second during peak times. Dynamic performance views hold these metrics, and the AWR can also store them in its repository.

You can consider statistics such as the number of user transactions and the number of physical reads in the system as the *base statistics* from which database metrics are derived. The manageability monitor (MMON) background process updates metric data on a minute-by-minute basis after collecting the necessary base statistics.

All the Oracle management advisors use database metrics for diagnosing performance problems and making tuning recommendations. Database metrics can be used to check the health of various resources like the CPU, memory, and I/O. The OEM Database Control's All Metrics page, shown in Figure 18-1, offers an excellent way to view metrics. To access this page, start at the Database Control home page and click All Metrics under the Related Links heading. For details about the metrics, click the Expand All link in the left corner of the page. From here, you can drill down to the details of any metric by simply clicking a specific metric.

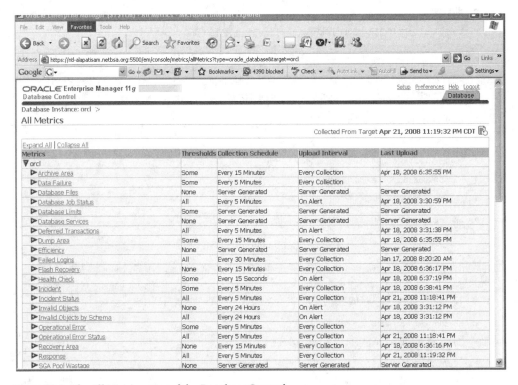

Figure 18-1. *The All Metrics page of the Database Control*

Oracle Database 11*g* uses several metric groups, with each group representing items like a wait event, service, or session. Table 18-1 lists the basic metric groups in Oracle Database 11*g*.

Table 18-1. *Oracle Database 11g Metric Groups*

Metric	Description
Event class metrics	Metrics collected at the wait event class level, such as DB_TIME_WAITING
Event metrics	Metrics collected on various wait events
File metrics long duration	Metrics collected at the file level, such as AVERAGE_FILE_WRITE_TIME
Service metrics	Metrics collected at the service level, such as CPU_TIME_PER_CALL
Session metrics short duration	Metrics collected at the session level, such as BLOCKED_USERS
System metrics long duration	Metrics collected at the system level
Tablespace metrics long duration	Metrics collected at the tablespace level, such as TABLESPACE_PCT_FULL

You can view the Oracle metrics in two ways: by using V$ dynamic views, you can view the in-memory metrics; by using the DBA_HIST* views, you can view the metrics that are stored by the AWR. I explain these two types of views in the following sections.

In-Memory Metrics

The MMON background process collects database metrics and saves them in the SGA for one hour by default. You can adjust this time by changing the AWR snapshot settings. You can view system-related metrics by using views like V$SYSMETRIC_HISTORY and V$SYSMETRIC.

Here are some of the system metrics maintained in the V$SYSMETRIC view:

- Buffer cache hit ratio

- CPU usage per second

- Database CPU time ratio

- Database wait time ratio

- Disk sort per second

- Hard parse count per second

- Host CPU utilization percent

- Library cache hit ratio

- SQL service response time

- Shared pool free percent

The V$SERVICEMETRIC and V$SERVICEMETRIC_HISTORY views provide details about service-level metrics. V$SERVICEMETRIC shows metric values measured on the most recent time interval for database services, in five-second and one-minute intervals, and V$SERVICEMETRIC_HISTORY gives the recent history of the metric values measured in five-second and one-minute intervals for the services running inside the database.

Saved Metrics

Using the AWR snapshots, Oracle saves the metric information that is being continuously placed in the SGA by the MMON process. After saving performance metrics in memory for an hour, the MMON process flushes metric data from the SGA to disk, where it is stored permanently in the DBA_HIST_* views, such as DBA_HIST_SUMMARY_HISTORY, DBA_HIST_SYSMETRIC_HISTORY, and DBA_HIST_METRICNAME. Each of these views actually represents snapshots of the corresponding V$ view, with, for example, the DBA_HIST_SYSMETRIC_HISTORY view containing snapshots of the V$SYSMETRIC_HISTORY view.

Oracle metrics serve as the foundation of the server-generated alerts feature, which is the next topic.

Server-Generated Alerts

Oracle DBAs generally use SQL scripts to alert them when abnormal conditions occur. Oracle Database 11g provides a built-in system of alerts, formally called *server-generated alerts*, which automatically alert you when problem conditions occur. The database generates alerts based on the occurrence of specific events, or when certain database metrics exceed their threshold values.

Oracle calls the threshold-based alerts *stateful alerts*, and they can be set off at either a warning threshold or a critical threshold. Threshold-based alerts thus are based on *metrics*, not *events*. Unlike in the old OEM alert-notification system, the database itself collects all alert-related metrics instead of the OEM. The warning and critical threshold values can be set by the DBA, or you can accept Oracle's internal settings for the thresholds.

The nonthreshold Oracle alerts are problem-related alerts, and they are based on the occurrence of certain predetermined events (usually bad ones) occurring in the database. Oracle calls these *stateless alerts*—here are some examples:

- Recovery area space usage exceeded
- Resumable session suspended
- Snapshot too old

Thus, there are altogether three situations when a database can send an alert:

- A metric crosses a critical threshold value
- A metric crosses a warning threshold value
- A nonthreshold (problem) type of alert occurs

When you use threshold-based alerts, Oracle distinguishes between a warning alert (severity level 5) and a critical alert (severity level 1). For example, by default, the database will send you a warning alert when any tablespace hits an 85 percent space use threshold. When the usage reaches the 97 percent level, you get a critical alert.

Default Server-Generated Alerts

Oracle provides several server-generated default alerts, which could be either threshold-based or problem alerts. These are some of the out-of-the-box server-generated alerts in an Oracle Database 11g database:

- Snapshot too old
- Tablespace space usage (warning alert at 85 percent usage; critical alert at 97 percent usage)
- Resumable session suspended
- Recovery area running out of free space

Note Oracle automatically sets thresholds on all metrics with the object type SYSTEM.

In addition to the default alerts, you can choose to use other alerts, and you can also change the thresholds for the default alerts. You can perform these tasks with the help of the OEM Database Control or with Oracle-supplied PL/SQL packages. You can also use the Database Control to set up notification rules; for example, you could specify a blackout period for the alerts, during which no alerts would be sent out by the database.

When the database issues an alert, you can see it in the Database Control Alerts table (see Figure 18-2), which is located at the bottom of the Database Control home page, and you'll receive a notification if you've configured the system to send you one. The alert data is, by default, updated every 60 seconds. To get the details of an alert, click the alert message in the Message column of the Alerts table. The alerts usually are accompanied by a recommendation to fix the problem as well.

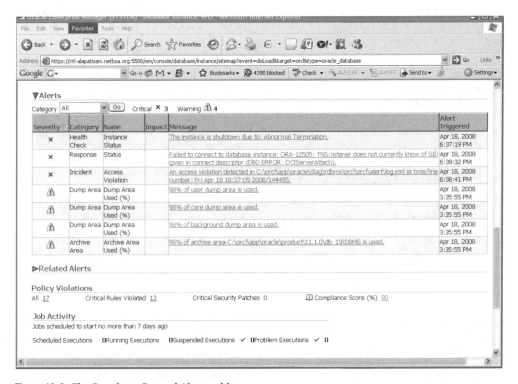

Figure 18-2. *The Database Control Alerts table*

Make sure you set the STATISTICS_LEVEL parameter to TYPICAL or ALL in order to use the server-generated alerts feature. In addition, you can display alerts directly by subscribing to the alert queue.

Baseline Metrics and Adaptive Thresholds

You can use the AWR baseline metrics for setting alert thresholds. Alert thresholds tell the database when to issue an alert, because a certain performance metric is at an unexpected value. In order to set alert thresholds, you must know how to tell that a certain metric's value is at an unexpected level.

You use a baseline to capture the metric values for a specific period, and the database uses the baseline to set the threshold values for various metrics. A static baseline computes metric value statistics manually over a time period. A system moving window automatically captures the metric value statistics.

You can use baseline metrics for computing alert thresholds. You can use three different methods to compare baseline statistics to current activity in the database:

- *Significance level*: Thresholds based on significance level use a statistical level to determine whether current levels of a metric are unusual. For example, if you set the significance level to 0.99 for a critical threshold, the database will issue an alert when more than 1% percent of the current metric values fall outside the metric value.

- *Percentage of maximum*: These are thresholds that are calculated based on the maximum value captured by the baseline.

- *Fixed values*: Fixed values are those set by the DBA, independent of any baselines.

Adaptive thresholds, which use AWR baselines as sources of metric statistics, are ideal for creating alert thresholds. Once you select a group of metrics that represent your database workload, the database automatically configures and evolves adaptive thresholds by basing them on the SYSTEM_MOVING_WINDOW baseline.

Managing Alerts

The best way to manage database alerts and related metrics is to use the OEM Database Control. You can also use the DBMS_SERVER_ALERT package to manage alerts, or you can access the alert queue directly. The following sections explain the default server-generated alerts and how to manage them.

Using the Database Control to Manage Alerts

Oracle automatically sends an alert message to a persistent queue named ALERT_QUE, and OEM reads this queue and sends out notifications about the outstanding server alerts. The Database Control (as well as the Grid Control) displays the alerts and can also send e-mail or pager notifications regarding the alerts.

If you've used the Oracle9*i* OEM, you're familiar with the Enterprise Manager alerts. Server-generated alerts work in a similar fashion. In addition to having Oracle send alerts, now you can configure alert thresholds as well.

Setting Alert Thresholds

It is very easy to set your own warning and critical thresholds for any database metric. To set alert thresholds, go to the Database Control home page and click the Manage Metrics link, which you'll find under the Related Links group. On the Manage Metrics page, click the Edit Thresholds button. You'll see the Edit Thresholds page, as shown in Figure 18-3. For each metric on the Edit Thresholds page, you can set the following:

- *Warning and critical thresholds*: You can set an arbitrary threshold or compute a threshold based on a set of baselines for a metric. For example, you might specify that the database should generate a threshold alert if use of a particular resource is 15 percent higher than its normal baseline values. You can also specify multiple thresholds.

- *Response action*: This action can be a SQL script or an operating system command. Oracle will automatically execute this response action immediately when the alert is generated. Make sure that you provide the complete path to the SQL script or operating system command, so the OEM Agent can find it.

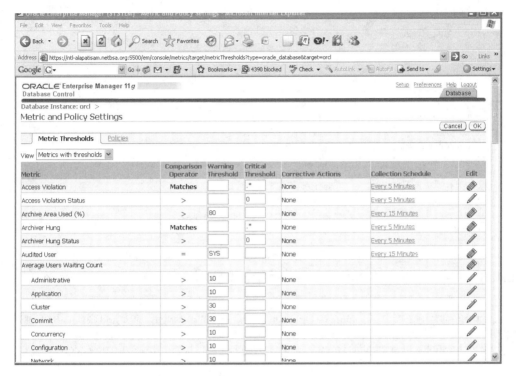

Figure 18-3. *Using the OEM Database Control to set alert thresholds*

Setting Notification Rules

Notification rules enable you to control the conditions under which you want to receive a message from the OEM. For example, you may not want to be awakened at 2:00 a.m. just because a tablespace with 100GB of allocated space has reached an 80 percent usage level. On the other hand, you would surely want to know immediately when a 200MB tablespace has crossed the 97 percent usage level.

You can use the OEM Database Control to set notification rules through the Preferences page. On the Database Control home page, click the Preferences link (at the very bottom of the page) to go to the Preferences page. Then click the Rules link in the Notification section. Select any metric, such as Listener Availability, and click the Edit button. From here, you can set notification rules for a selected event.

Using the DBMS_SERVER_ALERT Package to Manage Alerts

Although the OEM Database Control interface provides an easy way to manage database alerts, there may be times when you need to incorporate certain changes inside a PL/SQL program. At times like this, you can use the Oracle-supplied DBMS_SERVER_ALERT package to set up and modify thresholds on various database metrics. The DBMS_SERVER_ALERT package has two main procedures: GET_THRESHOLD and SET_THRESHOLD.

You use the SET_THRESHOLD procedure to define threshold settings for a database metric. Listing 18-1 shows the structure of the SET_THRESHOLD procedure.

Listing 18-1. *The SET_THRESHOLD Procedure of the DBMS_SERVER_ALERT Package*

```
SQL> DESC DBMS_SERVER_ALERT.SET_THRESHOLD

PROCEDURE dbms_server_alert.set_threshold
 Argument Name                    Type                In/Out     Default?
 ------------------------         ---------------     ---------  ---------
 METRICS_ID                       BINARY_INTEGER      IN
 WARNING_OPERATOR                 BINARY_INTEGER      IN
 WARNING_VALUE                    VARCHAR2            IN
 CRITICAL_OPERATOR                BINARY_INTEGER      IN
 CRITICAL_VALUE                   VARCHAR2            IN
 OBSERVATION_PERIOD               BINARY_INTEGER      IN
 CONSECUTIVE_OCCURRENCES          BINARY_INTEGER      IN
 INSTANCE_NAME                    VARCHAR2            IN
 OBJECT_TYPE                      BINARY_INTEGER      IN
 OBJECT_NAME                      VARCHAR2            IN
```

■**Tip** You can turn off all metric-based alerts by setting both the warning value and the critical value to NULL.

In the SET_THRESHOLD procedure described in Listing 18-1, the WARNING_VALUE and CRITICAL_VALUE refer to the warning and critical threshold values for an alert. To find out the current warning and critical thresholds for a database metric, you use the DBMS_ALERT.GET_THRESHOLD procedure.

Using the Alert Queue Directly

In addition to using the DBMS_SERVER_ALERT package, you can also use procedures from the DBMS_AQ and DBMS_AQADM packages to directly access and read alert messages in the alert queue. The DBMS_AQADM package lets you subscribe to the alert queue, set thresholds, and display alert notifications using various procedures. The DBMS_AQ package lets you manage alert notifications. See the Oracle documentation for more details. Besides displaying alerts on the database home page, the Database Control also will send you e-mail notifying you about alerts, so long as you set up your e-mail information using the Setup link in the Database Control.

Proactive Tablespace Alerts

All Oracle Database 11*g* tablespaces have built-in alerts that will notify you if their free space drops below a set threshold. The two default thresholds are *critical* and *warning*. The MMON background process monitors the free space in each tablespace and sends out the alerts.

Oracle will, by default, alert you with a warning when your tablespace is at 85 percent of capacity and will send a critical alert when the tablespace is at 97 percent of capacity. However, you can turn the alerting mechanism off if you want. To view information on your thresholds, see the DBA_THRESHOLDS view.

■**Tip** If you are migrating to Oracle Database 11*g*, Oracle turns off the automatic tablespace alerting mechanism by default. If you want to set the alert thresholds, use the DBMS_SERVER_ALERT package.

Here's a simple example that shows how to use the DBMS_SERVER_ALERT package to set warning and critical thresholds and trigger alerts when either of the thresholds is crossed. You'll see how to set, view, and clear an alert.

1. Create a small tablespace to use for testing the Oracle alert mechanism:

```
SQL> CREATE TABLESPACE test DATAFILE 'test01.dbf' size 10M
     EXTENT MANAGEMENT LOCAL UNIFORM SIZE 3M;

Tablespace created.
```

2. Set your tablespace alert thresholds as follows (warning alert at 80 percent full and critical at 95 percent full):

```
SQL> EXECUTE DBMS_SERVER_ALERT.SET_THRESHOLD(-
  >  dbms_server_alert.tablespace_pct_full,dbms_server_alert.operator_ge,'80',-
  >  dbms_server_alert.operator_ge,'95',1,1,null,-
  >  dbms_server_alert.object_type_tablespace,'TEST');

PL/SQL procedure successfully completed.
SQL>
```

3. Create a new table using the following SQL statement. (This will set off an alert because the MINEXTENTS 3 clause for the new table will cause the tablespace to cross its warning threshold of 80 percent full.)

```
SQL> CREATE TABLE test_table (name varchar2(30))
     TABLESPACE test
     STORAGE (MINEXTENTS 3);

Table created.
SQL>
```

4. You can verify the tablespace alert as follows (though you may not see the alert immediately, since the MMON process has to gather the alert information first):

```
SQL> SELECT reason FROM dba_outstanding_alerts;

REASON
--------------------------------------
Tablespace [TEST] is [88 percent] full
SQL>
```

5. You can clear the alert by increasing the size of the datafile that is part of the test tablespace and see what happens to the alert by querying the DBA_OUTSTANDING_ALERTS view. You'll find that the alert is gone from that view, since it has been cleared.

```
SQL> ALTER TABLESPACE test ADD DATAFILE 'test02.dbf' size 5M;

Tablespace altered.
SQL>
SQL> SELECT reason FROM dba_outstanding_alerts;

no rows selected
SQL>
```

6. All cleared alerts will show up in the DBA_ALERT_HISTORY view. You can verify that the cleared tablespace alert is in that view by using the following query:

```
SQL> SELECT reason, resolution FROM dba_alert_history;

REASON                                       RESOLUTION
--------------------------------------       -----------
Tablespace [TEST] is [88 percent] full           cleared
SQL>
```

Using the Alert Logs and Trace Files for Monitoring

You can use the database alert log and trace files for monitoring errors in the data set. Server and background processes write error information to trace files, which can be used by Oracle Support to help you. The alert log contains informational messages such as database startup and shutdown statement processing as well as tablespace creation statement processing. In addition, the alert log contains messages regarding internal errors and corruption errors.

You can check the alert log as well as the instance trace files to investigate background process errors. For example, when the log writer process is unable to write to a log group, it creates a trace file and puts a message in the alert log at the same time.

You can control the size of the individual trace files by setting the initialization parameter MAX_DUMP_FILE_SIZE. The database appends new data to the alert log. You can copy and move the alert log to tape periodically and delete the alert log after it reaches a certain limit. The database automatically creates a new alert log in the place of the deleted alert log.

Data Dictionary Views Related to Metrics and Alerts

There are several data dictionary views that provide information about database metrics and alerts. I've already mentioned the V$SYSMETRIC, V$SERVICEMETRIC, and V$SYSMETRIC_HISTORY views earlier in this chapter. Following are some of the other key views:

- V$METRICNAME shows the mapping of metric names to metric IDs.

- V$ALERT_TYPES displays information about server alert types.

- DBA_HIST_SYSMETRIC_HISTORY contains snapshots of V$SYSMETRIC_HISTORY.

- DBA_ALERT_HISTORY provides a history of alerts that are no longer outstanding; that is, all alerts that you have already resolved.

- DBA_OUTSTANDING_ALERTS contains all the threshold alerts that have yet to be resolved.

- DBA_THRESHOLDS shows the names as well as the critical and warning values for all thresholds in the database.

I'll describe a couple of the important views in more detail in the following sections.

V$ALERT_TYPES

The V$ALERT_TYPES view provides information about all system alert types. Three columns in this view are noteworthy:

- *STATE*: Holds two possible values: stateful or stateless. Stateful alerts are those alerts that clear automatically when the alert threshold that prompted the alert is cleared. The database considers all nonthreshold alerts as stateless alerts. A stateful alert first appears in the DBA_OUTSTANDING_ALERTS view and goes to the DBA_ALERT_HISTORY view when it is cleared. A stateless alert goes straight to DBA_ALERT_HISTORY.

- *SCOPE*: Classifies alerts into *database-wide* and *instance-wide*.

- *GROUP_NAME*: Oracle aggregates the various database alerts into some common groups: space, performance, and configuration.

DBA_THRESHOLDS

The DBA_THRESHOLDS view provides the current threshold settings for all alerts. This view is useful when you want to find out the current threshold settings for any alert:

```
SQL> SELECT metrics_name, warning_value, critical_value,
     consecutive_occurrences
     FROM DBA_THRESHOLDS
     WHERE metrics_name LIKE '%CPU Time%';
```

■**Tip** If you get a snapshot-too-old alert, you may need to increase the size of your undo tablespace. In addition, you may consider increasing the length of the undo retention period. Note that you'll get a maximum of only one undo alert during any 24-hour period.

The Automatic Workload Repository

The dynamic performance views V$SYSSTAT and V$SESSTAT hold many of the important cumulative statistics for the Oracle database. Dynamic performance views are very useful in judging database performance, but unfortunately, when you shut down the database, the data in the dynamic performance views disappears completely! If you wish to track database performance over time, or if you wish to compare the performance effects of database changes, you need to store the performance data in a repository, which is where the Automatic Workload Repository comes in.

AWR automatically collects and stores database performance statistics relating to problem detection and tuning, and it lies at the heart of the new database self-tuning mechanisms. The AWR was designed by Oracle as a replacement for the traditional Statspack utility, which helps you gather database performance statistics (the Statspack utility is still available, but Oracle strongly recommends using the AWR instead). Note that you must pay additional licensing fees if you want to use AWR.

The AWR generates snapshots of key performance data, such as system and session statistics, segment-usage statistics, time-model statistics, and high-load-SQL statistics, and it stores the snapshots in the Sysaux tablespace. By default, the database will generate a performance snapshot every hour. You can customize the snapshot interval, the types of statistics the AWR collects, and the length of time the snapshots are retained in the AWR.

AWR provides performance statistics in two formats:

- A *temporary* in-memory collection of statistics in the SGA, accessible through dynamic performance (V$) views or the OEM interface.

- A *persistent* type of performance data in the form of regular AWR *snapshots,* which you access either through data dictionary (DBA_*) views or the OEM Database Control. The persistent data in the AWR snapshots helps in historical comparisons of performance.

MMON is a background process that performs mostly management-related tasks, including issuing database alerts and capturing statistics for recently modified database objects. The MMON process transfers the memory version of AWR statistics to disk on a regular basis (in the form of snapshots).

Oracle DBAs traditionally have needed to maintain special database tables to collect historical performance data. The AWR automatically collects performance statistics for you and maintains historical data for analysis. You can view the data in the snapshots with the help of the V$ views or create reports to examine the data in detail. Various database components and features use the data from these AWR snapshots to monitor and diagnose performance issues. For example, as you saw in Chapter 17, the ADDM relies on these snapshots for the diagnosis of performance problems. In addition, the SQL Tuning Advisor, the Undo Advisor, and the Segment Advisor all use AWR data.

Types of Data Collected by the AWR

The AWR facility collects a large number of performance statistics, including the following:

- Base statistics that are also part of the V$SYSSTAT and V$SESSSTAT views

- SQL statistics that aid in the identification of resource-intensive SQL statements

- Database object-usage statistics that inform you about how the database is currently accessing various objects

- Time-model statistics, which tell you how much time each database activity is taking

- Wait statistics, which provide information about session waits (In previous versions, you needed to join the V$SESSION view with the V$SESSION_WAIT view to gather information on session waits; now several new columns have been added to the V$SESSION view, so you can query the view directly.)

- ASH statistics, which are flushed to the AWR on a regular basis

- Database feature-usage statistics that tell you whether and how intensively your database is utilizing various features

- The results of various management advisory sessions, such as the Segment Advisor and the SQL Access Advisor

- Operating system statistics such as disk I/O and memory usage within the database

As explained in Chapter 17, the ADDM will automatically run after each AWR snapshot, analyzing the time period between the last two snapshots. By comparing the difference in statistics between snapshots, for example, the ADDM knows which SQL statements are contributing significantly to your system load. It then focuses on these SQL statements.

AWR Data Handling

It is important to understand that the AWR isn't a permanent repository for Oracle performance statistics. By default, the AWR captures performance statistics on an hourly basis and retains them for eight days. Oracle estimates that with about ten concurrent sessions, these default settings would require about 200–300MB of storage space for AWR data.

The space used by AWR depends on the following:

- *Data-retention period*: The longer the retention period, the more space is used.

- *Snapshot interval*: The more frequently the snapshots are taken, the more space is used.

- *Number of active sessions*: The higher the number of user sessions, the more data is collected by the AWR.

By default, the AWR saves the data for a period of eight days, but you can modify this period. Oracle recommends that you retain the AWR data to cover at least one complete workload cycle.

Managing the AWR

Snapshots provide you values for key performance statistics at a given point in time. By comparing snapshots from different periods, you can compute the rate of change of a performance statistic. Most of the Oracle advisors depend on these AWR snapshots for their recommendations.

Managing the AWR essentially involves managing the regular snapshots that AWR collects from your database. The default interval for snapshot collection is 60 minutes, and the minimum interval is 10 minutes. If you think this isn't an appropriate length of time for your purposes, you can easily change the default snapshot interval by changing the INTERVAL parameter.

■**Note** You can take manual snapshots of the system any time you wish.

To make good use of the AWR feature, you need to select a truly representative baseline, which is a pair or range of AWR snapshots. When database performance is slow, you can compare the baseline snapshot statistics with current performance statistics and figure out where the problems are.

You can manage the AWR snapshots either with the help of the OEM Database Control or with the Oracle-supplied DBMS_WORKLOAD_REPOSITORY package, which lets you manage snapshots and baselines. Let's first look at how you can use this package to manage AWR snapshots.

Using the DBMS_WORKLOAD_REPOSITORY Package to Manage AWR Snapshots

You can use the DBMS_WORKLOAD_REPOSITORY package to create, drop, and modify snapshots, as well as to create and drop snapshot baselines.

To create a snapshot manually, use the CREATE_SNAPSHOT procedure, as follows:

```
SQL> BEGIN
    dbms_workload_repository.create_snapshot ();
    END;
```

In order to drop a range of snapshots, use the DROP_SNAPSHOT procedure. When you drop a set of snapshots, Oracle automatically purges the AWR data that is part of this snapshot range. The following example drops all snapshots whose snap IDs fall in the range of 40 to 60:

```
SQL> BEGIN
    dbms_workload_repository,drop_snapshot_range(
    low_snap_id => 40,
    high_snap_id => 60, dbid => 2210828132);
    END;
```

■**Tip** If you set the snapshot interval to 0, the AWR will stop collecting snapshot data. Of course, this means that the ADDM, the SQL Tuning Advisor, the Undo Advisor, and the Segment Advisor will all be adversely affected, because they depend on the AWR data.

Using the Database Control to Manage AWR Snapshots

You can manage AWR snapshots from the AWR page of the OEM Database Control, shown in Figure 18-4. To access this page, go to the Database Control home page, click the Administration link, and click the Automatic Workload Repository link, which is under the Statistics Management group. This page has two main sections: the General section and the Manage Snapshots and Preserved Snapshot Sets section.

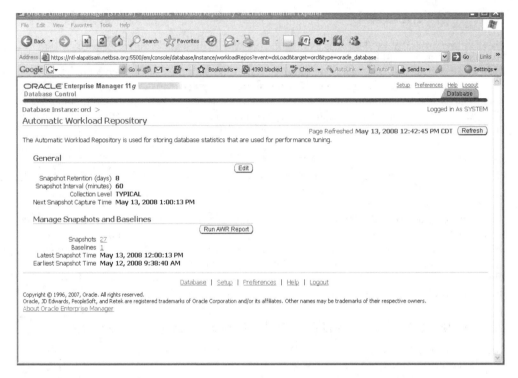

Figure 18-4. *The main AWR page*

If you want to change the general settings of the AWR, you can do so by clicking the Edit button in the General section. This will take you to the Edit Settings page, where you can modify the following:

- Snapshot retention intervals
- Snapshot collection intervals
- Snapshot collection levels (Typical or All)

Under the Manage Snapshots and Baselines section on the main AWR page, the first line lists the total number of snapshots. This listing is a link, which you click to get to the Manage Snapshots page, which lists all the snapshots in the AWR. You can click an individual snapshot to view complete details about it, including the capture time and the collection level. Figure 18-5 shows the snapshot details for a single AWR snapshot. If you have established an AWR baseline (which is a representative time period), you'll also see how a particular snapshot compares with that baseline.

From the Manage Snapshots page, you can do the following:

- Create a snapshot spontaneously (using the Create button).
- View a list of the snapshots collected over a specific period.
- Establish a range of snapshots to use as a baseline (using the Create Preserved Snapshot Set button).
- Delete a defined range of snapshots from the list of snapshots collected over a period of time (using the Delete Snapshot Range button).

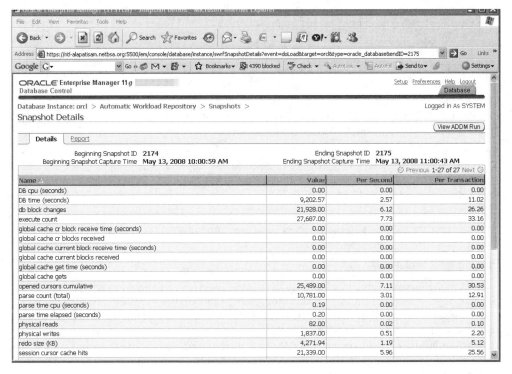

Figure 18-5. *Viewing the details of an AWR snapshot*

■**Note** The range of snapshots you use for a baseline is the same as a preserved snapshot set.

Creating and Deleting AWR Snapshot Baselines

AWR baselines enable you to perform comparative performance analysis between two periods. An AWR baseline consists of a set of AWR snapshots for a reference period. The purpose of using baselines is to have a valid measuring stick for acceptable database performance, as well as to have a reference point for various system statistics. When you say database performance is bad, you must know that it's bad compared to something you know to be good performance. If your database processes a certain number of transactions during a representative (baseline) period, it becomes easy to tell whether your current performance is normal or not. AWR baselines are defined by default, as long as you make sure that the STATISTICS_LEVEL initialization parameter is set to TYPICAL or ALL. You define an AWR baseline on a pair of snapshots taken when you know that the period covered represents typical good database performance. The baseline then serves as a valid representative sample to compare with current system database performance. When you create a baseline, the AWR retains the baseline snapshots indefinitely (it won't purge these snapshots after the default period of seven days), unless you decide to drop the baseline itself.

You can create a new snapshot baseline by using the CREATE_BASELINE procedure of the DBMS_WORKLOAD_REPOSITORY package. You identify the snapshots to use with the snap ID, which uniquely and sequentially identifies each snapshot. You can get the snap IDs you need to create baselines from the DBA_HIST_SNAPSHOT view.

The following example creates a snapshot baseline named PEAK_TIME baseline:

```
SQL> BEGIN
     DBMS_WORKLOAD_REPOSITORY.CREATE_BASELINE
     (START_SNAP_ID => 125,
     END_SNAP_ID => 185,
     BASELINE_NAME => 'peak_time baseline',
     DBID => 2210828132);
     END;
```

You can drop a snapshot baseline by using the DROP_BASELINE procedure of the DBMS_WORKLOAD_REPOSITORY package, as shown here:

```
SQL> BEGIN
     DBMS_WORKLOAD_REPOSITORY.DROP_BASELINE(BASELINE_NAME => 'peak_time
     baseline',
     CASCADE => FALSE, DBID => 2210828132);
     END;
```

By setting the CASCADE parameter to TRUE, you can drop the actual snapshots as well.

Purging AWR Snapshots

As you know, the AWR runs every hour by default, and the AWR statistics are saved for a default period of eight days. After the eight-day period, Oracle removes the snapshots, starting with the oldest ones first (excluding the baseline snapshots). Oracle estimates that if you have ten concurrent sessions, it will take between 200MB and 300MB of disk space to store the data that it saves over the standard seven-day period. You must therefore ensure that your Sysaux tablespace has at least this much free space. The number of user sessions is a key determinant of the space required for the AWR statistics.

■**Note** If your Sysaux tablespace runs out of space, Oracle will automatically delete the oldest set of snapshots to make room for new snapshots.

As mentioned earlier, in addition to the number of active user sessions, the period of time for which you want to retain the AWR data and the snapshot interval are the key determinants of the volume of statistics retained in the Sysaux tablespace. You can change the retention time period with the RETENTION parameter and the snapshot interval with the INTERVAL parameter. Here are some details on the role of these two important parameters in snapshot creation and maintenance:

- RETENTION: As you know, the default retention period for AWR statistics is eight days. The minimum retention period is one day. The longer the retention period, the more space the AWR will need in the Sysaux tablespace. However, if there is no room in the Sysaux tablespace, that fact will override all other retention settings. Oracle will start deleting snapshots, over-writing the oldest ones first with new data.

- INTERVAL: By default, the AWR collects data every 60 minutes, and the minimum interval value is 10 minutes. The more frequently you schedule the AWR snapshots, the more data the AWR will collect; the less frequent the AWR snapshots, the greater the chance that you may miss short bursts in disk or memory usage that may occur in your database.

You can use the DBMS_WORKLOAD_REPOSITORY package to modify the snapshot settings, as shown here:

```
SQL> BEGIN
    DBMS_WORKLOAD_REPOSITORY.MODIFY_SNAPSHOT_SETTINGS(
    RETENTION => 43200,
    INTERVAL => 30,
    DBID => 3310949047);
    END;
```

Oracle recommends that you make the retention period the same as your database workload cycle. If your database is like many typical OLTP databases, you probably have OLTP transactions throughout the weekdays, with batch jobs scheduled during nights and weekends. If this is the case, your workload is considered to span a week, in which case the default AWR retention period of eight days is just fine.

■**Note** If you set the value of the RETENTION parameter to 0, you disable the automatic purging of the AWR. If you set the value of the INTERVAL parameter to 0, you disable the automatic capturing of AWR snapshots.

Moving Window Baselines

The database always maintains a system-defined moving window baseline. The window size of the moving window baseline matches the current AWR baseline period, which is eight days by default. You can resize moving window baselines by setting the number of days in the moving widow equal to or less than the AWR retention period. You must first increase the AWR retention period before you can adjust the size of the moving window baseline

AWR Baseline Templates

Your ability to use AWR baselines isn't limited to already existing snapshots that you can compare. You can also create templates for how the data set should create baselines for time periods in the future. You can schedule the creation of AWR baselines by using baseline templates. You can create templates that create baselines for a single time period or according to a schedule. For example, if you know that a holiday weekend is coming up, you can use a single-baseline template to schedule the creation of a baseline for that period. Or, you can use a repeating-baseline template for creating a baseline every Friday afternoon from 3 p.m. to 5 p.m., for example. The background process MMON creates the baselines called for all the baseline templates you create.

You can create AWR baselines through the Enterprise Manager. I explain how to create them manually in the following sections.

Single-Baseline Templates

A single-baseline template creates a single baseline with a fixed time interval, for example, from January 1, 2008, at 10:00 a.m., to January 1, 2009, at 12:00 p.m. I show how to create a single baseline template in the following example, using the CREATE_BASELINE_TEMPLATE procedure:

```
SQL> begin
  2  dbms_workload_repository.create_baseline_template (
  3  start_time => '2008-12-31 22:00:00 CST',
  4  end_time => '2009-01-01 08:00:00 CST',
  5  baseline_name => 'test_baseline1',
  6  template_name => 'test_template1',
  7  expiration => 30);
  8* end;
SQL> /
```

The one-time baseline template will create an AWR baseline covering the period between 10 p.m. on December 31, 2008, and 8 a.m. on January 1, 2009. The example shown here creates a template for a single time period in the future. By default, AWR baselines never expire. You can, however, specify the EXPIRATION parameter to set the expiration duration, which is the number of days the database will maintain a baseline. In the example, the EXPIRATION parameter has a value of 30 days.

Repeating-Baseline Templates

A repeating-baseline template creates a repeating baseline, with a time interval that repeats over a time period, for example, every Friday from 10:00 a.m. to 12:00 p.m. during the year 2008. Here's how you create a repeating baseline template:

```
SQL> begin
dbms_workload_repository.create_baseline_template(
day_of_week            => 'Friday',
hour_in_day            =>  15,
duration               =>  4,
expiration             =>  30,
start_time             => '2008-10-01 22:00:00 PST'.
end_time               => '2007812-31   22:00:00 PST',
baseline_name_prefix   => 'Friday_Baseline',
template_name          => Friday_Template',
dbid                   => 1234567899);
     end;
SQL> /
```

Again, you specify the EXPIRATION parameter to set the length of time for which to retain a baseline.

Creating AWR Reports

Oracle provides a script named awrrpt.sql (located in the $ORACLE_HOME/rdbms/admin directory) to generate summary reports about the statistics collected by the AWR facility. The results of running the awrrpt.sql script are very similar to the output of the traditional Statspack reports. In order to run an AWR report, you must have the DBA privilege.

■**Caution** Make sure you don't confuse the AWR report with the ADDM report that you obtain by running the addmrpt.sql script. The ADDM report is also based on the AWR snapshot data, but it highlights both the problems in the database and the recommendations for resolving them.

When you run the awrrpt.sql script, you'll need to make the following choices:

• Choose between an HTML or plain text report.

• Specify the beginning and ending snap IDs.

If you prefer, you can use the awrsqrpt.sql SQL script, located in the $ORACLE_HOME/rdbms/admin directory, to generate a report focusing on the performance of *a single SQL statement* over a range of snapshot IDs. This may be the right script to run if you're trying to analyze the performance of a specific SQL statement, instead of the entire database.

■**Tip** You can also use the functions AWR_REPORT_TEXT and AWR_REPORT_HTML (both belonging to the DBMS_WORKLOAD_REPOSITORY package) to get AWR reports in text and HTML format, respectively. However, Oracle recommends that you use the awrrpt.sql script (which uses the preceding two functions) to get your reports instead of directly using these functions.

The AWR reports include voluminous information, including the following:

- Load profile
- Top five timed events
- Wait events and latch activity
- Time-model statistics
- Operating system statistics
- SQL ordered by elapsed time
- Tablespace and file I/O statistics
- Buffer pool and PGA statistics and advisories

Here's how you create a typical AWR report. First, run the awrrpt.sql script as shown here:

```
SQL> @$ORACLE_HOME/rdbms/admin/awrrpt.sql

Current Instance
~~~~~~~~~~~~~~~~~

   DB Id    DB Name   Inst Num Instance
----------- -------- -------- ------------
877170029   ORCL         1       orcl
```

In the next step, specify the report type, as shown in Listing 18-2.

Listing 18-2. *Specifying the Report Type for an AWR Report*

```
Specify the Report Type
~~~~~~~~~~~~~~~~~~~~~~~~~
Would you like an HTML report, or a plain text report?
Enter 'html' for an HTML report, or 'text' for plain text
Defaults to 'html'
Enter value for report_type: text
Type Specified:               text
Instances in this Workload Repository schema
~~~~~~~~~~~~~~~~~~~~~~~~~~~~~~~~~~~~~~~~~~~~~~~
   DB Id     Inst Num DB Name     Instance     Host
----------- -------- ------------ ------------ ------------
* 877170029        1 ORCL         orcl         prod5
Using  877170029 for database Id
Using          1 for instance number
```

Next, you must specify the range you want the AWR report to cover by specifying the beginning and ending snapshots for the time period you chose, as in Listing 18-3.

Listing 18-3. *Specifying the Report Range for an AWR Report*

```
Specify the number of days of snapshots to choose from
~~~~~~~~~~~~~~~~~~~~~~~~~~~~~~~~~~~~~~~~~~~~~=============
Entering the number of days (n) will result in the most recent
(n) days of snapshots being listed.  Pressing <return> without
specifying a number lists all completed snapshots.
Listing the last 3 days of Completed Snapshots
Instance        DB Name      Snap Id        Snap Started     Snap Level
------------    ---------    ---------    --------------------  -----
orcl            ORCL          3254         30 Mar 2008 00:00     1
                              3307         01 Apr 2008 05:00     1
                              3308         01 Apr 2008 06:00     1
                              3309         01 Apr 2008 07:00     1
                              3310         01 Apr 2008 08:01     1
                              3311         01 Apr 2008 09:00     1
                              3312         01 Apr 2008 10:00     1
                              3313         01 Apr 2008 11:00     1
Specify the Begin and End Snapshot Ids
Specify the Begin and End Snapshot Ids
~~~~~~~~~~~~~~~~~~~~~~~~~~~~~~~~~~~~~~~

Enter value for begin_snap: 3309
Begin Snapshot Id specified: 3309
Enter value for end_snap: 3313
End   Snapshot Id specified: 3313
Specify the Report Name
```

Finally, select a name for the report, as shown in Listing 18-4. You can either choose the default name that's offered or specify your own name for the AWR report.

Listing 18-4. *Specifying the Report Name for an AWR Report*

```
The default report file name is awrrpt_1_3309_3313.txt.  To use this name,
press <return> to continue, otherwise enter an alternative.
Enter value for report_name:
Using the report name awrrpt_1_3309_3313.txt
WORKLOAD REPOSITORY report for
DB Name      DB Id         Instance      Inst Num    Release       Cluster   Host
-----------  ----------    ------------  ----------  -----------   -------   -----------
ORCL         877170026       orcl          1         11.1.0.6.0      NO      prod2

Snap Id        Snap Time                  Sessions    Curs/Sess
---------    --------------------        --------   -------------
Begin Snap:    3309 01-Apr-08 07:00:28      480        7,795.3
  End Snap:    3313 01-Apr-08 11:00:58    1,179        3,239.7
  Elapsed:           240.49 (mins)
  DB Time:         7,999.88 (mins)
```

The first meaningful part of the AWR report shows the size of the buffer cache and the shared pool, as shown here:

```
Cache Sizes (end)
~~~~~~~~~~~~~~~~~

Buffer Cache:        2,304M        Std Block Size:     8K
Shared Pool Size:    1,424M        Log Buffer:     4,096K
```

The Load Profile segment of the AWR report, shown in Listing 18-5, indicates the amount of logical and physical reads in the database between the two snapshots you chose, as well as the number of parses, executions, and transactions. The load analysis is shown both on a per-second and per-transaction basis. This section should give you a quick idea about the load being carried by the instance, and it will be more useful if you have some baseline figures from a representative period to compare it with.

Listing 18-5. *The Load Profile Section of an AWR Report*

```
Load Profile           Per Second      Per Transaction
---------------------  -----------     ----------------
Redo size:             209,042.04          19,549.50
Logical reads:         181,753.19          16,997.46
Block changes:           1,470.90             137.56
Physical reads:          6,473.32             605.38
Physical writes:            46.45               4.34
User calls:              2,189.05             204.72
Parses:                    225.36              21.08
Hard parses:                 1.93               0.18
Sorts:                   2,462.09             230.25
Logons:                      0.91               0.09
Executes:                2,224.24             208.01
Transactions:               10.69
```

The Instance Efficiency segment, shown next, displays the buffer cache, library cache hit ratios, and the percentage of sorting in memory. If this value is low, you should investigate why disk sorting is high.

```
Instance Efficiency Percentages (Target 100%)
~~~~~~~~~~~~~~~~~~~~~~~~~~~~~~~~~~~~~~~~~~~~~~~~
            Buffer Nowait %:   99.91      Redo NoWait %:  100.00
            Buffer  Hit   %:   96.44    In-memory Sort %:  100.00
            Library Hit   %:   99.81       Soft Parse %:   99.14
         Execute to Parse %:   89.87        Latch Hit %:   99.55
 Parse CPU to Parse Elapsd %:   29.23    % Non-Parse CPU:   99.04
```

The Top 5 Timed Events section shows the wait situation in your instance during the specified period. In the following example, user I/O is contributing a vast majority of the instance waits:

```
Top 5 Timed Events
```

			% Total	
Event	Waits	Time (s)	DB Time	Wait Class
---------------------------	------------	-----------	---------	-----------
db file sequential read	30,650,078	308,185	64.21	User I/O
CPU time		63,520	13.23	
db file scattered read	3,641,607	34,740	7.24	User I/O
read by other session	2,256,127	15,262	3.18	User I/O
wait for SGA component shrink	14,012	14,079	2.93	Other

The Time Model Statistics section shows what the instance is spending its time on, as you can see in Listing 18-6.

Listing 18-6. *The Time Model Statistics Section of an AWR Report*

```
Time Model Statistics  DB/Inst: ORCL/orcl  Snaps: 3309-3313
-> ordered by Time (seconds) desc
                                              Time      % Total
Statistic Name                             (seconds)   DB Time
-------------------------------------- --------------- -----------
DB time                                    10,860.27    100.00
sql execute elapsed time                    9,989.24     91.98
DB CPU                                       6,605.53     60.82
background elapsed time                      1,693.64     15.59
parse time elapsed                             991.06      9.13
hard parse elapsed time                        977.66      9.00
background cpu time                             837.48      7.71
PL/SQL compilation elapsed time                385.77      3.55
Java execution elapsed time                    268.49      2.47
PL/SQL execution elapsed time                  246.51      2.27
failed parse elapsed time                       84.06       .77
inbound PL/SQL rpc elapsed time                 43.14       .40
connection management call elapsed time         17.47       .16
hard parse (sharing criteria) elapsed time       4.25       .04
hard parse (bind mismatch) elapsed time           .50       .00
```

You can review SQL statements in the SQL Ordered by Elapsed Time section. This section of the report, shown in Listing 18-7, shows the top SQL statements during the period of analysis, ranked according to the total elapsed time, the CPU time consumed, and the percentage of total DB time used.

Listing 18-7. *The SQL Ordered by Elapsed Time Section of an AWR Report*

```
SQL ordered by Elapsed Time  DB/Inst: ORCL/orcl  Snaps: 3309-3313
-> Resources reported for PL/SQL code includes the resources used by all SQL
   statements called by the code.
-> % Total DB Time is the Elapsed Time of the SQL statement divided
   into the Total Database Time multiplied by 100
  Elapsed      CPU                    Elap per  % Total
  Time (s)   Time (s)  Executions   Exec (s)  DB Time    SQL Id
---------- ---------- ------------ ---------- ------- -------------
   15,970    3,769         24         665.4     3.3    dvycj85pfmb1b
Module: PRNTREPORT
UPDATE UNIT_USERS UR SET UR.CARD_PRINTED_FLAG = 'Y' WHERE UR.CHARTER_ID IN
(SELECT DISTINCT CHARTER_ID FROM PS_LASER_CARDS WHERE BATCH_ID = :B1 ) AND UR.P
OSNTYP_CODE IN ('V','M','O') AND UR.POSN_CODE NOT IN ('AP','IH') AND UR.REGISTRA
NT_STATUS IN ('X','R','N') AND UR.CARD_PRINTED_FLAG = 'N'
```

Operating system statistics are listed next:

```
Operating System Statistics
Statistic Name                                Value
------------------------------------- ------------------
AVG_BUSY_TICKS                              989,293
AVG_IDLE_TICKS                            1,971,976
AVG_IOWAIT_TICKS                            125,186
AVG_SYS_TICKS                               447,993
AVG_USER_TICKS                              540,353
BUSY_TICKS                               15,845,441
IDLE_TICKS                               31,567,835
```

The Segments by Physical Reads section, shown in Listing 18-8, lists the database objects (tables and indexes) that have the highest percentage of physical reads.

Listing 18-8. *The Segments by Physical Reads Section of an AWR Report*

```
Segments by Physical Reads  DB/Inst: ORCL/orcl  Snaps: 3309-3313
            Tablespace                   Subobject  Obj.      Physical
Owner         Name       Object Name       Name     Type       Reads  %Total
----------  ----------  --------------------  ----------  -----  ------------  -------
PAS         UNIT_REGIS  UNIT_REGISTRANTS                  TABLE  18,003,616   21.08
PAS         CAMPAIGN_P  CAMPAIGN_POSITIONS                TABLE  15,319,556   17.94
PAS         OT_DO1      PAYMENT_CATEGORY_BAT              TABLE  11,799,007   13.81
PAS         PERSONNEL_D PERSONNEL                         TABLE   7,189,914    8.42
            ----------------------------------------------------------------------
. . .
End of Report
```

■**Note** I only highlighted a few of the categories of information contained in a typical AWR report. Run the `awrrpt.sql` script to get a full picture of your instance performance over a specified period of time. In addition to the information listed previously, you get important wait information, as well as detailed logical and physical reads analysis based on SQL statements and on a per-datafile basis.

Managing AWR Statistics with Data Dictionary Views

The best way to view AWR data is by using the OEM Database Control. Of course, you can also run the `awrrpt.sql` script, as shown earlier, to view a summary of the AWR data.

The following data dictionary views are very helpful in viewing AWR data:

- The DBA_HIST_SNAPSHOT view shows all snapshots saved in the AWR.

- The DBA_HIST_WR_CONTROL view displays the settings to control the AWR.

- The DBA_HIST_BASELINE view shows all baselines and their beginning and ending snap ID numbers.

Active Session History

AWR snapshots are very useful, but Oracle takes the snapshots only every 60 minutes by default. If you are interested in analyzing a performance problem that happened 10 minutes ago, the AWR snapshots aren't of any help to you. However, you do have a way to get that information. Oracle Database collects the new Active Session History statistics (mostly the wait statistics for different events) for all active sessions *every second,* and stores them in a circular buffer in the SGA. Thus, ASH records very recent session activity (within the past five or ten minutes).

The MMNL process (Oracle calls this *manageability monitor light,* although this process shows up as "manageability monitor process 2" when you query the V$BGPROCESS view) performs light-weight manageability tasks, including computing metrics and capturing session history information for the ASH feature under some circumstances. For example, MMNL will flush ASH data to disk if the ASH memory buffer fills up before the one-hour interval that would normally cause the MMON to flush it.

ASH analysis provides you with effective performance data, since it focuses strictly on active sessions. You can perform an analysis of the current active sessions by using the V$ACTIVE_SESSION_HISTORY view and older session history by using the DBA_HIST_ACTIVE_SESSION_HISTORY view.

■Note The extra statistics in Oracle Database described in this chapter won't have a detrimental effect on performance, since the statistics mostly come directly from the SGA via background processes. The ASH feature uses
about 2MB of SGA memory per CPU.

Current Active Session Data

As you are aware, the V$SESSION view holds all the session data for all current sessions. It contains
72 columns of information, so it's unwieldy when you are trying to analyze session data. That's why
ASH samples the V$SESSION view and gets the most critical wait information from it. Oracle provides
the new V$ACTIVE_SESSION_HISTORY view, which contains one row for each active session that
ASH samples and returns the latest session rows first.

The V$ACTIVE_SESSION_HISTORY view is where the database stores a sample of all active
session data. In this view, there's a column called SESSION_STATE, which indicates whether a session
is active. The SESSION_STATE column can take two values: ON CPU or WAITING. A session is defined as
an active session in the following cases:

- The session state is ON CPU, meaning that it is actively using the CPU to perform a database
  chore.

- The session state is WAITING, but the EVENT column indicates that the session isn't waiting for
  any event in the IDLE class.

Note that ASH is really a rolling buffer in the SGA; it is an *in-memory* active session history. Thus,
in a busy database, older information is frequently overwritten, since ASH collects data every second
from the V$SESSION view.

■Note Chapter 20 shows you how to use ASH statistics to tune instance performance.

Older Active Session History Data

The DBA_HIST_ACTIVE_SESSION_HISTORY data dictionary view provides historical information
about recent active session history. In other words, this view is nothing but a collection of snapshots
from the V$ACTIVE_SESSION_HISTORY view, which itself is a sample of active session data.

There are two ways in which the DBA_HIST_ACTIVE_SESSION_HISTORY view is populated:

- During the course of the regular (by default, hourly) snapshots performed by the AWR, the
  MMON background process flushes the ASH data to the AWR.

- Oracle may also need to transfer data to the DBA_HIST_ACTIVE_SESSION_HISTORY view in
  between the regular snapshots if the memory buffer is full and the database can't write new
  session activity data to it. In this case, the new MMNL background process will perform the
  flushing of data from the memory buffer to the data dictionary view.

Producing an ASH Report

You can use the ashrpt.sql script, located in the $ORACLE_HOME/rdbms/admin directory, to get an
ASH report. The use of the script is similar to the AWR script awrrpt.sql described earlier in this
chapter. The script generates information about the SQL that ran during the time you specify, and it
includes blocking and wait details. Here's how you run the ashrpt.sql script to get an ASH report:

```
$ $ORACLE_HOME/rdbms/admin/ashrpt.sql
```

You are prompted for the time frame for collecting ASH information, whether you'd like an HTML or text report, and the name of the report. Listing 18-9 shows a portion of an ASH report.

Listing 18-9. *The Beginning of an ASH Report*

```
ASH Report For NICKO/nicko
DB Name  DB Id      Instance     Inst Num Release   Cluster Host
------------ ----------- ------------- -------- ----------- -------
NICKO   1974138210  nicko         1     11.1.0  NO   localhost
CPUs    SGA Size    Buffer Cache   Shared Pool  ASH Buffer Size
----  ------------------  ------------------ ------------------ -----
1      304M (100%) 100M (32.9%)   184M (60.5%) 2.0M (0.7%)
             Analysis Begin Time:  28-Jun-08 12:29:55
             Analysis End Time:    28-Jun-08 13:30:00
                 Elapsed Time:        60.1 (mins)
                 Sample Count:          81
     Average Active Sessions:        0.02
  Avg. Active Session per CPU:       0.02
             Report Target:    None specified
```

The first section of the ASH report provides information about the top user events, as shown in Listing 18-10.

Listing 18-10. *The Top User Events Part of the ASH Report*

```
Top User Events           DB/Inst: NICKO/nicko  (Jun 28 12:29 to 13:30)
                                                 Avg Active
Event                     Event Class    % Activity  Sessions
-------------------------------- --------------- ---------- ----------
null event                Other            19.75      0.00
CPU + Wait for CPU        CPU              18.52      0.00
SQL*Net break/reset to client  Application      18.52      0.00
log file switch completion  Configuration     1.23      0.00
log file sync             Commit            1.23      0.00
              -------------------------------------------------------
```

The Top Background Events section, shown in Listing 18-11, shows the wait events in the database.

Listing 18-11. *The Top Background Events Part of the ASH Report*

```
Top Background Events      DB/Inst: NICKO/nicko  (Jun 28 12:29 to 13:30)
                                                 Avg Active
Event                     Event Class    % Activity  Sessions
-------------------------------- --------------- ---------- ----------
os thread startup         Concurrency      20.99      0.00
control file parallel write  System I/O        9.88      0.00
CPU + Wait for CPU        CPU               6.17      0.00
db file sequential read   User I/O          1.23      0.00
log file parallel write   System I/O         1.23      0.00
```

The Top Service/Module section, shown in Listing 18-12, displays the activity broken down according the services or modules in the instance.

Listing 18-12. *The Top Service/Module Part of the ASH Report*

```
Top Service/Module          DB/Inst: NICKO/nicko  (Jun 28 12:29 to 13:30)
                                                            Avg Active
Service              Module                       % Activity  Sessions
-------------------  -----------------------------  ----------  ----------
SYS$BACKGROUND       UNNAMED                          35.80       0.01
nicko                OEM.SystemPool                   20.99       0.00
SYS$USERS            UNNAMED                          17.28       0.00
nicko                OEM.BoundedPool                   7.41       0.00
SYS$USERS            EM_PING                           6.17       0.00
```

Listing 18-13 shows information on the top SQL command types executed in the database during the last hour.

Listing 18-13. *The Top SQL Command Types Part of the ASH Report*

```
Top SQL Command Types       DB/Inst: NICKO/nicko  (Jun 28 12:29 to 13:30)
                                                    Avg Active
SQL Command Type                          % Activity  Sessions
----------------------------------------  ----------  ----------
PL/SQL EXECUTE                               19.75       0.00
SELECT                                        9.88       0.00
INSERT                                        1.23       0.00
UPDATE                                        1.23       0.00
```

Listing 18-14 identifies the top SQL statements during the time period of the ASH analysis.

Listing 18-14. *The Top SQL Statements Part of the ASH Report*

```
Top SQL Statements          DB/Inst: NICKO/nicko  (Jun 28 12:29 to 13:30)

        SQL ID % Activity Event                        % Event
--------------- ---------- ----------------------------  ----------
 2b064ybzkwf1y      18.52 SQL*Net break/reset to client     18.52
BEGIN EMD_NOTIFICATION.QUEUE_READY(:1, :2, :3); END;
```

After this, you'll also see a section called Top SQL Using Literals that helps you identify SQL that's not using bind variables.

The next two segments, shown in Listing 18-15, relate to Top Sessions and Top Blocking Sessions based on enqueue waits and buffer busy wait statistics.

Listing 18-15. *The Top Sessions and Blocking Sessions Part of the ASH Report*

```
Top Sessions                DB/Inst: NICKO/nicko  (Jun 28 12:29 to 13:30)
-> '# Samples Active' shows the number of ASH samples in which the session
      was found waiting for that particular event. The percentage shown
      in this column is calculated with respect to wall clock time
      and not total database activity.
Top Blocking Sessions       DB/Inst: NICKO/nicko  (Jun 28 12:29 to 13:30)
-> Blocking session activity percentages are calculated with respect to
      waits on Enqueues and "buffer busy" only
```

The next three segments summarize the top database objects, the top database files, and the top latches in the instance. In the end, the ASH report provides a summary of the wait events in the database, distributed over smaller time slots than the aggregate period of analysis, as shown in Listing 18-16.

In this example, the one-hour time period is broken up into ten six-minute intervals. This analysis helps you pinpoint performance deterioration more accurately.

Listing 18-16. *Summary of Wait Events over Time Intervals*

```
Activity Over Time              DB/Inst: NICKO/nicko  (Jun 28 12:29 to 13:30)
-> Analysis period is divided into smaller time slots
-> Top 3 events are reported in each of those slots
-> 'Slot Count' shows the number of ASH samples in that slot
-> 'Event Count' shows the number of ASH samples waiting for
   that event in that slot
-> '% Event' is 'Event Count' over all ASH samples in the analysis period
                          Slot                          Event
Slot Time (Duration)      Count Event                   Count % Event
-------------------- -------- ------------------------------ -------- -------
   12:30:00 (6.0 min)      6 SQL*Net break/reset to client      3    3.70
                            null event                          2    2.47
                            os thread startup                   1    1.23
   12:36:00 (6.0 min)      4 CPU + Wait for CPU                 3    3.70
                            null event                          1    1.23
   12:42:00 (6.0 min)      7 CPU + Wait for CPU                 2    2.47
                            null event                          2    2.47
                            os thread startup                   2    2.47
   12:48:00 (6.0 min)      9 SQL*Net break/reset to client      3    3.70
                            CPU + Wait for CPU                  2    2.47
                            control file parallel write         2    2.47
   12:54:00 (6.0 min)     13 control file parallel write        4    4.94
                            os thread startup                   4    4.94
                            CPU + Wait for CPU                  2    2.47
   13:00:00 (6.0 min)     16 CPU + Wait for CPU                 5    6.17
                            SQL*Net break/reset to client       4    4.94
                            null event                          3    3.70
   13:06:00 (6.0 min)      9 CPU + Wait for CPU                 3    3.70
                            SQL*Net break/reset to client       2    2.47
                            os thread startup                   2    2.47
   13:12:00 (6.0 min)      5 null event                         2    2.47
                            CPU + Wait for CPU                  1    1.23
                            SQL*Net break/reset to client       1    1.23
   13:18:00 (6.0 min)      4 SQL*Net break/reset to client      1    1.23
                            control file parallel write         1    1.23
                            null event                          1    1.23
   13:24:00 (6.0 min)      8 os thread startup                  4    4.94
                            CPU + Wait for CPU                  2    2.47
                            SQL*Net break/reset to client       1    1.23
End of Report
```

The Management Advisory Framework

Oracle Database 11*g* includes several management advisors to provide you with automatic performance details about various subsystems of the database. These advisors are specialized tools that help in the performance tuning of various database components, identifying bottlenecks and suggesting optimal sizes for key database resources. For example, the Undo Advisor tells you what the optimal undo tablespace size might be for your database. Each of these advisors bases its actions on a specific Oracle PL/SQL package like the DBMS_ADVISOR package.

Each time an advisor runs a task, it performs an analysis and provides you with recommendations. Note that the ADDM and the Automatic Segment Advisor are the only advisors that are scheduled to run automatically. To get recommendations from any of the other advisors, you must manually schedule or perform an advisor task.

The management advisory framework offers you a uniform interface for all Oracle advisors. Some of these advisors have been around since Oracle9i. What is new is that Oracle has built a common management advisory framework to make it easy to manage the advisors. The new framework allows you to use a similar method to invoke all the advisors, and the advisors provide their reports in a consistent format as well. All the advisors get their raw data from the AWR and store their analysis results in the AWR.

The advisory framework's primary function is to help the database improve its performance. The ADDM recommends using the management advisors on an ad hoc basis, whenever a performance problem needs a deeper analysis. DBAs can also use the advisors for performing what-if analyses.

The Management Advisors

You can group the automatic advisors into the following groups: memory-related, tuning-related, and space-related. Let's briefly look at the advisors that fall into these three groups.

Memory- and Instance-Related Advisors

There are two memory- and instance-related management advisors:

- *Memory Advisor.* This advisor provides recommendations regarding the optimal sizing of total memory allocation as well as SGA and the PGA memory. The Allocation History chart shows the history of the memory allocation for the various SGA components over time.

- *MTTR Advisor:* This advisor lets you configure instance recovery by enabling you to adjust the mean time to recover (MTTR) setting for an instance.

■**Tip** Obviously, if you are using automatic shared memory and program global area management, you don't need the Memory Advisor to tell you how to size these memory components, since the database will manage these by itself.

Tuning-Related Advisors

The ADDM, of course, is the most important all-around tuning advisor in the database, and it provides access to the automatic diagnostic capabilities of the Oracle database. Apart from the ADDM, there are two purely SQL-tuning-related and SQL-performance-related advisors:

- *SQL Tuning Advisor.* This advisor analyzes complex SQL statements and recommends ways to improve performance. The SQL Tuning Advisor bases all its work on internal statistics and may include suggestions to collect new statistics as well as to restructure SQL code. In Oracle Database 11g, the SQL Tuning Advisor runs automatically during the daily maintenance windows. This advisor is referred to as the Automatic SQL Tuning Advisor during these runs, and it selects high-load SQL statements and generates recommendations on tuning them. I discuss the SQL Tuning Advisor in Chapter 19.

- *SQL Access Advisor.* This advisor mainly provides you advice on creating new indexes, materialized views, or materialized view logs. You provide the advisor with a representative workload in order to get its advice. I discuss the SQL Access Advisor in Chapter 7.

■**Note** Most of the database alert messages in the OEM also contain a link to specific management advisors. Thus, you can invoke a management advisor directly from the alert message itself.

Space-Related Advisors

Oracle Database 11*g* has two space-related advisors:

- *Segment Advisor.* This advisor allows you to perform growth-trend analyses on various database objects. This advisor also helps you perform object shrinkage, thus helping you reclaim unused space in your database. The Segment Advisor automatically runs during the maintenance window and recommends candidate objects for shrinking, as well as objects that are candidates for a reorganization operation due to issues such as excessive row chaining.

- *Undo Advisor.* This advisor bases its activities on system usage statistics, including the length of the queries as well as the rate of undo generation. The Undo Advisor facilitates Oracle's Automatic Undo Management (AUM) feature. It helps you to correctly size your undo tablespace and to correctly size the undo retention interval.

Managing the Advisory Framework

You can manage all aspects of the management advisory framework easily using the Database Control interface. You can also use the DBMS_ADVISOR package to create and manage tasks for each of the management advisors.

Using the DBMS_ADVISOR Package

You can invoke any of the management advisors through the OEM interface, using various wizards like the SQL Access Advisor Wizard, and this is my suggested way to use any of the advisors. However, there are times when you may need to invoke an advisor programmatically, in which case you can use the DBMS_ADVISOR package to manage modules in the advisory framework. The methods for creating a task, adjusting task parameters, performing the analysis, and reviewing the recommendations are common to all advisors.

■**Note** You must grant a user the ADVISOR privilege for the user to use the DBMS_ADVISOR package.

These are the steps you must follow to use the DBMS_ADVISOR package to manage various advisors:

1. Create a task.

2. Set the task parameters.

3. Generate the recommendations.

4. Review the advisor's recommendations.

I describe these steps in detail in the following sections.

Creating a Task

The first step in using an advisor is creating a task. A task is where the advisor stores all its recommendation-related information.

You create a task using the CREATE_TASK procedure, as shown here:

```
SQL> VARIABLE task_id NUMBER;
SQL> VARIABLE task_name VARCHAR2(255);
SQL> EXECUTE DBMS_ADVISOR.CREATE_TASK ('SQL Access Advisor', :task_id, :task_name);
```

Setting the Task Parameters

After you create a new task, the next step is to set the parameters for this task. The task parameters control the recommendation process. The parameters that you can modify belong to four groups: workload filtering, task configuration, schema attributes, and recommendation options.

Here is an example showing how you can set various task parameters using the SET_TASK_PARAMETER procedure:

```
SQL> EXECUTE DBMS_ADVISOR.SET_TASK_PARAMETER ( -
     'TEST_TASK', 'VALID_TABLE_LIST', 'SH.SALES, SH.CUSTOMERS');
```

In this example, the VALID_TABLE_LIST parameter belongs to the workload-filtering group of parameters. You are instructing the advisor (the SQL Access Advisor) to exclude all tables from the analysis except the sales and customers tables from the SH schema.

The following example uses the STORAGE_CHANGE parameter from the recommendation-options group to add 100MB of space to the recommendations:

```
SQL> EXECUTE DBMS_ADVISOR.SET_TASK_PARAMETER('TEST_TASK',
     'STORAGE_CHANGE', 100000000);
```

■**Tip** The V$ADVISOR_PROGRESS view lets you monitor the progress of advisor tasks as they execute.

Generating the Recommendations

To generate a set of recommendations by any advisor, you *execute* the task that you created earlier, using the EXECUTE_TASK procedure of the DBMS_ADVISOR package. The EXECUTE_TASK procedure will generate recommendations, which consist of one or more actions. For example, executing the SQL Access Advisor may provide a recommendation to create a materialized view and a materialized view log.

Here's how you execute a task named TEST_TASK:

```
SQL> EXECUTE DBMS_ADVISOR.EXECUTE_TASK('TEST_TASK');
```

Viewing the Recommendations

You can view the recommendations made by a certain task by using the GET_TASK_REPORT procedure. You can also use the DBA_ADVISOR_RECOMMENDATIONS view to check the recommendations related to a particular advisor task name:

```
SQL> SELECT rec_id, rank, benefit
     FROM DBA_ADVISOR_RECOMMENDATIONS
     WHERE task_name = 'TEST_TASK';
```

```
    REC_ID      RANK      BENEFIT
----------  ----------  ----------
         1         2         2754
         2         3         1222
         3         1         5499
         4         4          594
```

In this example, the RANK column shows how the four recommendations stack up against each other. The BENEFIT column shows the decrease in the execution cost for each of the four recommendations.

Using the OEM Database Control to Manage the Advisory Framework

The best way to use the management advisors is through the OEM Database Control. All you need to do is click the Advisor Central link on the Database Control home page. From the Advisor Central page, shown in Figure 18-6, you can select any of the management advisors in the database.

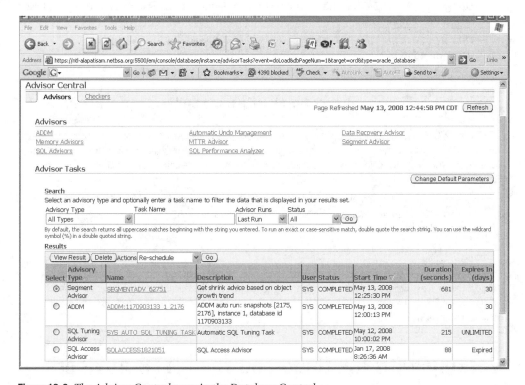

Figure 18-6. *The Advisor Central page in the Database Control*

The Advisor Central page is your starting point to using the advisory framework through the OEM Database Control or Grid Control. You use the Advisor Tasks sections to review the results of running an advisor task. The Results table on the main Advisor Central page shows the output of the last run of the advisor.

After creating a new database, the first time you check this page you'll see a single ADDM task result. This is because the ADDM runs automatically after you create the database. As you invoke the other advisors, the Results table will gather other results.

Using Data Dictionary Views to Manage the Advisory Framework

Several new data dictionary views provide information about managing tasks and recommendations made by the various advisors. These are the main advisor-related dictionary views:

- *DBA_ADVISOR_TASKS*: This view shows information about all tasks in the database, including the task name, data of creation, and frequency of usage. The ACTIVITY_COUNTER column indicates whether useful work is being done by a task.

- *DBA_ADVISOR_PARAMETERS*: This view shows the names and values of all parameters for all advisor tasks in the database.

- *DBA_ADVISOR_FINDINGS*: This view shows the findings reported by all the advisors, including the finding's impact value.

- *DBA_ADVISOR_RECOMMENDATIONS*: This view contains an analysis of all the recommendations in the database. You can also view the benefits of implementing each recommendation and a ranking of all recommendations based on their benefit value.

- *DBA_ADVISOR_ACTIONS*: This view shows the remedial actions associated with each advisor recommendation.

- *DBA_ADVISOR_RATIONALE*: This view shows you the rationale for all advisor recommendations.

USING THE SEGMENT ADVISOR

The Segment Advisor is automatically scheduled to run during the default maintenance window by the Scheduler. The Segment Advisor will provide you with recommendations regarding objects that might need compacting to reclaim unused space, as well as recommendations about object reorganization to eliminate problems such as excessive row chaining.

You can view the details of the Segment Advisor's recommendations through the DBA_AUTO_SEGADV_CTL view. By using the ASA_RECOMMENDATIONS built-in pipelined function (located in the DBMS_SPACE package), you can find out which segments have reclaimable space and excessive row chaining. Here's how you would use it:

```
SELECT * FROM TABLE (DBMS_SPACE.ASA_RECOMMENDATIONS());
```

You can also view the Segment Advisor's recommendations and the reasons for them by going to the Advisor Central page in the Database Control and clicking the Segment Advisor Recommendations link at the top of the page. At the bottom of the Segment Advisor Recommendations page, click the link entitled Recommendations from Last Run of the Automatic Segment Advisor Job.

Working with the Undo and the MTTR Advisors

I've discussed how to use the most important advisors like the ADDM, SQL Tuning Advisor, SQL Access Advisor, and Segment Advisor in other chapters. I'll briefly summarize the use of the Undo and MTTR Advisors here.

Using the Undo Advisor

The database automatically tunes undo retention to ensure the successful completion of the longest running queries. However, you can set your own undo threshold value, which then becomes the minimum value, below which Oracle can't set its automatically tuned undo retention period.

You can get to the Undo Advisor by following these steps:

1. From the Database Control home page, click the Advisor Central link.

2. On the Advisor Central page, click the Undo Management link.

3. Click the Undo Advisor button at the top of the page.

Using the Undo Advisor, you can do the following:

- Set the low threshold value for undo retention.

- Figure out the size of the undo tablespace size you'll need for a new undo retention setting.

- Use different analysis time periods representing different levels of system activity to get recommendations, in the form of a graph, about the right undo tablespace size for varying undo retention length.

Using the MTTR Advisor

To control database recovery time, you use the FAST_START_MTTR_TARGET initialization parameter to set the MTTR from a crash. To optimize performance, set the size of the redo log files so they are just large enough that Oracle isn't performing more checkpoints than required by the value of FAST_START_MTTR_TARGET.

Note The FAST_START_MTTR_TARGET parameter is discussed in detail in Chapter 16.

If your log files are small, Oracle may perform incremental checkpointing more often than the MTTR value specifies. As has been mentioned, frequent log switching tends to promote incremental checkpoint activity, meaning that the database writer will perform excessive disk I/O. In an ideal setup, the MTTR target should govern this activity.

You can access the MTTR Advisor through the Database Control, as follows:

1. From the Database Control home page, click the Advisor Central link under the Related Links section.

2. Click the MTTR Advisor link under the Advisors group.

The main page of the MTTR Advisor is titled Configure Recovery Settings. You can do the following things with the help of the MTTR Advisor:

- Look up the tradeoff between a certain MTTR and total I/O in the Instance Recovery section.

- Turn archive logging on and off and enable and disable the automatic archiving of the redo logs, both through the Media Recovery section.

- Manage the flash recovery area (discussed in detail in Chapter 15), including its location and size, and enable and disable Flashback Database logging for fast database point-in-time recovery. You do all this from the Flash Recovery Area section.

Managing Online Redo Logs

The online redo logs are Oracle's means of ensuring that all the changes made by the users are logged, in case there's a failure before those changes can be written to permanent storage. Thus, redo logs are fundamental for the recovery process.

Oracle organizes its redo log files in redo log groups, and you need to have at least two different groups of redo logs with at least one member in each. You need to have at least two redo groups, because even when one redo log is being archived, the log writer should be able to write to an active redo log.

Although your database will run just fine with only one member in each redo log group, Oracle strongly recommends that you multiplex the online redo logs. *Multiplexing* simply means that you maintain more than one member in each of your redo log groups. All members of a redo log group are identical—multiplexing is designed to protect against the loss of a single copy of a log file. When you multiplex the online redo log files, the log writer writes simultaneously to all the members of a group.

■**Tip** Always multiplex the online redo log, as you can lose data if one of the active online redo logs is lost due to a disk problem. The multiplexed redo logs should ideally be located on different disk drives under different disk controllers.

Hardware Mirroring vs. Oracle Multiplexing

Mirroring will protect you from a disk failure, but it will not protect you against an accidental deletion of files. Multiplexing ensures that your files are protected soundly against such errors.

If you lose an online redo log, you may lose valuable data, so under a multiplexed redo log system, the LGWR background process, which is in charge of writing redo log data from the redo log buffer, writes simultaneously to all the (identical) members of a multiplexed group. If there are problems writing to one member of a multiplexed group of redo logs, the writes to the other members continue unhindered.

Online Redo Log Groups

When you multiplex redo log files, you are maintaining identical copies of the same files. Let's say you create two copies of a redo log file. You need to create a redo log *group* to contain these two identical files, which are called *members* of the group. At any given time, the LGWR process will write to a single group of redo log files, and the members of that group are then said to be *current*.

Here are some basic conditions for Oracle redo log groups:

- All redo log files in a group must be identically sized.

- Although you can put both members of an online redo log group on the same physical disk, it's smart to locate them on different disks so one identical member can survive a disk crash that involves another member of the same group. Oracle will continue to write to the surviving members of the online redo log group when one member is not writable (perhaps due to a problem involving the disk drive).

Creating Online Redo Log Groups

You can create online redo log groups when you create a database for the first time. Here's an example showing just the redo log creation statement as part of the database creation process. Note that the three redo log groups each have only a single member—they are not multiplexed at this point.

```
SQL> CREATE DATABASE
    . . .
    LOGFILE GROUP 1 ('/u01/app/oracle/nicko/redo01.log') SIZE 100M,
            GROUP 2 ('/u01/app/oracle/nicko/redo02.log') SIZE 100M,
            GROUP 3 ('/u01/app/oracle/nicko/redo03.log') SIZE 100M,
    . . .
Database created.
SQL>
```

Adding Redo Log Groups

Although you need a minimum of two online redo log groups, the ideal number of online redo log groups for your database can only be worked out from the transaction activity in your database.

■**Tip** Start with two or three online redo log groups and monitor your alert log for any redo log errors. If the alert log frequently shows that the log writer was waiting to write to an online redo log, you have to increase the number of redo groups.

The following statement, which uses the ADD LOGFILE GROUP syntax, adds a new group of redo logs to your database. Note that this new redo log group is duplexed; two redo log files are being created in the group, not one:

```
SQL> ALTER DATABASE
    ADD LOGFILE GROUP 4 ('/u01/app/oracle/nicko/log4a.rdo',
                        ('/u01/app/oracle/nicko/log4b.rdo') SIZE 500M;
Database altered.
SQL>
```

In the example in the previous section, we created three online log groups, but each of them had only a single member. To duplex those groups to provide additional safety, we need to add a member to each group. To add a single member to an existing group, you use the ADD LOGFILE MEMBER statement:

```
SQL> ALTER DATABASE ADD LOGFILE MEMBER
    '/u01/app/oracle/nicko/log1b.rdo'
    TO GROUP 2;
Database altered.
SQL>
```

Note that we didn't have to specify a size for the new redo log member being added to group 2—the new member will simply be sized the same as the existing members of the group.

Renaming Redo Log Files

If you need to rename your redo log file, follow these steps:

1. Shut down the database and start it up in mount mode:

    ```
    SQL> STARTUP MOUNT
    ```

2. Move the files to the new location with an operating system command:

    ```
    SQL> host mv /u10/app/oracle/oradata/nina/log01.rdo
        /a10/app/oracle/oradata/nina/log01.rdo
    ```

3. Use the ALTER DATABASE RENAME *datafile* TO command to rename the file within the control file (you must rename the database after renaming the file):

```
SQL> ALTER DATABASE RENAME
        '/u10/app/oracle/oradata/nina/log01.rdo' TO
        '/a10/app/oracle/oradata/nina/log01.rdo';
```

Dropping Online Redo Logs

You can drop an entire redo log group by using the following command:

```
SQL> ALTER DATABASE DROP LOGFILE GROUP 3;
```

To drop a single member of an online redo log group, use this command:

```
SQL> ALTER DATABASE DROP LOGFILE MEMBER
        '/u01/app/oracle/oradata/nina/log01.rdo';
```

If the redo log file you want to drop is active or current, Oracle won't let you drop it. You need to use the following command to switch the log file first, after which you can drop it:

```
SQL> ALTER SYSTEM SWITCH LOGFILE;
```

Online Redo Log Corruption

You can set the DB_BLOCK_CHECKSUM initialization parameter to on to make sure Oracle checks for corruption in the redo logs before they're archived. If the online redo logs are corrupted, the file can't be archived, and one solution is to just drop and re-create them. But if there are only two log groups, you can't do this, as Oracle insists on having a minimum of two online redo log groups at all times. However, you can create a new (third) redo log group, and then drop the corrupted redo log group.

Also, you can't drop an online redo log file if the log file is part of the current group. Your strategy then would be to reinitialize the log file by using the following statement:

```
SQL> ALTER DATABASE CLEAR LOGFILE GROUP 1;
```

If the log group has not been archived yet, you can use the following statement:

```
SQL> ALTER DATABASE CLEAR UNARCHIVED LOGFILE GROUP 1;
```

Monitoring the Redo Logs

You can use two key dynamic views, V$LOG and V$LOGFILE, to monitor the online redo logs.

The V$LOGFILE view provides the full filename of the redo logs, their status, and type, as shown here:

```
SQL> SELECT * FROM V$LOGFILE;
 GROUP #     STATUS    TYPE              MEMBER
--------    --------   ------   ----------------------------------------
    3        STALE     ONLINE   /u10/app/oracle/oradata/nina/log01.rdo
    2                  ONLINE   /u10/app/oracle/oradata/nina/log01.rdo
    1                  ONLINE   /u10/app/oracle/oradata/nina/log01.rdo
3 rows selected.
```

The V$LOG view gives detailed information about the size and status of the redo logs, as well as showing whether the logs have been archived:

```
SQL> SELECT group#, sequence#, bytes, archived, members, status
  2* FROM V$LOG;

  GROUP#   SEQUENCE#    BYTES    ARCHIVED  MEMBERS   STATUS
---------- ---------- ---------- --- ---------- -------------
     1          8     104857600    NO         1     INACTIVE
     2         10     104857600    NO         1      CURRENT
     3          7     104857600    NO         1     INACTIVE
     4          9      10485760    NO         3     INACTIVE
SQL>
```

Managing Database Links

A *database link* enables a one-way connection to a remote database from a local database. The link is one-way only. The remote database users can't use this link to connect to the local database—they must create a separate database link for that.

A database link allows you to gain access to a different database though a remote database user account; you don't have to be a user in the remote database. Your privileges on that database will be identical to the privileges of the user account you use when creating the database link. Database links are useful when you want to query a table in a distributed database or even insert data from another database's table into a local table. Database links allow users to access multiple databases as a single logical database.

You can create private and public database links. In the following sections, we'll look at examples of how to create both types of database links.

Creating a Private Database Link

A *private* database link is owned by the user that creates the link. In the following statement, the SYSTEM user creates a private database link. The database link enables a connection to the remote database using the hr user's username and password in that database.

```
SQL> CONNECT system/system_passwd@finance
Connected.
SQL>
SQL> CREATE DATABASE LINK MONITOR
  2   CONNECT TO hr IDENTIFIED BY hr
  3   USING 'monitor';

Database link created.
SQL>
```

After the link is created, the SYSTEM user can query the hr.employees table in the remote database.

```
SQL> SELECT COUNT(*) FROM hr.employees@monitor;

  COUNT(*)
----------
       107
SQL>
```

■**Note** To create a database link, a user must have the CREATE PRIVATE DATABASE LINK privilege or the CREATE PUBLIC DATABASE LINK privilege in the local database.

In the preceding statement, note that the database link's name is MONITOR, which is the same as the remote database's TNS name alias (Oracle Net Service alias), but it could be anything you want. The CONNECT TO . . . IDENTIFIED BY clause means that the user of this database link will use that username and password to enter the remote database. The USING 'monitor' clause simply specifies the TNS name alias for the linked remote database.

Because this is a private database link, only the SYSTEM user can use it. When the hr user tries to use this link to a remote database, this is what happens:

```
SQL> CONNECT hr/hr;
Connected.
SQL> SELECT count(*) FROM hr.employees@monitor;
select count(*) from hr.employees@monitor
                               *
ERROR at line 1:
ORA-02019: connection description for remote database not found
SQL>
```

Creating a Public Database Link

A *public* database link, unlike a private database link, enables any user or any PL/SQL program unit to access the remote database objects. The creation statement is very similar to that for a private database link. You just add the PUBLIC keyword to the CREATE DATABASE LINK statement:

```
SQL> connect system/system_passwd as sysdba;
Connected.
SQL> CREATE PUBLIC DATABASE LINK MONITOR
  2  CONNECT TO hr IDENTIFIED BY hr
  3  USING 'monitor';
Database link created.
SQL>
```

■**Tip** You can create a public database link if several users require access to a remote Oracle database from a local database. Otherwise, create a private database link, which will allow only the owner of the private database link to access database objects in the remote database.

Once the public MONITOR link is created, any user can log into a remote database using that link. In the following example, the user tester uses the public database link to query the remote database, MONITOR.

```
SQL> CONNECT tester/tester1;

Connected.
SQL> SELECT COUNT(*) FROM hr.employees@monitor;

  COUNT(*)
----------
       107
SQL>
```

■Note The user tester can access the remote database, even without being a user in the remote database, because tester is using a public database link, which enables any user to use the hr user's username/password combination to access the remote database. Of course, from a security point of view, a public database link isn't a great idea, and it is bound to be frowned upon by your database auditors!

Using the Database Control to Create Database Links

It's very easy to create a database link using the OEM Database Control. On the Database Control home page, click the Administration tab. Then click the Database Links link in the Schema group. You can create a database link from this page by answering various prompts.

Comparing and Converging Database Objects

It's typical for replication environments to share database objects such as tables and indexes. These objects are known as *shared database objects*, since multiple databases share them. Shared database objects are commonly used by materialized views and Oracle Streams components, which maintain copies of the same tables and other objects in multiple databases. Replication environments such as these strive to keep the common database objects synchronized at the multiple sites. However, it's not uncommon for shared database objects to become unsynchronized, with the result that a table will have a different number of rows and/or different data in the rows when compared to the same table in another database. These data divergences, caused by network problems, user errors, configuration changes, materialized view refresh problems, and so on, may result in a failure to capture data changes on a database or to successfully transfer them to all databases in the configuration.

Oracle Database 11g provides the new DBMS_COMPARISION package, which lets you compare database objects on different objects. If the comparison process shows there are important differences in data between two databases, you can use the same package to converge the data in both databases so the two databases are consistent datawise. You can compare and converge the following types of data:

- Tables
- Views on single tables
- Materialized views
- Synonyms for the previous three types of objects

In an example a little later, I compare two tables on different databases that have the same name and the same columns. However, you can compare two tables that have different names, as well as tables that have different columns, as long as the columns share the same data type. You can also compare (and converge) a subset of columns and rows, instead of an entire table or materialized view.

Comparing Data

In the following example, we compare a simple shared database object (table employees) which is a table in the user HR's schema. To ensure that we can show how to converge data, we first change the data in three rows of the shared database object (table departments) in the remote database. We then use the DBMS_COMPARE package to perform a comparison of the two tables on the two databases, and then use the same package to merge the differences so the two tables are in sync once again.

The only requirement for using the DBMS_COMPARE package is that the two tables we're comparing have at least one column that the package can identify as an index column. This index column must uniquely identify each row that's part of the comparison, meaning the index has to be either a primary key constant or a unique constraint on a non-null column. Otherwise, the package can't compare the two objects. The table employees has a primary key column in both databases, so we're OK here.

1. Create a database link from the primary database (or11) to the secondary database (tenner). In the example, we use the user system as the owner of the database link to ensure that the user has the necessary privileges to execute the procedures in the DBMS_COMPARISION package and the privileges to access and modify tables in both databases. The remote database is named tenner and so is our database link to that database from the primary database or11.

```
SQL> create database link tenner
     connect to system identified by sammyy1
     using 'tenner';
Database link created.
SQL>
```

The next step is to create a divergence between the data in an identical table on the two databases.

2. On the secondary table, make some changes in the hr.employees table so the data diverges from the hr.employees table on the secondary database:

```
SQL> delete from hr.employees where ename='MILLER';
1 row deleted.
SQL> update hr.employees set sal=10000 where ename='FORD';
1 row updated.
SQL> insert into hr.employees values (9999,'ALAPATI','DBA',7792,'20-JUN-
     00',50000,10000,30);
1 row created.
SQL> commit;
Commit complete.
SQL>
```

Now that we made sure the hr.employees table in the two databases diverges, it's time to run the CREATE_COMPARISON procedure to trap the data divergence between the two tables.

3. Create a comparison for the hr.employees table on the two databases by running the CREATE_COMPARISON procedure, as shown here:

```
SQL> begin
  2  dbms_comparison.create_comparison(
  3  comparison_name => 'compare1',
  4  schema_name     => 'hr',
  5  object_name     => 'employees',
  6  dblink_name     => 'tenner');
  7* end;
SQL> /

PL/SQL procedure successfully completed.
SQL>
```

4. Execute the COMPARE function to see whether the CREATE_COMPARISON procedure has found any differences between the two tables.

```
SQL> declare
  2  consistent boolean;
  3  scan_info dbms_comparison.comparison_type;
  4  begin
  5  consistent := dbms_comparison.compare(
  6  comparison_name => 'comp1',
  7  scan_info => scan_info,
  8  perform_row_dif => TRUE);
  9  DBMS_OUTPUT.PUT_LINE('Scan ID: '||scan_info.scan_id);
 10  IF consistent=TRUE THEN
 11  DBMS_OUTPUT.PUT_LINE('No differences were found.');
 12  ELSE
 13  DBMS_OUTPUT.PUT_LINE('Differences were found.');
 14  end if;
 15* end;
SQL> /
Scan ID: 4
Differences were found.

PL/SQL procedure successfully completed.

SQL>
```

The compare function uses the scan ID 4 and prints the statement "Differences were found."

5. Since there are differences, you can run the following query, which uses the views DBA_COMPARISON and DBA_COMPARISION_SCAN_SUMMARY to tell how many differences were found during the table comparison:

```
SQL> select c.owner,
  2  c.comparision_name,
  3  c.schema_name,
  4  c.object_name,
  5  s.current_diff_count
  6  from dba_comparison , dba_comparison_scan_summary s
  7  where c.comparison_name = s.comparison_name and
  8  c.owner = s.owner and
  9  s.scan_id  = 1;
```

OWNER	COMP_NAME	SCHEMA_NAME	OBJECT_NAME	CURRENT_DIF_COUNT
SYSTEM	COMP1	HR	EMPLOYEES	3

```
SQL>
```

The current_diff_count column from the DBA_COMPARISON_SCAN_SUMMARY shows that there are three rows that are different between the hr.employees table in the or11 database and the hr.employees table in the tenner database. The differences could be because a row is present in one but not the other database, or the row is present in both databases but with different data in the row.

Converging Data

Since we've discovered a data divergence between the local and the remote databases, we may want to synchronize the hr.employees table in the two databases so they have identical data. You do this by using the CONVERGE procedure of the DBMS_COMPARISON package, as shown here:

1. Connect to the remote database from the local database as the system owner, who happens to be the owner of the database link that we created earlier between the two databases:

```
$ sqlplus sytem/sammyy1@or11
SQL>
```

2. Execute the converge procedure of the DBMS_COMPARISON package to synchronize the data between the two databases:

```
SQL> declare
  2    scan_info    DBMS_COMPARISON.COMPARISON_TYPE;
  3  begin
  4    DBMS_COMPARISON.CONVERGE(
  5      comparison_name  => 'comp1',
  6      scan_id          => 4,
  7      scan_info        => scan_info,
  8      converge_options => DBMS_COMPARISON.CMP_CONVERGE_LOCAL_WINS);
  9    DBMS_OUTPUT.PUT_LINE('Local Rows Merged:
                             '||scan_info.loc_rows_merged);
 10    DBMS_OUTPUT.PUT_LINE('Remote Rows Merged:
                             '||scan_info.rmt_rows_merged);
 11    DBMS_OUTPUT.PUT_LINE('Local Rows Deleted:
                             '||scan_info.loc_rows_deleted);
 12    DBMS_OUTPUT.PUT_LINE('Remote Rows Deleted:
                             '||scan_info.rmt_rows_deleted);
 13* end;
SQL> /
Local Rows Merged: 0
Remote Rows Merged: 2
Local Rows Deleted: 0
Remote Rows Deleted: 1

PL/SQL procedure successfully completed.

SQL>
```

In this example, we chose to replace the data in the hr.employees table at the remote database with the data from the hr.employees table on the local database. That way, we use cmp_converge_local_wins as the converge option, meaning that the data from the local database trumps that in the remote database. However, we could also have chosen to do the reverse by specifying cmp_converge_remote_wins instead, which would have required that the remote database table's data replace the local database table's data.

The converge procedure may modify or delete data from one of the databases to synchronize the data in both databases. The output that is printed after the converge procedure finished its execution shows that two rows in the remote database were merged, because they were different from the rows in the local database. Merging here means the local table's rows replace the rows in the remote table. One row shows up under the Remote Rows Deleted column. This was a row that was found in the remote database, but not in the local database. Since we chose to make the remote database data conform to the local database data, the converge procedure deletes that row from the remote database. Assuming there were no further changes made during the data synchronization process, the two tables in the local and remote databases are now completely synchronized.

Note that you can also compare and converge different types of database objects at two databases. For example, you can compare and converge a table at one database and a materialized view on the other.

Copying Files with the Database Server

You can copy binary files directly by using the database server, bypassing the operating system. The DBMS_FILE_TRANSFER package allows you to copy binary files in the same server or transfer them between different Oracle databases.

Requirements for the File Copy

There are some conditions to using the DBMS_FILE_TRANSFER package to copy files:

- The source files must be of the same type as the destination files. That is, the files on the two systems should all be operating system files or all be ASM files.

- The files can't be larger than 2 terabytes, and each file's size has to be a multiple of 512 bytes.

- You can't perform a character set conversion while you copy the files.

- You must grant explicit privileges to all nonprivileged users of the database before they can use files transferred by the DBMS_FILE_TRANSFER package.

Copying Files on a Local System

You copy files between directories on the same server using the DBMS_FILE_TRANSFER package's COPY_FILE procedure. Suppose you wanted to copy a file named example.txt from the /u01/app/oracle directory to the /u01/app/oracle/dba directory. Here are the steps you would follow:

1. Create a source directory object that points to a source directory (source_dir):

   ```
   SQL> CREATE DIRECTORY source_dir AS '/u01/app/oracle';
   Directory created.
   ```

2. Create a destination directory object that points to the destination directory (dest_dir):

   ```
   SQL> CREATE DIRECTORY dest_dir AS '/u01/app/oracle/test';
   Directory created.
   SQL>
   ```

3. Use COPY_FILE to copy the example.txt file (DESTINATION_FILE_NAME) from the source directory to the destination directory (and you can rename the file during the copy process if you wish):

   ```
   SQL> BEGIN
       DBMS_FILE_TRANSFER.COPY_FILE(
       SOURCE_DIRECTORY_OBJECT       => 'source_dir',
       SOURCE_FILE_NAME              => 'example.txt',
       DESTINATION_DIRECTORY_OBJECT  => 'dest_dir',
       DESTINATION_FILE_NAME         => 'example.txt');
       END;
   SQL> /
   PL/SQL procedure successfully completed.
   SQL>
   ```

If you now check in the destination directory (/u01/app/oracle/test), you'll find a copy of the original file from the source directory (/u01/app/oracle).

■**Tip** You must have the READ privilege on the source directory and the WRITE privilege on the destination directory to execute the DBMS_FILE_TRANSFER.COPY_FILE procedure.

The new OEM Database Control Load Data Wizard automates the process of creating SQL*Loader control files. You specify the datafiles and provide information about their structure, and the Load Data Wizard uses this information to automatically generate a SQL*Loader control file, as well as create the SQL*Loader job for loading the datafile into the database.

Transferring a File to a Different Database

The DBMS_FILE_TRANSFER package can send copies of files on a server to a remote server using the PUT_FILE procedure. You follow the same steps as in the previous section, but you use an additional parameter, DESTINATION_DATABASE, to point to the remote server:

```
SQL> BEGIN
    DBMS_FILE_TRANSFER.PUT_FILE(
    SOURCE_DIRECTORY_OBJECT      => 'source_dir',
    SOURCE_FILE_NAME             => 'example.txt',
    DESTINATION_DIRECTORY_OBJECT => 'dest_dir',
    DESTINATION_FILE_NAME        => 'e.txt',
    DESTINATION_DATABASE         => 'finance');
    END;
SQL> /
PL/SQL procedure successfully completed.
SQL>
```

■**Tip** You must first ensure that a database link exists between the local and the remote server before using the PUT_FILE procedure to send files to the remote server.

The PUT_FILE procedure first reads the specified file on the local server. It then creates a copy of that file on the remote server you specify in the DESTINATION_DATABASE parameter. Thus, the source directory is on the local server, and the destination directory will be located on the remote server.

The GET_FILE procedure is analogous to the PUT_FILE procedure, and it enables you to copy files on remote servers to your local server. In this procedure, the destination directory and the destination file are on the local server, and the source directory and the source file are on the remote server. Here's the structure of GET_FILE:

```
DBMS_FILE_TRANSFER.GET_FILE(
SOURCE_DIRECTORY_OBJECT       IN    VARCHAR2,
SOURCE_FILE_NAME              IN    VARCHAR2,
SOURCE_DATABASE               IN    VARCHAR2,
DESTINATION_DIRECTORY_OBJECT  IN    VARCHAR2,
DESTINATION_FILE_NAME         IN    VARCHAR2);
```

Mapping Oracle Files to Physical Devices

If your Oracle files are operating system files or if you're using a raw file system, it's no big deal to map datafiles to the devices that host them. If you aren't mapping UNIX mount points directly to physical disks, however, it's hard to tell where in the disk system a particular Oracle datafile is located. More commonly, organizations use Logical Volume Managers (LVMs) and RAID-based storage systems, and if you're interested in finding out where particular files are located in the storage system, you're normally out of luck.

You can use the V$DATAFILE and V$TABLESPACE dynamic views, along with some other views, to glean information about datafiles. When you're using host-based LVMs and RAID-based storage systems, you'll quickly find out that an I/O on a datafile can involve multiple storage devices that are part of a complex storage system. As a DBA, it's impossible for you to tell where your objects are located in the I/O stack.

However, you can come up with a physical mapping of all the datafiles in your database using the Oracle file-mapping feature. Oracle provides storage-mapping APIs, which are used by the storage vendors to provide corresponding mapping libraries that provide a complete mapping of the datafiles. Using the file-mapping feature, you can link datafiles to the logical devices and the physical drives. You can also map individual objects, including their file and the specific blocks on which they reside. This kind of detailed information helps you really understand and evaluate I/O performance.

Architecture of File Mapping

When you use the file-mapping feature, there will be an additional Oracle background process, FMON, that will run as part of your instance background processes. This FMON background process will run only if you set the FILE_MAPPING initialization parameter to TRUE in the init.ora file or SPFILE. You can also set this parameter dynamically by using the ALTER SYSTEM statement.

The FMON process starts an operating system process called FMPUTL, which communicates with mapping libraries that contain detailed information about where the files are located. Vendors of the storage systems provide mapping libraries, although Oracle provides the mapping library for storage systems made by EMC, a leading storage vendor. The FMPUTL process supplies FMON with the mapping information for various levels of the I/O stack, and FMON stores this information in the Oracle data dictionary.

Oracle uses *mapping structures* to map datafiles to their physical counterparts. At the foundation of the mapping structure are components that Oracle calls *elements*, which can be RAID 0, RAID 1, or RAID 5 disks or just whole disks. The FMON process gathers information about files and their elements through the FMPUTL process, and it saves this information in the SGA and some data dictionary views. Whenever you add, drop, or change the size of a datafile, FMON changes the information in the SGA and in the related V$ tables.

Setting Up File Mapping

Now let's look at the steps that are necessary to set up file mapping in your database.

Providing the Mapping Library

You must first have a mapping library from your storage system vendor, if it is not EMC (EMC's mapping library is supplied by Oracle). Then you should edit the filemap.ora file, which is located in the $ORACLE_HOME/rdbms/filemap/etc directory, to make it specific to your system. The mapping library path and the vendor name should be added to the filemap.ora file using a line like the following:

```
lib:vendor_name:mapping_library_path
```

For example, you might use the following line for a VERITAS mapping library:

```
Lib=VERITAS:/opt/VRTSdbed/lib/libvxoramap_32.so
```

Once you edit the `filemap.ora` file, either restart the database (if you are using the `init.ora` file instead of the `SPFILE`), or use the `ALTER SYSTEM` command to set the `FILE_MAPPING` initialization parameter to `TRUE`.

```
SQL> ALTER SYSTEM SET FILE_MAPPING=TRUE;
```

Starting the File Mapping

When you set the `FILE_MAPPING` initialization parameter to `TRUE`, Oracle doesn't automatically start mapping the files. You do this by invoking the DBMS_STORAGE_MAP package, which, by communicating with the Oracle FMON background process, invokes mapping operations that populate mapping views. If you invoke the MAP_ALL procedure in this package, mapping information about all the datafiles in your database will be collected.

Three dynamic performance tables, VMAP_FILE, VMAP_ELEMENT, and V$MAP_FILE_IO_STACK, can then be joined to see the mapping between Oracle datafiles and physical elements in the storage system. You can see the storage hierarchy all the way from an individual table down to a disk in any storage system.

Using the Oracle Scheduler

Oracle Database 11*g* offers the new built-in Scheduler feature that helps you automate jobs from within the Oracle database. The DBMS_SCHEDULER package contains various functions and procedures that help manage the Scheduler, although you can also schedule jobs very easily through the Database Control interface as well. The most important architectural feature of the Scheduler is its modular approach to managing tasks, which enables the reuse of similar jobs.

You can also use the Scheduler along with the Database Resource Manager to fine-tune the allocation of resources among various jobs. The Scheduler is not only a job-specification tool; it also helps you control resource usage and prioritize jobs within the database.

One of the limitations of the DBMS_JOB package is that it can only schedule PL/SQL-based jobs, and you can't use it to schedule operating system scripts or an executable. To run these non-database-type jobs, you must use the crontab in UNIX or the AT facility in Windows servers, or a third-party tool. The Oracle Scheduler lets you use PL/SQL scripts, operating system shell scripts, Java programs, and native binary executables to perform scheduled jobs.

Basic Scheduler Components

The Scheduler consists of five basic components—jobs, schedules, programs, events, and chains. Jobs are pretty similar to the jobs used in the DBMS_JOB package, but schedules, programs, events, and chains are new concepts, leading to a modular approach to the management of tasks. A program, for example, enables several users to perform similar tasks.

Let's examine the basic Scheduler components in more detail.

Jobs

A *job* is a task that you schedule to run one or more times A job contains a specification of what is to be executed, and when it should be executed. A Scheduler job can execute a PL/SQL block of code, a native binary executable, a Java application, or a shell script. You can create a new job by specifying the job details such as the actions that the job performs and time and frequency of the execution, just as you can with the traditional DBMS_JOB package. In the Scheduler, you can abstract all the job execution and timing details by using the *program* and *schedule* modules.

Schedules

A *schedule* is a specification of when and how frequently the database executes a job. You can use the same schedule for several jobs. You can also have schedules that specify job execution when a specific event occurs in the database.

Programs

A *program* contains metadata about a Scheduler job. A program includes the program name, the program type (PL/SQL code or a UNIX shell script, for example), and the program action, which is the actual name of a procedure or executable script, for example. Several jobs can use the same program. Note that a job can specify what the job is executing directly in the job definition, or it can use a preexisting program for that purpose.

Events

The Scheduler uses the Oracle Streams Advanced Queuing feature to raise *events* and start database jobs based on the events. An event is a message sent by an application or process when it notices some action or occurrence.

There are two types of events—Scheduler-raised events and application-raised events. Scheduler-raised events are caused by changes in the functioning of the Scheduler, so the successful completion of a job by the Scheduler may be an event. Application-raised events are "consumed" or used by the Scheduler to start a job. In fact, you have the option of using just an event instead of a schedule as the means of starting a job. You can also base a schedule on an event, in which case the schedule is known as an *event schedule*.

Chains

You can use the concept of a Scheduler *chain* to link related programs together. Thus, the running of a specific program could be made contingent on the successful running of certain other programs. You can also start a job based on a chain rather than on a single scheduler program. When you have interrelated jobs, a chain makes it easy to run all the programs necessary to complete the entire transaction.

Types of Scheduler Jobs

The Scheduler offers you a choice of the following types of jobs: database jobs, chain jobs, external jobs, detached jobs, and lightweight jobs. Let's take a closer look at these job types.

Database Jobs

Database jobs are the most common Scheduler jobs, and I refer to them as just jobs in this chapter. A database job runs program units such as a PL/SQL anonymous block or a stored procedure, in addition to Java stored procedures. You must set the JOB_TYPE attribute to PLSQL_BLOCK or STORED_PROCEDURE. You must specify the anonymous block or the stored procedure name as a value for the JOB_ACTION attribute.

Chain Jobs

Chain jobs enable you to use dependency-based scheduling. A chain defines a set of programs and their dependencies. Your job can point to a chain, thus setting off a set of jobs.

External Jobs

You use external jobs to run operating system executables outside the database. You specify the JOB_TYPE as EXECUTABLE for external jobs.

Detached Jobs

You use a detached job to run a script or application as an independent process. The program for a detached job has the DETACHED attribute set to TRUE.

Lightweight Jobs

Lightweight jobs are different from regular Scheduler jobs in that they depend on a template to derive their privileges and the job metadata. Lightweight jobs involve less overhead and are quick to create and drop, thus making them ideal when you have a large number of short jobs to run.

Unless otherwise specified, when I refer to a database job (regular jobs), I mean the regular Scheduler job and not a specialized type of job such as an external or lightweight job. I explain the various types of Scheduler jobs in more detail in this chapter.

Advanced Scheduler Components

In addition to the five basic Scheduler components—jobs, schedules, programs, chains, and events—the Scheduler also uses several advanced concepts: job classes, windows, and window groups. These advanced features set apart the Scheduler from its predecessor, the DBMS_JOB package. It's these advanced concepts that enable the prioritizing of jobs in the database and the allocation of resources in accordance with the organization's priorities. Let's look at the advanced Scheduler components briefly.

Job Classes

A *job class* groups a set of jobs that share common characteristics, such as resource requirements. Job classes enable you to allocate resources among jobs by grouping similar types of jobs together. You use job classes to do a couple of things:

- Assign job priority levels for individual jobs, with a higher-priority job always starting before a lower-priority job.
- Specify common attributes for a set of jobs.

You use the Database Resource Manager in coordination with the Scheduler to allocate scarce resources in your database. In the Database Resource Manager, the concept of a resource consumer group lets you group users according to their resource usage. Oracle controls resource allocation by assigning each job class to a specific resource consumer group. By default, a job class is assigned to the default consumer group.

Windows

Scheduler *windows* offer a link to the Oracle Resource Manager. A window represents an interval of time during which you can schedule jobs, and the purpose of using windows is to change resource allocation during specific time periods. Each window is associated with a specific resource plan, which you create through the Database Resource Manager. Using windows, you can activate different resource plans during different time periods, thus providing differential prioritizing for jobs.

Window Groups

A *window group* is a collection of similar windows. For example, you can create a window for your weekends and a window for your holidays, and group both these windows into a single maintenance window group.

Scheduler Architecture

The Scheduler architecture consists of the job table, job coordinator, and the job workers (or *slaves*, as Oracle calls them).

The *job table* contains information about jobs, such as the job name, program name, and job owner. You can examine the job table by using the DBA_SCHEDULER_JOBS view. The *job coordinator* regularly looks in the job table to find out what jobs to execute. The job coordinator creates and manages the *job worker* processes, which actually execute the job.

When you create a new job or execute a job, a background process (cjq*nnn*) wakes up and coordinates the running of the job. When the job coordinator tells a job worker to execute a job, the worker process starts a new database session and starts a transaction. It executes the job, and once completed, it commits and ends the transaction and terminates the database session. The job worker updates the job table, the run count, and the job log table.

Scheduler Privileges

Oracle creates all jobs, programs, and schedules in the schema of the user that creates these objects, but it creates all the advanced Scheduler components, like job classes, windows, and window groups, at the database level, and their owner is the SYS schema.

The SCHEDULER_ADMIN role contains all Scheduler system privileges, with the WITH ADMIN OPTION clause. The DBA role contains the SCHEDULER_ADMIN role.

The MANAGE SCHEDULER system privilege lets you do the following:

- Create, drop, and alter job classes, windows, and window groups.

- Stop any job.

- Start and stop windows prematurely.

■**Note** All Scheduler objects are of the form [*schema*.]*name*. By default, all scheduler object names are in uppercase, unless you wrap the lowercase names in double quotes, as in "test_job".

You must have the CREATE JOB privilege to create Scheduler components (jobs, schedules, programs, chains, and events). To use the advanced Scheduler components (windows, window groups, and job classes), you need the MANAGE SCHEDULER system privilege.

You can assign other users the right to use one of your components by giving them EXECUTE privileges on that component:

- The EXECUTE ANY PROGRAM privilege lets a user execute any program under any schema.

- The EXECUTE ANY CLASS privilege lets you assign a job to any job class.

In order for users to modify Scheduler components, they must use the GRANT ALTER SQL statement for each Scheduler component.

Note To be able to create a job in a job class you generate, you must have a separate EXECUTE privilege on that job class.

Note the following basic points regarding Scheduler privileges:

- To create a job, you must have the CREATE JOB privilege.
- You don't need any special privileges to specify a schedule, a window or window group, or a program that you own.
- If you specify a program owned by a different user, you must have the EXECUTE privilege on that program, or the EXECUTE ANY PROGRAM system privilege.

Managing the Basic Scheduler Components

The basic Scheduler components—jobs, programs, schedules, chains, and events—have several common manageability features. You create, alter, and drop all the components with the same procedure from the DBMS_SCHEDULER package. The following sections describe how to manage these components.

Managing Jobs

Creating and managing jobs is at the heart of the Scheduler feature. You can create and run jobs independently, or you can create a job using schedules and programs. Using saved programs and schedules saves you having to redefine a program or schedule each time you create a new job.

Creating Jobs

You create a Scheduler job using the CREATE_JOB procedure of the DBMS_SCHEDULER package. Listing 18-17 shows a simple example of how to create a basic Scheduler job, without using a program or schedule. This is the most straightforward way to specify a job, with all pertinent information being specified in the job-creation statement itself, without using programs and schedules.

Listing 18-17. *Creating a Basic Scheduler Job Without a Program or Schedule*

```
SQL> BEGIN
  2  DBMS_SCHEDULER.CREATE_JOB(
  3  JOB_NAME            => 'test_job',
  4  JOB_TYPE            => 'PLSQL_BLOCK',
  5  JOB_ACTION          => 'insert into persons select * from new_persons;',
  6  START_DATE          => '28-JUNE-08 07.00.00 PM ',
  7  REPEAT_INTERVAL     => 'FREQ=DAILY; INTERVAL=2',
  8  END_DATE            => '20-NOV-08 07.00.00 PM ',
  9  COMMENTS            => 'Insert new customers into the persons table',
 10  ENABLED             => TRUE,
 11* END;
/
PL/SQL procedure successfully completed.
SQL>
```

> **Note** You'll be the owner of a job if you create it in your own schema. However, if you create it in another schema, that schema owner will be the owner of the job. Thus, the fact that you create a job doesn't mean that you are necessarily its owner.

Let's look at the parameters of the CREATE_JOB procedure:

- JOB_NAME: Provides a way to specify a name for your job.
- JOB_TYPE: Specifies the type of job that you're creating. Jobs can include a PL/SQL block, a stored procedure, an executable, or a Java program.
- JOB_ACTION: Specifies the exact procedure, command, or script that the job will execute.
- START_DATE and END_DATE: Specifies the date that a new job should start and end. (If a job is ongoing, it may not have an END_DATE parameter.)
- REPEAT_INTERVAL: Specifies how often a job should be executed by the Scheduler. In Listing 18-17, the repeat interval is 'FREQ=DAILY; INTERVAL=2', which means that you run the job every other day. There are two ways to specify a repeat interval (both of which are discussed in the next section):
  - Use a database calendaring expression.
  - Use a PL/SQL date/time expression.
- COMMENTS: Allows you to include any comments about the scheduled job.
- ENABLED: Specifies whether the job is enabled or not when it is created. The default value is FALSE, meaning it is not enabled; to enable the job immediately, set this to TRUE.

Setting the Repeat Interval

Let's look at the two ways of specifying a repeat interval. A *calendaring expression* is a straightforward, English-like expression consisting of the following three components:

- *Frequency*: This is a mandatory component of a calendaring expression, identified by the keyword FREQ. Possible values are YEARLY, MONTHLY, WEEKLY, DAILY, HOURLY, MINUTELY, and SECONDLY.
- *Repeat interval*: This interval is identified by the INTERVAL keyword, and it specifies how often the database must repeat the job.
- *Specifiers*: These provide detailed information about when a job should be run; the possible values are BYMONTH, BYWEEKNO, BYYEARDAY, BYMONTHDAY, BYDAY, BYHOUR, BYMINUTE, and BYSECOND. For example, BYMONTHDAY specifies the day of the month when a job should be run, and BYDAY specifies the day of the week.

Note that specifiers are optional, but the repeat interval and frequency components of a calendaring expression are mandatory. Here are some typical calendaring expressions:

- FREQ=DAILY; INTERVAL=3: Executes a job every three days
- FREQ=HOURLY; INTERVAL=2: Executes a job every other hour
- FREQ=WEEKLY; BYDAY=MON: Executes a job every Monday
- FREQ=WEEKLY; INTERVAL=2; BYDAY=FRI: Executes a job every other Friday
- FREQ=MONTHLY; BYMONTHDAY=1: Executes a job on the last day of the month

You can also create more complex repeat intervals using *PL/SQL expressions*, with the proviso that all such expressions must evaluate to a date or a timestamp data type. When you use a date/time expression for specifying the repeat interval, you end up with a date/time data type as the value of the interval, as shown here:

```
repeat_interval  =>  'FREQ=MINUTELY INTERVAL=30'
```

The preceding PL/SQL expression states that Oracle will execute the job every half hour.

Administering Jobs

You use the DBMS_SCHEDULER package to perform job-related administrative tasks.

You can enable, and thus activate, a job as follows:

```
SQL> EXEC DBMS_SCHEDULER.ENABLE('TEST_JOB1');
PL/SQL procedure successfully completed.
```

You disable a job this way:

```
SQL> EXEC DBMS_SCHEDULER.DISABLE('TEST_JOB1');
PL/SQL procedure successfully completed.
```

You drop a job by using the DROP_JOB procedure, as shown here:

```
SQL> BEGIN
    DBMS_SCHEDULER.DROP_JOB( JOB_NAME => 'TEST_JOB1');
    END;
```

You can run a job manually (at other than the regularly scheduled times) using the RUN_JOB procedure, as shown here:

```
SQL> EXEC DBMS_SCHEDULER.RUN_JOB('TEST_JOB');
```

Finally, you can stop a job immediately using the STOP_JOB procedure, as shown here:

```
SQL> EXEC DBMS_SCHEDULER.STOP_JOB('TEST_JOB');
```

■**Tip** In both the STOP_JOB and RUN_JOB procedures, you can use the FORCE attribute, which will determine whether an active job can be stopped or dropped. By setting FORCE=TRUE, you can stop or drop a running job. The default for the FORCE attribute is FALSE.

Managing Lightweight Jobs

When you need to use the Scheduler to execute a short running job frequently, you can use lightweight jobs instead of the default database jobs, to gain performance benefits. Lightweight jobs aren't free-standing jobs. Since lightweight jobs aren't really schema objects, you incur far less overhead in creating and dropping them. You can also create lightweight jobs quicker than regular jobs; the lightweight jobs also take up less space for storing their metadata and runtime data. Thus, you gain in both time and space available when you use lightweight jobs for jobs that you run thousands of times in the database. Regular jobs do offer more flexibility and more job execution choices, and therefore, if you're going to execute a job only infrequently, you should use a regular job instead of a lightweight job.

You must use a job template when creating a lightweight job, with the template containing the metadata for the lightweight job as well as the privileges to be inherited by the lightweight job. You can use a stored procedure or a Scheduler program as a job template. You must reference a Scheduler program in order to specify a job action. The program type must be a PLSQL_BLOCK or STORED_ PROCEDURE. If a user has privileges on the program, that user will automatically have privileges on the lightweight job.

You can use the following query to find out the details about lightweight jobs in your database:

```
SQL> SELECT job_name, program_name FROM dba_scheduler_jobs
     WHERE job_style='LIGHTWEIGHT';

JOB_NAME                PROGRAM_NAME
-----------             -------------


TEST_JOB1               TEST_PROG1
```

Unlike the regular database jobs, lightweight jobs aren't shown in the DBA_SCHEDULER_JOBS view, since lightweight jobs aren't schema objects like regular jobs.

You create a lightweight job in a manner similar to how you create a regular job, by executing the CREATE_JOB procedure. Just specify the value LIGHTWEIGHT for the JOB_STYLE parameter, instead of REGULAR, the default value for this parameter. Here's an example showing how to create a light-weight job:

```
begin
dbms_scheduler.create_job (
job_name          => 'test_ltwtjob1',
program_name      => 'test_prog',
repeat_interval   => 'freq=daily,by_hour=10',
end_time          => '31-DEC-08 06:00:00 AM Australia/Sydney',
job_style_        => 'lightweight',
comments          => 'A lightweight job based on a program');
end;
```

In this example, the program test_prog serves as the template for the lightweight job TEST_ LTWTJOB1. You can also specify a schedule instead of the REPEAT_INTERVAL and the END_TIME attributes

You can use a job array to create a set of Scheduler lightweight jobs. The job array comes in handy when you have to create a large number of Scheduler jobs. The following example shows how to create a set of lightweight jobs using a job array:

1. Create two variables, one to define the Scheduler job and the other for the job array definition.

   ```
   declare
   testjob sys.job;
   testjobarr sys.job_array;
   ```

2. Use the sys.job_array constructor to initialize the job array.

   ```
   begin
   testjobarr := sys.job_array();
   ```

   When you initialize the job array testjobarr, which is an array of JOB object types, the database creates a slot for a single job in that array.

3. You must set the size of the job array to the number of jobs you expect to create.

```
testjobarr.extend(500);
```

The statement shown here allocates space in the job array to hold information for 500 jobs.

4. The following code creates the 500 jobs and places them in the job array:

```
for I in 1 . . . 500 loop
testjob := sys.job(job_name => 'TESTJOB'||TO_CHAR(I),
job_style    => 'LIGHTWEIGHT',
job_template => 'TEST_PROG',
enabled      => TRUE);
testjobarr(i) := TESTJOB;
end loop;
```

The code shown here creates all 500 jobs using the TEST_PROG template. The jobs are added to the job array by the assignment operator `testjobarr(i)`.

5. Use the CREATE_JOBS procedure to submit the array consisting of 500 jobs.

```
dbms_scheduler.create_jobs (testjobarr, 'transactional');
```

The CREATE_JOBS procedure creates all 500 jobs at once. In this example, I chose to create lightweight jobs as part of the array, by specifying LIGHTWEIGHT as the value for the JOB_STYLE parameter when I created the job array. By not specifying the JOB_STYLE parameter, I can create a job array of regular database jobs instead of lightweight jobs. This is so, because the default value of the JOB_STYLE parameter is REGULAR.

Managing External Jobs

External jobs are operating system executables that you run outside the database. You specify EXECUTABLE as the value for the JOB_TYPE parameter for an external job. If you use a named program for an external job, you must specify the complete directory path, for example, /usr/local/bin/perl, where you stored the executable, either in the JOB_ACTION attribute or the PROGRAM_ACTION attribute.

You can create local external jobs and remote external jobs. A *local external job* runs on the same server as the job-originating database, and a *remote external job* runs on a remote host. You can use remote external jobs to manage jobs across your entire network from a single database. The interesting thing about remote external jobs is that you don't need to have an Oracle database instance running on the remote hosts. You'll just need to install a Scheduler Agent on each of the remote hosts where you wish to run external jobs, to accept job requests from the job-originating database, execute them on the remote host, and transmit the job results to the job-originating database.

Running local external jobs is straightforward. All you need to do is to specify EXECUTABLE as the value for the JOB_TYPE or PROGRAM_TYPE arguments. To run remote external jobs, you'll need to install and configure the Scheduler Agent as well as assign credentials for executing the remote jobs. I explain the steps involved in setting up remote external jobs in the following sections.

Setting Up the Database

You must set up the database from where you want to issue external job requests by doing the following:

1. Since you'll need the Oracle XML DB to run a remote external job, first check whether the Oracle XML DB option has been successfully installed in your database by issue the following `DESCRIBE` command:

```
SQL> desc resource_view
```

```
Name                 Null?    Type
-----------------    -----    ----------------------------
RES
XMLTYPE                       (XMLSchema "http://xm
                             lns.oracle.com/xdb/XDBResour
                             ce.xsd" Element "Resource")
ANY_PATH                      VARCHAR2(4000)
RESID                         RAW(16)
```

```
SQL>
```

The `DESCRIBE` command shows that the Oracle XML DB option is correctly installed. If the query shows that Oracle XML DB isn't an option, you must install it before you can proceed.

2. Execute the Oracle-provided `prvtsch.plb` script, located in the `$ORACLE_HOME/rdbms/admin` directory.

```
SQL> connect sys/sammyy1 as sysdba
SQL> @$ORACLE_HOME/rdbms/admin/prvtrsch.plb
PL/SQL procedure successfully completed.
. . .
PL/SQL procedure successfully completed.
no rows selected
Package created.
Package body created.
No errors.
. . .
User altered.
```

```
SQL>
```

3. Finally, set a registration password for the Scheduler Agent.

```
SQL> EXEC dbms_scheduler.set_agent_registration_pass(
registration_password => 'sammyy1'.-
expiration_date        => systimestamp + interval '7' day,-
max_uses               => 25)
```

```
PL/SQL procedure successfully completed.
```

```
SQL>
```

The Scheduler Agent uses the password to register with the database. The `EXPIRATION_DATE` and the `MAX_USES` parameters show the date when the password expires and the number of times the password can be used, respectively.

Installing and Configuring the Scheduler Agent

You must install the Scheduler Agent on every remote host where you plan on running external jobs. You can either download the software for installation from Oracle or use the Database CD pack. In either case, you'll need to use the installation media for the Oracle Database Gateway. Here are the steps to install the Scheduler Agent:

1. Log in as the Oracle software owner (usually the user Oracle).

2. Go to where the Oracle Database Gateway installation files are stored and issue the following command to start up the Oracle Universal Installer:

   ```
   $ /oracle11g/gateways/runInstaller
   ```

3. On the Welcome screen, click Next.

4. On the Select a Product page, select Oracle Scheduler Agent 11.1.0.6.0, and click Next.

5. On the Specify Home Details page, select a name and provide the directory path for the Oracle Scheduler Agent home. Click Next.

6. On the Oracle Scheduler Agent page, provide the host name and the port number the agent must use to communicate with the external job request originating database. Click Next.

7. On the Summary page, review the selections you made and click Install.

■**Note** You can also use a silent install to automate the installation of the Scheduler Agent on a larger number of hosts.

---

8. When the installer prompts you to run the root.sh script as the root user, do so and click OK.

9. Click Exit after you see the End of Installation page.

You need to use the schagent executable to invoke the Scheduler Agent. But first, you must register the agent with the database from where you want run an external job on the host where you installed the Scheduler Agent. Here's how you register the Scheduler Agent with a database:

```
$ schagent –registerdatabase prod1  1522
```

In the example, the database host is named prod1, and the port number assigned to the Scheduler Agent is 1522. Once you issue this command, you'll be prompted to supply the agent registration password you created earlier:

```
$./schagent -registerdatabase localhost.localdomain 1522
Agent Registration Password ?  ******
$
```

You start the Scheduler Agent by issuing the following command:

```
$./schagent –start
Scheduler agent started
$
```

Stop the agent by issuing the following command:

```
$./schagent –stop
Scheduler agent stopped
$
```

The preceding examples show how to work with the Scheduler Agent on a UNIX/Linux system. You must install the OracleSchedulerExecutionAgent service before you can use the agent. You can install the service in the following way:

```
$ schagent -installagentservice
```

The OracleSchedulerExecutionAgent service is different from the Oracle service that you use to start and stop an Oracle instance on a Windows server.

Creating and Enabling Remote External Jobs

Since an external job must execute as an operating system user's job, the Scheduler lets you assign operating system credentials to an external job. You use a credential, which is a schema object that contains a username and password combination, to designate the credentials for an external job. Use the CREDENTIAL_NAME attribute when you create an external job to specify the credentials for executing that job.

You aren't required to specify credentials for a local external job, although Oracle recommends that you do so. Before you can create a remote external job, you must first create a credential. You can then assign that credential object to the user under whose account the remote external executable will be run. Note that a user must have the execute privilege on a credential object before the user can use that credential to execute a job.

Here are the steps you must follow to create a remote external job:

1. First, execute the CREATE_CREDENTIAL procedure to create a credential object.

   ```
   SQL> exec dbms_scheduler.create_credential('hrcredential,
        'hr','sammyy1');
   ```

2. Grant privileges on the newly created credential to the user who'll need to use the credential.

   ```
   SQL> grant execute on system.hrcrdential to sam;
   ```

   You can query the DBA_SCHEDULER_VIEW to examine all credentials in the database.

3. Create a remote external job by executing the CREATE_JOB procedure.

   ```
   SQL> begin
     2  dbms_scheduler.create_job(
     3  job_name => 'remove_logs',
     4  job_type => 'executable',
     5  job_action => '/u01/app/oracle/logs/removelogs',
     6  repeat_interval => 'freq=daily; byhour=23',
     7  enabled => false);
     8* end;
   SQL> /

   PL/SQL procedure successfully completed.
   SQL>
   ```

4. Once you create the remote external job REMOVE_LOGS, set the CREDENTIAL_NAME attribute of the remote job by executing the SET_ATTRIBUTE procedure.

   ```
   SQL> exec dbms_scheduler.set_attribute('remove_logs',
        'credential_name','hrcredential');

   PL/SQL procedure successfully completed.

   SQL>
   ```

5. Execute the SET_ATTRIBUTE procedure again, this time to set the DESTINATION attribute.

```
SQL> exec dbms_scheduler.set_attribute('remove_logs',

    'destination', 'localhost.localdomain:1521');

PL/SQL procedure successfully completed.

SQL>
```

6. Execute the ENABLE procedure to enable the external job.

```
SQL> exec dbms_scheduler.enable('remove_logs');

PL/SQL procedure successfully completed.
SQL>
```

You can disable the capability to run external jobs in a database by dropping the user remote_scheduler_agent, who is created by the prvtsch.plb script that you ran earlier.

```
SQL> drop user remote_scheduler_agent cascade;
```

You must reexecute the prvtrch.plb script for the database to run a remote external job, once you drop the remote_scheduler_agent.

Managing Programs

A program contains metadata about what the Scheduler will run, including the name and type of the program, and what a job will execute. Different jobs can share a single program.

Creating a Program

You create a new program using the CREATE_PROGRAM procedure of the DBMS_SCHEDULER package, as shown here:

```
SQL> BEGIN
  2  DBMS_SCHEDULER.CREATE_PROGRAM(
  3  PROGRAM_NAME   => 'MY_PROGRAM',
  4  PROGRAM_ACTION => 'UPDATE_SCHEMA_STATS',
  5  PROGRAM_TYPE   => 'STORED_PROCEDURE',
  6  enabled        => TRUE);
  7* end;
 SQL> /
PL/SQL procedure successfully completed.
SQL>
```

Once you create a program, you can simplify your job creation statement by replacing the JOB_TYPE and JOB_ACTION attributes with the name of the program that already contains the specification of these attributes. The PROGRAM_TYPE and PROGRAM_ACTION attributes thus replace the job attributes that you normally provide when creating a new job. You can see why this type of modular approach is beneficial—different jobs can use the same program, thus simplifying the creation of new jobs.

The following example re-creates the TEST_JOB job that was created in Listing 18-17, but using the program component this time:

```
SQL> BEGIN
  2  DBMS_SCHEDULER.CREATE_JOB(
  3  JOB_NAME          => 'TEST_JOB',
  4  PROGRAM_NAME      => 'TEST_PROGRAM',
  5  REPEAT_INTERVALl  => 'FREQ=DAILY;BYHOUR=12',ENABLED => TRUE);
  7* END;
SQL> /
PL/SQL procedure successfully completed.
SQL>
```

In the preceding example, using a program lets you avoid specifying the JOB_TYPE and JOB_ACTION parameters in the CREATE_JOB statement.

Administering Programs

You can enable, disable, and drop Scheduler programs using various procedures from the DBMS_SCHEDULER package, as shown in the following examples.

The ENABLE procedure is used to enable a Scheduler program:

```
SQL> EXEC DBMS_SCHEDULER.ENABLE('TEST_PROGRAM');
PL/SQL procedure successfully completed.
```

You use the DISABLE procedure to disable a program:

```
SQL> EXEC DBMS_SCHEDULER.DISABLE('TEST_PROGRAM');
PL/SQL procedure successfully completed.
SQL>
```

The DROP_PROGRAM procedure is used to drop a program:

```
SQL> EXEC DBMS_SCHEDULER.DROP_PROGRAM('TEST_PROGRAM');
PL/SQL procedure successfully completed.
SQL>
```

Managing Schedules

Let's say you have a number of jobs, all of which execute at the same time. By using a common schedule, you can simplify the creation and managing of such jobs. The following sections explain how you can manage schedules.

Creating a Schedule

You use the CREATE_SCHEDULE procedure of the DBMS_SCHEDULER package to create a schedule, as shown here:

```
SQL> BEGIN
  2  DBMS_SCHEDULER.CREATE_SCHEDULE(
  3  SCHEDULE_NAME    => 'TEST_SCHEDULE',
  4  START_DATE       => SYSTIMESTAMP,
  5  END_DATE         => SYSTIMESTAMP + 90,
  6  REPEAT_INTERVAL  => 'FREQ=HOURLY;INTERVAL= 4',
  7  COMMENTS         => 'Every 4 hours');
  8* END;
SQL> /
PL/SQL procedure successfully completed
SQL>
```

The TEST_SCHEDULE schedule states that a job with this schedule will be executed immediately and then be reexecuted every 4 hours, for a period of 90 days. Note the following things about this new schedule:

- The CREATE_SCHEDULE procedure has three important parameters: START_DATE, END_DATE, and REPEAT_INTERVAL.

- You specify the start and end times using the TIMESTAMP WITH TIME ZONE data type.

- You *must* use a calendaring expression when creating the repeat interval.

Once you create the TEST_SCHEDULE schedule, you can simplify the job creation process even further by using both a program and a schedule when creating a new job, as shown here:

```
SQL> BEGIN
  2  DBMS_SCHEDULER.CREATE_JOB(
  3  JOB_NAME       => 'MY_JOB',
  4  PROGRAM_NAME   => 'MY_PROGRAM',
  5  SCHEDULE_NAME  => 'MY_SCHEDULE');
  6  END;
  7  /
PL/SQL procedure successfully completed.
SQL>
```

As you can see, using saved schedules and programs makes creating new jobs a breeze.

Administering Schedules

You can alter various attributes of a schedule by using the SET_ATTRIBUTE procedure of the DBMS_SCHEDULER package. You can alter all attributes except the name of the schedule itself.

You can drop a schedule by using the DROP_SCHEDULE procedure, as shown here:

```
SQL> BEGIN
  2  DBMS_SCHEDULER.DROP_SCHEDULE (SCHEDULE_NAME => 'TEST_SCHEDULE');
  3  END;
  4  /
PL/SQL procedure successfully completed.
SQL>
```

If a job or window is using the schedule you want to drop, your attempt to drop the schedule will result in an error instead, by default. You can force the database to drop the schedule anyway, by using an additional FORCE parameter in the preceding example and setting it to TRUE.

▪**Tip** When you create a schedule, Oracle provides access to PUBLIC, thus letting all users use your schedule by default.

Managing Chains

A Scheduler chain consists of a set of related programs that run in a specified sequence. The successive positions in the chain are referred to as "steps" in the chain, and each step can point to another chain, a program, or an event. The chain includes the "rules" that determine what is to be done at each step of the chain.

We'll create a simple Scheduler chain by first creating a Scheduler chain object, and then the chain steps and the chain rules.

Creating a Chain

Since Scheduler chains use Oracle Streams Rules Engine objects, a user must have both the CREATE JOB privilege and the Rules Engine privileges to create a chain. You can grant all the necessary Rules Engine privileges by using a statement like this, which grants the privileges to the user nina:

```
SQL> BEGIN
    DBMS_RULE_ADM.GRANT_SYSTEM_PRIVILEGE(DBMS_RULE_ADM.CREATE_RULE_OBJ, 'nina'),
    DBMS_RULE_ADM.GRANT_SYSTEM_PRIVILEGE (
    DBMS_RULE_ADM.CREATE_RULE_SET_OBJ, 'nina'),
    DBMS_RULE_ADM.GRANT_SYSTEM_PRIVILEGE (
    DBMS_RULE_ADM.CREATE_EVALUATION_CONTEXT_OBJ, 'nina')
    END;
```

Now that you have the necessary privileges, let's create a Scheduler chain called TEST_CHAIN using the CREATE_CHAIN procedure:

```
SQL> BEGIN
    DBMS_SCHEDULER.CREATE_CHAIN (
    chain_name              =>    'test_chain',
    rule_set_name           =>    NULL,
    evaluation_interval     =>    NULL,
    comments                =>    NULL);
    END;
```

Next, define the steps for the new chain using the DEFINE_CHAIN_STEP procedure. Note that a chain step can point to a program, an event, or another chain:

```
SQL> BEGIN
    DBMS_SCHEDULER.DEFINE_CHAIN_STEP('test_chain', 'step1', 'program1');
    DBMS_SCHEDULER.DEFINE_CHAIN_STEP('test_chain', 'step2', 'program2');
    DBMS_SCHEDULER.DEFINE_CHAIN_STEP('test_chain', 'step3', 'program3');
    END;
```

Finally, to make the chain operative, you must add rules to the chain using the DEFINE_CHAIN_RULE procedure. Chain rules determine when a step is run and specify the conditions under which a step is run. Usually, a rule specifies that a step be run based on the fulfillment of a specific condition. Here's an example:

```
SQL> BEGIN
    DBMS_SCHEDULER.DEFINE_CHAIN_RULE('test_chain', 'TRUE', 'START step1');
    DBMS_SCHEDULER.DEFINE_CHAIN_RULE('test_chain', 'step1 COMPLETED',
    'Start step2, step3');
    DBMS_SCHEDULER.DEFINE_CHAIN_RULE('test_chain',
    'step2 COMPLETED AND step3 COMPLETED', 'END');
    END;
```

The first rule in the preceding example specifies that step1 be run, which means that the Scheduler will start program1. The second rule specifies that step2 (program2) and step3 (program3) be run if step1 has completed successfully ('step1 COMPLETED'). The final rule says that when step2 and step3 finish, the chain will end.

Enabling a Chain

You must enable a chain before you can use it. Here's how to do so:

```
SQL> BEGIN
    DBMS_SCHEDULER.ENABLE ('test_chain');
    END;
```

Embedding Jobs in Chains

In order to run a job within a Scheduler chain, you must create a job with the JOB_TYPE attribute set to CHAIN, and the JOB_ACTION attribute pointing to the name of the particular chain you wish to use. Of course, this means that you must first create the chain.

Here's the syntax for creating a job for a Scheduler chain:

```
SQL> BEGIN
    DBMS_SCHEDULER.CREATE_JOB (
    JOB_NAME         => 'test_chain_job',
    JOB_TYPE         => 'CHAIN',
    JOB_ACTION       => 'test_chain',
    REPEAT_INTERVAL  => 'freq=daily;byhour=13;byminute=0;bysecond=0',
    ENABLED          => TRUE);
    END;
```

You also have the option of using the RUN_CHAIN procedure to run a chain without creating a job first. The procedure will create a temporary job and immediately run the chain. Here's how you do this:

```
SQL> BEGIN
    DBMS_SCHEDULER.RUN_CHAIN (
    CHAIN_NAME   => 'my_chain1',
    JOB_NAME     => 'quick_chain_job',
    START_STEPS  => 'my_step1, my_step2');
    END;
```

As with the other components of the Scheduler, there are procedures that enable you to drop a chain, drop rules from a chain, disable a chain, alter a chain, and so on. For the details, please refer to the section about the DBMS_SCHEDULER package in the Oracle manual, *PL/SQL Packages and Types Reference*.

Managing Events

So far, you've seen how to create jobs with and without a schedule. When you create a job without a schedule, you'll have to provide the start time and the frequency, whereas using a schedule enables you to omit these from a job specification. In both cases, the job timing is based on calendar time. However, you can create both jobs and schedules that are based strictly on events, not calendar time. We'll briefly look at event-based jobs and schedules in the following sections.

Creating Event-Based Jobs

The following example shows how to create a Scheduler job using a program and an event. The job will start when the event, FILE ARRIVAL, occurs:

```
SQL> BEGIN
    dbms_scheduler.create_job(
    JOB_NAME          =>  test_job,
    PROGRAM_NAME      =>  test_program,
    START_DATE        =>  '01-AUG-08 5.00.00AM US/Pacific',
    EVENT_CONDITION   =>  'tab.user_data.event_name = ''FILE_ARRIVAL''',
    QUEUE_SPEC        =>  'test_events_q',
    ENABLED           =>  TRUE,
    COMMENTS          =>  'An event based job');
    END;
```

There are two unfamiliar attributes in the preceding CREATE_JOB procedure, both of which are unique to event-based jobs:

- EVENT_CONDITION: The EVENT_CONDITION attribute is a conditional expression that takes its values from the event source queue table and uses Oracle Streams Advanced Queuing rules. You specify object attributes in this expression and prefix them with tab.user_data. Review the DBMS_AQADM package to learn more about Oracle Streams Advanced Queuing and related rules.

- QUEUE_SPEC: The QUEUE_SPEC attribute determines the queue into which the job-triggering event will be queued. In the preceding example, test_events_q is the name of the queue.

Creating Event-Based Schedules

The following example shows how to create an event-based schedule. Whenever an event (FILE_ARRIVAL) occurs, the Scheduler will start a job based on the schedule created in this example. In this case, the event indicates that a file has arrived before noon.

```
SQL> BEGIN
    dbms_scheduler.create_event_schedule(
    SCHEDULE_NAME      =>  'appowner.file_arrival',
    START_DATE         =>  systimestamp,
    EVENT_CONDITION    =>  'tab.user_data.object_owner = ''APPOWNER''
                            AND tab.user_data.event_name = ''FILE_ARRIVAL''
    AND extract hour FROM tab.user_data.event_timestamp < 12',
    QUEUE_SPEC         =>  'test_events_q');
    END;
```

You were introduced to the EVENT_CONDITION and QUEUE_SPEC attributes in the previous example.

Managing Advanced Scheduler Components

So far, you've learned how to manage the basic Scheduler components—jobs, programs, schedules, chains, and events. In this section, let's look at how to manage the advanced Scheduler components— job classes and windows (and window groups).

You'll also learn how the Scheduler makes good use of the Database Resource Manager features, such as resource consumer groups and resource plans, to efficiently allocate scarce OS and database resources. Too often, heavy batch jobs run past their window and spill over into the daytime, when OLTP transactions demand the lion's share of the resources. Prioritizing jobs to ensure that they are guaranteed adequate resources to perform along accepted lines is an essential requirement in production databases. The Scheduler uses the concepts of job classes and windows to prioritize jobs.

Managing Job Classes

Using job classes helps you prioritize jobs by allocating resources differently among various groups of jobs. The scheduler associates each job class with a *resource consumer group*, which lets the Scheduler determine the appropriate resource allocation for each job class. The ability to associate job classes with the resource consumer groups created by the Database Resource Manager helps in prioritizing jobs.

Note All jobs must belong to a job class. There is a default job class, DEFAULT_JOB_CLASS, to which all jobs will belong by default, if they aren't assigned to any other job class. A job class will be associated with the DEFAULT_ CONSUMER_GROUP by default if you don't expressly assign it to a specific resource consumer group.

Creating a Job Class

All job classes are created in the SYS schema, regardless of which user creates it. The following example uses the CREATE_JOB_CLASS procedure to create a new job class called ADMIN_JOBS.

```
SQL> BEGIN
        DBMS_SCHEDULER.CREATE_JOB_CLASS(
        JOB_CLASS_NAME             =>  'admin_jobs'
        RESOURCE_CONSUMER_GROUP    =>  'admin_group',
        LOGGING_LEVEL              =>  dbms_scheduler.logging_runs
        LOG_HISTORY                =>  15);
        END;
```

These are the attributes in the preceding example:

- JOB_CLASS_NAME: This is the name of the job class.

- RESOURCE_CONSUMER_GROUP: This attribute specifies that all jobs that are members of this class will be assigned to the ADMIN_GROUP resource consumer group.

- LOGGING_LEVEL: This attribute can take the following three values:

  - DBMS_SCHEDULER.LOGGING_OFF: Specifies no logging of any kind for the jobs in the job class

  - DBMS_SCHEDULER.LOGGING_RUNS: Specifies detailed log entries for each run of a job

  - DBMS_SCHEDULER.LOGGING_FULL: Specifies detailed entries for each run of a job in the job class, as well as for all other operations on the jobs, including the creation, dropping, altering, enabling, or disabling of jobs

---

Note The DBMS_SCHEDULER.LOGGING_FULL value for the LOGGING_LEVEL attribute provides the most information about jobs in a job class; the default logging level is DBMS_SCHEDULER.LOGGING_RUNS.

- LOG_HISTORY: This attribute specifies the number of days that the database will retain the logs before purging them using the automatically scheduled PURGE_LOG job. You can also manually clear the logs using the PURGE_LOG procedure of the DBMS_SCHEDULER package.

The PURGE_LOG procedure of the DBMS_SCHEDULER package takes two important parameters—LOG_HISTORY and WHICH_LOG. You use the LOG_HISTORY parameter to specify the number of days to keep logs before the Scheduler purges them. The WHICH_LOG parameter enables you to specify whether you want to purge job or window logs. For example, to purge all job logs more than 14 days old, you would use the following statement:

```
SQL> EXEC DBMS_SCHEDULER.PURGE_LOG(LOG_HISTORY=14, WHICH_LOG='JOB_LOG');
```

Dropping a Job Class

You drop a job class using the DROP_JOB_CLASS procedure, as shown here:

```
SQL> BEGIN
        DBMS_SCHEDULER.DROP_JOB_CLASS('TEST_CLASS');
        END;
```

Tip You must specify the force=true option to drop job classes with jobs in them. If the job is already running, it will be allowed to complete before the dropped job class is disabled.

Changing Job Class Attributes

You can change job class attributes with the ALTER_ATTRIBUTES procedure. The following example will change the START_DATE attribute, and its new value is specified by the VALUE parameter:

```
SQL> BEGIN
  2  DBMS_SCHEDULER.ALTER_ATTRIBUTES(
  3  NAME          => 'ADMIN_JOBS',
  4  ATTRIBUTE     => 'START_DATE',
  5  VALUE         => '01-JUL-2008 9:00:00 PM US/Pacific');
  6* END;
SQL>
```

Changing Resource Plans Using Windows

A window is an interval with a specific start and end time, such as "from 12 midnight to 6:00 a.m." However, a window is not merely a chronological device like a schedule, specifying when a job will run; every window is associated with a resource plan. When you create a window, you specify a resource plan as a parameter. This ability to activate different resource plans at different times is what makes windows special scheduling devices that enable you to set priorities.

The basic purpose of a window is to switch the active resource plan during a certain time frame. All jobs that run during a window will be controlled by the resource plan that's in effect for that window. Without windows, you would have to manually switch the resource manager plans. Windows enable the automatic changing of resource plans based on a schedule.

■**Note** All windows are created in the SYS schema, no matter which user creates them. To manage windows, you must have the MANAGE SCHEDULER system privilege.

A Scheduler window consists of the following three major attributes:

- *Start date, end date, and repeat interval attributes*: These determine when and how frequently a Window will open and close (thus, these attributes determine when a window is in effect).

- *Duration*: This determines the length of time a window stays open.

- *Resource plan*: This determines the resource priorities among the job classes.

■**Note** The V$RSRC_PLAN view provides information on currently active resource plans in your database.

On the face of it, both a schedule and a window seem to be serving the same purpose, since both enable you to specify the start and end times and the repeat interval for a job. However, it's the resource plan attribute that sets a window apart from a simple schedule. Each time a window is open, a specific active resource plan is associated with it. Thus, a given job will be allocated different resources if it runs under different windows.

You can specify what resources you want to allocate to various job classes during a certain time period by associating a resource plan with the window you create for this period. When the window opens, the database automatically switches to the associated resource plan, which becomes the active resource plan. The systemwide resource plan associated with the window will control the resource allocation for all jobs and sessions that are scheduled to run within this window. When the window closes, there will be another switch to the original resource plan that was in effect, provided no other window is in effect at that time.

You can see which window is currently active and which resource plan is associated with that window by using the following query:

```
SQL> SELECT window_name, resource_plan, enabled, active
  2  FROM DBA_SCHEDULER_WINDOWS;

WINDOW_NAME            RESOURCE_PLAN          ENABLED      ACTIVE
--------------------   -------------------    --------     -------
TEST_WINDOW            TEST_RESOURCEPLAN      TRUE         FALSE
. . .
SQL>
```

You can see that the window TEST_WINDOW is enabled, but not currently active.

Creating a Window

You create a window by using the CREATE_WINDOW procedure. Let's look at two examples using this procedure, one with an inline specification of the start and end times and the repeat interval, and the other where you use a saved schedule instead to provide these three scheduling attributes.

In the first example, the window-creation statement specifies the schedule for the window:

```
SQL> BEGIN
     DBMS_SCHEDULER.CREATE_WINDOW(
     WINDOW_NAME        =>  'MY_WINDOW',
     START_DATE         =>  '01-JUN-08 12:00:00AM',
     REPEAT_INTERVAL    =>  'FREQ=DAILY',
     RESOURCE_PLAN      =>  'TEST_RESOURCEPLAN',
     DURATION           =>  interval '60' minute,
     END_DATE           =>  '31-DEC-08 12:00:00AM',
     WINDOW_PRIORITY    =>  'HIGH',
     COMMENTS           =>  'Test Window');
     END;
```

Let's look at the individual attributes of the new window created by the preceding statement:

- RESOURCE_PLAN: This attribute specifies that while this window is open, resource allocation to all the jobs that run in this window will be guided by the resource plan directives in the TEST_RESOURCEPLAN resource plan.

- WINDOW_PRIORITY: This attribute is set to HIGH, and the default priority level is LOW; these are the only two values possible. If two windows overlap, the window with the high priority level has precedence. Since only one window can be open at a given time, when they overlap, the high-priority window will open and the low-priority window doesn't open.

- START_DATE: The setting for this attribute specifies that the window first becomes active at 12:00 a.m. on June 1, 2008. You can also say that the window will *open* at this time.

- DURATION: This attribute is set so that the window will remain open for a period of 60 minutes, after which it will close.

- REPEAT_INTERVAL: This attribute specifies the next time the window will open again. In this example, it is 12:00 a.m. on June 2, 2008.

- END_DATE: This attribute specifies that this window will open for the last time on December 31, 2008, after which it will be disabled and closed.

■**Note** Since the Scheduler doesn't check to make sure that there are prior windows for any given schedule, windows can overlap sometimes.

The following example creates a window using a saved schedule. Obviously, it is much simpler to create a window this way:

```
SQL> BEGIN
     DBMS_SCHEDULER.CREATE_WINDOW(
     WINDOW_NAME        => 'TEST_WINDOW',
     SCHEDULE_NAME      => 'TEST_SCHEDULE',
     RESOURCE_PLAN      => 'TEST_RESOURCEPLAN',
     DURATION           => interval '180' minute,
     COMMENTS           => 'Test Window');
     END;
```

In the preceding CREATE_WINDOW procedure, the use of the TEST_SCHEDULE schedule lets you avoid specifying the START_DATE, END_DATE, and REPEAT_INTERVAL parameters.

■**Tip** A window is automatically enabled upon creation.

Once you create a window, you must associate it with a job or job class, so the jobs can take advantage of the automatic switching of the active resource plans.

Managing Windows

You can open, close, alter, enable, disable, or drop a window using the appropriate procedure in the DBMS_SCHEDULER package, and you need the MANAGE SCHEDULER privilege to perform any of these tasks. Note that since all windows are created in the SYS schema, you must always use the [SYS].window_name syntax when you reference any window.

A window will automatically open at a time specified by its START_TIME attribute. You can also open a window manually anytime you wish by using the OPEN_WINDOW procedure. Even when you manually open a window, that window will still open at its regular opening time as specified by its interval.

Here's an example that shows how you can open a window manually:

```
SQL> EXECUTE DBMS_SCHEDULER.OPEN_WINDOW(
     WINDOW_NAME  => 'BACKUP_WINDOW',
     DURATION     => '0 12:00:00');
SQL>
```

Look at the DURATION attribute in the preceding statement. When you specify the duration, you can specify days, hours, minutes, and seconds, in that order. Thus, the setting means 0 days, 12 hours, 0 minutes, and 0 seconds.

You can also open an already open window. If you do this, the window will remain open for the time specified in its DURATION attribute. That is, if you open a window that has been running for 30 minutes, and its duration is 60 minutes, that window will last be open for the initial 30 minutes plus an additional 60 minutes, for a total of 90 minutes.

To close a window, you use the CLOSE_WINDOW procedure, as illustrated by the following example:

```
SQL> EXECUTE DBMS_SCHEDULER.CLOSE_WINDOW('BACKUP_WINDOW');
```

If a job is running when you close a window, the job will continue to run to its completion. However, if you created a job with the STOP_ON_WINDOW_CLOSE attribute set to TRUE, that running job will close upon the closing of its window.

To disable a window, you use the DISABLE procedure, as shown here:

```
SQL> EXECUTE DBMS_SCHEDULER.DISABLE (NAME  =>  'BACKUP_WINDOW');
```

You can only disable a window if no job uses that window or if the window isn't open. If the window is open, you can disable it by using the DISABLE procedure with the FORCE=TRUE attribute.

You can drop a window by using the DROP_WINDOW procedure. If a job associated with a window is running, a DROP_WINDOW procedure will continue to run through to completion, and the window is disabled after the job completes. If you set the job's STOP_ON_WINDOW_CLOSE attribute to TRUE, however, the job will immediately stop when you drop an associated window. If you use the FORCE=TRUE setting, you'll disable all jobs that use that window.

Prioritizing Jobs

You can map each Scheduler job class to a specific resource consumer group. A resource plan is assigned to a resource consumer group, and thus indirectly to each job class as well, by the Database Resource Manager. The active resource plan (as determined by the currently open window) will apportion resources to groups, giving different levels of resources to different jobs, based on their job class.

The Scheduler works closely with the Database Resource Manager to ensure proper resource allocation to the jobs. The Scheduler will start a job only if there are enough resources to run it.

Within each Scheduler window, you can have several jobs running, with varying degrees of priority. You can prioritize jobs at two levels—*class* and *job*. The prioritization at the class level is based on the resources allocated to each resource consumer group by the currently active resource plan. For example, the FINANCE_JOBS class might rank higher than the ADMIN_JOBS class, based on the resource allocations dictated by its active resource plan.

Within the FINANCE_JOBS and ADMIN_JOBS classes, there will be several individual jobs. Each of these jobs has a job priority, which can range from 1 to 5, with 1 being the highest priority. You can use the SET_ATTRIBUTES procedure to change the job priority of any job, as shown here:

```
SQL> BEGIN
    dbms_scheduler.SET_ATTRIBUTE(
    NAME        =>    'test_job',
    ATTRIBUTE   =>    'job_priority',
    VALUE       =>    1);
    END;
```

The default job priority for a job is 3, which you can verify with the following query:

```
SQL> SELECT job_name, job_priority FROM dba_scheduler_jobs;

JOB_NAME                            JOB_PRIORITY
------------------------------ ---------------------
ADV_SQLACCESS1523128                            3
ADV_SQLACCESS5858921                            3
GATHER_STATS_JOB                                3
PURGE_LOG                                       3
TEST_JOB03                                      3
TEST_JOB1                                       3
6 rows selected
SQL>
```

When you have more than one job within the same class scheduled for the same time, the job_priority of the individual jobs determines which job starts first.

Window Priorities

Since windows might have overlapping schedules, you may frequently have more than one window open at the same time, each with its own resource plan. At times like this, the Scheduler will close all windows except one, using certain rules of precedence. Here is how the precedence rules work:

- If two windows overlap, the window with the higher priority opens and the window with the lower priority closes.
- If two windows of the same priority overlap, the active window remains open.
- If you are at the end of a window and you have other windows defined for the same time period with the same priority, the window that has the highest percentage of time remaining will open.

Window Groups

A window group is a collection of windows, and it is part of the SYS schema. Window groups are optional entities, and you can make a window a part of a window group when you create it, or you can add windows to a group at a later time. You can specify either a single window or a window group as the schedule for a job.

As explained earlier in this chapter, you can take two or more windows that have similar characteristics—for example, some night windows and a holiday window—and group them together to create a downtime window group. Window groups are used for convenience only, and their use is purely optional.

Managing Scheduler Attributes

In earlier sections in this chapter, you've seen how you can use the SET_ATTRIBUTE procedure to modify various components of the Scheduler. Attributes like JOB_NAME and PROGRAM_NAME are unique to the job and program components. You can retrieve the attributes of any Scheduler component with the GET_SCHEDULER_ATTRIBUTE procedure of the DBMS_SCHEDULER package.

Unsetting Component Attributes

You can use the SET_ATTRIBUTE_NULL procedure to set a Scheduler component's attributes to NULL. For example, to unset the COMMENTS attribute of the TEST_PROGRAM program, you can use the following code:

```
SQL> EXECUTE dbms_scheduler.SET_ATTRIBUTE_NULL('TEST_PROGRAM', 'COMMENTS');
```

Altering Common Component Attributes

There are some attributes that are common to all Scheduler components. The SET_SCHEDULER_ATTRIBUTE procedure lets you set these common, or *global*, attribute values, which affect all Scheduler components. The common attributes include the default time zone, the log history retention period, and the maximum number of job worker processes.

Monitoring Scheduler Jobs

There are several dynamic performance views you can use to monitor Scheduler jobs, and I briefly discuss the important views here.

DBA_SCHEDULER_JOBS

The DBA_SCHEDULER_JOBS view provides the status and general information about scheduled jobs in your database. Here's a simple query using the view:

```
SQL> SELECT job_name, program_name
  2  FROM DBA_SCHEDULER_JOBS;

JOB_NAME                          PROGRAM_NAME
----------------                  -----------------
PURGE_LOG                            PURGE_LOG_PROG
GATHER_STATS_JOB                  GATHER_STATS_PROG
. . .
SQL>
```

DBA_SCHEDULER_RUNNING_JOBS

The DBA_SCHEDULER_RUNNING_JOBS view provides information regarding currently running jobs.

DBA_SCHEDULER_JOB_RUN_DETAILS

You can use the DBA_SCHEDULER_JOB_RUN_DETAILS view to check the status and the duration of execution for all jobs in your database, as the following example shows:

```
SQL> SELECT job_name, status, run_duration
  2* FROM DBA_SCHEDULER_JOB_RUN_DETAILS;

JOB_NAME               STATUS          RUN_DURATION
-----------------      ----------      -------------
PURGE_LOG              SUCCEEDED       +000 00:00:02
PURGE_LOG              SUCCEEDED       +000 00:00:04
GATHER_STATS_JOB       SUCCEEDED       +000 00:31:18
SQL>
```

DBA_SCHEDULER_SCHEDULES

The DBA_SCHEDULER_SCHEDULES view provides information on all current schedules in your database, as shown here:

```
SQL> SELECT schedule_name, repeat_interval
  2* FROM dba_scheduler_schedules;

SCHEDULE_NAME                     REPEAT_INTERVAL
--------------------              -------------------------------------------
DAILY_PURGE_SCHEDULE              freq=daily;byhour=12;byminute=0;bysecond=0
SQL>
```

DBA_SCHEDULER_JOB_LOG

The DBA_SCHEDULER_JOB_LOG view enables you to audit job-management activities in your database. The data that this view contains depends on how you set the logging parameters for your jobs and job classes.

In the "Creating a Job Class" section, earlier in the chapter, you saw how to set the logging level for a job at the job class level. In order to set the logging levels at the individual job level, you use the

SET_ATTRIBUTE procedure of the DBMS_SCHEDULER package. In the SET_ATTRIBUTE procedure, you can set the LOGGING_LEVEL attribute to two different values:

```
DBMS_SCHEDULER.LOGGING_FULL
DBMS_SCHEDULER.LOGGING_RUNS
```

The DBMS_SCHEDULER.LOGGING_RUNS option will merely record the job runs, while the DBMS_SCHEDULER.LOGGING_FULL option turns on full job logging.

Here is an example showing how you can turn on full job logging at the job level:

```
SQL> EXECUTE dbms_scheduler.set_attribute ('TESTJOB',
     'LOGGING_LEVEL', dbms_scheduler.LOGGING_FULL);
```

Purging Job Logs

By default, once a day, the Scheduler will purge all window logs and job logs that are older than 30 days. You can also manually purge the logs by executing the PURGE_LOG procedure, as shown here:

```
SQL> EXECUTE DBMS_SCHEDULER.PURGE_LOG(
     LOG_HISTORY   => 1,
     JOB_NAME      => 'TEST_JOB1');
```

Default Scheduler Jobs

By default, all Oracle Database 11.1 databases use the Scheduler to run the following jobs, though you can, of course, disable any of these jobs if you wish:

```
SQL> SELECT owner, job_name, job_type FROM dba_scheduler_jobs;
```

OWNER	JOB_NAME	JOB_TYPE
SYS	ADV_SQLACCESS1821051	PLSQL_BLOCK
SYS	XMLDB_NFS_CLEANUP_JOB	STORED_PROCEDURE
SYS	FGR$AUTOPURGE_JOB	PLSQL_BLOCK
SYS	BSLN_MAINTAIN_STATS_JOB	
SYS	DRA_REEVALUATE_OPEN_FAILURES	STORED_PROCEDURE
SYS	HM_CREATE_OFFLINE_DICTIONARY	STORED_PROCEDURE
SYS	ORA$AUTOTASK_CLEAN	
SYS	PURGE_LOG	
ORACLE_OCM	MGMT_STATS_CONFIG_JOB	STORED_PROCEDURE
ORACLE_OCM	MGMT_CONFIG_JOB	STORED_PROCEDURE
EXFSYS	RLM$SCHDNEGACTION	PLSQL_BLOCK
EXFSYS	RLM$EVTCLEANUP	PLSQL_BLOCK

```
12 rows selected.
SQL>
```

The Scheduler is a welcome addition to the Oracle DBA's arsenal of tools. By providing a sophisticated means of scheduling complex jobs, it does away with the need for third-party tools or complex shell scripts to schedule jobs within the database.

Automated Maintenance Tasks

Automated maintenance tasks are jobs that run automatically in the database to perform maintenance operations. Following are the automated maintenance tasks in Oracle Database 11*g*:

- Automatic Optimizer Statistics Collection
- Automatic Segment Advisor
- Automatic SQL Tuning Advisor

All three automated maintenance tasks run during the default system maintenance window on a nightly basis. I discuss predefined maintenance windows next.

Predefined Maintenance Windows

In Oracle Database 11*g*, there are seven predefined maintenance windows, as shown here:

```
MONDAY_WINDOW          Starts and 10 P.M. on Monday and ends at 2 A.M.
TUESDAY_WINDOW         Starts and 10 P.M. on Tuesday and ends at 2 A.M.
WEDNESDAY_WINDOW       Starts and 10 P.M. on Wednesday and ends at 2.A.M.
THURSDAY_WINDOW        Starts and 10 P.M. on Thursday and ends at 2 A.M.
FRIDAY_WINDOW          Starts and 10 P.M. on Friday and ends at 2 A.M.
SATURDAY_WINDOW        Starts at 6 A.M on Saturday and ends at 2 A.M.
SUNDAY_WINDOW          Starts and 6 A.M. on Sunday and ends at 2 A.M.
```

The weekday maintenance windows are open for 4 hours and the weekend windows for 20 hours. The seven maintenance windows come under the group named MAINTENANCE_WINDOW_GROUP. You can manage the maintenance windows by altering their start and end times. You can also create new maintenance widows and remove or disable the default maintenance windows. I explain these tasks in the following sections.

Managing Automated Maintenance Tasks

Since the database doesn't assign permanent Scheduler jobs to the three automated maintenance tasks, you can't manage these tasks with the DBMS_SCHUDULER package. If you want to perform fine-grained management tasks that modify the automated maintenance tasks, you must use the DBMS_AUTO_TASK_ADMIN package.

Monitoring Automated Maintenance Tasks

Query the DBA_AUTOTASK_CLIENT and the DBA_AUTOTASK_OPERATION views to get details about the automated maintenance task execution in the database. The two views share several columns. Here's a query on the DBA_AUTOTASK_CLIENT view:

```
SQL> SELECT client_name, status,
  2  attributes, window_group,service_name
  3  FROM dba_autotask_client;


CLIENT_NAME           STATUS     ATTRIBUTES
--------------------  --------   --------------------------------------
auto optimizer        ENABLED    ON BY DEFAULT, VOLATILE, SAFE TO KILL
statistics collection
auto space advisor    ENABLED    ON BY DEFAULT, VOLATILE, SAFE TO KILL
sql tuning advisor    ENABLED    ONCE PER WINDOW, ON BY DEFAULT;
                                 VOLATILE, SAFE TO KILL

SQL>
```

The ATTRIBUTES column shows that all three automated maintenance tasks are enabled by default, as evidenced by the attribute ON BY DEFAULT. When a maintenance window opens, the database automatically creates the three automated maintenance tasks and executes those jobs. However, only the SQL Tuning Advisor task shows the ONCE PER WINDOW attribute. This is because the database executes both the Automatic Optimizer Statistics Collection and the Auto Space Advisor tasks more than once, if the maintenance window is long enough, while it executes the SQL Tuning Advisor just once during any maintenance window.

The database assigns a client name to each of the three automated maintenance tasks, which it deems clients. The Scheduler job associated with the three clients is given an operation name, since the jobs are considered operations. Here are the operation names associated with each of the three automated maintenance tasks:

```
SQL> SELECT client_name, operation_nameFROM dba_autotask_operation;

CLIENT_NAME                            OPERATION_NAME
--------------------------------       ------------------------
auto optimizer stats collection        auto optimizer stats job
auto space advisor                     auto space advisor job
sql tuning advisor                     automatic sql tuning task

SQL>
```

Enabling a Maintenance Task

Execute the ENABLE procedure to enable a previously disabled client or operation, as shown here:

```
SQL> begin
  2  dbms_auto_task_admin.enable
  3  (client_name  => 'sql tuning advisor',
  4  operation     => 'automatic sql tuning task',
  5  window_name   => 'monday_window');
  6* end;
SQL> /

PL/SQL procedure successfully completed.
SQL>
```

You can retrieve the CLIENT_NAME and the OPERATION_NAME attributes by querying the DBA_AUTOTASK-CLIENT and the DBA_AUTOTASK_OPERATION views.

Disabling a Maintenance Task

You can disable any of the three automated maintenance jobs during a specific maintenance window by executing the DISABLE procedure.

```
SQL> begin
  2  dbms_auto_task_admin.disable
  3  (client_name  => 'sql tuning advisor',
  4  operation     => 'automatic sql tuning task',
  5  window_name   => 'monday_window');
  6* end;
SQL> /

PL/SQL procedure successfully completed.

SQL>
```

The example shown here disables the SQL Tuning Advisor task only during the MONDAY_WINDOW but keeps the task enabled during all other windows.

Implementing Automated Maintenance Tasks

The Autotask Background Process (ABP) is responsible for implementing the three automated main-tenance tasks by converting the tasks into Scheduler jobs. For each automated task, ABP creates a task list and assigns a priority. The three priority levels are high, medium, and urgent. The Scheduler also creates job classes and maps a consumer group to the appropriate job class. The ABP assigns jobs to each of the job classes, and the job classes map the jobs to a consumer group based on the job priority level. The MMON background process spawns restarts and monitors the ABP process. The DBA_AUTOTASK view shows the tasks stored in the ABP repository, which is in the SYSAUX tablespace.

You can view the ABP repository by querying the DBA_AUTOTASK_TASK view.

Resource Allocation for Automatic Tasks

The default resource plan assigned to all maintenance windows is the DEFAULT_MAINTENANCE _ PLAN. When a maintenance window opens, the database actives the DEFAULT_MAINTENANCE_PLAN to control the CPU resources used by the automated maintenance tasks. The three automated maintenance tasks are run under the ORA$AUTOTASK_SUB_PLAN, a subplan for the DEFAULT_ MAINTENANCE_PLAN. You can change the resource allocation for automated tasks by changing the resource allocations for this subplan in the resource plan for a specific maintenance window.

Fault Diagnosability

Oracle Database 11g uses a built-in fault diagnosability infrastructure that helps you detect, diag-nose, and resolve problems in your database. The fault diagnosability infrastructure focuses on trapping and resolving critical errors such as data corruption and database code bugs. The goal is to proactively detect problems and limit damage to the databases, while reducing the time it takes to diagnose and resolve problems. The fault diagnosability feature also contains elements that make it easier to interact with Oracle Support. Here are the key components of the new fault diagnosability infrastructure:

- *Automatic Diagnostic Repository*: This is a file-based repository for storing database diagnostic data. You can access the ADR through the command line or the Enterprise Manager. It includes trace files, alert logs, and health monitor reports, among other things. Each database instance has its own ADR home directory, but the directory structure is uniform across instances and products, thus enabling Oracle Support to correlate and analyze diagnostic data from multiple products and instances. Immediately after a problem occurs in the database, the diagnostic information is captured and stored within the ADR. You use this diagnostic data to send what are called *incident packages* to Oracle Support.

- *The ADR Command Interpreter (ADRCI)*: This is a command-line tool to manage diagnostic information and create and manage incident reports.

- *Health Monitor*: This tool runs automatic diagnostic checks following database errors. You can also run manual health checks.

- *The Support Workbench*: This is an Enterprise Manager wizard that helps you diagnose critical errors and process and package diagnostic data for transmittal to Oracle Support and filing of technical assistance requests.

- *Incident packaging service*: This is a brand-new tool that enables you to easily create, edit, and modify incident information into physical packages for transmittal to Oracle Support for diagnosing purposes.

- *Data Recovery Advisor*: This tool automatically diagnoses data failures such as missing or corrupt datafiles and reports appropriate repair options. I discuss this in Chapter 16, so I won't include a section on it in this chapter.

- *SQL Repair Advisor*: This is a new tool that generates a failed SQL statement and recommends a patch to repair it.

- *SQL Test Case Builder*: This tool helps Oracle Support reproduce a failure.

Automatic Diagnostic Repository

Database instances as well as other Oracle products and components store various types of diagnostic data in the ADR. You can always access the ADR, even when the instance is down, thus leading some to compare the ADR to a plane's black box, which helps diagnose plane crashes.

Setting the Automatic Diagnostic Repository Directory

You set the location of the ADR with the initialization parameter DIAGNOSTIC_DEST. Setting the DIAGNOSTIC_DEST parameter means you don't have to set the traditional initialization parameters such as CORE_DUMP_DEST. If you omit the DIAGNOSTIC_DEST parameters, the database assigns the default location of the ADR base directory in the following manner:

- If you've set the ORACLE_BASE variable, the ADR base will be the same as the directory you assigned for the ORACLE_BASE directory.

- If you haven't set the ORACLE_BASE variable, the value of the DIAGNOSTIC_DEST parameter defaults to $ORACLE_HOME/log.

The DIAGNOSTIC_DEST parameter sets the location of the ADR base on a server. An ADR home represents the ADR home directory for an individual database instance. An ADR base may consist of multiple ADR homes, each for a different database instance or Oracle product.

The ADR home for an instance is relative to the ADR base. The following is the general directory structure of the ADR home for an instance, starting from the ADR base:

```
diag/product_type/product_id/instance_id
```

So, if your database has a database name and SID of orcl1, and the ADR base is /u01/app/oracle/ , the ADR home for the database orcl1 would be

```
/u01/app/oracle/diag/rdbms/orcl1/orcl1
```

Structure of the ADR

The various subdirectories under the ADR home for an instance store different types of diagnostic data, such as alert logs, Health Monitor reports, incident reports, and trace files for errors. Note that you have two types of alert logs in Oracle Database 11*g*: a normal text file and an XML-formatted log. You can query the V$DIAG_INFO view to see the different subdirectories of the ADR for an instance:

```
SQL> select * from v$diag_info;

INST_ID  NAME            VALUE
-------  --------------  ---------------------------------
1        Diag Enabled    TRUE
1        ADR Base        /u01/app/oracle
1        Diag Trace      /u01/app/oracle/diag/rdbms/orcl2/
                           orcl2/trace
```

```
1       Diag Alert      /u01/app/oracle/diag/rdbms/orcl2/
                            orcl2/alert
1       Diag Incident   /u01/app/oracle/diag/rdbms/orcl2/
                            orcl2/incident
1       Diag Cdump      /u01/app/oracle/diag/rdbms/orcl2/
                            orcl2/cdump
1       Health Monitor  /u01/app/oracle/diag/rdbms/orcl2/
                            orcl2/hm1
1       Def Trace File  /u01/app/oracle/diag/rdbms/orcl2/
                            orcl2/trace
                            /orcl2_ora_4813.trc
1       Active Problem  Count            2
1       Active Incident Count            4

11 rows selected.

SQL>
```

The following directories bear examination:

- ADR Base is the directory path for the ADR base.

- ADR Home is the ADR home for the instance.

- Diag Trace contains the text-based alert log.

- Diag Alert contains the XML-formatted alert log.

- Diag Incident is the directory for storing incident packages that you create.

ADRCI

The new ADRCI is a command-line utility to help you interact with the ADR. You can use ADRCI to view diagnostic data, create incident packages, and view Health Monitor reports.

You invoke ADRCI by simply typing **adrci** at the command line:

```
$ adrci

ADRCI: Release 11.1.0.6.0 - Beta on Thu Sep 27 16:59:27 2007
Copyright (c) 1982, 2007, Oracle.  All rights reserved.

ADR base = "/u01/app/oracle"

adrci>
```

Type the **help** command to view the commands you can use at the ADRCI prompt. When you would like to leave the ADRCI utility, type **exit** or **quit**.

You can also use ADRCI in batch mode, which lets you use ADRCI commands within shell scripts and batch files. You must use the command-line parameters exec and script to execute ADRCI in batch mode, as shown here:

```
adrci exec 'command [; comamnd]. . . '
adrci script=file_name
```

The ADR Homepath

If you have multiple Oracle instances, all of them will be current when you log into ADRCI. There are some ADRCI commands that work when you have multiple ADR homes current, but others require only a single instance to be current. The default behavior for the ADR homepath is for it to be null when you start up ADRCI. When the ADR home is null, all ADR homes are current. Here's an example:

```
adrci> show homes
adrci>
ADR Homes:
diag/rdbms/orcl/orcl
diag/rdbms/orcl2/orcl2
diag/rdbms/eleven/eleven
diag/rdbms/nina/nina

adrci>
```

All ADR homes are always shown relative to the ADR base. Thus, if the ADR base is /u01/app/oracle and the database name and SID are both named orcl1, the ADR homepath's complete directory path would be /u01/app/oracle/diag/rdbms/orcl1/orcl1.

In the example shown here, the ADR homepath indicates that multiple ADR homes are current. You can set the ADR path to point to a single instance by executing the SET HOMEPATH command.

■**Tip** Always set the ADR homepath as the first thing after logging into ADRCI.

```
adrci> set homepath diag/rdbms/orcl1/orcl1
adrci> show homes
ADR Homes:
diag/rdbms/orcl1/orcl1
adrci>
```

Now, when you issue an adrci command, the database will fetch diagnostic data only from the orcl1 instance.

Viewing the Alert Log

You can view the alert log using the ADRCI utility, as shown here:

```
adrci> show alert -tail

2008-10-17 16:49:50.579000 -
Starting background process FBDA
Starting background process SMCO
. . .
Completed: ALTER DATABASE OPEN
adrci>
```

Before you issue this command, make sure you set the homepath for the correct instance. You can return to the ADRCI prompt by pressing Ctrl+C.

Besides ADRCI, there are other ways to view the contents of the alert log. You can view the traditional text-based alert log by going to the directory path listed under the `Diag Trace` entry in the V$DIAG_INFO view. Of course, you can also view the alert log contents from the database home page in Enterprise Manager. Click Alert Log Contents under Related Links to view the alert log.

Incident Packaging Service

Oracle bases its diagnostic infrastructure on two key concepts: problems and incidents. A *problem* is a critical error such as the one accompanied by the Oracle error ORA-4031, which is issued when there isn't enough shared memory. An *incident* is a single occurrence of a problem; thus, if a problem occurs multiple times, there will be different incidents to mark the events, each identified by a unique incident ID. When an incident occurs in the database, the database collects diagnostic data for it and attaches an incident ID to the event and stores it a subdirectory in the ADR. An incident is connected to a problem with the help of a problem key. The database creates incidents automatically when a problem occurs, but you can also create your own incidents when you want to report errors that don't raise and send a critical error alert to Oracle Support.

The ADR uses a flood-controlled incident system, which allows a limited number of incidents for a given problem. This is done to avoid a large number of identical incidents from flooding the ADR with identical information. The database allows each problem to log the diagnostic data for only a certain number of incidents in the ADR. For example, after 25 incidents occur for the same problem during a day, the ADR won't record any more incidents for the same problem key. The ADR employs two types of retention policies, one governing the retention of the incident metadata and the other governing the retention of incident and dump files. By default, the ADR retains the incident metadata for a month and the incident and dump files for a period of one year.

Viewing Incidents

You can check the current status of an incident by issuing the SHOW INCIDENT command, as shown here:

```
adrci> show incident

ADR Home = /u01/app/oracle/diag/rdbms/orcl1/orcl1:
****************************************************************

INCIDENT_ID    PROBLEM_KEY       CREATE_TIME
------------ --------------- -----------------------------------
17060          ORA 1578     2007-09-25 17:00:18.019731 -04:00
14657          ORA 600      2007-09-09 07:01:21.395179 -04:00

2 rows fetched

adrci>
```

You can view detailed incident information by issuing the SHOW INCIDENT . . . MODE DETAIL command as shown here:

```
adrci> show incident -mode DETAIL -p "incident_id=1234"
```

The previous command shows detailed information for the incident with the ID 1234.

An incident package contains all diagnostic data relating to an incident or incidents (it can cover one or more problems). An incident package enables you to easily transmit diagnostic information to Oracle Support. You can create incident packages with either the Support Workbench or from the command line using the ADRCI tool. You send an incident package to Oracle Support when you are seeking Oracle's help in resolving problems and incidents. After creating an incident package, you can edit the package by adding and deleting diagnostic files to it.

Creating an Incident Package

The incident packaging service enables you to create an incident package. Using IPS, you gather diagnostic data for an error, such as trace files, dump files, and health-check reports, SQL test cases, and other information, and package this data into a zip file for sending to Oracle Support. IPS tracks and gathers diagnostic information for an incident by using incident numbers. You may add, delete, or scrub the diagnostic files before transmitting the zip file to Oracle Support. Here are the key things you must know about incident packages:

- An incident package is a logical entity that contains problem metadata only. By default, the database includes the first and the last three incidents for a problem in a zip package.

- The zip file that you'll actually send to Oracle is, of course, a physical package and contains the diagnostic files specified by the metadata in the logical incident package.

- You can send incremental or complete zip files to Oracle Support.

Here are the steps you must follow to create an incident packaging service using IPC commands in the ADRCI:

1. Create a logical package that'll be used to store incident metadata. You can create an empty or a non-empty logical package. A non-empty package requires an incident number, problem number, or problem key and will automatically contain diagnostic information for the specified incident or problem. In the following example, I create an empty package using the IPS CREATE PACKAGE command:

```
adrci> ips create package

Created package 4 without any contents,

correlation level typical

adrci>
```

In order to create a non-empty package, specify the incident number, as shown here:

```
adrci> ips create package incident 17060

Created package 5 based on incident id 17060,
correlation level typical

adrci>
```

You may also choose to create a package that spans a time interval:

```
adrci> ips create package time '2007-09-20 00:00:00 -12:00' to
       '2007-09-30 00:00:00 -12:00'
```

2. If you've created an empty logical package in the first step, you must add diagnostic data to it as shown here:

```
adrci> ips add incident 17060 package 4

Added incident 17060 to package 4

adrci>
```

You can add diagnostic files to the package in the following way:

```
adrci> ips add file <file_name> package <package_number>
```

3. Generate the physical package that you'll be transmitting to Oracle Support.

```
adrci> ips generate package 4 in /u01/app/oracle/support

Generated package 4 in file
/u01/app/oracle/diag/IPSPKG_20070929163401_COM_1.zip,
mode complete

adrci>
```

The `COM_1` in the filename indicates that it's a complete file, not incremental, in order to create an incremental physical incident package. Use the following command:

```
adrci> ips generate package 4 in /u01/app/oracle/diag
    incremental
Generated package 4 in file
/u01/app/oracle/diag/IPSPKG_20070929163401_INC_2.zip,
mode incremental

adrci>
```

4. Before you can send your incident package to Oracle Support for diagnosis and help, you must formally finalize the incident package, as shown here:

```
adrci> ips finalize package 4

Finalized package 4

adrci>
```

You can now transmit the finalized zip file to Oracle Support by manually uploading it. In the next section, which discusses the Support Workbench, I'll show how to automate the transmission of incident packages to Oracle Support.

The Support Workbench

The Support Workbench, which you can access from Enterprise Manager, enables you to automate the management of incidents including the process of filing service requests with Oracle Support and tracing their progress. Besides viewing problems and incidents, you can also generate diagnostic data for a problem as well as run advisors to fix the problem. You can create incident packages easily with the Support Workbench and automatically send them in to Oracle Support.

In order to enable the Support Workbench to upload IPS zip files to Oracle Support, you must install and configure the Oracle Configuration Manager. You can install the Oracle Configuration Manager during the installation of the Oracle software, as shown in Figure 18-7.

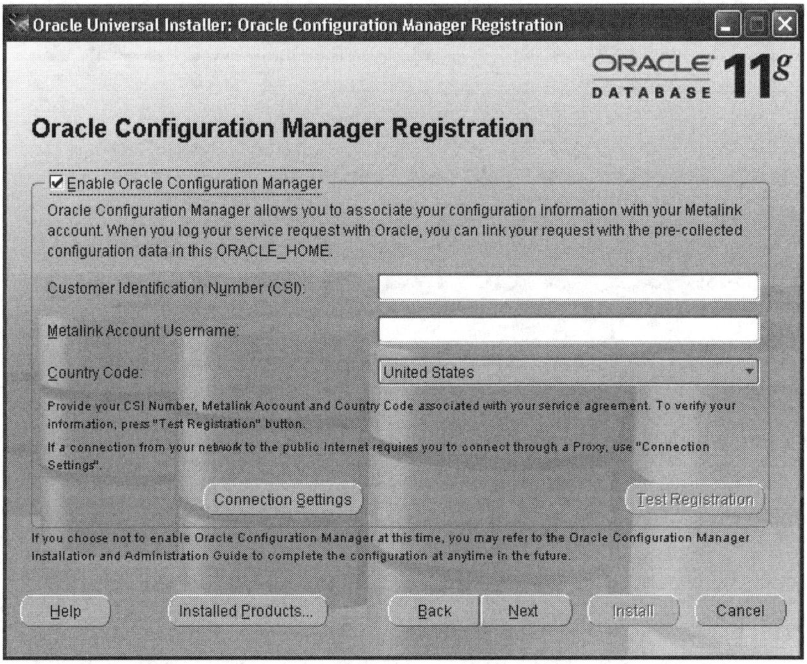

Figure 18-7. *Registering the Oracle Configuration Manager*

You can install and configure the Oracle Configuration Manager after the server installation as well, by invoking the Oracle Universal Installer.

The following sections summarize how you can use the Support Workbench to resolve problems.

■**Tip** Although the database automatically tracks all critical errors by storing the diagnostic data in the ADR, you can also create a *user-created problem* through the Support Workbench for errors that aren't automatically tracked by the database as critical errors. To do this, click Create User-Reported Problems under Related Links.

Viewing Error Alerts

You can view outstanding problems from the Support Workbench home page. You can check for critical alerts on the Database Home page in the Diagnostic Summary section by clicking the Active Incidents link there or by going to the Critical Alerts section under the Alerts section. To access the Support Workbench, click the Software and Support link and then click the Support Workbench link under the Support section. Figure 18-8 shows the Support Workbench page.

On the Support Workbench home page, select All from the View list to examine all problems.

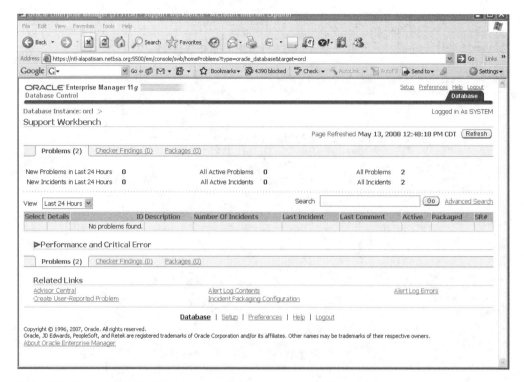

Figure 18-8. *The Support Workbench page*

Examining Problem Details

To view the details of any problem, click View Incident Details on the Incident page.

Collecting Additional Data

Besides the automatic collection of diagnostic data following a critical error in the database, you can also use the Support Workbench to invoke a health check to collect additional diagnostic data. I explain health checks later in this chapter in the section "Running a Health Check."

Creating Service Requests

From the Support Workbench, you can create service requests with MetaLink. For further reference, you may note down the service request number.

Creating Incident Packages

You can choose either the Quick Packaging method or the Custom Packaging method to create and submit incident packages. The Quick Packaging method is simpler but won't let you edit or customize the diagnostic data you're sending to Oracle Support. The Custom Packaging method is more elaborate but enables you customize your incident package.

Following are the steps you must take to create an incident package and send it to Oracle Support using the Custom Packaging method:

1. On the Incident Details page, click the Package link.

2. In the Select Packaging Mode page, select Custom Packaging and click OK.

3. On the Select Package page, select the Create New Package option. Enter the package name and click OK.

4. The Support Workbench takes you to the Customize Package page, confirming that your package was created. Figure 18-9 shows the Customize Package page.

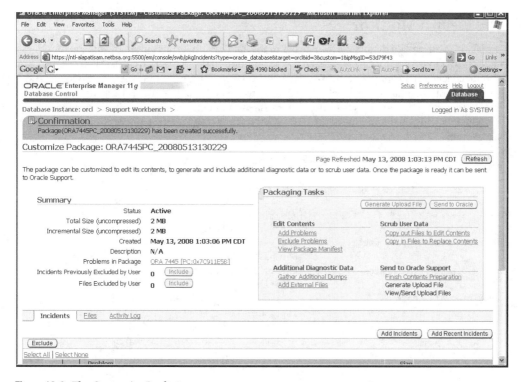

Figure 18-9. *The Customize Package page*

5. Once you finish tasks such as editing the package contents or adding diagnostic data, finalize the package by clicking Finish Contents Preparation under the Send to Oracle Support section (in the Packaging Tasks section of the Customize Package page).

6. Generate an upload file by clicking Generate Upload File. Click Immediately or Later followed by Submit to schedule the incident package submission for Oracle Support.

7. Once you submit the package to Oracle Support, IPS processes the zip file and confirms it, before returning you to the Custom Package page. Click Send to Oracle to send the confirmed zip file to Oracle. You must then fill in your MetaLink credentials and choose whether to create a new service request. Click Submit to send the file to Oracle Support.

Tracking Service Requests

After submission of an incident package to Oracle Support, you can still add new incidents to the package. You can also let the other DBAs at your organization get the details of the incident package by adding comments to the problem activity log.

Implementing Repairs and Closing Incidents

If the recommendations for repair involve the use of an Oracle advisor, you can make the repair directly from the Support Workbench itself. For example, you can run the Data Recovery Advisor and the SQL Repair Advisor (which I explain later in this chapter in the section "Repairing SQL Statements with the SQL Repair Advisor") from the Support Workbench.

You can close a resolved incident, or let Oracle purge it; Oracle purges all incidents after 30 days by default.

The Health Monitor

The Health Monitor is a diagnostic framework in the database that runs automatic diagnostic checks when the database encounters critical errors. In addition to these reactive checks, you can also run manual checks whenever you want. You can use either the Enterprise Manager or the DBMS_HM package to run manual health checks. In response to a reactive or a manual check, the database examines components such as memory and transaction integrity and reports back to you.

The following query on the V$HM_CHECK view shows the various types of health checks that can be run:

```
SQL> SELECT name, description FROM v$hm_check;
```

NAME	DESCRIPTION
HM Test Check	Check for HM Functionality
DB Structure Integrity Check	Checks integrity of all Database files
Data Block Integrity Check	Checks integrity of a datafile block
Redo Integrity Check	Checks integrity of redo log content
Logical Block Check	Checks logical content of a block
Transaction Integrity Check	Checks a transaction for corruptions
Undo Segment Integrity Check	Checks integrity of an undo segment
All Control Files Check	Checks all control files in the database
CF Member Check	Checks a multiplexed copy of the control file
All Datafiles Check	Check for all datafiles in the database
Single Datafile Check	Checks a datafile
Log Group Check	Checks all members of a log group
Log Group Member Check	Checks a particular member of a log group
Archived Log Check	Checks an archived log
Redo Revalidation Check	Checks redo log content
IO Revalidation Check	Checks file accessibility
Block IO Revalidation Check	Checks file accessibility
Txn Revalidation Check	Revalidate corrupted txn
Failure Simulation Check	Creates dummy failures

Dictionary Integrity Check   Checks dictionary
                                        integrity

21 rows selected.

SQL>

You can run all checks except the redo check and the data cross-check when the database is in the open or mount mode.

Running a Health Check

You can run a health check from the Health Monitor interface in the Enterprise Manager console, which you can access by clicking the Checkers tab in the Advisor Central page. You can also run a health check by using the DBMS_HM package. The following example shows how to run a health check with the RUN_CHECK procedure:

```
BEGIN

dbms_hm run_check (
    check_name   => 'Transaction Integrity Check',
    run_name     => 'testrun1',
    input_params => 'TXN_ID=9.44.1');
END;
/
PL/SQL procedure successfully completed.

SQL>
```

The example shown here runs a transaction integrity check for a specified transaction.

Viewing the Results of a Health Check

The Health Monitor stores all its execution results in the ADR. You can query the V$HM_RECOMMENDATION, V$HM_FINDING, and the V$HM_RUN views to view the recommendations and findings of a health check. But the easiest way to view a health check result is through the GET_RUN_REPORT function, as shown in the following example:

```
SQl> SET LONG 100000

SQL> SELECT dbms_hm.get_run_report('TestCheck1') FROM DUAL;

    DBMS_HM.GET_RUN_REPORT('TESTCHECK1')
-------------------------------------------------------------
Basic Run Information
 Run Name           : TestCheck1
 Run Id             : 42721
 Check Name         : Dictionary Integrity Check
 Mode               : MANUAL
 Status             : COMPLETED
 Start Time         : 2008-10-03 16:40:47.464989 -04:00
 End Time           : 2008-10-03 16:41:23.068746 -04:00
 Error Encountered  : 0
 Source Incident Id    : 0
 Number of Incidents Created  : 0
```

```
Input Paramters for the Run
 TABLE_NAME=ALL_CORE_TABLES
 CHECK_MASK=ALL

Run Findings And Recommendations
 Finding
 Finding Name   : Dictionary Inconsistency
 Finding ID     : 42722
 Type           : FAILURE
 Status         : OPEN
 Priority       : CRITICAL
 Message        : SQL dictionary health check:
dependency$.dobj# fk 126 on object DEPENDENCY$ failed
 Message        : Damaged rowid is AAAABnAABAAAOiHABI –
description: No further damage description available

SQL>
```

You can also use ADRCI to view the results of a Health Monitor check. First, issue the SHOW HM_RUN command to view the results of a health check:

```
adrci> SHOW hm_run

*****************************************************************
HM RUN RECORD 2131
*****************************************************************
    RUN_ID                  42721
    RUN_NAME                TestCheck1
    CHECK_NAME              Dictionary Integrity Check
    NAME_ID                 24
    MODE                    0
    START_TIME              2008-10-03 16:40:47.4649 -04:00
    RESUME_TIME             <NULL>
    END_TIME                2008-10-03 16:41:23.0687 -04:00
    MODIFIED_TIME           2008-10-03 16:41:59.7867 -04:00
    TIMEOUT                 0
    FLAGS                   0
    STATUS                  5
    SRC_INCIDENT_ID         0
    NUM_INCIDENTS           0
    ERR_NUMBER              0
    REPORT_FILE
    /u01/app/oracle/diag/rdbms/orcl2/orcl2/hm/HMREPORT_TestCheck1
2131 rows fetched

adrci>
```

In this example, the SHOW HM_RUN command shows the report filename under the REPORT_FILE column. Once you see the filename, you can view the report itself by issuing the SHOW REPORT HM_RUN command, as shown here:

```
adrci> SHOW REPORT hm_run TestCheck1
```

If the REPORT_FILE column shows a NULL value, you must first generate the report file in the following manner:

```
adrci> CREATE REPORT hm_run TestCheck1
```

Once you generate the report as shown here, you can use the SHOW REPORT HM_RUN command to view the report's contents.

Repairing SQL Statements with the SQL Repair Advisor

The SQL Repair Advisor is a new tool that helps you navigate situations where a SQL statement fails with a critical error. For example, if there's a known bug that's causing a critical error, you can use the SQL Repair Advisor. Contrary to what its name indicates, the SQL Repair Advisor doesn't really rewrite or repair the offending SQL statement—it recommends a patch that'll keep the SQL statement from erroring out. In other words, the advisor provides you a workaround for a problem SQL statement. Note that a SQL patch in this case is very similar to a SQL profile, and adopting the patch results in a change in the query execution plan. You can invoke the SQL Repair Advisor from the Support Workbench or with the help of the DBMS_SQLDIAG package. I explain both methods in the following sections.

Invoking the SQL Repair Advisor from the Support Workbench

Follow these steps to invoke the SQL Repair Advisor from the Support Workbench:

1. In the Support Workbench home page, click the ID of the problem you're trying to fix.
2. In the Problem Details page, click the problem message from the failed SQL statement.
3. In the Investigate and Resolve section on the Self Service tab, click SQL Repair Advisor.
4. Select the schedule for running the advisor and click Submit. Click View in the SQL Repair results page to view the Report Recommendations page.
5. Click Implement if you want the advisor to implement its recommendations. The SQL Repair Advisor presents a confirmation page after it implements the recommendations.

When you migrate to a new release of the database, you can easily drop the patches you applied through the SQL Repair Advisor.

Invoking the SQL Repair Advisor with the DBMS_SQLDIAG Package

The following example illustrates how to create a SQL Repair Advisor task and to apply a SQL patch recommended by the advisor to fix a bad SQL statement.

A WORD ABOUT THE FOLLOWING EXAMPLE

I have adapted the following example from the Oracle University course materials. If you try to execute the example as is, you won't really see any errors. In the Oracle course, an error is induced by using the fix control mechanism, which lets you turn off fixes for optimizer-related bugs. You control the fix control mechanism by setting the undocumented initialization parameter _FIX_CONTROL.

You can query the V$SESSION_FIX_CONTROL view to find out for which bugs you can turn the fixes off. You'd use the query SELECT DISTINCT BUGNO FROM V$SESSION_FIX_CONTROL to do this. Once you decide for which bugs you want to turn the fixes off for testing purposes, you can issue the query ALTER SESSION SET "_FIX_CONTROL"='4728348:OFF'; to turn the bug fix off temporarily while you're testing the code in our example.

Once you finish testing, don't forget to execute the statement ALTER SESSION SET "_FIX_CONTROL"= '4728348:ON'; to turn the bug fix on again. As you can tell, this is a somewhat cumbersome procedure, besides requiring you to use an undocumented parameter on your own without Oracle Support helping you along. I've mentioned the testing strategy here if you want to test the following code, but it may be smarter not to use any undocumented initialization parameter, due to potential harm to your database.

Let's say you identify the following SQL statement as the one responsible for a critical error in the database:

```
SQL> DELETE FROM t  t1
        WHERE t1.a = 'a'
        AND rowid <> (select max(rowid)
        FROM t t2 WHERE t1.a= t2.a AND t1.b = t2.b AND t1.d=t2.d);
```

You can use the SQL Repair Advisor to fix this problem by following these steps:

1. Execute the CREATE_DIAGNSOTIC_TASK procedure from the DBMS_SQLDIAG package to create a SQL Repair Advisor task.

```
SQL> declare
  2  report_out clob;
  3  task_id  varchar2(50);
  4  begin
  5  task_id := dbms_sqldiag.create_diagnosis_task(
  6  sql_text=>' delete from t t1 where t1.a = ''a''
                and rowid <> (select max(rowid) from t t2
                where t1.a= t2.a and t1.b = t2.b
                and t1.d=t2.d)',
  8  task_name   =>'test_task1',
  9  problem_type=>dbms_sqldiag.problem_type_compilation
                _error);
 10* end;
SQL> /

PL/SQL procedure successfully completed.
SQL>
```

I chose PROBLEM_TYPE_COMPILATION as the value for the PROBLEM_TYPE parameter in the CREATE_DIAGNOSIS_TASK procedure. You can also choose PROBLEM_TYPE_EXECUTION as the value for the PROBLEM_TYPE parameter.

2. Execute the SET_TUNING_TASK_PARAMETERS procedure to supply the task parameters for the new task you created in the previous step.

```
SQL> exec dbms_sqltune.set_tuning_task_parameter('task_id,
    '-SQLDIAG_FINDING_MODE', dbms_sqldiag.SQLDIAG_FINDING_
    FILTER_PLANS);
```

3. Execute the new task, after supplying a task name as the parameter to the EXECUTE_DIAGNOSTIC_TASK procedure.

```
SQL> exec dbms_sqlldiag.execute_diagnosis_task('test_task1');

PL/SQL procedure successfully completed.

SQL>
```

Note that you only need the TASK_NAME parameter to execute the EXECUTE-DIAGNOSTIC_TASK procedure.

4. You can get the report of the diagnostic task by executing the REPORT_DIAGNOSTIC_TASK function.

```
SQL> declare rep_out clob;
  2 begin
  3  rep_out := dbms_sqldiag.report_diagnosis_task
  4             ('test_task1',dbms_sqldiag.type_text);
  5  dbms_output.put_line ('Report  :  '  ||  rep_out);
  6*end;
SQL> /


Report                   : GENERAL INFORMATION
SECTION
-------------------------------------------------
Tuning Task Name         : test_task1
Tuning Task Owner        : SYS
Tuning Task ID           : 3219
Workload Type            : Single SQL Statement
Execution Count          : 1
Current Execution        : EXEC_3219
Execution Type           : SQL DIAGNOSIS
Scope                    : COMPREHENSIVE
Time Limit(seconds)      : 1800
Completion Status        : COMPLETED
Started at               : 10/20/2007 06:33:42
Completed at             : 10/20/2007 06:36:45
Schema Name              : SYS
SQL ID                   : 44wx3x03jx01v
SQL Text                 : delete from t t1 where t1.a = 'a'
                           and rowid <> (select max(rowid)
                           from t t2 where t1.a= t2.a
                           and t1.b = t2.b and t1.d=t2.d)
. . .
PL/SQL procedure successfully completed.

SQL>
```

5. You can accept the patch recommended by the SQL Repair Advisor by executing the ACCEPT_SQL_PATCH procedure.

```
SQL> exec dbms_sqldiag.accept_sql_patch (
        task_name   =>     'test_task1',
        task_owner  =>     'SYS')
```

If you execute the SQL statement after accepting the recommended patch, you'll see a different execution plan for the statement. Use the DBA_SQL_PATCHES view to find out the names of all patch recommendations made by the SQL Repair Advisor. You can drop a patch by executing the DROP_SQL_PATCH procedure. You can also export a SQL patch to a different database by using a staging table.

The SQL Test Case Builder

You can quickly create a test case for submission to Oracle Support by using the new SQL Test Case Builder. The SQL Test Case Builder provides information about the SQL query, object definitions, procedures, functions and packages, optimizer statistics, and initialization parameter settings. The SQL Test Case Builder creates a SQL script that you can run in a different system to re-create the database objects that exist in the source database. You can invoke the SQL Test Case Builder by executing the DBMS_SQLDIAG.EXPORT_SQL_TESTCASE_DIR_BY_INC function. This function will generate a SQL Test Case corresponding to the incident ID you pass to the function. You can instead use the DBMS_SQLDIAG.EXPORT_SQL_TESTCASE_DIR_BY_TEXT function to generate a SQL test case that corresponds to the SQL text you pass as an argument. However, as usual, it's a lot easier to access the SQL Test Case Builder through the Enterprise Manager, where you can get to it from the Support Workbench page by following these steps:

1. Go to the Problem Details page by clicking the relevant problem ID.

2. Click Oracle Support.

3. Click Generate Additional Dumps and Test Cases.

4. Click the icon in the Go to Task column in the Additional Dumps and Test Cases page. This'll start the SQL Test Case Builder analysis for the relevant SQL statement.

PART 7

■ ■ ■

Performance Tuning

■ ■ ■

Improving Database Performance: SQL Query Optimization

Performance tuning is the one area in which the Oracle DBA probably spends most of his or her time. If you're a DBA helping developers to tune their SQL, you can improve performance by suggesting more efficient queries or table- and index-organization schemes. If you're a production DBA, you'll be dealing with user perceptions of a slow database, batch jobs taking longer and longer to complete, and so on.

Performance tuning focuses primarily on writing efficient SQL, allocating appropriate computing resources, and analyzing wait events and contention in the system. This chapter focuses on SQL query optimization in Oracle. You'll learn about the Oracle optimizer and how to collect statistics for it. You'll find an introduction to the new Automatic Optimizer Statistics Collection feature. You can also manually collect statistics using the DBMS_STATS package, and this chapter shows you how to do that. You'll learn the important principles that underlie efficient code. I present a detailed discussion of the various tools, such as the EXPLAIN PLAN and SQL Trace utilities, with which you analyze SQL and find ways to improve performance.

Oracle provides several options to aid performance, such as partitioning large tables, using materialized views, storing plan outlines, and many others. This chapter examines how DBAs can use these techniques to aid developers' efforts to increase the efficiency of their application code. This chapter introduces the SQL Tuning Advisor to help you tune SQL statements. You can then use the recommendations of this advisor to rewrite poorly performing SQL code. I begin the chapter with a discussion of how to approach performance tuning. More than the specific performance improvement techniques you use, your approach to performance tuning determines your success in tuning a recalcitrant application system.

An Approach to Oracle Performance Tuning

Performance tuning is the 800-pound gorilla that is constantly menacing you and that requires every bit of your ingenuity, knowledge, and perseverance to keep out of harm's way. Your efforts to increase performance or to revive a bogged-down database can have a major impact on your organization, and users and management will monitor and appreciate your results.

Unlike several other features of Oracle database management, performance tuning isn't a cut-and-dried subject with clear prescriptions and rules for every type of problem you may face. This is one area where your technical knowledge must be used together with constant experimentation and observation. Practice does make you better, if not perfect, in this field.

Frustrating as it is at times, performance tuning is a rewarding part of the Oracle DBA's tasks. You can automate most of the mundane tasks such as backup, export and import, and data loading—the simple, everyday tasks that can take up so much of your valuable time. Performance tuning is one area that requires a lot of detective work on the part of application programmers and DBAs to see why some process is running slower than expected, or why you can't scale your application to a larger number of users without problems.

A Systematic Approach to Performance Tuning

It's important to follow a systematic approach to tuning database performance. Performance problems commonly come to the fore only after a large number of users start working on a new production database. The system seems fine during development and rigorous testing, but it slows down to a crawl when it goes to production. This could be because the application isn't easily scalable for a number of reasons.

The seeds of the future performance potential of your database are planted when you design your database. You need to know the nature of the applications the database is going to support. The more you understand your application, the better you can prepare for it by creating your database with the right configuration parameters. If major mistakes were made during the design stage and the database is already built, you're left with tuning application code on one hand and the database resources such as memory, CPU, and I/O on the other. Oracle suggests a specific design approach with the following steps:

1. Design the application correctly.

2. Tune the application SQL code.

3. Tune memory.

4. Tune I/O.

5. Tune contention and other issues.

Reactive Performance Tuning

Although the preceding performance tuning steps suggest that you can follow the sequence in an orderly fashion, the reality is completely different. Performance tuning is an iterative process, not a sequential one where you start at the top and end up with a fully tuned database as the product. As a DBA, you may be involved in a new project from the outset, when you have just the functional requirements. In this case, you have an opportunity to be involved in the tuning effort from the beginning stages of the application, a phase that is somewhat misleadingly dubbed *proactive tuning* by some. Alternatively, you may come in after the application has already been designed and implemented, and is in production. In this case, your performance efforts are categorized as *reactive performance tuning*. What you can do to improve the performance of the database depends on the stage at which you can have input, and on the nature of the application itself.

In general, developers are responsible for writing the proper code, but the DBA has a critical responsibility to ensure that the SQL is optimal. Developers and QA testers may test the application conscientiously, but the application may not scale well when exposed to heavy-duty real-life production conditions. Consequently, DBAs are left scrambling to find solutions to a poorly performing SQL statement after the code is running in production. Reactive performance tuning comprises most of the performance tuning done by most DBAs, for the simple reason that most problems come to light only after real users start using the application.

In many cases, you're experiencing performance problems on a production instance that was designed and coded long ago. Try to fix the SQL statements first if that's at all possible. Many people have pointed out that if the application is seriously flawed, you can do little to improve the overall performance of the database, and they're probably correct. Still, you can make a significant difference in performance, even when the suboptimal code can't be changed for one reason or another. You can use several techniques to improve performance, even when the code is poorly written but can't be changed in the immediate future. The same analysis, more or less, applies to performance-tuning packaged systems such as PeopleSoft and SAP, where you can't delve into the code that underlies the system. You can make use of the SQL Advisor tool's SQL Profiles to improve performance, even though you can't touch the underlying SQL code. *SQL tuning*, which is the topic of this chapter, is how you improve the performance in both of the aforementioned situations. In the next chapter, you'll learn ways to tune database resources such as memory, disks, and CPU.

Optimizing Oracle Query Processing

When a user starts a data-retrieval operation, the user's SQL statement goes through several sequential steps that together constitute *query processing*. One of the great benefits of using the SQL language is that it isn't a procedural language in which you have to specify the steps to be followed to achieve the statement's goal. In other words, you don't have to state how to do something; rather, you just state what you need from the database.

Query processing is the transformation of your SQL statement into an efficient execution plan to return the requested data from the database. *Query optimization* is the process of choosing the most efficient execution plan. The goal is to achieve the result with the least cost in terms of resource usage. Resources include the I/O and CPU usage on the server where your database is running. This also means that the goal is to reduce the total execution time of the query, which is simply the sum of the execution times of all the component operations of the query. This optimization of throughput may not be the same as minimizing response time. If you want to minimize the time it takes to get the first *n* rows of a query instead of the entire output of the query, the optimizer may choose a different plan. If you choose to minimize the response time for all the query data, you may also choose to parallelize the operation.

A user's SQL statement goes through the *parsing*, *optimizing*, and *execution* stages. If the SQL statement is a query, data has to be retrieved, so there's an additional *fetch* stage before the SQL statement processing is complete. In the next sections you'll examine what Oracle does during each of these steps.

Parsing

Parsing primarily consists of checking the syntax and semantics of the SQL statements. The end product of the parse stage of query compilation is the creation of the *parse tree*, which represents the query's structure.

The SQL statement is decomposed into a relational algebra query that's analyzed to see whether it's syntactically correct. The query then undergoes semantic checking. The data dictionary is consulted to ensure that the tables and the individual columns that are referenced in the query do exist, as well as all the object privileges. In addition, the column types are checked to ensure that the data matches the column definitions. The statement is normalized so it can be processed more efficiently. The query is rejected if it is incorrectly formulated. Once the parse tree passes all the syntactic and semantic checks, it's considered a valid parse tree, and it's sent to the logical query plan generation stage. All these operations take place in the library cache portion of the SGA.

Optimization

During the optimization phase, Oracle uses its optimizer—the Cost-Based Optimizer (CBO)—to choose the best access method for retrieving data for the tables and indexes referred to in the query. Using statistics that you provide and any hints specified in the SQL queries, the CBO produces an optimal execution plan for the SQL statement.

The optimization phase can be divided into two distinct parts: the query rewrite phase and the physical execution plan generation phase. Let's look at these two optimization phases in detail.

Query Rewrite Phase

In this phase, the parse tree is converted into an abstract logical query plan. This is an initial pass at an actual query plan, and it contains only a general algebraic reformulation of the initial query. The various nodes and branches of the parse tree are replaced by operators of relational algebra. Note that the query rewriting here isn't the same as the query rewriting that's involved in using materialized views.

Execution Plan Generation Phase

During this phase, Oracle transforms the logical query plan into a physical query plan. The optimizer may be faced with a choice of several algorithms to resolve a query. It needs to choose the most efficient algorithm to answer a query, and it needs to determine the most efficient way to implement the operations. In addition to deciding on the best operational steps, the optimizer determines the order in which it will perform these steps. For example, the optimizer may decide that a join between table A and table B is called for. It then needs to decide on the type of join and the order in which it will perform the table join.

The physical query or execution plan takes into account the following factors:

- The various operations (for example, joins) to be performed during the query
- The order in which the operations are performed
- The algorithm to be used for performing each operation
- The best way to retrieve data from disk or memory
- The best way to pass data from one operation to another during the query

The optimizer may generate several valid physical query plans, all of which are potential execution plans. The optimizer then chooses among them by estimating the cost of each possible physical plan based on the table and index statistics available to it, and selecting the plan with the lowest estimated cost. This evaluation of the possible physical query plans is called *cost-based query optimization*. The cost of executing a plan is directly proportional to the amount of resources such as I/O, memory, and CPU necessary to execute the proposed plan. The optimizer passes this low-cost physical query plan to Oracle's query execution engine. The next section presents a simple example to help you understand the principles of cost-based query optimization.

A Cost Optimization Example

Let's say you want to run the following query, which seeks to find all the supervisors who work in Dallas. The query looks like this:

```
SQL> SELECT * FROM employee e, dept d
     WHERE e.dept_no = d.dept_no
     AND(e.job = 'SUPERVISOR'
     AND d.city = 'DALLAS');
SQL>
```

Now, you have several ways to arrive at the list of the supervisors. Let's consider three ways to arrive at this list, and compute the cost of accessing the results in each of the three ways.

Make the following simplifying assumptions for the cost computations:

- You can only read and write data one row at a time (in the real world, you do I/O at the block level, not the row level).

- The database writes each intermediate step to disk (again, this may not be the case in the real world).

- No indexes are on the tables.

- The employee table has 2,000 rows.

- The dept table has 40 rows. The number of supervisors is also 40 (one for each department).

- Ten departments are in the city of Dallas.

In the following sections, you'll see three different queries that retrieve the same data, but that use different access methods. For each query, a crude cost is calculated, so you can compare how the three queries stack up in terms of resource cost. The first query uses a Cartesian join.

Query 1: A Cartesian Join

First, form a Cartesian product of the employee and dept tables. Next, see which of the rows in the Cartesian product satisfies the requirement. Here's the query:

```
WHERE e.job=supervisor AND d.dept=operations AND e.dept_no=d.dept_no.
```

The following would be the total cost of performing the query:

The Cartesian product of employee and dept requires a read of both tables: 2,000 + 40 = 2,040 reads

Creating the Cartesian product: 2,000 * 40 = 80,000 writes

Reading the Cartesian product to compare against the select condition: 2,000 * 40 = 80,000 reads

Total I/O cost: 2,040 + 80,000 + 80,000 = 162,040

Query 2: A Join of Two Tables

The second query uses a join of the employee and dept tables. First, join the employee and dept tables on the dept_no column. From this join, select all rows where e.job=supervisor and city=Dallas.
The following would be the total cost of performing the query:

Joining the employee and dept tables first requires a read of all the rows in both tables: 2,000 + 40 = 2,040

Creating the join of the employee and dept tables: 2,000 writes

Reading the join results costs: 2,000 reads

Total I/O cost: 2,040 + 2,000 + 2,000 = 6,040

Query 3: A Join of Reduced Relations

The third query also uses a join of the employee and dept tables, but not all the rows in the two tables—only selected rows from the two tables are joined. Here's how this query would proceed to retrieve the needed data. First, read the employee table to get all supervisor rows. Next, read the dept table to get all Dallas departments. Finally, join the rows you derived from the employee and the dept tables.

The following would be the total cost of performing the query:

Reading the employee table to get the supervisor rows: 2,000 reads

Writing the supervisor rows derived in the previous step: 40 writes

Reading the dept table to get all Dallas departments: 40 reads

Writing the Dallas department rows derived from the previous step: 10 writes

Joining the supervisor rows and department rows derived in the previous steps of this query execution: A total of 40 + 10 = 50 writes

Reading the join result from the previous step: 50 reads

Total I/O cost: $2,000 + 2(40) + 10 + 2(50) = 2,190$

This example, simplified as it may be, shows you that Cartesian products are more expensive than more restrictive joins. Even a selective join operation, the results show, is more expensive than a selection operation. Although a join operation is in query 3, it's a join of two reduced relations; the size of the join is much smaller than the join in query 2. Query optimization often involves early selection (picking only some rows) and projection (picking only some columns) operations to reduce the size of the resulting outputs or row sources.

Heuristic Strategies for Query Processing

The use of the cost-based optimization technique isn't the only way to perform query optimization. A database can also use less systematic techniques, known as *heuristic strategies*, for query processing. A join operation is called a *binary* operation, and an operation such as selection is called a *unary* operation. A successful strategy in general is to perform the unary operation early on, so the more complex and time-consuming binary operations use smaller operands. Performing as many of the unary operations as possible first reduces the row sources of the join operations. Here are some of the common heuristic query-processing strategies:

- Perform selection operations early so you can eliminate a majority of the candidate rows early in the operation. If you leave most rows in until the end, you're going to do needless comparisons with the rows that you're going to get rid of later anyway.

- Perform projection operations early so you limit the number of columns you have to deal with.

- If you need to perform consecutive join operations, perform the operation that produces the smaller join first.

- Compute common expressions once and save the results.

Query Execution

During the final stage of query processing, the optimized query (the physical query plan that has been selected) is executed. If it's a SELECT statement, the rows are returned to the user. If it's an INSERT, UPDATE, or DELETE statement, the rows are modified. The SQL execution engine takes the execution plan provided by the optimization phase and executes it.

Of the three steps involved in SQL statement processing, the optimization process is the crucial one because it determines the all-important question of how fast your data will be retrieved. Understanding how the optimizer works is at the heart of query optimization. It's important to know what the common access methods, join methods, and join orders are in order to write efficient SQL. The next section presents a detailed discussion of the all-powerful Oracle CBO.

Query Optimization and the Oracle CBO

In most cases, you have multiple ways to execute a SQL query. You can get the same results from doing a full table scan or using an index. You can also retrieve the same data by accessing the tables and indexes in a different order. The job of the optimizer is to find the optimal or best plan to execute your DML statements such as SELECT, INSERT, UPDATE, and DELETE. Oracle uses the CBO to help determine efficient methods to execute queries.

The CBO uses statistics on tables and indexes, the order of tables and columns in the SQL statements, available indexes, and any user-supplied access hints to pick the most efficient way to access them. The most efficient way, according to the CBO, is the least costly access method, cost being defined in terms of the I/O and the CPU expended in retrieving the rows. Accessing the necessary rows means Oracle reads the database blocks on the file system into the buffer pool. The resulting I/O cost is the most expensive part of SQL statement execution because it involves reading from the disk. You can examine these access paths by using tools such as the EXPLAIN PLAN. The following sections cover the tasks you need to perform to ensure that the optimizer functions efficiently.

Choosing Your Optimization Mode

In older versions of Oracle, you had a choice between a rule-based and a Cost-Based Optimizer. In a rule-based approach, Oracle used a heuristic method to select among several alternative access paths with the help of certain rules. All the access paths were assigned a rank, and the path with the lowest rank was chosen. The operations with a lower rank usually executed faster than those with a higher rank. For example, a query that uses the ROWID to search for a row has a cost of 1. This is expected because identifying a row with the help of the ROWID, an Oracle pointer-like mechanism, is the fastest way to locate a row. On the other hand, a query that uses a full table scan has a cost of 19, the highest possible cost under rule-based optimization. The CBO method almost always performs better than the older rule-based approach because, among other things, it takes into account the latest statistics about the database objects.

Providing Statistics to the Optimizer

By default, the database itself automatically collects the necessary optimizer statistics. Every night, the database schedules a statistics collection job during the maintenance window of the Oracle Scheduler. The maintenance window, by default, extends from 10 p.m. to 6 a.m. on weekdays and all weekend as well. The job is named GATHER_STATS_JOB and runs by default in every Oracle Database 11g database. You have the ability to disable the GATHER_STATS_JOB if you wish. You can get details about this default GATHER_STATS_JOB by querying the DBA_SCHEDULER_JOBS view.

The GATHER_STATS_JOB collects statistics for all tables that either don't have optimizer statistics or have stale (outdated) statistics. Oracle considers an object's statistics stale if more than 10 percent of its data has changed since the last time it collected statistics for that object. By default, Oracle monitors all DML changes such as inserts, updates, and deletes made to all database objects. You can also view the information about these changes in the DBA_TAB_MODIFICATIONS view. Based on this default object monitoring, Oracle decides whether to collect new statistics for an object.

To check that the GATHER_STATS_JOB is indeed collecting statistics on a regular basis, use the following:

```
SQL> SELECT last_analyzed, table_name, owner, num_rows, sample_size
  2  FROM dba_tables
  3* ORDER by last_analyzed;
```

TABLE_NAME	LAST_ANALYZED	OWNER	NUM_ROWS	SAMPLE_SIZE
iR_LICENSE	22/JUN/2008 12:38:56 AM	APSOWNER	142	142
ROLL_AUDIT	06/JUN/2008 11:34:29 PM	APSOWNER	8179264	5444
HISTORY_TAB	04/JUN/2008 07:28:40 AM	APSOWNER	388757	88066
YTDM_200505	04/JUN/2008 07:23:21 AM	APSSOWNER	113582	6142
REGS163X_200505	04/JUN/2008 07:23:08 AM	APSSOWNER	115631	5375
UNITS	07/JUN/2008 01:18:48 AM	APSOWNER	33633262	5144703
CAMPAIGN	16/JUN/2008 02:01:45 AM	APSOWNER	29157889	29157889
FET$	30/JUN/2008 12:03:50 AM	SYS	5692	5692

. . .
SQL>

Note the following points about the preceding output:

- The job collects statistics during the maintenance window of the database, which is, by default, scheduled between 10 p.m. and 6 a.m. during weekdays and all weekend.
- The statistics are collected by the nightly GATHER_STATS_JOB run by the Scheduler.
- If a table is created that day, the job uses all the rows of the table the first time it collects statistics for the table.
- The sampling percentage varies from less than 1 percent to 100 percent.
- The size of the table and the percentage of the sample aren't correlated.
- The job doesn't collect statistics for all the tables each day.
- If a table's data doesn't change after it's created, the job never collects a second time.

Oracle determines the sample size for each object based on its internal algorithms; there is no standard sample size for all objects. Once you verify the collection of statistics, you can pretty much leave statistics collection to the database and focus your attention elsewhere. This way, you can potentially run huge production databases for years on end, without ever having to run a manual statistics collection job using the DBMS_STATS package. Of course, if you load data during the day, or after the GATHER_STATS_JOB starts running, you'll miss the boat and the object won't have any statistics collected for it. Therefore, keep any eye on objects that might undergo huge changes during the day. You might want to schedule a statistics collection job right after the data changes occur.

In addition, you can provide the necessary statistics to the optimizer with the DBMS_STATS package yourself (the automatic statistics collection process managed by the GATHER_STATS_JOB uses the same package internally to collect statistics), which you'll learn about later on in this chapter. The necessary statistics are as follows:

- The number of rows in a table
- The number of rows per database block
- The average row length
- The total number of database blocks in a table
- The number of levels in each index
- The number of leaf blocks in each index
- The number of distinct values in each column of a table
- Data distribution histograms

- The number of distinct index keys

- Cardinality (the number of columns with similar values for each column)

- The minimum and maximum values for each column

- System statistics, which include I/O characteristics of your system; and CPU statistics, which include CPU speed and other related statistics

The key to the CBO's capability to pick the best possible query plan is its capability to correctly estimate the cost of the individual operations of the query plan. These cost estimates are derived from the knowledge about the I/O, CPU, and memory resources needed to execute each operation based on the table and index statistics. The estimates are also based on the operating system statistics that I enumerated earlier, and additional information regarding the operating system performance.

The database stores the optimizer statistics that it collects in its data dictionary. The DBA_TAB_STATISTICS table shows optimizer statistics for all the tables in your database. You can also see column statistics by querying the DBA_TAB_COL_STATISTICS view, as shown here:

```
SQL> SELECT  column_name, num_distinct
     FROM  dba_tab_col_statistics
     WHERE table_name='PERSONNEL';


COLUMN_NAME                      NUM_DISTINCT
-------------------------------- ------------
PERSON_ID                            22058066
UPDATED_DATE                          1200586
DATE_OF_BIRTH                           32185
LAST_NAME                                7281
FIRST_NAME                               1729
GENDER                                      2
HANDICAP_FLAG                               1
CREATED_DATE                          2480278
MIDDLE_NAME                             44477
SQL>
```

As you can see, more than 22 million PERSON_ID numbers are in the PERSONNEL table. However, there are only 7,281 distinct last names and 1,729 distinct first names. Of course, the GENDER column has only two distinct values. The optimizer takes into account these types of information regarding your table data, before deciding on the best plan of execution for a SQL statement that involves the table's columns.

■**Tip** Optimizer statistics include both object (table and index) statistics and system statistics. Without accurate system statistics, the optimizer can't come up with valid cost estimates to evaluate alternative execution plans.

Setting the Optimizer Mode

Oracle optimizes the throughput of queries by default. Optimizing throughput means using the fewest resources to process the entire SQL statement. You can also ask Oracle to optimize the response time, which usually means using the fewest resources to get the first (or first *n*) row(s). For batch jobs, response time for individual SQL statements is less important than the total time it takes to complete the entire operation. For interactive applications, response time is more critical.

You can use any of the following three modes for the optimizer with the CBO. The value you set for the OPTIMIZER_MODE initialization parameter is the default mode for the Oracle optimizer. The rule-based optimizer is a deprecated product, and I don't even mention it here.

- ALL_ROWS: This is the default optimizer mode, and it directs Oracle to use the CBO whether you have statistics on any of the tables in a query (derived by you through using the DBMS_STATS package or automatically by the Oracle database) or not, with the express goal of maximizing throughput.

■**Tip** In the case of all three values for the optimizing mode discussed here, I state that cost optimization is used regardless of whether there are any statistics on the objects that are being accessed in a query. What this means is that in the absence of any statistics collected with the help of the DBMS_STATS package, Oracle uses dynamic sampling techniques to collect the optimizer statistics at run time. For certain types of objects, such as external tables and remote tables, Oracle uses simple default values, instead of dynamic sampling, for the optimizer statistics. For example, Oracle uses a default value of 100 bytes for row length. Similarly, the number of rows in a table is approximated by using the number of storage blocks used by a table and the average row length. However, neither dynamic sampling nor default values give results as good as using comprehensive statistics collected using the DBMS_STATS package. Whether you collect statistics manually, or rely on Oracle's Automatic Optimizer Statistics Collection feature (which uses the DBMS_STATS package internally), optimizer statistics are collected through the DBMS_STATS package.

- FIRST_ROWS_n: This optimizing mode uses cost optimization regardless of the availability of statistics. The goal is the fastest response time for the first *n* number of rows of output, where *n* can take the value of 10, 100, or 1000.

- FIRST_ROWS: The FIRST_ROWS mode uses cost optimization and certain heuristics (rules of thumb), regardless of whether you have statistics or not. You use this option when you want the first few rows to come out quickly so response time can be minimized. Note that the FIRST_ROWS mode is retained for backward compatibility purposes only, with the FIRST_ROWS_n mode being the latest version of this model.

Setting the Optimizer Level

You can set the optimizer mode at the instance, session, or statement level. You set the optimizer mode at the instance level by setting the initialization parameter OPTIMIZER_MODE to ALL_ROWS, FIRST_ROWS_n, or FIRST_ROWS, as explained in the previous section. For example, you can set the goal of the query optimizer for the entire instance by adding the following line in your initialization parameter file:

```
OPTIMIZER_MODE = ALL_ROWS
```

Setting the initialization parameter OPTIMIZER_MODE to ALL_ROWS ensures that we can get the complete result set of the query as soon as feasible.

You can also set the optimizer mode for a single session by using the following ALTER SESSION statement:

```
SQL> ALTER SESSION SET optimizer_mode = first_rows_10;
Session altered.
SQL>
```

The previous statement directs the optimizer to base its decisions on the goal of the best response time for getting the first ten rows of the output of every SQL statement that is executed.

■**Tip** Note that the optimizer mode you choose applies only to SQL statements that are issued directly. If you use an ALTER SESSION statement to change the optimizer mode for SQL that's part of a PL/SQL code block, it'll be ignored. You must use optimizer hints, which I discuss in the section titled "Using Hints to Influence the Execution Plan," to set the optimizer mode for any SQL statement that's part of a PL/SQL block.

To determine the current optimizer mode for your database, you can run the following query:

```
SQL> SELECT name, value FROM V$PARAMETER
  2 WHERE name = 'optimizer_mode';

NAME                     VALUE
---------------          --------
optimizer_mode           ALL_ROWS
SQL>
```

Any SQL statement can override the instance- or session-level settings with the use of *optimizer hints*, which are directives to the optimizer for choosing the optimal access method. By using hints, you can override the instance-wide setting of the OPTIMIZER_MODE initialization parameter. See the section "Using Hints to Influence the Execution Plan" later in this chapter for an explanation of optimizer hints.

What Does the Optimizer Do?

The CBO performs several intricate steps to arrive at the optimal execution plan for a user's query. The original SQL statement is most likely transformed, and the CBO evaluates alternative access paths (for example, full-table or index-based scans). If table joins are necessary, the optimizer evaluates all possible join methods and join orders. The optimizer evaluates all the possibilities and arrives at the execution plan it deems the cheapest in terms of total cost, which includes both I/O and CPU resource usage cost.

SQL Transformation

Oracle hardly ever executes your query in its original form. If the CBO determines that a different SQL formulation will achieve the same results more efficiently, it transforms the statement before executing it. A good example is where you submit a query with an OR condition, and the CBO transforms it into a statement using UNION or UNION ALL. Or your statement may include an index hint, but the CBO might transform the statement so it can do a full table scan, which can be more efficient under some circumstances. In any case, it's good to remember that the query a user wishes to be executed may not be executed in the same form by Oracle, but the query's results are still the same. Here are some common transformations performed by the Oracle CBO:

- Transform IN into OR statements.
- Transform OR into UNION or UNION ALL statements.
- Transform noncorrelated nested selects into more efficient joins.
- Transform outer joins into more efficient inner joins.
- Transform complex subqueries into joins, semijoins, and antijoins.
- Perform star transformation for data warehouse tables based on the star schema.
- Transform BETWEEN to greater than or equal to and less than or equal to statements.

Choosing the Access Path

Oracle can often access the same data through different paths. For each query, the optimizer evaluates all the available paths and picks the least expensive one in terms of resource usage. The following sections present a summary of the common access methods available to the optimizer. If joins are involved, then the join order and the join method are evaluated to finally arrive at the best execution plan. You'll take a brief look at the steps the optimizer goes through before deciding on its choice of execution path.

Full Table Scans

Oracle scans the entire table during a full table scan. Oracle reads each block in the table sequentially, so the full table scan can be efficient if the database uses a high default value internally for the DB_FILE_MULTIBLOCK_READ_COUNT initialization parameter. The parameter determines the maximum number of blocks the database reads during a sequential scan. However, for large tables, full table scans are inefficient in general.

Table Access by ROWID

Accessing a table by ROWID retrieves rows using unique ROWIDs. ROWIDs in Oracle specify the exact location in the datafile and the data block where the row resides, so ROWID access is the fastest way to retrieve a row in Oracle. Often, Oracle obtains the ROWID through an index scan of the table's indexes. Using these ROWIDs, Oracle swiftly fetches the rows.

Index Scans

An index stores two things: the column value of the column on which the index is based and the ROWID of the rows in the table that contain that column value. An index scan retrieves data from an index using the values of the index columns. If the query requests only the indexed column values, Oracle will return those values. If the query requests other columns outside the indexed column, Oracle will use the ROWIDs to get the rows of the table.

Choosing the Join Method

When you need to access data that's in two or more tables, Oracle joins the tables based on a common column. However, there are several ways to join the row sets returned from the execution plan steps. For each statement, Oracle evaluates the best join method based on the statistics and the type of unique or primary keys on the tables. After Oracle has evaluated the join methods, the CBO picks the join method with the least cost.

The following are the common join methods used by the CBO:

- *Nested loop join*: A nested loop join involves the designation of one table as the *driving table* (also called the *outer table*) in the join loop. The other table in the join is called the *inner table*. Oracle fetches all the rows of the inner table for every row in the driving table.

- *Hash join*: When you join two tables, Oracle uses the smaller table to build a hash table on the join key. Oracle then searches the larger table and returns the joined rows from the hash table.

- *Sort-merge join*: The sort join operation sorts the inputs on the join key, and the merge join operation merges the sorted lists. If the input is already sorted by the join column, there's no need for a sort join operation for that row source.

Choosing the Join Order

Once the optimizer chooses the join method, it determines the order in which the tables are joined. The goal of the optimizer is always to join tables in such a way that the driving table eliminates the largest number of rows. A query with four tables has a maximum of 4 factorial, or 24, possible ways in which the tables can be joined. Each such join order would lead to a number of different execution plans, based on the available indexes and the access methods. The search for an optimal join strategy could take a long time in a query with a large number of tables, so Oracle depends on an *adaptive search strategy* to limit the time it takes to find the best execution plan. An adaptive search strategy means that the time taken for optimization is always a small percentage of the total time that is taken for execution of the query itself.

Drawbacks of the CBO

The CBO is systematic, but the optimizer is not guaranteed to follow the same plan in similar cases. However, the CBO isn't always perfect, and you need to watch out for the following:

- The CBO isn't fixed across Oracle versions. Execution plans can change over time as versions change. Later in this chapter, you'll see how to use stored outlines so the optimizer always uses a known plan to maintain plan stability.

- Application developers may know more than the CBO when it comes to choosing the best access path. Application developers know the needs of the users, of which the CBO is completely unaware. This could lead to a situation where the CBO may be optimizing throughput, when the users would rather have a quick set of results on their screen. By using hints such as FIRST_ROWS_*n*, you can overcome this drawback in the CBO.

- The CBO depends enormously on correct statistics gathering. If the statistics are absent or outdated, the optimizer can make poor decisions.

Providing Statistics to the CBO

The CBO can follow optimal execution paths only if it has detailed knowledge of the database objects. Starting with Oracle Database 10*g*, the recommended way to provide these statistics is by letting the database automatically collect statistics for you. This is known as the Automatic Optimizer Statistics Collection feature, which I explained in Chapter 17. You can also manually provide statistics to the optimizer with the DBMS_STATS package. Note that whether you rely on automatic collection of statistics or collect them yourself manually, Oracle uses the DBMS_STATS package to collect statistics.

Using DBMS_STATS to Collect Statistics

Although letting the database automatically collect optimizer statistics is the recommended approach, you can still manually collect optimizer statistics using the DBMS_STATS package.

■**Tip** For large tables, Oracle recommends just sampling the data, rather than looking at all of it. Oracle lets you specify row or block sampling, and it sometimes seems to recommend sampling sizes as low as 5 percent. The default sampling size for an estimate is low too. Oracle also recommends using the DBMS_STATS automatic sampling procedure. However, statistics gathered with sampled data aren't reliable. The difference between collecting optimizer statistics with the estimate at 30 percent and 50 percent is startling at times in terms of performance. Always choose the option of collecting full statistics for all your objects, even if the frequency is not as high as it could be if you just sampled the data.

As I explained in Chapter 17, you *must* manually collect optimizer statistics under the following conditions:

- When you use external tables

- When you need to collect system statistics

- To collect statistics on fixed objects, such as the dynamic performance tables (For dynamic tables, you should use the GATHER_FIXED_OBJECTS_STATS procedure to collect optimizer statistics.)

- Immediately after you run a bulk load job, because this makes your automatically collected statistics unrepresentative

The following sections show you how to make use of the DBMS_STATS package to gather statistics.

■**Note** Oracle recommends that you not use the older ANALYZE statement to collect statistics for the optimizer, but rather use the DBMS_STATS package. The ANALYZE command is retained for backward compatibility, and you must use it for non-optimizer statistics collection tasks, such as verifying the validity of an object (using the VALIDATE clause), or identifying migrated and chained rows in a table (using the LIST CHAINED ROWS clause).

Storing the Optimizer Statistics

You use various DBMS_STATS package procedures to collect optimizer statistics. Most of these procedures have three common attributes—STATOWN, STATTAB, and STATID—which enable you to save the collected statistics in a database table owned by a user. By default, these attributes are null, and you shouldn't provide a value for any of these attributes if your goal is to collect statistics for the optimizer. When you ignore these attributes, optimizer statistics you collect are stored in the data dictionary tables by default, where they're accessible to the Oracle optimizer.

Collecting the Statistics

The DBMS_STATS package has several procedures that let you collect data at different levels. The main data collection procedures for database table and index data are as follows:

- GATHER_DATABASE_STATISTICS gathers statistics for all objects in the database.

- GATHER_SCHEMA_STATISTICS gathers statistics for an entire schema.

- GATHER_TABLE_STATISTICS gathers statistics for a table and its indexes.

- GATHER_INDEX_STATISTICS gathers statistics for an index.

Let's use the DBMS_STATS package to collect statistics first for a schema, and then for an individual table.

- Collecting statistics at the schema level:

```
SQL> EXECUTE DBMS_STATS.GATHER_SCHEMA_STATS (ownname => 'hr');
PL/SQL procedure successfully completed.
SQL>
```

- Collecting statistics at the table level:

```
SQL> EXECUTE DBMS_STATS.GATHER_TABLE_STATS ('hr','employees');
PL/SQL procedure successfully completed.
SQL>
```

The GATHER_DATABASE_STATISTICS procedure collects optimizer statistics for the entire database. This is probably the most common way of using the DBMS_STATS package, as you can use this procedure to collect statistics for all database objects with a single statement. Here's an example:

```
SQL> EXECUTE dbms_stats.gather_database_stats (-
    > ESTIMATE_PERCENT => NULL, -
    > METHOD_OPT => 'FOR ALL COLUMNS SIZE AUTO', -
    > GRANULARITY => 'ALL', -
    > CASCADE => 'TRUE',-
    > OPTIONS => 'GATHER AUTO');

PL/SQL procedure successfully completed.
SQL>
```

■**Tip** Although you can use the ESTIMATE_PERCENT attribute to collect optimizer statistics for a sample ranging from 0.000001 to 100 percent of the rows in a table, you should strive to collect statistics for all the rows (by using null as the value for this attribute). Collecting statistics based on a sample is fraught with dangers. Unless the tables are so huge that you can't collect all statistics within your maintenance window, strive to collect full statistics on all objects, especially those that have heavy DML changes.

Let me explain the preceding GATHER_DATABASE_STATS procedure briefly here:

- The example shows only some of the various attributes or parameters that you can specify. You can see the complete list of attributes by typing in this command:

  ```
  SQL> DESCRIBE DBMS_STATS.GATHER_DATABASE_STATS
  ```

- If you don't specify any of the attributes, Oracle uses the default values for those attributes. Even when I use a default value, I list the attribute here, for exposition purposes.

- The ESTIMATE_PERCENT attribute refers to the percentage of rows that should be used to estimate the statistics. I chose null as the value. Null here, contrary to intuition, means that Oracle collects statistics based on *all* rows in a table. This is the same as using the COMPUTE STATISTICS option in the traditional ANALYZE command. The default for this attribute is to let Oracle estimate the sample size for each object, using the DBMS_STATS.AUTO_SAMPLE_SIZE procedure.

- You can use the METHOD_OPT attribute to specify several things, including whether histograms should be collected. Here, I chose FOR ALL COLUMNS SIZE AUTO, which is the default value for this attribute.

- The GRANULARITY attribute applies only to tables. The ALL value collects statistics for subpartitions, partitions, and global statistics for all tables.

- The CASCADE=>YES option specifies that statistics be gathered on all indexes, along with the table statistics.

- The OPTIONS attribute is critical. The most important values for this attribute are as follows:

  - GATHER gathers statistics for all objects, regardless of whether they have stale or fresh statistics.

  - GATHER AUTO collects statistics for only those objects that Oracle deems necessary.

  - GATHER EMPTY collects statistics only for objects without statistics.

  - GATHER STALE results in collection of statistics for only stale objects, the determination as to the object staleness being made by checking the DBA_TAB_MODIFICATIONS view.

Note that you could also execute the GATHER_DATABASE_STATS procedure in the following format, which produces equivalent results:

```
SQL> BEGIN
        dbms_stats.gather_database_stats (ESTIMATE_PERCENT => NULL, METHOD_OPT =>
        'FOR ALL COLUMNS SIZE AUTO',
        GRANULARITY => 'ALL',  CASCADE => 'TRUE', OPTIONS => 'GATHER AUTO');
        END;
PL/SQL procedure successfully completed.

SQL>
```

You can check when a table has last been analyzed by using the following query:

```
SQL> SELECT table_name, last_analyzed FROM dba_tables;

TABLE_NAME            LAST_ANALYZED
-----------           --------------
TEST1                    07/08/2008
TEST2                    07/08/2008
TEST3                    07/08/2008
. . .
SQL>
```

You can use a similar query for indexes, using the DBA_INDEXES view.

■**Tip** Make sure you have the initialization parameter JOB_QUEUE_PROCESSES set to a positive number. If this param-eter isn't set, it takes the default value of 0, and your DBMS_STATS.GATHER_SYSTEM_STATS procedure won't work. You can do this dynamically; for example, issue the command ALTER SYSTEM SET JOB_QUEUE_PROCESSES = 20.

Deferred Statistics Publishing

By default, the database publishes the statistics it collects for immediate use by the optimizer. However, there may be times when you don't want this to happen. Instead, you may wish to first test the statis-tics and release them for public use only if you're satisfied with them. Oracle lets you save new statistics collected by the database as pending statistics, which you can publish or not ultimately, based on your testing of the statistics. Current or published statistics are meant to be used by the optimizer, and pending or deferred statistics are private statistics, which are kept from the optimizer.

Determining and Setting the Status of the Statistics

Execute the DBMS_STATS.GET_PREFS procedure to determine the publishing status of statistics in your database:

```
SQL> select dbms_stats.get_prefs('PUBLISH') publish from dual;

PUBLISH
--------
TRUE

SQL>
```

The value TRUE indicates that the database automatically publishes all statistics after it collects them. This is the default behavior of the database. If the query had returned the value FALSE, it means that the database will keep new statistics pending until you decide to formally publish them. You can also execute the GET_PREFS function to find out the publishing mode for a single table:

```
SQL> SELECT dbms_stats.get_prefs('PUBLISH','stats','test_table')
     FROM dual;
```

You can change the publishing settings for objects at the database or at the object (table) level by executing the SET_TABLE_PREFS function. For example, to keep the database from automatically publishing the statistics it collects for the table EMPLOYEES, execute this function:

```
SQL> exec dbms_stats.set_table_prefs ('HR','EMPLOYEES',
     'PUBLISH','FALSE');
```

The database stores pending statistics in the DBA_TAB_PENDING_STATS view and it stores the published statistics in the DBA_TAB_STATS view.

Making Pending Statistics Public

You can test any pending statistics in your database to see how they affect performance. If they help performance, you can publish them for use by the optimizer; otherwise, just drop the statistics. You publish the pending statistics, that is, make them available to the optimizer for testing purposes, by setting the initialization parameter OPTIMIZER_USE_PENDING_STATISTICS. By default, this parameter is set to FALSE, which means the optimizer will bypass the pending statistics, as shown here:

```
SQL> show parameter optimizer_use_pending_statistics
```

NAME	TYPE	VALUE
optimizer_use_pending_statistics	boolean	FALSE

```
SQL>
```

You can make the optimizer take the pending statistics into account by setting the OPTIMIZER_USE_PENDING_STATISTICS parameter to TRUE, as shown here:

```
SQL> ALTER SESSION SET optimizer_use_pending_statistics=TRUE ;
```

The optimizer will use the pending statistics once you run the previous statement. Once your tests confirm that the new statistics are OK, you can make the pending statistics public by executing the PUBLISH_PENDING_STATS procedure:

```
SQL> EXEC dbms_stats.publish_pending_stats (NULL,NULL);
```

If you want to publish statistics for a single table, you can do so as well:

```
SQL> EXEC dbms_stats.publish_pending_stats('HR','EMPLOYEES');
```

If you conclude, on the other hand, that the pending statistics aren't helpful, delete them by executing the DELETE_PENDING_STATS procedure:

```
SQL> EXEC dbms_stats.delete_pending_stats ('HR','EMPLOYEES');
```

You can also test the pending statistics you collect in one database in another database, by using the EXPORT_PENDING_STATS procedure:

```
SQL> EXEC dbms_stats.export_pending_stats ('HR', 'EMPLOYEES');
```

Extended Statistics

The statistics that the database collects are sometimes unrepresentative of the true data. Oracle provides the capability for collecting extended statistics under some circumstances to mitigate the problems in statistics collection. Extended statistics include the collection of multicolumn statistics for groups of columns and expression statistics that collect statistics on function-based columns. I explain both types of extended optimizer statistics in the following sections.

Multicolumn Statistics

When Oracle collects statistics on a table, it estimates the selectivity of each column separately, even when two or more columns may be closely related. Oracle assumes that the selectivity estimates of the individual columns are independent of each other and simply multiplies the independent predicates' selectivity to figure out selectivity of the group of predicates. This approach leads to an underestimation of the true selectivity of the group of columns. You can collect statistics for a group of columns to avoid this underestimation.

I use a simple example to show why collecting statistics for column groups instead of individual columns is a good idea when the columns are related. In the SH.CUSTOMERS table, the CUST_STATE_PROVINCE and the COUNTRY_ID columns are correlated, with the former column determining the value of the latter column. Here's a query that shows the relationship between the two columns:

```
SQL> SELECT count(*)
       FROM sh.customers
       WHERE cust_state_province = 'CA';

COUNT(*)
----------
    3341

SQL>
```

The previous query uses only a single column, CUST_STATE_PROVINCE, to get a count of the number of customers from the province named "CA." The following query also involves the COUNTRY_ID column, but returns the same count, 3341.

```
SQL> SELECT count(*)
       FROM customers
       WHERE cust_state_province = 'CA'
       AND country_id=52790;

COUNT(*)
----------
    3341

SQL>
```

Obviously, the same query with a different value for the COUNTRY_ID column will return a different count (most likely zero, since CA stands for California and it's unlikely that a city of the same name is present in other countries). You can collect statistics on a set of related columns such as CUST_STATE_PROVINCE and COUNTRY_ID by estimating the combined selectivity of the two columns. The database can collect statistics for column groups based on the database workload, but you create column groups by using the DBMS_STATS.CREATE_EXTENDED_STATS function, as I explain next.

Creating Column Groups

You create a column group by executing the CREATE_EXTENDED_STATS function, as shown in this example:

```
declare
  cg_name varchar2(30);
begin
  cg_name := dbms_stats.create_extended_stats(null,'customers',
  '(cust_state_province,country_id)');
end;
/
```

Once you create a column group as shown here, the database will automatically collect statistics for the column group instead of the two columns as individual entities. The following query verifies the successful creation of the new column group:

```
SQL> SELECT extension_name, extension
     FROM dba_stat_extensions
     WHERE table_name='CUSTOMERS';


EXTENSION_NAME                      EXTENSION
-----------------------------       -----------------------------------
SYS_STU#S#WF25Z#QAHIHE#MOFFMM_      ("CUST_STATE_PROVINCE","COUNTRY-ID")

SQL>
```

You can drop a column group by executing the DROP_EXTENDED_STATS function:

```
SQL> exec dbms_stats.drop_extended_stats('sh','customers','
     (cust_state_province, country_id)');
```

Collecting Statistics for Column Groups

You can execute the GATHER_TABLE_STATS procedure with the METHOD_OPT argument set to the value for all columns . . . to collect statistics for column groups. By adding the FOR COLUMNS clause, you can have the database create the new column group as well as collect statistics for it, all in one step, as shown here:

```
SQL> exec dbms_Stats.gather_table_stats(
     ownname=>null,-
     tabname=>'customers',-
     method_opt=>'for all columns size skewonly,-
     for columns (cust_state_province,country_id) size skewonly');

PL/SQL procedure successfully completed.
SQL>
```

Expression Statistics

If you apply a function to a column, the column value changes. For example, the LOWER function in the following example returns a lowercase string:

```
SQL> SELECT count(*)
     FROM customers
     WHERE LOWER(cust_state_province)='ca';
```

Although the LOWER function transforms the values of the CUST_STATE_PROVINCE column by making them lowercase, the optimizer has only the original column estimates and not the changed columns estimates. So, the optimizer really doesn't have an accurate idea about the true selectivity of the transformed values of the column. You can collect expression statistics on some types of column expressions, in those cases where the function preserves the original data distribution characteristics of the original column. This is true when you apply a function such as TO_NUMBER to a column. You can use function-based expressions for user-defined functions as well as function-based indexes.

The expression statistics feature relies on Oracle's virtual column capabilities. You execute the CREATE_EXTENDED_STATS function to create statistics on column expressions, as shown here:

```
SQL> SELECT
        dbms_stats.create_extended_stats(null,'customers',
        '(lower(cust_state_province))')
     FROM dual;
```

Alternatively, you can execute the GATHER_TABLE_STATS function to create expression statistics:

```
SQL> exec dbms_stats.gather_table_stats(null,'customers',
        method_opt=>'for all columns size skewonly,
        for columns (lower(cust_state_province)) size skewonly');
```

As with the column group statistics, you can query the DBA_STAT_EXTENSIONS view to find out details about expression statistics.

The Cost Model of the Oracle Optimizer

The cost model of the optimizer takes into account both I/O cost and CPU cost, both in units of time. The CBO evaluates alternative query costs by comparing the total time it takes to perform all the I/O operations, as well as the number of CPU cycles necessary for the query execution. The CBO takes the total number of I/Os and CPU cycles that will be necessary according to its estimates, and converts them into execution time. It then compares the execution time of the alternative execution paths and chooses the best candidate for execution.

For the CBO to compute the cost of alternative paths accurately, it must have access to accurate system statistics. These statistics, which include items such as I/O seek time, I/O transfer time, and CPU speed, tell the optimizer how fast the system I/O and CPU perform. It's the DBA's job to provide these statistics to the optimizer. I show how to collect system statistics in the following section.

Collecting System Statistics

Although Oracle can automatically collect optimizer statistics for you regarding your tables and indexes, you need to collect operating system statistics with the GATHER_SYSTEM_STATS procedure. When you do this, Oracle populates the SYS.AUX_STATS$ table with various operating system statistics, such as CPU and I/O performance. Gathering system statistics at regular intervals is critical, because the Oracle CBO uses these statistics as the basis of its cost computations for various queries. System statistics enable the optimizer to compare more accurately the I/O and CPU costs of alternative execution. The optimizer is also able to figure out the execution time of a query more accurately if you provide it with accurate system statistics.

You can run the GATHER_SYSTEM_STATS procedure in different modes by passing values to the GATHERING_MODE parameter. There's a no-workload mode you can specify to quickly capture the I/O system characteristics. You can also specify a workload-specific mode by using the INTERVAL, START, and STOP values for the GATHERING_MODE parameter. Here's a brief explanation of the different values you can specify for the GATHERING_MODE parameter:

- *No-workload mode*: By using the NOWORKLOAD keyword, you can collect certain system statistics that mostly pertain to general I/O characteristics of your system, such as I/O seek time (IOSEEKTIM) and I/O transfer speed (IOTFRSPEED). You should ideally run the GATHER_ SYSTEM_STATS procedure in no-workload mode right after you create a new database. The procedure takes only a few minutes to complete and is suitable for all types of workloads.

Note If you collect both workload and no-workload statistics, the optimizer will use the workload statistics.

- *Workload mode*: To collect representative statistics such as CPU and I/O performance, you must collect system statistics during a specified interval that represents a typical workload for your instance. You can use the INTERVAL keyword to specify statistics collection for a certain interval of time. You can alternatively use the START and STOP keywords to collect system statistics for a certain length of time. Under both workload settings for the GATHERING_MODE parameter (INTERVAL, or START and STOP), the database collects the following statistics: MAXTHR, SLAVETHR, CPUSPEED, SREADTIM, MREADTIM, and MBRC.

Here's what the various system statistics I mentioned stand for:

- IOTFRSPEED: I/O transfer speed (bytes per millisecond)
- IOSEEKTIM: Seek time + latency time + operating system overhead time (milliseconds)
- SREADTIM: Average time to (randomly) read a single block (milliseconds)
- MREADTIM: Average time to (sequentially) read an MBRC block at once (milliseconds)
- CPUSPEED: Average number of CPU cycles captured for the workload (statistics collected using the INTERVAL or START and STOP options)
- CPUSPEEDNW: Average number of CPU cycles captured for the no-workload mode (statistics collected using NOWORKLOAD option)
- MBR: Average multiblock read count for sequential read, in blocks
- MAXTHR: Maximum I/O system throughput (bytes/second)
- SLAVETHR: Average slave I/O throughput (bytes/second)

Here's the structure of the GATHER_SYSTEM_STATS procedure:

```
DBMS_STATS.GATHER_SYSTEM_STATS (
    gathering_mode    VARCHAR2 DEFAULT 'NOWORKLOAD',
    interval          INTEGER  DEFAULT NULL,
    stattab           VARCHAR2 DEFAULT NULL,
    statid            VARCHAR2 DEFAULT NULL,
    statown           VARCHAR2 DEFAULT NULL);
```

Here's an example that shows how to use the procedure to collect system statistics:

```
SQL> EXECUTE dbms_stats.gather_system_stats('start');
PL/SQL procedure successfully completed.
SQL>
SQL> EXECUTE dbms_stats.gather_system_stats('stop');
PL/SQL procedure successfully completed.
SQL>
SQL> SELECT * FROM sys.aux_stats$;
```

```
SNAME              PNAME           PVAL1      PVAL2
-------------      -------------   ---------- -----------------
SYSSTATS_INFO      STATUS                     COMPLETED
SYSSTATS_INFO      DSTART                     04-25-2008 10:44
SYSSTATS_INFO      DSTOP                      04-26-2008 10:17
SYSSTATS_INFO      FLAGS                   1
SYSSTATS_MAIN      CPUSPEEDNW         67.014
SYSSTATS_MAIN      IOSEEKTIM          10.266
SYSSTATS_MAIN      IOTFRSPEED      10052.575
SYSSTATS_MAIN      SREADTIM            5.969
SYSSTATS_MAIN      MREADTIM            5.711
SYSSTATS_MAIN      CPUSPEED              141
SYSSTATS_MAIN      MBRC                   18
SYSSTATS_MAIN      MAXTHR           17442816
SYSSTATS_MAIN      SLAVETHR

13 rows selected.
SQL>
```

■**Note** You can view system statistics by using the GET_SYSTEM_STATISTICS procedure of the DBMS_STATS package.

Collecting Statistics on Dictionary Objects

You should collect optimizer statistics on data dictionary tables to maximize performance. The two types of dictionary tables are *fixed* and *real*. You can't change or delete dynamic performance tables, which means they are fixed. Real dictionary tables belong to schemas such as sys and system.

Collecting Statistics for Fixed Objects

Oracle recommends that you gather statistics for dynamic performance tables (fixed objects) only once for every database workload, which is usually a week for most OLTP databases. You can collect fixed object statistics in a couple ways, as follows:

- You can use the DBMS_STATS_GATHER_DATABASE_STATS procedure and set the GATHER_ SYS argument to TRUE (the default is FALSE).

- You can use the GATHER_FIXED_OBJECTS_STATS procedure of the DBMS_STATS package, as shown here:

```
SQL> SHO USER
USER is "SYS"
SQL> EXECUTE DBMS_STATS.GATHER_FIXED_OBJECTS_STATS;
```

■**Tip** Before you can analyze any dictionary objects or fixed objects, you need the SYSDBA or ANALYZE ANY DICTIONARY system privilege.

You can use the procedures from the DBMS_STATS package that enable table-level statistics collection to collect statistics for an individual fixed table.

Collecting Statistics for Real Dictionary Tables

You can use the following methods to collect statistics for real dictionary tables:

- Set the GATHER_SYS argument of the DBMS_STATS.GATHER_DATABASE_STATS procedure to TRUE. You can also use the GATHER_SCHEMA_STATS ('SYS') option.

- Use the DBMS_STATS.GATHER_DICTIONARY_STATS procedure, as shown here:

```
SQL> SHO user
USER is "SYS"
SQL> EXECUTE dbms_stats.gather_dictionary_stats;
```

The GATHER_DICTIONARY_STATS procedure helps you collect statistics for tables owned by the SYS and SYSTEM users as well as the owners of all database components.

■**Note** You can also use the DBMS_STATS package to delete, import, restore, and set optimizer statistics that you have previously collected.

Frequency of Statistics Collection

Theoretically, if your data is static, you may only need to collect statistics once. If your database performs only a small amount of DML activities, you may collect statistics at relatively longer intervals, say weekly or monthly. However, if your database objects go through changes on a daily basis, you need to schedule the statistics collection jobs much more frequently, say daily or even more often. You can avoid having to decide on the frequency of the statistics collection by letting the database itself decide when to collect new statistics. Remember that the database bases its statistics collection on whether the statistics are "fresh" or "stale." Thus, you can relax and let the database be the arbiter of how often to collect statistics.

What Happens When You Don't Have Statistics

You've seen how the Oracle database can automatically collect optimizer statistics for you. You've also learned how to use the DBMS_STATS package to collect the statistics manually yourself. But what happens if you disable the automatic statistics collection process, or if you don't collect statistics in a timely fashion? Even with automatic statistics collection, under which necessary statistics are collected on a nightly basis, you may have a situation where table data is altered after the statistics collection process is over. In situations such as this, Oracle uses data, such as the number of blocks taken up by the table data and other ancillary information, to figure out the optimizer execution plan.

You can also use the initialization parameter OPTIMIZER_DYNAMIC_SAMPLING to let Oracle estimate optimizer statistics on the fly, when no statistics exist for a table, or when the statistics exist but are too old or otherwise unreliable. Of course, sampling statistics dynamically would mean that the compile time for the SQL statement involved would be longer. Oracle smartly figures out if the increased compile time is worth it when it encounters objects without statistics. If it's worth it, Oracle will sample a portion of the object's data blocks to estimate statistics. Note that the additional compile time is really not relevant because it happens only once at the initial parsing stage and not for all the subsequent executions for a SQL statement. You need to set the value of the OPTIMIZER_DYNAMIC_ SAMPLING initialization parameter to 2 or higher to enable dynamic sampling of all unanalyzed tables. Because the default for this parameter is 2, dynamic sampling is turned on by default in your database. Thus, you need not spend sleepless nights worrying about objects with missing or outdated statistics. In any case, if you adhere to Oracle's recommendation and use the Automatic Optimizer Statistics Collection feature, the GATHER_STATS_JOB will automatically collect your database's statistics.

The GATHER_STATS_JOB is created at database creation time and is managed by the Oracle Scheduler, which runs the job when the maintenance window is opened. By default, the maintenance window opens every night from 10 p.m. to 6 a.m., and all day on weekends. Oracle will collect statistics for all objects that need them if you adopt the Automatic Optimizer Statistics Collection feature. The feature is turned on by default in a new Oracle 11g database or when you upgrade to the 11g release from an older release–based database.

Using the OEM to Collect Optimizer Statistics

As with so many other DBA tasks in Oracle Database 11g, you're better off simply using the OEM Database Control or the Grid Control to schedule the collection of optimizer statistics. Here are the steps to collect optimizer statistics using the Database Control or Grid Control interfaces of the OEM:

1. From the Database Control home page, click the Administration tab.

2. In the Administration page, click the Manage Optimizer Statistics link under the Statistics Management group.

3. You're now in the Manage Optimizer Statistics page. Click the Gather Statistics link to start collecting statistics and follow the instructions for the five steps you must implement.

Figure 19-1 shows part of the optimizer statistics collection process using the OEM Grid Control interface.

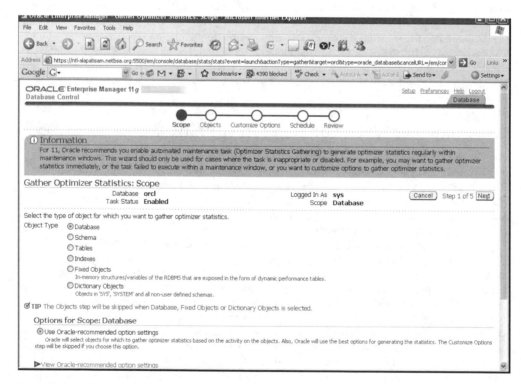

Figure 19-1. *Collecting optimizer statistics through the OEM*

■**Note** Oracle strongly recommends that you just use the Oracle-created GATHER_STATS_JOB, run by the Scheduler during the scheduled maintenance window, to collect optimizer statistics. You may want to collect optimizer statistics manually under an extreme situation, such as the database not being up during the scheduled maintenance window, or if you want to analyze a newly created table right away.

Writing Efficient SQL

One of the trickiest and most satisfying aspects of a DBA's job is helping to improve the quality of SQL code in the application. Efficient code means fast performance, and an easy way to decrease the I/O your query requires is to try to lower the number of rows that the optimizer has to examine. The optimizer is supposed to find the optimal plan based on your query. This means the optimizer won't rewrite an inefficiently written query—it only produces the execution plan for that query. Also, even if your query is efficiently written, the optimizer may not always end up producing the best execution plan. You have better knowledge of your application and data than the optimizer does, and you can, with hints, force the optimizer to use that knowledge. The following sections cover some of the best guidelines for writing good SQL.

Efficient WHERE Clauses

Selective criteria in your WHERE clauses can dramatically decrease the amount of data Oracle has to consider during a query. You can follow some simple principles to ensure that the structure of your SQL statements is not inherently inefficient. Your join methods may be fine, but overlooking some of these principles could doom your statement from a performance point of view.

Careful specification of WHERE conditions can have a significant bearing on whether the optimizer will choose existing indexes. The principle of *selectivity*—the number of rows returned by a query as a percentage of the total number of rows in a table—is the key idea here. A low percentage means high selectivity and a high percentage means the reverse. Because more selective WHERE clauses mean fewer I/Os, the CBO tends to prefer to choose those kinds of WHERE clauses over others in the same query. The following example makes this clear:

```
SQL> SELECT * FROM national_employees
    WHERE ss_no = 515086789
    AND city='DALLAS';
```

Two WHERE clauses are in this example, but you can see that the first WHERE clause that uses ss_no requires fewer I/Os. The column ss_no is the primary key and is highly selective—only one row with that ss_no is in the entire table. The optimizer determines the selectivity of each of the two columns in the query by looking at the index statistics, which tell it how many rows in the table contain each of the two column values in the query. If neither of the columns has an index, Oracle will use a full table scan to retrieve the answer to the query. If both of them have indexes, it will use the more selective (and hence more efficient) index on the ss_no column.

If you think that the optimizer should have used an index instead of doing a full table scan, then perform the following steps:

1. Views in a query sometimes prevent the use of indexes. Check to make sure that the execution plan shows that the correct indexes are being used.

2. If you think heavy data skew is in the table, use histograms to provide Oracle with a more accurate representation of the data distribution in the table. The CBO assumes a uniform distribution of column data. The CBO may forego the use of an index even when a column value is selective, because the column itself is unselective in nature. Histograms help by providing the CBO with an accurate picture of the column data distribution. I discuss histograms later in this chapter, in the section "Using Histograms."

3. If Oracle is still refusing to use the index, force it to do so by using an index hint, as explained in the section "Using Hints to Influence the Execution Plan" later in this chapter.

■**Note** It isn't always obvious why Oracle doesn't use an index. For example, Oracle may not use an index because the indexed columns are part of an IN list, and the consequent transformation prevents the use of an index.

If you use a WHERE clause such as WHERE *last_name* LIKE '%MA%', the optimizer might just decide to skip the index and do a full scan of the table because it needs to perform a pattern match of the entire LAST_NAME column to retrieve data. The optimizer correctly figures that it will go ahead and look up just the table, instead of having to read both the index and the table values. For example, if a table has 1,000 rows placed in 200 blocks, and you perform a full table scan assuming that the database has set the DB_FILE_MULTIBLOCK_READ_COUNT to 8, you'll incur a total of 25 I/Os to read in the entire table. If your index has a low selectivity, most of the index has to be read first. If your index has 40 leaf blocks and you have to read 90 percent of them to get the indexed data first, your I/O is already at 32. On top of this, you have to incur additional I/O to read the table values. However, a full table scan costs you only 25 I/Os, making that a far more efficient choice than using the index. Be aware that the mere existence of an index on a column doesn't guarantee that it will be used all the time.

You'll look at some important principles to make your queries more efficient in the following sections.

Using SQL Functions

If you use SQL functions in the WHERE clause (for example, the SUBSTR, INSTR, TO_DATE, and TO_NUMBER functions), the Oracle optimizer will ignore the index on that column. Make sure you use a function-based index if you must use a SQL function in the WHERE clause.

Using the Right Joins

Most of your SQL statements will involve multitable joins. Often, improper table-joining strategies doom a query. Here are some pointers regarding joining tables wisely:

- Using the *equi join* leads to a more efficient query path than otherwise. Try to use equi joins wherever possible.

- Performing filtering operations early reduces the number of rows to be joined in later steps. Fop example, a WHERE condition applied early reduces the row source that needs to be joined to another table. The goal is to use the table that has the most selective filter as the driving table, because this means fewer rows are passed to the next step.

- Join in the order that will produce the least number of rows as output to the parent step.

Using the CASE Statement

When you need to calculate multiple aggregates from the same table, avoid writing a separate query for each aggregate. With separate queries, Oracle has to read the entire table for each query. It's more efficient to use the CASE statement in this case, as it enables you to compute multiple aggregates from the table with just a single read of the table.

Efficient Subquery Execution

Subqueries perform better when you use IN rather than EXISTS. Oracle recommends using the IN clause if the subquery has the selective WHERE clause. If the parent query contains the selective WHERE clause, use the EXISTS clause rather than the IN clause.

Using WHERE Instead of HAVING

Wherever possible, use the WHERE clause instead of the HAVING clause. The WHERE clause restricts the number of rows retrieved at the outset. The HAVING clause forces the retrieval of a lot more rows than necessary. It then also incurs the additional overhead of sorting and summing.

Minimizing Table Lookups

One of the primary mottos of query writing is "Visit the data as few times as possible." This means getting rid of SQL that repeatedly accesses a table for different column values. Use multicolumn updates instead.

Using Hints to Influence the Execution Plan

The assumption that underlies the use of the CBO is that the optimizer knows best. That is, by evaluating the various statistics, the CBO will come to the best decision in terms of choosing the optimal execution plan. However, the optimizer is based on rules, and a good application developer has knowledge about the application and data that the CBO can't exploit. You can provide *hints* to the optimizer to override the CBO's execution plans. For example, if you know that a certain index is more selective than another, you can force Oracle to use that index by providing the hint in your query.

Hints can alter the join method, join order, or access path. You can also provide hints to parallelize the SQL statement operations. The following are some of the common hints that you can use in SQL statements:

- ALL_ROWS: The ALL_ROWS hint instructs Oracle to optimize throughput (that is, minimize total cost), not optimize the response time of the statement.

- FIRST_ROWS(n): The FIRST_ROWS(n) hint dictates that Oracle return the first *n* rows quickly. Low response time is the goal of this hint.

■**Note** When you specify ALL_ROWS or the FIRST_ROWS(n) hint, it overrides the current value of the OPTIMIZER_MODE parameter, if it's different from that specified by the hint.

- FULL: The FULL hint requires that a full scan be done on the table, ignoring any indexes that may be present. You would want to do this when you have reason to believe that using an index in this case will be inefficient compared to a full table scan. To force Oracle to do a full table scan, you use the FULL hint.

- ORDERED: This hint forces the join order for the tables in the query.

- INDEX: This hint forces the use of an index scan, even if the optimizer was going to ignore the indexes and do a full table scan for some reason.

- INDEX_FFS: An index fast full scan (INDEX_FFS) hint forces a fast full scan of an index, just as if you did a full table scan that scans several blocks at a time. INDEX_FFS scans all the blocks in an index using multiblock I/O, the size of which is determined by the DB_FILE_MULTIBLOCK_READ_COUNT parameter. You can also parallelize an INDEX_FFS hint, and it's generally preferable to a full table scan.

The OPTIMIZER_MODE settings determine the way the query optimizer performs optimization throughout the database. However, at times, due to lack of accurate statistics, the optimizer can be mistaken in its estimates, leading to poor execution plans. In cases such as this, you can use optimizer hints to override this database optimization setting at the individual SQL statement level. Oracle Database 11*g* also provides the SQL Profile feature. This feature enables you to collect auxiliary information using sampling and partial execution techniques, thereby avoiding the use of optimizer hints. I discuss SQL profiles in the section titled "Using the SQL Tuning Advisor on SQL Statements," later in this chapter.

Selecting the Best Join Method

Choose a join method based on how many rows you expect to be returned from the join. The optimizer generally tries to choose the ideal join condition, but it may not do so for various reasons. It's up to you to see what join method the optimizer will adopt and change it if necessary. The following guidelines will help you when you're analyzing output produced by an EXPLAIN PLAN.

Avoiding Cartesian Joins

Cartesian joins usually aren't the result of intentional planning; rather, they happen due to logical mistakes in the query. Cartesian joins are produced when your joins don't have any WHERE clauses. If you're joining several tables, make sure that each table in the join is referenced by a WHERE condition. Even if the tables being joined are small, avoid Cartesian joins because they're inefficient. For example, if the employee table has 2,000 rows and the dept table has 100 rows, a Cartesian join of employee and dept will have 2,000 * 100 = 200,000 rows.

Nested Loops

If you're joining small subsets of data, the nested loop (NL) method is ideal. If you're returning fewer than, say, 10,000 rows, the NL join may be the right join method. If the optimizer is using hash joins or full table scans, force it to use the NL join method by using the following hint:

```
SELECT /*+ USE_NL (TableA, TableB) */
```

Hash Join

If the join will produce large subsets of data or a substantial proportion of a table is going to be joined, use the hash join hint if the optimizer indicates it isn't going to use it:

```
SELECT /* USE_HASH */
```

Merge Join

If the tables in the join are being joined with an inequality condition (not an equi join), the merge join method is ideal:

```
SELECT /*+ USE_MERGE (TableA, TableB) */
```

Using Bitmap Join Indexes

Bitmap join indexes (BJIs) *prestore* the results of a join between two tables in an index, and thus do away with the need for an expensive runtime join operation. BJIs are specially designed for data warehouse star schemas, but any application can use them as long as there is a primary key/foreign key relationship between the two tables.

Typically, in a data warehouse setting, the primary key is in a dimension table and the fact table has the foreign key. For example, customer_id in the customer dimension table is the primary key, and customer_id in the fact table is the foreign key. Using a BJI, you can avoid a join between these two tables because the rows that would result from the join are already stored in the BJI. Let's look at a simple example of a BJI here.

Say you expect to use the following SQL statement frequently in your application:

```sql
SQL> SELECT SUM((s.quantity)
     FROM sales s, customers c
     WHERE s.customer_id = c.customer_id
     AND c.city = 'DALLAS';
```

In this example, the sales table is the fact table with all the details about product sales, and the customers table is a dimension table with information about your customers. The column customer_id acts as the primary key for the customers table and as the foreign key for the sales table, so the table meets the requirement for creating a BJI.

The following statement creates the BJI. Notice line 2, where you're specifying the index on the city column (c.city). This is how you get the join information to place in the new BJI. Because the sales table is partitioned, you use the clause LOCAL in line 5 to create a locally partitioned index:

```sql
SQL> CREATE BITMAP INDEX cust_city_BJI
  2 ON city (c.city)
  3 FROM sales s, customers c
  4 WHERE c.cust_id = s.cust_id
  5 LOCAL
  6*TABLESPACE users;

Index created.
SQL>
```

You can confirm that the intended index has been created with the help of the following query. The first index is the new BJI index you just created:

```sql
SQL> SELECT index_name, index_type, join_index
  2  FROM dba_indexes
  3 *WHERE table_name='SALES';
```

INDEX_NAME	INDEX_TYPE	JOIN_INDEX
CUST_CITY_BJI	BITMAP	YES
SALES_CHANNEL_BIX	BITMAP	NO
SALES_CUST_BIX	BITMAP	NO

```
3 rows selected.
 SQL>
```

Being a bitmap index, the new BJI uses space extremely efficiently. However, the real benefit of using this index is that when you need to find out the sales for a given city, you don't need to join the sales and customers tables. You only need to use the sales table and the new BJI that holds the join information already.

Selecting the Best Join Order

When your SQL statement includes a join between two or more tables, the order in which you join the tables is extremely important. The driving table in a join is the first table that comes after the WHERE clause. The driving table in the join should contain the filter that will eliminate the most rows. Choose the join order that gives you the least number of rows to be joined to the other tables. That is, if you're joining three tables, the one with the more restrictive filter should be joined first to one of the other two tables. Compare various join orders and pick the best one after you consider the number of rows returned by each join order.

Indexing Strategy

An index is a data structure that takes the value of one or more columns of a table (the key) and returns all rows (or the requested columns in a row) with that value of the column quickly. The efficiency of an index comes from the fact that it lets you find necessary rows without having to scan all the rows of a table. As a result, indexes are more efficient in general, because they need fewer disk I/Os than if you had to scan the table.

■**Note** For a quick summary of indexing guidelines, please refer to the section "Guidelines for Creating Indexes" in Chapter 7.

Developers are content when the EXPLAIN PLAN indicates that a query was using indexes. However, there's more to query optimization than simply using an index for speeding up your queries. If you don't use good indexes, your queries could slow down the database significantly. Important things to consider are whether you have the right indexes or even if the index is necessary in a certain query. In the next sections you'll look at some of the issues you should consider regarding the use of indexes.

■**Caution** A common problem is that an index that performs admirably during development and testing phases simply won't perform well on a production database. Often, this is due to the much larger amounts of data in the "real" system than in the development system. Ideally, you should develop and test queries on an identical version of the production database.

When to Index

You need to index tables only if you think your queries will be selecting a small portion of the table. If your query is retrieving rows that are greater than 10 or 15 percent of the total rows in the table, you may not need an index. Remember that using an index prevents a full table scan, so it is inherently a faster means to traverse a table's rows. However, each time you want to access a particular row in an indexed table, first Oracle has to look up the column referenced in your query in its index. From the index, Oracle obtains the ROWID of the row, which is the logical address of its location on disk.

If you choose to enforce uniqueness of the rows in a table, you can use a *primary index* on that table. By definition, a column that serves as a primary index must be non-null and unique. In addition to the primary index, you can have several *secondary indexes*. For example, the attribute LAST_NAME may serve as a primary index. However, if most of your queries include the CITY column, you may choose to index the CITY column as well. Thus, the addition of secondary indexes would enhance query performance. However, a cost is associated with maintaining additional secondary indexes. In addition to the additional disk space needed for large secondary indexes, remember that all inserts and updates to the table require that the indexes also be updated.

If your system involves a large number of inserts and deletes, understand that too many indexes may be detrimental, because each DML causes changes in both the table and its indexes. Therefore, an OLTP-oriented database ought to keep its indexes to a minimum. A data warehouse, on the other hand, can have a much larger number of indexes because there is no penalty to be paid. That's because the data warehouse is a purely query-oriented database, not a transactional database.

What to Index

Your goal should be to use as few indexes as possible to meet your performance criteria. There's a price to be paid for having too many indexes, especially in OLTP databases. Each INSERT, UPDATE, and DELETE statement causes changes to be made to the underlying indexes of a table, and can slow down an application in some cases. The following are some broad guidelines you can follow to make sure your indexes help the application instead of hindering it:

- Index columns with high selectivity. Selectivity here means the percentage of rows in a table with a certain value. High selectivity, as you learned earlier in this chapter, means that there are few rows with identical values.

- Index all important foreign keys.

- Index all predicate columns.

- Index columns used in table joins.

Proper indexing of tables involves carefully considering the type of application you're running, the number of DML operations, and the response time expectations. Here are some additional tips that can aid you in selecting appropriate indexes for your application:

- Try to avoid indexing columns that consist of long character strings, unless you're using the Oracle Text feature.

- Wherever possible, use index-only plans, meaning a query that can be satisfied completely by just the data in the index alone. This requires that you pay attention to the most common queries and create any necessary composite indexes (indexes that include more than one column attribute).

- Use secondary indexes on columns frequently involved in ORDER BY and GROUP BY operations, as well as sorting operations such as UNION or DISTINCT.

Using Appropriate Index Types

The B-tree index (sometimes referred to as the B*tree index) is the default or normal type of Oracle index. You're probably going to use it for almost all the indexes in a typical OLTP application. Although you could use the B-tree index for all your index needs, you'll get better performance by using more specialized indexes for certain kinds of data. Your knowledge of the type of data you have and the nature of your application should determine the index type. In the next few sections, you'll see several alternative types of indexes.

Bitmap Indexes

Bitmap indexes are ideal for column data that has a *low cardinality*, which means that the indexed column has few distinct values. The index is compact in size and performs better than the B-tree index for these types of data. However, the bitmap index is going to cause some problems if a lot of DML is going on in the column being indexed.

Index-Organized Tables

Index-organized tables (IOTs) are explained in Chapter 7. The traditional Oracle tables are called heap-organized tables, where data is stored in the order in which it is inserted. Indexes enable fast access to the rows. However, indexes also mean more storage and the need for accessing both the index and the table rows for most queries (unless the query can be selected just by the indexed columns themselves). IOTs place all the table data in its primary key index, thus eliminating the need for a separate index.

IOTs are more akin to B-tree indexes than tables. The data in an IOT is sorted, and rows are stored in primary key order. This type of organization of row values gives you faster access in addition to saving space. To limit the size of the row that's stored in the B-tree leaf blocks, IOTs use an overflow area to store infrequently accessed non-key columns, which leads to lower space consumption in the B-tree.

Concatenated Indexes

Concatenated or composite indexes are indexes that include more than one column, and are excellent for improving the selectivity of the WHERE predicates. Even in cases where the selectivity of the individual columns is poor, concatenating the index improves selectivity. If the concatenated index contains all the columns in the WHERE list, you're saved the trouble of looking up the table, thus reducing your I/O. However, you have to pay particular attention to the order of the columns in the composite index. If the WHERE clause doesn't specify the leading column of the concatenated index first, Oracle may not use the index at all.

Up until recently, Oracle used a composite index only if the leading column of the index was used in the WHERE clause or if the entire index was scanned. The *index skip scan* feature lets Oracle use a composite index even when the leading column isn't used in the query. Obviously, this is a nice feature that eliminates many full table scans that would have resulted in older versions of Oracle.

Function-Based Indexes

A function-based index contains columns transformed either by an Oracle function or by an expression. When the function or expression used to create the index is referenced in the WHERE clause of a query, Oracle can quickly return the computed value of the function or expression directly from the index, instead of recalculating it each time. Function-based indexes are efficient in frequently used statements that involve functions or complex expressions on columns. For example, the following function-based index lets you search for people based on the last_name column (in all uppercase letters):

```
SQL> CREATE INDEX upper_lastname_idx ON employees (UPPER(last_name));
```

Reverse-Key Indexes

If you're having performance issues in a database with a large number of inserts, you should consider using reverse-key indexes. These indexes are ideal for insert-heavy applications, although they suffer from the drawback that they can't be used in index range scans. A reverse-key index looks like this:

Index value	Reverse_Key Index Value
9001	1009
9002	2009
9003	3009
9004	4009

When you're dealing with columns that sequentially increase, the reverse-key indexes provide an efficient way to distribute the index values more evenly and thus improve performance.

Partitioned Indexing Strategy

As you saw in Chapter 7, partitioned tables can have several types of indexes on them. Partitioned indexes can be local or global. In addition, they can be prefixed or nonprefixed indexes. Here's a brief summary of important partitioned indexes:

- *Local partitioned indexes* correspond to the underlying partitions of the table. If you add a new partition to the table, you also add a new partition to the local partitioned index.

- *Global partitioned indexes* don't correspond to the partitions of the local table.

- *Prefixed indexes* are partitioned on a left prefix on the index columns.

- *Nonprefixed indexes* are indexes that aren't partitioned on the left prefix of the index columns.

In general, local partitioned indexes are a good indexing strategy if the table has been indexed primarily for access reasons. If your queries include columns that aren't a part of the partitioned table's key, global prefixed indexes are a good choice. Using global prefixed indexes is a good indexing strategy if the table has been indexed primarily for access reasons. Local nonprefixed indexes are good if you're using parallel query operations.

■**Note** In Chapter 5, I showed how to use the SQL Access Advisor to get advice concerning the creation of indexes and materialized views (and materialized view logs). Use the SQL Access Advisor on a regular basis to see if you need to create any new indexes or materialized views (or materialized view logs).

Monitoring Index Usage

You may have several indexes on a table, but that in itself is no guarantee that they're being used in queries. If you aren't using indexes, you might as well get rid of them, as they just take up space and time to manage them. You can use the V$OBJECT_USAGE view to gather index usage information. Here's the structure of the V$OBJECT_USAGE view:

```
SQL> DESC V$OBJECT_USAGE
        Name                    Null?        Type
 -----------------        --------     ------------
  INDEX_NAME              NOT NULL     VARCHAR2(30)
  TABLE_NAME              NOT NULL     VARCHAR2(30)
  MONITORING                          VARCHAR2(3)
  USED                                VARCHAR2(3)
  START_MONITORING                    VARCHAR2(19)
  END_MONITORING                      VARCHAR2(19)
SQL>
```

Chapter 7 shows how to use the V$OBJECT_USAGE view to find out if a certain index is being used.

Removing Unnecessary Indexes

The idea of removing indexes may seem surprising in the beginning, but you aren't being asked to remove just any index on a table. By all means, keep the indexes that are being used and that are also selective. If an index is being used but it's a nonselective index, you may be better off in most cases getting rid of it, because the index will slow down the DML operations without significantly increasing performance. In addition, unnecessary indexes just waste space in your system.

Using Similar SQL Statements

As you know by now, reusing already parsed statements leads to a performance improvement, besides conserving the use of the shared pool area of the SGA. However, the catch is that the SQL statements must be identical in all respects, white space and all.

Reducing SQL Overhead Via Inline Functions

Inline stored functions can help improve the performance of your SQL statements. Here's a simple example to demonstrate how you can use an inline function to reduce the overhead of a SQL statement. The following code chunk shows the initial SQL statement without the inline function:

```
SQL> SELECT r.emp_id,
     e.name, r.emp_type,t.type_des,
     COUNT(*)
     FROM employees e, emp_type t, emp_records r
     WHERE r.emp_id = e.emp_id
     AND r.emp_type = t.emp_type
     GROUP BY r. emp_id, e.name, r.emp_type, t.emp_des;
```

You can improve the performance of the preceding statement by using an inline function call. First, you create a couple of functions, which you can call later on from within your SQL statement. The first function is called SELECT_EMP_DETAIL, and it fetches the employee description if you provide emp_type as an input parameter. Here's how you create this function:

```
SQL> CREATE OR REPLACE FUNCTION select_emp_detail (type IN) number
  2  RETURN varchar2
  3  AS
  4  detail varchar2(30);
  5  CURSOR a1 IS
  6  SELECT emp_detail FROM emp_type
  7  WHERE emp_type = type;
  8  BEGIN
  9  OPEN a1;
 10  FETCH a1 into detail;
 11  CLOSE a1;
 12  RETURN (NVL(detail,'?'));
 13  END;
Function created.
SQL>
```

Next, create another function, SELECT_EMP, that returns the full name of an employee once you pass it employee_id as a parameter:

```
SQL> CREATE OR REPLACE FUNCTION select_emp (emp IN number) RETURN varchar2
  2  AS
  3  emp_name varchar2(30);
  4  CURSOR a1 IS
  5  SELECT name FROM employees
  6  WHERE employee_id = emp;
  7  BEGIN
  8  OPEN a1;
  9  FETCH a1 INTO emp_name;
 10  CLOSE a1;
 11  RETURN (NVL(emp_name,'?'));
 12  END;
```

```
 Function created.
SQL>
```

Now that you have both your functions, it's a simple matter to call them from within a SQL statement, as the following code shows:

```
SQL> SELECT r.emp_id, select_emp(r.emp_id),
  2   r.emp_type, select_emp_desc(r.emp_type),
  3   COUNT(*)
  4   FROM emp_records  r
  5* GROUP BY r.emp_id, r.emp_type;
SQL>
```

Using Bind Variables

The parsing stage of query processing consumes resources, and ideally you should parse just once and use the same parsed version of the statement for repeated executions. Parsing is a much more expensive operation than executing the statement. You should use bind variables in SQL statements instead of literal values to reduce the amount of parsing in the database. Bind variables should be identical in terms of their name, data type, and length. Failure to use bind variables leads to heavy use of the shared pool area and, more often than not, contention for latches and a general slowing down of the database when a large number of queries are being processed. Sometimes your application may not be changeable into a form where bind variables are used.

In Chapter 20, you'll see how to use Oracle configuration parameters to force statements that fail to use bind variables to do so.

Avoiding Improper Use of Views

Views have several benefits to offer, but faster performance may not necessarily be one of them. Views are useful when you want to present only the relevant portions of a table to an application or a user. Whenever you query a view, it has to be instantiated at that time. Because the view is just a SQL query, it has to perform this instantiation if you want to query the view again. If your query uses joins on views, it could lead to substantial time for executing the query.

Avoiding Unnecessary Full Table Scans

Full table scans can occur sometimes, even when you have indexed a table. The use of functions on indexed columns is a good example for when you unwittingly can cause Oracle to skip indexes and go to a full table scan. You should avoid the use of inequality and the greater than or equal to predicates, as they may also bypass indexes.

How the DBA Can Help Improve SQL Processing

Performance tuning involves the optimization of SQL code and the calibration of the resources used by Oracle. The developers generally perform SQL tuning, and the DBA merely facilitates their tuning efforts by setting the relevant initialization parameters, turning tracing on, and so on. Nevertheless, the DBA can implement several strategies to help improve SQL processing in his or her database.

In some cases, you and the developers might be working together to optimize the application. What if you can't modify the code, as is the case when you're dealing with packaged applications? Alternatively, what if even the developers are aware that major code changes are needed to improve performance, but time and budget constraints make the immediate revamping of the application difficult? There are several ways you can help without having to change the code itself.

It's common for DBAs to bemoan the fact that the response times are slow because of poorly written SQL. I've heard this in every place I've worked, so I assume this is a universal complaint of DBAs who have to manage the consequences of bad code. A perfectly designed and coded application with all the right joins and smart indexing strategies would be nice, but more often than not, that perfect state of affairs doesn't happen. The theory of the next best option dictates that you should do everything you can to optimize within the limitations imposed by the application design.

That said, let's look at some of the important ways in which you can help improve query performance in an application, even when you can't change the code right away.

Using Partitioned Tables

Partitioned tables usually lead to tremendous improvements in performance, and they're easy to administer. By partitioning a table into several subpartitions, you're in essence limiting the amount of data that needs to be examined to satisfy your queries. If you have large tables, running into tens of millions of rows, consider partitioning them.

Five table partitioning schemes are available to you in Oracle Database 11g, and I explain them in Chapter 7. You can index partitioned tables in a variety of ways, depending on the needs of the application. Partition maintenance is also easy, and it's well worth the additional effort when you consider the tremendous gains partitioned tables provide.

Using Compression Techniques

The Oracle database lets you use *table compression* to compress tables, table partitions, and materialized views. Table compression helps reduce space requirements for the tables and enhances query performance. Oracle compresses the tables by eliminating the duplicate values in a data block and replacing those values with algorithms to re-create the data when necessary. The table compression technique is especially suitable for data warehouse and OLAP databases, but OLTP databases can also use the technique fruitfully. The larger the table that is compressed, the more benefits you'll achieve with this technique. Here's a simple table compression statement:

```
SQL> CREATE table sales_compress
  2   COMPRESS
  3   AS SELECT * FROM sh.sales;
Table created.
SQL>
```

You can also use *index key compression* to compress the primary key columns of IOTs. This compression not only saves you storage space, but also enhances query performance. Index compression works by removing duplicate column values from the index.

To compress an index, all you have to do is add the keyword COMPRESS after the index-creation statement, as shown here:

```
SQL> CREATE INDEX item_product_x
  2   ON order_items(product_id)
  3   TABLESPACE order_items_indx_01
  4   COMPRESS;
Index created.
SQL>
```

Perform some tests to confirm the space savings and the time savings during the creation statements. Later, you can test query performance to measure the improvement.

Using Materialized Views

If you're dealing with large amounts of data, you should seriously consider using materialized views to improve response time. *Materialized views* are objects with data in them—usually summary data from the underlying tables. Expensive joins can be done beforehand and saved in the materialized view. When users query the underlying table, Oracle automatically rewrites the query to access the materialized view instead of the tables.

Materialized views reduce the need for several complex queries because you can precalculate aggregates with them. Joins between large tables and data aggregation are expensive in terms of resource usage, and materialized views significantly reduce the response time for complex queries on large tables. If you aren't sure which materialized views to create, not to worry—you can use the DBMS_OLAP package supplied by Oracle to get recommendations on ideal materialized views.

Chapter 7 discusses materialized views in more detail, and also shows you how to use the SQL Access Advisor tool to get recommendations for creating materialized views and materialized view logs.

Using Stored Outlines to Stabilize the CBO

As I mentioned earlier in this chapter, the CBO doesn't always use the same execution strategies. Changes in Oracle versions or changes in the initialization parameters concerning memory allocation may force the CBO to modify its plans. You can use Oracle's plan stability feature to ensure that the execution plan remains stable regardless of any changes in the database environment.

The plan stability feature uses stored outlines to preserve the current execution plans, even if the statistics and optimizer mode are changed. The CBO uses the same execution plan with identical access paths each time you execute the same query. The catch is that the query must be exactly identical each time if you want Oracle to use the stored plan.

■**Caution** When you use stored outlines to preserve a currently efficient execution plan, you're limiting Oracle's capability to modify its execution plans dynamically based on changes to the database environment and changes to the statistics. Ensure you use this feature for valid purposes, such as maintaining similar plans for distributed applications.

On the face of it, the stored outline feature doesn't seem impressive. Let's consider a simple example to see how a stored outline could be useful in a real production environment.

Suppose you have a system that's running satisfactorily and, due to a special need, you add an index to a table. The addition of the new index could unwittingly modify the execution plans of the CBO, and your previously fast-running SQL queries may slow down. It could conceivably take a lot of effort, testing, and time to fix the problem by changing the original query. However, if you had created stored outlines, these kinds of problems wouldn't arise. Once Oracle creates an outline, it stores it until you remove it. In the next section you'll examine how to implement planned stability in a database.

When to Use Outlines

Outlines are useful when you're planning migrations from one version of Oracle to another. The CBO could behave differently between versions, and you can cut your risk down by using stored outlines to preserve the application's present performance. You can also use them when you're upgrading your applications. Outlines ensure that the execution paths the queries used in a test instance successfully carry over to the production instance.

Stored outlines are especially useful when the users of an application have information about the environment that the Oracle CBO doesn't possess. By enabling the direct editing of stored outlines, Oracle lets you tune SQL queries without changing the underlying application. This is especially useful when you're dealing with packaged applications where you can't get at the source code.

Implementing Plan Stability

Implementing plan stability is a simple matter. You have to ensure that the following initialization parameters are consistent in all the environments. You must set the value of the first two parameters to TRUE. The default value for OPTIMIZER_FEATURES_ENABLE is 11.1.0.6, and if you change it, make sure it's the same in all environments. Here are the relevant initialization parameters:

- QUERY_REWRITE_ENABLED

- STAR_TRANSFORMATION_ENABLED

- OPTIMIZER_FEATURES_ENABLE

Creating Outlines

The outlines themselves are managed through the DBMS_OUTLN and DBMS_OUTLN_EDIT Oracle packages. To create outlines for all your current SQL queries, you simply set the initialization parameter CREATE_STORED_OUTLINES to TRUE.

The OUTLN user is part of the database when it is created and owns the stored outlines in the database. The outlines are stored in the table OL$. Listing 19-1 shows the structure of the OL$ table.

Listing 19-1. *The OL$ Table*

```
SQL> DESC OL$
 Name              Null?      Type
 -----------       -----      -----------
 OL_NAME                      VARCHAR2(30)
 SQL_TEXT                     LONG
 TEXTLEN                      NUMBER
 SIGNATURE                    RAW(16)
 HASH_VALUE                   NUMBER
 HASH_VALUE2                  NUMBER
 CATEGORY                     VARCHAR2(30)
 VERSION                      VARCHAR2(64)
 CREATOR                      VARCHAR2(30)
 TIMESTAMP                    DATE
 FLAGS                        NUMBER
 HINTCOUNT                    NUMBER
 SPARE1                       NUMBER
 SPARE2                       VARCHAR2(1000)
SQL>
```

The SQL_TEXT column has the SQL statement that is outlined. In addition to the OL$ table, the user OUTLN uses the OL$HINTS and OL$NODES tables to manage stored outlines.

Create a special tablespace for the user OUTLN and the tables OL$, OL$HINTS, and OL$NODES. By default, they're created in the System tablespace. After you create a new tablespace for user OUTLN, you can use the export and import utilities to move the tables.

Creating Outlines at the Database Level

To let Oracle automatically create outlines for all SQL statements, use the CREATE_STORED_OUTLINES initialization parameter, as shown here:

```
CREATE_STORED_OUTLINES = TRUE
```

You can also dynamically enable the creation of stored outlines for the entire database by using the ALTER SYSTEM statement, as shown here:

```
SQL> ALTER SYSTEM SET CREATE_STORED_OUTLINES=TRUE;
System altered.
SQL>
```

In both the preceding cases, the outlines that Oracle creates are assigned to a category called DEFAULT. You also have the option of specifying a named category for your stored outlines. Setting the CREATE_STORED_OUTLINES parameter means that the database creates a stored outline for every distinct SQL statement. This means that the System tablespace could potentially run out of space if you have a large number of SQL statements that are being processed. For this reason, use the CREATE_STORED_OUTLINES initialization parameter with care. To keep the overhead low, you may instead use the option to create stored outlines at the session level, or just for a lone SQL statement, as shown in the next section.

Creating Outlines for Specific Statements

You can create outlines for a specific statement or a set of statements by using the ALTER SESSION statement, as shown here:

```
SQL> ALTER SESSION SET create_stored_outlines = true;
Session altered.
SQL>
```

Any statements you issue after the ALTER SESSION statement is processed will have outlines stored for them.

To create a stored outline for a specific SQL statement, you use the CREATE OUTLINE statement. The user issuing this command must have the CREATE OUTLINE privilege. The following statement shows how to create a simple outline for a SELECT operation on the employees table:

```
SQL> CREATE OUTLINE test_outline
  2  ON SELECT employee_id, last_name
  3  FROM hr.employees;
Outline created.
SQL>
```

You can use the DROP OUTLINE statement to drop an outline, as shown here:

```
SQL> DROP OUTLINE test_outline;
Outline dropped.
SQL>
```

Using the Stored Outlines

After you create the stored outlines, Oracle won't automatically start using them. You have to use the ALTER SESSION or ALTER SYSTEM statement to set USE_STORED_OUTLINES to TRUE. The following example uses the ALTER SYSTEM statement to enable the use of the stored outlines at the database level:

```
SQL> ALTER SYSTEM SET use_stored_outlines=true;
System altered.
SQL>
```

You can also set the initialization parameter USE_STORED_OUTLINES to TRUE, to enable the use of the stored outlines. Otherwise, the database won't use any stored outlines it has created.

Editing Stored Outlines

You can easily change the stored access paths while using the plan stability feature. You can use either the DBMS_OUTLN_EDIT package or OEM to perform the changes.

SQL Plan Management

Changes such as database upgrades, or even minor changes such as adding or deleting an index, could affect SQL execution plans. I explained the Oracle stored outlines feature earlier in this chapter as a way to preserve SQL execution plans to prevent performance deterioration when the database undergoes major changes such as a database upgrade. Oracle recommends that you use the new feature called SQL Plan Management (SPM) to keep performance from being affected by major system changes. SQL Plan Management preserves database performance under the following types of system changes:

- Database upgrades
- New optimizer version
- Changes in optimizer parameters
- Changes in system settings
- Changes in schema and metadata definitions
- Deployment of new application modules

Although you can tune SQL statements using the SQL Tuning Advisor and ADDM, that's at best a reactive mechanism and requires the DBA to intervene. SPM is designed as a preventative mechanism. The database controls the evolution of SQL plans using the new SQL plan baselines, which are sets of efficient execution plans captured by the database over a period of time. The database allows a new execution plan to become part of a SQL plan baseline for a statement only if the new plan doesn't cause a regression in performance. The database uses only those execution plans that are part of a SQL plan baseline to execute SQL statements, and thus the database achieves the key goal of preserving database performance in the face of major system changes such as database upgrades.

The SPM comes in very handy when you're upgrading to Oracle Database 11g. After you upgrade to Oracle Database 11g from, say, the Oracle Database 10g release, first leave the OPTIMIZER_FEATURES_ ENABLE parameter at 10.2. Once the SPM mechanism collects the execution plans and stores them as SQL plan baselines, you can switch to the 11.1 setting for the OPTIMIZER_FEATURES_ENABLE parameter. This way, you ensure that you're using all the new capabilities of the 11g release, without compromising SQL performance: performance is safeguarded through the use of SQL plan baselines, which are similar in this regard to the stored outlines maintained by the database.

SQL Plan Baselines

Under SQL Plan Management, the database maintains a plan history, which is a record of all SQL plans generated over time for a SQL statement by the optimizer. The optimizer uses the plan history to figure out the optimal execution plan for a statement. Not all plans in the plan history for a statement are acceptable plans, however. The database defines as acceptable only those execution plans that don't lead to deterioration in performance relative to other plans in the plan history. The SQL plan baseline for a SQL statement is the set of all accepted plans in the plan history for a statement.

The very first plan for a statement is always an accepted plan, because there's nothing to compare it with. So, the SQL plan baseline and the plan history for a new SQL statement are identical at this point. Newer execution plans for the statement will automatically be a part of the statement's plan history, but are added to the SQL plan baseline for the statement only if the new plans are verified not to cause a regression in performance. The Automatic SQL Tuning Adviser task, which is a part of the automate maintenance tasks, verifies SQL plans. The advisor looks for high-load SQL statements and stores the accepted plans for those statements in that's statement's SQL plan baseline.

You can manage SQL plan baselines by using the DBMS_SPM package or through Enterprise Manager. I explain the steps in the following sections.

Capturing SQL Plan Baselines

There are two ways to capture the SQL plan baselines: have the database automatically capture the plans or load them in the database yourself. I explain both techniques in this section.

Capturing Plans Automatically

By default, the database doesn't maintain a plan history for SQL statements you execute. You must set the initialization parameter OPTIMIZER_CAPTURE_SQL_PLAN_BASELINES to TRUE (the default value is FALSE) for the database to start capturing the SQL plan baselines. When you set the parameter to TRUE, the database automatically creates and maintains a plan history for all repeatable SQL statements that are executed in the database.

■**Tip** By using the SQL Performance Analyzer (see Chapter 20), you can find out which SQL statements are likely to regress following a database upgrade to, say, Oracle Database 11*g* Release 1 from Oracle Database 10*g* Release 2. You can capture the execution plans for these statements and load them into the SQL management base of the upgraded database, thus avoiding the performance regression.

Manual Plan Loading

You can also load SQL plans manually into the SQL plan baselines. When you load plans manually, the database loads them automatically as accepted plans, without verifying the performance of the plans. You can bulk load SQL plans you captured before upgrading the database into a SQL plan baseline after upgrading your database to a new release.

You can use either a SQL Tuning Set (STS) or load the plans from the database cursor cache. I show both techniques in the following sections.

Execute the DBMS_SPM function LOAD_PLANS_FROM_SQLSET in order to load SQL plans from an STS. First create an empty STS as shown here:

```
begin
dbms_sqltune.create_sqlset(
sqlset_name => 'testset1',
description => 'Test STS to capture AWR Data');
end;
/
```

Next, load the new STS with SQL statements from the Automatic Workload Repository (AWR) snapshots.

```
declare
baseline_cur dbms_sqltune.sqlset_cursor;
begin
open baseline_cur for
select value(p) from table (dbms_sqltune.select_workload_repository(
'peak baseline',null,null,'elapsed_time',null,null,null,20)) p;
dbms_sqltune.load_sqlset (
sqlset_name  => 'testset1',
populate_cursor => baseline_cur);
end;
/
```

The STS shown in this example includes the top 20 statements from the AWR peak baseline, selected based in the criterion of elapsed time. The ref cursor and the table function help select the top 20 statements from the AWR baseline.

Load the SQL plans from the STS into the SQL plan baseline by executing the LOAD_PLANS_FROM_SQLSET function.

```
declare
test_plans pls_integer;
begin
test_plans := dbms_spm.load_plans_from_sqlset(
sqlset_name => 'testset1');
end;
/
```

You can also use the cursor cache instead of an STS as the source of the SQL plans you want to load into a SQL plan baseline. The following example shows how to load SQL plans from the cursor cache using the LOAD_PLANS_FROM_CURSOR_CACHE function.

```
declare
test_plans pls_integer;
begin
test_plans := dbms_spm.load_plans_from_cursor_cache (
sql_id => '123456789999')
return pls_integer;
end;
/
```

Selecting SQL Plan Baselines

Regardless of whether you collect SQL plans using the AWR as a source or from the cursor cache of the database, you must enable the use of those plans by setting the initialization parameter OPTIMIZER_USE_SQL_PLAN_BASELINES to TRUE. Since the parameter's default value is TRUE, it means the plan baselines are enabled by default.

When the database encounters a new repeatable SQL statement, it sees whether it can match it to a plan in the SQL plan baseline. If there's a match, it uses the best cost plan to execute the statement. If there's no match, the database adds the new plan to the plan history as a nonaccepted plan. The database will then choose the least costly plan from the set of accepted plans in the SQL plan baseline and execute the statement using that plan. If the database can't reproduce an accepted plan for some reason (such as the dropping of an index), it selects the least costly plan to execute the SQL statement.

■Tip Execute the DBMS_XPLAN DISPLAY_SQL_PLAN_BASELINE function to view the execution plan for a specific SQL_HANDLE in a SQL plan baseline.

The end result is that the optimizer will always produce an execution plan that's either the best cost plan or an accepted plan from the SQL plan baseline. The OTHER_XML column in the PLAN_TABLE's EXPLAIN PLAN output reveals the exact final strategy adopted by the optimizer

Evolving SQL Plan Baselines

The database routinely checks new plans so as to evolve the SQL plan baselines, which involves changing a nonaccepted plan into an accepted plan and this part of the SQL plan baseline. As mentioned earlier, a nonaccepted plan must show superior performance to an accepted plan in order to be converted into an accepted plan in the baseline. If you're manually loading SQL plans, there is no need to formally evolve the plans, as every plan you load is automatically deemed an accepted plan. However, any plans that the database captures automatically must be formally evolved into the SQL plan baseline.

You can evolve SQL plan baselines either by executing the EVOLVE_SQL_PLAN_BASELINE function or with the help of the SQL Tuning Advisor. The following example shows how to execute the EVOLVE_SQL_PLAN_BASELINE function to add new accepted plans to the baseline.

```
SQL> exec dbms_spm.evolve_sql_plan_baseline (sql_handle =>
'123456789111');
```

The example uses the SQL_HANDLE attribute to specify the plan for a specific SQL statement, but by ignoring this attribute, you can make the database evolve all nonaccepted plans in the database. You can also submit a list of SQL plans if you wish, by specifying the PLAN_LIST attribute.

■Tip You can export SQL plan baselines from one database to another by using a staging table.

The SQL Tuning Advisor evolves SQL plan baselines by automatically adding all plans for which you have implemented the advisor's SQL profile recommendations to the SQL plan baseline for a statement.

Fixed SQL Plan Baselines

You can limit the set of possible accepted plans for SQL statements by setting the FIXED attribute to YES for a SQL plan. When you fix a plan in a baseline, the optimizer prefers it to other nonfixed plans in the baseline, even if some of the other plans are actually cheaper to execute. The database stops evolving a fixed SQL plan baseline, but you can always evolve the baseline by adding a new plan to the baseline.

The following query on the DBA_SQL_PLAN_BASELINES view shows important attributes of SQL plans in the baseline:

```
SQL> SELECT sql_handle, sql_text, plan_name,    origin, enabled, accepted,
     fixed, autopurge
     FROM dba_sql_plan_baselines;
```

```
SQL_HANDLE      SQL_TEXT        PLAN_NAME        ORIGIN          ENA  ACC  FIX  AUT
----------      ----------      -------------    ------------    ---- ---  ---  ---
SYS_SQL_02a     delete from...  SYS_SQL_PLAN_930 AUTO-CAPTURE    YES  YES  NO   YES
SYS_SQL_a6f     SELECT...       SYS_SQL_PLAN_ael AUTO-CAPTURE    YES  YES  NO   YES
SQL>
```

The optimizer only uses those plans that are enabled and have the accepted status.

Managing SQL Plan Baselines

Execute the DISPLAY_SQL_PLAN_BASELINE function of the DBMS_XPLAN package to view all the SQL plans stored in the SQL plan baseline for a SQL statement. Here's an example:

```
SQL> set serveroutput on

SQL> set long 100000
SQL> SELECT * FROM table(
  2  dbms_xplan.display_sql_plan_baseline(
  3  sql_handle => 'SYS_SQL_ba5e12ccae97040f',
  4* format => 'basic'));
PLAN_TABLE_OUTPUT
-------------------------------------------------------------------------------


-------------------------------------------------------------------------------
SQL handle: SYS_SQL_ba5e12ccae97040f
SQL text: select t.week_ending_day, p.prod_subcategory, sum(s.amount_sold) as
 dollars, s.channel_id,s.promo_id from sales s,times t, products p where
 s.time_id = t.time_id and s.prod_id = p.prod_id and s.prod_id>10 and
 s.prod_id <50 group by t.week_ending_day, p.prod_subcategory,
PLAN_TABLE_OUTPUT
--------------------
s.channel_id,s.promo_id

Plan name: SYS_SQL_PLAN_ae97040f6b60c209
Enabled: YES   Fixed: NO   Accepted: YES   Origin: AUTO-CAPTURE
Plan hash value: 1944768804

PLAN_TABLE_OUTPUT

| Id  | Operation         | Name  |

|   0 | SELECT STATEMENT            |     |
|   1 |  HASH GROUP BY        |     |
|   2 |   HASH JOIN       |     |
|   3 |    TABLE ACCESS FULL        | TIMES |
|   4 |    HASH JOIN      |     |
|   5 |     TABLE ACCESS BY INDEX ROWID| PRODUCTS    |
|   6 |      INDEX RANGE SCAN       | PRODUCTS_PK |
|   7 |     TABLE ACCESS FULL       | SALES     |

29 rows selected.

SQL>
```

The output shows that the SQL plan was captured automatically and is enabled and accepted. It also reveals that the plan isn't fixed.

■Tip When the SQL Tuning Advisor finds execution plans that are superior to the plans in the SQL plan baseline for that statement, it recommends a SQL profile. Once you accept the recommendation for implementing the SQL profile, the SQL Tuning Advisor adds the tuned plan to the SQL plan baseline.

The SQL Management Base

The database stores SQL plan baseline information in the SQL Management Base (SMB), which is stored in the Sysaux tablespace. You can control the sizing and retention period of the SMB by setting the parameters SPACE_BUDGE_PERCENT and PLAN_RETENTION_WEEKS, using the DBMS_SPM package. The following query reveals the current values of the two parameters:

```
SQL> SELECT parameter_name, parameter_value
     FROM dba_sql_management_config;
```

```
PARAMETER_NAME               PARAMETER_VALUE
----------------------       ------------------
SPACE_BUDGET_PERCENT              30
PLAN_RETENTION_WEEKS             53
```

SQL>

The SPACE_BUDGET_PERCENT parameter controls the percentage of space the SMB can occupy in the Sysaux tablespace. The default is 10 percent, and you can set it anywhere between 1 and 50 percent. You can purge outdated SQL plan baselines or SQL profiles from the SMB to clear up space, or you can increase the size of the Sysaux tablespace. You can change the value of the SPACE_BUDGET_PERCENT parameter by executing the CONFIGURE parameter, as shown here:

```
SQL> EXEC dbms_spm.configure ('space_budget_percent', 40);
```

The CONFIGURE procedure specifies that the SPM can use up to 40 percent of the space in the Sysaux tablespace.

The database executes a weekly purging job to remove unused SQL baselines. The database removes any SQL baselines that it hasn't used in over a year (53 weeks). You can adjust the plan retention period by executing the CONFIGURE procedure as shown here:

```
SQL> exec dbms_spm.configure ('plan_retention_weeks', 105);
```

You can also remove specific baselines from the SMBA, as shown in the following example:

```
SQL> exec
dbms_spm.purge_sql_plan_baseline(''SYS_SQL_PLAN_b5429511dd6ab0f');
```

You can query the DBA_SQL_MANAGEMENT_CONFIG view for the current space and retention settings of the SMB.

Using Parallel Execution

Parallel execution of statements can make SQL run more quickly, and it's especially suitable for large warehouse-type databases. You can set the parallel option at the database or table level. If you increase the degree of parallelism of a table, Oracle could decide to perform more full table scans instead of using an index, because the cost of a full table scan may now be lower than the cost of an index scan. If you want to use parallel operations in an OLTP environment, make sure you have enough processors on your machine so the CPU doesn't become a bottleneck.

Other DBA Tasks

The DBA must perform certain tasks regularly to optimize the performance of the application. Some of these fall under the routine administrative chores, and the following sections cover some of the important DBA tasks related to performance tuning.

Collecting System Statistics

Even if you're using the Automatic Optimizer Statistics Collection feature, Oracle won't collect system statistics. As explained earlier in this chapter, you must collect system statistics yourself, so the Oracle optimizer can accurately evaluate alternate execution plans.

Refreshing Statistics Frequently

This section applies only if you have turned off the automatic statistics collection process for some reason. Refreshing statistics frequently is extremely important if you're using the CBO and your data is subject to frequent changes.

How often you run the DBMS_STATS package to collect statistics depends on the nature of your data. For applications with a moderate number of DML transactions, a weekly gathering of statistics will suffice. If you have reason to believe that your data changes substantially daily, schedule the statistics collection on a daily basis.

Using Histograms

Normally, the CBO assumes that data is uniformly distributed in a table. There are times when data in a table isn't distributed in a uniform way. If you have an extremely skewed data distribution in a table, you're better off using *histograms* to store the column statistics. If the table data is heavily skewed toward some values, the presence of histograms provides more efficient access methods. Histograms use buckets to represent distribution of data in a column, and Oracle can use these buckets to see how skewed the data distribution is.

You can use the following types of histograms in an Oracle database:

- *Height-based histograms* divide column values into bands, with each band containing a roughly equal number of rows. Thus, for a table with 100 rows, you'd create a histogram with 10 buckets if you wanted each bucket to contain 10 rows.

- *Frequency-based histograms* determine the number of buckets based on the distinct values in the column. Each bucket contains all the data that has the same value.

Creating Histograms

You create histograms by using the METHOD_OPT attribute of the DBMS_STATS procedure such as GATHER_TABLE_STATS, GATHER_DATABASE_STATS, and so on. You can either specify your own histogram creation requirements by using the FOR COLUMNS clause, or use the AUTO or SKEWONLY values for the METHOD_OPT attribute. If you choose AUTO, Oracle will decide which columns it should collect histograms for, based on the data distribution and workload. If you choose SKEWONLY, Oracle will base the decision only on the data distribution of the columns. In the two examples that follow, I use the FOR COLUMNS clause to specify the creation of the histograms.

The following example shows how to create a height-based histogram while collecting the optimizer statistics:

```
SQL> BEGIN
    DBMS_STATS.GATHER_table_STATS (OWNNAME => 'HR', TABNAME => 'BENEFITS',
    METHOD_OPT => 'FOR COLUMNS SIZE 10 Number_of_visits');
    END;
```

The following example shows how to create a frequency-based histogram:

```
SQL> BEGIN
    DBMS_STATS.GATHER_table_STATS(OWNNAME => 'HR', TABNAME => 'PERSONS',
    METHOD_OPT => 'FOR COLUMNS SIZE 20 department_id');
    END;
```

Viewing Histograms

You can use the DBA_TAB_COL_STATISTICS view to view histogram information. Following are the two queries that show the number of buckets (num_buckets) and the number of distinct values (num_distinct), first for the height-balanced and then for the frequency-based histogram created in the previous section:

```
SQL> SELECT column_name, num_distinct, num_buckets, histogram
    FROM USER_TAB_COL_STATISTICS
    WHERE table_name = 'BENEFITS' AND column_name = 'NUMBER_OF_VISITS';
```

COLUMN_NAME	NUM_DISTINCT	NUM_BUCKETS	HISTOGRAM
NUMBER_OF_VISITS	320	10	HEIGHT BALANCED

```
SQL> SELECT column_name, num_distinct, num_buckets, histogram
    FROM USER_TAB_COL_STATISTICS
    WHERE table_name = 'PERSONS' AND column_name = 'DEPARTMENT_ID';
```

COLUMN_NAME	NUM_DISTINCT	NUM_BUCKETS	HISTOGRAM
DEPARTMENT_ID	8	8	FREQUENCY

Adaptive Cursor Sharing

Although using bind variables improves performance and scalability by reducing parse time and memory usage, literal values actually produce better execution plans than bind values for variables. When you force cursor sharing in the database by setting the CURSOR_SHARING parameter to EXACT or SIMILAR, some SQL statements end up with suboptimal plans for some bind variable values. The Cost-Based Optimizer may very well create a suboptimal plan if it happens to peek at the bind values and if the bind values used by the first SQL statements to go into the shared pool are unrepresentative of the true values of the variable. Developers and DBA's sometimes resort to setting the unofficial Oracle initialization parameter _OPTIM_PEEK_USER_BINDS (ALTER SESSION SET "_optim_peek_user_binds"=FALSE;) to prevent the database from peeking at the bind values. Adaptive cursor sharing provides a much more elegant way to prevent the optimizer from creating suboptimal execution plans caused by bind peeking.

Oracle relies on its "bind peeking" technique when it first parses a SQL statement. The optimizer will always hard parse a new statement and peek at the bind variable values to get a sense of what the values look like. The initial bind values it sees during the bind peeking have an inordinate influence on the execution plan it chooses for the statement. If, for example, the bind peeking dictates using an index, Oracle will continue to do so, even if later values would actually dictate a full scan instead. Since bind peeking actually leads to suboptimal execution plans in cases such as these, hard-coded variable values would be preferable to bind values.

As the preceding discussion indicates, cursor sharing using bind variables may not always lead to the best (optimal) execution plans. Hard-coded values for variables may actually provide more optimal execution plans than using bind variables, especially when dealing with heavily skewed data. Oracle provides you the adaptive cursor sharing feature, which is an attempt to resolve the conflict between cursor sharing using bind variables and query optimization. Using adaptive cursor sharing, whenever the database estimates that it's cheaper to produce a new execution plan for a statement than reusing the same cursors, it'll do so, generating new child cursors for the statement. The database strives to minimize the number of child cursors to take advantage of cursor sharing. However, the database won't blindly try to reuse cursors.

▪**Tip** Adaptive cursor sharing is automatic, and it's always on and you can't switch it off.

How Adaptive Cursor Sharing Works

Two concepts—the bind sensitivity of a cursor and a bind-aware cursor—play a critical role in how adaptive cursor sharing works. If changing a bind variable's values leads to different execution plans, a cursor is called a *bind-sensitive cursor*. Whenever the database figures that it must create new execution plans because the bind values vary considerably, the variable is deeded bind sensitive. Once the database marks a cursor as bind sensitive, the cursor is termed *bind aware*.

▪**Note** The adaptive cursor sharing feature is independent of the cursor sharing feature.

Here's an example that illustrates how adaptive cursor sharing works. Suppose you execute the following query several times in your database:

```
SQL> select * from hr.employees where salary = :1
    and department_id = :2;
```

The SQL statement uses two bind variables, SALARY and DEPARTMENT_ID.

During the very first execution of a new SQL statement, the database makes the cursor bind sensitive if it peeks at the bind values and computes the selectivity of the predicate. The database assigns each execution plan with a set of selectivity values such as (0.25, 0.0050), which indicates the selectivity range of the execution plan. If new bind variables fall within the selectivity range, the optimizer reuses the execution plan, and if not, it creates a new execution plan.

The next step is to evaluate whether the cursor is a bind-aware cursor. After the first hard parse, the database performs soft parses for the subsequent executions and compares the execution statistics with the hard parse execution statistics. If the database decides that the cursor is bind aware, it uses bind-aware cursor matching when it executes the query again. If the new pair of bind values falls inside the selectivity range, the database reuses the plan; otherwise, it performs a hard parse, thus generating a new child cursor with a different plan. If the new execution produces a similar plan, the database merges the child cursors, which means that if the bind values are roughly the same, the statements will share the execution plan.

Monitoring Adaptive Cursor Sharing

The V$SQL view contains two columns, named IS_BIND_SENSITIVE and IS_BIND_AWARE, that help you monitor adaptive cursor sharing in the database. The IS_BIND_SENSITIVE column lets you know whether a cursor is bind sensitive, and the IS_BIND_AWARE column shows whether the database has marked a cursor for bind-aware cursor sharing. The following query, for example, tells you which SQL statements are binds sensitive or bind aware:

```
SQL> SELECT sql_id, executions, is_bind_sensitive, is_bind_aware
     FROM v$sql;

SQL_ID             EXECUTIONS     I     I
--------------     -----------    ---   ---
57pfs5p8xcO7w      21             Y     N
1gfaj4z5hn1kf      4              Y     N
1gfaj4z5hn1kf      4              N     N
...
294 rows selected.

SQL>
```

In this query, the IS_BIND_SENSITIVE column shows whether the database will generate different execution plans based on bind variable values. Any cursor that shows an IS_BIND_SENSITIVE column value of Y is a candidate for an execution plan change. When the database plans to use multiple execution plans for a statement based on the observed values of the bind variables, it marks the IS_BIND_AWARE column Y for that statement. This means that the optimizer realizes that different bind variable values would lead to different data patterns, which requires the statement to be hard-parsed during the next execution. In order to decide whether to change the execution plan, the database evaluates the next few executions of the SQL statement. If the database decides to change a statement's execution plan, it marks the cursor bind aware and puts a value of Y in the IS_BIND_AWARE column for that statement. A bind-aware cursor is one for which the database has actually modified the execution plan based on the observed values of the bind variables.

You can use the following views to manage the adaptive cursor sharing feature:

- *V$SQL_CS_HISTOGRAM*: Shows the distribution of the execution count across the execution history histogram

- *V$SQL_CS_SELECTIVITY*: Shows the selectivity ranges stored in cursors for predicates with bind variables

- *V$SQL_CS_STATISTICS*: Contains the execution statistics of a cursor using different bind sets gathered by the database

Rebuilding Tables and Indexes Regularly

The indexes could become unbalanced in a database with a great deal of DML. It's important to rebuild such indexes regularly so queries can run faster. You may want to rebuild an index to change its storage characteristics or to consolidate it and reduce fragmentation. Use the ALTER INDEX . . . REBUILD statement, because the old index is accessible while you're re-creating it. (The alternative is to drop the index and re-create it.)

When you rebuild the indexes, include the COMPUTE STATISTICS statement so you don't have to gather statistics after the rebuild. Of course, if you have a 24/7 environment, you can use the ALTER INDEX . . . REBUILD ONLINE statement so that user access to the database won't be affected. It is important that your tables aren't going through a lot of DML operations while you're rebuilding online, because the online feature may not work as advertised under such circumstances. It might even end up unexpectedly preventing simultaneous updates by users.

Reclaiming Unused Space

The Segment Advisor runs automatically during the scheduled nightly maintenance and provides you with recommendations about objects you can shrink to reclaim wasted space. Just remember that you need to use locally managed tablespaces with Automatic Segment Space Management in order to use the Segment Advisor. Shrinking segments saves space, but more importantly, improves performance by lowering the high-water mark of the segments and eliminating the inevitable fragmentation that occurs over time in objects with heavy update and delete operations.

Caching Small Tables in Memory

If the application doesn't reuse a table's data for a long period, the data might be aged out of the SGA and need to be read from disk. You can safely pin small tables in the buffer cache with the following:

```
SQL> ALTER TABLE hr.employees CACHE;
Table altered.
SQL>
```

SQL Performance Tuning Tools

SQL performance tuning tools are extremely important. Developers can use the tools to examine good execution strategies, and in a production database they're highly useful for reactive tuning. The tools can give you a good estimate of resource use by queries. The SQL tools are the EXPLAIN PLAN, Autotrace, SQL Trace, and TKPROF utilities.

Using EXPLAIN PLAN

The EXPLAIN PLAN facility helps you tune SQL by letting you see the execution plan selected by the Oracle optimizer for a SQL statement. During SQL tuning, you may have to rewrite your queries and experiment with optimizer hints. The EXPLAIN PLAN tool is great for this experimentation, as it immediately lets you know how the query will perform with each change in the code. Because the utility gives you the execution plan without executing the code, you save yourself from having to run untuned software to see whether the changes were beneficial or not. Understanding an EXPLAIN PLAN is critical to understanding query performance. It provides a window into the logic of the Oracle optimizer regarding its choice of execution plans.

The output of the EXPLAIN PLAN tool goes into a table, usually called PLAN_TABLE, where it can be queried to determine the execution plan of statements. In addition, you can use GUI tools, such as OEM or TOAD, to get the execution plan for your SQL statements without any fuss. In OEM, you can view the explain statements from the Top Sessions or the Top SQL charts.

A walkthrough of an EXPLAIN PLAN output takes you through the steps that would be undertaken by the CBO to execute the SQL statement. The EXPLAIN PLAN tool indicates clearly whether the optimizer is using an index, for example. It also tells you the order in which tables are being joined and helps you understand your query performance. More precisely, an EXPLAIN PLAN output shows the following:

- The tables used in the query and the order in which they're accessed.

- The operations performed on the output of each step of the plan. For example, these could be sorting and aggregation operations.

- The specific access and join methods used for each table mentioned in the SQL statement.
- The cost of each operation.

Oracle creates the PLAN_TABLE as a global temporary table, so all the users in the database can use it to save their EXPLAIN PLAN output. However, you can create a local plan table in your own schema by running the utlxplan.sql script, which is located in the $ORACLE_HOME/rdbms/admin directory. The script, among other things, creates the plan table, where the output of the EXPLAIN PLAN utility is stored for your viewing. You are free to rename this table. Here's how you create the plan table so you can use the EXPLAIN PLAN feature:

```
SQL> @$ORACLE_HOME/rdbms/admin/utlxplan.sql
Table created.
SQL>
```

Creating the EXPLAIN PLAN

To create an EXPLAIN PLAN for any SQL data manipulation language statement, you use a SQL statement similar to that shown in Listing 19-2.

Listing 19-2. *Creating the EXPLAIN PLAN*

```
SQL> EXPLAIN PLAN
  2  SET statement_id = 'test1'
  3  INTO plan_table
  4  FOR select p.product_id,i.quantity_on_hand
  5  FROM oe.inventories i,
  6  oe.product_descriptions p,
  7  oe.warehouses w
  8  WHERE p.product_id=i.product_id
  9  AND i.quantity_on_hand > 250
 10  AND w.warehouse_id = i.warehouse_id;
Explained.
SQL>
```

Producing the EXPLAIN PLAN

You can't easily select the columns out of the PLAN_TABLE table because of the hierarchical nature of relationships among the columns. Listing 19-3 shows the code that you can use so the EXPLAIN PLAN output is printed in a form that's readable and shows clearly how the execution plan for the statement looks.

Listing 19-3. *Producing the EXPLAIN PLAN*

```
SQL> SELECT lpad(' ',level-1)||operation||' '||options||' ||
  2  object_name "Plan"
  3  FROM plan_table
  4  CONNECT BY prior id = parent_id
  5  AND prior statement_id = statement_id
  6  START WITH id = 0 AND statement_id = '&1'
  7  ORDER BY id;
Enter value for 1: test1
old   6:   START WITH id = 0 AND statement_id = '&1'
new   6:   START WITH id = 0 AND statement_id = 'test1'
Plan
```

```
--------------------------------------------------------
SELECT STATEMENT
 HASH JOIN
  NESTED LOOPS
   TABLE ACCESS FULL INVENTORIES
   INDEX UNIQUE SCAN WAREHOUSES_PK
  INDEX FAST FULL SCAN PRD_DESC_PK
6 rows selected.
SQL>
```

Other Ways of Displaying the EXPLAIN PLAN Results

You can also use the DBMS_XPLAN package to display the output of an EXPLAIN PLAN statement in an easily readable format. You use a table function from this package to display the EXPLAIN PLAN output. You use the DISPLAY table function of the DBMS_XPLAN package to display the output of your most recent EXPLAIN PLAN. You can use the table function DISPLAY_AWR to display the output of the SQL statement's execution plan from the AWR. Here's an example that shows how to use the DBMS_XPLAN package to produce the output of the most recent EXPLAIN PLAN statement.

First, create the EXPLAIN PLAN for a SQL statement:

```
SQL> EXPLAIN PLAN FOR
  2   SELECT * FROM persons
  3   WHERE PERSONS.last_name LIKE '%ALAPATI%'
  4   AND created_date < sysdate -30;
Explained.
SQL>
```

Make sure you set the proper line size and page size in SQL*Plus:

```
SQL> SET LINESIZE 130
SQL> SET PAGESIZE 0
```

Display the EXPLAIN PLAN output:

```
SQL> SELECT * FROM table (DBMS_XPLAN.DISPLAY);
---------------------------------------------------------------------------
| Id  | Operation          | Name    | Rows | Bytes | Cost (%CPU)| Time     |
---------------------------------------------------------------------------
|   0 | SELECT STATEMENT   |         |    1 |   37  |   3    (0) | 00:00:01 |
|*  1 |   TABLE ACCESS FULL| PERSONS |    1 |   37  |   3    (0) | 00:00:01 |
---------------------------------------------------------------------------

Predicate Information  (identified by operation id) :
---------------------------------------------------

-  filter ("ENAME" LIKE '%ALAPATI%' AND "CREATED_DATE">SYSDATE@!-30)

13 rows selected.
SQL>
```

If you wish, you can use the Oracle-provided utlxpls.sql script to get nicely formatted output. The utlxpls.sql script is an alternative to using the DBMS_XPLAN package directly, and it relies on the same package. The utlxpls.sql script is located in the $ORACLE_HOME/rdbms/admin directory, as I mentioned earlier, and uses the DBMS_XPLAN package to display the most recent EXPLAIN PLAN in the database. Of course, you must make sure that the table PLAN_TABLE exists before you can use the utlxpls.sql script. Here's how you'd run this script:

```
$ @$ORACLE_HOME/rdbms/admin/utlxpls.sql
```

The output of the `utlxpls.sql` script is exactly identical to that of the `DBMS_XPLAN.DISPLAY`, which was presented a few paragraphs prior.

Interpreting the EXPLAIN PLAN Output

Reading an EXPLAIN PLAN is somewhat confusing in the beginning, and it helps to remember these simple principles:

- Each step in the plan returns output in the form of a set of rows to the parent step.
- Read the plan outward starting from the line that is indented the most.
- If two operations are at the same level in terms of their indentation, read the top one first.
- The numbering of the steps in the plan is misleading. Start reading the EXPLAIN PLAN output from the inside out. That is, read the most *indented* operation first.

In the example shown earlier in Listing 19-3 (I reproduce the plan output after the code), Oracle uses the INVENTORIES table as its driving table and uses the following execution path:

```
SELECT STATEMENT
 HASH JOIN
  NESTED LOOPS
   TABLE ACCESS FULL INVENTORIES
   INDEX UNIQUE SCAN WAREHOUSES_PK
  INDEX FAST FULL SCAN PRD_DESC_PK
```

The plan output is as follows:

1. Oracle does a full table scan of the INVENTORIES table.
2. Oracle performs an index unique scan of the WAREHOUSES table using its primary key index.
3. Oracle performs a nested loop operation to join the rows from steps 1 and 2.
4. Oracle performs an index fast full scan of the product_descriptions table using its primary key, `PRD_DESC_PK`.
5. In the final step, Oracle performs a hash join of the set from step 3 and the rows resulting from the index full scan of step 4.

Using the output of the EXPLAIN PLAN, you can quickly see why some of your queries are taking much longer than anticipated. Armed with this knowledge, you can fine-tune a query until an acceptable performance threshold is reached. The wonderful thing about the EXPLAIN PLAN is that you never have to execute any statement in the database to trace the execution plan of the statement. The next section presents a few examples so you can feel more comfortable using the EXPLAIN PLAN utility.

More Plan Examples

In this section, you'll learn how to interpret various kinds of execution plans derived by using the EXPLAIN PLAN utility.

In the first example, consider what happens when you use a function on an indexed column. Oracle completely ignores the index! As you can see, the optimizer can make mistakes. Good programmers can help the optimizer get it right by using methods such as proper indexing of tables, optimizer hints, and so on.

```
SQL> EXPLAIN PLAN set statement_id = 'example_plan1'
  2  FOR
  3  SELECT last_name FROM hr.employees
  4  WHERE upper(last_name) = 'FAY';

Explained.
SQL>

example_plan1
-----------------------------
SELECT STATEMENT
 TABLE ACCESS FULL EMPLOYEES
SQL>
```

The next example is a query similar to the preceding one, but without the upper function on last_name. This time, Oracle uses the index on the last_name column:

```
SQL> EXPLAIN PLAN SET  statement_id = 'example_plan1'
  2 FOR
  3 SELECT last_name FROM hr.employees
  4*WHERE last_name='FAY';
Explained.

SQL>
example_plan1
-----------------------------
SELECT STATEMENT
 INDEX RANGE SCAN EMP_NAME_IX
SQL>
```

In the third example, two tables (customers and orders) are joined to retrieve the query results:

```
SQL> EXPLAIN PLAN SET statement_id 'newplan1'
  2  FOR
  3  SELECT o.order_id,
  4  o.order_total,
  5  c.account_mgr_id
  6  FROM customers c,
  7  orders o
  8  WHERE o.customer_id=c.customer_id
  9  AND o.order_date > '01-JUL-05'
Explained.
SQL>
```

Listing 19-4 shows the EXPLAIN PLAN from the plan table.

Listing 19-4. *Another EXPLAIN PLAN Output*

```
 SQL> SELECT lpad(' ',level-1)||operation||' '||options||' '||
   2  object_name "newplan"
   3  FROM plan_table
   4  CONNECT BY prior id = parent_id
   5  AND prior statement_id = statement_id
   6  START WITH id = 0 AND statement_id = '&1'
   7* ORDER BY id;
Enter value for 1: newplan1
old   6:    START WITH id = 0 AND statement_id = '&1'
```

```
new    6:   START WITH id = 0 AND statement_id = 'newplan1'
newplan
SELECT STATEMENT
 HASH JOIN                                  /* step 4 */
  TABLE ACCESS FULL CUSTOMERS            /* step 2 */
  TABLE ACCESS BY INDEX ROWID ORDERS    /* step 3 */
   INDEX RANGE SCAN ORD_ORDER_DATE_IX /* step 1 */
Elapsed: 00:00:00.01
SQL>
```

In step 1, the query first does an index range scan of the orders table using the ORD_ORDER_
DATE_IX index. Why an index range scan? Because this index isn't unique—it has multiple rows with
the same data value—the optimizer has to scan these multiple rows to get the data it's interested in.
For example, if the indexed column is a primary key, it will be unique by definition, and you'll see the
notation "Unique Scan" in the EXPLAIN PLAN statement.

In step 2, the customers table is accessed through a full table scan, because account_
manager_id in that table, which is part of the WHERE clause, isn't indexed.

In step 3, the query accesses the orders table by INDEX ROWID, using the ROWID it derived in the
previous step. This step gets you the order_id, customer_id, and order_total columns from the orders
table for the date specified.

In step 4, the rows from the orders table are joined with the rows from the customers table based
on the join condition WHERE o.customer_id=c.customer_id.

As you can see from the preceding examples, the EXPLAIN PLAN facility provides you with a
clear idea as to the access methods used by the optimizer. Of course, you can do this without having
to run the query itself. Often, the EXPLAIN PLAN will provide you with a quick answer as to why your
SQL may be performing poorly. The plan's output can help you determine how selective your
indexes are and let you experiment with quick changes in code.

Using Autotrace

The Autotrace facility enables you to produce EXPLAIN PLANs automatically when you execute a
SQL statement in SQL*Plus. You automatically have the privileges necessary to use the Autotrace
facility when you log in as SYS or SYSTEM.

First, if you plan to use Autotrace, you should create a plan table in your schema. Once you
create this plan table, you can use it for all your future executions of the Autotrace facility. If you
don't have this table in your schema, you'll get an error when you try to use the Autotrace facility,
as shown here:

```
SQL> SET AUTOTRACE ON SP2-0618: Cannot find the Session Identifier
.  Check PLUSTRACE role is enabled
SP2-0611: Error enabling STATISTICS report
SQL>
```

You can create the PLAN_TABLE table by using the CREATE TABLE statement, as shown in
Listing 19-5. You can also create this table by executing the utlxplan.sql script, as I explained
earlier.

Listing 19-5. *Manually Creating the Plan Table*

```
SQL> CREATE TABLE PLAN_TABLE(
  2  STATEMENT_ID      VARCHAR2(30), TIMESTAMP       DATE,
  3  REMARKS           VARCHAR2(80), OPERATION       VARCHAR2(30),
  4  OPTIONS           VARCHAR2(30), OBJECT_NODE     VARCHAR2(128),
  5  OBJECT_OWNER      VARCHAR2(30), OBJECT_NAME     VARCHAR2(30),
```

```
 6  OBJECT_INSTANCE  NUMERIC,         OBJECT_TYPE         VARCHAR2(30),
 7  OPTIMIZER        VARCHAR2(255),SEARCH_COLUMNS         NUMBER,
 8  ID               NUMERIC,         PARENT_ID           NUMERIC,
 9  POSITION         NUMERIC,         COST                NUMERIC,
10  CARDINALITY      NUMERIC,         BYTES               NUMERIC,
11  OTHER_TAG        VARCHAR2(255),PARTITION_START        VARCHAR2(255),
12  PARTITION_STOP   VARCHAR2(255),PARTITION_ID           NUMERIC,
13  OTHER            LONG,            DISTRIBUTION        VARCHAR2(30));
Table created.
SQL>
```

Next, the SYS or SYSTEM user needs to grant you the PLUSTRACE role, as shown here:

```
SQL> GRANT PLUSTRACE TO salapati;
                 *
ERROR at Line 1:
ORA-1919: role 'PLUSTRACE' does not exist.
```

If, as in the preceding case, the PLUSTRACE role doesn't already exist in the database, the SYS user needs to run the plustrace.sql script, as shown in Listing 19-6, to create the PLUSTRACE role.

Listing 19-6. *Creating the PLUSTRACE Role*

```
SQL> @ORACLE_HOME/sqlplus/admin/plustrce.sql
SQL> DROP ROLE plustrace;
drop role plustrace
          *
ERROR at line 1:
ORA-01919: role 'PLUSTRACE' does not exist
SQL> CREATE ROLE plustrace;
Role created.
SQL>
SQL> GRANT SELECT ON v_$sesstat TO plustrace;
Grant succeeded.
SQL> GRANT SELECT ON v_$statname TO plustrace;
Grant succeeded.
SQL> GRANT SELECT ON v_$mystat TO plustrace;
Grant succeeded.
SQL> GRANT plustrace TO dba WITH ADMIN OPTION;
Grant succeeded.
SQL>
```

Third, the user who intends to use Autotrace should be given the PLUSTRACE role, as shown here:

```
SQL> GRANT plustrace TO salapati;
Grant succeeded.
SQL>
```

The user can now set the Autotrace feature on and view the EXPLAIN PLAN for any query that is used in the session. The Autotrace feature can be turned on with different options:

- SET AUTOTRACE ON EXPLAIN: This generates the execution plan only and doesn't execute the query itself.

- SET AUTOTRACE ON STATISTICS: This shows only the execution statistics for the SQL statement.

- SET AUTOTRACE ON: This shows both the execution plan and the SQL statement execution statistics.

All SQL statements issued after the Autotrace feature is turned on will generate the execution plans (until you turn off the Autotrace facility with the command SET AUTOTRACE OFF), as shown in Listing 19-7.

Listing 19-7. *Using the Autotrace Utility*

```
SQL> SET AUTOTRACE ON;
SQL> SELECT * FROM EMP;
no rows selected
Execution Plan
    0       SELECT STATEMENT Optimizer=CHOOSE (Cost=2 Card=1 Bytes=74)
    1    0  TABLE ACCESS (FULL) OF 'EMP' (Cost=2 Card=1 Bytes=74)
Statistics
          0  recursive calls
          0  db block gets
          3  consistent gets
          0  physical reads
          0  redo size
        511  bytes sent via SQL*Net to client
        368  bytes received via SQL*Net from client
          1  SQL*Net roundtrips to/from client
          0  sorts (memory)
          0  sorts (disk)
          0  rows processed
SQL>
```

After showing the execution plan for the SQL statement, the Autotrace feature shows the details about the number of SQL recursive calls incurred in executing the original statement; the number of physical and logical reads, in memory and on disk sorts; and the number of rows processed.

I provide a few simple examples to show how Autotrace helps you optimize SQL queries. In the following examples, the same query is used twice in the courses table, once without an index and once with an index. After the table is indexed, you run the query before you analyze the table. The results are instructive.

In the first example, whose output is shown in Listing 19-8, you run the test query before you create an index on the courses table.

Listing 19-8. *The Execution Plan for a Query Without an Index*

```
SQL> SET AUTOTRACE ON
SQL> SELECT COUNT(*) FROM courses
  2  WHERE course_subject='medicine'
  3* AND course_title = 'fundamentals of human anatomy';
  COUNT(*)
    98304
Execution Plan
----------------------------------------------------
    0       SELECT STATEMENT Optimizer=CHOOSE
    1    0  SORT (AGGREGATE)
    2    1    TABLE ACCESS (FULL) OF 'COURSES'
Statistics
----------------------------------------------------
          0  recursive calls
          0  db block gets
        753  consistent gets
```

```
  338  physical reads
    0  redo size
  381  bytes sent via SQL*Net to client
  499  bytes received via SQL*Net from client
    2  SQL*Net roundtrips to/from client
    0  sorts (memory)
    0  sorts (disk)
    1  rows processed
SQL>
```

As you can see, the query used a full table scan because there are no indexes. There were a total of 338 physical reads. Note that the total number of rows in the courses table is 98,384. Out of this total, the courses with medicine as the course subject were 98,304. That is, the table values aren't distributed evenly among the courses at all. Now let's see what happens when you use an index.

The following example uses a query with an index. However, no statistics are collected for either the table or the index. When you create an index on the courses table and run the same query, you'll see some interesting results. Listing 19-9 tells the story.

Listing 19-9. *The Execution Plan for a Query with an Index*

```
SQL> CREATE INDEX title_idx ON courses (course_title);
Index created.
SQL> SELECT count(*) FROM courses
  2  WHERE course_subject='medicine'
  3  AND course_title = 'fundamentals of human anatomy';
  COUNT(*)
     98304
Execution Plan
----------------------------------------------------------------
   0       SELECT STATEMENT Optimizer=CHOOSE
   1    0   SORT (AGGREGATE)
   2    1    TABLE ACCESS (BY INDEX ROWID) OF 'COURSES'
   3    2     INDEX (RANGE SCAN) OF 'TITLE_IDX' (NON-UNIQUE)
Statistics
----------------------------------------------------------------
     0  recursive calls
     0  db block gets
  1273  consistent gets
  1249  physical reads
     0  redo size
   381  bytes sent via SQL*Net to client
   499  bytes received via SQL*Net from client
     2  SQL*Net roundtrips to/from client
     0  sorts (memory)
     0  sorts (disk)
     1  rows processed
SQL>
```

After you created the index, the physical reads went from 338 to 1,249! The EXPLAIN PLAN shows that Oracle is indeed using the index, so you would expect the physical reads to be lower when compared to the no-index case. What happened here is that even if a table has an index, this doesn't mean that it's always good to use it under all circumstances. The CBO always figures the best way to get a query's results, with or without using the index. In this case, the query has to look at almost all the rows of the table, so using an index isn't the best way to go. However, you haven't collected statistics for the table and the index, so Oracle has no way of knowing the distribution of the actual data in the courses table. Lacking any statistics, it falls back to a rule-based approach. Under a rule-based optimization, using an index occupies a lower rank and therefore indicates that this is the optimal approach here. Let's see the results after analyzing the table.

The third example is a query with an index executed after collecting optimizer statistics for the table. Oracle has the complete statistics, and it uses the CBO this time around. The CBO decides to use an index only if the cost of using the index is lower than the cost of a full table scan. The CBO decides that it won't use the index, because the query will have to read 98,304 out of a total of 98,384 rows. It rightly decides to do a full table scan instead. The results are shown in Listing 19-10.

Listing 19-10. *The Execution Plan with an Index After Analyzing the Table*

```
SQL> ANALYZE TABLE  courses COMPUTE STATISTICS;
Table analyzed.
SQL> SELECT count(*) FROM courses
  2  WHERE course_subject='medicine'
  3  AND course_title = 'fundamentals of human anatomy';
  COUNT(*)
-----------
   98304
Execution Plan
----------------------------------------------------------
   0      SELECT STATEMENT Optimizer=CHOOSE (Cost=74 Card=1 Bytes=39)
   1    0   SORT (AGGREGATE)
   2    1     TABLE ACCESS (FULL) OF 'COURSES' (Cost=74 Card=24596 Bytes=959244)
Statistics
----------------------------------------------------------
        290  recursive calls
          0  db block gets
        792  consistent gets
        334  physical reads
          0  redo size
        381  bytes sent via SQL*Net to client
        499  bytes received via SQL*Net from client
          2  SQL*Net roundtrips to/from client
          6  sorts (memory)
          0  sorts (disk)
          1  rows processed
SQL>
```

In this listing, the first item, recursive calls, refers to additional statements Oracle needs to make when it's processing a user's SQL statement. For example, Oracle issues recursive calls (or recursive SQL statements) to make space allocations or to query the data dictionary tables on disk. In our example, Oracle made 290 internal calls during the SQL Trace period.

Using SQL Trace and TKPROF

SQL Trace is an Oracle utility that helps you trace the execution of SQL statements. TKPROF is another Oracle utility that helps you format the trace files output by SQL Trace into a readable form. Although the EXPLAIN PLAN facility gives you the expected execution plan, the SQL Trace tool gives you the actual execution results of a SQL query. Sometimes, you may not be able to identify the exact code, say, for dynamically generated SQL. SQL Trace files can capture the SQL for dynamic SQL. Among other things, SQL Trace enables you to track the following variables:

- CPU and elapsed times
- Parsed and executed counts for each SQL statement
- Number of physical and logical reads
- Execution plan for all the SQL statements
- Library cache hit ratios

■**Tip** If your application has a lot of dynamically generated SQL, the SQL Trace utility is ideal for tuning the SQL statements.

Although the EXPLAIN PLAN tool is important for determining the access path that the optimizer will use, SQL Trace gives you a lot of hard information on resource use and the efficacy of the statements. You'll get a good idea of whether your statement is being parsed excessively. The statement's execute and fetch counts illustrate its efficiency. You get a good sense of how much CPU time is consumed by your queries and how much I/O is being performed during the execution phase. This helps you identify the resource-guzzling SQL statements in your application and tune them. The EXPLAIN PLAN, which is an optional part of SQL Trace, gives the row counts for the individual steps of the EXPLAIN PLAN, helping you pinpoint at what step the most work is being done. By comparing resource use with the number of rows fetched, you can easily determine how productive a particular statement is.

In the next sections you'll use SQL Trace to trace a simple SQL statement and interpret it with the TKPROF utility. You start by setting a few initialization parameters to ensure tracing.

Setting the Trace Initialization Parameters

Collecting trace statistics imposes a performance penalty, and consequently the database doesn't automatically trace all sessions. Tracing is purely an optional process that you turn on for a limited duration to capture metrics about the performance of critical SQL statements. You need to look at four initialization parameters to set up Oracle correctly for SQL tracing, and you have to restart the database after checking that the following parameters are correctly configured. Three of these parameters are dynamic session parameters, and you can change them at the session level.

STATISTICS_LEVEL

The STATISTICS_LEVEL parameter can take three values. The value of this parameter has a bearing on the TIMED_STATISTICS parameter. You can see this dependency clearly in the following summary:

- If the STATISTICS_LEVEL parameter is set to TYPICAL or ALL, timed statistics are collected automatically for the database.
- If STATISTICS_LEVEL is set to BASIC, then TIMED_STATISTICS must be set to TRUE for statistics collection.
- Even if STATISTICS_LEVEL is set to TYPICAL or ALL, you can keep the database from tracing by using the ALTER SESSION statement to set TIMED_STATISTICS to FALSE.

TIMED_STATISTICS

The TIMED_STATISTICS parameter is FALSE by default, if the STATISTICS_LEVEL parameter is set to BASIC. In a case like this, to collect performance statistics such as CPU and execution time, set the value of the TIMED_STATISTICS parameter to TRUE in the init.ora file or SPFILE, or use the ALTER

SYSTEM SET TIMED_STATISTICS=TRUE statement to turn timed statistics on instance-wide. You can also do this at the session level by using the ALTER SESSION statement as follows:

```
SQL> ALTER SESSION SET timed_statistics = true;
Session altered.
SQL>
```

USER_DUMP_DEST

USER_DUMP_DEST is the directory on your server where your SQL Trace files will be sent. By default you use the $ORACLE_HOME/admin/*database_name*/udump directory as your directory for dumping SQL trace files. If you want non-DBAs to be able to read this file, make sure the directory permissions authorize reading by others. Alternatively, you can set the parameter TRACE_FILES_PUBLIC=TRUE to let others read the trace files on UNIX systems. Make sure the destination points to a directory that has plenty of free space to accommodate large trace files. USER_DUMP_DEST is a dynamic parameter, so you can also change it using the ALTER SYSTEM command, as follows:

```
SQL> ALTER SYSTEM SET user_dump_dest='c:\oraclent\oradata';
System altered.
SQL>
```

■**Note** In Oracle Database 11*g*, if you set the new DIAGNSOTIC_DEST initialization parameter, the database ignores the USER_DUMP_DEST setting. The directory you set for the DIAGNOSTIC_DEST parameter determines where the database will place the trace files.

MAX_DUMP_FILE_SIZE

Some traces could result in large trace files in a big hurry, so make sure your MAX_DUMP_FILE_SIZE initialization parameter is set to a high number. The default size of this parameter may be too small for some traces. If the trace fills the dump file, it won't terminate, but the information in the file will be truncated.

Enabling SQL Trace

To use SQL Trace and TKPROF, first you need to enable the Trace facility. You can do this at the instance level by using the ALTER SESSION statement or the DBMS_SESSION package. You can trace the entire instance by either including the line SQL_TRACE=TRUE in your init.ora file or SPFILE or by using the ALTER SYSTEM command to set SQL_TRACE to TRUE. Tracing the entire instance isn't recommended, because it generates a huge amount of tracing information, most of which is useless for your purpose. The statement that follows shows how to turn tracing on from your session using the ALTER SESSION statement:

```
SQL> ALTER SESSION SET sql_trace=true;
Session altered.
SQL>
```

The following example shows how you set SQL_TRACE to TRUE using the DBMS_SESSION package:

```
SQL> EXECUTE sys.dbms_session.set_sql_trace(true);
PL/SQL procedure successfully completed.
SQL>
```

Often, users request the DBA to help them trace their SQL statements. You can use the DBMS_
SYSTEM.SET_SQL_TRACE_IN_SESSION procedure to set tracing on in another user's session. Note
that usage of the DBMS_SYSTEM package has never actually been supported by Oracle. The recommended way is to use the DBMS_MONITOR package to trace a session. Regardless of the method you
use, once you start tracing a session, all statements are traced until you use the ALTER SESSION statement or the DBMS_SESSION package to turn tracing off (replace true with false in either of the
preceding statements). Alternatively, when the user logs off, tracing is automatically stopped for
that user.

Interpreting the Trace Files with TKPROF

Once you set tracing on for a session, any SQL statement that is issued during that session is traced
and the output stored in the directory (udump) specified by the USER_DUMP_DEST parameter in your
init.ora file or SPFILE. The filename has the format *db_name_ora_nnnnn.trc*, where *nnnnn* is usually
a four- or five-digit number. For example, the sample trace file in our example is named pasx_ora_
16340.trc. If you go to the user dump destination directory immediately after a trace session is
completed, the most recent file is usually the session trace file you just created.

You can also differentiate the trace file output by a SQL Trace execution from the other files in
the dump directory, by its size—these trace files are much larger in general than the other files
output to the directory. These trace files are detailed and complex. Fortunately, the easy-to-run
TKPROF utility formats the output into a readable format. The TKPROF utility uses the trace file as
the input, along with several parameters you can specify.

Table 19-1 shows the main TKPROF parameters you can choose to produce the format that suits
you. If you type **tkprof** at the command prompt, you'll see a complete listing of all the parameters
that you can specify when you invoke TKPROF.

Table 19-1. *TKPROF Command-Line Arguments*

Parameter	Description
FILENAME	The input trace file produced by SQL Trace
EXPLAIN	The EXPLAIN PLAN for the SQL statements
RECORD	Creates a SQL script with all the nonrecursive SQL statements
WAITS	Records a summary of wait events
SORT	Presents sort data based on one or more items, such as PRSCPU (CPU time parsing), PRSELA (elapsed time parsing), and so on
TABLE	Defines the name of the tables into which the TKPROF utility temporarily puts the execution plans
SYS	Enables and disables listing of SQL statements issued by SYS
PRINT	Lists only a specified number of SQL statements instead of all statements
INSERT	Creates a script that stores the trace information in the database

Let's trace a session by a user who is executing two SELECT statements, one using tables with
indexes and the other using tables without any indexes. In this example, you're using only a few
parameters, choosing to run TKPROF with default sort options. The first parameter is the name of
the output file and the second is the name for the TKPROF-formatted output. You're specifying that
you don't want any analysis of statements issued by the user SYS. You're also specifying that the
EXPLAIN PLAN for the statement be shown in addition to the other statistics.

■Tip By just typing **tkprof** at the operating system prompt, you can get a quick help guide to the usage of the TKPROF utility.

```
$ tkprof finance_ora_16340.trc test.txt sys=no explain=y


TKPROF: Release 11.1.0.6.0 - Production on Mon Apr 28 12:49:38 2008

Copyright (c) 1982, 2007, Oracle.  All rights reserved.
$
```

The test.txt file contains the output of the SQL trace, now nicely formatted for you by the TKPROF utility.

Examining the Formatted Output File

Listing 19-11 shows the top portion of the test.txt file, which explains the key terms used by the utility.

Listing 19-11. *The Top Part of the TKPROF-Formatted Trace File*

```
TKPROF: Release 11.1.0.6.0 - Production on Mon Apr 28 12:49:38 2008

Copyright (c) 1982, 2007, Oracle.  All rights reserved.
Trace file: finance_ora_16340.trc
Sort options: default
********************************************************************************
count    = number of times OCI procedure was executed
cpu      = cpu time in seconds executing
elapsed  = elapsed time in seconds executing
disk     = number of physical reads of buffers from disk
query    = number of buffers gotten for consistent read
current  = number of buffers gotten in current mode (usually for update)
rows     = number of rows processed by the fetch or execute call
********************************************************************************
```

Each TKPROF report shows the following information for each SQL statement issued during the time the user's session was traced:

- The SQL statement
- Counts of parse, execute, and fetch (for SELECT statements) calls
- Count of rows processed
- CPU seconds used
- I/O used
- Library cache misses
- Optional execution plan
- Row-source operation listing
- A report summary analyzing how many similar and distinct statements were found in the trace file

Let's analyze the formatted output created by TKPROF. Listing 19-12 shows the parts of the TKPROF output showing the parse, execute, and fetch counts.

Listing 19-12. *The Parse, Execute, and Fetch Counts*

```
SQL> select e.last_name,e.first_name,d.department_name
     from teste e,testd d
     where e.department_id=d.department_id;
call     count  cpu elapsed disk     query   current      rows
-------  ------ ------ ---------- -- ---------- ---------- --------
Parse        1  0.00   0.00   0          0         0         0
Execute      1  0.00   0.00   0          0         0         0
Fetch    17322  1.82   1.85   3        136         5    259806
-------  ------ -------- ---------- ---------- ---------- ----------
total    17324  1.82   1.85   3        136         5    259806

Misses in library cache during parse: 0
Optimizer goal: CHOOSE
Parsing user id: 53
```

In Listing 19-12

- *CPU* stands for total CPU time in seconds.

- *Elapsed* is the total time elapsed in seconds.

- *Disk* denotes total physical reads.

- *Query* is the number of consistent buffer gets.

- *Current* is the number of database block gets.

- *Rows* is the total number of rows processed for each type of call.

From Listing 19-12, you can draw the following conclusions:

- The SQL statement shown previously was parsed once, so a parsed version wasn't available in the shared pool before execution. The Parse column shows that this operation took less than 0.01 seconds. Note that the lack of disk I/Os and buffer gets indicates that there were no data dictionary cache misses during the parse operation. If the Parse column showed a large number for the same statement, it would be an indicator that bind variables weren't being used.

- The statement was executed once and execution took less than 0.01 seconds. Again, there were no disk I/Os or buffer gets during the execution phase.

- It took me a lot longer than 0.01 seconds to get the results of the SELECT statement back. The Fetch column answers this question of why that should be: it shows that the operation was performed 17,324 times and took up 1.82 seconds of CPU time.

- The Fetch operation was performed 17,324 times and fetched 259,806 rows. Because the number of rows is far greater than the number of fetches, you can deduce that Oracle used array fetch operations.

- There were three physical reads during the fetch operation. If there's a large difference between CPU time and elapsed time, it can be attributed to time taken up by disk reads. In this case, the physical I/O has a value of only 3, and it matches the insignificant gap between CPU time and elapsed time. The fetch required 136 buffer gets in the consistent mode and only 5 DB block gets.

- The CBO was being used, because the optimizer goal is shown as CHOOSE.

The following output shows the execution plan that was explicitly requested when TKPROF was invoked. Note that instead of the cost estimates that you get when you use the EXPLAIN PLAN tool, you get the number of rows output by each step of the execution.

```
Rows     Row Source Operation
-------  -----------------------
259806     MERGE JOIN
  1161     SORT JOIN
  1161     TABLE ACCESS FULL TESTD
259806     SORT JOIN
```

Finally, TKPROF summarizes the report, stating how many SQL statements were traced. Here's the summary portion of the TKPROF-formatted output:

```
Trace file: ORA02344.TRC
Trace file compatibility: 9.00.01
Sort options: default
       2  sessions in trace file.
      18  user  SQL statements in trace file.
     104  internal SQL statements in trace file.
      72  SQL statements in trace file.
      33  unique SQL statements in trace file.
   18182  lines in trace file.
```

The TKPROF output makes it easy to identify inefficient SQL statements. TKPROF can order the SQL statements by elapsed time (time taken for execution), which tells you which of the SQL statements you should focus on for optimization.

The SQL Trace utility is a powerful tool in tuning SQL, because it goes far beyond the information produced by using EXPLAIN PLAN. It provides you with hard information about the number of the various types of calls made to Oracle during statement execution, and how the resource use was allocated to the various stages of execution.

■**Note** It's easy to trace individual user sessions using the OEM Database Control. I explain how you can trace and view user sessions using the Database Control in the section "Using the Database Control for End-to-End Tracing." You can trace a session as well as read the output file directly from the Database Control.

End-to-End Tracing

In multitier environments, the middle tier passes a client's request through several database sessions. It's hard to keep track of the client across all these database sessions. Similarly, when you use shared server architecture, it's hard to identify the user session that you're tracing at any given time. Because multiple sessions may use the same shared server connection, when you trace the connection, you can't be sure who the user is exactly at any given time—the active sessions using the shared server connection keep changing throughout.

In the cases I described earlier, tracing a single session becomes impossible. Oracle Database 10*g* introduced *end-to-end tracing*, with which you can uniquely identify and track the same client through multiple sessions. The attribute CLIENT_IDENTIFIER uniquely identifies a client and remains the same through all the tiers. You can use the DBMS_MONITOR package to perform end-to-end tracing. You can also use the OEM Database Control to set up end-to-end tracing easily. Let's look at both approaches in the following sections.

Using the DBMS_MONITOR Package

You use the Oracle PL/SQL package DBMS_MONITOR to set up end-to-end tracing. You can trace a user session through multiple tiers and generate trace files using the following three attributes:

- Client identifier
- Service name
- Combination of service name, module name, and action name

You can specify a combination of service name, module name, and action name. You can also specify service name alone, or a combination of service name and module name. However, you can't specify an action name alone. Your application must use the DBMS_APPLICATION_INFO package to set module and action names. The service name is determined by the connect string you use to connect to a service. If a user's session isn't associated with a service specifically, the sys$users service handles it.

Let's use two procedures belonging to the DBMS_MONITOR package. The first one, SERV_MOD_ACT_TRACE_ENABLE, sets the service name, module name, and action name attributes. The second, CLIENT_ID_TRACE_ENABLE, sets the client ID attribute. Here's an example:

```
SQL> EXECUTE dbms_monitor.serv_mod_act_trace_enable
     (service_name=>'myservice', module_name=>'batch_job');
PL/SQL procedure successfully completed.
SQL> EXECUTE dbms_monitor.client_id_trace_enable
     (client_id=>'salapati');
PL/SQL procedure successfully completed.
SQL>
```

You can use the SET_IDENTIFIER procedure of the DBMS_SESSION package to get a client's session ID. Here's an example showing how you can use a logon trigger and the SET_IDENTIFIER procedure together to capture the user's session ID immediately upon the user's logging into the system:

```
SQL> CREATE OR REPLACE TRIGGER logon_trigger
     AFTER LOGON
     ON DATABASE
     DECLARE
     user_id VARCHAR2(64);
     BEGIN
     SELECT ora_login_user ||':'||SYS_CONTEXT('USERENV','OS_USER')
     INTO user_id
     FROM dual;
     dbms_session.set_identifier(user_id);
     END;
```

Using the value for the client_id attribute, you can get the values for the SID and SERIAL# columns in the V$SESSION view for any user and set up tracing for that client_id. Here's an example:

```
SQL> EXECUTE dbms_monitor.session_trace_enable
     (session_id=>111, serial_num=>23, waits=>true, binds=>false);
```

You can now ask the user to run the problem SQL and collect the trace files so you can use the TKPROF utility to analyze them. In a shared server environment especially, there may be multiple trace files. By using the trcsess command-line tool, you can consolidate information from multiple trace files into one single file. Here's an example (first navigate to your user dump or udump directory):

```
$ trcsess output="salapati.trc" service="myservice
  "module="batch job" action="batch insert"
```

You can then run your usual TKPROF command against the consolidated trace file, as shown here:

```
$ tkprof salapati.trc output=salapati_report SORT=(EXEELA, PRSELA, FCHELA)
```

■**Note** In this chapter, you saw how to enable SQL tracing using the SQL Trace facility, the DBMS_SESSION package, and the DBMS_MONITOR package. You should use one of the two packages, rather than SQL Trace, to trace SQL statements. You can use any one of these three methods to set up a session-level or instance-wide trace. Be careful about tracing the entire instance, because it'll lead to excessive load on your instance, as well as produce too many voluminous trace files.

Using the Database Control for End-to-End Tracing

The best approach, as well as the recommended one, to end-to-end tracing is to use the OEM Database Control. This way, you don't have to bother with manual runs of the DBMS_MONITOR package. Here are the steps:

1. From the Database Control home page, click the Performance link.

2. In the Performance page, click the Top Consumers link under the Additional Management Links section.

3. In the Top Consumers page, you'll see the tabs for Top Services, Top Modules, Top Actions, Top Clients, and Top Sessions, as shown in Figure 19-2. Click the Top Clients tab.

4. To enable aggregation for a client, select the client and click Enable Aggregation.

If you wish, you can use the Database Control to trace a normal SQL session instead of using the SET_TRACE command and the TKPROF utility. To trace a user command, in step 3 of the preceding sequence, click the Top Sessions tab. You then click the Enable SQL Trace button. You can then use the Disable SQL Trace button to stop the session tracing and view the output by clicking the View SQL Trace File button.

■**Note** You can view all outstanding trace information in your instance by examining the DBA_ENABLED_TRACES view, or use a trace report generated through the Database Control.

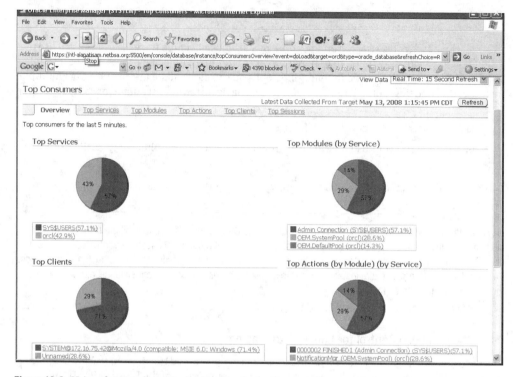

Figure 19-2. *Using the Database Control for tracing*

Using the V$SQL View to Find Inefficient SQL

The V$SQL view is an invaluable tool in tracking down wasteful SQL code in your application. The V$SQL view gathers information from the shared pool area on every statement's disk reads and memory reads, in addition to other important information. The view holds all the SQL statements executed since instance startup, but there's no guarantee that it will hold every statement until you shut down the instance. For space reasons, the older statements are aged out of the V$SQL view. It's a good idea for you to grant your developers select rights on this view directly if you haven't already granted them the "select any catalog" role. You can use the V$SQL view to perform ad hoc queries on disk and CPU usage, but remember that the AWR report includes summaries of these kinds of information.

The V$SQL view includes, among other things, the following columns, which help in assessing how many resources a SQL statement consumes:

- *rows_processed* gives you the total number of rows processed by the statement.
- *sql_text* is the text of the SQL statement (first 1,000 characters).
- *sql_fulltext* is a CLOB column that shows the full text of a SQL statement.
- *buffer_gets* gives you the total number of logical reads (indicates high CPU use).
- *disk_reads* tells you the total number of disk reads (indicates high I/O).
- *sorts* gives the number of sorts for the statement (indicates high sort ratios).
- *cpu_time* is the total parse and execution time.
- *elapsed_time* is the elapsed time for parsing and execution.

- *parse_calls* is the combined soft and hard parse calls for the statement.
- *executions* is the number of times a statement was executed.
- *loads* is the number of times the statement was reloaded into the shared pool after being flushed out.
- *sharable_memory* is the total shared memory used by the cursor.
- *persistent_memory* is the total persistent memory used by the cursor.
- *runtime_memory* is the total runtime memory used by the cursor.

> ■**Note** In previous versions, DBAs used the V$SQLAREA view to gather information shown earlier. However, the V$SQL view supplants the V$SQLAREA view by providing all information in that view, plus other important tuning-related information as well.

Finding SQL That Uses Most of Your Resources

You can query the V$SQL view to find high-resource-using SQL. You can determine resource-intensive SQL on the basis of the number of logical reads or buffer gets, or high disk reads, high parse calls, large number of executions, or combinations of these factors. It's obvious that a high number of disk reads is inefficient because a high amount of physical I/O slows query performance. However, a high number of memory reads (buffer gets) is also expensive because they consume CPU resources. You normally have high buffer gets because you're using the wrong index, the wrong driving table in a join, or a similar SQL-related error. One of the primary goals of SQL tuning should be to lower the number of unnecessary logical reads. If buffer gets and disk reads are at identical levels, it could indicate a missing index. The reasoning is this: if you don't have an index, Oracle is forced to do a full table scan. However, full table scans can't be kept in the SGA for too long because they might force a lot of other data to be cleared out. Consequently, the full table won't get to stay in the SGA for too long unless it's a small table.

The following simple query shows how the V$SQL view can pinpoint problem SQL statements; both high disk reads and high logical reads are used as the criteria for flagging down poor SQL statements captured by the V$SQL view. The SQL_TEXT column shows the exact SQL statement that's responsible for the high disk reads and logical reads:

```
SQL> SELECT sql_text, executions, buffer_gets, disk_reads,
  2  FROM V$SQL
  3  WHERE buffer_gets > 100000
  4  OR disk_reads > 100000
  5  ORDER BY buffer_gets + 100*disk_reads DESC;
```

SQL_TEXT	EXECUTIONS	BUFFER_GETS	DISK_READS
BEGIN dbms_job.run(1009133);	726216	1615283234	125828
BEGIN label_sc_pkg.launch_sc;	34665	1211625422	3680242
SELECT COUNT(*) AV_YOUTHS...	70564	152737737	7186125
SELECT UC.CHART_ID...	37849	96590083	5547319
SELECT MAX(REC_NUM) FROM...	5163242	33272842	6034715

```
SQL>
```

The following query is a slight variation on the preceding query. It seeks to find out the number of rows processed for each statement:

```
SQL> SELECT sql_text, rows_processed,
  2 buffer_gets, disk_reads, parse_calls
  3 FROM V$SQL
  4 WHERE buffer_gets > 100000
  5 OR disk_reads > 100000
  6*ORDER BY buffer_gets + 100*disk_reads DESC;
```

SQL_TEXT	ROWS_PROCESSED	BUFFER_GETS	DISK_READS	PARSE_CALLS
BEGIN dbms_job.run(1009133);	9659	1615322749	125830	2078
BEGIN label_sc_pkg.launch_sc;	3928	1214405479	3680515	4
SELECT COUNT(*) AV_YOUTHS...	70660	152737737	7186125	3863
SELECT UC.CHART_ID...	37848	96590083	5547319	5476
SELECT MAX(REC_NUM) FROM...	5163236	33272842	6034715	606

```
SQL>
```

The V$SQL view helps you find out which of your queries have high *logical I/O* (LIO) and high *physical I/O* (PIO). By also providing the number of rows processed by each statement, it tells you whether a statement is efficient or not. By providing the disk reads and the number of executions per statement, the view helps you determine whether the number of disk reads per execution is reasonable. If CPU usage is your concern, look at the statements that have a high number of buffer gets. If I/O is your primary concern, focus on the statements that perform the most disk reads. Once you settle on the statement you want to investigate further, examine the complete SQL statement and see whether you (or the developers) can improve it.

One of the best ways to find poorly performing SQL queries is by using the Oracle *wait interface*, which I explain in detail in Chapter 20.

Here's a query that uses the V$SQL view to sort the top five queries that are taking the most CPU time and the most elapsed time to complete:

```
SQL> SELECT sql_text, executions,
  2 ROUND(elapsed_time/1000000, 2) elapsed_seconds,
  3 ROUND(cpu_time/1000000, 2) cpu_secs from
  4 (select * from v$sql order by elapsed_time desc)
  5* WHERE rownum <6;
```

SQL_TEXT	EXECUTIONS	ELAPSED_SECONDS	CPU_SECS
DELETE MS_DASH_TRANLOGS...	2283	44.57	43.04
UPDATE PERSONS SET...	14132	19.74	20.52
SELECT /*+ INDEX(ud)...	9132	9.95	9
SELECT PROG_ID FROM UNITS ...	14132	5.26	5.81
SELECT NVL(SUM(RECHART),0)...	2284	4.13	4.43

```
SQL>
```

Using Other Dictionary Views for SQL Tuning

The V$SQL_PLAN and V$SQL_PLAN_STATISTICS views are highly useful for tracking the efficiency of execution plans. You should be wary of quick changes in code to fix even the worst-performing query in the system. Let's say you create an extra index on a table or change the order of columns in a composite key to fix this problem query. How do you know these aren't going to impact other queries in the application adversely? This happens more often than you think, and therefore you must do your due diligence to rule out unintended consequences of your fixes.

The SQL Tuning Advisor

You can use the SQL Tuning Advisor to improve poorly performing SQL statements. The SQL Tuning Advisor provides the following to help you tune bad SQL statements:

- Advice on improving the execution plan
- Reasons for the SQL improvement recommendations
- Benefits you can expect by following the Advisor's advice
- Details of the commands to tune the misbehaving SQL statements

Using the SQL Tuning Advisor

The SQL Tuning Advisor can use the following sources:

- New SQL statements. When working with a development database, this may be your best source of SQL statements.
- High-load SQL statements.
- SQL statements from the AWR.
- SQL statements from the database cursor cache.

The Advisor can tune sets of SQL statements called SQL Tuning Sets. An STS is a set of SQL statements combined with execution information, which includes the average elapsed time. An STS has the advantage of capturing the information about a database's workload as well as allowing you to tune several large SQL statements at once.

How the SQL Tuning Advisor Works

As mentioned previously, the optimizer will try to find the optimal execution plan for each statement you provide. However, this process happens under production conditions, so the optimizer can only devote a short amount of time to working out a solution. The optimizer uses heuristics to generate an estimate of the best solution. This is called the *normal mode* of the optimizer.

You can also run the optimizer in *tuning mode*, which means that the optimizer carries out in-depth analysis to come up with ways to optimize execution plans. While in this mode, the optimizer can take several minutes and produces recommendations instead of the best SQL execution plan. You, in turn, use these recommendations to optimize the SQL statements' execution plans. You get the added advantage of advice that details the rationale behind the recommendations and what you will gain from implementing them. The Oracle optimizer running in tuning mode is called the Automatic Tuning Optimizer (ATO). The ATO does the following tasks:

- Statistics analysis
- SQL profiling
- Access path analysis
- SQL structure analysis

I describe each of these tasks in the following sections, along with the types of recommendations that the SQL Tuning Advisor makes.

Statistics Analysis

The ATO makes sure that there are representative, up-to-date statistics for all the objects in the SQL statement, which you need for efficient execution plans. If the ATO finds any statistics that are missing or stale, it suggests that you collect new statistics for the objects in question. During this process, the ATO collects other information that it can use to fill in any missing statistics. It can also correct stale statistics.

SQL Profiling

At this stage the ATO tries to verify the validity of its estimates of factors such as column selectivity and cardinality of database objects. It can use three methods to verify its estimates:

- *Dynamic data sampling*: The ATO can use a data sample to check its estimates. The ATO can apply correction factors if the data-sampling process shows its estimates to be significantly wrong.

- *Partial execution*: The ATO can carry out the partial execution of a SQL statement. This process allows it to check whether its estimates are close to what really happens. It does not check whether its estimates are correct, but rather it checks whether a plan derived from those statistics is the best possible plan.

- *Past execution history statistics*: The ATO can use the SQL statement's execution history to help with its work.

If there's enough information from statistics analysis or SQL profiling, the ATO suggests you create a SQL profile, which is supplementary information about a SQL statement.

If you accept this advice and are running the optimizer in tuning mode, Oracle will store the SQL profile in the data dictionary. Once you have done this, the optimizer uses it to produce optimal execution plans, even when it is running in normal mode.

Tip   Remember that a SQL profile is not the same thing as a stored execution plan.

The SQL profile will continue to apply if you make small changes to your database and allow your objects to grow normally. One of the big advantages of SQL profiles is the ability to tune packaged applications. These are hard to tune because you can't easily access and modify the code. Because SQL profiles are saved in the data dictionary, you can use them to tune packaged applications.

Analyzing Access Paths

The ATO analyzes how using an improved access method, such as working with an index, will affect queries. These are important considerations, because adding an index can substantially increase the speed of a query. However, adding new indexes can adversely affect other SQL statements; the SQL Advisor knows this and makes its recommendations as follows:

- If an index is effective, it will advise you to create it.

- It can advise you to run the SQL Access Advisor (see Chapter 7 for details) to analyze the wisdom of adding the new index.

SQL Structure Analysis

The ATO can make recommendations to modify the structure (both the syntax and semantics) of poorly performing SQL statements. The ATO considers issues such as the following:

- Design mistakes; for example, performing full table scans because you didn't create indexes.
- Using inefficient SQL; for example, the NOT IN construct, which is known to be much slower than the NOT EXISTS construct in general.

■**Note** The ATO only identifies poorly written SQL, but it won't rewrite it for you. You will know your application better than the ATO, so Oracle only provides advice, which you can implement or not.

Recommendations

Here are some recommendations that the SQL Tuning Advisor will give you:

- Creating indexes will speed up access paths.
- Using SQL profiles will allow you to generate a better execution plan.
- Gathering optimizer statistics for objects that do not have any, or renewing stale statistics, will be of benefit.
- Rewriting SQL as advised will improve its performance.

The SQL Tuning Advisor in Practice

You can use the SQL Tuning Advisor through packages or through the web interface of the OEM Database Control.

Using the DBMS_SQLTUNE Package to Run the SQL Tuning Advisor

The main SQL package for tuning SQL statements is DBMS_SQLTUNE. The first example will be creating and managing tasks that tune SQL statements.

■**Note** You must have the ADVISOR privilege to use the DBMS_SQLTUNE package. Ensure that you do before running any of the following examples.

Performing Automatic SQL Tuning

Here's how to tune SQL statements using the DBMS_SQLTUNE package:

1. *Create a task*: The CREATE_TUNING_TASK procedure creates a task to tune a single statement or several statements (a SQL tuning set or STS). You can also use a SQL statement (using the SQL identifier) from the AWR or from the cursor cache. In the following example, I show how to create a task using a single SQL statement as input. First, I pass the SQL statement as a CLOB argument, as shown here:

```
DECLARE
  my_task_name VARCHAR2(30);
  my_sqltext    CLOB;
BEGIN
  my_sqltext := 'SELECT /*+ ORDERED */ *
                 FROM employees e, locations l, departments d
                 WHERE e.department_id = d.department_id AND
                 l.location_id = d.location_id AND
                 e.employee_id < :bnd';
```

Next, I create the following tuning task:

```
my_task_name := DBMS_SQLTUNE.CREATE_TUNING_TASK(
          sql_text     => my_sqltext,
          bind_list    => sql_binds(anydata.ConvertNumber(90)),
          user_name    => 'HR',
          scope        => 'COMPREHENSIVE',
          time_limit   => 60,
          task_name    => 'my_sql_tuning_task',
          description  => 'Task to tune a query on a specified employee');
END;
/
```

In the preceding task, sql_text refers to the single SQL statement that I'm tuning. The bind_list shows that 90 is the value of the bind variable bnd. The tuning task's scope is comprehensive, meaning that it analyzes the SQL Profile, and the task_limit parameter sets a limit of 60 seconds on the total time for analysis.

2. *Execute the task*: To execute the task, run the EXECUTE_TUNING_TASK procedure:

```
BEGIN
  DBMS_SQLTUNE.EXECUTE_TUNING_TASK( task_name => 'my_sql_tuning_task' );
END;
/
```

3. *Get the tuning report*: You can view the tuning process with the REPORT_TUNING_TASK procedure:

```
SQL> SET LONG 1000
SQL> SET LONGCHUNKSIZE 1000
SQL> SET LINESIZE 100
SQL> SELECT DBMS_SQLTUNE.REPORT_TUNING_TASK( 'my_sql_tuning_task')
       FROM DUAL;
```

The report consists of findings and recommendations. The Tuning Advisor provides the rationale and the expected benefits for each recommendation. It also provides you with the SQL to implement the recommendations.

You can use the following views to manage your automatic SQL tuning efforts:

- DBA_ADVISOR_TASKS
- DBA_ADVISOR_FINDINGS
- DBA_ADVISOR_RECOMMENDATIONS
- DBA_ADVISOR_RATIONALE
- DBA_SQLTUNE_STATISTICS
- DBA_SQLTUNE_PLANS

Managing SQL Profiles

Once the ATO has made its recommendations, you can accept its findings and run the DBMS_ SQLTUNE.ACCEPT_SQL_PROFILE procedure to create an appropriate SQL profile, though you must ensure you have the CREATE_ANY_PROFILE privilege first.

The preceding may seem to say that a SQL profile is an inevitable consequence of an ATO process, but it will only recommend that you create a SQL profile if it has built one as a result of its scan. However, it will only do this if it collected auxiliary information while analyzing statistics and profiling SQL (as detailed previously). Oracle will apply the new profile to the SQL statement when you execute it.

Managing SQL Tuning Categories

You may find that you have a number of different SQL profiles for a single SQL statement. Oracle has to manage them in some way, so it assigns each one to a SQL tuning category. The same process occurs when a user logs in, meaning that Oracle will assign a user to a tuning category. The category is selected according to the SQLTUNE_CATEGORY initialization parameter.

If you do not change it, SQLTUNE_CATEGORY takes the value DEFAULT. This means that any SQL profiles belonging to the default category apply to everyone who logs in. You can alter the SQL tuning category for every user with the ALTER SYSTEM command. You can also alter a session's tuning category with the ALTER SESSION command. For example, take the PROD and DEV categories. To change the SQL tuning category for every user, do the following:

```
SQL> ALTER SYSTEM SET SQLTUNE_CATEGORY = PROD;
```

If you wanted to change a session's tuning category, you could do this:

```
SQL> ALTER SESSION SET SQLTUNE_CATEGORY = DEV;
```

■**Note** You may also use the DBMS_SQLTUNE.ALTER_SQL_PROFILE procedure to alter the SQL tuning category.

Using the OEM to Run the SQL Tuning Advisor

To use the OEM to run the Advisor, click Related Links ➤ Advisor Central ➤ SQL Tuning Advisor. This is the SQL Tuning Advisor page. Here you can specify the SQL statements that the SQL Advisor will analyze, which can be one of two kinds:

- *Top SQL*: These SQL statements could be top SQL from the cursor cache or saved high-load SQL statements that have come from the AWR.

- *SQL Tuning Sets*: You can create an STS from any set of SQL statements.

Choosing one of the four links on the SQL Tuning Advisor page will take you to your selected data source. You can now launch the SQL Tuning Advisor if you wish.

The Automatic SQL Tuning Advisor

I explained the Automatic Tuning Optimizer earlier in this chapter. This is what Oracle calls the optimizer when it runs in tuning mode. The Automatic Tuning Optimizer performs the following types of analysis for high-load SQL statements, with a goal of isolating poorly written SQL statements and making recommendations to improve them: statistics analysis, SQL profiling, access path analysis, and SQL structure analysis. When you execute a SQL Tuning Advisor session, it invokes the Automatic Tuning Optimizer to tune the SQL statements. The SQL Tuning Advisor provides recommendations, but can't implement them for you.

The Automatic Tuning Optimizer also runs regularly as an automated maintenance task called the (Automatic) SQL Tuning Advisor task. The advisor can identify poorly running SQL statements by picking them from the AWR, make recommendations to improve them, and also implement any recommendations that invoke the use of SQL profiles. The SQL Tuning Advisor task conducts statistics analysis, SQL profiling, access path analysis, and SQL structure analysis.

The Automatic SQL Tuning process consists of the identification of candidates for tuning, tuning the statements and making recommendations, testing the recommendations, and automatic implementation of the SQL profile recommendations. I describe each of the steps in the following sections.

Identifying SQL Tuning Candidates

The Automatic SQL Tuning Advisor uses the AWR Top SQL identification process for selecting candidates for automatic tuning. The database takes into account the CPU time and I/O time utilized by SQL statements to select these candidates. The goal is to select statements that offer a large potential for improvement. The advisor prepares a list of candidate statements by organizing the top SQL queries in the past week into the following "buckets":

- Top for the week
- Top for any day in the week
- Top for any hour during the week
- Highest average single execution

By assigning weights to each of the buckets, the SQL Tuning Advisor combines the four buckets into a single group of statements and ranks the statements according to their impact on performance. Subsequently, during the maintenance window, the advisor automatically tunes each of the candidate SQL statements selected by it.

A SQL profile consists of addition statistics beyond those collected by the optimizer, to help evolve better execution plans. The additional information gathered via SQL profiles may include customized optimizer settings, adjustments to compensate for missing or stale statistics, and adjustments for estimation errors in optimization statistics. Since you don't need to change the SQL query when you implement a SQL profile, they are ideal for use in packaged applications. Implementation of a SQL profile would normally lead to the generation of more efficient execution plans for SQL statements.

Tuning and Making Recommendations

The SQL Tuning Advisor tunes statements in the order of their performance impact. If the advisor finds stale or missing statistics, it lets the GATHER_STATS_JOB know about this fact, so it can collect statistics for it when the database collects statistics the next time.

The advisor makes different types of recommendations to improve the poorly performing SQL statements, including the creation of indexes, refreshing of the optimizer statistics, restructuring SQL statements, and creation of SQL profiles. The advisor can automatically implement only the SQL profile creation recommendations. The advisor creates and tests the SQL profiles it recommends before implementing them. You can decide whether to retain the new SQL profiles that are automatically implemented by the advisor or not, based on an analysis of the SQL Tuning Advisor report.

Testing the Recommendations for New SQL Profiles

For any SQL profile recommendation it makes, the SQL Tuning Advisor runs the statement with and without the profile and compares the performance. The advisor will recommend adopting a profile only if implementing the profile leads to at least a threefold increase in improvement in performance, as shown by a reduction in the sum of the CPU and I/O usage.

Implementing the SQL Profiles

The setting of the `ACCEPT_SQL_PROFILES` attribute of the SET_TUNING_TASK_PARAMETERS view determines whether the database automatically accepts the SQL profile recommendations made by the Automatic SQL Tuning Advisor. The DBA_SQL_PROFILES view shows all the automatically implemented SQL profiles. If a SQL profile was automatically implemented, it'll have a value of `AUTO` in the TYPE column.

Limitations

You can't tune the following types of statements with the Automatic SQL Tuning Advisor:

- Parallel queries
- Ad hoc queries
- Recursive statements
- SQL statements that use the `INSERT` and `DELETE` statements
- SQL statements that use DDL statements such as `CREATE TABLE AS SELECT`

If a query takes a long time to execute after implementing a SQL profile, the advisor will reject the implementation of the SQL profile, since it can't test-execute the query. Note that with the exception of ad hoc statements, you can manually tune all the preceding types of statements with a manual invocation of the SQL Tuning Advisor.

Configuring Automatic SQL Tuning

Use the DBMS_SQLTUNE package to configure and manage the automatic SQL tuning task. Manage the SYS_AUTO_TUNING_TASK, which controls the automatic SQL tuning job, with the following procedures:

- *SET_TUNING_TASK_PARAMETERS*: Use this procedure to test task parameters controlling items such as whether to automatically implement SQL profiles.
- *EXECUTE_TUNING_TASK*: Use this procedure to run the tuning task in the foreground.
- *EXPORT_TUNING_TASK*: This procedure helps produce a task execution report.

The Automatic SQL Tuning Advisor job runs for a maximum of one hour by default, but you can change the execution time limit by executing the SET_TUNING_TASK_PARAMETERS procedure, as shown here:

```
SQL> exec dbms_sqltune.set_tuning_task_parameter
    ('SYS_AUTO _SQL_TUNING_TASK', 'TIME_LIMIT', 14400);
```

The previous example shows how to raise the maximum run time for the SQL tuning task to four hours, from its default value of one hour.

The SET_TUNING_TASK_PARAMETERS procedure enables you to configure the tuning task by specifying the following parameters:

- `ACCEPT_SQL_PROFILES` determines whether the database must automatically accept a SQL profile.
- `REPLACE_USER_SQL_PROFILES` determines whether the task should replace the SQL profiles created by the user.
- `MAX_SQL_PROFILES_PER_EXEC` specifies the maximum number of SQL profiles that can be accepted for a single automatic SQL tuning task.

- MAX_AUTO_SQL_PROFILES determines the total number of SQL profiles that are accepted by the database.

- EXECUTION_DAYS_TO_EXPIRE specifies the maximum number of days for which the database saves the task history. The default is 30 days.

The following example shows how to configure a SQL tuning task that'll automatically accept all SQL profile recommendations:

```
SQL> begi
  2  dbms_sqltune.set_tuning_task_parameters(
  3  task_name => 'SYS_AUTO_SQL_TUNING_PROG',
  4  parameter => 'accept_sql_profiles', value => 'true');
  5* end;

SQL> /
```

The previous example sets the value for the ACCEPT_SQL_PROFILES parameter to TRUE, which makes the advisor automatically accept SQL profile recommendations.

The SYS_AUTO_SQL_TUNING_TASK procedure runs the automatic SQL tuning job every night during the maintenance window of the Oracle Scheduler. It tunes SQL statements according to the priority ranking in the SQL candidates. It creates necessary SQL profiles for a statement and tests them before tuning the next statement in the candidate list.

Managing Automatic SQL Tuning

Use the DBMS_AUTO_TASK_ADMIN package to enable and disable the Automatic SQL Tuning Advisor job during the Scheduler maintenance window. The ENABLE procedure helps you enable the Automatic SQL Tuning Advisor task:

```
begin
dbms_auto_task_admin.enable (
client_name => 'sql tuning advisor',
operation => 'NULL',
window_name='NULL');
end;
```

The value NULL for the WINDOW_NAME parameter will enable the task in all maintenance windows. To specify the task in a specific maintenance window, specify a window name, as shown here:

```
begin
dbms_auto_task_admin.enable (
client_name => 'sql tuning advisor',
operation => 'NULL',
window_name='monday_night_window');
end;
```

To disable the Automatic SQL Tuning Advisor task, execute the DISABLE procedure, as shown here:

```
begin
dbms_auto_task_admin.disable (
client_name => 'sql tuning advisor',
operation => 'NULL',
window_name='NULL');
end;
```

The previous code will disable the automatic SQL tuning tasks in all maintenance windows, since I didn't specify a value for the WINDOW_NAME parameter.

■Tip By setting the TEST_EXECUTE parameter when you execute the SET_TUNING_TASK_PARAMETER procedure, you can run the SQL Tuning Advisor in test execute mode to save time.

You can also configure all Automatic SQL Tuning parameters easily through the Database control (or the Grid Control). Go to the Automatic SQL Tuning Settings page, accessible by clicking the Configure button in the Automated Maintenance Tasks page. You can configure all automated tasks from the Automated Maintenance Tasks configuration page. Here's a simple example that shows how to get recommendations for fixing a SQL statement:

1. Click the finding with the highest impact on database time in the Database Home page.

2. Click Schedule SQL Tuning Advisor on the SQL Details page.

3. Click Submit on the Scheduler Advisor page.

4. Click Implement if you want to adopt the advisor's recommendations.

5. Click Yes on the Confirmation page, and the database creates a new SQL profile.

6. View the tuning benefits by going to the Performance page after the database executes the tuned statement again.

Go to the Automated Maintenance Task page to view information about the latest executions of the Automatic SQL Tuning Advisor. Click the Server tab in the Database Control home page first. Click the Automated Maintenance Tasks link under the Tasks section in the Server page, and then click the most recent execution icon or the Automatic SQL Tuning task link to view the Automatic SQL Tuning Result Summary page.

Interpreting Automatic SQL Tuning Reports

You can get a report of the Automatic SQL Tuning Advisor tasks by executing the REPORT_AUTO_TUNING_TASK function, as shown here:

```
SQL> begin
  2  :test_report :=dbms_sqltune. report_auto_tuning_task (
  3  type        => 'text',
  4  level       => 'typical',
  5  section     => 'all');
  6* end;
SQL> /
PL/SQL procedure successfully completed.
SQL>
print :test_report
```

The report produced by the previous code contains information about all the statements analyzed by the advisor in its most recent execution and includes both the implemented and unimplemented advisor recommendations. The report also contains EXPLAIN PLANs before and after implementing the tuning recommendations.

You can use the following views to get information about the Automatic SQL Tuning Advisor jobs:

- *DBA_ADVISOR_EXECUTIONS*: Shows metadata information for each task
- *DBA_ADVISOR_SQLSTATS*: Shows a list of all SQL compilation and execution statistics
- *DBA_ADVISOR_SQLPLANS*: Shows a list of all SQL execution plans

The following code, for example, provides information about all Automatic SQL Tuning Advisor tasks:

```
SQL> SELECT execution_name, status, execution_start, execution_end
     FROM dba_advisor_executions
     WHERE task_name='SYS_AUTO_SQL_TUNING_TASK';
```

Using Other GUI Tools

The EXPLAIN PLAN and SQL Trace utilities aren't the only tools you have available to tune SQL statements. Several GUI-based tools provide the same information much more quickly. Just make sure that statistics collection is turned on in the initialization file before you use these tools. One of the well-known third-party tools is the free version of TOAD software, which is marketed by Quest Software (http://www.quest.com). From this tool you get not only the execution plan, but also memory usage, parse calls, I/O usage, and a lot of other useful information, which will help you tune your queries. The use of GUI tools helps you avoid most of the drudgery involved in producing and reading EXPLAIN PLANs. Note that whether you use GUI tools or manual methods, the dynamic performance views that you use are the same. How you access them and use the data makes the difference in the kind of tool you use.

Using the Result Cache

You can improve the response times of frequently executed SQL queries by using the result cache. The result cache stores results of SQL queries and PL/SQL functions in a new component of the SGA called the Result Cache Memory. The first time a repeatable query executes, the database caches its results. On subsequent executions, the database simply fetches the results from the result cache instead of executing the query again. The database manages the result cache. You can turn result caching on only at the database level. If any of the objects that are part of a query are modified, the database invalidates the cached query results. Ideal candidates for result caching are queries that access many rows to return a few rows, as in many data warehousing solutions.

The result cache consists of two components, the SQL Query Result Cache that stores SQL query results and the PL/SQL Function Result Cache that stores the values returned by PL/SQL functions, with both components sharing the same infrastructure. I discuss the two components of the result cache in the following sections.

Managing the Result Cache

The result cache is always enabled by default, and its size depends on the memory the database allocates to the shared pool. If you specify the MEMORY_TARGET parameter for allocating memory, Oracle allocates 0.25% of the MEMORY_TARGET parameter value to the result cache. If you specify the SGA_TARGET parameter instead, Oracle allocates 0.5% of the SGA_TARGET value to the result cache.

You can change the memory allocated to the result cache by setting the RESULT_CACHE_MAX_SIZE initialization parameter. This parameter can range from a value of zero to a system-dependent maximum. You disable result caching by setting the parameter to zero, as shown here:

```
SQL> ALTER SYSTEM SET result_cache_max_size=0;
```

Since result caching is enabled by default, it means that the RESULT_CACHE_MAX_SIZE parameter has a positive default value as well, based on the size of the MEMORY_TARGET parameter (or the SGA_TARGET parameter if you have that parameter instead).

In addition to the RESULT_CACHE_MAX_SIZE parameter, two other initialization parameters have a bearing on the functioning of the result cache: the RESULT_CACHE_MAX_RESULT parameter specifies the maximum amount of the result cache a single result can use. By default, a single cached result can occupy up to 5 percent of the result cache, and you can specify a percentage between 1 and 100. The RESULT_CACHE_REMOTE_EXPIRATION parameter determines the length of time for which a cached result that depends on remote objects is valid. By default, this parameter is set to zero, meaning you aren't supposed to use the result cache for queries involving remote objects. The reason for this is over time remote objects could be modified, leading to invalid results in the cache.

Setting the RESULT_CACHE_MODE Parameter

Whether the database caches a query result or not depends on the value of the RESULT_CACHE_MODE initialization parameter, which can take two values: MANUAL or FORCE. Here's how the two values affect result caching behavior in the database:

- If you set the parameter to FORCE, the database will try to use the cache for all results, wherever it's possible to do so. You can, however, skip the cache by specifying NO_RESULT_CACHE hint within a query.

- If you set the parameter to MANUAL, the database caches the results of a query only if you include the RESULT_CACHE hint in the query.

By default, the RESULT_CACHE_MODE parameter is set to MANUAL and you can change the value dynamically as shown here:

```
SQL> alter session set result_cache_mode=force scope=spfile;
```

Using the RESULT_CACHE and NO_RESULT_CACHE Hints

Using the RESULT_CACHE hint as a part of a query adds the ResultCache operator to a query's execution plan. The ResultCache operator will search the result cache to see whether there's a stored result in there for the query. It retrieves the result if it's already in the cache; otherwise, the ResultCache operator will execute the query and store its results in the result cache. The no_result_cache operator works the opposite way. If you add this hint to a query, it'll lead the ResultCache operator to bypass the result cache and reexecute the query to get the results.

The following example shows how to incorporate the RESULT_CACHE hint in a SQL query:

```
SQL> select /*+ result_cache +*/
  2  department_id, avg(salary)
  3  from hr.employees
  4* group by department_id;

SQL>
```

The RESULT_CACHE hint in line 1 of the query adds the ResultCache operator, which looks in the result cache for the cached results and, if they aren't there already, executes the query and stores its results in the result cache. The EXPLAIN PLAN for the query shows that the query will utilize the result cache:

```
SQL> EXPLAIN PLAN FOR select /*+ result_cache +*/
  2   department_id,avg(salary)
  3   from hr.employees
  4*  group by department_id
SQL> /
Explained.

SQL>
SQL> SELECT plan_table_output FROM table(DBMS_XPLAN.DISPLAY());
PLAN_TABLE_OUTPUT
-------------------------------------------------------------
Plan hash value: 1192169904
-------------------------------------------------------------
| Id  | Operation      | Name | Rows  | Bytes | Cost
(%CPU)| Time |
-------------------------------------------------------------
PLAN_TABLE_OUTPUT
-------------------------------------------------------------
|   0 | SELECT STATEMENT   ||   11 | 77 |     4
  (25)| 00:00:01 |
|   1 |   RESULT CACHE     | 8nk7a7rfhymzy0s0b89ksn9bfz | ||
|   2 |    HASH GROUP BY   | |   11 |   77 |     4
  (25)| 00:00:01 |
|   3 |     TABLE ACCESS FULL| EMPLOYEES  |   107 |  749 |     3
   (0)| 00:00:01 |
PLAN_TABLE_OUTPUT
-------------------------------------------------------------
-------------------------------------------------------------
Result Cache Information (identified by operation id):
-----------------------------------------------------
   1 - column-count=2; dependencies=(HR.EMPLOYEES);
name="select /*+ result_cache +*/
department_id,avg(salary)
from hr.employees
group by department_id"

15 rows selected.

SQL>
```

■Tip The RESULT_CACHE and the NO_RESULT_CACHE hints always take precedence over the value you set for the RESULT_CACHE_MODE initialization parameter.

The EXPLAIN PLAN output reveals the use of the result cache by the query in our example. Since I used the RESULT_CACHE hint to use the result cache, the RESULT_CACHE_MODE parameter is set to MANUAL. If it is set to FORCE, I don't have to set the RESULT_CACHE hint inside the queries. The database will simply cache results for all repeatable SQL statements, unless I specify the NO_RESULT_CACHE hint in a query.

Managing the Result Cache

Use the DBMS_RESULT_CACHE package to manage the result cache, such as checking the status of the cache and flushing the cache. The following example shows how to check the memory allocation to the cache by executing the MEMORY_REPORT function:

```
SQL> set serveroutput on
SQL> exec dbms_result_cache.memory_report
R e s u l t    C a c h e    M e m o r y    R e p o r t
[Parameters]
Block Size          = 1K bytes
Maximum Cache Size  = 672K bytes (672 blocks)
Maximum Result Size = 33K bytes (33 blocks)
[Memory]
Total Memory = 5132 bytes [0.005% of the Shared Pool]
... Fixed Memory = 5132 bytes [0.005% of the Shared Pool]
... Dynamic Memory = 0 bytes [0.000% of the Shared Pool]

PL/SQL procedure successfully completed.
SQL>
```

Execute the STATUS function to check the current status of the result cache, which could be ENABLED or DISABLED. You can purge the contents of the result cache by executing the FLUSH procedure or the FLUSH function. You may have to purge the result cache if the database ends up filling up the result cache, as the result cache doesn't automatically flush its contents. If you load a new version of a function, for example, you can get rid of the older function's results from the result cache by purging the results with the FLUSH procedure or function. Before you execute the FLUSH procedure or FLUSH function, you must first put the result cache in bypass mode by executing the BYPASS procedure with the TRUE value. Once you purge the result cache, execute the BYPASS procedure again, now with the FALSE value, as shown here:

```
BEGIN
EXEC dbms_result_cache.bypass (FALSE);
END;
 /
PL/SQL procedure successfully completed.
SQL>
```

You can use the following views to manage the result cache:

- *V$RESULT_CACHE_STATISTICS*: Lists cache settings and memory usage statistics

- *V$RESULT_CACHE_OBJECTS*: Lists all cached objects and their attributes

- *V$RESULT_CACHE_DEPENDENCY*: Lists the dependency information between the cached results and dependencies

- *V$RESULT_CACHE_MEMORY*: Lists all memory blocks and their statistics

- *V$RESULT_CACHE_OBJECTS*: Lists both cached results and all dependencies

For example, you can use the following query on the V$RESULT_CACHE_OBJECTS view to find out which results are part of the result cache:

```
SQL> select type,status,name from v$result_cache_objects;

TYPE           STATUS        NAME
-----------    -----------   ------------------------------------
Dependency     Published     HR.COUNT_EMP
Result         Published     select  /* + result_cache
                             query name(q1) */
                             last_name, salary from hr.employees
                             order by salary
SQL>
```

The previous query shows there are currently two results in the result cache.

Restrictions on Using the SQL Query Result Cache

You can't cache results in the SQL Query Result Cache for the following objects:

- Temporary tables

- Dictionary tables

- Nondeterministic PL/SQL functions

- The curval and nextval pseudo functions

- The SYSDATE, SYS_TIMESTAMP, CURRENT_DATE, CURRENT_TIMESTAMP, LOCAL_TIMESTAMP, USERENV, SYS_CONTEXT, and SYS_QUID functions

You also won't be able to cache subqueries, but you can use the RESULT_CACHE hint in an inline view.

The PL/SQL Function Result Cache

The SQL Query Result Cache shares the result cache infrastructure with the PL/SQL Function Result Cache, which caches the results of PL/SQL functions. Candidates for PL/SQL function caching are those functions that the database uses frequently that depend on fairly static information. You can choose to specify that the database invalidate the cached results of a PL/SQL function when there's a change in any of the objects the functions depends on.

Creating a Cacheable Function

Include the RESULT_CACHE clause in a PL/SQL function definition to make the database cache the function results in the PL/SQL Function Result Cache. Here's an example:

```
SQL> CREATE OR REPLACE function
     get_dept_info (dept_id number) RETURN dept_info_record
     result_cache relies_on (employees)
     IS
     rec dept_info_record;
     BEGIN
       SELECT AVG(salary), COUNT(*) INTO rec
       FROM employees
       WHERE department_id = dept_id;
       RETURN rec;
     END get_dept_info;
/
```

The RELIES ON clause is optional. The clause specifies that the database must invalidate the function results if any of the tables or other objects that the function depends on undergoes a modification.

The first time the database executes the GET_DEPT_INFO function, the function will execute as usual. On subsequent executions of the function, the database fetches the function values directly from the PL/SQL Function Result Cache instead of reexecuting the function. The database reexecutes the function only when

- You bypass the result cache by not specifying the RESULT_CACHE hint.
- You execute the DBMS_RESULT_CACHE_BYPASS procedure to make functions and queries bypass the result cache, regardless of the setting of the RESULT_CACHE_MODE parameter or the specification or the RESULT_CACHE hint.
- Any of the objects underlying a function change and you've specified the RELIES_ON clause in the function definition.
- The database ages out cached results because the system needs additional memory.

Restrictions

A PL/SQL function must satisfy the following requirements in order for the database to cache its results. A function cannot

- Have any IN/OUT parameters
- Be an anonymous block
- Be defined in a module that has invoker's rights
- Have parameters that belong to the collection, object, ref cursor, or LOB types
- Be a pipelined table function

Besides meeting these requirements, the function must not depend on session-specific settings or application contexts and must also not have any side effects.

The Client Query Result Cache

If you are using any OCI applications and drivers such as JDBC and ODP.NET, you can also use Oracle's client-side caching of SQL result sets in the Client Query Result Cache that's located on the server. The database keeps the result sets consistent with changes in session attributes. If you've frequently repeated statements in your applications, client-side caching could offer tremendous improvement in query performance benefits. Since the database caches results on the clients, server round-trips are minimized and scalability improves as a result, with lower I/O and CPU load.

Unlike server-side caching, client-side caching isn't enabled by default. If your applications produce small result sets that are static over a period of time, client-side caching may be a good thing to implement. Frequently executed queries and queries involving lookup tables are also good candidates for client-side caching.

Enabling and Disabling the Client Query Result Cache

As with server-side caching, you use the RESULT_CACHE_MODE initialization parameter to enable and disable client-side caching. The RESULT_CACHE and the NO_RESULT_CACHE hints work the same way as they do for server-side caching. If you choose to specify the MANUAL setting for the RESULT_CACHE_MODE parameter, you must use the RESULT_CACHE hint in a query for the query's results to be cached. Also, the two hints override the setting of the RESULT_CACHE_MODE parameter, as in the case of server-side caching. You pass the RESULT_CACHE and the NO_RESULT_CACHE hints to SQL statements by using the OCIStatementPrepare() and the OCIStatementPrepare2() calls.

Managing the Client Result Cache

There are two initialization parameters that control how the Client Query Result Cache works. Here's a brief description of these parameters:

- CLIENT_RESULT_CACHE_SIZE: Determines the maximum client per-process result set cache size (in bytes). If you set this parameter to zero, you disable the Client Query Result Cache. The database allocates the maximum-size memory to every OCI client process by default.

■**Tip** You can override the setting of the CLIENT_RESULT_CACHE_SIZE parameter with the server-side parameter OCI_RESULT_CACHE_MAX_SIZE. By setting the latter to zero, you can disable the Client Query Result Cache.

- CLIENT_RESULT_CACHE_LAG: Determines the Client Query Result Cache lag time. A low value means more round-trips to the database from the OCI client library. Set this parameter to a low value if your application accesses the database infrequently.

An optional client configuration file overrides any client caching configuration parameters you set. You can set the client-side configuration parameters in the sqlnet.ora file on the client. You can set the following client-side configuration parameters:

- OCI_RESULT_CACHE_MAX_SIZE: Specifies the maximum size of the query cache for a single process
- OCI_RESULT_CACHE_MAX_RSET_SIZE: Enables you to specify the maximum size of a single result in bytes for a process
- OCI_RESULT_CACHE_MAX_RST_ROWS: Sets the maximum size of a query result in rows for a single process

You can also insert the RESULT_CACHE and NO_RESULT_CACHE hints in OCI applications. Use the CLIENT_RESULT_CACHE view to see the settings of the result cache and the usage statistics for the Client Query Result Cache.

Restrictions

You can't cache queries that use the following types of objects, even though you may be able to cache them in a server-side result cache:

- Views
- Remote objects
- Complex types in the select list
- Flashback queries
- Queries that include PL/SQL functions
- Queries that reference VPD policies on the tables

A Simple Approach to Tuning SQL Statements

Whether you use manual methods such as EXPLAIN PLAN, SQL Trace, and TKPROF, or more sophisticated methods such as the SQL Tuning Advisor, you need to understand that optimizing SQL statements can improve performance significantly. In the following sections, I summarize a simple methodology you can follow to tune your SQL statements.

Identify Problem Statements

This chapter has shown you many ways you can identify your slow-running or most resource-intensive SQL statements. For instance, you can use dynamic performance views such as V$SQL to find out your worst SQL statements, as shown earlier. Statements with high buffer gets are the CPU-intensive statements and those with high disk reads are the high I/O statements. Alternatively, you can rely on the AWR report and the ADDM analysis to figure out which of your SQL statements need to be written more efficiently. Obviously, you want to start (and maybe end) with tuning these problem statements.

Locate the Source of the Inefficiency

The next step is to locate the inefficiency in the SQL statements. To do this, you need to collect information on how the optimizer is executing the statement. That is, you must first walk through the EXPLAIN PLAN for the statement. This step helps you find out if there are any obvious problems, such as full table scans due to missing indexes.

In addition to analyzing the EXPLAIN PLAN output or using the V$SQL_PLAN view, collect the performance information, if you can, by using the SQL Trace and TKPROF utilities.

Review each EXPLAIN PLAN carefully to see that the access and join methods and the join order are optimal. Specifically, check the plans with the following questions in mind:

- Are there any inefficient full table scans?
- Are there any unselective range scans?
- Are the indexes appropriate for your queries?
- Are the indexes selective enough?
- If there are indexes, are all of them being used?
- Are there any later filter operations?
- Does the driving table in the join have the best filter?
- Are you using the right join method and the right join order?
- Do your SQL statements follow basic guidelines for writing good SQL statements (see the section "Writing Efficient SQL" in this chapter)?

In most cases, a structured analysis of the query will reveal the source of the inefficiency.

Tune the Statement

Use the Database Control's SQL Access Advisor to get index and materialized view recommendations. Review the access path for the tables in the statement and the join order. Consider the use of hints to force the optimizer to use a better execution plan. You can also use the SQL Tuning Advisor to get recommendations for more efficient SQL statements.

Compare Performance

Once you generate alternative SQL, it's time to go through the first three steps again. Use the EXPLAIN PLAN facility and performance statistics to compare the new statement with the older one. After you ensure that your new statements perform better, it's time to replace the inefficient SQL. Oracle Database 11g has a much wider array of automatic SQL tuning capabilities than ever before. Once you get familiar with the various automatic tuning tools, such as the SQL Tuning Advisor and the ADDM, you should be able to harness the database's capabilities to tune your recalcitrant SQL statements.

■ ■ ■

Performance Tuning: Tuning the Instance

In the previous chapter, you learned how to write efficient SQL to maximize an application's performance. The use of optimal SQL and efficient design of the layout of the database objects are parts of a planned or proactive tuning effort. This chapter focuses on the efficient use of the resources Oracle works with: memory, CPU, and storage disks.

The chapter discusses how to monitor and optimize memory allocation for the Oracle instance. In this context, you'll learn about the traditional database hit ratios, such as the buffer cache hit ratios. However, focusing on the hit ratios isn't necessarily the smartest way to maintain efficient Oracle databases because you need to focus on the user's response time. Investigating factors that are causing processes to spend excessive time waiting for resources is a better approach to performance tuning. This chapter provides you with a solid introduction to Oracle wait events and tells you how to interpret them and reduce the incidence of these wait events in your system.

A fairly common problem in many production systems is that of a database *hang*, when things seem to come to a standstill for some reason. This chapter shows you what to do during such events.

The chapter explains the key dynamic performance tables that you need to be familiar with to understand instance performance issues. Although you've encountered the Automatic Database Diagnostic Monitor (ADDM) and Automatic Workload Repository (AWR) in earlier chapters, this chapter reviews their role in instance tuning. You can also use the Active Session History (ASH) feature to understand recent session history. Analyzing ASH information helps solve numerous performance issues in a running instance.

Although it's nice to be able to design a system proactively for high performance, more often than not, the DBA has to deal with reactive tuning when performance is unsatisfactory and a fix needs to be found right away. The final part of this chapter deals with a simple methodology to follow when your system performance deteriorates and you need to fine-tune the Oracle instance.

I begin this chapter with a short introduction to instance tuning and then turn to cover in detail the tuning of crucial resources such as memory, disk, and CPU usage. Later on in the chapter, I review the important Oracle wait events, which will help you get a handle on several kinds of database performance issues.

An Introduction to Instance Tuning

Oracle doesn't give anything but minimal and casual advice regarding the appropriate settings of key resources, such as total memory allocation or the sizes of the components of memory. Oracle has some general guidelines about the correct settings for several key initialization parameters that have a bearing on performance. However, beyond specifying wide ranges for the parameters, the company's guidelines aren't helpful to DBAs deciding on the optimal levels for these parameters.

Oracle says this is because all these parameters are heavily application dependent. All of this means that you as a DBA have to find out the optimal sizes of resource allocations and the ideal settings of key initialization parameters through trial and error. As a DBA, you're often called in to tune the instance when users perceive slow response caused by a bottleneck somewhere in the system. This bottleneck can be the result of either an excessive use of or insufficient provision of some resource. In addition, database locks and latches may cause a slowdown. You have to remember, though, that in most cases, the solution isn't simply to increase the resource that seems to be getting hit hard—that may be the symptom, not the cause of a problem. If you address the performance slowdown by fixing the symptoms, the root causes will remain potential troublemakers.

Performance tuning an Oracle database instance involves tuning memory and I/O as well as operating system resources such as CPU, the operating system kernel, and the operating system memory allocation. When you receive calls from the help desk or other users of the system complaining that the system is running slowly, you can only change what's under your direct control—mainly, the allocation of memory and its components and some dynamic initialization parameters that have a bearing on instance performance. Depending on what the various indicators tell you, you may adjust the shared pool and other components of memory to improve performance. You can also change the operating system priority of some processes, or quickly add some disk drives to your system.

One of the main reasons for a slow response time in a production system is due to user processes waiting for a resource. Oracle provides several ways of monitoring waits, but you need to understand their significance in your system. Long wait times aren't the problem themselves; they're symptoms of deep-seated problems. The DBA should be able to connect different types of waits with possible causes in the application or in the instance.

Although some manuals tell you that you should do performance tuning before application tuning—before you proceed to tuning areas such as memory, I/O, and contention—real life isn't so orderly. Most of the time, you don't have the opportunity to have the code revised, even if there are indications that it isn't optimal. Instead of being an orderly process, tuning databases is an iterative process, where you may have to go back and forth between stages.

More often than not, DBAs are forced to do what they can to fix the performance problem that's besetting them at that moment. In this sense, most performance tuning is a reactive kind of tuning. Nevertheless, DBAs should endeavor to understand the innards of wait issues and seek to be proactive in their outlooks.

There are two big advantages to being in a proactive mode of tuning. First, you have fewer sudden performance problems that force hurried reactions. Second, as your understanding of your system increases, so does your familiarity with the various indicators of poor performance and the likely causes for them, so you can resolve problems that do occur much more quickly.

If you're fortunate enough to be associated with an application during its design stages, you can improve performance by performing several steps, including choosing automatic space management and setting correct storage options for your tables and indexes. Sizing the table and indexes correctly doesn't hurt, either. However, if you're stuck with a database that has a poor design, all is not lost. You can still tune the instance using techniques that I show later in this chapter to improve performance.

When response time is slower than usual, or when throughput falls, you'll notice that the Oracle instance isn't performing at its usual level. If response times are higher, obviously there's a problem somewhere in one of the critical resources Oracle uses. If you can rule out any network slowdowns, that leaves you with memory (Oracle's memory and the system's memory), the I/O system, and CPUs. One of these resources is usually the bottleneck that's slowing down your system.

In the next few sections, you'll learn how to tune key system resources such as memory, I/O, and CPU to improve performance. You'll also see how to measure performance, detect inefficient waits in the system, and resolve various types of contention in an Oracle database. The next section presents a discussion of how tuning Oracle's memory can help improve database performance.

PATCHES AND NEW VERSIONS OF SOFTWARE

Oracle Corp., like the other software vendors, releases periodic *patches* or *patch sets*, which are a set of fixes for bugs discovered by either Oracle or its customers. When you get in touch with Oracle technical support, one of the things the technical support representative will commonly ask you to do is make sure you have applied the latest patch set to your Oracle software. Similarly, UNIX operating systems may have their own patch sets that you may have to apply to fix certain bugs.

Each of Oracle's patch sets could cover fixes for literally hundreds of bugs. My recommendation is to apply a patch set as soon as it's available. One of the primary reasons for this is to see whether your bug is unique to your database or if a general solution has already been found for the problem. When you ask Oracle technical support to resolve a major problem caused by a bug, Oracle usually provides you with a workaround. Oracle recommends that you upgrade your database to the latest versions and patch sets because some Oracle bugs may not have any workarounds or fixes. Oracle will continue to support older versions of its server software throughout their support life cycle, which is usually about two to three years after the next major release. Many organizations see no urgency to move to newer versions, as Oracle continues to support the older versions after the release of the new versions.

The question regarding how quickly you should convert to a new version is somewhat tricky to answer. Traditionally, people have shied away from being early adopters of new Oracle software versions. Oracle, like most other software companies, has a reputation for buggy initial releases of its major software versions. DBAs and managers in general prefer to wait a while until a "stable version" comes out. Although the logic behind this approach is understandable, you must also figure in the cost of not being able to use the many powerful features Oracle introduces in each of its major releases.

Because nobody likes to jeopardize the performance of a production system, the ideal solution is to maintain a test server where the new software is tested thoroughly before being moved into production as early as possible. However, don't wait forever to move to a new version—by the time some companies move to the new version, an even newer Oracle version is already out!

Some of your good SQL statements may not be so good after you migrate to a new version, due to the way a hint might behave in the new version, for example. That's why it's extremely important to test the whole system on the new version before cutting over production systems. A smart strategy is to collect a set of performance statistics that can serve as a baseline before you make any major changes in the system. These system changes may include the following:

- Migrating or upgrading a database
- Applying a new database or operating system patch set
- Adding a new application to your database
- Substantially increasing the user population

Automatic Performance Tuning vs. Dynamic Performance Views

Traditionally, Oracle DBAs relied heavily on the use of dynamic performance views (V$ views) to gather performance statistics and diagnose instance performance problems. You have access to all the traditional views in Oracle Database 11*g*. However, you now also have powerful automatic performance tuning features that provide a faster and more painless way to approach instance performance tuning. Most of these tools use the same V$ dynamic performance views that you use in manual performance tuning. Although I provide several examples of manual performance tuning in this chapter, I must emphasize the importance of understanding and using the powerful set of automatic performance features that are already a part of your database. Here's a brief summary of the automatic performance tuning features:

- The AWR collects all the performance data necessary for tuning as well as diagnosing instance problems.

- The ADDM automatically diagnoses database performance by analyzing the AWR data.

- The Automatic SQL Tuning Advisor provides SQL tuning recommendations.

- The database automatically runs the statistics collection job, thus keeping all statistics up to date.

- The Segment Advisor runs automatically during the maintenance interval and makes recommendations about which segments to shrink and which to reorganize (for example, due to excessive row chaining).

- The SQL Access Advisor provides recommendations about the ideal indexes and materialized views to create.

- The Memory Advisor, MTTR Advisor, and Undo Advisor help you tune memory, redo logs, and undo segments, respectively.

In this chapter, I present the major dynamic performance views that you can use to diagnose instance performance. Traditionally, Oracle DBAs relied heavily on scripts using these views to monitor and tune instance performance. However, the best way to diagnose and tune Oracle performance issues is through the OEM Database Control (or Grid Control). I thus show you a simple approach to tuning using the OEM Database Control.

■**Note** The AWR and ADDM are Oracle products that need special licensing through the purchase of the Diagnostic Pack. If you haven't purchased this licensing, you aren't supposed to use these features.

Tuning Oracle Memory

A well-known fact of system performance is that fetching data that's stored in memory is a lot faster than retrieving data from disk storage. Given this, Oracle tries to keep as much of the recently accessed data as possible in its SGA. In addition to data, shared parsed SQL code and necessary data dictionary information are cached in memory for quick access. You can easily adjust the memory allocation of Oracle, by simply changing a single initialization parameter—MEMORY_TARGET.

There's a two-way relationship between memory configuration and the application's use of that memory. The correct memory allocation size depends on the nature of your application, the number of users, and the size of transactions. If there isn't enough memory, the application will have to perform time-consuming disk I/Os. However, the application itself might be using memory unnecessarily, and throwing more memory at it may not be the right strategy. As a DBA, you must not view memory and its sizing in isolation. This can lead to some poor choices, as you address the symptoms instead of the causes for what seems like insufficient memory. The tendency on a DBA's part is to allocate as much memory as possible to the shared pool, hoping that doing so will resolve the problem. However, sometimes this only exacerbates the problem. It's wise to manage the database with as little memory as necessary, and no more. The system can always use the free memory to ensure there's no swapping or paging. Performance slowdowns caused by paging outweigh the benefits of a larger SGA under most operating systems.

Tuning the Shared Pool

In a production database, the shared pool is going to command most of your attention because of its direct bearing on application performance. The shared pool is a part of the SGA that holds almost all the necessary elements for execution of the SQL statements and PL/SQL programs. In addition to caching program code, the shared pool caches the data dictionary information that Oracle needs to refer to often during the course of program execution.

Proper shared pool configuration leads to dramatic improvements in performance. An improperly tuned shared pool leads to problems such as the following:

- Increased latch contention with the resulting demand for more CPU resources
- Greater I/O because executable forms of SQL aren't present in the shared pool
- Higher CPU usage because of unnecessary parsing of SQL code

The general increase in shared pool waits and other waits observed during a severe slowdown of the production database is the result of SQL code that fails to use bind variables (I explain the important concept of bind variables in the following section).

As the number of users increases, so does the demand on shared pool memory and latches, which are internal locks for memory areas. If there are excessive latches, the result might be a higher wait time and a slower response time. Sometimes the entire database seems to hang.

The shared pool consists of two major areas: the library cache and the data dictionary cache. You can't allocate or decrease memory specifically for one of these components. If you increase the total shared pool memory size, both components will increase in some ratio that Oracle determines. Similarly, when you decrease the total shared pool memory, both components will decrease in size. Let's look at these two important components of the shared pool in detail.

The Library Cache

The *library cache* holds the parsed and executable versions of SQL and PL/SQL code. As you may recall from Chapter 19, all SQL statements undergo the following steps during their processing:

- *Parsing*, which includes syntactic and semantic verification of SQL statements and checking of object privileges to perform the actions.
- *Optimization*, where the Oracle optimizer evaluates how to process the statement with the least cost, after it evaluates several alternatives.
- *Execution*, where Oracle uses the optimized physical execution plan to perform the action stated in the SQL statement.
- *Fetching*, which only applies to SELECT statements where Oracle has to return rows to you. This step isn't necessary in any nonquery-type statements.

Parsing is a resource-intensive operation, and if your application needs to execute the same SQL statement repeatedly, having a parsed version in memory will reduce contention for latches, CPU, I/O, and memory usage. The first time Oracle parses a statement, it creates a *parse tree*. The optimization step is necessary only for the first execution of a SQL statement. Once the statement is optimized, the best access path is encapsulated in the *access plan*. Both the parse tree and the access plan are stored in the library cache before the statement is executed for the first time. Future invocation of the same statement will need to go through only the last stage, execution, which avoids the overhead of parsing and optimizing as long as Oracle can find the parse tree and access plan in the library cache. Of course, if the statement is a SQL query, the last step will be the fetch operation.

The library cache, being limited in size, discards old SQL statements when there's no more room for new SQL statements. The only way you can use a parsed statement repeatedly for multiple executions is if a SQL statement is identical to the parsed statement. Two SQL statements are identical if they use exactly the same code, including *case* and *spaces*. The reason for this is that when Oracle compares a new statement to existing statements in the library cache, it uses simple string comparisons. In addition, any bind variables used must be similar in *data type* and *size*. Here are a couple of examples that show you how picky Oracle is when it comes to considering whether two SQL statements are identical.

In the following example, the statements aren't considered identical because of an extra space in the second statement:

```
SELECT * FROM employees;
SELECT *  FROM employees;
```

In the next example, the statements aren't considered identical because of the different case used for the table Employees in the second statement. The two versions of employees are termed *literals* because they're literally different from each other.

```
SELECT * FROM employees;
SELECT * FROM Employees;
```

Let's say users in the database issue the following three SQL statements:

```
SELECT * FROM persons WHERE person_id = 10
SELECT * FROM persons WHERE person_id = 999
SELECT * FROM persons WHERE person_id = 6666
```

Oracle uses a different execution plan for the preceding three statements, even though they seem to be identical in every respect, except for the value of person_id. Each of these statements has to be parsed and executed separately, as if they were entirely different. Because all three are essentially the same, this is inherently inefficient. As you can imagine, if hundreds of thousands of such statements are issued during the day, you're wasting database resources and the query performance will be slow. Bind variables allow you to reuse SQL statements by making them "identical," and thus eligible to share the same execution plan.

In our example, you can use a bind variable, which I'll call :var, to help Oracle view the three statements as identical, thus requiring a single execution instead of multiple ones. The person_id values 10, 99, and 6666 are "bound" to the bind variable, :var. Your replacement SQL statement using a bind variable, then, would be this:

```
SELECT * FROM persons WHERE person_id = :var
```

Using bind variables can dramatically increase query performance, and I explain in the section "Using the CURSOR_SHARING (Literal Replacement) Parameter" how you can "force" Oracle to use bind variables, even if an application doesn't use them.

The Dictionary Cache

The dictionary cache, as mentioned earlier, caches data dictionary information. This cache is much smaller than the library cache, and to increase or decrease it you modify the shared pool accordingly. If your library cache is satisfactorily configured, chances are that the dictionary cache is going to be fine too. You can get an idea about the efficiency of the dictionary cache by using the following query:

```
SQL> SELECT (sum(gets - getmisses - fixed)) / SUM(gets)
  2 "data dictionary hit ratio" from v$rowcache;
data dictionary hit ratio
-------------------------
      .936781093
SQL>
```

Usually, it's a good idea to shoot for a dictionary hit ratio as high as 95 to 99 percent, although Oracle itself sometimes seems to refer to a figure of 85 percent as being adequate. To increase the library cache ratio, you simply increase the shared pool size for the instance.

Hard Parsing and Soft Parsing

You may recall from the last chapter that all SQL code goes through the parse, optimize, and execute phases. When an application issues a statement, Oracle first sees whether a parsed version of the statement already exists. If it does, the result is a so-called soft parse and is considered a library cache hit. If, during a parse phase or the execution phase, Oracle isn't able to find the parsed version or the executable version of the code in the shared pool, it will perform a *hard parse*, which means that the SQL statement has to be reloaded into the shared pool and parsed completely.

During a hard parse, Oracle performs syntactic and semantic checking, checks the object and system privileges, builds the optimal execution plan, and finally loads it into the library cache. A hard parse involves a lot more CPU usage and is inefficient compared to a soft parse, which depends on reusing previously parsed statements. Hard parsing involves building all parse information from scratch, and therefore it's more resource intensive. Besides involving a higher CPU usage, hard parsing involves a large number of latch gets, which may increase the response time of the query. The ideal situation is where you parse once and execute many times. Otherwise, Oracle has to perform a hard parse.

■**Caution** High hard parse rates lead to severe performance problems, so it's critical that you reduce hard parse counts in your database.

A soft parse simply involves checking the library cache for an identical statement and reusing it. The major step of optimizing the SQL statement is completely omitted during a soft parse. There's no parsing (as done during a hard parse) during a soft parse, because the new statement is hashed and its hash value is compared with the hash values of similar statements in the library cache. During a soft parse, Oracle only checks for the necessary privileges. For example, even if there's an identical statement in the library cache, your statement may not be executed if Oracle determines during the (soft) parsing stage that you don't have the necessary privileges. Oracle recommends that you treat a hard parse rate of more than 100 per second as excessive.

Using SQL Trace and TKPROF to Examine Parse Information

In Chapter 19, you learned how to use the SQL Trace and TKPROF utilities to trace SQL statement execution. One of the most useful pieces of information the SQL Trace utility provides concerns the hard and soft parsing information for a query. The following simple example demonstrates how you can derive the parse information for any query:

1. Enable tracing in the session by using the following command:

```
SQL> ALTER SESSION SET SQL_TRACE=TRUE;
Session altered.
SQL>
```

To make sure none of your queries were parsed before, flush the shared pool, which removes all SQL statements from the library cache:

```
SQL> ALTER SYSTEM FLUSH SHARED_POOL;
System altered.
SQL>
```

2. Use the following query to create a trace in the user dump directory:

```
SQL> SELECT * FROM comp_orgs WHERE created_date > SYSDATE-5;
```

The SQL Trace output shows the following in the output file:

```
PARSING IN CURSOR #1 len=63 dep=0 uid=21 oct=3
lid=21 tim=1326831345 hv=71548308
SELECT * FROM comp_orgs WHERE created_date > SYSDATE-:"SYS_B_0"
END OF STMT
PARSE #1:c=4,e=4,p=0,cr=57,cu=3,mis=1,r=0,dep=0,og=0,tim=1326831345
```

Note that mis=1 indicates a hard parse because this SQL isn't present in the library cache.

3. Use a slightly different version of the previous query next. The output is the same, but Oracle won't use the previously parsed version, because the statements in steps 2 and 3 aren't identical.

```
SQL> SELECT * FROM comp_orgs WHERE created_date > (SYSDATE -5);
```

Here's the associated SQL Trace output:

```
PARSING IN CURSOR #1 len=77 dep=0 uid=21 oct=3 lid=21 tim=1326833972
SELECT /* A  Hint */ * FROM comp_orgs WHERE
created_date > SYSDATE-:"SYS_B_0"
END OF STMT
PARSE #1:c=1,e=1,p=0,cr=0,cu=0,mis=1,r=0,dep=0,og=0,tim=1326833972
```

Again, a hard parse, indicated by mis=1, shows a library cache miss. This isn't a surprise, as this statement isn't identical to the one before, so it has to be parsed from scratch.

4. Use the original query again. Now Oracle performs only a soft parse, because the statements here and in the first step are the same. Here's the SQL Trace output:

```
PARSING IN CURSOR #1 len=63 dep=0 uid=21 oct=3 lid=21 tim=1326834357
SELECT * FROM comp_orgs WHERE created_date > SYSDATE-:"SYS_B_0"
END OF STMT
PARSE #1:c=0,e=0,p=0,cr=0,cu=0,mis=0,r=0,dep=0,og=4,tim=1326834357
```

The statement in step 4 is identical in all respects to the statement in step 1, so Oracle reuses the parsed version. Hence mis=0 indicates there wasn't a hard parse but merely a soft parse, which is a lot cheaper in terms of resource usage.

If you now look at the TKPROF output, you'll see the following section for the SQL statements in step 2 and step 4 (identical statements):

```
********************************************************************
SELECT * FROM comp_orgs WHERE created_date > SYSDATE - 5
call     count    cpu   elapsed     disk    query   current   rows
-------  ------  ------  --------  -------  -------  --------  -------
Parse     2      0.03    0.01        0        1        3        0
Execute   2      0.00    0.00        0        0        0        0
Fetch     4      0.07    0.10       156      166       24       10
total     8      0.10    0.11       156      167       27       10
Misses in library cache during parse: 1
********************************************************************
```

As you can see, there was one miss in the library cache when you first executed the statement. The second time around, there was no hard parse and hence no library cache miss.

Measuring Library Cache Efficiency

You can use simple ratios to see if your library cache is sized correctly. The V$LIBRARYCACHE data dictionary view provides you with all the information you need to see whether the library cache is efficiently sized. Listing 20-1 shows the structure of the V$LIBRARYCACHE view.

Listing 20-1. *The V$LIBRARYCACHE View*

```
SQL> DESC V$LIBRARYCACHE
Name                                      Null?     Type
----------------------------------------- --------- ------------
NAMESPACE                                           VARCHAR2(15)
GETS                                                NUMBER
GETHITS                                             NUMBER
GETHITRATIO                                         NUMBER
PINS                                                NUMBER
PINHITS                                             NUMBER
PINHITRATIO                                         NUMBER
RELOADS                                             NUMBER
INVALIDATIONS                                       NUMBER
DLM_LOCK_REQUESTS                                   NUMBER
DLM_PIN_REQUESTS                                    NUMBER
DLM_PIN_RELEASES                                    NUMBER
DLM_INVALIDATION_REQUESTS                           NUMBER
DLM_INVALIDATIONS                                   NUMBER
SQL>
```

The following formula provides you with the library cache hit ratio:

```
SQL> SELECT SUM(pinhits)/sum(pins)  Library_cache_hit_ratio
  2  FROM V$LIBRARYCACHE;

LIBRARY_CACHE_HIT_RATIO
------------------------
      .993928013
SQL>
```

The formula indicates that the library cache currently has a higher than 99 percent hit ratio, which is considered good. However, be cautious about relying exclusively on high hit ratios for the library cache and the buffer caches, such as the one shown here. You may have a hit ratio such as 99.99 percent, but if significant waits are caused by events such as excessive parsing, you're going to have a slow database. Always keep an eye on the wait events in your system, and don't rely blindly on high hit ratios such as these.

Listing 20-2 shows how to determine the number of reloads and pinhits of various statements in your library cache.

Listing 20-2. *Determining the Efficiency of the Library Cache*

```
SQL> SELECT namespace, pins, pinhits, reloads
  2  FROM V$LIBRARYCACHE
  3  ORDER BY namespace;
```

```
NAMESPACE              PINS      PINHITS    RELOADS
------------------    ------    ----------  -------
BODY                     25         12         0
CLUSTER                 248        239         0
INDEX                    31          0         0
JAVA DATA                 6          4         0
JAVA RESOURCE             2          1         0
JAVA SOURCE               0          0         0
OBJECT                    0          0         0
PIPE                      0          0         0
SQL AREA             390039     389465        14
TABLE/PROCEDURE        3532       1992         0
TRIGGER                   5          3         0
11 rows selected.
SQL>
```

   If the RELOADS column of the V$LIBRARYCACHE view shows large values, it means that many
SQL statements are being reloaded into the library pool after they've been aged out. You might want
to increase your shared pool, but this still may not do the trick if the application is large, the number
of executions is large, or the application doesn't use bind variables. If the SQL statements aren't
exactly identical and/or if they use constants instead of bind variables, more hard parses will be
performed, and hard parses are inherently expensive in terms of resource usage. You can force the
executable SQL statements to remain in the library cache component of the shared pool by using the
Oracle-provided DBMS_SHARED_POOL package. The package has the KEEP and UNKEEP procedures;
using these you can retain and release objects in the shared pool.

   You can use the V$LIBRARY_CACHE_MEMORY view to determine the number of library cache
memory objects currently in use in the shared pool and to determine the number of freeable library
cache memory objects in the shared pool. The V$SHARED_POOL_ADVICE view provides you with
information about the parse time savings you can expect for various sizes of the shared pool.

Optimizing the Library Cache

You can configure some important initialization parameters so the library cache areas are used efficiently. You'll look at some of these initialization parameters in the following sections.

Using the CURSOR_SHARING (Literal Replacement) Parameter

The key idea behind optimizing the use of the library cache is to reuse previously parsed or executed
code. One of the easiest ways to do this is to use *bind variables* rather than literal statements in the
SQL code. Bind variables are like placeholders: they allow binding of application data to the SQL
statement. Using bind variables enables Oracle to reuse statements when the only things changing
in the statements are the values of the input variables. Bind variables enable you to reuse the cached,
parsed versions of queries and thus speed up your application. Here's an example of the use of bind
variables. The following code sets up a bind variable as a number type:

```
SQL> VARIABLE bindvar NUMBER;
SQL> BEGIN
  2  :bindvar :=7900;
  3  END;
  4  /
PL/SQL procedure successfully completed.
SQL>
```

You can now issue the following SQL statement that makes use of the bind variable you just created:

```
SQL> SELECT ename FROM scott.emp WHERE empid = :bindvar;
ENAME
JAMES
```

You can execute this statement multiple times with different values for the bind variable. The statement is parsed only once and executes many times. Unlike when you use a literal value for the emp_id column (7499, for example), Oracle reuses the execution plan it created the first time, instead of creating a separate execution plan for each such statement. This cuts hard parsing (and high latch activity) and the attendant CPU usage drastically, and dramatically reduces the time taken to retrieve data. For example, all the following statements can use the parsed version of the query that uses the bind variable:

```
SELECT ename FROM scott.emp WHERE empid = 7499;
SELECT ename FROM scott.emp WHERE empid = 7788;
SELECT ename FROM scott.emp WHERE empid = 7902;
```

Unfortunately, in too many applications, literal values rather than bind values are used. You can alleviate this problem to some extent by setting up the following initialization parameter:

```
CURSOR_SHARING=FORCE
```

Or you could use the following parameter:

```
CURSOR_SHARING=SIMILAR
```

By default, the CURSOR_SHARING initialization parameter is set to EXACT, meaning that only statements that are identical in all respects will be shared among different executions of the statement. Either of the alternative values for the CURSOR_SHARING parameter, FORCE or SIMILAR, ensures Oracle will reuse statements even if they aren't identical in all respects.

For example, if two statements are identical in all respects and differ only in literal values for some variables, using CURSOR SHARING=FORCE will enable Oracle to reuse the parsed SQL statements in its library cache. Oracle replaces the literal values with bind values to make the statements identical. The CURSOR_SHARING=FORCE option forces the use of bind variables under all circumstances, whereas the CURSOR SHARING=SIMILAR option does so only when Oracle thinks doing so won't adversely affect optimization. Oracle recommends the use of CURSOR_SHARING=SIMILAR rather than CURSOR_SHARING=FORCE because of possible deterioration in the execution plans. However, in reality, the benefits provided by the CURSOR_SHARING=FORCE parameter far outweigh any possible damage to the execution plans. You can improve the performance of your database dramatically when you notice a high degree of hard parsing due to failing to use bind variables by moving from the default CURSOR_SHARING=EXACT option to the CURSOR_SHARING=FORCE option. You can change the value of this parameter in the init.ora file or SPFILE, or you can do so dynamically by using the ALTER SYSTEM (instance-wide) statement or the ALTER SESSION (session-level) statement.

By allowing users to share statements that differ only in the value of the constants, the CURSOR_SHARING parameter enables the Oracle database to scale easily to a large number of users who are using similar, but not identical, SQL statements. This major innovation started in the Oracle8*i* version.

Sessions with a High Number of Hard Parses

The query in Listing 20-3 enables you to find out how the hard parses compare with the number of executions since the instance was started. It also tells you the session ID for the user using the SQL statements.

Listing 20-3. *Determining Sessions with a High Number of Parses*

```
SQL> SELECT s.sid, s.value "Hard Parses",
  2  t.value "Executions Count"
  3  FROM v$sesstat s, v$sesstat t
  4  WHERE s.sid=t.sid
  5  AND s.statistic#=(select statistic#
  6  FROM v$statname where name='parse count (hard)')
  7  AND t.statistic#=(select statistic#
  8  FROM v$statname where name='execute count')
  9  AND s.value>0
 10* ORDER BY 2 desc;

      SID   Hard Parses   Executions Count
----------   -----------   ----------------
     1696        70750            3638104
     1750        12188             262881
     1759         3555            5895488
     1757         3265            2758185
     1694         1579            2389953
. . .
SQL>
```

Using the CURSOR_SPACE_FOR_TIME Parameter

By default, cursors can be deallocated even when the application cursors aren't closed. This forces an increase in Oracle's overhead because of the need to check whether the cursor is flushed from the library cache. The parameter that controls whether this deallocation of cursors takes place is the CURSOR_SPACE_FOR_TIME initialization parameter, whose default value is FALSE. If you set this parameter to TRUE, you ensure that the cursors for the application cannot be deallocated while the application cursors are still open. The initialization parameter in the init.ora file should be as follows:

```
CURSOR_SPACE_FOR_TIME=TRUE
```

■**Tip** If you want to set this parameter, make sure that you have plenty of free shared pool memory available, because this parameter will use more shared pool memory for saving the cursors in the library cache.

Using the SESSION_CACHED_CURSORS Parameter

Ideally, an application should have all the parsed statements available in separate cursors, so that if it has to execute a new statement, all it has to do is pick the parsed statement and change the value of the variables. If the application reuses a single cursor with different SQL statements, it still has to pay the cost of a soft parse. After opening a cursor for the first time, Oracle will parse the statement, and then it can reuse this parsed version in the future. This is a much better strategy than re-creating the cursor each time the database executes the same SQL statement. If you can cache all the cursors, you'll retain the server-side context, even when clients close the cursors or reuse them for new SQL statements.

You'll appreciate the usefulness of the SESSION_CACHED_CURSORS parameter in a situation where users repeatedly parse the same statements, as happens in an Oracle Forms-based application when users switch among various forms. Using the SESSION_CACHED_CURSORS parameter ensures that for any cursor for which more than three parse requests are made, the parse requests are automatically cached in the session cursor cache. Thus new calls to parse the same statement avoid the parsing overhead. Using the initialization parameter SESSION_CACHED_CURSORS and setting it to a high number makes the query processing more efficient. Although soft parses are cheaper than hard parses, you can reduce even soft parsing by using the SESSION_CACHED_CURSORS parameter and setting it to a high number.

You can enforce session caching of cursors by setting the SESSION_CACHED_CURSORS in your initialization parameter file, or dynamically by using the following ALTER SESSION command:

```
SQL> ALTER SESSION SET SESSION_CACHED_CURSORS = value;
```

You can check how good your SESSION_CACHED_CURSORS parameter value is by using the V$SYSSTAT view. If the value of session cursor cache hits is low compared to the total parse count for a session, then the SESSION_CACHED_CURSORS parameter value should be bumped up.

The perfect situation is where a SQL statement is soft parsed once in a session and executed multiple times. For a good explanation of bind variables, cursor sharing, and related issues, please read the Oracle white paper "Efficient use of bind variables, cursor_sharing and related cursor parameters" (http://otn.oracle.com/deploy/performance/pdf/cursor.pdf).

Parsing and Scaling Applications

When the number of users keeps increasing, some systems have trouble coping. Performance slows down dramatically in many systems as a result of trying to scale to increased user populations. When your user counts are increasing, focus on unnecessary parsing in your system. A high level of parsing leads to latch contention, which slows down the system. Here are some guidelines that help summarize the previous discussion about the library cache, parsing, and the use of special initialization parameters:

- A standard rule is to put as much of the code as possible in the form of stored code—packages, procedures, and functions—so you don't have the problems caused by *ad hoc* SQL. Use of ad hoc SQL could wreak havoc with your library cache, and it's an inefficient way to run a large application with many users. Using stored code guarantees that code is identical and thus reused, thereby enhancing scalability.

- Lower the number of hard parses, as they could be expensive. One way to convert a hard parse to a soft parse is to use bind variables, as you saw earlier in this chapter. Reducing hard parsing reduces shared-pool latch contention.

- If bind variables aren't being used in your system, you can use the CURSOR_SHARING=FORCE parameter to force the sharing of SQL statements that differ only in the value of literals.

- Pay attention to the *amount* of soft parsing, not the *per unit* cost, which is much lower than that of a hard parse. A high amount of soft parsing increases contention for the library cache latch and could lead to a slow-performing database. The point to note here is to avoid any *unnecessary* soft parsing, which will end up costing you.

- Use the SESSION_CACHED_CURSORS initialization parameter to reuse the open cursors in a session. If repeated parse calls are used for a SQL statement, Oracle moves the session cursor for that statement into the session cursor cache. This, as you've seen, reduces the amount of soft parsing. Set the value of this parameter to somewhere between the value of the OPEN_CURSORS initialization parameter and the number of cursors that are being used in the session.

- Use the CURSOR_SPACE_FOR_TIME initialization parameter (set it to TRUE) to prevent the early deallocation of cursors. If you don't mind the extra cost of using more memory, this feature will enhance your application's scalability level.

- Reduce the amount of session logging on/off activity by users. This may reduce scalability due to the increased amount of overhead involved in authenticating the user, verifying privileges, and so on, leading to a waste of time and resources. Furthermore, the users may be spending more time trying to log into the system than executing their SQL statements. Frequent logging off and logging back on might also cause contention for the web server and other resources, and increase the time it takes to log into your system.

- To increase scalability, you must also ensure that applications share sessions. If you only have shared SQL, your hard parses will go down, but your soft parses might still be high. If an application program can maintain a persistent connection to the Oracle server, it doesn't have to perform repeated soft parsing to reuse code.

Sizing the Shared Pool

The best way to set the size of the shared pool in Oracle Database 11g is to let Oracle do all the work for you by using the MEMORY_TARGET initialization parameter, thus automating the management of SGA. You can initially set the SGA_TARGET parameter at something close to the total SGA you would have allocated under a manual management mode. Review the material in Chapter 17 for guidance on setting your initial MEMORY_TARGET value.

Pinning Objects in the Shared Pool

As I have discussed, if code objects have to be repeatedly hard-parsed and executed, database performance will deteriorate eventually. Your goal should be to see that as much of the executed code remains in memory as possible so compiled code can be reexecuted. You can avoid repeated reloading of objects in your library cache by pinning objects using the DBMS_SHARED_POOL package. (The library cache is a component of the shared pool, as you've seen earlier.) Listing 20-4 shows how you can determine the objects that should be pinned in your library cache (shared pool).

Listing 20-4. *Determining the Objects to Be Pinned in the Shared Pool*

```
SQL> SELECT type, COUNT(*) OBJECTS,
  2  SUM(DECODE(KEPT,'YES',1,0)) KEPT,
  3  SUM(loads) - count(*) reloads
  4  FROM V$DB_OBJECT_CACHE
  5  GROUP BY type
  6* ORDER BY objects DESC;
```

TYPE	OBJECTS	KEPT	RELOADS
CURSOR	41143	0	136621
NOT LOADED	37522	0	54213
TABLE	758	24	133742
PUB_SUB	404	0	135
SYNONYM	381	0	7704
JAVA CLASS	297	296	317
VIEW	181	0	11586
INVALID TYPE	139	48	11
PACKAGE	137	0	8352
TRIGGER	136	0	8515
PACKAGE BODY	121	0	218
SEQUENCE	81	0	3015
INDEX	61	7	0
PROCEDURE	41	0	219

FUNCTION	35	0	825
NON-EXISTENT	31	0	1915
TYPE	13	0	1416
CLUSTER	10	6	6
TYPE BODY	3	0	5
LIBRARY	2	0	99
RSRC CONSUMER GROUP	2	0	0
QUEUE	2	0	96
JAVA SHARED DATA	1	1	0
JAVA SOURCE	1	0	0

```
24 rows selected.
SQL>
```

If the number of reloads in the output shown in Listing 20-4 is high, you need to make sure that the objects are pinned using the following command:

```
SQL> EXECUTE SYS.DBMS_SHARED_POOL.KEEP(object_name,object_type);
```

You can use the following statements to pin a package first in the shared pool and then remove it, if necessary:

```
SQL> EXECUTE SYS.DBMS_SHARED_POOL.KEEP(NEW_EMP.PKG, PACKAGE);
SQL> EXECUTE SYS.DBMS_SHARED_POOL.UNKEEP(NEW_EMP.PKG,PACKAGE);
```

Of course, if you shut down and restart your database, the shared pool won't retain the pinned objects. That's why most DBAs use scripts with all the objects they want to pin in the shared pool and schedule them to run right after every database start. Most of the objects usually are small, so there's no reason to be too conservative about how many you pin. For example, I pin all my packages, including Oracle-supplied PL/SQL packages.

Look at the following example, which gives you an idea about the total memory taken up by a large number of packages. This query shows the total number of packages in my database:

```
SQL> SELECTCOUNT(*)
  2  FROM V$DB_OBJECT_CACHE
  3* WHERE type='PACKAGE';

   COUNT(*)
---------------
      167
SQL>
```

The following query shows the total amount of memory needed to pin all my packages in the shared pool:

```
SQL> SELECT SUM(sharable_mem)
  2  FROM V$DB_OBJECT_CACHE
  3* WHERE type='PACKAGE';

   SUM(SHARABLE_MEM)
------------------
      4771127
SQL>
```

As you can see, pinning every single package in my database takes up less than 5MB of a total of several hundred megabytes of memory allocated to the shared pool.

Tuning the Buffer Cache

When users request data, Oracle reads the data from the disks (in terms of Oracle blocks) and stores it in the buffer cache so it may access the data easily if necessary. As the need for the data diminishes, eventually Oracle removes the data from the buffer cache to make room for newer data. Note that some operations don't use the buffer cache (SGA); rather, they read directly into the PGA area. Direct sort operations and parallel reads are examples of such operations.

How to Size the Buffer Cache

As with the shared pool component, the best way to manage the buffer cache is to choose automatic SGA management. However, if you choose to manage the SGA manually, you can use a process of trial and error to set the buffer cache size. You assign an initial amount of memory to the pool and watch the buffer cache hit ratios to see how often the application can retrieve the data from memory, as opposed to going to disk. The terminology used for calculating the buffer hit ratio can be somewhat confusing on occasion. Here are the key terms you need to understand:

- *Physical reads*: These are the data blocks that Oracle reads from disk. Reading data from disk is much more expensive than reading data that's already in Oracle's memory. When you issue a query, Oracle always first tries to retrieve the data from memory—the database buffer cache—and not disk.

- *DB block gets*: This is a read of the buffer cache, to retrieve a block in *current* mode. This most often happens during data modification when Oracle has to be sure that it's updating the most recent version of the block. So, when Oracle finds the required data in the database buffer cache, it checks whether the data in the blocks is up to date. If a user changes the data in the buffer cache but hasn't committed those changes yet, new requests for the same data can't show these interim changes. If the data in the buffer blocks is up to date, each such data block retrieved is counted as a DB block get.

- *Consistent gets*: This is a read of the buffer cache, to retrieve a block in *consistent* mode. This may include a read of undo segments to maintain the read consistency principle (see Chapter 8 for more information about read consistency). If Oracle finds that another session has updated the data in that block since the read began, then it will apply the new information from the undo segments.

- *Logical reads*: Every time Oracle is able to satisfy a request for data by reading it from the database buffer cache, you get a logical read. Thus logical reads include both DB block gets and consistent gets.

- *Buffer gets*: This term refers to the number of database cache buffers retrieved. This value is the same as the logical reads described earlier.

The following formula gives you the buffer cache hit ratio:

```
1 - ('physical reads cache') /
   ('consistent gets from cache' + 'db block gets from cache')
```

You can use the following query to get the current values for all three necessary buffer cache statistics:

```
SQL> SELECT name, value FROM v$sysstat
    WHERE where name IN ('physical reads cache',
                         'consistent gets from cache',
                         'db block gets from cache');
```

NAME	VALUE
db block gets from cache	103264732
consistent gets from cache	5924585423
physical reads cache	50572618

3 rows selected.
SQL>

The following calculation, based on the statistics I derived in the preceding code from the V$SYSSTAT view, show that the buffer cache hit ratio for my database is a little over 91 percent:

$$1 - (505726180)/(103264732 + 5924585494) = .916101734$$

As you can see from the formula for the buffer cache hit ratio, the lower the ratio of physical reads to the total logical reads, the higher the buffer cache hit ratio.

You can use the V$BUFFER_POOL_STATISTICS view, which lists all buffer pools for the instance, to derive the hit ratio for the buffer cache:

```
SQL> SELECT NAME, PHYSICAL_READS, DB_BLOCK_GETS, CONSISTENT_GETS,
        1 - (PHYSICAL_READS/(DB_BLOCK_GETS + CONSISTENT_GETS)) "HitRatio"
        FROM V$BUFFER_POOL_STATISTICS;
```

NAME	PHYSICAL_READS	DB_BLOCK_GETS	CONSISTENT_GETS	HitRatio
DEFAULT	50587859	103275634	5924671178	.991607779

SQL>

In addition, you can use the Database Control's Memory Advisor to get advice regarding the optimal buffer cache size. The advice is presented in a graphical format, showing the trade-off between increasing the SGA and the reduction in DB time. You can use the V$DB_CACHE_ADVICE view (use V$SGA_TARGET_ADVICE to size the SGA_TARGET size) to see how much you need to increase the buffer cache to lower the physical I/O by a certain amount. Essentially, the output of the V$DB_CACHE_ADVICE view shows you how much you can increase your buffer cache memory before the gains in terms of a reduction in the amount of physical reads (estimated) are insignificant. The Memory Advisor simulates the miss rates in the buffer cache for caches of different sizes. In this sense, the Memory Advisor can keep you from throwing excess memory in a vain attempt at lowering the amount of physical reads in your system.

Oracle blocks used during a full table scan involving a large table are aged out of the buffer cache faster than Oracle blocks from small-table full scans or indexed access. Oracle may decide to keep only part of the large table in the buffer cache to avoid having to flush out its entire buffer cache. Thus, your buffer cache hit ratio would be artificially low if you were using several large-table full scans. If your application involves many full table scans for some reason, increasing the buffer cache size isn't going to improve performance. Some DBAs are obsessed about achieving a high cache hit ratio, such as 99 percent or so. A high buffer cache hit ratio is no guarantee that your application response time and throughput will also be high. If you have a large number of full table scans or if your database is more of a data warehouse than an OLTP system, your buffer cache may be well below 100 percent, and that's not a bad thing. If your database consists of inefficient SQL, there will be an inordinately high number of logical reads, making the buffer cache hit ratio look good (say 99.99 percent), but this may not mean your database is performing efficiently. Please read the interesting article by Cary Millsap titled "Why a 99%+ Database Buffer Cache Hit Ratio Is Not Ok" (http://www.hotsos.com/e-library/abstract.php?id=6).

Using Multiple Pools for the Buffer Cache

You don't have to allocate all the buffer cache memory to a single pool. As Chapter 10 showed you, you can use three separate pools: the *keep* buffer pool, the *recycle* buffer pool, and the *default* buffer pool. Although you don't have to use the keep and default buffer pools, it's a good idea to configure all three pools so you can assign objects to them based on their access patterns. In general, you follow these rules of thumb when you use the multiple buffer pools:

- Use the recycle cache for large objects that are infrequently accessed. You don't want these objects to occupy a large amount of space unnecessarily in the default pool.

- Use the keep cache for small objects that you want in memory at all times.

- Oracle automatically uses the default pool for all objects not assigned to either the recycle or keep cache.

Since version 8.1, Oracle has used a concept called *touch count* to measure how many times an object is accessed in the buffer cache. This algorithm of using touch counts for managing the buffer cache is somewhat different from the traditional modified LRU algorithm that Oracle used to employ for managing the cache. Each time a buffer is accessed, the touch count is incremented. A low touch count means that the block isn't being reused frequently, and therefore is wasting database buffer cache space. If you have large objects that have a low touch count but occupy a significant proportion of the buffer cache, you can consider them ideal candidates for the recycle pool. Listing 20-5 contains a query that shows you how to find out which objects have a low touch count. The TCH column in the x$bh table owned by the user SYS indicates the touch count.

Listing 20-5. *Determining Candidates for the Recycle Buffer Pool*

```
SQL> SELECT
  2   obj object,
  3   count(1)  buffers,
  4   (count(1)/totsize) * 100 percent_cache
  5   FROMx$bh,
  6   (select value totsize
  7   FROM v$parameter
  8   WHERE name ='db_block_buffers')
  9   WHERE tch=1
 10   OR (tch = 0 and lru_flag <10)
 11   GROUP BY obj, totsize
 12*  HAVING (count(1)/totsize)  *  100 > 5

    OBJECT   BUFFERS  PERCENT_CACHE
 ----------  -------  -------------
      1386    14288    5.95333333
      1412    12616    5.25666667
    613114    22459    9.35791667
SQL>
```

The preceding query shows you that three objects, each with a low touch count, are taking up about 20 percent of the total buffer cache. Obviously, they're good candidates for the recycle buffer pool. In effect, you're limiting the number of buffers the infrequently used blocks from these three tables can use up in the buffer cache.

The following query on the DBA_OBJECTS view gives you the names of the objects:

```
SQL> SELECT object_name FROM DBA_OBJECTS
  2  WHERE object_id IN (1386,1412,613114);

OBJECT_NAME
-----------------
EMPLOYEES
EMPLOYEE_HISTORY
FINANCE_RECS
SQL>
```

You can then assign these three objects to the reserved buffer cache pool. You can use a similar criterion to decide which objects should be part of your keep buffer pool. Say you want to pin all objects in the keep pool that occupy at least 25 buffers and have an average touch count of more than 5. Listing 20-6 shows the query that you should run as the user SYS.

Listing 20-6. *Determining Candidates for the Keep Buffer Cache*

```
SQL> SELECT obj object,
  2  count(1) buffers,
  3  AVG(tch) average_touch_count
  4  FROM x$bh
  5  WHERE lru_flag = 8
  6  GROUP BY obj
  7  HAVING avg(tch) > 5
  8* AND count(1) > 25;

    OBJECT     BUFFERS     AVERAGE_TOUCH_COUNT
---------- ----------  --------------------
   1349785         36                      67
4294967295         87               57.137931
SQL>
```

Again, querying the DBA_OBJECTS view provides you with the names of the objects that are candidates for the keep buffer cache pool.

Here's a simple example to show how you can assign objects to specific buffer caches (keep and recycle). First, make sure you configure the keep and recycle pools in your database by using the following set of initialization parameters:

```
DB_CACHE_SIZE=256MB
DB_KEEP_CACHE_SIZE=16MB
DB_RECYCLE_CACHE_SIZE=16MB
```

In this example, the keep and recycle caches are 16MB each. Once you create the keep and recycle pools, it's easy to assign objects to these pools. All tables are originally in the default buffer cache, where all tables are cached automatically unless specified otherwise in the object creation statement.

You can use the ALTER TABLE statement to assign any table or index to a particular type of buffer cache. For example, you can assign the following two tables to the keep and recycle buffer caches:

```
SQL> ALTER TABLE test1 STORAGE (buffer_pool keep);
Table altered.

SQL> ALTER TABLE test2 STORAGE (buffer_pool recycle);
Table altered.
SQL>
```

■**Note** For details about Oracle's touch-count buffer management, please download Craig A. Shallahamer's interesting paper "All About Oracle's Touch-Count Data Block Buffer Algorithm" using this URL: `http://resources.orapub.com/product_p/tc.htm`.

Tuning the Large Pool, Streams Pool, and Java Pool

You mainly use the large pool, an optional component of the SGA, in shared server systems for session memory, for facilitating parallel execution for message buffers, and for backup processes for disk I/O buffers. Oracle recommends the use of the large pool if you're using shared server processes so you can keep the shared pool fragmentation low. If you're using shared server configurations, you should configure the large pool. The streams pool is relevant only if you're using the Oracle Streams feature. You don't have to bother with tuning the Java pool allocation unless you're using heavy Java applications.

■**Note** You size the large pool based on the number of active simultaneous sessions in a shared server environment. Remember that if you're using the shared server configuration and you don't specify a large pool, Oracle will allocate memory to the shared sessions out of your shared pool.

Tuning PGA Memory

Each server process serving a client is allocated a private memory area, the PGA, most of which is dedicated to memory-intensive tasks such as group by, order by, rollup, and hash joins. The PGA area is a nonshared area of memory created by Oracle when a server process is started, and it's automatically deallocated upon the end of that session. Operations such as in-memory sorting and building hash tables need specialized work areas. The memory you allocate to the PGA determines the size of these work areas for specialized tasks, such as sorting, and determines how fast the system can finish them. In the following sections you'll examine how you can decide on the optimal amount of PGA for your system.

Automatic PGA Memory Management

The management of the PGA memory allocation is easy from a DBA's point of view. You can set a couple of basic parameters and let Oracle automatically manage the allocation of memory to the individual work areas. You need to do a couple things before Oracle can automatically manage the PGA. You need to use the PGA_AGGREGATE_TARGET parameter to set the memory limit, and you need to use the V$PGA_TARGET_ADVICE view to tune the target's value. In the next sections I discuss those tasks.

Using the PGA_AGGREGATE_TARGET Parameter

The PGA_AGGREGATE_TARGET parameter in the init.ora file sets the maximum limit on the total memory allocated to the PGA. Oracle offers the following guidelines on sizing the PGA_AGGREGATE_TARGET parameter:

- For an OLTP database, the target should be 16 to 20 percent of the total memory allocated to Oracle.

- For a DSS database, the target should be 40 to 70 percent of the total memory allocated to Oracle.

The preceding guidelines are just that—guidelines. The best way to determine the ideal size of the PGA_AGGREGATE_TARGET parameter is to use the V$PGA_TARGET_ADVICE or V$PGASTAT view, which I explain in the following sections.

Using the V$PGA_TARGET_ADVICE View

Once you've set the initial allocation for the PGA memory area, you can use the V$PGA_TARGET_ADVICE view to tune the target's value. Oracle populates this view with the results of its simulations of different workloads for various PGA target levels. You can then query the view as follows:

```
SQL> SELECT ROUND(pga_target_for_estimate/1024/1024) target_mb,
  2  estd_pga_cache_hit_percentage cache_hit_perc,
  3  estd overalloc_count
  4* FROM V$PGA_TARGET_ADVICE;
```

Using the estimates from the V$PGA_TARGET_ADVICE view, you can then set the optimal level for PGA memory.

Setting the Value of the PGA_AGGREGATE_TARGET Parameter

Remember that the memory you provide through setting the PGA_AGGREGATE_TARGET parameter is what determines the efficiency of sorting and hashing operations in your database. If you have a large number of users who perform heavy-duty sort or hash operations, your PGA_AGGREGATE_TARGET must be set at a high level. When you set the SGA_TARGET at, say 2GB, the instance takes the 2GB from the total OS memory as soon as you start it. However, the PGA_AGGREGATE_TARGET is merely a target. Oracle doesn't take all the memory you assign to the PGA_AGGREGATE_TARGET when the instance starts. The PGA_AGGREGATE_TARGET only serves as the upper bound on the total private or work-area memory the instance can allocate to all the sessions combined.

The ideal way to perform sorts is by doing the entire job in memory. A sort job that Oracle performs entirely in memory is said to be an *optimal* sort. If you set the PGA_AGGREGATE_TARGET too low, some of the sort data is written out directly to disk (temporary tablespace) because the sorts are too large to fit in memory. If only part of a sort job spills over to disk, it's called a *one-pass sort*. If the instance performs most of the sort on disk instead of in memory, the response time will be high. Luckily, as long as you have enough memory available, you can monitor and avoid problems due to the undersizing of the PGA memory (PGA_TARGET).

You can examine the PGA usage within your database by using the following query. The value column shows, in bytes, the amount of memory currently allocated to the various users:

```
SQL> SELECT
  2  s.value,s.sid,a.username
  3  FROM
  4  V$SESSTAT S, V$STATNAME N, V$SESSION A
  5  WHERE
  6  n.STATISTIC# = s.STATISTIC# and
  7  name = 'session pga memory'
  8  AND s.sid=a.sid
  9* ORDER BY s.value;
```

```
VALUE        SID     USERNAME
----------   -------  ---------
  5561632     1129    BSCOTT
  5578688     1748    VALAPATI
  5627168      878    DHULSE
  5775296      815    MFRIBERG
  5954848     1145    KWHITAKE
  5971904     1182    TMEDCOFF                . . .
SQL>
```

An important indicator of the efficiency of the PGA_TARGET parameter is the PGA "hit ratio," shown in the last row of the following query, which uses the V$PGASTAT view:

```
SQL> SELECT * FROM V$PGASTAT;
```

NAME	VALUE	UNIT
aggregate PGA target parameter	49999872	bytes
aggregate PGA auto target	4194304	bytes
global memory bound	2499584	bytes
total PGA inuse	67717120	bytes
total PGA allocated	161992704	bytes
maximum PGA allocated	244343808	bytes
total freeable PGA memory	16121856	bytes
PGA memory freed back to OS	6269370368	bytes
total PGA used for auto workareas	0	bytes
maximum PGA used for auto	6843392	bytes
total PGA used for manual workareas	0	bytes
maximum PGA used for manual workareas	530432	bytes
over allocation count	1146281	bytes
processed	4.4043E+10	bytes
extra bytes read/written	7744561152	bytes
cache hit percentage	85.04	percent

```
16 rows selected.
SQL>
```

In this example, the cache hit percentage (PGA) is more than 85 percent, which is good enough for an OLTP or data warehouse application. In fact, if you have a large data-warehousing type of database, you may even have to be content with a much smaller PGA cache hit ratio.

Another way to look at PGA efficiency is by using the following query, which involves the V$SQL_WORKAREA_HISTOGRAM view. The view contains information about the number of work areas executed with optimal, one-pass, and multipass memory size. The work areas are divided into groups, whose optimal requirement varies from 0KB to 1KB, 1KB to 2KB, 2KB to 4KB—and so on. Listing 20-7 shows the results of a query using the V$SQL_WORKAREA_HISTOGRAM view.

Listing 20-7. *Using the V$SQL_WORKAREA_HISTOGRAM View*

```
SQL> SELECT
  2  low_optimal_size/1024 "Low (K)",
  3  (high_optimal_size + 1)/1024 "High (K)",
  4  optimal_executions "Optimal",
  5  onepass_executions "1-Pass",
  6  multipasses_executions ">1 Pass"
  7  FROM v$sql_workarea_histogram
  8* WHERE total_executions <> 0;
```

Low (K)	High (K)	Optimal	1-Pass	>1 Pass
2	4	7820241	0	0
32	64	0	2	0
64	128	9011	1	0
128	256	4064	14	0
256	512	3782	13	0
512	1024	18479	58	4
1024	2048	3818	53	0
2048	4096	79	241	67
4096	8192	1	457	26
8192	16384	0	11	44
16384	32768	3	1	2
32768	65536	0	2	0
65536	131072	0	0	1
131072	262144	0	0	1

```
14 rows selected.
SQL>
SQL>
```

An overwhelming number of the sorts in this instance were done optimally, with only a few sorts using the one-pass approach. This why you have the 85 percent PGA hit ratio in the previous example. Here's an instance that's in trouble, as shown by the significant number of sorts in the one-pass and the multipass (> 1 Pass) group. Right now, most of your customers will be complaining that the database is slow.

Note that the query is the same as in the previous example. Here's the output:

Low (K)	High (K)	Optimal	1-Pass	>1 Pass
2	4	2	3	0
4	8	2	7	5
8	16	129866	3	19
16	32	1288	21	3
64	128	2	180	61
128	256	6	2	44
256	512	44	0	16
512	1024	1063	0	35
1024	2048	31069	11	12
2048	4096	0	0	18
8192	16384	986	22	0
16384	32768	0	0	2

As you can see, there are significant multiple pass sorts in this example, and you can bet that the cache hit ratio is going to be low, somewhere in the 70 percent range. Fortunately, all you have to do to speed up the instance is to increase the value of the PGA_AGGREGATE_TARGET parameter in the following manner:

```
SQL> ALTER SYSTEM SET pga_aggregate_target=500000000;
System altered.
SQL>
```

The new V$PROCESS_MEMORY view lets you view dynamic PGA memory usage for each Oracle process, and shows the PGA usage by each process for categories such as Java, PL/SQL, OLAP, and SQL. Here's a simple query on that view:

```
SQL> SELECT pid, category, allocated, used from v$process_memory;

PID         CATEGORY      ALLOCATED    USED
----        ---------     ----------   -----
22          PL/SQL             2068     136
22          Other           360367
27          SQL              23908    15120
. . .
SQL>
```

You can also use the V$PROCESS view to monitor PGA usage by individual processes. If you're running out of memory on your server, it's a good idea to see whether you can release some PGA memory for other uses. Here's a query that shows you the allocated, used, and freeable PGA memory for each process currently connected to the instance:

```
SQL> SELECT program, pga_used_mem, pga_alloc_mem,
     pga_freeable_mem,pga_max_mem V$PROCESS;
```

You can use the following SQL statement to estimate quickly the proportion of work areas since you started the Oracle instance, using optimal, one-pass, and multipass PGA memory sizes:

```
SQL> SELECT name PROFILE, cnt COUNT,
     DECODE(total, 0, 0, ROUND(cnt*100/total)) PERCENTAGE
     FROM (SELECT name, value cnt, (sum(value) over ()) total
     FROM V$SYSSTAT
     WHERE name like 'workarea exec%');

PROFILE                               COUNT       PERCENTAGE
------------------------------------  ---------   ----------
workarea executions - optimal          7859595          100
workarea executions - onepass              853            0
workarea executions - multipass            145            0

SQL>
```

In the preceding example, the PGA cache hit percentage for optimal executions is 100 percent, which, of course, is excellent. Oracle DBAs have traditionally paid a whole lot more attention to tuning the SGA memory component because the PGA memory tuning in its present format is relatively new. DBAs in charge of applications requiring heavy-duty hashing and sorting requirements are well advised to pay close attention to the performance of the PGA. It's easy to tune the PGA, and the results of a well-tuned PGA show up in dramatic improvements in performance.

Evaluating System Performance

The instance-tuning efforts that you undertake from within Oracle will have only a limited impact (they may even have a negative impact) if you don't pay attention to the system performance as a whole. System performance includes the CPU performance, memory usage, and disk I/O. In the following sections you'll look at each of these important resources in more detail.

CPU Performance

You can use operating system utilities such as System Activity Reporter (sar) or vmstat to find out how the CPU is performing. Don't panic if your processors seem busy during peak periods—that's what they're there for, so you can use them when necessary. If the processors are showing a heavy load during low usage times, you do need to investigate further. Listing 20-8 shows a sar command output indicating how hard your system is using the CPU resources right now.

Listing 20-8. *sar Command Output Showing CPU Usage*

```
$ sar -u 10 5
HP-UX finance1  B.11.00 A 9000/800    07/03/05
13:39:17    %usr      %sys      %wio     %idle
13:39:27     34        23         7        36
13:39:37     37        17         8        38
13:39:47     34        18         6        41
13:39:57     31        16         9        44
13:40:07     38        19        11        32
Average      35        19         8        38
```

In the preceding listing, the four columns report on the following CPU usage patterns:

- %usr shows the proportion of total CPU time taken up by the various users of the system.

- %sys shows the proportion of time the system itself was using the CPU.

- %wio indicates the percentage of time the system was waiting for I/O.

- %idle is the proportion of time the CPU was idle.

If the %wio or %idle percentages are near zero during nonpeak times, it indicates a CPU-bound system.

Remember that an intensive CPU usage level may mean that an operating-system process is hogging CPU, or an Oracle process may be doing the damage. If it is Oracle, a background process such as PMON may be the culprit, or an Oracle user process may be running some extraordinarily bad ad hoc SQL query on the production box. You may sometimes track down such a user and inform the person that you're killing the process in the interest of the welfare of the entire system. Imagine your surprise when you find that the user's Oracle process is hale and hearty, while merrily continuing to devastate your system in the middle of a busy day. This could happen because a child process or a bequeath process continued to run even after you killed this user. It pays to double-check that the user is gone—lock, stock, and barrel—instead of assuming that the job has been done.

That said, let's look at some of the common events that could cause CPU-related slowdowns on your system.

The Run Queue Length

One of the main indicators of a heavily loaded CPU system is the length of the run queue. A longer run queue means that more processes are lined up, waiting for CPU processing time. Occasional blips in the run-queue length aren't bad, but prolonged high run-queue lengths indicate that the system is CPU bound.

CPU Units Used by Processes

You can determine the number of CPU units a UNIX process is using by using the simple process (ps) command, as shown here:

```
$ ps -ef | grep f60
    UID    PID  PPID    C    STIME  TTY  TIME    CMD
  oracle 20108  4768    0  09:11:49   ?  0:28    f60webm
  oracle   883  4768    5  17:12:21   ?  0:06    f60webm
  oracle  7090  4768   16  09:18:46   ?  1:08    f60webm
  oracle 15292  4768  101  15:49:21   ?  1:53    f60webm
  oracle 18654  4768    0  14:44:23   ?  1:18    f60webm
  oracle 24316  4768    0  15:53:33   ?  0:52    f60webm
$
```

The key column to watch is the fourth one from the left, which indicates the CPU units of processing that each process is using. If each CPU on a server has 100 units, the Oracle process with PID 15292 (the fourth in the preceding list) is occupying more than an entire CPU's processing power. If you have only two processors altogether, you should worry about this process and why it's so CPU intensive.

Finding High CPU Users

If the CPU usage levels are high, you need to find out which of your users are among the top CPU consumers. Listing 20-9 shows how you can easily identify those users.

Listing 20-9. *Identifying High CPU Users*

```
SQL> SELECT n.username,
  2  s.sid,
  3  s.value
  4  FROM v$sesstat s,v$statname t, v$session n
  5  WHERE s.statistic# = t.statistic#
  6  AND n.sid = s.sid
  7  AND t.name='CPU used by this session'
  8  ORDER BY s.value desc;

USERNAME          SID    VALUE
---------------   -----  --------
JOHLMAN           152    20745
NROBERTS          103     4944
JOHLMAN           167     4330
LROLLINS           87     3699
JENGMAN           130     3694
JPATEL             66     3344
NALAPATI           73     3286
SQL>
```

Listing 20-9 shows that CPU usage isn't uniformly spread across the users. You need to investigate why one user is using such a significant quantity of resources. If you need to, you can control CPU usage by a single user or a group of users by using the Database Resource Manager. You can also find out session-level CPU usage information by using the V$SESSTAT view, as shown in Listing 20-10.

Listing 20-10. *Determining Session-Level CPU Usage*

```
SQL> SELECT sid, s.value "Total CPU Used by this Session"
  2  FROM V$SESSTAT S
  3  WHERE S.statistic# = 12
  4* ORDER BY S,value DESC;

     SID                Total CPU Used by this Session
     -----              ------------------------------
     496                        27623
     542                        21325
     111                        20814
     731                        17089
     424                        15228
SQL>
```

What Is the CPU Time Used For?

It would be a mistake to treat all CPU time as equal. CPU time is generally understood as the processor time taken to perform various tasks, such as the following:

- Loading SQL statements into the library cache
- Searching the shared pool for parsed versions of SQL statements
- Parsing the SQL statements
- Querying the data dictionary
- Reading data from the buffer cache
- Traversing index trees to fetch index keys

The total CPU time used by an instance (or a session) can be viewed as the sum of the following components:

```
total CPU time = parsing CPU usage + recursive CPU usage + other CPU usage
```

Ideally, your total CPU usage numbers should show a small proportion of the first two categories of CPU usage—parsing and recursive CPU usage. For example, for a session-wide estimate of CPU usage, you can run the query shown in Listing 20-11.

Listing 20-11. *Decomposition of Total CPU Usage*

```
SQL> SELECT name,value FROM V$SYSSTAT
  2  WHERE NAME IN ('CPU used by this session',
  3  'recursive cpu usage',
  4 *'parse time cpu');

NAME                         VALUE
-------------------------    ---------
recursive cpu usage          4713085
CPU used by this session     98196187
parse time cpu                132947
3 rows selected.
SQL>
```

In this example, the sum of recursive CPU usage and parse time CPU usage is a small proportion of total CPU usage. You need to be concerned if the parsing or recursive CPU usage is a significant part of total CPU usage. Let's see how you can go about reducing the CPU usage attributable to these various components.

■**Note** In the following examples, you can examine CPU usage at the instance level by using the V$SYSSTAT view or at an individual session level by using the V$SESSTAT view. Just remember that the column "total CPU used by this session" in the V$SYSSTAT view refers to the *sum* of the CPU used by all the sessions combined.

Parse Time CPU Usage

As you learned at the beginning of this chapter, parsing is an expensive operation that you should reduce to a minimum. In the following example, the parse time CPU usage is quite low as a percentage of total CPU usage. The first query tells you that the total CPU usage in your instance is 49159124:

```
SQL> SELECT name, value FROM V$SYSSTAT
  2* WHERE name LIKE '%CPU%';
```

NAME	VALUE
CPU used when call started	13220745
CPU used by this session	49159124

```
2 rows selected.
SQL>
```

The next query shows that the parse time CPU usage is 96431, which is an insignificant proportion of total CPU usage in your database:

```
SQL> SELECT name, value FROM V$SYSSTAT
  2 WHERE name LIKE  '%parse%';
```

NAME	VALUE
parse time cpu	96431
parse time elapsed	295451
parse count (total)	3147900
parse count (hard)	29139

```
4 rows selected.
SQL>
```

Listing 20-12 shows an example of a session whose CPU usage is predominantly due to high parse time.

Listing 20-12. *Determining Parse Time CPU Usage*

```
SQL> SELECT a.value   " Tot_CPU_Used_This_Session",
  2 b.value "Total_Parse_Count",
  3 c.value "Hard_Parse_Count",
  4 d.value "Parse_Time_CPU"
  5 FROM v$sysstat a,
  6 v$sysstat b,
  7 v$sysstat c,
  8 v$sysstat d
```

```
 9  WHERE a.name = 'CPU used by this session'
10  AND b.name = 'parse count (total)'
11  AND c.name = 'parse count (hard)'
12* AND d.name = 'parse time cpu';

Tot_CPU_Used  Total_Parse_Count  Hard_Parse_Count  Parse_Time_CPU
This_Session
------------- ------------------ ----------------- ---------------
         2240              53286               281            1486
SQL>
```

Parse time CPU in the preceding example is fully two-thirds of the total CPU usage. Obviously, you need to be concerned about the high rates of parsing, even though most of the parses are soft parses. The next section shows you what you can do to reduce the amount of parsing in your database.

Reducing Parse Time CPU Usage

If parse time CPU is the major part of total CPU usage, you need to reduce this by performing the following steps:

1. Use bind variables and remove hard-coded literal values from code, as explained in the "Optimizing the Library Cache" section earlier in this chapter.

2. Make sure you aren't allocating *too much memory* for the shared pool. Remember that even if you have an exact copy of a new SQL statement in your library cache, Oracle has to find it by scanning all the statements in the cache. If you have a zillion relatively useless statements sitting in the cache, all they're doing is slowing down the instance by increasing the parse time.

3. Make sure you don't have latch contention on the library cache, which could result in increased parse time CPU usage.

4. If your TKPROF output or one of the queries shown previously indicates that total parse time CPU is as high as 90 percent or more, check to make sure all the tables in the queries have been analyzed recently. If you don't have statistics on some of the tables, the parsing process generates the statistics, but the parse CPU usage time goes up dramatically.

Recursive CPU Usage

Recursive CPU usage is mostly for data dictionary lookups and for executing PL/SQL programs. Thus, if your application uses a high number of packages and procedures, you'll see a significant amount of recursive CPU usage.

In the following example, there's no need for alarm, because the percentage of recursive CPU usage is only about 5 percent of total CPU usage:

```
SQL> SELECT name, value FROM V$SYSSTAT
  2  WHERE name IN ('CPU used by this session',
  3*               'recursive cpu usage');

NAME                             VALUE
------------------------------  ---------
recursive cpu usage            4286925
CPU used by this session       84219625
2 rows selected.
SQL>
```

If the recursive CPU usage percentage is a large proportion of total CPU usage, you may want to make sure the shared pool memory allocation is adequate. However, a PL/SQL-based application will always have a significant amount of recursive CPU usage.

■**Note** A high number of recursive SQL statements may also indicate that Oracle is busy with space management activities, such as allocating extents. This has a detrimental effect on performance. You can avoid this problem by increasing the extent sizes for your database objects. This is another good reason to choose locally managed tablespaces, which cut down on the number of recursive SQL statements.

Memory

Operating system physical memory holds all the data and programs by loading them from disk. System CPU executes programs only if they're loaded into the physical memory. If excessive memory usage occurs, the operating system will use virtual memory, which is storage space on secondary storage media such as disks, to hold temporarily some of the data and/or programs being used. The space for the virtual memory is called *swap space*. When the system needs room in the physical or main memory, it "swaps out" some programs to the swap area, thus freeing up additional physical memory for an executing program.

The operating system swaps out data in units called *pages*, which are the smallest units of memory that can be used in transferring memory back and forth between physical memory and the swap area. When the operating system needs a page that has been swapped out to the swap area, a page fault is said to occur. Page faults are commonly referred to as simply "paging," and involve the transfer of data from virtual memory back to the physical memory. An excessive amount of paging results in degradation of operating system performance, and thus affects Oracle instance performance as well.

One of the best ways to check operating system memory performance is by using the vmstat utility, which was explained in Chapter 3.

Disk I/O

The way you configure your disk system has a profound impact on your I/O rates. You have to address several issues when you're planning your disk system. Important factors that have a bearing on your I/O are as follows:

- *Choice of RAID configuration*: Chapter 3 covered RAID system configuration in detail. Just remember that a RAID 5 configuration doesn't give you ideal I/O performance if your application involves a large number of writes. For faster performance, make sure you use a configuration that involves striping your disks, preferably according to the Oracle guidelines.

- *Raw devices or operating system file systems*: Under some circumstances, you can benefit by using raw devices, which bypass the operating system buffer cache. Raw devices have their own drawbacks, though, including limited backup features, and you want to be sure the benefits outweigh the drawbacks. Raw devices in general provide faster I/O capabilities and give better performance for a write-intensive application. You might also want to consider alternative file systems such as VERITAS's VXFSS, which helps large I/O operations through its direct I/O option.

- *I/O size*: I/O size is in terms of the Oracle block size. The minimum size of I/O depends on your block size, and the maximum size depends on the DB_FILE_MULTIBLOCK_READ_COUNT initialization parameter. If your application is OLTP based, the I/O size needs to be small, and if your application is oriented toward a DSS, the I/O size needs to be much larger. As of Oracle Database 10.2, the database automatically tunes this parameter, if you don't set it.

- *Logical volume stripe sizes*: Stripe size (or stripe width) is a function of the stripe depth and the number of drives in the striped set. If you stripe across multiple disks, your database's I/O performance will be higher and its load balancing will be enhanced. Make sure that the stripe size is larger than the average I/O request; otherwise, you'll be making multiple I/Os for a single I/O request by Oracle. If you have multiple concurrent I/O requests, your stripe size should be much larger than the I/O size. Most modern LVMs can dynamically reconfigure the stripe size.

- *Number of controllers and disks*: The number of spindles and the number of controllers are both important variables in determining disk performance. Even if you have a large number of spindles, you could conceivably run into contention at the controller level.

- *Distribution of I/O*: Your goal should be to avoid a lopsided distribution of I/O in your disk system. If you're using an LVM or using striping at the hardware level, you don't have a whole lot to worry about in this area. However, if you aren't using an LVM or using striping at the hardware level, you should manually arrange your datafiles on the disks such that the I/O rate is fairly even across the system. Note that your tables and indexes are usually required to be in different tablespaces, but there is no rule that they have to be placed on different disks. Because the index is read before the table, they can coexist on the same disk.

Measuring I/O Performance

You have a choice of several excellent tools to measure I/O performance. Several operating system utilities are easy to use and give you information about how busy your disks are. Iostat and sar are two of the popular operating system utilities that measure disk performance. I explained how to use both these tools in Chapter 3.

Is the I/O Optimally Distributed?

From the sar output, you can figure out whether you're using the storage subsystem heavily. If the number of waits is higher than the number of CPUs, or if the service times are high (say, greater than 20 milliseconds), then your system is facing contention at the I/O level. One of the most useful pieces of information you can get is by using the sar -d command to find out if you're using any of your disks excessively compared to other disks in the system. Once you identify such hot spots, you can move the datafiles to less busy drives, thereby spreading the load more evenly.

The following is the output of a sar -d command that shows extremely high queue values. Even at peak levels, the avque column value should be less than 2. Here, it is 61.4. Obviously, something is happening on the file system named c2t6d0 that's showing up as a high queue value:

```
$ sar -d 10 5
HP-UX finance1 B.11.00 A 9000/800    07/03/08
17:27:13   device   %busy   avque   r+w/s   blks/s   avwait   avserv
17:27:23   c2t6d0   100     61.40    37     245      4.71     10.43
           c5t6d0   20.38   0.50     28     208      4.92     9.54
           c2t6d0   100     61.40    38     273      4.55     9.49
           c5t6d0   18.28   0.50     27     233      4.46     7.93
           c0t1d0   0.10    0.50      4      33      4.99     0.81
. . .
$
```

You can obtain an idea about the I/O distribution in your system by using the query in Listing 20-13.

Listing 20-13. *Determining I/O Distribution in the Database*

```
SQL> SELECT d.name,
  2  f.phyrds reads,
  3  f.phywrts wrts,
  4  (f.readtim / decode(f.phyrds,0,-1,f.phyrds)) readtime,
  5  (f.writetim / decode(f.phywrts,0,-1,phywrts)) writetime
  6  FROM
  7  v$datafile d,
  8  v$filestat f
  9  WHERE
 10  d.file# = f.file#
 11  ORDER BY
 12* d.name;

NAME                              READS  WRTS  READTIME     WRITETIME
------------------------------    -----  ----  ----------   ----------
/pa01/oradata/pa/lol_i_17.dbf       23     9  .608695652   .222222222
/pa01/oradata/pa/lol_i_18.dbf       18     7  .277777778            0
. . .
SQL>
```

■**Caution** Excessive reads and writes on some disks indicate that there might be disk contention in your I/O system.

Reducing Disk Contention

If there's severe I/O contention in your system, you can undertake some of the following steps, depending on your present database configuration:

- Increase the number of disks in the storage system.
- Separate the database and the redo log files.
- For a large table, use partitions to reduce I/O.
- Stripe the data either manually or by using a RAID disk-striping system.
- Invest in cutting-edge technology, such as file caching, to avoid I/O bottlenecks.
- Consider using the new Automatic Storage Management system, which is discussed in Chapter 17.

The Oracle SAME Guidelines for Optimal Disk Usage

Oracle provides you with the Stripe and Mirror Everything (SAME) guidelines for optimal disk usage. This methodology advocates striping all files across all disks and mirroring all data to achieve a simple, efficient, and highly available disk configuration. Striping across all the available disks aims to spread the load evenly and avoid hot spots. The SAME methodology also recommends placing frequently accessed data on the outer half of the disks. The goal of the SAME disk storage strategy is to eliminate I/O hot spots and maximize I/O bandwidth.

Network Performance

You may want to rule out the network as the culprit during a poor performance period by checking whether it's overloaded and exhibiting excessive latency. You can use the operating system tool netstat to check your network performance, as I explained in Chapter 3. Excessive network round-trips necessitated by client messages could clog your network and increase the latency, thus indirectly affecting the CPU load on your system. In cases such as this, you must try and reduce the network round-trips by using array inserts and array fetches.

Measuring Instance Performance

One of the trickiest parts of the DBA's job is to judge the performance of the Oracle instance accurately. Trainers and the manuals advise you to perform diligent proactive tuning, but in reality most tuning efforts are reactive—they're intensive attempts to fix problems that perceptibly slow down a database and cause user complaints to increase. You look at the same things whether you're doing proactive or reactive tuning, but proactive tuning gives you the luxury of making decisions in an unhurried and low-stress environment. Ideally, you should spend more than two-thirds of your total tuning time on proactive planning. As you do so, you'll find that you're reacting less and less over time to sudden emergencies.

Oracle Database 11g uses the concept of DB time (discussed in detail in Chapter 17) to determine how well the instance is performing. You can look at some statistics to see how well the database is performing. These statistics fall into two groups: database hit ratios and database wait statistics. If you're consistently seeing numbers in the high 90s for the various hit ratios you saw earlier in this chapter, you're usually doing well, according to this approach.

However, the big question is this: Do high hit ratios automatically imply a perfectly tuned and efficient database? The surprising answer is no. To understand this confusing fact, you need to look at what hit ratios indicate. The following sections examine the two main groups of performance statistics.

Database Hit Ratios

Database hit ratios are the most commonly used measures of performance. These include the buffer cache hit ratio, the library cache and dictionary cache hit ratios, the latch hit ratio, and the disk sort ratios. These hit ratios don't indicate how well your system is performing. They're broad indicators of proper SGA allocation, and they may be high even when the system as a whole is performing poorly. The thing to remember is that the hit ratios only measure such things as how physical reads compare with logical reads, and how much of the time a parsed version of a statement is found in memory. As to whether the statements themselves are efficient or not, the hit ratios can't tell you anything. When your system is slow due to bottlenecks, the hit ratios are of little help, and you should turn to a careful study of wait statistics instead.

■**Caution** Even if you have a 99.99 percent buffer cache hit ratio, you may still have major inefficiencies in your application. What if you have an extremely high number of "unnecessary" logical reads? This makes your buffer cache hit ratio look good, as that hit ratio is defined as physical reads over the sum of logical reads. Although you may think your application should run faster because you're doing most of your reads from memory instead of disk, this may well not happen. The reason is that even if you're doing logical reads, you're still burning up the CPU units to do the unnecessary logical reads. In essence, by focusing zealously on the buffer cache hit ratio to relieve the I/O subsystem, you could be an unwitting party to a CPU usage problem. Please read Cary Millsap's interesting article, "Why You Should Focus on LIOs Instead of PIOs" (http://www.hotsos.com/e-library/abstract.php?id=7), which explains why a high logical I/O level could be a major problem.

When faced with a slow-performing database or a demand for shorter response times, Oracle DBAs have traditionally looked to increase their database hit ratios and tune the database by adjusting a host of initialization parameters (such as SGA allocations). More recently, there's been awareness that the key area to focus on is clearing up database bottlenecks that contribute to a higher response time.

The total response time for a query is the time Oracle takes to execute it, plus the time the process spends waiting for resources such as latches, data buffers, and so on. For a database instance to perform well, ideally your application should spend little time waiting for access to critical resources.

Let's now turn to examining the critical wait events in your database, which can be real show-stoppers on a busy day in a production instance.

Database Wait Statistics

When your users complain that the database is crawling and they can't get their queries returned fast enough, there's no use in your protesting that your database is showing high hit ratios for the shared pool and the buffer cache (and the large pool and redo log buffer as well). If the users are waiting for long periods of time to complete their tasks, then the response time will be slow, and you can't say that the database is performing well, the high hit ratios notwithstanding.

■**Note** For an interesting review of the Oracle wait analysis (the wait interface), please read one of the early papers in this area, titled "Yet Another Performance Profiling Method (or YAPP-Method)," by Anjo Kolk, Shari Yamaguchi, and Jim Viscusi. It's available at the OraPerf web site at http://www.oraperf.com (a free registration is required).

Once it starts executing a SQL statement, an Oracle process doesn't always get to work on the execution of the statement without any interruptions. Often, the process has to pause or wait for some resource to be released before it can continue its execution. Thus, an active Oracle process is doing one of the following at any given time:

- The process is executing the SQL statement.

- The process is waiting for something (for example, a resource such as a database buffer or a latch). It could be waiting for an action such as a write to the buffer cache to complete.

That's why the response time—the total time taken by Oracle to finish work—is correctly defined as follows:

```
response time = service time + wait time
```

When you track the total time taken by a transaction to complete, you may find that only part of that time was taken up by the Oracle server to actually "do" something. The rest of the time, the server may have been waiting for some resource to be freed up or waiting for a request to do something. This busy resource may be a slow log writer or a database writer process. The wait event may also be due to unavailable buffers or latches. The wait events in the V$SYSTEM_EVENT view (instance-level waits) and the V$SESSION_EVENT view (session-level waits) tell you what the wait time is due to (full table scans, high number of library cache latches, and so on). Not only do the wait events tell you what the wait time in the database instance is due to, but they also tell you a lot about bottlenecks in the network and the application.

■**Note** It's important to understand that the wait events are only the *symptoms* of problems, most likely within the application code. The wait events show you what's slowing down performance, but not why a certain wait event is showing up in large numbers. It's up to you to investigate the SQL code to find out the real cause of the performance problems.

Four dynamic performance views contain wait information: V$SESSION, V$SYSTEM_EVENT, V$SESSION_EVENT, and V$SESSION_WAIT. These four views list just about all the events the instance was waiting for and the duration of these waits. Understanding these wait events is essential for resolving performance issues.

Let's look at the common wait events in detail in the following sections. Remember that the four views show similar information but focus on different aspects of the database, as you can see from the following summary. The wait events are most useful when you have timed statistics turned on. Otherwise, the wait events only have the number of times they occurred, not the length of time they consumed. Without timing the events, you can't tell if a wait event was indeed a contributing factor in a system slowdown.

■**Tip** Use the wait event views (wait interface) for examining current and recent performance issues in your instance. For comprehensive analysis of most performance problems, you need to use the ADDM, which analyzes the AWR hourly snapshots.

Oracle wait interface analysis has garnered quite a bit of attention in the last few years. There are entire books dedicated to Oracle waits. I discuss the important performance topic of Oracle wait analysis later in this chapter, in the section "Analyzing Instance Performance." Ideally, all sessions should be on the CPU, with zero time spent waiting for resources such as I/O. However, remember that every working instance will have some kind of wait. It's unrealistic to expect to work toward a zero wait system. The key question should not be whether you have any Oracle wait events occurring, but rather if there are *excessive waits*.

Wait Events and Wait Classes

Any time a server process waits for an event to complete, it's classified as a *wait event*. There are more than 950 Oracle wait events in Oracle Database 11g. The most common wait events are those caused by resource contention such as latch contention, buffer contention, and I/O contention.

A wait class is a grouping of related wait events, and every wait event belongs to a wait class. Important wait classes include Administrative, Application, Concurrency, Configuration, Idle, Network, System I/O, and User I/O. For example, the Administrative wait class includes lock waits caused by row-level locking. The User I/O class of waits refers to waits for blocks to be read off a disk. Using wait classes helps you move quickly to the root cause of a problem in your database by limiting the focus of further analysis. Here's a summary of the main wait classes in Oracle Database 11g:

- *Administrative*: Waits caused by administrative commands, such as rebuilding an index, for example.

- *Application*: Waits due to the application code.

- *Cluster*: Waits related to Real Application Cluster management.

- *Commit*: The single wait event log file sync, which is a wait caused by commits in the database.

- *Concurrency*: Waits for database resources that are used for locking, for example, latches.

- *Idle*: Waits that occur when a session isn't active, for example, the 'SQL*Net message from client' wait event.

- *Network*: Waits incurred during network messaging.

- *Other*: Miscellaneous waits.

- *Scheduler*: Resource Manager–related waits.

- *System I/O*: Waits for background-process I/O, including the database writer background process's wait for the db file parallel write event. Also included are archive-log–related waits and redo log read-and-write waits.

- *User I/O*: Waits for user I/O. Includes the db file sequential read and db file scattered read events.

Analyzing Instance Performance

One of the first things you can do to measure instance performance efficiency is to determine the proportion of total time the database is spending working compared to the proportion of time it's merely waiting for resources. The V$SYSMETRIC view displays the system metric values for the most current time interval. The following query using the V$SYSMETRIC view reveals a database instance where waits are taking more time than the instance CPU usage time:

```
SQL> SELECT  METRIC_NAME, VALUE
      FROM V$SYSMETRIC
      WHERE METRIC_NAME IN ('Database CPU Time Ratio',
      'Database Wait Time Ratio') AND
      INTSIZE_CSEC =
      (select max(INTSIZE_CSEC) from V$SYSMETRIC);

METRIC_NAME                          VALUE
-----------------------            ------
Database Wait Time Ratio             72
Database CPU Time Ratio              28
SQL>
```

Once you realize that the total instance wait time ratio is much higher than the CPU time ratio, you can explore things further. Wait classes provide a quick way to figure out why the database instance is performing poorly. In the example shown in Listing 20-14, you can easily see that user I/O waits are responsible for most of the wait time. You can establish this fact by looking at the PCT_TIME column, which gives you the percentage of time attributable to each wait class. Total waits are often misleading, as you can see by looking at the NETWORK wait class. In percentage terms, network waits are only 1 percent, although total network waits constitute more than 51 percent of total waits in this instance.

Listing 20-14. *Determining Total Waits and Percentage Waits by Wait Class*

```
SQL> SELECT WAIT_CLASS,
  2   TOTAL_WAITS,
  3   round(100 * (TOT_WAITS / SUM_WAITS),2) PCT_TOTWAITS,
  4   ROUND((TIME_WAITED / 100),2) TOT_TIME_WAITED,
  5   round(100 * (TOT_TIME_WAITED / SUM_TIME),2) PCT_TIME
  6   FROM
  7   (select WAIT_CLASS,
  8   TOT_WAITS,
  9   TOT_TIME_WAITED
 10   FROM V$SYSTEM_WAIT_CLASS
 11   WHERE WAIT_CLASS != 'Idle'),
 12   (select  sum(TOT_WAITS) SUM_WAITS,
 13   sum(TOT_TIME_WAITED) SUM_TIME
 14   from     V$SYSTEM_WAIT_CLASS
 15   where    WAIT_CLASS != 'Idle')
 16* ORDER BY PCT_TIME DESC;
```

WAIT_CLASS	TOTAL_WAITS	PCT_TOT_WAITS	TOT_TIME_WAITED	PCT_TIME
User I/O	6649535191	45.07	46305770.5	84.42
Other	394490128	2.67	5375324.17	9.8
Concurrency	78768788	.53	1626254.9	2.96
Network	7546925506	51.15	547128.66	1
Application	2012092	.01	449945.5	.82
Commit	15526036	.11	351043.3	.64
Configuration	12898465	.09	116029.85	.21
System I/O	53005529	.36	78783.64	.14
Administrative	25	0	7.6	0
Scheduler	1925	0	.15	0

```
10 rows selected.
SQL>
```

Using V$ Tables for Wait Information

The key dynamic performance tables for finding wait information are the V$SYSTEM_EVENT, V$SESSION_EVENT, V$SESSION_WAIT, and the V$SESSION views. The first two views show the waiting time for different events.

The V$SYSTEM_EVENT view shows the total time waited for all the events for the entire system since the instance started up. The view doesn't focus on the individual sessions experiencing waits, and therefore it gives you a high-level view of waits in the system. You can use this view to find out what the top instance-wide wait events are. You can calculate the top *n* waits in the system by dividing the event's wait time by the total wait time for all events.

The three key columns of the V$SYSTEM_EVENT view are total_waits, which gives the total number of waits; time_waited, which is the total wait time per session since the instance started; and average_wait, which is the average wait time by all sessions per event.

The V$SESSION_EVENT view is similar to the V$SYSTEM_EVENT view, and it shows the total time waited per session. All the wait events for an individual session are recorded in this view for the duration of that session. By querying this view, you can find out the specific bottlenecks encountered by each session.

The third dynamic view is the V$SESSION_WAIT view, which shows the current waits or just-completed waits for sessions. The information on waits in this view changes continuously based on the types of waits that are occurring in the system. The real-time information in this view provides you with tremendous insight into what's holding up things in the database *right now*. The V$SESSION_WAIT view provides detailed information on the wait event, including details such as file number, latch numbers, and block number. This detailed level of information provided by the V$SESSION_WAIT view enables you to probe into the exact bottleneck that's slowing down the database. The low-level information helps you zoom in on the root cause of performance problems.

The following columns from the V$SESSION_WAIT view are important for troubleshooting performance issues:

- EVENT: These are the different wait events described in the next section (for example, latch free and buffer busy waits).

- P1, P2, P3: These are the additional parameters that represent different items, depending on the particular wait event. For example, if the wait event is db file sequential read, P1 stands for the file number, P2 stands for the block number, and P3 stands for the number of blocks. If the wait is due to a latch free event, P1 stands for the latch address, P2 stands for the latch number, and P3 stands for the number of attempts for the event.

- WAIT_CLASS_ID: This identifies the wait class.

- WAIT_CLASS#: This is the number of the wait class.
- WAIT_CLASS: This is the name of the wait class.
- WAIT_TIME: This is the wait time in seconds if the state is waited known time.
- SECONDS_IN_WAIT: This is the wait time in seconds if the state is waiting.
- STATE: The state could be waited short time, waited known time, or waiting, if the session is waiting for an event.

The fourth wait-related view is the V$SESSION view. Not only does this view provide many details about the session, it also provides significant wait information as well. The V$SESSION view contains all the columns of the V$SESSION_WAIT view, plus a number of other important session-related columns. Because of this overlap of wait information in the V$SESSION and the V$SESSION_WAIT views, you can use the V$SESSION view directly to look for most of the wait-related information, without recourse to the V$SESSION_WAIT view. You can start analyzing the wait events in your system by first querying the V$SYSTEM_EVENT view to see if any significant wait events are occurring in the database. You can do this by running the query shown in Listing 20-15.

Listing 20-15. *Using the V$SYSTEM_EVENT View to View Wait Events*

```
SQL> SELECT event, time_waited, average_wait
  2  FROM V$SYSTEM_EVENT
  3  GROUP BY event, time_waited, average_wait
  4* ORDER BY time_waited DESC;
```

EVENT	TIME_WAITED	AVERAGE_WAIT
rdbms ipc message	24483121	216.71465
SQL*Net message from client	18622096	106.19049
PX Idle Wait	12485418	205.01844
pmon timer	3120909	306.93440
smon timer	3093214	29459.18100
PL/SQL lock timer	3024203	1536.68852
db file sequential read	831831	.25480
db file scattered read	107253	.90554
free buffer waits	52955	43.08787
log file parallel write	19958	2.02639
latch free	5884	1.47505

```
. . .
58 rows selected.
SQL>
```

This example shows a simple system with hardly any waits other than the idle type of events and the SQL*Net wait events. There aren't any significant I/O-related or latch-contention–related wait events in this database. The db file sequential read (caused by index reads) and the db file scattered read (caused by full table scans) wait events do seem somewhat substantial, but if you compare the total wait time contributed by these two events to the total wait time since the instance started, they don't stand out. Furthermore, the AVERAGE_WAIT column shows that both these waits have a low average wait time (caused by index reads). I discuss both these events, along with several other Oracle wait events, later in this chapter, in the section "Important Oracle Wait Events." However, if your query on a real-life production system shows significant numbers for any nonidle wait event, it's probably a good idea to find out the SQL statements that are causing the waits. That's where you have to focus your efforts to reduce the waits. You have different ways to obtain the associated SQL for the waits, as explained in the following section.

Obtaining Wait Information

Obtaining wait information is as easy as querying the related dynamic performance tables. For example, if you wish to find out quickly the types of waits different user sessions (session-level wait information) are facing and the SQL text of the statements they're executing, you can use the following query:

```
SQL> SELECT s.username,
  2  t.sql_text, s.event
  3  FROM V$SESSION s, V$SQLTEXT t
  4  WHERE s.sql_hash_value = t.hash_value
  5  AND s.sql_address  = t.address
  6  AND s.type  <> 'BACKGROUND'
  7* ORDER BY s.sid,t.hash_value,t.piece;
```

■**Note** You need to turn on statistics collection by either setting the initialization parameter TIMED_STATISTICS to TRUE or setting the initialization parameter STATISTICS_LEVEL to TYPICAL or ALL.

If you want a quick instance-wide wait event status, showing which events were the biggest contributors to total wait time, you can use the query shown in Listing 20-16 (several idle events are listed in the output, but I don't show them here).

Listing 20-16. *Instance-Wide Waits Sorted by Total Wait Time*

```
SQL> SELECT event, total_waits,time_waited
  2  FROM V$SYSTEM_EVENT
  3  WHERE event NOT IN
  4  ('pmon timer','smon timer','rdbms ipc reply','parallel deque
  5  wait','virtual circuit','%SQL*Net%','client message','NULL    event')
  6* ORDER BY time_waited DESC;
```

EVENT	TOTAL_WAITS	TIME_WAITED
db file sequential read	35051309	15965640
latch free	1373973	1913357
db file scattered read	2958367	1840810
enqueue	2837	370871
buffer busy waits	444743	252664
log file parallel write	146221	123435

```
SQL>
```

The preceding query shows that waits due to the db file scattered read wait event account for most of the waits in this instance. The db file sequential read wait event, as you'll learn shortly, is caused by full table scans. It's somewhat confusing in the beginning when you're trying to use all the wait-related V$ views, which all look similar. Here's a quick summary of how you go about using the key wait-related Oracle Database 11g dynamic performance views.

First, look at the V$SYSTEM_EVENT view and rank the top wait events by the total amount of time waited, as well as the average wait time for that event. Start investigating the top waits in terms of the percentage of total wait time. You can also look at any AWR reports you may have, because the AWR also lists the top five wait events in the instance.

Next, find out more details about the specific wait event that's at the top of the list. For example, if the top event is buffer busy waits, look in the V$WAITSTAT view to see which type of buffer block (data block, undo block, and so on) is causing the buffer busy waits (a simple SELECT * from V$WAITSTAT gets you all the necessary information). For example, if the undo-block buffer waits make up most of your buffer busy waits, then the undo segments are at fault, not the data blocks.

Finally, use the V$SESSION view to find out the exact objects that may be the source of a problem. For example, if you have a high amount of db file scattered read–type waits, the V$SESSION view will give you the file number and block number involved in the wait events. In the following example, the V$SESSION view is used to find out who is doing the full table scans showing up as the most important wait events right now. As explained earlier, the db file scattered read wait event is caused by full table scans.

```
SQL> SELECT sid, sql_address, sql_hash_value
     FROM V$SESSION WHERE event = 'db file scattered read';
```

Here's an example that shows how to find out the current wait event for a given session:

```
SQL> SELECT sid, state, event, wait_time, seconds_in_wait
  2 FROM v$session
  3*WHERE sid=1418;
```

SID	STATE	EVENT	WAIT_TIME	SECONDS_IN_WAIT
1418	WAITING	db file sequential read	0	0

SQL>

The value of 0 under the WAIT_TIME column indicates that the wait event db file sequential read is occurring for this session. When the wait event is over, you'll see values for the WAIT_TIME and the SECONDS_IN_WAIT columns.

You can also use the V$SQLAREA view to find out which SQL statements are responsible for high disk reads. If latch waits predominate, you should be looking at the V$LATCH view to gain more information about the type of latch that's responsible for the high latch wait time:

```
SQL> SELECT sid, blocking_session, username,
  2 event, seconds_in_wait siw
  3 FROM V$SESSION
  4* WHERE blocking_session_status = 'VALID';
```

SID	BLOCKING_SESS	USERNAME	EVENT	SIW
1218	1527	UCR_USER	enq: TX - row lock contention	23
1400	1400	APPOWNER	latch free	0

SQL>

The V$SESSION_WAIT_HISTORY View

The V$SESSION_WAIT_HISTORY view holds information about the *last ten wait events* for each active session. The other wait-related views, such as the V$SESSION and the V$SESSION_WAIT, show you only the wait information for the most recent wait. This may be a short wait, thus escaping your scrutiny. Here's a sample query using the V$SESSION_WAIT_HISTORY view:

```
SQL> SELECT seq#, event, wait_time, p1, p2, p3
  2 FROM V$SESSION_WAIT_HISTORY
  3 WHERE sid = 988
  4* ORDER BY seq#;
```

SEQ#	EVENT	WAIT_TIME	P1	P2	P3
1	db file sequential read	0		52	21944
2	db file sequential read	0		50	19262
3	latch: shared pool	0	1.3835E+19	198	0
4	db file sequential read	0		205	21605
5	db file sequential read	4		52	13924
6	db file sequential read	1		49	29222
7	db file sequential read	2		52	14591
8	db file sequential read	2		52	12723
9	db file sequential read	0		205	11883
10	db file sequential read	0		205	21604

```
10 rows selected.
SQL>
```

Note that a zero value under the WAIT_TIME column means that the session is waiting for a specific event. A nonzero value represents the time waited for the last event.

Analyzing Waits with Active Session History

The V$SESSION_WAIT view tells you what resource a session is waiting for. The V$SESSION view also provides significant wait information for active sessions. However, neither of these views provides you with *historical* information about the waits in your instance. Once the wait is over, you can no longer view the wait information using the V$SESSION_WAIT view. The waits are so fleeting that by the time you query the views, the wait in most times is over. The new Active Session History feature, by recording session information, enables you to go back in time and review the history of a performance bottleneck in your database. Although the AWR provides hourly snapshots of the instance by default, you won't be able to analyze events that occurred five or ten minutes ago, based on AWR data. This is where the ASH information comes in handy. ASH samples the V$SESSION view every second and collects the wait information for all *active* sessions. An active session is defined as a session that's on the CPU or waiting for a resource. You can view the ASH session statistics through the view V$ACTIVE_SESSION_HISTORY, which contains a single row for each active session in your instance. ASH is a rolling buffer in memory, with older information being overwritten by new session data.

Every 60 minutes, the MMON background process flushes filtered ASH data to disk, as part of the hourly AWR snapshots. If the ASH buffer is full, the MMNL background process performs the flushing of data. Once the ASH data is flushed to disk, you won't be able to see it in the V$ACTIVE_SESSION_HISTORY view. You'll now have to use the DBA_HIST_ACTIVE_SESS_HISTORY view to look at the historical data.

In the following sections, I show how you can query the V$ACTIVE_SESSION_HISTORY view to analyze current (recent) Active Session History.

Using the V$ACTIVE_SESSION_HISTORY View

The V$ACTIVE_SESSION_HISTORY view provides a window on the ASH data held in memory by the Oracle instance before it's flushed as part of the hourly AWR snapshots. You can use it to get information on things such as the SQL that's consuming the most resources in the database, the particular objects causing the most waits, and the identities of the users who are waiting the most.

In the following sections I show how to use the ASH information to gain valuable insights into the nature of the waits in your instance, including answering such questions as the objects with the highest waits, the important wait events in your instance, and the users waiting the most.

Objects with the Highest Waits

The following query identifies the objects causing the most waits and the type of events the objects waited for during the last 15 minutes:

```
SQL> SELECT o.object_name, o.object_type, a.event,
  2  SUM(a.wait_time +
  3  a.time_waited) total_wait_time
  4  FROM v$active_session_history a,
  5  dba_objects o
  6  WHERE a.sample_time between sysdate - 30/2880 and sysdate
  7  AND a.current_obj# = o.object_id
  8  GROUP BY o.object_name, o.object_type, a.event
  9* ORDER BY total_wait_time;
```

OBJECT_NAME	OBJECT_TYPE	EVENT	TOTAL_WAIT_TIME
UC_ADDRESS	TABLE	SQL*Net message to client	2
PERS_PHONES	TABLE	db file sequential read	8836
PAY_FK_I	INDEX	db file sequential read	9587
UC_STAGING	TABLE	log file sync	23633
PERSONNEL	TABLE	db file sequential read	43612

```
SQL>
```

Most Important Wait Events

The following query lists the most important wait events in your database in the last 15 minutes:

```
SQL> SELECT a.event,
  2  SUM(a.wait_time +
  3  a.time_waited) total_wait_time
  4  FROM v$active_session_history a
  5  WHERE a.sample_time between
  6  sysdate - 30/2880 and sysdate
  7  GROUP BY a.event
  8* ORDER BY total_wait_time DESC;
```

EVENT	TOTAL_WAIT_TIME
wait for SGA component shrink	878774247
smon timer	300006992
PL/SQL lock timer	210117722
SQL*Net message from client	21588571
db file scattered read	1062608
db file sequential read	105271
log file sync	13019
latch free	274
SQL*Net more data to client	35
null event	6

```
17 rows selected.
SQL>
```

Users with the Most Waits

The following query lists the users with the highest wait times within the last 15 minutes:

```
SQL> SELECT s.sid, s.username,
  2  SUM(a.wait_time +
  3  a.time_waited) total_wait_time
  4  FROM v$active_session_history a,
  5  v$session s
  6  WHERE a.sample_time between sysdate - 30/2880 and sysdate
  7  AND a.session_id=s.sid
  8  GROUP BY s.sid, s.username
  9* ORDER BY total_wait_time DESC;
```

SID	USERNAME	TOTAL_WAIT_TIME
1696	SYSOWNER	165104515
885	SYSOWNER	21575902
1087	BLONDI	5019123
1318	UCRSL	569723
1334	REBLOOM	376354
1489	FRAME	395

```
15 rows selected.
SQL>
```

Identifying SQL with the Highest Waits

Using the following query, you can identify the SQL that's waiting the most in your instance. The sample time covers the last 15 minutes.

```
SQL> SELECT a.user_id,d.username,s.sql_text,
  2  SUM(a.wait_time + a.time_waited) total_wait_time
  3  FROM v$active_session_history a,
  4  v$sqlarea s,
  5  dba_users d
  6  WHERE a.sample_time between sysdate - 30/2880 and sysdate
  7  AND a.sql_id = s.sql_id
  8  AND a.user_id = d.user_id
  9* GROUP BY a.user_id,s.sql_text, d.username;
```

USER_ID	USERNAME	SQL_TEXT	TOTAL_WAIT_TIME
0	SYS	BEGIN dbms_stats . . .; END;	9024233

```
. . .
SQL>
```

Wait Classes and the Wait-Related Views

The V$SESSION_WAIT view shows the events and resources that active sessions are waiting for. Using the V$SESSION_WAIT view, you can also see what types of wait classes your session waits belong to. Here's an example:

```
SQL> SELECT wait_class, event, sid, state, wait_time, seconds_in_wait
     FROM v$session_wait
     ORDER BY wait_class, event, sid;
```

WAIT_CLASS	EVENT	SID	STATE	WAIT_TIM	SEC_IN_WAIT
Application	enq: TX - row lock contention	269	WAITING	0	73
Idle	Queue Monitor Wait	270	WAITING	0	40
Idle	SQL*Net message from client	265	WAITING	0	73
Idle	jobq slave wait	259	WAITING	0	8485
Idle	pmon timer	280	WAITING	0	73
Idle	rdbms ipc message	267	WAITING	0	184770
Idle	wakeup time manager	268	WAITING	0	40
Network	SQL*Net message to client	272	WAITED SHORT TIME		1

```
SQL>
```

The previous query indicates that the most important wait lies within the Application wait class. The V$SYSTEM_WAIT_CLASS view gives you a breakdown of waits by wait classes, as shown here:

```
SQL> SELECT wait_class, time_waited
     FROM v$system_wait_class
     ORDER BY time_waited DESC;
```

WAIT_CLASS	TIME_WAITED
Idle	1.0770E+11
User I/O	4728148400
Other	548221433
Concurrency	167154949
Network	56271499
Application	46336445
Commit	35742104
Configuration	11667683
System I/O	8045920
Administrative	760
Scheduler	16

```
11 rows selected.
SQL>
```

The V$SESSION_WAIT_CLASS view shows the total time spent in each type of wait class by an individual session. Here's an example:

```
SQL> SELECT wait_class, time_waited
  2  FROM v$session_wait_class
  3  WHERE    sid = 1053
  4* ORDER BY time_waited DESC;
```

WAIT_CLASS	TIME_WAITED
Idle	21190
User I/O	8487
Other	70
Concurrency	13
Application	0
Network	0

```
6 rows selected.
SQL>
```

The V$WAITCLASSMETRIC view shows metric values of wait classes for the most recent 60-second interval. The view keeps information for up to one hour. Here's an example of using the query:

```
SQL> SELECT WAIT_CLASS#, WAIT_CLASS_ID
  2  dbtime_in_wait,time_waited,wait_count
  3  FROM v$waitclassmetric
  4* ORDER BY time_waited DESC;

WAIT_CLASS# DBTIME_IN_WAIT TIME_WAITED WAIT_COUNT
----------- -------------- ----------- ----------
          6     2723168908      170497      51249
          0     1893977003        5832         58
          8     1740759767         717       1351
          5     3386400367          11         68
          7     2000153315           8      52906
          9     4108307767           6         99
          1     4217450380           0          4
          2     3290255840           0          0
          3     4166625743           0          0
         11     3871361733           0          0
         10     2396326234           0          0
          4     3875070507           0          0
12 rows selected.

SQL>
```

As you can see, `WAIT_CLASS` 6 tops the list, meaning that idle class waits currently account for most of the wait time in this instance.

Looking at Segment-Level Statistics

Whether you use the AWR or the wait-related V$ views, you're going to find no information about where a certain wait event is occurring. For example, you can see from the V$SYSTEM_EVENT view that buffer busy waits are your problem, and you know that you reduce these waits by switching from manual segment space management to Automatic Segment Space Management (ASSM). However, neither AWR nor the V$ view indicates which tables or indexes you should be looking at to fix the high wait events. Oracle provides three V$ views to help you drill down to the *segment level*.

The segment-level dynamic performance views are V$SEGSTAT_NAME, V$SEGSTAT, and V$SEGMENT_STATISTICS. Using these, you can find out which of your tables and indexes are being subjected to high resource usage or high waits. Once you're aware of a performance problem due to high waits, you can use these segment-level views to find out exactly which table or index is the culprit and fix that object to reduce the waits and increase database performance. The V$SEGMENT_NAME view provides you with a list of all the segment levels that are being collected, and tells you whether the statistics are sampled or not.

Let's see how you can use these segment-level views to your advantage when you're confronted with a high number of wait events in your system. Say you look at the V$SYSTEM_EVENT view and realize that there are a large number of buffer busy waits. You should now examine the V$SEGMENT_STATISTICS view with a query such as the following to find out which object is the source of the high buffer busy waits. You can then decide on the appropriate corrective measures for this wait event, as discussed in the section "Important Oracle Wait Events" later in this chapter.

```
SQL> SELECT owner, object_name, object_type, tablespace_name
  2  FROM V$SEGMENT_STATISTICS
  3  WHERE statistic_name='buffer busy waits'
  4* ORDER BY value DESC;

OWNER          OBJECT_NAME      OBJECT_TYPE      TABLESPACE_NAME
---------      --------------   -----------      ----------------
SYSOWNER       LAB_DATA         TABLE            LAB_DATA_D
SYSOWNER       LAB_ADDR_I       INDEX            LAB_DATAS_I
SYSOWNER       PERS_SUMMARIES   TABLE            PERS_SUMMARIES_D
. . .
SQL>
```

Collecting Detailed Wait Event Information

Selecting data from V$ dynamic performance views and interpreting them meaningfully isn't always so easy to do. Because the views are dynamic, the information that they contain is constantly changing as Oracle updates the underlying tables for each wait event. Also, the wait-related dynamic performance views you just examined don't provide crucial data such as bind variable information. For a more detailed level of wait information, you can use one of the methods described in the following sections.

Method 1: Using the Oracle Event 10046 to Trace SQL Code

You can get all kinds of bind variable information by using a special trace called the 10046 trace, which is much more advanced than the SQL Trace utility you saw in Chapter 19. The use of this trace causes an output file to be written to the trace directory. You can set the 10046 trace in many ways by specifying various levels, and each higher level provides you with more detailed information. (Level 12 is used in the following case as an example only—it may give you much more information than necessary. Level 4 gives you detailed bind value information, and Level 8 gives you wait information.)

You can use the ALTER SESSION statement as follows:

```
SQL> ALTER SESSION SET EVENTS '10046 trace name context forever level 12';
Session altered.
SQL>
```

You can also incorporate the following line in your init.ora file:

```
event = 10046 trace name context forever, level 12
```

Method 2: Using the Oradebug Utility to Perform the Trace

You can use the oradebug utility as shown in the following example:

```
SQL> ORADEBUG SETMYPID
Statement processed.
SQL> ORADEBUG EVENT 10046 TRACE NAME CONTEXT FOREVER LEVEL 8;
Statement processed.
SQL>
```

In this example, SETMYPID indicates that you want to trace the current session. If you want a different session to be traced, you replace this with SETOSPID <Process Id>.

Method 3: Using the DBMS_SYSTEM Package to Set the Trace

Use the SET_EV procedure of the DBMS_SYSTEM package so you can set tracing on in any session, as shown in the following example:

```
SQL> EXECUTE SYS.DBMS_SYSTEM.SET_EV (9,271,10046,12,'');

PL/SQL procedure successfully completed.
SQL>
```

Method 4: Using the DBMS_MONITOR Package

The DBMS_MONITOR package provides you with an easy way to collect extended session trace information. You enable tracing of a user's session using the DBMS_MONITOR.SESSION_TRACE_ENABLE package. Here's the structure of the procedure:

```
DBMS_MONITOR.SESSION_TRACE_ENABLE(
    session_id   IN  BINARY_INTEGER DEFAULT NULL,
    serial_num   IN  BINARY_INTEGER DEFAULT NULL,
    waits        IN  BOOLEAN DEFAULT TRUE,
    binds        IN  BOOLEAN DEFAULT FALSE)
```

If you set the WAITS parameter to TRUE, the trace will contain wait information. Similarly, setting the BINDS parameter to TRUE will provide bind information for the session being traced.

If you don't set the SESSION_ID parameter or set it to NULL, your own session will be traced. Here's how you trace your session using the DBMS_MONITOR package:

```
SQL> EXECUTE dbms_monitor.session_trace_enable (waits=>TRUE, binds=>TRUE);
```

In addition to all the preceding methods of gathering wait information, you have the handy OEM Database Control tool, which lets you drill down to various items from the Database Control home page.

■**Note** Both the AWR report that you can obtain by using the `awrrpt.sql` script and the ADDM report that you can obtain with the `addmrpt.sql` script contain copious amounts of wait information.

Important Oracle Wait Events

The wait events listed in the sections that follow have a significant impact on system performance by increasing response times. Each of these events (and several other events) indicates an unproductive use of time because of an excessive demand for a resource, or contention for Oracle structures such as tables or the online redo log files.

■**Note** The query `SELECT NAME FROM V$EVENT_NAME` gives you the complete list of all Oracle wait events.

Buffer Busy Waits

The buffer busy waits event occurs in the buffer cache area when several processes are trying to access the same buffer. One session is waiting for another session's read of a buffer into the buffer cache. This wait could also occur when the buffer is in the buffer cache, but another session is changing it.

■**Note** Starting with the Oracle Database 10.2 release, the buffer busy wait has been divided into several events: you can have very few buffer busy waits, but a huge number of read by other session waits, which were previously reported as buffer busy waits.

You should observe the V$SESSION_WAIT view while this wait is occurring to find out exactly what type of block is causing the wait.

Two of the common causes of high buffer busy waits are contention on data blocks belonging to tables and indexes, and contention on segment header blocks. If you're using dictionary managed tablespaces or locally managed tablespaces with manual segment space management (see Chapter 7), you should proceed as follows:

- If the waits are primarily on data blocks, try increasing the PCTFREE parameter to lower the number of rows in each data block. You may also want to increase the INITRANS parameter to reduce contention from competing transactions.

- If the waits are mainly in segment headers, increase the number of freelists or freelist groups for the segment in question, or consider increasing the extent size for the table or index.

The best way to reduce buffer busy waits due to segment header contention is to use locally managed tablespaces with ASSM. ASSM also addresses contention for data blocks in tables and indexes.

Besides the segment header and data block contention, you could also have contention for rollback segment headers and rollback segment blocks. However, if you're using Automatic Undo Management (AUM), you don't have to do anything other than make sure you have enough space in your undo management tablespace to address the rollback (undo) headers and blocks, leaving table and index data blocks and segment headers as the main problem areas. The following query clearly shows that in this database, the buffer busy waits are in the data blocks:

```
SQL> SELECT class, count FROM V$WAITSTAT
  2  WHERE COUNT > 0
  3* ORDER BY COUNT DESC;

CLASS                 COUNT
---------------    ----------
data block            519731
undo block              5829
undo header             2026
segment header            25
SQL>
```

If data-block buffer waits are a significant problem even with ASSM, this could be caused by poorly chosen indexes that lead to large index range scans. You may try using global hash-partitioned indexes, and you can also tune SQL statements as necessary to fix these waits. Oracle seems to indicate that if you use AUM instead of traditional rollback segments, then two types of buffer busy waits, undo block and undo header, will go away. However, that's not the case in practice, as the following example from a database with AUM shows:

```
CLASS                 COUNT
---------------    ---------
undo header            29891
data block                52
segment header             1
```

Occasionally, you may have a situation where the buffer busy waits spike suddenly, seemingly for no reason. The sar utility (use the sar -d option) might indicate high request queues and service times. This often happens when the disk controllers get saturated by a high amount of I/O. Usually, you see excessive core dumps during this time, and if core dumps are choking your I/O subsystem, do the following:

- Move your core dump directory to a less busy file system, where it resides by itself.
- Use the following init.ora or SPFILE parameters to control core dumps in your system. Setting these parameters' values could reduce the size of a core dump to a few megabytes from a gigabyte or more:

```
SHADOW_CORE_DUMP = PARTIAL /* or NONE */
BACKGROUND_CORE_DUMP = PARTIAL /* or NONE */
```

- Investigate the core dumps and see whether you can fix them by applying necessary Oracle and operating-system patch sets.

Checkpoint Completed

The CHECKPOINT COMPLETED wait event means that a session is waiting for a checkpoint to complete. This could happen when you're shutting the database down or during normal checkpoints.

Db File Scattered Read

The db file scattered read wait event indicates that full table scans (or index fast full scans) are occurring in the database. The initialization parameter DB_FILE_MULTIBLOCK_READ_COUNT sets the number of blocks read at one time by Oracle. The database will automatically tune this parameter if you don't set any value for it in your parameter file. Although Oracle reads data in multiblock chunks, it scatters the data into noncontiguous cache buffers. If you don't have many full table scans and if they mainly consist of smaller tables, don't worry about it.

However, if this event is showing up as an important wait event, you need to look at it as an I/O-related problem—the database isn't able to cope with an excessive request for physical I/Os. There are two possible solutions. You can either reduce the demand for physical I/Os or increase the capacity of the system to handle more I/Os. You can reduce the demand for physical I/O by drilling down further to see whether one of the following solutions will work. Raising the buffer cache component of the SGA would normally contribute to lowering physical I/Os. However, I'm assuming that you're using Automatic Shared Memory Management by setting the SGA_TARGET initialization parameter, in which case your buffer cache is already optimally set by the database:

- Add missing indexes on key tables (unlikely in a production system).
- Optimize SQL statements if they aren't following an efficient execution plan.

If you don't see any potential for reducing the demand for physical I/O, you're left with no choice but to increase the number of disks on your system. You also need to make sure you're reducing the hot spots in your system by carefully distributing the heavily hit tables and indexes across the available disks. You can identify the datafiles where the full table or index fast full scans are occurring with the help of a query using the V$FILESTAT view. In this view, two columns are of great use:

- *phyrds*: The number of physical reads done
- *phyblkrd*: The number of physical blocks read

Obviously, the number of phyrds is equal to or close to the number of phyblkrds because almost all reads are single block reads. If the column phyrds shows a much smaller value than the phyblkrds column, Oracle is reading multiple blocks in one read—a full table scan or an index fast full scan, for example. Here's a sample query on the V$FILESTAT view:

```
SQL> SELECT file#, phyrds,phyblkrd
  2  FROMV$FILESTAT
  3* WHERE phyrds != phyblkrd;

     FILE#     PHYRDS    PHYBLKRD
--------- ------ --------
         1       4458       36533
         7      67923      494433
        15      28794      378676
        16      53849      408981
SQL>
```

Db File Sequential Read

The db file sequential read wait event signifies that a single block is being read into the buffer cache. This event occurs when you're doing an indexed read and you're waiting for a physical I/O call to return. This is nothing to be alarmed about, because the database has to wait for file I/O. However, you should investigate disk I/O if this statistic seems extraordinarily high. If disk sorts are high, you can make them lower by increasing the value of the PGA_AGGREGATE_TARGET initialization parameter. Because the very occurrence of this event proves that your application is making heavy use of an index, you can't do much to reduce the demand for physical I/Os in this case, unlike in the case of the db file scattered read event. Increasing the number of disks and striping indexes across them may be your best bet to reduce db file sequential read waits. If the objects aren't too large, you can use the DEFAULT and KEEP buffer pools to retain them in memory. However, if the objects are large, you may not have this option. Indexed reads are going to show up in most systems as a wait, and it's not necessarily a bad thing, because indexes are required in most cases for faster data retrieval.

Direct Path Read and Direct Path Write

The direct path read and direct path write events are waits that occur while performing a direct read or write into the PGA, bypassing the SGA buffer cache. Direct path reads indicate that sorts are being done on disk instead of in memory. They could also result from a busy I/O system. If you use automatic PGA tuning, you shouldn't encounter this problem too often.

Automatic tuning of the PGA by Oracle should reduce your disk sorts due to a low PGA memory allocation. Another solution may be to increase the number of disks, as this problem also results in an I/O system that can't keep up with the increased requests for reading blocks into the PGA. Of course, tuning the SQL statements themselves to reduce sorting wouldn't hurt in this case.

Free Buffer Waits

Free buffer waits usually show up when the database writer process is slow. The database writer process is simply unable to keep up with the requests to service the buffer cache. The number of dirty buffers in cache waiting to be written to disk is larger than the number of buffers the database writer process can write per batch. Meanwhile, sessions have to wait because they can't get free buffers to write to. First, you need to rule out whether the buffer cache is too small, and check the I/O numbers on the server, especially the write time, using an operating system tool. A check of the database buffer cache and a quick peek at the Database Control's Memory Advisor will show you the pattern of usage of the various memory components and if you're below the optimal buffer cache level, in which case you can increase the size of the buffer cache. Of course, if you're using Automatic Shared Memory Management, the database will size the SGA allocations for you.

The other reason for a high number of free buffer waits in your system is that the number of database writer processes is inadequate to perform the amount of work your instance needs to get done. As you know, you can add additional database writer processes to the default number of processes, which is one database writer process for every eight processors on your host machine. If your database performs heavy data modifications and you determine that the database writer is responsible for wait events, you can reduce these waits in most cases by increasing the number of database writer processes. You can choose a value between 2 and 20 for the DB_WRITER_PROCESSES initialization parameter. Oracle recommends that you use one database writer process for every four CPUs on your system. You can't change this variable on the fly, so you'll need to perform a system restart to change the number of database writer processes.

Enqueue Waits

Enqueues are similar to locks in that they are internal mechanisms that control access to resources. High enqueue waits indicate that a large number of sessions are waiting for locks held by other sessions. You can query the dynamic performance view V$ENQUEUE_STAT to find out which of the enqueues have the most wait times reported. You can do this by using the cum_wait_time (shows the cumulative time spent waiting for the enqueue) column of the view.

Note that the use of locally managed tablespaces eliminates several types of enqueues such as space transactions (ST) enqueues. In a system with a massive concurrent user base, most common enqueues are due to infrequent commits (or rollbacks) by transactions that force other transactions to wait for the locks held by the early transactions. In addition, there may be a problem with too few interested transactions list (ITL) slots, which also show up as transaction (TX) enqueues. Locally managed tablespaces let you avoid the most common types of space-related enqueues.

Latch Free

Latches are internal serialization mechanisms used to protect shared data structures in Oracle's SGA. You can consider a latch as a type of lock that's held for an extremely short time period. Oracle has several types of latches, with each type guarding access to a specific set of data. The latch free wait event is incremented when a process can't get a latch on the first attempt. If a required Oracle latch isn't available, the process requesting it keeps spinning and retrying to gain the access. This spinning increases both the wait time and the CPU usage in the system. Oracle uses about 500 latches, but two of the important latches that show up in wait statistics are the shared pool latch (and the library cache latches) and the cache buffers LRU chain. It's normal to see a high number of latch free events in an instance. You should worry about this wait event only if the total time consumed by this event is high.

High latch waits will show up in your AWR reports, or you can use the query shown in Listing 20-17 to find out your latch hit ratio.

Listing 20-17. *Determining the Latch Hit Ratio*

```
SQL> SELECT a.name "Latch Name",
     a.gets "Gets (Wait)",
     a.misses "Misses (Wait)",
     (1 - (misses / gets)) * 100 "Latch Hit Ratio %"
     FROM    V$LATCH a
     WHERE a.gets   != 0
     UNION
     SELECT a.name "Latch Name",
     a.gets "Gets (Wait)",
     a.misses "Misses (Wait)",
     100 "Latch Hit Ratio"
```

```
        FROM    V$LATCH a
        WHERE   a.gets   = 0
        ORDER BY 1;
SQL>
```

If the ratio isn't close to 1, it's time to think about tuning the latch contention in your instance. There's only one shared pool latch for the database, and it protects the allocation of memory in the library cache. The library cache latch regulates access to the objects present in the library cache. Any SQL statement, PL/SQL code, procedure, function, or package needs to acquire this latch before execution. If the shared pool and library cache latches are high, more often than not that's because the parse rates in the database are high. The high parse rates are due to the following factors:

- An undersized shared pool
- Failure to use bind variables
- Using dissimilar SQL statements and failing to reuse statements
- Users frequently logging off and logging back into the application
- Failure to keep cursors open after each execution
- Using a shared pool size that's too large

The cache buffers LRU chain latch free wait is caused by high buffer cache throughput, either due to full table scans or the use of unselective indexes, which lead to large index range scans. Unselective indexes can also lead to yet another type of latch free wait: the cache buffer chain latch free wait. These wait events are often due to the presence of hot blocks, so you need to investigate why that might be happening. If you see a high value for row cache object latch waits, it indicates contention for the dictionary cache, and you need to increase the shared pool memory allocation.

In most instances, latch waits tend to show up as a wait event, and DBAs sometimes are alarmed by their very presence in the wait event list. As with the other Oracle wait events, ask yourself this question: "Are these latch waits a significant proportion of my total wait time?" If the answer is no, don't worry about it—your goal isn't to try and eliminate all waits in the instance, because you can't do it.

Log Buffer Space

The log buffer space wait event indicates that a process waited for space in the log buffer. Either the log buffer is too small or the redo is being written faster than the log writer process can write it to the redo log buffer. If the redo log buffer is already large, then investigate the I/O to the disk that houses the redo log files. There's probably some contention for the disk, and you need to work on reducing the I/O contention. This type of wait usually shows up when the log buffer is too small, in which case you increase the log buffer size. A large log buffer tends to reduce the redo log I/O in general. Note that Oracle's default value for this parameter is several megabytes in size. If you have a large number of huge transactions, you might want to bump up the value of the LOG_BUFFER initialization parameter from its default value, although too high a value means that too much data may have to be written to the redo log files at one time.

Log File Switch

The log file switch wait event can occur when a session is forced to wait for a log file switch because the log file hasn't yet been archived. It can also occur because the log file switch is awaiting the completion of a checkpoint.

If the problem isn't due to the archive destination getting full, it means that the archive process isn't able to keep up with the rate at which the redo logs are being archived. In this case, you need to increase the number of archiver (ARC*n*) processes to keep up with the archiving work. The default for the ARC*n* process is 2. This is a static parameter, so you can't use this fix to resolve a slowdown right away.

You also need to investigate whether too-small redo log files are contributing to the wait for the log file switch. If the log file switch is held up pending the completion of a checkpoint, obviously the log files are too small and hence are filling up too fast. You need to increase the size of the redo log files in this case. Redo log files are added and dropped online, so you can consider this a dynamic change.

If you see high values for redo log space requests in V$SYSSTAT, that means that user processes are waiting for space in the redo log buffer. This is because the log writer process can't find a free redo log file to empty the contents of the log buffer. Resize your redo logs, with the goal of having a log switch every 15 to 30 minutes.

Log File Sync

You'll see a high number of waits under the log file sync category if the server processes are frequently waiting for the log writer process to finish writing committed transactions (redo) to the redo log files from the log buffer. This is usually the result of too-frequent commits, and you can reduce it by adopting batch commits instead of a commit after every single transaction. This wait event may also be the result of an I/O bottleneck.

Idle Events

You can group some wait events under the category *idle events*. Some of these may be harmless in the sense that they simply indicate that an Oracle process was waiting for something to do. These events don't indicate database bottlenecks or contention for Oracle's resources. For example, the system may be waiting for a client process to provide SQL statements for execution. The following list presents some common idle events:

- Rdbms ipc message: This is used by the background process, such as the log writer process and PMON, to indicate they are idle.

- SMON timer: The SMON process waits on this event.

- PMON timer: This indicates the PMON process idle event.

- SQL*Net message from client: This is the user process idle event.

You should ignore many idle events during your instance performance tuning. However, some events, such as the SQL*Net message from client event, may indicate that your application isn't using an efficient database connection strategy. In this case, you need to see how you can reduce these waits, maybe by avoiding frequent logging on and off by applications.

Examining System Performance

You can use the various operating system tools, such as vmstat, to examine system performance. You can also use the new V$OSSTAT dynamic view to figure out the performance characteristics of your system. The V$OSSTAT view provides operating system statistics in the form of busy ticks.

Here are some of the key system usage statistics:

- NUM_CPUS: Number of processors

- IDLE_TICKS: Number of hundredths of a second that all processors have been idle

- BUSY_TICKS: Number of hundredths of a second that all processors have been busy executing code

- USER_TICKS: Number of hundredths of a second that all processors have been busy executing user code

- SYS_TICKS: Number of hundredths of a second that all processors have been busy executing kernel code

- IOWAIT_TICKS: Number of hundredths of a second that all processors have been waiting for I/O to complete

The AVG_IDLE_WAITS, AVG_BUSY_TICKS, AVG_USER_TICKS, AVG_SYS_TICKS, and AVG_IOWAIT_TICKS columns provide the corresponding information average over all the processors. Here's a simple example that shows how to view the system usage statistics captured in the V$OSSTAT view:

```
SQL> SELECT * FROM V$OSSTAT;
```

STAT_NAME	VALUE	OSSTAT_ID
NUM_CPUS	16	0
IDLE_TICKS	17812	1
BUSY_TICKS	2686882247	2
USER_TICKS	1936724603	3
SYS_TICKS	750157644	4
IOWAIT_TICKS	1933617293	5
AVG_IDLE_TICKS	545952047	7
AVG_BUSY_TICKS	167700614	8
AVG_USER_TICKS	120815895	9
AVG_SYS_TICKS	46655696	10
AVG_IOWAIT_TICKS	120621649	11
OS_CPU_WAIT_TIME	5.3432E+13	13
RSRC_MGR_CPU_WAIT_TIME	0	14
IN_BYTES	6.2794E+10	1000
OUT_BYTES	0	1001
AVG_IN_BYTES	1.7294E+19	1004
AVG_OUT_BYTES	0	1005

```
17 rows selected.

SQL>
```

Know Your Application

Experts rely on hit ratios or wait statistics, or sometimes both, but there are situations in which both the hit ratios and the wait statistics can completely fail you. Imagine a situation where all the hit ratios are in the 99 percent range. Also, imagine that the wait statistics don't show any significant waiting for resources or any contention for latches. Does this mean that your system is running optimally? Well, your system is doing what you asked it to do extremely well, but there's no guarantee that your SQL code is processing things efficiently. If a query is performing an inordinate number of logical reads, the hit ratios are going to look wonderful. The wait events also won't show you a whole lot, because they don't capture the time spent while you were actually using the CPU. However, you'll be burning a lot of CPU time, because the query is making too many logical reads.

This example shows why it's important not to rely only on the hit ratios or the wait statistics, but also to look at the major consumers of resources on your instance with an intense focus. Check the Top Sessions list (sorted according to different criteria) on your instance and see if there's justification for the major consumers to be in that list.

Above all, try not to confuse the symptoms of poor performance with the causes of poor performance. If your latch rate is high, you might want to adjust some initialization parameters right away—after all, isn't Oracle a highly configurable database? You may succeed sometimes by relying solely on adjusting the initialization parameters, but it may be time to pause and question why exactly the latch rate is so high. More than likely, the high latch rate is due to application coding issues rather than a specific parameter setting. Similarly, you may notice that your system is CPU bound, but the reason may not be slow or inadequate CPU resources. Your application may again be the real culprit because it's doing too many unnecessary I/Os, even if they're mostly from the database buffer cache and not disk.

When you're examining wait ratios, understand that your goal isn't to make all the wait events go away, because that will never happen. Learn to ignore the unimportant, routine, and unavoidable wait events. As you saw in the previous section, wait events such as the SQL*Net message from client event reflect waits outside the database, so don't attribute these waits to a poorly performing database. Focus on the total wait time rather than the number of wait events that show up in your performance tables and AWR reports. Also, if the wait events make up only a small portion of response time, there's no point in fretting about them. As Einstein might say, the significance of wait events is relative—relative to the total response time and relative to the total CPU execution time.

Recently, there has been a surge in publications expounding the virtues of the wait event analysis-based performance approach (also called the *wait interface* approach). You can always use the buffer hit ratios and the other ratios for a general idea about how the system is using Oracle's memory and other resources, but an analysis of wait events is still a better bet in terms of improving performance. If you take care of the wait issues, you'll have taken care of the traditional hit ratios as well. For example, if you want to fix a problem that's the result of a high number of free buffer waits, you may need to increase the buffer cache. Similarly, if latch free wait events are troublesome, one of the solutions is to check whether you need to add more memory to the shared pool. You may fix a problem due to a high level of waits caused by the direct path reads by increasing the value of the PGA_AGGREGATE_TARGET parameter.

EXAMINING SQL RESPONSE TIME WITH THE DATABASE CONTROL

You can use the OEM Database Control to examine quickly the current SQL response time compared to a normal "baseline" SQL response time. The Database Control computes the SQL response time percentage by dividing the baseline SQL response time by the current SQL response time, both expressed in microseconds. If the SQL response time percentage exceeds 100 percent, then the instance is processing SQL statements slower than the baseline times. If the percentage is approximately equal to 100 percent, then the current response time and the baseline response time are equal, and your instance is performing normally. The SQL Response Time section is right on the Database Control home page.

Using the ADDM to Analyze Performance Problems

There's no question that the new ADDM tool should be the cornerstone of your performance-tuning efforts. In Chapter 17, I showed how you can manually get an ADDM report or use the OEM Database Control to view the ADDM analysis. Use the findings and recommendations of the ADDM advisor to fine-tune database performance. Here's the partial output from an ADDM analysis (invoked by running the addmrpt.sql script located in the $ORACLE_HOME/rdbms/admin directory). Listing 20-18 shows part of an ADDM report.

Listing 20-18. *An Abbreviated ADDM Report*

```
DETAILED ADDM REPORT FOR TASK 'TASK_1493' WITH ID 1493
-------------------------------------------------------------------------
                Analysis Period: 22-JUL-2008 from 07:01:02 to 17:00:36
            Database ID/Instance: 877170026/1
          Database/Instance Names: NINA/nina
                      Host Name: finance1
                Database Version: 10.2.0.0
                 Snapshot Range: from 930 to 940
                  Database Time: 801313 seconds
            Average Database Load: 22.3 active sessions
~~~~~~~~~~~~~~~~~~~~~~~~~~~~~~~~~~~~~~~~~~~~~~~~~~~~~~~~~~~~~~~~~~~~~~~~~~~~~~
FINDING 1: 24% impact (193288 seconds)
----------------------------------------
The buffer cache was undersized causing significant additional read I/O.

   RECOMMENDATION 1: DB Configuration, 24% benefit (193288 seconds)
      ACTION: Increase SGA target size by increasing the value of parameter
         "sga_target" by 1232 M.
   SYMPTOMS THAT LED TO THE FINDING:
      Wait class "User I/O" was consuming significant database time. (54%
      impact [436541 seconds])
FINDING 2: 19% impact (150807 seconds)
----------------------------------------
SQL statements consuming significant database time were found.
   RECOMMENDATION 1: SQL Tuning, 4.4% benefit (34936 seconds)
      ACTION: Run SQL Tuning Advisor on the SQL statement with SQL_ID
         "b3bkjk3ybcp5p".
         RELEVANT OBJECT: SQL statement with SQL_ID b3bkjk3ybcp5p and
         PLAN_HASH 954860671
. . .
```

ADDM may sometimes recommend that you run the Segment Advisor for a certain segments, or the Automatic SQL Advisor for a specific SQL statement. See Chapter 17 for a detailed analysis of an ADDM performance report.

Using AWR Reports for Individual SQL Statements

In Chapter 17, you learned how to use AWR reports to analyze the performance of the database during a time period encompassed by a pair of snapshots. As explained in that chapter, AWR reports are an excellent source of information for wait-related as well as other instance performance indicators. You can also use the AWR to produce reports displaying performance statistics *for a single SQL statement*, over a range of snapshot IDs. Listing 20-19 shows how you can get an AWR report for a particular SQL statement.

■**Note** The awrsqrpt.sql script seems to run slower than the instance-wide report-generating AWR script, awrrpt.sql, that you encountered in Chapter 17 during the introduction to AWR.

Listing 20-19. *Producing an AWR Report for a Single SQL Statement*

```
SQL> @$ORACLE_HOME/rdbms/admin/awrsqrpt.sql
Current Instance
~~~~~~~~~~~~~~~~

  DB Id      DB Name      Inst Num Instance
----------- ------------ -------- ------------
  877170026 PASPROD             1 pasprod
Specify the Report Type
~~~~~~~~~~~~~~~~~~~~~~~~

Would you like an HTML report, or a plain text report?
Enter 'html' for an HTML report, or 'text' for plain text
Defaults to 'html'
Enter value for report_type: text

Type Specified:                  text
Instances in this Workload Repository schema
~~~~~~~~~~~~~~~~~~~~~~~~~~~~~~~~~~~~~~~~~~~~~~

  DB Id      Inst Num DB Name      Instance      Host
----------- -------- ------------ ------------ ------------
* 877170026        1 PASPROD       pasprod       prod1
Using  877170026 for database Id
Using            1 for instance number
Specify the number of days of snapshots to choose from
~~~~~~~~~~~~~~~~~~~~~~~~~~~~~~~~~~~~~~~~~~~~~~~~~~~~~~~~~~

Entering the number of days (n) will result in the most recent
(n) days of snapshots being listed.  Pressing <return> without
specifying a number lists all completed snapshots.

Enter value for num_days: 3
Listing the last 3 days of Completed Snapshots
Instance  DB Name  Snap Id   Snap Started           Level
--------- -------- --------- ------------------- -----

pasprod   PASPROD   1        3829 23 Apr 2008 00:01       1
                            3830 23 Apr 2008 02:00       1
                            3832 23 Apr 2008 03:00       1
                            3833 23 Apr 2008 04:00       1
                            3834 23 Apr 2008 05:00       1
                            3835 23 Apr 2008 06:00       1
                    Specify the Begin and End Snapshot Ids
~~~~~~~~~~~~~~~~~~~~~~~~~~~~~~~~~~~~~~~~~~~~~~~

Enter value for begin_snap: 3830
Begin Snapshot Id specified: 3830
Enter value for end_snap: 3835
End    Snapshot Id specified: 3835
Specify the Report Name
~~~~~~~~~~~~~~~~~~~~~~~~~

The default report file name is 1_3830_3835.  To use this name,
press <return> to continue, otherwise enter an alternative.
Enter value for report_name
Using the report name 1_3830_3835
Specify the SQL Id
~~~~~~~~~~~~~~~~~~~

Enter value for sql_id: 9a64dvpzyrzza:
```

Operating System Memory Management

You can use the vmstat utility, as explained in Chapter 3, to find out whether enough free memory is on the system. If the system is paging and swapping, database performance will deteriorate and you need to investigate the causes. If the heavy consumption of memory is due to a non-Oracle process, you may want to move that process off the peak time for your system. You may also want to consider increasing the size of the total memory available to the operating system. You can use the vmstat command to monitor virtual memory on a UNIX system. The UNIX tool *top* shows you CPU and memory use on your system.

Analyzing Recent Session Activity with an ASH Report

The V$ACTIVE_SESSION_HISTORY view records active session activity by sampling all active sessions on a per-second basis. The V$ACTIVE_SESSION_HISTORY view's column data is similar to that of the V$SESSION history view, but contains only sample data from active sessions. An active session could be on the CPU, or could be waiting for a wait event that's not part of the idle wait class. When the AWR performs its snapshot, the data in the V$ACTIVE_SESSION_HISTORY view is flushed to disk as part of the AWR snapshot data. However, the data in the V$ACTIVE_SESSION_HISTORY VIEW isn't permanently lost when the AWR flushes the view's contents during its snapshots. Another view, the DBA_HIST_ACTIVE_SESS_HISTORY, stores snapshots of the V$ACTIVE_SESSION_HISTORY view.

You don't have to use either of the two ACTIVE_SESSION_HISTORY–related views to analyze session history. You can simply produce an ASH report, which contains both the current active session data from the V$ACTIVE_SESSION_HISTORY view as well as the historical active session data stored in the DBA_HIST_ACTIVE_SESS_HISTORY view. The ASH report shows you the SQL identifier of SQL statements, object information, session information, and relevant wait event information.

You can produce an ASH report by simply going to the OEM Database Control, or by running an Oracle-provided script. In fact, Oracle provides you with two ASH-related scripts, as follows:

- The ashrpt.sql script produces an ASH report for a specified duration for the default database.
- The ashrpti.sql script produces the same report as the ashrpt.sql script, but lets you specify a database instance.

Actually, the ashrpt.sql script defaults the DBID and instance number to those of the current instance, and simply runs the ashrpti.sql script. Both of the preceding described scripts are available in the $ORACLE_HOME/rdbms/admin directory. Here's how you get an ASH report for your instance:

```
SQL> @ORACLE_HOME/rdbms/admin/ashrpt.sql
```

You can then look at the ASH report, which is placed in the directory from which you ran the ashrpt.sql script. Chapter 18 explains a typical ASH report, in the section titled "Producing an ASH Report."

When a Database Hangs

So far in this chapter, you've looked at ways to improve performance—how to make the database go faster. Sometimes, however, your problem is something much more serious: the database seems to have stopped all of a sudden! The following sections describe the most important reasons for a hanging or an extremely slow-performing database, and how you can fix the problem ASAP.

One of the first things I do when the database seems to freeze is check and make sure that the archiver process is doing its job. The following sections describe the archiver process.

Handling a Stuck Archiver Process

If your archive log destination is full and there isn't room for more redo logs to be archived, the archiver process is said to be *stuck*. The database doesn't merely slow down—it freezes in its tracks. As you are aware, in an archive log mode the database simply won't overwrite redo log files until they're archived successfully. Thus, the database starts hanging when the archive log directory is full. It stays in that mode until you move some of the archive logs off that directory manually.

The Archiver Process

The archiver process is in charge of archiving the filled redo logs. It reads the control files to find out if there are any unarchived redo logs that are full, and then it checks the redo log headers and blocks to make sure they're valid before archiving them. You may have archiving-related problems if you're in the archive log mode but the archiver process isn't running for some reason. In this case, you need to start the archiver process by using the following command:

```
SQL> ALTER SYSTEM ARCHIVE LOG START;
```

If the archiver process is running but the redo logs aren't being archived, then you may have a problem with the archive log destination, which may be full. This causes the archiver process to become stuck, as you'll learn in the next section.

Archiver Process Stuck?

When the archiver process is stuck, all database transactions that involve any changes to the tables can't proceed any further. You can still perform SELECT operations, because they don't involve the redo logs.

If you look in the alert log, you can see the Oracle error messages indicating that the archiver process is stuck due to lack of disk space. You can also query the V$ARCHIVE view, which holds information about all the redo logs that need archiving. If the number of these logs is high and increasing quickly, you know your archiver process is stuck and that you need to clear it manually. Listing 20-20 shows the error messages you'll see when the archiver process is stuck.

Listing 20-20. *Database Hang Due to Archive Errors*

```
$ sqlplus system/system_passwd
ERROR:
ORA-00257: archiver error. Connect internal only, until freed.
$
$ oerr ora 257
00257, 00000, "archiver error. Connect internal only, until freed."
//*Cause: The archiver process received an error while trying to
// archive a redo log. If the problem is not resolved soon, the
// database will stop executing transactions. The most likely cause
// of this message is the destination device is out of space to
// store the redo log file.
// *Action: Check archiver trace file for a detailed description
// of the problem. Also verify that the device specified in the
// initialization parameter ARCHIVE_LOG_DEST is set up properly for
// archiving.
$
```

You can do either of the following in such a circumstance:

- Redirect archiving to a different directory.

- Clear the archive log destination by removing some archive logs. Just make sure you back up the archive logs to tape before removing them.

Once you create more space in the archive log directory, the database resumes normal operations, and you don't have to do anything further. If the archiver process isn't the cause of the hanging or frozen database problem, then you need to look in other places to resolve the problem.

If you see too many "checkpoint not complete" messages in your alert log, then the archiver process isn't causing the problem. The redo logs are causing the database slowdown, because they're unable to keep up with the high level of updates. You can increase the size of the redo logs online to alleviate the problem.

■**Note** The database logs all connections as SYS in the default audit trail, which is usually the $ORACLE_HOME/ rdbms/audit directory. If you don't have adequate space in that directory, it may fill up eventually, and you'll get an error when you try logging in as the SYS user. Delete the old audit trail files or choose an alternative location for them.

System Usage Problems

You need to check several things to make sure there are no major problems with the I/O subsystem or with the CPU usage. Here are some of the important things you need to examine:

- Make sure your system isn't suffering from a severe paging and swapping problem, which could result in a slower-performing database.

- Use top, sar, vmstat, or similar operating-system–level tools to check resource usage. Large queries, sorting, and space management operations could all lead to an increase in CPU usage.

- Runaway processes and excessive snapshot processes (SNPs) could gobble excessive CPU resources. Monitor any replication (snapshot) processes or DBMS_JOB processes, because they both use resource-hungry SNP processes. If CPU usage spikes, make sure no unexpected jobs are running in the database. Even if no jobs are executing currently, the SNP processes consume a great deal of CPU because they have to query the job queue constantly.

- High run queues indicate that the system is CPU bound, with processes waiting for an available processor.

- If your disk I/O is close to or at 100 percent and you've already killed several top user sessions, you may have a disk controller problem. For example, the 100 percent busy disk pack might be using a controller configured to 16-bit, instead of 32-bit like the rest of the controllers, causing a severe slowdown in I/O performance.

Excessive Contention for Resources

Usually when people talk about a database hang, they're mistaking a severe performance problem for a database hang. This is normally the case when there's severe contention for internal kernel-level resources such as latches and pins. You can use the following query to find out what the contention might be:

```
SQL> SELECT event, count(*)
  2  from v$session_wait
  3  group by event;
```

```
EVENT                             COUNT(*)
-----------------------------     --------
PL/SQL lock timer                    2
Queue Monitor Wait                   1
SQL*Net message from client         61
SQL*Net message to client            1
jobq slave wait                      1
pmon timer                           1
rdbms ipc message                   11
smon timer                           1
wakeup time manager                  1

9 rows selected.

SQL>
```

The previous query doesn't reveal any significant contention for resources—all the waits are for idle events.

If your database is performing an extremely high number of updates, contention for resources such as undo segments and latches could potentially be a major source of database-wide slowdowns, making it seem sometimes like the database is hanging. In the early part of this chapter, you learned how to analyze database contention and wait issues using the V$SESSION_WAIT view and the AWR output. On Windows servers, you can use the Performance Monitor and Event Monitor to locate possible high resource usage.

Check for excessive library cache contention if you're confronted by a database-wide slowdown.

Locking Issues

If a major table or tables are locked unbeknownst to you, the database could slow down dramatically in short order. Try running a command such as SELECT * FROM persons, for example, where persons is your largest table and is part of just about every SQL statement. If you aren't sure which tables (if any) might be locked, you can run the following statement to identify the table or index that's being locked, leading to a slow database:

```
SQL> SELECT l.object_id, l.session_id,
  2  l.oracle_username, l.locked_mode,
  3  o.object_name
  4  FROM V$LOCKED_OBJECT l,
  5  DBA_OBJECTS o
  6* WHERE  o.object_id=l.object_id;

OBJECT_ID   SESSION_ID   ORACLE_USERNAME   LOCKED_MODE   OBJECT_NAME
---------   ----------   ---------------   -----------   -----------
  6699         22        NICHOLAS               6        EMPLOYEES
SQL>
```

As the preceding query and its output show, user Nicholas has locked up the Employees table. If this is preventing other users from accessing the table, you have to remove the lock quickly by killing the locking user's session. You can get the locking user's SID from the session_id column in the preceding output, and the V$SESSION view gives you the SERIAL# that goes with it. Using the ALTER SYSTEM KILL . . . command, you can then kill the offending session. The same analysis applies to a locked index, which prevents users from using the base table. For example, an attempt to create an index or rebuild it when users are accessing the table can end up inadvertently locking up the table.

If there's a table or index corruption, that could cause a problem with accessing that object(s). You can quickly check for corruption by running the following statement:

```
SQL> ANALYZE TABLE employees VALIDATE STRUCTURE CASCADE;
Table analyzed.
SQL>
```

Abnormal Increase in Process Size

On occasion, there might be a problem because of an alarming increase in the size of one or more Oracle processes. You have to be cautious in measuring Oracle process size, because traditional UNIX-based tools can give you a misleading idea about process size. The following sections explain how to measure Oracle process memory usage accurately.

What Is Inside an Oracle Process?

An Oracle process in memory has several components:

- *Shared memory*: This is the SGA that you're so familiar with.

- *The executable*: Also known as TEXT, this component consists of the machine instructions. The TEXT pages in memory are marked read-only.

- *Private data*: Also called DATA or heap, this component includes the PGA and the User Global Area (UGA). The DATA pages are writable and aren't shared among processes.

- *Shared libraries*: These can be private or public.

When a new process starts, it requires only the DATA (heap) memory allocation. Oracle uses the UNIX implementation of shared memory. The SGA and TEXT components are visible to and shared by all Oracle processes, and they aren't part of the cost of creating new Oracle processes. If 1,000 users are using Oracle Forms, only one set of TEXT pages is needed for the Forms executable.

Unfortunately, most operating system tools such as ps and top give you a misleading idea as to the process size, because they include the common shared TEXT sizes in individual processes. Sometimes they may even include the SGA size. Solaris's pmap and HP's glance are better tools from this standpoint, as they provide you with a more accurate picture of memory usage at the process level.

■**Note** Even after processes free up memory, the operating system may not take the memory back, indicating larger process sizes as a result.

Measuring Process Memory Usage

As a result of the problems you saw in the previous section, it's better to rely on Oracle itself for a true indication of its process memory usage. If you want to find out the total DATA or heap memory size (the biggest nonsharable process memory component), you can do so by using the following query:

```
SQL> SELECT value, n.name|| '('||s.statistic#||')', sid
     FROM v$sesstat s, v$statname n
     WHERE s.statistic# = n.statistic#
     AND n.name like '%ga memory%'
     ORDER BY value;
```

If you want to find out the total memory allocated to the PGA and UGA memory together, you can issue the command in the next example. The query reveals that a total of more than 367MB of memory is allocated to the processes. Note that this memory is in addition to the SGA memory allocation, so you need to make allowances for both types of memory to avoid paging and swapping issues.

```
SQL> SELECT SUM(value)
     FROM V$SESSSTAT s, V$STATNAME n
     WHERE s.statistic# = n.statistic#
     AND n.name like '%ga memory%';

SUM(VALUE)
---------------
3674019536
1 row selected.
SQL>
```

If the query shows that the total session memory usage is growing abnormally over time, you might have a problem such as a memory leak. A telltale sign of a memory leak is when Oracle's memory usage is way outside the bounds of the memory you've allocated to it through the initialization parameters. The Oracle processes are failing to return the memory to the operating system in this case. If the processes continue to grow in size, eventually they may hit some system memory barriers and fail with the ora 4030 error:

```
$ oerr ora 4030
04030, 00000, "out of process memory when trying to allocate %s bytes (%s,%s)"
// *Cause:  Operating system process private memory has been exhausted
$
```

Note that Oracle tech support may request that you collect a *heap dump* of the affected Oracle processes (using the oradebug tool) to fix the memory leak problem.

If your system runs out of swap space, the operating system can't continue to allocate any more virtual memory. Processes fail when this happens, and the best way to get out of this mess is to see whether you can quickly kill some of the processes that are using a heavy amount of virtual memory.

Delays Due to Shared Pool Problems

Sometimes, database performance deteriorates dramatically because of inadequate shared pool memory. Low shared pool memory relative to the number of stored procedures and packages in your database could lead to objects constantly aging out of the shared pool and having to be executed repeatedly.

Problems Due to Bad Statistics

As you know by now, the Oracle Cost-Based Optimizer (CBO) needs up-to-date statistics so it can pick the most efficient method of processing queries. If you're using the Automatic Optimizer Statistics Collection feature, Oracle will naturally keep optimizer statistics up to date for you without any effort on your part. However, if you have deactivated the automatic statistics collection process, you could run the risk of not providing representative statistics to the CBO.

If you don't collect statistics regularly while lots of new data is being inserted into tables, your old statistics will soon be out of date, and the performance of critical SQL queries could head south. DBAs are under time constraints to collect statistics overnight or over a weekend. Sometimes, they may be tempted to use a small sample size while using the DBMS_STATS package to collect statistics. This could lead to unreliable statistics, resulting in the slowing down of query processing.

Collecting Information During a Database Hang

It can sometimes be downright chaotic when things come to a standstill in the database. You might be swamped with phone calls and anxious visitors to your office who are wondering why things are slow. Oftentimes, especially when serious unknown locking issues are holding up database activity, it's tempting just to bounce the database because usually that clears up the problem. Unfortunately, you don't know what caused the problem, so when it happens again, you're still just as ignorant as you were the first time. Bouncing the database also means that you're disconnecting all active users, which may not always be a smart strategy.

It's important that you collect some information quickly for two reasons. First, you might be able to prevent the problem next time or have someone in Oracle tech support (or a private firm) diagnose the problem using their specialized tools and expertise in these matters. Second, most likely a quick shutdown and restart of the database will fix the problem for sure (as in the case of some locking situations, for example). But a database bounce is too mighty a weapon to bring to bear on every similar situation. If you diagnose the problem correctly, simple measures may prevent the problem or help you fix it when it does occur. The following sections describe what you need to do to collect information on a slow or hanging database.

Using the Database Control's Hang Analysis Page

You can use OEM's Database Control during an instance slowdown to see a color-coded view of all sessions in the database. The Hang Analysis page provides the following information:

- Instantaneously blocked sessions
- Sessions in a prolonged wait state
- Sessions that are hung

Figure 20-1 shows the Database Control Hang Analysis page, which you can access from the Performance page. Click the Hang Analysis link under the Additional Monitoring Links section.

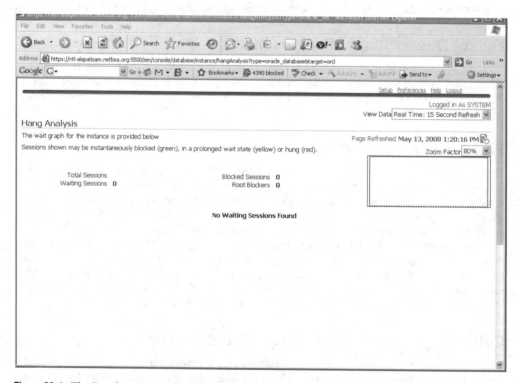

Figure 20-1. *The Database Control Hang Analysis page*

Gathering Error Messages

The first thing you do when you find out the database suddenly slowed down or is hanging is to look in some of the log files where Oracle might have sent a message. Quickly look in the alert log file to see whether there are any Oracle error messages or any other information that could pinpoint any problems. You can check the directory for background dumps for any other trace files with error messages. I summarize these areas in the following discussion.

Getting a Systemstate Dump

A systemstate dump is simply a trace file that is output to the user dump directory. Oracle (or a qualified expert) can analyze these dumps and tell you what was going on in the database when the hanging situation occurred. For example, if logons are slow, you can do a systemstate dump during this time, and it may reveal that most of the waits are for a particular type of library cache latch. To get a systemstate dump (for level 10), run the following command:

```
SQL> ALTER SESSION SET EVENTS 'immediate trace name systemstate level 10';
Session altered.
SQL>
```

■**Caution** Oracle Corp. strongly warns against customers setting events on their own. You may sometimes end up causing more severe problems when you set events. Please contact Oracle technical support before you set any event. For example, the event 10235 has been known to cause heavy latch contention.

You can send the resulting output to Oracle so it can analyze the output for you. Note that at this stage, you need to open a technical assistance request (TAR) with Oracle technical support through MetaLink (http://metalink.oracle.com). (The hanging database problem gets you a priority level 1 response, so you should hear from an analyst within minutes.) Oracle technical support may ask you for more information, such as a core dump, and ask you to run a debugger or another diagnostic tool and FTP the output to them.

Using the Hanganalyze Utility

The systemstate dumps, although useful, have several drawbacks, including the fact that they dump out too much irrelevant information and take too much time to complete, leading to inconsistencies in the dump information. The newer hanganalyze utility is more sophisticated than a systemstate dump. Hanganalyze provides you with information on resources each session is waiting for, and what is blocking access to those resources. The utility also provides you with a dependency graph among the active sessions in the database. This utility isn't meant to supplant the systemstate dumps; rather, you should use it to help make systemstate dumps more meaningful. Again, use this utility in consultation with Oracle technical support experts. Here's a typical HANGANALYZE command:

```
SQL> ALTER SESSION SET EVENTS 'immediate trace name HANGANALYZE level 3';
```

THE PROMISE AND THE PERFORMANCE

A few years ago, the Immigration and Naturalization Service (INS) of the United States created a new $36 million Student and Exchange Visitor Information System (SEVIS) to replace the old paper-based methods the INS had used for years to track foreign students in U.S. educational institutions. More than 5,400 high schools, colleges, and universities have to use SEVIS to enter the necessary information about enrolled students from other countries.

The INS had imposed a deadline by which all educational institutions had to switch over fully to the SEVIS system. However, it extended the deadline by at least two weeks amid several complaints about the system working slowly, if at all. Here are a few of those complaints from users across the country:

- Some employees in Virginia could enter data only in the mornings, before the West Coast institutions logged onto the system. In the afternoons, the system slowed to a crawl.

- From the University of Minnesota came complaints that that the officials were "completely unable" to use the system at all. The users mentioned that the system "was really jammed with users trying to get on." They also complained that the system was "unbelievably slow." An INS spokesperson admitted that the system had been "somewhat sluggish" and that schools were having trouble using the SEVIS system.

- The University of North Carolina complained that the situation, if it continued any further, was going to be "a real nightmare" and that it was already "starting to cause some problems."

- One worker at a college in Michigan was quoted as saying this in frustration: "Please tell me what I'm doing wrong, or I am going to quit."

The INS realized the colleges and universities weren't going to meet the deadline, and they announced a grace period after saying that "upgrades to the system" had greatly improved performance.

Behind the SEVIS system is an Oracle database that was performing awfully slowly. The system apparently couldn't scale well enough. When a large number of users got on, it ground to a halt. Obviously, the system wasn't configured to handle a high number of simultaneous operations. Was the shared server approach considered, for example? How were the wait statistics? I don't know the details. I do know that the Oracle database is fully capable of meeting the requirements of an application such as this. I picked this example to show that even in high-profile cases, DBAs sometimes have to eat humble pie when the database isn't tuned properly and consequently performance doesn't meet expectations.

A Simple Approach to Instance Tuning

Most of the instance tuning that DBAs perform is in response to a poorly performing database. The following sections present a brief summary of how you can start analyzing the instance to find out where the problem lies.

First, examine all the major resources such as the memory, CPUs, and storage subsystem to make sure your database isn't being slowed down by bottlenecks in these critical areas.

■**Note** Collecting baseline data about your database statistics, including wait events, is critically important for troubleshooting performance issues. If you have baseline data, you can immediately check whether the current resource-usage patterns are consistent with the load on the system.

What's Happening in the Database?

It isn't rare for a single user's SQL query to cause an instance-wide deterioration in performance if the query is bad enough. SQL statements are at the root of all database activity, so you should look at what's going on in the database right now. The following are some of the key questions to which you need to find answers:

- Who are the top users in your Top Sessions display?

- What are the exact SQL statements being executed by these users?

- Is the number of users unusually high compared to your baseline numbers for the same time period?

- Is the load on the database higher than what your baseline figures show for the time of the day or the time of the week or month?

- What top waits can you see in the V$SESSION or the V$SESSION_WAIT view? These real-time views show the wait events that are happening right now or that have just happened in the instance. You have already seen how you can find out the actual users responsible for the waits by using other V$ views.

A critical question here is whether the performance problem *du jour* is something that's sudden without any forewarnings or if it's caused by factors that have been gradually creeping up on you. Under the latter category are things such as a growing database, a larger number of users, and a larger number of DML operation updates than what you had originally designed the system for. These types of problems may mean that you need to redesign at least some of your tables and indexes with different storage parameters, and other parameters such as freelists. If, on the other hand, the database has slowed down suddenly, you need to focus your attention on a separate set of items.

Your best bet for analyzing what's happening in the database currently is to probe the ASH. You can easily find out the users, the objects, and the SQL causing the waits in your instance by using the queries based on V$ACTIVE_SESSION_HISTORY, which I explained in the section "Using the V$ACTIVE_SESSION_HISTORY View" earlier in this chapter. You can also run a quick ASH report encompassing the past few minutes to see where the bottlenecks may lie, and who is causing them.

Tip The OEM Database Control provides the Gather Statistics Wizard, which you can use if there are performance issues due to out-of-date statistics for fixed and dictionary objects.

Using the OEM Database Control to Examine Database Performance

I reviewed the OEM Database Control and Grid Control in Chapter 19. It's nice to learn about all the different V$ views regarding waits and performance, but nothing beats the Database Control when it comes to finding out quickly what's happening in your database at any given time. I present a simple approach to using the Database Control's various performance-related pages in the following sections.

The Database Control Home Page

Start your performance analysis by looking at the following three instance performance charts on the Database Control's home page. Figure 20-2 shows the Database Control home page.

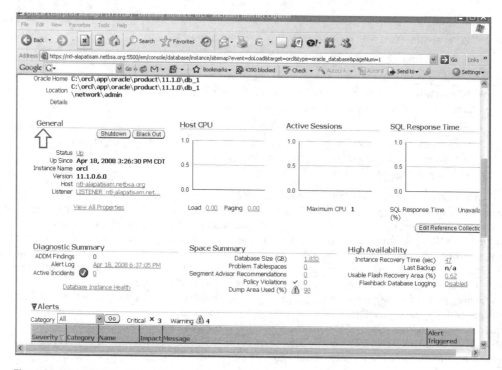

Figure 20-2 the *OEM Database Control home page*

Host CPU

The CPU consumption on the host server is shown in the form of a bar chart. The chart shows two categories: the *instance* and another category called *other*, which represents all the processes that don't belong to the database instance.

Active Sessions

The Active Sessions chart is a key chart, because it shows the extent of performance bottlenecks in your database instance. The chart consists of three components:

- CPU
- User I/O
- Wait

The Active Sessions chart shows the time consumed by the three items: CPU, User I/O, and Wait. You can drill down to each of these categories by clicking on the respective links. Note that the Wait category includes all waits in the instance except User I/O, which is shown in a separate category by itself.

SQL Response Time

The SQL Response Time chart provides a quick idea about how efficiently the instance is executing SQL statements. If the current SQL response ratio exceeds the baseline response ratio of 100 percent, then the SQL statements are executing slower than "normal." If the SQL Response Time shows a small response percentage, then you have inefficient SQL statement processing in the instance.

■ Note If you have a pre-Oracle Database 10*g* database, you may have to configure certain things for the SQL activity metrics to show up in the SQL Response Time chart. You do this by using the Database Configuration wizard, which you activate by clicking the Configure button in the SQL Activity Monitoring file under the Diagnostic Summary.

Using the ADDM Analysis in the Performance Analysis Section

The Performance Analysis section of the Database Control home page summarizes the most recent ADDM analysis. Figure 20-3 shows the Performance Analysis section. From here, you can click any of the findings to analyze any performance issues further. ADDM reports, which use the AWR statistics, provide you with a quick top-down analysis of instance activity.

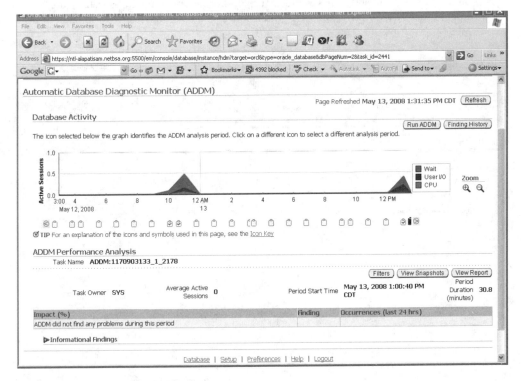

Figure 20-3. *Summary of ADDM findings*

Using the Database Performance Page

The Database Performance page is your jump-off point for evaluating instance performance. This page helps you do the following:

- Check for problems both within the database and the system.
- Run the ASH report to get a quick session-sampling data-based performance diagnostic report.
- Quickly see what bottlenecks exist within the system.
- Run ADDM reports.
- For slow or hung systems, access the Memory Access Mode.

Using the Memory Access Mode

You can view the Performance page in the default mode, which is called the SQL Access Mode, or the new Memory Access Mode. The SQL Access Mode works through SQL statements that mostly query the V$ dynamic performance view to obtain instance performance data. However, when the database is running painfully slowly, or is completely hung, running in the SQL Access Mode puts further stress due to the additional parsing and execution load of the SQL statements run by the OEM interface to diagnose instance performance. If your instance is already facing heavy library cache contention, your attempt to diagnose the problem will exacerbate the situation.

Oracle recommends that you switch to the Memory Access Mode while diagnosing slow or hung systems. Under this mode, the database gets its diagnostic information straight from the SGA, using more lightweight system calls than the resource-intensive SQL statements that are employed during the default SQL Access Mode. Because the data is sampled more frequently under the Memory Access Mode, you're less likely to miss events that span short intervals of time as well. Figure 20-4 shows how to use the drop-down window to switch between the Memory Access Mode and the SQL Access Mode.

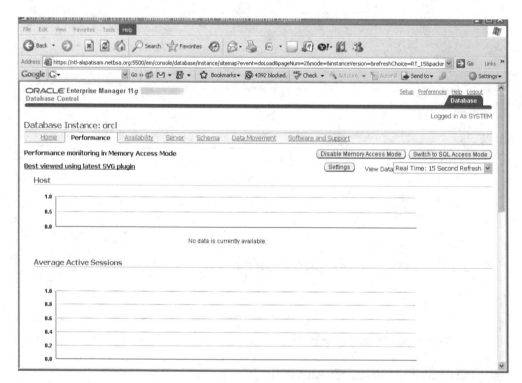

Figure 20-4. *Using the Performance page in the Memory Access Mode*

The following sections describe the main charts you'll see on the Database Performance page.

Host

The Host chart indicates whether there is a CPU bottleneck. If the number of users is low while the Host section shows a high run-queue length, it means that the database users may not be the main contributing factor for high CPU consumption. Look at what else may be running on your system and consuming the CPU resources.

Average Active Sessions

The Average Active Sessions chart shows performance problems within your instance, by focusing on the wait events in your instance. This is the key chart in the Performance page and should be the starting point of a performance analysis using the OEM. Figure 20-5 shows the Average Active Sessions chart. The chart shows you which of the active sessions are waiting on CPU and which are waiting on an event.

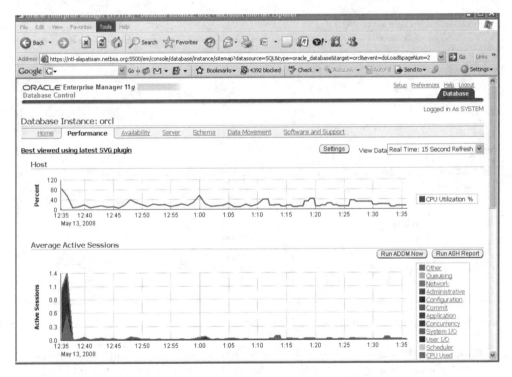

Figure 20-5. *The Average Active Sessions page of the Database Control*

The Average Active Sessions chart is color coded for your benefit. Green represents users on the CPU and the other colors show users waiting on various events such as disk I/O, locks, or network communications. Here's how you can tell whether you have too many waits in your instance: if the level of waits is twice the Max CPU line, you have too many waits, and should look at tuning the instance.

To the right of the Average Active Sessions screen, you can see the breakdown of the components that contribute to session time. For example, if you see user I/O as the main culprit for high
waits, you can click this component to find out details about the wait. Figure 20-5 also shows the
buttons you can click to run the ADDM or get an ASH report.

You can also click the link for Top Activity to find out details about the sessions that are most
responsible for waits in your instance right now. Figure 20-6 shows the Top Activity page of the Database Control. Database activity is ranked into Top SQL and Top Sessions. You can run the SQL Tuning
Advisor from here to get tuning recommendations about the top SQL statements.

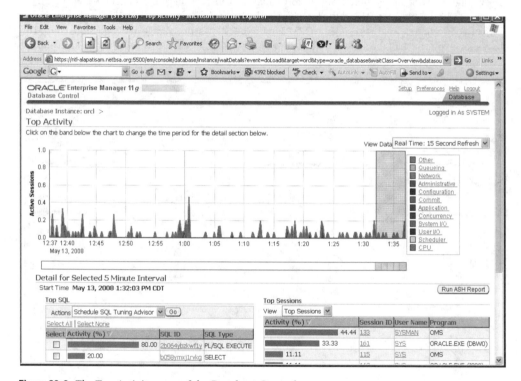

Figure 20-6. *The Top Activity page of the Database Control*

If you suspect that an individual session is wait bound or you get complaints from particular
users that their sessions are running slowly, you can examine the Top Sessions page. You can go the
Top Sessions page by clicking the Top Sessions link under the Additional Monitoring Links group on
the Performance page. Once you get to the Top Sessions page, click the username and SID you're
interested in. That takes you to the Session Details page for that session. By clicking the Wait Event
History tab in the Session Details page, you can see the nature of the recent waits for that session.
Figure 20-7 shows the Wait Event History for a session.

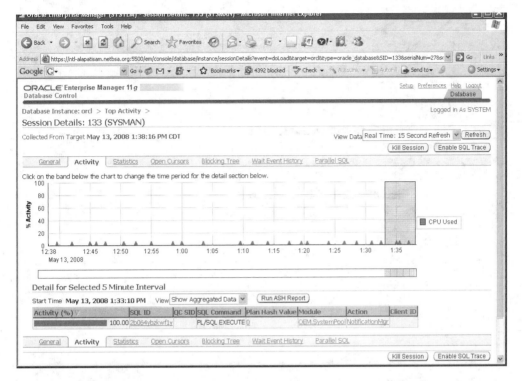

Figure 20-7. *The Wait Event History for a session*

The Performance Data Report Page

You can get to the Performance Data Report page by clicking the Create ASH Report button in the Average Active Sessions screen on the Database Control's Performance home page. The AWR reports are good for analyzing instance performance, but they're usually collected at 30-minute or 1-hour intervals. What if you have a three-to-four-minute performance spike that's not shown in the aggregated AWR report? ASH reports focus on session-sampling data over a recent period of time.

When you click the Create ASH Report button, you're given a choice as to the time period over which you want to create your ASH report. You can choose a time period that lies within the last seven days, because that's how long the AWR saves its statistics. Remember that ASH statistics are saved in the AWR repository. Figure 20-8 shows the ASH report, which relies on the V$ACTIVE_SESSION_HISTORY view. This is the same ASH report that you can produce by running the ashrpt.sql script. It contains information about the following items:

- Top Events

- Load Profile

- Top SQL

- Top Sessions, including Top Blocking Sessions

- Other entities causing contention in the instance, including Top Database Objects, Top Database Files, and Top Latches

- Activity Over Time

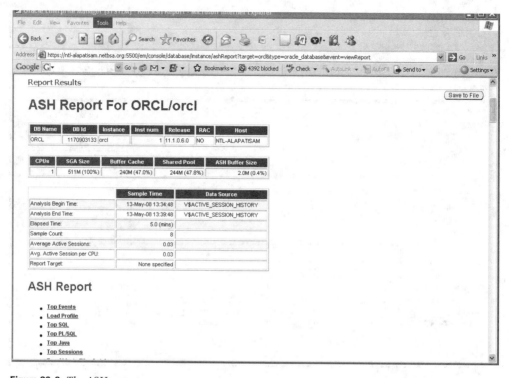

Figure 20-8. *The ASH report*

Are There Any Long-Running Transactions?

You can use the V$SQL view, as shown in the following example, to find out which of the SQL statements in the instance are taking the most time to finish and are the most resource intensive. The query ranks the transactions by the total number of elapsed seconds. You can also rank the statements according to CPU seconds used.

```
SQL> SELECT hash_value, executions,
  2  ROUND (elapsed_time/1000000, 2) total_time,
  3  ROUND (cpu_time/1000000, 2) cpu_seconds
  4  FROM (SELECT * FROM V$SQL
  5  ORDER BY elapsed_time desc);

HASH_VALUE EXECUTIONS   TOTAL_TIME  CPU_SECONDS
---------- ----------   ----------  -----------
 238087931    168          9.51        9.27
1178035321    108          4.98        5.01
. . .
SQL>
```

Once you have the value for the HASH_VALUE column from the query you just ran, it's a simple matter to find out the execution plan for this statement, which is in your library cache. The following query uses the V$SQL_PLAN view to get you the execution plan for your longest-running SQL statements:

```
SQL> SELECT * FROM V$SQL_PLAN WHERE hash_value = 238087931;
```

Is Oracle the Problem?

Just because your database users are complaining, you shouldn't be in a hurry to conclude that the problem lies within the database. After all, the database doesn't work in a vacuum—it runs on the server and is subject to the resource constraints and bottlenecks of that server. If the non-Oracle users on the server are using up critical resources such as CPU processing and disk I/O, your database may be the victim of circumstances, and you need to look for answers outside the database. That's why it's critical that DBAs understand how to measure general system performance, including memory, the disk storage subsystem, the network, and the processors. In the following sections you'll take a look at the system resources you should focus on.

Is the Network Okay?

One of the first things you need to do when you're investigating slowdowns is to rule out network-related problems. Quite often, users complain of being unable to connect to the system, or being abruptly disconnected from the system. Check your round-trip ping times and the number of collisions. Your network administrator should check the Internet connections and routers.

On the Oracle end, you can check the following dynamic views to find out if there's a slowdown due to a network problem. The V$SESSION_EVENT view shows the average amount of time Oracle waits between messages in the average wait column. The V$SESSION_WAIT view, as you've seen, shows what a session is waiting for, and you can see whether waits for network message transport are higher than normal.

If the time for SQL round-trips is extremely long, it could reflect itself as a high amount of network-related wait time in the V$ views. Check to see whether your ping time for network round-trips has gone up appreciably. You should discuss with your network administrator what you can do to decrease the waits for network traffic.

You may explore the possibility of setting the parameter TCP,NODELAY=TRUE in your sqlnet.ora file. This results in TCP sending packets without waiting, thus increasing response time for real-time applications.

If the network seems like one of your constant bottlenecks, you may want to investigate the possibility of using the shared server approach instead of the dedicated server approach for connecting users to your database. By using a shared server and its connection pooling feature, you can reduce the number of physical network connections and thus help your application scale more efficiently to large user bases.

Is the System CPU Bound?

Check the CPU performance to make sure a runaway process or a valid Oracle process isn't hogging one or more processes and contributing to the system slowdown. Often, killing the runaway processes or the resource-hogging sessions will bring matters to a more even keel. Using the OEM Database Control, you can get a quick idea about the breakdown of CPU usage among parse, recursive, and other usage components.

Normally, you should expect to see no more than 20 to 25 percent of total CPU usage by the system itself, and about 60 to 65 percent usage by the Oracle application. If the system usage is close to 50 percent, it's an indication that there are too many system calls, for example, which leads to excessive use of the processors.

As you learned earlier in this chapter, the V$SESSTAT view shows CPU usage by session. Using the following query, you can find out the top CPU-using Oracle sessions. You may want to look into the actual SQL that these sessions are executing.

```
SQL> SELECT a.sid,a.username, s.sql_text
     FROM V$SESSION a, V$SQLTEXT s
     WHERE a.sql_address = s.address
     AND a.sql_hash_value = s.hash_value
     AND a.username  = '&USERNAME'
     AND A.STATUS='ACTIVE'
     ORDER BY a.username,a.sid,s.piece;
```

Is the System I/O Bound?

Before you go any further analyzing other wait events, it's a good idea to rule out whether you're limited by your storage subsystem by checking your I/O situation. Are the read and write times on the host system within the normal range? Is the I/O evenly distributed, or are there hot spots with one or two disks being hit hard? If your normal, healthy I/O rates are 40–50/ms and you're seeing an I/O rate of 80/ms, obviously something is amiss. The AWR and ASH reports include I/O times (disk read and disk write) by datafile. This will usually tip you off about what might be causing the spike. For example, if the temporary tablespace datafiles are showing up in the high I/O list often, that's usually an indication that disk sorting is going on, and you need to investigate that further.

You can use the V$SYSTEM_EVENT view to verify whether the top wait events include events such as db file scattered read, db file sequential read, db file single write, and Logfile parallel write, which are database file, log file, and redo log file-related wait events. You can run an AWR report and identify the tablespaces and datafiles causing the I/O contention. Use the V$SQLAREA view, as shown in this chapter, to identify SQL statements that lead to high disk reads and have them tuned.

Too often, a batch program that runs into the daytime could cause spikes in the I/O rates. Your goal is to see whether you can rule out the I/O system as the bottleneck. Several of the wait events that occur in the Oracle database, such as the db file sequential read and db file scattered read waits, can be the result of extremely heavy I/O in the system. If the average wait time for any of these I/O-related events is significant, you should focus on improving the I/O situation. You can do two things to increase the I/O bandwidth: reduce the I/O workload or increase the I/O bandwidth. In Chapter 21, you learned how you can reduce physical I/Os by proper indexing strategies and the use of efficient SQL statements.

Improving SQL statements is something that can't happen right away, so you need to do other things to help matters in this case. This means you need to increase the I/O bandwidth by doing either or both of the following:

- Make sure that the key database objects that are used heavily are spread evenly on the disks.

- Increase the number of disks.

Storage disks are getting larger and larger, but the I/O rates aren't quite keeping up with the increased disk sizes. Thus, servers are frequently I/O bound in environments with large databases. Innovative techniques such as file caching might be one solution to a serious I/O bottleneck. On average, about 50 percent of I/O activity involves less than 5 percent of the total datafiles in your database, so caching this limited number of hot files should be a win. Caching gives you the benefit of read/write operations at memory speeds, which could be 200 times faster than disk speed. You can include your temp, redo log, and undo tablespace files, as well as the most frequently used table and index datafiles on file cache accelerators.

It's possible for large segments to waste a lot of disk space due to fragmentation caused by update and delete operations over time. This space fragmentation could cause severe performance degradation. You can use the Segment Advisor to find out which objects are candidates for a space reclamation exercise due to excessive fragmentation within the segment.

Is the Database Load Too High?

If you have baseline numbers for the database load, you can see whether the current load on the database is relatively too high. Pay attention to the following data, which you can obtain from the V$SYSSTAT view: physical reads and writes, redo size, hard and soft parse counts, and user calls. You can also check the Load Profile section of the AWR report for load data that's normalized over transactions and over time.

Checking Memory-Related Issues

As you saw earlier in this chapter, high buffer cache and shared pool hit ratios aren't guarantees of efficient instance performance. Sometimes, an excessive preoccupation with hit ratios can lead you to allocate too much memory to Oracle, which opens the door to serious problems such as paging and swapping at the operating-system level. Make sure that the paging and swapping indicators don't show anything abnormal. High amounts of paging and swapping slow down everything, including the databases on the server.

Due to the virtual memory system used by most operating systems, a certain amount of paging is normal and to be expected. If physical memory isn't enough to process the demand for memory, the operating system will go to the disk to use its virtual memory, and this results in a page fault. Processes that result in high page faults are going to run slowly.

When it comes to Oracle memory allocation, don't forget to pay proper attention to PGA memory allocation, especially if you're dealing with a DSS-type environment. Databases that perform a large number of heavy sorting and hashing activities need a high amount of PGA memory allocation. The database self-tunes the PGA, but you still have to ensure that the pga_aggregate_target value is high enough for Oracle to perform its magic.

■Tip Unlike the SGA, the PGA memory allocation isn't immediately and permanently allocated to the Oracle database. Oracle is allowed to use PGA memory up to the limit specified by the PGA_TARGET parameter. Once a user's job finishes executing, the PGA memory used by the job is released back to the operating system. Therefore, you shouldn't hesitate to use a high value for the PGA_TARGET initialization parameter. There's absolutely no downside to using a high number, and it guarantees that your instance won't suffer unnecessary disk sorting and hashing.

See whether you can terminate a few of the Top Sessions that seem to be consuming inordinate amounts of memory. It's quite possible that some of these processes are orphan or runaway processes.

Are the Redo Logs Sized Correctly?

If the redo logs are too few or if they are too small relative to the DML activity in the database, the archiver process will have to work extra hard to archive the filled redo log files. This may cause a slowdown in the instance. It's easy to resize the redo logs or add more redo log groups. When you use the FAST_START_MTTR_TARGET parameter to impose a ceiling on instance recovery time, Oracle will checkpoint as frequently as necessary to ensure the instance can recover from a crash within the MTTR setting. You must ensure that the redo logs are sized large enough to avoid additional checkpointing. You can get the optimal redo log size from the OPTIMAL_LOGFILE_SIZE column from the V$INSTANCE_RECOVERY view. You can also use the Database Control's Redo Log Groups page to get advice on sized redo logs. As a rule of thumb, Oracle recommends that you size the log files so they switch every 20 minutes.

Is the System Wait Bound?

If none of the previous steps indicated any problems, chances are that your system is suffering from a serious contention for some resource such as library cache latches. Check to see whether there's contention for critical database resources such as locks and latches. For example, parsing similar SQL statements leads to an excessive use of CPU resources and affects instance performance by increasing the contention for the library cache or the shared pool. Contention for resources manifests itself in the form of wait events. The wait event analysis earlier in this chapter gave you a detailed explanation of various critical wait events. You can use AWR and ASH reports to examine the top wait events in your database.

The V$SESS_TIME_MODEL (and the V$SYS_TIME_MODEL) view is useful in finding out accumulated time for various database operations at the individual session level. This view helps you understand precisely where most of the CPU time is being spent. As explained in Chapter 17, the V$SESS_TIME_MODEL view shows the following things, among others:

- *DB time*, which is the elapsed time spent in performing database user-level calls.

- *DB CPU* is the amount of CPU time spent on database user-level calls.

- *Background CPU time* is the amount of CPU time used by the background processes.

- *Hard parse elapsed time* is the time spent hard parsing SQL statements.

- *PL/SQL execution elapsed time* is the amount of time spent running the PL/SQL interpreter.

- *Connection management call elapsed time* is the amount of time spent making session connect and disconnect calls.

You can use segment data in the V$SEGMENT_STATISTICS view to find out the hot table and index segments causing a particular type of wait, and focus on eliminating (or reducing, anyway) that wait event.

The Compare Periods Report

Let's say you encounter a situation where one of your key nightly batch jobs is running past its time window and continuing on into the daytime, where it's going to hurt the online OLTP performance. You *know* the batch job used to finish within the stipulated time, but now it's tending to take a much longer time. As of Oracle Database 10g Release 2, you can use the Database Control's Compare Periods Report to compare the changes in key database metrics between two time intervals. As you know, an AWR snapshot captures information between two points in time. However, you can use the Time Periods Comparison feature to examine the difference in database metrics between two different time intervals or periods, by analyzing performance statistics captured by *two sets* of AWR snapshots. If your nightly batch job ran just fine on Tuesday but was slow on Wednesday, you can find out why, using the Compare Periods Report.

To use the Compare Periods Report, use the following steps:

1. In the Database Control home page, click the Performance tab.

2. Under the Additional Monitoring Links group, click the Snapshots link.

3. In the drop-down list for Actions, select Compare Periods and click Go.

4. The Compare Periods: First Period End page appears. You must select the start time for the comparison analysis by selecting an ending snapshot ID for the first period. You may also choose a time period, if you wish, instead of the ending snapshot ID. Click Next.

5. The Compare Periods: Second Period Start page is next. You must select a snapshot ID to mark the beginning of the second period. Click Next.

6. The Compare Periods: Second Period End page is next. You select the ending snapshot for the second period on this page and click Next.

7. The Compare Periods: Review page is next, as shown in Figure 20-9. It shows the first period and second period beginning and ending snapshot IDs. After confirming that the first and second period ranges are correct, click Finish.

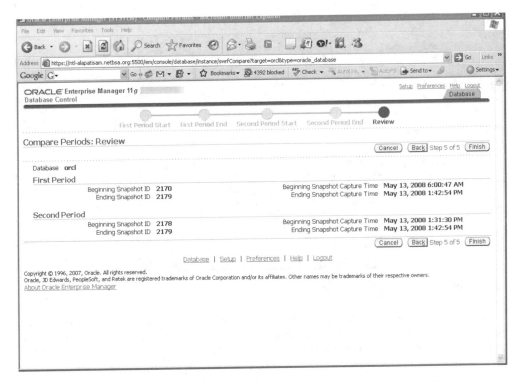

Figure 20-9. *The Compare Periods: Review page*

8. You'll now get the Compare Period: Results page, which summarizes the differences in key database metrics between the two periods.

Going through the differences in key database metrics between the two periods helps you identify the root causes of the performance slowdown in the latter period when compared to the earlier "good" period. You can also view the database configuration differences between the two periods as well.

To compare the two periods in detail and to drill down into various items such as SQL statements executed, SGA usage, and so on, click the Report link in the Compare Periods: Results page. You can see a nicely formatted report comparing the two periods on the basis of configuration, top five timed events, and the load profile. By viewing the various statistics for the two periods, you can determine whether there was excessive load or some such thing during the second period.

At the bottom of the report, you'll find the Report Details section, with links for various items like wait events, I/O statistics, segment statistics, and SGA statistics. You can click any of these links to drill down into what exactly went on inside the database during the two periods. For example, by clicking the SQL Statistics link, you can get to the top ten SQL statements compared by execution time, CPU time, buffer gets, physical reads, and so on. For example, Figure 20-10 shows the top ten SQL statements compared on the basis of physical reads during each period.

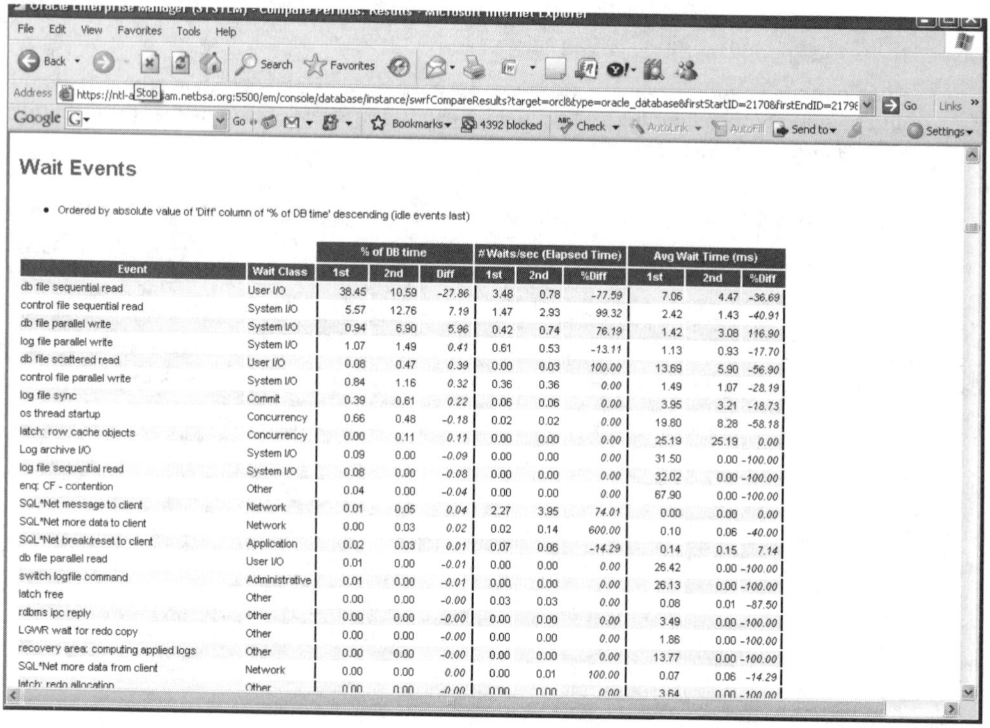

Figure 20-10. *The top 10 SQL comparison report*

Instead of running myriad SQL scripts and manually examining various statistics, as is the tradition, you can use the Compare Periods feature to zoom in quickly on the reasons for deterioration in recent database performance compared to a past period of time.

Eliminating the Contention

Once you identify wait events due to contention in the system, you need to remove the bottleneck. Of course, this is easier said than done in the short run. You may be able to fix some contention problems right away, whereas you may need more time with others. Problems such as high db file scattered read events, which are due to full table scans, may indicate that the I/O workload of the system needs to be reduced. However, if the reduction in I/O requires creating new indexes and rewriting SQL statements, obviously you can't fix the problem right away. You can't add disks and rearrange objects to reduce hot spots right away either. Similarly, most latch contention requires changes at the application level. Just make sure you don't perform a whole bunch of changes at once—you'll never be able to find out what fixed the problem (or in some cases, what made it worse).

The trick, as usual, is to go after the problems you can fix in the short run. Problems that you can fix by changing the memory allocation to the shared pool or the buffer cache you can easily handle almost immediately by dynamically adjusting the cache values. You can also take care of any changes that concern the redo logs right away. If you notice one or two users causing a CPU bottleneck, it may be a smart idea to kill those sessions so the database as a whole will perform better. As you know, prevention is much better than a cure, so consider using the Oracle Database Resource Manager tool (Chapter 12 shows you in detail how to use the Database Resource Manager) to create resource groups and prevent a single user or group from monopolizing the CPU usage.

If intense latch contention is slowing your database down, you probably should be setting the CURSOR_SHARING initialization parameter's value to FORCE or SIMILAR to ameliorate the situation.

Most other changes, though, may require more time-consuming solutions. Some changes may even require major changes in the code or the addition or modification of important indexes. However, even if the problem isn't fixed immediately, you have learned your craft, and you're on the right path to improving instance performance.

Although I've discussed various methods and techniques that use SQL scripts to analyze instance performance, try to make the OEM Database Control (or Grid Control) the center of your database performance monitoring, and use Oracle's powerful tools, such as the ADDM, to save time. The AWR and ASH reports are also highly useful when searching for root causes of performance problems.

Real Application Testing

One of the biggest problems facing a DBA is how to figure out the potential performance impact of a major system change, such as an upgrade to a new release of the database server, for example. Several third-party tools can help you test the changes, but Oracle provides you the new Real Application Testing option, also known as Total Recall, which is an easy-to-use solution that enables you to test the impact of system changes in a test environment before introducing those changes in the production system. You can thus safely introduce changes into your system without any adverse impact. Real Application Testing consists of two distinct features, Database Replay and the SQL Performance Analyzer, that together provide a complete solution to assess the impact of major system changes. I explain these features in the following sections.

Database Replay

When you're planning a major system change, you spend a significant amount of time testing your system before cutting over to production. No matter how much prior testing you perform, there's no guarantee that the production cutover to the new system will be trouble free, as you've never had the chance to "test" in the production environment itself. Oracle offers two brand-new tools called Database Replay and the SQL Performance Analyzer as part of the new Real Application Testing, or Total Recall, feature, to help test your application performance before an actual system change, thus providing you great change management support. I discuss the Database Replay feature first in this section and explain the SQL Performance Analyzer feature toward the end of the chapter.

Database Replay offers you a way to test your system changes on a test system where you can simulate the actual production workload. You first capture the actual production workload over a representative period such as a peak period and replay it on a test system, thus re-creating your production system on a test system. The replay adheres to the original production concurrency and timing characteristics. The replay executes the RDBMS code in a way similar to how it was executed on the production system. The way it does this is by replaying all external client requests made to the RDBMS. The testing process will reveal whether there are any significant performance differences or errors between the before and after system change performance. Database Replay will also recommend fixes to the problems it encounters during the production workload replay. Database Replay offers a powerful, easy-to-implement system that lets you test system changes with confidence. If you're moving from a single instance to an Oracle RAC environment, for example, you can test the database performance on a test system first before making the production cut over.

You can use Database Replay to test operating system and database upgrades, configuration changes such as a switch to a RAC system from a single-instance system and changes in the storage system. Database Replay captures all external requests such as SQL queries, PL/SQL code blocks, logins and logoffs, and DML/DDL statements. It ignores background jobs and requests made by internal clients such as the Enterprise Manager. Database Replay ignores the following types of client requests:

- SQL*Loader direct path load of data
- Oracle Streams
- Data Pump Import and Export
- Advanced replication streams
- Non–PL/SQL-based Advanced Queuing (AQ)
- Flashback Database and Flashback Queries
- Distributed transactions and remote describe/commit operations
- Shared server

You can use either Enterprise Manager or APL/SQL APIs to run Database Replay. I show the manual steps in the following sections.

Capturing the Production Workload

Use the DBMS_WORKLOAD_CAPTURE package to capture the database workload. The database uses binary files called *capture files* to stop all captured external client requests to the database. The capture files hold client request–related information such as SQL statements and bind values. Here are the steps you must follow to capture the database workload:

1. Restart the database; although this isn't mandatory, it will minimize the errors and data divergence due to uncommitted or partial transactions at the time of the start of the data capture. You want to restart the database in restricted mode. Once you start the workload capture, the database automatically switches to an unrestricted mode of operation.

■**Tip** You can use a physical restore method using an SCN or a point in time, a logical restore method, or a flashback or snapshot standby technique to re-create the production system on the test server.

---

2. Define workload filters. You can use exclusion or inclusion filters to capture only a part of the actual workload and ignore the rest, as shown in the following example:

```
SQL> begin

        dbms_workload_capture.add_filter (
                        fname      => 'user_salapati',
                        fattribute => 'USER',
                        fvalue     => 'salapati'
    end;

    /
```

In this example, I restrict the workload capture to external calls made by the user SALAPATI.

3. Set up a capture directory before starting the workload capture, making sure this directory is large enough to hold the workload. You can use a new or a preexisting directory.

4. Capture the production workload using a representative period. Execute the START_CAPTURE procedure to capture the workload:

```
begin

    dbms_workload_capture.start_capture (name => '2008Jan',
                                         dir => 'jan08',
                                         duration => 1200);

end;
```

Only the DIR parameter, which specifies the capture directory, is mandatory. If you omit the DURATION parameter, the workload capture will continue until you manually stop it as shown here:

```
begin
    dbms_workload.capture.finish_capture ();
end;
;
/
```

You can use the DBA_WORKLOAD_CAPTURES view to get information about the workload capture.

Preprocessing the Workload

You must preprocess the captured workload before you can replay it. Preprocessing is the step that converts the captured workload into replay files. As long as the database version is identical, you can preprocess the workload on the production system or a test system. Here's how to preprocess the workload:

```
begin
dbms_workload_replay.process_capture (capture_dir => 2008jan');
end;
```

Preprocessing the workload produces the metadata for the captured workload and transforms the captured workload datafiles into replay streams called *replay files*.

Making the System Change

At this point, make the system change you want to test on the test system. Once you make the change such as upgrading the database release, you can replay the captured production workload in the changed system to test the impact of the system change on performance, errors, and other related areas.

Replaying the Captured Workload

Create a test system that's identical in every respect to the production system to run the captured production workload. You can duplicate the database on a test server to do this. Replaying the workload on the test system involves the following steps:

Setting Up the Test System Restore the production system on the test server, making sure it has the same application state as the production system. To avoid date-related errors, make sure the system time on the test system is set to the same time as prevailed at the start of the workload capture. Start the test system in the restricted mode to avoid errors.

Resolving External References External references include objects such as database links, directory objects, and URLs. Before starting the replay, resolve all external references from the database. For example, all database links must be fully functional on the test system and point to the test system instead of the production database.

Setting Up the Replay Clients

Database Replay relies on a special application called the *replay driver* to send workload replay requests to the database. The replay driver is made up of replay clients that connect to the test system and simulate the external requests. So, the replay clients replace all external client interactions by sending requests that seem as if they came from the external clients themselves. You can have more than one replay client to share the replay workload, in which case it's best to install the multiple replay clients on separate servers.

After ensuring that you've moved the workload files to the appropriate replay directory, start the replay client as shown here:

```
$ wrc [user/password[$server]] mode=[value] [keyword=[value]]
```

You can execute the wrc executable in different modes such as REPLAY, CALIBRATE, or LIST_HOSTS, by setting the MODE parameter. The parameter KEYWORD lets you specify execution options. You can find out the options available to you by typing in **wrc** at the command line:

```
$ wrc

Workload Replay Client: Release 11.1.0.6.0 - Production on Wed
April 30 12:45:01 2007
Copyright (c) 1982, 2007, Oracle.  All rights reserved.
FORMAT:
=======
 wrc [user/password[@server]] [MODE=mode-value] KEYWORD=value
Example:
========
   wrc  REPLAYDIR=.
   wrc  scott/tiger@myserver REPLAYDIR=.
   wrc  MODE=calibrate REPLAYDIR=./capture
 The default privileged user is: SYSTEM

Mode:
=====
wrc can work in different modes to provide additional
Functionalities.
The default MODE is REPLAY.

Mode       Description
-------------------------------------------------------------------
REPLAY     Default mode that replays the workload in REPLAYDIR
CALIBRATE  Estimate the number of replay clients and CPUs
           needed to replay the workload in REPLAYDIR.
LIST_HOSTS List all the hosts that participated in the capture
           or replay.
```

```
Options (listed by mode):
==========================
MODE=REPLAY (default)
---------------------

Keyword     Description
------------------------------------------------------------------
USERID      username (Default: SYSTEM)
PASSWORD    password (Default: default password of SYSTEM)
SERVER      server connection identifier (Default: empty string)
REPLAYDIR   replay directory (Default:.)
WORKDIR     work directory (Default:.)
DEBUG       FILES, STDOUT, NONE  (Default: NONE)
            FILES  (write debug data to files at WORKDIR)
            STDOUT (print debug data to stdout)
            BOTH   (print to both files and stdout)
            NONE   (no debug data)
CONNECTION_OVERRIDE  TRUE, FALSE (Default: FALSE)
            TRUE   All replay threads connect using SERVER,
                   settings in DBA_WORKLOAD_CONNECTION_MAP
                   will be ignored!
            FALSE  Use settings from DBA_WORKLOAD_CONNECTION_MAP
SERIALIZE_CONNECTS  TRUE, FALSE (Default: FALSE)
            TRUE   All the replay threads will connect to
                   the database in a serial fashion one after
                   another. This setting is recommended when
                   the replay clients use the bequeath protocol
                   to communicate to the database server.
            FALSE  Replay threads will connect to the database
                   in a concurrent fashion mimicking the
                   original capture behavior.
MODE=CALIBRATE
,,,
MODE=LIST_HOSTS
. . .
```

If you have a large number of user sessions, you'll need multiple wrc clients on different hosts. Each replay thread from a replay client represents a single stream from the captured workload.

Although the default mode is REPLAY, it may be a good idea to first execute the wrc in CALIBRATE mode to estimate the number of replay clients and hosts you'll need to replay the workload. After you run the wrc in CALIBRATE mode, you can execute wrc in REPLAY mode, as shown here:

```
$ wrc system/<system_password> mode=replay replay_dir=./test_dir
```

Initializing the Replay Data

Your next step is to initialize the workload data by executing the INITIALIZE_REPLAY procedure:

```
SQL> exec dbms_workload_replay.initialize_replay(replay_name =>
    'test_replay',replay_dir => 'test_dir');
```

Initializing the data loads the metadata into tables that are used by Database Replay.

Remapping External Connections

Before you start the workload replay, you must remap all external connections by executing the REMAP_CONNECTION procedure as shown here.

```
SQL> exec dbms_workload_replay.remap_connection (connection_id =>999,
     replay_connection => 'prod1:1521/testdb');
```

Remapping connections ensures users can connect to all the external databases. If you leave the REPLAY_CONNECTION parameter out, all replay sessions will automatically try connecting to the default host.

Setting Workload Options

The next step is the setting of various workload replay options. You can select from one of the following four options:

- SYNCHRONIZATION: The default for this parameter is true. This option preserves the commit order of the workload during the replay. With this parameter set to true, you can eliminate data divergence caused by not following the commit order among dependent transactions.

- CONNECTION_TIME_SCALE: This parameter lets you adjust the time between the beginning of the workload capture and the time when a session connects with the specified value. By adjusting this parameter, you can control the number of concurrent users during the replay.

- THINK_TIME_SCALE: This parameter enables you to calibrate the elapsed time between user calls in the same session. The smaller the value, the faster the client requests are sent to the database.

■**Note** During a workload capture, elapsed time consists only of user time and user think time, whereas during a workload replay, elapsed time also includes the synchronization time component.

- THINK_TIME_AUTO_CORRECT: If you set this parameter to true, the database automatically corrects the think time specified by the THINK_TIME_SCALE parameter. For example, if the replay is moving slowly, the database reduces the value of the THINK_TIME_SCALE parameter. By default, this parameter is set to false.

Preparing the Workload for Replay

Before replaying the captured workload, prepare the workload by executing the PREPARE_REPLAY procedure:

```
SQL> dbms_workload_replay.prepare_replay (replay_name =>
     'replay1',replay_dir => 'test_dir',
     synchronization= FALSE);
```

If the workload consists mostly of independent transactions, it's better to ignore the commit order by setting the SYNCHRONIZATION parameter to false, as shown in the example.

Starting the Workload Replay

Execute the START_REPLAY procedure to begin the workload replay, as shown here:

```
SQL> exec dbms_workload_replay.start_replay();
```

You can cancel the workload replay in midstream by doing this:

```
SQL> exec dbms_workload_replay.cancel_replay();
```

Analyzing Workload Capture and Replay

Once the database completes the workload replay, you can analyze the replay report to find out about any errors and performance differences, as well as possible data anomalies between the original workload and the replayed workload. Here's how you'd get a replay report by executing the GET_REPLAY_INFO function:

```
declare
        cap_id     number;
        rep_id     number;
        rep_rpt    clob;
begin
    cap_id  := dbms_workload_replay.get_replay_info (dir =>
                 'mytestdir');
    select max(id) into rep_id
     from dba_workload_replays
     where capture_id = cap_id;
    rep_rpt  := dbms_workload_replay.report(
                  replay_id  => rep_id,
                  format      => dbms_workload_replay.type_text);
end;
/
```

The REPLAY_REPORT function produces the following text report:

```
Error Data

(% of total captured actions)
New errors:
 12.3%
Not reproduced old errors: 1.0%
Mutated errors:
 2.0%
Data Divergence

Percentage of row count diffs:
 7.0%
Average magnitude of difference (% of captured):
4.0%
Percentage of diffs because of error (% of diffs):
20.0%
Result checksums were generated for 10% of all
actions(% of checKSUMS)
Percentage of failed checksums:
0.0%
Percentage of failed checksums on same row count:
0.0%
Replay Specific Performance Metrics
Total time deficit (-)/speed up (+):
-32 min
```

```
Total time of synchronization:
44 min
Average elapsed time difference of calls:
0.1 sec
Total synchronization events:
```

3675119064

You can also get a report in the HTML or XML format. You can query the DBA_WORKLOAD_ REPLAYS view for the history of the replays performed by the database.

You must pay attention to any significant divergence between the captured workload and the replay of that workload. Any data divergence such as a smaller or larger result set in one of the two executions of the analyzer is a serious issue and merits further investigation. You must also check the performance deviation between the replay and the original workload. If the replay is taking longer to complete, you must consider this a serious issue. Any errors during the workload replay are good things for you to focus on as well. You can also use the ADDM to analyze the performance differences between the capture and the replay systems. Note that the presence of any of the following in the workload will exacerbate data or error divergence:

- Implicit session dependencies due to things such as the use of the DBMS_PIPE package
- Multiple commits within PL/SQL
- User locks
- Using nonrepeatable functions
- Any external interaction with URLs or database links

Use the following views to manage Database Replay:

- *DBA_WORKLOAD_CAPTURES* shows all workload captures you performed in a database.
- *DBA_WORKLOAD_FILTERS* shows all workload filters you defined in a database.
- *DBA_WORKLOAD_REPLAYS* shows all workload replays you performed in a database.
- *DBA_WORKLOAD_REPLAY_DIVERGENCE* helps monitor workload divergence.
- *DBA_WORKLOAD_THREAD* helps monitor the status of external replay clients.
- *DBA_WORKLOAD_CONNECTION_MAP* shows all connection strings used by workload replays.

Database Replay tests almost all of the database workload, unlike third-party tools, which can only simulate part of the real workload in an Oracle database. Compared to the third-party tools, the Database Replay tool is faster, and therefore you can compile the replay in a much shorter time period.

SQL Performance Analyzer

The SQL Performance Analyzer, which together with the Database Replay feature forms the Total Replay feature offered by Oracle, enables you to test the impact of major system changes such as a database upgrade on SQL workload response time. The SQL Performance Analyzer analyzes and compares SQL performance before and after the system change and provides suggestions to improve any deterioration in performance. You can use the SQL Performance Analyzer to analyze potential changes in SQL performance following system changes such as database, application, operating system, or hardware upgrades; changes in initialization parameter settings; SQL tuning actions; and statistics gathering and schema changes.

The SQL Performance Analyzer lets you know, ahead of an actual database upgrade, which of your SQL statements is possibly going to regress in performance, so you can take care of them. You can take steps to preserve SQL performance by using SQL Plan Management (SPM), which I discussed in Chapter 19. Or, you can employ the SQL Tuning Advisor to tune the potentially negatively impacted SQL statements.

You can use either the production system or a test system to run the SQL Performance Analyzer. Of course, if you run the analysis on a test system, you can avoid overhead on your production system. You can capture the SQL workload on a production system and run the analyzer on the test system. You can use either the Enterprise Manger or components of the DBMS_SQLPA package to use the SQL Performance Analyzer. You capture the SQL workload in the production system by using a SQL Tuning Set (STS). Once you capture SQL information in the STS, you can export the STS to the test system to provide the data for the SQL Performance Analyzer analysis. You can use any of the following as sources of the statements you load into the STS:

- AWR snapshots
- AWR baselines
- A cursor cache
- Another STS

The SQL Performance Analyzer executes SQL serially on the test server, ignoring the concurrency characteristics. It analyzes performance differences in the before- and after-change SQL workloads. The analyzer is integrated with the SQL Tuning Advisor for easy tuning of regressed statements.

I explain the workflow of a SQL Performance Analyzer analysis by showing how to predict changes in SQL performance following an upgrade to Oracle Database 11*g* from Oracle Database Release 10.2.

Capturing the Production SQL Workload

Select a representative period to capture the SQL workload from the production database. The workload that you collect consists of the SQL text and information pertaining to bind variable values and execution frequency. Following are the steps in capturing the production SQL workload:

Creating the SQL Tuning Set

Create the STS by executing the CREATE_SQLSET procedure as shown here:

```
SQL> exec dbms_sqltune.create_sqlset(sqlset_name => 'test_set',
        description  => '11g upgrade workload';
```

The next step is to load the empty STS you created in this step.

Loading the SQL Tuning Set

Execute the DBMS_SQLTUNE SELECT_CURSOR_CACHE procedure to load the empty STS.

```
declare
  mycur dbms_sqltune.sqlset_cursor;
begin
  open  mycur for
    select value (P)
    from table (dbms_sqltune.select_cursor_cache(
      'parsing_schema_name <> ''SYS'' AND elapsed_time >
      2500000',null,null,null,null,1,null,
      'ALL')) P;
```

```
         dbms_sqltune.load_sqlset(sqlset_name => 'upgrade_set',
                                  populate_cursor => cur);
end;
/

PL/SQL procedure successfully completed.
SQL>
```

The database incrementally loads the STS from the cursor cache over a period of time.

Transporting the SQL Tuning Set

Create a staging table first, in order to transport the STS to the test system.

```
SQL> exec dbms_sqltune.create_stgtb_sqlset ( table_name =>
    'stagetab');
```

Export the STS to the staging table using the PACK_STGTAB_SQLSEET procedure.

```
SQL> exec dbms_sqltune.pack_stgtab_sqlset(sqlset_name =>
    'test_sts',
    staging_table_name => 'stagetab');
```

In the next step, you'll import the staging table you created into the test system. Use Data Pump to import the staging table stagetab into the test system. Execute the UNPACK_STGTAB_SQLSET procedure to the import the STS into the test database.

```
SQL> exec dbms_sqltune.unpack_stgtab_sqlset (sqlset_name = '%',
        replace => true, staging_table_name => ('stagetab');
```

Next, you'll create the SQL Performance Analyzer task.

Creating the SQL Performance Analyzer Task

Use the CREATE_ANALYSIS_TASK procedure to create a new SQL Performance Analyzer task, as shown here:

```
SQL> exec dbms_sqlpa.create_analysis_task(sqlset_name => 'sts1',
        task_name => 'spa_task1');
```

The procedure you execute here enables you to create an analyzer job to analyze one or more SQL statements.

Analyzing the Prechange SQL Workload

The before-change SQL workload analysis analyzes the performance of SQL statements in an Oracle 10.2 environment. Make sure that the OPTIMIZER_FEATURES_ENABLE initialization parameter is correctly set.

```
optimizer_features_enable=10.2.0
```

Execute the EXECUTE_ANALYSIS_TASK procedure to analyze the preupgrade performance of the SQL workload, as shown here:

```
SQL> exec dbms_sqlpa.execute_analysis_task (task_name =>
            'spa_task1',
            execution_type => 'test_execute',
            execution_name= 'before_change');
```

Note that the value of the EXECUTION_TYPE parameter is set to TEST_EXECUTE. This value ensures that the database executes all SQL statements in the workload and generates both the execution plans and execution statistics such as disk reads. You can assign two other values for the EXECUTION_TYPE parameter. The COMPARE_PERFORMANCE parameter will compare the performance based on a comparison of two different analyses. The value EXPLAIN_PLAN will generate SQL plans without executing them.

Get a report of the preupgrade SQL performance by executing the REPORT_ANALYSIS_TASK function:

```
SQL> select dbms_sqlpa.report_analysis_task (task_name =>
     'spa_task1',
     type => 'text',
     section=> 'summary') from dual;
```

You now have a performance baseline with which to compare the after-upgrade SQL performance.

Analyzing the After-Upgrade SQL Workload

Set the value of the OPTIMIZER_FEATURES_ENABLE parameter to match the Oracle Database 11g release:

```
optimizer_features_enable=11.1
```

Execute the SPA task again, this time to analyze the after-upgrade performance of the SQL workload.

```
SQL> exec dbms_sqlpa.execute_analysis_task (task_name  => 'spa_task2',
        execution_type => 'test_execute',
        execution_name => 'after_change')
```

Get a report of the after-upgrade performance as shown here:

```
SQL> select dbms_sqlpa.report_analysis_task (task_name =>   'spa_task2',
     type => 'text', section=> 'summary') from dual;
```

Comparing the SQL Performance

Execute the EXECUTE_ANALYSIS_TASK procedure once again, but with the value COMPARE_PERFORMANCE for the EXECUTION_TYPE parameter, in order to analyze and compare the SQL performance data before and after the database upgrade.

```
SQL> exec dbms_sqltune.execute_analysis_task (task_name =>
        'spa_task3',
        execution_type   => 'compare performance',
        execution_params =>
        dbms_advisor.arglist('execution_name1','before_change',
        execution_name2','after_change''comparision_metric',
         'disk_reads',)
```

In addition to DISK READS, you can specify metrics such as ELAPSED_TIME, PARSE TIME, or BUFFER GETS when comparing the performance.

Generating the Analysis Report

Execute the REPORT_ANALYSIS_TASK function to get a report of the performance comparison:

```
var report clob;

exec :report := dbms_sqlpa.report_analysis_task('spa_task1',
                'text',
                'typical','summary');
```

```
set long 100000 longchunksize 100000 linesize 120

print :report
```

During the compare and analysis phase, you can do the following:

- Calculate the impact of the change on specific SQL statements.
- Calculate the impact of the change on the SQL workload as a whole.
- Assign weights to important SQL statements in the workload.
- Detect performance regression and improvements.
- Detect changes in the execution plans of the SQL statements.
- Recommend the running of the SQL Tuning Advisor to tune regressed SQL statements.

You can use the following views when working with the SQL Performance Analyzer:

- *DBA_ADVISOR_TASKS* shows details about the analysis task.
- *DBA_ADVISOR_FINDINGS* shows analysis findings, which are classified as performance regression, symptoms, informative messages, and errors.
- *DBA_ADVISOR_EXECUTIONS* shows metadata information for task executions.
- *DBA_ADVISOR_SQLPLANS* shows a list of SQL execution plans.
- *DBA_ADVISOR_SQLSTATS* shows a list of SQL compilation and execution statistics.

Analyzing the Performance Report

The SQL Performance Analyzer contains both a result summary and a result details section. The former shows quickly whether the database upgrade in our example will result in any performance deterioration or improvement. The advisor also provides recommendations to avoid any potential performance deterioration.

Since the SQL Performance Analyzer is an integral part of the Oracle database, it can take advantage of tools such as the SQL Tuning Advisor as well as features such as SQL Plan Management to fine-tune database performance.

Oracle Database 11*g* SQL and PL/SQL: A Brief Primer

I'm sure most of you are already familiar with SQL to some extent. However, I present in this appendix a quick introduction to Oracle Database 11*g* SQL and its programmatic cousin, PL/SQL, as a starting point for those new to programming Oracle databases. My goal here is simply to present a short summary of the classic DML and DDL commands and to discuss the newer SQL and PL/SQL concepts in greater detail.

Your need to know SQL or PL/SQL depends somewhat on the type of DBA you are—a production support DBA won't need to know as much about Oracle programming as a DBA assisting in developmental efforts. It's becoming increasingly important, however, for DBAs to learn a number of advanced SQL and PL/SQL concepts, including the new Java and XML-based technologies. The reason is simple: even when you aren't developing applications yourself, you're going to be assisting people who are doing so, and it helps to know what they're doing.

This appendix aims to summarize some of the most important Oracle Database 11*g* SQL and PL/SQL features so you and the developers you work with can take advantage of them. Oracle SQL and PL/SQL represent an enormously broad topic, so this appendix lightly covers several important topics without attempting any detailed explanation due to space considerations. Please refer to the Oracle manuals *Application Developer's Guide—Fundamentals* and *PL/SQL User's Guide and Reference* for a comprehensive introduction to SQL and PL/SQL.

The Oracle Database 11*g* Sample Schemas

The examples in this appendix use the demo schemas provided by Oracle as part of the Oracle Database 11*g* server software. The demo data is for a fictitious company and contains the following five schemas:

- *HR* is the human resources division, which contains information on employees. It is the most commonly used schema, with its familiar employees and dept tables. The schema uses scalar data types and simple tables with basic constraints.

- *OE* is the order entry department, which contains inventory and sales data. This schema covers a simple order-entry system and includes regular relational objects as well as object-relational objects. Because the OE schema contains synonyms for HR tables, you can query HR's objects from the OE schema.

- *PM* is the product media department, which covers content management. You can use this schema if you're exploring Oracle's Multimedia option. The tables in the PM schema contain audio and video tracks, images, and documents.

- *IX* is the information exchange department in charge of shipping using various B2B applications.
- *SH* is the sales history department in charge of sales data. It is the largest sample schema, and you can use it for testing examples with large amounts of data. The schema contains partitioned tables, an external table, and Online Analytical Processing (OLAP) features. The SALES and COSTS tables contain 750,000 rows and 250,000 rows, respectively, as compared to 107 rows in the employees table from the HR schema.

In order to install the SH schema, you must have the partitioning option installed in your Oracle database; this option lets you use table and index partitioning in your database. Ideally, you should install the Oracle demo schemas in a test database where you can safely practice the parts of SQL you aren't familiar with. The Oracle *Sample Schemas* documentation manual provides detailed information about the sample schemas.

If you've created a starter database using the Database Configuration Assistant (DBCA) as part of your Oracle software installation (the Basic Installation option), it will have automatically created the sample schemas in the new starter database.

If you've chosen to not create the starter database (by selecting a Software Only installation option), you can run the DBCA to install the sample schemas. Choose the Sample Schemas option when you use the DBCA to create the sample schemas in an existing database. By default, all the sample schema accounts are locked, and you must use the ALTER USER . . . ACCOUNT UNLOCK statement to unlock them.

If you want to create the sample schemas in a database without using the DBCA, you can run Oracle-provided scripts to install the sample schemas.

Oracle Data Types

Data in an Oracle database is organized in rows and columns inside tables. The individual columns are defined with properties that limit the values and format of the column contents. Let's review the most important Oracle built-in data types before we look at Oracle SQL statements.

Character Data Types

The CHAR data type is used for fixed-length character literals:

```
SEX     CHAR(1)
```

The VARCHAR2 data type is used to represent variable-length character literals:

```
CITY    VARCHAR2 (20)
```

The CLOB data type is used to hold large character strings and the BLOB and BFILE data types are used to store large amounts of binary data.

Numeric Data Types

There are two important SQL data types used to store numeric data:

- The NUMBER data type is used to store real numbers, either in a fixed-point or floating-point format.
- The BINARY FLOAT and BINARY DOUBLE data types store data in a floating-point format.

Date and Time Data Types

There are a couple of special data types that let you handle date and time values:

- The DATE data type stores the date and time (such as year, month, day, hours, minutes, and seconds).
- The TIMESTAMP data type stores time values that are precise to fractional seconds.

Conversion Functions

Oracle offers several conversion functions that let you convert data from one format to another. The most common of these functions are the TO_CHAR, TO_NUMBER, TO_DATE, and TO_TIMESTAMP functions. The TO_CHAR function converts a floating number to a string, and the TO_NUMBER function converts a floating number or a string to a number. The TO_DATE function converts character data to a DATE data type. Here are some examples:

```
SQL> SELECT TO_CHAR(TO_DATE('20-JUL-08', 'DD-MON-RR') ,'YYYY') "Year" FROM DUAL;

Year
------------------------------------------------------------------------
2008
SQL>

SQL> SELECT TO_CHAR(SYSDATE, 'DD-MON-YYYY')
     FROM DUAL;

TO_CHAR(SYSDATE
--------------
20-JUL-2008
SQL>
```

SQL

In Chapter 7 you saw how Oracle SQL statements include DDL, DML, and other types of statements. Let's begin with a review of the basic SQL statements.

The SELECT Statement

The SELECT statement is the most common SQL statement (it is also called a *projection*). A SELECT statement retrieves all or some of the data in a table, based on the criteria that you specify.

The most basic SELECT statement is one that retrieves all the data in the table:

```
SQL> SELECT * FROM employees;
```

To retrieve only certain columns from a table, you specify the column names after the SELECT keyword, as shown in the following example:

```
SQL> SELECT first_name, last_name, hiredate FROM employees;
```

If you want only the first ten rows of a table, you can use the following statement:

```
SQL> SELECT * FROM employees WHERE rownum <11;
```

If you want just a count of all the rows in the table, you can use the following statement:

```
SQL> SELECT COUNT(*) FROM employees;
```

If a table has duplicate data, you can use the DISTINCT clause to eliminate the duplicate values, as shown here:

```
SQL> SELECT DISTINCT username FROM V$SESSION;
```

The optional WHERE clause in a SELECT statement uses conditions to help you specify that only certain rows be returned. Table A-1 lists some of the common conditions you can use in a WHERE clause.

Table A-1. *Common Conditions Used in WHERE Clauses*

Symbol	Condition
=	Equal
>	Greater than
<	Less than
<+	Less than or equal to
>=	Greater than or equal to
<> or !	Not equal to

Here are some examples of using the WHERE clause:

```
SQL> SELECT employee_id WHERE salary = 50000;
SQL> SELECT employee_id WHERE salary < 50000;
SQL> SELECT employee_id WHERE salary > 50000;
SQL> SELECT employee_id WHERE salary <= 50000;
SQL> SELECT employee_id WHERE salary >= 50000;
SQL> SELECT employee_id WHERE salary ! 50000;
```

The LIKE Condition

The LIKE condition uses pattern matching to restrict rows in a SELECT statement. Here's an example:

```
SQL> SELECT employee_id, last_name FROM employees
  2* WHERE last_name LIKE 'Fa%';
EMPLOYEE_ID    LAST_NAME
-----------    ----------
    109        Faviet
    202        Fay
SQL>
```

The pattern that you want the WHERE clause to match should be enclosed in single quotes (' '). In the preceding example, the percent sign (%) indicates that the letters Fa can be followed by any character string. Thus, the percent sign acts as a wildcard for one or more characters, performing the same job as the asterisk (*) in many operating systems. Note that a single underscore character (_) acts as a wildcard for one and only one character.

The INSERT Statement

The INSERT statement enables you to add new data to a table, including duplicate data if there are no unique requirements enforced by a primary key or an index. The general form of the INSERT statement is as follows:

```
INSERT INTO <table>  [(<column i, . . . , column j>)]
VALUES (<value i, . . . ,value j>);
```

Here is an example of the insert command:

```
SQL> INSERT INTO employees(
  2   employee_id,last_name,email,hire_date,job_id)
  3   VALUES
  4* (56789,'alapati','salapati@netbsa.org', sysdate,98765);
1 row created.
SQL>
```

In the preceding list, the column names were specified because only some columns were being populated in the row being inserted. The rest of them are left blank, which is okay, provided the column isn't defined as a "not null" column.

If you're inserting values for all the columns of a table, you can use the simpler INSERT statement shown here:

```
SQL> INSERT INTO department
     VALUES
       (34567, 'payroll', 'headquarters', 'dallas');
  1 row created.
SQL>
```

If you want to insert all the columns of a table into another table, you can use the following INSERT statement:

```
SQL> INSERT INTO b SELECT * FROM a
     WHERE city='DALLAS';
```

If table b doesn't exist, you can use the CREATE TABLE table_name AS SELECT * FROM (CTAS) statement, as shown here:

```
SQL> CREATE table b as SELECT * FROM a;
```

The DELETE Statement

You use the DELETE statement to remove rows from a table. The DELETE statement has the following structure:

```
DELETE FROM <table> [WHERE ,condition>];
```

For example, if you want to delete employee Fay's row from the employees table, you would use the following DELETE statement:

```
SQL> DELETE FROM employees
  2* WHERE last_name='Fay';
1 row deleted.
```

If you don't have a limiting WHERE condition, the DELETE statement will result in the removal of all the rows in the table, as shown here:

```
SQL> DELETE FROM X;
```

You can also remove all rows in a table using the TRUNCATE command, but you can't undo or roll back the TRUNCATE command's effects. You can undo a delete by using the ROLLBACK statement:

```
SQL> ROLLBACK;
```

The UPDATE Statement

The UPDATE statement changes the value (or values) of one or more columns of a row (or rows) in a table. The expression to which a column is being set or modified can be a constant, arithmetic, or string operation, or the product of a SELECT statement.

The general structure of the UPDATE statement is as follows (note that the elements in square brackets are optional):

```
UPDATE <table>
SET <column i> = <expression i>, . . . , <column j> = <expression j>
[WHERE  <condition> ];
```

If you want to change or modify a column's values for all the rows in the table, you use an UPDATE statement without a WHERE condition:

```
SQL> UPDATE persons SET salary=salary*0.10;
```

If you want to modify only some rows, you need to use the WHERE clause in your UPDATE statement:

```
SQL> UPDATE persons SET salary = salary * 0.10
    WHERE review_grade > 5;
```

Filtering Data

The WHERE clause in a SELECT, INSERT, DELETE, or UPDATE statement lets you filter data. That is, you can restrict the number of rows on which you want to perform a SQL operation. Here's a simple example:

```
SQL> INSERT INTO a
    SELECT * FROM b
    WHERE city='DALLAS';
```

Sorting the Results of a Query

Frequently, you'll have to sort the results of a query in some order. The ORDER BY clause enables you to sort the data based on the value of one or more columns. You can choose the sorting order (ascending or descending) and you can choose to sort by column aliases. You can also sort by multiple columns. Here's an example:

```
SQL> SELECT employee_id, salary FROM employees
    ORDER BY salary;
```

Changing the Sorting Order

Be default, an ORDER BY clause sorts in ascending order. If you want to sort in descending order, you need to specify the DESC keyword:

```
SQL> SELECT employee_id, salary FROM employees
    ORDER BY salary desc;
```

Sorting by Multiple Columns

You can sort results based on the values of more than one column. The following query sorts on the basis of two columns, salary and dept:

```
SQL> SELECT employee_id, salary FROM employees
     ORDER BY salary, dept;
```

Operators

SQL provides you with a number of operators to perform various tasks, such as comparing column values and performing logical operations. The following sections outline the important SQL operators: comparison operators, logical operators, and set operators.

Comparison Operators

Comparison operators compare a certain column value with several other column values. These are the main comparison operators:

- BETWEEN: Tests whether a value is between a pair of values
- IN: Tests whether a value is in a list of values
- LIKE: Tests whether a value follows a certain pattern, as shown here:

```
SQL> SELECT employee_id from employees
     WHERE dept LIKE 'FIN%';
```

Logical Operators

The *logical operators*, also called *Boolean operators*, logically compare two or more values. The main logical operators are AND, OR, NOT, GE (greater than or equal to), and LE (less than or equal to). Here's an example that illustrates the use of some of the logical operators:

```
SQL> SELECT last_name, city
     WHERE salary GT 100000 and LE 200000;
```

When there are multiple operators within a single statement, you need rules of precedence. Oracle always evaluates arithmetical operations such as multiplication, division, addition, and subtraction before it evaluates conditions. The following is the order of precedence of operators in Oracle, with the most important first:

```
=, !=, <, >, <=, >=
IS NULL, LIKE, BETWEEN, IN, EXISTS
NOT
AND
OR
```

The Set Operators

Sometimes your query may need to combine results from more than one SQL statement. In other words, you need to write a *compound* query. *Set operators* facilitate compound SQL queries. Here are the important Oracle set operators:

- **UNION**: The UNION operator combines the results of more than one SELECT statement after removing any duplicate rows. Oracle will sort the resulting set of data. Here's an example:

```
SQL> SELECT emp_id FROM old_employees
     UNION
     SELECT emp_id FROM new_employees;
```

- **UNION ALL**: The UNION ALL operator is similar to UNION, but it doesn't remove the duplicate rows. Oracle doesn't sort the result set in this case, unlike the UNION operation.

- **INTERSECTION**: The INTERSECTION operator gets you the common values in two or more result sets derived from separate SELECT statements. The result set is distinct and sorted.

- **MINUS**: The MINUS operator returns the rows returned by the first query that aren't in the second query's results. The result set is distinct and sorted.

SQL Functions

Oracle functions manipulate data items and return a result, and built-in Oracle functions help you perform many transformations quickly, without your having to do any coding. In addition, you can build your own functions. Functions can be divided into several groups: single-row functions, aggregate functions, number and date functions, general and conditional functions, and analytical functions.

Single-Row Functions

Single-row functions are typically used to perform tasks such as converting a lowercase word to uppercase or vice versa, or replacing a portion of text in a row. Here are the main single-row functions used in Oracle:

- **CONCAT**: The CONCAT function concatenates or puts together two or more character strings into one string.

- **LENGTH**: The LENGTH function gives you the length of a character string.

- **LOWER**: The LOWER function transforms uppercase letters into lowercase, as shown in the following example:

```
SQL> SELECT LOWER('SHANNON ALAPATI') from dual;

LOWER('SHANNONALAPATI')
-----------------------
shannon alapati
SQL>
```

- **SUBSTR**: The SUBSTR function returns part of a string.

- **INSTR**: The INSTR function returns a number indicating where in a string a certain string value starts.

- **LPAD**: The LPAD function returns a string after padding it for a specified length on the left.

- **RPAD**: The RPAD function pads a string on the right side.

- **TRIM**: The TRIM function trims a character string.

- **REPLACE**: The REPLACE function replaces every occurrence of a specified string with a specified replacement string.

Aggregate Functions

You can use *aggregate functions* to compute things such as averages and totals of a selected column in a query. Here are the important aggregate functions:

- MIN: The MIN function returns the smallest value. Here's an example:

  SELECT MIN(join_date) FROM employees;

- MAX: The MAX function returns the largest value.

- AVG: The AVG function computes the average value of a column.

- SUM: The SUM function computes the sum of a column:

  SQL> SELECT SUM(bytes) FROM dba_free_space;

- COUNT: The COUNT function returns the total number of columns.

- COUNT(*): The COUNT(*) function returns the number of rows in a table.

Number and Date Functions

Oracle includes several *number functions,* which accept numeric input and return numeric values. The *date functions* help you format dates and times in different ways. Here are some of the important number and date functions:

- ROUND: This function returns a number rounded to the specified number of places to the right of the decimal point.

- TRUNC: This function returns the result of a date truncated in the specified format.

- SYSDATE: This commonly used function returns the current date and time:

  SQL> SELECT sysdate FROM dual;

  SYSDATE

  07/AUG/2008
  SQL>

- TO_TIMESTAMP: This function converts a CHAR or VARCHAR(2) data type to a timestamp data type.

- TO_DATE: You can use this function to change the current date format. The standard date format in Oracle is DD-MMM-YYYY, as shown in the following example:

  07-AUG-2008

- The TO_DATE function accepts a character string that contains valid data and converts it into the default Oracle date format. It can also change the date format, as shown here:

  SQL> SELECT TO_DATE('August 20,2008', 'MonthDD,YYYY') FROM dual;

  TO_DATE('AUGUST20,2008'

  08/20/2008
  SQL>

- TO_CHAR: This function converts a date into a character string, as shown in the following example:

```
SQL> SELECT SYSDATE FROM dual;

SYSDATE
-----------
04-AUG-2008
SQL>

SQL> SELECT TO_CHAR(SYSDATE, 'DAY, DDTH MONTH YYYY') FROM DUAL;

TO_CHAR(SYSDATE,'DAY,DDTHMON
--------------------------------
THURSDAY , 04TH AUGUST     2008

SQL>
```

- TO_NUMBER: This function converts a character string to a number format:

```
SQL> UPDATE employees SET salary = salary +
     TO_NUMBER('100.00', '9G999D99')
     WHERE last_name = 'Alapati';
```

General and Conditional Functions

Oracle provides some very powerful *general* and *conditional functions* that enable you to extend the power of simple SQL statements into something similar to a traditional programming language construct. The conditional functions help you decide among several choices. Here are the important general and conditional Oracle functions:

- NVL: The NVL function replaces the value in a table column with the value after the comma if the column is null. Thus, the NVL function takes care of column values if the column values are null and converts them to non-null values:

```
SQL> SELECT last_name, title,
     salary * NVL (commission_pct,0)/100 COMM
     FROM employees;
```

- COALESCE: This function is similar to NVL, but it returns the first non-null value in the list:

```
SQL> COALESCE(region1, region2, region3, region4)
```

- DECODE: This function is used to incorporate basic if-then functionality into SQL code. The following example assigns a party name to all the voters in the table based on the value in the affiliation column. If there is no value under the affiliation column, the voter is listed as an independent:

```
SQL> SELECT DECODE(affiliation, 'D', 'Democrat',
     'R', 'Republican', 'Independent') FROM voters;
```

- CASE: This function provides the same functionality as the DECODE function, but in a much more intuitive and elegant way. Here's a simple example of using the CASE statement, which helps you incorporate if-then logic into your code:

```
SQL> SELECT ename,
     (CASE deptno
     WHEN 10 THEN 'Accounting'
     WHEN 20 THEN 'Research'
     WHEN 30 THEN 'Sales'
```

```
WHEN 40 THEN 'Operations'
ELSE 'Unknown'
END)
department
FROM employees;
```

Analytical Functions

Oracle's SQL analytical functions are powerful tools for business intelligence applications. Oracle claims a potential improvement of 200 to 500 percent in query performance with the use of the SQL analytical functions. The purpose behind using analytical functions is to perform complex summary computations without using a lot of code. Here are the main SQL analytical functions of the Oracle database:

- *Ranking functions*: These enable you to rank items in a data set according to some criteria. Oracle has several types of ranking functions, including RANK, DENSE_RANK, CUME_DIST, PERCENT_RANK, and NTILE. Listing A-1 shows a simple example of how a ranking function can help you rank some sales data.

Listing A-1. *An Example of a Ranking Function*

```
SQL> SELECT sales_type,
    TO_CHAR(SUM(amount_sold), '9,999,999,999') SALES,
    RANK() OVER (ORDER BY SUM(amount_sold) ) AS original_rank,
    RANK() OVER (ORDER BY SUM(amount_sold)
    DESC NULLS LAST) AS derived_rank
    FROM sales, products, customers, time_frame, sales_types
    WHERE sales.prod_id=products.prod_id AND
    sales.cust_id=customers.cust_id AND
    sales.time_id=time_frame.time_id AND
    sales.sales_type_id=sales_types.sales_type_id AND
    timeframe.calendar_month_desc IN ('2008-07', '2008-08')
    AND country_id='INDIA'
    GROUP BY sales_type;
```

SALES_TYPE	SALES	ORIGINAL_RANK	DERIVED_RANK
Direct Sales	5,744,263	5	1
Internet	3,625,993	4	2
Catalog	1,858,386	3	3
Partners	1,500,213	2	4
Tele Sales	604,656	1	5

```
SQL>
```

- *Moving-window aggregates*: These functions provide cumulative sums and moving averages.

- *Period-over-period comparisons*: These functions let you compare two periods (for example, "How does the first quarter of 2008 compare with the first quarter of 2006 in terms of percentage growth?").

- *Ratio-to-report comparisons*: These make it possible to compare ratios (for example, "What is August's enrollment as a percentage of the entire year's enrollment?").

- *Statistical functions*: These functions calculate correlations and regression functions so you can see cause-and-effect relationships among data.

- *Inverse percentiles*: These help you find the data corresponding to a percentile value (for example, "Get me the names of the salespeople who correspond to the median sales value.").

- *Hypothetical ranks and distributions*: These help you figure out how a new value for a column fits into existing data in terms of its rank and distribution.

- *Histograms*: These functions return the number of the histogram data appropriate for each row in a table.

- *First/last aggregates*: These functions are appropriate when you are using the GROUP BY clause to sort data into groups. Aggregate functions let you specify the sort order for the groups.

Hierarchical Retrieval of Data

If a table contains hierarchical data (data that can be grouped into levels, with the parent data at higher levels and child data at lower levels), you can use Oracle's hierarchical queries. Hierarchical queries typically use the following structure:

- The START WITH clause denotes the root row or rows for the hierarchical relationship.

- The CONNECT BY clause specifies the relationship between parent and child rows, with the prior operator always pointing out the parent row.

Listing A-2 shows a hierarchical relationship between the employees and manager columns. The CONNECT BY clause describes the relationship. The START WITH clause specifies where the statement should start tracing the hierarchy.

Listing A-2. *A Hierarchical Relationship Between Data*

```
SQL> SELECT employee_id, last_name, manager_id
     FROM employees
     START WITH manager_id = 100
     CONNECT BY PRIOR employee_id = manager_id;

EMPLOYEE_ID  LAST_NAME       MANAGER_ID
-----------  --------------  ----------
        101  Reddy                  100
        108  Greenberg              101
        109  Faviet                 108
        110  Colon                  108
        111  Chowdhary              108
        112  Urman                  108
        113  Singh                  108
        200  Whalen                 101
SQL>
```

Selecting Data from Multiple Tables

So far, we've mostly looked at how to perform various DML operations on single tables, including using SQL functions and expressions. However, in real life, you'll mostly deal with query output retrieved from several tables or views. When you need to retrieve data from several tables, you need to *join* the tables. A join is a query that lets you combine data from tables, views, and materialized views. Note that a table can be joined to other tables or to itself.

The Cartesian product or Cartesian join is simply a join of two tables without a selective WHERE clause. Therefore, the query output will consist of all rows from both tables. Here's an example of a Cartesian join:

```
SQL> SELECT * FROM employees, dept;
```

Cartesian products of two large tables are almost always the result of a mistaken SQL query that omits the *join condition*. By using a join condition when you're combining data from two or more tables, you can limit the number of rows returned. A join condition can be used in the WHERE clause or the FROM clause, and it limits the data returned by selecting only data that satisfies the condition stipulated by the join condition.

Here's an example of a join statement that uses a join condition:

```
SQL> SELECT * FROM employees, dept
     WHERE dept='HR';
```

Types of Oracle Joins

Oracle offers various types of joins based on the way you combine rows from two or more tables or views. The next sections discuss the most commonly used types of Oracle joins.

Equi-Join

With an *equi-join*, two or more tables are joined based on an equality condition between two columns. In other words, the same column has the same value in all the tables that are being joined. Here's an example:

```
SQL> SELECT e.last_name, d.dept
     FROM emp e, dept d WHERE e.emp_id = d.emp_id;
```

You can also use the following new syntax for the preceding join statement:

```
SQL> SELECT e.last_name, d.dept
     FROM emp e JOIN dept d
     USING (emp_id);
```

If you want to join multiple columns, you can do so by using a comma-delimited list of column names, as in USING (dept_id, emp_name).

Natural Join

A *natural join* is an equi-join where you don't specify any columns to be matched for the join. Oracle will automatically determine the columns to be joined, based on the matching columns in the two tables. Here's an example:

```
SQL> SELECT e.last_name, d.dept
     FROM emp e NATURAL JOIN dept d;
```

In the preceding example, the join is based on identical values for the last_name column in both the emp and dept tables.

Self Join

A *self join* is a join of a table to itself through the use of table aliases. In the following example, the employees table is joined to itself using an alias. The query deletes duplicate rows in the employees table.

```
SQL> DELETE FROM employees X WHERE ROWID >
  2  (select MIN(rowid) FROM employees Y
  3  where X.key_values = Y.key_values);
```

Inner Join

An *inner join*, also known as a *simple join*, returns all rows that satisfy the join condition. The traditional Oracle inner join syntax used the WHERE clause to specify how the tables were to be joined. Here's an example:

```
SQL> SELECT e.flast_name, d.dept
     FROM emp e, dept d WHERE e.emp_id = d.emp_id;
```

The newer Oracle inner joins (or simply joins) specify join criteria with the new ON or USING clause. Here's a simple example:

```
SQL> SELECT DISTINCT NVL(dname, 'No Dept'),
        COUNT(empno) nbr_emps
        FROM emp JOIN DEPT
        ON emp.deptno = dept.deptno
        WHERE emp.job IN ('MANAGER', 'SALESMAN', 'ANALYST')
        GROUP BY dname;
```

Outer Join

An *outer join* returns all rows that satisfy the join condition, *plus* some or all of the rows from the table that doesn't have matching rows that meet the join condition. There are three types of outer joins: left outer join, right outer join, and full outer join. Usually, the word "outer" is omitted from the full outer join statement.

Oracle provides the outer join operator, wherein you use a plus sign (+) to indicate missing values in one table, but it recommends the use of the newer ISO/ANSI join syntax. Here's a typical query using the full outer join:

```
SQL> SELECT DISTINCT NVL(dept_name, 'No Dept') deptname,
        COUNT(empno) nbr_emps
        FROM emp FULL JOIN dept
        ON dept.deptno = emp.deptno
        GROUP BY dname;
```

Grouping Operations

Oracle provides the GROUP BY clause so you can group the results of a query according to various criteria. The GROUP BY clause enables you to consider a column value for all the rows in the table fulfilling the SELECT condition.

A GROUP BY clause commonly uses aggregate functions to summarize each group defined by the GROUP BY clause. The data is sorted on the GROUP BY columns, and the aggregates are calculated. Here's an example:

```
SQL> SELECT department_id, MAX(salary)
  2    FROM employees
  3*   GROUP BY department_id;

    DEPARTMENT_ID    MAX(SALARY)
    -------------    -----------
             10           4400
             20          13000
             30          11000
             40           6500
             50           8200
    5 rows selected.
SQL>
```

Oracle also allows you to nest group functions. The following query gets you the minimum average budget for all departments (the AVG function is nested inside the MIN function here):

```
SQL> SELECT MIN(AVG(budget))
     FROM dept_budgets
     GROUP BY dept_no;
```

The GROUP BY Clause with a ROLLUP Operator

You've seen how you can derive subtotals with the help of the GROUP BY clause. The GROUP BY clause with a ROLLUP operator gives you subtotals and total values. You can thus build subtotal aggregates at any level. In other words, the ROLLUP operator gets you the aggregates at each group by level. The subtotal rows and the grand total row are called the superaggregate rows.

Listing A-3 shows an example of using the ROLLUP operator.

Listing A-3. *A GROUP BY Clause with a ROLLUP Operator*

```
SQL> SELECT Year,Country,SUM(Sales) AS Sales
     FROM Company_Sales
     GROUP BY ROLLUP (Year,Country);
```

YEAR	COUNTRY	SALES
1997	France	3990
1997	USA	13090
1997		17080
1998	France	4310
1998	USA	13900
1998		18210
1999	France	4570
1999	USA	14670
1999		19240
		54530 /*This is the grand total */

```
SQL>
```

The GROUP BY Clause with a CUBE Operator

You can consider the CUBE operator to be an extension of the ROLLUP operator, as it helps extend the standard Oracle GROUP BY clause. The CUBE operator computes all possible combinations of subtotals in a GROUP BY operation. In the previous example, the ROLLUP operator gave you yearly subtotals. Using the CUBE operator, you can get countrywide totals in addition to the yearly totals. Here's a simple example:

```
SQL> SELECT department_id, job_id, SUM(salary)
  4  FROM employees
  5  GROUP BY CUBE (department_id, job_id);
```

DEPARTMENT_ID	JOB_ID	SUM(SALARY)
10	AD_ASST	44000
20	MK_MAN	130000
20	MK_REP	60000
30	PU_MAN	110000
30	PU_CLERK	139000

. . .

```
SQL>
```

The GROUP BY Clause with a GROUPING Operator

As you've seen, the ROLLUP operator gets you the superaggregate subtotals and grand totals. The GROUPING operator in a GROUP BY clause helps you distinguish between superaggregated subtotals and the grand total column from the other row data.

The GROUP BY Clause with a GROUPING SETS Operator

The GROUPING SETS operator lets you group multiple sets of columns when you're calculating aggregates such as sums. Here's an example that shows how you can use this operator to calculate aggregates over three groupings: (year, region, item), (year, item), and (region, item). The GROUPING SETS operator eliminates the need for inefficient UNION ALL operators.

```
SQL> SELECT year, region, item, sum(sales)
     FROM regional_salesitem    GROUP BY
     GROUPING SETS (( year, region, item),
     (year, item), (region, item));
```

The GROUP BY Clause with a HAVING Operator

The HAVING operator lets you restrict or exclude the results of a GROUP BY operation, in essence putting a WHERE condition on the GROUP BY clause's result set. In the following example, the HAVING operator restricts the query results to only those departments that have a maximum salary greater than 20,000:

```
SQL> SELECT department_id, max(salary)
  2   FROM employees
  3   GROUP BY department_id
  4*  HAVING MAX(salary)>20000;

DEPARTMENT_ID    MAX(SALARY)
-------------    -----------
          90          24000
SQL>
```

Writing Subqueries

Subqueries resolve queries that have to be processed in multiple steps—where the final result depends on the results of a child query or subquery to the main query. If the subquery occurs in the WHERE clause of the statement, it's called a *nested subquery*.

Top-N Analysis

The following query gives you the top ten employees in a firm ranked by salary. You can just as easily retrieve the bottom ten employees by using the ORDER BY clause instead of the ORDER BY DESC clause.

```
SQL> SELECT emp_id, emp_name, job, manager, salary
     FROM
     (SELECT emp_id, emp_name, job, manager, salary,
     RANK() OVER
     (ORDER BY SALARY DESC NULLS LAST) AS Employee_Rank
     FROM employees
     ORDER BY SALARY DESC NULLS LAST)
     WHERE employee_Rank < 5;
```

Subqueries can be single-row or multiple-row SQL statements. Let's take a quick look at both types of subqueries.

Single-Row Subqueries

Subqueries are useful when you need to answer queries on the basis of as-yet unknown values, such as "Which employees have a salary higher than the employee with the employee ID 9999?" To answer such a question, a subquery or inner query is executed first (and only once). The result of this subquery is then used by the main or outer query. Here's the query:

```
SQL> SELECT first_name||last_name, dept
  2  FROM employee
  3  WHERE sal >
  4  (SELECT sal
  5  FROM emp
  6  WHERE empno= 9999);
```

Multiple-Row Subqueries

A *multiple-row subquery* returns multiple rows in the output, so you need to use multiple-row comparison operators, such as IN, ANY, and ALL. Using a single-row operator with a multiple-row subquery returns this common Oracle error:

```
ERROR:
ORA-01427: single-row subquery returns more than one row
```

Multiple-Column Subqueries

Multiple-column subqueries are queries where the inner query retrieves the values of more than one column. The rows in the subquery are then evaluated in the main query in pair-wise comparison, column by column and row by row.

Advanced Subqueries

Correlated subqueries are more complex than regular subqueries and answer questions such as "What are the names of all employees whose salary is below the average salary of their department?" The inner query computes the average salary, and the outer or main query gets the employee information. However, for each employee in the main (outer) query, the inner query has to be computed, because department averages depend on the department number of the employee in the outer query.

The Exists and Not Exists Operators

The EXISTS operator tests for the existence of rows in the inner query or subquery when you're using subqueries. The NOT EXISTS operator tests for the nonexistence of rows in the inner query. In the following statement, the EXISTS operator will be TRUE if the subquery returns at least one row:

```
SQL> SELECT department_id
     FROM departments d
     WHERE EXISTS
     (SELECT * FROM employees e
     WHERE d.department_id
     = e.department_id);
```

Using Regular Expressions

Oracle Database 11g provides support for regular expressions that you can use as part of SQL statements. Regular expressions let you use special operators to manipulate strings or carry out a search.

Traditionally, developers used operators such as LIKE, REPLACE, and SUBSTRING in their search expressions. However, these expressions forced you to write lengthy SQL and PL/SQL code when performing complex searches. Oracle Database 11g lets you perform complex searches and string manipulations easily with regular expressions.

Note Oracle's regular expression features follow the popular POSIX standards.

A regular expression searches for patterns in character strings. The character string has to be one of CHAR, VARCHAR2, NCHAR, or NVARCHAR2, and the regular expression function can be one of the following:

- REGEXP_LIKE
- REGEXP_REPLACE
- REGEXP_INSTRING
- REGEXP_SUBSTRING

The REGEXP_LIKE function evaluates strings using a specified set of characters. The regular expression function searches for a pattern in a string, which is specified with the SOURCE_STRING parameter in the function. The PATTERN variable represents the actual *regular expression*, which is the pattern to search for. A regular expression is usually a text literal; it can be one of CHAR, VARCHAR2, NCHAR, or NVARCHAR2, and it can be a maximum of 512 bytes long. You can also specify an optional match parameter to modify the matching behavior. For example, a value of i specifies case-insensitive matching, while c specifies case-sensitive matching.

Here is the syntax of the REGEXP_LIKE function:

```
REGEXP_LIKE(source_string, pattern [,match_parameter])
```

If you want to carry out string-manipulation tasks, you can use the REGEXP_INSTR, REGEXP_REPLACE, or REGEXP_SUBSTR built-in functions. These are really extensions of the normal SQL INSTR, REPLACE, and SUBSTR functions.

Regular expression features use characters like the period (.), asterisk (*), caret (^), and dollar sign ($), which are common in UNIX and Perl programming. The caret character (^), for example, tells Oracle that the characters following it should be at the beginning of the line. Similarly, the $ character indicates that a character or a set of characters must be at the very end of the line. Here's an example using the REGEXP_LIKE function that picks up all names with consecutive vowels:

```
SQL> SELECT last_name
     FROM employees
     WHERE REGEXP_LIKE (last_name, '([aeiou])\1', 'i');

LAST_NAME
-----------
Freedman
Greenberg
Khoo
Gee
Lee
. . .
SQL>
```

Here's another example that quickly searches for employees who were hired between the years 2000 and 2008.

```
SQL> SELECT emp_name, salary,
  2   TO_CHAR(hire_date,'yyyy') year_of_hire
  3   FROM emp
  4* WHERE REGEXP_LIKE (TO_CHAR (hire_date, 'yyyy'), '^200[0-8]$');
```

LAST_NAME	FIRST_NAME	SALARY	YEAR
Austin	David	4800	2007
Chen	John	8200	2007
Alapati	Shannon	7700	2007
Baida	Shelli	2900	2007
Tobias	Sigal	2800	2007
Weiss	Matthew	8000	2007

Abstract Data Types

This section briefly reviews the important Oracle features that facilitate object-oriented programming. *Abstract types*, also called *object types*, are at the heart of Oracle's object-oriented programming. Unlike a normal data type, an abstract data type contains a data structure along with the functions and procedures needed to manipulate the data; thus, data and behavior are coupled.

Object types are like other schema objects, and they consist of a name, attributes, and methods. Object types are similar to the concept of classes in C++ and Java. Oracle support for object-oriented features, such as types, makes it feasible to implement object-oriented features, such as encapsulation and abstraction, while modeling complex real-life objects and processes. Oracle also supports single inheritance of user-defined SQL types.

The CREATE TYPE Command

Object types are created by users and stored in the database like Oracle data types such as VARCHAR2, for example. The CREATE TYPE command lets you create an abstract template that corresponds to a real-world object. Here's an example:

```
SQL> CREATE TYPE person AS object
  2   (name varchar2(30),
  3   phone varchar2(20));

Type created.
SQL>
```

Object Tables

Object tables contain objects such as the person type that was created in the previous section. Here's an example:

```
SQL> CREATE TABLE person_table OF person;

Table created.
SQL>
```

Here's the interesting part. The person_table table doesn't contain single-value columns like a regular Oracle table—its columns are types, which can hold multiple values. You can use object tables to view the data as a single-column table or a multicolumn table that consists of the components of the object type. Here's how you would insert data into an object table:

```
SQL> INSERT INTO person_table
  2  VALUES
  3  ('john smith', '1-800-555-9999');

1 row created.
SQL>
```

Collections

Collections are ideal for representing one-to-many relationships among data. Oracle offers you two main types of collections: varrays and nested tables. We'll look at these two types of collections in more detail in the following sections.

Varrays

A varray is simply an ordered collection of data elements. Each element in the array is identified by an index, which is used to access that particular element. Here's how you declare a VARRAY type:

```
SQL> CREATE TYPE prices AS VARRAY (10) OF NUMBER (12,2);
```

Nested Tables

A *nested table* consists of an ordered set of data elements. The ordered set can be of an object type or an Oracle built-in type. Here's a simple example:

```
SQL> CREATE TYPE lineitem_table AS TABLE OF lineitem;
```

To access the elements of a collection with SQL, you can use the TABLE operator, as shown in the following example. Here, history is a nested table and courses is the column you want to insert data into:

```
SQL> INSERT INTO
        TABLE(SELECT courses FROM department WHERE name = 'History')
        VALUES('Modern India');
```

Type Inheritance

You can create not just types, but also *type hierarchies*, which consist of parent supertypes and child subtypes connected to the parent types by inheritance. Here's an example of how you can create a subtype from a supertype. First, create the supertype:

```
SQL> CREATE TYPE  person_t AS OBJECT (
        name varchar2(80),
        social_sec_no number,
        hire_date date,
        member function age() RETURN number,
        member function print() RETURN varchar2) NOT FINAL;
```

Next, create the subtype, which will inherit all the attributes and methods from its supertype:

```
SQL> CREATE TYPE employee_t UNDER person_t
     (salary number,
     commission number,
     member function wages () RETURN number,
     OVERRIDING member function print () RETURN varchar2);
```

The Cast Operator

The CAST operator enables you to do two things. It lets you convert built-in data types and also convert a collection-type value into another collection-type value.

Here's an example of using CAST with built-in data types:

```
SQL> SELECT product_id,
     CAST(description AS VARCHAR2(30))
     FROM product_desc;
```

PL/SQL

Although SQL is easy to learn and has a lot of powerful features, it doesn't allow the procedural constructs of third-generation languages such as C. PL/SQL is Oracle's proprietary extension to SQL, and it provides you the functionality of a serious programming language. One of the big advantages of using PL/SQL is that you can use program units called procedures or packages in the database, thus increasing code reuse and performance.

The Basic PL/SQL Block

A PL/SQL *block* is an executable program. A PL/SQL code block, whether encapsulated in a program unit such as a procedure or specified as a free-form anonymous block, consists of the following structures, with a total of four key statements, only two of which are mandatory:

- DECLARE: In this optional section, you declare the program variables and cursors.
- BEGIN: This mandatory statement indicates that SQL and PL/SQL statements will follow it.
- EXCEPTION: This optional statement specifies error handling.
- END: This mandatory statement indicates the end of the PL/SQL code block.

Here's an example of a simple PL/SQL code block:

```
SQL> DECLARE isbn  NUMBER(9)
     BEGIN
     isbn := 123456789;
     insert into book values (isbn, 'databases', 59.99);
     COMMIT;
     END;
SQL>
```

Declaring Variables

You can declare both variables and constants in the DECLARE section. Before you can use any variable, you must first declare it. A PL/SQL variable can be a built-in type such as DATE, NUMBER, VARCHAR2, or CHAR, or it can be a composite type such as VARRAY. In addition, PL/SQL uses the BINARY_INTEGER and BOOLEAN data types.

Here are some common PL/SQL variable declarations:

```
hired_date      DATE;
emp_name        VARCHAR2(30);
```

In addition to declaring variables, you can also declare constants, as shown in the following example:

```
tax_rate   constant     number := 0.08;
```

You can also use the %TYPE attribute to declare a variable that is of the same type as a specified table's column, as shown here:

```
emp_num        employee.emp_id%TYPE;
```

The %ROWTYPE attribute specifies that the record (row) is of the same data type as a database table. In the following example, the DeptRecord record has all the columns contained in the department table, with identical data types and length:

```
declare
v_DeptRecord        department%ROWTYPE;
```

Writing Executable Statements

After the BEGIN statement, you can enter all your SQL statements. These look just like your regular SQL statements, but notice the difference in how you handle a SELECT statement and an INSERT statement in the following sections.

A SELECT Statement in PL/SQL

When you use a SELECT statement in PL/SQL, you need to store the retrieved values in variables, as shown here:

```
DECLARE
name  VARCHAR2(30);
BEGIN
SELECT employee_name INTO name FROM employees WHERE emp_id=99999;
END;
/
```

DML Statements in PL/SQL

Any INSERT, DELETE, or UPDATE statements in PL/SQL work just as they do in regular SQL. You can use the COMMIT statement after any such operation, as shown here:

```
BEGIN
DELETE FROM employee WHERE emp_id = 99999;
COMMIT;
END;
/
```

Handling Errors

In PL/SQL, an error or a warning is called an *exception*. PL/SQL has some internally defined errors, and you can also define your own error conditions. When any error occurs, an exception is raised and program control is handed to the exception-handling section of the PL/SQL program. If you define your own error conditions, you have to raise exceptions by using a special RAISE statement.

The following example shows an exception handler using the RAISE statement:

```
DECLARE
    acct_type INTEGER := 7;
BEGIN
    IF acct_type NOT IN (1, 2, 3) THEN
        RAISE INVALID_NUMBER;  -- raise predefined exception
    END IF;
EXCEPTION
    WHEN INVALID_NUMBER THEN
    ROLLBACK;
END;
/
```

PL/SQL Control Structures

PL/SQL offers you several types of control structures, which enable you to perform iterations of code or conditional execution of certain statements. The various types of control structures in PL/SQL are covered in the following sections.

Conditional Control

The main type of conditional control structure in PL/SQL is the IF statement, which enables conditional execution of statements. You can use the IF statement in three forms: IF-THEN, IF-THEN-ELSE, and IF-THEN-ELSEIF. Here's an example of a simple IF-THEN-ELSEIF statement:

```
BEGIN
    . . .
    IF total_sales > 100000 THEN
        bonus := 5000;
    ELSEIF total_sales > 35000 THEN
        bonus := 500;
    ELSE
        bonus := 0;
    END IF;
    INSERT INTO new_payroll VALUES (emp_id, bonus . . .);
END;
/
```

PL/SQL Looping Constructs

PL/SQL loops provide a way to perform iterations of code for a specified number of times or until a certain condition is true or false. The following sections cover the basic types of looping constructs.

The Simple Loop

The simple loop construct encloses a set of SQL statements between the keywords LOOP and END LOOP. The EXIT statement ends the loop. You use the simple loop construct when you don't know how many times the loop should execute. The logic inside the LOOP and END LOOP statements decides when the loop is terminated.

In the following example, the loop will be executed until a quality grade of 6 is reached:

```
LOOP
  . . .
  if quality_grade > 5  then
  . . .
  EXIT;
  end if;
END LOOP;
```

Another simple loop type is the LOOP . . . EXIT . . . WHEN construct, which controls the duration of the loop with a WHEN statement. A condition is specified for the WHEN statement, and when this condition becomes true, the loop will terminate. Here's a simple example:

```
DECLARE
  count_num  NUMBER(6);
BEGIN
  count_num := 1;
  LOOP
  dbms_output.put_line(' This is the current count  '|| count_num);
  count_num := count_num + 1;
  Exit when count_num > 100;
  END LOOP;
END;
```

The WHILE Loop

The WHILE loop specifies that a certain statement be executed while a certain condition is true. Note that the condition is evaluated outside the loop. Each time the statements within the LOOP and END LOOP statements are executed, the condition is evaluated. When the condition no longer holds true, the loop is exited. Here's an example of the WHILE loop:

```
WHILE total <= 25000
LOOP
 . . .
 SELECT sal INTO salary FROM emp WHERE . . .
 total := total + salary;
END LOOP;
```

The FOR Loop

The FOR loop is used when you want a statement to be executed a certain number of times. The FOR loop emulates the classic do loop that exists in most programming languages. Here's an example of the FOR loop:

```
BEGIN
    FOR count_num IN 1..100
    LOOP
      dbms_output.put_line('The current count is :  '|| count_num);
    END LOOP;
END;
```

PL/SQL Records

Records in PL/SQL let you treat related data as a single unit. Records contain fields, with each field standing for a different item. You can use the %ROWTYPE attribute to declare a table's columns as a record, which uses the table as a cursor template, or you can create your own records. Here's a simple example of a record:

```
DECLARE
      TYPE MeetingTyp IS RECORD (
      date_held DATE,
      location  VARCHAR2(20),
      purpose   VARCHAR2(50));
```

To reference an individual field in a record, you use dot notation, as shown here:

```
MeetingTyp.location
```

Using Cursors

An Oracle *cursor* is a handle to an area in memory that holds the result set of a SQL query, enabling you to individually process the rows in the result set. Oracle uses *implicit cursors* for all DML statements. *Explicit cursors* are created and used by application coders.

Implicit Cursors

Implicit cursors are automatically used by Oracle every time you use a SELECT statement in PL/SQL. You can use implicit cursors in statements that return just one row. If your SQL statement returns more than one row, an error will result.

In the following PL/SQL code block, the SELECT statement makes use of an implicit cursor:

```
DECLARE
  emp_name  varchar2(40);
  salary    float;
BEGIN
  SELECT emp_name, salary FROM employees
  WHERE employee_id=9999;
  dbms_output.put_line('employee_name : '||emp_name||'
  salary :'||salary);
END;
/
```

Explicit Cursors

Explicit cursors are created by the application developer, and they facilitate operations with a set of rows, which can be processed one by one. You always use explicit cursors when you know your SQL statement will return more than one row. Notice that you have to declare an explicit cursor in the DECLARE section at the beginning of the PL/SQL block, unlike an implicit cursor, which you never refer to in the code.

Once you declare your cursor, the explicit cursor will go through these steps:

1. The OPEN clause will identify the rows that are in the cursor and make them available for the PL/SQL program.

2. The FETCH command will retrieve data from the cursor into a specified variable.

3. The cursor should always be explicitly closed after your processing is completed.

Listing A-4 shows how a cursor is first created and then used within a loop.

Listing A-4. *Using an Explicit Cursor*

```
DECLARE
/* The cursor select_emp is explicitly declared */
     CURSOR  select_emp IS
     select emp_id, city
     from employees
     where city = 'DALLAS';
     v_empno  employees.emp_id%TYPE;
     v_empcity employees.city%TYPE;
BEGIN
  /* The cursor select_emp is opened */
   Open select _emp;
    LOOP
  /* The select_emp cursor data is fetched into v_empno variable */
     FETCH select_emp into v_empno;
     EXIT WHEN select_emp%NOTFOUND;
     dbms_output.put_line(v_empno|| ','||v_empcity);
    END LOOP;
       /* The cursor select_emp is closed */
    Close select_emp;
END;
/
```

Cursor Attributes

In the example shown in Listing A-4, a special cursor attribute, %NOTFOUND, is used to indicate when the loop should terminate. Cursor attributes are very useful when you're dealing with explicit cursors. Here are the main cursor attributes:

- %ISOPEN is a Boolean attribute that evaluates to false after the SQL statement completes execution. It returns true as long as the cursor is open.

- %FOUND is a Boolean attribute that tests whether the SQL statement matches any row—that is, whether the cursor has any more rows to fetch.

- %NOTFOUND is a Boolean attribute that tells you that the SQL statement doesn't match any row, meaning there are no more rows left to fetch.

- %ROWCOUNT gives you the number of rows the cursor has fetched so far.

Cursor FOR Loops

Normally when you use explicit cursors, cursors have to be opened, the data has to be fetched, and finally the cursor needs to be closed. A cursor FOR loop automatically performs the open, fetch, and close procedures, which simplifies your job. Listing A-5 shows an example that uses a cursor FOR loop construct.

Listing A-5. *Using the Cursor FOR Loop*

```
DECLARE
  CURSOR emp_cursor IS
  SELECT emp_id, emp_name, salary
  FROM employees;
  v_emp_info    employees%RowType;
```

```
Begin
  FOR emp_info IN emp_cursor
  LOOP
  dbms_output.put_line ('Employee id : '||emp_id||'Employee
  name : '|| emp_name||'Employee salary :'||salary);
  END LOOP;
END;
/
```

Cursor Variables

Cursor variables point to the current row in a multirow result set. Unlike a regular cursor, though, a cursor variable is dynamic—that is, you can assign new values to a cursor variable and pass it to other procedures and functions. Let's look at how you can create cursor variables in PL/SQL.

First, define a REF CURSOR type, as shown here:

```
DECLARE
TYPE EmpCurTyp IS REF CURSOR RETURN dept%ROWTYPE;
```

Next, declare cursor variables of the type DeptCurTyp in an anonymous PL/SQL code block or in a procedure (or function), as shown in the following code snippet:

```
DECLARE
    TYPE EmpRecTyp IS RECORD (
        Emp_id NUMBER(9),
        emp_name VARCHAR2(30),
        sal    NUMBER(7,2));
    TYPE EmpCurTyp IS REF CURSOR RETURN EmpRecTyp;
    emp_cv EmpCurTyp;   -- declare cursor variable
```

Procedures, Functions, and Packages

A PL/SQL procedure can be used to perform various DML operations. The following is a simple Oracle procedure:

```
create or replace procedure new_employee (emp_id number,
last_name varchar(2), first_name varchar(2))
is
begin
    insert into employees values ( emp_id, last_name, first_name);
end new_employee;
/
```

Unlike a PL/SQL procedure, a function returns a value, as shown in the following example:

```
CREATE OR REPLACE FUNCTION sal_ok (salary REAL, title VARCHAR2) RETURN BOOLEAN IS
    min_sal REAL;
    max_sal REAL;
BEGIN
    SELECT losal, hisal INTO min_sal, max_sal FROM sals
        WHERE job = title;
    RETURN (salary >= min_sal) AND (salary <= max_sal);
END sal_ok;
```

Oracle *packages* are objects that usually consist of several related procedures and functions, and the package is usually designed to perform an application function by invoking all the related procedures and functions within the package. Packages are extremely powerful, because they can contain large amounts of functional code and be repeatedly executed by several users.

A package usually has two parts: a *package specification* and a *package body*. The package specification declares the variables, cursors, and subprograms (procedures and functions) that are part of the package. The package body contains the actual cursors and subprogram code.

Listing A-6 shows a simple Oracle package.

Listing A-6. *A PL/SQL Package*

```
/* First, the Package Specification /*
 create or replace package emp_pkg as
 type list is varray (100) of number (5);
 procedure new_employee  (emp_id number, last_name
 varchar2, first_name varchar2);
 procedure salary_raise ( emp_id number, raise number);
end emp_pkg;
/
/* The Package Body follows */
create or replace package body emp_pkg as
procedure new_employee  (emp_id number,
last_name varchar(2), first_name varchar(2) is
  begin
    insert into employees values ( emp_id, last_name, first_name);
  end new_employee;
  procedure salary_raise ( emp_num number, raise_pct real)  is
  begin
    update employees set salary = salary * raise_pct
    where emp_id = emp_num;
  end salary_raise;
end emp_pkg;
/
```

If you want to use emp_pkg to award a raise to an employee, all you have to do is execute the following:

```
SQL> EXECUTE emp_pkg.salary_raise(99999, 0.15);
```

Oracle XML DB

A typical organization has information stored in multiple formats, some of which may be organized in relational databases, but most of which is stored outside the database. The nondatabase information may be stored in application-specific formats, such as Excel spreadsheets. Storing the nondatabase information in XML format instead makes it easier to access and update nonstructured organizational information.

Oracle XML DB isn't really a special type of database for XML. It simply refers to the set of built-in XML storage and retrieval technologies for the manipulation of XML data. Oracle XML DB provides the advantages of object-relational database technology and XML technology. For example, one of the major problems involved in dealing with XML data from within a relational database is that most XML data is hierarchical in nature, whereas the Oracle database is based on the relational model. Oracle manages to deal effectively with the hierarchical XML data by using special SQL operators and methods that let you easily query and update XML data in an Oracle database. Oracle XML DB builds the XML Document Object Model (DOM) into the Oracle kernel. Thus, most XML operations are treated as part of normal database processing.

Oracle XML DB provides the ability to view both structured and nonstructured information as relational data. You can view the data as either rows in a table or nodes in an XML document.

Here is a brief list of the benefits offered by Oracle XML DB:

- You can access XML data using regular SQL queries.

- You can use Oracle's OLTP, data warehousing, test, spatial data, and multimedia features to process XML data.

- You can generate XML from an Oracle SQL query.

- You can transform XML into HTML format easily.

Storing XML in Oracle XML DB

Oracle uses a special native data type called XMLType to store and manage XML data in a relational table. XMLType and XDBURIType, which is another built-in type for XML data, enable you to leave the XML parsing, storage, and retrieval to the Oracle database. You can use the XMLType data type just as you would the usual data types in an Oracle database. You can now store a well-formed XML document in the database as an XML test using the CLOB base data type.

Here's an example of using the XMLType data type:

```
SQL> CREATE TABLE sales_catalog_table
  2  (sales_num  number(18),
  3  sales_order xmltype);
Table created.
SQL> DESC sales_catalog_table
 Name                    Null? Type
 --------------------- ----- --------
 SALES_NUM                     NUMBER(18)
 SALES_ORDER                   XMLTYPE
SQL>
```

The XMLType data type comes with a set of XML-specific methods, which you use to work with XMLType objects. You can use these methods to perform common database operations, such as checking for the existence of a node and extracting a node. The methods also support several operators that enable you to access and manipulate XML data as part of a regular SQL statement. These operators follow the emerging SQL/XML standard. Using the well-known XPath notation, the SQL/XML operators traverse XML structures to find the node or nodes on which they should use the SQL operations. Here are some of the important SQL/XML operators:

- Extract() extracts a subset of the nodes contained in the XMLType.

- ExistsNode() checks whether a certain node exists in the XMLType.

- Validating() validates the XMLType contents against an XML schema.

- Transform() performs an XSL transformation.

- ExtractValue() returns a node corresponding to an XPath expression.

XML is in abstract form compared to the normal relational table entries. To optimize and execute statements that involve XML data, Oracle uses a query-rewrite mechanism to transform an XPath expression into an equivalent regular SQL statement. The optimizer then processes the transformed SQL statement like any other SQL statement.

You can store XML in Oracle XML DB in the following ways:

- You can use SQL or PL/SQL to insert the data. Using XMLType constructors, you must first convert the sourced data into an XMLType instance.

- You can use the Oracle XML DB repository to store the XML data.

Here's a simple example using the sales_catalog_table table to demonstrate how to perform SQL-based DML operations with an XML-enabled table. In Listing A-7, an XML document is inserted into sales_catalog_table.

Listing A-7. *Inserting an XML Document into an Oracle Table*

```
SQL>    INSERT INTO sales_catalog_table
  2     VALUES (123456,
  3     XMLTYPE(
  4     '<SalesOrder>
  5     <Reference>Alapati - 200302201428CDT</Reference>
  6     <Actions/>
  7     <Reject/>
  8     <Requestor>Nina U. Alapati</Requestor>
  9     <User>ALAPATI</User>
 10     <SalesLocation>Dallas</SalesLocation>
 11     <ShippingInstructions/>
 12     <DeliveryInstructions>Bicycle Courier</DeliveryInstructions>
 13     <ItemDescriptions>
 14        <ItemDescription  ItemNumber="1">
 15        <Description>Expert Oracle DB Administration</Description>
 16        <ISBN Number="1590590228"Price="59.95"Quantity="5"/>
 17        </ItemDescription>
 18     </ItemDescriptions>
 19*  </SalesOrder>'));
1 row created.
SQL>
```

You can query the sales_catalog_table table's sales_order column, as shown in Listing A-8, to view the XML document in its original format.

Listing A-8. *Viewing XML Data Stored in an Oracle Table*

```
SQL> SELECT sales_order FROM
  2 sales_catalog_table;
   <SalesOrder>
 <Reference>Alapati - 200302201428CDT</Reference>
 <Actions/>
 <Reject/>
 <Requestor>Sam R. Alapati</Requestor>
 <User>ALAPATI</User>
 <SalesLocation>Dallas</SalesLocation>
 <ShippingInstructions/>
 <DeliveryInstructions>Bicycle Courier</DeliveryInstructions>
 <ItemDescriptions>
   <ItemDescription ItemNumber="1">
     <Description>Expert Oracle DB Administration</Description>
     <ISBN Number="9999990228" Price="59.95" Quantity="2"/>
   </ItemDescription>
```

```
  </ItemDescriptions>
</SalesOrder>
SQL>
```

Once you create the sales_catalog_table table, it's very easy to retrieve data using one of the methods I just described. The following example shows how to query the table using the extract() method. Note that the query includes XPath expressions and the SQL/XML operators extractValue and existsNode to find the requestor's name where the value of the /SalesOrder/SalesLocation/ text() node contains the value Dallas.

```
SQL> SELECT extractValue(s.sales_order,'/SalesOrder/Requestor')
  2    FROM sales_catalog_table s
  3    WHERE existsNode(s.SALES_ORDER,
  4* '/SalesOrder[SalesLocation="Dallas"]') = 1;

EXTRACTVALUE(S.SALES_ORDER,'/SALESORDER/REQUESTOR')
--------------------------------------------------
Nina U. Alapati
SQL>
```

The Oracle XML DB Repository

The best way to process XML documents in Oracle XML DB is to first load them into a special repository called the Oracle XML DB repository. The XML repository is hierarchical, like most XML data, and it enables you to easily query XML data. The paths and URLs in the repository represent the relationships among the XML data, and a special hierarchical index is used to traverse the folders and paths within the repository. The XML repository can hold non-XML data such as JPEG images, Word documents, and more.

You can use SQL and PL/SQL to access the XML repository. XML authoring tools can directly access the documents in the XML repository using popular Internet protocols such as HTTP, FTP, and WebDAV. For example, you can use Windows Explorer, Microsoft Office, and Adobe Acrobat to work with the XML documents that are stored in the XML repository. XML is by nature document-centric, and the XML repository provides applications with a file abstraction when dealing with XML data.

Setting Up an XML Schema

Before you can start using Oracle XML DB to manage XML documents, you need to perform the following tasks:

1. Create an XML schema. For example, SalesOrder, shown in Listing A-7, is a simple XML schema that reflects a simple XML document. Within the SalesOrder schema are elements such as ItemDescription, which provides details about the attributes of the component items.

2. Register the XML schema. After the XML schema is created, you must register it with the Oracle database using a PL/SQL procedure. When you register the XML schema, Oracle will create the SQL objects and the XMLType tables that are necessary to store and manage the XML documents. For the example shown in Listing A-6, registering the XML schema will create a table called SalesOrder automatically, with one row in the table for each SalesOrder document loaded into the XML repository. The XML schema is registered under the URL http://localhost:8080/home/SCOTT/xdb/salesorder.xsd, and it contains the definition of the SalesOrder element.

Creating a Relational View from an XML Document

Even if a developer doesn't know much XML, he or she can use the XML documents stored in the Oracle database by creating relational views based on the XML documents. The following example maps nodes in an XML document to columns in a relational view called salesorder_view:

```
SQL> CREATE OR REPLACE VIEW salesorder_view
  2  (requestor,description,sales_location)
  3  AS SELECT
  4  extractValue(s.sales_order,'/SalesOrder/Requestor'),
  5  extractValue(s.sales_order,'/SalesOrder/Sales_Location')
  6* FROM sales_Catalog_Table s ;

 View created.
SQL>
```

You can query salesorder_view like you would any other view in an Oracle database, as shown here:

```
SQL> SELECT requestor,sales_location FROM salesorder_view;

REQUESTOR
SALES_LOCATION
Aparna Alapati
Dallas
SQL>
```

Oracle and Java

You can use both PL/SQL and Java to write applications that need Oracle database access. Although PL/SQL has several object-oriented features, the Java language is well known as an object-oriented programming language. If your application needs heavy database access and must process large amounts of data, PL/SQL is probably a better bet. However, for open distributed applications, Java-based applications are more suitable.

The Oracle database contains a Java Virtual Machine (JVM) to interpret Java code from within the database. Just as PL/SQL enables you to store code on the server and use it multiple times, you can also create Java stored procedures and store them in the database. These Java stored procedures are in the form of Java classes. You make Java files available to the Oracle JVM by loading them into the Oracle database as schema objects.

You can use the Java programming language in several ways in an Oracle database. You can invoke Java methods in classes that are loaded in the database in the form of Java stored procedures. You can also use two different application programming interfaces (APIs), Java Database Connectivity (JDBC) or SQLJ, to access the Oracle database from a Java-based application program. In the sections that follow, we'll briefly look at the various ways you can work with Java and the Oracle database.

Java Stored Procedures

Java stored procedures are, of course, written using Java, and they facilitate the implementation of data-intensive business logic using Java. These procedures are stored within the database like PL/SQL stored procedures. Java stored procedures can be seen as a link between the Java and non-Java environments.

You can execute Java stored procedures just as you would PL/SQL stored procedures. Here's a summary of the steps involved in creating a Java stored procedure:

1. Define the Java class.

2. Using the Java compiler, compile the new class.

3. Load the class into the Oracle database. You can do this by using the loadjava command-line utility.

4. Publish the Java stored procedure.

Once you've completed these steps, you can invoke the Java stored procedure.

JDBC

JDBC is a popular method used to connect to an Oracle database from Java. Chapter 10 contains a complete example of a Java program. JDBC provides a set of interfaces for querying databases and processing SQL data in the Java programming language.

Listing A-9 shows a simple JDBC program that connects to an Oracle database and executes a simple SQL query.

Listing A-9. *A Simple JDBC Program*

```
import java.sql.*;
public class JDBCExample {
  public static void main(String args[]) throws SQLException
/* Declare the type of Oracle Driver you are using */
   {DriverManager.registerDriver(new oracle.jdbc.driver.OracleDriver());
/* Create a database connection for the JDBC program */
Connection conn=
DriverManager.getConnection(
                "jdbc:oracle:thin:@nicholas:1521:aparna","hr","hr");
Statement stmt = conn.createStatement();
/* Pass a query to SQL and store the results in the result set rs */
ResultSet rs =
stmt.executeQuery("select emp_id, emp_name,salary from employees");
/* Using the while loop, result set rs is accessed row by row */
while(rs.next()){
int number = rs.getInt(1);
String name= rs.getString(2);
System.out.println(number+" "+name+" "+salary);
        }
/* Close the JDBC result set and close the database connection */
rs.close();
conn.close();
        }
}
```

JDBC is ideal for dynamic SQL, where the SQL statements aren't known until run time.

SQLJ

SQLJ is a complementary API to JDBC, and it's ideal for applications in which you're using static SQL (SQL that's known before the execution). Being static, SQLJ enables you to trap errors before they occur during run time. Keep in mind that even with SQLJ, you still use JDBC drivers to access the database.

There are three steps involved in executing a SQLJ program:

1. Create the SQLJ source code.

2. Translate the SQLJ source code into Java source code using a Java compiler.

3. Execute the SQLJ runtime program after you connect to the database.

Listing A-10 contains a simple SQLJ example that shows how to execute a SQL statement from within Java.

Listing A-10. *A Simple SQLJ Program*

```
import java.sql.*;
import sqlj.runtime.ref.DefaultContext;
import oracle.sqlj.runtime.Oracle;
/* Declare the variables here */
/* Define an Iterator type to store query results */
#sql iterator ExampleIter (int emp_id, String emp_name,float salary);
public class MyExample
/* The main method */
    { public static void main (String args[]) throws SQLException
    {
/* Establish the database connection for SQLJ */
    Oracle.connect
      ("jdbc:oracle:thin:@shannon:1234:nicholas1", "hr", "hr");
/* Insert a row into the employees table */
    #sql { insert into employees  (emp_id, emp_name, salary)
        values (1001, 'Nina Alapati', 50000) };
/* Create an instance of the iterator ExampleIter */
    ExampleIter iter;
/* Store the results of the select query in the iterator ExampleIter */
    #sql iter={ select emp_id, emp_name, salary from  employees };
/* Access the data stored in the iterator, using the next() method */
    while (iter.next()) {
        System.out.println
        (iter.emp_id,()+" "+iter.emp_name()+" "+iter.salary());
        }
    }
}
```

As you can see from the SQLJ example in Listing A-10, SQLJ is nothing more than embedded SQL in a Java program. Using SQLJ, you can easily make calls to the database from Java. For a wealth of information on Oracle and Java, please visit Oracle's Java Center web site (http://otn.oracle.com/tech/java/content.html).

This appendix just provided a very brief introduction to the Oracle Database 11g SQL and PL/SQL capabilities. Although Oracle DBAs aren't always expected be very proficient in SQL and PL/SQL, the more you know about them, the better off you'll be as a professional Oracle DBA.

Index

You Need the Companion eBook

Your purchase of this book entitles you to buy the companion PDF-version eBook for only $10. Take the weightless companion with you anywhere.

We believe this Apress title will prove so indispensable that you'll want to carry it with you everywhere, which is why we are offering the companion eBook (in PDF format) for $10 to customers who purchase this book now. Convenient and fully searchable, the PDF version of any content-rich, page-heavy Apress book makes a valuable addition to your programming library. You can easily find and copy code — or perform examples by quickly toggling between instructions and the application. Even simultaneously tackling a donut, diet soda, and complex code becomes simplified with hands-free eBooks!

Once you purchase your book, getting the $10 companion eBook is simple:

❶ Visit **www.apress.com/promo/tendollars/**.

❷ Complete a basic registration form to receive a randomly generated question about this title.

❸ Answer the question correctly in 60 seconds, and you will receive a promotional code to redeem for the $10.00 eBook.

Apress®
THE EXPERT'S VOICE™

233 Spring Street, New York, NY 10013

Offer valid through 2/01/2011.